LAW OF EMPLOYEE PENSION AND WELFARE BENEFITS

Third Edition

LEXISNEXIS LAW SCHOOL ADVISORY BOARD

LAW OF EMPLOYEE PENSION AND WELFARE BENEFITS

Third Edition

Lawrence A. Frolik
Professor of Law
University of Pittsburgh School of Law

Kathryn L. Moore
Everett H. Metcalf, Jr. Professor of Law
University of Kentucky College of Law

LexisNexis®

ISBN: 978-0-7698-5280-5 (casebound)
ISBN: 978-0-7698-5300-0 (looseleaf)
ISBN: 978-0-3271-7754-8 (eBook)

Library of Congress Cataloging-in-Publication Data

Frolik, Lawrence A.
Law of employee pension and welfare benefits / Lawrence A. Frolik, professor of law, University of Pittsburgh School of Law, Kathryn L. Moore, Everett H. Metcalf, Jr. Professor of Law, University of Kentucky. — 3rd ed.
p. cm.
Includes index.
ISBN 978-0-7698-5280-5
1. Employee fringe benefits—Law and legislation—United States. 2. Pension trusts—Law and legislation—United States.
I. Moore, Kathryn L., 1961- II. Title.
KF3509.F76 2012
344.7301'252—dc23

2012029412

NOTE TO USERS

To ensure that you are using the latest materials available in this area, please be sure to periodically check the LexisNexis Law School web site for downloadable updates and supplements at www.lexisnexis.com/lawschool.

Editorial Offices
121 Chanlon Rd., New Providence, NJ 07974 (908) 464-6800
201 Mission St., San Francisco, CA 94105-1831 (415) 908-3200
www.lexisnexis.com

MATTHEW BENDER

(2012–Pub.3158)

PREFACE

The Law of Employee Pension and Welfare Benefits, 3rd Edition, integrates new statutory and case law developments into the framework of the previous edition. Private employer-sponsored retirement plans hold trillions of dollars in assets, and more than half of all Americans depend upon employer-sponsored plans for their health care coverage. In light of the size, diversity, and complexity of employee benefit plans, it should come as no surprise that the federal law governing employee benefit plans is also diverse and complex.

The complex nature of pension and welfare benefits law affords attorneys a variety of practice opportunities. For example, some benefits lawyers are principally litigators focusing their practice on enforcing the benefits promised by such plans. Other benefits attorneys are principally tax lawyers who, among other things, draft and amend plans to ensure that they comply with the extensive requirements that plans must satisfy to "qualify" for favorable federal income tax treatment. Some benefits lawyers work for one of three federal agencies that regulate employee benefits: the Department of Labor, the Internal Revenue Service, or the Pension Benefit Guaranty Corporation. The breadth of employee benefits practice is aptly illustrated by the fact that six different sections of the American Bar Association have committees on employee benefits and executive compensation: the Business Law Section, the Health Law Section, the Labor and Employment Law Section, the Real Property, Trust and Probate Law Section, the Taxation Section, and the Tort Trial and Insurance Practice Section.

This book is designed to introduce readers to the breadth and the depth of employee benefits law. Its goal is to give the reader an appreciation of why the federal government regulates employee benefit plans, how it does so, and the policy and social justice questions raised by the manner and effectiveness of that regulation.

The book begins with a brief history of employee benefit plans and explains how they came to have such importance in our society. It then offers a broad overview of how the two most significant federal statutes, the Employee Retirement Income Security Act of 1974 (ERISA) and the Internal Revenue Code (IRC), regulate employee benefit plans. The creation and operation of pension and welfare benefit plans is examined, followed by an analysis of the federal preemption of state regulation in this area. The statutory and case law that governs plan administration and enforcement of plan benefits is next considered. The book then turns to the complex regulatory scheme that determines whether a plan qualifies for favorable tax treatment. It concludes with the issues that arise if a plan is terminated, and the role of the Pension Benefit Guaranty Corporation in insuring certain plan benefits.

Employee benefit law is an amalgam of statutory and case law with some aspects, such as preemption, dominated by case law, while others, such as the nondiscrimination rules, are almost exclusively creatures of statutes and regulations. The book, therefore, necessarily reflects these differences in the presentation of the material. Some of the chapters, such as Chapters Five, Six, and Seven on ERISA Preemption, Plan Administration, and Enforcement Issues, are case oriented. Because the law in these areas is developed principally by judicial decisions interpreting the law, the book reproduces many of the significant decisions on these topics. Other chapters, such as Chapters Eight and Nine on the Tax Nondiscrimination Rules, and Plan Operation, where case law plays a relatively minor role, focus on the statute and its application. These chapters contain many problems designed to enhance the reader's appreciation and understanding of the governing statute.

Throughout the book, we cite both ERISA and the Internal Revenue Code with the expectation that the reader will consult and read the statutes. The reader of the book should have a comprehensive statutory supplement at hand and consult it frequently. A paraphrase of a statute is no substitute for the "real thing." While we believe that the statutes and cases are the best sources of understanding the material, we have by necessity often resorted to descriptive prose. Fortunately, we were able to use excerpts of many of the fine writings that describe and analyze the world of employee benefits, and we urge the user of this book to seek out the complete articles.

In editing cases, we have deleted some, but not all, case citations and citations to secondary sources. For ease of reading, we have not disclosed each omission with a "citations omitted." Case citations and footnotes from excerpted material have usually been omitted without disclosure. The footnotes that are included have been renumbered as indicated with brackets, [ ], around the numbers. We have indicated substantive deletions from cases or excerpted materials with ellipses. Any material bracketed, [ ], is an editorial insertion by the authors.

ERISA is codified in the U.S. Code, specifically in Title 29, § 1001 et seq. Many of those who work with ERISA, however, refer to its sections not by the U.S. Code, but by the original section numbers with which it was enacted. And so it is with those original section numbers that we refer to ERISA in this book. In the cases, where the courts usually use U.S. Code section cites, we have renumbered the ERISA citations with the original section numbers and so indicated with brackets, i.e. [ ].

This book represents a collaborative effort by the two authors. Each has contributed to every chapter. Primary responsibility for some of the chapters was allocated, however, as follows: Professor Frolik, Chapters 2, 5, 6, and 7; Professor Moore, Chapters 3, 4, 8 and 9. Excellent research assistance was provided by Stephanie Gallo and Danielle Hodnicki, students at the University of Pittsburgh School of Law, and Eric Smith, Tai Tucker, Stephen Barnes, Catherine Barrett and Gwendolyn Junge, students at the University of Kentucky College of Law. We thank these students for their contributions to this book. Our thanks also to the Document Technology Center of the University of Pittsburgh School of Law under the direction of LuAnn Driscoll, to Nancy Fritz, Amy Osborne, Carol Parris, and Susan Wild of the University of Kentucky College of Law Library, and to Adam Cohen, Brian Jones, and especially Carol Weiser for helpful discussions and comments on portions of the text.

Special thanks are due to the many authors and journals who have generously permitted us to reprint excerpts from their work. Citations to the material is found with the material in the book.

Lawrence A. Frolik
frolik@pitt.edu
Kathryn L. Moore
kmoore@uky.edu

ACKNOWLEDGMENTS

Chapter 1

Dilley, Patricia E. *Hidden in Plain View: The Pension Shield Against Creditors*, 74 Ind. L.J. 355, 376-79 (1999). Copyright © 1999. Reprinted with permission.

Gregory, David. *The Scope of ERISA Preemption of State Law: A Study in Effective Federalism*, 48 U. Pitt. L. Rev. 427, 437-40 (1987). Copyright © 1987. Reprinted with permission.

Matthew, Dayna Bowen. *Controlling the Reverse Agency Costs of Employment-Based Health Insurance: Of Markets, Courts and a Regulatory Quagmire*, 31 Wake Forest L. Rev. 1037, 1041-47 (1996). Copyright © 1996. Reprinted with permission.

Moore, Kathryn L. *The Future of Employment-Based Health Insurance After the Patient Protection and Affordable Care Act*, 89 Univ. of Nebraska L. Rev. 885, 893-99 (2011). Copyright ©2011. Reprinted with permission.

Roe, Mark J. *The Modern Corporation and Private Pension* s, 41 U.C.L.A. L. Rev. 75, 82-83 (1993). Copyright © 1993. Reprinted with permission.

Van Zante, Peter M. *Mandated Vesting: Suppression of Voluntary Retirement Benefits*, 75 Notre Dame L. Rev. 125-130 (October 1999). Copyright © 1999 Notre Dame Law Review. Reprinted with permission.

Chapter 2

Cannon, Coleman J. F. *Cashing In on Older Workers: Age Discrimination Claims in Cash-Balance Pension Plans*, 19 Law & Ineq. 31, 37-39 (2001). Copyright © 2001. Reprinted with permission.

Moore, Kathryn L., *Eligible Employees: Owners, Partners, Independent Contractors, Leased Employees*, in Alvin D. Lurie et al., *Federal Income Taxation of Retirement Plans* § 12.01 (Matthew Bender 2012).

Stabile, Susan J. *The Behavior of Defined Contribution Plan Participants*, 77 N.Y.U. L. Rev. 71, 88 (2002). Copyright © 2002. Reprinted with permission.

Stein, Norman P.; Dilley, Patricia E. *Leverage, Linkage, and Leakage: Problems with the Private Pension System and How They Should Inform the Social Security Reform Debate*, 58 Wash. & Lee L. Rev. 1369, 1374 (2001). Copyright © 2001. Reprinted with permission.

Vanderploeg, Frank P. *Role-Playing Under ERISA: The Company as "Employer" and "Fiduciary"*, 9 DePaul Bus. L.J. 259, 281 (1997). Copyright © 1997. Reprinted with permission.

Chapter 3

Befort, Stephen F.; Kopka, Christopher J. *The Sounds of Silence: The Libertarian Ethos of ERISA Preemption*, 52 Fla. L. Rev. 1, 4, 7 (2000). Copyright © 2000. Reprinted with permission.

Monahan, Amy B. *The Promise and Peril of Ownership Society Health Care Policy*, 80 Tul. L. Rev. 777 (2006). Copyright © 2006. Reprinted with permission.

Moore, Kathryn L. *The New Retiree Health VEBAs*, NYU Review of Employee Benefits and Executive Compensation 7-1, 7-2-7-4 (2008) Copyright ©2008. Reprinted with permission.

Pratt, David A. *The Past, Present and Future of Retiree Health Benefits*, 3 J. Health & Biomedical L. 103 (2007). Copyright © 2007. Reprinted with permission.

Chapter 4

Zelinsky, Edward A. *The Cash Balance Controversy*, 19 Va. Tax Rev. 683, 719-21 (2000). Copyright © 2000. Reprinted with permission.

Chapter 5

Fox, Daniel M.; Schaffer, Daniel C. *Semi-Preemption in ERISA: Legislative Process and Health Policy*, 7 Am. J. Tax Pol'y 47, 48-51 (1988). Copyright © 1988. Reprinted with permission.

Gregory, David. *The Scope of ERISA Preemption of State Law: A Study in Effective Federalism*, 48 U. Pitt. L. Rev. 427, 457-58 (1987). Copyright © 1987. Reprinted with permission.

Paredes, Troy. Note, *Stop-Loss Insurance, State Regulation, and ERISA: Defining the Scope of Federal Preemption*, 34 Harv. J. on Legis. 233, 249-50 (1997). Copyright © 1997. Reprinted with permission.

Sherman, Jeffrey G. *Domestic Partnership and ERISA Preemption*, 76 Tul. L. Rev. 373-429 (2001). Copyright © 2001. Reprinted with permission.

Zelinsky, Edward A. Travelers, *Reasoned Textualism, and the New Jurisprudence of ERISA Preemption*, 21 Cardozo L. Rev. 807, 812-14 (1999). Copyright © 1999. Reprinted with permission.

Chapter 6

Conison, Jay. *Suits for Benefits under ERISA*, 54 U. Pitt. L. Rev. 1, 9-14 (1992). Copyright © 1992. Reprinted with permission.

Hatamyar, Patricia Wick. *See No Evil? The Role of the Directed Trustee under ERISA*, 64 Tenn. L. Rev. 1, 12-14 (1996). Copyright © 1996. Reprinted with permission.

Millon, David. *Enron and the Dark Side of Worker Ownership*, 1 Seattle J. Soc. Just. 113, 115, 117-19 (2002). Copyright © 2002. Reprinted with permission.

Phillips Jr., W. Brantley Note, *Chasing Down the Devil: Standards of Prudent Investment under the Restatement (Third) of Trusts*, 54 Wash. & Lee L. Rev. 335, 348-50 (1997). Copyright © 1997. Reprinted with permission.

Chapter 8

Bankman, Joseph. *Tax Policy and Retirement Income: Are Pension Plan Anti-Discrimination Provisions Desirable?*, 55 U. Chi. L. Rev. 790, 800-03 (1988). Copyright © 1988. Reprinted with permission.

Berger, Mark. *The Contingent Employee Benefits Problems*, 32 Ind. L. Rev. 301, 346-47 (1999). Copyright © 1999. Reprinted with permission.

Moore, Kathryn L. *The Effects of Partial Privatization of Social Security Upon Private Pensions*, N.Y.U. Rev. Emp. Benefits & Executive Compensation 5-1, 5-5–5-17 (2003). Copyright © 2003. Reprinted with permission.

Van Zante, Peter M. *Mandated Vesting: Suppression of Voluntary Retirement* 75 Notre

Dame L. Rev. 125, 193n.225 (October 1999). Copyright © 1999 Notre Dame Law Review. Reprinted with permission.

Chapter 9

Stein, Norman P. *Simplification and I.R.C. § 415*, 2 Fla. Tax Rev. 69, 82 (1994). Copyright © 1994. Reprinted with permission.

TABLE OF CONTENTS

TABLE OF CONTENTS

Chapter 1

ORIGINS AND REASONS FOR EMPLOYEE BENEFITS AND ERISA

According to the Employee Benefit Research Institute, in 2009, in addition to salaries, wages and other forms of employee compensation, American employers paid over $1.5 trillion for employee benefits, such as pensions and health care insurance. According to the same source, in 2009, employee benefits made up 19.6 percent of the cost of employee compensation.

Not only do employee benefits represent a high percentage of payroll costs, but because such benefits generally receive favorable federal income tax treatment, they represent enormous tax expenditures — that is, federal income tax revenue losses attributable to the failure to tax or to defer the taxation on what would otherwise be currently taxable income. The exclusion of employer contributions for health care, health insurance premiums, and long-term care insurance premiums represents the single largest tax expenditure, estimated to be $659.4 billion between 2010 and 2014. The net exclusion of pension contributions and earnings for employer plans represents the second largest tax expenditure, estimated to be $515.4 billion of foregone income tax revenues between 2010 and 2014.

Because employee benefits play such a critical role in our national economy and enjoy such favorable tax treatment, they are subject to a complex system of federal statutes and regulations that have resulted in seemingly endless litigation. The Employee Retirement Income Security Act (ERISA), enacted in 1974 and amended multiple times since, together with the pension law sections of the Internal Revenue Code, § 401(a) *et seq.*, provide the principal regulation of employee benefits. Other federal laws, such as securities laws, also play a role in regulating employee benefits.

This book examines the federal law that regulates employee benefits, focusing principally on voluntary benefits, particularly employer-provided retirement and health care benefits.

1-1 QUESTIONS AND PROBLEMS

Imagine that you have been offered jobs with two large companies. The two jobs are identical except for the differences in compensation described in each scenario below. For each scenario, decide which job you would accept, assuming that you are yourself — that is, that you are a male or female (as the case may be), single or married, with or without children, etc. Then consider which job you would accept if you were a single parent, age 40, with two children, ages 12 and 9.

a. Alpha Co. which offers a salary of $55,000 a year with no health insurance; or

Beta Inc., which offers a salary of $44,000 a year and a health insurance package for you, your spouse or life partner, and children that costs the company $10,000 a year.

b. Delta Co., which offers a salary of $55,000 a year with no paid maternity leave program; or

Epsilon Co., which offers a salary of $53,000 a year and six months of paid maternity leave.

c. Sigma Inc., which offers a salary of $55,000 a year with no pension plan; or

Tau Co., which offers a salary of $50,000 a year and promises to deposit $4,000 a year into a retirement account on your behalf each year that you are employed. You will have no access to the account until you retire at age 65.

d. Nu Co., which offers a salary of $55,000 a year with no pension plan; or

Omega Inc., which offers a salary of $50,000 a year and, if you stay with the company for at least 5 years, promises to pay a pension of $1,000 a month for life beginning when you retire at age 65.

A. INTRODUCTION TO RETIREMENT BENEFITS

As individuals age, their participation rates in the work force decline. In 2010, four out of five men between the ages of 55 and 59 participated in the labor force. By ages 60 to 64, 60 percent of men participated in the labor force, while only 36.5 percent of men ages 65 to 69 participated in the labor force and only 22 percent of men ages 70 to 74 participated in the labor force. Women's labor force participation rates also decline dramatically with age, although their labor force participation rates are lower than those of similarly aged men in all age groups.

While work force participation rates decline dramatically by age 65, most individuals live well beyond age 65. Indeed, at age 65, the life expectancy of the average female is just under twenty years, while the life expectancy for the average male is just over seventeen years. (African-Americans have somewhat shorter life expectancies. At age 65, black men have a life expectancy of 15.2 years compared to 17.3 years for white men, and black women have a life expectancy of 18.7 years compared to 19.9 years for white women.) Because most Americans live many years after retirement, they must rely on our national retirement income system for support during their long years of retirement. That system, frequently referred to as a three-legged stool, consists of Social Security, employer-sponsored pensions, and individual savings/family support.

The first of these legs, Social Security, is almost universal. In 2011, Social Security covered about 94 percent of the workforce, and 9 out of 10 people aged 65 or over received Social Security benefits. For more than half of these beneficiaries, Social Security represented at least half of their retirement income. Social Security, however, was never expected to be the sole source of retirement income. Consequently, the federal government, by its income tax policies, promotes employer-sponsored pensions that supplement Social Security.

The amount of wealth held by private pensions is staggering. In 2009, employer-sponsored pensions were estimated to hold about $9.6 *trillion* in assets. Not surprisingly, the value of the assets of pension plans gives them considerable economic influence. For example, in 2003, pensions owned over 40 percent of all equities and almost 12 percent of all corporate and other taxable bonds.

The tremendous wealth of pension funds and their critical role in providing retirement income did not just happen. The success of pensions has been spurred by an interplay of political, economic and social innovations. In the 1930s, Murray Latimer, economist and pension analyst for a private research council created by John D. Rockefeller, identified several reasons why employers implemented pensions: pensions helped replace older workers with younger, more productive, workers, discouraged union organization, helped the firm compete for and retain skilled employees, and encouraged employee goodwill and loyalty. The greatest contributor, though, to the popularity of pension plans has been their enjoyment of substantial federal income tax advantages, which make pensions the preferred manner of saving for retirement.

The federal government's encouragement of private pensions has also resulted in a complex web of statutory, regulatory and case law designed to mold private pensions into forms that meet national priorities. In particular, the government seeks to protect the rights of pension plan participants and to see that in return for their income tax advantages, pension plans are secure and treat participants in a fair manner.

B. WHAT ARE RETIREMENT BENEFITS?

Retirement benefits are a form of deferred income, that is, payment tomorrow for work done today. Pensions are not gifts or evidence of employer largess, nor are they an acknowledgment of an obligation of the employer to provide income support for retirees. Pensions merely represent a decision by the employer, and possibly by the employee, that the employer, and perhaps the employee, is better served if part of the employee's compensation is not paid until after the employee retires, or at least until the employee reaches a specified age such as age 65. Pensions, consequently, represent compensation earned by the employee, and should be due to him or her as a matter of right. Conversely, an employer or the employee might decide that current payment of compensation is preferable to a pension. The employer, therefore, may not offer a pension. In fact, many employers do not provide their employees with a pension.

C. A BRIEF HISTORY OF RETIREMENT BENEFITS

DAVID GREGORY, THE SCOPE OF ERISA PREEMPTION OF STATE LAW: A STUDY IN EFFECTIVE FEDERALISM

48 U. PITT. L. REV. 427, 437–440 (1987)

The first major private sector pension plan in the United States was provided by the American Express Company in 1875. A few unions sporadically began to provide pension plans for their members. However, for the most part, unions were not interested in pension plan initiatives. Some state and local governments also began to provide pensions to public sector employees in the early twentieth century. These early pension plan initiatives were isolated and fitful. However, imperceptible early growth in pension plans eventually took on significant dimensions. By 1935, half of the states provided minimal pension plans for state employees, with strict work and residency requirements. Military personnel were the first beneficiaries of federal pension plans.

At the same time, the national economy was shifting from an agrarian to an industrial base. Employers saw pensions as a means to attract and retain younger, more energetic workers. However, employers also regarded early pension plans solely as gratuities, rather than as accrued vested rights or as forms of deferred compensation. Employees were not perceived as owners of property claims to pensions; their legal status as beneficiaries was very tenuous. Pension plans at the beginning of the century were off to a rocky, perilous start.

Early private pension plans were usually unfunded. No viable safeguards insured that current employees would ever receive pensions upon retirement, or that retirees would continue to receive their benefits. Employers reinforced paternalism with express exculpatory language, disavowing all liability for pension plan terminations or deficiencies. Only a small minority of the national workforce, concentrated primarily in a few large corporations, was covered by pension plans. Despite these marked shortcomings, four million employees were subject to some form of private pension plan coverage by 1925. Four hundred private pension plans were in operation by that time. Of the four million workers covered, one-third were employed by four large corporations — U.S. Steel, AT&T, and the New York and Pennsylvania Central Railroads. Gradually, various trusts were established to administer pension plans, with federal government stimulation via tax incentives for employer pension and profit sharing plans. Otherwise, pension regulation was governed by individual state law.

The Great Depression accented the need for comprehensive minimum social welfare legislation. The Social Security Act of 1935, which included old-age provisions, was the first partial systemic response to this national problem by the federal government. The Internal Revenue Act of 1942 provided comprehensive favorable income tax treatment of pension plans. In part, the federal tax legislation was designed to broaden employer pension coverage to lower-level employees. In the wake of the labor and employment law changes affected by World War II, pension plans continued to expand during the next two decades. Pensions, considered fringe benefits, were exempt from the federal wage controls and therefore were powerful, attractive job inducements in a very tight civilian labor market. These pre-World War II pension plans had severe drawbacks. Because most of them permitted the employer to unilaterally modify the plan at any time, the promised pension often proved illusory, particularly if the employer came upon economic hard times. If the employer went bankrupt or ceased to exist, the pension was usually lost. Moreover, the plans usually only paid benefits if the worker remained with the employer until retirement. Early case law upheld the employers' contentions that pensions were unilateral promises that could not be enforced. For example, in *McNevin v. Solvay Process Co.*, 53 N.Y.S. 98 (App. Div. 1898), *aff'd per curiam*, 60 N.E. 1115 (N.Y. 1901), the court stated:

> "It is conceded that this pension fund has been created voluntarily, and is a gift by the defendant . . . an employee cannot, in any case, demand payment of the sum credited to his account, except when the defendant shall adjudge the account to be payable . . . according to the rules and regulations established . . . " 53 N.Y.S. at 99–100.

During the Great Depression of the 1930s, employees learned the value of pension "gifts" as most employers, faced with greatly diminished profits or losses, were unable to pay the promised pensions. The enactment of Social Security in 1935 was, in part, a response to the massive failure of private pensions.

After World War II, because of inflation, changes in the federal income tax law, and wage controls, both employers and employees, particularly those represented by unions, had a renewed interest in pensions. After 1950, pension coverage grew rapidly among both unionized and nonunionized employees. This period also saw the creation of collectively bargained for multiemployer pension plans in which many employers contribute to a single union negotiated pension plan. Such plans were particularly popular in the construction, transportation and mining industries. By the 1960s pension plans were a common aspect of employee compensation.

D. WHO HAS RETIREMENT BENEFITS?

Of the 153 million Americans who worked in 2010, about 54 percent worked for an employer or union that sponsored a retirement plan while just under 45 percent of all workers participated in such a plan. Participation, however, is not divided evenly across the population. Rather, participation depends on factors such as income, gender, the size of the employer, employment status (whether full-time or part-time), age, and industry.

The participation rate of higher income workers is much greater than that of lower income workers. To illustrate, in 2010 only 6.7 percent of workers with an income of less than $10,000 per year participated in an employment-based retirement plan while 32.8 percent of workers earning $20,000–$29,000 participated in an employment-based retirement plan, and 68.9 percent of worker earning 50,000 or more participated in such a plan.

Among all workers, men are more likely to participate in a retirement plan than women, but among full-time, full-year workers, women are more likely to participate than men. Specifically, 55.5 percent of full-time, full-year female workers participated in a retirement plan in 2010 compared to 53.6 percent of full-time, full-year male workers. Women's overall lower participation rates are due to their overall lower earnings and/or lower rates of full-time work relative to men.

Individuals working for large employers are more likely to participate in an employment-based retirement plan than are individuals who work for a small employer. For example, 51.9 percent of employees working for employers with 1,000 or more employees participated in a retirement plan in 2010, compared to 43.6 percent of employees working for employers with 100–499 employees and 11.5 percent of employees working for an employer with fewer than 10 employees.

Individuals who work full-time are more likely to participate in a retirement plan than are individuals who work part-time. For example, 51.5 percent of full-time, full-year workers participated in a retirement plan, compared to 17.8 percent of part-time, full-year workers and only 8.8 percent of part-time, part-year workers.

Older workers are more likely to participate in a retirement plan than are younger workers. For example, 48.8 percent of workers between 45 and 54 participated in a retirement plan in 2010, compared to 16.9 percent of workers between 21 and 24.

Finally, employees in some industries are more likely to participate in a retirement plan than are employees in other industries. For example, among full-time, full-year workers 81.8 percent of workers employed in the public sector participated in a retirement plan in 2010, compared to only 48.8 percent of workers in the private sector. Among private sector workers, participation rates were higher in manufacturing (52.5 percent) and transportation, utilities, information, and financial (47.1 percent), and professional services (38.7 percent) than wholesale and retail trade (30.3 percent), agriculture, mining, and construction (23.1 percent) and other services (14.5 percent).

(All of the statistics in this section are drawn from Craig Copeland, *Employment-Based Retirement Plan Participation: Geographic Differences and Trends, 2010*, EMPLOYEE BENEFIT RESEARCH INSTITUTE Issue Brief No. 363 (Nov. 2011).)

E. WHY DO EMPLOYERS OFFER RETIREMENT BENEFITS?

For over one hundred years, employers have either initiated or accepted pension plans. They do so for many reasons. This section explores those reasons.

[1] Federal Income Tax Advantages

First and foremost, by offering a pension plan, an employer can take advantage of federal tax law, which grants significant tax advantages to retirement plans that meet the complex federal statutory requirements. As noted at the beginning of this chapter, the net exclusion of pension contributions and earnings for employer plans represents the second largest federal tax expenditure, and is estimated to be $515.4 billion between 2010 and 2014.

There are four basic tax advantages for "qualified" retirement plans. First, the employer may deduct contributions to the pension plan at the time they are made, regardless of when the participants include the benefits in income. IRC § 404. Second, even though the employer can deduct contributions to the pension plan in the year made, employees participating in the plans do not include the pension benefits in income until the benefits are actually distributed to them. IRC § 402(a)(1). Third, earnings on the contributions held by the pension plan are exempt from income taxation. IRC § 501(a). Finally, a participant who receives a lump-sum distribution from the plan can elect to roll the proceeds into an individual retirement account or another qualified plan without incurring any income tax and continue to defer taxation until the proceeds are distributed from the individual retirement account or the new qualified plan. IRC § 402(c).

The manner in which the federal tax rules interact with pension plans are discussed in more detail throughout this book.

[2] Reducing Employee Turnover

Employers often favor retirement plans because such plans can help reduce employee turnover, which spares the employer the cost of recruiting and training new employees and protects the employer's investment in employee training and education. Retirement plans also encourage long-term employees who are more productive because they have mastered the skills needed to perform their jobs.

Retirement plans can reduce employee turnover in several ways. First, retirement plans can reduce employee turnover by requiring that employees work for an employer for a minimum number of years, for example, 30 years, or by requiring that employees work for the employer until reaching a minimum age, such as 65, or both, before employees are eligible for a retirement benefit. Such requirements were common before the enactment of ERISA, but ERISA added vesting and participation rules (discussed in detail in Chapter 4), which strictly limit employers' ability to bind employees by imposing long participation and vesting requirements.

Second, some types of retirement plans can be designed to "backload" benefits; that is, the value of the retirement benefits increases significantly the longer the employee remains with the employer. For example, Fred, who worked for Gamma Co. for 10 years, receives a pension of $5,000 a year, while Faith, who worked for Gamma for twice as long, 20 years, receives a pension of $15,000 a year, triple the value of Fred's pension. While some retirement plans are inherently backloaded, both ERISA and the Internal Revenue Code limit the degree to which employers can backload retirement benefits.

[3] Encouraging Older Employees to Retire

"One of the earliest and principal purposes of employers in adopting pension plans was to promote economy and efficiency by replacing older employees with younger, more energetic and alert employees." (MERTON C. BERNSTEIN, THE FUTURE OF PRIVATE PENSIONS 10 (1964).) As employees age, they may become less productive. At some age, depending on the job requirements, almost everyone is less productive. Moreover, because of the custom of increasing wages along with job seniority and age, older employees are usually paid more even if their level of productivity does not justify it. When older employees retire, the employer can often replace them with younger workers who are as productive, but are paid lower salaries.

To avoid a homogenous workforce, some employers prefer a periodic influx of new employees, which may not be possible unless some of the older ones retire. With the passage in 1967 of the federal Age Discrimination in Employment Act and subsequent amendments, employers are largely prohibited from terminating employees merely because of age. Because individually evaluating older employees and discharging those who do not measure up can be very destructive to employee morale, employers often prefer the carrot of a pension plan that encourages voluntary retirement.

Just as retirement plans typically encourage employees to remain with their employers, they often encourage employees to leave when they reach normal retirement age. Plans may require employees to terminate service with the employer in order to receive retirement benefits. If the employee continues to work for the employer, the value of the employee's compensation is reduced by the foregone retirement benefit. For example, Gordon has reached age 65, at which time his retirement plan will pay him $15,000 a year if he terminates service with the employer. If Gordon continues at his job, he will be paid $28,000 a year. However, since Gordon could collect $15,000 a year if he quits, if he continues to work for his employer he is effectively working for $13,000 ($28,000–$15,000). Faced with such a choice, most workers elect to retire and claim their retirement benefits.

Retirement plans also help employers to predict when older employees are likely to retire, and so enable them to plan for hiring and training of replacement employees. A large manufacturer, for example, can estimate very accurately when the workers on the assembly line will retire — at the earliest date that they qualify for their pension being the usual answer. Absent the inducement of a retirement plan, the employer would be faced with a random and unpredictable pattern of retirement by older workers.

F. WHY DO EMPLOYEES VALUE PENSIONS?

Most employees value their pensions, although not all do, and certainly the degree to which they value their pensions varies considerably. How an employer chooses between paying current wages or a deferred pension is determined by balancing the desires of the employer with what may be inchoate and misinformed desires of the employee.

PETER M. VAN ZANTE, MANDATED VESTING: SUPPRESSION OF VOLUNTARY RETIREMENT BENEFITS

75 Notre Dame L. Rev. 125, 132–33 (1999)

The formality of the employer's apparently unilateral control over the retirement plan obscures a more important reality: a retirement plan reflects the preferences and choices of the employees who participate in the plan. The plan is one component of the entire relationship between an employer and its employees, and retirement benefits are but one form among the many in which compensation may be paid to employees. Wages typically comprise the largest portion of employees' compensation packages, but those packages usually include several types of in-kind compensation. When an employee earns rights, whether vested or unvested, to (perhaps) receive retirement benefits in the future, the employee has received in-kind compensation. The total cost of employees' compensation packages, including wages and fringe benefits, is limited by an employer's compensation budget. When employees receive compensation in the form of retirement benefits, they will necessarily receive lesser amounts of other forms of compensation.

An employer will create a plan to provide retirement benefits, and employees will receive compensation in that form when the employees participating in the plan prefer retirement benefits to other forms of compensation. Different employees will have different preferences about retirement benefits as a form of compensation. A sponsoring employer aims to provide that level and structure of retirement benefits that its workforce values most highly. An employer does not gratuitously provide retirement benefits to its employees, nor can it unilaterally dictate the portion of employees' compensation that will be received in the form of retirement benefits. Instead, a retirement plan is a device by which both the employer and employees can realize additional value from the resources available to compensate employees. From this perspective, it can be seen that a particular retirement plan structure reflects the compensation preferences of the employer's workforce. While as a matter of form, the sponsoring employer seems to control a retirement plan, in substance, the employer must satisfy the preferences of its workforce by providing that level and structure of retirement benefits that its workforce values most highly.

Professor Van Zante points out that different employees place different values upon a pension. Some of the causes of those differences are the relative financial sophistication of the employees, their ability to empathize with their older selves, and whether they have other sources of retirement income such as a working spouse or an expected inheritance. There are a variety of reasons how and why employees value a pension, although it must be noted that many employees give little or no thought to their pension, and merely accept it as a given.

1-2 QUESTIONS AND PROBLEMS

Jen, age 26, has just graduated from Wise University Business School. She has job offers from two companies for similar jobs. Acme Co. offers to pay her $56,000 a year and no benefits. Beta Co. will pay $50,000 a year plus each year put an amount equal to 10 percent of Jen's salary into a qualified, tax exempt pension plan. When she retires at age 65, the accumulated pension fund will be paid to Jen as an annuity. However, she must work at least four years for Beta or forfeit the plan. If she leaves after four years, but before age 65, the Beta pension plan will hold the money, invest it, and then provide Jen with an annuity at age 65.

Jen asks you to advise her as to whether to take the Acme or Beta offer. She reminds you that she has $20,000 of student loans, owes $10,000 on her car, a year old Jetta, and has a $1,500 balance due on her credit card. What advice would you give Jen?

[1] Belief that the Pension Does Not Displace Wages

Some employees may not realize that a pension is merely deferred wages and so not recognize the trade-off between current income and retirement income. They may not perceive that the pension depresses their current wage income because they think of a pension as an add-on or extra benefit, rather than the transformation of cash wages into the in-kind benefit of forced savings. An employer who pays an employee $30,000 and contributes another $2,000 into a pension fund for that employee's retirement benefit knows that the employee costs the employer $32,000. From the employer's perspective, the total cost of $32,000 is a given. The issue is how to divide that $32,000 between current wages and retirement benefits in light of the fact that the retirement benefits help insure that the employee will remain with the employer. If the employer concludes that the value of loyal employees is not worth the trouble of operating a pension plan or that the employee places little value on retirement benefits, the employer will reduce or eliminate the retirement benefits and simply pay the employee the $32,000. The employee, however, may believe that his or her pay is $30,000 with the retirement benefits an extra benefit, but one of uncertain value, since the employee is unlikely to consider $2,000 put in a pension trust that is not payable for many years to be equal in value to an immediate extra $2,000 in cash.

Employees who are represented by unions in collective bargaining may be more cognizant of the trade-off between current income and greater fringe benefits including retirement benefits. Even though they are quite aware that pensions depress current wages, unions have been the leaders in demanding pension benefits for their members. Though the individual union member may be uncertain as to how benefits displace higher wages, the union bargaining agent is quite likely keenly aware of the present discounted value of retirement benefits when the union and the employer negotiate a contract.

[2] Desire for Forced Savings

Pensions are a form of forced savings. The employee gives up current income that could either be consumed or saved in favor of a pension, which is of course a form of non-electable savings. Individuals save either to create capital or to set aside wealth for later consumption. To illustrate: Hajib saves $200 a month with the goal of saving $10,000 with which he plans to buy a lemonade stand that he will operate on weekends. Hajib is saving to accumulate capital. Iris saves $500 a month to amass $10,000 to buy a car. For Iris, saving is merely deferred consumption. Both Hajib and Iris invest $350 in the stock market each month hoping to accumulate $100,000 to help finance their retirements. They are saving the $350 to accumulate capital that will create income to replace the loss of wage income upon retirement. They also expect to spend some or all of that $100,000 during their retirement years. To the extent that they do, the savings of $350 a month is a form of deferred consumption.

While employees know that they need to save both to create wealth to be used for deferred consumption and to accumulate capital to provide for their retirement, most find it very difficult to do so. America is a consumer society. Bathed in advertising, lured by installment credit, tempted by ever new products and seduced by the status of spending, employees quite naturally find it difficult to save for their old age. Even if they do manage to save for retirement, their plans could be upset by unexpected expenses, divorce, or even by a lawsuit.

Even if an employee can resist the enticement of current consumption, he or she is likely to save less than is needed to provide for a comfortable retirement. Some give up when they realize just what percent of their income they must set aside. Others assume that they can save less when young because they somehow will be able to accumulate enough when they are older. Most underestimate how much income they will need when retired or overestimate how much they will receive from Social Security.

1-3 QUESTIONS AND PROBLEMS

Jeff, age 30, earns $30,000 a year. He has no pension plan. He wants to retire when he is age 60 with an annual retirement income of $24,000. Ignoring any possible Social Security retirement benefits and inflation, how can Jeff determine how much he should save each month until he is age 60 to assure a lifetime monthly income of $2,000?

[3] Advantage of Professional Management of Pensions

A major source of the wealth of pension funds arises from the success the fund has in investing the pension assets. Professional financial advisors often advise the plan management (trustees) on how best to invest the plan assets, how to balance risk and possible return on the investment. Most large pension funds hold a mix of equity (stocks) and debt (bonds), while some pension funds invest in real estate or other property and debt instruments, such as mortgages. Many employees are happy to leave the investment decisions to the experts who have the training and the time to make wise choices. Also, because the pension fund often owns assets of significant value, it can lower investment risk by diversification to a degree that would be less feasible for an individual investor with fewer dollars to invest. The pension fund also profits from economies of scale as it invests and manages the funds and so has lower investment costs than the individual investor. The fund may also have investment opportunities such as buying stock at an initial stock offering that normally are not available to the individual investor.

[4] Preference for Self-Directed Retirement Accounts

Many employees participate in 401(k) retirement accounts that permit the employee to direct how the account will be invested subject to certain choices offered by the plan. Increasingly, employees believe that they are capable of handling how their retirement fund is invested and, in fact, many enjoy the challenge. They feel confident that they can craft an investment plan that best meets their needs and tolerance for risk. Whether that confidence is well-placed is not always clear, but still, many employees would rather be the master of the investment fate of their retirement account.

[5] Tax Advantages

The tax advantages of qualified pension plans are probably the single greatest advantage for the employee. That advantage, however, can be recreated outside of a pension plan by granting immediate tax deductions for employee retirement savings accounts and by exempting the earnings of the retirement saving account from taxation until they are distributed. These tax advantages do exist in the form of Individual Retirement Accounts (IRAs), which come in several different forms, but the annual limits on contributions to an IRA are typically much lower than those for an employer-sponsored plan, and many higher income employees with pension plans are not eligible for the tax advantages offered by these accounts. Interestingly, the existence of employer-provided pensions does not seem to have discouraged individuals from saving for retirement on their own without the tax subsidy enjoyed by qualified pension plans. In fact, the mere existence of a pension apparently alerts the employee to the need to save for retirement and so actually encourages more savings for retirement.

G. INTRODUCTION TO WELFARE BENEFITS

In addition to retirement benefits, many employers offer other benefits to employees and their dependents as a form of supplemental compensation. Typically, employers offer benefits such as health care, disability, and life insurance to their active employees. A few offer similar benefits to retired employees. These benefits, known as "welfare benefits," may include any of a host of benefits ranging from health, accident and disability benefits, to life insurance, vacation pay, prepaid legal services, severance pay, day care centers, and scholarship funds. *See* ERISA § 3(1).

Most workers view their health benefits as their most important benefit. According to data from 2007, 75 percent of workers considered their health benefits their most important non-cash compensatory benefit. Retirement benefits were ranked next, with life insurance, long-term care insurance, disability insurance, and stock options ranking far behind health and retirement benefits in importance. Because of the importance of health benefits, this section will focus principally on health benefits.

[1] Health Benefits

In 2010, 59 percent of U.S. workers participated in an employer-provided health care benefit plan. In addition, 21 percent of the nonelderly American population had health insurance through the government, and 7 percent of the nonelderly population was covered by an insurance policy purchased directly from an insurer.

DAYNA BOWEN MATTHEW, CONTROLLING THE REVERSE AGENCY COSTS OF EMPLOYMENT-BASED HEALTH INSURANCE: OF MARKETS, COURTS AND A REGULATORY QUAGMIRE

31 Wake Forest L. Rev. 1037, 1041–43 (1996)

Employment-based health insurance is a relatively recent innovation; it is one that developed, arguably, quite by accident . . . . In a real sense, World War II was responsible for the expansion of employer-based health insurance in this country.

The Second World War brought both prosperity and a large military population conditioned to receive government-issued health insurance. When the armed forces returned to civilian life, they sought a similar arrangement. More important, the

Office of Price Administration froze wages in an effort to stabilize the economy, but the War Labor Board permitted fringe benefits to continue to expand in lieu of wages . . . . The popularity of employer-based plans exploded as employers, facing tax rates as high as 85% during the Second World War, were able to spend fifteen cents on each after-tax dollar in order to offer health benefits. These benefits were considered by the IRS to be "in kind" compensation, deductible as a business expense and excluded from employees' taxable income . . . .

There is no statutory mandate requiring that employers must provide health insurance for their employees. It is a voluntary system. Nonetheless, dependency upon the employer agency model appears to be an immutable fixture on the landscape of health insurance coverage and reform in this country. It is an arrangement supported and encouraged by lucrative tax subsidies, allowing the exclusion of health insurance benefits received from employees' taxable income, as well as from the tax base for Social Security and other payroll taxes. Also, employers may deduct the cost of health insurance premiums paid on behalf of employees as a business expense.

As noted above, 59 percent of the American population has employer-sponsored health insurance. Just as participation in an employer-sponsored retirement plan is not divided evenly across the population, participation in an employer-sponsored health care plan is not evenly divided across the population. Rather, participation depends on factors such as the size of the employer, the industry, the employee's wages, job status (full-time or part-time), tenure, gender, and race.

Individuals who work for a large employer are more likely to have employer-sponsored health insurance through their job than are individuals who work for a smaller employer. For example, in 2010 only 25 percent of individuals who worked for firms with 10 or fewer employees had health insurance through their employer, compared to 63 percent of individuals working for employers with 1,000 or more employees.

Workers in certain industries, such as the public sector, manufacturing and professional services, are more likely to have employer-sponsored health insurance through their job than are workers in other industries, such as agriculture, arts, entertainment, recreation, accommodation, and food service. For example, 72 percent of full-time workers in the public sector workers have employer-based health insurance through their job compared to 51 percent in the private sector. Within the private sector, 66 percent of full-time workers in finance, insurance, real estate, and rental leasing have such insurance compared to 70 percent in manufacturing, 76 percent in mining, 25 percent in arts, entertainment, recreation, accommodation, and food service, and 24 percent in agriculture.

Individuals who work full-time are much more likely to have employer-sponsored health insurance through their job than are individuals who work part-time. For example, in 2009 only 30 percent of part-time public sector employees had employer-sponsored health insurance through their job, compared to 80 percent of full-time public sector employees, and 17 percent of part-time private sector employees had employer-sponsored health insurance compared to 60 percent of full-time private sector employees.

(All of the statistics in this section refer to the year 2009 and are drawn from Chapter 27 of the EBRI Databook on Employee Benefits.)

1-4 QUESTIONS AND PROBLEMS

1. How do the participation rates for employer-sponsored health insurance compare to those for employer-sponsored retirement benefits?

2. Why do you think some employees, such as higher-income workers and full-time workers, are more likely to have employer-sponsored health insurance through their job than are other employees?

The American system of employment-based health care benefits has both advantages and disadvantages. The following excerpt discusses those advantages and disadvantages.

KATHRYN L. MOORE, THE FUTURE OF EMPLOYMENT-BASED HEALTH INSURANCE AFTER THE PATIENT PROTECTION AND AFFORDABLE CARE ACT

89 NEB. L. REV. 885, 893-899 (2011)

A. Favorable Tax Treatment

One of the principal advantages of employment-based health insurance is that, as discussed above, employment-based health insurance is eligible for favorable tax treatment. The value of the tax exemption to an individual worker depends on the worker's marginal tax rate, with the exemption being more valuable to a higher-income worker with a higher marginal tax rate than to a lower-income worker with a lower marginal tax rate. There is general agreement that this favorable tax treatment encourages employers to offer health insurance, but economists disagree as to how significant a role tax treatment plays in employers' decisions to offer employment-based health insurance.

The tax preference accorded employment-based health insurance has been subject to a great deal of criticism. Critics contend that it is inequitable because (1) individuals who do not have employment-based health insurance do not benefit from the tax exclusion, and (2) the tax subsidy is more valuable for higher-income workers than it is for lower-income workers. In addition, critics contend that the tax subsidy creates an incentive to purchase too much insurance, which distorts the health services market, causes inefficient allocation of scarce resources, and increases health care costs.

B. Cost

A second advantage of employment-based health insurance is that it is typically much less expensive than health insurance individual workers can purchase on the private market. This lower cost can be attributed to three separate factors. First, administrative costs are typically much lower for employment-based insurance than for individual insurance. According to David Hyman and Mark Hall, the largest employer groups typically have administrative costs of 5 percent or less, while the administrative costs for smaller groups may reach about 20 percent, and the administrative costs for individual purchasers may exceed 30 percent. Second, through "pooling," employment-based health insurance avoids, or at least reduces, the problem of adverse selection. Third, workers tend to be healthier, on average, than non-workers, and thus the cost of insuring them tends to be lower.

Relative to private, individual health insurance, the administrative costs and limited coverage of employment-based health insurance may be viewed as advantages because they reduce the cost of employment-based insurance. Proponents of universal health care, on the other hand, view the administrative costs and limited coverage as disadvantages of employment-based health insurance. For example, Ewe Reinhardt has noted that the administrative costs under the American health care system were $360 higher per capita than under the German health care system. Alain Enthoven and Victor Fuchs, strong proponents of a universal health care system, contend that under the voluntary employment-based system, "[t]he need for more than 850 health insurance companies to sell and contract with millions of employers underwriting each one, adds greatly to administrative costs." Enthoven and Fuchs assert that typical administrative costs under the voluntary employment-based system are about 11 percent compared to costs of 0.5 percent for the California's Public Employees Retirement System's (CalPERS) coverage of 400,000 employees and dependents through its single annual contract with Kaiser Permanente.

Ethicists contend that health care is a fundamental public good that should not depend on a voluntary system. By its very nature, voluntary employment-based health insurance cannot and does not cover the entire working population, let alone the entire U.S. population. For example, lower-income workers are less likely to have employment-based health insurance than are higher-income workers, and individuals who work for small employers are less likely to have employment-based health insurance than are individuals employed by large firms. In addition, workers in certain industries, such as manufacturing, professional services, and the public sector, are more likely to have health insurance than are workers in other industries, such as agriculture, food services, and entertainment. Indeed, under the country's voluntary employment-based health insurance system, almost 19 percent of the U.S. population under the age of 65 was uninsured in 2008. According to proponents of universal health care, this is a fundamental failure of voluntary employment-based health insurance.

C. The Employer as Agent for Its Employees

A third advantage of employment-based health insurance, from the standpoint of employees, is that employers, acting as agents for their employees, can help employees avoid transaction costs in the selection of their health insurance. Shopping for individual health insurance can be time consuming because employees may be required to assess and compare the benefits of many different plans. Employers assist employees by offering employees a limited choice among plans. In addition, employers, acting as agents for their employees, can aggressively bargain for discounts for their employees, effectively advocate for employees in the case of coverage disputes, and generally obtain more valuable coverage for the same money than employees could on their own.

In a focus group study of large employers in Pittsburgh and Cleveland, four researchers found that employers generally do a good job as agents for their employees in the health insurance market. For these purposes, an employer was considered to be a good agent if (1) the employer understood its employees' health plan preferences, (2) the employer incorporated its employees' preferences into its health plan designs, and (3) employees valued their employer's role as an agent in purchasing health insurance benefits.

On the other hand, the fact that employers act as agents for their employees is sometimes viewed as a fault of employment-based health insurance. According to

David Hyman and Mark Hall, staunch supporters of employment-based health insurance, most of the problems associated employment-based health insurance arise, at least in theory, from the fact that employers rather than employees — the ultimate consumers of health care — are responsible for making most of the decisions with respect to coverage and cost. The fear is that employers, particularly in a weak economy, may be more motivated by cost considerations than employees' wishes in negotiating health care contracts. Indeed, a few critics contend that agency cost problems are a significant cause of the health care crisis. Specifically, they contend that incentives under the voluntary employment-based system create a zero sum game where employers and insurers lose when employees are granted benefits.

D. Labor Incentives

A fourth potential advantage of employment-based health insurance is that it may help employers attract and retain high-quality workers. To the extent that workers value employment-based health insurance, they may be better, more productive, and more loyal employees. Indeed, employers report that they believe that offering health insurance has a positive impact on the overall success of their business.

Whether employment-based health insurance leads to a better, more productive workforce and has a positive impact on the employer's bottom line is subject to debate. In 2000, Thomas Buchmueller reviewed the existing literature and concluded that there was little evidence that employment-based health insurance dramatically increases worker productivity or reduces workers' compensation costs and employee absenteeism. On the other hand, Ellen O'Brien reviewed the literature and found some support for the proposition that offering health insurance results in gains in worker quality and productivity. Nevertheless, O'Brien recognized that there are substantial gaps in the research and contended that economists should make more of an effort to assess the relationship between health insurance coverage and its effect on overall business success.

1-5 QUESTIONS AND PROBLEMS

Kareem, a 45-year old employee, is married with two teenaged children. Assume that Kareem is taxed at a marginal rate of 25 percent and that his employer pays $10,000 a year in premiums for medical insurance for Kareem and his two children. If his employer discontinued paying the premiums, how much would Kareem's wages have to be increased so that he could purchase the same level of coverage without any loss of disposable income?

[2] Life Insurance

Although health care benefits are the most popular employee benefit, employers often provide other significant benefits. For example, more than 50 percent of employers offer life insurance to their full-time employees. The most common plans are group life insurance plans that make lump-sum payments to whomever the employee designates as beneficiary. Less frequently, employers provide survivor income plans, which pay regular, usually monthly, income benefits for a specified period of time to an employee-identified survivor. These benefits are in addition to any rights that the survivors of the deceased employee might have under the employer's pension plan.

Usually the employer contracts with an insurance company for group-term life insurance, which is less expensive than an individually purchased policy. Typically the employer pays the premiums, but under some plans the employee pays a portion or all of the premium. Term insurance means that coverage is bought for a designated period of time, most often a year, is renewable up to a certain age, and remains in effect only so long as the premiums are paid. Usually the life insurance for the employee is terminated if the employee quits or when the employee retires. Unlike whole life insurance, term insurance has no cash surrender value as it is pure insurance and, unlike whole life, has no savings component. It pays only upon the death of the insured during the period of the payment of the premiums.

The cost of group-term life insurance depends on the risk factors, i.e. the morbidity rate of the covered group. For small groups, the insurer will use a standard rate table, but for larger groups the insurer will set the rate based upon the death rate (claims experience) of the group. For employers with a great many employees, the insurer will attempt to segregate the employees into smaller groups with more homogeneous morbidity rates. In this way the insurer can best calibrate the rates to insure that the premiums are sufficient to pay the claims, cover administrative expenses and return a profit to the insurance company. For the employer, however, the smaller groups may mean that the cost of insuring some employees who have higher death rates may be prohibitive.

The amount of insurance per employee will either be a flat sum, such as $25,000 per employee, or some percentage of the employee's compensation, e.g. 50 percent of employee's pay for the year. The latter is popular as a way of using insurance as temporary replacement for the loss of income.

The premiums paid by the employer are tax deductible, but are not income to the employees for a death benefit of up to $50,000. (IRC § 79.) If the death benefit exceeds $50,000, the employee is taxed on cost of the premiums for the excess benefit. The death benefit that is paid to the beneficiary is not income. (IRC § 101.) To qualify for the income tax advantages, the group-term life insurance must not discriminate in favor of key employees.

H. HISTORY AND PURPOSES OF ERISA

Pension and welfare plans are regulated by the federal Employee Retirement Income Security Act ("ERISA"), which was signed into law by President Ford on September 2, 1974, and has been significantly amended over the years. ERISA states that it exists for the purposes of "assuring the equitable character of [employee benefit] plans and their financial soundness." ERISA § 2(a). ERISA attempts to do so by a complex statutory scheme that, among other things, sets forth detailed eligibility, benefit, and distribution rules. ERISA is enforced by the Department of Labor, the Internal Revenue Service, the Pension Benefit Guaranty Corporation, and by individual litigants.

DAVID GREGORY, THE SCOPE OF ERISA PREEMPTION OF STATE LAW: A STUDY IN EFFECTIVE FEDERALISM

48 U. Pitt. L. Rev. 427, 443–448 (1987)

ERISA's Formation, Legislative History, and Congressional Intent

Throughout the 1960's, pension plan abuses increased dramatically. Existing regulations proved dysfunctional and unable to protect pension rights. Case law and common law were not effective remedial or enforcement instruments.

Congress was faced with the compelling need to provide an effective national solution for this pressing national problem. On March 28, 1962, President Kennedy created a cabinet-level presidential task force to study the national pension problem. Although no remedial legislation was immediately forthcoming, in January, 1965 the Committee on Corporate Pension Funds and Other Private Retirement and Welfare Programs recommended federal legislation to require and to safeguard realistic vesting standards and to enunciate fiduciary responsibilities to protect plan beneficiaries.

Approximately thirty million persons in the private sector, both unionized and non-unionized employees, were subject to pension plans in 1970. An additional eleven million public sector employees in state, local, and federal governments were covered by pensions. Still, however, less than half the national workforce was covered by pension plans less than two decades ago. Adverse experiences were demonstrating that pension plan coverage was no guarantee that pension benefits would actually ever be paid. Vesting provisions, for example, were often harsh and incapable of attainment. Employees' breaks in service or employees' lengthy service terminated only days before the normal retirement age usually precluded pension vesting. Employees' forfeited funds reverted to the pension plans, which continued to amass staggering amounts of capital with distressingly few proportionate payouts. Business terminations, employers' temporary reductions in force, layoffs, and bankruptcies also wreaked havoc with pension rights. To compound this bleak situation, many pensions were inadequately funded and not invested in diversified markets. In the early 1970's, the stock market plummeted. Correspondingly, pension funds were seriously debilitated. Less than half of the national work force ever received the benefits to which they were entitled.

In 1967, Senator Javits of New York introduced a comprehensive private pension reform bill. Other bills soon followed from a variety of congressional sponsors. Congressional emphasis on the need for comprehensive pension plan reform grew throughout the decade. These efforts culminated in the Employee Retirement Income Security Act of 1974 (ERISA).

ERISA provides adequate statutory mechanisms to effectuate congressional policies. The law federalizes pension law and grounds primary regulatory and enforcement responsibilities in the federal government, no longer leaving it to the private parties or to happenstance state regulation. Congress' major concerns in passing ERISA were to set forth realistic vesting provisions based on employee age and length of service, to strengthen fiduciary duties, to mandate minimum funding requirements and pension plan insurance, and to provide effective remedies in the event of statutory violations.

Interestingly, ERISA does not compel employers to provide pension plans to employees. Congress chose to maintain a voluntary, essentially private pension regime, eschewing government imposition of mandatory pensions. Congress sought to encourage pension plan development. However, wherever pension plans are made available by employers, ERISA has done a reasonably good job of safeguarding employee pension rights and of guaranteeing that employees receive the pension benefits to which they are entitled in a timely fashion. ERISA also established the Pension Benefit Guaranty Corporation (PBGC) within the Department of Labor to guarantee payment of pension benefits for vested employees of defunct employers. Detailed reporting and disclosure requirements are imposed on ERISA fiduciaries. The PBGC and the Departments of Labor and Treasury share responsibilities for monitoring fiduciary compliance with ERISA.

What did the proponents of the ERISA legislation hope to accomplish?

SENATE REPORT NO. 127

93d Congress, 1st Session 13 (1973)

[E]xpeditious enactment of S. 4 will institute a program which will achieve a strengthening of the role played by private retirement plans within the fabric of our economic and social structures. Its most important purpose will be to assure American workers that they may look forward with anticipation to a retirement with financial security and dignity, and without fear that this period of life will be lacking in the necessities to sustain them as human beings within our society. The enactment of progressive and effective pension legislation is also certain to increase stability within the framework of our nation's economy, since the tremendous resources and assets of the private pension plan system are an integral part of our economy. It will also serve to restore credibility and faith in the private pension plans designed for American working men and women, and this should serve to encourage rather than diminish efforts by management and industry to expand pension plan coverage and to improve benefits for workers.

The voluntary nature of pension and welfare plans cannot be over emphasized. No private employer is required to offer a pension or welfare benefit plan. (But if an employer adopts an employee benefit plan, it will be subject to ERISA's regulatory requirements.) While ERISA certainly protects employees, it also deters some employers from offering employee benefit plans, particularly pension plans, because employers do not want to become ensnared in the world of pension regulation. It is unclear, however, how many more employers would offer pension plans if ERISA did not exist. Competitive labor markets may require even the most regulation-averse employer to offer retirement benefits. Nevertheless, ERISA, together with the IRC, have certainly affected the type of pensions employers offer, which employees receive pension benefits, and the amount, type and timing of such benefits.

MARK J. ROE, THE MODERN CORPORATION AND PRIVATE PENSIONS

41 UCLA L. Rev. 75, 82–83 (1993)

ERISA responded to two public interest problems: unfunded pensions and unvested pensions. Unfunded unvested pensions left some workers without security for their old age. Many plans had no vesting until retirement, creating insecurity: Lose your job and you lose the pension. The General Motors plan — a prototype for others — had ten year "cliff" vesting: nothing unless the employee worked ten years for GM. Cliff vesting made workers overly dependent on the firm in the few years before vesting; if they quit or were fired, they lost the pension. Half of the employees covered by plans never got a pension because they never vested. Even if the employee vested, if the firm disappeared, so might the pension if the firm's obligations were unfunded. Although most pensions were funded — money was set aside to pay the pension, due largely to pre-ERISA tax rules — some were not. Employees counted on having their pensions when they retired. They presumably lacked the skills to negotiate details about funding or financial guarantees.

ERISA was the solution to these perceived public interest problems. To get a tax deduction, the firm had to shorten the cliff or vest employees in steps, so that dismissal or quitting would not lead to total loss of the pension. To deal with the risk of employees losing their unfunded pension if the firm went bankrupt, ERISA required funding of normal expected costs with minimal funding standards and set up an insurance fund, to pay workers with unfunded pensions from bankrupt companies.

Prior to the enactment of ERISA, if the employer's enterprise failed, the workers could only hope that the pension plan had sufficient assets to meet all of its obligations. For example, in 1963 when the automobile manufacturer, Studebaker, closed its South Bend, Indiana plant, several thousand employees who had been promised a pension learned that the company could not afford to pay all of the promised benefits. In the end, only about a third of the employees, those age 60 or older, received full benefits. Many younger employees lost all their promised retirement benefits. (For a fuller discussion of the galvanizing effect of the Studebaker collapse for pension reform, *see* James A. Wooten, *"The Most Glorious Story of Failure in the Business": The Studebaker-Packard Corporation and the Origins of ERISA*, 49 Buffalo L. Rev. 683 (2001).)

ERISA attempts to protect employees against the loss of a pension due to the employer's economic misfortune by imposing minimum funding requirements that are designed to keep the pension fund fiscally solvent, i.e. able to pay the contracted pension obligations, and by the creation of the Pension Benefit Guaranty Corporation (PBGC). Certain pension plans are required to pay premiums to the PBGC, which guarantees at least nominal benefits for plan participants in the event the plan is unable to pay the promised retirement benefits.

I. WHAT IS ERISA?

[1] ERISA Coverage

The Employee Retirement Insurance Security Act, ERISA, was enacted in 1974. Though it has been amended many times in the following years, the basic structure remains intact. The statute contains four titles:

Title I	Protection of Employee Benefit Rights
Title II	Amendments to the Internal Revenue Code Relating to Retirement Plans
Title III	Jurisdiction and Miscellaneous Issues
Title IV	Plan Termination Insurance

With the exception of Title II, ERISA is codified in 29 U.S.C. § 1001 *et seq.* For example, definitions of the terms used in the statute are found in ERISA § 3 or 29 U.S.C. § 1002. Title II of ERISA is found in the Internal Revenue Code (IRC). When courts cite to the non-tax sections of ERISA, they often, but not always, use the ERISA section number reference rather than U.S.C. section. Commentators almost always cite to the ERISA reference. In this book, references are to ERISA rather than to the U.S.C., and cases and other sources have been edited to refer to ERISA section numbers.

Title I of ERISA, commonly referred to as the labor title, is enforced by the Secretary of Labor by way of the Department of Labor (DOL) and, more importantly, by private rights of action by plan participants and beneficiaries as well as plans. Title II, which contains the tax aspects, is enforced by the Secretary of the Treasury through the Internal Revenue Service (IRS). The plan termination insurance created by Title IV is operated by the Pension Benefit Guaranty Corporation (PBGC).

The IRS enforces the tax provisions that decide whether a plan is "qualified" and thus eligible to enjoy the considerable tax advantages afforded to pension plans. The IRC also has many sections that significantly overlap sections of Title I, such as funding requirements and vesting terms. The result is that the DOL and the IRS have concurrent jurisdiction over some aspects of ERISA enforcement. In such cases, the IRS has jurisdiction unless the matter involves an area traditionally within the purview of the DOL. (For a fuller discussion of the interplay of ERISA, the IRC, and the respective responsibilities of the DOLs and the IRS, *see* Russell Osgood, *Qualified Pension and Profit-Sharing Plan Vesting: Revolution Not Reform*, 59 Boston U. L. Rev. 452 n.2 (1979).)

PATRICIA E. DILLEY, HIDDEN IN PLAIN VIEW: THE PENSION SHIELD AGAINST CREDITORS

74 Ind. L.J. 355, 376–379 (1999)

There seems to be a substantial and persistent level of confusion, at least among commentators in the bankruptcy literature, about the relationship between ERISA and the provisions of the IRC governing employee benefit plans. This situation was probably created by the duplication of existing and amended IRC provisions in Title II of ERISA when the latter was enacted in 1974. Many of these IRC provisions had already been in existence for thirty to fifty years by then, having established the tax treatment for qualified pension plans dealing with employee benefits and pensions as early as 1921. Notwithstanding the close links between the pension provisions of the IRC and the pension regulatory provisions of Title I of ERISA, the tax provisions remain part of the IRC and the rest of ERISA is codified in the U.S. Code as part of the labor laws. Strictly speaking, there is no single statute that can be identified as "ERISA."

. . .

The Treasury established specific tax treatment for employee pensions and pension trusts very soon after enactment of the income tax in 1913, and preferential tax treatment for them has been a part of the IRC since the 1920s. Employers were not required to actually set aside funds to pay for promised pensions, or provide more than minimal pensions for all but the longest-tenured rank and file employees, until passage of ERISA in 1974.

As a result, the main purpose and function of ERISA was to enforce the pension promises that employers make to employees. In addition, ERISA was intended to limit the ability of employers to require extraordinarily long periods of service before an employee is entitled to benefits. The focus of Titles I, III, and IV of ERISA is on vesting requirements, disclosure of information to participants and employees, fiduciary responsibilities of plan administrators and sponsors, (including employee and Department of Labor rights to sue plan sponsors and fiduciaries), and funding requirements for defined benefit plans, including the mechanism and funding institution (the Pension Benefit Guaranty Corporation) to provide a federal system of insurance for underfunded pension plans.

ERISA also contained a tax title, Title II, which reproduced, amended, and expanded the provisions of the IRC dealing with tax qualification rules for qualified plans. However, those provisions remained part of and continue to be amended as part of the IRC and are not codified as part of ERISA. Moreover, ERISA applies to all employee benefit plans, including "welfare benefit plans," which provide fringe benefits such as health insurance and have either different or no qualification rules comparable to those applicable to pension plans. In addition, ERISA may apply to deferred compensation arrangements that do not qualify for special tax treatment under the IRC, with the result that the employer providing such a plan may be subject to reporting, disclosure and fiduciary duty rules without any tax benefit at all.

In short, ERISA is best understood as a body of law providing certain rights to beneficiaries and placing specific duties on sponsors and fiduciaries of employee benefit arrangements including, but not limited to, qualified plans under the IRC However, the favorable tax treatment of qualified plans, which is the entire point of qualification, depends solely on compliance with the relevant provisions of the IRC.

ERISA regulates both pension benefits (retirement benefits) and welfare benefits such as employee health insurance. An "employee pension benefit plan" is statutorily defined as "any plan, fund, or program which was . . . established or maintained . . . [that] (i) provides retirement income to employees or (ii) results in a deferral of income by employees for periods extending to the termination of covered employment or beyond." ERISA § 3(2)(A).

ERISA defines an "employee welfare benefit plan" as one that provides participants though the purchase of insurance or otherwise "medical, surgical, or hospital care or benefits, or benefits in the event of sickness, accident, disability, death or unemployment, or vacation benefits, apprenticeship or other training programs or day care centers, scholarship funds, or prepaid legal services." ERISA § 3(1)(A).

Pension and welfare benefits are two very different forms of employee benefits. Pensions are promises of benefits that will be paid in the future, possibly years hence. For the employee, the biggest worry about a pension is whether some event, such as being fired, can cause its loss and, when the employee finally retires, whether the pension fund will be able to pay the promised benefits. In contrast, most welfare benefits are identified with current employment and with events that might happen soon, even tomorrow. With welfare benefits, the employee wants to be sure that if something untoward should occur, he or she will be eligible for benefits. The employee is not so much worried about the ability of the employer or the employer's insurer to pay the benefit, but about the willingness of the employer or insurer to pay. Whether these two different forms of employee benefits should both be subject to ERISA governance, has been questioned by many. In particular, ERISA's regulation of employee medical benefit plans has caused considerable controversy.

[2] ERISA Covers Only Private Employer Plans

ERISA applies to any employee benefit plan established or maintained by any *private* employer. It does not apply to governmental plans, federal, state or local. ERISA § 4(b). Attempts to extend ERISA to governmental pensions have failed despite the great number of public pension plans and covered employees.

J. DOES ERISA GO FAR ENOUGH?

The enactment of ERISA signaled the nation's continuing reliance on regulated but voluntary pension plans. If an employer chooses to offer such benefits, it must adhere to the elaborate requirements of ERISA. Because ERISA is so complex, the cost to employers who operate pension plans is considerable. Employees are often clueless as to their pension rights, while the employer is equally at sea as to its responsibilities. In the face of the complex regulatory environment, many smaller employers have given up offering pensions.

The voluntary nature of employer pensions is almost taken for granted in this country, but that need not be the case. Employers are subject to many other requirements, such as a duty to recognize union representation of employees and collectively bargain with the union about wages and fringe benefits. Yet ERISA does not mandate that employers provide pension plans or require that they offer any particular level of benefits. Congress could mandate pensions, though such a requirement would raise significant regulatory problems, including extensive monitoring to insure that employers were meeting their responsibilities. Mandated pensions would also raise the cost of hiring employees, possibly lowering employment and encouraging demands for exemptions or federal subsidies for marginally profitable employers who might claim they could not afford the cost of the mandated pensions.

Of course, the nation does have a mandatory old age pension program, Social Security, which was created in 1935 during the Great Depression, in recognition that many elderly retired individuals were destitute or nearly so. At the time, state poorhouses and local or private relief efforts were totally inadequate to the need, and worse, they were demeaning and dispiriting. Social insurance in the form of Social Security was seen as the solution to elderly poverty, as well as providing an economic encouragement to retirement, thereby creating jobs for younger workers. Over the years Social Security became an almost universal program whose existence as a economic "safety net" has quelled any significant demand for mandated private pensions.

Although complicated, Social Security is based upon a few basic principles.

PROGRAM PRINCIPLES

54 SOCIAL SECURITY BULLETIN 9–10 (Sept. 1991)

Work related. Economic security for the worker and his or her family grows out of the individual's own work history. A worker's entitlement to benefits is based on past employment, and the amount of cash benefits the worker and his or her family will receive is related to earnings in covered work. In general, the higher the worker's average amount of taxable earnings, the greater the protection. [Ed. — Both benefits and payroll taxes are based on wages up to a maximum taxable wage base, adjusted annually for inflation. In 2012, the maximum taxable wage base is $110,100. In 2011 the average monthly benefit for a retired worker was $1,164, while the maximum monthly benefit for an individual retiring at the normal retirement age that year was $2,366. Social Security benefits are adjusted annually for inflation.]

No means test. Benefits are an insured worker's earned right and are paid regardless of income from savings, pensions, private insurance, or other forms of nonwork income. . . .

Contributory. The concept of an earned right is reinforced by the fact that workers pay earmarked Social Security taxes to help finance current benefits. . . .

Universal compulsory coverage. Another important principle is that, with minor exception, coverage is universal and compulsory. . . .

Rights defined in the law. An additional principle is that a person's rights to Social Security benefits — how much he or she gets and under what conditions — are clearly defined in the law and are generally related to facts that can be objectively determined. The area of administrative discretion is thus severely limited. A person who meets the conditions in the law must be paid.

1-6 QUESTIONS AND PROBLEMS

1. Consider carefully the pros and cons of mandated retirement benefits. What values are served by the current reliance upon regulation of voluntary plans? What is lost by not mandating minimum pension benefits? Who "wins" in our ERISA world? Who would "win" in a mandated benefit world?

2. What about welfare benefits, particularly health care benefits? Should employers be required to provide health care benefits?

3. Why are pension plans voluntary while other employment dependent benefits such as Social Security and unemployment insurance are mandatory?

4. Why should employee health and safety concerns justify a statute such as OSHA, but not justify mandatory health care insurance?

Chapter 2
EMPLOYEE PENSION PLANS

ERISA pension plans come in two basic forms: defined benefit plans and defined contribution plans with the latter including the very popular 401(k) plans. While ERISA governs the creation and operation of pension plans, it is the Internal Revenue Code (IRC) that grants them their income tax advantages. To qualify for favorable income tax treatment, a pension plan must meet the exacting standards of the IRC. This Chapter begins with an examination of the characteristics of ERISA-governed pension plans and the corresponding IRC requirements. Next, the Chapter looks at the ERISA definition of the term "plan." At times, employers have inadvertently created a "plan" subject to ERISA regulation by informally offering certain employee benefits. The Chapter concludes with an analysis of just who qualify as "employees" under ERISA and the IRC. Although the Chapter covers many of the ERISA and IRC requirements for pension plans, the rules are very complex and extensive. Consequently, this Chapter does not cover all of the statutory and regulatory requirements applicable to pension plans.

A. PENSION PLANS

ERISA §§ 3(3), 3(34), 3(35).

IRC §§ 414(i), 414(j).

ERISA regulates "employee benefit plans," which consist of "employee pension benefit plans" or "pension plans" and "employee welfare benefit plans" or "welfare plans." ERISA § 3(3). "Pension plans" are defined as plans, funds, or programs established or maintained by employers for the purpose of providing employees with retirement income or deferring income until the employee terminates employment or later. ERISA § 3(2). "Welfare plans" are defined as plans, funds, or programs established or maintained by employers for the purpose of providing participants with benefits such as reimbursement for health care costs, insurance for disability and death, and vacation and unemployment benefits. ERISA § 3(1).

The Internal Revenue Code (IRC) also regulates "employee benefits plans." Many of the requirements under the IRC and ERISA overlap. For example, both the IRC and ERISA impose vesting and funding standards on pension plans. Yet there are regulatory aspects of ERISA and the IRC that are independent of one another, such as the IRC nondiscrimination requirements, that have no counterpart in ERISA.

Pension plans are either defined benefit plans, ERISA § 3(35), IRC § 414(j) or defined contribution plans, ERISA § 3(34), IRC § 414(i). Technically, a defined benefit plan is defined as any pension plan that is not a defined contribution plan. ERISA § 3(34), IRC § 414(i). In popular parlance, however, a defined benefit plan is a plan in which the benefit is expressed as a certain amount to be paid at the participant's retirement. The promised benefit may be an exact dollar amount, such as $600 a month, or, more commonly, the benefit is calculated by a formula that takes into account the participant's compensation and the number of years the employee worked for the employer (known as "years of service"). Defined benefit plan assets are pooled together in a common fund, invested, and paid out as needed to meet the benefits promised to the participant. The employer, in its capacity as plan sponsor, assumes the responsibility that the fund will have sufficient assets to pay all promised benefits. The employer therefore bears the risk of the rate of investment return on the assets of the defined benefit plan.

Defined contribution plans do not promise participants a specified benefit upon retirement. Instead, benefits under a defined contribution plan are based on contributions to the plan on behalf of the employee and any earnings and losses on those contributions. Contributions to the plan are credited to an individual account on behalf of each participant. The amount of the contribution is usually based on a set rate, such as five percent of the participant's annual compensation. Because the individual account is invested in stocks, bonds, and the like, the value of each account fluctuates with changes in the value of the investments held by the account. The participant's pension benefit is based upon the amount held in his or her individual account, rather than a fixed benefit based upon the employee's years of service and compensation. Consequently, a participant in a defined contribution plan bears the investment risk.

[1] Defined Benefit Plans

Under ERISA, defined benefit plans are broadly defined as any plan that is not a defined contribution plan. In actuality, most defined benefit plans share common characteristics, such as a formula that determines the benefits to be paid to participants. A defined benefit plan must also satisfy IRC requirements if it is to be qualified for favorable federal income tax treatment.

[a] Benefit Formulas

While a few defined benefit plans merely promise participants a fixed amount at retirement, such as $20,000 a year for life, the great majority of plans determine benefits according to a benefit formula, using either a flat benefit formula or a unit credit formula.

A flat benefit formula promises participants a benefit that is based solely on a percentage of the employee's compensation, e.g., a pension equal to 50 percent of the employee's average annual compensation during his or her last three years of employment. The promised benefit is not affected by the employee's years of service with the employer.

For example, Sean participates in the Alpha Co. defined benefit plan that provides a pension equal to 60 percent of the employee's average annual compensation during the last three years of employment. Sean's average annual compensation for the last three years of employment was $60,000. Consequently, his pension benefit will be $36,000 a year ($60,000 x 60%).

A unit credit formula promises a pension benefit that depends on the participant's years of service as well as his or her compensation. The most common type of defined benefit formula is the "final average pay" formula. A final average pay formula promises participants a pension starting at some age (e.g., age 65) equal to some percent (e.g., 2 percent) times the employee's years of service times the employee's average annual compensation for some period, such as the three years preceding retirement. For example, Charleen, who works for Beta Inc., participates in its defined benefit plan, which uses a unit credit formula equal to two percent times the participant's years of service times the average pay of the participant for the final three years of employment. Charleen, age 65, has worked for Beta Inc. and participated in its defined benefit pension plan for 40 years. Her average pay for the last three years is $40,000. If Charleen, who is single, retires at age 65, her pension benefit will be calculated as 2 percent times 40 years (80%) times $40,000, or a benefit of $32,000 per year for her life.

A career average pay plan promises participants an annual retirement benefit starting at some age (again, usually age 65) equal to some percent (e.g., two percent) times the participant's years of service times the participant's average compensation over his or her entire career with the employer. Alternatively, a unit credit plan might provide an employee with a retirement benefit starting at some age (e.g., age 65) equal to a flat amount (e.g., $2,000) times the employee's years of service.

About 25 percent of both defined benefit and defined contribution plans are "integrated" with Social Security, meaning the benefit formula usually provides participants with a smaller benefit for wages up to the maximum taxable wage base under the Social Security Act, i.e. the maximum wages subject to the Social Security tax ($110,100 in 2012, adjusted annually for inflation) and disregards employee compensation that exceeds the maximum Social Security wage base. Integration is defended, in part, on the basis that because employers pay one-half of the Social Security wage tax, integrated plans permit employers to offset at least part of this cost. Also, because Social Security replaces approximately 40 percent of the wages of lower-paid workers, it is possible that absent integration some lower-paid workers might otherwise receive combined pension and Social Security benefits that would exceed 100 percent of their pre-retirement wages. Plans that integrate benefits with Social Security are subject to complex statutory and regulatory requirements as to the extent and manner of such integration.

[b] Normal Retirement Age

ERISA § 3(24).

Every defined benefit plan must specify a "normal retirement age" (NRA) that cannot be later than age 65 or five years after the employee commenced participation in the plan. For example, Laura, age 63, begins to work for Theta Co. and immediately begins to participate in the plan. Her NRA can be as late as age 68. The NRA is the age at which "full benefits" are payable under the terms of the plan, not the age at which the participant must retire or, in the language of ERISA, separate from service. Employees are free to continue to work for the employer past the NRA. In fact, under the Age Discrimination in Employment Act (ADEA), almost all employees are protected from mandatory retirement because of age. 29 U.S.C. §§ 621–634. The participant, however, is almost always required to terminate employment with the employer who sponsors the plan in order to collect his or her pension, though the participant does not have to leave the work force. The participant could retire from Alpha Inc., collect a pension from the Alpha Inc. defined benefit plan, and commence employment with Beta Co.

A participant who continues to work for the plan sponsor (employer) beyond the plan's NRA must continue to accrue benefits under the terms of the plan, though the plan may cap the number of years of service for which it grants credit. For example, suppose that Chi Corp. has a defined benefit plan with a unit credit formula that promises employees at the NRA of age 65 an annual benefit equal to 2 percent times years of service times the average final three years of compensation, capped at 30 years. Yang, who has worked for Chi for 27 years, retires at age 65. His annual benefit will be equal to 2 percent times 27 years of service times his final three years average salary. If he continues to work until age 68, his annual benefit beginning at age 68 will be equal to 2 percent times 30 years of service times his final three years average salary. If he continues to work until he reaches age 70, despite having worked for the company for 32 years, his annual benefit beginning at age 70 will only equal 2 percent times 30 years of service times his final three years average salary. If his salary at ages 69 and 70 is higher than in the preceding years, his annual benefit at age 70 will be somewhat higher than his annual benefit at age 68 because it will be based on the higher final average salary, but he will be limited to 30 years of credit.

Many defined benefit plans also specify an "early retirement age," which is the earliest age at which participants can begin to receive benefits under the terms of the plan. For example, some defined benefit plans provide that participants may retire at age 55 if they have at least ten years of service. Defined benefit plans typically provide that the benefit payable at early retirement will be actuarially reduced to reflect the fact that benefits that begin at the early retirement age will be paid over a longer period of time than benefits that begin at the normal retirement age. Plans, however, may subsidize early retirement benefits either by reducing early retirement benefits by less than an actuarially fair amount or by not reducing early retirement benefits at all. For example, a plan may subsidize early retirement benefits by providing that participants who reach some age, such as 60, are entitled to full benefits if they have 30 years of service. Alternatively, participants may be entitled to full benefits if the sum of their age and years of service equals some number such as 90. For example, a 58-year-old participant with 32 years of service would be eligible for full benefits, even though he or she had not reached the plan's NRA of 65.

[c] Distributions

Pension benefits under a defined benefit plan are normally distributed in the form of an annuity for life beginning at the plan's NRA. IRC § 411(a)(7), although a plan may provide the participant the option of taking a lump sum distribution that is actuarially the equivalent of an annuity for life. ERISA § 205(g); IRC § 415(b)(2)(E). A life annuity pays the participant a fixed amount at regular intervals for the participant's lifetime (e.g. $600 per month for life). If the participant is married, the plan must distribute benefits in the form of a "qualified joint and survivor annuity" or "optional survivor annuity" unless the participant elects otherwise with the consent of the participant's spouse. ERISA §§ 205(a)(1) & 205(c)(1)(A)(i); IRC §§ 401(a)(11)(A)(i) & 417(a)(1)(A)(i). A joint and survivor annuity provides payments for as long as the participant or his or her surviving spouse is alive. In order to qualify as a "qualified joint and survivor annuity," the amount payable to the surviving spouse (survivor continuation percentage) must not be less than 50 percent nor more than 100 percent of the amount payable to the participant during his or her lifetime (e.g., $600 per month for the participant's life and, upon the death of the participant, $300 per month for the surviving spouse's life), and the total amount payable must be at least the actuarial equivalent of a single life annuity for the life of the participant. ERISA § 205(d)(1), IRC § 417(b).

If benefits are paid in the form of a joint and survivor annuity, the amount of the monthly payment is often actuarially reduced to reflect the projected payout for a greater number of years. For example, Leo and Mary have both been employed by Sigma Inc. for 30 years and have identical pay histories. They share the same birthday and retire on the same date. Leo is single. According to the plan benefit formula, he is entitled to $25,000 a year for life. If Mary were single, she would receive the same amount. (Because gender cannot be used to calculate pension benefits, the fact that Mary is a female with a longer life expectancy than Leo is irrelevant in calculating the amount of her pension.) Mary, however, is married to Mort, and will receive a joint and 50 percent survivor annuity of $22,000 a year for her life. Upon her death, Mort will receive $11,000 a year. If Mort predeceases

Mary, she will continue to receive $22,000 a year for her life. Mary's annual benefit is less than Leo's because together Mary and Mort have a longer life expectancy than does Leo. Employers are not required to actuarially reduce joint and survivor life annuities, but they typically do.

If the participant has the option to accept a lump sum distribution rather than an annuity, the lump sum will represent the present, discounted value of the potential annuity payments as calculated according to the interest rate and life expectancy assumptions as defined in ERISA § 205(g)(3) and IRC § 417(e)(3). Because the receipt of a lump sum distribution from a defined benefit plan usually represents taxable income, many recipients elect a direct rollover payment from the plan. A direct rollover is a non-taxable distribution from the plan to an individual retirement account (IRA) or to another tax exempt retirement plan. As the participant takes out money from the IRA, each distribution represents taxable income, but the amounts are usually taxed at lower marginal income tax rates.

If a participant continues to work for the plan sponsor beyond the plan's NRA, the plan may, and typically does, "suspend" the payment of benefits until the participant terminates employment with the plan sponsor. If benefits are "suspended," the participant must continue to accrue benefits for the period of time during which the participant continues to work, but the plan need not pay the participant any benefits during that period of time nor does the plan need to compensate the participate for foregoing those benefits. Thus, once an employee reaches the plan's NRA, the employee is often financially better off changing employers and beginning to collect benefits rather than continuing to work for that employer.

For example, assume that Theta Inc. has a defined benefit plan with a benefit formula equal to $1,000 a year for each year of credited service. At age 65, Luis has 15 years of credited service. If Luis retires that year, he will receive an annual benefit of $15,000 ($1,000 x 15 years = $15,000) beginning that year. If he continues to work for Theta, Theta may suspend the payment of the retirement benefit and not pay Luis the $15,000 pension. If he retires at age 66, Luis' annual benefit will be slightly higher at $16,000 ($1,000 x 16 years = $16,000), but the plan does not need to compensate Luis for the $15,000 in benefits he did not receive the preceding year. If Luis wants to continue to work, he may be better off terminating employment with Theta and looking for another job — even if it means taking a pay cut or working part-time — rather than continuing to work for Theta and delaying his pension.

A defined benefit plan must provide the participant's spouse with a preretirement survivor annuity if the participant dies before the commencement of benefits unless the participant waived this right with the consent of his or her spouse. Benefit payments to the surviving spouse are based upon the benefits earned by the participant, and must begin no later than the date the participant would have reached the NRA or early retirement age, if available. ERISA § 205(a)(2); IRC § 401(a)(11)(A)(ii).

Defined benefit plans may and often do provide certain supplemental benefits, such as disability and death benefits. For example, some plans pay a lump-sum death benefit to surviving spouses or heirs if the employee dies before separation from service. Plans may also pay a disability benefit to a disabled participant until he or she reaches the NRA, at which time the participant qualifies for the retirement benefit. Defined benefit plans, however, generally may not provide layoff benefits or benefits for sickness, accident, hospitalization, or medical expenses. Treas. Reg. § 1.401-1(b)(1)(i). These benefits are typically provided through separate welfare benefit plans.

Although an annuity is the typical form of a defined benefit pension, a defined benefit plan may offer participants the option of electing a lump-sum distribution equal to the present or discounted value of the annuity. (Defined benefit plans that are significantly underfunded, however, may not pay benefits except as a life annuity. ERISA § 206(g)(3); IRC § 436(d)(1).) For example, Nina, who is about to retire, has a right under her defined benefit plan to an annual pension of $27,000 per year. Under the plan, she has the option to elect a lump-sum distribution of $320,000, the present value of the annuity. Whether Nina should elect the lump-sum distribution or the annuity depends on a number of factors, including her individual life expectancy, tolerance for risk, investment acumen, and interest in leaving an estate. An annuity is a guaranteed monthly payment that the retiree cannot outlive. Yet a lump-sum distribution, if invested wisely, may provide more disposable income or a sizable estate. Still, a participant who elects a lump-sum distribution and who lives a long time risks spending all of it before dying.

In determining the present value of an annuity, average life expectancy is taken into account, not the individual participant's life expectancy. If Nina has a shorter life expectancy than the average person her age because she is ill and expects to die soon, a lump-sum distribution is probably worth more than the alternative of receiving an annuity for only a short period of time. On the other hand, if Nina is healthy and expects to live longer than the average person her age, the actual payout under an annuity may be worth more than a lump-sum distribution.

[d] Funding and Investment Risk

Defined benefit plans are typically funded solely by employer contributions. ERISA and the IRC set forth complex minimum funding rules that determine how much employers must contribute each year to fund their defined benefit plans. ERISA §§ 302, 303; IRC §§ 412, 430. The minimum funding rules are designed to ensure that defined benefit plans have sufficient assets to pay the promised benefits. Plans employ actuaries, who determine each year the amount the employer must contribute to the plan. The amount of the annual employer contribution depends upon factors such the number of employees, their respective ages, how many years they can be expected to remain with the employer, the current and anticipated compensation paid to the employees, and the expected rate of investment return on the plan assets.

The employer does not have to fund a dollar into the pension fund for every dollar that the fund expects to pay out to retired employees, because the fund invests its assets. The return on those investments is a significant source of funds to pay the pensions. The higher the rate of return on the pension fund, the less money the employer need pay into the fund. In some years, the fund may be so successful in its investments that the employer need not pay any money into the fund. Conversely, if the fund's investments produce less income than anticipated, the employer will have to make up the difference by contributing more money into the fund. Hence, defined benefit plans are said to place investment risk on the employer. Sometimes that can prove to be very advantageous. If the plan investments earn a high rate of return, the plan can become overfunded; that is, have more value than is necessary to fulfill its pension obligations. If that occurs, the employer can cease making contributions until the plan returns to actuarial balance. Alternatively, the employer can use the surplus pension assets to pay for health care expenses for retirees, IRC § 420, or to increase pension benefits for employees who accept early retirement. *Lockheed Corp. v. Spink*, 517 U.S. 882, 885 (1996). Conversely, if the defined benefit plan fund does not meet its investment goals or actually loses money, the employer will be required to make larger contributions to the fund in order to insure the fund's ability to meet its obligations.

If a defined benefit plan is terminated and has insufficient assets to pay its promised pensions, the promised benefits may be paid by the federal insurance plan, the Pension Benefit Guaranty Corporation (PBGC). (*See* Chapter 10, *infra.*)

[e] Multiemployer Pension Plans

The traditional, single-employer pension plan is a poor fit for employees, such as construction workers, who often work for a variety of employers over their careers. In unionized industries in which employment is episodic and usually for a number of different employers, such as construction, the employees often participate in a "multiemployer" pension plan. ERISA § 3(37). A multiemployer plan operates much like any other defined benefit plan, except that contributions are made to it by a number of employers. The employee is credited with participation in the plan during the period that he or she works for a participating employer. Over the working life of the employee, the various employers contribute to the defined benefit pension plan. For example, Darius is a union bricklayer. Over his career he has worked for five different construction companies. His employment time with each construction company is credited towards his retirement plan participation just as though he had worked for a single employer. While generally subject to defined benefit rules, multiemployer benefit plans have flexibility with respect to certain requirements, such as the funding and tax nondiscrimination rules. They are regulated not only by ERISA and the IRC, but also by the Labor Management Relations Act of 1947, commonly called the Taft-Hartley Act.

[f] Vesting

ERISA requires all pension benefits to vest, i.e. become nonforfeitable, after an employee has worked for the company for a prescribed number of years. (*See* Chapter 4, *infra.*) Once the employee's benefit is vested, typically after three to five years of service with the employer, termination of employment will not result in the loss of the pension. For example, Luellen worked for Theta Inc. from 1980 to 1990. She then worked for Sigma Co. from 1990 to 2010, when she retired at age 65. Both Theta and Sigma offered defined benefit plans with a NRA of 65. Because Luellen worked for Theta for 10 years, her benefit was vested, meaning that her termination of employment did not affect her right to a pension. Although the amount of her benefit was frozen as of the date of her departure, she was entitled to it at age 65. The Theta plan's benefit formula promised her an annual retirement benefit beginning at age 65 equal to 1.5 percent times her years of service times her average compensation for the last three years of employment. Luellen's compensation for the years 1988, 1989 and 1990 averaged $25,000. Her pension from Theta is thus $3,750 (1.5% x 10 x $25,000). The Sigma plan uses the same benefit formula, but her average compensation for 2008, 2009, and 2010, was $75,000. Her Sigma pension is $22,500 (1.5% x 20 x $75,000). Together her pensions from Theta and Sigma total $26,250.

[g] The Rise and Fall of Defined Benefit Plans

Historically, defined benefit plans were the most common form of pension plan because both employers and employees liked the certainty of the retirement benefit. Employers favored defined benefit plans because they encouraged employees to remain with the company and thereby accrue greater retirement benefits. Employees also preferred defined benefit plans, because they knew that if they stayed with the employer until retirement age, they would receive a predetermined pension for life. Because the pension was usually related to the employee's pay in the final years of employment, the employee was protected against preretirement inflation eroding the value of the pension. Perhaps the greatest attraction of a defined benefit plan was the sense for the employee that the pension increased along with the employee's age, wages, and years of service. To many employees, a defined benefit pension seemed just compensation for their contribution over the years to the enterprise of the employer.

Defined benefits plans were so dominant that in 1970 they enrolled over 70 percent of all participants in pension plans. By 1983, that had declined to 57 percent. In 2004, the percentage had declined to less than 20 percent. By 2004 there were fewer than 12,000 defined benefit plans with more than 100 participants though those plans represented over 20 million participants. In 2008, there were still about 20 million defined benefit plan participants, but they represented only about a third of workers who participated in a retirement plan. The other two-thirds participated solely in a 401(k) plan.

The reasons for the decline in defined benefit plans are many. In part they are less attractive compared to defined contribution plans because they are more costly to administer due to more complex legal requirements. Most defined benefit plans are offered by employers with a unionized workforce. Consequently, as union membership declines, so does the number of defined benefit plans. The increasing mobility of employees in the workforce has also eroded support for defined benefit plans that typically were seen as an inducement to the employee to stay with the same employer for as long as possible in order to maximize the value of the retirement annuity. Today, however, most employees do not expect to remain with one employer for life, and so often prefer a defined contribution plan. Employers also prefer to offer defined contribution plans, which they perceive as a more efficient form of pension in a transient employment world. Although defined benefit plans promise a secure and predictable level of retirement benefits, they are less attractive to today's younger, more mobile and sophisticated work force, and particularly to employees of rapidly growing enterprises, who prefer defined contribution plans that can be funded at least in part by the employer's stock.

Some commentators point to fundamental changes in the economy to account for the decline in defined benefit plans.

JEFFREY N. GORDON, ESSAY: EMPLOYEES, PENSIONS, AND THE NEW ECONOMIC ORDER

97 Colum. L. Rev. 1519, 1544–1546 (1997)

The New Economic Order has undermined the effectiveness of defined benefit plans in two important respects. First, as job tenure becomes less stable in the sectors of the economy where defined benefit plans have been dominant, particularly manufacturing, portability and mobility have emerged as problems. In the past, vesting patterns caused serious troubles, since most plans required ten years service for full vesting; displacement from one employer to another could mean forfeiture of substantial pension benefits. This problem has been significantly mitigated by legislative changes taking effect in 1989 that have reduced the standard period for full vesting to five years. Nevertheless, under the customary defined benefits formula, the mobile employee will still receive a lower pension than the stationary employee. This is because benefits increase with tenure at the paying firm. Consider this example: An employee works ten years each for three firms and is fully vested at each, and so receives three pensions based on ten years service and his final salary average at each firm. Assuming that salary increases with total work experience, this means that his last and presumably highest final average salary is multiplied by ten, not thirty, as would be the case for the stationary employee.

The second challenge to the defined benefit plan of the New Economic Order is more fundamental. The connection between salary and pension payout levels means that constrained wage growth depresses future as well as present welfare. In the halcyon 1950s and 1960s the defined benefit plan was a vehicle for sharing economic gains because increasing wages led to increasing future pension payouts. But flat average real wages, especially pronounced since 1980, conversely mean no real growth in the eventual pension payouts. Wage growth for an average employee is a function of two variables: the tenure ladder and upward shifts of the entire tenure ladder. That is, salary increases come first from movement (or promotion) on a tenure ladder — a wage curve that exists at a given moment in time — and second from wage increases that move the entire wage curve upwards. It is the latter shift upwards that represents increased average wages, a sharing of economic gains. Flat wages (in real terms) mean that the curve is not shifting upward (except, as noted above, for the top quintile). Thus the implications of the New Economic Order for average employee welfare are twofold: since employee wealth (in defined benefit plans) is tied to wage growth, a pattern of flat real wages affects not only current consumption (or savings) but also future consumption. Mobility and lack of portability at a time of less stable employment further reduce pension wealth and future consumption.

---

[2] Defined Contribution Plans

In recent years, defined contribution plans have become increasingly popular as many employers have either supplemented or replaced their defined benefit plans with a defined contribution plan. As a result, the majority of American workers who participate in a retirement plan do so in a defined contribution plan. Today, more than 42 million workers participate in defined contribution plans. These plans hold assets in excess of $3 trillion.

[a] Types of Defined Contribution Plans

Defined contribution plans come in four basic types: (1) money purchase plans, (2) profit-sharing plans, (3) stock bonus plans, and (4) Employee Stock Ownership Plans (ESOPs). What all have in common is the lack of any assured pension. The employee is only promised that the employer will fund the retirement plan, invest the assets of the plan and distribute the employee's share to the employee when the employee becomes eligible for his or her distribution from the plan.

Money purchase plans are the most basic form. These plans require the employer to make fixed, annual contributions to an individual account for each participant. The amount of the contribution is based upon a formula, usually some percentage of the employee's annual compensation.

Profit-sharing plans, the most common type of defined contribution plan, originally required that employer contributions to the plan be contingent upon profits, but that requirement was eliminated by the Tax Reform Act of 1986. Under present law, contributions are permitted regardless of whether the employer has profits. The plan can either provide for regular employer contributions to the plan or it can give the employer discretion whether and how much to contribute to the plan each year. The plan must have a formula that determines how the employer contributions to the plan are allocated to the participating employees and must specify what events trigger distributions to participants. Treas. Reg. § 1.401-1(b)(ii).

A stock bonus plan is like a profit-sharing plan in that contributions can be at the discretion of the employer and do not depend on the existence of profits. But under a stock bonus plan contributions to the plan can be in the form of the stock of the employer. Alternately, the employer can contribute cash, which in turn is used to purchase the employer's stock. Distributions to the plan participants can be either in cash or the employer's stock. Treas. Reg. § 1.401-1(b)(iii).

Employee Stock Ownership Plans (ESOPs) are a special form of a stock bonus plan. An ESOP creates individual participant pension accounts funded primarily with the stock of the employer. Upon retirement, the participants' retirement benefits are generally paid in the form of employer stock. Although pension plans are typically prohibited from borrowing from the plan sponsor (employer), ESOPs enjoy a special right to do so. IRC § 4975(d)(3). Because an ESOP may be financed with borrowed funds, typically the ESOP will borrow money from a bank to purchase the stock of the employer. The loan is guaranteed by the employer with the purchased stock pledged as security. One particularly attractive feature of an ESOP is the possible deductibility of dividends issued by the employer. Dividends paid by the employer to the ESOP on account of the employer's stock held by the ESOP are deductible by the employer if the dividends are used by the ESOP to repay a loan, reinvested by the ESOP in employer stock, or if distributed to the plan participants.

[b] Distributions

The rules governing distributions by defined contribution plans are quite complex. In summary, most defined contribution plans pay participants benefits in the form of a lump-sum cash distribution. Plans other than money purchase plans may offer additional distribution options, such as installment payments and annuities. Stock bonus plans and ESOPs may make distributions in the form of employer stock. If the participant requests, ESOPs must make distributions in the form of employer stock. Treas. Reg. § 1.401-1(b)(1)(iii); IRC § 409(h)(1)(A).

Profit-sharing plans, stock bonus plans, and ESOPs are required to have a formula that determines distributions from the participant's account "after a fixed number of years, the attainment of a stated age, or upon the prior occurrence of some event such as layoff, illness, disability, retirement, death, or severance of employment." Treas. Reg. § 1.401-1(b)(1)(ii). Thus, profit-sharing plans, stock bonus plans, and ESOPs can make "in-service" distributions, that is, distributions to participants while they remain employed by the plan sponsor. If, however, a participant elects to receive a distribution from any kind of pension plan before age 59½, the distribution is not only taxed as ordinary income, but is also subject to a 10 percent excise tax. IRC § 72(t). However, the participant may avoid this excise tax by rolling the distribution over into an Individual Retirement Account (IRA) or another qualified retirement plan. In addition to paying retirement benefits, the amounts allocated to participants' accounts by a profit-sharing plan, stock bonus plan, or ESOP can pay for incidental life or accident or health insurance for the participant and his or her family. Treas. Reg. § 1.401-1(b)(1)(ii). In contrast, money purchase plans, which are treated like defined benefit plans for this purpose, generally cannot make "in-service" distributions or provide benefits for sickness, accident, hospitalization, or medical expenses. Treas. Reg. § 1.401-1(b)(1)(i).

Money purchase plans are also subject to the same joint and survivor annuity rules as defined benefit plans. IRC § 401(a)(11)(B)(ii). If a participant in a money purchase plan is married, distributions must be in the form of a qualified joint and survivor annuity or optional survivor annuity, unless the participant elects otherwise with the consent of his or her spouse. IRC §§ 401(a)(11); 417(a)(1). Profit-sharing plans, stock bonus plans, and ESOPs, on the other hand, are not subject to the joint and survivor annuity rules, so long as the plan provides that the account balance of a deceased participant will be paid to the participant's spouse unless the spouse has consented to a different beneficiary. IRC § 401(a)(11)(B)(iii).

[c] Funding and Investment Risk

All contributions to a defined contribution plan are allocated to individual participant accounts. In most 401(k) plans, individual participants determine how the funds in their accounts are invested. In other defined contribution plans, the participant accounts are pooled and invested by the plan sponsor or an investment advisor, with the individual participant accounts credited with their proportionate share of the earnings or losses of the plan investment pool. Regardless of who makes the investment decisions, the participant's benefit in a defined contribution plan is based on contributions to the participant's account and any earnings or losses on investments made on those contributions. Consequently, the participant is said to bear the investment risk in a defined contribution plan.

To illustrate, assume, for example, that Jose is employed by Acme Inc. and Jackie is employed by Beta Inc. Both companies offer money purchase pension plans to which they promise to contribute $2,000 a year per participant, and for both plans the plan's investment advisor makes the investment decisions. For the last ten years, the Acme plan has had an 8 percent annual return on its investments, while the Beta fund has averaged 4 percent. Both Jose and Jackie have been employed by their companies for the entire ten years. At 8 percent compounded annually, Jose's account totals $33,828 at the end of 10 years. Jackie's account, however, compounding at an annual rate of 4 percent, totals only $27,077 at the end of ten years. Though each company contributed $2,000 a year for the 10 years, because Jose's defined contribution account had a much higher rate of return on its investments, his account is worth 25 percent more than Jackie's. Yet Beta Inc. has no obligation to pay Jackie additional amounts, even though her account suffered from the lower rate of earnings that was a result of the financial investment choices made by the pension plan controlled and operated by her employer, Beta Inc.

Because defined contribution plans do not promise participants any particular benefit, benefits under a defined contribution plan are not guaranteed by the PBGC. Unlike a participant in a defined benefit plan, a participant in a defined contribution plan has no assurance or certainty as to the value of his or her retirement benefit.

[d] Prevalence of Defined Contribution Plans

Defined benefit plans are increasingly being replaced or supplemented by defined contribution plans. Twenty-five years ago, defined benefit plans prevailed. For example, in 1985, defined benefit plans held $813 billion worth of assets and defined contribution plans held $508 billion. In contrast by 2010, defined benefit plans held $2.2 billion in assets while defined contribution plans held $4.5 billion.

Employers favor defined contribution plans in part because they have fewer costs and administrative burdens than defined benefit plans. For example, defined contribution plans do not incur premiums for PBGC insurance and there is no need to hire actuaries to determine the employer's annual contribution. Defined contribution plans are not as burdened with regulations and are less likely to be sued for violations of those regulations or ERISA. In addition, employers prefer defined contribution plans because their contributions to such plans are usually stable and predictable because they are almost always based upon some percentage of employee compensation. At the beginning of the fiscal year, an employer can estimate the likely amount of its contribution to a defined contribution plan. Contributions to defined benefit plans, in contrast, can be less stable and predictable because they are dependent on a variety of factors, including the plan's investment return. If investment earnings suddenly decline, employers may need to make much greater contributions to their defined benefits plans than they had anticipated. Since contributions to pension plans reduce company profits, these unexpected contributions can cause employers to experience unexpected decreases in their profitability. They prefer that their employees bear the investment risk.

In contrast, employees may prefer defined contribution plans in part precisely because they not only bear the investment risk, but in most 401(k) plans, they enjoy the right to manage that risk through their investment choices. To some employees, the essence of a 401(k) plan contribution plan is not its "risk," but rather the opportunity to reap the benefits of a successful investment. Some employees may also be more comfortable with the greater transparency of defined contribution plans. The employee knows how much is contributed to his or her defined contribution account each year and the current value of that account.

---

[3] Summary of Distinctions Between Defined Benefit and Defined Contribution Plans

The most important differences between defined benefit plans and defined contribution plans are summarized below:

Defined Benefit Plans	Defined Contribution Plans
• Benefits determined by a formula.	• There are no predetermined benefits.
• Employer contributions are based upon actuarial requirements needed to pay the promised benefits.	• Employer contributions are based upon the amount fixed in the plan document or as determined by the employer each year.

Defined Benefit Plans	Defined Contribution Plans
• Favor long-term employees who retire at peak of earnings.	• Favor younger employees who can accumulate tax free earnings for longer periods of time than older employees.
• Employer bears investment risk and plan can potentially be underfunded.	• Employee bears investment risk. Plan always fully funded.
• Vesting only preserves benefits based upon lower wages that do not reflect inflation after termination of employment.	• Vesting preserves amounts in trust accounts that grow with inflation even after termination of employment.
• Generally not portable.	• Portable.
• Preferred by employees who want guaranteed financial security.	• Preferred by employees who accept the risk of financial investments.
• Employee is unlikely to understand current valuation of retirement benefits.	• Employee is always aware of current account balance.
• Benefits are usually in the form of an annuity. Plan may contain preretirement death benefits.	• Benefits are often in the form of a lump-sum distribution. Death benefits usually limited to the accumulated value of the employee's individual account.
• Most benefits are guaranteed by the PBGC.	• No PBGC guarantee of benefits.

2-1 QUESTIONS AND PROBLEMS

1. Identify the type of plan or plans that could contain the following language:

a. Subject to the rights of the Employer under Article XI, the Employer may make a contribution to the Trust beginning with the first Plan Year ending on or after the effective date of the Plan.

b. Each Plan Year prior to the time required by law for filing the Employer's federal income tax return (including extensions) for the year with respect to which the contribution is made, the Employer shall make contributions to the Employer Account of each Participant who has a Year of Service for Accrual of Benefits for the Plan Year which shall be an amount equal to 10% of Compensation of each Participant.

c. A Participant's Accrued Benefit at Normal Retirement Age shall be 10% of the Average Annual Compensation of a Participant.

d. The Employer shall contribute all amounts needed to provide the benefits under this plan. The amount of Employer contribution shall be based on the recommendation of the Enrolled Actuary, using such methods and assumptions as he may deem advisable and consistent with the minimum funding standards of ERISA.

2. Omega Corp. is considering instituting a qualified pension plan, but is uncertain whether it should adopt a defined contribution plan or a defined benefit plan. In light of the following variables, what type of plan should Omega adopt?

a. The corporation, an advertising firm, is only three years old, with 12 employees, none of whom is over the age of 40.

b. The corporation is five years old, manufactures plastic kitchen utensils, has ten managers or sales personnel and 50 blue collar workers. It hopes to double in size in the next five years. The owner believes that she needs a pension plan to discourage her employees from joining a union.

c. The corporation operates a restaurant, Big, Fast & Good, that seats over one hundred customers. It employs between 30 and 40 employees, depending on how good business is. Employee turnover is high. The owner hopes that he can retain more employees with a pension plan.

d. The corporation operates a warehouse and is negotiating with its union about instituting a pension plan for the 55 employees who are not part of management. The average age of the unionized employees is 45. Many have worked for the corporation for more than ten years.

[4] 401(k) Plans: Cash or Deferred Arrangements (CODAs)

In 1978 Congress added IRC § 401(k), which created a particular type of defined contribution plan called a "401(k) plan." Although initially enacted as a means of supplementing other forms of pension plans, 401(k) plans soon became the most widely adopted form of retirement plan. In 1984, there were a little over 17,000 401(k) plans. By 2000, the number of plans had grown to 322,000. Between 1984 and 2004, 401(k) plans grew from about 3 percent of all private sector retirement plans to about almost half of all plans, and over 80 percent of all defined contribution plans. By 2010, over 650,000 401(k) plans enrolled over 52 million employees and held over $3 trillion dollars worth of assets. The amount of funds in these accounts varies greatly; the average value of a 401(k) account in 2010 was estimated at about $75,000.

[a] The Cash or Deferred Arrangement (CODA)

A 401(k) plan is a cash or deferred arrangement (CODA) that permits participating employees to choose between receiving a cash payment or having a contribution made on their behalf to a qualified plan (usually a profit-sharing plan). Under the income tax constructive receipt doctrine, employees normally would be taxed whether they elected to receive cash or have a contribution made on their behalf because they had the choice of receiving cash. The constructive receipt doctrine, however, does not apply to 401(k) contributions. If the plan satisfies the requirements of IRC § 401(k), the employee will be currently taxed on any cash payment the employee elects to receive, but any amounts the employee elects to defer, that is, amounts contributed to the plan, will not be considered taxable income and will not be taxed until distributed.

An employee cannot contribute more than $17,000 to a 401(k) plan in 2012. IRC § 402(g). (The limit is adjusted for inflation as measured by the cost of living index in $500 increments.) If permitted by the terms of their employer's plan, employees age 50 or older can contribute up to an additional $5,500 per year. Most employees do not contribute the maximum amount to their account, though the higher the compensation the greater the percentage of wages that is contributed. It is estimated that fewer than one percent of employees earning under $60,000 contribute the maximum compared with almost 60 percent of those earning $100,000 or more.

As with any defined contribution plan, the investment risk of the 401(k) account is with the employee. Unlike the traditional defined benefit plan, in almost all 401(k) plans, each employee directs the investment of his or her account. The plan sponsor, the employer, selects a limited number of investment alternatives subject to the fiduciary rules of ERISA § 404(c). Subject to those limitations, employees have the on-going responsibility to manage their 401(k) account. (See discussion in section [d] below.)

The 401(k) plan is designed to encourage employees to reject current disposable income and instead elect to have contributions made to their retirement 401(k) accounts. Yet about 20 percent of eligible employees do not participate in their 401(k) plan, preferring instead to receive more current income. Not surprisingly, higher paid employees, who are subject to higher income tax rates and can better afford the loss of current income, are more likely to participate in a 401(k) plan. (Like all qualified plans, 401(k) plans are subject to nondiscrimination rules that prohibit disproportionate participation and contribution rates by higher income workers. *See* Chapter 8, *infra.*) Just as predictable, younger employees are much less likely to participate.

The failure of an employee to participate can be costly for the employee. For example, Kim's salary is $90,000 per year. If she contributes, $9,000 to her 401(k) plan, she will not pay federal income tax on the $9,000. If she had not participated in the 401(k) plan, she would have been taxed on the $9,000 — perhaps at a tax rate of 30 percent or in the amount of $2,700 (30% x $9,000). After taxes, she would have $6,300 to spend. Her choice is whether to spend $6,300 or save $9,000 for her retirement by contributing it to her 401(k).

The employee contribution limits do not include amounts contributed by the employer. Some employers make contributions not related to the employee's contributions. More commonly, however, to overcome employee reluctance to participate, employers provide matching funds. The typical employer contribution is a maximum 3 percent match if the employee contributes 6 percent of his or her compensation, that is the employer contributes one dollar for every two dollars contributed by the employee. Naturally, plans with matching employer contributions have significantly higher participation rates in terms of number of employees participating and the percentage contribution by those employees. Not all employers provide matching funds, however, and the matching rate varies from employer to employer. And many employees still do not contribute despite the employer matching funds. Apparently, for these employees the desire for current consumption greatly outweighs the future value of income during retirement.

Researchers have found that employee participation rates in 401(k) plans increase if the employee is automatically enrolled even though the employee can easily withdraw from the plan. Studies have shown that if the default is to not participate, fewer employees participate in the 401(k) plan than if the default is reversed so that the employee is enrolled unless he or she withdraws. Though enrollment or withdrawal requires essentially the same effort of filing the appropriate document with the employer, inertia apparently is strong enough to cause some employees not to take the effort to enroll or withdraw.

To increase participation and contributions by employees, the Pension Protection Act of 2006 (PPA) added IRC §§ 410(k)(13), 401(m)(12), and 412(w) to facilitate and encourage automatic enrollment in 401(k) plans. Automatic enrollment, also known as an automatic contribution arrangement, provides that in the absence of an affirmative election by an eligible employee, a default election applies under which the employee is treated as having made an election to have a specified contribution made to a 401(k) account. Employees must be given notice of the right for 90 days to opt out of the automatic enrollment without any penalty for doing so. The employee also must receive written notification of the automatic enrollment, be notified of the right to not have elective contributions made on his or her behalf or to elect to have the contributions made at a different percentage, to have a reasonable time to make the election whether to permit the enrollment, and be informed as to how the automatic contributions will be invested in the absence of the employee making any investment decisions. The PPA also amended ERISA § 514 to preempt any State laws that prohibit or restrict automatic enrollment.

An automatic enrollment or contribution plan must provide a specified schedule of automatic contributions — called qualified percentages — for each eligible employee beginning with an initial minimum qualified percentage of 3 percent of compensation. IRC § 401(k)(13). That initial percentage continues until the last day of the year following the year of enrollment in the plan or a maximum of two years. After this initial period, the minimum qualified percentage increases by 1 percent for each of the next three plan years so that after four years 6 percent is the minimum qualified percentage. These are minimum percentages. A plan could provide for more rapid raises in the percentage or for higher percentages, though the maximum permitted percentage is 10 percent. IRC § 401(k)(13)(C). Whatever the percentage, it must be uniform for all eligible employees. The employer is permitted, but not required, to make contributions to an automatic enrollment 401(k) plan of either 3 percent of compensation or 100 percent of the first 1 percent of compensation plus 50 percent of the next 5 percent of compensation for a total of 3.5 percent.

One issue for employers with 401(k) plans is the need to comply with the tax nondiscrimination rules. Under these rules, a sufficient percentage of nonhighly compensated employees must participate in the plan relative to the participation rate of highly compensated employees, and the contribution rates of the highly compensated employees must not be too great rate relative to the contribution rates of the lower paid. IRC §§ 401(a)(4), 410(b) (discussed in Chapter 8, Nondiscrimination Rules.) Compliance with the highly technical nondiscrimination rules can be difficult, and failure to comply can result in the highly compensated employees not receiving favorable federal income tax treatment for their contributions to the plan. To assist with compliance, the Internal Revenue Code sets forth two different types of safe harbors by which a 401(k) plan will automatically satisfy the nondiscrimination requirements.

The first type of safe harbor, the matching contribution safe harbor, encourages employees to contribute to 401(k) plans by providing employer matching contributions. Under the basic matching contribution safe harbor, a 401(k) plan will automatically satisfy the nondiscrimination requirement if the employer makes a matching contribution equal to 100 percent of each nonhighly compensated employee's elective 401(k) contribution in an amount up to 3 percent of compensation plus 50 percent of the amount the employee contributes that is greater than 3 percent but does not exceed 5 percent of compensation. IRC § 401(k)(12)(B)(i).

An employer can meet the second safe harbor requirement by electing to contribute for all nonhighly compensated employees an amount equal to at least 3 percent of the employees compensation to a 401(k) account for the employee whether the employee elects to contribute to the account. IRC § 401(k)(12)(C).

The nondiscrimination requirements can also be met by an election to use the automatic enrollment plan. As with regular 401(k) plans, automatic enrollment plans may satisfy either a matching or nonelective contribution safe harbor. Under the basic matching contribution safe harbor, the plan must provide matching contributions equal to 100 percent of elective deferrals up to 1 percent of compensation, plus 50 percent of elective deferrals between 1 percent and 6 percent of compensation. IRC § 401(k)(13)(D)(i). Under the nonelective contribution safe harbor, the plan must provide for an employer nonelective contribution of at least 3 percent of compensation of all nonhighly compensated employees eligible to participate in the plan, regardless of whether the employees make elective contributions. IRC § 401(k)(13)(D)(i)(II).

[b] Reasons for Popularity of 401(k) Plans

401(k) plans are very popular. Employers often prefer 401(k) plans because they are relatively simple to administer and so avoid many of the administrative costs associated with defined benefit plans. The portability of 401(k) plans is also a selling point. The employer can assure the employee that termination of employment will not affect the employee's right to the 401(k) account since the employee's contributions to the account cannot be forfeited despite the time or cause of the employee's termination from the employer.

Many employees like 401(k) plans because they give the employee the choice of whether to contribute to their retirement fund or to accept more current compensation. The challenge and opportunity of directing the investment of their accounts is also attractive to many employees. When the stock market is rising, the employee can see and enjoy the sense of a growing retirement account. Of course, there is no guarantee that an individual employee's investment choices will prove to be successful. When the stock market declines or the employee's investment choices prove inept, the employee experiences the pain of a shrinking retirement account. Still, many employees prefer the right to control the investment of their retirement fund. Whether the right to control the 401(k) investments is an opportunity or a potential pitfall depends on the financial acumen, foresight, and luck of the individual employee.

Employee participation is 401(k) plans varies by race and ethnicity. Between 2001 and 2007, among eligible employees white participation was 77.4 percent, Black participation was 69.9 percent, Hispanic participation 69.8 percent and Asian participation was 83.1 percent. The average percent of wages contributed varied similarly with Asian employees contributing the highest at 7.8 percent while Hispanic employees averaged the lowest rate at 5.9 percent. Participation also varies by earnings with the higher paid employee participating in 401(k) plans at significantly higher rates. In 2008 the upper third of eligible income earners eligible to participate did so at a rate of 83 percent. The lowest third of eligible income earners participated at a rate of 64 percent.

[c] Distributions

Distributions from a 401(k) plan can, but need not, begin when the employee terminates service (employment) with the sponsoring employer. An employee who terminates service and takes a 401(k) distribution before age 59½, however, is subject to a 10 percent excise tax in addition to any regular federal income tax. IRC § 72(t). Fortunately a terminating employee can avoid taking a taxable distribution. For example, Peter, age 40, has worked for Delta Inc. and participated in its 401(k) plan for the last ten years. His retirement account has a value of $100,000. Upon termination from Delta, Peter has several choices. First, he can leave his funds in the 401(k) plan with Delta and continue to manage his account investments subject to the options provided by the Delta plan. He can withdraw the funds in the account at any time subject to the tax implications. Second, Peter can withdraw all the funds in the account, but the withdrawal will result in the distribution being as current income plus the ten percent excise tax because he is not yet age 59½. IRC § 72(t). Third, Peter can withdraw the account and roll it over free of federal income taxes into a tax-exempt Individual Retirement Account (IRA). The funds in the IRA will continue to enjoy tax-exempt status until the funds are withdrawn.

Unfortunately, more than one-half of employees covered by a 401(k) plan take taxable distributions from their accounts when they change jobs. Sometimes referred to as the lure of a new bass boat, these withdrawals account, in part, for the relatively low value of many employee retirement savings.

An employer can adopt a 401(k) plan that permits a plan loan feature, whereby the participant can borrow money from his or her 401(k) account. The plan may limit borrowing for only prescribed events such as the purchase of a home or for educational costs. Many plans permit loans without limiting conditions. IRC § 72(p)(1) provides that such loans are not income if they do not exceed certain dollar limits: $50,000 or the greater of $10,000 or 50 percent of the nonforfeitable balance. Loans from a 401(k) account must carry an interest rate that is set by the employer in the plan description.

Although 401(k) plans are designed as sources of retirement income, even without terminating service, an employee can draw down funds in his or her account without penalty before age 59½, if disabled or upon the occurrence of a hardship, defined as an immediate and pressing financial need. Treas. Reg. § 1.401(k)-1(d)(2)(i). The death of an employee permits the estate or heirs to withdraw the funds in the 401(k) account without penalty although withdrawals will be subject to the federal income tax.

[d] Funding and Plan Investment

What is distinct about 401(k) plans is that they permit the participant to direct the investments of the funds in the account. Over 90 percent of 401(k) plans permit the participants to control the investment of their accounts subject to the options provided by the plan. Department of Labor regulations permit the employer or plan administrator to avoid the fiduciary responsibility for plan investments if the plan offers at least three investment options. If each of the investment options is diversified, presents materially different possibilities of risk and return potential, and in the aggregate permit the employee to create an appropriate investment portfolio, the employer is not responsible if the investments lose value. DOL Reg. § 2550.404c-1(b)(3)(i)(B). The effect is to shift not only the investment risk but also the investment responsibility for 401(k) accounts to the plan participants.

The wisdom of making 401(k) plan participants responsible for making investment decisions about their 401(k) accounts has been questioned. Studies suggest that employees are not well suited to bear this responsibility.

SUSAN J. STABILE, THE BEHAVIOR OF DEFINED CONTRIBUTION PLAN PARTICIPANTS

77 N.Y.U. L. Rev. 71, 88 (2002)

Apart from the theoretical problem with the statutory regime, investment decisions by plan participants are a poor substitute for investment decisions made by professional asset managers. Empirically this is clear — investment returns by defined contribution plan participants are 2% per year lower than those achieved by institutional investors. This is not a surprising result. Study findings reveal that substantial numbers of plan participants are financially illiterate, including a lack of knowledge and understanding of financial concepts and common financial instruments as well as inadequate "general knowledge regarding retirement planning and savings issues." Indeed, one survey found that almost one-half of the 401(k) plan participants surveyed couldn't name a single investment option in their plan. Another found that 40% of participants did not know how their investments were allocated . . . .

The problem of excessive investment of 401(k) funds in the stock of the employer is compounded by many participants believing it is to their advantage to own the company stock, partly as an expression of loyalty and support for the company, and partly because they think they understand their own company's financial prospects better than any other's. Unfortunately, there is no constraint on what percentage of a 401(k) can be invested in the stock of the employer as there is no mandatory diversification requirement. ERISA § 407(b). Most commentators believe that excessive investment in the employer's stock is unwise.

One study found that over 16 percent of all 401(k) accounts are invested in employer stock with many accounts having a majority of their value so invested. In contrast, a defined benefit plan cannot invest more than 10 percent of the plan assets in the stock or real estate of the employer. ERISA § 407(a)(2).

[e] 401(k) Fees

A 401(k) plan requires payment of a variety of fees. The administration of the plan requires record-keeping, transaction processing, and trustee services, all of which must be paid for by the plan. Because of the plan participant's right to determine whether to participate, how much to participate and how to invest the amounts in the plan, and the plan must pay for the cost of communicating with participants on a regular basis. The plan must also pay for the management of the funds, including the right of participants to buy and sell securities and the right of employees to borrow money from the plan. The statutory and regulatory compliance requirements also incur fees, including audits, accounting and legal services. The plan sponsor and the plan participants share these costs.

There are also fees related to the investment of participants' accounts including sales charges such as commissions, management fees, and record keeping fees. The investment related fees average about 1 percent per year of the plan assets, although they vary considerably with smaller plans usually paying higher fees than larger plans. The investment fees are usually paid by the plan participants.

[5] Cash Balance Plans

Over the years, a number of employers have adopted cash balance plans. Although technically defined benefit plans, cash balance plans partake of characteristics of both defined benefit plans and defined contribution plans. In a cash balance plan, each employee has a hypothetical individual account. The employer makes monthly or annual contributions to the plan that are credited according to the plan formula to the hypothetical individual accounts. For example, each employee's individual account might be credited with an amount equal to six percent of the employee's annual compensation. To this extent, the cash balance plan operates very much like a traditional defined contribution plan. Unlike a defined contribution plan, however, in which the growth in the individual account is a function of the actual rate of return on the plan investments, in a cash balance plan, each account is credited with a rate of return determined by the plan. The credited rate is unrelated to the actual return on the plan's assets. For example, the plan may announce that it will credit employees' accounts with an annual compounded rate of return of 6 percent. Alternatively, the plan can credit each account with a market rate of return such as the return on long-term United States Treasury bonds.

In reality, the employee's individual retirement accounts are only bookkeeping fictions, because the plan has but a single fund, much like a defined benefit plan, which it uses to pay the promised retirement benefits. While each employee's account will be credited with the announced rate of return, the actual rate of investment return on the collective fund could be higher or lower depending how successful are its investments. Upon retirement the employee will be credited with a pension benefit equal in value to the annual contributions to the account increased as if the amounts had been invested at the announced rate of return. If the actual rate of return is higher than the announced rate of return, the excess investment income does not benefit the employees but rather reduces the contribution required to be made by the employer. If actual earnings are lower than the announced rate, the employer must make up the difference. To avoid this outcome, the plan will select a rate of return that it is confident that it can earn on the investment of the plan assets.

Many cash balance plans come about by the conversion of existing overfunded, traditional defined benefit plans into cash balance plans. The following case describes one such conversion.

CIGNA CORPORATION v. AMARA (PART I)

131 S. Ct. 1866 (2011)

Justice Breyer delivered the opinion of the Court.

In 1998, petitioner CIGNA Corporation changed the nature of its basic pension plan for employees. Previously, the plan provided a retiring employee with a defined benefit in the form of an annuity calculated on the basis of his preretirement salary and length of service. The new plan provided most retiring employees with a (lump sum) cash balance calculated on the basis of a defined annual contribution from CIGNA as increased by compound interest. Because many employees had already earned at least some old-plan benefits, the new plan translated already-earned benefits into an opening amount in the employee's cash balance account.

* * *

I

* * *

A

Under CIGNA's pre-1998 defined-benefit retirement plan, an employee with at least five years service would receive an annuity annually paying an amount that depended upon the employee's salary and length of service. Depending on when the employee had joined CIGNA, the annuity would equal either (1) 2 percent of the employee's average salary over his final three years with CIGNA, multiplied by the number of years worked (up to 30); or (2) 1 2/3 percent of the employee's average salary over his final five years with CIGNA, multiplied by the number of years worked (up to 35). Calculated either way, the annuity would approach 60 percent of a longtime employee's final salary. A well-paid longtime employee, earning, say, $160,000 per year, could receive a retirement annuity paying the employee about $96,000 per year until his death. The plan offered many employees at least one other benefit: They could retire early, at age 55, and receive an only-somewhat-reduced annuity.

In November 1997, CIGNA sent its employees a newsletter announcing that it intended to put in place a new pension plan. The new plan would substitute an "account balance plan" for CIGNA's pre-existing defined-benefit system. The newsletter added that the old plan would end on December 31, 1997, that CIGNA would introduce (and describe) the new plan sometime during 1998, and that the new plan would apply retroactively to January 1, 1998.

Eleven months later CIGNA filled in the details. Its new plan created an individual retirement account for each employee. (The account consisted of a bookkeeping entry backed by a CIGNA-funded trust.) Each year CIGNA would contribute to the employee's individual account an amount equal to between 3 percent and 8.5 percent of the employee's salary, depending upon age, length of service, and certain other factors. The account balance would earn compound interest at a rate equal to the return on 5-year treasury bills plus one-quarter percent (but no less than 4.5 percent and no greater than 9 percent). Upon retirement the employee would receive the amount then in his or her individual account-in the form of either a lump sum or whatever annuity the lump sum then would buy. As promised, CIGNA would open the accounts and begin to make contributions as of January 1, 1998.

But what about the retirement benefits that employees had already earned prior to January 1, 1998? CIGNA promised to make an initial contribution to the individual's account equal to the value of that employee's already earned benefits. And the new plan set forth a method for calculating that initial contribution. The method consisted of calculating the amount as of the employee's (future) retirement date of the annuity to which the employee's salary and length of service already (i.e., as of December 31, 1997) entitled him and then discounting that sum to its present (i.e., January 1, 1998) value.

An example will help: Imagine an employee born on January 1, 1966, who joined CIGNA in January 1991 on his 25th birthday, and who (during the five years preceding the plan changeover) earned an average salary of $100,000 per year. As of January 1, 1998, the old plan would have entitled that employee to an annuity equal to $100,000 times 7 (years then worked) times 1 2/3 percent, or $11,667 per year-when he retired in 2031 at age 65. The 2031 price of an annuity paying $11,667 per year until death depends upon interest rates and mortality assumptions at that time. If we assume the annuity would pay 7 percent until the holder's death (and we use the mortality assumptions used by the plan), then the 2031 price of such an annuity would be about $120,500. And CIGNA should initially deposit in this individual's account on January 1, 1998, an amount that will grow to become $120,500, 33 years later, in 2031, when the individual retires. If we assume a 5 percent average interest rate, then that amount presently (i.e., as of January 1, 1998) equals about $24,000. And (with one further mortality-related adjustment that we shall describe infra,) that is the amount, more or less, that the new plan's transition rules would have required CIGNA initially to deposit. Then CIGNA would make further annual deposits, and all the deposited amounts would earn compound interest. When the employee retired, he would receive the resulting lump sum.

The new plan also provided employees a guarantee: An employee would receive, upon retirement, either (1) the amount to which he or she had become entitled as of January 1, 1998, or (2) the amount then in his or her individual account, whichever was greater. Thus, the employee in our example would receive (in 2031) no less than an annuity paying $11,667 per year for life.

B

1

The District Court found that CIGNA's initial descriptions of its new plan were significantly incomplete and misled its employees. In November 1997, for example, CIGNA sent the employees a newsletter that said the new plan would "significantly enhance" its "retirement program," would produce "an overall improvement in . . . retirement benefits," and would provide "the same benefit security" with "steadier benefit growth." App. 990a, 991a, 993a. CIGNA also told its employees that they would "see the growth in [their] total retirement benefits from CIGNA every year," id., at 952a, that its initial deposit "represent[ed] the full value of the benefit [they] earned for service before 1998," Record E-503 (Exh. 98), and that "[o]ne advantage the company will not get from the retirement program changes is cost savings." App. 993a.

In fact, the new plan saved the company $10 million annually (though CIGNA later said it devoted the savings to other employee benefits). Its initial deposit did not "represen[t] the full value of the benefit" that employees had "earned for service before 1998." And the plan made a significant number of employees worse off in at least the following specific ways:

First, the initial deposit calculation ignored the fact that the old plan offered many CIGNA employees the right to retire early (beginning at age 55) with only somewhat reduced benefits. This right was valuable. For example, as of January 1, 1998, respondent Janice Amara had earned vested age-55 retirement benefits of $1,833 per month, but CIGNA's initial deposit in her new-plan individual retirement account (ignoring this benefit) would have allowed her at age 55 to buy an annuity benefit of only $900 per month.

Second, as we previously indicated but did not explain the new plan adjusted CIGNA's initial deposit downward to account for the fact that, unlike the old plan's lifetime annuity, an employee's survivors would receive the new plan's benefits (namely, the amount in the employee's individual account) even if the employee died before retiring. The downward adjustment consisted of multiplying the otherwise-required deposit by the probability that the employee would live until retirement-a 90 percent probability in the example of our 32-year-old. And that meant that CIGNA's initial deposit in our example-the amount that was supposed to grow to $120,500 by 2031-would be less than $22,000, not $24,000 (the number we computed). The employee, of course, would receive a benefit in return-namely, a form of life insurance. But at least some employees might have preferred the retirement benefit and consequently could reasonably have thought it important to know that the new plan traded away one-tenth of their already-earned benefits for a life insurance policy that they might not have wanted.

Third, the new plan shifted the risk of a fall in interest rates from CIGNA to its employees. Under the old plan, CIGNA had to buy a retiring employee an annuity that paid a specified sum irrespective of whether falling interest rates made it more expensive for CIGNA to pay for that annuity. And falling interest rates also meant that any sum CIGNA set aside to buy that annuity would grow more slowly over time, thereby requiring CIGNA to set aside more money to make any specific sum available at retirement. Under the new plan CIGNA did not have to buy a retiring employee an annuity that paid a specific sum. The employee would simply receive whatever sum his account contained. And falling interest rates meant that the account's lump sum would earn less money each year after the employee retired. Annuities, for example, would become more expensive (any fixed purchase price paying for less annual income). At the same time falling interest meant that the individual account would grow more slowly over time, leaving the employee with less money at retirement.

Of course, interest rates might rise instead of fall, leaving CIGNA's employees better off under the new plan. But the latter advantage does not cancel out the former disadvantage, for most individuals are risk averse. And that means that most of CIGNA's employees would have preferred that CIGNA, rather than they, bear these risks.

The amounts likely involved are significant. If, in our example, interest rates between 1998 and 2031 averaged 4 percent rather than the 5 percent we assumed, and if in 2031 annuities paid 6 percent rather than the 7 percent we assumed, then CIGNA would have had to make an initial deposit of $35,500 (not $24,000) to assure that employee the $11,667 annual annuity payment to which he had already become entitled. Indeed, that $24,000 that CIGNA would have contributed (leaving aside the life-insurance problem) would have provided enough money to buy (in 2031) an annuity that assured the employee an annual payment of only about $8,000 (rather than $11,667).

We recognize that the employee in our example (like others) might have continued to work for CIGNA after January 1, 1998; and he would thereby eventually have earned a pension that, by the time of his retirement, was worth far more than $11,667. But that is so because CIGNA made an additional contribution for each year worked after January 1, 1998. If interest rates fell (as they did), it would take the employee several additional years of work simply to catch up (under the new plan) to where he had already been (under the old plan) as of January 1, 1998, a phenomenon known in pension jargon as "wear away."

* * *

COLEMAN J. F. CANNON, CASHING IN ON OLDER WORKERS: AGE DISCRIMINATION CLAIMS IN CASH-BALANCE PENSION PLANS

19 LAW & INEQ. 31, 37–38 (2001)

Today, the traditional model of employer-sponsored defined benefit pensions is somewhat of an endangered species among the various types of retirement plans. Changes in the economy and the workforce have altered the format of plans that employers find meet their dual goals of minimizing costs and attracting desired employees. While traditional defined benefit plans still exist, the number in existence has been static for many years. In addition to relying more on defined contribution plans, many employers are moving away from the traditional model and toward the cash-balance model.

Unlike the traditional model, cash-balance plans define their benefits not in terms of a retirement annuity, but rather as a lump-sum amount. Cash-balance plans make a "contribution" to the employees' account on a regular basis, and the account balance grows at a stated rate of interest. The account, however, is simply a record-keeping device. A plan sponsor still pays for benefits out of one pension fund, but the account mechanism is used to show employees how their pensions grow while they are working. If an employee has met the vesting requirements when she ends her employment, the balance of the account is hers to take with her. Thus, instead of averaging pay in the later, more lucrative years of employment as most traditional defined benefit pensions do, cash-balance plans require employees to accrue a flat percentage of pay annually over their careers.

Older employees often fare less well when an employer adopts a cash balance plan. As a result, a number of lawsuits have been filed against employers who have instituted a cash balance plan by older employees who allege that such plans unlawfully discriminate against older workers. In the following case, cash balance plans were held not to discriminate against older employees.

COOPER v. IBM PERSONAL PENSION PLAN

457 F.3d 636 (7th Cir. 2006), *cert. denied*, 127 S. Ct. 1143 (2007)

EASTERBROOK, CIRCUIT JUDGE.

The IBM Personal Pension Plan is a cash-balance defined-benefit plan. It is almost, but not quite, a defined-contribution plan. Although each employee in a defined-contribution plan has a fully funded individual account, the personal account in a cash-balance plan is not separately funded. Instead IBM imputes value to the account in the form of "credits": there are pay credits (set at 5% of the employee's gross taxable income) and interest credits (set at 100 basis points above the rate of interest on one-year Treasury bills). A trust holds assets that may (or may not) be enough to fund all of the individual accounts when workers quit or retire. IBM's plan permits an employee who quits or retires after working long enough for pension benefits to vest (a maximum of five years) to withdraw the balance in cash or roll it over into a fully funded annuity. During the time before cash-out the employee takes the risk that IBM will suffer business reverses and be unable to pay the full stated value of the account (if th e amount already in trust for participants as a group turns out to be insufficient); otherwise IBM's plan is economically identical to a defined-contribution plan funded the same way and invested in a bond fund that returns 1% above the Treasury rate.

Plaintiffs in this class-action litigation contend that IBM's plan violates a subsection of ERISA (the Employee Retirement Income Security Act) that prohibits age discrimination. The district court ruled in plaintiffs' favor . . . .

All terms of IBM's plan are age-neutral. Every covered employee receives the same 5% pay credit and the same interest credit per annum. The basis of the plaintiffs challenge — and the district court's holding — is that younger employees receive interest credits for more years. The language on which plaintiffs rely was added to ERISA in 1986; Congress also enacted a parallel provision covering defined-contribution plans. We set these out alongside to facilitate comparison:

Defined-benefit plans: ERISA § 204(b)(1)(H)(i)

> [A] defined benefit plan shall be treated as not satisfying the requirements of this paragraph if, under the plan, an employee's benefit accrual is ceased, or the rate of an employee's benefit accrual is reduced, because of the attainment of any age.

Defined-contribution plans: ERISA § 204(b)(2)(A)

> A defined contribution plan satisfies the requirements of this paragraph if, under the plan, allocations to the employee's account are not ceased, and the rate at which amounts are allocated to the employee's account is not reduced, because of the attainment of any age.

These appear to say the same thing, except that the rule for defined-benefit plans tells us what is not allowed, while the rule for defined-contribution plans tells us what works. Either way, the employer can't stop making allocations (or accruals) to the plan or change their rate on account of age. The IBM plan does neither of these things and therefore, one would suppose, complies with the statute. If this were a real, rather than a phantom, defined-contribution plan, that much would be taken for granted. Yet if the 5%-plus-interest formula is non-discriminatory when used in a defined-contribution plan, why should it become unlawful because the account balances are book entries rather than cash?

Plaintiffs persuaded the district court, however, that the two subsections are radically different. That difference is attributable to the phrase "benefit accrual," which appears in the subsection for defined-benefit plans but not the one for defined-contribution plans. Neither ERISA nor any regulation defines this phrase, so the district judge went looking for some equivalent elsewhere in the statute. It found the phrase "accrued benefit," which is defined in § 3(23)(A). An "accrued benefit" is an amount "expressed in the form of an annual benefit commencing at normal retirement age." Plug this back into § 204(b)(1)(H)(i), and the rule against discrimination then refers not to what IBM puts into the plan, but what the employee takes out on retirement. Someone who leaves IBM at age 50, after 20 years of service, will have a larger annual benefit at 65 than someone whose 20 years of service conclude with retirement at age 65. The former receives 15 years' more interest than the latter — and the judge assumed that this is not counterbalanced by the fact that older workers generally draw higher salaries. Under the district court's analysis, compound interest becomes a scourge, for the younger the employee when any given year's salary is earned, the greater the payout "expressed in the form of an annual benefit commencing at normal retirement age."

This approach treats the time value of money as age discrimination. Yet the statute does not require that equation. Interest is not treated as age discrimination for a defined-contribution plan, and the fact that these subsections are so close in both function and expression implies that it should not be treated as discriminatory for a defined-benefit plan either. The phrase "benefit accrual" reads most naturally as a reference to what the employer puts in (either in absolute terms or as a rate of change), while the defined phrase "accrued benefit" refers to outputs after compounding. That's where this litigation went off the rails: a phrase dealing with inputs was misunderstood to refer to outputs. As long as we think of "benefit accrual" as referring to what the employer imputes to the account — an understanding reinforced by the use of the word "allocation" in the subsection addressing defined-contribution plans — there is no statutory difference between the treatment of economically equivalent defined-benefit and defined-contribution plans. For defined-benefit plans, where the account is an accounting entry rather than cash, "benefit accrual" matches the money "allocated" to a defined-contribution plan.

Nothing in the language or background of § 204(b)(1)(H)(i) suggests that Congress set out to legislate against the fact that younger workers have (statistically) more time left before retirement, and thus a greater opportunity to earn interest on each year's retirement savings. Treating the time value of money as a form of discrimination is not sensible. *Cf. Hazen Paper Co. v. Biggins*, 507 U.S. 604, 611 (1993) (variables correlated with age must be kept "analytically distinct" from age when searching for discrimination). The parallel between the subsections for defined-benefit and defined-contribution plans shows as much. All sorts of things go wrong unless we treat both § 204(b)(1)(H)(i) and § 204(b)(2)(A) as addressing the rate at which value is added (or imputed) to an account, rather than the annual pension at retirement age. Consider a formula that adds $500 to annual pension benefits for every year worked. This setup economically favors older workers (as does a top-five-year-salary multiplier) because it ignores the time value of money and treats the last year of work as contributing equally with the first. Yet on the plaintiffs' understanding it would be a form of discrimination against the old, because the $500 is a smaller "rate of benefit accrual" as time passes. Someone who worked two years would get a "100% rate of increase" in his second year (his annual benefits on retirement would jump from $500 to $1,000), while someone who works 20 years receives only a 2.56% increase (from $19,500 to $20,000) in Year 20.

Our conclusion that "benefit accrual" (for defined-benefit plans) and "allocation" (for defined-contribution plans) both refer to the employer's contribution rather than the time value of money between contribution and retirement has the support of regulations that the Treasury Department proposed. (Appropriations riders have prevented the Treasury from taking final action on the draft regulations, but they still help to inform our understanding of the statute.) The draft regulations treat the "rate of benefit accrual" as "the increase in the participant's accrued normal retirement benefit for the year." 67 Fed. Reg. 76123, 76125 (Dec. 11, 2002). For cash-balance plans in particular the phrase would have been defined as "the additions to the participant's hypothetical account for the plan year." 67 Fed. Reg. at 76126. The draft specifies that interest credits must accrue "at a reasonable rate of interest that does not decrease because of the attainment of age" and be provided "for all future periods, including after normal retirement age." *Ibid.*

Thus the Treasury's view, like our independent reading, looks at the rate of contribution (what goes into the account) rather than the annual rate of withdrawal at retirement. The Treasury asks: "if this employee were younger, would the hypothetical balance have grown more this year?" For IBM's plan, the answer is no. When an employee is 20, his account is increased monthly by 5% of his salary plus credits based on the account's balance multiplied by a prescribed interest rate. The same is true when the employee turns 50, 60, or 70. Neither the contribution rate nor the interest rate changes with age. (No one contests the rate at which interest is credited-though 100 basis points over the Treasury rate looks low compared with what investments could earn in the private market and therefore could be understood to disfavor younger employees.)

Plaintiffs propose a different definition of "benefit accrual": annual pension (at retirement age) divided by salary. Contributions at age 25 produce an annual pensio n benefit that equals about 3% of each year's income in nominal dollars, while contributions at 65 produce annual benefits only 0.4% of the year's income. Not surprising, and hardly illuminating; this is just another illustration of the power of compound interest. The example depends on (a) allowing the pension to be increased by compounding, while (b) failing to discount the pension to present value. Stated another way, this example compares 1966 dollars (when the 25-year-old earned the salary) with 2006 dollars (when that person turns 65 and starts to draw a pension); of course the return on investment looks good, but much of it is inflation and the rest is real interest rates. The person who earns a salary in 2005 and retires in 2006 is (materially) unaffected by both inflation and compound interest. Nothing depends on age. Someone who earns a salary at age 65 and waits 40 years to start drawing a pension would receive the same 3%-of-salary-per-retirement-year as the illustrative 25-year-old who retires at 65; and someone who earns wages at 25 and retires the next year gets the same 0.4%-of-salary annual pension, if not less (because of discounting).

Much of the plaintiffs' argument rests on the idea that the account of a 25-year-old worker does not get 5% plus periodic interest, but instead is immediately credited with 5% of salary plus 40 years' interest. That makes the contributions look discriminatory: the 25-year-old worker's account receives 40 times as much interest credit in the year the contributions accrue as a 65-year-old worker's account. Once again, however, this perspective misunderstands both the statute and the time value of money.

Nothing in either ERISA or the IBM plan requires 40 years of interest to be credited to the account as soon as the young worker earns wages. What plaintiffs have in mind is the rule that, when any beneficiary (young or old) elects to take a cash distribution or roll the account into an annuity before reaching age 65, the plan must distribute a lump sum calculated to be the "actuarial equivalent" of the annuity that would be available at normal retirement age. ERISA § 204(c)(3). To derive the "actuarial equivalent" of a pension at age 65, a plan must (a) add all interest that would accrue through age 65, then (b) discount the resulting sum to its present value. *Berger v. Xerox Corp. Retirement Income Guarantee Plan*, 338 F.3d 755, 762–763 (7th Cir. 2003). Plaintiffs characterize step (a) as extra interest credits for the young, but they ignore step (b). The discount rate may be close to (if it does not exceed) the rate at which interest is imputed, so the amount paid out in cash may be close to if not below the nominal balance in the account. Berger did not consider § 204(b)(1)(H)(i) and does not hold that the process of grossing up the balance and then discounting is a form of age discrimination. To the contrary: *Berger* described this process as the means to *avoid* age discrimination.

. . .

Here, as so often, it is essential to separate age discrimination from other characteristics that may be correlated with age. [A] plaintiff alleging age discrimination must demonstrate that the complained-of effect is *actually* on account of age. One need only look at IBM's formula to rule out a violation. It is age-neutral.

Now this may give a clue about why plaintiffs (a class of older workers) have sued. The cash-balance plan replaced a more traditional arrangement under which the annual pension on retirement was a function of closing salary (say, an average of the last five years before retirement) multiplied by the number of years of service. Because wages rise with seniority, such a formula favors older workers. Workers who quit or retire early not only miss out on the rising wages that accompany seniority but also don't receive credit for the time value of money: years of service at age 30 and at age 70 count equally in the traditional formula. Many employers design such back-loaded systems to give the most-experienced members of the labor force a reason (even beyond rising salary) to stay on the job. Like a defined-contribution plan, a cash-balance plan removes the back-loading of the pension formula; older workers (accurately) perceive that they are worse off under a cash-balance approach than under a traditional years-of-service-times-final-salary plan. But removing a feature that gave extra benefits to the old differs from discriminating against them. Replacing a plan that discriminates against the young with one that is age-neutral does not discriminate against the old.

There is a transition issue. When IBM moved employees from a more traditional plan to a cash-balance system, it gave them the greater of the present value of their pension entitlements as of the transition date or the account balance that they would have had if IBM had a cash-balance plan in effect since the employee came to work. Plaintiffs complain that this gives the younger workers too much credit for interest (because more time passes between their work and retirement dates), but that rehashes arguments that we've already rejected. Every employee with the same salary and service record receives the same opening account balance under the new plan. That the change disappointed expectations is not material. An employer is free to move from one legal plan to another legal plan, provided that it does not diminish vested interests — and this transition did not. *Cf. Lockheed Corp. v. Spink*, 517 U.S. 882 (1996) (employers are not fiduciaries under ERISA when they create or amend pension plans).

. . .

The judgment of the district court is reversed, and the case is remanded with directions to enter judgment in IBM's favor.

A claim of age discrimination was also rejected by the Third Circuit in *Register v. PNC Financial Services*, 477 F.3d 56 (3d Cir. 2007) and the Sixth Circuit in *Drutis v. Rand McNally & Co.*, 499 F.3d 608 (6th Cir. 2007). In contrast, in 2006 a federal district judge ruled that Citigroup Inc.'s cash balance pension plan discriminated against older workers. *In re Citigroup Pension Plan ERISA Litigation*, 470 F. Supp. 2d 323 (S.D.N.Y. 2006).

The Pension Protection Act of 2006 amended and clarified the law by providing that cash balance and other hybrid plans do not violate ERISA, fail to qualify for favorable tax treatment, or discriminate on the basis of age if a number of requirements are satisfied. Primarily to avoid influencing past and current litigation, the rules set forth in the Act only apply to cash balance plans created on or after June 29, 2005.

The first requirement imposed by the Pension Protection Act is that a participant's accrued benefit under a cash balance or hybrid plan must be at least as great as that of any similarly situated younger individual, defined as any individual who is identical in every respect, including period of service, compensation, date of hire, work history, etc., except age — who is or could be a participant in the plan. PPA § 701(a), adding IRC § 411(b)(5)(A); ERISA § 204(b)(5)(A); and ADEA § 4(i)(10)(A).

Second, the "interest credits" provided under the plan must not be at a rate that exceeds a "market rate of return"; although, the plan may provide for a reasonable minimum guaranteed rate of return or for interest crediting at the greater of a fixed or variable rate. PPA § 701(a), adding IRC § 411(b)(5)(B)(i); ERISA § 204(b)(5)(B)(i); and ADEA § 4(i)(10)(B)(i).

Third, the Pension Protection Act prohibits the use of wear-away provisions in conversions from defined benefit plans to cash balance plans. Thus, if a traditional defined benefit plan is converted to a cash balance or other hybrid plan, a participant's accrued benefit must be the sum of (1) his or her accrued benefit determined prior to the conversion, plus (2) the benefit accrued for years of service after the conversion. PPA § 701(a), adding IRC § 411(b)(5)(B)(iii); ERISA § 204(b)(5)(B)(iii); and ADEA § 4(i)(10)(B)(iii).

Finally, the Pension Protection Act eliminates the whipsaw problem by providing that, for purposes of calculating lump sums and certain other optional forms of benefits, a plan can treat the present value of a participant's accrued benefit as being equal to his or her hypothetical account balance. PPA § 701(a), adding IRC § 411(a)(13) and ERISA § 203(f).

2-2 QUESTIONS AND PROBLEMS

1. What are the advantages of a cash balance plan relative to a traditional defined contribution plan? To a traditional defined benefit plan? What are the disadvantages?

2. Why might an employer adopt a cash balance plan rather than a 401(k) plan?

B. TAX QUALIFIED PLANS

Retirement plans are generally either "qualified" or "nonqualified." Qualified plans must meet the strict requirements set forth in the Internal Revenue Code (primarily in IRC § 401(a)) in order to receive favorable federal income tax treatment. Nonqualified plans, which do not meet those requirements, do not receive favorable tax treatment. Qualified plans come in a wide variety of forms and include defined benefit plans, defined contribution plans, including 401(k) plans, and hybrid plans, such as cash balance plans.

[1] Tax Advantages of Qualified Plans

Qualified plans enjoy four significant federal income tax advantages.

1. The employer may deduct contributions to the plan at the time they are made, regardless of when the participants include the benefits in their income. IRC § 404. Under general tax law, an employer cannot take a deduction for salary related expenses until the employee includes the payment in income. IRC § 404, however, provides an exception to that rule and permits employers an accelerated deduction for contributions to qualified retirement plans.

2. Even though the employer is permitted a current tax deduction for contributions, employees who participate in the plans do not include the contributions in current income and so delay taxation until the contributions are distributed to them. IRC § 402(a)(1).

3. The pension plan trust that receives and invests the contributions is a tax exempt entity. It does not pay income taxes on contributions or upon the earnings from the investments of those contributions. IRC §§ 401(a); 501(a). The tax-free build-up of investment income is the essence of the favorable treatment of qualified pension plans.

4. To avoid taxation upon the receipt of a lump-sum distribution from the plan, a participant can roll over the distribution into an individual retirement account (IRA) or another qualified plan, thereby continuing to defer taxation until the proceeds are distributed from the IRA or new qualified plan. IRC § 402(c).

To demonstrate: in 2011 the employer, Rho Co, contributes $1,000 to a qualified profit-sharing plan on behalf of its employee, Clarissa. In 2011, Rho Co deducts the $1,000 contribution from its taxable income as an ordinary and necessary business expense. The plan is not taxed upon receipt of the $1,000, nor does Clarissa have to report the $1,000 as income even though it is irrevocably set aside for her. The plan invests the $1,000 in corporate bonds that earn $70 per year, but is not taxed on that income. In 2020, Clarissa retires, and the plan makes a lump-sum distribution to her of $1,700, which is taxable income to Clarissa upon its receipt in 2020. If Clarissa had rolled the lump-sum distribution over into an IRA, she could have delayed the taxation of the lump-sum distribution until it was distributed from the IRA.

Though the employee is not taxed on the employer contribution, the employee will be taxed when the amount is distributed from the pension plan. Assuming that tax rates do not change, the eventual tax burden is the same. The real benefit enjoyed by a qualified plan is the deferral of taxation on the investment income earned by the trust that holds the plan assets.

To demonstrate, assume a constant income tax rate of 20 percent. Emily earns $1,000 in 2010 and so pays a tax of $200, leaving her with $800 which she places in a drawer. This continues for the next two years, through 2012, at which time Emily has $2,400 (3 x $800) in the drawer, which she then withdraws to help pay for her retirement. Suppose, however, that instead of paying Emily the $1,000, her employer contributes $1,000 to a pension fund, which puts the money a drawer for Emily's benefit. At the end of three years, the trust fund drawer contains $3,000, at which time Emily retires. The trust fund gives her the $3,000. She is taxed at 20 percent or $600 and so has $2,400, the same amount as if she had been taxed each year upon receipt. Assuming a constant tax rate, the tax deferral provides no advantage to Emily.

Now assume that each year Emily receives the $1,000, pays the $200 in taxes, and invests the remaining $800 at a annual rate of 10 percent. Because she is taxed on the interest income at a 20 percent rate, she has an after-tax rate of return of 8 percent. Assuming she receives the $1,000 ($800 after taxes) on January 1, over three years her $800 a year savings will grow as follows:

End of -				Interest earned after taxes	Total
Year 1	$800	*	8% =	$64	$864
Year 2	$1,664	*	8% =	$133.12	$1,797.12
Year 3	$2,597.12	*	8% =	$207.77	$2,804.89

Assume that instead of paying Emily the $1,000, her employer pays it to a qualified plan. The plan's trust fund receives the $1,000 each year and does not pay taxes on either the $1,000 or the interest at 10 percent that it earns on the investment. Emily, however, is taxed on the entire amount when it is distributed to her upon her retirement. The result is:

End of	Total Savings			Interest (Tax Free)	Total
Year 1	$1,000	*	10% =	$100	$1,100
Year 2	$2,100	*	10% =	$210	$2,310
Year 3	$3,310	*	10% =	$331	$3,641

The fund distributes the $3,641 to Emily who pays an income tax at a rate of 20 percent, or $728.20, leaving her with $2,912.80. Compare that with the $2,804.89 that she would had if she had received the $1,000 each year. A difference of $107.91 or four percent more. If we increase the number of years that the money is held by the tax-exempt pension fund, the percentage of additional income available to Emily increases significantly.

Assuming constant tax rates, the tax deferral granted to qualified plans is economically identical to not taxing the investment earnings of the plan. To illustrate, suppose that Emily receives the same $1,000 each year subject to a 20 percent tax rate. She earns the same 10 percent on the plan assets but those earnings are not subject to tax. The result is:

End of	Total Savings		Interest (Tax Free)	Total
-				
Year 1	$800	* 10% =	$80	$880
Year 2	$1,680	* 10% =	$168	$1,848
Year 3	$2,648	* 10% =	$264.80	$2,912.80

At the end of three years, this total ($2,912.80) is identical to the amount she would have received from a tax qualified plan after taxes were paid on the distribution.

Currently, some IRAs (known as Roth IRAs) follow this form of taxation. Specifically, contributions to the IRA must be made with after-tax dollars (the contributions are not deductible), but all earnings on the Roth IRA accumulate tax free and all distributions from the IRA are tax free. Beginning in 2006, 401(k) plans were able to incorporate a "qualified Roth program," pursuant to which participants may elect to have all or a portion of their elective deferrals to the plan designated as after-tax "Roth contributions." IRC § 402A. Like Roth IRAs, Roth 401(k) contributions will be subject to tax, but the earnings on those taxes will be tax free and there will be no tax imposed on distributions. Economically, the tax treatment of Roth 401(k) plans will be identical to that of traditional qualified plans (except that the contribution limits for Roth 401(k) plans may be higher).

The wisdom of granting favorable tax treatment to qualified pension plans is questioned by some commentators.

NORMAN P. STEIN, PATRICIA E. DILLEY, LEVERAGE, LINKAGE, AND LEAKAGE: PROBLEMS WITH THE PRIVATE PENSION SYSTEM AND HOW THEY SHOULD INFORM THE SOCIAL SECURITY REFORM DEBATE

58 Wash. & Lee L. Rev. 1369, 1374 (2001)

The orthodox explanation for the subsidy is the provision of retirement income security for employees who would not otherwise save adequately for retirement. The intended primary beneficiaries of the tax expenditure, then, are low- and moderate-income employees, who often find it difficult to save on their own for retirement because of immediate consumption demands. More affluent individuals have greater capacity to save for their retirement on their own, without governmental assistance.

Given that the intended primary beneficiaries of the subsidy are low- and moderate-income workers, the structure of the Internal Revenue Code's subsidy of retirement plans might strike us as irrational, for its architecture is one of unreconstructed tax deferral for plan participants. The value of the tax deferral to a given taxpayer correlates directly to that taxpayer's marginal tax rate. Thus, the Code provides the greatest retirement tax subsidy to the people with the greatest capacity to save for their own retirement, and the smallest to those with the smallest capacity. Understood another way, this upside-down tax subsidy is an arguably rational component of a two-part governmental strategy to enlist the private sector in building retirement savings for low- and moderate-income workers.

This strategy is first, to make the tax benefits of qualified plans sufficiently attractive to the tax-sensitive people who own and manage businesses that they decide to set up plans to capture tax benefits for themselves; and second, to require such plans, once established, to provide meaningful benefits not only to the people who set them up but also to their low- and moderate-income employees. The Code effects the latter part of the strategy through a series of statutory provisions, most prominently the nondiscrimination rules. Professor Dan Halperin has used a (tax) carrot and (regulatory) stick metaphor to describe the strategy. Some have labeled this simply trickle-down benefits policy. This is, in any event, the idea that we refer to as leverage. As the pension economist Alicia Munnell put it, "The rationale for favorable tax treatment of qualified plans is that retirement benefits for rank-and-file employees will exist if Congress provides tax incentive that induce higher paid employees to support the establishment of employer-sponsored pension plans."

The tax treatment of qualified plans has been subject to criticism, and indeed, its rationale is only arguably rational. Firms do respond to the incentives by establishing plans. But firms often do not want to cover low- and moderate-income employees because those employees, at least as a group, do not value deferred compensation at its cost to the firm. Accordingly, some employers who participate in the system play a game of statutory limbo, bending under the regulatory sticky by manipulating the complexities of the nondiscrimination rules to minimize benefits for rank-and-file employees, while maximizing benefits for the highly compensated. Moreover, many employers simply do not respond to the incentives and fail to sponsor pension plans. Thus, the system is both overinclusive in that it provides benefits for those who can save for their own retirement without governmental incentive, and underinclusive because it fails to cover many low- and moderate-income workers and often pays such employees trivial benefits, if that.

---

[2] Tax Qualification Requirements

Section 401(a) of the IRC sets forth a host of requirements that qualified plans must satisfy. IRC § 401(a) includes 37 separate subsections, many of which cross reference other sections of the IRC. Generally speaking, two policy goals can be said to underlie these requirements. The first, and perhaps most important, goal, is to protect plan participants and their beneficiaries. This is a goal that ERISA shares and many, if not all, of the tax qualification requirements that further this purpose are duplicated in ERISA. For example, qualified plans must be created "for the exclusive benefit of [an employer's] employees or their beneficiaries" and must be in writing. IRC § 401(a), ERISA § 404(a)(1)(A). Treas. Reg. § 401-1(a)(2), ERISA § 402(a)(1). The IRC § 401 qualification requirements include a set of rules that are often referred to as the "pension benefit security" rules. They include vesting requirements, minimum participation standards, benefit accrual rules that prohibit defined benefit plans from backloading benefits (that is, having participants earn most of their benefits in their later years of employment), and an "anti-cutback rule" that prohibits pension plans from reducing accrued, i.e. earned, benefits. These rules are discussed in more detail in later Chapters.

Not all of the plan qualification requirements are designed to protect plan participants. The favorable tax treatment that is accorded to qualified plans results in the federal government's second largest tax expenditure, valued at $515.4 billion of foregone income tax revenues between 2010 and 2014. Consequently, some of the tax qualification requirements are designed to insure that benefits do not go disproportionately to higher paid employees and that benefits are used for retirement plan purposes. Unlike the tax qualification requirements that protect plan participants and beneficiaries, the tax qualification requirements that target the tax subsidy are not duplicated in ERISA.

The nondiscrimination rules are the primary means employed to insure that the tax subsidy of benefits is not disproportionally enjoyed by higher paid employees or owners of enterprises that sponsor a pension plan. Convoluted, detailed and complicated, the nondiscrimination rules are perhaps the most complex set of rules in the entire IRC. Despite their complexity, they have a simple purpose: ensure that tax qualified plans provide benefits to the lesser paid as well as to the higher paid. There are two principal nondiscrimination requirements: the IRC § 410(b) minimum coverage rules and the IRC § 401(a)(4) prohibition on discrimination in contributions or benefits. The minimum coverage rules mandate that the percentage of highly compensated employees participating in a plan not be excessive relative to the percentage of participating nonhighly compensated employees. The nondiscrimination in contributions or benefits rules require that the contributions and benefits provided to nonhighly compensated employees be roughly comparable to the benefits provided to highly compensated employees. In addition, IRC § 401(a)(26) requires that defined benefit plans cover a minimum number of employees, essentially the lesser of 50 employees or 40 percent of the employer's workforce. (These rules are discussed in Chapter 8.)

Tax qualified plans that are "top heavy," that is, provide more than 60 percent of their benefits to "key employees," must satisfy certain minimum vesting and benefit requirements set forth in IRC § 416. Key employees are defined as: 1) officers with compensation in excess of $130,000 (indexed to $165,000 in 2012); 2) 5-percent owners; and 3) 1-percent owners with compensation in excess of $150,000. IRC § 416(i)(1)(A). Like the nondiscrimination rules, the top heavy rules are designed to ensure benefits of qualified plans are enjoyed by the lower paid as well as the higher paid and corporate officers. (The vesting rules applicable to top heavy plans are discussed in Chapter 4.)

The tax qualification requirements also target the tax subsidy by limiting the benefits payable to highly compensated employees. For example, under IRC § 401(a)(17), the amount of compensation which a qualified plan can take into account for plan purposes is limited to $250,000, indexed for inflation, in 2012. To illustrate, if a qualified profit-sharing plan promises to make a contribution on behalf of each participant equal to two percent of compensation per year, a participant who earns $500,000 per year is only entitled to receive a contribution of $5,000 (2% x $250,000 = $5,000) rather than $10,000 (2% x $500,000 = $10,000). (This limit is discussed in Chapter 9.) IRC § 415(b) limits the annual benefit that a participant may receive under a defined benefit plan to the lesser of $160,000, indexed for inflation ($200,000 in 2008), or 100 percent of the participant's average compensation for the three consecutive years of the participant's highest compensation. IRC § 415(b)(1). (IRC § 415 is discussed in Chapter 9.) To ensure that the benefits of the deferral of income taxes benefits participants rather than the employer, IRC § 411(d)(3) requires that the plan fully vest all participants in their plan benefits upon termination or partial termination of the plan. (The termination rules are discussed in Chapter 10.)

To ensure that the tax subsidy accorded qualified plans is used for retirement purposes rather than estate accumulation purposes, IRC § 401(a)(9) contains minimum distribution requirements of benefits, which generally require that plan participants begin receiving benefits under a qualified plan no later than age 70½. (These rules are discussed in Chapter 9.)

2-3 QUESTIONS AND PROBLEMS

1. To provide additional benefits for their executives, employers often create nonqualified plans that are not eligible for favorable tax treatment. Why do employers establish these plans? Why do they typically benefit only highly paid executives?

2. Is there any way to simplify the current qualified plan system while still insuring that the advantages of the favorable income tax treatment will not be limited to the highly paid employees or the owners of the entity that sponsors the plan?

[3] Determination Letter Process and Correction Programs

Because of the technical complexity of qualified plans, most plans sponsors request that the IRS review their qualified plans under its "determination letter process." The cost of obtaining a determination letter depends upon the type of plan submitted. The fees for pre-approved plans are substantially lower than those for individually designed plans. In the determination letter process, the IRS reviews the submitted plan for drafting defects and whether it meets all technical requirements. An IRS issuance of a favorable determination letter protects the plan against any subsequent IRS challenge to whether the plan is qualified in form. A determination letter, however, does not protect against a later finding that the plan failed to operate in compliance with the qualification requirements. Although it is not required for a plan to be tax qualified, it is prudent to submit a plan for a determination letter to insure that it will enjoy favorable tax treatment.

Because of the number and complexity of qualification requirements, it is relatively easy for a plan to violate one or more qualification requirements. Indeed, one commentator contends,

> It is virtually administratively impossible to operate a plan in complete compliance with the law. Even where a plan is procedurally in compliance with the law simple administrative errors will inevitably occur and arguably could disqualify the plan. For example, the simple transposition of numbers can lead to incorrect birth dates being maintained by employers. This can lead to inaccurate participation records, and may result in employees having delayed or accelerated participation. Roger C. Siske, IRS Voluntary Compliance Programs, *Ali-Aba Advance Law Of Pensions, Welfare Plans, and Deferred Compensation* (July 2002).

The Internal Revenue Service (IRS) has taken the position that any error in form or operation of a plan, no matter the size or significance, disqualifies the plan. If a plan is disqualified, it loses its tax benefits. The plan's income becomes taxable, the employer's deductions for contributions to defined contribution plans are disallowed to the extent participants' benefits are not vested, and plan participants are taxed on their vested benefits.

In light of the draconian nature of plan disqualification, the IRS has created the Employee Plans Compliance Resolution System (EPCRS), pursuant to which plan defects can be corrected without disqualifying the plan. The EPCRS consists of three separate programs: (1) a voluntary self-correction program (the Self-Correction Program or SCP); (2) a voluntary correction program with IRS approval (the Voluntary Correction Program or VCP); and (3) a closing agreement program to resolve defects found on audit (the Audit Closing Agreement Program or Audit Program). The program pursuant to which the defect can be corrected and the applicable sanctions depend on the type of defect, whether the plan has received a favorable determination letter, and whether the defect was identified by the plan sponsor or by the IRS in an audit of the plan.

C. THE CREATION AND OPERATION OF A PENSION PLAN

[1] Plan Design Options

ERISA does not require employers to sponsor pension plans, nor does it prevent employers from amending or terminating their plans. And although ERISA regulates pension plans once they have been created, employers who adopt plans, known as plan sponsors, ERISA § 3(16)(B), have a great deal of flexibility in the choice and form of the plan. Typically, employers will hire experts to help them make these important decisions regarding the design of their plan. (If the plan is created pursuant to a collective bargaining agreement, then the decisions regarding plan design will be made pursuant to the collective bargaining process.)

The initial decision is what type of plan to create: a defined benefit plan, a defined contribution plan, or a hybrid such as a cash balance plan. Next, the employer must decide which employees will participate in the plan. For example, the employer might limit coverage to certain job classifications, such as sales associates. The employer has a great deal of latitude as to who to include in the plan, so long as the plan coverage comports with the IRC § 410(b) minimum coverage rules and does not discriminate in favor of highly compensated employees. The employer can exclude union members so long as retirement benefits were the subject of good-faith bargaining with the union. IRC § 410(b)(3).

Next, if the plan is a defined benefit plan, the employer must select the benefit formula; if the plan is a defined contribution plan, it must select the contribution formula. If the plan is a profit-sharing plan, the contribution formula may simply be a statement that the employer reserves the right to determine whether and how much to contribute to the plan each year. Other plan design decisions include whether employee contributions will be permitted or required, the vesting schedule, and what will trigger plan distributions and what form they will take. If the plan is a 401(k) plan, the employer must decide whether employees will direct their investments, and if so, what investment vehicles will be permitted.

[2] Plan Administration

Every pension plan must have a plan administrator, who may be a single individual or several persons who collectively as a committee act as the plan administrator. The plan administrator can be identified by name or by position, e.g., the Chief Executive Officer. ERISA § 3(16)(A), IRC § 414(g). The plan administrator is responsible for managing the day-to-day affairs of the plan and commonly does so by hiring accountants, actuaries, attorneys and other professionals. The plan administrator, relying on the plan documents, determines who is eligible, sees that the benefits are properly distributed, prepares and files required governmental reports and maintains the plan records.

The employer, as plan sponsor, selects the plan administrator, unless the plan was adopted pursuant to a collective bargaining agreement, in which case the selection of the administrator will be determined as part of the collective bargaining process. The employer may choose to serve as the plan administrator, but when the employer is both plan sponsor and plan administrator confusion with serious legal consequences can arise. When acting as a plan administrator, the employer has fiduciary obligations to the plan and its participants and beneficiaries. ERISA 3(14)(A). But when acting as the plan sponsor, the employer has no such fiduciary obligations. Thus, if the plan sponsor amends the plan, it may legally do so without regard to the interests of the participants, so long as the amendment does not retroactively reduce accrued benefits nor adversely affect a participant's vested interests.

In addition to a plan administrator, most pension plans have a trustee who either manages and controls the plan's assets or is subject to the direction and control of an investment committee or other fiduciary who directs how the plan assets should be invested. As described below, many plans employ a bank or other financial services company to act as trustee of the plan's funds.

FRANK P. VANDERPLOEG, ROLE-PLAYING UNDER ERISA: THE COMPANY AS "EMPLOYER" AND "FIDUCIARY"

9 DePaul Bus. L.J. 259, 281 (1997)

Since the typical employer lacks trust powers, the employer almost invariably appoints a separate committee, or an institutional trustee, to be the trustee of its funded plans for which a trust is required. However, it is unusual for an independent institutional trustee to assume the additional responsibilities of plan administrator. For unfunded (or fully insured) plans, no trustee is required. Accordingly, the employer, or its officer committee, will typically be the plan administrator. Since the committee members generally are, or include, the same employees that have human resources responsibilities on behalf of the employer in the normal corporate hierarchy, they themselves will be wearing "two hats."

The plan trustee holds and invests the plan funds, but is not necessarily the plan administrator, a position that creates fiduciary obligations to the plan and the plan participants. If, however, a trustee is granted sufficient discretion over the plan investments and operations, the trustee may have fiduciary obligations to the plan and its participants. ERISA § 3(21)(A). Pension plans commonly employ investment advisors who under ERISA are fiduciaries and so, like the plan administrators, owe a special duty of care to the plan and its participants and beneficiaries. ERISA § 3(21)(A).

The plan will also employ other professionals who ERISA defines as "parties in interest." ERISA § 3(14)(A). They include attorneys, plan custodians, and persons providing services to the plan such as accountants, actuaries, and even relatives (spouses, ancestors, and descendants) of those who provide services to the plan. Although not fiduciaries, parties in interest also owe certain duties to the plan and its participants. (Discussed in Chapter 6).

D. WHAT IS A PENSION PLAN?

Because ERISA regulates pension *plans*, the question can arise as to just what is a "plan." Typically, an employer will know when it has created a pension plan subject to ERISA's regulation. Occasionally, however, an employer may find that by offering certain benefits it has inadvertently created an ERISA governed pension plan.

MUSMECI v. SCHWEGMANN GIANT SUPER MARKETS

332 F.3d 339 (5th Cir. 2003)

Davis, Circuit Judge.

Defendants . . . appeal the district court's adverse money judgment, in favor of the Plaintiff class, holding, *inter alia*, that a grocery voucher plan established by Schwegmann Giant Super Market Partnership (SGSM) was a pension plan under [ERISA] . . .

Until 1997, SGSM operated a chain of over forty grocery stores, employing over 5000 employees, primarily in the New Orleans, Louisiana area. SGSM is a partnership comprised of SGSM, Inc., G.G. Schwegmann, and Schwegmann Trust. SGSM, Inc. owned a seventy percent interest in the partnership and was its managing partner. Mr. Schwegmann was the majority stockholder of SGSM, Inc. and its chief executive officer. As such, Mr. Schwegmann was responsible for the daily operations of SGSM and was the primary policy maker for the partnership.

Mr. Schwegmann conceived a plan for SGSM to give its retirees groceries and other goods free of charge. Mr. Schwegmann then worked with Mr. Sam Levy, president of SGSM, Inc., and Mr. Joe Warnke, SGSM director of human resources, to create a voucher program for long-term SGSM employees at their retirement. In 1985, SGSM implemented this grocery voucher plan (the "Voucher Plan") designed to supply SGSM retirees with a portion of their monthly food needs. Under this plan, SGSM issued vouchers to retirees, and these vouchers could then be used in lieu of cash to purchase goods in SGSM stores. It is this Voucher Plan which is the subject of this lawsuit.

In 1985, Joe Warnke prepared a memorandum memorializing the eligibility requirements for participation in the Voucher Plan. To qualify for the vouchers, an employee must have completed twenty years of service with SGSM, have reached the age of sixty, and have been employed in a supervisory position for at least one year at the time of retirement. SGSM informed qualifying employees of the program at the time of their retirement. Each month, SGSM sent qualifying employees a set of four vouchers worth a total of $216. These vouchers were valid for a period of thirty days, redeemable only at SGSM stores and could not be transferred. Although SGSM intended the vouchers to be used only for in-kind purchases with no cash redemption, store personnel, including managers, were largely unaware of this proscription, and retirees were often given change in cash when using the vouchers for grocery purchases.

SGSM had no written procedures for administering the Voucher Plan. The Voucher Plan was nonetheless run in a systematic manner. When a manager or supervisor retired, the SGSM human resources department prepared a form with information used to determine whether the employee qualified for the Voucher Plan. The form was then sent to Sam Levy who reviewed the form and decided whether a retiree qualified for the program. Levy would sign the forms of qualified retirees and forward the forms to the SGSM controller, Gene Lemoine, who issued the vouchers. Lemoine performed this task two to three days before the month in which they were to be used. Once used, the vouchers were routed back to Lemoine who retained them for five years.

SGSM did not set up a trust to fund the Voucher Plan. Rather, the Voucher Plan was funded out of the partnership's general revenue. Each year, SGSM deducted the total face value of the vouchers as a business expense on its tax returns under the category of "retirement plans, etc." SGSM also issued an Internal Revenue Service form 1099-R to every retiree receiving vouchers, reflecting the face value of the vouchers received by the retiree that year.

By the early 1990's, SGSM experienced declining profits due to competition from well-financed national supermarket chains. In 1995, Mr. Schwegmann decided to aggressively expand SGSM to compete with these stores. SGSM acquired the 28-store National Tea Company chain and, in doing so, undertook a sizable debt. After this acquisition, SGSM continued to suffer from financial losses, and in 1997, it sold the business. A week before the sale, Mr. Schwegmann sent a letter to all voucher recipients informing them that they would no longer receive vouchers because of the sale of the business. Because Mr. Schwegmann considered the Voucher Plan a gratuity subject to termination at will, he made no provision for the continuation of the Voucher Plan after the sale.

. . .

After being informed of the termination of the Voucher Plan, Plaintiffs filed this suit on behalf of themselves and other similarly situated individuals under ERISA and Louisiana state law claiming that they were vested in a pension benefit plan.

After a bench trial, the court dismissed the Plaintiffs' state law claims. After taking the remaining claims under advisement, the court issued findings of fact and conclusions of law, ruling that the grocery Voucher Plan was a pension benefit plan under ERISA, that SGSM breached its fiduciary duty under ERISA, that Mr. Schwegmann was liable as a fiduciary to the plan, that the Plaintiffs were entitled to monetary relief for benefits denied after SGSM's sale . . . .

While not disputing the underlying facts [defendant] first argues that the district court committed legal error in concluding that the in-kind Voucher Plan constituted a pension benefit plan under ERISA . . . . Specifically, the Defendants contend that ERISA does not apply to any program providing a non-cash benefit . . . .

ERISA does not regulate all benefits paid by an employer, but only those paid pursuant to an "employee benefit plan." *Fort Halifax Packing v. Coyne*, 482 U.S. 1, 11 [ERISA] § 4. Two different types of benefit programs are regulated by ERISA: welfare plans and pension plans. [ERISA] § 3. The district court determined that the Voucher Plan was a pension benefit plan and not a welfare benefit plan. The Plaintiffs have not challenged this ruling. The Defendants, however, challenge the district court's determination that it is a pension benefit plan.

To determine whether ERISA applies to the Voucher Plan, we begin our analysis with an examination of the language of the statute itself. ERISA defines an "employee pension benefit" plan as:

> any plan, fund, or program which was heretofore or is hereafter established or maintained by an employer or by an employee organization, or by both, to the extent that by its express terms or as a result of surrounding circumstances such plan, fund, or program . . . provides retirement income to employees . . . [ERISA] § 3(2)(A)(i).

The parties agree that SGSM established a "program." Thus, the primary issue

this court must resolve is whether the vouchers issued pursuant to SGSM's Voucher Plan provided the Plaintiffs with "retirement income."

Neither ERISA's statutory provisions nor the federal regulations define the term "income." However, they do not affirmatively require that the pension benefit be paid in cash.

. . .

Relying on the definition of "income" used for the purposes of determining taxable income under the Internal Revenue Code (IRC), 26 U.S.C. § 1, et seq., the district court found that the grocery vouchers constituted retirement income. We believe that the district court's analysis is sound given the close connection between ERISA and the IRC.

. . .

This court has interpreted the term income broadly under the IRC to include anything that can be valued in terms of currency. The district court was entitled to infer that when SGSM deducted the vouchers' face value as a business expense on its tax returns under the category of "retirement plans" and issued Internal Revenue Service form 1099-R's to the recipients of the vouchers, SGSM considered the vouchers as income under the IRC. The cash value of the grocery vouchers is readily ascertainable from the face of the vouchers. The district court correctly concluded that the vouchers constitute income and the Voucher Plan is governed by ERISA.

Even if we were to adopt the plain or ordinary meaning of "income," our conclusion would be the same. As noted by the Supreme Court in *Lukhard v. Reed*, the term "income" is commonly understood to mean a "gain or recurrent benefit usually measured in money." *Lukhard v. Reed*, 481 U.S. 368, 374, citing *Webster's Third International Dictionary* 1143 (1976). Because the vouchers provided a gain or benefit to SGSM employees and could readily be measured in money, they would constitute income as the term is generally understood.

. . .

2-4 QUESTIONS AND PROBLEMS

1. Did Schwegmann intend for its voucher program to be a pension plan? Does Schwegmann's intent matter? Should it matter?

2. What difference does it make whether the voucher program was a "pension plan?"

3. Would Schwegmann have created the voucher program if it had known that it had created an ERISA governed pension plan?

What happens if an employer promises its employees a pension plan but does not go through the necessary steps to create such a plan?

GUILBERT v. GARDNER

480 F.3d 140 (2d Cir. 2007)

HALL, CIRCUIT JUDGE.

Plaintiff-Appellant Thomas R. Guilbert ("plaintiff") appeals from an order of the district court (Jones, J.) granting the summary judgment motion of Defendants-

Appellees Charles Gardner III, Douglas Gardner, and Marianne Gardner ("moving defendants") on plaintiff's claims under the Employee Retirement Income Security Act ("ERISA" or "the Act"), as well as his claims for breach of contract, promissory estoppel, and fraud.

* * *

BACKGROUND

For purposes of this appeal from summary judgment, we accept as true the following facts and allegations. In December 1991, Charles Gardner Jr. ("Charles Jr.") and his sons Douglas Gardner ("Douglas") and Charles Gardner III ("Charles III") approached plaintiff, a former co-worker and family friend, about joining their new print brokerage business. Plaintiff later met with defendants to discuss the details of plaintiff's prospective employment. Plaintiff informed defendants that he had accumulated approximately $39,000 in pension funds at his present job. Charles Jr. allegedly told plaintiff that if he joined the company, in addition to his salary, defendants would establish a pension fund for him with an initial deposit of $39,000 and subsequent annual deposits of $10,000.

Plaintiff accepted the terms of the agreement ("the employment agreement") and began work in January of 1992. He worked for the company until it collapsed in 2000. In early 1992, plaintiff alleges that Charles Jr. wrote down the terms of the pension on a legal writing pad. This document has not been produced in discovery. In the summer of 1992, and on a number of occasions thereafter, plaintiff requested documentation of his pension, but none was provided. Plaintiff alleges that defendants orally assured him on numerous occasions that they had "taken care of" his pension benefits.

On August 24, 2000, August 31, 2000, and September 7, 2000, defendants tendered three checks, each in the amount of $1,178.98, to plaintiff as part of his salary. In addition, on August 28, 2000, defendants tendered a check for $9,131.00 as reimbursement for plaintiff's car lease. Each of these checks bounced. In September 2000, it became clear to plaintiff that defendants were not going to pay his past salary and had not established pension benefits for him.

Plaintiff brought this action in August of 2002. Plaintiff's amended complaint set forth nine causes of action. Plaintiff's first cause of action alleged that defendants were liable to him for his pension benefits under ERISA.

* * *

In an opinion entered February 9, 2004, the district court granted summary judgment to all defendants. First, the district court rejected Plaintiff's ERISA claims. The court found there were "no surrounding circumstances other than defendants' alleged oral assurances from which a reasonable person could ascertain that defendants intended to set up the pension fund for Plaintiff." The district court held that oral assurances of a plan's existence are unenforceable and that therefore defendants had not "established or maintained" a pension program within the meaning of ERISA § 4(a).

DISCUSSION

I. ERISA Claims

Plaintiff first contends the district court erred in granting summary judgment on his ERISA claims. We are unpersuaded. ERISA covers "any employee benefit plan if it is established or maintained — (1) by any employer engaged in commerce or in any industry or activity affecting commerce." ERISA § 4(a) In a case involving an alleged employee welfare benefit plan, this Court held that a plan, fund, or program under ERISA " 'is established if from the surrounding circumstances a reasonable person can ascertain the intended benefits, a class of beneficiaries, the source of financing, and procedures for receiving benefits.' " *Grimo v. Blue Cross/Blue Shield of Vermont*, 34 F.3d 148, 151 (2d Cir. 1994) (quoting *Donovan v. Dillingham*, 688 F.2d 1367, 1373 (11th Cir. 1982) (in banc)). A plan "need not be a formal written document," however. *Id.* (citing *Donovan*, 688 F.2d at 1372–1373); *see also* ERISA § 4(a) (ERISA covers "*any* employee benefit plan" (emphasis added)).

In *Donovan*, the Eleventh Circuit rejected the proposition that the term " 'establish' means no more than an ultimate decision by an employer . . . to provide the type of benefits described in ERISA." *Donovan*, 688 F.2d at 1372–1373. The court held that "[a] decision to extend benefits is not the establishment of a plan or program." *Id.* at 1373. Instead, "[a]cts or events that record, exemplify or implement the decision" can be introduced as "direct or circumstantial evidence that the decision has become reality." *Id.* The court emphasized that "it is the reality of a plan, fund or program and not the decision to extend certain benefits that is determinative." *Id.*; *see also Scott v. Gulf Oil Corp.*, 754 F.2d 1499, 1504 (9th Cir. 1985) ("We . . . agree with Donovan . . . that a mere allegation that an employer or employee organization ultimately decided to provide an employee welfare benefit is not enough to invoke ERISA's coverage. Such an allegation fails to allege the 'establishment' of a plan. Something more is needed." (internal citation omitted)). Although neither *Donovan* nor *Scott* is binding on this Court, their logic is persuasive. We therefore look to whether there is a genuine issue of material fact as to "the reality" of an employee pension benefit plan.

In support of his claim that defendants established an employee pension benefit plan covered by ERISA, plaintiff presented his own deposition testimony to the following effect. Charles Jr. promised him a pension fund with an initial deposit of $39,000 and annual contributions of $10,000 thereafter. In early 1992, Charles Jr. wrote the terms of the pension plan on a legal pad and told plaintiff it would be filed in the company's records. On numerous occasions defendants assured him that the pension plan was established. Plaintiff also submitted deposition testimony from two other employees stating that plaintiff was owed money other than his salary. Finally, plaintiff submitted the company's tax returns indicating the company took certain tax deductions for "employee benefit programs." Viewing, as we must, this evidence in the light most favorable to plaintiff, we conclude that no reasonable fact finder could find that defendants "established or maintained" a pension plan under ERISA. Accordingly, the district court's grant of summary judgment on the ERISA claims is affirmed.

2-5 QUESTIONS AND PROBLEMS

1. Why should an employer's oral promise to create a pension plan be unenforceable?

2. What, if anything, should the participant have done to ensure that a plan was established?

E. WHO IS AN EMPLOYEE?

ERISA § 3(6), 3(7).

Even if the parties agree that an ERISA plan exists, they may not agree as to which individuals are eligible to participate. ERISA limits plan participation to employees, former employees, and members and former members of employee organizations. ERISA § 3(7). Yet ERISA's definition of the term employee, "any individual employed by an employer," ERISA § 3(6), is not particularly helpful. Consequently courts look to sources outside of ERISA for guidance on the meaning of the term.

NATIONWIDE MUTUAL INSURANCE COMPANY v. DARDEN

503 U.S. 318 (1992)

JUSTICE SOUTER delivered the opinion of the Court.

In this case we construe the term "employee" as it appears in § 3(6) of the Employee Retirement Income Security Act of 1974 (ERISA), and read it to incorporate traditional agency law criteria for identifying master-servant relationships.

I

From 1962 through 1980, respondent Robert Darden operated an insurance agency according to the terms of several contracts he signed with petitioners Nationwide Mutual Insurance Co. et al. Darden promised to sell only Nationwide insurance policies, and, in exchange, Nationwide agreed to pay him commissions on his sales and enroll him in a company retirement scheme called the "Agent's Security Compensation Plan" (Plan). The Plan consisted of two different programs: the "Deferred Compensation Incentive Credit Plan," under which Nationwide annually credited an agent's retirement account with a sum based on his business performance, and the "Extended Earnings Plan," under which Nationwide paid an agent, upon retirement or termination, a sum equal to the total of his policy renewal fees for the previous 12 months.

Such were the contractual terms, however, that Darden would forfeit his entitlement to the Plan's benefits if, within a year of his termination and 25 miles of his prior business location, he sold insurance for Nationwide's competitors. The contracts also disqualified him from receiving those benefits if, after he stopped representing Nationwide, he ever induced a Nationwide policyholder to cancel one of its policies.

In November 1980, Nationwide exercised its contractual right to end its relationship with Darden. A month later, Darden became an independent insurance agent and, doing business from his old office, sold insurance policies for several of Nationwide's competitors. The company reacted with the charge that his new business activities disqualified him from receiving the Plan benefits to which he would have been entitled otherwise. Darden then sued for the benefits, which he claimed were nonforfeitable because already vested under the terms of ERISA.

Darden brought his action under [ERISA § 502(a)], which enables a benefit plan "participant" to enforce the substantive provisions of ERISA. The Act elsewhere defines "participant" as "any employee or former employee of an employer . . .

who is or may become eligible to receive a benefit of any type from an employee benefit plan . . . ." [ERISA § 3(7).] Thus, Darden's ERISA claim can succeed only if he was Nationwide's "employee," a term the Act defines as "any individual employed by an employer." [ERISA § 3(6).]

It was on this point that the District Court granted summary judgment to Nationwide. After applying common-law agency principles and, to an extent unspecified, our decision in *United States v. Silk*, 331 U.S. 704 (1947), the court found that " 'the total factual context' of Mr. Darden's relationship with Nationwide shows that he was an independent contractor and not an employee."

The United States Court of Appeals for the Fourth Circuit vacated. After observing that "Darden most probably would not qualify as an employee" under traditional principles of agency law, it found the traditional definition inconsistent with th e " 'declared policy and purposes' " of ERISA, and specifically with the congressional statement of purpose found in § 2 of the Act. It therefore held that an ERISA plaintiff can qualify as an "employee" simply by showing "(1) that he had a reasonable expectation that he would receive [pension] benefits, (2) that he relied on this expectation, and (3) that he lacked the economic bargaining power to contract out of [benefit plan] forfeiture provisions." The court remanded the case to the District Court, which then found that Darden had been Nationwide's "employee" under the standard set by the Court of Appeals. The Court of Appeals affirmed.

We now reverse.

II

We have often been asked to construe the meaning of "employee" where the statute containing the term does not helpfully define it. Most recently we confronted thi s problem in *Community for Creative Non-Violence v. Reid*, 490 U.S. 730 (1989), a case in which a sculptor and a nonprofit group each claimed copyright ownership in a statue the group had commissioned from the artist. The dispute ultimately turned on whether, by the terms of § 101 of the Copyright Act of 1976, 17 U.S.C. § 101, the statute had been "prepared by an employee within the scope of his or her employment." Because the Copyright Act nowhere defined the term "employee," we unanimously applied the "well established" principle that

> [w]here Congress uses terms that have accumulated settled meaning under . . . the common law, a court must infer, unless the statute otherwise dictates, that Congress means to incorporate the established meaning of these terms . . . . In the past, when Congress has used the term "employee" without defining it, we have concluded that Congress intended to describe the conventional master-servant relationship as understood by common-law agency doctrine.

While we supported this reading of the Copyright Act with other observations, the general rule stood as independent authority for the decision.

So too should it stand here. ERISA's nominal definition of "employee" as "any individual employed by an employer," ERISA 3(6), is completely circular and explains nothing. As for the rest of the Act, Darden does not cite, and we do not find, any provision either giving specific guidance on the term's meaning or suggesting that construing it to incorporate traditional agency law principles would thwart the congressional design or lead to absurd results. Thus, we adopt a common-law test for determining who qualifies as an "employee" under ERISA, a test we most recently summarized in *Reid:*

> In determining whether a hired party is an employee under the general common law of agency, we consider the hiring party's right to control the manner and means by which the product is accomplished. Among the other factors relevant to this inquiry are the skill required; the source of the instrumentalities and tools; the location of the work; the duration of the relationship between the parties; whether the hiring party has the right to assign additional projects to the hired party; the extent of the hired party's discretion over when and how long to work; the method of payment; the hired party's role in hiring and paying assistants; whether the work is part of the regular business of the hiring party; whether the hiring party is in business; the provision of employee benefits; and the tax treatment of the hired party.

Cf. Restatement (Second) of Agency § 220(2) (1958) (listing nonexhaustive criteria for identifying master-servant relationship); Rev. Rul. 87-41, 1987-1 Cum. Bull. 296, 298–299 (setting forth 20 factors as guides in determining whether an individual qualifies as a common-law "employee" in various tax law contexts). Since the common-law test contains "no shorthand formula or magic phrase that can be applied to find t he answer, . . . all of the incidents of the relationship must be assessed and weighed with no one factor being decisive." *NLRB v. United Ins. Co. of America*, 390 U.S. at 258, 88 S. Ct. at 991.

In taking its different tack, the Court of Appeals cited *NLRB v. Hearst Publications, Inc.*, 322 U.S. at 120–129, and *United States v. Silk*, 331 U.S. at 713, for the proposition that "the content of the term 'employee' in the context of a particular federal statute is to be construed "in the light of the mischief to be corrected and the end to be attained." *Darden*, 796 F.2d at 706, quoting *Silk, supra*, 331 U.S. at 713, in turn quoting *Hearst, supra*, 322 U.S. at 124. But *Hearst* and *Silk*, which interpreted "employee" for purposes of the National Labor Relations Act and Social Security Act, respectively, are feeble precedents for unmooring the term from the common law. In each case, the Court read "employee," which neither statute helpfully defined, to imply something broader t han the common-law definition; after each opinion, Congress amended the statute so construed to demonstrate that the usual common-law principles were the keys to meaning.

To be sure, Congress did not, strictly speaking, "overrule" our interpretation of those statutes, since the Constitution invests the Judiciary, not the Legislature, with the final power to construe the law. But a principle of statutory construction can endure just so many legislative revisitations, and *Reid*'s presumption that Congress means an agency law definition for "employee" unless it clearly indicates otherwise signaled our abandonment of *Silk*'s emphasis on construing that term " 'in the light of the mischief to be corrected and the end to be attained.' " *Silk, supra*, 331 U.S. at 713, quoting *Hearst, supra*, 322 U.S. at 124.

. . .

Quite apart from its inconsistency with our precedents, the Fourth Circuit's analysis reveals an approach infected with circularity and unable to furnish predictable results. Applying the first element of its test, which ostensibly enquires into an employee's "expectations," the Court of Appeals concluded that Nationwide had "created a reasonable expectation on the 'employees' part that benefits would be paid to them in the future," *Darden*, 796 F.2d at 706, by establishing "a comprehensive retirement benefits program for its insurance agents," *id.* at 707. The court thought it was simply irrelevant that the forfeiture clause in Darden's contract "limited" his expectation of receiving pension benefits, since "it is precisely that sort of employer-imposed condition on the *employee's* anticipations that

Congress intended to outlaw with the enactment of ERISA." *Id.* at 707 n.7 (emphasis added). Thus, the Fourth Circuit's test would turn not on a claimant's actual "expectations," which the court effectively deemed inconsequential, *ibid.*, but on his statutory entitlement to relief, which itself depends on his very status as an "employee." This begs the question.

This circularity infects the test's second prong as well, which considers the extent to which a claimant has relied on his "expectation" of benefits by "remaining for 'long years,' or a substantial period of time, in the 'employer's' service, and by foregoing other significant means of providing for [his] retirement." *Id.* at 706. While this enquiry is ostensibly factual, we have seen already that one of its objects may not be: to the extent that actual "expectations" are (as in Darden's case) unnecessary to relief, the nature of a claimant's required "reliance" is left unclear. Moreover, any enquiry into "reliance," whatever it might entail, could apparently lead to different results for claimants holding identical jobs and enrolled in identical plans. Because, for example, Darden failed to make much independent provision for his retirement, he satisfied the "reliance" prong of the Fourth Circuit's test, *see* 922 F.2d at 206, whereas a more provident colleague who signed exactly the same contracts, but saved for a rainy day, might not.

Any such approach would severely compromise the capacity of companies like Nationwide to figure out who their "employees" are and what, by extension, their pension-fund obligations will be. To be sure, the traditional agency law criteria offer no paradigm of determinacy. But their application generally turns on factual variable s within an employer's knowledge, thus permitting categorical judgments about the "employee" status of claimants with similar job descriptions. Agency law principles comport, moreover, with our recent precedents and with the common understanding, reflected in those precedents, of the difference between an employee and an independent contractor.

III

While the Court of Appeals noted that "Darden most probably would not qualify as an employee" under traditional agency law principles, *Darden, supra*, at 705, it did not actually decide that issue. We therefore reverse the judgment and remand the case to that court for proceedings consistent with this opinion.

2-6 QUESTIONS AND PROBLEMS

1. Was Darden an employee of Nationwide? Why does it matter if he was?

2. Do you agree with the Court that the ERISA definition of "employee" is "completely circular and explains nothing"?

3. How might ERISA better define the term "employee"?

IRS GUIDANCE ON DISTINGUISHING BETWEEN EMPLOYEES AND INDEPENDENT CONTRACTORS

In Revenue Ruling 87-41, to which the Court referred in *Darden*, the IRS identified twenty factors that are relevant in determining whether the hiring party has sufficient control over the worker to establish an employer-employee relationship. In October 1996, the IRS published a 160 page training book on distinguishing between independent contractors and employees. In the training materials, the IRS emphasized that the twenty factors identified in Rev. Rul. 87-41 are an analytical tool, not the legal test, for determining whether a worker is an employee or independent contractor. The legal test is whether there is a right to direct and control the means and details of the work. According to the training manual, every piece of information that helps determine the extent to which the business retains the right to control the worker is important, and the factors may change over time, as business relationships change over time.

The IRS separates the relevant factors into three categories: (1) behavioral control, (2) financial control, and (3) type of relationship. Behavioral control addresses whether the hiring party has a right to direct and control and considers whether the worker receives instructions and training. Financial control focuses on whether the hiring party has a right to control the business aspects of the worker's job, including whether the worker has unreimbursed expenses and whether the worker can realize a profit or loss. The type of relationship focuses on, among other things, written contracts describing the relationship the parties intended to create and whether the worker is provided benefits.

The following example, drawn from the IRS' training materials, illustrates how the IRS applies these factors:

> Aaron, a computer programmer, is laid off when Supercompute Corporation downsizes. Supercompute agrees to pay Aaron $10,000 to complete a one-time project to create a certain product. It is not clear how long it will take to complete the project and Aaron is not guaranteed any minimum payment for hours spent on the project. Aaron does the work on a new high-end computer, which cost him $5,000. Aaron works at home and is not expected or allowed to attend meetings of the software development group. Supercompute provides Aaron with no instructions beyond the specifications for the project itself. Aaron and Supercompute have a written contract, which provides that Aaron is considered to be an independent contractor, is required to pay federal and state taxes, and receives no employee benefits from Supercompute. Supercompute will file a Form 1099.
>
> The fact that Aaron was laid off and hired back for the same kind of job suggests that he is an employee. The following three factors are of neutral value: (1) Aaron purchased a $5,000 computer to do the work; (2) Aaron works from home; and (3) there is no length of time specified for the project. The following seven factors suggest that Aaron is an independent contractor: (1) he was hired for a one-time project; (2) he is not guaranteed any minimum payment; (3) he is not expected or allowed to go to meetings; (4) he has a written contract with Supercompute; (5) Supercompute filed a Form 1099 showing intent that he be characterized as an independent contractor; (6) Aaron is required to pay federal and state taxes; and (7) Aaron receives no instructions on how to perform his job. According to the IRS training materials, Aaron is clearly an independent contractor with respect to services provided to Supercompute.

2-7 QUESTIONS AND PROBLEMS

In each of the following situations, determine which factors suggest that the worker is an employee, which suggest that the worker is an independent contractor, and which are neutral. Based on these factors, determine whether the individual worker is an employee or independent contractor.

(a) Bob, a manufacturer's representative, is the sole proprietor of a building supplies business and has an exclusive contract with ABC Construction, a building supplies manufacturer. Bob has the sole right to the territory covered, sells only ABC's products, but did not pay anything for the right to the territory. Bob has a bachelors degree in civil engineering and belongs to several professional associations for which Bob pays the membership dues. Bob has an office and secretary; ABC does not reimburse Bob for these expenses. Bob's name appears in the yellow page advertisements under both Bob's name and ABC's name. Bob is required to provide regular trip reports to ABC and attend sales meetings and trade shows conducted on Bob's territory. Bob bids on portions of major commercial construction contracts. These jobs require engineering skills and design work to adapt the building materials to the project plans. All bids are subject to ABC's post-review. Upon winning a bid, Bob engages and pays the workers who will install the building materials, and Bob provides the necessary construction bonds. Bob submits invoices to the general contractor for payment directly to Bob on forms prescribed by ABC. If the general contractor fails to pay, Bob is responsible for collecting and is liable to ABC for payment.

(b) Connie, an attorney, is a sole practitioner who rents office space and pays for her telephone, computer, on-line legal research linkup, fax machine, and photocopier. She also buys her own office supplies and pays bar dues and membership for three other professional organizations. She has a part-time receptionist who also does the bookkeeping. Connie pays the receptionist, withholds and pays federal and state employment taxes, and files a Form W-2 each year. For the past two years, Connie has had one client, a corporation with which she has had a long-standing relationship. She charges the corporation an hourly rate for services and sends monthly bills detailing the work performed for the prior month. The bills include charges for long distance calls, on-line research time, fax charges, photocopies, mailing costs, and travel costs which the corporation has agreed to reimburse.

KATHRYN L. MOORE, OTHER ELIGIBLE EMPLOYEES: OWNERS, PARTNERS, INDEPENDENT CONTRACTORS, LEASED EMPLOYEES IN FEDERAL INCOME TAXATION OF RETIREMENT PLANS

(Published as Alvin D. Lurie et al., *Federal Income Taxation of Retirement Plans* Ch. 12 (Matthew Bender 2012).)

In recent years, the use of independent contractors has increased. In 1995, there were an estimated 8.3 million independent contractors (or about 6.7 percent of the U.S. workforce); by 2005, that number had grown to an estimated 10.3 million workers (or about 7.4 percent of the workforce). Employers may use independent contractors rather than employees for a variety of reasons, including to accommodate workload fluctuations, fill temporary employee absences, and save on wage and benefit costs. Among the reasons why using an independent contract may save on wage and benefits costs is that generally an employer may not provide employee benefits to an independent contractor.

In light of the cost savings, an employer may be tempted to misclassify employees as independent contractors. In its last comprehensive estimate on the subject, the IRS estimated that 15 percent of employers misclassified 3.4 million employees as independent contractors in 1984.

In the most publicized recharacterization case, *Vizcaino v. Microsoft*, [97 F.3d 1187 (9th Cir. 1996),] the Ninth Circuit addressed the possible consequences an employer faces under ERISA when the employer misclassifies an employee as an independent contractor.

VIZCAINO v. MICROSOFT CORPORATION [I]

97 F.3d 1187 (9th Cir. 1996)

REINHARDT, CIRCUIT JUDGE.

Large corporations have increasingly adopted the practice of hiring temporary employees or independent contractors as a means of avoiding payment of employee benefits, and thereby increasing their profits. This practice has understandably led to a number of problems, legal and otherwise. One of the legal issues that sometimes arises is exemplified by this lawsuit. The named plaintiffs, who were classified by Microsoft as independent contractors, seek to strip that label of its protective covering and to obtain for themselves certain benefits that the company provided to all of its regular or permanent employees. After certifying the named plaintiffs as representatives of a class of "common-law employees," the district court granted summary judgment to Microsoft on all counts. The named plaintiffs and the class they represent now appeal as to two of their claims: a) the claim, made pursuant to section 502(a) of the Employee Retirement Income Security Act (ERISA), that they are entitled to savings benefits under Microsoft's Savings Plus Plan (SPP); and b) the claim, made pursuant to Washington state law, that they are entitled to stock-option benefits under Microsoft's Employee Stock Purchase Plan (ESPP). In both cases, the claims are based on their contention that they are common-law employees.

I

Microsoft, one of the country's fastest growing and most successful corporations and the world's largest software company, produces and sells computer software internationally. It employs a core staff of permanent employees. It categorizes them as "regular employees" and offers them a wide variety of benefits, including paid vacations, sick leave, holidays, short-term disability, group health and life insurance, and pensions, as well as the two benefits involved in this appeal. Microsoft supplements its core staff of employees with a pool of individuals to whom it refuses to pay fringe benefits. It previously classified these individuals as "independent contractors" or "freelancers," but prior to the filing of the action began classifying them as "temporary agency employees." Freelancers were hired when Microsoft needed to expand its workforce to meet the demands of new product schedules. The company did not, of course, provide them with any of the employee benefits regular employees receive.

The named plaintiffs worked for Microsoft in the United States between 1987 and 1990 as freelancers in the company's international division. Some were still working for the company when the suit was filed in 1993, and may still be doing so today. Although hired to work on specific projects, seven of the eight named plaintiffs had worked on successive projects for a minimum of two years prior to the time the action was filed, while the eighth had worked for more than a year. During that time, they performed services as software testers, production editors, proofreaders, formatters and indexers. Microsoft fully integrated the plaintiffs into its workforce: they often worked on teams along with regular employees, sharing the same supervisors, performing identical functions, and working the same core hours. Because Microsoft required that they work on site, they received admittance card keys, office equipment and supplies from the company.

Freelancers and regular employees, however, were not without their obvious distinctions. Freelancers wore badges of a different color, had different electronic-mail addresses, and attended a less formal orientation than that provided to regular employees. They were not permitted to assign their work to others, invited to official company functions, or paid overtime wages. In addition, they were not paid through Microsoft's payroll department. Instead, they submitted invoices for their services, documenting their hours and the projects on which they worked, and were paid through the accounts receivable department.

The plaintiffs were told when they were hired that, as freelancers, they would not be eligible for benefits. None has contended that Microsoft ever promised them any benefits individually . . .

In 1989 and 1990, the Internal Revenue Service (IRS) examined Microsoft's employment records to determine whether the company was in compliance with the tax laws. Applying common-law principles defining the employer-employee relationship, it concluded that Microsoft's freelancers were not independent contractors but employees for withholding and employment tax purposes, and that Microsoft would thereafter be required to pay withholding taxes and the employer's portion of Federal Insurance Contribution Act (FICA) tax. Microsoft agreed to pay overdue employer withholding taxes and issue retroactive W-2 forms to allow the freelancers to recover Microsoft's share of FICA taxes, which they had been required to pay. It apparently also agreed to pay freelancers retroactively for any overtime they may have worked.

In response to the IRS rulings, Microsoft began "converting" its freelancers. That is, it tendered offers to some freelancers to become permanent employees; it gave other freelancers the option of terminating their employment relationship with Microsoft completely or continuing to work at the company but in the capacity of employees of a new temporary employment agency, which would provide payroll services, withhold federal taxes, and pay the employer's portion of FICA taxes . . .

After learning of the IRS rulings, the plaintiffs sought various employee benefits, including those now at issue: the ESPP and SPP benefits. The SPP, which became effective January 1, 1987, is a cash or deferred salary arrangement under § 401k of the Internal Revenue Code that permits Microsoft's employees to save and invest up to fifteen percent of their income through tax-deferred payroll deductions. Under the plan, Microsoft matches fifty percent of the employee's contribution in any year, with a maximum matching contribution of three percent of the employee's yearly compensation. The ESPP, established in January, 1986, permits employees to purchase company stock at eighty-five percent of the lower of the fair market value on the first or on the last day of each six-month offering period through payroll deductions of from two to ten percent. Employees may purchase shares having a value not exceeding ten percent of their gross compensation for the offering period.

Microsoft rejected the plaintiffs' claims for benefits, maintaining that they were independent contractors who were personally responsible for all their own benefits. The plaintiffs sought review of the denial of benefits from the Microsoft plan administrator, who determined that the plaintiffs were ineligible because they contractually waived any rights to benefits and, in any event, they were not " 'regular, full time employees' in approved headcount positions." Although ruling "technically" only on the denial of ERISA benefits, the plan administrator concluded, for the same reasons, that the plaintiffs were ineligible to receive non-ERISA benefits.

. . .

VIZCAINO v. MICROSOFT CORPORATION [II]

120 F.3d 1006 (9th Cir. 1997) *(on rehearing en banc), cert. denied,* 522 U.S. 1098 (1998), *on remand,* 21 E.B.C. 2821 (W.D. Wash. 1998)

FERNANDEZ, CIRCUIT JUDGE.

. . .

DISCUSSION

Although the Workers [the term the court uses to refer to the plaintiffs and the court-certified class] challenge both their exclusion from the SPP and their exclusion from the ESPP, the two plans are subject to rather different legal regimes. The former is a[n IRC] § 401(k) plan, which is governed by ERISA; the latter is a[n IRC] § 423 plan, which is not governed by ERISA. It, instead, is governed, at least in large part, by principles arising out of the law of the State of Washington. Nevertheless, certain issues, perhaps the most critical ones, cut across both regimes, and we will address them first.

I. GENERAL CONSIDERATIONS

A. *The Workers' Status*

It is important to recognize that there is no longer any question that the Workers were employees of Microsoft, and not independent contractors. The IRS clearly determined that they were. In theory one could argue that what the IRS said was fine for withholding and FICA purposes, but that is as far as it goes.

. . . . both Microsoft and the SPP have conceded for purposes of this appeal that the Workers were common law employees. In fact, they have asserted that the Workers' status is a "nonissue" because they concede that the Workers were common law employees. That is to say, they were employees of Microsoft.

B. *The Employment Agreements*

The concession that the Workers were employees would, at first blush, appear to dispose of this case. It means that for legal purposes they, along with the other employees of Microsoft, were subject to Microsoft's control as to both "the manner and means" of accomplishing their job, that they worked for a substantial period, that they were furnished a workplace and equipment, that they were subject to discharge, and the like. *See id.*; *see also* 26 C.F.R. § 31.3401(c)-1(b). If that were all, this would be an exceedingly easy case. Of course, it is not at all.

Microsoft also entered into special agreements with the Workers, and it is those which complicate matters to some extent. Each of the Workers and Microsoft signed agreements which stated, among other things not relevant here, that the worker was "an Independent Contractor for [Microsoft]," and nothing in the agreement should be construed as creating an "employer-employee relationship." As a result, the worker agreed "to be responsible for all of [his] federal and state taxes, withholding, social security, insurance, and other benefits." At the same time, Microsoft had the Workers sign an information form, which explained: "[A]s an Independent Contractor to Microsoft, you are self employed and are responsible to pay all your own insurance and benefits . . . . Microsoft . . . will not subject your payments to any withholding . . . . You are not either an employee of Microsoft, or a temporary employee of Microsoft." We now know beyond peradventure that most of this was not, in fact, true because the Workers actually were employees rather than independent contractors. What are we to make of that?

We now know that as a matter of law Microsoft hired the Workers to perform their services as employees and that the Workers performed those services. Yet we are also obligated to construe the agreements. In doing so, we could take either a negative or a positive view of Microsoft's intent and motives. We could decide that Microsoft knew that the Workers were employees, but chose to paste the independent contractor label upon them after making a rather amazing series of decisions to violate the law. Or we could decide that Microsoft mistakenly thought that the Workers were independent contractors and that all else simply seemed to flow from that status.

Were we to take the former approach, we would have to determine that Microsoft, with the knowledge that the Workers were simply a group of employees, decided to engage in the following maneuvers:

(1) Despite the requirements of federal law that amounts be withheld from employee wages, Microsoft decided it would not withhold. *See* 26 U.S.C. §§ 3102, 3401–3406.

(2) Despite the fact that the SPP states that "employee" means "any common law employee . . . who is on the United States payroll of the employer," Microsoft decided to manipulate the availability of that benefit by routing the wages of these employees through the accounts payable department, so that it could argue that they were not on the United States payroll. Beyond that, it also determined that it would tell the IRS in its "Application for Determination for Defined Contribution Plan," that Microsoft did, indeed, basically include all employees, a category that it knew included the Workers, even though it had contrived to exclude them. Beyond even that, Microsoft excluded these employees when it filed its tax returns for the SPP, even though it knew better.

(3) Despite the fact that the ESPP must, essentially, be made available to all employees, Microsoft excluded these employees and thereby intentionally risked the possibility that the plan would not qualify for favorable tax treatment. It did that, even though the plan itself stated that it covered all regular employees and that it was to be construed to comply with IRC § 423, a law which basically requires that all employees be covered. The officers of Microsoft also decided to eliminate one group of common law employees from the benefits, even though the board of directors and the shareholders had already made the benefits of the ESPP available to those employees. In doing that, the officers intentionally violated the corporate law of Delaware, to which Microsoft was subject, because

the terms of coverage of stock option plans are not in the hands of corporate officers; they are in the hands of the board itself. *See* Del. Code Ann. tit. 8, § 157.

On the other hand, in construing the agreements we can view the label as a simple mistake. That is, Microsoft honestly thought that the Workers were independent contractors and took its various actions and inactions based upon that misapprehension. Its actions and the conclusions conveyed to the Workers in the agreements and in the explanation in the information form, which accompanied the agreements, were simply an explication of what the effect of independent contractor status would be and had no separate purpose or effect aside from that explanatory function. That is to say, of course there could neither be withholding from wages nor participation in the benefit plans because those keyed on common law employment status. If the Workers were independent contractors, those would be the inevitable results, even if nothing were said about them in the agreement or the information form. Explaining the meaning of independent contractor status was simply a helpful disclosure.

Absent evidence that the officers of Microsoft used their daedalian talents to follow the first route we have just outlined, we must decide that the second route is a more accurate portrayal of what occurred here. In other words, we should, and we do, consider what the parties did in the best light. In so doing, we do not believe that we are being panglossian; we are merely acting in accordance with the ancient maxim which assumes that "the law has been obeyed." *See, e.g.*, Cal. Civ. Code § 3548.

. . .

In short, Microsoft has already recognized that the Workers were employees and that the "no withholding" consequence of the independent contractor label has fallen; we now hold that the "benefit" consequence has fallen also. Having thus burned off the brumes which threatened to obscure our view, we will now turn to the plans themselves.

II. THE PLANS

A. *The SPP*

The SPP is an ERISA plan. *See* [ERISA § 3(2)(A)(ii); IRC § 401(k)]. The Workers seek enforcement of the terms of that plan. That is, they seek to have us review the determination of the plan administrator and to require that the plan make its benefits available to them. *See* [ERISA 502(a)(1)(B)]. As we have already pointed out, the administrative panel of the SPP determined that the Workers are not entitled to benefits. The reasons appear to have been that the Workers were independent contractors and that they waived the benefits. We must review those determinations to see if they were arbitrary or capricious. Based upon what we have already said, it is pellucid that they were. To the extent that the decision was based upon the supposed independent contractor status of the Workers, the plan conceded that the decision was wrong when it conceded that the Workers were, in fact, employees. To the extent that the decision was based upon a supposed waiver of benefits, the plan administrator purported to construe the agreements rather than the plan itself. But, as we have pointed out, our construction is the opposite. We, therefore, determine that the reasons given for denying benefits were arbitrary and capricious because they were based upon legal errors which "misconstrued the Plan and applied a wrong standard to a benefits determination."

The SPP now concedes as much, but it and the Workers asked the district court, and ask us, to decide a different issue of plan construction, one on which the administrator has not opined. The district court accepted that invitation, so did the panel. We are tempted to do the same, but upon reflection we have determined that we should not allow ourselves to be seduced into making a decision which belongs to the plan administrator in the first instance.

We are asked to decide what is meant by the SPP's restriction of benefits to common law employees who are "on the United States payroll of the employer." The panel explored some of the reasonably possible meanings of that phrase and construed the apparent ambiguity in favor of the Workers. No doubt the plan administrator should pay careful attention to what was said there. We have also pointed out that we are dubious about the proposition that Microsoft would manipulate plan coverage by assigning recognized common law employees to its accounts payable department or to its payroll department, as it saw fit. We have our doubts that it could properly do so. But it is the terms of the SPP which control, and the plan is separate from Microsof t itself. Thus, we cannot, and will not, predict how the plan administrator, who has the primary duty of construction, will construe the terms of the SPP.

We do not know whether he will rely upon an "is" construction — you must actually be on the payroll — or upon an "ought" construction — you must be a person who should be on the payroll. Nor do we know if he will accept the domestic versus foreign gloss on the provision in question. What we do know is that the decision is his in the first instance. We would set a poor precedent were we to intrude upon that exercise of discretion before he has even considered and ruled upon the issue. We would encourage the dumping of difficult and discretionary decisions into the laps of the courts, although one of the very purposes of ERISA is to avoid that kind of complication and delay. Of course, should he rule in favor of the Workers' position, he must then go on to determine what benefits they are entitled to and under what conditions, but that, too, is exactly the kind of decision that he should be making for each of the Workers in the first instance.

. . . . this is simply a case where a wholly new issue, which was never put to the SPP administrator, has been raised. He has both the right and the duty to decide it, and we must then review his ultimate decision regarding the Workers by the usual standard. " 'It is not the court's function *ab initio* to apply the correct standard to [the participant's] claim. That function, under the Plan, is reserved to the Plan administrator.' " *Saffle*, 85 F.3d at 461.

. . .

CONCLUSION

Microsoft, like other advanced employers, makes certain benefits available to all of its employees, who meet minimum conditions of eligibility. For some time, it did not believe that the Workers could partake of certain of those benefits because it thought that they were independent contractors. In that it was mistaken, as it now knows and concedes.

The mistake brought Microsoft difficulties with the IRS, but it has resolved those difficulties by making certain payments and by taking other actions. The mistake has also brought it difficulties with the Workers, and the time has come to resolve those.

Therefore, we now determine that the reasons for rejecting the Workers' participation in the SPP and the ESPP were invalid. Any remaining issues regarding the rights of a particular worker in the ESPP and his available remedies must be decided by the district court upon remand. However, any remaining issues regarding the right of any or all of the Workers to participate in the SPP must be decided by the plan administrator upon remand.

Reversed and Remanded to the district court as to the ESPP. Reversed and Remanded to the district court for further remand to the plan administrator as to the SPP.

FLETCHER, CIRCUIT JUDGE, with whom HUG, CHIEF JUDGE, and PREGERSON, MICHAEL DALY HAWKINS and THOMAS, CIRCUIT JUDGES, join, concurring in part and dissenting in part:

We concur in the substance of Judge Fernandez' opinion except that we would not remand the issue of eligibility to participate in the SPP to the Plan Administrator and would hold that the Workers are eligible to participate. Remand is inappropriate and further unnecessary in that we conclude that interpretation of the phrase "on the United States payroll of the employer" is not required.

In its denial of the Workers' claim, the administrative panel convened by the Plan Administrator stated:

> "The denial is affirmed for the reasons that: (1) claimants had agreed and/or acknowledged upon first working for Microsoft that they would not receive employee benefits; (2) claimants specifically waived (by contract) any rights to benefits and (3) even if claimants had been employees and had not "waived rights to benefits," they were not "regular, full-time employees" in an approved headcount position."

We agree with Judge Fernandez that these determinations were arbitrary and capricious. On appeal, as Judge Fernandez has also properly noted, the Plan abandoned all of its prior positions in favor of a new tack: that the Workers are not eligible for SPP benefits based on a construction of the phrase "on the United States payroll of the employer." Our disagreement with Judge Fernandez, therefore, concerns (1) whether the Plan can properly raise a theory on judicial review not raised in the administrative process, and (2) if a new theory can be raised, whether the appropriate course is for the court to remand to the Plan Administrator to interpret the phrase in the first instance or for the court to decide the issue *de novo.* We would hold that the Plan waived any arguments not raised in the administrative process. Second, we conclude that because of their conduct in this litigation the defendants should be estopped from asserting that remand is appropriate. Third, were we to reach the U.S. payroll question, we would conclude that the issue was resolved by the administrative panel's factual determinations. Finally, were we required to interpret the phrase, we would affirm the interpretation of the original three-judge panel of our court.

* * *

O' SCANNLAIN, CIRCUIT JUDGE, joined by CYNTHIA HOLCOMB HALL and T.G. NELSON, CIRCUIT JUDGES, concurring in part and dissenting in part:

I respectfully dissent from all but Part II-A of the court's opinion because Microsoft and the plaintiffs never formed a valid contract under Washington law for the benefits now claimed. I concur in the result of Part II-A of the court's opinion but not in its analysis.

I

I do not disagree with the court's statement of facts, but it has failed to mention some and may leave a mistaken impression of others. Thus, I suggest that the following additional facts from the record be taken into account.

The plaintiffs were temporary "freelancers" for Microsoft. Instead of calling them by this label — which was ubiquitously used within the Microsoft community and by the plaintiffs themselves — the court styles the plaintiffs as "workers." It then engages in a long discussion of why they were in fact "common law employees" of Microsoft. Both labels may be true — the plaintiffs did work, and Microsoft has conceded that the plaintiffs satisfy the definition of common law employees for some purposes. Neither of these labels are relevant to the question before us, however, and both are potentially misleading. Both labels imply that the plaintiffs were just like any other regular Microsoft employees, and hence should be eligible for the same benefits as regular staff. The evidence in the record, however, points to the contrary. I will refer to the plaintiffs by the same term the plaintiffs themselves use "freelancers."

. . . For the sake of clarity, I note that all we decide today is whether the freelancers should have been allowed to participate in the ESPP and the SPP during the period leading up to the 1989–90 conversion. All agree that those freelancers who were converted into employees of outside employment agencies have no valid claim for participation in the ESPP and SPP after the date of their conversion.

When the freelancers were originally retained by contract with Microsoft, they were expressly told that they were not eligible for any Microsoft employee benefits, and that they would have to provide their own benefits. Indeed, the named plaintiffs admit that they did not think they were entitled to benefits, and did not think benefits were a part of their compensation package.

Moreover, the freelancers each signed contractual documents which expressly stated that they would not receive any benefits, and would have to pay their own taxes and benefits. Specifically, Microsoft required that each plaintiff sign an "Independent Contractor Agreement" ("ICA"). I think it is appropriate to set out the complete text of the relevant ICA provision:

> "CONTRACTOR is an independent contractor for MS [Microsoft]. Nothing in this Agreement shall be construed as creating an employer-employee relationship, or as a guarantee of a future offer of employment. CONTRACTOR further agrees to be responsible for all federal and state taxes, withholding, social security, insurance and other benefits."

Attached to the ICA was a one-page document entitled "independent contractor/freelancer information," which the freelancers also signed. It stated:

> "[A]s an Independent Contractor to Microsoft, you are self-employed and are responsible to pay all your own insurance and benefits."

In the district court, Microsoft's uncontested extrinsic evidence established that the plaintiffs were told, and knew, that benefits were not a part of their compensation. Instead of providing benefits, Microsoft paid the freelancers at a higher hourly rate than Microsoft's regular employees. The freelancers were also treated differently in a host of other ways. They had different color employee badges, different e-mail addresses, and were not invited to company parties and functions. Instead of receiving a regular paycheck from Microsoft's Payroll department (like Microsoft's regular employees), freelancers submitted invoices for their services to the Accounts Payable department.

With these additional relevant facts in mind, we may consider the merits.

. . .

III

The freelancers also claim that Microsoft should have allowed them to participate in its Savings Plus Plan ("SPP"), which is governed by ERISA. The SPP provides that "[e]ach employee who is 18 years of age or older and who has been employed for six months shall be eligible to participate in this Plan." It then defines "employee" as "any common law employee who receives remuneration for personal services rendered to the employer and who is on the United States payroll of the employer." The freelancers argue that they fit this definition of employee; Microsoft retorts that the freelancers were not "on the United States payroll of the employer." Our first task, therefore, is ascertaining what that phrase means.

We cannot immediately set about this task, however, because the SPP grants discretion to the plan administrator to construe the plan. The Supreme Court has instructed us that when the plan vests discretion in the administrator, principles of trust law require that we leave the plan administrator's interpretation undisturbed if reasonable. *Firestone Tire & Rubber Co. v. Bruch*, 489 U.S. 101, 111 (1989). Indeed, ERISA encourages plan fiduciaries to exercise properly the discretion they have been granted; courts should not be second-guessing the discretionary decisions of fiduciaries without a very good reason. Thus, we are not to impose our view of a provision on the plan, but are confined to reviewing the administrator's construction to determine whether it is reasonable.

In order for this rule protecting a plan administrator's discretion to be meaningful, however, the administrator must be given an opportunity to interpret the meaning of plan provisions before the court rules. In this case, the plan administrator did not overtly construe the phrase "on the United States payroll of the employer," at least so far as I can tell from the record. The district court believed that the administrator impliedly rested its decision on a particular interpretation of that phrase. Although there is a colorable argument in support of the district court's belief, I believe that the judicially stated preference that the plan administrator interpret the plan, subject to a limite d review by courts, requires us to remand to the plan administrator explicitly to construe the meaning of that phrase. I agree with the court's conclusion on this point.

I write separately to clarify that I do not concur in the court's analysis of the meaning and implications of "on the United States payroll of the employer," and, as dicta, the court's statements do not bind the plan administrator in any way. In my view, that phrase is a term of art with significance within the Microsoft community. Further, I do not agree with the ill-advised suggestion that Microsoft might not have been able properly to classify employees for participation or non-participation in an ERISA plan based on whether the employees were regular hires paid through the Payroll department or "freelancers" paid through the Accounts Payable department. Microsoft could choose to offer the SPP to whichever classes of employees it wishes. It is certainly free to decide not to offer positions satisfying the SPP's criteria to these plaintiffs.

I respectfully concur in the result of Part II-A of the court's opinion but otherwise dissent.

2-8 QUESTIONS AND PROBLEMS

1. Does Microsoft's 401(k) plan cover the plaintiffs?

2. Must Microsoft's 401(k) plan cover the plaintiffs if they are common law employees of Microsoft?

3. Could Microsoft's 401(k) plan cover the plaintiffs if they were not common law employees? *See* IRC § 401(a)(2).

4. Why did Microsoft want to treat the plaintiffs as independent contractors rather than common law employees?

5. In *Vizcaino I*, Judge Trott quoted a 1996 General Accounting Office Report which declared, "Until the classification rules are clarified, we are not optimistic that the confusion over who is an independent contractor and who is an employee can be avoided." Does *Vizcaino II* clarify the distinction between employees and independent contractors?

6. How might Microsoft have drafted its plan to avoid this litigation?

In March 2001, the *Microsoft* case was settled. Microsoft agreed to create a $97 million fund to compensate both the freelancers and their attorneys. Between 8,000 and 12,000 class members were expected to receive payments from the settlement fund. The amount of compensation the freelancers were entitled to receive depended on when they worked for Microsoft, the duration of their freelancer status, and the total number of individuals who filed claims under the settlement. The law firm representing the freelancers was awarded more than $27 million from the settlement fund for attorneys' fees and costs for its representation of the freelancers.

Owners as "Employees"

In *Yates v. Hendon*, 541 U.S. 1 (2004), the Supreme Court held that if a pension plan covers not only the working owner of a business but also one or more other employees, the working owner qualifies as an "employee" for purposes of ERISA. In that case, the working owner took out a loan from his pension plan and paid it back three weeks before his creditors filed an involuntary bankruptcy petition against him. The working owner sought to take advantage of ERISA's antialienation provision (discussed in Chapter 4) that prevents creditors from reaching participants' benefits prior to retirement. The Court held that the working owner qualified as an employee and thus a plan "participant" and so was entitled to ERISA's protections.

Chapter 3
WELFARE BENEFITS

ERISA regulates two principal types of employee benefit plans: "employee pension benefit plans" or "pension plans," and "employee welfare benefit plans" or "welfare plans." ERISA § 3(3). Welfare plans may offer a wide variety of benefits, including health, accident and disability benefits, life insurance, vacation pay, apprenticeship and training, day care centers, scholarship funds, pre-paid legal services, and severance pay. ERISA § 3(1). Among these benefits, paid time off is the most common, with 77 percent of workers in private establishments receiving paid vacations in 2011. The next most common benefits were life insurance (with 56 percent of workers receiving such benefits), medical care benefits (51 percent), and short-term disability benefits (37 percent). Most workers view medical care as their most important benefit, and for most employers, medical insurance premiums are the most costly benefit they offer.

Since its inception, ERISA has regulated welfare plans through its reporting and disclosure rules (discussed in Chapter 4), fiduciary rules (discussed in Chapter 6), and enforcement provisions (discussed in Chapter 7). When ERISA was enacted, however, pension plans were much more important than welfare plans, and consequently most of ERISA's substantive regulation, such as the funding rules (discussed in Chapter 9) and vesting rules (discussed in Chapter 4), was directed exclusively at pension plans. Free of funding requirements and vesting rules, welfare plans are typically financed on a pay-as-you-go basis with the employer's general assets, and employees have no assurance that their current welfare benefits will be provided in the future. Absent any contractual obligation, the employer can amend, reduce, or eliminate welfare benefits at any time. For example, an employer who offers health care insurance, and whose employees are not represented by a union, can typically unilaterally announce that it is terminating the health care benefits.

ERISA's lack of substantive regulation combined with its broad preemption provision (discussed in Chapter 5) led to some serious inadequacies in the welfare benefit arena, particularly with respect to self-funded health care plans. As welfare benefits in general, and health care benefits in particular, have grown in importance over the years, Congress began to expand ERISA's substantive regulation of welfare benefit plans. This regulation began in 1985 with the enactment of the Consolidated Omnibus Budget Reconciliation Act (COBRA), which requires group health plans to make coverage available to employees and dependents who might otherwise lose their benefits due to changes in employment or job status. Eleven years later, with the enactment of the Health Insurance Portability and Accountability Act of 1996 (HIPAA), Congress further extended the substantive regulation of employer-sponsored health care plans by limiting the ability of such plans to impose pre-existing coverage exclusions. Between 1996 and 2010, Congress amended ERISA a few other times in response to very specific shortcomings in the health care system. Then, in 2010, Congress enacted sweeping reform of health insurance with enactment of the Patient Protection and Affordable Care Act (Affordable Care Act). Many of those changes extend to employment-based health care plans.

This chapter begins by considering what is a welfare benefit plan for purposes of ERISA. It then considers ERISA's and the Affordable Care Act's regulation of health care benefits and retiree health plans. Finally, it concludes with the taxation of welfare benefits.

A. WHAT IS A WELFARE BENEFIT PLAN?

ERISA § 3(1).

Although ERISA § 3(1) regulates welfare benefit plans, it does not clearly define the term "plan." The following case remains the leading case for establishing the standards that determine when an employer has created an employee benefit plan for purposes of ERISA.

DONOVAN v. DILLINGHAM

688 F.2d 1367 (11th Cir. 1982)

GOBOLD, CHIEF JUDGE.

The Secretary of Labor pursuant to his authority under ERISA § 502(a) brought this action against the trustees of Union Insurance Trust (UIT) and businesses owned and operated by them, alleging they are fiduciaries subject to the fiduciary responsibility provisions contained in Part 4 of Title I of ERISA, § 401 *et seq.* Fiduciary duties under ERISA, however, arise only if there are employee benefit plans as defined by the Act. The district court . . . dismissed for lack of subject matter jurisdiction because there were no employee benefit plans involved. A panel of this court agreed. Upon reconsideration en banc we find there was subject matter jurisdiction and reverse.

Congress enacted ERISA to protect working men and women from abuses in the administration and investment of private retirement plans and employee welfare plans. Broadly stated, ERISA established minimum standards for vesting of benefits, funding of benefits, carrying out fiduciary responsibilities, reporting to the government and making disclosures to participants.

With a few specific exceptions not pertinent to this decision, Title I of ERISA applies to any "employee benefit plan" if it is established or maintained by any employer or employee organization engaged in commerce or in any industry or activity affecting commerce, or by both an employer and an employee organization . . . .

UIT is a group insurance trust, commonly known as a multiple employer trust ("MET"), whose purpose is to allow employers of small numbers of employees to secure group health insurance coverage for their employees at rates more favorable than offered directly by an insurer. UIT obtained a group health insurance policy from Occidental Life Insurance Company of California to furnish specified insurance benefits. Employers and various employee organizations "subscribe" to UIT to receive the coverage of the blanket Occidental Life policy. Appellees contend that ERISA does not apply because there is involved only the "bare purchase of health insurance" and that no employee welfare benefit plans are implicated . . . .

ERISA § 3(1) defines "employee welfare benefit plan" or "welfare plan" as any plan, fund, or program which was heretofore or is hereafter established or maintained by an employer or by an employee organization, or by both, to the extent that such plan, fund, or program was established or is maintained for the purpose of providing for its participants or their beneficiaries, through the purchase of insurance or otherwise, (A) medical, surgical, or hospital care or benefits, or benefits in the event of sickness, accident, disability, death or unemployment, or vacation benefits, apprenticeship or other training programs, or day care centers, scholarship funds, or prepaid legal services, or (B) any benefit described in § 302(c) of the Labor Management Relations Act, 1947 (other than pensions on retirement or death, and insurance to provide such pensions).

By definition, then, a welfare plan requires (1) a "plan, fund, or program" (2) established or maintained (3) by an employer or by an employee organization, or by both, (4) for the purpose of providing medical, surgical, hospital care, sickness, accident, disability, death, unemployment or vacation benefits, apprenticeship or other training programs, day care centers, scholarship funds, prepaid legal services or severance benefits (5) to participants or their beneficiaries.

Prerequisites (3), (4) and (5) are either self-explanatory or defined by statute. A plan, fund, or program must be established or maintained "for the purpose of providing for its participants or their beneficiaries, through the purchase of insurance or otherwise," health, accident, disability, death, or unemployment or vacation benefits or apprenticeship or other training programs, day care centers, scholarship funds, prepaid legal services, or severance benefits.

The gist of ERISA's definitions of employer, employee organization, participant, and beneficiary is that a plan, fund, or program falls within the ambit of ERISA only if the plan, fund, or program covers ERISA participants because of their employee status in an employment relationship, and an employer or employee organization is the person that establishes or maintains the plan, fund, or program . . . .

. . .

Not so well defined are the first two prerequisites: "plan, fund, or program" and "established or maintained." Commentators and courts define "plan, fund, or program" by synonym — arrangement, scheme, unitary scheme, program of action, method of putting into effect an intention or proposal, design — but do not specify the prerequisites of a "plan, fund, or program." At a minimum, however, a "plan, fund, or program" under ERISA implies the existence of intended benefits, intended beneficiaries, a source of financing, and a procedure to apply for and collect benefits.

"Established or maintained" appears twice in the definition of an employee welfare benefit plan: first, an employer or employee organization or both must establish or maintain a plan, fund, or program, and, second, the plan, fund, or program must be established or maintained for specified purposes. In many instances a plan is established or maintained, or both, in writing. It is obvious that a system of providing benefits pursuant to a written instrument that satisfies ERISA §§ 102 and 402, would constitute a "plan, fund or program."

ERISA does not, however, require a formal, written plan. ERISA's coverage provision reaches "any employee benefit plan if it is established or maintained" by an employer or an employee organization, or both, who are engaged in any activities or industry affecting commerce. ERISA § 4(a). There is no requirement of a formal, written plan in either ERISA's coverage section, ERISA § 4(a), or its definitions section, ERISA § 3(1). Once it is determined that ERISA covers a plan, the Act's fiduciary and reporting provisions do require the plan to be established pursuant to a written instrument, ERISA §§ 102 and 402, but clearly these are only the responsibilities of administrators and fiduciaries of plans covered by ERISA and are not prerequisites to coverage under the Act. Furthermore, because the policy of ERISA is to safeguard the well-being and security of working men and women and to apprise them of their rights and obligations under any employee benefit plan, *see* ERISA § 2, it would be incongruous for persons establishing or maintaining informal or unwritten employee benefit plans, or assuming the responsibility of safeguarding plan assets, to circumvent the Act merely because an administrator or other fiduciary failed to satisfy reporting or fiduciary standards.

The Secretary contends that "establish" means no more than an ultimate decision by an employer or an employee organization to provide the type of benefits described in ERISA § 3(1). This sweeps too broadly. A decision to extend benefits is not the establishment of a plan or program. Acts or events that record, exemplify, or implement the decision will be direct or circumstantial evidence that the decision has become reality — e.g., financing or arranging to finance or fund the intended benefits, establishing a procedure for disbursing benefits, assuring employees that the plan or program exists — but it is the reality of a plan, fund, or program and not the decision to extend certain benefits that is determinative.

In determining whether a plan, fund or program (pursuant to a writing or not) is a reality a court must determine whether from the surrounding circumstances a reasonable person could ascertain the intended benefits, beneficiaries, source of financing, and procedures for receiving benefits. Some essentials of a plan, fund, or program can be adopted, explicitly or implicitly, from sources outside the plan, fund, or program — e.g., an insurance company's procedure for processing claims, (qualified health maintenance organization) — but no single act in itself necessarily constitutes the establishment of the plan, fund, or program . . . .

In summary, a "plan, fund, or program" under ERISA is established if from the surrounding circumstances a reasonable person can ascertain the intended benefits, a class of beneficiaries, the source of financing, and procedures for receiving benefits . . . .

The record indicates that subscribers to UIT included single-employer, collectively bargained programs, multi-employer health and welfare funds, and union-sponsored funds . . . .

Without inquiring into other assets or purposes of the subscribers, the purpose stated in the Agreement and Declaration of Trust establishing UIT and thus the purpose of those who subscribed to UIT, was "to provide, through policies issued by insurers, life, accident-and-health, sickness-and-health, disability-income, hospital benefits, surgical-benefits, dental-care, and pre-paid-legal-expenses insurance for the use and the benefit of insured employees and of their families and dependents." The group health insurance policy UIT obtained from Occidental Life Insurance Company of California may provide less benefits than those listed in the UIT trust agreement, but clearly employers and employee organizations subscribe to UIT with the intent to provide health insurance, which is covered by ERISA § 3(1), It is equally clear from participation agreements found in the record that the persons benefitting from the group hospitalization are employees of employers or members of the employee organizations that subscribed to UIT and are financing the participation.

Many of the subscriptions were methods of fulfilling collective bargaining agreements between employers and unions to furnish health insurance benefits to employees. In these situations the employer or employee organization, or both, were committed to providing benefits to employees or members through the purchase of health insurance on a continuing basis. In some cases, as noted above, unions or employers were already furnishing insurance benefits and merely substituted UIT for other METs or carriers while continuing to furnish health insurance coverage.

. . .

Thus, it appears that employers or unions that subscribed to UIT to furnish health insurance for employees or members (either pursuant to an agreement or pursuant to a continuing practice of purchasing the insurance for a class of employees) established employee welfare benefit plans. It also appears that some subscribers that previously had not furnished health insurance to their employees or members, and that did not subscribe to UIT pursuant to an agreement to furnish health benefits, nevertheless did purchase benefits for a substantial percentage of a class of employees or members under circumstances tending to show an anticipated continuing furnishing of such benefits (either through an MET or insurance carrier or otherwise); these subscribers too established employee welfare benefit plans. Thus, it appears that numerous subscribers to UIT established employee welfare benefit plans; with respect to each of these, ERISA conferred subject matter jurisdiction on the district court.

. . .

The judgment of the district court dismissing the case is Reversed and the case is Remanded for proceedings not inconsistent with this opinion.

3-1 QUESTIONS AND PROBLEMS

1. Why is the Secretary of Labor involved in the *Donovan* lawsuit?

2. The issue in *Donovan* is whether the Federal District Court has jurisdiction. Why the discussion of what is a plan under ERISA?

3. Explain why there is no need for a writing to establish a plan, but a writing is required after the plan is established.

4. If the employer offers a fringe benefit but there is no ERISA plan, in what court can an employee sue to enforce the right to the fringe benefit?

5. Under what circumstances would an employer prefer that a plan be found?

6. In 1980, prior to *Donovan*, the Fifth Circuit held in *Taggart Corp. v. Life & Health Benefits Administration*, 617 F.2d 1208 (5th Cir. 1980), *cert. denied*, 450 U.S. 1030 (1981), that the mere purchase of a health insurance plan for the sole employee of Taggart Corporation did not constitute an ERISA plan. The court noted that the supposed "plan" had "no assets and is liable for no benefits." Thus, there were no assets to be protected, which the court held was the principal purpose of ERISA — protection of pension plan assets. In 1991, the Sixth Circuit, when asked to determine whether the purchase of group health insurance constituted an ERISA welfare benefit plan, relied on *Donovan* and rejected *Taggart*, stating that, "We agree with the *Donovan* analysis and find that the *Donovan* court's construction of ERISA is more consistent with the Act's broad scope than *Taggart*." *International Resources Inc. v. New York Life Insurance Company*, 950 F.2d 294, 297 (6th Cir. 1991). Is the holding in *Donovan* more consistent with ERISA?

Determining whether there is a plan is of considerable significance. If there is a plan, ERISA preempts state law, ERISA § 514(a) (discussed in Chapter 5), and governs. Of course, in the welfare benefit arena, ERISA may not provide any regulation or remedy because ERISA provides relatively little substantive regulation of welfare benefit plans. Thus, in many cases, the employer may argue that it has created a welfare benefit plan so as to preempt state law that would otherwise control.

MASSACHUSETTS v. MORASH

490 U.S. 107 (1989)

JUSTICE STEVENS delivered the opinion of the Court.

This case requires us to determine whether a company's policy of paying its discharged employees for their unused vacation time constitutes an "employee welfare benefit plan" within the meaning of § 3(1) of the Employee Retirement Income Security Act of 1974 (ERISA or Act) and whether a criminal action to enforce that policy is foreclosed by the Act's broad pre-emption provision.

In May 1986, petitioner, the Commonwealth of Massachusetts, issued two complaints in the Boston Municipal Court against respondent, Richard N. Morash, president of the Yankee Bank for Finance and Savings (Bank). The complaints charged Morash with criminal violations of the Massachusetts Payment of Wages Statute, Mass. Gen. Laws c. 149 § 148 (1987).

Under the Massachusetts law, an employer is required to pay a discharged employee his full wages, including holiday or vacation payments, on the date of discharge. Similar wage payment statutes have been enacted by 47 other States, the District of Columbia, and the United States, and over half of these include vacation pay. The complaints filed in the Boston Municipal Court alleged that respondent had failed to compensate two discharged bank vice presidents for vacation time they accrued but did not use.

Respondent moved to dismiss the criminal complaints on the ground that the Massachusetts statute, insofar as it applied to these complaints, had been pre-empted by ERISA. He argued that the Bank's vacation policy constituted an "employee welfare benefit plan" under the Act, and that the State's prosecution of him for failure to comply with the policy therefore ran afoul of § 514(a) of the Act, which pre-empts "any and all State laws insofar as they . . . relate to any employee benefit plan." Without ruling on the motion, the trial judge reported the preemption question to the Massachusetts Appeals Court for decision; the Supreme Judicial Court then transferred the case to its docket on its own initiative.

The Supreme Judicial Court held that the policy constituted an employee welfare benefit plan and that the prosecution was pre-empted by ERISA. 522 N.E.2d 409 (1988) . . . . The fact that it would be necessary for an employer to maintain records relating to its employees' unused vacation time, plus the need to accumulate funds to pay the benefits, made it appropriate to treat the employer's promise to its employees as a "plan." The court concluded that the Massachusetts statute related to the plan within the meaning of § 514, and was not excluded from its coverage by the provision saving from preemption a "generally applicable criminal law." ERISA § 514(b)(4).

Because the federal question decided by the Supreme Judicial Court is an important one over which the courts have disagreed, we granted certiorari. We now reverse.

. . .

The precise coverage of ERISA is not clearly set forth in the Act. ERISA covers "employee benefit plans," which it defines as plans that are either "an employee welfare benefit plan," or "an employee pension benefit plan," or both.

The Act does not further define "plan, fund, or program" or "vacation benefits" and does not specify whether every policy to provide vacation benefits falls within its ambit.

. . .

The interpretation of § 3(1) is governed by the familiar principles that "words grouped in a list should be given related meaning," and that "in expounding a statute, we [are] not . . . guided by a single sentence or member of a sentence, but look to the provision of the whole law, and to its object and policy." *Pilot Life Ins. Co. v. Dedeaux*, 481 U.S. 41 (1987). In enacting ERISA, Congress' primary concern was with the mismanagement of funds accumulated to finance employee benefits and the failure to pay employees benefits from accumulated funds. To that end, it established extensive reporting, disclosure, and fiduciary duty requirements to insure against the possibility that the employee's expectation of the benefit would be defeated through poor management by the plan administrator. Because ordinary vacation payments are typically fixed, due at known times, and do not depend on contingencies outside the employee's control, they present none of the risks that ERISA is intended to address. If there is a danger of defeated expectations, it is no different from the danger of defeated expectations of wages for services performed — a danger Congress chose not to regulate in ERISA.

This conclusion is supported by viewing the reference to vacation benefits not in isolation but in light of the words that accompany it and give the provision meaning. Section 3(1) subjects to ERISA regulation plans to provide medical, sickness, accident, disability, and death benefits, training programs, day care centers, scholarship funds, and legal services. The distinguishing feature of most of these benefits is that they accumulate over a period of time and are payable only upon the occurrence of a contingency outside of the control of the employee. Thus, for example, plans to pay employees severance benefits, which are payable *only* upon termination of employment, are employee welfare benefit plans within the meaning of the Act. The reference to vacation payments in § 3(1) should be understood to include within the scope of ERISA those vacation benefits funds, analogous to other welfare benefits, in which either the employee's right to a benefit is contingent upon some future occurrence or the employee bears a risk different from his ordinary employment risk. It is unlikely that Congress intended to subject to ERISA's reporting and disclosure requirements those vacation benefits which by their nature are payable on a regular basis from the general assets of the employer and are accumulated over time only at the election of the employee.

. . .

A contrary interpretation, including routine vacation pay policies with ERISA would have profound consequences. Most employers in the United States provide some type of vacation benefit to their employees. ERISA coverage would put all these employers to the choice of complying with the statute's detailed requirements for reporting and disclosure or discontinuing the practice of compensating employees for unused vacation time. In addition, the extension of ERISA to claims for vacation benefits would vastly expand the jurisdiction of the federal courts, providing a federal forum for any employee with a vacation grievance. Finally, such an interpretation would also displace the extensive state regulation of the vesting, funding, and participation rights of vacation benefits; because ERISA's vesting and funding requirements do not apply to welfare benefit plans, ERISA §§ 201(1), 301(a), as amended, employees would actually receive less protection if ERISA were applied to ordinary vacation wages paid from the employer's general assets. The States have traditionally regulated the payment of wages, including vacation pay. Absent any indication that Congress intended such far-reaching consequences, we are reluctant to so significantly interfere with "the separate spheres of governmental authority preserved in our federalist system." *Fort Halifax Packing Co. v. Coyne*, 482 U.S. at 19.

. . .

The judgment of the Massachusetts Supreme Judicial Court is reversed, and the case is remanded for further proceedings not inconsistent with this opinion.

3-2 QUESTIONS AND PROBLEMS

1. Is the Court's decision in *Mass. v. Morash* consistent with *Donovan*? Would the vacation benefits constitute a welfare benefit plan under the four-factor *Donovan* test?

2. If the *Mass. v. Morash* Court had considered the facts in *Donovan* would it have reached a different result than the *Donovan* court did?

3. Do you think the Court would have reached a different result if the case had arisen because participants were trying to enforce ERISA's substantive protections rather than because the employer was trying to avoid culpability under a state statute?

In *James v. Fleet/Norstar Financial Group*, 992 F.2d 463 (2d Cir. 1993), the issue was whether an employer's promise to give employees sixty days of pay following their last day of work if the employees would remain on the job until an internal consolidation was completed created an employee welfare benefit plan under ERISA. The employer later revoked the promised benefit. The employees sued for the value of the promised severance pay asserting state law claims including breach of contract and negligent misrepresentation. In response, the employer, Fleet, claimed that because the promised severance pay constituted an ERISA plan, all claims based on state law were preempted. On appeal, the court held that the promise was not an ERISA plan. It pointed out that if Fleet's claim of an ERISA plan was upheld, the result

> . . . would be that even if Fleet's actions violated the employees' rights under state law (on which we, of course, intimate no views), the employees could not obtain any redress therefor. They could not prevail on their state law claims because ERISA preempts those claims; and they could not prevail on their ERISA claim because ERISA permits what Fleet did. It is difficult to believe that Congress, which enacted ERISA to protect employees' benefit rights, intended the preemption provision of that statute to produce such an anomalous result. *Id.* at 468.

3-3 QUESTIONS AND PROBLEMS

1. Why would a finding that the severance benefits constituted an ERISA plan have left the plaintiffs with no relief?

2. Suppose the court in *Fleet* had determined that the promise of the severance benefits did constitute an ERISA plan. Assume that Nancy was an employee of Fleet. In May of 2011, she was informed by a letter from Fleet that it expected to close the service center where she worked. She began to look for another job, and on September 10, 2011, she was offered employment by Beta Bank and given two weeks to report to work. On September 15, 2011, she learned of the Fleet offer to pay 60 days pay to those employees who remained at the service center until it ceased operations. Based on the Fleet offer, on September 16 Nancy declined the

job offer from Beta Bank. On November 15, 2011, Fleet canceled the 60 day severance pay offer and instead offered the employees 60 more days of employment. Nancy remained with Fleet for the 60 days, until January 15, 2012, when the service center closed. She finally found another job that began on March 15, 2012. Does it make sense that Nancy has no cause of action against Fleet under ERISA? Has Nancy detrimentally relied upon Fleet's promise of severance pay?

3. If an employer offers a severance plan providing two to twelve months of severance pay to employees who are involuntarily terminated with the amount based on the employee's age and length of service, would that constitute a welfare benefit plan subject to ERISA?

Suppose an employer labels a plan an "ERISA plan." Is the employer bound by that determination? Should it be? The following case addresses this issue.

LANGLEY v. DAIMLERCHRYSLER CORPORATION

502 F.3d 475 (6th Cir. 2007)

McKeague, Circuit Judge.

I

Langley began working for DaimlerChrysler as a production worker, and eventually moved up to production supervisor. Langley had difficulty working with some of the employees she supervised, including Lobzun. In April 2004, Langley was summoned to meet with the members of the company's Local Response Team ("LRT"), which investigates troublesome employees and situations. The LRT told Langley that Lobzun had reported that "someone was going to pull a Daryl Richardson" on Langley. Richardson was a supervisor who was beaten with a baseball bat in an incident well-known to employees, including Langley. The LRT's investigation revealed, however, that no employee had actually threatened Langley. The team reported its findings to Langley.

After her meeting with the LRT, Langley felt unable to return to her job. She went to her family doctor, who advised her to take some time off work due to the stress she was experiencing. She took a leave of absence from the company, but has since returned.

During her leave of absence, Langley sought short-term disability benefits through DaimlerChrysler's Disability Absence Plan ("DAP"), which provides salary payments to employees who are unable to perform all the duties of their occupation. DaimlerChrysler denied her claim.

Langley then brought suit against DaimlerChrysler and Lobzun in Ohio state court. DaimlerChrysler removed the case to federal court. Langley's Second Amended Complaint set forth claims against DaimlerChrysler for: wrongful discharge in violation of Ohio public policy; age discrimination in violation of *Ohio Revised Code* § 4112.02 and Ohio public policy; sex discrimination in violation of *Ohio Revised Code* § 4112.02 and Ohio public policy; intentional infliction of emotional distress; violation of ERISA; breach of contract; and disability discrimination in violation of *Ohio Revised Code* § 4112.02. She also made a claim against Lobzun for intentional infliction of emotional distress.

After the close of discovery, the defendants moved for summary judgment. Langley filed her own motion for partial summary judgment. The district court granted the defendants' motions, denied Langley's motion, and entered judgment in favor of the defendants on all counts.

II

B. *Langley's DAP Claim*

Langley asserted an ERISA claim for benefits under the company's DAP. ERISA provides an eligible employee the right to bring a cause of action against a plan administrator, but only for violating a plan governed by that statute. See ERISA § 502(a)(1)(B). The district court concluded that DaimlerChrysler's DAP was not an ERISA plan, but rather a payroll practice, even though the company's summary plan description ("SPD") included statements from which an employee might conclude the company represented the DAP to be covered by ERISA. Langley argues that the district court committed reversible error.

"Determining the existence of an ERISA plan is a question of fact to be answered in light of all the surrounding circumstances and facts from the point of view of a reasonable person, which is reviewed for clear error." In general, courts apply a three-part test to determine whether ERISA covers a particular plan or practice: (1) first, does a "safe harbor" exception apply; (2) if not, do "the surrounding circumstances" suggest that "a reasonable person could ascertain the intended benefits, the class of beneficiaries, the source of financing, and the procedures for receiving benefits"; and 3) has "the employer established or maintained the plan with the intent of providing benefits to its employees." Here, the district court's analysis started and ended at the first step.

Under ERISA, the terms "employee welfare benefit plan" and "welfare plan" are defined as:

> any plan, fund, or program which has heretofore or is hereafter established or maintained by an employer or by an employee organization, or by both, to the extent that such plan, fund, or program was established or is maintained for the purpose of providing for its participants or their beneficiaries, through the purchase of insurance or otherwise . . . benefits in the event of sickness, accident, disability, death or unemployment, ...

ERISA § 3(1). Under the Department of Labor's regulations, however, "normal compensation" paid to an employee as a result of a disability and from "the employer's general assets" does not constitute an employee welfare benefit plan, but instead is considered a "payroll practice." 29 C.F.R. § 2510.3-1(b)(2). Such practices are not regulated by ERISA.

Langley does not dispute that DaimlerChrysler made DAP payments entirely out of its general assets. Nor does she assert that recipients received anything other than "normal" compensation under the plan. Accordingly, the DAP falls squarely within the plain meaning of a payroll practice. This is not, however, the end of our analysis.

Langley correctly points out that DaimlerChrysler made statements in its SPD from which an employee might conclude that the DAP was an ERISA plan (which is presumably why she pleaded an ERISA claim). DaimlerChrysler argues on appeal that it does not conflate the group insurance benefits (covered under ERISA) with the DAP, as the benefits are described in the SPD. The company fails, however, to address any of the specific statements relied upon by the district court for finding otherwise. For example, the SPD states that "[t]hese plans are designed to meet the legal requirements for employee benefit plans" under ERISA. The company does not refer us to any statement in the SPD which excludes the DAP from "[t]hese plans" — in fact, the DAP is listed directly above the "[t]hese plans" statement. As DaimlerChrysler has pointed to no clear error by the district court, the next step is to consider whether, as Langley argues, the district court erred in attaching little weight to this and other statements in the SPD.

A review of the case law and record confirms that the district court did not err. Although we have not had occasion to address the issue, several of our sister circuits have considered whether an employer's description of a plan as one governed by ERISA is determinative. In *McMahon v. Digital Equipment Corporation*, the First Circuit affirmed a lower court's finding that a disability benefit plan was covered by ERISA. 162 F.3d 28 (1st Cir. 1998). The company had held the plan out to its employees and the federal government as an ERISA plan. Moreover, the company funded the disability payments with insurance as well as general assets. The First Circuit concluded that the combination of these facts weighed in favor of an ERISA plan, not a payroll practice. The court emphasized, however, the limitations of its holding:

> We do not hold that an employer's *mere labeling* of a plan determines whether a plan is an ERISA plan, since this also could lead to a form of "regulation shopping." But where, as here, an employer partially funds a plan from sources outside of its general assets, files documents with the Department of Labor and the IRS consistent with the plan's ERISA status, and informs employees that the plan is subject to ERISA regulation, we find that the plan is an ERISA plan and not a payroll practice.

Id. at 38 (emphasis added).

Several years later, the Eleventh Circuit faced a similar issue, but concluded the payroll-practice exception did apply. In *Stern v. IBM*, the company argued that its disability benefit program was an ERISA plan because it held the benefit out as such to employees and the federal government. The Eleventh Circuit rejected this argument:

> The way in which an employer characterizes its plan may be one factor, among others, in determining ERISA coverage. Nevertheless, even if IBM has treated the Program as an ERISA plan with respect to government filings, its mere labeling of the plan should not determine whether ERISA applies. Allowing this could lead to a form of "regulation shopping." Where, as here, an employer pays an employee's normal compensation for periods of mental or physical disability entirely from its general assets, the program constitutes an exempted payroll practice under 29 C.F.R. § 2510.3-1(b) and not an ERISA plan.

326 F.3d 1367, 1374 (11th Cir. 2003).

* * *

There are sound reasons supporting this approach. As first alluded to in *McMahon*, a contrary ruling would enable employers to engage in regulation shopping. If, by merely labeling a particular benefit an "ERISA plan," an employer could convert an otherwise exempt benefit into one covered under ERISA, it could avoid state tort liability under ERISA-preemption doctrine.

Moreover, when benefits are paid solely from general assets, the protections of ERISA are not necessary. ERISA is intended to protect employees from abuses and mismanagement of private retirement and welfare funds controlled by employers or third parties. "Where an employer pays occasional, temporary benefits from its general assets, there is no benefits fund to abuse or mismanage and no special risk of loss or nonpayment of benefits." Rather, employees face the same general risk with their disability payments as they do with their wages or salaries: the company might not have enough general assets to pay them.

We agree with the approach in *McMahon* and *Stern*, and adopt it here: mere labeling by a plan sponsor or administrator is not determinative on whether a plan is governed by ERISA. Other than the arguably ambiguous description of the DAP in the SPD, Langley points to no other aspect of the DAP that would bring it under the ERISA rubric. There is no evidence that DaimlerChrysler treated the DAP as an ERISA plan in its filings with the federal government, nor is there any evidence that the company partially funded benefits from a source other than general assets. Further, whether, as alleged by Langley, the company used the same notice requirements for the initial denial of DAP benefits as it did for ERISA-governed benefits has negligible import here. Accordingly, as the DAP plainly falls under the definition of a payroll practice, it was not covered by ERISA and the district court properly denied Langley's claim for disability-absence benefits.

3-4 QUESTIONS AND PROBLEMS

1. Why did the short term disability benefits not constitute an ERISA plan?

2. Why was DaimlerChrysler not bound by its characterization of the short term disability benefits as a plan?

3. Was the court's decision in *Langley v. DaimlerChrysler Corporation* consistent with *Donovan*?

4. The plaintiff filed suit claiming a variety of state law claims as well as a violation of ERISA. What effect does the court's finding that the plan is not governed by ERISA have on these state law claims?

B. HEALTH CARE BENEFITS

Employment-based insurance is the leading source of health care coverage in the United States. In 2010, 84 percent of the U.S. population had health insurance coverage. Most Americans (55 percent) were covered by a private employer-sponsored health insurance plan while 31 percent had health insurance through the government.

The United States is unique in its heavy reliance on employer-sponsored health care plans. All other advanced industrial countries provide health care through a publicly financed national health care system that covers the country's entire population. In 2010, Congress fundamentally reformed the American health care system with the enactment of the Patient Protection and Affordable Care Act (Affordable Care Act). The Affordable Care Act, however, does not eliminate the system's reliance on employer-sponsored health insurance. Instead, it builds on, and arguably strengthens, the employment-based system.

The Affordable Care Act was enacted to address two significant shortcomings in the U.S. health care system: coverage and cost. Whether the law will succeed in expanding coverage and controlling cost is subject to considerable debate.

Health Care Coverage

In 2010, about 16 percent of the U.S. population was uninsured. Not surprisingly, lower-income individuals were more likely to be uninsured than were higher-income individuals. For example, in 2010, 27 percent of people with household incomes below $25,000 were uninsured compared with only 8 percent of people with household income above $75,000. Perhaps more surprisingly, more than three-quarters of the uninsured were in working families. Workers were typically uninsured for one of three reasons: (1) their employer did not offer health insurance coverage; (2) although their employer offered health insurance, they were not eligible for coverage because they had not worked for their employer for a sufficient period of time or they did not work enough hours; or (3) they declined coverage under their employer's plan because it was too expensive.

As discussed in more detail below, the Affordable Care Act addresses coverage concerns in a number of specific ways. For example, beginning in 2014, it requires large employers to offer their employees "essential health coverage" or pay an excise tax. Similarly, in the most controversial aspect of the law, it requires all individual to enroll in "essential health coverage" or pay an excise tax beginning in 2014. Subsidies are available for lower-income individuals.

Health Care Cost

The cost of health care has long been a problem in this country. The United States spends more per capita on health care than other countries. Moreover, the United States has one of the highest growth rates in health care spending in the world.

Over the years, employers have addressed escalating health care costs in two principal ways. First, employers have expressly shifted costs to employees by requiring employees to pay a portion of the premiums for health insurance. To illustrate, in 1980, 72 percent of employees had single coverage health benefits that were paid entirely by their employer. By 2011, 84 percent of employees were required to contribute to the cost of single coverage with an average flat monthly contribution of $77. Moreover, 94 percent of employees were required to contribute to the cost of family coverage with an average flat monthly contribution of $344.

Second, the type of health care plans employers offer their employees has evolved over the years in response to escalating costs. In the 1950s, employers typically offered major medical coverage, often referred to as indemnity plans. Indemnity plans usually covered a wide variety of services but required insured individuals to meet an annual deductible before the plan provided benefits, and the insured were required to pay for a portion of costs (referred to as coinsurance) once the deductible was satisfied. Service providers (doctors and hospitals) were paid directly for their services. Thus, the more services they provided, the more money they received. There was no incentive for service providers to ration their care. The insured had some incentive to limit their demand because they had to pay a deductible and coinsurance. The insured, however, generally only paid for a small portion of the cost of their health care and health care costs escalated.

In the 1980s, HMOs were introduced in response to escalating costs. HMOs stressed preventive care and removed the financial barriers to health care access. Specifically, HMOs generally eliminated deductibles and significantly reduced coinsurance costs. HMOs also introduced changes to the supply-side of health care. Specifically, they rationed health care by (1) capping the amount of money health care providers were paid, and (2) requiring preauthorization by the HMO for any treatment beyond routine medical care. Despite their great promise, HMOs were quite unpopular in practice.

In the 1990s, two new types of managed care became popular: (1) preferred provider organization (PPO) plans, and (2) point-of-service (POS) plans. Under these plans, the insured pay less for services provided by service providers who have contracted with the plan to provide services at discounted rates. The insured pay more for services provided by service providers who have not contracted with the plans. Insured are generally happier with services provided by PPO and POS plans, but the costs are generally quite high.

In 2001, a new type of plan was introduced, the "consumer-driven health plan." This type of plan generally consists of a health savings account combined with a high-deductible medical plan, similar to an indemnity plan. Typically, the employer funds the health savings account, but with less than the deductible under the medical plan. The employee first uses the money in the health savings account to pay for health care. If the money in the health savings account is exhausted, the employee must pay for medical services until the deductible is satisfied. Once the deductible is satisfied, the plan operates like a typical indemnity plan. If the employee does not use all of the money in the health savings account, the balance can be rolled over to the next plan year. These plans are intended to create a demand-side incentive for employees to ration health care. (For a more detailed discussion of the evolution of health insurance over the years, see Amy B. Monahan, *The Promise and Peril of Ownership Society Health Care Policy*, 80 Tul. L. Rev. 777, 787–91 (2006).)

The Affordable Care Act contains a number of provisions intended to rein in health care costs. For example, it regulates insurance company rate setting and expands preventive health care efforts. Whether the Affordable Care Act will manage to control health care costs is debatable. Indeed, many critics of the law contend that it will increase health care costs rather than reduce them.

Health Care Financing

Employers typically finance health care benefits in one of two fundamentally different ways: (1) by contracting with an insurance company or (2) by self-funding. Under a traditional insurance contract, the employer pays a premium to the insurance company based on the number of individuals covered by the plan, and the insurance company pays for the agreed-upon benefits. The premiums the insurance company charges may vary each year depending on the number of claims made in the preceding year, but the insurance company bears the risk that in any given year it may be required to pay more in claims than it received as a premium from the employer. In contrast, under a self-funded plan, or a self-insured plan as it is also known, the employer pays the benefits directly from its own assets and bears the risk that claims may exceed expectations in any given year. (The employer may limit the risk it faces by purchasing a stop-loss insurance policy to cover costs above a stated level. Self-funded plans with stop-loss policy are typically treated like all other self-funded plans.)

The employee typically does not know whether a plan is financed through an insurance company or self-funded by the employer. This is because employers usually enter into administrative-services-only (ASO) contracts with conventional insurers or with third party administrators (TPAs) who process benefit claims. From the standpoint of ERISA, however, the financing of the plan can make a significant difference.

Historically, health insurance has been regulated by the states, and employer-provided health benefits funded through insurance continue to be regulated by state law. As discussed in Chapter 5, ERISA Preemption, however, self-funded plans are exempt from state regulation. As of 2010, slightly more than half (59 percent) of covered employees were covered by a self-funded health care plan. Workers in large firms were far more likely to have a self-funded plan than employees in small firms. (In 2010, 83 percent of covered workers employed by firms with 200 or more employees were covered by a self-funded plan compared to 16 percent of covered workers employed by firms with fewer than 200 employees.)

Historically, ERISA has imposed only limited regulation on employer-provided health plans. Prior to the enactment of the Affordable Care Act, employers were generally free to select the types of benefits they would provide and the deductibles and co-pays that they would charge. Some states mandated that certain benefits be provided, but those mandates only applied to insured plans. Employers could avoid state regulation by self-funding their plans because of ERISA's broad preemption rules.

The Affordable Care Act has fundamentally reformed health care insurance in this country and, for the first time in the country's history, health insurance is subject to significant federal regulation. The Affordable Care Act, however, does not eliminate the distinction between insured and self-funded plans. Moreover, the Affordable Care Act creates distinctions between small and large group plans. Thus, large employer plans, whether self-funded or insured, are exempt from some of the Affordable Care Act's mandates, but only insured plans are subject to state regulation.

[1] ERISA's Regulation of Health Care Benefits

Because health insurance has traditionally been regulated by the states, when ERISA was originally enacted it did not contain any substantive regulation aimed exclusively at health benefits. It was not until 1985 that Congress amended ERISA to provide direct regulation of health care benefits for the first time. That year, with the enactment of the Consolidated Omnibus Budget Reconciliation Act (COBRA), Congress amended ERISA to require employers with health insurance plans to offer qualified beneficiaries, who would otherwise lose coverage under a plan, the opportunity to continue coverage under the plan. ERISA § 601 *et seq.* COBRA was not intended to provide comprehensive reform of the American health care system or even employer-provided health insurance. Instead, it was designed to address a specific problem arising from employer-provided health care: "job lock." Job lock refers to the phenomenon that employees often found it difficult to change jobs because changing jobs meant losing their health care coverage. COBRA was intended to help employees with the transition between jobs by permitting them to continue coverage under their old employer's health insurance until they were eligible for health insurance under their new employer's plan.

Although COBRA helped to reduce job lock, it had drawbacks. First, COBRA requires that former employees pay the plan premiums, but many employees cannot take advantage of COBRA because they find the premiums prohibitively expensive. Moreover, even if employees can afford the premiums, COBRA only provides coverage for a limited period of time. Until 1996, employees could still be stuck in their old job if they (or their family members) had pre-existing health conditions because new employers could exclude health care coverage for such employees (or their family members) through the use of pre-existing condition provisions. In 1996, Congress again amended ERISA to improve the portability of employer-based health insurance and thus reduce job lock by enacting the Health Insurance Portability and Accountability Act of 1996 (HIPAA), which imposes a limit on the length of time for which pre-existing health condition clauses can restrict coverage.

Over the next decade or so, Congress amended ERISA a number of times in response to very specific shortcomings in the health care system. For example, in response to the so-called "drive-through" delivery, where some managed care organizations routinely required that new mothers be discharged from the hospital shortly after giving birth, Congress enacted the Newborns' and Mothers' Health Protection Act of 1996 (NMHPA), which established minimum hospital stay requirements for group health plans that offer maternity benefits. The Women's Health and Cancer Rights Act, enacted in 1998, requires group health plans, insurance companies, and health maintenance organizations that offer mastectomy coverage to also provide coverage for reconstructive surgery.

In 2010, Congress fundamentally reformed health insurance in this country with the enactment of the Affordable Care Act. Among other things, beginning in 2014, the Affordable Care Act prohibits insurers from imposing preexisting condition exclusions and requires states to establish Health Insurance Exchanges. Once these changes go into effect, assuming the Affordable Care Act is neither repealed nor overturned by the U.S. Supreme Court, COBRA and HIPAA will be of little importance. Until then, COBRA and HIPAA impose significant requirements on employer-sponsored plans.

[a] COBRA Continuation Coverage

ERISA §§ 601–608.

COBRA requires an employer who sponsors a group health plan to give the plan's "qualified beneficiaries" the opportunity to elect "continuation coverage" under the plan when the beneficiaries might otherwise lose coverage upon the occurrence of certain "qualifying events." ERISA § 601. "Qualified beneficiaries" entitled to make a COBRA election include the covered employee, the covered employee's spouse, and the covered employee's dependent child. ERISA § 607. "Qualifying events" include the death of the covered employee, the termination (except in the case of gross misconduct) or reduction in the hours of the covered employee's employment, and divorce or legal separation from the covered employee. ERISA § 603. The continuation coverage offered to qualified beneficiaries must be identical to what the plan provides to plan beneficiaries who have not suffered a qualifying event. ERISA § 602(1).

ERISA requires plans to advise beneficiaries of their rights under COBRA both at the commencement of coverage and within 14 days of learning of a qualifying event. ERISA § 606(a). The qualified beneficiary then has 60 days to elect continuation coverage. ERISA § 605(a). If the qualifying event is termination or reduced hours, the maximum period of continuation coverage is 18 months. ERISA § 602(2)(A)(i). In other cases, the maximum period of coverage is generally 36 months. ERISA § 602(A)(iv). The plan sponsor may charge the beneficiary up to 102 percent of the applicable premium for the first 18 months of continuation coverage and up to 150 percent thereafter. ERISA § 602(3). The "applicable premium" is typically the cost to the plan of providing continuation coverage, regardless of who usually pays for the insurance benefit. ERISA § 604.

COBRA coverage may be terminated if "the employer ceases to provide any group health plan" or if the qualified beneficiary fails to pay applicable premiums. ERISA § 602(2)(B) & (C). In addition COBRA coverage may be terminated on the date the qualified beneficiary "first becomes, after the date of election covered under any other group plan (as an employee or otherwise which does not contain any exclusion or limitation with respect to any preexisting condition of such beneficiary)." ERISA § 602(2)(D)(i).

To ensure that employees are notified of their COBRA continuation rights, the DOL may impose a $100 per day penalty for each participant the plan administrator fails to notify of his or her COBRA rights. ERISA § 502(c)(1)(A). The IRS may also impose an excise tax on employers of $100 per day for each qualified beneficiary affected by a COBRA violation. IRC § 4980B(b)(1). If there is more than one qualified beneficiary with respect to the same qualifying event, the maximum excise tax is $200 per day. IRC § 4980B(c)(3)(B).

3-5 QUESTIONS AND PROBLEMS

1. Fran, a bank employee who was covered by her employer's health plan, was discharged for cashing a check for a fellow employee and holding the check in her cash drawer until the fellow employee was paid and could cover the check. Is Fran eligible for COBRA coverage upon termination? If so, how long must the coverage last?

2. Geraldo filed for divorce from his wife, Nina. Prior to the divorce, he had been covered by Nina's employer's health insurance plan. Is Geraldo entitled to COBRA coverage upon filing for divorce? If so, how long must the coverage last?

3. If Geraldo had not been covered by his wife's plan at the time of the divorce, would he be entitled to COBRA coverage?

4. Suppose that Geraldo had been covered by his wife's plan until two weeks before he filed for divorce when she terminated his coverage in anticipation of his filing for divorce. Would he be entitled to COBRA coverage? *See* Treas. Reg. § 54.4980 B-4 Q&A-1(c).

5. The Theta Corporation Health Insurance plan covers the biological children of participants even if they are born out of wedlock. Hank, a Theta employee, enrolled Isabella, a child born out of wedlock, because Hank believed that Isabella was Hank's child. Relations between Hank and Jasmine, Isabella's mother, became strained, and Hank contested paternity. Hank obtained a blood test which showed conclusively that Isabella was not his biological child. Accordingly, Isabella ceased to qualify as a dependent child of Hank under the terms of the Theta plan. Is Isabella entitled to COBRA coverage? If so, for how long?

6. Justin resigned from the Iota Corporation on September 1, 2011, and elected COBRA coverage for himself and his wife. On February 1, 2012, Justin and his wife, Kayla, divorced. How long is Justin entitled to COBRA coverage? How long is Kayla entitled to COBRA coverage?

7. After experiencing several years of adverse experience, the Kappa Corporation terminated its health insurance plan. Must it offer COBRA coverage to the employees who lost health coverage as a result of the termination of the plan?

8. Why did Congress allow plans to charge up to 102 percent, rather than 100 percent, of the applicable premium for COBRA continuation coverage?

Suppose that an employee has two forms of health care coverage: primary health care coverage through his employer's plan and secondary coverage through his wife's employer's plan. If the employee's employment terminates, must his employer offer him COBRA continuation coverage? Courts have looked to ERISA § 602(2)(D)(i) for guidance. That section provides, in relevant part, that COBRA continuation coverage may be terminated on the date the qualified beneficiary "first becomes, after the date of election covered under any other group plan (as an employee or otherwise which does not contain any exclusion or limitation with respect to any preexisting condition of such beneficiary)."

In interpreting this language, some courts held that ERISA § 602(2)(D)(i) does not apply to such beneficiaries because they do not "first become, after the date of election covered" by the second plan but instead are covered by that plan before the date of election. According to these courts, the employer must offer such beneficiaries COBRA continuation coverage. *See, e.g.*, *Lutheran Hosp. of Indiana, Inc. v. Business Men's Assurance Co.*, 51 F.3d 1308 (7th Cir. 1995); *Oakley v. City of Longmont*, 890 F.2d 1128 (10th Cir. 1989). Other courts, citing Congress' general intent in enacting COBRA, held that a qualified beneficiary who is covered by two plans at the time of the qualifying event is only entitled to COBRA continuation coverage if there is a "significant gap" between the coverage of the COBRA plan and that of the preexisting plan. *See, e.g.*, *National Companies Health Benefit Plan v. St. Joseph Hospital of Atlanta, Inc.*, 929 F.2d 1558 (11th Cir. 1991); *Brock v. Primedica, Inc.*, 904 F.2d 295 (5th Cir. 1990).

In the following case, the Supreme Court granted certiorari to resolve the issue of whether an employer can deny COBRA continuation coverage to a qualified beneficiary who has preexisting coverage.

GEISSAL v. MOORE MEDICAL CORPORATION

524 U.S. 74 (1998)

JUSTICE SOUTER delivered the opinion of the Court.

The Employee Retirement Income Security Act of 1974 (ERISA), as amended by the Consolidated Omnibus Budget Reconciliation Act of 1985 (COBRA), authorizes a qualified beneficiary of an employer's group health plan to obtain continued coverage under the plan when he might otherwise lose that benefit for certain reasons, such as the termination of employment. The issue in this case is whether [ERISA § 602(2)(D)(i)] allows an employer to deny COBRA continuation coverage to a qualified beneficiary who is covered under another group health plan at the time he makes his COBRA election. We hold that it does not.

On July 16, 1993, respondent Moore Medical Corporation fired James Geissal, who was suffering from cancer. While employed, Geissal was covered under Moore's group health plan as well as the health plan provided by his wife's employer, Trans World Airlines (TWA), through Aetna Insurance Company.

According to Geissal, soon after he lost his job, Moore told him that he had a right under COBRA to elect to continue coverage under Moore's plan. Geissal so elected, and made the necessary premium payments for six months. On January 27, 1994, however, Moore informed Geissal it had been mistaken: he was not actually entitled to COBRA benefits because on the date of his election he was already covered by another group health plan, through his wife's employer. Geissal then brought this suit against Moore, the Group Benefit Plan of Moore Medical Group, Herbert Walker (an administrator of the plan), and Sedgick Lowndes (another administrator) (collectively Moore). Geissal charged Moore with violating COBRA by renouncing an obligation to provide continuing health benefits coverage (Count I) . . . .

After limited discovery, Geissal moved for partial summary judgment on Count I . . . of the complaint. He argued that Moore's reliance upon [ERISA § 602(D)(i)] as authority to deny him COBRA continuation coverage was misplaced. Although the subsection provides that an employer may cancel COBRA continuation coverage as of "[t]he date on which the qualified beneficiary first becomes, after the date of the election . . . covered any other group health plan (as an employee or otherwise)," Geissal was first covered under the TWA plan before he elected COBRA continuation coverage, not after . . . . While the summary judgment motion was pending, Geissal died of cancer, and petitioner Bonnie Geissal, his wife and personal representative of his estate, replaced him as plaintiff . . . .

The Magistrate denied summary judgment for Geissal, however, and instead *sua sponte* granted partial summary judgment on Count[] I . . . in favor of Moore, concluding that an employee with coverage under another group health plan as of the date he elects COBRA continuation coverage is ineligible for COBRA coverage under [ERISA § 602(2)(D)(i)] . . . .

The Court of Appeals for the Eighth Circuit affirmed, and we granted certiorari, to resolve a conflict among the Circuits on whether an employer may deny COBRA continuation coverage under its health plan at the time he elects coverage under COBRA . . . .

II

B

Moore, like the Magistrate, believes that James Geissal's coverage under the TWA plan defeats the claim for COBRA coverage after his election to receive it. As Moore reads [ERISA § 602(2)(D)(i)], it is not relevant when a qualified beneficiary first obtains other health insurance coverage; instead, Moore submits, all that matters is whether, at any time after the date of election, the beneficiary is covered by another group health plan. In any event, Moore claims, James Geissal first became covered under the TWA plan only after his COBRA election, because it was only at that moment that his TWA coverage became primary.

Moore's reading, however, will not square with the text. [ERISA § 602(2)(D)(i)] does not provide that the employer is excused if the beneficiary "is" covered or "remains" covered on or after the date of the election. Nothing in [ERISA § 602(2)(D)(i)] says anything about the hierarchy of policy obligations, or otherwise suggests that it might matter whether the coverage of another group health plan is primary. So far as this case is concerned, what is crucial is that [ERISA § 602(2)(D)(i)] does not speak in terms of "coverage" that might exist or continue; it speaks in terms of an event, the event of "becom[ing] covered." This event is significant only if it occurs, and "first" occurs, at a time "after the date of the election." It is undisputed that both before and after James Geissal elected COBRA continuation coverage he was continuously a beneficiary of TWA's group health plan. Because he was thus covered before he made his COBRA election, and so did not "first become" covered under the TWA plan after the date of election, Moore could not cut off his COBRA coverage under the plain meaning of [ERISA § 602(2)(D)(i)].

Moore argues, to the contrary, that there is a reasonable sense in which a beneficiary does "first becom[e]" covered under a pre-existing plan "after the date of the election," even when prior coverage can be said to persist after the election date: the first moment of coverage on the day following the election is the moment of first being covered after the date of the election. *See National Cos. Health Benefit Plan v. St. Joseph's Hosp., Inc.*, 929 F.2d 1558, 1570 (11th Cir. 1991) ("[I]t is immaterial when the employee acquires other group health coverage; the only relevant question is when, after the election date, does that other coverage take effect. In the case of an employee covered by preexisting group health coverage, . . . the first time after the election date that the employee becomes covered by a group health plan other than the employer's plan is the moment after the election date."). But that reading ignores the condition that the beneficiary must "first becom[e]" covered after the election, robbing the modifier "first" of any consequence, thereby equating "first becomes . . . covered" with "remains covered." It transforms the novelty of becoming covered for the first time into the continuity of remaining covered over time.

Moore argues, further that even if our reading of the statute is more faithful to its plain language, Congress could not have meant to give a qualified beneficiary something more than the right to preserve the status quo as of the date of the qualifying event.[1] Moore points out that if the phrase "first becomes covered . . . after" the date of election does not apply to any coverage predating election, then the beneficiary is quite free to claim continuation coverage even if he has obtained entirely new group coverage between the qualifying event and the election; in that case, on our reading, COBRA would not be preserving the circumstances as of the date of the qualifying event.

That the plain reading does not confine COBRA strictly to guardianship of the status quo is, of course, perfectly true, though it is much less certain whether this fact should count against the plain reading (even assuming that the obvious reading would be vulnerable to such an objection, *see Ardestani v. INS*, 502 U.S. 129 (1991)). The statute is neither cast expressly in terms of the status quo, nor does it speak to the status quo on the date of the qualifying event except with reference to the coverage subject to election. Nor does a beneficiary's decision to take advantage of another group policy not previously in effect carry any indicia of the sort of windfall Congress presumably would have disapproved. Since the beneficiary has to pay for whatever COBRA coverage he obtains, there is no reason to assume he will make an election for coverage he does not need, whether he is covered by another plan in place before the qualifying event or one obtained after it but before his election.

Still, it is true that if during the interim between the qualifying event and election a beneficiary gets a new job, say, with health coverage (having no exclusion or limitation for his condition), he will have the benefit of COBRA, whereas he will not have it if his new job and coverage come after the election date. Do we classify this as an anomaly or merely a necessary consequence of the need to draw a line somewhere? For the sake of argument we might call it an anomaly, but that would only balance it against the anomaly of Moore's own position, which defies not only normal language usage but the expectations of common sense: since an election to continue coverage is retroactive to the date of the qualifying event, under Moore's reading of [ERISA § 602(2)(D)(i)] an election that is ineffective to bring about continuation coverage for the roughly 18 (or 36) month statutory period would nonetheless have the surprising effect of providing continuation coverage for the period of weeks, or even days, between the event and the election. One wonders why Congress would have wanted to create such a strange scheme. Thus, assuming

[1] Moore also argues that Congress could not have intended to render COBRA eligible those individuals with pre-existing coverage under another health plan at the time of election, because such individuals who in fact elect COBRA coverage are typically high risk. As a result, Moore contends, covering them under COBRA tends to increase an employer's overall cost of providing a group health plan, and may cause some employers to cease offering a group health plan entirely. This may or may not be true. If substantiated, the argument would be considered in construing the scope of a vague provision; [ERISA 602(2)(D)(i)], however, is not vague.

that our reading of [ERISA § 602(2)(D)(i)] produces an anomaly, so does Moore's.

But this is not all, for the anomalous consequences of Moore's position are not exhausted without a look at the interpretative morass to which it has led in practice. To support its thesis that Congress meant individuals situated like James Geissal to be ineligible for COBRA benefits, Moore points to a statement in the House Reports on the original COBRA bill, that "[t]he Committee [on Ways and Means] is concerned with reports of the growing number of Americans without any health insurance coverage and the decreasing willingness of our Nation's hospitals to provide care to those who cannot afford to pay." H.R. Rep. No. 99-241, pt. 1, 44 (1985); U.S. Code Cong. & Admin. News 1986, 42, 622. Of course, if this concern (expressed in one House Committee Report) were thought to be a legitimate limit on the meaning of the statute as enacted, there would be no COBRA coverage for any beneficiary who had "any health insurance" on the date of election, or obtained "any" thereafter. But neither Moore nor any court rejecting the plain meaning has gone quite so far. Instead, that draconian alternative has been averted by a nontextual compromise.

The compromise apparently alludes to the proviso that [ERISA § 602(2)(D)(i)] applies so as to authorize termination of COBRA coverage only if the coverage provided by the other group health plan "does not contain any exclusion or limitation with respect to any preexisting condition of such beneficiary." Moore urges us to hold, as some Courts of Appeals have done, that although Congress generally intended to deny COBRA coverage to individuals with other group insurance on the election date, there will still be COBRA eligibility in such cases if there is a "significant gap" between the coverage offered by the employer's plan and that offered by the beneficiary's other group health plan.[2] *See* 114 F.3d at 1464–1465; *accord, National Cos. Health Benefit Plan v. St. Joseph's Hosp., Inc.*, 904 F.2d 295, 297 (5th Cir. 1990). When there is such a gap, some courts have explained, it cannot be said that the employee is truly "covered" by his pre-existing insurance coverage. *See* 114 F.3d at 1463; *National Cos. Health Benefit Plan v. St. Joseph's Hosp., Inc., supra*, at 1571.

This "significant gap" approach to [ERISA § 602(2)(D)(i)] is plagued with difficulties, however, beginning with the sheer absence of any statutory support for it. [ERISA § 602(2)(D)(i)] makes no mention of what to do when a person's other coverage is generally inadequate or inferior; instead, it provides merely that coverage under a later acquired group health plan will not terminate COBRA rights when the plan limits or excludes coverage for a pre-existing condition of the beneficiary. The proviso applies not when there is a "gap" or difference between the respective coverages of the two policies, but when the later acquired group coverage excludes or limits coverage specific to the beneficiary's pre-existing condition. It is this "gap" between different coverage provisions of the non-COBRA plan, not a gap between the coverage provisions of the COBRA plan and the non-COBRA plan, that Congress was legislating about.

But even leaving textual inadequacy aside, there is further trouble under the "significant gap" approach. Needless to say, when the proviso (as written) arguably does apply, its applicability is easy to determine. Once the beneficiary's pre-existing condition is identified, a court need only look among the terms of the later

---

[2] The lower courts have disagreed about whether this "significant gap" interpretation should be made evaluating the actual expenses an employee incurs as a result of COBRA cancellation, or by comparing the policies' provisions in light of the information available to the employer on the day of the COBRA election. *See* 114 F.3d at 1464–1465 (comparing approaches).

policy for an exclusion or limitation peculiar to that condition. If either is found, COBRA continuation coverage is left undisturbed; if neither is found, the consequence of obtaining this later insurance is automatic. Applying the significant gap rule, on the other hand, requires a very different kind of determination, essentially one of social policy. Once a gap is found, the court must then make a judgment about the adequacy of medical insurance under the later group policy, for this is the essence of any decision about whether the gap between the two regimes of coverage is "significant" enough. This is a powerful point against the gap interpretation for two reasons. First, the required judgment is so far unsuitable for courts that we would expect a clear mandate before inferring that Congress meant to foist it on the judiciary. What is even more strange, however, is that Congress would have meant to inject the courts into the policy arena, evaluating the adequacy of non-COBRA coverage that happened to be in place prior to the COBRA election, while at the same time intending to limit the judicial intrusion, and leave the beneficiary to the unmediated legal consequences of the terms of the non-COBRA coverage that happened to become effective after the election. One just cannot credibly attribute such oddity to congressional intent.

In sum, there is no justification for disparaging the clarity of [ERISA § 602(2)(D)(i)]. The judgment of the Court of Appeals is vacated, and the case is remanded for further proceedings consistent with this opinion.

For a thorough analysis of *Geissal* and the issues it raises, *see* Jason R. Yungtum, *COBRA Preexisting Coverage After the Supreme Court's Decision in* Geissal v. Moore Medical Corp., 32 CREIGHTON L. REV. 1541 (1999).

3-6 QUESTIONS AND PROBLEMS

1. Geissal was already covered by his wife's health care plan when he was terminated. Why did he want to elect COBRA continuation coverage? Why wasn't his wife's coverage enough?

2. What role does legislative history play in the Court's opinion? What role should legislative history play in the Court's opinion?

3. Ethan has been covered by the Kappa Corp. health care plan since he started to work for the company in 1995. On January 15, 2012, Ethan terminates employment with Kappa Corp. He begins to work for Lambda Ltd. on January 25, 2012, and begins to be covered by the Lambda Ltd. health care plan on February 1, 2012.

   a. Must Kappa Corp. offer Ethan the opportunity to elect COBRA continuation coverage under the Kappa Corp. health care plan when he terminates employment on January 15, 2012?

   b. Would the answer to (a) change if Ethan had preexisting coverage through his wife's plan at the time he terminated employment?

   c. Suppose that Ethan elected to receive COBRA continuation coverage under the Kappa Corp. health care plan on January 15, 2012, and the Lambda Ltd. health care plan offers benefits that are identical to those provided by the Kappa Corp. health care plan. When can Kappa Corp. terminate Ethan's coverage?

d. Same facts as (c) except that Ethan waits until March 1, 2012, to elect COBRA continuation coverage under the Kappa Corp. health care plan. When can Kappa Corp. terminate Ethan's COBRA coverage?

e. Same facts as (c) except that the Lambda Corp. health care plan does not provide benefits for AIDS while the Kappa Corp. health care plan does. When can Kappa Corp. terminate Ethan's COBRA coverage? In answering this question, does it matter whether Ethan has a preexisting condition with respect to AIDS?

f. Same facts as (c) except that the Lamba Ltd. health care plan imposes a pre-existing condition limitation on AIDS. When can Kappa Corp. terminate Ethan's COBRA coverage? In answering this question, does it matter whether Ethan has a preexisting condition with respect to AIDS?

[b] Limitations on Preexisting Condition Exclusions and Prohibition Against Discrimination Based on Health Status

ERISA §§ 701–702.

Traditionally, many employer-sponsored health care plans limited or excluded coverage of conditions that were present prior to the time an individual enrolled in the health care plan. These types of limitations and exclusions are referred to as "preexisting condition exclusions." Effective for plan years beginning on or after September 23, 2010, the Affordable Care Act prohibits all employer-sponsored health care plans from imposing preexisting condition exclusions for enrollees under the age of 19. Effective for plan years beginning on or after January 1, 2014, the prohibition on preexisting condition exclusions will apply to all enrollees. The regulations define a preexisting condition exclusion as a limitation or exclusion of benefits (including a denial of coverage) based on the fact that the condition was present before the effective date of coverage, whether or not any medical advice, diagnosis, care, or treatment was recommended or received before that date. 29 C.F.R. § 2590.701-2.

Until the Affordable Care prohibition goes into effect, the restrictions on preexisting condition exclusions under the Health Insurance Portability and Accountability Act of 1996 (HIPAA), codified at ERISA §§ 701–702, will continue to apply. HIPAA limits preexisting condition exclusions in two ways. First, it limits the types of conditions that may be excluded. Second, it limits the length of time health care plans may impose preexisting condition exclusions.

HIPAA provides that unless "medical advice, diagnosis, care, or treatment was recommended or received" for a condition within six months prior to enrollment in the new plan, the health care plan cannot treat the condition as a preexisting condition. ERISA § 701(a)(1). HIPAA also explicitly exempts genetic information from the definition of a preexisting condition in the "absence of a diagnosis of the condition related to such information." ERISA § 701(b)(1)(B).

HIPAA limits the maximum period for a preexisting condition exclusion to twelve months (or eighteen months in the case of a late enrollee). ERISA § 701(a)(2). In addition, HIPAA permits individuals to offset the twelve (or eighteen) month period with any period of prior "creditable coverage." ERISA § 701(a)(3). Creditable coverage is defined broadly to include almost any type of health care coverage, such as coverage through a private employer, federal or state government group health plan, individual health insurance, COBRA coverage, and

Medicare and Medicaid coverage. ERISA § 701(c)(1). Prior creditable coverage is forfeited, however, if there was a sixty-three day period during which time the individual did not have any health care coverage. ERISA § 701(c)(2)(A). Thus, under HIPAA, if an individual has at least twelve months of prior health care coverage, enrolls in the new plan at the first opportunity, and did not experience a sixty-three consecutive day lapse in coverage, the plan is prohibited from imposing any preexisting condition exclusion.

Regardless of prior creditable coverage, HIPAA prohibits the imposition of any preexisting condition exclusion: (1) in the case of newborn children enrolled in the plan within thirty days of birth; (2) for adopted children under age eighteen enrolled in the plan within thirty days of adoption or placement for adoption; and (3) for any condition relating to pregnancy. ERISA § 701(d).

HIPAA also prohibits discrimination based on health status in two ways. First, it prohibits group health plans from establishing "rules for eligibility" on the basis of any of the following "health status related factors": (a) health status, (b) medical condition (including both physical and mental illness), (c) claims experience, (d) receipt of health care, (e) medical history, (f) genetic information, (g) evidence of insurability, and (h) disability. ERISA § 702(a)(1). Second, HIPAA prohibits group health plans from charging one individual a higher premium than the premium charged to a "similarly situated individual" already enrolled in the plan on the basis of any of these health status related factors. ERISA § 702(b)(1).

Professor Medill explains how these two sections operate in unison to ensure the effectiveness of the limitation of preexisting condition exclusions:

> "Section 701(a) limits or, in some cases, eliminates the imposition of a pre-existing condition coverage exclusion upon a new plan participant. In the absence of section 702(a)(1), a group health plan could, rather than admit an individual with a pre-existing condition (but with no pre-existing condition coverage exclusion) as a participant in the plan, simply declare the individual ineligible to participate in the plan due to the individual's pre-existing health condition. Section 702(a)(1) prevents such tactics by prohibiting a group health plan from basing eligibility on the enumerated health status related factors. Finally, faced with the admission, by virtue of sections 701(a) and 702(a)(1), of a new plan participant with a pre-existing health condition (but no pre-existing condition coverage exclusion), a group health plan could discourage the new participant's enrollment in the plan by charging a prohibitively higher premium for that particular participant due to the foreseeable additional cost attributable to coverage and benefits for the pre-existing condition. Section 702(b)(1) likewise prevents such tactics by prohibiting the practice of charging a greater premium or contribution to an individual than to "similarly situated" individuals based upon a health status related factor. Colleen E. Medill, *HIPAA and Its Related Legislation: A New Role for ERISA in the Regulation of Private Health Care Plans?*, 65 TENN. L. REV. 485, 497–501 (1998)."

The Genetic Information and Nondiscrimination Act (GINA) extended the HIPAA nondiscrimination requirements to prohibit group health plans from discriminating in group premiums based on genetic information. ERISA § 702(b)(3).

HIPAA does not require group health plans to provide particular benefits, nor does it restrict the premiums plans may charge to all participants in the plan. It allows group health plans to establish limits or place restrictions on the amount, level, extent, or nature of the plan's coverage and benefits for "similarly situated individuals" enrolled in the plan.

3-7 QUESTIONS AND PROBLEMS

1. On July 1, 2004, Jamal was hired by Alpha Corp. and enrolled in its health care plan. His employment terminated on January 2, 2012, and he elected COBRA coverage for himself and his wife. On May 10, 2012, his wife became pregnant. On May 15, 2012, he was diagnosed with cancer. On June 1, 2012, he was hired by Beta Company and immediately enrolled in the Beta Company health care plan. The Beta Company plan offers dependent care coverage but excludes all preexisting conditions to the extent permissible by HIPAA.

a. Can the Beta Company health care plan impose a preexisting condition exclusion with respect to Jamal's cancer and his wife's pregnancy? If so, how long can the exclusions last?

b. Would the answer to (a) change if Jamal had not elected COBRA coverage on January 2, 2012, and thus he and his wife had no health care insurance between January 2, 2012, and June 1, 2012?

c. Would the answer to (a) change if Jamal had elected COBRA coverage on January 2, 2012, but let the coverage lapse on April 15, 2012, so that he and his wife had no health care insurance between April 15, 2012, and June 1, 2012?

d. Can the Beta Company health care plan impose a three month waiting period and thus require Jamal and his wife to wait until September 1, 2012, to be covered under the plan? Assuming the plan can impose a three month waiting period, would that change any of your answers above?

2. Gino worked for DeltaCo from January 1, 2010, until December 20, 2011. DeltaCo did not offer health insurance and Gino was not enrolled in any other health care plan. On December 20, 2011, Gino quit working for DeltaCo. On January 1, 2012, Gino was hired by Epsilon Corp. and was immediately enrolled in its health care plan. Gino's employment with Epsilon Corp. terminated on April 1, 2012, and he did not elect COBRA coverage. On April 11, 2012, he was diagnosed with cancer. On May 1, 2012, Gino was hired by ZetaCo and immediately enrolled in the ZetaCo plan. The ZetaCo plan excludes all preexisting conditions to the extent permissible by HIPAA.

Can the ZetaCo plan impose a preexisting condition exclusion with respect to Gino's cancer? If so, how long can the exclusion last?

3. The Nu Company sponsors a health care plan.

a. Must the Nu Company plan provide coverage for dependent children?

b. Norbert, a Nu employee, is covered by the plan and plans to adopt his two year old nephew, Oscar, who has a congenital heart defect. Oscar's parents died two months ago in a car accident. They had health insurance when Oscar was born but lost that coverage six months after his birth. A doctor diagnosed Oscar's condition when he was an infant but Oscar was never treated for it. Assuming the Nu Company plan covers dependent children, must the plan provide coverage for Oscar as an adopted child?

c. Can the Nu Company plan exclude coverage for Oscar's heart defect because it is a preexisting condition? Suppose that Oscar had been diagnosed with the heart defect two months before his parents died. Would that change the answer?

d. Would any of the answers above be different if Oscar's mother died shortly after Oscar was born and Norbert adopted Oscar as an infant rather than as a two year old?

e. Can the Nu Company plan charge Norbert a higher premium after he adopts Oscar because Oscar has a congenital heart defect? Can the plan increase the premium it charges all employees to help cover the cost of the congenital heart defect?

f. May the plan wait until Oscar is formally adopted to cover Oscar?

4. COBRA and HIPAA represent two different approaches to financing health care reform. COBRA requires the entire cost of the benefit to be borne by the individual employee. The HIPAA approach requires the plan to contain certain benefits if the plan sponsor chooses to have a health care plan. The plan sponsor (usually the employer) can decide whether to absorb the additional cost of the required benefits or allocate all or part of the additional costs to all of the participants in the plan. Which approach is better and why?

[c] Other Health Care Regulation

ERISA §§ 609, 711, 712, 713.

Since the 1990s, Congress has amended parts 6 and 7 of title I of ERISA a number of times to provide for very discrete and specific health care regulation. For example, in the Omnibus Reconciliation Act of 1993, Congress added three new requirements related to benefits for children. First, it provided an exception to ERISA's preemption provisions for qualified medical child support orders. ERISA § 609(a). Second, it provided that group health plans that provide benefits for dependent children of plan participants must provide benefits for adopted children of plan participants on the same terms and conditions as for children born to plan participants. ERISA § 609(b). Third, it prohibited group health plans from reducing coverage for pediatric vaccines costs below the plan coverage provided as of May 1, 1993.

As noted above, Congress enacted the Newborns' and Mothers' Health Protection Act of 1996 (NMHPA) in response to concerns with "drive-through" deliveries. NMHPA does not require that group health plans offer maternity benefits, ERISA § 711(c)(2), but if a group health plan does offer such benefits, NMHPA requires that the plan provide minimum hospital stays. ERISA § 711(a).

The Paul Wellstone and Pete Domenici Mental Health Parity and Addiction Equity Act of 2008 (MHPAEA) does not require that group health plans offer mental health or substance abuse benefits. ERISA § 712(b)(1). If, however, a group health plan does offer such benefits, MHPAEA prohibits group health plans from imposing more restrictive financial requirements, such as deductibles, copayments, coinsurance, and out-of-pocket expenses, on mental health and substance abuse disorder benefits than the most common or frequent financial requirements applicable to medical and surgical benefits. ERISA § 712(a)(3)(i). Similarly, MHPAEA prohibits group health plans from imposing different treatment limitations on mental health or substance abuse disorder benefits, such as limits on frequency of treatment or number of visits or days of coverage, than the most common or frequent limitations imposed on medical and surgical benefits. ERISA § 712(a)(3)(i). Different aggregate lifetime and annual limits for mental health or substance abuse disorder benefits are also prohibited. ERISA § 712(a)(1) & (2).

The Women's Health and Cancer Rights Act of 1998 (WHCRA) requires that group health plans offering mastectomy coverage also provide coverage for reconstructive surgery in a manner determined in consultation with the attending physician and patient. ERISA § 713. The WHCRA is also referred to as "Janet's Law," after Janet Franquet, a woman who was denied reconstructive surgery following a mastectomy. Janet was diagnosed with an extremely aggressive form of breast cancer in 1997 and required a mastectomy and very intricate reconstruction of her breast. Her insurance provider refused to cover the breast reconstruction on the ground that it was cosmetic surgery. Her doctor agreed to perform the surgery without compensation. After a lengthy appeal process, the insurer ultimately agreed to cover the expenses as medically necessary. The WHCRA was enacted "so that other women with breast cancer need not go through what Janet Franquet went through." Joanne L. Grimes, *New Law Expands Women's Medical Coverage for Breast Reconstruction*, 3 No. 6 Pacific Employment Law Letter 2 (Dec. 1998).

3-8 QUESTIONS AND PROBLEMS

1. What do these provisions say about Congress' willingness to regulate the content of employer-sponsored health care plans?

2. How effective are the provisions likely to be in that they do not require that employers provide dependent care, maternity benefits, mental health benefits, or mastectomy coverage?

3. Why did Congress regulate the terms of dependent care, maternity benefits, mental health benefits, and mastectomy coverage without requiring that employers provide such benefits?

[d] The Patient Protection and Affordable Care Act (Affordable Care Act)

In March 2010, Congress enacted sweeping national reform of health insurance with the Affordable Care Act. The fundamental purpose of the Act is to ensure that all individuals are covered by health insurance. To ensure that individuals can purchase health insurance at a reasonable cost, the law requires the states to establish Health Insurance Exchanges, which are essentially new insurance marketplaces for individuals and small employers. The legislation creates tax credits to help lower-income individuals pay for the cost of health insurance coverage and imposes tax penalties on covered employers who fail to provide covered employees with "minimum essential coverage." In addition, it provides a tax credit for small employers who elect to provide coverage while imposing a tax penalty on individuals who fail to obtain "minimum essential coverage."

The Affordable Care Act includes a number of employer mandates, such as extending coverage for children up to age 26, prohibiting preexisting condition exclusions, prohibiting lifetime limits on the dollar value of "essential health benefits" for any participant or beneficiary, and requiring plans to provide certain preventive services without imposing any cost-sharing on these benefits. Some of the requirements, such as the prohibition on lifetime limits, are effective in 2010 while others, such as the prohibition on preexisiting condition exclusions, will not be effective until as late as 2014. Some of the mandates apply to all employer-sponsored plans, such as the prohibition on preexisting condition exclusions; others, such as the requirement that certain preventive services be provided without any cost-sharing, do not apply to "grandfathered" plans, generally defined as plans that were in existence at the time the legislation was enacted in March 2010.

Prior to the Affordable Care Act, most legislation regulating employer-sponsored health care benefits was codified in parallel provisions of ERISA, the Internal Revenue Code, and the Public Health Services Act (PHSA) (codified in chapter 42 of the U.S. Code). The Affordable Care Act broke with this tradition. Instead of having separate parallel provisions in ERISA, the Internal Code, and the PHSA, the Affordable Care Act simply added ERISA § 715 and IRC § 9815 to incorporate the relevant provisions of the PHSA. To the extent that the applicable provisions of the PHSA conflict with existing provisions of ERISA and the IRC, the PHSA provisions control. ERISA § 715(a)(2); IRC § 9815(a)(2).

At the time this book went to press, the U.S. Supreme Court had heard oral argument on the constitutionality of the Affordable Care Act but had not yet decided the issue.

[1] Employer Mandates

PHSA §§ 2708, 2711, 2712, 2713, 2714.

Effective for plan years beginning after September 23, 2010, all employer plans that offer dependent coverage must extend dependent coverage to adult children up to age 26, regardless of the child's marital or student status. PHSA § 2714. Prior to 2014, grandfathered plans are only required to provide coverage for an adult child if he or she is not eligible to enroll in an eligible employer-sponsored health plan other than the grandfathered health plan. Coverage provided to the adult child is not taxable to the employee. IRC § 105(b).

Effective for plan years beginning after September 23, 2010, the Affordable Care Act prohibits all employer-sponsored health plans from imposing any lifetime limits on "essential health benefits." PHSA § 2711(a)(1)(A). The Affordable Care Act does not define the term "essential health benefits." Instead, it directs the Secretary of the Department of Health and Human Services to define the term, but requires that the following general categories and items and services be included among "essential health benefits:" ambulatory patient services, emergency services, hospitalization, maternity and newborn care, mental health and substance abuse disorder services, including behavioral health treatment, prescription drugs, rehabilitative and habilitative services and devices, laboratory services, preventive and wellness services and chronic disease management, and pediatric services, including oral and vision care. 42 U.S.C. § 18022. Beginning in 2014, annual caps on essential health benefits will be prohibited. PHSA § 2711(a)(1)(B). Lifetime and annual limits may be imposed on specific covered benefits that are not considered essential health benefits. PHSA § 2711(b).

Effective for plan years beginning after September 23, 2010, all employer-sponsored health care plans are prohibited from rescinding coverage from a covered individual in the absence of fraud or material misrepresentation. PHSA § 2712.

Employer-sponsored group health plans that are adopted after March 23, 2010, must provide certain preventive care coverage without cost to covered employees. PHSA § 2713. The preventive care coverage must include, among other things, certain immunizations for children and certain preventive care and screenings for women and children. *Id.*

Effective in 2014, all employer-sponsored plans are prohibited from applying a waiting period that exceeds 90 days. PHSA § 2708.

3-9 QUESTIONS AND PROBLEMS

1. Why are there delayed effective dates for many of the Affordable Care Act's mandates?

2. Why are "grandfathered" plans exempt from some of the Affordable Care Act mandates? What effect do the exemptions have on employers' willingness to change the terms of their plans?

3. Historically, plans sponsors have used annual and lifetime dollar limits to cap their exposure to medical costs. What effect is the prohibition on dollar limits likely to have on employer costs? On employers' willingness to offer health care plans?

[2] Employer "Pay-or-Play" Mandate

IRC § 4980H.

The Affordable Care Act imposes an excise tax on "applicable large employers" who fail to satisfy their "shared responsibility" of offering employees the opportunity to enroll in "minimum essential coverage" under an eligible employer-sponsored plan. IRC § 4980H. For these purposes, an "applicable large employer" is generally defined as an employer who employed an average of at least fifty full-time employees during the preceding calendar year. IRC § 4980H(c)(2)(A). Full-time employees are generally defined as employees who perform, on average, at least thirty hours of service per week. IRC 4980H(c)(4)(A).

An employer may fail to meet its "shared responsibility" if (1) the employer does not offer its full-time employees and their dependents the opportunity to enroll in minimum essential coverage under an eligible employer-sponsored group health plan for a month, and at least one full-time employee is certified as having claimed a premium assistance tax credit or cost sharing reduction, IRC § 4980H(a), or (2) the employer offers its full-time employees and their dependents the opportunity to enroll in minimum essential coverage under an eligible employer-sponsored group health plan for a month, and at least one full-time employee is certified to have claimed the premium assistance tax credit or cost-sharing reduction. IRC § 4980H(b).

Generally, an employee will be eligible for a tax premium credit or cost sharing reduction for health coverage purchased through the exchange if (1) the employee's household income is between 100% and 400% of the federal poverty level, and (2) either (a) the employee is not eligible to participate in an employer-sponsored group health plan, or (b) the employee is eligible to participate in such a plan, but (i) the coverage under the employer's plan is "unaffordable," that is, the premium required to be paid exceeds 9.5 of the employee's household income, or (ii) the coverage consists of a plan under which the plan's share of the total allowed cost of benefits is less than 60%. IRC § 36B; 42 U.S.C. § 1402.

If an employer fails to meet its "shared responsibility" because it does not offer coverage and at least one employee obtains a premium tax credit or cost sharing reduction, the employer is subject to an excise tax for the month equal to one-twelfth of $2,000, or about $167, per full-time employee. IRC § 4980H(a) & (c). Thus, if an applicable large employer does not offer coverage to its workforce, its penalty is based on its entire workforce. IRC § 4980H(a). Nevertheless, up to thirty full-time employees may be disregarded in calculating the penalty. IRC § 4980H(c)(2)(D). The penalty is indexed to the rate of premium growth after 2014. IRC § 4980H(c)(5).

If an employer offers coverage but still fails to meet its "shared responsibility" because at least one employee obtains a premium tax credit or cost sharing reduction, the employer is subject to an excise tax for the month equal to one-twelfth of $3,000, or about $250, per full-time employee who opts out of the employer's plan and receives the credit or cost sharing reduction. IRC § 4980H(b). Thus, if an applicable large employer offers coverage to its workforce, its penalty is based the number of employees who opt out of the employer plan (and receive a premium tax credit or cost sharing reduction) rather than the employer's entire workforce. The penalty is limited to the amount the employer would owe if it did not offer any coverage, IRC § 4980H(b)(2), and it is indexed to the rate of premium growth after 2014, IRC § 4980H(c)(5).

3-10 QUESTIONS AND PROBLEMS

1. Why does the excise tax only apply to employers with 50 or more employees?

2. Why is the premium assistance tax credit and cost sharing reduction based on the employee's household income? How easy will it be for the employer to know the employee's household income?

3. In 2011, the average annual cost to employers of providing single coverage was $4,508 while the annual average cost of providing family coverage was $10,944. (On average, employees contributed $921 for single coverage and $4,129 for family coverage.) In contrast, the annual nondeductible excise tax for employers that fail to offer coverage is generally $2,000 per worker, while the annual nondeductible excise tax for employers that offer coverage is $3,000 for each employee for whom the coverage is "unaffordable." How influential is the excise tax likely to be for employers trying to decide whether to offer coverage?

4. Company, which employs 75 full-time workers, does not offer its employees and their dependents coverage under an eligible employer-sponsored plan for a month in 2014. Two employees are certified to claim a premium tax credit or cost sharing reduction. How much excise tax is imposed on Company? Suppose instead that Company offered coverage but the same two employees opted out. How much excise tax would Company owe?

[3] Small Employer Tax Credit

IRC § 45R.

While the Affordable Care Act uses a "stick" approach to encourage large employers to offer health care coverage to their employees, it employs a "carrot" method to encourage small employers with low- and moderate-income employees to provide their employees with health care coverage. Specifically, it creates a small employer tax credit. IRC § 45R.

In order to qualify for the tax credit, small employers must satisfy three requirements. First, the employer must have fewer than twenty-five full-time equivalent employees (FTE) for the taxable year. IRC § 45R(d)(1)(A). Second, the average annual wages of the employees for the year must be less than $50,000 per FTE. IRC § 45R(d)(1)(B), (d)(3)(B). Third, the employer must maintain a "qualifying arrangement" under which the employer pays a uniform percentage of at least 50% of the premium cost of the health coverage for each employee covered under the employer-provided health insurance. IRC § 45R(d)(1)(C), (d)(4). Beginning in 2014, the small tax credit is only available if the insurance is provided through a state-sponsored exchange. IRC § 45R(s)(4), (g)(3).

For tax years through 2013, small employers are eligible for a tax credit of up to 35%. IRC § 45R(g)(2)(A). Beginning in 2014, the full credit will increase to 50%, IRC § 45R(b), but employers will only be eligible for the credit for two years. IRC § 45R(a), (e)(2). Employers with ten or fewer FTEs with average taxable wages of $25,000 or less are eligible for the full credit. The credit is phased out as the number of FTEs increases from 10 to 25, and annual average compensation increases from $25,000 to $50,000. IRC § 45R(c)(1) & (2). In addition, the credit is limited to the applicable percentage of "the average premium (as determined by the Secretary of Health and Human Services) for the small group market in the rating area in which the employee enrolls for coverage." IRC § 45R(b)(2). Thus, if an employer purchases insurance with higher than average premiums, the employee will not receive a credit with respect to premiums that exceed the average.

3-11 QUESTIONS AND PROBLEMS

1. Why is the small employer tax credit limited to employers with 25 or fewer employees?

2. How effective is the small employer tax credit likely to be in encouraging small employers to offer health insurance coverage for the first time or to maintaining coverage they already have?

[4] Cadillac Tax

IRC § 4980I.

Employment-based health insurance is accorded favorable tax treatment, principally under sections 105 and 106 of the Internal Revenue Code. See Section C *infra*. Critics of this favorable tax treatment contend that, among other things, it leads to over-insurance which distorts the health services market, causes inefficient allocations of scarce resources, and inflates health care costs. The Affordable Care Act creates a nondeductible excise tax on so-called "Cadillac" health care plans, IRC § 4980I, to address this problem.

The excise tax applies to any "excess benefit" provided under "applicable employer-sponsored coverage." IRC § 4980I(a). Generally, a health plan qualifies as "applicable employer-sponsored coverage" if the value of coverage is excludable from the employee's income under Section 106 of the Internal Revenue Code. IRC § 4980I(d)(1)(A). An "excess benefit" arises if the annual cost of coverage exceeds $10,200 in the case of individual coverage, or $27,500, in the case of family coverage, multiplied by a "health cost adjustment percentage." IRC § 4980I(b). The "health cost adjustment percentage" increases the dollar limits to the extent that the 2018 per-employee cost under the Blue Cross/Blue Shield standard option under the Federal Employees Health Benefits Plan exceeds the 2010 cost by more than 55%. IRC § 4980I(b)(3)(C)(ii). After 2018, the dollar limits will be adjusted for inflation. IRC § 4980I(b)(3)(C)(v). The dollar limits are also adjusted for age and gender and increased for retirees and plans that primarily cover employees in high-risk professions. IRC § 4980I(b)(3)(C)(iii) & (iv).

The excise tax is imposed on the "coverage provider." IRC § 4980I(c). In the case of a group health plan, the coverage provider is the health insurance issuer. IRC § 4980I(c)(2)(A). In the case of a health savings account (HSA) and medical savings account (MSA) contributions, the employer is the coverage provider. IRC § 4980I(c)(2)(B). In all other instances, the coverage provider is the person who administers the plan, IRC § 4980I(c)(2)(C), which will often be the employer.

3-12 QUESTIONS AND PROBLEMS

1. Why is coverage under a collectively bargained multiemployer plan deemed to be family coverage, IRC § 4980I(b)(3)(B)(ii), and thus always eligible for the higher limit?

2. Why doesn't the so-called Cadillac tax go into effect until 2018?

3. What effect is it likely to have on employers' willingness to offer "Cadillac" plans?

[2] Retiree Health Care Benefits

Medicare, a federal health insurance program for the elderly, is the principal source of health care coverage for most individuals aged 65 or older. Medicare, however, does not cover all medical expenses. For example, it has limited prescription drug coverage, has deductibles for hospitalization, limits the number of days of hospitalization that it will cover, and imposes co-pays for a variety of services. In fact, according to estimates by the Employee Benefit Research Institute, Medicare only covers about 51 percent of covered individuals' health expenses. Many individuals supplement their Medicare coverage by individually purchasing supplemental insurance, known as Medigap. In addition, some Medicare-eligible retirees have additional retiree health care coverage provided by a former employer, and some retirees between the ages of 55 and 64 (who are not yet eligible for Medicare) receive retiree health coverage from a former employer.

The following excerpt provides some perspective on retiree health care coverage.

KATHRYN L. MOORE, THE NEW RETIREE HEALTH VEBAs

N.Y.U. Review of Employee Benefits and Executive Compensation 7-1, 7-2 to 7-4 (2008)

Employers first began to offer retiree health benefits on a wide scale in the late 1940s and early 1950s. When retiree health benefits were first introduced they were viewed as an inexpensive, "throway benefit" that was "lightly granted." For most companies, those were plush years; they needed workers and had relatively few retirees.

Although never universal, retiree health benefits became increasingly common through the 1980s. For example, while a majority of collective bargaining agreements did not provide retiree health benefits in the early 1960s, by 1980 more than half of private collective bargaining agreements provided such benefits. According to calculations by the Employee Benefit Research Institute, 43 percent of Americans aged 40 and over had retiree health coverage in 1988. Covered individuals tended to work for large companies or public employers and were more likely to be unionized.

Although retiree benefits began as an inexpensive benefit, as health care costs soared in the 1980s, so too did the cost of retiree health benefits. According to a survey by Wyatt Company, from 1987 to 1989, expenditures for active and retiree medical benefit plans by the nation's largest industrial companies increased at an annual rate of 21 percent, which was, in turn, increasing more than two percentage points faster than the Gross National Product. "What had started out as a throw-away benefit had become a formidable commitment."

* * *

Since [1993], many employers have terminated their retiree health benefits. According to one survey, while 46 percent of large employers offered medical benefits to early retirees in 1993, that number had fallen to 29 percent by 2005. Over that same time period, the percentage of large employers offering benefits to Medicare-eligible retirees fell from 40 percent to 20 percent. According to another study, over the last ten years, the percentage of private sector companies that provide retiree health benefits has fallen from 2.1 percent to 12.7 percent.

Because ERISA does not require welfare benefits to be vested, an employer is generally free to reduce or eliminate retiree health benefits if the employer expressly retains the right in the plan to do so. Suppose, however, that the employer promises the benefits pursuant to the terms of a contract. Is the employer still free to amend or terminate the benefits? The following case was one of the first and most influential cases to address an employer's right under ERISA to terminate retiree health benefits promised pursuant to a collective bargaining agreement.

UAW v. YARD-MAN, INC.

716 F.2d 1476 (6th Cir. 1983), *cert. denied*, 465 U.S. 1007 (1984)

CORNELIA G. KENNEDY, CIRCUIT JUDGE.

Yard-Man appeals the District Court's grant of summary judgment that it breached its collective bargaining agreement with appellees, United Automobile, Aerospace and Agricultural Implement Workers of America (UAW or Union) and its Local 134, UAW, by terminating the life and health insurance benefits of Yard-Man's retired employees at the expiration of the collective bargaining agreement . . . . We affirm the District Court's holding that the retirees are entitled to continued insurance benefits . . . .

In August 1974, Yard-Man and the UAW entered into a collective bargaining agreement covering employees at Yard-Man's Jackson, Michigan, plant. The contract bore a stated expiration date of June 1, 1977. Less than a year after the signing of the contract the plant closed.

In April 1977, Yard-Man notified its Jackson retirees that existing health and life insurance benefits would terminate upon the collective bargaining agreement's expiration. Soon thereafter, the UAW filed grievances claiming that Yard-Man's unilateral action in terminating the retirees' life and health insurance violated that agreement . . . .

. . .

Relying solely upon the language of the collective bargaining agreement, the District Court found that Yard-Man breached its contractual obligations when it cancelled the retirees' insurance upon expiration of that agreement. Yard-Man was ordered to provide health and life insurance for its retirees and their dependents, and to reimburse employers for losses due to termination of this insurance . . . .

The District Court certified its judgment under 28 U.S.C. § 1292(b) as a decision involving a controlling question of law as to which there is substantial ground for difference of opinion. This court permitted Yard-Man's appeal from the summary judgment, granting specific performance on both counts . . . .

. . .

The District Court properly recognized that whether retiree insurance benefits continue beyond the expiration of the collective bargaining agreement depends upon the intent of the parties. Clearly the parties to a collective bargaining agreement may provide for rights which will survive termination of their collective bargaining relationship. The parties may, for example, provide retiree insurance benefits which survive the expiration of the collective bargaining agreement. Any such surviving benefit must necessarily find its genesis in the collective bargaining agreement.

The enforcement and interpretation of collective bargaining agreements under § 301 [of the National Labor Management Relations Act] is governed by substantive federal law. However, traditional rules for contractual interpretation are applied as long as their application is consistent with federal labor policies . . . .

Many of the basic principles of contractual interpretation are fully appropriate for discerning the parties' intent in collective bargaining agreements. For example, the court should first look to the explicit language of the collective bargaining agreement for clear manifestations of intent. The intended meaning of even the most explicit language can, of course, only be understood in light of the context which gave rise to its inclusion. The court should also interpret each provision in question as part of the integrated whole. If possible, each provision should be construed consistently with the entire document and the relative positions and purposes of the parties. As in all contracts, the collective bargaining agreement's terms must be construed so as to render none nugatory and avoid illusory promises. Where ambiguities exist, the court may look to other words and phrases in the collective bargaining agreement for guidance. Variations in language used in other durational provisions of the agreement may, for example, provide inferences of intent useful in clarifying a provision whose intended duration is ambiguous. Finally, the court should review the interpretation ultimately derived from its examination of the language, context and other indicia of intent for consistency with federal labor policy. This is not to say that the collective bargaining agreement should be construed to affirmatively promote any particular policy but rather that the interpretation rendered not denigrate or contradict basic principles of federal labor law.

Application of these basic rules of construction to the present case demonstrates the correctness of the District Court's conclusion that the parties intended to create nonterminating lifelong insurance benefits for the Yard-Man retirees.

The key provision of the collective bargaining agreement, Article XVII, Section 4, states:

> "When the former employee has attained the age of 65 years then:
>
> *(1) The Company will provide insurance benefits equal to the active group benefits . . . for the former employee and his spouse.*"

(Emphasis added.)

. . .

We agree with the District Court that the key provision of the collective bargaining agreement is ambiguous. The language "will provide insurance benefits equal to the active group" could reasonably be construed, if read in isolation, as either solely a reference to the nature of retiree benefits or as an incorporation of some durational limitation as well. This phrase is no less ambiguous as to intended duration than language construed as creating continuing benefits in the various cases and arbitration decisions cited by the parties.

This ambiguity requires that we look to other provisions of the collective bargaining agreement for evidence of intent and an interpretation which is harmonious with the entire document. This examination persuades us that Yard-Man and the Union intended to create vested insurance benefits in the Yard-Man retirees which continue beyond the life of the collective bargaining agreement.

First, termination of insurance benefits for active employees was explicitly and clearly set out and yet under conditions — the layoff of seniority employees — typically inapplicable to retirees. Moreover, there are variations in the duration of insurance benefits available to active employees dependent upon their seniority. These variations and the impracticality of hinging retiree benefits to events as unpredictable and unstable as active worker layoffs make it improbable that retiree benefits were intended to depend in duration upon the fortunes of the active employees. Yard-Man's own course of conduct in continuing retiree insurance benefits after plant closure beyond the point as [sic] which insurance benefits could have been terminated for active employees indicates that it did not consider retiree benefits to be tied to the durational limitations of that active group.

Second, the insurance provisions limit health insurance coverage for a retiree's spouse and dependent children in case of the retiree's death to expiration of the collective bargaining agreement. While this limitation does not preclude an intent to also terminate the retiree's benefits with the expiration of the collective bargaining agreement in any event, it is more reasonable to infer that the spouse-dependent child provision was meant as an exception to the anticipated continuation of benefits beyond the life of the collective bargaining agreement.

Third, the retiree insurance provisions, Article XVII, Section 1, contain a promise that the company will pay an early retiree's insurance upon such retiree reaching age 65 but that the retiree must bear the cost of company insurance until that time. Since an employee is entitled under the collective bargaining agreement to retire at 55, the company's promise could remain outstanding for a ten-year period. If retiree insurance benefits were terminated at the end of the collective bargaining agreement's three-year term, this promise is completely illusory for many early retirees under age 62.

Fourth, the inclusion of specific durational limitations in other provisions of the current collective bargaining agreement suggests that retiree benefits, not so specifically limited, were intended to survive the expiration of successive agreements in the parties' contemplated long term relationship. Article XIX, for example, provides that "savings and pension plan programs" continue only for the duration of the collective bargaining agreement. No such specific limitation was provided to similarly restrict payment of retiree insurance benefits to the life of the collective bargaining agreement.

Finally, examination of the context in which these benefits arose demonstrates the likelihood that continuing insurance benefits for retirees were intended. Benefits for retirees are only permissive not mandatory subjects of collective bargaining. As such, it is unlikely that such benefits, which are typically understood as a form of delayed compensation or reward for past services, would be left to the contingencies of future negotiations. The employees are presumably aware that the union owes no obligation to bargain for continued benefits for retirees. If they forego wages now in expectation of retiree benefits, they would want assurance that once they retire they will continue to receive such benefits regardless of the bargain reached in subsequent agreements. Contrary to Yard-Man's assertions, the finding of an intent to create interminable rights to retiree insurance benefits in the absence of explicit language, is not, in any discernible way, inconsistent with federal labor law.

Further, retiree benefits are in a sense "status" benefits which, as such, carry with them an inference that they continue so long as the prerequisite status is maintained. Thus, when the parties contract for benefits which accrue upon achievement of retiree status, there is an inference that the parties likely intended those benefits to continue as long as the beneficiary remains a retiree. This is not to say that retiree insurance benefits are necessarily interminable by their nature. Nor does any federal labor policy identified to this Court presumptively favor the finding of interminable rights to retiree insurance benefits when the collective bargaining agreement is silent. Rather, as part of the context from which the collective bargaining agreement arose, the nature of such benefits simply provides another inference of intent. Standing alone, this factor would be insufficient to find an intent to create interminable benefits. In the present case, however, this contextual factor buttresses the already sufficient evidence of such intent in the language of this agreement itself.

Yard-Man urges that a general duration clause which provided that the collective bargaining agreement should remain in force until June 1, 1977 demonstrates an intent that all benefits described in the agreement also terminate at that date. We do not agree. The clause does not specifically refer to the duration of benefits. The persuasive considerations we have discussed demonstrate that retiree benefits were intended to outlive the collective bargaining agreement's life and outweigh any contrary implications derived from a routine duration clause terminating the agreement generally. Such an intent takes precedence over a non-specific, general clause.

Yard-Man's exhaustive analysis of the contract language greatly influenced subsequent decisions, with courts nearly unanimous in following Yard-Man's general contract analysis. Yard-Man's observation that retiree benefits constitute "status benefits" that carry "an inference that they will continue so long as the prerequisite status is maintained" has proven more controversial. Some Circuits, such as the First, Fourth and Eleventh, have followed this inference, while others, such as the Third, Fifth, Seventh, and Eighth, have rejected the inference.

3-13 QUESTIONS AND PROBLEMS

1. Was the language in the collective bargaining agreement ambiguous? What difference does it make whether the language was ambiguous?

2. What role does intent play in the court's analysis? How is intent determined? Whose intent is relevant?

3. What factors supported the court's inference that retiree benefits will continue so long as the prerequisite status is maintained? Does the inference create a presumption in favor of vested benefits in every case? Is this inference consistent with or contrary to the purpose of ERISA?

Although retiree health benefits often arise from a collective bargaining agreement, not all do. The following case addresses an employer's termination of retiree health benefits provided to non-union employees.

SPRAGUE v. GENERAL MOTORS CORPORATION

133 F.3d 388 (6th Cir.) (en banc), *cert denied*, 524 U.S. 923 (1998)

David A. Nelson, Circuit Judge.

This is a purported class action in which the plaintiffs — retired employees of the defendant, General Motors Corporation — allege that GM violated [ERISA] by denying them fully "paid-up" lifetime health care benefits. The district court certified a class of some 50,000 employees who had taken early retirement, but the court declined to grant class status to about 34,000 "general retirees" who had retired in accordance with the company's normal criteria. As to the general retiree plaintiffs, the court held that the benefits in question did not vest under the pertinent plan documents. As to the early retirees, however, the district court held that each of the 50,000 members of the class had entered into a separate contract that called for the benefits in question to be furnished for life at no cost to the recipient. In the alternative, the court ruled that GM was estopped to rely on the terms of the plan documents to defeat the claims of any early retiree.

We shall affirm the judgment of the district court as to the general retirees, but reverse the court's certification of the class of early retirees. Insofar as the merits of the claims asserted by the named plaintiffs are concerned, we conclude that the claims fail as a matter of law.

A

In 1961 General Motors began paying part of the cost of health insurance for its salaried retirees [Ed. non-union employees receiving a salary rather than an hourly wage] and their surviving spouses. Three years later GM assumed the full cost of basic health insurance for its salaried retirees, and in 1968 it extended this benefit to surviving spouses as well. (In the interest of simplicity, further reference to surviving spouses will generally be omitted.)

In addition to basic health insurance, GM offered its salaried retirees supplemental coverage under what was called the Comprehensive Medical Expense Insurance Program. Participants in this optional program were required to pay a share of the premiums, and co-payment was required for certain medical services. There were also annual deductibles.

Prior to 1985 the health care benefits were provided through arrangements with private insurers. The insurers issued each covered person a certificate of insurance describing the terms and conditions of the underlying policy.

GM became fully self-insured in 1985. At that time the company prepared a document, entitled "The General Motors Health Care Insurance Program for Salaried Employees," that set forth the terms and conditions of GM's self-insured health care program . . . . The new plan gave participants a choice between traditional fee-for-service coverage and enrollment in a managed care organization. GM continued its supplemental coverage program, shortening the name to the Comprehensive Medical Expense Program.

GM has long made it a practice to inform its salaried employees and retirees of their health care coverage by providing them booklets containing summaries of the company's health insurance policies and programs. Prior to 1974 GM put out a booklet entitled "The GM Insurance Program for Salaried Employees." After ERISA took effect in 1974 the booklet became "Highlights of Your GM Benefits." Beginning in 1977 GM also issued a booklet called "Your Benefits in Retirement." Each of these publications went through a series of different editions.

A number of the booklets contained language informing plan participants that the health care plan called for GM to pay health insurance costs during retirement:

> • "If you retire . . . and are eligible to receive retirement benefits under the provisions of the GM Retirement Program for Salaried Employees, you may keep your basic hospital, surgical and medical expense coverages in effect . . . . GM will pay the full monthly premium or subscription charge for such coverages." The General Motors Insurance Program for Salaried Employees (1968)."

The 1971 version was nearly identical.

> • "Hospital-Medical Coverages: Your basic coverages will be provided at Corporation expense for your lifetime . . . ." Highlights of Your GM Benefits (1974).
>
> • "Your basic health care coverages will be provided at GM's expense for your lifetime . . . ." Your Benefits in Retirement (1977).
>
> • "General Motors pays the full cost of any basic health care coverages that are continued for most retired employees and for eligible surviving spouses and children of deceased retirees." Your Benefits in Retirement (1977)."

However, most of the booklets also put plan participants on notice of GM's right to change or terminate the health care plan at any time:

> . . .
>
> • "The Corporation reserves the right to amend, modify, suspend, or terminate its benefit Plans or Programs by action of its Board of Directors." Your Benefits in Retirement (1985)."

B

For more than two decades GM has engaged in systematic reductions in the size of its salaried workforce. In this connection the company has launched special early retirement programs designed to induce salaried workers to retire before reaching normal retirement age. The inducements have included, among other things, offers to provide pension benefits to early retirees at levels not reduced to reflect the longer periods over which such benefits can be expected to accrue. Some of the early retirement programs were company-wide initiatives, while others applied to a particular plant, division, or group of plants or divisions.

Salaried employees who accepted early retirement were often asked to sign documents evincing their acceptance of the terms of the particular program under which they were retiring. From 1974 until 1984 GM utilized a so-called "short form" statement of acceptance . . . .

In 1984 GM adopted the "long form" statement of acceptance . . . .

Both forms had numerous variants, but all stated in essence that the early retiree had "reviewed the benefits applicable" and "accept[ed] them." In return for such benefits, the early retirees agreed to waive certain causes of action they might have had against GM.

Not all early retirees signed a statement of acceptance. Some merely signed a "statement of intent" to retire, while others apparently signed nothing.

In the course of explaining its special early retirement programs, GM made numerous oral and written representations about the health care benefits available to early retirees. Most of the early retirees participated in exit interviews where a particular early retirement program was described. These interviews were conducted by plant supervisors, members of the benefits staff, and others. Many of the early retirees also received documents summarizing applicable retirement benefits. These summaries often informed retirees that their health insurance would be paid by GM for life. Again, however, such documents sometimes put the retirees on notice of GM's right to change benefits. Certain summaries advised, for example, that "General Motors Corp. reserves the right to amend, change or terminate the Programs described."

Some early retirees received individualized letters about early retirement programs. And a small number of early retirees explicitly asked GM representatives about future changes to health care benefits. The answers given, it seems, were accurate — benefits could be changed in the future.

C

Late in 1987 GM announced that early in the following year significant changes would become effective in health care coverage for both salaried employees and retirees . . . . By reason of these two changes, fee-for-service participants could find themselves responsible for paying as much as $700 a year (with individual coverage) or $750 (with family coverage) that would previously have been paid by GM.

. . .

D

The present lawsuit was commenced in August of 1989 by 114 salaried retirees who challenged the legality of the changes to the health care plan that took effect in 1988. The main thrust of the plaintiffs' complaint was that GM had bound itself to provide salaried retirees and their spouses basic health coverage for life, entirely at GM's expense. The right to such coverage vested upon retirement, according to the plaintiffs, so the coverage could never be changed or revoked.

. . .

The named plaintiffs purported to represent a class of some 84,000 similarly-situated individuals, about 50,000 of whom were early retirees and 34,000 of whom were general retirees.

. . .

III

A

The plaintiffs' first theory of recovery is that GM committed a breach of the terms of the plan documents when it implemented the changes in 1988. Under the plan documents, according to the plaintiffs, their health care benefits were vested — and having vested, the benefits could not be altered without the plaintiffs' consent.

The district court rejected this theory, holding that the plan documents, including the summary plan descriptions, effectively reserved a right on GM's part to amend or terminate the plan. The court's holding, in our view, was manifestly correct; we shall affirm the summary judgment that was entered in favor of GM on this issue.

ERISA distinguishes between pension plans and welfare plans. A pension plan "provides retirement income to employees" or "results in a deferral of income by employees for periods extending to the termination of . . . employment or beyond . . . ." [ERISA § 3(2).] Welfare plans, in contrast, include plans "established or . . . maintained for the purpose of providing . . . medical, surgical, or hospital care or benefits . . . ." [ERISA § 3(1).] Because the plan in question here provided health insurance to its participants, it was a welfare plan. *See Musto v. American Gen. Corp.*, 861 F.2d 897, 901 n.2 (6th Cir. 1988) (a medical insurance plan is a welfare plan), *cert. denied*, 490 U.S. 1020 (1989).

Welfare plans are specifically exempted from vesting requirements to which pension plans are subject. [ERISA § 201(1).] Therefore, employers "are generally free under ERISA, for any reason at any time, to adopt, modify, or terminate welfare plans." *Curtiss-Wright Corp. v. Schoonejongen*, 514 U.S. 73, 78 (1995) . . . . Employers may vest welfare benefits if they choose to do so, however. *See Inter-Modal Rail Employees Ass'n v. Atchison, Topeka & Santa Fe Ry. Co.*, 117 S. Ct. 1513, 1516 (1997) . . . .

To vest benefits is to render them forever unalterable. Because vesting of welfare plan benefits is not required by law, an employer's commitment to vest such benefits is not to be inferred lightly; the intent to vest "must be found in the plan documents and must be stated in clear and express language." *Wise v. El Paso Natural Gas Co.*, 986 F.2d 929, 937 (5th Cir. 1993) . . . . It is the plaintiffs' burden to prove GM's intent to vest. *Id.*

The plaintiffs have not seriously disputed that the plan itself permitted GM to amend or terminate benefits. Instead the plaintiffs focus on the plan summaries, which must "be written in a manner calculated to be understood by the average plan participant, and shall be sufficiently accurate and comprehensive to reasonably apprise such participants and beneficiaries of their rights and obligations under the plan." [ERISA § 102(a)(1).]

In *Edwards v. State Farm Mut. Auto. Ins. Co.*, 851 F.2d 134, 136 (6th Cir. 1988), we held that "statements in a summary plan are binding and if such statements conflict with those in the plan itself, the summary shall govern." Application of the *Edwards* principle, the plaintiffs say, compels a judgment in their favor. We disagree.

. . .

Most of the summary plan descriptions unambiguously reserved GM's right to amend or terminate the plan . . . .

The plaintiffs counter by pointing out that these summaries also told them that their health coverage would be paid "at no cost to" them and "for [their] lifetime[s]." Such language, they argue created an ambiguity within the summaries that must be resolved by extrinsic evidence.

We have rejected this argument in the past, and we reject it again now. We see no ambiguity in a summary plan description that tells participants both that the terms of the current plan entitle them to health insurance at no cost throughout retirement and that the terms of the current plan are subject to change.

. . .

Not all of the summaries clearly stated that GM could amend or terminate the plan. But the failure to allude to this power in some of the booklets did not prejudice

GM's right, clearly stated in the plan itself, to change the plan's terms.

In the first place, the principle announced in *Edwards* does not apply to silence. An omission from the summary plan description does not, by negative implication, alter the terms of the plan itself. *Jensen*, 38 F.3d at 952 . . . . The reason is obvious: by definition, a summary will not include every detail of the thing it summarizes. GM's failure to include in some summaries a notice of its right to change the plan does not trump the clearly-stated right to do so in the plan itself.

In the second place, GM was not required to disclose in the summary plan descriptions that the plaintiffs' benefits were not vested. *See Jensen*, 38 F.3d at 952 . . .

ERISA specifies in detail the information that every summary plan description "shall contain." *See* [ERISA § 102(b).] Among the items a summary must include is "a description of the provisions providing for nonforfeitable pension benefits." *Id.* Despite having required that summaries inform plan participants about the vesting of benefits under *pension* plans, Congress did not require such information for *welfare* plans; neither did the Department of Labor in its ERISA reporting and disclosure regulations . . . .

. . .

B

We turn next to the theory that GM bilaterally contracted with each early retiree to vest benefits. All of the early retirees took retirement under one of the special early retirement programs offered by GM between 1974 and 1988. The early retirees argue that, as the district court held, the statements, promises, and representations GM made to them in connection with these programs, and the documents that they signed, created binding bilateral contracts. The alleged contracts, which supposedly provided for vesting of the early retirees' health care benefits, are said to be enforceable either as modifications to the general plan, or as ERISA plans themselves, or as a matter of federal common law.

ERISA "has an elaborate scheme in place for beneficiaries to learn their rights and obligations at any time, a scheme that is built around reliance on the face of written plan documents." *Curtiss-Wright*, 514 U.S. at 83. To implement this scheme, ERISA requires that every plan "shall be established and maintained pursuant to a written instrument." [ERISA § 402(a)(1).] ERISA also requires, as we have said, a written summary plan description that will "reasonably apprise . . . participants and beneficiaries of their rights and obligations under the plan." ERISA § 102(a).

The writing requirement ensures that "every employee may, on examining the plan documents, determine exactly what his rights and obligations are under the plan." *Curtiss-Wright*, 514 U.S. at 83 (quoting H. Rep. No. 1280, 93d Cong., 2d Sess. 297). And the requirement lends predictability and certainty to employee benefit plans. *Gable*, 53 F.3d at 857 . . . This serves the interests of both employers and employees. *See Gordon v. Barnes Pumps, Inc.*, 999 F.2d 133, 136 (6th Cir. 1993) . . .

"Congress intended that plan documents and SPDs exclusively govern an employer's obligations under ERISA plans." *Moore*, 856 F.2d at 492. We recognize that "[t]his may not be a foolproof informational scheme, although it is quite thorough. Either way, it is the scheme that Congress devised." *Curtiss-Wright*, 514 U.S. at 84.

Our court has consistently refused to recognize oral modifications to written plan documents . . . . The plaintiffs may not invoke oral statements by GM personnel in order to modify the terms of the written plan.

Neither can we accept the argument that the plan was modified or superseded either by the written "statements of acceptance" signed by some of the named plaintiffs or by the written representations received by some from GM . . . . None of GM's representations suggested that the plan was being modified. The statements of acceptance, moreover, merely said that the employee "ha[d] reviewed the benefits applicable to [him]" and "accept[ed] them." Far from modifying the terms of the welfare plan, it seems to us, this language incorporated the plan's terms.

. . .

For us to sanction informal "plans" or plan "amendments" — whether oral or written — would leave the law of employee benefits in a state of uncertainty and would create disincentives for employers to offer benefits in the first place. Such a result is not in the interests of employees generally, and it is certainly not compatible with the goals of ERISA . . . .

. . .

Boyce F. Martin, Jr., Chief Judge, with whom Judges Moore and Cole join, dissenting.

The question before this Court is whether General Motors has created a lifetime right to basic health care for its retirees. The en banc majority found that former General Motors salaried employees do not have any vested right in free lifetime health care, which they were promised at their retirement . . .

. . .

The early retirees' claims are founded on the early retirement agreements they signed and other representations General Motors made to them at retirement. These agreements, they argue, constitute binding, bilateral contracts with General Motors for lifetime health care — a bargained-for agreement. The early retirees not only gave up their jobs, but some also surrendered the right to bring causes of action, including civil rights and age discrimination claims, against the company. They argue that this mutual consideration entitles them to bring a breach of bilateral contract claim. Typically a breach of contract claim falls under state law, and ERISA preempts state law. ERISA § 514. Preemption need not sound the death knell for a contract-based claim, though. As the district court recognized, plaintiffs can make claims beyond state law.

The district court in *Sprague II* found the early retirement agreements for early retiree subclasses (1) and (2) "enforceable under ERISA as independent bilateral contracts, or as modifications of GM's health care benefit plan." 843 F. Supp. at 299 . . . The district court in *Sprague II* found enforceable contracts for the subclass (1) and (2) early retirees, 843 F. Supp. at 299, and the district court noted in its Final Judgment that the subclass (4) early retirees also had enforceable contracts. That judgment should have been affirmed.

For an interesting critique of the *Sprague* opinion, *see* Steven J. Sacher and William Payne, *Sixth Circuit Holds that a Reservation of Rights in the Plan and in Some of the SPDs Trumps "Lifetime" Statement in SPDs*, 14 Lab. Law. 475, 489 (1999).

3-14 QUESTIONS AND PROBLEMS

1. Was the language in the summary plan descriptions unambiguous? The Highlights of Your GM Benefits' Booklet in 1974 stated "Your basic coverages will be provided at Corporation expense for your lifetime . . ." Were they? How did the majority justify its decision finding in favor of GM?

2. What role did the *Yard-Man* inference play in the court's opinion? What role should it have played?

3. The fact that welfare benefits need not be vested is generally justified by the fact that they are current benefits; that is, paid currently. Is that true with respect to retiree health benefits? Should retiree health benefits be vested? If they were, how would that work? Would it merely mean that the employer could not reduce retiree health benefits for current retirees? Or would the employer also be prohibited from reducing retiree health benefits for future retirees?

4. Would it be correct to say that absent an express reservation of the right to amend a welfare benefit plan, an employer can lower an employee's wages or even fire the employee, but is not permitted to reduce the employee's retiree health care benefits?

5. If the decision in *Yard-Man* is congruous with the idea that retiree benefits represent deferred compensation, how is the *Sprague* decision justified? Were the health care benefits merely gratuitous promises by GM?

6. Is the *Sprague* decision fair to the employees who took early retirement with the expectation that they would have health benefits for life? Conversely, why shouldn't the salaried employees be expected to read and pay attention to the GM reservation of the right to amend the plan?

7. Tau Co. is considering providing retiree health benefits to its current nonunionized salaried employees as a means of attracting qualified workers in a tight, competitive labor market. Should the company reserve the right to amend or terminate the plan or would that right make the promise illusory? If it does retain that right, can the company "afford" to invoke it? Are there any alternatives to promising health care benefits to retirees?

[3] Retiree Health Benefits and the Accounting Rules

In the past, retiree health benefit costs were viewed as immaterial, and few employers tracked or analyzed them. Employers typically did not pre-fund retiree health benefits and accounted for them on a cash basis; that is, they only recognized current benefits paid and included the existence of future liabilities in a footnote in their financial statements. As the cost of retiree health care became much more significant in the 1980s and early 1990s, the Financial Accounting Board changed the rules governing the accounting of retiree health benefits and adopted Financial Accounting Standard 106 (FAS 106), "Employer's Accounting for Postretirement Benefits Other Than Pensions," effective December 15, 1992.

FAS 106 requires companies to report retiree health benefit liabilities in their financial reports on the accrual method rather than the cash method. When FAS 106 took effect, employers could either report their unfunded liability as a one-time nonrecurring charge or report it through annual charges taken over a period of up to 20 years. Many companies chose to recognize the expense immediately. For example, in 1992, Ford Motor Co. reported a $7.5 billion charge against income and General Motors a charge of $20.8 billion in order to comply with the rule. Some estimate that implementation of FAS 106 resulted in total reductions in current income of American corporations of about $1.5 trillion.

In 2004, the Governmental Accounting Standards Board (GASB) issued GASB Statement No. 45, which, similar to FAS 106, requires governmental employers to recognize their retiree health benefit liabilities on an accrual basis rather than a pay-as-you-go basis. One report estimated that there are over $1.5 trillion in unfunded liabilities. Implementation of the rule is expected to have a significant impact on many governmental employers.

For a more detailed discussion of these accounting rules and their impact on retiree health benefits, see David A. Pratt, *The Past, Present and Future of Retiree Health Benefits*, 3 J. Health & Biomedical L. 103 (2007); Susan E. Cancelosi, *VEBAs to the Rescue: Evaluating One Alternative for Public Sector Retiree Health Benefits*, 42 J. Marshall L. Rev. 879 (2009).

3-15 QUESTIONS AND PROBLEMS

1. Not surprisingly, as a result of FAS 106, a number of employers eliminated their retiree health plans in order to avoid reporting a significant liability. Indeed, according to one survey, the percentage of large employers offering medical benefits to early retirees decreased from 46 percent in 1993 to 29 percent in 2005, and the percentage of large employers offering medical benefits to Medicare-eligible retirees decreased from 40 percent to 21 percent over the same time period. Does this mean that FAS 106 is bad policy?

2. Much of the problem with FAS 106 arises from the fact that retiree health benefits are generally unfunded. Should ERISA be amended to require that retiree health benefits be funded? If so, should the Internal Revenue Code be amended to provide a tax favorable means of prefunding retiree health benefits?

[4] Funding Retiree Health Benefits Through Voluntary Employees' Beneficiary Associations (VEBAs)

IRC § 501(c)(9).

Although Voluntary Employees' Beneficiary Associations (VEBAs) have existed in some form since 1928, in recent years, VEBAs have become a very popular vehicle for funding retiree health benefits for employers who have collective bargaining agreements with unions. For example, in the fall of 2007, Ford agreed to put $13.2 million into a VEBA to fund retiree health benefits for its union workers. Similarly, GM agreed to contribute $24.1 billion to another VEBA, and Chrysler agreed to pay $8.8 billion in cash and securities to a third VEBA.

VEBAs are governed by IRC § 501(c)(9) . To qualify as a VEBA, the following requirements must be satisfied: (1) the organization must be an employee's association; (2) membership must be voluntary; (3) the organization must provide life, sickness, accident, or similar benefits; and (4) the earnings must not inure to the benefit of a private shareholder or individual. Treas. Reg. § 1.501(c)(9)-1. If the VEBA satisfies the requirements of IRC § 501(c)(9) and the nondiscrimination requirements set forth in IRC § 505, income earned by the VEBA will not be taxed. Retiree health benefits paid to VEBA members will be usually be tax exempt under IRC §§ 105 and 106.

Sections 419 and 419A of the Internal Revenue Code impose significant limitations on an employer's ability to deduct contributions to fund retiree health benefits for nonunion employees. Specially, private employers may only deduct the "qualified" cost for nonunion employees in any year. The qualified cost, in turn, is generally one year's expected claims and expenses plus certain limited reserves for post-retirement medical benefits that may be funded over the working lives of covered employees.

The deduction limits, however, do not apply to contributions for union employees. Thus, not only can employers deduct contributions to fund current retiree health care benefits for these employees, but they can currently deduct contributions to fund future payment obligations. As a result, the use of VEBAs to prefund retiree health benefits has become popular among employers whose employees are represented by a union.

When the employer agrees to pre-fund retiree health benefits through a VEBA, the obligation to pay the retiree health care benefits shifts from the employer to the VEBA. The employer in turn promises to make a fixed payment to the VEBA from which all future health care benefits for the current retirees will be paid. These are essentially closed funds with a fixed number of members. When the last member (beneficiary) of the VEBA dies off, the VEBA terminates. Some VEBAs continue to add members as employees retire, and the employer agrees to continue to fund the VEBA over time according to an agreed upon formula.

Closed membership VEBAs cap the employer's liability and shift the risk of future payment of their health care costs to the current retired employees. Whether the VEBA will be able to pay all promised health care depends on the rate of return on the VEBA assets, the rate of increase in health care costs, and the demand for health care by the retired employees. The employer may or may not provide health care benefits for future retirees or may provide greatly reduced benefits. The reduced financial obligation will be at a level that the employer believes it can afford to pay out of its current revenues.

> In many ways, this arrangement is analogous to how the legal system dealt with companies' mass-tort liabilities during the 1980s and 1990s. In those cases, the companies would admit that they had future liabilities that were significant. The problem was, these companies could not successfully operate as ongoing entities with the size and scope of those liabilities still unknown. If these giant uncertain future liabilities would force a company to liquidate in the short-term, then everyone would lose, including future victims.
>
> The solution was to shift a portion of the company's assets into a separate financial entity that would be solely responsible for that category of liability. In that way, future victims would have some source of funds from which to recover, and the companies would continue to operate without the specter of unlimited future liability holding them back.

Daniel Keating, *Harsh Realities and Silver Linings for Retirees*, 15 Am. Bankr. Inst. L. Rev. 437, 452 (2007).

VEBAs are operated as trusts with trustee fiduciaries responsible for the management of the VEBA. The employees' union will usually demand the right to appoint the trustees, who are typically a mix of union members and outside, independent trustees with the latter responsible for selecting their replacements. The trustees are responsible for investing the VEBA assets and operating it in a manner that permits it to pay health care benefits for the lives of all participating members. That may require less generous benefits and higher deductibles and copays to ensure that the VEBA is not exhausted while there are surviving member beneficiaries.

3-16 QUESTIONS AND PROBLEMS

1. In funding retiree health care VEBAs, union employers are shifting responsibility for health care costs from the employer to the VEBA, a trust with a limited amount of assets. Why would a union agree to a VEBA rather than insist that the employer live up to its previously agreed upon obligation to pay retiree health care benefits?

2. In funding retiree health care VEBAs, employers typically contribute less than the entire cost of their liability. For example, in 2006, Goodyear agreed to create a VEBA and fund it with $1 billion to offset a $1.2 billion liability. Why would a union agree to accept $1 billion to fund a $1.2 billion liability? What happens if the VEBA runs out of money?

[5] Retiree Health Benefits and the Age Discrimination in Employment Act

On December 26, 2007, the Equal Employment Opportunity Commission (EEOC) published a final rule permitting employers to coordinate retiree health benefits with Medicare or comparable state programs. 72 Fed. Reg. 72,938. Specifically, the regulation provides a narrow exemption from the Age Discrimination in Employment Act (ADEA) to permit employers to alter, reduce, or eliminate health benefits for retirees who are eligible for Medicare or a comparable state health benefit plan. 29 C.F.R. § 1625.32. The regulation also permits employers to alter, reduce, or eliminate health benefits for spouses or dependents of such retirees. 29 C.F.R. § 1625.32, APP. Q&A-4. It does not, however, permit employers to coordinate benefits for active employees who are eligible for Medicare, nor does it permit coordination of retiree health benefits with Medicaid eligibility. 29 C.F.R. § 1625.32, APP. Q&A-7.

Without this exemption, the ADEA would require that the health insurance benefits received by Medicare-eligible retirees be the same, or cost the same, as the health insurance benefits received by younger retirees. Such a rule would make retiree health benefits cost prohibitive. The Commission adopted the rule because it "believes that it is in the best interest of both employers and employees for the Commission to pursue a policy that permits employers to offer [retiree health] benefits to the greatest extent possible." 29 C.F.R. § 1625.32, APP. Q&A-1.

3-17 QUESTIONS AND PROBLEMS

1. Does the EEOC's final rule makes sense from a policy standpoint? Who benefits from the rule? Who is harmed?

2. AARP unsuccessfully challenged this rule. Why would AARP challenge the rule?

[6] Early Retiree Reinsurance Program

The Affordable Care Act created the Early Retiree Reinsurance Program to provide a temporary subsidy for employer-sponsored health plans that cover early retirees and their dependents. 42 U.S.C. § 18002. Under the program, employers can obtain a reimbursement equal to 80% of the claim costs between $15,000 and $90,000 for early retirees who are age 55 or older and not yet eligible for Medicare.

42 U.S.C. § 18002(c)(2) & (3). Reimbursements also apply to coverage for the employees' spouses and/or dependents. 42 U.S.C. § 18002(c)(1)(B). The plan must use the proceeds it receives to lower health costs for enrollees. 42 U.S.C. § 18002(c)(4). The program became effective in June 2010 and funds are available on a first-come first-served basis. The program is scheduled to end upon the earlier of January 1, 2014, or when the $5 billion funding for the program runs out. On May 6, 2011, the Department of Health and Human Services stopped accepting new applications to participate in the program, and just under $4.1 million had been disbursed by November 18, 2011.

C. FEDERAL TAXATION OF WELFARE BENEFITS

[1] General Taxation of Welfare Benefits

IRC §§ 79(a), 105(b), 106(a).

Section 61 of the Internal Revenue Code defines the term "gross income" broadly to include "compensation for services, including fees, commissions, fringe benefits, and similar items" except to the extent otherwise provided. IRC § 61(a)(1). Thus, unless specifically exempted, welfare benefits are generally includible in gross income. The Internal Revenue Code specifically exempts a number of welfare benefits from taxation. First, and most significantly, the Internal Revenue Code generally excludes employer contributions to fund health care benefits from income. IRC § 106(a). In addition, it excludes benefits paid by employer-sponsored health care plans to the extent that the benefits are paid to reimburse the cost of the employee's medical care or the medical care of the employee's spouse or dependents. IRC § 105(b). Although these benefits are excludable from the employee's income, the employer generally may deduct its contributions to fund the benefits as ordinary business expenses. IRC § 162. Treas. Reg. § 1.162.10(a).

Section 79 of the Internal Revenue Code excludes from an employee's income employer contributions to fund group-term life insurance providing a death benefit for an employee of up to $50,000. IRC § 79(a). The cost of any additional insurance is includible in the employee's income. Id. For example, if an employer pays the premiums for $75,000 worth of group-term life insurance, the employee can exclude the premiums for $50,000 worth of insurance but must include in income the cost of the remaining $25,000 worth of coverage. Just as employer contributions to fund health care insurance are deductible as ordinary business expenses, so too are employer payments for group-term life insurance. IRC § 162. Treas. Reg. § 1.162-10(a).

The Internal Revenue Code also excludes benefits from a number of other welfare plans, such as educational assistance programs, IRC § 127, dependent care assistance programs, IRC § 129, and adoption assistance programs, IRC § 137. Employer's contributions to fund those benefits are generally deductible as ordinary business expenses. IRC § 162. Treas. Reg. § 1.162-10(a). Similarly, employer payments for disability benefits are excludable from an employee's income, IRC § 106(a), and the employer's contributions are deductible. IRC § 162. Treas. Reg. § 1.162-10(a). The disability benefits themselves, however, are includible in an employee's income if paid for with employer contributions. IRC §§ 104(a)(3) and 105.

The favorable tax treatment afforded welfare benefits differs fundamentally from that afforded to pension benefits. As indicated in Chapter 2, the principal tax advantage of traditional qualified plans arises from the deferral of taxation. Under a traditional qualified plan, the employer may deduct contributions to the plan at the time the contributions are made even though the employee does not recognize the contributions in income until they are distributed to the employee. In addition, earnings on the contributions are exempt from tax until they are distributed to the employee. The principal tax advantage of welfare benefit plans, in contrast, is exemption from tax, not tax deferral. So long as the Internal Revenue Code requirements are satisfied (such as life insurance coverage not exceeding $50,000), the benefits are never included in taxable income.

Just as the Internal Revenue Code imposes nondiscrimination requirements on qualified pension plans (*see* Chapter 8), it also imposes nondiscrimination requirements on most welfare plans under the specific sections of the Internal Revenue Code that govern the taxation of each type of benefit. The nondiscrimination requirements are designed to ensure that plans do not discriminate in favor of highly compensated employees; that is, that plans do not benefit principally — or exclusively — highly compensated employees. For example, IRC § 79 prohibits "key employees" from excluding from income the cost of group-term life insurance coverage if the plan discriminates in favor of key employees. IRC § 79(d)(1)(A). Key employees are generally defined as employees who earn more than $130,000 or own 5 percent or more of the employer. IRC §§ 79(d)(6), 416(i)(1)(A). Section 105(h) imposes a nondiscrimination requirement on self-insured health plans. If an employer's self-funded health plan only provides certain benefits to highly compensated employees, a highly compensated employee receiving those benefits must include the benefits in income. Prior to the enactment of the Affordable Care in March 2010, the nondiscrimination requirements only applied to self-funded health plans. The Affordable Care Act extends the nondiscrimination rules to insured health plans. PHSA § 2716. If an insured plan violates the nondiscrimination requirements, highly compensated employees will not be required to include the benefits in income. Instead, if an insured plan fails to satisfy the nondiscrimination requirements, the plan is subject to a civil action to compel it to provide nondiscriminatory benefits or the plan sponsor may be subject to an excise tax or civil monetary penalty of $100 per day per individual discriminated against. IRS Notice 2010-63. The nondiscrimination rules do not apply to grandfathered plans. Treas. Reg. § 54.9815T; 29 C.F.R. § 2590.715-1251; 45 C.F.R. § 147.140.

3-18 QUESTIONS AND PROBLEMS

1. Why doesn't the Internal Revenue Code simply defer taxation of welfare benefits rather than exempting them from taxation altogether?

2. What is the justification for tax exemption for particular employee benefits such as life insurance and health care reimbursements?

3. Dylan recently accepted a job where the employer provides all employees with group-term life insurance equal to $50,000. How will Dylan be taxed on this benefit? Would the answer be different if the coverage were for $100,000 worth of group-term life insurance? Suppose that Dylan earned $150,000, and only employees who earned $130,000 or more were eligible for coverage. How would Dylan be taxed on his group-term life insurance benefits? Suppose that the insurance were whole life rather than group-term insurance. Would that change the answer?

[2] Cafeteria Plans

IRC § 125.

The modern workforce is quite diverse, and different employees often desire different benefits. For example, an employee with dependent children has a much greater need for life insurance than does an employee with no dependents. Similarly, a married employee with a dependent spouse may have different benefits needs than a married employee with a working spouse. In order to permit employees flexibility in selecting their employee benefits, and thus maximize the perceived value of the benefits, employers often establish cafeteria plans.

A cafeteria plan, or flexible benefit plan, is a plan that permits each employee to choose between cash and one or more benefits offered by the plan. Under the constructive receipt doctrine, any benefit the employee selects would be subject to income tax because the employee had the choice between that benefit and cash. Section 125 of the Internal Revenue Code, however, establishes an exception to the constructive receipt doctrine; if a cafeteria plan satisfies the requirements of that section, participants are only taxed on the value of any taxable benefits they select under the plan, even though the employer's contributions to the plan are generally deductible.

To qualify under IRC § 125, the plan must be in writing, available only to employees, and each participant must have the choice between cash (or a taxable benefit that is treated like cash) and a "qualified benefit." IRC § 125(d)(1). A qualified benefit is any benefit (with a few expressly enumerated exceptions) attributable to employer contributions that is excludable from income under a specific provision of the Internal Revenue Code. For example, qualified benefits include the first $50,000 of group-term life insurance (excludable under IRC § 79) and coverage under an accident and health plan to the extent such coverage is excludable under IRC § 106.

Employers typically use one of four basic structures or some combination of the structures for their cafeteria plans: (1) a pretax conversion plan, (2) a multiple option pretax conversion plan, (3) a medical plan plus flexible spending arrangement, or (4) an employer credit cafeteria plan. Most employer-sponsored health care plans require employees to contribute to the cost of that plan. Those contributions are generally paid with after-tax dollars because individuals are only entitled to deduct medical expenses to the extent that they exceed 7.5 percent of adjusted gross income (10 percent effective for tax years beginning on or after January 1, 2013), IRC § 213, and few employees' medical expenses exceed 7.5 percent of adjusted gross income. A pretax conversion plan, however, converts employees' after-tax contributions to pretax contributions, through salary reduction, so long as the plan satisfies the requirements of IRC § 125.

A multiple option pretax conversion plan permits an employee to select benefit options, such as between a health indemnity plan and one or more HMOs or PPOs with differing amounts of employee contributions. If the plan satisfies the requirements of IRC § 125, the employee's contributions to the plan will be made on a pretax basis rather than an after-tax basis.

A medical plan plus flexible spending arrangement converts employees' after-tax contributions to fund an employer-sponsored health care plan to pretax contributions and offers employees the opportunity to participate in a flexible spending arrangement (FSA). An FSA is a bookkeeping account to which the employee pretax salary reduction contributions are credited. The amounts credited to the FSA can be used during the coverage period to pay out-of-pocket medical or dependent care expenses, such as deductibles, co-pays, and day care expenses for dependents, which the participant would otherwise have to pay with after-tax dollars. The FSA permits employees to use pretax dollars to fund those expenses. Generally, an employee must elect before the beginning of the coverage period what amount he or she will contribute to a health FSA or dependent care FSA for the year. The employee will have only limited opportunities to change his or her election during the year, and no amounts can be transferred from one type of FSA to the other.

An employer credit cafeteria plan gives each employee a specified number of credits which the employee can "spend" on different employee benefits or contribute to an FSA. Usually, the plan provides sufficient credits so that an employee can choose a low-cost medical plan and limited life insurance coverage without having to make any additional contributions. If the employee chooses a more costly benefits package, the employee will have to make contributions out of his or her own money, usually through a pretax conversion feature.

A cafeteria plan cannot provide for deferred compensation, other than pretax contributions to a 401(k) plan. IRC § 125(d)(2). The IRS has interpreted this requirement to prohibit amounts held by a cafeteria plan from being carried over into a subsequent year. It has also interpreted this requirement to prohibit a cafeteria plan from permitting participants to use contributions for one plan year to purchase a benefit that will be provided in a subsequent plan year. This requirement, often referred to as the "use it or lose it" rule, is most significant with respect to flexible spending arrangements (FSAs). Thus, under the "use it or lose it" rule, if an employee sets aside more in the FSA than the employee can use that year, the employee forfeits any remaining balance because the employee cannot carry the unused contribution forward to the next year. The Treasury Regulations also require that the amount of an employee's salary reduction contributions for the entire plan year be available to pay benefits from a health FSA as of the first day of the plan year. Thus, if an employee elects to have his or her salary reduced by $50 per month for payment of medical bills, the employee's health FSA must be credited with $600 as of the first day of the plan year. This requirement does not apply to dependent care FSAs.

One of the most frequent complaints about FSAs is the "use it or lose it" forfeiture rule. Critics have long argued that it should be eliminated so that outstanding balances could be rolled over from year to year. The IRS has responded that it does not have the authority to change the rule because IRC § 125 provides that the term "cafeteria plan" does not include any plan which provides for deferred compensation and the carrying forward or rolling over of unused contributions from one plan year to another operates to defer compensation.

In an effort to compromise with the rule's critics, the IRS issued Notice 2005-42 which modifies the "use it or lose it" forfeiture rule applicable to FSAs. Under the modified rule, plans may allow for an additional period of time (or "grace period") of up to 2½ months following the end of the each plan year to incur expenses before the "use it or lose it" rule applies. Thus, plans can provide that expenses incurred within 2½ months after the plan year can be reimbursed with funds carried over from the prior plan year. Any unused amounts from the prior plan year that are not used to reimburse expenses by the end of the grace period remain subject to the "use it or lose it" rule and must be forfeited.

The IRS bases its authority for the new rule on the premise that the grace period does not result in the deferral of compensation because it is only for a "brief" period of time (2½ months). The IRS maintains that any further extension of the grace period or a complete elimination of the "use it or lose it" rule must come from a Congressional amendment to IRC § 125.

Like most welfare benefits, cafeteria plans are subject to nondiscrimination rules. Specifically, a cafeteria plan may not discriminate in favor of highly compensated employees, as defined in IRC § 125(e), as to (1) eligibility to participate, or (2) contributions and benefits. IRC § 125(b)(1). In addition, nontaxable benefits provided to key employees, as defined in IRC § 416(i)(1), may not exceed 25% of the total nontaxable benefits provided to all employees under a cafeteria plan. IRC § 125(b)(2). If a cafeteria plan violates these nondiscrimination rules, either the highly compensated participants or key employees, depending on the nondiscrimination rule violated, will generally not be eligible for favorable treatment on benefits provided by the plan and may also be subject to excise taxes and penalties. A collectively bargained cafeteria plan is automatically treated as nondiscriminatory if the plan is maintained under a collective bargaining agreement between an employee representative and one or more employers. IRC § 125(g)(1). Any benefits offered by a cafeteria plan must also satisfy any separate nondiscrimination requirements applicable to those benefits. Thus, for example, if a cafeteria plan offers group-term life insurance coverage, the cafeteria plan must satisfy the IRC § 125(b) nondiscrimination rules as well as the separate IRC § 79(d) nondiscrimination rules applicable to group-term life insurance plans.

3-19 QUESTIONS AND PROBLEMS

1. If an employer establishes a cafeteria plan, the employee may use pretax dollars to pay his or her share of employer-sponsored health care plan premiums. If, however, an employer does not establish a cafeteria plan, or an employer does not offer a health care plan at all, individuals must use after-tax dollars to pay for health care coverage until their total medical expenses exceed 7.5 percent of adjusted gross income. Is this fair?

2. If an employer establishes a cafeteria plan with an FSA, an employee may use pretax dollars to pay for out-of-pocket medical expenses. If, however, an employer does not offer a cafeteria plan with an FSA, the employee must use after-tax dollars to pay for out-of-pocket medical expenses. Is this fair?

3. The Beta Company offers an FSA to which Brian, a Beta employee, elects to contribute $100 per month or $1,200 for the year. The FSA is a calendar year plan, and by the beginning of March, Brian has contributed $300 to the plan. On March 15, Brian has elective surgery and incurs $1,400 in out-of-pocket expenses. On March 25, Brian submits a claim to the FSA administrator for $1,400. How much is Brian entitled to receive as of March 25? What happens if Brian quits his job on April 25?

[3] Consumer-Driven Health Plans (CDHPs)

IRC § 223

The consumer-driven health plan (CDHP) combines a tax-favored health savings account or health reimbursement account with high-deductible medical insurance and requires the individual "consumer" to pay for the cost of any health care once the balance in the account has been depleted and before the deductible for the medical insurance has been met.

> The concept of CDHPs grew out of the belief that traditional health insurance plans are flawed because the high levels of coverage and small out-of-pocket expenses create no incentive for covered individuals to spend medical care dollars wisely, thereby contributing to high medical costs. CDHPs attempt to address this problem by sensitizing individuals to the costs of their medical expenses, while still shielding individuals from catastrophic medical costs. By giving an individual ownership of the tax-favored savings account, and by making the individual responsible for any "gap" between the savings account balance and coverage under an insurance plan, individuals will be incentivized to spend their medical dollars more judiciously. Whereas health maintenance organizations (HMOs) attempted to control medical spending through supply-side control, CDHPs attempt to control medical spending through demand-side control. Amy B. Monahan, *The Promise and Peril of Ownership Society Health Care Policy*, 80 TULANE L. REV. 777, 780–81 (2006).

The "savings" component of a CDHP may take one of two different forms: a health reimbursement arrangement (HRA) or a health savings accounts (HSA). HRAs were first approved by the IRS and the Treasury Department in 2002. An HRA reimburses employees for medical care expenses incurred by the employee and his or her spouse and dependents up to a maximum dollar amount. To the extent that the HRA qualifies as an employer-provided health plan, coverage and reimbursements of medical care expenses are generally excludable from the employee's gross income under IRC §§ 106 and 105.

To be eligible for favorable tax treatment, the HRA must be funded solely by the employer and not by salary reductions, and may only provide benefits for substantiated medical expenses. A plan that, directly or indirectly, allows an employee to receive cash or other benefits regardless of whether the employer or his or her family have incurred equivalent medical expenses, loses eligibility and all payments — including prior medical reimbursements — become taxable. Rev. Rul. 2002-41, 2002 IRB Lexis 291.

HRAs differ significantly from FSAs in that the "use it or lose it rule" does not apply to HRAs. Unused amounts can be carried forward to another year and remain excludable from tax. Notice 2002-45, 2002 IRB Lexis 290. In addition, unlike FSAs, the maximum annual dollar amount for HRAs does not have to be made available to the employee on the first day of the plan year. Instead, the total employer contribution can accrue throughout the plan year. Unless the plan document provides otherwise, the amounts contained in the HRA must be used before employees can receive reimbursements for medical expenses from their medical FSAs.

Health savings accounts (HSAs), authorized by IRC § 223, were introduced in the Medicare Prescription Drug Improvement and Modernization Act of 2003. HSAs are similar to IRAs except they are intended to be used to pay for health care expenses. Unlike HRAs, which limit contributions to employers, both individuals and their employers can make tax deductible contributions to HSAs. Earnings on HSA funds are not taxable, and distributions used to pay for qualified medical expenses are excludable from income.

Generally, any individual who is covered by a high deductible health plan (HDHP) is eligible to participate in an HSA so long as the individual is not covered by another health plan. As originally enacted, a plan qualified as a HDHP if it had an annual deductible of at least $1,000 for individual coverage and $2,000 for family coverage, and limited annual out-of-pocket expenses to no more than $5,000 for individuals and $10,000 for families. IRC § 223(c)(2). These thresholds were indexed to future increases in the cost of living. IRC § 223(g)(1). In 2012, the HDHP must have annual deductible of at least $1,200 for individual coverage and $2,400 for family coverage, and must limit annual out-of-pocket expenses to no more than $6,050 for individuals and $12,100 for families. Annual contributions to an HSA are limited to the lesser of the annual deductible amount or a statutory dollar amount, IRC § 223(b)(2), which is also indexed to the cost of living, IRC § 223(g)(1). In 2012, the statutory dollar amount is $3,100 for a single-coverage HDHP and $6,250 for a family-coverage HDHP. Although HSA distributions may be used to pay for nonmedical expenses, such distributions are includable in income. IRC § 223(f)(2). In addition, such distributions are subject to a ten percent penalty unless the distributions are made on account of death, disability, or to a person who is age 65 or older. IRC § 223(f)(4).

HSAs have a number of distinct advantages over FSAs (flexible spending accounts) and HRAs (health reimbursement arrangements). First, unlike FSAs, HSAs are not subject to a use-it-or-lose-it rule. Unused contributions to HSAs can be carried forward to a future year and there is no accumulation limit on HSA balances. Second, HSA contributions belong to the employee, not the employer, and may be "rolled over" to another HSA if the participant terminates employment with his or her employer. Finally, unlike distributions from FSAs and HRAs, distributions from HSAs may be used for non-medical expenses, although such distributions are includable in income and may be subject to a ten percent penalty.

Thirty-three percent of firms that participated in a national survey planned to offer a CDHP in 2007; at firms where CDHPs were offered, median enrollment was seven percent.

For a comprehensive discussion of the advantages and disadvantages of CDHPs, see Amy B. Monahan, *The Promise and Peril of Ownership Society Health Care Policy*, 80 Tulane L. Rev. 777 (2006).

3-20 QUESTIONS AND PROBLEMS

1. Just as defined contribution pension plans shift investment risk to employees, CDHPs shift risk to employees. From a policy standpoint, is this risk shifting a good thing or a bad thing?

2. Why is enrollment in CDHPs so low? What kind of employees are likely to be attracted to CDHPs?

3. Are CDHPs likely to contain the soaring cost of health care in this country?

Chapter 4

REGULATION OF EMPLOYEE BENEFIT PLANS

Although employee benefit plans are voluntary, once adopted, they must conform to the regulatory requirements of ERISA. This chapter introduces a number of those requirements and analyzes the legal issues that they raise. ERISA's protections include disclosure and reporting requirements to which all plans must adhere as well as a number of substantive requirements that are designed to protect the rights of the plan participants. Among the substantive requirements are benefit security or benefit building rules that regulate the participation, vesting or nonforfeitability, and benefit accruals of pension plans. Section 510 of ERISA, which applies to both pension and welfare plans, protects plan participants from employer attempts to interfere with the enjoyment of plan benefits. ERISA and the Internal Revenue Code require that certain retirement plans provide automatic survivor benefits to a participant's spouse. Finally, ERISA contains an anti-alienation rule that prohibits the assignment of pension plan benefits. ERISA expressly authorizes an exception to that rule for qualified domestic relations orders.

A. REPORTING AND DISCLOSURE REQUIREMENTS

ERISA §§ 101-111.

ERISA's principal reporting and disclosure requirements, which apply to both pension and welfare benefit plans, are set forth in ERISA §§ 101-111. Additional reporting and disclosure requirements are interspersed throughout ERISA and the Internal Revenue Code. *See, e.g.*, ERISA §§ 204(h); 205(c)(3); 606; 713; IRC §§ 402(f); 417(a)(3). The reporting and disclosure requirements are intended to ensure that participants and beneficiaries are aware of their rights under ERISA and have the necessary information to make informed decisions regarding their benefit options. The requirements also encourage employers to comply with ERISA by making the plan's transactions public and assist government agencies in enforcing ERISA.

ERISA's disclosure and reporting requirements center on adequate disclosure of the plan and its benefits to the participants and annual information reports to the government and participants. Sections 101–111 of ERISA require three primary forms of disclosure to participants: 1) the summary plan description, ERISA § 102(a)(1), and summary of material modifications, ERISA § 102(a)(1); 2) the summary annual report, ERISA § 103(a)(1); and 3) individual benefits statements, ERISA § 105(a). The summary plan description and summary of material modifications explain how the plan works and the benefits it promises. The summary annual report and individual benefits statements provide participants with the figures needed to determine whether the plan is working and providing the promised benefits.

ERISA requires that pension and welfare plan information be reported to three separate government agencies: 1) the Department of Labor (DOL), 2) the Internal Revenue Service (IRS), and 3) the Pension Benefit Guaranty Corporation (PBGC). ERISA and the Internal Revenue Code require that an annual report be filed with each agency, ERISA § 104(a)(1); IRC §§ 6058(a), 6039D; and ERISA § 4065. The three agencies have developed a single form that satisfies each agency's annual reporting requirement. In addition, ERISA and the Internal Revenue Code require that a variety of other forms of notice be made to the three agencies. For example,

ERISA requires that, upon request, plan administrators provide the Secretary of Labor with the latest summary plan description, summary of material modifications, and the bargaining agreement, trust agreement, contract or other instrument under which the plan is established or operated. ERISA § 104(a)(6). The Patient Protection and Affordable Care Act imposes a new reporting requirement on employer-sponsored health plans. PHSA § 2715(d), as added by PPACA § 1001. Specifically, it requires that plan participants be provided with a summary of benefits and coverage at the time of plan enrollment or reenrollment. The summary is to be limited to four pages and provided in non-technical language. PHSA § 2715(b), as added by PPACA § 1001. The Departments of Health and Human Services, Labor, and Treasury are working together to develop uniform standards and definitions for this summary.

[1] Summary Plan Descriptions

The summary plan description (SPD) is the cornerstone of ERISA's disclosure requirements. The SPD must be written "in a manner calculated to be understood by the average plan participant" and must be accurate and comprehensive in informing participants and beneficiaries of their rights and obligations under the plan. ERISA § 102(a). The Department of Labor regulations mandate that the SPD avoid or at least minimize technical jargon and complex, lengthy sentences and prohibit SPDs from minimizing or making to appear unimportant descriptions of exceptions, limitations, or other restrictions of plan benefits. DOL Reg. § 2520.102-2(a) & (b).

Section 102(b) of ERISA specifies the information that must be included in the SPD. In addition to fundamental information such as the name of the plan and its trustees and administrators, the SPD must describe the plan's criteria for participation and vesting, what circumstances might result in the loss of benefits, how to claim benefits, and how to appeal if a claim is denied. If properly drafted, an SPD should provide a participant with an accurate and understandable description of his or her rights under the plan.

Section 104(b)(1) of ERISA requires the plan administrator to furnish each participant with an SPD within 90 days after he or she becomes a participant in the plan. What happens if the plan administrator fails to provide a participant with an SPD? The following case addresses this issue.

SIMEON v. THE MOUNT SINAI MEDICAL CENTER

150 F. Supp. 2d 598 (S.D.N.Y. 2001)

KOELTL, DISTRICT JUDGE.

Plaintiff Daphne Simeon ("Simeon") brings this action pursuant to section 502(a)(3) of the Employee Retirement Income Security Act of 1974, ("ERISA"), against defendants The Mount Sinai Medical Center ("Mount Sinai"), the Mount Sinai Tax Sheltered Annuity Plan a/k/a Mount Sinai NYU Health 403(b) Plan (the "Plan"), the Mount Sinai Hospital, and Mount Sinai School of Medicine. The Plan is an ERISA regulated tax sheltered annuity plan that allows Mount Sinai employees to make tax deferred contributions to an account to save for their retirement. If an employee enrolls in the Plan, Mount Sinai also makes an annual contribution equal to ten percent (10%) of the employee's salary to the employee's Plan account. Simeon alleges that the defendants breached their duties under ERISA by failing to give her adequate notice of the existence of the Plan. As a result, Simeon failed to enroll in the Plan for approximately five years and was unable to take advantage of the Plan benefits for that period of time. The defendants have moved pursuant to Fed. R. Civ. P. 12(b)(6) to dismiss the complaint for failure to state a claim upon which relief can be granted. For the following reasons, the defendants' motion to dismiss is denied.

. . .

B

The plaintiff's complaint is based on the following allegations . . . . As an employee of Mount Sinai, Simeon has been eligible to participate in the Plan and to have Mount Sinai make annual contributions to her account in an amount equal to ten percent (10%) of her salary. Simeon has also been eligible to make additional annual contributions to her Plan account from her own funds. Simeon alleges that she did not enroll in the Plan after beginning her employment because she was not notified of the Plan and was not aware that the Plan existed. In or about the Spring of 1998, Simeon phoned the Mount Sinai Benefits Office after a co-worker informed Simeon about the Plan. A Mount Sinai representative at the benefits office allegedly informed her that no such plan existed. On or about March 29, 1999, after another co-worker informed Simeon about the Plan, Simeon met with a Mount Sinai representative and was advised that she was eligible for the Plan. At that meeting, Simeon was advised that Mount Sinai had informed her about the Plan in a letter mailed to her home on or about August 15, 1994 and that no contributions had been made to her Plan account because she had not returned a signed copy of the enrollment forms included in the mailing. Simeon claims that she did not receive this letter and that the letter was the only attempt by Mount Sinai to inform her that she was eligible for the Plan. Simeon then completed enrollment forms for the Plan. Simeon has received annual contributions to the Plan for her account in the amount of 10% of her salary since about April 1, 1999.

By letter dated July 22, 1999, Simeon submitted a written appeal to Mount Sinai's Benefits Office. In that letter, her counsel argued that the denial of benefits was "an unlawful denial of a benefit and a breach of fiduciary duty" in violation of ERISA. By letter postmarked October 27, 1999, Diane Tucker, the Director of Human Resources, informed Simeon that she was not entitled to retroactive contributions because she had not submitted an enrollment form by September 23, 1994 as was required by the August 1994 letter. By letter delivered December 17, 1999, Simeon appealed the denial of her claim to Mount Sinai's Vice President of Human Resources and Labor Relations. Mount Sinai has not replied to Simeon's appeal. The plaintiff brings a cause of action pursuant to [ERISA § 502(a)(3)] against the defendants for violating provisions of ERISA. The plaintiff alleges that the defendants breached their fiduciary duty to her by failing to advise her of her right to enroll in the Plan and by failing to facilitate her enrollment in the Plan. The plaintiff seeks equitable relief, specifically a contribution to the Plan of an amount equal to the economic loss she incurred as a result of the defendants' conduct. The plaintiff estimates that this loss is in excess of $60,000. Alternatively, the plaintiff seeks direct compensation in excess of $200,000 for the economic loss she incurred. The plaintiff also seeks to recover the reasonable costs and attorneys fees incurred in this action pursuant to [ERISA § 502(g)(1).]

II

A

The defendants first move to dismiss the complaint on the grounds that they satisfied their duties under ERISA by sending Simeon a certified letter dated August 14, 1994 informing her that she would have to enroll in the Plan to be eligible for Plan benefits. The plaintiff's complaint alleges that the defendants violated their duties under ERISA by failing to give her adequate notice of the existence of the Plan. An administrator of an ERISA benefit plan has a duty to provide participants with certain information about the plan. [ERISA § 101(a).] Specifically, "[t]he administrator shall furnish to each participant . . . a copy of the summary plan description . . . within 90 days after he becomes a participant . . . ." [ERISA § 104(b)(1).] A summary plan description must include information such as the name and type of plan, the plan's requirements with respect to eligibility for participation and benefits, and circumstances that may result in disqualification, ineligibility, or denial or loss of benefits. [ERISA § 102.] Simeon qualified as an ERISA "participant," which ERISA defines as "any employee or former employee of an employer . . . who is or may become eligible to receive a benefit of any type from an employee benefit plan which covers employees of such employer or members of such organization . . . ." [ERISA § 3(7)], in July 1994 when she became an employee of Mount Sinai and was eligible to join the Plan. Thus, she was entitled to a summary plan description within 90 days of the date in July 1994 that she became a participant.

When ERISA requires a plan administrator to furnish certain materials to a participant or beneficiary:

> the plan administrator shall use measures reasonably calculated to ensure actual receipt of the material by plan participants and beneficiaries. Material which is required to be furnished to all participants covered under the plan . . . must be sent by a method or methods of delivery likely to result in full distribution . . . . Material distributed through the mail may be sent by first, second, or third-class mail . . . . Any material sent by second or third-class mail which is returned with an address correction shall be sent again by first-class mail or personally delivered to the participant at his or her worksite. 29 C.F.R. § 2520.104b-1(b)(1) . . . .

[The certified letter sent on August 15, 1994, and other document] that were submitted in support of the defendants' motion to dismiss do not establish that the defendants satisfied their duties under ERISA. ERISA not only requires that notice be reasonably calculated to reach the participant but also requires that the participant receive a copy of the summary plan description. The failure to provide participants with a Plan description in violation of a statutory obligation can support a breach of fiduciary duty claim. The certified letter dated August 15, 1994, contains some description of the Plan including Mount Sinai's 10% contribution and informs the participant to attend a 45 minute enrollment session in order to receive a detailed description of the Plan; enrollment was required by September 23, 1994. It is only at the enrollment session that details of the Plan, including information about the participant's rights, investment options, and tax benefits are explained. The certified letter of August 15, 1994 is therefore not a summary plan description. *See, e.g., Gridley v. Cleveland Pneumatic Co.*, 924 F.2d 1310, 1316–18 (3d Cir. 1991) (holding that overview brochure was not a summary plan description). The contents of the mailing are important because the full summary plan description would contain greater information about the benefits of enrollment in the Plan than a brief letter stating that the employee has an option of affirmatively enrolling in the Plan. The letter does note that it included enclosures but there is no way on this motion of determining what those enclosures were or what information they provided. The papers submitted by the defendants do not establish that they met their statutory obligations to send the plaintiff a summary plan description.

The defendants claimed at oral argument that they cannot be liable under [ERISA § 502(a)(3)] even if they failed to send the plaintiff a copy of the summary plan description because [ERISA § 502(c)(1)] provides a specific penalty for failing to provide a summary plan description upon request, which would preclude granting further equitable relief because any further relief would not be "appropriate equitable relief." *See Varity Corp. v. Howe*, 516 U.S. 489, 515 (1996). This argument is without merit. The claim is not that the defendants failed to respond to a request for a summary plan description. The defendants are obligated to provide the summary plan description within 90 days even without a request under [ERISA § 104(b)(1)]. There is no specific provision providing specific relief for a violation of this duty. Therefore, there is nothing that precludes equitable relief for a violation of [ERISA § 104(b)(1)].

The defendants also argued that the failure to provide a summary plan description is only a "technical violation" under *Andersen v. Chrysler Corp.*, 99 F.3d 846, 859 (7th Cir. 1996) . . . . In this case, the claim is that no summary plan description was furnished and it is simply not possible on this motion to dismiss to determine what information was provided. The defendants' interpretation contradicts language by the Court of Appeals for the Second Circuit that the failure to provide a plan description can breach statutory and fiduciary duties. *See Lee v. Burkhart*, 991 F.2d at 1011. The failure to provide a summary plan description is not merely a technical violation.

Moreover, it cannot be decided on this motion whether the defendants satisfied their fiduciary duties by allegedly sending one certified letter to a participant and obtaining no response in light of the fact that the Plan requires the participants affirmatively to opt into the Plan and when it appears that the employer was prepared to make a substantial contribution to the Plan.

Therefore, the defendants have not established that the plaintiff can prove no set of facts in support of her claim that would entitle her to relief. The defendants' motion to dismiss is therefore denied . . . .

4-1 QUESTIONS AND PROBLEMS

1. Absent the reporting and disclosure requirements, why might an employer not inform all of its employees about its employee benefit plans?
2. What is the purpose of an SPD? Why didn't the letter qualify as an SPD?
3. What remedy was the plaintiff seeking?
4. Did the defendants violate ERISA?

[2] Conflict Between Terms of Plan and Summary Plan Description

Employees who want to know about their benefits almost always turn to the SPD. The exception is union members, who may ask their union representative, who in turn may consult union officials familiar with the actual plan language.

Normally, the SPD accurately describes the plan, but what happens if the SPD conflicts with the plan document? The following case addresses that question.

CIGNA CORPORATION v. AMARA (PART II)

131 S. Ct. 1866 (2011)

Justice Breyer delivered the opinion of the Court.

[In 1998 CIGNA converted its final average pay defined benefit plan into a cash balance plan. The accrued benefits of participants under the final average pay plan were converted into cash balance benefits with participants being provided the greater of their final average pay benefit or their cash balance benefit, sometimes referred to as a "greater of A and B" benefit. As a result, some plan participants did not accrue any additional benefits for a period of time - until their cash balance benefit exceeded their final average pay benefit. The district court found that CIGNA's descriptions of the new plan were incomplete and misleading and that plan participants who read the descriptions believed that their benefit under the converted plan was equal to the value of their final average pay benefit plus additional accruals under the cash balance plan, sometimes referred to as an "A plus B" benefit.]

* * *

The District Court concluded, as a matter of law, that CIGNA's representations (and omissions) about the plan, made between November 1997 (when it announced the plan) and December 1998 (when it put the plan into effect) violated:

* * *

> (b) ERISA §§ 102(a) and 104(b), which require a plan administrator to provide beneficiaries with summary plan descriptions and with summaries of material modifications, "written in a manner calculated to be understood by the average plan participant," that are "sufficiently accurate and comprehensive to reasonably apprise such participants and beneficiaries of their rights and obligations under the plan."

* * *

II

* * *

A

The District Court ordered relief in two steps. Step 1: It ordered the terms of the plan reformed (so that they provided an "A plus B," rather than a "greater of A or B" guarantee). Step 2: It ordered the plan administrator (which it found to be CIGNA) to enforce the plan as reformed. One can fairly describe step 2 as consistent with § 502(a)(1)(B), for that provision grants a participant the right to bring a civil action to "recover benefits due . . . under the terms of his plan." And step 2 orders recovery of the benefits provided by the "terms of [the] plan" as reformed.

But what about step 1? Where does § 502(a)(1)(B) grant a court the power to change the terms of the plan as they previously existed? The statutory language speaks of "enforc[ing] " the "terms of the plan," not of changing them. The provision allows a court to look outside the plan's written language in deciding what those terms are, i.e., what the language means. See UNUM Life Ins. Co. of America v. Ward, 526 U.S. 358, 377-379 (1999) (permitting the insurance terms of an ERISA-governed plan to be interpreted in light of state insurance rules). But we have found nothing suggesting that the provision authorizes a court to alter those terms, at least not in present circumstances, where that change, akin to the reform of a contract, seems less like the simple enforcement of a contract as written and more like an equitable remedy.

Nor can we accept the Solicitor General's alternative rationale seeking to justify the use of this provision. The Solicitor General says that the District Court did enforce the plan's terms as written, adding that the "plan" includes the disclosures that constituted the summary plan descriptions. In other words, in the view of the Solicitor General, the terms of the summaries are terms of the plan.

Even if the District Court had viewed the summaries as plan "terms" (which it did not), however, we cannot agree that the terms of statutorily required plan summaries (or summaries of plan modifications) necessarily may be enforced (under § 502(a)(1)(B)) as the terms of the plan itself. For one thing, it is difficult to square the Solicitor General's reading of the statute with ERISA § 102(a), the provision that obliges plan administrators to furnish summary plan descriptions. The syntax of that provision, requiring that participants and beneficiaries be advised of their rights and obligations "under the plan," suggests that the information about the plan provided by those disclosures is not itself part of the plan. Nothing in § 502(a)(1)(B) (or, as far as we can tell, anywhere else) suggests the contrary.

Nor do we find it easy to square the Solicitor General's reading with the statute's division of authority between a plan's sponsor and the plan's administrator. The plan's sponsor (e.g., the employer), like a trust's settlor, creates the basic terms and conditions of the plan, executes a written instrument containing those terms and conditions, and provides in that instrument "a procedure" for making amendments. ERISA § 402. The plan's administrator, a trustee-like fiduciary, manages the plan, follows its terms in doing so, and provides participants with the summary documents that describe the plan (and modifications) in readily understandable form. §§ 3(21)(A), 101(a), 102, 104. Here, the District Court found that the same entity, CIGNA, filled both roles. But that is not always the case. Regardless, we have found that ERISA carefully distinguishes these roles. See, e.g., Varity Corp., 516 U.S., at 498. And we have no reason to believe that the statute intends to mix the responsibilities by giving the administrator the power to set plan terms indirectly by including them in the summary plan descriptions. See Curtiss-Wright Corp. v. Schoonejongen, 514 U.S. 73, 81-85 (1995).

Finally, we find it difficult to reconcile the Solicitor General's interpretation with the basic summary plan description objective: clear, simple communication. See ERISA § 102(a). To make the language of a plan summary legally binding could well lead plan administrators to sacrifice simplicity and comprehensibility in order to describe plan terms in the language of lawyers. Consider the difference between a will and the summary of a will or between a property deed and its summary. Consider, too, the length of Part I of this opinion, and then consider how much longer Part I would have to be if we had to include all the qualifications and nuances that a plan drafter might have found important and feared to omit lest they lose all legal significance. The District Court's opinions take up 109 pages of the Federal Supplement. None of this is to say that plan administrators can avoid providing complete and accurate summaries of plan terms in the manner required by ERISA and its implementing regulations. But we fear that the Solicitor General's rule might bring about complexity that would defeat the fundamental purpose of the summaries.

For these reasons taken together we conclude that the summary documents, important as they are, provide communication with beneficiaries about the plan, but that their statements do not themselves constitute the terms of the plan for purposes of § 502(a)(1)(B). We also conclude that the District Court could not find authority in that section to reform CIGNA's plan as written.

* * *

III

Section 502(a)(3) invokes the equitable powers of the District Court. We cannot know with certainty which remedy the District Court understood itself to be imposing, nor whether the District Court will find it appropriate to exercise its discretion under § 502(a)(3) to impose that remedy on remand. We need not decide which remedies are appropriate on the facts of this case in order to resolve the parties' dispute as to the appropriate legal standard in determining whether members of the relevant employee class were injured.

The relevant substantive provisions of ERISA do not set forth any particular standard for determining harm. They simply require the plan administrator to write and to distribute written notices that are "sufficiently accurate and comprehensive to reasonably apprise" plan participants and beneficiaries of "their rights and obligations under the plan." ERISA § 102(a); see also ERISA §§ 104(b), 204(h). Nor can we find a definite standard in the ERISA provision, § 502(a)(3) (which authorizes the court to enter "appropriate equitable relief" to redress ERISA "violations"). Hence any requirement of harm must come from the law of equity.

Looking to the law of equity, there is no general principle that "detrimental reliance" must be proved before a remedy is decreed. To the extent any such requirement arises, it is because the specific remedy being contemplated imposes such a requirement. Thus, as CIGNA points out, when equity courts used the remedy of estoppel, they insisted upon a showing akin to detrimental reliance, i.e., that the defendant's statement "in truth, influenced the conduct of" the plaintiff, causing "prejudic[e]." Eaton § 61, at 175; see 3 Pomeroy § 805. Accordingly, when a court exercises its authority under § 502(a)(3) to impose a remedy equivalent to estoppel, a showing of detrimental reliance must be made.

But this showing is not always necessary for other equitable remedies. Equity courts, for example, would reform contracts to reflect the mutual understanding of the contracting parties where "fraudulent suppression[s], omission[s], or insertion[s]," 1 Story § 154, at 149, "material[ly] . . . affect[ed]" the "substance" of the contract, even if the "complaining part[y]" was negligent in not realizing its mistake, as long as its negligence did not fall below a standard of "reasonable prudence" and violate a legal duty. 3 Pomeroy §§ 856, 856b, at 334, 340-341; see Baltzer, 115 U.S., at 645; Eaton § 307(b).

Nor did equity courts insist upon a showing of detrimental reliance in cases where they ordered "surcharge." Rather, they simply ordered a trust or beneficiary made whole following a trustee's breach of trust. In such instances equity courts would "mold the relief to protect the rights of the beneficiary according to the situation involved." Bogert § 861, at 4. This flexible approach belies a strict requirement of "detrimental reliance."

To be sure, just as a court of equity would not surcharge a trustee for a nonexistent harm, 4 Scott & Ascher § 24.9, a fiduciary can be surcharged under § 502(a)(3) only upon a showing of actual harm-proved (under the default rule for civil cases) by a preponderance of the evidence. That actual harm may sometimes consist of detrimental reliance, but it might also come from the loss of a right protected by ERISA or its trust-law antecedents. In the present case, it is not difficult to imagine how the failure to provide proper summary information, in violation of the statute, injured employees even if they did not themselves act in reliance on summary documents-which they might not themselves have seen-for they may have thought fellow employees, or informal workplace discussion, would have let them know if, say, plan changes would likely prove harmful. We doubt that Congress would have wanted to bar those employees from relief.

The upshot is that we can agree with CIGNA only to a limited extent. We believe that, to obtain relief by surcharge for violations of §§ 102(a) and 104(b), a plan participant or beneficiary must show that the violation injured him or her. But to do so, he or she need only show harm and causation. Although it is not always necessary to meet the more rigorous standard implicit in the words "detrimental reliance," actual harm must be shown.

We are not asked to reassess the evidence. And we are not asked about the other prerequisites for relief. We are asked about the standard of prejudice. And we conclude that the standard of prejudice must be borrowed from equitable principles, as modified by the obligations and injuries identified by ERISA itself. Information-related circumstances, violations, and injuries are potentially too various in nature to insist that harm must always meet that more vigorous "detrimental harm" standard when equity imposed no such strict requirement.

IV

We have premised our discussion in Part III on the need for the District Court to revisit its determination of an appropriate remedy for the violations of ERISA it identified. Whether or not the general principles we have discussed above are properly applicable in this case is for it or the Court of Appeals to determine in the first instance. Because the District Court has not determined if an appropriate remedy may be imposed under § 502(a)(3), we must vacate the judgment below and remand this case for further proceedings consistent with this opinion.

It is so ordered.

Justice SOTOMAYOR took no part in the consideration or decision of this case.

Justice SCALIA, with whom Justice THOMAS joins, concurring in the judgment.

I agree with the Court that § 502(a)(1)(B) of ERISA does not authorize relief for misrepresentations in a summary plan description (SPD). I do not join the Court's opinion because I see no need and no justification for saying anything more than that.

Section 502(a)(1)(B) of ERISA states that a plan participant or beneficiary may bring a civil action "to recover benefits due to him under the terms of his plan, to enforce his rights under the terms of the plan, or to clarify his rights to future benefits under the terms of the plan." ERISA defines the word "plan" as "an employee welfare benefit plan or an employee pension benefit plan or a plan which is both," ERISA § 3(3), and it requires that a "plan" "be established and maintained pursuant to a written instrument," § 402(a)(1). An SPD, in contrast, is a disclosure meant "to reasonably apprise [plan] participants and beneficiaries of their rights and obligations under the plan." § 102(a). It would be peculiar for a document meant to "apprise" participants of their rights "under the plan" to be itself part of the "plan." Any doubt that it is not is eliminated by ERISA's repeated differentiation of SPDs from the "written instruments" that constitute a plan, see, e.g., §§ 109(c), 104(b)(2) and ERISA's assignment to different entities of responsibility for drafting and amending SPDs on the one hand and plans on the other, see ERISA §§ 3(1), (2)(A); 104(b)(1); Beck v. PACE Int'l Union, 551 U.S. 96, 101, (2007). An SPD, moreover, would not fulfill its purpose of providing an easily accessible summary of the plan if it were an authoritative part of the plan itself; the minor omissions appropriate for a summary would risk revising the plan.

Nothing else needs to be said to dispose of this case. The District Court based the relief it awarded upon ERISA § 502(a)(1)(B), and that provision alone. It thought that the "benefits" due "under the terms of the plan," ERISA § 502(a)(1)(B), could derive from an SPD, either because the SPD is part of the plan or because it is capable of somehow modifying the plan. Under either justification, that conclusion is wrong. An SPD is separate from a plan, and cannot amend a plan unless the plan so provides. See Curtiss-Wright Corp. v. Schoonejongen, 514 U.S. 73, 79, 85 (1995). I would go no further.

* * *

I agree with the Court that an SPD is not part of an ERISA plan, and that, as a result, a plan participant or beneficiary may not recover for misrepresentations in an SPD under § 502(a)(1)(B). Because this is the only question properly presented for our review, and the only question briefed and argued before us, I concur only in the judgment.

4-2 QUESTIONS AND PROBLEMS

1. Which is the plan participant more likely to see, the SPD or the plan document?

2. How easy is it to draft an SPD that accurately reflects the terms of the plan yet is written in language that is "calculated to be understood by the average plan participant."

3. Prior to the Court's decision in *Amara*, many lower courts held that when the terms of an SPD conflicted with the terms of the plan, the participant was entitled to enforce the terms of the SPD if they were more favorable. Under *Amara*, which terms control in the case of a conflict? Why? What remedy, if any, is a plan participant entitled to in the case of a conflict?

4. Health and welfare benefit plans often use SPDs as plan documents or incorporate SPDs into plan documents by reference under the terms of a "wrap plan." After *Amara*, can a single document serve as both the plan and the SPD?

B. PENSION BENEFIT SECURITY RULES

In enacting ERISA, Congress found, among other things, that "many employees with long years of employment are losing anticipated retirement benefits owing to the lack of vesting provisions in such plans." ERISA § 2(a). In order to reduce the number of employees losing expected pension benefits, ERISA instituted detailed rules regarding vesting, participation, and benefit accrual. These rules, contained in

Title I of ERISA, are duplicated in the Internal Revenue Code as qualification requirements. They only apply to pension plans; they do not apply to welfare benefit plans.

The vesting rules require that benefits become vested, i.e., nonforfeitable, after a prescribed number of years of service with the employer. The participation rules dictate when an employee must become eligible to participate in the plan, and the benefit accrual rules regulate how pension benefits are earned.

The following example illustrates the differences between vesting, participation, and benefit accrual. The Alpha Pension Plan provides that employees may begin to participate in the plan after one year of service, that benefits will be fully vested after three years of service, and that participants will receive an annual benefit at normal retirement age equal to two percent per year of participation multiplied by the employee's average annual salary over the final three years of employment. Ariel, an Alpha employee, joins the Alpha Company on July 1, 2012. She will be eligible to participate (and thus earn benefits) in the Alpha Pension Plan on July 1, 2013. On July 1, 2015, after three years of service, she will be fully vested in the plan, and thus will have the right to receive her accrued benefit at the normal retirement age, even if she quits Alpha Company before then. On July 1, 2017, after having participated in the plan for four years, her annual accrued benefit (the amount receivable at normal retirement age) will equal eight percent (two percent per year for four years) multiplied by her average annual salary over the final three years of her employment.

This example also illustrates why regulation of vesting also requires regulation of participation and benefit accruals. Suppose that ERISA only imposed a three year cliff vesting rule; that is, it required that benefits be nonforfeitable after three years of service. If ERISA did not also regulate participation and benefit accruals, an employer could evade the purpose of the vesting rules by providing that an employee could not participate in the plan until the employee had thirty years of service with the employer or by providing that benefits would accrue at the rate of 0 percent per year for the first 29 years of service and 60 percent of the employee's average annual salary over the final three years of employment for the 30th year of service.

4-3 QUESTIONS AND PROBLEMS

1. Why don't the vesting, participation, and benefit accrual rules apply to welfare benefit plans?

2. Are the pension benefit security rules necessary in a tight labor market? Why can't employees just bargain for appropriate protection?

3. Do the pension benefit security rules discourage employers from offering pension plans?

[1] Vesting

ERISA § 203, IRC § 411(a).

> Prior to the enactment of [ERISA] many employee retirement plans lacked any concept of vesting. Employers were free to discontinue the plans at any time, and even long-term employees on the verge of retirement often had no enforceable pension claims. Plans that included vesting provisions tended to make the required service periods so long, and

disqualifying events so numerous, that very few participants — fewer than 10% — ever attained benefit eligibility. Mary E. O'Connell, *On the Fringe: Rethinking the Link Between Wages and Benefits*, 67 Tul. L. Rev. 1422, 1454–55 (1993).

ERISA's vesting rules dramatically altered this landscape by imposing minimum vesting requirements. Benefits derived from an employee's own contributions must be immediately fully vested. ERISA § 203(a)(1); IRC § 411(a)(1). The vesting rules for benefits attributable to employer contributions depend on the type of plan.Benefits attributable to employer contributions to defined benefit plans must satisfy one of two alternative vesting schedules. Under the first, the so-called cliff vesting schedule, an employee must be fully vested in benefits attributable to employer contributions after five years of service. ERISA § 203(a)(2)(A)(ii); IRC § 411(a)(2)(A)(ii). Under the alternative, graded vesting schedule, an employee's benefit attributable to employer contributions must begin to vest after three years of service and be fully vested after seven years of service according to the following schedule:

Years of Service	Nonforfeitable percentage
3	20
4	40
5	60
6	80
7 or more	100

ERISA § 203(a)(2)(A)(iii); IRC § 411(a)(2)(A)(iii).

Benefits attributable to employer contributions to defined contribution plans must either fully vest after three years of service, ERISA § 203(a)(2)(B)(ii); IRC § 411(a)(B)(ii), or begin to vest after two years of service and be fully vested after six years of service, ERISA § 203(a)(2)(b)(iii); IRC § 411(a)(2)(B)(iii), according to the following schedule:

Years of Service	Nonforfeitable percentage
2	20
3	40
4	60
5	80
6 or more	100

Note that the vesting rules are based on years of service, not participation, although certain types of service may be excluded. *See* ERISA § 203(b)(1); IRC § 411(a)(4). Of course, neither ERISA nor the Internal Revenue Code prevent a plan from providing a more generous vesting schedule. Thus, a plan may provide that benefits attributable to employer contributions will be fully vested after two years of service.

To illustrate the vesting rules, suppose that Beta Company has a profit-sharing plan with a 401(k) feature. The profit-sharing plan provides that Beta Company will contribute 2 percent of pay on behalf of each employee each year. In addition, the plan authorizes employees to contribute up to an additional 4 percent of pay each year and provides for employer matching contributions equal to 100 percent of each employee's elective contribution. The plan uses a three year cliff vesting schedule for employer contributions. In 2012, Barry, a new Beta employee, earns $50,000 and elects to contribute 4 percent of his pay (or $2,000) to the plan. Barry will be credited with a total of $5,000 for the year (a 2 percent or $1,000 regular employer contribution, a 4 percent or $2,000 employee elective contribution, and a 4 percent or $2,000 employer matching contribution). Barry's $2,000 elective contribution will be immediately fully vested. Beta Company's $1,000 regular contribution and $2,000 matching contribution will be fully vested after three years. Thus, if Barry leaves after two years of service, he will not lose his $2,000 elective contribution, but he will forfeit the $3,000 Beta contributed on his behalf. If he leaves after three or more years of service, he will be entitled to the entire $5,000 contribution made on his behalf in 2012.

In the case of a defined contribution plan, forfeitures may be used to reduce future employer contributions or administrative expenses or may be reallocated to the account balances of the remaining participants to increase their benefits. In the case of a qualified defined benefit plan, forfeitures may only be used to reduce future employer contributions or administrative expenses. They may not be used to increase the benefits of the remaining participants. IRC § 401(a)(8).

In addition to the basic vesting rules, ERISA requires that pension plans provide that an employee's right to his normal retirement benefit be nonforfeitable upon the attainment of the normal retirement age (NRA). ERISA § 203(a); IRC § 411(a). If, for example, a plan has a normal retirement age of 65, all participants who reach 65 must be fully vested in their retirement benefit regardless of how many years they have worked for the company.

4-4 QUESTIONS AND PROBLEMS

1. Gamma Enterprises, a non-unionized company with no part-time employees, is considering adopting one of the following profit-sharing plans for the benefit of all of its employees. Which plan or plans, if any, satisfy the minimum vesting requirements of ERISA § 203(a)? Assume that none of the plans provide for employer matching contributions.

a. Plan I provides that employees are eligible to participate after the completion of one year of service and an employee's accrued benefit derived from employer contributions is 100 percent nonforfeitable after three years of service. Prior to that, the employee's accrued benefit derived from employer contributions is completely forfeitable.

b. Plan II is identical to Plan I except that it provides that an employee's accrued benefit derived from employer contributions is 100 percent nonforfeitable after three years of participation in the plan, rather than three years of service with the employer.

c. Plan III provides that employees are eligible to participate after one year of service and contains the following vesting schedule for accrued benefits derived from employer contributions:

Years of Service	Nonforfeitable Percentage
1	10
2	20
3 or more	100

d. Plan IV provides that employees are eligible to participate after six months of service and contains the following vesting schedule for accrued benefits derived from employer contributions:

Years of Service	Nonforfeitable Percentage
1	10
2	20
3	40
4	50
5	75
6 or more	100

e. Plan VI provides that employees are eligible to participate after one year of service and participants have a vested right to the greater of:

1) A percentage of the participant's entire account balance (including benefits derived from the employee's own contributions) determined in accordance with the following schedule:

Years of Service	Nonforfeitable Percentage
2	20
3	40
4	60
5	80
6 or more	100

or,

2) 100 percent of the portion of the participant's account balance that was derived from the employee's own contributions.

2. Would the answers to question 1 be different if the plan were a defined benefit plan?

3. Why is there a faster vesting schedule for defined contribution plans than for defined benefit plans?

4. Why doesn't ERISA require immediate full vesting of accrued benefits derived from employer contributions?

5. Delta Corporation suffers from a high turnover rate and would like to establish a retirement plan to encourage longevity, reward longer service, and minimize costs. Which vesting schedule should Delta Corporation use and why?

6. The Epsilon Profit-Sharing Plan provides that an employee is fully vested in his or her employer-derived accrued benefit after the completion of three years of service. The plan further states an employee who works for a competitor forfeits all of his or her rights in the plan. Does the plan satisfy ERISA's vesting requirements? What if the plan limited forfeitures to employees who completed less than three years of service?

[2] Additional Vesting Rules for Qualified Plans

Section 416 of the Internal Revenue Code imposes accelerated vesting requirements, like the vesting schedules applicable to defined contribution plans, on top-heavy plans. IRC § 416(b)(1). Top-heavy plans are plans for which 60 percent or more of benefits or contributions are held for the benefit of key employees. IRC § 416(g)(1)(A). Key employees are defined as: 1) officers with compensation in excess of $130,000, as adjusted for inflation; 2) 5 percent owners; and 3) 1 percent owners who receive compensation in excess of $150,000. IRC

§ 416(i)(1)(A). In 2012, the IRC § 416(i)(1)(A)(i) threshold, as adjusted for inflation, is $165,000.

Section 411(d)(3) of the Internal Revenue Code adds a special vesting requirement for qualified plans. It requires that upon plan termination, all employees become fully vested in their plan benefits "to the extent funded." This special vesting rule also applies in the event that there is a "partial termination" of a qualified plan. This special vesting rule is discussed in more detail in Chapter 10.

[3] Minimum Age and Service Requirements

ERISA § 202; IRC § 410.

Prior to the enactment of ERISA, retirement plans often required that employees satisfy long periods of continuous service before they were eligible to participate in the plan. For example, plans typically required that employees be continuously employed for five years before they were eligible to participate in the plan. Moreover, many plans did not permit employees to participate in the plan if they had reached a specific age, such as 55, before they were eligible to participate in the plan. Thus, employees hired at or after age 50 could be permanently excluded from participation in the plan if the plan imposed a five year service requirement.

ERISA changed the law by limiting the minimum age and service requirements. ERISA generally requires that a pension plan permit an employee to participate once the employee has reached age 21 or completed one year of service, whichever occurs later. Alternatively, a plan (other than a 401(k) plan) may impose a 2 years of service requirement if benefits are immediately fully vested. In addition, tax exempt educational institutions may set age 26 as the minimum participation age if the plan provides immediate, full vesting. ERISA § 202(a)(1); IRC § 410(a)(1).

ERISA and its regulations contain lengthy rules defining years and hours of service and regulating breaks in service. *See, e.g.*, ERISA §§ 202(a)(3), 202(a)(4); IRC §§ 410(a)(3), 410(a)(4); DOL Reg. §§ 2530.200b-2 and 2530.200b-4 and Treas. Reg. §§ 1.410(a)-5 and 1.410(a)-7. For administrative ease, ERISA permits employers to delay the employee's "entry date" until the earlier of the first day of the plan year beginning after the employee satisfies the minimum age and service requirements or six months after the employee satisfies these requirements. ERISA § 202(a)(4); IRC § 410(a)(4).

In addition to the minimum age and service requirements, ERISA also prohibits plans from establishing a maximum age for participation. ERISA § 202(a)(2); IRC § 410(a)(2). Employees who elect to continue working past the plan's normal retirement age must continue to accrue benefits.

4-5 QUESTIONS AND PROBLEMS

1. The Zeta Corporation Pension Plan provides that an employee will be eligible to participate in the plan once the employee has both: (i) completed six months of service, and (ii) attained age 21. The plan further provides that participants will be fully vested after 4 years of service. Does the plan satisfy ERISA's minimum age and participation requirements?

2. The Eta Corporation Profit Sharing Plan provides than an employee will be eligible to participate in the plan once the employee has completed one year of service, and that participants will be fully vested after three years of service.

Courtney was hired on June 1, 2012, when she was 19 years of age. When will she be eligible to participate in the Eta Corporation Profit Sharing Plan?

3. Private University, a tax exempt educational institution, offers a defined contribution plan that sets 25 as the minimum participation age and provides 100 percent vesting after three years of service. Does Private University's plan satisfy ERISA's minimum age and service requirements?

4. Why does ERISA permit employers to exclude all workers under age 21 from participating in a plan regardless of how many years they have worked for the employer?

5. What types of employers would likely elect to offer immediate full vesting and impose a two-year period of service requirement on participation?

[4] Benefit Accrual Rules

ERISA § 204; IRC § 411(b).

Benefit accrual refers to the rate at which participants accumulate benefits under a plan. In a defined contribution plan, a participant's accrued benefit is the participant's individual account balance. ERISA § 3(23)(B); IRC § 411(a)(7)(A)(ii). In a defined benefit plan, the participant's accrued benefit is expressed in the form of an annual benefit commencing at normal retirement age. ERISA § 3(23)(A). For example, an accrued benefit might read: "Upon reaching the normal retirement age of 65, an employee who has been a plan participant for 25 years is eligible for retirement benefits equal to 50 percent of his or her average wages for the three years prior to retirement."

EDWARD A. ZELINSKY, THE CASH BALANCE CONTROVERSY

19 VA. TAX REV. 683, 719–721 (2000)

In essentially identical terms, the Code and ERISA regulate the rate at which participants earn their retirement entitlements under defined benefit arrangements. The purpose of these provisions is to prevent excessive backloading (i.e. postponing) of accrued benefits. As we have seen, a certain amount of backloading is inherent in conventional defined benefit arrangements. Older participants tend to earn more of their traditional annuity-type benefits in their later years because these are their years of highest salary and greatest seniority as well as years proximate to retirement. On the other hand, the Code and ERISA preclude more egregious forms of backloading.

Consider, in this context, the extreme (but heuristically useful) possibility that a defined benefit plan would provide an annuity at retirement equal to fifty percent of the employee's final average salary, but that the benefit would accrue at the rate of one dollar per year of service until age sixty-five when the entire remaining balance of the benefit would be earned in one fell swoop. Suppose further that a sixty-four year-old employee has been making $40,000 per year, has twenty years of service, and terminates her employment one year short of the normal retirement age of sixty-five.

In this theoretical circumstance, the employee undoubtedly (and quite reasonably) expects a retirement benefit in the vicinity of $20,000 annually, discounted for the year she quit early. However, if the plan is permitted to accrue benefits at the rate of one dollar per year until retirement, this employee is instead entitled to only twenty dollars annually, one dollar for each year worked. Only with the final year of participation would the employee have actually earned the benefit based on her final average salary.

One way of understanding this example is that the plan's hypothetical accrued benefit formula emasculates the vesting schedules promulgated in the Code and ERISA. This theoretical employee has a fully nonforfeitable interest in the pension benefit she earned through age sixty-four. However, that interest is de minimis since the pattern of benefit accrual effectively postpones the participant's opportunity to earn her benefit until her last year of employment. To prevent this evisceration of the vesting rules, the Code and ERISA regulate the minimum pace at which defined benefit plans must permit participants to earn their benefits and thereby preclude excessive backloading.

ERISA and the Internal Revenue Code require that defined benefit plans satisfy one of three alternative benefit accrual schedules. Those schedules are: 1) the 3 percent method, 2) the 133⅓ percent method, and 3) the fractional method.

The 3 percent method measures the accrual of benefits for plan participants against the maximum accrual that participants might expect if they continued to participate until the actual retirement age. The 3 percent method requires that the accrued benefit be no less than 3 percent of the pension the employee would receive at normal retirement age if he or she joined the plan at the youngest possible age and remained in covered service until the earlier of age 65 or the normal retirement age multiplied by the employee's actual years of participation in the plan, but not to exceed 33⅓ years. ERISA § 204(b)(1)(A); IRC § 411(b)(1)(A). To apply the 3 percent method, first determine the amount a participant could theoretically accrue under the plan if the participant entered the plan at the earliest possible entry date and remained in the plan until the earlier of the normal retirement age or 65. Once the theoretical maximum accrued benefit is determined, calculate 3 percent of that benefit. Finally, compare that 3 percent figure with the benefit, at any given time, to which the participant is entitled. With limited exceptions, a participant must, at any given time, have an accrued benefit equal to at least the three percent figure times the participant's years of service.

For example, suppose that a defined benefit plan provides an annual retirement benefit commencing at age 65 equal to $200 for each year of participation, imposes a minimum age requirement of 25, and provides for no limit on the number of years of credited service. To determine whether the plan satisfies the 3 percent method for a plan participant Daniel, age 40, who has participated in the plan for five years, first determine the maximum amount Daniel could theoretically accrue under the plan if he entered on the earliest possible entry date (age 25) and remained until the plan's normal retirement age 65, which is $200 × (65-25), or $8,000. Then calculate 3 percent of that theoretical maximum benefit, which is 3% × $8,000 or $240. Finally, compare the three percent figure with the benefit to which David is entitled. Since David's benefit (5 × $200) or $1,000, is less than the 3 percent figure times David's years of service (5 × $240), or $1,200, the plan does not satisfy the 3 percent method.

If, on the other hand, the plan were only to take the first 30 years of participation into account, the plan would satisfy the 3 percent method. For example, first, the theoretical maximum amount David could accrue under the plan if he entered at the earliest entry day (25) and remained until the plan's normal retirement age of 65 is 30 × $200, or $6,000. Three percent of the $6,000 theoretical maximum benefit is $180. Since David's benefit (5 × $200), or $1000, is more than the 3 percent figure times his years of service (5 × $180), or $900, the plan satisfies the 3 percent method.

The 133⅓ percent method measures a plan's benefit accrual rate in a given year against the benefit accrual rate for all subsequent years. Under the 133⅓ percent method, (a) the plan's accrued benefit at normal retirement age must equal the plan's normal retirement benefit, and (b) the annual rate at which any individual who is, or could be, a participant can accrue the retirement benefit payable at normal retirement age must not be more than 133⅓ percent of the annual rate at which the participant can accrue benefits in any prior plan year. ERISA § 204(b)(1)(B); IRC § 411(b)(1)(B).

For example, suppose that a plan provides that in the first 10 years of service an employee will accrue benefits at an annual rate of 2 percent of compensation, for the second 10 years of participation, the employee will accrue benefits at the rate of 2½ percent of compensation, and for the following five years of participation, the employee will accrue benefits at the rate of 3 percent of compensation, with a maximum of 25 years of participation taken into account in calculating benefits. In addition, the accrued benefits payable at normal retirement age are equal to the normal retirement benefit. Although benefit accruals in years 11–20 (2½ percent) are not more than 133⅓ percent (specifically 125 percent) of benefit accrual accruals in years 1-10 (2 percent), the plan does not satisfy the 133⅓ percent method because benefit accruals in years 21–25 (3 percent) are more than 133⅓ percent (specifically 150 percent) of the benefit accruals in years 1–10.

Under the fractional method, the annual benefit to which a participant is entitled if the participant separates from service before reaching the plan's normal retirement age must be at least a ratable portion of the benefit that the participant would have earned under the plan had the participant worked until normal retirement age, considering the number of actual years of participation and the total years the participant could have been expected to participate if the participant had not terminated employment before the normal retirement age. ERISA § 204(b)(1)(C); IRC § 411(b)(1)(C). The fraction may described as follows:

$$\text{Annual benefit to which entitled on separation} = \text{Annual benefit commencing at normal retirement age to which would have been entitled} \times \frac{\text{Total years of participation}}{\text{Total years would have participated if had terminated at normal retirement age}}$$

For example, suppose that an employee who has participated in a plan for 10 years terminates at age 50. If the annual retirement benefit commencing at normal retirement age 65 would have been $5,000, the employee must be entitled to an annual benefit of at least $2,000 to satisfy the fractional method. The following fraction illustrates that requirement:

$$\text{Annual benefit required by fractional method } (\$2{,}000) = \$5{,}000 \times \frac{10}{25}$$

The following sample plan language is designed to satisfy the fractional benefit rule:

> Section 4.2 Accrued Benefit if Terminated Prior to Normal Retirement Age.
>
> If a Participant's employment is terminated prior to Normal Retirement Age, the Accrued Benefit shall be the benefit the Participant would have received in accordance with Section 4.1 multiplied by the following fraction

and subject to the provisions of Article VIII (Vesting) and IX (Distribution of Benefits): The numerator of the fraction is the number of Years of Service for Accrual of Benefits a Participant has as of his Termination Date; the denominator is the number of Years of Service for Accrual of Benefits a Participant would have had if he had remained an Employee to his Normal Retirement Age.

4-6 QUESTIONS AND PROBLEMS

1. Why do the three minimum accrual methods set forth in ERISA § 204 and IRC § 411(b) only apply to defined benefit plans, and not to defined contribution plans?

2. Suppose that the Alpha Pension Plan provides an annual retirement benefit commencing at age 65 equal to $100 for each year of participation, provides for no limit on the number of years of credited service, and does not specify a minimum entry age. Does the Alpha plan satisfy the three percent method with respect to Emma, age 45, who began to participate in the plan at age 30?

3. Would the Alpha plan satisfy the three percent method with respect to Emma if the plan were to specify an entry age of 25?

4. Would the Alpha plan satisfy the three percent method if the plan were to specify an entry age of 25 and take a maximum of 32 years of service into account?

5. Suppose that Beta Pension Plan provides that for the first 10 years of service an employee will accrue benefits at an annual rate of 2 percent of compensation, that for the second 10 years of participation, the employee will accrue benefits at the rate of 2¼ percent of compensation, and that for the following 10 years of participation, the employee will accrue benefits at the rate of 2⅓ percent of compensation, with a maximum of 30 years of participation taken into account in calculating benefits. In addition, the accrued benefits payable at normal retirement age are equal to the normal retirement benefit. Does the Beta plan satisfy the 133⅓ percent method?

6. Suppose that the Omega Pension Plan provides that for the first 10 years of service an employee will accrue benefits at an annual rate of 2⅓ percent of compensation, that for the second 10 years of participation, the employee will accrue benefits at the rate of 3 percent of compensation, and that for the following 10 years of participation, the employee will accrue benefits at the rate of 4 percent of compensation, with a maximum of 30 years of participation taken into account in calculating benefits. In addition, the accrued benefits payable at normal retirement age are equal to the normal retirement benefit. Does the Omega plan satisfy the 133⅓ percent method?

7. Suppose that the Theta Pension Plan provides that for the first 10 years of service an employee will accrue benefits at an annual rate of 4 percent of compensation, that for the second 10 years of participation, the employee will accrue benefits at the rate of 3 percent of compensation, and that for the following 10 years of participation, the employee will accrue benefits at the rate of 2 percent of compensation, with a maximum of 30 years of participation taken into account in calculating benefits. In addition, the accrued benefits payable at normal retirement age are equal to the normal retirement benefit. Does the Theta plan satisfy the 133⅓ percent method?

C. ERISA § 510

Section 510 of ERISA prohibits employers from discharging or discriminating against plan participants for exercising their rights under an employee benefit plan or under ERISA. Section 510, which applies to both pension and welfare benefit plans, prohibits two distinct types of acts. First, it prohibits employers (or any other persons) from discharging or in any other way discriminating against plan participants and beneficiaries in retaliation for exercising rights under an employee benefit plan or under the statute. Second, it prohibits "interference with the attainment of any right to which the participant may become entitled."

Should an employer's right to modify or terminate a plan be taken into account in determining the "right[s] to which the participant may become entitled"? The following case addresses that issue.

MCGANN v. H & H MUSIC COMPANY

946 F.2d 401 (5th Cir. 1991)

GARWOOD, CIRCUIT JUDGE.

McGann, an employee of H & H Music, discovered that he was afflicted with AIDS in December 1987. Soon thereafter, McGann submitted his first claims for reimbursement under H & H Music's group medical plan, provided through Brook Mays, the plan administrator, and issued by General American, the plan insurer, and informed his employer that he had AIDS. McGann met with officials of H & H Music in March 1988, at which time they discussed McGann's illness. Before the change in the terms of the plan, it provided for lifetime medical benefits of up to $1,000,000 to all employees.

In July 1988, H & H Music informed its employees that, effective August 1, 1988, changes would be made in their medical coverage. These changes included, but were not limited to, limitation of benefits payable for AIDS-related claims to a lifetime maximum of $5,000. No limitation was placed on any other catastrophic illness. H & H Music became self-insured under the new plan and General American became the plan's administrator. By January 1990, McGann had exhausted the $5,000 limit on coverage for his illness.

In August 1989, McGann sued H & H Music, Brook Mays and General American under section 510 of ERISA . . .

McGann claimed that defendants discriminated against him in violation of both prohibitions of section 510. He claimed that the provision limiting coverage for AIDS-related expenses was directed specifically at him in retaliation for exercising his rights under the medical plan and for the purpose of interfering with his attainment of a right to which he may become entitled under the plan.

Defendants, conceding the factual allegations of McGann's complaint, moved for summary judgment. These factual allegations include no assertion that the reduction of AIDS benefits was intended to deny benefits to McGann for any reason which would not be applicable to other beneficiaries who might then or thereafter have AIDS, but rather that the reduction was prompted by the knowledge of McGann's illness, and that McGann was the only beneficiary then known to have AIDS.[1] On June 26, 1990, the district court granted defendants'

---

[1] We assume, for purposes of this appeal that the defendants' knowledge of McGann's illness was a motivating factor in their decision to reduce coverage for AIDS-related expenses, that this knowledge

motion on the ground that they had an absolute right to alter the terms of the plan, regardless of their intent in making the alterations. The district court also held that even if the issue of discriminatory motive were relevant, summary judgment would still be proper because the defendants' motive was to ensure the future existence of the plan and not specifically to retaliate against McGann or to interfere with his exercise of future rights under the plan.

McGann contends that defendants violated both clauses of section 510 by discriminating against him for two purposes: (1) "for exercising any right to which [the beneficiary] is entitled," and (2) "for the purpose of interfering with the attainment of any right to which such participant may become entitled." In order to preclude summary judgment in defendants' favor, McGann must make a showing sufficient to establish the existence of a genuine issue of material fact with respect to each material element on which he would carry the burden of proof at trial. *Celotex Corp. v. Catrett*, 477 U.S. 317 (1986).

At trial, McGann would bear the burden of proving the existence of defendants' specific discriminatory intent as an essential element of either of his claims . . . . Thus, in order to survive summary judgment McGann must make a showing sufficient to establish that a genuine issue exists as to defendants' specific intent to retaliate against McGann for filing claims for AIDS-related treatment or to interfere with McGann's attainment of any right to which he may have become entitled.

Although we assume there was a connection between the benefits reduction and either McGann's filing of claims or his revelations about his illness, there is nothing in the record to suggest that defendants' motivation was other than as they asserted, namely to avoid the expense of paying for AIDS treatment (if not, indeed, also for other treatment), no more for McGann than for any other present or future plan beneficiary who might suffer from AIDS. McGann concedes that the reduction in AIDS benefits will apply equally to all employees filing AIDS-related claims and that the effect of the reduction will not necessarily be felt only by him. He fails to allege that the coverage reduction was otherwise specifically intended to deny him particularly medical coverage except "in effect." He does not challenge defendants' assertion that their purpose in reducing AIDS benefits was to reduce costs.

Furthermore, McGann has failed to adduce evidence of the existence of "any right to which [he] may become entitled under the plan." The right referred to in the second clause of section 510 is not simply any right to which an employee may conceivably become entitled, but rather any right to which an employee may become entitled pursuant to an existing, enforceable obligation assumed by the employer. "Congress viewed [section 510] as a crucial part of ERISA because, without it, employers would be able to circumvent the provision of *promised* benefits." *Ingersoll-Rand Co. v. McClendon*, 498 U.S. 133 (1990) (emphasis added).

McGann's allegations show no *promised* benefit, for there is nothing to indicate that defendants ever promised that the $1,000,000 coverage limit was permanent. The H & H Music plan expressly provides: "Termination or Amendment of Plan: The Plan Sponsor may terminate or amend the Plan at any time or terminate any benefit under the Plan at any time." There is no allegation or evidence that any oral or written representations were made to McGann that the $1,000,000 coverage limit would never be lowered. Defendants broke no promise to McGann. The continued availability of the $1,000,000 limit was not a right to which McGann may

---

was obtained either through McGann's filing of claims or his meetings with defendants, and that McGann was the only plan beneficiary then known to have AIDS.

have become entitled for the purposes of section 510. To adopt McGann's contrary construction of this portion of section 510 would mean that an employer could not effectively reserve the right to amend a medical plan to reduce benefits respecting subsequently incurred medical expenses, as H & H Music did here, because such an amendment would obviously have as a purpose preventing participants from attaining the right to such future benefits as they otherwise might do under the existing plan absent the amendment. But this is plainly not the law, and ERISA does not require such "vesting" of the right to a continued level of the same medical benefits once those are ever included in a welfare plan. *See Moore v. Metropolitan Life Insurance Co.*, 856 F.2d 488, 492 (2d Cir. 1988).

McGann appears to contend that the reduction in AIDS benefits alone supports an inference of specific intent to retaliate against him or to interfere with his future exercise of rights under the plan. McGann characterizes as evidence of an individualized intent to discriminate the fact that AIDS was the only catastrophic illness to which the $5,000 limit was applied and the fact that McGann was the only employee known to have AIDS. He contends that if defendants reduced AIDS coverage because they learned of McGann's illness through his exercising of his rights under the plan by filing claims, the coverage reduction therefore could be "retaliation" for McGann's filing of the claims.[2] Under McGann's theory, any reduction in employee benefits would be impermissibly discriminatory if motivated by a desire to avoid the anticipated costs of continuing to provide coverage for a particular beneficiary. McGann would find an implied promise not to discriminate for this purpose; it is the breaking of this promise that McGann appears to contend constitutes interference with a future entitlement.

McGann cites only one case in which a court has ruled that a change in the terms and conditions of an employee-benefits plan could constitute illegal discrimination under section 510. *Vogel v. Independence Federal Sav. Bank*, 728 F. Supp. 1210 (D. Md. 1990). In *Vogel*, however, the plan change at issue resulted in the plaintiff and only the plaintiff being excluded from coverage. McGann asserts that the *Vogel* court rejected the defendant's contention that mere termination of benefits could not constitute unlawful discrimination under section 510, but in fact the court rejected this claim not because it found that mere termination of coverage could constitute discrimination under section 510, but rather because the termination at issue affected only the beneficiary. *Id.* at 1225. Nothing in *Vogel* suggests that the change there had the potential to then or thereafter exclude any present or possible future plan beneficiary other than the plaintiff. *Vogel* therefore provides no support for the proposition that the alteration or termination of a medical plan could alone sustain a section 510 claim. Without necessarily approving of the holding in *Vogel*, we note that it is inapplicable to the instant case. The post-August 1, 1988 $5,000 AIDS coverage limit applies to any and all employees.

McGann effectively contends that section 510 was intended to prohibit any discrimination in the alteration of an employee benefits plan that results in an identifiable employee or group of employees being treated differently from other employees. The First Circuit rejected a somewhat similar contention in *Aronson v. Servus Rubber, Div. of Chromalloy*, 730 F.2d 12 (1st Cir.), *cert. denied*, 469 U.S. 1017 (1984). In *Aronson*, an employer eliminated a profit sharing plan with respect to employees at only one of two plants. The disenfranchised employees sued their

---

[2] We assume that discovery of McGann's condition — and realization of the attendant, long-term costs of caring for McGann — did in fact prompt defendants to reconsider the $1,000,000 limit with respect to AIDS-related expenses and to reduce the limit for future such expenses to $5,000.

employer under section 510, claiming that partial termination of the plan with respect to employees at one plant and not at the other constituted illegal discrimination. The court rejected the employees' discrimination claim, stating in part:

> [Section 510] relates to discriminatory conduct directed against individuals, not to actions involving the plan in general. The problem is with the word 'discriminate.' An overly literal interpretation of this section would make illegal any partial termination, since such terminations obviously interfere with the attainment of benefits by the terminated group, and, indeed, are expressly intended so to interfere . . . . This is not to say that a plan could not be discriminatorily modified, intentionally benefitting, or injuring, certain identified employees or a certain group of employees, but a partial termination cannot constitute discrimination per se. A termination that cuts along independently established lines — here separate divisions — and that has a readily apparent business justification, demonstrates no invidious intent. *Id.* at 16 (citation omitted).

The Supreme Court has observed in dictum: "ERISA does not mandate that employers provide any particular benefits, and does not itself proscribe discrimination in the provision of employee benefits." *Shaw v. Delta Air Lines, Inc.*, 463 U.S. 85 (1983) . . . . To interpret "discrimination" broadly to include defendants' conduct would clearly conflict with Congress's intent that employers remain free to create, modify and terminate the terms and conditions of employee benefits plans without governmental interference.

The Sixth Circuit, in rejecting a challenge to an employer's freedom to choose the terms of its employee pension plan, stated that:

> [i]n enacting ERISA, Congress continued its reliance on *voluntary* action by employers by granting substantial tax advantages for the creation of qualified retirement programs. Neither Congress nor the courts are involved in either the decision to establish a plan or in the decision concerning which benefits a plan should provide. In particular, courts have no authority to decide which benefits employers must confer upon their employees; these are decisions which are more appropriately influenced by forces in the marketplace and, when appropriate, by federal legislation. Absent a violation of federal or state law, a federal court may not modify a substantive provision of a pension plan. *Id.* (citation omitted) (emphasis in original).

The Sixth Circuit has subsequently declared that "the principle articulated in [*Reynolds Metals*] applies with at least as much force to welfare plans . . ." *Musto v. American General Corp.*, 861 F.2d 897, 912 (6th Cir. 1988), *cert. denied*, 490 U.S. 1020 (1989).

As persuasively explained by the Second Circuit, the policy of allowing employers freedom to amend or eliminate employee benefits is particularly compelling with respect to medical plans:

> With regard to an employer's right to change medical plans, Congress evidenced its recognition of the need for flexibility in rejecting the automatic vesting of welfare plans. Automatic vesting was rejected because the costs of such plans are subject to fluctuating and unpredictable variables. Actuarial decisions concerning fixed annuities are based on fairly stable data, and vesting is appropriate. In contrast, medical insurance must take account of inflation, changes in medical practice and technology, and increases in the costs of treatment independent of inflation. These unstable

> variables prevent accurate predictions of future needs and costs. *Moore v. Metropolitan Life Ins. Co.*, 856 F.2d 488, 492 (2d Cir. 1988) (*Metropolitan Life*).

In *Metropolitan Life*, the court rejected an ERISA claim by retirees that their employer could not change the level of their medical benefits without their consent. The court stated that limiting an employer's right to change medical plans increased the risk of "decreas[ing] protection for future employees and retirees." *Id.* at 492 . . .

McGann's claim cannot be reconciled with the well-settled principle that Congress did not intend that ERISA circumscribe employers' control over the content of benefits plans they offered to their employees. McGann interprets section 510 to prevent an employer from reducing or eliminating coverage for a particular illness in response to the escalating costs of covering an employee suffering from that illness. Such an interpretation would, in effect, change the terms of H & H Music's plan. Instead of making the $1,000,000 limit available for medical expenses on an as-incurred basis only as long as the limit remained in effect, the policy would make the limit *permanently* available for all medical expenses as they might thereafter be incurred because of a single event, such as the contracting of AIDS. Under McGann's theory, defendants would be effectively proscribed from reducing coverage for AIDS once McGann had contracted that illness and filed claims for AIDS-related expenses. If a federal court could prevent an employer from reducing an employee's coverage limits for AIDS treatment once that employee contracted AIDS, the boundaries of judicial involvement in the creation, alteration or termination of ERISA plans would be sorely tested.

. . .

Proof of defendants' specific intent to discriminate among plan beneficiaries on grounds not proscribed by section 510 does not enable McGann to avoid summary judgment. ERISA does not broadly prevent an employer from "discriminating" in the creation, alteration or termination of employee benefits plans; thus, evidence of such intentional discrimination cannot alone sustain a claim under section 510. That section does not prohibit welfare plan discrimination between or among categories of diseases. Section 510 does not mandate that if some, or most, or virtually all catastrophic illnesses are covered, AIDS (or any other particular catastrophic illness) must be among them. It does not prohibit an employer from electing not to cover or continue to cover AIDS, while covering or continuing to cover other catastrophic illnesses, even though the employer's decision in this respect may stem from some "prejudice" against AIDS or its victims generally. The same, of course, is true of any other disease and its victims. That sort of "discrimination" is simply not addressed by section 510. Under section 510, the asserted discrimination is illegal only if it is motivated by a desire to retaliate against an employee or to deprive an employee of an existing right to which he may become entitled. The district court's decision to grant summary judgment to defendants therefore was proper. Its judgment is accordingly Affirmed.

4-7 QUESTIONS AND PROBLEMS

1. Would the court have reached a different result if H & H Music had terminated McGann rather than amending its plan?

2. Would the court have reached a different result if H & H Music had simply excluded McGann from plan coverage?

3. Was McGann's suit an attempt to transform ERISA § 510 into a vesting provision for welfare benefits?

4. In October 2011, shortly after his divorce, Randall started his position with BetaCo as a Software Quality Assurance Engineer. The following year, Randall's former wife sued BetaCo in state court alleging that she was entitled to coverage under BetaCo's medical plan. While this suit was pending, Randall was asked by his supervisor, Sam, to call in his location when not in the office. Before a month elapsed, Sam sent Randall a memorandum instructing him to report to the department's secretary each morning. These two requirements were not imposed on any other employee under Sam's supervision. Randall also was informed by a BetaCo staff attorney that if BetaCo lost the pending suit instituted by Randall's former wife, the decision could affect hundreds of other pending cases involving medical coverage. Thus, the attorney "advised" Randall to secure a private health plan for his former wife. A few weeks after this conversation, Randall was notified of his discharge. The stated reason for the termination was Randall's alleged failure to complete a certain assignment. At another meeting with BetaCo's representatives, however, Randall was told that he was being terminated due to the elimination of his position. Nevertheless, at the time of discharge, BetaCo had an open requisition for Randall's position, which was filled after Randall's termination. Randall's work at BetaCo was at a satisfactory or above satisfactory level. Is Randall entitled to relief under ERISA § 510?

5. In 2002, GammaCo closed one of its manufacturing facilities and many employees lost their jobs. Ten years later, when the company's production needs increased, it sought to rehire its displaced employees. The company, however, quickly realized that hiring employees with credited service under its pension plan would result in increased pension liabilities. Accordingly, it adopted a conscious policy of not hiring former employees with credited service under its pension plan. Fifty former employees filed suit challenging this practice as a violation of ERISA § 510. What result?

6. Suppose that rather than electing not to rehire former employees, GammaCo intentionally elected to lay off employees who were just short of vesting. Would this policy violate ERISA § 510?

INTER-MODAL RAIL EMPLOYEES ASSOCIATION v. ATCHISON, TOPEKA AND SANTA FE RAILWAY COMPANY

520 U.S. 510 (1997)

JUSTICE O'CONNOR delivered the opinion of the Court.

Section 510 of the Employee Retirement Income Security Act of 1974 (ERISA), 88 Stat. 895, makes it unlawful to "discharge, fine, suspend, expel, discipline, or discriminate against a participant or beneficiary [of an employee benefit plan] for the purpose of interfering with the attainment of any right to which such participant may become entitled under the plan." [ERISA § 510.] The Court of Appeals for the Ninth Circuit held that § 510 only prohibits interference with the attainment of rights that are capable of "vesting," as that term is defined in ERISA. We disagree.

The individual petitioners are former employees of respondent Santa Fe Terminal Services, Inc. (SFTS), a wholly owned subsidiary of respondent The Atchison, Topeka and Santa Fe Railway Co. (ATSF), which was responsible for transferring cargo between railcars and trucks at ATSF's Hobart Yard in Los Angeles, California. While petitioners were employed by SFTS, they were entitled to retirement benefits under the Railroad Retirement Act of 1974, and to pension, health, and welfare benefits under collective bargaining agreements involving SFTS and the Teamsters Union. SFTS provided its workers with pension, health, and welfare benefits through employee benefit plans subject to ERISA's comprehensive regulations.

In January 1990, ATSF entered into a formal "Service Agreement" with SFTS to have SFTS do the same "inter-modal" work it had done at the Hobart Yard for the previous 15 years without a contract. Seven weeks later, ATSF exercised its right to terminate the newly formed agreement and opened up the Hobart Yard work for competitive bidding. Respondent In-Terminal Services (ITS) was the successful bidder, and SFTS employees who declined to continue employment with ITS were terminated. ITS, unlike SFTS, was not obligated to make contributions to the Railroad Retirement Account under the Railroad Retirement Act. ITS also provided fewer pension and welfare benefits under its collective bargaining agreement with the Teamsters Union than had SFTS. Workers who continued their employment with ITS "lost their Railroad Retirement Act benefits" and "suffered a substantial reduction in Teamsters benefits." 80 F.3d 348, 350 (C.A. 9 1996) (*per curiam*).

Petitioners sued respondents SFTS, ATSF, and ITS in the United States District Court for the Central District of California, alleging that respondents had violated § 510 of ERISA by "discharg[ing]" petitioners "for the purpose of interfering with the attainment of . . . right[s] to which" they would have "become entitled" under the ERISA pension and welfare plans adopted pursuant to the SFTS-Teamsters collective bargaining agreement. Had SFTS remained their employer, petitioners contended, they would have been entitled to assert claims for benefits under the SFTS-Teamsters benefit plans, at least until the collective bargaining agreement that gave rise to those plans expired. The substitution of ITS for SFTS, however, precluded them from asserting those claims and relegated them to asserting claims under the less generous ITS-Teamsters benefit plans. According to petitioners, the substitution "interfer[ed] with the attainment" of their "right" to assert those claims and violated § 510. Respondents moved to dismiss these § 510 claims, and the District Court granted the motion.

The Court of Appeals for the Ninth Circuit affirmed in part and reversed in part. The court reinstated petitioners' claim under § 510 for interference with their *pension* benefits, concluding that § 510 " 'protects plan participants from termination motivated by an employer's desire to prevent a pension from vesting.' " *Id.* at 350–351 (quoting *Ingersoll-Rand Co. v. McClendon*, 498 U.S. 133, 143 (1990)). But the Court of Appeals affirmed the dismissal of petitioners' claim for interference with their *welfare* benefits. "Unlike pension benefits," the Court of Appeals observed, "welfare benefits do not vest." 80 F.3d at 351. As a result, the Court of Appeals noted, "employers remain free to unilaterally amend or eliminate [welfare] plans," and "employees have no present 'right' to future, anticipated welfare benefits.' " *Ibid.* (emphasis deleted; internal quotation marks omitted). Because the "existence of a present 'right' is [a] prerequisite to section 510 relief," the Court of Appeals concluded that § 510 did not state a cause of action for interference with welfare benefits. *Ibid.* We granted certiorari to resolve a conflict among the Courts of Appeals on this issue, and now vacate the decision below and remand.

II

The Court of Appeals' holding that § 510 bars interference only with vested rights is contradicted by the plain language of § 510. As noted above, that section makes it unlawful to "discharge . . . a [plan] participant or beneficiary . . . for the purpose of interfering with the *attainment of any right* to which such participant may become entitled under *the plan.*" [ERISA § 510] (emphasis added). ERISA defines a "plan" to include both "an employee welfare benefit plan [and] an employee pension benefit plan," [ERISA § 3(3)], and specifically exempts "employee welfare benefit plan[s]" from its stringent vesting requirements, *see* [ERISA § 201(1)]. Because a "plan" includes an "employee welfare benefit plan," and because welfare plans offer benefits that do not "vest" (at least insofar as ERISA is concerned), Congress' use of the word "plan" in § 510 all but forecloses the argument that § 510's interference clause applies only to "vested" rights. Had Congress intended to confine § 510's protection to "vested" rights, it could have easily substituted the term "pension plan," *see* [ERISA § 3(2)], for "plan," or the term "nonforfeitable" right, *see* [ERISA § (19)], for "any right." But § 510 draws no distinction between those rights that "vest" under ERISA and those that do not.

The right that an employer or plan sponsor may enjoy in some circumstances to unilaterally amend or eliminate its welfare benefit plan does not, as the Court of Appeals apparently thought, justify a departure from § 510's plain language. It is true that ERISA itself "does not regulate the substantive content of welfare-benefit plans." *Metropolitan Life Ins. Co. v. Massachusetts*, 471 U.S. 724, 732 (1985). Thus, unless an employer contractually cedes its freedom, it is "generally free under ERISA, for any reason at any time, to adopt, modify, or terminate [its] welfare pla[n]." *Curtiss-Wright Corp. v. Schoonejongen*, 514 U.S. 73, 78 (1995).

The flexibility an employer enjoys to amend or eliminate its welfare plan is not an accident; Congress recognized that "requir[ing] the vesting of these ancillary benefits would seriously complicate the administration and increase the cost of plans." S. Rep. No. 93-383, p. 51 (1973). Giving employers this flexibility also encourages them to offer more generous benefits at the outset, since they are free to reduce benefits should economic conditions sour. If employers were locked into the plans they initially offered, "they would err initially on the side of omission." *Heath v. Varity Corp.*, 71 F.3d 256, 258 (CA 7 1995). Section 510 counterbalances this flexibility by ensuring that employers do not "circumvent the provision of promised benefits." *Ingersoll-Rand Co., supra*, 498 U.S. at 143 (1973). In short, "§ 510 helps to make promises credible." *Heath, supra*, at 258. An employer may, of course, retain the unfettered right to alter its promises, but to do so it must follow the formal procedures set forth in the plan. *See* [ERISA § 402 (b)(3)] (requiring plan to "provide a procedure for amending such plan"); *Schoonejongen, supra*, at 78, at 1228 (observing that the "cognizable claim [under ERISA] is that the company did not [amend its welfare benefit plan] in a permissible manner"). Adherence to these formal procedures "increases the likelihood that proposed plan amendments, which are fairly serious events, are recognized as such and given the special consideration they deserve." *Schoonejongen, supra*, at 82. The formal amendment process would be undermined if § 510 did not apply because employers could "informally" amend their plans one participant at a time. Thus, the power to amend or abolish a welfare benefit plan does not include the power to "discharge, fine, suspend, expel, discipline, or discriminate against" the plan's participants and beneficiaries "for the purpose of interfering with [their] attainment of . . . right[s] . . . under the plan." To be sure, when an employer acts without this purpose, as could be the case when making fundamental business decisions, such actions are not barred by § 510. But in the case where an employer acts with a purpose that triggers the protection of § 510, any tension that might exist between an employer's power to amend the plan and a participant's rights under § 510 is the product of a careful balance of competing interests, and is most surely not the type of "absurd or glaringly unjust" result, *Ingalls Shipbuilding v. Director, Office of Workers' Compensation Programs, DOL*, 519 U.S. 248, 261 (1997), that would warrant departure from the plain language of § 510.

Respondents argue that the Court of Appeals' decision must nevertheless be affirmed because § 510, when applied to benefits that do not "vest," only protects an employee's right to cross the "threshold of eligibility" for welfare benefits. *See* Brief for Respondent Atchison, Topeka & Santa Fe Railway Co. et al. 18. In other words, argue respondents, an employee who is eligible to receive benefits under an ERISA welfare benefit plan has already "attain[ed]" her "right[s]" under the plan, so that any subsequent actions taken by an employer cannot, by definition, "interfer[e]" with the "attainment of . . . right[s]" under the plan. According to respondents, petitioners were eligible to receive welfare benefits under the SFTS-Teamsters plan at the time they were discharged, so they cannot state a claim under § 510. The Court of Appeals' approach precluded it from evaluating this argument, and others presented to us, and we see no reason not to allow it the first opportunity to consider these matters on remand.

We therefore vacate the judgment of the Court of Appeals and remand the case for further proceedings consistent with this opinion.

4-8 QUESTIONS AND PROBLEMS

1. Why did STFS not simply amend its employee benefit plans to provide lower benefits?

2. Did the employers violate ERISA § 510?

3. Suppose that ITS has used different employees rather than hiring SFTS' former employees. What effect would that have on the employees' claim under ERISA § 510?

4. To what extent may employers consider benefit costs in making outsourcing decisions? What effect will the Court's decision have on employers' outsourcing decisions?

5. Does ERISA § 510's prohibition against interference with the "attainment of any [plan] right" apply only to employees who are not vested or eligible for benefits under an existing plan or does it extend to employees who are already vested or eligible for benefits as well?

6. Because Alpha Corporation's sales dramatically decreased over the last five years, its board of directors has decided to close one of its three manufacturing plants to reduce costs. Alpha Corporation offers a defined benefit pension plan. Because the average age and average seniority level of Plant One employees is significantly higher than those of Plant Two and Plant Three employees, the pension costs at Plant One are significantly higher than those of Plants Two and Three. If Alpha Corporation were to close Plant One because of its higher pension costs, would it violate ERISA § 510? Would Alpha Corporation violate ERISA § 510 if Plant One's higher pension costs were only one factor it considered in electing to close Plant One?

7. Rochelle, a real estate agent employed by NuCo Real Estate Agency, was entitled to health insurance coverage and participation in a 401(k) plan pursuant to her employment contract with NuCo. NuCo notified her that her employment contract would be terminated so that NuCo could eliminate the costs of providing health insurance and contributing to the 401(k) plan. NuCo offered Rochelle an independent contractor position that did not provide health or retirement benefits. When Rochelle refused to sign the new contract, NuCo fired her. Rochelle filed suit, claiming that her discharge resulted from her refusal to accept a change in status from an employee to an independent contractor and a concomitant loss of nonvested health benefits in violation of ERISA § 510. What result?

8. Recall *Vizcaino v. Microsoft Corporation* [I], 97 F.3d 1187 (9th Cir. 1996). In that case, the court noted:

> In response to the IRS rulings [that its freelancers were common law employees], Microsoft began "converting" its freelancers. That is, it tendered offers to some freelancers to become permanent employees; it gave other freelancers the option of terminating their employment relationship with Microsoft completely or continuing to work at the company but in the capacity of employees of a new temporary employment agency, which would provide payroll services, withhold federal taxes, and pay the employer's portion of FICA taxes. Most of the plaintiffs who were not given the opportunity to become permanent employees decided to become "temporary agency employees" rather than to be fired. However, Donna Vizcaino refused that option and was discharged. Those who elected "temporary employee status" noticed little change in the terms or conditions of their employment; they continued working the same hours on the same projects and under the same supervisors.

Did Microsoft's termination of Donna Vizcaino violate ERISA § 510?

Plaintiffs who sue under ERISA § 510 have the burden of proof to show that they were discriminated against because they attempted to exercise their rights under the employer's pension or welfare plan. For example, a discharged employee must prove that the reason for the discharge was an attempt by the employer to interfere with the employee's rights under the pension or welfare plan. Because direct evidence of intent to discriminate is rarely available, employees typically use circumstantial evidence to prove a *prima facie* case. If the plaintiff makes out a *prima facie* case, the burden shifts to the employer to articulate a legitimate, nondiscriminatory reason for the challenged action. If the employer articulates a legitimate, nondiscriminatory reason for the challenged action, the plaintiff must prove by a preponderance of the evidence that the reasons advanced are simply a pretext for discrimination.

CRAWFORD v. TRW AUTOMOTIVE U.S. LLC

560 F.3d 607 (6th Cir. 2009)

BOYCE F. MARTIN, JR., Circuit Judge.

Plaintiffs, a class of former TRW Automotive employees, allege that TRW violated the Employee Retirement and Income Security Act by closing the plant where they worked to interfere with the vesting of their retirement benefits. The district court disagreed, and granted the company's motion for summary judgment. We affirm.

I.

TRW, an indirect subsidiary of TRW Automotive Holdings Corporation, owned and operated the Van Dyke plant where plaintiffs worked. Van Dyke, a 370,000 square foot facility, was part of TRW's North American Braking and Suspension Group: workers there manufactured front suspension components for various car makers. Its employees, represented by the United Auto Workers, were covered by a collective bargaining agreement between TRW and the UAW, and a defined pension plan. Under the pension plan, employees who retired with thirty or more years of "benefit service" were entitled to retirement benefits; they earned benefit service for each year that they worked over 1680 hours, though if laid-off they only needed 170 hours to get a year's credit. Employees who retired with 10 years of service and were 55 or older were entitled to an early benefit.

TRW claims that, as of 2004, it faced overcapacity problems which hampered profits. In response, it organized a group to research the costs and benefits of shutting down some of its North American plants. That group identified the Van Dyke plant as a prime candidate for closure. But, before making that leap, TRW considered a few alternatives. Most significantly, it considered placing at Van Dyke work for DaimlerChrysler, though this was only assembly work and not the manufacturing kind typical of Van Dyke. Ultimately, however, the company decided that Van Dyke was in fact not the right place, and the DaimlerChrysler work wound up (the record is unclear precisely how) at a plant located on Mancini Drive owned by the Kelsey-Hayes Company, a separate subsidiary of TRW Holdings. (The Mancini plant employees are not represented by a union and they do not have a defined-benefit pension plan.) So Van Dyke's days became numbered.

Shortly before TRW shut Van Dyke down, however, the company discussed with the UAW the possibility of preferentially hiring laid-off Van Dyke employees to the Mancini plant and "bridging" the benefits of Van Dyke employees who were close to vesting. TRW also offered a severance to employees who opted out of their available retiree benefits. But the two sides failed to reach an agreement and TRW closed Van Dyke in January 2007. At that time, three employees missed the 30-year retirement mark by less than one year of benefit service (all three had been laid-off in 2005), and four others missed the 30-year mark by less than two years.

Plaintiffs, a certified class of former Van Dyke employees, sued, alleging that TRW violated ERISA § 510 by (1) failing to recall employees following a layoff, (2) refusing to transfer employees to the Mancini Drive facility, and (3) improperly discharging employees to interfere with their attainment of retirement eligibility. The district court granted summary judgment to TRW on all counts, and also later dismissed plaintiffs' motion for relief from the judgment on the basis of new evidence. Plaintiffs appeal.

II.

* * *

A.

Plaintiffs contend that the district court improperly granted TRW summary judgment because the company violated ERISA when it laid them off in connection with closing the Van Dyke plant. ERISA § 510 makes it "unlawful for any person to discharge, fine, suspend, expel, discipline, or discriminate against a participant or beneficiary . . . for the purpose of interfering with the attainment of any right to which such participant may become entitled under [an employee benefit plan]." This section was designed to prevent "employers from discharging or harassing" employees to preclude "them from obtaining vested pension rights." West v. Butler, 621 F.2d 240, 245 (6th Cir.1980). Of course, not only is this illegal, it is also bad business: because providing benefits is discretionary (and so part of total employee-compensation), firing older employees to reduce pension costs both creates animosity between employer and employee and makes employees' compensation less certain, and thus employees will demand higher wages to offset this heightened risk of being fired inopportunely; as a result, employers will have to pay employees higher wages to attract and keep them. See Maria O'Brien Hylton, Insecure Retirement Income, Wrongful Plan Administration and Other Employee Benefits Woes-Evaluating ERISA at Age Thirty, 53 Buff. L. Rev. 1193, 1204-11 (2005). But some employers are foolish, and thus Congress enacted § 510 to provide a remedy. Plaintiffs assert that TRW "discharge[d]" them to "interfer[e]" with their attainment of full retirement benefits in violation of § 510.

So the primary question here is whether the plaintiffs proffered enough evidence of this improper motive to get to a jury. But first we must dismiss two errant contentions: TRW asserts that ERISA interference claims in the plant sale or closing context are never actionable and plaintiffs assert that TRW violated section 510 by failing to recall or transfer them following their discharge. Neither is correct.

1.

TRW overreaches in stating that employees may never challenge discharges that result from a plant-closing decision. While "[e]mployers or other plan sponsors are generally free under ERISA . . . to adopt, modify or terminate" pension benefit plans, Coomer v. Bethesda Hosp. Inc., 370 F.3d 499, 508 (6th Cir.2004), this discretion does not permit them to discharge employees or alter their plan rights to "circumvent the provision of promised benefits." Inter-Modal Rail Emples. Ass'n v. Atchison, Topeka & Santa Fe Ry., 520 U.S. 510, 515 (1997) (internal quotations omitted).

Of course, the D.C. Circuit has pointed out that Congress's use of the term "discharge" in § 510 comes in the context of other individually focused terms like "fine, suspend, expel, [and] discipline." Andes v. Ford Motor Co., 70 F.3d 1332, 1337 (D.C.Cir.1995). TRW latches onto this to say that broad or class-based claims are never actionable. But, as the D.C. Circuit-and other courts-have routinely recognized, the term "discharge," by definition, is not so limited and thus covers employees fired or laid-off, either individually or as a group, and thus the statutory language gives any "discharged" employee a right to sue, whether via class-action or individually. See, e.g., Gavalik v. Cont'l Can Co., 812 F.2d 834, 838 (3d Cir.1987). Indeed, the Andes court explicitly pointed out the possibility that some employer might unscrupulously sell or close a plant to shake off employees on the cusp of establishing benefit eligibility. 70 F.3d at 1338.

2.

Plaintiffs similarly overreach in claiming that TRW was legally required to recall many of them back to or to transfer them to the Mancini plant. As stated above, § 510 includes a list of prohibited actions, including improperly "discharg[ing], fin[ing], expel[ling]," and "discriminat [ing]." But nowhere is "transferring" or "recalling" listed. Neither have plaintiffs identified case law giving effect to such a claim. This is not surprising: the sine qua non of a § 510 claim is the presence of some adverse action done to interfere with an employee's rights, and had plaintiffs not been laid-off, whether or not there was a transfer would have been irrelevant because plaintiffs would still have been accruing benefits; similarly, recall would have been irrelevant if there was no discharge or it was lawful, because employees would have no more right to be hired than someone who had never worked for TRW. In other words, the whole game is whether TRW unlawfully discharged plaintiffs.

Also, TRW's decision to recall some employees and not others was not discriminatory because those decisions were seniority based, and at least two employees accrued enough pension credits to retire with benefits after being recalled. Finally, the employees' collective bargaining agreement provided that benefits accrued only at the Van Dyke plant, so plaintiffs also lacked plan rights to be recalled. See McGath v. Auto-Body North Shore, Inc., 7 F.3d 665, 670 (7th Cir.1993).

* * *

B.

To defeat summary judgment, the plaintiffs must show that TRW fired them for the purpose of interfering with the attainment of their retirement benefits. ERISA § 510. Plaintiffs may make this showing either through direct or circumstantial evidence, with the latter via the ubiquitous burden-shifting framework that has, like some B-movie villain, devoured nearly every area of law with which it has come into contact. See Texas Dep't of Community Affairs v. Burdine, 450 U.S. 248, 253 (1981); McDonnell Douglas Corp. v. Green, 411 U.S. 792 (1973). Plaintiffs here rely on circumstantial evidence. In the ERISA context, the burden-shifting framework first requires the plaintiffs to establish their "prima facie" case "by showing the existence of (1) prohibited employer conduct (2) taken for the purpose of interfering (3) with the attainment of any right to which the employee may become entitled." Smith v. Ameritech, 129 F.3d 857, 865 (6th Cir.1997). Although some of the cases discuss, in reference to this "prima facie" case, the need for the plaintiff to prove the existence of the employer's "specific intent," see, e.g., Schweitzer v. Teamsters Local 100, 413 F.3d 533, 537 (6th Cir.2005); Humphreys v. Bellaire Corp., 966 F.2d 1037, 1043 (6th Cir.1992), that requirement is superfluous and not relevant (at this first stage at least) because it gets to the ultimate question of whether the employer purposefully interfered with the employee's pension rights. This confusion stems in part because the term "prima facie" as used here, does not comport with the traditional understanding of that term-namely, that plaintiffs have proven enough to get to a jury, see 9 WIGMORE ON EVIDENCE s 2494, 378-79 nn. 1, 3 (1981).

Instead, "prima facie" is Burdine/ McDonnell Douglas patois for the fact that the plaintiffs have shown enough to create a rebuttable presumption such that the employer must then produce evidence supporting a legitimate, non-discriminatory reason for the discharge. Humphreys, 966 F.2d at 1043; see also Majewski v. Automatic Data Processing, Inc., 274 F.3d 1106, 1113-14 (6th Cir.2001) ("A plaintiff's burden in establishing a prima facie case is not intended to be an onerous one."). If the employer makes this showing, the burden shifts back to the plaintiff to show that this proffered reason was a "pretext"-i.e. a phony reason-and instead that the intent to interfere with the plaintiff's ERISA rights was a "motivating factor." Id.

The plaintiffs easily satisfy the low-threshold for establishing their prima facie case. TRW's Vice President of Operations for the Suspension Group stated that pension costs-colloquially known within the company as "legacy" or "heritage" costs-were among the reasons to close down the plant. And that is no surprise: labor costs are often among the largest costs for a plant, and such "legacy" or retirement and benefits costs typically make up the largest portion of labor costs. Indeed, as the district court observed, the work done at Van Dyke was transferred to a non-union facility where such costs "were reduced or non-existent." This is enough to erect the presumption and require TRW to make an evidentiary showing.

TRW thus replies that it closed Van Dyke because of its overcapacity: only 30,000 square feet of its available 300,000 square feet was being used, so roughly 26% of every sales dollar went to fixed costs and overhead. This is a strong non-discriminatory reason, especially when coupled with the fact that there are necessarily a variety of concerns at play whenever a company decides to shut down a plant.

So we reach the "pretext" stage. Plaintiffs retort that TRW's proffered reason is phony because the plant was so poorly run; specifically, that the company could have kept Van Dyke going if it had cut a variety of possible costs and placed the DaimlerChrysler work there. Thus, plaintiffs argue, because they did not do those things, it must have been the company's desire to interfere with their pension benefits that motivated it to close their plant. TRW, predictably, retorts that, since its stated reason concerned "business judgment," then its reason is unassailable. In support, TRW quotes dicta from the cases, like: "Measures designed to reduce costs in general that also result in an incidental reduction in benefit expenses do not suggest discriminatory intent." Daughtrey v. Honeywell, Inc., 3 F.3d 1488, 1492 (11th Cir.1993).

But of course: the whole issue is whether reducing pension benefits by shutting down a plant with employees close to vesting was a "motivating factor" or was instead "incidental" because there were other, neutral, business reasons at play. See Smith, 129 F.3d at 865. "Business judgment" is not an aegis that deflects all ERISA interference liability; Congress, in enacting § 510, made clear its view that an employer may only discharge employees when neutral, non-pension right-interfering concerns animate the decision.

And, while plaintiffs may not second-guess every business decisions, the reasons supporting any decision to discharge an employee, either individually or in connection with a plant closing, may be considered "to the extent that such an inquiry sheds light on whether the employer's proper reason for the employment action was its actual motivation." Wexler v. White's Fine Furniture, Inc., 317 F.3d 564, 576 (6th Cir.2003) (en banc). In other words, business judgments are relevant insofar as plaintiffs can show that they are incredible or phony, which, while difficult, is not categorically barred, as TRW seems to think.

To support their claim that TRW's overcapacity justification was pretext, plaintiffs point to a variety of documents indicating TRW's desire to reduce pension costs and that reducing these costs played a definite role in TRW's decision to shut down Van Dyke. And, of course, TRW has not denied this. Nevertheless, plaintiffs cannot satisfy their burden of persuasion. At the pretext stage, judges must still bring their judgment to bear on whether or not plaintiffs have met their burden-in effect, the Burdine/ McDonnell Douglas framework has fallen away and the question reduces to whether plaintiffs can prove improper motivation. And, despite plaintiffs' evidence, we cannot say that TRW's reason was a mere pretext.

When the plant was shut down and the employees laid-off, only three employees were within a year of reaching eligibility, while another four were roughly two years away; a majority of the Van Dyke employees needed more than five more years for their benefits to fully vest. And two of the employees that TRW did recall-which was done on the basis of seniority per the bargaining agreement-established their benefits eligibility while working at the Mancini plant. This undercuts the plaintiffs' claim.

Although TRW vastly overstated the deference its business decisions are afforded, it is true that, when plants are shut down, there will necessarily be a variety of factors at play beyond how close certain employees might be to vesting, and thus plaintiffs have a lot to wade through to establish liability. This is not due to any presumption or legal threshold erected against their claims; the facts of these cases will always be myriad and complicated, and plaintiffs must show that the employer, in the midst of all this, in some way targeted certain employee benefits or rights for interference. This is not to say that employers always act properly-some are foolish-it is instead that the facts do not always make it obvious that this was so. To succeed, § 510 plaintiffs do not need "smoking gun" evidence, but, they do need more than plaintiffs have here. We thus affirm the district court's grant of summary judgment to TRW.

* * *

4-9 QUESTIONS AND PROBLEMS

1. April was a packaging operator whose duties required her to spend the entire day on her feet. After seven years she had bunions on both feet and required separate operations to remove each bunion. April took a 4½ month leave of absence after the first bunionectomy, came back to work for a year, and then underwent the second operation. During her first and second absences, she received benefits under TauCorp's short-term disability plan. TauCorp's human resource manager hired a private investigator to determine whether April was actually disabled during the second absence. The investigator produced a report stating that April had been "cleaning professional offices" during the second leave. Relying on this report, TauCorp fired April. April denied that she had been cleaning professional offices while she was on disability and filed a ERISA § 510 claim. TauCorp filed a motion for summary judgment. What result?

2. Adam was employed by Zeta Inc. for 22 years until fired at age 57. Near the end of his employment he suffered from diabetes, heart problems and serious kidney ailments. Due to his filing for health care cost reimbursements, his employer, who operated a self-insured medical plan for its employees, was aware of his condition. One week after Adam had taken a stress test to see if he might need a kidney transplant, he was fired. Zeta claims it terminated Adam after other employees reported observing him taking a company computer, a printer, and a scanner and placing it in his car. They believed he was stealing the equipment. Adam asserts that Zeta had fired him for the purpose of depriving him of participating in the company group health care plan in violation of ERISA § 510. At the trial of his ERISA claim, Adam proved that he had not stolen company property. He had, however, no evidence that Zeta fired him because of the high cost of his health care. What result?

D. JOINT AND SURVIVOR ANNUITY AND PRERETIREMENT ANNUITY RULES

ERISA § 205; IRC § 401(a)(11).

To protect the spouses of plan participants, ERISA § 205 requires that certain retirement plans provide automatic survivor benefits to a participant's spouse. The Internal Revenue Code imposes parallel requirements in IRC § 401(a)(11) as qualification requirements. "The legislative history of [the Retirement Equity Act, which added these requirements,] reflects that Congress viewed the marriage relationship as a partnership, and the retirement benefits resulting from that partnership as derived from the contributions of both partners." Ann. 95-33, 1995 IRB LEXIS 14.

These rules generally require pension plans to distribute benefits in the form of a "qualified joint and survivor annuity" or an "optional survivor annuity" payable to the participant during his or her lifetime and to his or her spouse after the participant's death, unless the participant elects otherwise with the consent of the participant's spouse. ERISA §§ 205(a)(1) & 205(c)(1)(A); IRC §§ 401(a)(11)(A)(i) & 417(a)(1)(A). If the participant dies before the distribution of benefits begins, plans must provide a "qualified preretirement survivor annuity" to the participant's surviving spouse, unless the participant waived this right with the consent of the participant's spouse. ERISA § 205(a)(2); IRC § 401(a)(11)(A)(ii). The automatic survivor benefit rules apply to defined benefit plans, money purchase plans, and target benefit plans. ERISA § 205(b)(1), IRC § 401(a)(11)(B). The rules also apply to all other defined contribution plans (such as profit-sharing plans and stock bonus plans) unless they satisfy the conditions set forth in ERISA § 205(b)(1)(C) and IRC § 401(a)(11)(B)(iii).

An annuity is a contractual commitment to provide periodic payments for an agreed-upon period of time; for example, $3,000 a month for ten years. A life annuity provides payments for as long as the annuitant is alive. A joint and survivor annuity provides payments for as long as the participant and his or her surviving spouse is alive. In order to qualify as a "qualified joint and survivor annuity," the amount payable to the surviving spouse must not be less than 50 percent nor more than 100 percent of the amount payable to the participant during his or her lifetime, and the total amount payable must be at least the actuarial equivalent of a single life annuity for the life of the participant. ERISA § 205(d)(1); IRC § 417(b). If the survivor continuation percentage under the qualified joint and survivor annuity is less than 75 percent, the survivor continuation percentage under "qualified optional survivor annuity" must be 75 percent. ERISA § 205(d)(2); IRC § 417(g). If the survivor continuation percentage under the plan's qualified joint and survivor annuity is at least 75 percent, the survivor continuation percentage under qualified optional survivor annuity must be 50 percent. ERISA § 205(d)(2); IRC § 417(g).

A preretirement survivor annuity pays a life annuity to the surviving spouse if the participant dies before distribution of benefits has begun. Generally, benefit payments to the surviving spouse must begin no later than the date the participant would have reached the NRA (or early retirement age, if available) and are based on the value of the benefit the participant earned under the terms of the plan. ERISA § 205(e)(1); IRC § 417(c)(1). In the case of a defined contribution plan, the annuity must begin within a reasonable time after the participant's death and the amount of payments must not be less than the actuarial equivalent of 50 percent of the portion of the account balance in which the participant (as of the date of death) was vested. ERISA § 205(e)(2); IRC § 417(c)(2); Treas. Reg. § 1.401(a)-20, Q&A-22(b).

A participant may elect, with the written consent of his or her spouse, to waive distribution in the form of a qualified joint and survivor annuity, qualified optional survivor annuity, or qualified preretirement annuity. ERISA § 205(c)(1) & (2); IRC § 417(a)(1) & (2). In addition, defined contribution plans (other than money purchase plans and target benefit plans) need not distribute benefits in the form of a qualified joint and survivor annuity, qualified optional survivor annuity, or qualified preretirement annuity if the plan satisfies the conditions set forth in ERISA § 205(b)(1)(C) and IRC § 401(a)(11)(B)(iii). Those conditions include a requirement that the plan provide that the participant's nonforfeitable accrued benefit be payable in full, on the participant's death, to the participant's surviving spouse (unless there is no spouse or the spouse consents to another beneficiary) and that the participant not elect the payment of benefits in the form of a life annuity. As a practical matter, most defined contribution plans satisfy these requirements and thus do not distribute benefits in the form of a qualified joint and survivor annuity, qualified optional survivor annuity, or qualified preretirement annuity.

4-10 QUESTIONS AND PROBLEMS

1. At age 65, Ethan retired and began receiving monthly benefits from the Zeta Company Pension Plan in the form of a single life annuity. Two years later, at age 67, Ethan married Victoria. Three years later, Ethan died. Is Victoria entitled to a survivor's annuity on Ethan's death?

2. Rachel, age 65, retired six months after marrying David. When she retired, she elected to receive her retirement benefits in the form of an annuity. Three weeks after retiring, Rachel died. Is David entitled to a survivor's annuity on Rachel's death? *See* ERISA § 205(b)(3); IRC § 417(d). Would your answer be different if Rachel died one year after retiring?

3. Brandon, a fully vested participant in the Theta Co. Pension Plan, died at age 45. He was survived by his wife of 15 years, Megan, and their three children. The normal retirement age under the plan is age 65, and plan participants are eligible for reduced benefits at age 60.

   a. When must the Theta Co. plan commence paying Megan benefits under her survivor annuity?

   b. Would your answer be any different if Brandon were 55 when he died?

   c. Would your answer be any different if Megan were 55 when Brandon died?

   d. Would your answer be any different if Megan remarried five years after Brandon's death?

   e. Would your answer be any different if Megan were divorced from Brandon when he died?

4. One month before they were married, Tina and Charles signed a premarital agreement waiving any rights to each other's property. Tina wanted to ensure that her holdings in her Beta Co. employee stock ownership plan would be passed on to her father. The agreement did not mention the Beta Co. ESOP by name, and neither Tina nor Charles included language designating a beneficiary for individually owned property. The premarital agreement did say that Charles "does hereby waive and release unto Tina, her heirs, executors, administrators and assigns . . . all rights and interest in property . . . which he has or may acquire by reason of Tina's death." A year after they were married, Tina began experiencing symptoms of Cruetzfeldt-Jakob Disease (mad cow's disease), which was mistaken for mental illness. Six months later, while Tina was hospitalized in a delusional state, Charles had Tina give him her power of attorney. Three months later, Charles designated himself as beneficiary of the Beta Co. ESOP. Two weeks later, Tina died at age 41.

Tina's father and her estate sued Charles and the Beta Co. ESOP, seeking to enforce the premarital agreement. What result?

E. ANTI-ALIENATION RULES

ERISA § 206(d); IRC § 401(a)(13).

Section 206(d) of ERISA prohibits pension plans from assigning or alienating benefits. Section 401(a)(13) of the Internal Revenue Code contains a parallel prohibition on qualified retirement plans. Referred to as anti-alienation rules, these provisions prevent a participant from bargaining away benefits or having them subject to creditors prior to retirement. They are designed to ensure that retirement benefits "are actually available for retirement purposes." H.R. Rep. No. 93-807, at 68 (1974). The anti-alienation rules only apply to pension plans; they do not apply to welfare benefit plans.

As originally enacted, the anti-alienation provisions contained two express exceptions. First, they excepted loans "secured by the participant's accrued nonforfeitable benefit" so long as the loan satisfied the prohibited transaction rules. ERISA § 206(d)(2); IRC § 401(a)(13)(A). In addition, they excepted any "voluntary and revocable assignment of not to exceed 10 percent of any benefit payment . . ." *Id.* In the intervening years, Congress has created two additional express exceptions to the anti-alienation provisions. Those exceptions are for (1) amounts paid to spouses and children under "qualified domestic relations orders," ERISA § 206(d)(3)(A); IRC § 401(a)(13)(B), and (2) amounts paid for fiduciary breaches of trust, IRC § 206(d)(4); ERISA § IRC § 401(a)(13)(C).

Courts have generally been reluctant to expand on the express exceptions to the anti-alienation rules. As a result, a number of seemingly worthy creditors have been unable to reach pension benefits, and one commentator has referred to the anti-alienation rules as "the gilded gates of pension protection." *See* Sharon Reece, *The Gilded Gates of Pension Protection: Amending the Anti-Alienation Provision ofERISA Section 206(d)*, 80 Or. L. Rev. 379 (2001). Of course, the anti-alienation rules do not prohibit creditors from attaching benefits once they are actually distributed to a participant.

4-11 QUESTIONS AND PROBLEMS

1. Why do the anti-alienation rules not apply to welfare benefit plans?

2. When the anti-alienation provisions of both ERISA and the Internal Revenue Code were enacted with ERISA in 1974, both provisions were included in the section of the bill that established minimum vesting requirements. How do the anti-alienation provisions relate to the minimum vesting requirements?

3. What is the purpose of the two original exceptions to the anti-alienation rules (contained in ERISA § 206(d)(2) and IRC § 401(a)(13)(A))? Do they interfere with the goal that retirement benefits "actually [be] available for retirement purposes"?

[1] Qualified Domestic Relations Orders

ERISA § 206(d)(3); IRC § 414(p).

Because pension savings represent one of the most significant assets for most Americans, whether and how to divide a participant's interest in a pension plan are often important considerations in separation, divorce, or other domestic relations proceedings. Though the division of marital property is generally governed by state domestic relations law, any assignment of pension interests must also comply with ERISA and the Internal Revenue Code to be enforceable.

Prior to 1984, the courts were divided as to whether the anti-alienation rules applied to state domestic relations orders imposing family support obligations. In the Retirement Equity Act of 1984, Congress amended ERISA and the Internal Revenue Code to expressly exempt "qualified domestic relations orders" or "QDROs" from the anti-alienation rules. ERISA § 206(d)(3); IRC § 401(a)(13)(B).

A QDRO is defined as a "judgment, decree, order" which "is made pursuant to a state domestic relations law," that provides "child support, alimony payments, or marital property rights to a spouse, former spouse, child, or other dependant of a participant." ERISA § 206(d)(3)(B)(ii); IRC § 414(p)(1)(B). To qualify as a QDRO, the order must contain the name and addresses of the plan participant and the alternative payee (that is, the spouse, former spouse, or other dependent), the name of the affected plan, and to whom and how the payments are to be made. The payment of benefits can be expressed either in dollar amounts, e.g. $200 a month, or as a percentage, e.g. 40% of the monthly benefit. The order can neither mandate benefits that are not provided in the plan nor can it increase benefits.

Because a QDRO must strictly comply with the statutory requirements to be enforceable, divorce counsel often contact plan administrators before drawing up the QDRO to insure that they understand all the plan benefits, and do not draft an order that inadvertently omits benefits or requires the payment of benefits not provided by the plan. The QDRO is submitted to the plan administrator, who must determine its validity within a reasonable time period and notify the participant and the alternative payee of that determination. ERISA § 206(d)(3)(G); IRC § 414(p)(6)(A).

Interestingly, a QDRO can require the plan to make payments to the alternate payee when the participant reaches the earliest retirement age under the plan, regardless of whether the plan participant has actually begun to receive benefits under the plan. The QDRO, however, can only require payment of the actuarial value of the early retirement benefit, which cannot include any early retirement subsidy benefits. ERISA § 206(d)(3)(E); IRC § 414(p)(4). If, however, the participant subsequently retires early and is granted an early retirement benefit, the QDRO may be modified to award part of that early retirement benefit to the alternate payee.

A QDRO may provide that the former spouse is to be treated as the participant's surviving spouse for purposes of the qualified joint and survivor annuity and pre-retirement survivor annuity rules (discussed in the preceding section). If a QDRO so provides and the participant later remarries, the participant's subsequent remarriage will not affect the former spouse's rights. For example, Dora, who is a participant in a defined benefit plan, and her husband, Jules, divorce. The QDRO provides that Jules is to be treated as Dora's surviving spouse for purposes of all of the survivor annuity rules. If Dora dies before she has begun to receive benefits under the plan and Jules is still alive, Jules will be entitled to a pre-retirement survivor annuity. If Dora is alive when the payment of benefits commence, the benefits must be paid in the form of a joint and survivor annuity (with Jules entitled to the survivor annuity) unless Jules consents to another form of distribution. If Dora predeceases Jules, Jules will receive a survivor annuity after Dora's death. If Dora had married Ed before she died, Ed would have no survivor rights because the rights given to Jules by the QDRO would trump the survivor rights that Ed would otherwise have. IRC § 414(p)(5)(A).

The alternate payee who is awarded benefits under a defined contribution plan will usually not receive any benefits until the date the participant is entitled to a distribution from the plan or when the participant could begin to receive payments if he or she were to terminate employment. ERISA § 206(d)(3)(E); IRC § 414(p)(4). Some plans, however, permit an alternate payee to receive an immediate distribution of plan benefits upon presentation of the QDRO to the plan administrator. For example, Kim, age 49, divorces Chang, age 52. Chang participates in the Chi Co. defined contribution plan. The QDRO awards Kim 50 percent of the value of Chang's plan account. At the date of the issuance of the QDRO, Chang is credited with $100,000. The plan has a provision that permits a QDRO to order immediate distribution of a participant's account to an alternate payee. Kim submits the QDRO to the plan administrator, who distributes $50,000 to her. Thereafter, Kim has no further rights in Chang's account, which is now worth $50,000. By the time Chang reaches age 65, his account is worth $170,000, all of which belongs to him.

4-12 QUESTIONS AND PROBLEMS

1. Why did Congress provide an exception from the anti-alienation rules for QDROs?

2. Tyler, age 45, is a participant in the Beta profit-sharing plan. Tyler and his wife, Alexis, age 43, are divorced. The QDRO issued by the state court awards Alexis 50 percent of Tyler's plan account as of the date of their divorce. The Beta profit-sharing plan provides for payment of benefits on separation from service (but not before then).

   a. If Alexis remains with the Beta Company until retiring at age 65, what is the earliest the QDRO can require that payments be made to Alexis? *See* 206(d)(3)(E)(ii); IRC § 414(p)(4)(B).

   b. Suppose that Tyler separates from service at age 48 and Alexis receives a distribution from the Beta profit-sharing plan pursuant to the QDRO at that time. Is the distribution to Alexis subject to an IRC § 72(t) 10 percent additional income tax?

3. Cole, age 45, is a participant in the Zeta Pension Plan, when he and his wife, Jocelyn, are divorced. The QDRO states that Jocelyn shall be treated as Cole's current spouse with respect to all of Cole's benefits under the Zeta Pension Plan — unless Cole obtains Jocelyn's consent to waive the QJSA or QPSA or both.

   a. If, after the divorce, Cole marries Lea, and then dies prior to reaching the earliest eligibility age under the terms of the plan, is Lea, Cole's second wife, eligible for any benefits under the plan? *See* ERISA § 206(d)(3)(F)(i); IRC § 414(p)(5)(A); Treas. Reg. § 1.401(a)-13(g)(4)(i)(B)(1).

   b. Would your answer be different if the QDRO provided that Jocelyn shall be treated as Cole's current spouse only with respect to benefits that accrued prior to their divorce?

In the following case, the Court addressed the question whether ERISA's QDRO provision is the only valid way a divorcing spouse can waive his or her right to receive an ex-spouse's pension benefits under ERISA.

KENNEDY v. PLAN ADMINISTRATOR FOR DuPONT SAVINGS AND INVESTMENT PLAN et al.

129 S. Ct. 865 (2009)

JUSTICE SOUTER delivered the opinion of the Court.

The Employee Retirement Income Security Act of 1974 (ERISA), 29 U.S.C. § 1001 *et seq.*, generally obligates administrators to manage ERISA plans "in accordance with the documents and instruments governing" them. ERISA § 404(a)(1)(D). At a more specific level, the Act requires covered pension benefit plans to "provide that benefits . . . under the plan may not be assigned or alienated," ERISA § 206(d)(1), but this bar does not apply to qualified domestic relations orders (QDROs), ERISA § 206(d)(3). The question here is whether the terms of the limitation on assignment or alienation invalidated the act of a divorced spouse, the designated beneficiary under her ex-husband's ERISA pension plan, who purported to waive her entitlement by a federal common law waiver embodied in a divorce decree that was not a QDRO. We hold that such a waiver is not rendered invalid by the text of the antialienation provision, but that the plan administrator properly disregarded the waiver owing to its conflict with the designation made by the former husband in accordance with plan documents.

I

The decedent, William Kennedy, worked for E.I. DuPont de Nemours & Company and was a participant in its savings and investment plan (SIP), with power both to "designate any beneficiary or beneficiaries . . . to receive all or part" of the funds upon his death, and to "replace or revoke such designation." The plan requires "[a]ll authorizations, designations and requests concerning the Plan [to] be made by employees in the manner prescribed by the [plan administrator]," and provides forms for designating or changing a beneficiary. If at the time the participant dies "no surviving spouse exists and no beneficiary designation is in effect, distribution shall be made to, or in accordance with the directions of, the executor or administrator of the decedent's estate." *Id.* at 48.

The SIP is an ERISA " 'employee pension benefit plan,' " 497 F.3d 426, 427 (C.A.5 2007); ERISA § 3(2), and the parties do not dispute that the plan satisfies ERISA's antialienation provision, ERISA § 206(d)(1), which requires it to "provide that benefits provided under the plan may not be assigned or alienated." The plan does, however, permit a beneficiary to submit a "qualified disclaimer" of benefits as defined under the Tax Code, see 26 U.S.C. § 2518, which has the effect of switching the beneficiary to an "alternate . . . determined according to a valid beneficiary designation made by the deceased." Supp. Record 86–87 (Exh. 15).

In 1971, William married Liv Kennedy, and, in 1974, he signed a form designating her to take benefits under the SIP, but naming no contingent beneficiary to take if she disclaimed her interest. 497 F.3d at 427. William and Liv divorced in 1994, subject to a decree that Liv "is . . . divested of all right, title, interest, and claim in and to . . . [a]ny and all sums . . . the proceeds [from], and any other rights related to any . . . retirement plan, pension plan, or like benefit program existing by reason of [William's] past or present or future employment." William did not, however, execute any documents removing Liv as the SIP beneficiary, 497 F.3d at 428, even though he did execute a new beneficiary-designation form naming his daughter, Kari Kennedy, as the beneficiary under DuPont's Pension and Retirement Plan, also governed by ERISA.

On William's death in 2001, petitioner Kari Kennedy was named executrix and asked DuPont to distribute the SIP funds to William's Estate. *Ibid.* DuPont, instead, relied on William's designation form and paid the balance of some $400,000 to Liv. *Ibid.* The Estate then sued respondents DuPont and the SIP plan administrator (together, DuPont), claiming that the divorce decree amounted to a waiver of the SIP benefits on Liv's part, and that DuPont had violated ERISA by paying the benefits to William's designee.

So far as it matters here, the District Court entered summary judgment for the Estate, to which it ordered DuPont to pay the value of the SIP benefits. The court relied on Fifth Circuit precedent establishing that a beneficiary can waive his rights to the proceeds of an ERISA plan 'provided that the waiver is explicit, voluntary, and made in good faith.'

The Fifth Circuit nonetheless reversed, distinguishing prior decisions enforcing federal common law waivers of ERISA benefits because they involved life-insurance policies, which are considered " 'welfare plan[s]' " under ERISA and consequently free of the antialienation provision. 497 F.3d at 429. The Court of Appeals held that Liv's waiver constituted an assignment or alienation of her interest in the SIP benefits to the Estate, and so could not be honored. *Id.* at 430. The court relied heavily on the ERISA provision for bypassing the antialienation provision when a marriage breaks up: under § 206(d)(3),[3] a court order that satisfies certain statutory requirements is known as a qualified domestic relations order, which is exempt from the bar on assignment or alienation. Because the Kennedys' divorce decree was not a QDRO, the Fifth Circuit reasoned that it could not give effect to Liv's waiver incorporated in it, given that "ERISA provides a specific mechanism-the QDRO-for addressing the elimination of a spouse's interest in plan benefits, but that mechanism is *not* invoked." 497 F.3d at 431.

We granted certiorari to resolve a split among the Courts of Appeals and State Supreme Courts over a divorced spouse's ability to waive pension plan benefits through a divorce decree not amounting to a QDRO. We subsequently realized that this case implicates the further split over whether a beneficiary's federal common law waiver of plan benefits is effective where that waiver is inconsistent with plan documents, and after oral argument we invited supplemental briefing on that latter issue, upon which the disposition of this case ultimately turns. We now affirm, albeit on reasoning different from the Fifth Circuit's rationale.

II

A

By its terms, the antialienation provision, ERISA § 206(d)(1), requires a plan to provide expressly that benefits be neither "assigned" nor "alienated," the operative verbs having histories of legal meaning: to "assign" is "[t]o transfer; as to assign property, or some interest therein," Black's Law Dictionary 152 (4th rev. ed. 1968), and to "alienate" is "[t]o convey; to transfer the title to property," *id.* at 96. We think it fair to say that Liv did not assign or alienate anything to William or to the Estate later standing in his shoes.

---

[3] Section 206(d)(3)(A) provides that the antialienation provision "shall apply to the creation, assignment, or recognition of a right to any benefit payable with respect to a participant pursuant to a domestic relations order, except that paragraph (1) shall not apply if the order is determined to be a qualified domestic relations order."

The Fifth Circuit saw the waiver as an assignment or alienation to the Estate, thinking that Liv's waiver transferred the SIP benefits to whoever would be next in line; without a designated contingent beneficiary, the Estate would take them. The court found support in the applicable Treasury Department regulation that defines "assignment" and "alienation" to include

> [a]ny direct or indirect arrangement (whether revocable or irrevocable) whereby a party acquires from a participant or beneficiary a right or interest enforceable against the plan in, or to, all or any part of a plan benefit payment which is, or may become, payable to the participant or beneficiary. 26 C.F.R. § 1.401(a)–13(c)(1)(ii) (2008).

See *Boggs v. Boggs*, 520 U.S. 833, 851–52, (1997) (relying upon the regulation to interpret the meaning of "assignment" and "alienation" in [ERISA § 206(d)(1)]). The Circuit treated Liv's waiver as an " 'indirect arrangement' " whereby the Estate gained an " 'interest enforceable against the plan.' " 497 F.3d at 430.

Casting the alienation net this far, though, raises questions that leave one in doubt. Although it is possible to speak of the waiver as an "arrangement" having the indirect effect of a transfer to the next possible beneficiary, it would be odd usage to speak of an estate as the transferee of its own decedent's property, just as it would be to speak of the decedent in his lifetime as his own transferee. And treating the estate or even the ultimate estate beneficiary as the assignee or transferee would be strange under the terms of the regulation: it would be hard to say the estate or future beneficiary "acquires" a right or interest when at the time of the waiver there was no estate and the beneficiary of a future estate might be anyone's guess. If there were a contingent beneficiary (or the participant made a subsequent designation) the estate would get no interest; as for an estate beneficiary, the identity could ultimately turn on the law of intestacy applied to facts as yet unknown, or on the contents of the participant's subsequent will, or simply on the participant's future exercise of (or failure to invoke) the power to designate a new beneficiary directly under the terms of the plan. Thus, if such a waiver created an "arrangement" assigning or transferring anything under the statute, the assignor would be blindfolded, operating, at best, on the fringe of what "assignment" or "alienation" normally suggests.

The questionability of this broad reading is confirmed by exceptions to it that are apparent right off the bat. Take the case of a surviving spouse's interest in pension benefits, for example. Depending on the circumstances, a surviving spouse has a right to a survivor's annuity or to a lump-sum payment on the death of the participant, unless the spouse has waived the right and the participant has eliminated the survivor annuity benefit or designated a different beneficiary. See *Boggs, supra*, at 843; [ERISA §§ 205(a), (b)(1)(C), (c)(2)]. This waiver by a spouse is plainly not barred by the antialienation provision. Likewise, DuPont concedes that a qualified disclaimer under the Tax Code, which allows a party to refuse an interest in property and thereby eliminate federal tax, would not violate the antialienation provision. See Brief for Respondents 21–23; 26 U.S.C. § 2518. In each example, though, we fail to see how these waivers would be permissible under the Fifth Circuit's reading of the statute and regulation.

Our doubts, and the exceptions that call the Fifth Circuit's reading into question, point us toward authority we have drawn on before, the law of trusts that "serves as ERISA's backdrop." *Beck v. Pace Int'l Union*, 551 U.S. 96, 101 (2007). We explained before that § 206(d)(1) is much like a spendthrift trust provision barring assignment or alienation of a benefit, see *Boggs, supra*, at 852, and the cognate trust law is highly suggestive here. Although the beneficiary of a spendthrift trust traditionally lacked the means to transfer his beneficial interest to anyone else, he did have the power to disclaim prior to accepting it, so long as the disclaimer made no attempt to direct the interest to a beneficiary in his stead . . . .

We do not mean that the whole law of spendthrift trusts and disclaimers turns up in § 206(d)(1), but the general principle that a designated spendthrift can disclaim his trust interest magnifies the improbability that a statute written with an eye on the old law would effectively force a beneficiary to take an interest willy-nilly. Common sense and common law both say that "[t]he law certainly is not so absurd as to force a man to take an estate against his will." *Townson v. Tickell*, 3 Barn. & Ald. 31, 36, 106 Eng. Rep. 575, 576–77 (K.B. 1819).

The Treasury is certainly comfortable with the state of the old law, for the way it reads its own regulation "no party 'acquires from' a beneficiary a 'right or interest enforceable against the plan' pursuant to a beneficiary's waiver of rights where the beneficiary does not attempt to direct her interest in pension benefits to another person." Brief for United States as *Amicus Curiae* 18. And, being neither "plainly erroneous [n]or inconsistent with the regulation," the Treasury Department's interpretation of its regulation is controlling. *Auer v. Robbins*, 519 U.S. 452, 461 (1997).

The Fifth Circuit found "significant support" for its contrary holding in the QDRO subsections, reasoning that "[i]n the marital-dissolution context, the QDRO provisions supply the *sole* exception to the anti-alienation provision," 497 F.3d at 430, a point that echoes in DuPont's argument here. But the negative implication of the QDRO language is not that simple. If a QDRO provided a way for a former spouse like Liv merely to waive benefits, this would be powerful evidence that the antialienation provision was meant to deny any effect to a waiver within a divorce decree but not a QDRO, else there would have been no need for the QDRO exception. But this is not so, and DuPont's argument rests on a false premise. In fact, a beneficiary seeking only to relinquish her right to benefits cannot do this by a QDRO, for a QDRO by definition requires that it be the "creat[ion] or recogni[tion of] the existence of an alternate payee's right to, or assign[ment] to an alternate payee [of] the right to, receive all or a portion of the benefits payable with respect to a participant under a plan." ERISA § 206(d)(3)(B)(i)(I). There is no QDRO for a simple waiver; there must be some succeeding designation of an alternate payee. Not being a mechanism for simply renouncing a claim to benefits, then, the QDRO provisions shed no light on whether a beneficiary may waive by a non-QDRO.

In sum, Liv did not attempt to direct her interest in the SIP benefits to the Estate or any other potential beneficiary, and accordingly we think that the better view is that her waiver did not constitute an assignment or alienation rendered void under the terms of § 206(d)(1).

B

DuPont has three other reasons for saying that Liv's waiver was barred by ERISA. They are unavailing.

First, it argues that even if the waiver is not an assignment or alienation barred under the terms of § 206(d)(1), § 206(d)(3)(A) still prohibits it, in providing that § 206(d)(1) "shall apply to the creation, assignment, or recognition of a right to any benefit payable with respect to a participant pursuant to a domestic relations order [that is not a QDRO]." At the very least, DuPont reasons, Liv's waiver included a "recognition" of William's rights with respect to the SIP benefits. But DuPont overlooks the point that when subsection (d)(3)(A) provides that the bar to assignments or alienations extends to non-QDRO domestic relations orders, it does nothing to expand the scope of prohibited assignment and alienation under subsection (d)(1). Whether Liv's action is seen as a waiver or as a domestic relations order that incorporated a waiver, subsection (d)(1) does not cover it and § 206(d)(3)(A) does not independently bar it.

Second, DuPont relies upon § 206(d)(3)(H)(iii)(II), providing that if a domestic relations order is not a QDRO, "the plan administrator shall pay the segregated amounts (including any interest thereon) to the person or persons who would have been entitled to such amounts if there had been no order." According to DuPont, because the divorce decree was not a QDRO this provision calls for paying benefits as if there had been no order. But DuPont has wrenched this language out of its setting, reading clause (iii) of subparagraph (H) as if there were no clause (i):

> During any period in which the issue of whether a domestic relations order is a qualified domestic relations order is being determined . . . the plan administrator shall separately account for the amounts (hereinafter in this subparagraph referred to as the "segregated amounts") which would have been payable to the alternate payee during such period if the order had been determined to be a qualified domestic relations order. § 206(d)(3)(H)(i).

Thus it is clear that subparagraph (H) speaks of a domestic relations order that distributes certain benefits (the "segregated amounts") to an alternate payee, when the question for the plan administrator is whether the order is effective as a QDRO. That is the circumstance in which, for want of a QDRO, clause (iii) tells the plan administrator not to pay the alternate, but to distribute the segregated amounts as if there had been no order. Clause (iii) does not, as DuPont suggests, state a general rule that a non-QDRO domestic relations order is a nullity in any proceeding that would affect the determination of a beneficiary. And of course clause (iii) says nothing here at all; the divorce decree names no alternate payee, and there are consequently no "segregated amounts."

Third, DuPont claims that a plan cannot recognize a waiver of benefits in a non-QDRO divorce decree because ERISA preempts "any and all State laws insofar as they may now or hereafter relate to any employee benefit plan," with "State law" being defined to include "decisions" or "other State action having the effect of law." §§ 514(a), (c)(1). DuPont says that Liv's waiver, expressed in a state-court decision and related to an employee benefit plan, is thus preempted. But recognizing a waiver in a divorce decree would not be giving effect to state law; the argument is that the waiver should be treated as a creature of federal common law, in which case its setting in a state divorce decree would be only happenstance. A court would merely be applying federal law to a document that might also have independent significance under state law.

III

The waiver's escape from inevitable nullity under the express terms of the antialienation clause does not, however, control the decision of this case, and the question remains whether the plan administrator was required to honor Liv's waiver with the consequence of distributing the SIP balance to the Estate. We hold that it was not, and that the plan administrator did its statutory ERISA duty by paying the benefits to Liv in conformity with the plan documents.

ERISA requires "[e]very employee benefit plan [to] be established and maintained pursuant to a written instrument," § 402(a)(1), "specify[ing] the basis on which payments are made to and from the plan," § 402(b)(4). The plan administrator is obliged to act "in accordance with the documents and instruments governing the plan insofar as such documents and instruments are consistent with the provisions of [Title I] and [Title IV] of [ERISA]," § 404(a)(1)(D), and the Act provides no exemption from this duty when it comes time to pay benefits. On the contrary, § 502(a)(1)(B) (which the Estate happens to invoke against DuPont here) reinforces the directive, with its provision that a participant or beneficiary may bring a cause of action "to recover benefits due to him under the terms of his plan, to enforce his rights under the terms of the plan, or to clarify his rights to future benefits under the terms of the plan."

The Estate's claim therefore stands or falls by "the terms of the plan," § 502(a)(1)(B), a straightforward rule of hewing to the directives of the plan documents that lets employers " 'establish a uniform administrative scheme, [with] a set of standard procedures to guide processing of claims and disbursement of benefits.' " *Egelhoff v. Egelhoff*, 532 U.S. 141, 148, (2001) . . . The point is that by giving a plan participant a clear set of instructions for making his own instructions clear, ERISA forecloses any justification for enquiries into nice expressions of intent, in favor of the virtues of adhering to an uncomplicated rule: "simple administration, avoid[ing] double liability, and ensur[ing] that beneficiaries get what's coming quickly, without the folderol essential under less-certain rules." *Fox Valley & Vicinity Const. Workers Pension Fund v. Brown*, 897 F.2d 275, 283 (C.A.7 1990) (Easterbrook, J., dissenting).

And the cost of less certain rules would be too plain. Plan administrators would be forced "to examine a multitude of external documents that might purport to affect the dispensation of benefits," *Altobelli v. IBM Corp.*, 77 F.3d 78, 82–83 (C.A.4 1996) (Wilkinson, C.J., dissenting), and be drawn into litigation like this over the meaning and enforceability of purported waivers. The Estate's suggestion that a plan administrator could resolve these sorts of disputes through interpleader actions merely restates the problem with the Estate's position: it would destroy a plan administrator's ability to look at the plan documents and records conforming to them to get clear distribution instructions, without going into court.

The Estate of course is right that this guarantee of simplicity is not absolute. The very enforceability of QDROs means that sometimes a plan administrator must look for the beneficiaries outside plan documents notwithstanding § 404(a)(1)(D); § 206(d)(3)(J) provides that a "person who is an alternate payee under a [QDRO] shall be considered for purposes of any provision of [ERISA] a beneficiary under the plan." But this in effect means that a plan administrator who enforces a QDRO must be said to enforce plan documents, not ignore them. In any case, a QDRO enquiry is relatively discrete, given the specific and objective criteria for a domestic relations order that qualifies as a QDRO, see §§ 206(d)(3)(C), (D), requirements that amount to a statutory checklist working to "spare [an administrator] from litigation-fomenting ambiguities," *Metropolitan Life Ins. Co. v. Wheaton*, 42 F.3d 1080, 1084 (C.A.7 1994). This is a far cry from asking a plan administrator to figure out whether a claimed federal common law waiver was knowing and voluntary, whether its language addressed the particular benefits at issue, and so forth, on into factually complex and subjective determinations.

These are good and sufficient reasons for holding the line, just as we have done in cases of state laws that might blur the bright-line requirement to follow plan documents in distributing benefits. Two recent preemption cases are instructive here. *Boggs v. Boggs*, 520 U.S. 833, held that ERISA preempted a state law permitting the testamentary transfer of a nonparticipant spouse's community property interest in undistributed pension plan benefits. We rejected the entreaty to create "through case law . . . a new class of persons for whom plan assets are to be held and administered," explaining that "[t]he statute is not amenable to this sweeping extratextual extension." *Id.* at 850. And in *Egelhoff* we held that ERISA preempted a state law providing that the designation of a spouse as the beneficiary of a nonprobate asset is revoked automatically upon divorce. 532 U.S. at 143. We said the law was at fault for standing in the way of making payments "simply by identifying the beneficiary specified by the plan documents," *id.* at 148, and thus for purporting to "undermine the congressional goal of 'minimiz[ing] the administrative and financial burden[s]' on plan administrators," *id.* at 149–50. . .

What goes for inconsistent state law goes for a federal common law of waiver that might obscure a plan administrator's duty to act "in accordance with the documents and instruments." See *Mertens v. Hewitt Associates*, 508 U.S. 248, 259, (1993) ("The authority of courts to develop a 'federal common law' under ERISA . . . is not the authority to revise the text of the statute."). And this case does as well as any other in pointing out the wisdom of protecting the plan documents rule. Under the terms of the SIP Liv was William's designated beneficiary. The plan provided an easy way for William to change the designation, but for whatever reason he did not. The plan provided a way to disclaim an interest in the SIP account, but Liv did not purport to follow it. The plan administrator therefore did exactly what § 404(a)(1)(D) required: "the documents control, and those name [the ex-wife]." *McMillan v. Parrott*, 913 F.2d 310, 312 (C.A.6 1990).

It is no answer, as the Estate argues, that William's beneficiary-designation form should not control because it is not one of the "documents and instruments governing the plan" under § 404(a)(1)(D) and was not treated as a plan document by the plan administrator. That is beside the point. It is uncontested that the SIP and the summary plan description are "documents and instruments governing the plan." See *Curtiss-Wright Corp.*, 514 U.S. at 84, (explaining that ERISA §§ 104(b)(2) and (b)(4) require a plan administrator to make available the "governing plan documents"). Those documents provide that the plan administrator will pay benefits to a participant's designated beneficiary, with designations and changes to be made in a particular way. William's designation of Liv as his beneficiary was made in the way required; Liv's waiver was not.

IV

Although Liv's waiver was not rendered a nullity by the terms of § 206, the plan administrator properly distributed the SIP benefits to Liv in accordance with the plan documents. The judgment of the Court of Appeals is affirmed on the latter ground.

It is so ordered.

4-13 QUESTIONS AND PROBLEMS

1.Whom did William intend to receive his SIP benefits upon his death? What role did William's intent play in the Court's decision? Why?

2. Suppose that William had remarried. Who would have received the SIP benefits upon his death? Why?

3. If a divorce decree states that the participant is to keep 100 percent of his or her retirement benefits as his or her sole and separate property, is a QDRO necessary? Must a change in beneficiary designation form be completed?

4. The Airline Pilots Retirement Plan provides that, upon divorce, if a pilot is at least 50 years old and assigns his or her benefits to his or her ex-spouse, the ex-

spouse can elect to receive those benefits even though the pilot continues to work at The Airline. Martin, age 52, and his wife, Chloe, divorced and obtained a DRO from the state court which assigned 100 percent of Martin's Retirement Plan benefit to Chloe. Chloe has asked the plan administrator for a lump sum distribution of Martin's Retirement Plan benefit. The plan administrator has learned that Martin and Chloe still live together and have not informed any of their family or friends that they have gotten a divorce. Moreover, the plan administrator was told that Martin and Chloe will remarry as soon as she receives the lump sum distribution. Can the plan administrator refuse to distribute the lump sum to Chloe because the divorce is a "sham?"

[2] Participant Misconduct

Should a participant's behavior affect his or her rights to benefits?

GUIDRY v. SHEET METAL WORKERS NATIONAL PENSION FUND

493 U.S. 365 (1990)

Justice Blackmun delivered the opinion of the Court.

Petitioner Curtis Guidry pleaded guilty to embezzling funds from his union. The union obtained a judgment against him for $275,000. The District Court imposed a constructive trust on Guidry's pension benefits, and the United States Court of Appeals for the Tenth Circuit affirmed that judgment. Petitioner contends that the constructive trust violates the statutory prohibition on assignment or alienation of pension benefits imposed by [ERISA].

I

From 1964 to 1981, petitioner Guidry was the chief executive officer of respondent Sheet Metal Workers International Association, Local 9 (Union). From 1977 to 1981 he was also a trustee of respondent Sheet Metal Workers Local No. 9 Pension Fund. Petitioner's employment made him eligible to receive benefits from three union pension funds.

In 1981, the Department of Labor reviewed the Union's internal accounting procedures. That review demonstrated that Guidry had embezzled substantial sums of money from the Union. *See* App. 20. This led to petitioner's resignation. A subsequent audit indicated that over $998,000 was missing. *Id.* at 26. In 1982, petitioner pleaded guilty to embezzling more than $377,000 from the Union, in violation of § 501(c) of the Labor-Management Reporting and Disclosure Act of 1959 (LMRDA). Petitioner began serving a prison sentence. In April 1984, while still incarcerated, petitioner filed a complaint against two of the plans in the United States District Court for the District of Colorado, alleging that the plans had wrongfully refused to pay him the benefits to which he was entitled. The Union intervened, joined the third pension plan as a party, and asserted six claims against petitioner. On the first five claims, petitioner and the Union stipulated to the entry of a $275,000 judgment in the Union's favor. App. 52-58. Petitioner and the Union agreed to litigate the availability of the constructive trust remedy requested in the sixth claim. *Id.* at 58.

Petitioner previously had negotiated a settlement with the Local No. 9 Pension Fund. *Id.* at 44–46. The other two plans, however, contended that petitioner had forfeited his right to receive benefits as a result of his criminal misconduct. *Id.* at 47–50. In the alternative those plans contended that, if petitioner were found to have a right to benefits, those benefits should be paid to the Union rather than to Guidry. *Ibid.*

The District Court therefore was confronted with three different views regarding the disbursement of petitioner's pension benefits. Petitioner contended that the benefits should be paid to him. The two funds argued that the benefits had been forfeited. The Union asserted that the benefits had not been forfeited, but that a constructive trust should be imposed so that the benefits would be paid to the Union rather than to petitioner.

The District Court first rejected the funds' claim that petitioner had forfeited his right to benefits. 641 F. Supp. 360, 362 (Colo. 1986). The court relied on § 203(a) of ERISA, which declares that "[e]ach pension plan shall provide that an employee's right to his normal retirement benefit is nonforfeitable" if the employee meets the statutory age and years of service requirements. 641 F. Supp. at 361–362. The court noted other District Court and Court of Appeals decisions holding that pension benefits were not forfeitable even upon a showing of the covered employee's misconduct. *Id.* at 362.

The court concluded, however, that the prohibition on assignment or alienation of pension benefits contained in ERISA's § 206(d)(1) did not preclude the imposition of a constructive trust in favor of the Union. The court appeared to recognize that the anti-alienation provision generally prohibits the garnishment of pension benefits as a means of collecting a judgment. The court, nevertheless, stated: "ERISA must be read in pari materia with other important federal labor legislation." 641 F. Supp. at 362. In the Labor Management Relations Act and in the LMRDA, Congress sought to combat corruption on the part of union officials and to protect the interests of the membership. Viewing these statutes together with ERISA, the District Court concluded: "In circumstances where the viability of a union and the members' pension plans was damaged by the knavery of a union official, a narrow exception to ERISA's anti-alienation provision is appropriate." 641 F. Supp. at 363. The court therefore ordered that benefits payable to petitioner from all three funds should be held in constructive trust until the Union's judgment and interest thereon were satisfied. *Ibid.*

The United States Court of Appeals for the Tenth Circuit affirmed. 856 F.2d 1457 (1988). The court concluded that ERISA's anti-alienation provision could not be invoked to protect a dishonest pension plan fiduciary whose breach of duty injured the beneficiaries of the plan. The court deemed it "extremely unlikely that Congress intended to ignore equitable principles by protecting individuals such as [petitioner] from the consequences of their misconduct." *Id.* at 1460. The court concluded that "the district court's imposition of a constructive trust on [petitioner's] pension benefits both accorded with . . . principles of trust law and was well within its discretionary power as defined by the common law and ERISA." *Id.* at 1461.

Because Courts of Appeals have expressed divergent views concerning the availability of exceptions to ERISA's anti-alienation provision, we granted certiorari.

II

Both the District Court and the Court of Appeals presumed that § 206(d)(1) of ERISA erects a general bar to the garnishment of pension benefits from plans covered by the Act. This Court, also, indicated as much, although in dictum, in *Mackey v. Lanier Collection Agency & Service, Inc.*, 486 U.S. 825 (1988). In *Mackey* the Court held that ERISA does *not* bar the garnishment of welfare (*e.g.*, vacation) benefits. In reaching that conclusion, it noted that § 206(d)(1) proscribes the assignment or alienation of *pension* plan benefits, but that no comparable provision applies to ERISA *welfare* benefit plans. *Id.* at 836. It reasoned that "when Congress was adopting ERISA, it had before it a provision to bar the alienation or garnishment of ERISA plan benefits, and chose to impose that limitation only with respect to ERISA pension benefit plans, and *not* ERISA welfare benefit plans." *Id.* at 837 (emphasis in original). The view that the statutory restrictions on assignment or alienation of pension benefits apply to garnishment is consistent with applicable administrative regulations, with the relevant legislative history, and with the views of other federal courts. It is also consonant with other statutory provisions designed to safeguard retirement income. We see no meaningful distinction between a writ of garnishment and the constructive trust remedy imposed in this case. That remedy is therefore prohibited by § 206(d)(1) unless some exception to the general statutory ban is applicable.

A

The Court of Appeals, in holding that "the district court's use of a constructive trust to redress breaches of ERISA was proper," 856 F.2d at 1460, indicated that an exception to the anti-alienation provision can be made when a pension plan fiduciary breaches a duty owed to the plan itself. The court relied on § 409(a) of ERISA, which provides that a faithless pension plan fiduciary "shall be personally liable to make good to such plan any losses to the plan resulting from each such breach, . . . and shall be subject to such other equitable or remedial relief as the court may deem appropriate." 856 F.2d at 1459. We need not decide whether the remedial provisions contained in § 409(a) supersede the bar on alienation in § 206(d)(1), since petitioner has not been found to have breached any fiduciary duty *to the pension plans.* Respondents contend that, due to the nature of petitioner's scheme, there exists continuing uncertainty as to how much money was stolen from the Union and how much was taken from the pension funds. It is clear, however, that petitioner was convicted of stealing money only from the Union. Moreover, petitioner has negotiated a settlement with the fund of which he was a fiduciary, and only the Union has a judgment against him. Respondents' argument plays on the natural tendency to blur the distinctions between a fund and its related union (since an injury to either will hurt the union's membership). Respondents, however, cannot avoid the fact that the funds here and the Union are distinct legal entities. (Indeed, at an earlier stage of the litigation these parties took inconsistent positions: the funds argued that petitioner's benefits were subject to forfeiture, while the Union contended that petitioner retained his right to benefits but that the benefits should be placed in constructive trust). Although petitioner's actions may have harmed the Union's members who are the beneficiaries of the funds, petitioner has not been found to have breached any duty to the plans themselves. In our view, therefore, the Court of Appeals erred in invoking § 409(a)'s remedial provisions.

B

Recognizing the problem with the Court of Appeals' approach, respondents, like the District Court, rely principally on the remedial provisions of the LMRDA. Section 501(a) of that Act states that a union's officers "occupy positions of trust in relation to such organization and its members as a group" and therefore have a duty "to hold its money and property solely for the benefit of the organization and its members." Section 501(b) provides, under certain conditions, a private right of action "to recover damages or secure an accounting or other appropriate relief for the benefit of the labor organization." We assume, without deciding, that the statutory provision for "other appropriate relief" may authorize, in some circumstances, the imposition of a constructive trust. The question is whether that authorization may override ERISA's prohibition on the alienation of pension benefits.

Respondents point to § 514(d) of ERISA. It states: "Nothing in this title shall be construed to alter, amend, modify, invalidate, impair, or supersede any law of the United States . . . or any rule or regulation issued under any such law." In respondents' view, application of ERISA's anti-alienation provision to preclude a remedy that would otherwise be available would "modify, impair or supersede" the LMRDA. We do not believe, however, that the LMRDA will be modified, impaired, or superseded by our refusal to allow ERISA pension plans to be used to effectuate the remedial goals of the LMRDA. Were we to accept respondents' position, ERISA's anti-alienation provision would be inapplicable whenever a judgment creditor relied on the remedial provisions of a federal statute. Such an approach would eviscerate the protections of § 206(d), and we decline to adopt so broad a reading of § 514(d).

It is an elementary tenet of statutory construction that "[w]here there is no clear intention otherwise, a specific statute will not be controlled or nullified by a general one . . . ." *Morton v. Mancari*, 417 U.S. 535, 550–551 (1974). We do not believe that congressional intent would be effectuated by reading the LMRDA's general reference to "other appropriate relief" as overriding an express, specific congressional directive that pension benefits not be subject to assignment or alienation. In our view, the two statutes are more persuasively reconciled by holding that the LMRDA determines what sort of *judgment* the aggrieved party may obtain, while ERISA governs the narrow question whether that judgment may be collected through a particular means — a constructive trust placed *on the pension.*

C

Nor do we think it appropriate to approve any generalized equitable exception — either for employee malfeasance or for criminal misconduct — to ERISA's prohibition on the assignment or alienation of pension benefits. Section 206(d) reflects a considered congressional policy choice, a decision to safeguard a stream of income for pensioners (and their dependents, who may be, and perhaps usually are, blameless), even if that decision prevents others from securing relief for the wrongs done them. If exceptions to this policy are to be made, it is for Congress to undertake that task. [citing the exception for QDROs.]

As a general matter, courts should be loath to announce equitable exceptions to legislative requirements or prohibitions that are unqualified by the statutory text. The creation of such exceptions, in our view, would be especially problematic in the context of an antigarnishment provision. Such a provision acts, by definition, to hinder the collection of a lawful debt. A restriction on garnishment therefore can be defended *only* on the view that the effectuation of certain broad social policies sometimes takes precedence over the desire to do equity between particular parties. It makes little sense to adopt such a policy and then to refuse enforcement whenever enforcement appears inequitable. A court attempting to carve out an exception that would not swallow the rule would be forced to determine whether application of the rule in particular circumstances would be "especially" inequitable. The impracticability of defining such a standard reinforces our conclusion that the identification of any exception should be left to Congress.

Understandably, there may be a natural distaste for the result we reach here. The statute, however, is clear. In addition, as has been noted above, the malefactor often is not the only beneficiary of the pension.

The judgment of the Court of Appeals is reversed, and the case is remanded for further proceedings consistent with this opinion.

4-14 QUESTIONS AND PROBLEMS

1. Does the Court focus on the purpose or language of the statute?

2. Is the Court correct in stating that only Congress should create exceptions to the anti-alienation rules?

3. Bernard, the majority owner and chief executive officer of Beta Co., was a trustee of and participant in the Beta Co. Profit-Sharing Plan. Over a five year period, Bernard stole over million dollars from the Plan for the benefit of his other business interests. Fifteen of the Plan's participants brought suit against Bernard. The court granted summary judgment in favor of the Plan, finding that Bernard had breached his fiduciary duties as trustee of the Plan and had violated ERISA's prohibited transaction provisions by misusing Plan assets for his own benefit and for the benefit of others. Under the reasoning of *Guidry*, can Bernard's benefits under the Plan be offset against the equitable judgment obtained by the Plan beneficiaries? Do ERISA § 206(d)(4) and IRC § 401(a)(13)(C) permit the judgment to provide for the offset of all or part or the amount ordered or required to be paid to the Plan against Bernard's benefits provided under the Plan?

4. Sections 206(d)(4) of ERISA and 401(a)(13)(C) of the IRC were added in 1997, seven years after the Court rendered its decision in *Guidry*. Would the result in *Guidry* have been different had these sections been in effect?

5. Jackson was indicted on 46 counts of embezzling labor union assets in violation of section 501(c) of the Labor-Management Reporting and Disclosure Act of 1959. He pled guilty to six of these counts. As a condition of his plea, Jackson agreed to make full restitution for the losses caused by his crimes, in an amount to be determined by the district court based on his ability to pay. Taking into account the assets held in Jackson's tax-qualified retirement plan, the district court ordered that Jackson pay restitution in the amount of $220,000, and that he pay immediate restitution out of the proceeds of his undistributed tax-qualified retirement plan. Jackson appealed, claiming that the district court's order violated ERISA's anti-alienation rules. What result?

[3] Bankruptcy of Participants

PATTERSON v. SHUMATE
504 U.S. 753 (1992)

Justice Blackmun delivered the opinion of the Court.

The Bankruptcy Code excludes from the bankruptcy estate property of the debtor that is subject to a restriction on transfer enforceable under "applicable nonbankruptcy law." 11 U.S.C. § 541(c)(2). We must decide in this case whether an anti-alienation provision contained in an ERISA-qualified pension plan constitutes a restriction on transfer enforceable under "applicable nonbankruptcy law," and whether, accordingly, a debtor may exclude his interest in such a plan from the property of the bankruptcy estate.

Respondent Joseph B. Shumate, Jr., was employed for over 30 years by Coleman Furniture Corporation, where he ultimately attained the position of president and chairman of the board of directors. Shumate and approximately 400 other employees were participants in the Coleman Furniture Corporation Pension Plan (Plan). The Plan satisfied all applicable requirements of ERISA and qualified for favorable tax treatment under the Internal Revenue Code. In particular, Article 16.1 of the Plan contained the anti-alienation provision required for qualification under § 206(d)(1) of ERISA. Shumate's interest in the Plan was valued at $250,000.

In 1982, Coleman Furniture filed a petition for bankruptcy under Chapter 11 of the Bankruptcy Code. The case was converted to a Chapter 7 proceeding, and a trustee, Roy V. Creasy, was appointed. Shumate himself encountered financial difficulties and filed a petition for bankruptcy in 1984. His case, too, was converted to a Chapter 7 proceeding, and petitioner John R. Patterson was appointed trustee.

Creasy terminated and liquidated the Plan, providing full distributions to all participants except Shumate. Patterson then filed an adversary proceeding against Creasy in the Bankruptcy Court for the Western District of Virginia to recover Shumate's interest in the Plan for the benefit of Shumate's bankruptcy estate. Shumate in turn asked the United States District Court for the Western District of Virginia, which already had jurisdiction over a related proceeding, to compel Creasy to pay Shumate's interest in the Plan directly to him. The bankruptcy proceeding subsequently was consolidated with the District Court action.

The District Court rejected Shumate's contention that his interest in the Plan should be excluded from his bankruptcy estate. The court held that § 541(c)(2)'s reference to "nonbankruptcy law" embraced only state law, not federal law such as ERISA. Applying Virginia law, the court held that Shumate's interest in the Plan did not qualify for protection as a spendthrift trust. The District Court also rejected Shumate's alternative argument that even if his interest in the Plan could not be excluded from the bankruptcy estate under § 541(c)(2), he was entitled to an exemption under 11 U.S.C. § 522(b)(2)(A), which allows a debtor to exempt from property of the estate "any property that is exempt under Federal law." The District Court ordered Creasy to pay Shumate's interest in the Plan over to his bankruptcy estate.

The Court of Appeals for the Fourth Circuit reversed. The court relied on its earlier decision in *In re Moore*, 907 F.2d 1476 (1990), in which another Fourth Circuit panel was described as holding, subsequent to the District Court's decision in the instant case, that "ERISA-qualified plans, which by definition have a non-alienation provision, constitute 'applicable nonbankruptcy law' and contain enforceable restrictions on the transfer of pension interests." Thus, the Court of Appeals held that Shumate's interest in the Plan should be excluded from the bankruptcy estate under § 541(c)(2).The court then declined to consider Shumate's alternative argument that his interest in the Plan qualified for exemption under § 522(b).

We granted certiorari, to resolve the conflict among the Courts of Appeals as to whether an anti-alienation provision in an ERISA-qualified pension plan constitutes a restriction on transfer enforceable under "applicable nonbankruptcy law" for purposes of the § 541(c)(2) exclusion of property from the debtor's bankruptcy estate.

II

A

In our view, the plain language of the Bankruptcy Code and ERISA is our determinant. Section 541(c)(2) provides the following exclusion from the otherwise broad definition of "property of the estate" contained in § 541(a)(1) of the Code:

> "A restriction on the transfer of a beneficial interest of the debtor in a trust that is enforceable under *applicable nonbankruptcy law* is enforceable in a case under this title." (Emphasis added.)

The natural reading of the provision entitles a debtor to exclude from property of the estate any interest in a plan or trust that contains a transfer restriction enforceable under any relevant nonbankruptcy law. Nothing in § 541 suggests that the phrase "applicable nonbankruptcy law" refers, as petitioner contends, exclusively to *state* law. The text contains no limitation on "applicable nonbankruptcy law" relating to the source of the law.

Reading the term "applicable nonbankruptcy law" in § 541(c)(2) to include federal as well as state law comports with other references in the Bankruptcy Code to sources of law. The Code reveals, significantly, that Congress, when it desired to do so, knew how to restrict the scope of applicable law to "state law" and did so with some frequency. *See, e.g.*, 11 U.S.C. § 109(c)(2) (entity may be a debtor under chapter 9 if authorized "by State law"); § 522(b)(1) (election of exemptions controlled by "the State law that is applicab le to the debtor"); § 523(a)(5) (a debt for alimony, maintenance, or support determined "in accordance with State or territorial law" is not dischargeable); § 903(1) ("[A] State law prescribing a method of composition of indebtedness" of municipalities is not binding on nonconsenting creditors); *see also* §§ 362(b)(12) and 1145(a). Congress' decision to use the broader phrase "applicable nonbankruptcy law" in § 541(c)(2) strongly suggests that it did not intend to restrict the provision in the manner that petitioner contends.

The text of § 541(c)(2) does not support petitioner's contention that "applicable nonbankruptcy law" is limited to state law. Plainly read, the provision encompasses any relevant nonbankruptcy law, including federal law such as ERISA. We must enforce the statute according to its terms.

B

Having concluded that "applicable nonbankruptcy law" is not limited to state law, we next determine whether the anti-alienation provision contained in the ERISA-qualified Plan at issue here satisfies the literal terms of § 541(c)(2).

Section 206(d)(1) of ERISA, which states that "[e]ach pension plan shall provide that benefits provided under the plan may not be assigned or alienated," clearly imposes a "restriction on the transfer" of a debtor's "beneficial interest" in the trust. The coordinate section of the Internal Revenue Code, IRC § 401(a)(13), states as a general rule that "[a] trust shall not constitute a qualified trust under this section unless the plan of which such trust is a part provides that benefits provided under the plan may not be assigned or alienated," and thus contains similar restrictions.

Coleman Furniture's pension plan complied with these requirements. Article 16.1 of the Plan specifically stated: "No benefit, right or interest" of any participant "shall be subject to anticipation, alienation, sale, transfer, assignment, pledge, encumbrance or charge, seizure, attachment or other legal, equitable or other process."

Moreover, these transfer restrictions are "enforceable," as required by § 541(c)(2). Plan trustees or fiduciaries are required under ERISA to discharge their duties "in accordance with the documents and instruments governing the plan." ERISA § 404(a)(1)(D). A plan participant, beneficiary, or fiduciary, or the Secretary of Labor may file a civil action to "enjoin any act or practice" which violates ERISA or the terms of the plan. ERISA §§ 502(a)(3) and (5). Indeed, this Court itself vigorously has enforced ERISA's prohibition on the assignment or alienation of pension benefits, declining to recognize any implied exceptions to the broad statutory bar. *See Guidry v. Sheet Metal Workers Nat. Pension Fund*, 493 U.S. 365 (1990).

The anti-alienation provision required for ERISA qualification and contained in the Plan at issue in this case thus constitutes an enforceable transfer restriction for purposes of § 541(c)(2)'s exclusion of property from the bankruptcy estate.

III

Petitioner raises several challenges to this conclusion. Given the clarity of the statutory text, however, he bears an "exceptionally heavy" burden of persuading us that Congress intended to limit the § 541(c)(2) exclusion to restrictions on transfer that are enforceable only under state spendthrift trust law. *Union Bank v. Wolas*, 502 U.S. 151, 155–156 (1991).

A

Petitioner first contends that contemporaneous legislative materials demonstrate that § 541(c)(2)'s exclusion of property from the bankruptcy estate should not extend to a debtor's interest in an ERISA-qualified pension plan. Although courts "appropriately may refer to a statute's legislative history to resolve statutory ambiguity," *Toibb v. Radloff*, 501 U.S. at 162, the clarity of the statutory language at issue in this case obviates the need for any such inquiry. *See ibid.*

Even were we to consider the legislative materials to which petitioner refers, however, we could discern no "clearly expressed legislative intention" contrary to the result reached above. In his brief, petitioner quotes from House and Senate Reports accompanying the Bankruptcy Reform Act of 1978 that purportedly reflect "unmistakable" congressional intent to limit § 541(c)(2)'s exclusion to pension plans that qualify under state law as spendthrift trusts. Those reports contain only the briefest of discussions addressing § 541(c)(2). The House Report states: "Paragraph (2) of subsection (c) . . . preserves restrictions on transfer of a spendthrift trust to the extent that the restriction is enforceable under applicable nonbankruptcy law." H.R. Rep. No. 95-595, p. 369 (1977); *see also* S. Rep. No. 95-989, p. 83 (1978), U.S. Code Cong. & Admin. News 1978, pp. 5787, 5869, 6325 (§ 541(c)(2) "preserves restrictions on a transfer of a spendthrift trust"). A general introductory section to the House Report contains the additional statement that the new law "continues over the exclusion from property of the estate of the debtor's interest in a spendthrift trust to the extent the trust is protected from creditors under applicable State law." H.R. Rep. No. 95-595, p. 176, U.S. Code Cong. & Admin. News 1978, p. 6136. These meager excerpts reflect at best congressional intent to *include* state spendthrift trust law within the meaning of "applicable nonbankruptcy law." By no means do they provide a sufficient basis for concluding, in derogation of the statute's clear language, that Congress intended to *exclude* other state and federal law from the provision's scope.

B

Petitioner next contends that our construction of § 541(c)(2), pursuant to which a debtor may exclude his interest in an ERISA-qualified pension plan from the bankruptcy estate, renders § 522(d)(10)(E) of the Bankruptcy Code superfluous. Brief for Petitioner 24-33. Under § 522(d)(10)(E), a debtor who elects the federal exemptions set forth in § 522(d) may exempt from the bankruptcy estate his right to receive "a payment under a stock bonus, pension, profitsharing, annuity, or similar plan or contract. . . , to the extent reasonably necessary for the support of the debtor and any dependent of the debtor." If a debtor's interest in a pension plan could be *excluded* in full from the bankruptcy estate, the argument goes, then there would have been no reason for Congress to create a limited *exemption* for such interests elsewhere in the statute.

Petitioner's surplusage argument fails, however, for the reason that § 522(d)(10)(E) exempts from the bankruptcy estate a much broader category of interests than § 541(c)(2) excludes. For example, pension plans established by governmental entities and churches need not comply with Subchapter I of ERISA, including the anti-alienation requirement of § 206(d)(1). *See* ERISA §§ 4(b)(1) and (2); 26 CFR § 1.401(a)-13(a) (1991). So, too, pension plans that qualify for preferential tax treatment under § 408 of the IRC (individual retirement accounts) are specifically excepted from ERISA's anti-alienation requirement. *See* ERISA § 201(6). Although a debtor's interest in these plans could not be excluded under § 541(c)(2) because the plans lack transfer restrictions enforceable under "applicable nonbankruptcy law," that interest nevertheless could be exempted under § 522(d)(10)(E). Once petitioner concedes that § 522(d)(10)(E)'s exemption applies to more than ERISA-qualified plans containing anti-alienation provisions, *see* Tr. of Oral Arg. 10-11; Brief for Petitioner 31, his argument that our reading of § 541(c)(2) renders the exemption provision superfluous must collapse.

C

Finally, petitioner contends that our holding frustrates the Bankruptcy Code's policy of ensuring a broad inclusion of assets in the bankruptcy estate. *See id.* at 37; 11 U.S.C. § 541(a)(1) (estate composed of "all legal or equitable interests of the debtor in property as of the commencement of the case"). As an initial matter, we think that petitione r mistakes an admittedly broad definition of includable property for a "policy" underlying the Code as a whole. In any event, to the extent that policy considerations are even relevant where the language of the statute is so clear, we believe that our construction of § 541(c)(2) is preferable to the one petitioner urges upon us.

First, our decision today ensures that the treatment of pension benefits will not vary based on the beneficiary's bankruptcy status. We previously have declined to recognize any exceptions to ERISA's anti-alienation provision *outside* the bankruptcy context. *See Guidry v. Sheet Metal Workers Nat. Pension Fund*, 493 U.S. 365 (1990). Declining to recognize any exceptions to that provision *within* the bankruptcy context minimizes the possibility that creditors will engage in strategic manipulation of the bankruptcy laws in order to gain access to otherwise inaccessible funds.

Our holding also gives full and appropriate effect to ERISA's goal of protecting pension benefits. *See* ERISA §§ 2(b) and (c). This Court has described that goal as one of ensuring that "if a worker has been promised a defined pension benefit upon retirement — and if he has fulfilled whatever conditions are required to obtain a vested benefit — he actually will receive it." *Nachman Corp. v. Pension Benefit Guaranty Corporation*, 446 U.S. 359, 375 (1980). In furtherance of these principles, we recently declined in *Guidry*, notwithstanding strong equitable considerations to the contrary, to recognize an implied exception to ERISA's anti-alienation provision that would have allowed a labor union to impose a constructive trust on the pension benefits of a corrupt union official. We explained:

> "Section 206(d) reflects a considered congressional policy choice, a decision to safeguard a stream of income for pensioners (and their dependents, who may be, and perhaps usually are, blameless), even if that decision prevents others from securing relief for the wrongs done them. If exceptions to this policy are to be made, it is for Congress to undertake that task." 493 U.S. at 376.

These considerations apply with equal, if not greater, force in the present context.

Finally, our holding furthers another important policy underlying ERISA: uniform national treatment of pension benefits. *See Fort Halifax Packing Co. v. Coyne*, 482 U.S. 1, 9 (1987). Construing "applicable nonbankruptcy law" to include federal law ensures that the security of a debtor's pension benefits will be governed by ERISA, not left to the vagaries of state spendthrift trust law.

IV

In light of our conclusion that a debtor's interest in an ERISA-qualified pension plan may be excluded from the property of the bankruptcy estate pursuant to § 541(c)(2), we need not reach respondent's alternative argument that his interest in the Plan qualifies for exemption under § 522(b)(2)(A).

The judgment of the Court of Appeals is affirmed.

4-15 QUESTIONS AND PROBLEMS

1. Does the Court focus on the purpose or the language of the statute?

2. Is the Court's decision consistent with *Guidry*? Does the Court apply the same approach as it did in *Guidry*?

3. What is an "ERISA-qualified pension plan"? Does the exclusion apply to retirement accounts not covered by ERISA, such as IRAs and Keogh plans? To pension plans that fail to satisfy the tax qualification rules? To plan assets that are rolled over to an IRA? Following *Patterson v. Shumate*, there was some dispute over the meaning of the term "ERISA-qualified." On April 20, 2005, President Bush signed the Bankruptcy Abuse Prevention and Consumer Protection Act of 2005, which clarifie s and expands the type of plans that may be excluded from bankruptcy estates. Specifically, it permits debtors to exclude from the bankruptcy estate retirement funds or accounts that are exempt from tax under IRC §§ 401, 403, 408, 408A, 414, 547, or 501(a). While this Act was pending in Congress, the Supreme Court held that debtors may exempt IRA funds from their bankruptcy estate. *Rousey v. Jacoway*, 125 S. Ct. 1561 (2005). The new Bankruptcy Act expands on the Court's ruling by specifically extending bankruptcy protection to Roth IRAs.

The Bankruptcy Act imposes a $1 million cap on the amount of a debtor's interest in a traditional or Roth IRA that may be claimed as exempt. The $1 million cap may be increased if the "interests of justice so require." Assets that were "rolled over" to the IRA from a qualified plan or another IRA are disregarded for purposes of this $1 million limit.

4. The following excerpt briefly describes the policy goals of the Bankruptcy Code. Is the exclusion of "ERISA-qualified pension plans" consistent with these policy goals?

> [T]he Bankruptcy Code also attempts to further specific policy goals with respect to debtors in bankruptcy. The first is to give debtors a fresh start in economic life by cutting off creditors' access to future earnings (that is, those realized after the commencement of the bankruptcy proceedings) and any other interests that serve as a substitute for future earnings. The second, closely related to the fresh start principle, is to ensure that the debtor is left, after the creditors' claims have been satisfied, with the minimum income necessary for support — and "income maintenance" approach. [Patricia E. Dilley, *Hidden in Plain View: The Pension Shield Against Creditors*, 74 Ind. L.J. 355, 392–393 (1999).]

5. Does the exclusion of "ERISA-qualified pension plans" apply to plans that permit participants to borrow from the plan? Can a debtor who is a participant in a plan that permits loans be forced by her creditors to borrow from her plan to provide disposal income to fund obligations to the creditors?

6. Should there be an exception to the anti-alienation rules for participants in bankruptcy? If so, who should create this exception, the courts or Congress?

Chapter 5
PREEMPTION

The enactment of ERISA in 1974 federalized the law of employee benefits by preempting state governance or regulation of employee benefit plans. Specifically, ERISA § 514(a) states that the provisions of ERISA Titles I and IV "shall supersede any and all State laws insofar as they may now or hereafter relate to any employee benefit plan . . ." Because of ERISA preemption, regulation of employee benefit plans begins, and in most cases, ends with ERISA. The extent of the ERISA preemption is a frequently litigated issues, in part because of its "savings" clause that excludes state regulation of insurance from ERISA preemption. There are literally thousands of cases that have considered the application of ERISA preemption. One court compared ERISA preemption to a " 'Pac Man' that runs around the legal landscape, eating up other claims."[1] Although the Supreme Court has ruled on the parameters of ERISA preemption in over a dozen cases, the extent of ERISA preemption remains uncertain. This chapter reviews the statutory basis of ERISA preemption, its judicial interpretation, and the effects of preemption on the regulation of employee benefit plans.

A. INTRODUCTION

STEPHEN F. BEFORT, CHRISTOPHER J. KOPKA, THE SOUNDS OF SILENCE: THE LIBERTARIAN ETHOS OF ERISA PREEMPTION

52 Fla. L. Rev. 1, 4, 7 (2000)

A federal system of government necessarily involves a tension in the division of power between state and federal governments. Under the United States Constitution, this tension is principally resolved through the Supremacy Clause, which states, "This Constitution, and the laws of the United States . . . shall be the supreme law of the Land." This language authorizes, but does not compel, federal preemption of state law. Generally speaking, federal law supersedes state law where the two laws conflict or where Congress has otherwise indicated its desire to oust state regulation. Preemption analysis, therefore, is a matter of divining Congressional intent with respect to the particular federal statute at issue.

The federal courts primarily bear the responsibility of determining when federal preemption of state law is appropriate . . . .

The Supreme Court, through this evolving jurisprudence, has identified two functional categories of preemption: express and implied. The court uses express analysis to determine the effect of a direct statement within a federal law describing the appropriate scope of federal preemption. In other words, preemption is express when "Congress' command is explicitly stated in the statute's language . . . ." Express preemption clauses sometimes have been a cause of consternation, prompting one commentator to suggest that Congress instead should leave preemption issues to the judiciary. Still, because the ultimate goal of preemption analysis is to ascertain Congressional intent, an express statement serves at least to assist the courts in determining that intent.

. . .

---

[1] *Andrews-Clarke v. Travelers Insurance Co.*, 984 F. Supp. 49 (D. Mass. 1997), *quoting Nwogugu v. KPMG Peat Marwick*, Civil Action No. 97-10282 (June 19, 1997).

Prior to ERISA's adoption, relatively little legislation, either state or federal, governed employee benefits. State law predominated in the form of insurance regulation focused principally on issues of taxation and fiduciary duties.

With the enactment of ERISA in 1974, Congress crafted the first comprehensive law governing employee benefits in the United States. The findings and declaration of policy incorporated in ERISA reflect Congress' views on the importance of this step.

> The Congress finds . . . that the continued well being and security of millions of employees and their dependents are directly affected by these plans; that they are affected with a national public interest; that they have become an important factor in activities of their participants, and the employers, employee organizations, and other entities by which they are established or maintained . . . .

Congress clearly felt that the prior set of state and federal laws governing employee benefits were inadequate: "[O]wing to the lack of employee information and adequate safeguards concerning their operation, it is desirable in the interests of employees and their beneficiaries that disclosure be made and safeguards be provided with respect to the establishment, operation, and administration of such plans . . . ."

* * *

By having ERISA preempt state laws that regulate employee benefit plans, Congress attempted to create a single, uniform, national law governing employee benefit plan.

DANIEL M. FOX & DANIEL C. SCHAFFER, SEMI-PREEMPTION IN ERISA: LEGISLATIVE PROCESS, AND HEALTH POLICY

7 AM. J. TAX POL'Y 47, 48–51 (1988)

The preemption clause of ERISA is unusual because it forbids the states to regulate employee benefits even when federal law is silent. It preempts state laws touching on pensions, for which ERISA has set federal standards. But it also preempts state laws relating to other employee benefit plans, like health insurance, whose content federal law does not regulate.

The resulting "regulatory vacuum," as one participant in drafting ERISA recalled it in retrospect, was not a deeply considered result of the years of planning, negotiating, and drafting the bill that was passed by Congress in 1974. On the contrary, the preemption clause of 1974 was inserted during the final negotiations in the conference committee, in response to strong opinions voiced by House conferees speaking for powerful interest groups.

The preemption language that had survived, without controversy, until the conference simply prevented the states from legislating about the "subject matters regulated by this Act." The new language, preempting state laws relating to "any employee benefit plan" including matters not regulated by the Act, was disclosed when the conference committee report was filed ten days before Congress took final action on ERISA.

The House and Senate sponsors of the bill made very different claims about the significance of the revised preemption clause. Representative Dent called the new clause the "crowning achievement of this legislation" because it eliminated the "threat of conflicting and inconsistent state and local regulation." Senators Javits and Williams were less expansive, no doubt because they were rationalizing a change from a position they had held during the long period of drafting the legislation. Javits looked forward to a future refining of ERISA preemption, saying that the "desirability of further regulation — at either the State or Federal level — undoubtedly warrants further attention." The conferees had created a Joint Pension Task Force and ordered it to study ERISA's preemption of state law: Javits thought that this might lead to "appropriate modifications."

The influence of the lobbyists was also apparent in the final language of the preemption clause regarding the regulation of insurance. The bill had, from its earliest stages, provided as an exception to ERISA's preemption language that "nothing in this subchapter shall be construed to exempt or relieve any person from any law of any State which regulates insurance." This language, inserted at the request of the National Association of Insurance Commissioners, was consistent with the traditional arrangement in insurance regulation, expressed in the McCarran-Ferguson Act of 1946. In the final version, at the request of the House conferees, the insurance clause also provided that no "employee benefit plan . . . shall be deemed an insurance company." This clause would thwart a state which tried to impose its insurance premium tax or licensing law on a benefit plan jointly administered by labor and management. In combination with the conferees' language extending preemption to all employer provided benefits, it prevented these plans, or any self-insured plans, from being regulated by the states. Thus employers who provided health benefits through such plans could not be regulated on the grounds that they were in the business of providing health insurance.

Organized labor also pressed for preemption of state regulation relating to health insurance in order to prevent the states from mandating benefits. Unions representing workers in industries with national contracts — notably construction, mining, shipping, and garments — had two reasons to oppose mandates. They feared nonuniform regulation — state laws that would modify national contracts. More important, they wanted to preempt state interference in collective bargaining. As their chief lobbyist at the time, Robert J. Connerton, recalled in 1987, "We understood we were giving up good state mandated benefits but we wanted the freedom to give up particular benefits in return for cash wages, and to trade in one benefit for another." Although business firms and associations would defend ERISA preemption on the same grounds in later years, we have no evidence that they did so in 1974.

The insurance industry seems to have been relatively quiet in 1974 about the effects of preemption on health insurance. Some major companies were ambivalent. On the one hand, they favored the preemption of state law, especially mandates, because it made it easier to offer uniform policies to national employers. On the other hand, they had relied for many years on the arrangement whereby Congress left regulation of insurance to the states and the insurance companies cultivated the goodwill of the state insurance commissioners. Another segment of the insurance industry, smaller companies, generally operating in regional and state markets, who were losing business to self-insured benefit plans negotiated and administered by unions and management, however, favored state regulation of employee benefit plans. As a result of both ambivalence and internal conflict, the insurance industry did not actively seek to influence the final language of ERISA preemption.

The health insurers appear not to have been aware of the significance of the preemption clause for their markets. A high official of the Blue Cross Association recalled that "very little was going on because nobody saw it; nobody in the health industry understood the implications of preemption."

5-1 QUESTIONS AND PROBLEMS

Consider whether the following firms would prefer ERISA preemption of state law:

a. A large manufacturer with plants in several states and thousands of employees.

b. A small manufacturer with one plant and 35 employees.

c. A labor union with thousands of members working in a dozen states.

d. A construction firm with its headquarters in one state, but with construction operations in many states and collective bargaining agreements with several unions.

e. An insurance company that offers health insurance in 30 states.

ERISA preemption applies to both pension plans and welfare benefit plans. When it was enacted, most observers understood the effect of ERISA preemption of state regulation of pension plans. The drastic effect of preemption of state regulation of welfare benefit plans, however, was not generally perceived.

B. PLAN REQUIREMENT

ERISA § 514 manifests the Congressional use of "express preemption" because the statute specifically states that it supersedes "any and all laws" that "relate to any employee benefit plan." However, for ERISA preemption to arise, there must be an "employee benefit plan."

FORT HALIFAX PACKING CO. v. COYNE
482 U.S. 1 (1987)

JUSTICE BRENNAN delivered the opinion of the Court.

In this case we must decide whether a Maine statute requiring employers to provide a one-time severance payment to employees in the event of a plant closing is pre-empted by the Employee Retirement Income Security Act of 1974. The statute was upheld by the Maine Supreme Judicial Court . . . .

In 1972, Fort Halifax Packing Company (Fort Halifax or Company) purchased a poultry packaging and processing plant that had operated in Winslow, Maine, for almost two decades. The Company continued to operate the plant for almost another decade, until, on May 23, 1981, it discontinued operations at the plant and laid off all its employees except several maintenance and clerical workers. At the time of closing, over 100 employees were on the payroll. Forty-five had worked in the plant for over 10 years, 19 for over 20 years, and 2 for 29 years. [Maine law required a one-time payment to all workers terminated because of the closing of a plant or other facility.]

. . .

We hold that the Maine statute is not pre-empted by ERISA, not for the reason offered by the Maine Supreme Judicial Court, but because the statute neither establishes, nor requires an employer to maintain, an employee welfare benefit "plan" under that federal statute.

Appellant's basic argument is that any state law pertaining to a type of employee benefit listed in ERISA necessarily regulates an employee benefit plan, and therefore must be pre-empted. Because severance benefits are included in ERISA, appellant argues that ERISA pre-empts the Maine statute. In effect, appellant argues that ERISA forecloses virtually all state legislation regarding employee benefits. This contention fails, however, in light of the plain language of ERISA's pre-emption provision, the underlying purpose of that provision, and the overall objectives of ERISA itself.

The first answer to appellant's argument is found in the express language of the statute. ERISA's pre-emption provision does not refer to state laws relating to "employee benefits," but to state laws relating to "employee benefit plans" . . . :

We have held that the words "relate to" should be construed expansively: "[a] law 'relates to' an employee benefit plan, in the normal sense of the phrase, if it has a connection with or reference to such a plan." *Shaw v. Delta Airlines, Inc.*, 463 U.S. 85, 96–97 (1983). Nothing in our case law, however, supports appellant's position that the word "plan" should in effect be read out of the statute. Indeed, *Shaw* itself speaks of a state law's connection with or reference to a plan. The words "benefit" and "plan" are used separately throughout ERISA, and nowhere in the statute are they treated as the equivalent of one another. Given the basic difference between a "benefit" and a "plan," Congress' choice of language is significant in its pre-emption of only the latter.

Thus, as a first matter, the language of the ERISA presents a formidable obstacle to appellant's argument. The reason for Congress' [sic] decision to legislate with respect to plans rather than to benefits becomes plain upon examination of the purpose of both the pre-emption section and the regulatory scheme as a whole.

The second answer to appellant's argument is that pre-emption of the Maine statute would not further the purpose of ERISA pre-emption. In analyzing whether ERISA's pre-emption section is applicable to the Maine law, "as in any pre-emption analysis, 'the purpose of Congress is the ultimate touchstone.'" *Metropolitan Life Ins. Co. v. Massachusetts*, 471 U.S. 724 (1985) (quoting *Malone v. White Motor Corp.*, 435 U.S. 497, 504 (1978)). Attention to purpose is particularly necessary in this case because the terms "employee benefit plan" and "plan" are defined only tautologically in the statute, each being described as "an employee welfare benefit plan or employee pension benefit plan or a plan which is both an employee welfare benefit plan and an employee pension benefit plan." [ERISA § 3(3).]

Statements by ERISA's sponsors in the House and Senate clearly disclose the problem that the pre-emption provision was intended to address. In the House, Representative Dent stated that "with the preemption of the field [of employee benefit plans], we round out the protection afforded participants by eliminating the threat of conflicting and inconsistent State and local regulation." 120 Cong. Rec. 29197 (1974). Similarly, Senator Williams declared: "It should be stressed that with the narrow exceptions specified in the bill, the substantive and enforcement provisions of the conference substitute are intended to preempt the field for Federal regulations, thus eliminating the threat of conflicting or inconsistent State and local regulation of employee benefit plans." *Id.* at 29933.

These statements reflect recognition of the administrative realities of employee benefit plans. An employer that makes a commitment systematically to pay certain benefits undertakes a host of obligations, such as determining the eligibility of claimants, calculating benefit levels, making disbursements, monitoring the availability of funds for benefit payments, and keeping appropriate records in order to comply with applicable reporting requirements. The most efficient way to meet these responsibilities is to establish a uniform administrative scheme, which provides a set of standard procedures to guide processing of claims and disbursement of benefits.

Such a system is difficult to achieve, however, if a benefit plan is subject to differing regulatory requirements in differing States. A plan would be required to keep certain records in some States but not in others; to make certain benefits available in some States but not in others; to process claims in a certain way in some States but not in others; and to comply with certain fiduciary standards in some States but not in others.

We have not hesitated to enforce ERISA's pre-emption provision where state law created the prospect that an employer's administrative scheme would be subject to conflicting requirements . . .

This point was emphasized in *Shaw, supra,* where we said with respect to another form of State regulation: "Obligating the employer to satisfy the varied and perhaps conflicting requirements of particular state fair employment laws . . . would make administration of a nationwide plan more difficult." 463 U.S. at 105 n.25. Such a situation would produce considerable inefficiencies, which the employer might choose to offset by lowering benefit levels. As the Court in *Shaw* indicated, "ERISA's comprehensive pre-emption of state law was meant to minimize this sort of interference with the administration of employee benefit plans," *ibid.*, so that employers would not have to "administer their plans differently in each State in which they have employees." *Id.* at 105.

. . .

The purposes of ERISA's pre-emption provision make clear that the Maine statute in no way raises the types of concerns that prompted pre-emption. Congress intended pre-emption to afford employers the advantages of a uniform set of administrative procedures governed by a single set of regulations. This concern only arises, however, with respect to benefits whose provision by nature requires an ongoing administrative program to meet the employer's obligation. It is for this reason that Congress pre-empted state laws relating to plans, rather than simply to benefits. Only a plan embodies a set of administrative practices vulnerable to the burden that would be imposed by a patchwork scheme of regulation.

The Maine statute neither establishes, nor requires an employer to maintain, an employee benefit plan. The requirement of a one-time, lump-sum payment triggered by a single event requires no administrative scheme whatsoever to meet the employer's obligation. The employer assumes no responsibility to pay benefits on a regular basis, and thus faces no periodic demands on its assets that create a need for financial coordination and control. Rather, the employer's obligation is predicated on the occurrence of a single contingency that may never materialize. The employer may well never have to pay the severance benefits. To the extent that the obligation to do so arises, satisfaction of that duty involves only making a single set of payments to employees at the time the plant closes. To do little more than write a check hardly constitutes the operation of a benefit plan. Once this single event is over, the employer has no further responsibility. The theoretical possibility of a one-time obligation in the future simply creates no need for an ongoing administrative program for processing claims and paying benefits conflict. We hold that the statute is not pre-empted by ERISA.

. . .

We hold that the Maine severance pay statute is not pre-empted by ERISA, since it does not "relate to any employee benefit plan" under that statute. The judgment of the Maine Supreme Judicial Court is therefore Affirmed.

JUSTICE WHITE, with whom THE CHIEF JUSTICE, JUSTICE O'CONNOR, and JUSTICE SCALIA join, dissenting.

The Court rejects appellant's pre-emption challenge to Maine's severance pay statute by reasoning that the statute does not create a "plan" under ERISA because it does not require an "administrative scheme" to administer the payment of severance benefits. By making pre-emption turn on the existence of an "administrative scheme," the Court creates a loophole in ERISA's pre-emption statute, which will undermine Congress' decision to make employee-benefit plans a matter of exclusive federal regulation. The Court's rule requiring an established "administrative scheme" as a prerequisite for ERISA pre-emption will allow States to effectively dictate a wide array of employee benefits that must be provided by employers by simply characterizing them as non-"administrative." The Court has also chosen to ignore completely what precedent exists as to what constitutes a "plan" under ERISA. I dissent because it is incredible to believe that Congress intended that the broad pre-emption provision contained in ERISA would depend upon the extent to which an employer exercised administrative foresight in preparing for the eventual payment of employee benefits.

. . .

[The Maine statute] establishes no requirement that a "plan" meet any specific formalities or that there be some policy manual or employee handbook to effectuate it. In reading such a requirement . . . the majority ignores the obvious: when a Maine employer is called upon to discharge its legislatively mandated duty under the severance pay statute, the funds from which it pays the benefits do not materialize out of thin air. The Maine Legislature has presumed, as it is so entitled, that employers will comply with the dictates of the statute's requirements. That an employer's liability is contingent upon an event that may never happen does not make the plan that the legislature has imposed upon employers any less of a plan.

NADWORNY v. SHAW'S SUPERMARKETS, INC.

405 F. Supp. 2d 124 (D. Mass. 2005)

YOUNG, Chief Justice.

I. INTRODUCTION

The plaintiff Eric Nadworny ("Nadworny") initially filed a complaint in the Massachusetts Superior Court sitting in and for the County of Plymouth against the defendants Shaw's Supermarkets, Inc. ("Shaw's") and Albertson's, Inc. ("Albertson's"), alleging breach of contract. Nadworny alleges that his former employer, Shaw's, which was later acquired by Albertson's, breached its severance plan payment agreement with him by refusing to provide benefits enumerated in the agreement after Nadworny resigned from his position. Shaw's and Albertson's removed the action to this Court and now move to dismiss with prejudice pursuant to FED. R. CIV. P. 12(b)(6) and 12(b)(1). The basis for Shaw's and Albertson's Rule 12(b)(6) motion to dismiss is that Nadworny's breach of contract claim is preempted by the federal Employee Retirement Income Security Act ("ERISA"). Alternatively, they move to dismiss on Rule 12(b)(1) grounds, as federal subject matter jurisdiction is conditioned upon this Court's ruling that ERISA governs this dispute. Nadworny also has moved for remand to the Plymouth Superior Court on the ground that the severance agreement does not fall under ERISA and this Court, therefore, lacks jurisdiction.

The parties' motions present two questions to this Court. First, whether ERISA preempts the breach of contract claim because the parties' severance agreement constitutes an "employee benefit plan" within the meaning of ERISA. Second, whether the suit ought be dismissed for failure to state a claim upon which relief may be granted.

II. BACKGROUND

This action commenced on September 16, 2005, when Nadworny filed a complaint against Shaw's and Albertson's in Plymouth Superior Court. On October 14, 2005, Shaw's and Albertson's filed a notice of removal to the United States District Court for the District of Massachusetts on the basis of complete preemption by ERISA. On October 19, 2005, Shaw's and Albertson's filed a motion to dismiss for failure to state a claim, arguing that, due to ERISA preemption, Nadworny was owed no relief for breach of contract. On November 2, 2005, Nadworny filed an opposition to the motion to dismiss, and a motion for remand to the Plymouth County Superior Court, asserting that ERISA did not apply to the Shaw's severance agreement.

Nadworny was employed by Shaw's Human Resources Department from November 30, 1998 through February 4, 2005. On April 30, 2004, Albertson's acquired Shaw's, thus becoming Nadworny's employer. Prior to the acquisition, Nadworny's title was "Vice President, Associate & Labor Relations"; after the acquisition, his title became "Vice President, Labor Relations in the Legal Department." Nadworny alleges that his job responsibilities, in addition to his job title, changed after the Albertson's acquisition. He details the changes in his complaint, to illustrate what he alleges to be substantial and material changes to his position, entitling him to severance benefits under the severance agreement he entered into with Shaw's prior to the Albertson's acquisition.

Nadworny's supervisory responsibilities were diminished following the change in control. . . .

Nadworny contends that his responsibilities in other matters changed as well. Various other responsibilities assigned to Nadworny under the Shaw's structure were given instead to Walter subsequent to the Albertson's acquisition. *Id.* Under Albertson's structure, Nadworny also lost his previously held authority to hire his staff and other positions in the human resources department, the authority to make management decisions such as determining salaries and bonus targets and checking references, and opportunities to have input in hiring for various other positions not directly under his supervision. . . . Prior to the acquisition, Nadworny played an instrumental role in the strategic planning and design of the human resources department, afterwards, Walter assumed these responsibilities and Nadworny was excluded from departmental meetings about these matters. . . .

In anticipation of the Albertson's acquisition, Shaw's implemented a severance agreement, the purpose of which was to "provide certain severance benefits to Eligible Employees in the event that their employment with the Company or its successor is terminated under certain circumstances after the occurrence of the Change in Control." According to the agreement, an employee could be eligible for the benefits if terminated by the company "without Cause" within twelve months of the change in control, or if the employee resigned "for Good Reason" within twelve months of the change in control.

On January 21, 2005, Nadworny submitted his letter of resignation, indicating that he was ending his employment for "[g]ood [r]eason," under the terms of the severance agreement. He continued working until February 4, 2005. On January 21, 2005, Nadworny, in writing, requested benefits under the severance agreement. Albertson's denied his benefits claim on April 9, 2005. Nadworny appealed the benefits denial on May 18, 2005, and requested information to which he believed he was entitled pursuant to the severance agreement. Albertson's denied the appeal and refused to provide most of the information Nadworny had requested. Nadworny thus exhausted the administrative appeal procedure available under the agreement.

Nadworny maintains that he is entitled to his annual salary plus 150% of his annual bonus in severance, pursuant to the severance agreement. He maintains that he is an "[e]ligible [e]mployee," as he worked in a corporate management capacity, primarily at the company's headquarters. Nadworny asserts that he is eligible for the severance benefits because his resignation was for "[g]ood [r]eason," in that it was caused b y a material diminution in his title, duties, and responsibilities, and a material reduction or adverse change in his benefit plans. Nadworny is adamant in his contention that ERISA does not preempt the severance agreement, that he is owed relief under a breach of contract theory only, and that a federal court therefore lacks subject matter jurisdiction over the dispute.

III. DISCUSSION

A. Standard of Review for ERISA Preemption

All factual allegations in Nadworny's complaint are assumed to be true, and the Court draws inferences in Nadworny's favor when considering Shaw's and Albertson's motion to dismiss. "[D]ismissal is warranted only if 'it appears beyond doubt that [Nadworny] can prove no set of facts in support of [his] claim which would entitle [him] to relief.' " Nadworny, however, must put forth "factual allegations, either direct or inferential, specifying each material element necessary to sustain recovery under some actionable legal theory." This Court has determined that Nadworny has put forth factual allegations sufficient to support a claim against Shaw's and Albertson's. Although this Court has determined that ERISA preempts the breach of contract claim, it will not dismiss Nadworny's action as Shaw's and Albertson's have requested. Rather, Nadworny will be given leave to amend his complaint to request judicial review of his employer's denial of benefits under an employee benefit plan covered by ERISA.

Although this dispute began with Shaw's and Albertson's moving to dismiss for both failure to state a claim upon which relief can be granted and lack of subject matter jurisdiction, having determined that Nadworny has made factual allegations that support a cause of action, this Court need address only the jurisdictional issue raised under the Federal Rules of Civil Procedure.

Discerning whether federal jurisdiction over this matter is proper pursuant to Fed. R. Civ. P. 12(b)(1) is a mixed question of fact and law. Here, although the party seeking removal to federal court generally bears the burden of establishing that jurisdiction is proper, because ERISA Section 502(a)(1)(B) provides for exclusive original federal jurisdiction over ERISA matters, this Court's primary concern is not whether the removing party has met its burden of proof but rather whether Shaw's severance agreement *is* an employee benefit plan within the meaning of ERISA.

B. ERISA Preemption

Albertson's and Shaw's argue that the breach of contract claim is entirely preempted by ERISA, while Nadworny asserts that the severance benefit agreement is not an "employee benefits plan" within the meaning of ERISA, and therefore is not preempted.

ERISA § 514(a) provides that "the provisions of this title . . . shall supersede any and all State laws insofar as they may now or hereafter relate to any employee benefit plan. . . ." Thus, ERISA will supersede the breach of contract claim based upon Shaw's severance agreement insofar as the claim "relates to" an employee benefit plan. This raises two initial questions: (1) whether the severance agreement constitutes an "employee benefit plan," and, if so, (2) whether Nadworny's breach of contract claim "relates to" the employee benefit plan. The controversy in this matter focuses upon the first. If this Court determines that the severance agreement is an employee benefit plan, there is little doubt that the issue of its breach "relates to" that benefit plan.

Since the statutory language of ERISA is unclear on this point, the Court must resort to case law to discern whether a benefit program constitutes an ERISA plan. The leading case in this realm is *Fort Halifax Packing Co., Inc. v. Coyne*, 482 U.S. 1 (1987). While *Fort Halifax* and other case law provide useful guidance, each case requires an individualized analysis based upon its unique facts and circumstances. This often forces courts to make nuanced and discriminating determinations where precedent indicates the case could well be determined in either party's favor. In an ERISA case, this requires a conclusion that allowing a state cause of action to proceed would counter Congress's purposes for passing ERISA.

ERISA may preempt state court actions involving employee benefit *plans*, but will not reach adjudication of employee *benefits*, if the benefits are not part of a benefit *plan*. *Fort Halifax*, 482 U.S. at 6–7. Since "[t]here is no authoritative checklist that can be consulted to determine conclusively if an employer's obligations rise to the level of an ERISA plan[,]" the Court's analysis must focus on the "nature and extent" of the benefits. In comparing *Nadworny's* case with governing precedents in order to discern whether the parties' severance benefits constitutes an ERISA plan, this Court has considered a number of interrelated, overlapping factors.

Questions of ERISA preemption require a court to view the benefit program before it in light of Congress's purposes for enacting ERISA: the protection of employees' and employers' interests and rights with regard to employee benefits administration. A "[p]articularly germane" factor in this regard is the extent to which the administrator of the benefits must exercise discretion, as opposed to following a mechanical formula, in implementing the plan. The more that subjective judgments are required of the administrator, the more likely the plan is to fall within the purview of ERISA. Another factor, closely related to the question of whether the administrator must exercise discretion, is whether the benefits are disbursed on an ongoing, or one-time, basis. One-time, lump sum payments of benefits frequently are found to be too discrete and temporary to constitute a "plan," and deemed not to be preempted by ERISA. Third, where the employer's obligation to disburse benefits is triggered by a single event, *Fort Halifax* indicates that preemption is less likely to be appropriate. Also pertinent is whether the employer assumed a long-term obligation to review claims and make payments.

1. Purposes of ERISA

. . .

In the interest of protecting employers, Congress enacted the ERISA preemption provision to "ensure that plans and plan sponsors would be subject to a uniform body of benefits law . . . [in order to] minimize the administrative and financial burden of complying with conflicting directives among States or between States and the Federal Government." . . .

Congress also intended for ERISA preemption to protect the interests of employee — beneficiaries of benefit plans. Specifically, ERISA is geared toward "safeguard[ing] the financial integrity of employee benefit funds, . . . permit [ting] employee monitoring of earmarked assets, and . . . ensur[ing] that employers' promises are kept."

2. Ongoing versus One Time Payment Obligations, Lump Sum versus Periodic Payments and Span of Time During which Employer is Obligated.

A "very important" consideration in ERISA preemption disputes is whether, in light of all the facts and circumstances, the employee reasonably could believe that the employer has an ongoing commitment to provide benefits. A court's finding that an employer has an obligation to disburse benefits on a long-term or periodic basis weighs in favor of ERISA preemption, while a finding that a benefit plan consists solely of an obligation to make a single, lump sum payment of benefits weighs against preemption.

The Shaw's severance agreement indicates that an eligible beneficiary "will receive his/her severance payment in a lump sum." Lump sum payments weigh against finding preemption in part because the amounts to be paid usually are determined by a straightforward calculation based upon the employees' salaries and years of servic e with the organization. *See, e.g.*, *Fort Halifax*, 482 U.S. at 12. The force of this factor stems in large part from the fact that benefit plans that require only single, lump sum payments tend to demand less of the administrator in terms of rendering judgments of eligibility and managing the program and fund than do plans that entail ongoing or periodic payment schemes.

. . .

While Shaw's and Alberton's severance package similarly provides for a lump sum payment of benefits when an employee leaves the employ of the company, Nadworny's case is distinguishable from *Belanger*, *Rodowicz*, and *O'Connor* in that the circumstances under which each company offered the benefits speaks to the degree of discretion the plan administrator must exercise in determining employee eligibility for the benefits.

* * * * *

* * *

Indeed, Nadworny's charge against Shaw's and Albertson's stems from his disagreement with the administrator's determination, based upon the administrator's interpretation of the facts of Nadworny's case and the company's obligations under the agreement, that Shaw's and Albertson's are not obligated to disburse benefits to Nadworny. This is the very nature of a plan administrator's discretionary decision.

Nadworny also relies on the seminal *Fort Halifax* case to support his argument.

In *Fort Halifax,* the Supreme Court held that ERISA did not preempt a Maine state statute that obligated all employers who closed or transferred their facilities to pay employees a lump sum based upon each employee's weekly salary and years of service. . . .

Although Nadworny argues to the contrary, the *Fort Halifax* decision alone cannot serve as adequate guidance to this Court, because the Supreme Court's rationale for that ruling does not apply so readily here. In *Fort Halifax*, the Court ruled that the distribution of benefits in accordance with the Maine statute would not require employers to establish an administrative scheme; if the triggering event were to occur, the employer simply would have to pay benefits to all employees based upon a straightforward calculation. The *Fort Halifax* Court itself recognized this distinction, noting that in a previous case it had ruled preemption to be proper where the employer had committed to pay benefits "*as each person left employment*" because, in that case, the employer would have to establish an administrative scheme to pay benifits on an ongoing basis. . . .

Given that the Shaw's agreement does not provide for automatic disbursement of benefits to a broad class of employees upon the occurrence of a certain event, this Court rules the one-time, lump sum nature of benefits disbursement under the Shaw's severance agreement is not determinative of the question of ERISA preemption.

3. Triggering Event

When the employer's obligation to distribute benefits is triggered by the occurrence of a particular contingency, one-time, lump sum payments are an especially strong indication that the benefits do not fall within an employee benefit plan, within the meaning of ERISA. *Fort Halifax*, 482 U.S. at 12. Shaw's obligation to pay severance benefits to Nadworny is contingent, at minimum, upon Nadworny leaving the employ of Shaw's and Albertson's within twelve months of the change in control. Nadworny argues that this is a single triggering event, and that it warrants a ruling that preemption is not appropriate in this case.

. . .

. . . Under the Shaw's agreement, eligible employees might submit claims for benefits to Shaw's and Albertson's individually, over the course of a twelve-month period following the change in control. Although Nadworny points to the change in control as the "triggering effect," the events that ultimately might trigger an obligation to pay under the agreement would be either a dismissal of an employee without "cause" or an employee's resignation for "good reason." These factors render Nadworny's case meaningfully different from *Fort Halifax,* where the employer was required to pay benefits to all employees immediately after the occurrence of a single event.

. . . Like the statute at issue in *Simas,* the Shaw's severance agreement renders certain employees eligible for benefits within a specified period of time (twelve months) following a change in corporate control. There was no single triggering event of the kind in *Fort Halifax* giving rise to Shaw's obligation to pay benefits. Therefore, this factor of the ERISA preemption analysis leads this Court to rule that ERISA preempts the state cause of action.

4. Discretionary Functions of Benefits Administrator

The extent to which the benefits administrator must exercise discretion in the discharge of his duties is likewise a significant factor in determining a question of

ERISA preemption because it is indicative of the complexity of the benefit program. . . .

. . .

. . . The administration of benefits under the Shaw's agreement would entail more than mere mechanical calculations, as Nadworny suggests. That the agreement provides for "administration and appeal of decisions," and details the "claims procedure," also suggest that the administrator would be required to make individualized, discretionary assessments of each employee's qualifications to receive benefits under the agreement.

. . .

IV. CONCLUSION

As is the case in many similar disputes, the answer to the question whether the parties' severance agreement constitutes an employee benefit plan is an extremely close one. Were the existence of a one-time, lump sum payment of benefits upon the occurrence of a particular event the sole criterion to which this Court was directed to look, Nadworny might be correct in his argument that ERISA does not preempt his breach of contract claim. There are, however, various other factors for this Court to consider in making its ultimate determination, especially the extent to which the benefit plan administrator is required to exercise discretion in distributing benefits. Furthermore, here there is not truly one, single contingency triggering Albertson's and Shaw's obligation to pay benefits. That obligation to disburse benefits may be triggered each time an eligible employee is laid-off or resigns from the company within twelve months of the change in control.

While the fact that the Shaw's severance agreement provides for a lump sum payment weighs in favor of a holding that ERISA does not preempt, the fact that, under the terms of the agreement, the administrator must make decisions as to the eligibility of each employee claiming benefits on a case-by-case basis weighs more heavily in favor of ERISA preemption. In light of all of the facts and circumstances of this case and governed by First Circuit precedent, this Court holds that the Shaw's Severance Pay Plan is an employee benefit plan.

The result may seem perverse: this Court seemingly is saving Nadworny from himself, where Nadworny expressly does not want the protections of ERISA and the federal jurisdiction that Congress designed for such situations. Nevertheless, Congress did not draft ERISA so that it would be optional to each claimant. As this Court rules that the severance agreement meets the ERISA criteria of being an employee benefit plan, it must maintain jurisdiction over the matter.

Accordingly, Nadworny's Motion to Remand is DENIED.

This Court also DENIES Shaw's and Albertson's motion to dismiss, provided Nadworny, within 30 days of the date of this decision, amends his complaint to drop his claim for breach of contract and to request judicial review of Shaw's and Albertson's denial of benefits under the Severance Pay Plan, pursuant to ERISA.

While Nadworny's complaint will not be dismissed, it is important to focus on what he has lost now that ERISA governs. Most important, it appears he has lost his right to trial by jury, with all the concomitant public values that right ensures. . . .

5-2 QUESTIONS AND PROBLEMS

1. In *Fort Halifax*, the state was trying to protect workers from the effects of a plant closure. In *Nadworny*, the employees are protected by a "plan" unilaterally declared by the company. Should the state in *Fort Halifax* be able to create a benefit like the employer in *Nadworny* or should ERISA bar the state from offering such protection for workers?

2. In *Nadworny*, the employer cannot keep the possible merger secret and so has to offer incentives to discourage valued employees from quitting. But in *Fort Halifax*, the closure of the plant can be a closely guarded secret, thereby denying employees the choice to seek new employment or await the inevitable termination when the plant closes. Does this suggest that ERISA should not preempt the Maine requirement of termination pay?

3. Does the existence of an employee benefit plan depend upon a formal written document or an informal agreement? Or can the mere existence of benefits create a plan that triggers ERISA coverage and preemption?

4. If the dissent's argument in *Fort Halifax* had prevailed, would any state law that mandated an employee benefit survive ERISA preemption?

5. Did Congress intend that ERISA be the sole statute governing employee-employer relations or did it expect states to continue to have a role? If so, how extensive?

6. State X enacts legislation that requires employers to give employees the option of the day off without pay if the employee's birthday is a working day. Would such a law survive ERISA preemption?

The extended interpretation of an ERISA plan that preempts state law remedies is illustrated by "conversion policies" for health care. Under many plans an employee who terminates employment has the option to convert the group health care insurance policy offered by the plan to an individual policy. If the employee later sues the insurance company that issued the individual policy, the question is whether the individual policy is still considered part of an ERISA "plan." If it is, ERISA preemption applies to the employee's claims against the insurance company. In *Painter v. Golden Rule Ins. Co.*, 121 F.3d 436 (8th Cir. 1997), the court held that the plaintiff's state law claims against the insurance company were preempted because the individual policy (the "conversion" policy) came into being as a result of the plaintiff exercising her rights under the group policy. The plaintiff's right to the conversion policy was thus part of the ERISA plan, and her state claims were subject to preemption under ERISA § 502(a)(1)(B). Several other circuits seem to agree as to the preemption of state claims against conversion policies. However, in *Demars v. CIGNA Corp.*, 173 F.3d 443 (1st Cir. 1999) and in *Waks v. Empire Blue Cross/Blue Shield*, 263 F.3d 872 (9th Cir. 2001), the circuit courts held that while the *right* to convert a group policy into an individual policy was subject to ERISA, the converted policy was not. According to these courts, ERISA does reach the converted policy insurance contract between the insured and the insurance provider because that contract is independent of the employer's ERISA plan.

The other two leading cases defining what is a plan for ERISA purposes, *Donovan v. Dillingham* and *Massachusetts v. Morash*, are reprinted in Chapter 3, *supra*.

C. THE MEANING OF "RELATE TO" IN ERISA § 514(a)

ERISA § 514(a).

Section 514 states that ERISA preempts "any and all State laws" as they "relate to" employee benefit plans. But just what does the term "relate to" mean?

The Supreme Court first attempted to interpret the "relate to" language of § 514 preemption in *Alessi v. Raybestos-Manhattan, Inc.*, 451 U.S. 504 (1981). The Court considered the effect of ERISA preemption upon a New Jersey statute that prohibited pension plans from reducing benefits by the amount of any workers' compensation received by the employee. The question was whether a pension subject to ERISA preemption had to comply with the New Jersey anti-off-set law and pay full benefits without regard to any workers' compensation where the pension plan provided for reduced benefits in the event the ex-employee also received workers' compensation. The Court found the New Jersey law to be preempted. It was an impermissible intrusion on federal law because it attempted to override the provisions of the pension plan that were otherwise acceptable under ERISA.

Two years later, the Supreme Court revisited the meaning of § 514(a) preemption in *Shaw v. Delta Airlines*, 463 U.S. 85 (1983) when it considered whether New York laws that mandated sick leave for employees unable to work because of pregnancy and which forbade discrimination in employee benefits on the basis of pregnancy. In holding the laws preempted by ERISA, the court wrote:

> We have no difficulty in concluding that the [New York laws] "relate to" employee benefit plans. The breadth of § 514(a)'s pre-emptive reach is apparent from that section's language. A law "relates to" an employee benefit plan, in the normal sense of the phrase, if it has a connection with or reference to such a plan. Employing this definition, the Human Rights Law, which prohibits employers from structuring their employee benefit plans in a manner that discriminates on the basis of pregnancy, and the Disability Benefits Law, which requires employers to pay employees specific benefits, clearly "relate to" benefit plans. We must give effect to this plain language unless there is good reason to believe Congress intended the language to have some more restrictive meaning.
>
> Of course, § 514(a) pre-empts state laws only insofar as they relate to plans covered by ERISA. The Human Rights Law, for example, would be unaffected insofar as it prohibits employment discrimination in hiring, promotion, salary, and the like.
>
> In fact, however, Congress used the words "relate to" in § 514(a) in their broad sense. To interpret § 514(a) to preempt only state laws specifically designed to affect employee benefit plans would be to ignore the remainder of § 514. It would have been unnecessary to exempt generally applicable state criminal statutes from pre-emption in § 514(b), for example, if § 514(a) applied only to state laws dealing specifically with ERISA plans.
>
> Nor, given the legislative history, can § 514(a) be interpreted to pre-empt only state laws dealing with the subject matters covered by ERISA — reporting, disclosure, fiduciary responsibility, and the like. The bill that became ERISA originally contained a limited pre-emption clause, applicable only to state laws relating to the specific subjects covered by ERISA.

> The Conference Committee rejected these provisions in favor of the present language, and indicated that the section's pre-emptive scope was as broad as its language. *Shaw v. Delta Airlines*, 463 U.S. 85, 96–98 (1983).

In footnote 21 that has been often cited, the Court noted:

> Some state actions may affect employee benefit plans in too tenuous, remote or peripheral a manner to warrant a finding that the law "relates to" the plan. *Cf. American Telephone & Telegraph Co. v. Merry*, 592 F.2d 118, 121 (CA2 1979) (state garnishment of a spouse's pension income to enforce alimony and support orders is not pre-empted). The present litigation plainly does not present a borderline question, and we express no views about where it would be appropriate to draw the line.

The broad holdings of *Alessi* and *Shaw* were later cut back.

NEW YORK STATE CONFERENCE OF BLUE CROSS & BLUE SHIELD PLANS v. TRAVELERS INSURANCE CO.

514 U.S. 645 (1995)

JUSTICE SOUTER delivered the opinion of the Court.

A New York statute requires hospitals to collect surcharges from patients covered by a commercial insurer but not from patients insured by a Blue Cross/Blue Shield plan, and it subjects certain health maintenance organizations (HMO's) to surcharges that vary with the number of Medicaid recipients each enrolls. These cases call for us to decide whether the Employee Retirement Income Security Act of 1974 (ERISA) pre-empts the state provisions for surcharges on bills of patients whose commercial insurance coverage is purchased by employee health-care plans governed by ERISA, and for surcharges on HMO's insofar as their membership fees are paid by an ERISA plan. We hold that the provisions for surcharges do not "relate to" employee benefit plans within the meaning of ERISA's pre-emption provision, § 514(a), and accordingly suffer no pre-emption.

New York's Prospective Hospital Reimbursement Methodology (NYPHRM) regulates hospital rates for all in-patient care, except for services provided to Medicare beneficiaries. The scheme calls for patients to be charged not for the cost of their individual treatment, but for the average cost of treating the patient's medical problem, as classified under one or another of 794 Diagnostic Related Groups (DRG's). The charges allowable in accordance with DRG classifications are adjusted for a specific hospital to reflect its particular operating costs, capital investments, bad debts, costs of charity care, and the like.

Patients with Blue Cross/Blue Shield coverage, Medicaid patients, and HMO participants are billed at a hospital's DRG rate. Others, however, are not. Patients served by commercial insurers providing in-patient hospital coverage on an expense-incurred basis, by self-insured funds directly reimbursing hospitals, and by certain workers' compensation, volunteer firefighters' benefit, ambulance workers' benefit, and no-fault motor vehicle insurance funds, must be billed at the DRG rate plus a 13% surcharge to be retained by the hospital. For the year ending March 31, 1993, moreover, hospitals were required to bill commercially insured patients for a further 11% surcharge to be turned over to the State, with the result that these patients were charged 24% more than the DRG rate.

New York law also imposes a surcharge on HMO's, which varies depending on the number of eligible Medicaid recipients an HMO has enrolled, but which may run as high as 9% of the aggregate monthly charges paid by an HMO for its members' in-patient hospital care. This assessment is not an increase in the rates to be paid by an HMO to hospitals, but a direct payment by the HMO to the State's general fund.

. . .

On the claimed authority of ERISA's general preemption provision, several commercial insurers, acting as fiduciaries of ERISA plans they administer, joined with their trade associations to bring actions against state officials in United States District Court seeking to invalidate the 13%, 11%, and 9% surcharge statutes. The New York State Conference of Blue Cross and Blue Shield plans, Empire Blue Cross and Blue Shield (collectively the Blues), and the Hospital Association of New York State intervened as defendants, and the New York State Health Maintenance Organization Conference and several HMO's intervened as plaintiffs. The District Court consolidated the actions and granted summary judgment to the plaintiffs . . .

[The Court of Appeals affirmed. The Supreme Court reversed and remanded the case.]

. . .

As we have said before, § 514 indicates Congress's intent to establish the regulation of employee welfare benefit plans "as exclusively a federal concern." *Alessi v. Raybestos-Manhattan, Inc.*, 451 U.S. 504, 523 (1981) . . . . Congress intended "to ensure that plans and plans sponsors would be subject to a uniform body of benefits law . . . " *Ingersoll-Rand*, 498 U.S. at 142.

Accordingly in *Shaw*, for example, we had no trouble finding that New York's "Human Rights Law, which prohibit[ed] employers from structuring their employee benefit plans in a manner that discriminate[d] on the basis of pregnancy, and [New York's] Disability Benefits Law, which require[d] employers to pay employees specific benefits, clearly 'relate[d] to' benefit plans." 463 U.S. at 97. These mandates affecting coverage could have been honored only by varying the subjects of a plan's benefits whenever New York law might have applied, or by requiring every plan to provide all beneficiaries with a benefit demanded by New York law if New York law could have been said to require it for any one beneficiary . . .

In each of these cases, [ed. note — *Shaw*, *FMC Corp. v. Holliday*, 498 U.S. 52 (1990), and *Alessi*] ERISA pre-empted state laws that mandated employee benefit structures or their administration. Elsewhere, we have held that state laws providing alternative enforcement mechanisms also relate to ERISA plans, triggering pre-emption. *See Ingersoll-Rand*, *supra*.

Both the purpose and the effects of the New York surcharge statute distinguish it from the examples just given. The charge differentials have been justified on the ground that the Blues pay the hospitals promptly and efficiently and, more importantly, provide coverage for many subscribers whom the commercial insurers would reject as unacceptable risks. The Blues' practice, called open enrollment, has consistently been cited as the principal reason for charge differentials, whether the differentials resulted from voluntary negotiation between hospitals and payers as was the case prior to the NYPHRM system, or were created by the surcharges as is the case now. Since the surcharges are presumably passed on at least in part to those who purchase commercial insurance or HMO membership, their effects follow from their purpose. Although there is no evidence that the surcharges will drive every health insurance consumer to the Blues, they do make the Blues more attractive (or less unattractive) as insurance alternatives and thus have an indirect economic effect on choices made by insurance buyers, including ERISA plans.

An indirect economic influence, however, does not bind plan administrators to any particular choice and thus function as a regulation of an ERISA plan itself; commercial insurers and HMO's may still offer more attractive packages than the Blues. Nor does the indirect influence of the surcharges preclude uniform administrative practice or the provision of a uniform interstate benefit package if a plan wishes to provide one. It simply bears on the costs of benefits and the relative costs of competing insurance to provide them. It is an influence that can affect a plan's shopping decisions, but it does not affect the fact that any plan will shop for the best deal it can get, surcharges or no surcharges.

. . .

If the common character of rate differentials even in the absence of state action renders it unlikely that ERISA pre-emption was meant to bar such indirect economic influences under state law, the existence of other common state action with indirect economic effects on a plan's costs leaves the intent to pre-empt even less likely. Quality standards, for example, set by the State in one subject area of hospital services but not another would affect the relative cost of providing those services over others and, so, of providing different packages of health insurance benefits. Even basic regulation of employment conditions will invariably affect the cost and price of services.

Quality control and workplace regulation, to be sure, are presumably less likely to affect premium differentials among competing insurers, but that does not change the fact that such state regulation will indirectly affect what an ERISA or other plan can afford or get for its money. Thus, in the absence of a more exact guide to intended pre-emption than § 514, it is fair to conclude that mandates for rate differentials would not be pre-empted unless other regulation with indirect effects on plan costs would be superseded as well. The bigger the package of regulation with indirect effects that would fall on the respondents' reading of § 514, the less likely it is that federal regulation of benefit plans was intended to eliminate state regulation of health care costs.

. . . While Congress's extension of pre-emption to all "state laws relating to benefit plans" was meant to sweep more broadly than "state laws dealing with the subject matters covered by ERISA [,] reporting, disclosure, fiduciary responsibility, and the like," *Shaw*, 463 U.S. at 98, nothing in the language of the Act or the context of its passage indicates that Congress chose to displace general health care regulation, which historically has been a matter of local concern.

In sum, cost uniformity was almost certainly not an object of pre-emption, just as laws with only an indirect economic effect on the relative costs of various health insurance packages in a given State are a far cry from those "conflicting directives" from which Congress meant to insulate ERISA plans. Such state laws leave plan administrators right where they would be in any case, with the responsibility to choose the best overall coverage for the money. We therefore conclude that such state laws do not bear the requisite "connection with" ERISA plans to trigger pre-emption.

. . .

. . . We do not hold today that ERISA pre-empts only direct regulation of ERISA plans, nor could we do that with fidelity to the views expressed in our prior opinions on the matter. We acknowledge that a state law might produce such acute, albeit indirect, economic effects, by intent or otherwise, as to force an ERISA plan to adopt a certain scheme of substantive coverage or effectively restrict its choice of insurers, and that such a state law might indeed be pre-empted under § 514. But as we have shown, New York's surcharges do not fall into either category; they affect only indirectly the relative prices of insurance policies, a result no different from myriad state laws in areas traditionally subject to local regulation, which Congress could not possibly have intended to eliminate.

The judgment of the Court of Appeals is therefore reversed, and the cases are remanded for further proceedings consistent with this opinion.

Although in *Travelers* the Court did not address whether ERISA preempted the application of New York's hospital rate regulations to self-insured plans, on remand the United States Court of Appeals for the Second Circuit held that the New York statute was also valid when applied to self-insured plans, that is plans in which the employee accepts the risk of paying for the medical care benefits rather than purchasing health care insurance from an insurer such as Blue Cross.

The Supreme Court later held that *Travelers* did not depend upon the indirect nature of the tax. In *De Buono v. NYSA-ILA Medical and Clinical Services Fund*, 520 U.S. 806 (1997), the Court found a state tax on hospital gross receipts not to be preempted even though the tax applied to hospitals owned and operated by an ERISA plan. Any tax, according to the Court, whether direct or indirect, increased the cost to an ERISA plan of providing services to its plan participants. The Court noted that the direct tax was merely another state law of general applicability that imposed a burden on an ERISA plan, but it did not otherwise "relate to" such plans within the meaning of the preemption provision.

The Court continued in other cases to constrict the preemption of ERISA when faced with state laws that did not appear to have an intent to regulate pension or welfare benefit plans.

In *California Division of Labor Standards Enforcement v. Dillingham Construction, Inc.*, 519 U.S. 316 (1997), the Court considered a California law that required contractors to pay the prevailing wages on public works projects, but permitted contractors to pay less than the prevailing journey man wages to apprentices enrolled in state approved apprentice programs. In that case, the Dillingham Construction company employed apprentices who were not in a state approved program and paid them below prevailing wages. California sued, insisting that because the apprentices were not in an approved program that the contractor had to pay them prevailing wages. Dillingham countered that because an apprentice program is an employee benefit plan under ERISA § 3(1), California's prevailing wage statute was preempted by ERISA § 514(a).] The Court declared:

> In *Shaw v. Delta Air Lines, Inc.*, we held that the New York Human Rights Law, which prohibited "employers from structuring their employee benefit plans in a manner that discriminates on the basis of pregnancy," and New York's Disability Benefits Law, which required "employers to pay employees specific benefits," "relate[d] to" ERISA plans. 463 U.S. at 97 . . . .
>
> The state law at issue in *Travelers*, our most recent exercise in ERISA pre-emption, stands in considerable contrast. That statute regulated hospital rates, and required hospitals to exact surcharges (ranging from 9% to 24% of the rate set under the statute) from patients whose hospital bills were paid by any of a variety of non-Blue Cross/Blue Shield providers. . . .
>
> We upheld the statute. The "indirect economic influence" of the surcharge, we noted, did not "bind plan administrators to any particular choice

and thus function as a regulation of an ERISA plan itself." 514 U.S. at 659. Nor did the indirect influence of the surcharge "preclude uniform administrative practice or the provision of a uniform interstate benefit package if a plan wishe[d] to provide one." Indeed, if ERISA were concerned with any state action — such as medical-care quality standards or hospital workplace regulations — that increased costs of providing certain benefits, and thereby potentially affected the choices made by ERISA plans, we could scarcely see the end of ERISA's pre-emptive reach, and the words "relate to" would limit nothing. We also noted that several States regulated hospital charges at the time that ERISA was enacted, and yet neither ERISA's language nor legislative history made any mention of pre-empting these state efforts.

We think that, in every relevant respect, California's prevailing wage statute is indistinguishable from New York's surcharge program of apprenticeship. . . .

Like New York's surcharge requirement, the apprenticeship portion of the prevailing wage statute does not bind ERISA plans to anything. No apprenticeship program is required by California law to meet California's standards. . . . . The effect of § 1777.5 on ERISA apprenticeship programs, therefore, is merely to provide some measure of economic incentive to comport with the State's requirements, at least to the extent that those programs seek to provide apprentices who can work on public works projects at a lower wage . . .

The effect of the prevailing wage statute on ERISA-covered apprenticeship programs in California is substantially similar to the effect of New York law on ERISA plans choosing whether to provide health insurance benefits in New York through the Blues, or through a commercial carrier. The prevailing wage statute alters the incentives, but does not dictate the choices, facing ERISA plans. *California Division of Labor Standards Enforcement v. Dillingham Construction, Inc.*, 519 U.S. 316, 328-34 (1997).

5-3 QUESTIONS AND PROBLEMS

1. Why does an "indirect" effect not "relate to" a benefit plan?

2. Are there any fundamental differences between state laws that dictate plan benefits, impose a tax as in *Travelers*, or a penalty for noncompliance such as in *Dillingham*? Aren't all three statutes attempting to influence or control the substance of a benefit plan?

3. Is the *Travelers* reference to the objectives of ERISA more sensible than the *Shaw* use of a dictionary definition? Is it any more helpful or predictive?

4. *Travelers* claims that the preemption clause is designed to avoid the situation in which a plan is regulated by inconsistent or contradictory state regulation. Does this mean that states should be allowed to regulate benefit plans if the plan operates only in one state or if the state laws are consistent or not in conflict? Are there other reasons for preemption?

5. City Councilman Reich has proposed an ordinance that would require contractors with the city to offer pension and welfare benefits to their employees with domestic partners to the same extent as they do to married employees. Would such an ordinance be preempted by ERISA?

6. State Senator Chen introduced legislation in her state that would require all employers with 20 or more employees to offer retirement benefit plans that are consistent with ERISA. Would such a law be preempted by ERISA?

In recent years, a number of states and local jurisdictions have enacted "pay-or-play" mandates requiring employers to provide employees with health care coverage or pay a penalty. Although the specifics of the mandates vary from jurisdiction to jurisdiction, they all raise the fundamental issue of whether ERISA preempts such legislation. In *Retail Industry Leaders Assoc. v. Fielder*, 475 F.3d 180 (4th Cir. 2007), the Fourth Circuit held that ERISA preempted Maryland's "Fair Share Health Care Fund Act," and in *Retailer Industry Leaders Association v. Suffolk County*, 497 F. Supp. 2d 403 (E.D.N.Y. 2007), the District Court for the Eastern District of New York held that a Suffolk County ordinance was preempted by ERISA. In *Golden Gate Restaurant Association v. City and County of San Francisco*, 546 F.3d 639 (9th Cir. 2008), in contrast, the Ninth Circuit upheld a San Francisco ordinance.

> As with the courts, health law commentators are split on whether pay-or-play laws are likely to survive an ERISA preemption challenge. While the weight of the commentary suggests that these laws will be preempted, that assessment is not unanimous. Most of those concluding that pay-or-play laws will be preempted include such commentators as Edward Zelinsky, Kathlynn Polvino, Jon Shimabukuro, and Jennifer Staman, who largely adopt the Fourth Circuit's 'relate to' analysis. Amy Monahan largely agrees, but indicates that Massachusetts' "soft" pay-or-play law may offer the courts a way of avoiding preemption without burdening plan administration. In contrast, Pat Butler (along with Catherine Fisk and Michael Oswalt) argues that "ERISA should not preempt a well-designed pay-or-pay law that offers a dollar-for-dollar credit for employer health care spending because, under the reasoning of the *Travelers* case, it does not interfere with ERISA plan administration choices." This quote captures the essence of what is likely to be the crux of the argument: if the Supreme Court follows the *Travelers* line of cases, pay-or-play laws could survive. But if the Court reverts to the mean of preemption, as I expect, the laws will be preempted. Peter D. Jacobson, *The Role of ERISA Preemption in Health Reform: Opportunities and Limits*, 37 J. L. Med. & Ethics 88, 95 (2009).

The 2010 enactment of the Affordable Care Act (discussed in Chapter 3) adds an additional layer of complexity to the question of whether ERISA preempts state and/or local pay-or play mandates. The Affordable Care Act includes a federal pay-or-play mandate but is silent on the question of preemption. In June 2010, the Department of Justice submitted a brief to the Supreme Court opposing the grant of *certiorari* in *Golden Gate* because it was unclear what effect the Affordable Care Act would have on state and/or local pay-or-play mandates. The Court denied *certiorari* in the case, and more than a year and a half after the enactment of the Affordable Care Act, the effect of ERISA preemption on state and local pay-or-play mandates remains an important but unsettled question. *See* Mallory Jensen, *Is ERISA Preemption Superfluous in the New Age of Health Care Reform?*, 2011 Colum. Bus. L. Rev. 464; Mary Ann Chirba-Martin, *ERISA Preemption of State "Play or Pay" Mandates: How PPACA Clouds an Already Confusing Picture*, 13 J. Health Care L. & Pol'y 393 (2010).

D. THE "SAVINGS CLAUSE"

ERISA § 514(b)(2)(A).

Section 514(b)(2)(A) states that ERISA preemption does not apply to any state law that regulates "insurance, banking or securities." "Saving" state insurance laws from ERISA preemption is in accord with the McCarran-Ferguson Act of 1945 that declared that state rather than federal regulation of insurance was in the public interest. 15 U.S.C. §§ 1011, 1012(a). Prior to the enactment of the Affordable Care Act in 2010, Congress left the regulation of insurance up to the states,' As a result, every state has laws that regulate insurance. With the passage of ERISA and its complete preemption, determining when a state law regulates insurance and so escapes preemption became critical.

METROPOLITAN LIFE INSURANCE CO. v. MASSACHUSETTS

471 U.S. 724 (1985)

JUSTICE BLACKMUN delivered the opinion of the Court.

A Massachusetts statute requires that specified minimum mental-health-care benefits be provided a Massachusetts resident who is insured under a general insurance policy, an accident or sickness insurance policy, or an employee health-care plan that covers hospital and surgical expenses. The first question before us in these cases is whether the state statute, as applied to insurance policies purchased by employee health-care plans regulated by the federal Employee Retirement Income Security Act of 1974, is pre-empted by that Act.

General health insurance typically is sold as group insurance to an employer or other group. Group insurance presently is subject to extensive state regulation, including regulation of the carrier, regulation of the sale and advertising of the insurance, and regulation of the content of the contracts. Mandated-benefit laws, that require an insurer to provide a certain kind of benefit to cover a specified illness or procedure whenever someone purchases a certain kind of insurance, are a subclass of such content regulation.

While mandated-benefit statutes are a relatively recent phenomenon, statutes regulating the substantive terms of insurance contracts have become commonplace in all 50 States over the last 30 years. Perhaps the most familiar are those regulating the content of automobile insurance policies.

The substantive terms of group-health insurance contracts, in particular, also have been extensively regulated by the States. For example, the majority of States currently require that coverage for dependents continue beyond any contractually imposed age limitation when the dependent is incapable of self-sustaining employment because of mental or physical handicap; such statutes date back to the early 1960's. And over the last 15 years all 50 States have required that coverage of infants begin at birth, rather than at some time shortly after birth, as had been the prior practice in the unregulated market. Many state statutes require that insurers offer on an optional basis particular kinds of coverage to purchasers. Others require insurers either to offer or mandate that insurance policies include coverage for services rendered by a particular type of health-care provider.

Mandated-benefit statutes, then, are only one variety of a matrix of state laws that regulate the substantive content of health-insurance policies to further state health policy. Massachusetts Gen. Laws Ann., ch. 175 § 47B (West Supp. 1985), is typical of mandated-benefit laws currently in place in the majority of States. With respect to a Massachusetts resident, it requires any general health-insurance policy that provides hospital and surgical coverage, or any benefit plan that has such coverage, to provide as well a certain minimum of mental-health protection. In particular, § 47B requires that a health-insurance policy provide 60 days of coverage for confinement in a mental hospital, coverage for confinement in a general hospital equal to that provided by the policy for nonmental illness, and certain minimum outpatient benefits.

Section 47B was designed to address problems encountered in treating mental illness in Massachusetts. The Commonwealth determined that its working people needed to be protected against the high cost of treatment for such illness. It also believed that, without insurance, mentally ill workers were often institutionalized in large state mental hospitals, and that mandatory insurance would lead to a higher incidence of more effective treatment in private community mental-health centers . . . .

In addition, the Commonwealth concluded that the voluntary insurance market was not adequately providing mental-health coverage, because of "adverse selection" in mental-health insurance: good insurance risks were not purchasing coverage, and this drove up the price of coverage for those who otherwise might purchase mental-health insurance. The legislature believed that the public interest required that it correct the insurance market in the Commonwealth by mandating minimum-coverage levels, effectively forcing the good-risk individuals to become part of the risk pool, and enabling insurers to price the insurance at an average market rather than a market retracted due to adverse selection. *See* Findings of Fact of the Superior Court, App. to Juris. Statement in No. 84-325, pp. 50a–53a. Section 47B, then, was intended to help safeguard the public against the high costs of comprehensive inpatient and outpatient mental-health care, reduce nonpsychiatric medical-care expenditures for mentally related illness, shift the delivery of treatment from inpatient to outpatient services, and relieve the Commonwealth of some of the financial burden it otherwise would encounter with respect to mental-health problems. *Ibid.*

It is our task in these cases to decide whether such insurance regulation violates or is inconsistent with federal law.

. . .

To state the obvious, § 47B regulates the terms of certain insurance contracts, and so seems to be saved from pre-emption by the saving clause as a law "which regulates insurance . . ."

The insurers nonetheless argue that § 47B is in reality a health law that merely operates on insurance contracts to accomplish its end, and that it is not the kind of traditional insurance law intended to be saved by § 514(b)(2)(A). We find this argument unpersuasive.

Initially, nothing in § 514(b)(2)(A), or in the "deemer clause" which modifies it, purports to distinguish between traditional and innovative insurance laws. The presumption is against pre-emption, and we are not inclined to read limitations into federal statutes in order to enlarge their pre-emptive scope. Further, there is no indication in the legislative history that Congress had such a distinction in mind.

Appellants assert that state laws that directly regulate the insurer, and laws that regulate such matters as the way in which insurance may be sold, are traditional laws subject to the clause, while laws that regulate the substantive terms of insurance contracts are recent innovations more properly seen as health laws rather than as insurance laws, which § 514(b)(2)(A) does not save. This distinction reads the saving clause out of ERISA entirely, because laws that regulate only the insurer, or the way in which it may sell insurance, do not "relate to" benefit plans in the first instance. Because they would not be pre-empted by § 514(a), they do not need to be "saved" by § 514(b)(2)(A). There is no indication that Congress could have intended the saving clause to operate only to guard against too expansive readings of the general pre-emption clause that might have included laws wholly unrelated to plans. Appellants' construction, in our view, violates the plain meaning of the statutory language and renders redundant both the saving clause it is construing, as well as the deemer clause which it precedes, and accordingly has little to recommend it.

Moreover, it is both historically and conceptually inaccurate to assert that mandated-benefit laws are not traditional insurance laws. As we have indicated, state laws regulating the substantive terms of insurance contracts were commonplace well before the mid-70's, when Congress considered ERISA. The case law concerning the meaning of the phrase "business of insurance" in the McCarran-Ferguson Act, 15 U.S.C. § 1011 *et seq.*, also strongly supports the conclusion that regulation regarding the substantive terms of insurance contracts falls squarely within the saving clause as laws "which regulate insurance."

. . .

We therefore decline to impose any limitation on the saving clause beyond those Congress imposed in the clause itself and in the "deemer clause" which modifies it. If a state law "regulates insurance," as mandated-benefit laws do, it is not pre-empted. Nothing in the language, structure, or legislative history of the Act supports a more narrow reading of the clause, whether it be the Supreme Judicial Court's attempt to save only state regulations unrelated to the substantive provisions of ERISA, or the insurers' more speculative attempt to read the saving clause out of the statute.

. . .

Those who thought that *Metropolitan Life* meant that the Supreme Court was going to limit the application of ERISA preemption by a liberal interpretation of the Savings Clause, and so permit states to freely regulate insurance, were soon to learn otherwise.

PILOT LIFE INSURANCE CO. v. DEDEAUX

481 U.S. 41 (1987)

JUSTICE O'CONNOR delivered the opinion of the Court.

This case presents the question whether the Employee Retirement Income Security Act of 1974 (ERISA) pre-empts state common law tort and contract actions asserting improper processing of a claim for benefits under an insured employee benefit plan.

In March 1975, in Gulfport, Mississippi, respondent Everate W. Dedeaux injured his back in an accident related to his employment for Entex, Inc. (Entex). Entex had at this time a long term disability employee benefit plan established by purchasing a group insurance policy from petitioner, Pilot Life Insurance Co. (Pilot Life). Entex collected and matched its employees' contributions to the plan and forwarded those funds to Pilot Life; the employer also provided forms to its employees for processing disability claims, and forwarded completed forms to Pilot Life. Pilot Life bore the responsibility of determining who would receive disability benefits. Although Dedeaux sought permanent disability benefits following the 1975 accident, Pilot Life terminated his benefits after two years. During the following three years Dedeaux's benefits were reinstated and terminated by Pilot Life several times.

In 1980, Dedeaux instituted a diversity action against Pilot Life in the United States District Court for the Southern District of Mississippi. Dedeaux's complaint contained three counts: "Tortious Breach of Contract"; "Breach of Fiduciary Duties"; and "Fraud in the Inducement." Dedeaux sought "[d]amages for failure to provide benefits under the insurance policy in a sum to be determined at the time of trial," "[g]eneral damages for mental and emotional distress and other incidental damages in the sum of $250,000.00," and "[p]unitive and exemplary damages in the sum of $500,000.00." Dedeaux did not assert any of the several causes of action available to him under ERISA.

At the close of discovery, Pilot Life moved for summary judgment, arguing that ERISA pre-empted Dedeaux's common law claim for failure to pay benefits on the group insurance policy. The District Court granted Pilot Life summary judgment, finding all Dedeaux's claims pre-empted.

The Court of Appeals for the Fifth Circuit reversed, primarily on the basis of this Court's decision in *Metropolitan Life Ins. Co. v. Massachusetts*, 471 U.S. 724 (1985). We granted certiorari, and now reverse.

. . .

. . . If a state law "relate[s] to . . . employee benefit plan[s]," it is pre-empted. § 514(a). The saving clause excepts from the pre-emption clause laws that "regulat[e] insurance." § 514(b)(2)(A). The deemer clause makes clear that a state law that "purport[s] to regulate insurance" cannot deem an employee benefit plan to be an insurance company. § 514(b)(2)(B).

"[T]he question whether a certain state action is pre-empted by federal law is one of congressional intent. " 'The purpose of Congress is the ultimate touchstone.' " We have observed in the past that the express pre-emption provisions of ERISA are deliberately expansive, and designed to "establish pension plan regulation as exclusively a federal concern." As we explained in *Shaw v. Delta Air Lines, Inc.*, 463 U.S. 85, 98 (1983):

> The bill that became ERISA originally contained a limited pre-emption clause, applicable only to state laws relating to the specific subjects covered by ERISA. The Conference Committee rejected those provisions in favor of the present language, and indicated that section's pre-emptive scope was as broad as its language.

The House and Senate sponsors emphasized both the breadth and importance of the pre-emption provisions. Representative Dent described the "reservation to Federal authority [of] the sole power to regulate the field of employee benefit plans" as ERISA's "crowning achievement." 120 Cong. Rec. 29197 (1974). Senator Williams said:

> It should be stressed that with the narrow exceptions specified in the bill, the substantive and enforcement provisions of the conference substitute are intended to preempt the field for Federal regulations, thus eliminating the threat of conflicting or inconsistent State and local regulation of employee benefit plans. This principle is intended to apply in its broadest sense to all actions of State or local governments, or any instrumentality thereof, which have the force or effect of law.

In *Metropolitan Life*, this Court, noting that the pre-emption and saving clauses "perhaps are not a model of legislative drafting," 471 U.S. at 739, interpreted these clauses in relation to a Massachusetts statute that required minimum mental health care benefits to be provided Massachusetts residents covered by general health insurance policies. The appellants in *Metropolitan Life* argued that the state statute, as applied to insurance policies purchased by employee health care plans regulated by ERISA, was pre-empted.

The Court concluded, first, that the Massachusetts statute did "relate to . . . employee benefit plan[s]," thus placing the state statute within the broad sweep of the pre-emption clause, § 514(a). *Metropolitan Life, supra,* at 739. However, the Court held that, because the state statute was one that "regulate[d] insurance," the saving clause prevented the state law from being pre-empted. In determining whether the Massachusetts statute regulated insurance, the Court was guided by case law interpreting the phrase "business of insurance" in the McCarran-Ferguson Act, 59 Stat. 33, as amended, 15 U.S.C. § 101 *et seq.*

Given the "statutory complexity" of ERISA's three pre-emption provisions, *Metropolitan Life, supra,* at 740, as well as the wide variety of state statutory and decisional law arguably affected by the federal pre-emption provisions, it is not surprising that we are again called on to interpret these provisions.

There is no dispute that the common law causes of action asserted in Dedeaux's complaint "relate to" an employee benefit plan and therefore fall under ERISA's express pre-emption clause, § 514(a). In both *Metropolitan Life, supra,* and *Shaw v. Delta Air Lines, Inc., supra,* at 96–100, we noted the expansive sweep of the pre-emption clause. In both cases "the phrase 'relate to' was given its broad common-sense meaning, such that a state law 'relate[s] to' a benefit plan 'in the normal sense of the phrase, if it has a connection with or reference to such a plan.' " *Metropolitan Life, supra,* at 739, quoting *Shaw v. Delta Air Lines, supra,* at 97. In particular we have emphasized that the pre-emption clause is not limited to "state laws specifically designed to affect employee benefit plans." *Shaw v. Delta Air Lines, supra,* at 98. The common law causes of action raised in Dedeaux's complaint, each based on alleged improper processing of a claim for benefits under an employee benefit plan, undoubtedly meet the criteria for pre-emption under § 514(a).

Unless these common law causes of action fall under an exception to § 514(a), therefore, they are expressly pre-empted. Although Dedeaux's complaint pleaded several state common law causes of action, before this Court Dedeaux has described only one of the three counts — called "tortious breach of contract" in the complaint, and "the Mississippi law of bad faith" in respondent's brief — as protected from the pre-emptive effect of § 514(a). The Mississippi law of bad faith, Dedeaux argues, is a law "which regulates insurance," and thus is saved from pre-emption by § 514(b)(2)(A).

. . .

In the present case, the considerations weighed in Metropolitan Life argue against the assertion that the Mississippi law of bad faith is a state law that "regulates insurance."

As early as 1915 the Mississippi Supreme Court had recognized that punitive damages were available in a contract case when "the act or omission constituting the breach of the contract amounts also to the commission of a tort." In *American Railway Express Co. v. Bailey*, 107 So. 761, 763 (1926), a case involving a failure of a finance company to deliver to the plaintiff the correct amount of money cabled to the plaintiff through the finance company's offices, the Mississippi Supreme Court explained that punitive damages could be available when the breach of contract was "attended by some intentional wrong, insult, abuse, or gross negligence, which amounts to an independent tort." In *Standard Life Insurance Co. v. Veal*, 354 So. 2d 239 (1977), the Mississippi Supreme Court, citing *D. L. Fair Lumber Co. v. Weems*, 196 Miss. 201, 16 So. 2d 770 (1944) (breach of contract was accompanied by "the breaking down and destruction of another's fence"), *American Railway Express Co. v. Bailey*, *supra*, and *Hood v. Moffett*, *supra*, upheld an award of punitive damages against a defendant insurance company for failure to pay on a credit life policy. Since *Veal*, the Mississippi Supreme Court has considered a large number of cases in which plaintiffs have sought punitive damages from insurance companies for failure to pay a claim under an insurance contract, and in a great many of these cases the court has used the identical formulation, first stated in *Bailey*, of what must "attend" the breach of contract in order for punitive damages to be recoverable . . .

Certainly a common-sense understanding of the phrase "regulates insurance" does not support the argument that the Mississippi law of bad faith falls under the saving clause. A common-sense view of the word "regulates" would lead to the conclusion that in order to regulate insurance, a law must not just have an impact on the insurance industry, but must be specifically directed toward that industry. Even though the Mississippi Supreme Court has identified its law of bad faith with the insurance industry, the roots of this law are firmly planted in the general principles of Mississi ppi tort and contract law. Any breach of contract, and not merely breach of an insurance contract, may lead to liability for punitive damages under Mississippi law.

Neither do the McCarran-Ferguson Act factors support the assertion that the Mississippi law of bad faith "regulates insurance." Unlike the mandated-benefits law at issue in *Metropolitan Life*, the Mississippi common law of bad faith does not effect a spreading of policyholder risk. The state common law of bad faith may be said to concern "the policy relationship between the insurer and the insured." The connection to the insurer-insured relationship is attenuated at best, however. In contrast to the mandated- benefits law in *Metropolitan Life*, the common law of bad faith does not define the terms of the relationship between the insurer and the insured; it declares only that, whatever terms have been agreed upon in the insurance contract, a breach of that contract may in certain circumstances allow the policyholder to obtain punitive damages. The state common law of bad faith is therefore no more "integral" to the insurer-insured relationship than any State's general contract law is integral to a contract made in that State. Finally, as we have just noted, Mississippi's law of bad faith, even if associated with the insurance industry, has developed from general principles of tort and contract law available in any Mississippi breach of contract case . . .

The Solicitor General, for the United States as amicus curiae, argues that Congress clearly expressed an intent that the civil enforcement provisions of ERISA § 502(a) be the exclusive vehicle for actions by ERISA-plan participants and beneficiaries asserting improper processing of a claim for benefits, and that varying state causes of action for claims within the scope of § 502(a) would pose an obstacle to the purposes and objectives of Congress. We agree.

. . .

In sum, the detailed provisions of § 502(a) set forth a comprehensive civil enforcement scheme that represents a careful balancing of the need for prompt and fair claims settlement procedures against the public interest in encouraging the formation of employee benefit plans. The policy choices reflected in the inclusion of certain remedies and the exclusion of others under the federal scheme would be completely undermined if ERISA-plan participants and beneficiaries were free to obtain remedies under state law that Congress rejected in ERISA. "The six carefully integrated civil enforcement provisions found in § 502(a) of the statute as finally enacted . . . provide strong evidence that Congress did not intend to authorize other remedies that it simply forgot to incorporate expressly." *Russell, supra*, at 146 (emphasis in original).

The deliberate care with which ERISA's civil enforcement remedies were drafted and the balancing of policies embodied in its choice of remedies argue strongly for the conclusion that ERISA's civil enforcement remedies were intended to be exclusive . . .

. . .

In *Metropolitan Life Ins. Co. v. Massachusetts*, 471 U.S. at 746, this Court rejected an interpretation of the saving clause of ERISA's express pre-emption provisions, § 514(b)(2)(A), that saved from pre-emption "only state regulations unrelated to the substantive provisions of ERISA," finding that "nothing in the language, structure, or legislative history of the Act" supported this reading of the saving clause. *Metropolitan Life*, however, did not involve a state law that conflicted with a substantive provision of ERISA. Therefore the Court's general observation — that state laws related to ERISA may also fall under the saving clause — was not focused on any particular relationship or conflict between a substantive provision of ERISA and a state law. In particular, the Court had no occasion to consider in *Metropolitan Life* the question raised in the present case: whether Congress might clearly express, through the structure and legislative history of a particular substantive provision of ERISA, an intention that the federal remedy provided by that provision displace state causes of action. Our resolution of this different question does not conflict with the Court's earlier general observations in *Metropolitan Life*.

Considering the common-sense understanding of the saving clause, the McCarran-Ferguson Act factors defining the business of insurance, and, most importantly, the clear expression of congressional intent that ERISA's civil enforcement scheme be exclusive, we conclude that Dedeaux's state law suit asserting improper processing of a claim for benefits under an ERISA-regulated plan is not saved by § 514(b)(2)(A), and therefore is pre-empted by § 514(a). Accordingly, the judgment of the Court of Appeals is

Reversed.

Damages are the key to understanding what was at stake in *Pilot Life*. Dedeaux sought "[d]amages for failure to provide benefits under the insurance policy in a sum to be determined at the time of trial," "[g]eneral damages for mental and emotional distress and other incidental damages in the sum of $250,000.00," and "[p]unitive and exemplary damages in the sum of $500,000.00."

None of these damages would be available to Dedeaux under ERISA, which explains why he preferred to assert his state claims rather than sue for more limited remedies under ERISA (*see* Chapter 7). Though the lack of compensatory and punitive damages and the lack of a right to a jury trial makes suing under ERISA much less appealing than suing for damages for state law claims, in many instances the plaintiff has no choice but to sue under ERISA because potential state claims are preempted by ERISA. As a practical matter, the employer defends against the plaintiff's state claims by asking for summary judgment based upon ERISA preemption. The legal battle is thus fought on the proper scope of ERISA preemption rather than on the substantive merits of the plaintiff's claims.

5-4 QUESTIONS AND PROBLEMS

1. In what capacity was Pilot Life Insurance Co. being sued — as a plan fiduciary or an insurance carrier?

2. The Governor of your state wants "bad faith" to serve as a cause of action against insurers who sell policies to welfare benefit plans? She is aware of *Pilot Life* and asks you if there is a way to draft a statute that would avoid the *Pilot Life* holding. Is that possible?

In 2003, the Supreme Court by a unanimous decision formulated the current rule as to when a state law regulates insurance and thus is not preempted by § 514.

KENTUCKY ASSOCIATION OF HEALTH PLANS, INC. v. MILLER

538 U.S. 329 (2003)

Justice Scalia delivered the opinion of the Court.

Kentucky law provides that "[a] health insurer shall not discriminate against any provider who is located within the geographic coverage area of the health benefit plan and who is willing to meet the terms and conditions for participation established by the health insurer, including the Kentucky state Medicaid program and Medicaid partnerships." Ky. Rev. Stat. Ann. § 304.17A-270 (West 2001). Moreover, any "health benefit plan that includes chiropractic benefits shall . . . permit any licensed chiropractor who agrees to abide by the terms, conditions, reimbursement rates, and standards of quality of the health benefit plan to serve as a participating primary chiropractic provider to any person covered by the plan." § 304.17A-171(2). We granted certiorari to decide whether the Employee Retirement Income Security Act of 1974 (ERISA) pre-empts either, or both, of these "Any Willing Provider" (AWP) statutes.

Petitioners include several health maintenance organizations (HMOs) and a Kentucky-based association of HMOs. In order to control the quality and cost of health-care delivery, these HMOs have contracted with selected doctors, hospitals, and other health-care providers to create exclusive "provider networks." Providers in such networks agree to render health-care services to the HMOs' subscribers at discounted rates and to comply with other contractual requirements. In return, they receive the benefit of patient volume higher than that achieved by nonnetwork providers who lack access to petitioners' subscribers.

Kentucky's AWP statutes impair petitioners' ability to limit the number of providers with access to their networks, and thus their ability to use the assurance of high patient volume as the *quid pro quo* for the discounted rates that network membership entails. Petitioners believe that AWP laws will frustrate their efforts at cost and quality control, and will ultimately deny consumers the benefit of their cost-reducing arrangements with providers.

In April 1997, petitioners filed suit against respondent, the Commissioner of Kentucky's Department of Insurance, in the United States District Court for the Eastern District of Kentucky, asserting that ERISA, pre-empts Kentucky's AWP laws. ERISA pre-empts all state laws "insofar as they may now or hereafter relate to any employee benefit plan," [ERISA] § 514(a), but state "laws . . . which regulate insurance, banking, or securities" are saved from pre-emption, [ERISA] § 514(b)(2)(A). The District Court concluded that although both AWP statutes "relate to" employee benefit plans under [ERISA] § 514(a), each law "regulates insurance" and is therefore saved from pre-emption by [ERISA] § 514(b)(2)(A). In affirming the District Court, the Sixth Circuit also concluded that the AWP laws "regulate insurance" and fall within ERISA's savings clause. [T]he Sixth Circuit first held that Kentucky's AWP laws regulate insurance "as a matter of common sense, because they are "specifically directed toward 'insurers' and the insurance industry . . . ," The Sixth Circuit then considered, as "checking points or guideposts" in its analysis, the three factors used to determine whether a practice fits within "the business of health insurance" in our cases interpreting the McCarran-Ferguson Act. These factors are: "*first*, whether the practice has the effect of transferring or spreading a policyholder's risk; *second*, whether the practice is an integral part of the policy relationship between the insurer and the insured; and *third*, whether the practice is limited to entities within the insurance industry." *Union Labor Life Ins. Co. v. Pireno*, 458 U.S. 119, 129 (1982). The Sixth Circuit found all three factors satisfied. Notwithstanding its analysis of the McCarran-Ferguson factors, the Sixth Circuit reiterated that the "basic test" under ERISA's savings clause is whether, from a common-sense view, the Kentucky AWP laws regulate insurance. Finding that the laws passed both the "common sense" test and the McCarran-Ferguson "checking points," the Sixth Circuit upheld Kentucky's AWP statutes.

We granted certiorari, 536 U.S. 956 (2002).

II

To determine whether Kentucky's AWP statutes are saved from preemption, we must ascertain whether they are "laws . . . which regulate insurance" under [ERISA] § 514(b)(2)(A).

It is well established in our case law that a state law must be "specifically directed toward" the insurance industry in order to fall under ERISA's savings clause; laws of general application that have some bearing on insurers do not qualify. *Pilot Life Ins. Co. v. Dedeaux*, 481 U.S. 41, 50 (1987); *see also Rush Prudential HMO, Inc. v. Moran*, 536 U.S. 355, 366 (2002). *FMC Corp. v. Holliday*, 498 U.S. 52, 61 (1990). At the same time, not all state laws "specifically directed toward" the insurance industry will be covered by [ERISA] § 514(b)(2)(A), which saves laws that regulate *insurance*, not insurers. As we explained in *Rush Prudential*, insurers must be regulated "with respect to their insurance practices," 536 U.S. at 366. Petitioners contend that Kentucky's AWP laws fall outside the scope of [ERISA] § 514(b)(2)(A) for two reasons. First, because Kentucky has failed to "specifically direct" its AWP laws towards the insurance industry; and second, because the AWP laws do not regulate an insurance practice. We find neither contention persuasive.

A

Petitioners claim that Kentucky's statutes are not "specifically directed toward" insurers because they regulate not only the insurance industry but also doctors wh o seek to form and maintain limited provider networks with HMOs. That is to say, the AWP laws equally prevent *providers* from entering into limited network contracts with *insurers*, just as they prevent insurers from creating exclusive networks in the first place. We do not think it follows that Kentucky has failed to specifically direct its AWP laws at the insurance industry.

Neither of Kentucky's AWP statutes, by its terms, imposes any prohibitions or requirements on health-care providers. *See* Ky. Rev. Stat. Ann. § 304.17A-270 (West 2001) (imposing obligations only on "health insurers" not to discriminate against any willing provider); § 304.17A-171 (imposing obligations only on "health benefit plans that include chiropractic benefits"). And Kentucky health-care providers are still capable of entering exclusive networks with insurers who conduct business outside the Commonwealth of Kentucky or who are otherwise not covered by §§ 304.17A-270 or 304.17A-171. Kentucky's statutes are transgressed only when a "health insurer," or a "health benefit plan that includes chiropractic benefits," excludes from its network a provider who is willing and able to meet its terms.

It is of course true that as a *consequence* of Kentucky's AWP laws, entities outside the insurance industry (such as health-care providers) will be unable to enter into certain agreements with Kentucky insurers. But the same could be said about the state laws we held saved from pre-emption in *FMC Corp.* and *Rush Prudential.* Pennsylvania's law prohibiting insurers from exercising subrogation rights against an insured's tort recovery, *see FMC Corp.*, also prevented insureds from entering into enforceable contracts with insurers allowing subrogation. Illinois' requirement that HMOs provide independent review of whether services are "medically necessary," *Rush Prudential* likewise excluded insureds from joining an HMO that would have withheld the right to independent review in exchange for a lower premium. Yet neither case found the effects of these laws on noninsurers, significant though they may have been, inconsistent with the requirement that laws saved from pre-emption by [ERISA] § 514(b)(2)(A) be "specifically directed toward" the insurance industry. Regulations "directed toward" certain entities will almost always disable other entities from doing, with the regulated entities, what the regulations forbid; this does not suffice to place such regulation outside the scope of ERISA's savings clause.

B

Petitioners claim that the AWP laws do not regulate insurers with respect to an insurance practice because, unlike the state laws we held saved from pre-emption in *Metropolitan Life Ins. Co. v. Massachusetts*, 471 U.S. 724 (1985), *UNUM*, and *Rush Prudential*, they do not control the actual terms of insurance policies. Rather, they focus upon the relationship between an insurer and *third-party providers* — which in petitioners' view does not constitute an "insurance practice."

In support of their contention, petitioners rely on *Group Life & Health Ins. Co. v. Royal Drug Co.*, 440 U.S. 205 (1979), which held that third-party provider arrangements between insurers and pharmacies were not "the 'business of insurance' " under § 2(b) of the McCarran-Ferguson Act. ERISA's savings clause, however, is not concerned (as is the McCarran-Ferguson Act provision) with how to characteriz e *conduct* undertaken by private actors, but with how to characterize *state laws* in regard to what they "regulate." It does not follow from *Royal Drug* that a law mandating certain insurer-provider relationships fails to "regulate insurance." Suppose a state law required all licensed attorneys to participate in 10 hours of continuing legal education (CLE) each year. This statute "regulates" the practice of law — even though sitting through 10 hours of CLE classes does not constitute the practice of law — because the state has *conditioned* the right to practice law on certain requirements, which substantially affect the product delivered by lawyers to their clients. Kentucky's AWP laws operate in a similar manner with respect to the insurance industry: Those who wish to provide health insurance in Kentucky (any "health insurer") may no t discriminate against any willing provider. This "regulates" insurance by imposing conditions on the right to engage in the business of insurance; whether or not an HMO's contracts with providers constitute "the business of insurance" under *Royal Drug* is beside the point.

We emphasize that conditions on the right to engage in the business of insurance must also substantially affect the risk pooling arrangement between the insurer and the insured to be covered by ERISA's savings clause. Otherwise, any state law aimed at insurance companies could be deemed a law that "regulates insurance," contrary to our interpretation of [ERISA] § 514(b)(2)(A) in *Rush Prudential*, 536 U.S. at 364. A state law requiring all insurance companies to pay their janitors twice the minimum wage would not "regulate insurance," even though it would be a prerequisite to engaging in the business of insurance, because it does not substantially affect the risk pooling arrangement undertaken by insurer and insured. Petitioners contend that Kentucky's AWP statutes fail this test as well, since they do not alter or affect the terms of insurance policies, but concern only the relationship between insureds and third-party providers. We disagree. We have never held that state laws must alter or control the actual terms of insurance policies to be deemed "laws . . . which regulate insurance" under [ERISA] § 514(b)(2)(A); it suffices that they substantially affect the risk pooling arrangement between insurer and insured. By expanding the number of providers from whom an insured may receive health services, AWP laws alter the scope of permissible bargains between insurers and insureds in a manner similar to the mandated-benefit laws we upheld in *Metropolitan Life*, the notice-prejudice rule we sustained in *UNUM*, and the independent-review provisions we approved in *Rush Prudential*. No longer may Kentucky insureds seek insurance from a closed network of health-care providers in exchange for a lower premium. The AWP prohibition substantially affects the type of risk pooling arrangements that insurers may offer.

III

Our prior decisions construing [ERISA] § 514(b)(2)(A) have relied, to varying degrees, on our cases interpreting §§ 2(a) and 2(b) of the McCarran-Ferguson Act. In determining whether certain practices constitute "the *business of* insurance" under the McCarran-Ferguson Act (emphasis added), our cases have looked to three factors: "*first*, whether the practice has the effect of transferring or spreading a policyholder's risk; second, whether the practice is an integral part of the policy relationship between the insurer and the insured; and third, whether the practice is limited to entities within the insurance industry." *Pireno*, 458 U.S. at 129.

We believe that our use of the McCarran-Ferguson case law in the ERISA context has misdirected attention, failed to provide clear guidance to lower federal courts, and, as this case demonstrates, added little to the relevant analysis. That is unsurprising, since the statutory language of [ERISA] § 514(b)(2)(A) differs substantially from that of the McCarran-Ferguson Act. Rather than concerning itself with whether certain practices constitute "the business of insurance," or whether a state law was "enacted . . . *for the purpose of* regulating the business of insurance," [ERISA]. § 514(b)(2)(A) asks merely whether a state law is a "law . . . which regulate s insurance, banking, or securities." What is more, the McCarran-Ferguson factors were developed in cases that characterized *conduct* by private actors, not state laws . . .

Our holdings in *UNUM* and Rush Prudential — that a state law may fail the first McCarran-Ferguson factor yet still be saved from pre-emption under [ERISA] § 514(b)(2)(A) — raise more questions than they answer and provide wide opportunities for divergent outcomes. May a state law satisfy *any* two of the three McCarran-Ferguson factors and still fall under the savings clause? Just one? What happens if two of three factors are satisfied, but not "securely satisfied" or "clearly satisfied," as they were in *UNUM* and *Rush Prudential*? Further confusion arises from the question whether the *state law itself* or the *conduct regulated by that law* is the proper subject to which one applies the McCarran-Ferguson factors. In *Pilot Life*, we inquired whether Mississippi's *law of bad faith* has the effect of transferring or spreading risk, whether *that law* is integral to the insurer-insured relationship, and whether *that law* is limited to the insurance industry. *Rush Prudential*, by contrast, focused the McCarran-Ferguson inquiry on the *conduct regulated* by the state law, rather than the state law itself . . .

We have never held that the McCarran-Ferguson factors are an essential component of the [ERISA] § 514(b)(2)(A) inquiry. *Metropolitan Life* initially used these factors only to buttress its previously reached conclusion that Massachusetts' mandated-benefit statute was a "law . . . which regulates insurance" under [ERISA] § 514(b)(2)(A). *Pilot Life* referred to them as mere "considerations [to be] weighed" in determining whether a state law falls under the savings clause. *UNUM* emphasized that the McCarran-Ferguson factors were not ' "required" ' in the savings clause analysis, and were only "checking points" to be used after determining whether the state law regulates insurance from a "common-sense" understanding and *Rush Prudential* called the factors "guideposts," using them only to "confirm our conclusion" that Illinois' statute regulated insurance.

Today we make a clean break from the McCarran-Ferguson factors and hold that for a state law to be deemed a "law . . . which regulates insurance" under [ERISA] § 514(b)(2)(A), it must satisfy two requirements. First, the state law must be specifically directed toward entities engaged in insurance. *See Pilot Life*, *UNUM*, *Rush Prudential*. Second, as explained above, the state law must substantially affect the risk pooling arrangement between the insurer and the insured. Kentucky's law satisfies each of these requirements.

For these reasons, we affirm the judgment of the Sixth Circuit.

It is so ordered.

5-5 QUESTIONS AND PROBLEMS

1. With the holding in *Kentucky Association of Health Plans*, did the Supreme Court settle the issue of which state laws regulate insurance and so escape ERISA preemption?

2. How does the Kentucky AWP statute "affect the risk pooling arrangement between the insurer and the insured"?

3. Lilly is employed by Alpha Bank which offers a welfare benefit plan that includes disability insurance purchased from the Omega Insurance Co. The policy pays up to 24 months of disability benefits if the employee is "unable to perform all of the material and substantial duties of his or her occupation because of injury or sickness." Lilly came down with fibromyalgia, which causes pain in muscles and tendons. In time Lilly ceased work and applied for disability benefits. Omega approved her claim. Six months later, based on additional medical reports, Omega denied that Lilly qualified for disability under the policy. Lilly sued Omega in state

court citing state insurance regulations that impose upon insurance companies a duty of good faith and fair dealing. Omega filed for summary judgement claiming that the claims were preempted by § 514(a) because th e regulations do not affect the risk pooling arrangements that insurers may offer as required by *Miller*. Is Omega correct? Should Lilly's claim be preempted?

E. THE "DEEMER" CLAUSE

ERISA § 514(b)(2)(B).

The "deemer" clause, found in ERISA § 514(b)(2)(B), states that an employee benefit plan shall not be "deemed to be an insurance company . . . for purposes of any law of any State purporting to regulate insurance companies . . . " The inclusion of the deemer clause was a reaction to litigation taking place in Missouri at the time of the enactment of ERISA in which a lower court held that a company that operated a self-insured health plan was subject to state insurance regulation. (That decision was later reversed by the Missouri Supreme Court. *Farmer v. Monsanto Co.*, 517 S.W.2d 129 (Mo. 1974).) Consequently, ERISA preempts state regulation of self-insured, employer-sponsored benefit plans.

Self-insurance simply means that the employer does not purchase insurance, such as health care insurance, to pay for the promised benefits. Instead, the employer pays for the promised benefits out of its own assets and accepts the concurrent financial risk of paying for the benefits. Many employers self-insure because they have the financial capability of paying off employee medical claims, and so see no reason to incur the added cost of purchasing health care insurance. The deemer clause is an added incentive to self-insure because ERISA preemption will protect the employer's health care benefit plan from state regulation. For example, recall that *Metropolitan Life Insurance Co. v. Massachusetts*, *supra* held an employee health care plan could be required by the state to provide mental health care benefits. If, however, the Acme Corporation Employee Welfare Plan operates a self-insured health plan in Massachusetts, because of the deemer clause, it is not subject to the Massachusetts mental health requirement law, which is preempted by ERISA. Conversely, if Acme contracted with Beta Insurance Co. to offer its employees health care insurance, the plan would have to provide mental health benefits because the Beta Insurance Co. would be subject to the Massachusetts requirement of offering mental health benefits. This difference has been noted by the Supreme Court.

> State laws directed toward the [self-insured] plans are preempted because they relate to an employee benefit plan but are not "saved" because they do not regulate insurance. State laws that directly regulate insurance are "saved" but do not reach self-funded employee benefit plans because the plans may not be deemed to be insurance companies, other insurers, or engaged int the business of insurance for purposes of such state laws. *FMC Corp. v. Holliday*, 498 U.S. 51, 61 (1990).
>
> We are aware that our decision results in a distinction between insured and uninsured plans, leaving the former open to indirect regulation while the latter are not. *Metropolitan Life Insurance Co. v. Massachusetts*, p. 747.

Although many employers self-insure, commercial insurance companies still play an important role. Employers who self-insure typically engage traditional insurance companies to handle the administration of health care benefits. Self-insurance plans also contract with third party administrators or specialty concerns to perform a number of other activities including drafting the plan, advising on the scope of benefits, claims processing and payment, and negotiating with health care providers as to the cost of the covered services.

5-6 QUESTIONS AND PROBLEMS

1. Is there any policy justification for subjecting insured plans to state regulation while exempting self-insured plans?

2. Does the "deemer" clause encourage self-insurance?

Third-party insurance companies who administer self-insured plans have been held not subject to state regulation when acting in the capacity as plan administrator.

> The laws of the state of Alabama require insurers to cover chiropractic services . . .
>
> As noted, defendant Aetna is the administrator of the Plan. It processes claims filed by beneficiaries of the Plan in accordance with the terms of a contract with the employer. The Plan includes a provision for an ERISA appeal, and the wage agreement includes a provision for binding arbitration concerning benefit disputes. When their claims were turned down by Aetna, plaintiffs did not seek to appeal under the terms of the agreement. Instead, they filed a suit in state court for compensatory and punitive damages, alleging that the failure of Aetna to pay plaintiffs' medical benefits for chiropractic services was a breach of contract and a "bad faith" denial of claims in violation of the provisions of Alabama law.
>
> By answer, Aetna averred the self-insured status of the Plan, and alleged that plaintiffs' claims were preempted by the provisions of ERISA.
>
> This circuit, as well as the Fifth and Ninth Circuits, has relied on the language in the *Metropolitan* case to the effect that the "deemer clause" creates "a distinction between insured and uninsured plans, leaving the former open to indirect regulation while the latter are not." We have also concluded that *Metropolitan* and the "deemer clause" have the specific effect that uninsured or self-insured ERISA plans are not subject to state insurance regulation either directly or indirectly, and that a state insurance law purporting to apply to such a plan is preempted.
>
> The Alabama statute here clearly seeks to "regulate insurance," but in this case there is no insurance policy, insurance fund, or insurer which could be subject to state regulation directly or indirectly. The statute also purports to extend the state's regulatory authority to "any *plan or agreement* for health services" by providing that "insureds" have the right to chiropractic services "notwithstanding any provisions of such contract or policy of insurance or plan or agreement for health services to the contrary." (Emphasis supplied.) Such law is preempted under the provisions of [ERISA] § 514(b)(2)(B), *supra* . . . . *Mullenix v. Aetna Life and Casualty Company*, 912 F.2d 1406, 1407–08, 1413 (11th Cir. 1990).

The essence of insurance, to diminish risk, is lost by self-insuring. While an employer may be willing to accept the risk of the cost of "normal" health care, it may not wish to be exposed to the cost of an "extraordinary" expense, such as the cost of a liver transplant. To protect themselves from such risks, most self-insurers purchase stop-loss insurance.

Some stop-loss insurance covers a plan against the risk that a particular participant's claims will exceed a specified level. For example, if the insurance kicks in when an individual's claims exceed $50,000 per year and a participant submits has claims of $60,000, the plan's stop-loss insurer will pay $10,000, Other stop-loss insurance covers a plan against the risk that the sum of all of its participants' claims will exceed a specified level. For example, if the insurance kicks in when aggregate claims exceed $1 million per year and claims under the plan total $1.3 million, the stop-loss insurer will pay $300,000 of the claims.

The question arises whether a self-insurer who also purchases stop-loss insurance can be subject to state insurance laws or whether the deemer clause still preempts state regulation. In general, courts have upheld the application of the deemer clause to employers who use stop-loss insurance, thereby exempting their health care plans from state regulation.

AMERICAN MEDICAL SECURITY, INC. v. BARTLETT

111 F.3d 358 (4th Cir. 1997)

NIEMEYER, CIRCUIT JUDGE.

. . .

Stop-loss insurance provides coverage to self-funded plans above a certain level of risk absorbed by the plan. It provides protection to the plan, not to the plan's participants or beneficiaries, against benefits payments over the specified level, called the "attachment point." Attachment points may be "specific" or "aggregate." Specific attachment points define the level of benefits paid to individual beneficiaries beyond which the insurance company will indemnify the plan. Aggregate attachment points define the total amount of benefits paid to all participants or beneficiaries beyond which the insurance company will indemnify the plan. Stop-loss insurance is thus akin to "reinsurance" in that it provides reimbursement to a plan after the plan makes benefit payments.

The State of Maryland regulates health insurance, requiring that health insurance policies afford at least 28 specified benefits. Apparently not wishing to be subject to state-mandated health benefits, insurance companies and their ERISA plan clients have entered into arrangements under which plans self-fund benefits and purchase stop-loss insurance to insure themselves against benefits paid beyond designated attachment points. A stop-loss policy does not itself provide coverage for benefits. Since such a policy insures only those benefits defined and actually paid by the plan, the ERISA plan's sponsor, not state health insurance regulations, dictates the range of benefits provided. Thus, by absorbing a minimal amount of initial risk and insuring the remainder through stop-loss insurance, plans are able to provide health benefits of a kind or at a level different from what state law requires of health insurance.

Recognizing that such arrangements bypass Maryland's regulations for health insurance and intending to prevent such arrangements, the Maryland Insurance Commissioner adopted regulations that require plans to absorb the risk of at least the first $10,000 of benefits paid to each beneficiary. As the regulations' statement of purpose notes, the Commissioner seeks to protect Maryland residents "against acts by persons and insurers which deprive them of mandated health benefits." 22 Md. Reg. 91 3 (1995). Justifying the regulation and explaining how low attachment points permit self-funded ERISA plans to bypass state mandates, the Insurance Commissioner stated in his order:

> At very low attachment points, however, a "stop loss" policy is merely a substitution for health insurance. It does not insure only against catastrophic loss. The self-funded health benefit plan is not regulated by the Insurance Commissioner and is not required to provide any of the state-mandated benefits. The goal is obvious: As policies become available with attachment points lower than many deductibles, it became an increasingly attractive option to "self-insure" a health plan, but to continue to shift the majority of the risk to the insurance carrier by purchasing "stop loss" coverage.

In re Maryland Stop Loss Insurance Litigation, No. MIA-370-12195 at 4 (Dec. 8, 1995). The regulations accordingly provide that any stop-loss insurance policy with a specific attachment point below $10,000 is deemed to be a health insurance policy for purposes of Maryland's health insurance regulations and must therefore contain mandated benefits. *See* COMAR, § 09.31.02.03. On the other hand, if the specific attachment point is above $10,000 and the policy provides for payment only to the plan, and not to its participants and beneficiaries, it is considered to be traditional stop-loss insurance that essentially reinsures the risks defined by the plan. *See id.*

In summary, on one side of the issue before us, the Maryland Insurance Commissioner seeks to take advantage of his right under ERISA's savings clause to regulate the business of insurance. And on the other side, the insurance companies seek to take advantage of ERISA's preemption and deemer clauses to remove self-funded plans from the reach of state insurance regulation.

. . .

We recognize that the regulations are carefully drafted to focus directly on insurance companies issuing stop-loss insurance and not on the employee benefit plans themselves. Thus, the regulations purport to define stop-loss insurance as health insurance subject to state regulation if the stop-loss insurance meets specific criteria. Notwithstanding the regulations' wording, however, their purpose and effect are directed at self-funded employee benefit plans that attempt to provide fewer health benefits to Maryland residents than state law mandates for health insurance policies. The state asserts a need for this regulation because, in its absence, the loophole would allow every self-funded plan to provide coverage for fewer health benefits than state law mandates for health insurance policies. It argues that absorbing a minimal risk is simply a sham to circumvent state insurance regulation, the area carved out by ERISA in which states may act. But in seeking to address this perceived loophole, the state in fact ends up regulating self-funded employee benefit plans that are exclusively subject to ERISA.

In seeking to require self-funded plans to offer coverage consistent with state insurance law, Maryland crosses the line of preemption. Even though the regulatory language targets stop-loss insurance policies, the Commissioner's stated purpose is to protect Maryland residents from self-funded ERISA plans and insurers "which deprive them of mandated health benefits." 22 Md. Reg. 913 (1995). The regulations thus use stop-loss insurance policies as a vehicle to impose the requirements of Maryland health insurance law on self-funded ERISA plans. By aiming at the plan-participant relationship, Maryland law violates the ERISA provision that no ERISA plan "shall be deemed to be an insurance company . . . for purposes of any law of any State purporting to regulate insurance companies [or] insurance contracts." 29 U.S.C. § 1144(b)(2)(B).

The state's fear that plans will circumvent state regulation and offer citizens too few health benefits is understandable. But to state that fear reveals that Maryland is really concerned, not with the business of insurance and its coverage of risks, but with the benefits that ERISA plans can choose to provide their participants and beneficiaries. No matter how understandable this concern may be, only Congress may address it, not the State of Maryland through its insurance regulations. In attempting to address this concern through the regulation of stop-loss insurance, the state blurs the real distinction between self-funded plans, with or without stop-loss insurance, and fully insured plans. Maryland's regulations distinguish self-funded plans from insured plans solely based on the level of the attachment point of stop-loss insurance. Thus, when the attachment point becomes low, Maryland deems self-funded plans with stop-loss insurance to be insured plans. *See* COMAR, § 09.35.02.02. This distinction overlooks the real risks.

Under a self-funded plan, the employer who promises the benefit incurs the liability defined by the plan's terms. That liability remains the employer's even if it has purchased stop-loss insurance and even if the stop-loss insurer becomes insolvent. Conversely, if the employer becomes insolvent, the solvency of the stop-loss insurer may not benefit plan participants and beneficiaries. This is because their claims against the insurer would be derivative of the plan's claim against the insurer, which arises only after the plan actually makes benefit payments beyond the agreed attachment point. In contrast, when a plan buys health insurance for participants and beneficiaries, the plan participants and beneficiaries have a legal claim directly against the insurance company, thereby securing the benefits even in the event of the plan's insolvency. Participants and beneficiaries in self-funded plans may not have the security of the insurance company's assets because stop-loss insurance insures the plan and not the participants.

The state's regulations fail to recognize that in a self-funded plan, with or without stop-loss insurance and regardless of the attachment point, the provision of benefits depends on the plan's solvency, whereas the provision of benefits in an insured plan depends entirely on the insurer's solvency. It is this fundamental difference that precludes the Maryland Insurance Agency from regulating self-funded plans but permits them to regulate insurance companies that provide health benefits to plans for their participants. While ERISA's savings clause explicitly empowers states to adjust the obligations and incentives which bear on insurance companies' solvency, the combined effect of the preemption and deemer clauses is that ERISA plan solvency is the purview of federal law alone.

Maryland's stop-loss insurance regulations also directly and impermissibly affect ERISA plans' costs and choices in designing their own array of benefits. If a self-funded plan insured by stop-loss insurance having an attachment point of $5,000 provided no benefit for organ transplants, the regulations would either raise plan costs by including unwanted, state-mandated insurance coverage for organ transplants or convert the self-funded plan into a fully insured plan contrary to its preference. These effects impermissibly intrude on the relationship between an ERISA plan and its participants and beneficiaries.

While we recognize that self-funded plans may not be providing Maryland residents with the range of benefits mandated by state law and that such plans' benefits may not always be as secure as those offered by regulated insurance companies, the remedy for any such deficiency must be requested of Congress. When ERISA preempted state law relating to ERISA-covered employee benefit plans, it may have created a regulatory gap, but Maryland is without authority to fill that gap . . . we affirm the judgment of the district court.

5-7 QUESTIONS AND PROBLEMS

1. The court in *American Medical Security* stated: "Participants and beneficiaries in self-funded plans may not have the security of the insurance company's assets because stop-loss insurance insures the plan and not the participants." Does this offer any reason to apply the deemer clause to stop-loss insurance?

2. Does the amount of risk assumed by the employer matter? What if the employer purchased stop-loss insurance to cover all employee medical costs once the total exceeded $1,000 for all claims. Would the employer still be considered to be self-insured and thus safe from state regulation?

3. What is the practical effect of permitting the deemer clause to apply even when the plan sponsor purchases stop-loss insurance?

F. PREEMPTION PURSUANT TO § 502(A)

While many ERISA preemption cases arise under the express preemption found in § 514, state law can also be preempted by virtue of ERISA § 502(a). Recall the language of *Pilot Life:*

> The Solicitor General, for the United States as amicus curiae, argues that Congress clearly expressed an intent that the civil enforcement provisions of ERISA § 502(a) be the exclusive vehicle for actions by ERISA-plan participants and beneficiaries asserting improper processing of a claim for benefits, and that varying state causes of action for claims within the scope of § 502(a) would pose an obstacle to the purposes and objectives of Congress. We agree. The conclusion that § 502(a) was intended to be exclusive is supported, first, by the language and structure of the civil enforcement provisions, and second, by legislative history in which Congress declared that the pre-emptive force of § 502(a) was modeled on the exclusive remedy provided by § 301 of the Labor Management Relations Act.
>
> The civil enforcement scheme of § 502(a) is one of the essential tools for accomplishing the stated purposes of ERISA. The civil enforcement scheme is sandwiched between two other ERISA provisions relevant to enforcement of ERISA and to the processing of a claim for benefits under an employee benefit plan. Section 501, authorizes criminal penalties for violations of the reporting and disclosure provisions of ERISA. . . . Under the civil enforcement provisions of § 502(a), a plan participant or beneficiary may sue to recover benefits due under the plan, to enforce the participant's rights under the plan, or to clarify rights to future benefits. Relief may take the form of accrued benefits due, a declaratory judgment on entitlement to benefits, or an injunction against a plan administrator's improper refusal to pay benefits. A participant or beneficiary may also bring a cause of action for breach of fiduciary duty, and under this cause of action may seek removal of the fiduciary. §§ 502(a)(2), 409. In an action under these civil enforcement provisions, the court in its discretion may allow an award of attorney's fees to either party. § 502(g) . . .

> In sum, the detailed provisions of § 502(a) set forth a comprehensive civil enforcement scheme that represents a careful balancing of the need for prompt and fair claims settlement procedures against the public interest in encouraging the formation of employee benefit plans. The policy choices reflected in the inclusion of certain remedies and the exclusion of others under the federal scheme would be completely undermined if ERISA-plan participants and beneficiaries were free to obtain remedies under state law that Congress rejected in ERISA.

Three years after deciding *Pilot Life*, the Court had another occasion to discuss preemption under § 502.

INGERSOLL-RAND CO. v. MCCLENDON

498 U.S. 133 (1990)

JUSTICE O'CONNOR delivered the opinion of the Court.

This case presents the question whether the Employee Retirement Income Security Act of 1974 (ERISA), pre-empts a state common law claim that an employee was unlawfully discharged to prevent his attainment of benefits under a plan covered by ERISA.

Petitioner Ingersoll-Rand Company employed respondent Perry McClendon as a salesman and distributor of construction equipment. In 1981, after McClendon had worked for the company for nine years and eight months, the company fired him citing a companywide reduction in force. McClendon sued the company in Texas state court, alleging that his pension would have vested in another four months and that a principal reason for his termination was the company's desire to avoid making contributions to his pension fund. McClendon sought compensatory and punitive damages under various tort and contract theories; he did not assert any cause of action under ERISA. After a period of discovery, the company moved for, and obtained, summary judgment on all claims. The State Court of Appeals affirmed, holding that McClendon's employment was terminable at will.

In a 5-to-4 decision, the Texas Supreme Court reversed and remanded for trial. The majority reasoned that notwithstanding the traditional employment-at-will doctrine, public policy imposes certain limitations upon an employer's power to discharge at-will employees. Citing [Texas law] and § 510 of ERISA, the majority concluded that "the state has an interest in protecting employees' interests in pension plans." As support the court noted that "[t]he very passage of ERISA demonstrates the great significance attached to income security for retirement purposes." Accordingly, the court held that under Texas law a plaintiff could recover in a wrongful discharge action if he established that "the principal reason for his termination was the employer's desire to avoid contributing to or paying benefits under the employee's pension fund." The court noted that federal courts had held similar claims pre-empted by ERISA, but distinguished the present case on the basis that McClendon was "not seeking lost pension benefits but [was] instead seeking lost future wages, mental anguish and punitive damages as a result of the wrongful discharge."

Because this issue has divided state and federal courts, we granted certiorari and now reverse.

. . .

B.

Even if there were no express pre-emption in this case, the Texas cause of action would be pre-empted because it conflicts directly with an ERISA cause of action. McClendon's claim falls squarely within the ambit of ERISA § 510, which provides:

> "It shall be unlawful for any person to discharge, fine, suspend, expel, discipline, or discriminate against a participant or beneficiary for exercising any right to which he is entitled under the provisions of an employee benefit plan . . . *or for the purpose of interfering with the attainment of any right to which such participant may become entitled* under the plan . . . ." 29 U.S.C. § 1140 (emphasis added).

By its terms § 510 protects plan participants from termination motivated by an employer's desire to prevent a pension from vesting Congress viewed this section as a crucial part of ERISA because, without it, employers would be able to circumvent the provision of promised benefits. We have no doubt that this claim is prototypical of the kind Congress intended to cover under § 510.

[T]he mere existence of a federal regulatory or enforcement scheme," however, even a considerably detailed one, "does not by itself imply pre-emption of state remedies." Accordingly, " 'we must look for special features warranting pre-emption.' "

Of particular relevance in this inquiry is § 502(a) — ERISA's civil enforcement mechanism. That section, as set forth in [ERISA § 502] provides in pertinent part . . .

In *Pilot Life* we examined this section at some length and explained that Congress intended § 502(a) to be the exclusive remedy for rights guaranteed under ERISA, including those provided by § 510:

> "[T]he detailed provisions of § 502(a) set forth a comprehensive civil enforcement scheme that represents a careful balancing of the need for prompt and fair claims settlement procedures against the public interest in encouraging the formation of employee benefit plans. The policy choices reflected in the inclusion of certain remedies and the exclusion of others under the federal scheme would be completely undermined if ERISA-plan participants and beneficiaries were free to obtain remedies under state law that Congress rejected in ERISA. 'The six carefully integrated civil enforcement provisions found in § 502(a) of the statute as finally enacted . . . provide strong evidence that Congress did *not* intend to authorize other remedies that it simply forgot to incorporate expressly.' "

It is clear to us that the exclusive remedy provided by § 502(a) is precisely the kind of " 'special featur[e]' " that " 'warrant[s] pre-emption' " in this case. As we explained in *Pilot Life*, ERISA's legislative history makes clear that "the pre-emptive force of § 502(a) was modeled on the exclusive remedy provided by § 301 of the Labor Management Relations Act, 1947 (LMRA), 29 U.S.C. § 185." In *Metropolitan Life Ins. Co. v. Taylor*, 481 U.S. 58 (1987), we again drew upon the parallel between § 502(a) and § 301 of the LMRA to support our conclusion that the pre-emptive effect of § 502(a) was so complete that an ERISA pre-emption defense provides a sufficient basis for removal of a cause of action to the federal forum notwithstanding the traditional limitation imposed by the "well-pleaded complaint" rule.

We rely on this same evidence in concluding that the requirements of conflict pre-emption are satisfied in this case. Unquestionably, the Texas cause of action purports to provide a remedy for the violation of a right expressly guaranteed by § 510 and exclusively enforced by § 502(a). Accordingly we hold that "[w]hen it is clear or may fairly be assumed that the activities which a State purports to regulate are protected" by § 510 of ERISA, "due regard for the federal enactment requires that state jurisdiction must yield."

The preceding discussion also responds to the Texas court's attempt to distinguish this case as not one within ERISA's purview. Not only is § 502(a) the exclusive remedy for vindicating § 510-protected rights, but there is no basis in § 502(a)'s language for limiting ERISA actions to only those which seek "pension benefits." It is clear that the relief requested here is well within the power of federal courts to provide. Consequently, it is no answer to a pre-emption argument that a particular plaintiff is not seeking recovery of pension benefits.

The judgment of the Texas Supreme Court is reversed.

5-8 QUESTIONS AND PROBLEMS

1. Does ERISA § 502(a) provide a remedy for the wrongful termination?
2. Is the Court's decision influenced by whether ERISA provides a remedy?

In 2002 the Supreme Court appeared to retreat from its broad preemption announcements in *Pilot Life* and breathed new life into state law claims.

RUSH PRUDENTIAL HMO, INC. v. MORAN
536 U.S. 355 (2002)

JUSTICE SOUTER delivered the opinion of the Court.

Section 4-10 of Illinois's Health Maintenance Organization Act, 215 Ill. Comp. Stat., ch. 125, § 4-10 (2000), provides recipients of health coverage by such organizations with a right to independent medical review of certain denials of benefits. The issue in this case is whether the statute, as applied to health benefits provided by a health maintenance organization under contract with an employee welfare benefit plan, is preempted by [ERISA]. We hold it is not.

I

Petitioner, Rush Prudential HMO, Inc., is a health maintenance organization (HMO) that contracts to provide medical services for employee welfare benefit plans covered by ERISA. Respondent Debra Moran is a beneficiary under one such plan, sponsored by her husband's employer. Rush's "Certificate of Group Coverage," issued to employees who participate in employer-sponsored plans, promises that Rush will provide them with "medically necessary" services. The terms of the certificate give Rush the "broadest possible discretion" to determine whether a medical service claimed by a beneficiary is covered under the certificate. . . .

In 1996, when Moran began to have pain and numbness in her right shoulder, Dr. Arthur LaMarre, her primary care physician, unsuccessfully administered "conservative" treatments such as physiotherapy. In October 1997, Dr. LaMarre recommended that Rush approve surgery by an unaffiliated specialist, Dr. Julia Terzis, who had developed an unconventional treatment for Moran's condition. Although Dr. LaMarre said that Moran would be "best served" by that procedure,

Rush denied the request and, after Moran's internal appeals, affirmed the denial on the ground that the procedure was not "medically necessary." Rush instead proposed that Moran undergo standard procedure, performed by a physician affiliated with Rush.

In January 1998, Moran made a written demand for an independent medical review of her claim, as guaranteed by §§ 4-10 of Illinois's HMO Act . . .

When Rush failed to provide the independent review, Moran sued in an Illinois state court to compel compliance with the state Act. Rush removed the suit to Federal District Court, arguing that the cause of action was "completely preempted" under ERISA.

While the suit was pending, Moran had surgery by Dr. Terzis at her own expense and submitted a $94,841.27 reimbursement claim to Rush. Rush treated the claim as a renewed request for benefits and began a new inquiry to determine coverage. The three doctors consulted by Rush said the surgery had been medically unnecessary.

The Court of Appeals for the Seventh Circuit reversed. Although it found Moran's state-law reimbursement claim completely preempted by ERISA so as to place the case in federal court, the Seventh Circuit did not agree that the substantive provisions of Illinois's HMO Act were so preempted. The court noted that although ERISA broadly preempts any state laws that "relate to" employee benefit plans, [ERISA § 514(a)], state laws that "regulat[e] insurance" are saved from preemption, [ERISA § 514(b)(2)(A)]. The court held that the Illinois HMO Act was such a law, the independent review requirement being little different from a state-mandated contractual term of the sort this Court had held to survive ERISA preemption. The Seventh Circuit rejected the contention that Illinois's independent review requirement constituted a forbidden "alternative remedy" under this Court's holding in *Pilot Life Ins. Co. v. Dedeaux*, 481 U.S. 41 (1987), and emphasized that § 4-10 does not authorize any particular form of relief in state courts; rather, with respect to any ERISA health plan, the judgment of the independent reviewer is only enforceable in an action brought under ERISA's civil enforcement scheme, [ERISA § 502(a)].

Because the decision of the Court of Appeals conflicted with the Fifth Circuit's treatment of a similar provision of Texas law in *Corporate Health Ins., Inc. v. Texas Dept. of Ins.*, 215 F.3d 526 (2000), we granted certiorari. We now affirm.

. . . . Rush contends that seeing an HMO as an insurer distorts the nature of an HMO, which is, after all, a health care provider, too . . . .

The answer to Rush is, of course, that an HMO is both: it provides health care, and it does so as an insurer. Nothing in the saving clause requires an either-or choice between health care and insurance in deciding a preemption question, and as long as providing insurance fairly accounts for the application of state law, the saving clause may apply. There is no serious question about that here, for it would ignore the whole purpose of the HMO-style of organization to conceive of HMOs without their insurance element.

* * *

So Congress has understood from the start, when the phrase "Health Maintenance Organization" was established and defined in the HMO Act of 1973 . . . . This congressional understanding that it was promoting a novel form of insurance was made explicit in the Senate Report's reference to the practices of "health insurers to charge premium rates based upon the actual claims experience of a particular group of subscribers," thus "raising costs and diminishing the availability of health insurance for those suffering from costly illnesses," S. Rep. No. 93-129, at 29-30 . . . . The Senate explanation left no doubt that it viewed an HMO as an insurer; the subsidy was justified because "the same stringent requirements do not apply to other indemnity or service benefits insurance plans."

Given that § 4-10 regulates insurance, ERISA's mandate that "nothing in this subchapter shall be construed to exempt or relieve any person from any law of any State which regulates insurance," [ERISA § 514(b)(2)(A)], ostensibly forecloses preemption. Rush, however, does not give up. It argues for preemption anyway, emphasizing that the question is ultimately one of congressional intent, which sometimes is so clear that it overrides a statutory provision designed to save state law from being preempted.

In ERISA law, we have recognized one example of this sort of overpowering federal policy in the civil enforcement provisions, [ERISA § 502(a)], authorizing civil actions for six specific types of relief. In *Massachusetts Mut. Life Ins. Co. v. Russell*, 473 U.S. 134 (1985), we said those provisions amounted to an "interlocking, interrelated, and interdependent remedial scheme," which Pilot Life described as "represent[ing] a careful balancing of the need for prompt and fair claims settlement procedures against the public interest in encouraging the formation of employee benefit plans," 481 U.S. at 54. So, we have held, the civil enforcement provisions are of such extraordinarily preemptive power that they override even the "well-pleaded complaint" rule for establishing the conditions under which a cause of action may be removed to a federal forum. *Metropolitan Life Ins. Co. v. Taylor*, 481 U.S. at 63–64.

Although we have yet to encounter a forced choice between the congressional policies of exclusively federal remedies and the "reservation of the business of insurance to the States," *Metropolitan Life*, 471 U.S. at 744, n. 21, we have anticipated such a conflict, with the state insurance regulation losing out if it allows plan participants "to obtain remedies . . . that Congress rejected in ERISA," *Pilot Life*, *supra*, at 54.

In *Pilot Life*, an ERISA plan participant who had been denied benefits sued in a state court on state tort and contract claims. He sought not merely damages for breach of contract, but also damages for emotional distress and punitive damages, both of which we had held unavailable under relevant ERISA provisions. We not only rejected the notion that these common law contract claims "regulat[ed] insurance," *Pilot Life*, 481 U.S. at 50–51, but went on to say that, regardless, Congress intended a "federal common law of rights and obligations" to develop under ERISA, *id.* at 56, without embellishment by independent state remedies. As in AT & T, we said the saving clause had to stop short of subverting congressional intent, clearly expressed "through the structure and legislative history[,] that the federal remedy . . . displace state causes of action." 481 U.S. at 57.

Rush says that the day has come to turn dictum into holding by declaring that the state insurance regulation, § 4-10, is preempted for creating just the kind of "alternative remedy" we disparaged in *Pilot Life*. As Rush sees it, the independent review procedure is a form of binding arbitration that allows an ERISA beneficiary to submit claims to a new decisionmaker to examine Rush's determination *de novo*, supplanting judicial review under the "arbitrary and capricious" standard ordinarily applied when discretionary plan interpretations are challenged. *Firestone Tire & Rubber Co. v. Bruch*, 489 U.S. 101, 110–112 (1989). Rush says that the beneficiary's option falls within *Pilot Life*'s notion of a remedy that "supplement[s] or supplant[s]" the remedies available under ERISA.

We think, however, that Rush overstates the rule expressed in *Pilot Life*. The enquiry into state processes alleged to "supplemen[t] or supplan[t]" the federal scheme by allowing beneficiaries "to obtain remedies under state law that Congress rejected in ERISA," *id.* at 54, has, up to now, been far more straightforward than it is here. The first case touching on the point did not involve preemption at all; it arose from an ERISA beneficiary's reliance on ERISA's own enforcement scheme to claim a private right of action for types of damages beyond those expressly provided. Russell, 473 U.S. at 145. We concluded that Congress had not intended causes of action under ERISA itself beyond those specified in [§ 502(a)]. *Id.* at 148. Two years later we determined in *Metropolitan Life Ins. Co. v. Taylor, supra*, that Congress had so completely preempted the field of benefits law that an ostensibly state cause of action for benefits was necessarily a "creature of federal law" removable to federal court. Russell and Taylor naturally led to the holding in *Pilot Life* that ERISA would not tolerate a diversity action seeking monetary damages for breach generally and for consequential emotional distress, neither of which Congress had authorized in [§ 502(a)]. These monetary awards were claimed as remedies to be provided at the ultimate step of plan enforcement, and even if they could have been characterized as products of "insurance regulation," they would have significantly expanded the potential scope of ultimate liability imposed upon employers by the ERISA scheme.

Since Pilot Life, we have found only one other state law to "conflict" with [§ 502(a)] in providing a prohibited alternative remedy. In *Ingersoll-Rand Co. v. McClendon*, 498 U.S. 133 (1990), we had no trouble finding that Texas's tort of wrongful discharge, turning on an employer's motivation to avoid paying pension benefits, conflicted with ERISA enforcement; while state law duplicated the elements of a claim available under ERISA, it converted the remedy from an equitable one under [§ 502(a)(3)] (available exclusively in federal district courts) into a legal one for money damages (available in a state tribunal). Thus, *Ingersoll-Rand* fit within the category of state laws *Pilot Life* had held to be incompatible with ERISA's enforcement scheme; the law provided a form of ultimate relief in a judicial forum that added to the judicial remedies provided by ERISA. Any such provision patently violates ERISA's policy of inducing employers to offer benefits by assuring a predictable set of liabilities, under uniform standards of primary conduct and a uniform regime of ultimate remedial orders and awards when a violation has occurred.

But this case addresses a state regulatory scheme that provides no new cause of action under state law and authorizes no new form of ultimate relief. While independent review under § 4-10 may well settle the fate of a benefit claim under a particular contract, the state statute does not enlarge the claim beyond the benefits available in any action brought under [§ 502(a)]. And although the reviewer's determination would presumably replace that of the HMO as to what is "medically necessary" under this contract, the relief ultimately available would still be what ERISA authorizes in a suit for benefits under [§ 502(a)]. This case therefore does not involve the sort of additiona l claim or remedy exemplified in *Pilot Life, Russell*, and *Ingersoll-Rand*, but instead bears a resemblance to the claims-procedure rule that we sustained in *UNUM Life Ins. Co. of America v. Ward*, 526 U.S. 358 (1999), holding that a state law barring enforcement of a policy's time limitation on submitting claims did not conflict with [§ 502(a)], even though the state "rule of decision," *id.* at 377, could mean the difference between success and failure for a beneficiary. The procedure provided by § 4-10 does not fall within *Pilot Life*'s categorical preemption.

Rush still argues for going beyond *Pilot Life*, making the preemption issue here one of degree, whether the state procedural imposition interferes unreasonably with Congress's intention to provide a uniform federal regime of "rights and obligations" under ERISA. However, "[s]uch disuniformities . . . are the inevitable result of the congressional decision to 'save' local insurance regulation." *Metropolitan Life*, 471 U.S. at 747. Although we have recognized a limited exception from the saving clause for alternative causes of action and alternative remedies in the sense described above, we have never indicated that there might be additional justifications for qualifying the clause's application. Rush's arguments today convince us that further limits on insurance regulation preserved by ERISA are unlikely to deserve recognition.

In sum, § 4-10 imposes no new obligation or remedy like the causes of action considered in *Russell*, *Pilot Life*, and *Ingersoll-Rand*. Even in its formal guise, the State Act bears a closer resemblance to second-opinion requirements than to arbitration schemes. Deferential review in the HMO context is not a settled given; § 4-10 operates before the stage of judicial review; the independent reviewer's *de novo* examination of the benefit claim mirrors the general or default rule we have ourselves recognized; and its effect is no greater than that of mandated-benefit regulation.

In deciding what to make of these facts and conclusions, it helps to go back to where we started and recall the ways States regulate insurance in looking out for the welfare of their citizens. Illinois has chosen to regulate insurance as one way to regulate the practice of medicine, which we have previously held to be permissible under ERISA. While the statute designed to do this undeniably eliminates whatever may have remained of a plan sponsor's option to minimize scrutiny of benefit denials, this effect of eliminating an insurer's autonomy to guarantee terms congenial to its own interests is the stuff of garden variety insurance regulation through the imposition of standard policy terms. It is therefore hard to imagine a reservation of state power to regulate insurance that would not be meant to cover restrictions of the insurer's advantage in this kind of way. And any lingering doubt about the reasonableness of § 4-10 in affecting the application of [§ 502(a)] may be put to rest by recalling that regulating insurance tied to what is medically necessary is probably inseparable from enforcing the quintessentially state-law standards of reasonable medical care. See *Pegram v. Herdrich*, 530 U.S. at 236. "[I]n the field of health care, a subject of traditional state regulation, there is no ERISA preemption without clear manifestation of congressional purpose." *Id.* at 237. To the extent that benefit litigation in some federal courts may have to account for the effects of § 4-10, it would be an exaggeration to hold that the objectives of [§ 502(a)] are undermined. The saving clause is entitled to prevail here, and we affirm the judgment.

It is so ordered.

5-9 QUESTIONS AND PROBLEMS

1. How much of *Pilot Life* remains good law in light of *Rush Prudential*?

2. What if state "X" does not have a law requiring independent medical review. Would this mean that employees in state X would have a different medical plan than workers in Illinois? Would this defeat the Congressional intent that an employee benefit plan be uniform across the nation?

[1] Medical Malpractice Claims

A welfare plan sponsor who offers health care benefits, but is self-insured, will often contract with a health care provider such as a Health Maintenance Organization (HMO) to provide health care under the welfare benefit plan. The sponsor will pre-pay for employee health care based on a set dollar amount per plan participant and beneficiary. The employees will receive subsidized or free health care only if it is provided or approved by the provider with whom the employer has contracted. In theory the capitation (cost) per employee on average will cost the employer less than permitting the employees to seek out health care as they choose. The employer is still a self-insurer because the health care is purchased from the provider of health care rather than being paid for by an insurer.

One reason that a contracted health care provider such as an HMO may be able to provide health care more efficiently is its use of utilization review, by which initial recommended treatment is subject to oversight review. In theory, the oversight review should reduce or eliminate unnecessary or excessively costly health care. Unfortunately for patients who are participants in a self-insured, employer-provided welfare benefit plan, ERISA § 514(a) may preempt state law claims against the health care provider for mistakes incurred during the utilization review process. For example:

> The basic facts are undisputed. Florence Corcoran, a long-time employee of South Central Bell Telephone Company (Bell), became pregnant in early 1989. In July, her obstetrician, Dr. Jason Collins, recommended that she have complete bed rest during the final months of her pregnancy. Mrs. Corcoran applied to Bell for temporary disability benefits for the remainder of her pregnancy, but the benefits were denied. This prompted Dr. Collins to write to Dr. Theodore J. Borgman, medical consultant for Bell, and explain that Mrs. Corcoran had several medical problems which placed her "in a category of high risk pregnancy." . . . As Mrs. Corcoran neared her delivery date, Dr. Collins ordered her hospitalized so that he could monitor the fetus around the clock.
>
> Mrs. Corcoran was a member of Bell's Medical Assistance Plan (MAP or "the Plan") . . . Under a portion of the Plan known as the "Quality Care Program" (QCP), participants must obtain advance approval for overnight hospital admissions and certain medical procedures ("pre-certification"), and must obtain approval on a continuing basis once they are admitted to a hospital ("concurrent review"), or plan benefits to which they otherwise would be entitled are reduced.
>
> . . .
>
> In accordance with the QCP portion of the plan, Dr. Collins sought pre-certification from United for Mrs. Corcoran's hospital stay. Despite Dr. Collins's recommendation, United determined that hospitalization was not necessary, and instead authorized 10 hours per day of home nursing care. Mrs. Corcoran entered the hospital on October 3, 1989, but, because United had not pre-certified her stay, she returned home on October 12. On October 25, during a period of time when no nurse was on duty, the fetus went into distress and died.
>
> Mrs. Corcoran and her husband, Wayne, filed a wrongful death action in Louisiana state court alleging that their unborn child died as a result of various acts of negligence committed by Blue Cross and United. Both

> sought damages for the lost love, society and affection of their unborn child. In addition, Mrs. Corcoran sought damages for the aggravation of a pre-existing depressive condition and the loss of consortium caused by such aggravation, and Mr. Corcoran sought damages for loss of consortium. The defendants removed the action to federal court on grounds that it was pre-empted by ERISA and that there was complete diversity among the parties.
>
> . . .
>
> United's argument in favor of pre-emption is grounded in the notion that the decision it made concerning Mrs. Corcoran was not primarily a medical decision, but instead was a decision made in its capacity as a plan fiduciary about what benefits were authorized under the Plan. All it did, it argues, was determine whether Mrs. Corcoran qualified for the benefits provided by the plan by applying previously established eligibility criteria.
>
> . . .
>
> . . . Ultimately, we conclude that United makes medical decisions — indeed, United gives medical advice — but it does so in the context of making a determination about the availability of benefits under the plan. Accordingly, we hold that the Louisiana tort action asserted by the Corcorans for the wrongful death of their child allegedly resulting from United's erroneous medical decision is pre-empted by ERISA.

Corcoran v. United Healthcare, Inc., 965 F.2d 1321 (5th Cir. 1992).

The reaction of one United States District Court to the reality of § 514(a) preemption of state law claims in light of the lack of a meaningful federal remedy under § 502(a) for errors by HMOs is instructive.

> When Congress passed ERISA in 1974, traditional fee-for-service insurance plans dominated the American health care industry. Under this model of health care delivery, a plan beneficiary who was ill or injured would visit the doctor of her choice, receive treatment, and then send the bill to her health insurer. If the insurer improperly refused to pay, the beneficiary could be made whole by commencing suit to recover the cost of the treatment pursuant to ERISA.
>
> . . .
>
> ERISA's civil enforcement provision, however, does not authorize recovery for wrongful death, personal injury, or other consequential damages caused by an improper refusal of an insurer or utilization review provider to authorize treatment. ERISA permits a beneficiary to seek an injunction ordering an insurer to authorize the disputed treatment, but such action is often impractical, either because of time constraints or — as was the case here — the incapacity of the beneficiary brought on by his medical condition. Thus, if a beneficiary never receives treatment because of the insurer's failure to pre-approve, ERISA leaves him without any meaningful remedy.

Andrews-Clarke v. Travelers Insurance Company, 984 F. Supp. 49 (D. Mass. 1997).

A claimant who is limited to a suit under ERISA for wrongful denial of coverage may seek injunctive relief to compel the insurer to offer the benefit (*see Bast v. Prudential Insurance Co.*, 150 F.3d 1003 (9th Cir. 1998)). By the time the claimant can obtain a judicial decision as to whether the plan should pay for the requested medical procedure, however, the claimant may have suffered permanent injury or even death. Alternatively, the claimant can pay for the medical procedure and sue for reimbursement from the plan. This, of course, assumes that the claimant can afford to prepay the cost of the treatment. Most claimants lack the financial wherewithal to do so. Contrast this to traditional cost reimbursement insurance. If the medical provider, and perhaps a second provider (a second opinion requirement), thought the patient the procedure was medically needed, it was furnished. The provider then filed with the insurer for reimbursement. The provider bore the risk that the insurer might refuse to reimburse on the basis that the medical procedure was unnecessary, experimental, or otherwise not covered by the insurance plan. As a result, the provider, and not the patient, bore the risk. However, that risk was not great because medical insurance plans provided broad coverage that was almost certain to pay for the treatment, in part because in the past there were fewer very expensive procedures that might conceivably be classed as experimental or otherwise not covered by the plan.

In the context of health care decisions, ERISA preemption applies only to coverage determinations (the scope of the plan), not to medical decisions in cases when it is conceded that the plan should provide coverage. Typically the plan participant will allege that the health care provider negligently failed to provide the level or quality of care required by the participant's condition; in short, a claim for medical malpractice. In *Pegram v. Herdrich*, 530 U.S. 211 (2000), the Supreme Court implied that state malpractice claims against HMOs might be permissible if the lawsuit concerned the quality of care (treatment decisions) rather than whether the plan should have accepted responsibility for covering the care (eligibility decisions).

> What we will call pure "eligibility decisions" turn on the plan's coverage of a particular condition or medical procedure for its treatment. "Treatment decisions," by contrast, are choices about how to go about diagnosing and treating a patient's condition: given a patient's constellation of symptoms, what is the appropriate medical response?
>
> These decisions are often practically inextricable from one another, as amici on both sides agree. This is so not merely because, under a scheme like Carle's, treatment and eligibility decisions are made by the same person, the treating physician. It is so because a great many and possibly most coverage questions are not simple yes-or-no questions, like whether appendicitis is a covered condition (when there is no dispute that a patient has appendicitis), or whether acupuncture is a covered procedure for pain relief (when the claim of pain is unchallenged).
>
> The more common coverage question is a when-and-how question. Although coverage for many conditions will be clear and various treatment options will be indisputably compensable, physicians still must decide what to do in particular cases. The issue may be, say, whether one treatment option is so superior to another under the circumstances, and needed so promptly, that a decision to proceed with it would meet the medical necessity requirement that conditions the HMO's obligation to provide or pay for that particular procedure at that time in that case. In practical terms, these eligibility decisions cannot be untangled from physicians' judgments about reasonable medical treatment, and in the case before us, Dr. Pegram's decision was one of that sort. She decided (wrongly, as it turned out) that Herdrich's condition did not warrant immediate action; the consequence of that medical determination was that Carle would not cover immediate care, whereas it would have done so if Dr. Pegram had made the proper diagnosis and judgment to treat. The eligibility decision and the

treatment decision were inextricably mixed, as they are in countless medical administrative decisions every day. *Pegram v. Herdrich*, 530 U.S. at 228.

5-10 QUESTIONS AND PROBLEMS

Elroy is an adult diabetic. His physician since 2005 has been Dr. Carmen Levy. On July 1, 2011, Elroy took a job with Beta Inc., which has a self-insured health plan that has contracted with Sunrise HMO to provide care for the plan participants. The plan has no limit on preexisting conditions. Although Dr. Levy was not an approved primary care provider (PCP) under the Sunrise HMO, Elroy continued to see Dr. Levy. Sunrise paid Dr. Levy, which made Elroy believe that Dr. Levy was an approved PCP.

On March 1, 2012 Elroy begin to suffer painful swelling of his left foot. He visited Dr. Levy, who directed him to go the Hope Hospital Wound Care Center. When Elroy tried to check into Hope Hospital, he was told that Sunrise would not approve the costs unless Elroy was referred there by an approved PCP. Elroy contacted Sunrise, who gave him the names of three PCPs. Elroy could not make contact with any of them until March 15, 2012. On that day he met with Dr. Sung, who was an approved PCP for Sunrise. At that meeting Dr. Sung observed that the sore on the foot had opened and was draining blood and pus. He immediately sent Elroy to St. Mary's hospital, the usual hospital used by Sunrise PCPs. There a surgeon, Dr. Halley, amputated Elroy's left foot.

Elroy brought suit in the federal district court against Sunrise allegedly that the delay in obtaining treatment resulted in the need to amputate his foot. He alleged negligent care and management of his condition. Sunrise moved to dismiss on the basis that Elroy's claims were preempted under ERISA. How should the court rule on Sunrise's motion?

The hopes raised by *Pegram* that in the future, fact situations such as *Corcoran* would not be preempted were dashed in 2004 by the following Supreme Court case.

AETNA HEALTH INC. v. DAVILA
542 U.S. 200 (2004)

JUSTICE THOMAS delivered the opinion of the Court.

In these consolidated cases, two individuals sued their respective health maintenance organizations (HMOs) for alleged failures to exercise ordinary care in the handling of coverage decisions, in violation of a duty imposed by the Texas Health Care Liability Act (THCLA). We granted certiorari to decide whether the individuals' causes of action are completely pre-empted by the "interlocking, interrelated, and interdependent remedial scheme." We hold that the causes of action are completely pre-empted and hence removable from state to federal court. The Court of Appeals, having reached a contrary conclusion, is reversed.

I

A

Respondent Juan Davila is a participant, and respondent Ruby Calad is a beneficiary, in ERISA-regulated employee benefit plans. Their respective plan sponsors had entered into agreements with petitioners, Aetna Health Inc. and CIGNA Healthcare of Texas, Inc., to administer the plans. Under Davila's plan, for instance, Aetna reviews requests for coverage and pays providers, such as doctors, hospitals, and nursing homes, which perform covered services for members; under Calad's plan sponsor's agreement, CIGNA is responsible for plan benefits and coverage decisions.

Respondents both suffered injuries allegedly arising from Aetna's and CIGNA's decisions not to provide coverage for certain treatment and services recommended by respondents' treating physicians. Davila's treating physician prescribed Vioxx to remedy Davila's arthritis pain, but Aetna refused to pay for it. Davila did not appeal or contest this decision, nor did he purchase Vioxx with his own resources and seek reimbursement. Instead, Davila began taking Naprosyn, from which he allegedly suffered a severe reaction that required extensive treatment and hospitalization. Calad underwent surgery, and although her treating physician recommended an extended hospital stay, a CIGNA discharge nurse determined that Calad did not meet the plan's criteria for a continued hospital stay. CIGNA consequently denied coverage for the extended hospital stay. Calad experienced postsurgery complications forcing her to return to the hospital. She alleges that these complications would not have occurred had CIGNA approved coverage for a longer hospital stay.

Respondents brought separate suits in Texas state court against petitioners. Invoking THCLA § 88.002(a), respondents argued that petitioners' refusal to cover the requested services violated their "duty to exercise ordinary care when making health care treatment decisions," and that these refusals "proximately caused" their injuri es. Petitioners removed the cases to Federal District Courts, arguing that respondents' causes of action fit within the scope of, and were therefore completely pre-empted by, ERISA § 502(a). . . .

. . .

Congress enacted ERISA to "protect . . . the interests of participants in employee benefit plans and their beneficiaries" by setting out substantive regulatory requirements for employee benefit plans and to "provid[e] for appropriate remedies, sanctions, and ready access to the Federal courts." [ERISA § 1.] The purpose of ERISA is to provide a uniform regulatory regime over employee benefit plans. To this end, ERISA includes expansive pre-emption provisions.

ERISA's "comprehensive legislative scheme" includes "an integrated system of procedures for enforcement." *Russell*, 473 U.S. at 147. This integrated enforcement mechanism, ERISA § 502(a), is a distinctive feature of ERISA, and essential to accomplish Congress' purpose of creating a comprehensive statute for the regulation of employee benefit plans. . . .

. . .

Therefore, any state-law cause of action that duplicates, supplements, or supplants the ERISA civil enforcement remedy conflicts with the clear congressional intent to make the ERISA remedy exclusive and is therefore pre-empted.

. . .

ERISA § 502(a)(1)(B) provides:

> A civil action may be brought — (1) by a participant or beneficiary — . . . (B) to recover benefits due to him under the terms of his plan, to enforce his rights under the terms of the plan, or to clarify his rights to future benefits under the terms of the plan.

This provision is relatively straightforward. If a participant or beneficiary believes that benefits promised to him under the terms of the plan are not provided, he can bring suit seeking provision of those benefits. . . .

It follows that if an individual brings suit complaining of a denial of coverage for medical care, where the individual is entitled to such coverage only because of the terms of an ERISA-regulated employee benefit plan, and where no legal duty (state or federal) independent of ERISA or the plan terms is violated, then the suit falls "within the scope of" ERISA § 502(a)(1)(B). In other words, if an individual, at some point in time, could have brought his claim under ERISA § 502(a)(1)(B), and where there is no other independent legal duty that is implicated by a defendant's actions, then the individual's cause of action is completely pre-empted by ERISA § 502(a)(1)(B).

To determine whether respondents' causes of action fall "within the scope" of ERISA § 502(a)(1)(B), we must examine respondents' complaints, the statute on which their claims are based (the THCLA), and the various plan documents. Davila alleges that Aetna provides health coverage under his employer's health benefits plan. The only action complained of was Aetna's refusal to approve payment for Davila's Vioxx prescription. Further, the only relationship Aetna had with Davila was its partial administration of Davila's employer's benefit plan.

Similarly, Calad alleges that she receives, as her husband's beneficiary under an ERISA-regulated benefit plan, health coverage from CIGNA. . . . And, as in Davila's case, the only connection between Calad and CIGNA is CIGNA's administration of portions of Calad's ERISA-regulated benefit plan.

It is clear, then, that respondents complain only about denials of coverage promised under the terms of ERISA-regulated employee benefit plans. Upon the denial of benefits, respondents could have paid for the treatment themselves and then sought reimbursement through a § 502(a)(1)(B) action, or sought a preliminary injunction, see *Pryzbowski v. U.S. Healthcare, Inc.*, 245 F.3d 266, 274 (CA3 2001) (giving examples where federal courts have issued such preliminary injunctions).

Respondents contend, however, that the complained — of actions violate legal duties that arise independently of ERISA or the terms of the employee benefit plans at issue in these cases. . . .

The duties imposed by the THCLA in the context of these cases, however, do not arise independently of ERISA or the plan terms. The THCLA does impose a duty on managed care entities to "exercise ordinary care when making health care treatment decisions," and makes them liable for damages proximately caused by failures to abide by that duty. § 88.002(a). However, if a managed care entity correctly concluded that, under the terms of the relevant plan, a particular treatment was not covered, the managed care entity's denial of coverage would not be a proximate cause of any injuries arising from the denial. Rather, the failure of the plan itself to cover the requested treatment would be the proximate cause. More significantly, the THCLA clearly states that "[t]he standards in Subsections (a) and

(b) create no obligation on the part of the health insurance carrier, health maintenance organization, or other managed care entity to provide to an insured or enrollee treatment which is not covered by the health care plan of the entity." § 88.002(d). Hence, a managed care entity could not be subject to liability under the THCLA if it denied coverage for any treatment not covered by the health care plan that it was administering.

Thus, interpretation of the terms of respondents' benefit plans forms an essential part of their THCLA claim, and THCLA liability would exist here only because of petitioners' administration of ERISA-regulated benefit plans. Petitioners' potential liability under the THCLA in these cases, then, derives entirely from the particular rights and obligations established by the benefit plans. . . .

Hence, respondents bring suit only to rectify a wrongful denial of benefits promised under ERISA-regulated plans, and do not attempt to remedy any violation of a legal duty independent of ERISA. We hold that respondents' state causes of action fall "within the scope of" ERISA § 502(a)(1)(B), and are therefore completely pre-empted by ERISA § 502 and removable to federal district court.

. . .

Ultimately, the Court of Appeals rested its decision on one line from *Rush Prudential*. There, we described our holding in *Ingersoll-Rand* as follows: "[W]hile state law duplicated the elements of a claim available under ERISA, it converted the remedy from an equitable one under [ERISA § 502(a)(3)] (available exclusively in federal district courts) into a legal one for money damages (available in a state tribunal)." The point of this sentence was to describe why the state cause of action in *Ingersoll-Rand* was pre-empted by ERISA § 502(a): It was pre-empted because it attempted to convert an equitable remedy into a legal remedy. Nowhere in *Rush Prudential* did we suggest that the pre-emptive force of ERISA § 502(a) is limited to the situation in which a state cause of action precisely duplicates a cause of action under ERISA § 502(a).

Nor would it be consistent with our precedent to conclude that only strictly duplicative state causes of action are pre-empted. . . . In order to recover for mental anguish, for instance, the plaintiffs in *Ingersoll-Rand* and *Metropolitan Life* would presumably have had to prove the existence of mental anguish; there is no such element in an ordinary suit brought under ERISA § 502(a)(1)(B). This did not save these state causes of action from pre-emption. Congress' intent to make the ERISA civil enforcement mechanism exclusive would be undermined if state causes of action that supplement the ERISA § 502(a) remedies were permitted, even if the elements of the state cause of action did not precisely duplicate the elements of an ERISA claim.

. . .

Respondents, their amici, and some Courts of Appeals have relied heavily upon *Pegram v. Herdrich*, 530 U.S. 211 (2000), in arguing that ERISA does not pre-empt or completely pre-empt state suits such as respondents'. They contend that *Pegram* makes it clear that causes of action such as respondents' do not "relate to [an] employee benefit plan," ERISA § 514(a), and hence are not pre-empted.

Pegram cannot be read so broadly. In *Pegram*, the plaintiff sued her physician-owned-and-operated HMO (which provided medical coverage through plaintiff's employer pursuant to an ERISA-regulated benefit plan) and her treating physician, both for medical malpractice and for a breach of an ERISA fiduciary duty. The plaintiff's treating physician was also the person charged with administering plaintiff's benefits; it was she who decided whether certain treatments were covered. We reasoned that the physician's "eligibility decision and the treatment decision were inextricably mixed." We concluded that "Congress did not intend [the defendant HMO] or any other HMO to be treated as a fiduciary to the extent that it makes mixed eligibility decisions acting through its physicians."

A benefit determination under ERISA, though, is generally a fiduciary act. Hence, a benefit determination is part and parcel of the ordinary fiduciary responsibilities connected to the administration of a plan. The fact that a benefits determination is infused with medical judgments does not alter this result.

. . .

ERISA itself and its implementing regulations confirm this interpretation. ERISA defines a fiduciary as any person "to the extent . . . he has any discretionary authority or discretionary responsibility in the administration of [an employee benefit] plan." § 3(21)(A)(iii). . . .

Since administrators making benefits determinations, even determinations based extensively on medical judgments, are ordinarily acting as plan fiduciaries, it was essential to *Pegram*'s conclusion that the decisions challenged there were truly "mixed eligibility and treatment decisions," *i.e.*, medical necessity decisions made by the plaintiff's treating physician *qua* treating physician and *qua* benefits administrator. Put another way, the reasoning of *Pegram* "only make[s] sense where the underlying negligence also plausibly constitutes medical maltreatment by a party who can be deemed to be a treating physician or such a physician's employer." Here, however, petitioners are neither respondents' treating physicians nor the employers of respondents' treating physicians. Petitioners' coverage decisions, then, are pure eligibility decisions, and *Pegram* is not implicated.

V

We hold that respondents' causes of action, brought to remedy only the denial of benefits under ERISA-regulated benefit plans, fall within the scope of, and are completely pre-empted by, ERISA § 502(a)(1)(B), and thus removable to federal district court. The judgment of the Court of Appeals is reversed, and the cases are remanded for further proceedings consistent with this opinion.

5-11 QUESTIONS AND PROBLEMS

1. Does ERISA provide *Davila* and *Calad* with a remedy?

2. The Court states that upon the denial of benefits, the plaintiffs could have paid for the treatment themselves and then sought reimbursement or alternatively could have sought a preliminary injunction. Why did they not do so? Are these realistic options?

3. In light of the cases in this section, when is a malpractice claim preempted by ERISA?

4. Why doesn't Congress amend ERISA to deal with its apparent overreaching preemption of what have traditionally been state medical malpractice claims?

In *Roark v. Humana, Inc.*, 307 F.3d 298 (5th Cir. 2002), the court found that decisions by an HMO to limit a post-hysterectomy hospital stay despite the physician recommending a longer stay and to approve a different drug for a patient than the one recommended by the treating physician were "when and how" decisions that were not preempted by ERISA. According to the court, the plaintiffs' did not challenge the interpretation of the plan by the HMO, nor did they seek reimbursement for benefits denied them which would have been claims under ERISA § 502(a)(1)(B). Instead, the plaintiffs sued claiming that the decisions by the HMO violated its duty of ordinary care and thus was medical malpractice. Citing *Pegram*, the court concluded that ERISA did not preempt the claim because it was not intended to "federalize medical malpractice law under § 502(a)(1)(B)." *Roark* at 311.

In addition to citing *Pegram v. Herdrich*, the *Roark* decision also relied upon *Rush Prudential, HMO Inc. v. Moran*, 536 U.S. 355 (2002), which upheld state legislation that mandated independent appraisal of the appropriateness of the procedure requested by the patient but denied by an HMO.

G. UNANTICIPATED PREEMPTION OF STATE STATUTES AND COMMON LAW

The breath of ERISA preemption has led to unanticipated and perhaps undesirable nullification of state laws not intended to regulate employee benefit plans.

EGELHOFF v. EGELHOFF

532 U.S. 141 (2001)

Justice Thomas delivered the opinion of the Court.

A Washington statute provides that the designation of a spouse as the beneficiary of a nonprobate asset is revoked automatically upon divorce. We are asked to decide whether the Employee Retirement Income Security Act of 1974 (ERISA), pre-empts that statute to the extent it applies to ERISA plans. We hold that it does.

Petitioner Donna Rae Egelhoff was married to David A. Egelhoff. Mr. Egelhoff was employed by the Boeing Company, which provided him with a life insurance policy and a pension plan. Both plans were governed by ERISA, and Mr. Egelhoff designated his wife as the beneficiary under both. In April 1994, the Egelhoffs divorced. Just over two months later, Mr. Egelhoff died intestate following an automobile accident. At that time, Mrs. Egelhoff remained the listed beneficiary under both the life insurance policy and the pension plan. The life insurance proceeds, totaling $46,000, were paid to her.

Respondents Samantha and David Egelhoff, Mr. Egelhoff's children by a previous marriage, are his statutory heirs under state law. They sued petitioner in Washington state court to recover the life insurance proceeds. Respondents relied on a Washington statute that provides:

> If a marriage is dissolved or invalidated, a provision made prior to that event that relates to the payment or transfer at death of the decedent's interest in a nonprobate asset in favor of or granting an interest or power to the decedent's former spouse is revoked. A provision affected by this section must be interpreted, and the nonprobate asset affected passes, as if the former spouse failed to survive the decedent, having died at the time of entry of the decree of dissolution or declaration of invalidity. Wash. Rev. Code § 11.07.010(2)(a) (1994).

That statute applies to "all nonprobate assets, wherever situated, held at the time of entry by a superior court of this state of a decree of dissolution of marriage or a declaration of invalidity." It defines "nonprobate asset" to include "a life insurance policy, employee benefit plan, annuity or similar contract, or individual retirement account."

Respondents argued that they were entitled to the life insurance proceeds because the Washington statute disqualified Mrs. Egelhoff as a beneficiary, and in the absence of a qualified named beneficiary, the proceeds would pass to them as Mr. Egelhoff's heirs. In a separate action, respondents also sued to recover the pension plan benefits. Respondents again argued that the Washington statute disqualified Mrs. Egelhoff as a beneficiary and they were thus entitled to the benefits under the plan.

The trial courts, concluding that both the insurance policy and the pension plan "should be administered in accordance" with ERISA, granted summary judgment to petitioner in both cases. The Washington Court of Appeals concluded that the Washington statute was not pre-empted by ERISA. Applying the statute, it held that respondents were entitled to the proceeds of both the insurance policy and the pension plan. *Ibid.*

The Supreme Court of Washington affirmed. It held that the state statute, although applicable to "employee benefit plan[s]," does not "refe[r] to" ERISA plans to an extent that would require pre-emption, because it "does not apply immediately and exclusively to an ERISA plan, nor is the existence of such a plan essential to operation of the statute." It also held that the statute lacks a "connection with" an ERISA plan that would compel pre-emption. It emphasized that the statute "does not alter the nature of the plan itself, the administrator's fiduciary duties, or the requirements for plan administration."

Nor, the court concluded, does the statute conflict with any specific provision of ERISA, including the antialienation provision, [ERISA § 206(d)(1)], because it "does not operate to divert benefit plan proceeds from distribution under terms of the plan documents," but merely alters "the underlying circumstances to which the distribution scheme of [the] plan must be applied."

Courts have disagreed about whether statutes like that of Washington are pre-empted by ERISA. To resolve the conflict, we granted certiorari.

II

Petitioner argues that the Washington statute falls within the terms of ERISA's express pre-emption provision and that it is pre-empted by ERISA under traditional principles of conflict pre-emption. Because we conclude that the statute is expressly pre-empted by ERISA, we address only the first argument.

ERISA's pre-emption section, ERISA § 514, states that ERISA "shall supersede any and all State laws insofar as they may now or hereafter relate to any employee benefit plan" covered by ERISA. We have observed repeatedly that this broadly worded provision is "clearly expansive." But at the same time, we have recognized that the term "relate to" cannot be taken "to extend to the furthest stretch of its indeterminacy," or else "for all practical purposes pre-emption would never run its course."

. . .

We recognize that all state laws create some potential for a lack of uniformity. But differing state regulations affecting an ERISA plan's "system for processing claims and paying benefits" impose "precisely the burden that ERISA pre-emption was intended to avoid." And as we have noted, the statute at issue here directly conflicts with ERISA's requirements that plans be administered, and benefits be paid, in accordance with plan documents. We conclude that the Washington statute has a "connection with" ERISA plans and is therefore pre-empted.

III

Respondents suggest several reasons why ordinary ERISA pre-emption analysis should not apply here. First, they observe that the Washington statute allows employers to opt out. According to respondents, the statute neither regulates plan administration nor impairs uniformity because it does not apply when "[t]he instrument governing disposition of the nonprobate asset expressly provides otherwise." Wash. Rev. Cod e § 11.07.010(2)(b)(i) (1994). We do not believe that the statute is saved from pre-emption simply because it is, at least in a broad sense, a default rule.

Even though the Washington statute's cancellation of private choice may itself be trumped by specific language in the plan documents, the statute does "dictate the choice[s] facing ERISA plans" with respect to matters of plan administration. Plan administrators must either follow Washington's beneficiary designation scheme or alter the terms of their plan so as to indicate that they will not follow it. The statute is not any less of a regulation of the terms of ERISA plans simply because there are two ways of complying with it. Of course, simple noncompliance with the statute is not one of the options available to plan administrators. Their only choice is one of timing, *i.e.*, whether to bear the burden of compliance *ex post*, by paying benefits as the statute dictates (and in contravention of the plan documents), or *ex ante*, by amending the plan.

Respondents emphasize that the opt-out provision makes compliance with the statute less burdensome than if it were mandatory. That is true enough, but the burden that remains is hardly trivial. It is not enough for plan administrators to opt out of this particular statute. Instead, they must maintain a familiarity with the laws of all 50 States so that they can update their plans as necessary to satisfy the opt-out requirements of other, similar statutes. They also must be attentive to changes in the interpretations of those statutes by state courts. This "tailoring of plans and employer conduct to the peculiarities of the law of each jurisdiction" is exactly the burden ERISA seeks to eliminate.

Second, respondents emphasize that the Washington statute involves both family law and probate law, areas of traditional state regulation. There is indeed a presumption against pre-emption in areas of traditional state regulation such as family law. But that presumption can be overcome where, as here, Congress has made clear its desire for pre-emption. Accordingly, we have not hesitated to find state family law pre-empted when it conflicts with ERISA or relates to ERISA plans.

Finally, respondents argue that if ERISA pre-empts this statute, then it also must pre-empt the various state statutes providing that a murdering heir is not entitled to receive property as a result of the killing. In the ERISA context, these "slayer" statutes could revoke the beneficiary status of someone who murdered a plan participant. Those statutes are not before us, so we do not decide the issue. We note, however, that the principle underlying the statutes — which have been adopted by nearly every State — is well established in the law and has a long historical pedigree predating ERISA. And because the statutes are more or less uniform nationwide, their interference with the aims of ERISA is at least debatable.

The judgment of the Supreme Court of Washington is reversed, and the case is remanded for further proceedings not inconsistent with this opinion.

JUSTICE SCALIA, with whom JUSTICE GINSBURG joins, concurring.

I join the opinion of the Court, since I believe that the "relate to" pre-emptive provision of the Employee Retirement Income Security Act of 1974 (ERISA) is assuredly triggered by a state law that contradicts ERISA. As the Court notes, "the statute at issue here directly conflicts with ERISA's requirements that plans be administered, and benefits be paid, in accordance with plan documents." *Ante*, at 1328–1329. I remain unsure (as I think the lower courts and everyone else will be) as to what else triggers the "relate to" provision, which — if it is interpreted to be anything other than a reference to our established jurisprudence concerning conflict and field pre-emption — has no discernible content that would not pick up every ripple in the pond, producing a result "that no sensible person could have intended." I persist in the view that we can bring some coherence to this area, and can give the statute both a plausible and precise content, only by interpreting the "relate to" clause as a reference to our ordinary pre-emption jurisprudence.

JUSTICE BREYER, with whom JUSTICE STEVENS joins, dissenting.

Like Justice Scalia, I believe that we should apply normal conflict pre-emption and field pre-emption principles where, as here, a state statute covers ERISA and non-ERISA documents alike. Our more recent ERISA cases are consistent with this approach . . . .

I do not agree with Justice Scalia or with the majority, however, that there is any plausible pre-emption principle that leads to a conclusion that ERISA pre-empts the statute at issue here. No one could claim that ERISA pre-empts the entire *field* of state law governing inheritance — though such matters "relate to" ERISA broadly speaking. Neither is there any direct conflict between the Washington statute and ERISA, for the one nowhere directly contradicts the other.

The Court correctly points out that ERISA requires a fiduciary to make payments to a beneficiary "in accordance with the documents and instruments governing the plan." [ERISA § 404(a)(1)(D).] But nothing in the Washington statute requires the contrary. Rather, the state statute simply sets forth a default rule for interpreting documentary silence. The statute specifies that a nonprobate asset will pass at A's death "as if" A's "former spouse" had died first — *unless the "instrument governing disposition of the nonprobate asset expressly provides otherwise.*" Wash. Rev. Code § 11.07.010(2)(b)(i) (1994) (emphasis added). This state-law rule is a rule of interpretation, and it is designed to carry out, not to conflict with, the employee's likely intention as revealed in the plan documents.

There is no direct conflict or contradiction between the Washington statute and the terms of the plan documents here at issue. David Egelhoff's investment plan provides that when a "beneficiary designation" is "invalid," the "benefits will be paid" to a "surviving spouse," or "if there is no surviving spouse," to the "children in equal shares." The life insurance plan is silent about what occurs when a beneficiary designation is invalid. The Washington statute fills in these gaps, *i.e.*, matters about which the documents themselves say nothing. Thus, the Washington statute specifies that a beneficiary designation — here "Donna R. Egelhoff wife" in the pension plan — is invalid where there is no longer any such person as Donna R. Egelhoff, wife. And the statute adds that in such instance the funds would be paid to the children, who themselves are potential pension plan beneficiaries.

The Court's "direct conflict" conclusion rests upon its claim that "administrators must pay benefits to the beneficiaries chosen by state law, rather than to those identified in the plan documents." *Ante*, at 1327. But the Court cannot mean "identified *anywhere* in the plan documents," for the Egelhoff children were "identified" as recipients in the pension plan documents should the initial designation to "Donna R. Egelhoff wife" become invalid. And whether that initial designation became invalid upon divorce is a matter about which the plan documents are silent.

To refer to state law to determine whether a given name makes a designation that is, or has become, invalid makes sense where background property or inheritance law is at issue, say, for example, where a written name is potentially ambiguous, where it is set forth near, but not in, the correct space, where it refers to a missing person perhaps presumed dead, where the name was written at a time the employee was incompetent, or where the name refers to an individual or entity disqualified by other law, say, the rule against perpetuities or rules prohibiting a murderer from benefiting from his crime. Why would Congress want the courts to create an ERISA-related federal property law to deal with such problems? Regardless, to refer to background state law in such circumstances does not *directly* conflict with any explicit ERISA provision, for no provision of ERISA forbids reading an instrument or document in light of state property law principles. In any event, in this case the plan documents *explicitly* foresee that a beneficiary designation may become "invalid," but they do not specify the invalidating circumstances. To refer to state property law to fill in that blank cannot possibly create any direct conflict with the plan documents.

. . .

No one can seriously argue that Congress has *clearly* resolved the question before us. And the only damage to federal interests that the Court identifies consists of the added administrative burden the state statute imposes upon ERISA plan administrators.

The Court claims that the Washington statute "interferes with nationally uniform plan administration" by requiring administrators to "familiarize themselves with state statutes." *Ante*, at 1328. But administrators have to familiarize themselves with state law in any event when they answer such routine legal questions as whether amounts due are subject to garnishment, who is a "spouse," who qualifies as a "child," or when an employee is legally dead. And were that "familiarizing burden" somehow overwhelming, the plan could easily avoid it by resolving the divorce revocation issue in the plan documents themselves, stating expressly that state law does not apply. The "burden" thus reduces to a one-time requirement that would fall primarily upon the few who draft model ERISA documents, not upon the many who administer them. So meager a burden cannot justify pre-empting a state law that enjoys a presumption against pre-emption.

. . .

Professor T.P. Gallanis has observed that *Egelhoff* has the potential to interfere with state attempts to create consistent outcomes in state laws of survivorship, lapse, elective share provisions and in laws that revoke legacies if a beneficiary killed the decedent. By doing so, ERISA, as interpreted by *Egelhoff*, can create considerable mischief. For example, many, if not all states, have laws that require that in order in inherit, an heir must survive the decedent by some minimum amount of time, such as 120 hours. But *Egelhoff* might override such provisions. For example, Adam names his sister, Betty, as the beneficiary of his pension. Adam and Betty are killed in a car accident, though Betty survives Adam by 20 minutes. State laws, which require an heir to survive 120 hours, would treat Betty as predeceased, and so she would not inherit Adam's pension. But if *Egelhoff* overrides state law, Betty would inherit Adams's pension. Suppose that Adam had named as the alternate taker his alma mater, State University. If Betty inherits, however, her estate plan determines who takes the pension, and Betty's will leaves her estate to State University's bitter rival, Private College of the Elite. Hardly, the outcome that Adam would have wanted. See T.P. Gallinis, *ERISA and the Law of Succession*, 65 OHIO ST. L.J. 185 (2004).

Can an automatic restraining order that bars the change of a beneficiary under an ERISA plan in an attempt to enforce a Qualified Domestic Relations Order (QDRO) survive preemption?

UNICARE LIFE & HEALTH INS. CO. v. PHANOR

472 F. Supp. 2d 8 (D. Mass. 2007)

TAURO, District Judge.

Background

Joseph Pamphile ("Decedent") and Defendant Ruth Pamphile married in 1984. Decedent was a participant in his employer's group life insurance benefit plan. This life insurance policy was provided by Unicare Life & Health Insurance Company ("Plaintiff") and is governed by the federal Employment Retirement Income Security Act ("ERISA"). On November 1, 2001, the Pamphiles separated and Decedent initiated a divorce proceeding in Massachusetts Probate and Family Court.

At that time, the life insurance policy listed Ruth Pamphile as the sole beneficiary. When Decedent commenced the divorce proceeding, the state probate court issued a standard Automatic Restraining Order ("ARO") which prohibited either party from encumbering assets, incurring unreasonable additional debt, changing the beneficiary of any life insurance policy, pension or retirement plan, or causing the opposing part y or minor children to be removed from an existing insurance plan.[2] On November 12, 2004, March 10, 2005, and March 20, 2005, Decedent purportedly executed change of beneficiary forms. The first two changes specified various allocations of funds to Decedent's children (Beverly, Judy, Jeffrey and Brunel) and sisters (Sonia Pamphile and Widlene Cesar). The final change specified that all of the life insurance benefits would go to Defendant Chantal Phanor, Decedent's girlfriend.

Joseph Pamphile died on March 23, 2005. The divorce proceedings were never completed and no final judgment allocating matrimonial assets has ever issued.

On March 28, 2005, Defendant Phanor submitted her claim to Plaintiff Unicare. On April 8, 2005, Unicare received a letter from Defendant Ruth Pamphile claiming that the ARO, as well as Decedent's impaired mental competence, voided subsequent changes to the policy's beneficiary designation. Considering this dispute as to the proper beneficiary, Plaintiff Unicare brought this interpleader

---

[2] Specifically, the ARO provides in relevant part:

> The following order PROHIBITS either party to a complaint for divorce or separate support from:
>
> . . . .
>
> (3) Directly or indirectly changing the beneficiary of any life insurance policy, pension or retirement plan, or pension or retirement investment account, except with the written consent of the other party or by Order of the Court.

action on June 28, 2005, to force the Defendants to litigate the question of who is entitled to the life insurance proceeds. On April 12, 2006, this court allowed Plaintiff Unicare's *Motion to Deposit Funds* and subsequently dismissed it from the case. Now before the court is a *Motion for Summary Judgment* by Ruth Pamphile and her children ("Movants"), which Defendant Phanor opposes.

Discussion

. . . Movants contend that Ruth Pamphile should receive the entire policy benefit as a matter of law because changes made in violation of the ARO should not be given credit. In response, Phanor argues that ERISA preempts any such application of the ARO. Movants argue in the alternative that Ruth Pamphile would be entitled to an equitable constructive trust on any benefits paid to Phanor under the life insurance policy. Phanor argues that while the First Circuit has not addressed whether such a remedy is proper in an ERISA case, Massachusetts law indicates that an equitable remedy would be inappropriate. Without resort to any disputed fact, the court concludes as matter of law that Plaintiff is correct on both points.

ERISA requires the plan administrator to discharge duties in accordance with the plan documents. Here, the policy itself is not in the record. But there is no dispute that according to the plan, Plaintiff had the duty to pay benefits to the beneficiary ultimately designated by the Decedent. Movants argue that the ARO modified this obligation by ordering all parties to the divorce to essentially freeze their financial assets.

ERISA preempts "state laws insofar as they may now or hereafter relate to any employee benefit plan." It is well established "that designating a beneficiary of an ERISA plan has connections with or references to that plan" and that laws restricting such designation are therefore preempted. Congress created an exception for qualified domestic relations orders ("QDROs"), likely because it recognized the importance of allowing divorce courts to allocate all financial assets, including pensions and life insurance. Courts have held that this exemption applies to all types of ERISA plans.

A domestic relations order is "any judgment, decree, or order" which "(I) relates to the provision of child support, alimony payments, or marital property rights to a spouse, former spouse, child, or other dependent of a participant, and (II) is ma de pursuant to a State domestic relations law." The ARO (though not a final judgment) is a domestic relations order because it was issued pursuant to state law and freezes marital property rights pending determination of alimony and child support.

A domestic relations order is a QDRO if it "creates or recognizes the existence of an alternate payee's right to . . . receive all or a portion of the benefits payable with respect to a participant under a plan" and complies with other enumerated requirements. The ARO recognizes the existence of a potential right in Ms. Pamphile to ultimately receive some portion of her husband's life insurance benefit. Because such a right would be meaningless if the husband were allowed to simply change the beneficiary, the Massachusetts courts routinely order all parties to a divorce to refrain from such action. Phanor contends that the state court order created no rights, but simply imposed certain obligations under threat of contempt. As will be further explained below, this court does not accept this argument. The ARO exists to protect the rights of parties to a divorce and is an order which meets the first definition of a QDRO by recognizing the existence of an alternate right to benefits that exists outside the benefit plan documents.

. . .

The state court's ARO clearly states that all existing policies should be frozen while the order is in effect. The purpose of this freeze is preserve the assets so the court can properly distribute them. The effect of this freeze is that the existing beneficiaries receive all of the benefits until any divorce becomes final. This effect is necessary to accomplish the purpose, does not conflict with the goals of ERISA, and is not ambiguous. This court therefore concludes that the Automatic Restraining Order issued by the Massachusetts Probate and Family Court is a Qualified Domestic Relations Order under ERISA.

. . .

This result is preferable to the alternative of allowing Decedent to ignore the ARO without consequence. The probate court can only make a meaningful final division of assets if parties comply with the ARO and do not shelter their assets. Decedent should not be allowed to accomplish an unlawful modification of assets by dying before the entry of a final judgment. For this reason, it is appropriate to interpret the ARO as an order conferring enforceable and meaningful rights on the parties to a divorce.

. . .

The proper liberal reading of ERISA, 29 U.S.C. § 1056(d)(3)(C), shows that the Massachusetts Probate Court's ARO is sufficiently unambiguous to avoid preemption as a QDRO. Because such an ARO must be enforceable, and because Massachusetts courts likely would enforce it using equitable remedies, it is appropriate to allow the QDRO to undo subsequent unlawful changes in Decedent's life insurance policy. Accordingly, Movant's *Motion for Summary Judgment* is ALLOWED. Ruth Pamphile is entitled to the funds deposited with the court by Plaintiff Unicare. An order will issue.

5-12 QUESTIONS AND PROBLEMS

1. In *Egelhoff*, the Court stated, "There is indeed a presumption against pre-emption in areas of traditional state regulation such as family law. But that presumption can be overcome where, as here, Congress has made clear its desire for pre-emption." Isn't the very question before the Court: whether Congress meant to preempt a statute such as Washington's?

2. Should an abstract desire for "uniformity" in the regulation of employee benefits trump the desire of states to protect its citizens against the unexpected consequences of failing to amend the beneficiaries under a pension plan?

As suggested in the *Egelhoff* opinion, ERISA preemption can have unexpected consequences for state laws. For example, almost all states have "slayer statutes" tha t prevent an individual from inheriting from someone that they intentionally kill. Suppose Bob, the named beneficiary of Paula's pension plan, murders Paula? Does the state statute that would bar Bob from taking Paula's pension apply? Or is it overruled by virtue of *Egelhoff*? Several federal courts held prior to *Egelhoff* that public policy supported the slayer statutes and so such laws were not preempted by ERISA. E.g. *A.T.U. New York Employees Pension Fund & Plan*, 709 F. Supp. 329 (E.D.N.Y. 1989). In *Egelhoff*, the Court indicated that slayer statutes could avoid preemption because such laws are "well established in the law and [have] a long historical pedigree predating ERISA. And because the statutes are more or less uniform nationwide . . ." The argument is less than convincing given that slayer laws are not uniform. However, it seems very doubtful that the Supreme Court would want to go record as holding that ERISA mandates that the pension benefits of murder victims be paid to their assailants.

In 1984, ERISA was amended by the Retirement Equity Act to provide that it would not preempt state court ordered decrees that divided or transferred pensions to divorced spouses or for child support. Known as qualified domestic relations orders (QDROs), the orders are enforceable without regard to the preemption provisions of ERISA § 514. *See* Chapter 3, *infra*. Community property rights, however, were held preempted by ERISA in *Boggs v. Boggs*, 520 U.S. 833 (1997), in which the Court held that ERISA preempted a Louisiana community property law that would have permitted a nonparticipant spouse to transfer by her will her undistributed interest in a pension plan. The Court held that ERISA §§ 205 and 206 requirements provide the exclusive manner of naming a beneficiary under a pension plan. The attempt by the spouse to name her sons as plan beneficiaries was invalid because the sons were neither plan beneficiaries nor participants. According to the Court, Louisiana community property law could not grant the spouse a right to transfer her interest by will in contradiction to the ERISA distribution scheme.

ERISA preemption does not apply to any "generally applicable" state criminal law, § 514(b)(2), nor to plans excluded from ERISA coverage because they are "maintained solely for the purpose of complying with applicable workmen's compensation laws or unemployment compensation or disability insurance laws." ERISA § 514(b)(3).

Chapter 6
PLAN ADMINISTRATION

A. INTRODUCTION

The creation of a pension or welfare benefit plan necessitates the appointment of individuals or entities to administer the plan. ERISA § 402 requires that plans appoint "named fiduciaries" to "control and manage the operation" of the plan. The identification of the plan fiduciaries is critical, because the fiduciaries have special obligations to the plan. As discussed in this chapter, while some fiduciaries are specifically named, other individuals or entities are ERISA fiduciaries by virtue of their actions and authority. The obligations of plan fiduciaries are many and varied, and to some degree resemble the fiduciary duties owed by a trustee to a trust. But unlike the traditional common law of trusts, ERISA fiduciary duties arise from statutory requirements found in ERISA §§ 403, 404, and 406, which are addressed in this chapter. The interpretation of those statutes has resulted in extensive litigation. The cases have considered, for example, fiduciary duties arising from such obligations as the duty to disclose plan information and possible plan amendments to participants, the duty to avoid self-dealing with plan assets, the duty of loyalty to plan participants and beneficiaries, and the duty to productively, but prudently, invest plan assets.

B. PLAN ADMINISTRATION

ERISA §§ 3(16)(A), (21)(A), 402(a)(1), 403(a)(1).

Once an employer has established an ERISA pension or welfare benefit plan, it must appoint fiduciaries, administrators and trustees to manage the plan. ERISA § 402(a)(1) requires that every plan be created by a written instrument that provides for "one or more named fiduciaries" who have the "authority to control and manage the operation and administration of the plan." As part of the creation and drafting of the plan, the plan sponsor will name the plan fiduciaries or establish procedures for their appointment. If the plan sponsor does not name fiduciaries, the sponsor will be considered the plan fiduciary. Fiduciaries may also be appointed pursuant to a collective bargaining agreement with a labor union. The agreement may permit the union to name the fiduciaries to operate the plan or the agreement may call for the union and the employer to jointly operate the plan. Regardless of how named, the plan fiduciaries are responsible for the operation of the plan, and are subject to a variety of ERISA requirements and obligations.

Plan fiduciaries and their functions are as follows:

Board of Directors	Are fiduciaries if they appoint the plan administrator and plan trustee (or delegate appointment) and monitor their performance.
Plan Administrator	Primary authority to manage and control the plan operation. May delegate fiduciary responsibility, but has an ongoing duty to monitor appointed fiduciary.

Plan Trustee	Holds, invests and distributes plan assets. May be a directed trustee acting under direction of plan administrator.
Plan Investment Committee	Acts within delegated authority and determines general plan investment of assets.
Investment Manager	Acts according to specific investment responsibility granted by trustee or plan investment committee.
Investment Advisor	Advises the plan administrator and plan investment committee as to the selection of investment options and investment managers.

While ERISA § 402(a)(1) requires a plan to name fiduciaries, an individual or entity can also be a fiduciary if he or she exercises any "discretionary authority or discretionary control" over the management of the plan or "any authority or control" over the management or disposition of the plan assets. ERISA § 3(21)(A)(i). Anyone who, for a fee, renders investment advice to the plan is also a fiduciary. ERISA § 3(21)(A)(ii). In addition, anyone who has "discretionary authority or discretionary responsibility with respect to the administration of a plan is a plan fiduciary. ERISA § 3(21)(A)(iii). However identified, the plan fiduciaries must act for the exclusive benefit of the plan participants and beneficiaries, ERISA §§ 403(c), 404(a)(1)(A), and prudently invest the assets of the pension trust. ERISA § 404(a)(1)(B). Fiduciaries must also avoid violating the prohibited transactions rules of ERISA §§ 406–408, and face potential liability under ERISA §§ 409 and 502 for fiduciary misconduct.

For day-to-day operations, the plan requires plan administrators. The plan sponsor can appoint the plan administrators by name, by reference to individuals who hold a particular position, e.g., Vice President for Personnel, or the sponsor can create a procedure whereby the plan administrator is named, such as permitting the named plan fiduciaries to name or hire the plan administrator. If the plan does not name an administrator, ERISA § 3(16)(A) designates the plan sponsor as the administrator (for single-employer plans). ERISA § 402(a)(1) states that the plan fiduciaries shall "control and manage the operation and administration of the plan." Plan administrators, therefore, may be fiduciaries if they have sufficient discretion over the administration of the plan. Individuals who merely perform functions "within a framework of policies, interpretations, rules, practices, and procedures made by other persons" are not fiduciaries. 29 C.F.R. § 2509.75-8, D-2 (2007).

ERISA pension plans have assets that must be managed. Generally ERISA § 403(a) requires all plan assets, other than insurance contracts, to be held in trust by one or more trustees. The plan may name the trustees or may provide that the plan fiduciary will appoint the trustees. Once named, the trustees, who have "exclusive authority and discretion to manage and control" the plan assets, are fiduciaries. ERISA §§ 3(21), 403(a). If the plan expressly provides that the trustees' actions are subject to the direction of the fiduciary, however, such trustees are not fiduciaries and are referred to as "directed trustees." Also, trustees are not considered fiduciaries with respect to any assets for which management authority has been delegated to an investment manager, who, as stated above, is a fiduciary by virtue of his or her control over the plan assets.

C. WHO IS A PLAN FIDUCIARY?

ERISA § 3(21)(A).

Because of the responsibilities and potential liabilities associated with being a plan fiduciary, determination of just who is a fiduciary is critical. Even if the plan has a named entity or person(s) identified as a fiduciary, other unnamed entities or persons may also be found to be fiduciaries if they function as a fiduciary. ERISA § 3(21)(A). The following language is the standard case law description of how to identify non-named fiduciaries."To become a fiduciary, the person or entity must have control respecting the management of the plan or its assets, give investment advice for a fee, or have discretionary responsibility in the administration of the plan." *Arizona State Carpenters Pension Trust Fund v. Citibank*, 125 F.3d 715 (9th Cir. 1997).

[1] The Employer

The employer who creates the plan, the plan sponsor, is not a fiduciary merely by virtue of establishing the plan, amending it, designating benefits or terminating the plan. If the plan does not identify the employer as the fiduciary, its status as a fiduciary is determined by whether it exercises discretionary authority over the plan.

IN RE LUNA

406 F.3d 1192 (10th Cir. 2005)

Tyrmkovich, Circuit Judge.

The question in this case is whether the Employee Retirement Income Security Act of 1974 (ERISA) makes an employer a fiduciary to its employees if it agrees to make regular employer contributions to an ERISA-covered employee-benefit plan. The Plaintiff-Appellants (Trustees) are trustees of various employee-benefit funds (Funds) who sued the Defendant-Appellees (the Lunas) to recover promised but unpaid monthly employer contributions to the Funds. The payments were owed pursuant to a collective bargaining agreement to which the Lunas' company was a party.

The Trustees argue that the Lunas breached their fiduciary duties to the Funds under ERISA, and that therefore the unpaid contributions cannot be discharged in bankruptcy. Finding that the Lunas were not ERISA fiduciaries, we AFFIRM the district court's ruling that the debt is dischargeable in bankruptcy.

I. *Background*

Luna Steel Erectors, Inc. was an Oklahoma construction company that employed workers represented by Local 584 of the International Association of Bridge, Structural & Ornamental Iron Workers, AFL-CIO. The Lunas, whose family had been ironworkers for generations, each owned 50% of Luna Steel's stock, and Joyce Luna served as its President, Secretary, and record-keeper. Her son, Mark Luna, acted as Vice President.

The Trustees administer a number of multi-employer employee-benefit plans pursuant to a collective bargaining agreement (CBA) between various local unions, including Local 584, and various local employers and employer groups. In 1997, Joyce Luna signed the CBA as an owner of Luna Steel, and thereafter employed workers represented by Local 584. According to the CBA, Luna Steel agreed to submit monthly employer contributions to the Funds for the benefit of its Local 584-affiliated employees. . . .

In March 1999, the financial condition of Luna Steel considerably worsened, and from March until December it failed to make the requisite contributions to the Funds. . . . As of a March 2000 audit, over $121,000 was owing to the Funds. Joyce and Mark Luna both filed voluntary Chapter 7 bankruptcy petitions on August 1, 2000.

In November 2000, the Trustees brought an action in United States Bankruptcy Court seeking a determination that the Lunas were personally responsible for the unpaid contributions. The Trustees alleged the debt was nondischargeable under 11 U.S.C. § 523(a)(4) since the Lunas had committed "fraud or defalcation" while acting in a fiduciary capacity. The Trustees based this argument on the fact that the Lunas continued to take some income and personal expenses at a time when they should have been making contributions to the Funds. To prevail on this claim, the Trustees had to establish that the Lunas acted as fiduciaries. In an attempt to do so, the Trustees argued the Lunas were fiduciaries under ERISA § 3(21)(A), which states, in part, that a fiduciary is one who "exercises any authority or control respecting management or disposition of [plan] assets."

. . .

II. *Discussion*

To establish ERISA fiduciary status within the meaning of ERISA § 3(21)(A), the Trustees had to show: (1) that the unpaid contributions were plan assets; and (2) that the Lunas exercised authority and control over the management or disposition of these assets. The district court's holding addressed only the first issue, finding that unpaid contributions "do not become plan assets until they have been paid into the particular funds." Having concluded that unpaid contributions were not plan assets, the district court did not need to decide whether the Lunas exercised fiduciary — like authority or control. As explained below, although we disagree with the district court's conclusion that contributions are not plan assets, we nevertheless affirm the lower court's order because, in our view, the Lunas did not exercise authority or control respecting the management or disposition of a plan asset.

. . .

. . . [W]e conclude that the contractual right to the unpaid contributions is an "asset" under ERISA.

B. The Lunas are Not "Fiduciaries" Under ERISA § 3(21)(A)

We turn next to consider whether the Lunas acted as fiduciaries with respect to a plan asset. Based on our de novo review, we conclude the Lunas were not fiduciaries under ERISA.

1. Fiduciary Status Under ERISA

Under ERISA § 402(a), every employee benefit plan must appoint "one or more named fiduciaries who jointly or severally shall have authority to control and manage the operation and administration of the plan." In addition to these so-called "named fiduciaries," individuals may acquire fiduciary status if they exercise the fiduciary functions set forth in ERISA § 3(21)(A). . . .

Section 3(21)(A) of ERISA defines a person as a fiduciary of an ERISA plan to the extent that he:

> (i) [E]xercises any discretionary authority or discretionary control respecting management of such plan or *exercises any authority or control respecting management or disposition of its assets*; (ii) he renders investment advice for a fee or other compensation, direct or indirect, with respect to any moneys or other property of such plan, or has any authority or responsibility to do so; or (iii) he has any discretionary authority or discretionary responsibility in the administration of such plan.

(emphasis added). The definition, thus, encompasses a variety of duties commonly performed by fiduciaries, including the providing of investment advice, administrative control over a plan, advising on whom to retain as legal or investment advisors to a plan, and, ultimately, how to invest plan assets. Once deemed a fiduciary, either by express designation in the plan documents or the assumption of fiduciary obligations (the functional or de facto method), the fiduciary becomes subject to ERISA's statutory duties. These duties, as summarized by the Supreme Court, "relate to the proper management, administration, and investment of fund assets, the maintenance of proper records, the disclosure of specified information, and the avoidance of conflicts of interest." *Mass. Mut. Life Ins. Co. v. Russell*, 473 U.S. 134 (1985).

Assessing whether a person is a named fiduciary under the terms of a plan is, of course, a straightforward inquiry. Deciding whether a person has assumed functional or de facto fiduciary status, however, is a more difficult exercise. To overcome this difficulty, courts frequently interpret the statutory language in ERISA § 3(21)(A) by referencing the common law of trusts. This is because "ERISA abounds with the language and terminology of trust law." *Firestone Tire & Rubber Co. v. Bruch*, 489 U.S. 101, 110 (1989). Indeed, given the close relationship between the law of trusts and ERISA's fiduciary responsibility provisions, the Supreme Court has instructed the federal courts to consider the law of trusts in "develop[ing] a federal common law of rights and obligations under ERISA-regulated plans." *Firestone Tire & Rubber Co.*, 489 U.S. at 110.

2. Authority or Control Respecting Management or Disposition of Plan Assets

We now look to the specific language of ERISA § 3(21)(A). It is undisputed that the Lunas did not render investment advice under clause (ii) of the definition. Nor did the Lunas exercise discretionary responsibility under clause (iii) in the administration of the plans. Instead, this case focuses on clause (i) of the statutory definition. Specifically, the issue we face is whether the Lunas "exercise[d] any authority or control respecting management or disposition of [plan] assets."

The question of whether the Lunas exercised authority or control over the asset at issue almost answers itself: It is the Trustees, not the Lunas, who control the contractual right to collect unpaid contributions from the Lunas. Whether to enforce their contractual rights is entirely up to the Trustees; the Lunas, meanwhile, have no say over whether this right will be enforced or not.

Nonetheless, our analysis cannot stop here. Emphasizing the "mutual character" of the relationship between an employer and an ERISA plan, at least one court has held that an employer-contributor exercises "authority or control" of plan assets solely by virtue of its duty "to report the basis on which contributions will be made to an ERISA fund," i.e., to give an accurate accounting of how much the employer is contributing each month. *Northern Cal. Retail Clerks Unions & Food Employers Joint Pension Trust Fund v. Jumbo Markets, Inc.*, 906 F.2d 1371, 1372 (9th Cir. 1990). Under this view, even though an employer agrees only to a contractual duty to make contributions, its discretion to exercise prudence in upholding this duty — i.e., to pay or not to pay — is enough to make it an ERISA fiduciary. In other words, an employer automatically becomes a fiduciary of an ERISA plan as soon as it breaches its agreement to make employer contributions. We disagree with this logic.

In our view, an employer cannot become an ERISA fiduciary merely because it breaches its contractual obligations to a fund. ERISA's text and purpose, the law of trusts, Department of Labor regulatory pronouncements, and case law all lend support to our conclusion.

. . .

The language of ERISA § 3(21)(A) does not support a finding that the Lunas acted as fiduciaries. As noted, the relevant language states that a person assumes fiduciary status to the extent he or she "exercises any authority or control respecting management or disposition of its assets." The plain meaning of the operative words suggests that Congress envisioned a greater degree of responsibility than was exercised by the Lunas. The act of failing to make contributions to the Funds cannot reasonably be construed as taking part in the "management" or "disposition" of a plan asset. The asset in question, it must be remembered, is the Trustees' contractual right to collect the unpaid contributions, and the Lunas exercised no control over how the Trustees manage or dispose of that asset.

Even if, however, the asset were the unpaid contributions themselves, it is still not clear that the statutory definition would be met. For one, there were never any earmarked funds or segregated accounts for the contributions. And secondly, courts have noted that the "management or disposition" language "refers to the common transactions in dealing with a pool of assets: selecting investments, exchanging one instrument or asset for another, and so on." *Harris Trust & Sav. Bank v. John Hancock Mut. Life Ins. Co.*, 302 F.3d 18, 28 (2d Cir. 2002) (quoting *Johnson v. Georgia-Pacific Corp.*, 19 F.3d 1184, 1189 (7th Cir. 1994)). The Lunas exercised no such authority or control here. The statutory language, thus, does not support the Trustees' contention that the Lunas were fiduciaries under ERISA.

(b) Law of Trusts.

Our interpretation of the statutory language is also supported by the law of trusts. First, a trustee is almost always given powers of management over trust property, *see* George Gleason Bogert, TRUSTS & TRUSTEES § 50 (2d ed. 1984), which, as we have shown, the Lunas do not have. . . . SCOTT & W. FRATCHER, TRUSTS §§ 176, 181 (4th ed. 1987). "Trustees buy, sell, and lease investment property, lend and borrow, and do other things to conserve and nurture assets. They pay out income, choose beneficiaries, and distribute remainders at termination." Making contractually-owed contributions to an ERISA plan bears only a limited resemblance, if any, to these traditional fiduciary responsibilities.

In fact, given the context of the CBA whereby the Lunas agreed to make regular contributions to the Funds, as we have discussed above, the relationship between the Lunas and the Funds is best characterized as contractual, not fiduciary. This is well-supported by the law of trusts: A contract to convey property does not give rise to a fiduciary relationship. . . .

Thus, as with the statute's language, the law of trusts does not support the

Trustees' contention that the Lunas were fiduciaries under ERISA — in fact, it compels the opposite conclusion.

(c) Regulatory Interpretations.

Next, the Department of Labor's guidance with respect to ERISA's definition of "fiduciary" makes clear that persons who have "no power to make any decisions as to plan policy, interpretations, practices or procedures," but instead who perform only "administrative" or "ministerial functions" related to the plan, are not fiduciaries under ERISA § 3(21)(A). 29 C.F.R. § 2509.75-8 at D-2. The question, then, is whether the Lunas' obligation to make contributions under the CBA is more akin to a plan administrator's ability to make decisions as to plan policy, practices, or procedures, or whether it is closer to non-fiduciary ministerial functions. In our view, it is the latter. Ministerial functions include, among other things, the "[c]ollection of contributions and application of contributions as provided in the plan." *Id.* This ministerial function closely resembles the Lunas' obligation to make plan contributions according to the dictates of the CBA.

(d) Case Law.

Turning to ERISA case law, we begin with the noncontroversial position that the Lunas' status as employers, standing alone, is not enough to confer fiduciary status. . . .

A number of cases support the proposition, which we discussed above, that the true nature of the relationship between the Lunas and the Funds was contractual, and not fiduciary, in nature.

Following from this proposition is the conclusion that a delinquent employer-contributor is merely a debtor, not a fiduciary. Meanwhile, the benefit plan does not own the actual unpaid contributions, but only a contractual claim for damages. It is the Trustees, not the Lunas, that exercise control over the contractual right to unpaid contributions. Under the CBA, the Lunas had no duty other than to make monthly contributions, and no discretion other than to fail to make those required contributions. The mere discretion whether to pay debts owed to an employee benefit plan, however, does not suffice to confer fiduciary status under ERISA. . . .

Admittedly, there is contrary authority suggesting the discretion whether to pay contractually-owed monies to an employee benefit plan is sufficient to establish fiduciary status. *See Jumbo Markets, Inc.*, 906 F.2d at 1372. Such cases, however, are either easily distinguished on the facts, or otherwise identify the plan asset as the actual unpaid contributions — i.e., the pool of funds — rather than, as we have held, a contractual right belonging to the fund trustees. When the asset in question is properly identified as a contractual right to unpaid contributions, the issue of control over that asset is straightforward.

Another essential ingredient in this case is the fact that the Lunas, as owners of a closely-held corporation, were required to make business decisions with respect to general corporate funds. Such business decisions must not be confused with fiduciary actions. It is well-established that an ERISA fiduciary can "wear two hats," meaning an individual can be both an employer and a fiduciary. Therefore, as the Supreme Court has noted, the "threshold question" in an action for breach of fiduciary duty is whether the alleged fiduciary "was acting as a fiduciary (that is, was performing a fiduciary function) when taking the action subject to complaint." *Pegram v. Herdrich*, 530 U.S. 211, 226 (2000).

Because virtually every business decision an employer makes can have an adverse impact on an employee benefit plan, courts must "examine the conduct at issue to determine whether it constitutes management or administration of the plan, giving rise to fiduciary concerns, or merely a business decision that has an effect on an ERISA plan not subject to fiduciary duties."

Under the circumstances of this case, the Lunas' decision to use their limited funds to pay other business expenses rather than to make contributions to the Funds was a business decision, not a breach of fiduciary duty. . . .

(e) Statutory Purpose.

Finally, we are confident that our decision honors the statutory balance struck by Congress. As one court has stated,

> If ERISA did not limit the definition of fiduciaries to those with knowledge of their authority and discretion, then persons or entities could become subject to fiduciary liability without notice. Such a result would not only be unfair, but it would also disserve a core purpose of ERISA, which is to create a system whereby accountable fiduciaries are motivated by their accountability to protect the interests of participants in ERISA plans.

Herman v. NationsBank Trust Co., 126 F.3d 1354, 1366 (11th Cir. 1997).

ERISA's definition of "fiduciary" is broad but not all-encompassing. Every employer in some sense has discretion in meeting its obligations. But discretion alone does not confer fiduciary status under ERISA. If it did, any obligor to an employee benefit plan could become an ERISA fiduciary. . . . We recognize, of course, that Congress enacted ERISA because it found that prior law did not sufficiently protect the rights of plan beneficiaries. This does not mean, however, that Congress meant to impose fiduciary obligations on all employer-contributors. In the absence of Congressional direction, therefore, we are not inclined to expand ERISA beyond its plain meaning and hold that the officers of a company who contract with an ERISA-covered fund automatically become fiduciaries under the Bankruptcy Code.

III. *Conclusion*

For the foregoing reasons, the judgment of the district court is AFFIRMED.

CONFER v. CUSTOM ENGINEERING COMPANY

952 F.2d 34 (3d Cir. 1991)

MANSMANN, CIRCUIT JUDGE.

In this ERISA action, we are asked to decide whether corporate officers of a plan administrator, as individuals, are fiduciaries under section 3(21)(A) of the Employee Retirement Income Security Act (ERISA). We must also decide whether a "plan supervisor," who denies a claim on the basis of a written plan document, is a fiduciary under section 3(21)(A). We hold that individual officers of an ERISA plan's fiduciary are not fiduciaries by virtue of their offices, and that a plan supervisor who merely calculates claims according to a plan document is not a fiduciary.

Plaintiff Ricky Confer worked for Custom Engineering Company. Defendants Theodore Flower and Peter Traphagen own 94 percent of Custom Engineering. Flower is president and Traphagen, vice president.

Custom Engineering provided Confer with medical benefits through the Custom Engineering Company Employee Health Benefit Plan. The Plan designated Custom Engineering as administrator and named fiduciary. The Plan also provided that Custom Engineering could delegate day-to-day administrative tasks to a

"Plan Supervisor." The Plan Supervisor was Self-Funded Plans, Inc., whose responsibilities included drafting a new plan, handling claims, and arranging for excess insurance.

On June 1, 1985, Confer was injured in a motorcycle accident. *After* Confer's accident, Custom Engineering — through its officers — had Self-Funded prepare an amendment excluding motorcycle accidents from coverage. Sometime after Confer's accident and before July 31, 1985, Custom Engineering's president signed the amendment, backdating its effective date to April 10, 1985. In September of 1985, Self-Funded denied Confer's claim based on the backdated amendment; at that time, an officer of Self-Funded knew that the amendment had not been in effect when Confer's accident occurred on June 1, 1985.

Confer brought this action against the Plan to recover benefits, and against Custom Engineering, Flower, Traphagen and Self-Funded for breach of fiduciary duty. The district court held that the Plan covered Confer's claim and that Custom Engineering — through the actions of its officers Flower and Traphagen — had breached its fiduciary duty by backdating the amendment. That holding was the subject of a separate appeal; we have affirmed the judgment of the district court in a separate Per Curiam Opinion.

Confer here appeals from the district court's determination, on summary judgment, that, as a matter of law, Flower, Traphagen and Self-Funded were not fiduciaries . . . .

No court of appeals has addressed the question here before us: Whether officers who cause a corporate fiduciary to wrongfully deny claims are fiduciaries because, for purposes of section 3(21)(A)(iii), they have discretionary authority or responsibility "in the administration" of a plan.

We note that ERISA does not limit fiduciary status to individuals. A corporation may be a "person" for purposes of section 3(21)(A), which defines fiduciary. (definition of "person" includes corporation) . . . .

ERISA permits a plan to designate more than one fiduciary, [ERISA] § 402(a)(1), and ERISA permits a plan to provide for a procedure by which a named fiduciary can designate others as fiduciaries. [ERISA] § 405(c)(1)(B). Although either designation would lead to fiduciary status under section 3(21)(A), ERISA does not require a corporate fiduciary to make such a designation.

. . .

We thus hold that when an ERISA plan names a corporation as a fiduciary, the officers who exercise discretion on behalf of that corporation are not fiduciaries within the meaning of section 3(21)(A)(iii), unless it can be shown that these officers have *individual* discretionary roles as to plan administration. For example, if the plan designates an officer as plan administrator or if, pursuant to [ERISA] § 405(c)(1)(B), the corporation delegates some of its fiduciary responsibilities to an officer, then the designated individual would be a fiduciary under section 3(21)(A)(iii).

. . .

The Plan does not name Flower or Traphagen as a fiduciary or as a Trustee nor is there any indication that Custom Engineering delegated its fiduciary responsibility to Flower or Traphagen. Indeed, Confer does not point to any plan provision that would allow Custom Engineering to have done so. In sum, the plan document shows that Custom Engineering exercised the "discretionary authority" or the discretionary responsibility that would give rise to fiduciary status under section 3(21)(A)(iii). ERISA does not automatically extend that fiduciary status to the officers through whom Custom Engineering acted.

Although Flower backdated the amendment and Traphagen may have participated in the decision to do so, neither acted in an individual capacity. Flower and Traphagen exercised discretion and control over the Plan's administration, but only as officers of Custom Engineering. Their actions resulted in a breach by the corporation of its duty to administer the plan solely in the interest of beneficiaries. Flower and Traphagen certainly owed, and may have breached, a duty to Custom Engineering. Confer, however, has failed to demonstrate that either officer, *as an individual,* had discretionary authority or responsibility which gave rise to a fiduciary duty that either or both owed directly to Confer.

. . .

The holding in *Confer* was rejected by the Ninth Circuit Court of Appeals. The following case represents how most courts have determined whether a corporate officer is a plan fiduciary.

KAYES v. PACIFIC LUMBER CO.

51 F.3d 1449 (9th Cir. 1995)

Choy, Circuit Judge.

Fiduciary Status of Hurwitz and Leone as a Matter of Law

PLC argues that the district court erred in finding that, as a matter of law, Hurwitz and Leone were fiduciaries of the Plan. This court reviews the grant of summary judgment de novo, viewing all evidence in the light most favorable to PLC, the nonmoving party. The facts are not in question here; it is purely a question of law that we must determine.

PLC asserts that Hurwitz and Leone were not fiduciaries because they acted solely on behalf of PLC, who was the named fiduciary in the Plan. Under ERISA § 402(a)(1), every plan must have a named fiduciary with authority to administer the plan. ERISA permits corporations to be fiduciaries. *See* ERISA § 3(9) (definition of "person" includes corporation, and ERISA § 3(21)(A), defines fiduciary in terms of a "person"); *Confer v. Custom Eng'g Co.*, 952 F.2d 34, 36 (3d Cir. 1991).

The Plan at issue named the corporation PLC as the Plan fiduciary. Pacific Lumber Company Retirement Plan, § 11(b). It further went on to provide that the Company could delegate fiduciary responsibilities, but that "[t]he Company's duties and responsibilities under the Plan not delegated to other fiduciaries . . . shall be carried out by the Company directors, officers, and employees, acting on behalf of and in the name of the Company . . . and not as individual fiduciaries."

PLC's proffered ground for error rests on the contention that where a corporation is the named fiduciary, the persons who act on behalf of the corporation do not become individual fiduciaries by virtue of those acts, even under the functional definition of fiduciary set forth in ERISA § 3(21)(A). PLC's argument lacks merit.

ERISA § 3(21)(A) provides a functional definition of a fiduciary which depends, in part, upon whether a person "exercises any discretionary authority or discretionary control respecting management of such plan or exercises any authority or control respecting management or disposition of its assets. . . . " The Supreme Court has held that ERISA "defines 'fiduciary' not in terms of formal trusteeship, but in *functional* terms of control and authority over the plan, thus expanding the universe of persons subject to fiduciary duties — and to damages — under § 409(a)." *Mertens v. Hewitt Assocs.*, 113 S. Ct. 2063 (1993).

PLC does not claim that under this functional test Hurwitz and Leone are not fiduciaries. Instead, citing *Confer*, it asserts that because PLC acted solely on behalf of the corporation, only the corporation is a fiduciary, not its officers. In *Confer*, the Third Circuit held that "when an ERISA plan names a corporation as a fiduciary, the officers who exercise discretion on behalf of that corporation are not fiduciaries within the meaning of section 3(21)(A)(iii), unless it can be shown that these officers have *individual* discretionary roles as to plan administration." 952 F.2d at 37. The gist of the Third Circuit's holding is that where a corporation is designated as the plan fiduciary, an officer's actions will not render that officer a fiduciary where those actions are ones with which the designated named fiduciary is chargeable. In other words, when the named fiduciary does not designate the officer, either explicitly or impliedly, as a fiduciary, the officer is shielded from personally becoming a fiduciary, *id.*, so long as he acts within the corporate form.

Insofar as *Confer* holds that a corporate officer or director acting on behalf of a corporation is not acting in a fiduciary capacity if the corporation is the named plan fiduciary, we disagree with the Third Circuit's conclusion. The *Confer* holding is undermined by the decision of this court in *Yeseta v. Baima*, 837 F.2d 380 (9th Cir. 1988), the text of ERISA, and the agency interpretations of ERISA. This court has held officers to be liable as fiduciaries on the basis of their conduct and authority with respect to ERISA plans. In *Yeseta*, we held that by withdrawing funds from plan assets a corporate officer of a plan sponsor was a fiduciary, whether or not the sponsoring corporation authorized him to make such withdrawals:

> Under ERISA § 3(21), a fiduciary includes a person who "exercises any authority or control respecting management or disposition of [a plan's] assets."

Whether Yeseta was authorized to make the $14,200 and the $25,000 withdrawals or not, he did exercise control over and disposed of Plan assets. . . . On this basis, Yeseta is a fiduciary under § 3(21) whether or not he individually, or the business as an entity, incurred a benefit from the withdrawal.

Id. at 386. It was irrelevant for the purpose of § 3(21) whether Yeseta was acting on behalf of the corporation or outside of his authority. Either way, if he met the functional definition of § 3(21), Yeseta was a fiduciary. Thus, *Yeseta* rejected the distinction relied upon in *Confer*, 952 F.2d at 37, between officers exercising discretion "on behalf of a corporation" and officers "hav[ing] individual discretionary roles."

PLC claims that *Yeseta* is distinguishable from both this case and *Confer*, because unlike the situation in *Confer*, where the corporation was named as the plan fiduciary, in *Yeseta* the corporate employer was not a named fiduciary. Rather, in Yeseta, two of the corporate employees were named fiduciaries. Therefore, the argument runs, Yeseta could not claim to have been exercising the fiduciary duty of the corporation, since the corporation was not a named fiduciary. PLC points out that *Confer* is the only case entirely on point in any federal circuit court. No other cases present the analogous situation in which a corporation is the named fiduciary, but the person acting on behalf of the corporation is charged with being a fiduciary.

Even if *Yeseta* were distinguishable on the ground suggested by PLC, the language of ERISA itself undermines the Third Circuit's holding and PLC's contentions. ERISA specifically provides for personal, as well as corporate, liability. ERISA § 409(a) provides that "[a]ny person who is a fiduciary . . . who breaches any of the responsibilities, obligations, or duties imposed upon fiduciaries by this subchapter shall be personally liable. . . . " However, "fiduciary" and "named fiduciary" have separate definitions for purposes of the subchapter containing § 409. The term "fiduciary" is defined "[f]or purposes of this subchapter" at ERISA § 3(21)(A), and it is a functional definition as noted above. In contrast, "named fiduciary" is given a separate and formal definition in ERISA § 402(a)(2):

> For purposes of this subchapter, the term "named fiduciary" means a fiduciary who is named in the plan instrument, or who, pursuant to a procedure specified in the plan, is identified as a fiduciary (A) by a person who is an employer or employee organization with respect to the plan or (B) by such an employer and such an employee organization acting jointly.

There is no indication that an officer of a named fiduciary cannot be a fiduciary and the personal liability provision asserts that all fiduciaries will be held personally liable, without mention of named fiduciaries. ERISA § 409.

Moreover, ERISA § 410 states that "any provision in an agreement or instrument which purports to relieve a fiduciary from responsibility or liability for any responsibility, obligation, or duty under this part shall be void as against public policy." The section goes on to allow insurance of fiduciaries for potential liability, but not to permit relief from liability. *See* 29 C.F.R. § 2509.75-4 (1993) (interpreting the statute in the above manner). Here, PLC relies upon a statement in the Plan itself to establish that the officers of PLC are not acting as fiduciaries, but are acting on behalf of the corporation. Because that statement purports to relieve the officers from fiduciary responsibility or liability, under § 410 it is void as against public policy. Application of § 410 requires one to find first that the person in question is a fiduciary. However, the definition of who is a fiduciary under § 410 is based on the person's functions, not the title conferred by the Plan. If the Plan itself could not define who was or was not a fiduciary, the § 410 prohibition against relieving fiduciaries from liability would be rendered wholly ineffective. Therefore, we hold that any interpretation of the Plan which prevents individuals acting in a fiduciary capacity from being found liable as fiduciaries is void.

Agency interpretations of ERISA indicate fiduciary status depends on an individual's functional role rather than title. In an ERISA bulletin answering questions, fiduciary status is consistently defined by reference to ERISA § 3(21)(A):

> D-3 Q: Does a person automatically become a fiduciary with respect to a plan by reason of holding certain positions in the administration of such plans?
>
> A: Some offices or positions of an employee benefit plan by their very nature require persons who hold them to perform one or more of the functions described in section 3(21)(A) of the Act. . . . Persons who hold such positions will therefore be fiduciaries.
>
> Other offices and positions should be examined to determine whether they involve the performance of any of the functions described in section 3(21)(A) of the Act.

29 C.F.R. § 2509.75-8 (1993) (Department of Labor). The agency interpretations favor finding fiduciary status for discretionary actions and creating personal liability for breach of the fiduciary duties to which those actions necessarily give rise.

Accordingly, we reject the Third Circuit's interpretation in *Confer* that an officer who acts on behalf of a named fiduciary corporation cannot be a fiduciary if he acts within his official capacity and if no fiduciary duties are delegated to him individually. The broadly based liability policy underpinning ERISA and its functional definition of "fiduciary" compel the conclusion that the district court correctly found that Hurwitz and Leone were fiduciaries as a matter of law.

. . .

Were we to accept PLC's argument, a corporation would be able to shield its decision-makers from personal liability merely by stating in the plan documents that all their actions are taken on behalf of the company and not in a fiduciary capacity. We find that this was not Congress's intent when it included the "named fiduciary" provision of ERISA § 402(a)(1). We therefore affirm the district court on this point.

. . .

6-1 QUESTIONS AND PROBLEMS

1. In *Confer*, the court stated: "Confer, however, has failed to demonstrate that either officer, *as an individual*, had discretionary authority or responsibility which gave rise to a fiduciary duty that either or both owed directly to Confer." On what basis did the court conclude that the corporate officers, "as an individual," lacked discretionary authority?

2. Omega, Inc. sponsors an employee benefit plan. The minutes of the meeting of the Omega Board of Directors at which the plan was adopted state: "Rajesh Das, as Corporate Treasurer, shall serve as the plan fiduciary." If Rajesh fails in his duties as plan administrator, is he personally liable or does the holding in *Confer* relieve him from liability? Does the outcome depend on whether *Confer* or *Kayes* controls?

3. Pak owns 100 percent of the stock and is President of PhiCo, a company which has signed an agreement with its union to purchase health care insurance for its employees. Pursuant to that agreement, Pak had PhiCo purchase health care insurance from Healthguard, a health care insurer. Facing financial difficulties, Pak instructed the company Treasurer to stop paying the health care insurance premiums, and instead pay past due invoices. If the invoices had not been paid, PhiCo would not have been able to purchase needed inventory and would have had to close its doors. After not being paid for three months, Healthguard canceled the health care insurance, causing PhiCo employees to incur health care expenses. Two months later PhiCo went bankrupt. The ex-employees sued Pak as a fiduciary of the health care plan seeking reimbursement of their health care expenses. Pak claims that his acts were undertaken as President of PhiCo and not as a fiduciary, assuming that (a) there was a health care plan, and (b) he was a fiduciary. Is Pak personally liable as a fiduciary?

4. Acme Inc. is owned 50 percent by Maud and 50 percent by her husband, Mickey. Maud is the company President, Mickey the company Treasurer. The company pension plan for its 20 employees contains $200,000 of stocks and bonds. Acme is the named plan fiduciary. Fox Bank is the custodial Trustee. Acme Inc. instructs Fox Bank to sell $150,000 of the stocks and bonds and remit the funds to Acme. Fox Bank does so. Acme Inc. declares a bonus of $75,000 each to the President and Treasurer, i.e., Maud and Mickey. Acme Inc. pays each $75,000. A plan participant learns of these transactions and sues Acme Inc., as the plan

fiduciary, as well as Maud and Mickey individually, claiming they too are fiduciaries. Should Maud and Mickey be considered ERISA fiduciaries?

The employer as plan sponsor will be treated as the plan administrator unless the plan designates someone else. ERISA § 3(16)(A)(ii). Often the employer's board of directors will collectively act as the plan sponsor. The board in turn will usually name high level administrators or corporate officers as the plan administrators. If, however, the corporation (the plan sponsor) acts as the administrator, the corporate officers who carry out the administrative duties on behalf of the corporation are not necessarily considered to be fiduciaries.

[2] The Employer as Both Plan Sponsor and Plan Fiduciary

ERISA § 408(c)(3).

Because ERISA § 408(c)(3) specifically permits an officer, employee, agent, or representative of the employer to be a fiduciary, quite often the employer is the named plan fiduciary. When the employer wears "two hats," as both the plan sponsor (defined in ERISA § 3(16)(B)) and the plan fiduciary (administrator), there exists the potential for a significant conflict of interest because the employer's interests are not necessarily congruent with those of the plan participants. As the plan fiduciary, the employer owes a duty of loyalty and care toward the plan participants, but as the plan sponsor, the employer also owns duties to itself and its owners. At times employers find it difficult to balance these two divergent roles.

VARITY CORP. v. HOWE (PART 1)

516 U.S. 489 (1996)

Breyer, J.

A group of beneficiaries of a firm's employee welfare benefit plan, protected by the Employee Retirement Income Security (ERISA), have sued their plan's administrator, who was also their employer. They claim that the administrator, through trickery, led them to withdraw from the plan and to forfeit their benefits. They seek, among other things, an order that, in essence, would reinstate each of them as a participant in the employer's ERISA plan. The lower courts entered judgment in the employees' favor, and we agreed to review that judgment.

In conducting our review, we do not question the lower courts' findings of serious deception by the employer, but instead consider three legal questions. First, in the factual circumstances (as determined by the lower courts), was the employer acting in its capacity as an ERISA "fiduciary" when it significantly and deliberately misled the beneficiaries? Second, in misleading the beneficiaries, did the employer violate the fiduciary obligations that ERISA § 404 imposes upon plan administrators? Third, does ERISA § 502(a)(3) authorize ERISA plan beneficiaries to bring a lawsuit, such as this one, that seeks relief for individual beneficiaries harmed by an administrator's breach of fiduciary obligations?

We answer each of these questions in the beneficiaries' favor, and we therefore affirm the judgment of the Court of Appeals.

The key facts, as found by the District Court after trial, include the following: Charles Howe, and the other respondents, used to work for Massey-Ferguson, Inc., a farm equipment manufacturer, and a wholly owned subsidiary of the petitioner, Varity Corporation. (Since the lower courts found that *Varity* and

Massey-Ferguson were "alter egos," we shall refer to them interchangeably.) These employees all were participants in, and beneficiaries of, Massey-Ferguson's self-funded employee welfare benefit plan — an ERISA protected plan that Massey-Ferguson itself administered. In the mid-1980's, Varity became concerned that some of Massey-Ferguson's divisions were losing too much money and developed a business plan to deal with the problem.

The business plan — which Varity called "Project Sunshine" — amounted to placing many of Varity's money-losing eggs in one financially rickety basket. It called for a transfer of Massey-Ferguson's money-losing divisions, along with various other debts, to a newly created, separately incorporated subsidiary called Massey Combines. The plan foresaw the possibility that Massey Combines would fail. But it viewed such a failure, from Varity's business perspective, as closer to a victory than to a defeat. That is because Massey Combine's failure would not only eliminate several of Varity's poorly performing divisions, but it would also eradicate various debts that Varity would transfer to Massey Combines, and which, in the absence of the reorganization, Varity's more profitable subsidiaries or divisions might have to pay.

Among the obligations that Varity hoped the reorganization would eliminate were those arising from the Massey-Ferguson benefit plan's promises to pay medical and other nonpension benefits to employees of Massey-Ferguson's money-losing divisions. Rather than terminate those benefits directly (as it had retained the right to do), Varity attempted to avoid the undesirable fallout that could have accompanied cancellation by inducing the failing divisions' employees to switch employers and thereby voluntarily release Massey-Ferguson from its obligation to provide them benefits (effectively substituting the new, self-funded Massey Combines benefit plan for the former Massey-Ferguson plan). Insofar as Massey-Ferguson's employees did so, a subsequent Massey Combines failure would eliminate — simply and automatically, without distressing the remaining Massey-Ferguson employees — what would otherwise have been Massey-Ferguson's obligation to pay those employees their benefits.

To persuade the employees of the failing divisions to accept the change of employer and benefit plan, Varity called them together at a special meeting and talked to them about Massey Combines' future business outlook, its likely financial viability, and the security of their employee benefits. The thrust of Varity's remarks was that the employees' benefits would remain secure if they voluntarily transferred to Massey Combines. As Varity knew, however, the reality was very different. Indeed, the District Court found that Massey Combines was insolvent from the day of its creation and that it hid a $46 million negative net worth by overvaluing its assets and underestimating its liabilities.

After the presentation, about 1,500 Massey-Ferguson employees accepted Varity's assurances and voluntarily agreed to the transfer. (Varity also unilaterally assigned to Massey Combines the benefit obligations it owed to some 4,000 workers who had retired from Massey-Ferguson prior to this reorganization, without requesting permission or informing them of the assignment.) Unfortunately for these employees, Massey Combines ended its first year with a loss of $88 million, and ended its second year in a receivership, under which its employees lost their nonpension benefits. Many of those employees . . . brought this lawsuit, seeking the benefits they would have been owed under their old, Massey-Ferguson plan, had they not transferred to Massey Combines.

After trial, the District Court found, among other things, that Varity and Massey-Ferguson, acting as ERISA fiduciaries, had harmed the plan's beneficiaries through deliberate deception. The court held that Varity and Massey-Ferguson thereby violated an ERISA-imposed fiduciary obligation to administer Massey-Ferguson's benefit plan "solely in the interest of the participants and beneficiaries" of the plan. ERISA § 404(a). The court added that ERISA § 502(a)(3) gave the former Massey-Ferguson employees a right to "appropriate equitable relief . . . to redress" the harm that this deception had caused them individually. Among other remedies the court considered "appropriate equitable relief" was an order that Massey-Ferguson reinstate its former employees into its own plan (which had continued to provide benefits to employees of Massey-Ferguson's profitable divisions).

Varity has raised two additional issues. First, Varity points out that the relevant ERISA section imposes liability only upon plan fiduciaries; and it argues that it was acting only as an employer and not as a plan fiduciary when it deceived its employees. Second, it argues that, in any event, its conduct did not violate the fiduciary standard that ERISA imposes.

We begin with the question of Varity's fiduciary status. In relevant part, the statute says that a "person is a fiduciary with respect to a plan," and therefore subject to ERISA fiduciary duties, "to the extent" that he or she "exercises any discretionary authority or discretionary control respecting management" of the plan, or "has any discretionary authority or discretionary responsibility in the administration" of the plan. ERISA § 3(21)(A).

Varity was both an employer and the benefit plan's administrator, as ERISA permits. But, obviously, not all of Varity's business activities involved plan management or administration. Varity argues that when it communicated with its Massey-Ferguson workers about transferring to Massey Combines, it was not administering or managing the plan; rather, it was acting only in its capacity as an employer and not as a plan administrator.

The District Court, however, held that when the misrepresentations regarding employee benefits were made, Varity was wearing its "fiduciary," as well as its "employer," hat. In reviewing this legal conclusion, we give deference to the factual findings of the District Court, recognizing its comparative advantage in understanding the specific context in which the events of this case occurred. We believe that these factual findings (which Varity does not challenge) adequately support the District Court's holding that Varity was exercising "discretionary authority" respecting the plan's "management" or "administration" when it made these misrepresentations, which legal holding we have independently reviewed.

The relevant factual circumstances include the following: In the spring of 1986, Varity summoned the employees of Massey-Ferguson's money-losing divisions to a meeting at Massey-Ferguson's corporate headquarters for a 30-minute presentation. The employees saw a 90-second videotaped message from Mr. Ivan Porter, a Varity vice president and Massey Combines' newly appointed president. They also received four documents: (a) a several-page, detailed comparison between the employee benefits offered by Massey-Ferguson and those offered by Massey Combines; (b) a question-and-answer sheet; (c) a transcript of the Porter videotape; and (d) a cover letter with an acceptance form. Each of these documents discussed employee benefits and benefit plans, some briefly in general terms, and others at length and in detail:

> (a) The longest document, the side-by-side benefits comparison, contained a fairly detailed description of the benefit plans. Its object was to show that after transfer, the employees' benefits would remain the same. It says, for example, that, under Massey-Ferguson's plan, "[d]iagnostic x-ray

and laboratory expenses will be paid on the basis of reasonable and customary charges for such services." It then repeats the same sentence in describing Massey Combines' "[d]iagnostic x-ray and laboratory expenses" benefits. It describes about 20 different benefits in this way.

(b) The eight questions and answers on the question-and-answer sheet include three that relate to welfare benefits or to the ERISA pension plan Varity also administered:

"Q. 3. What happens to my benefits, pension, etc.?

"A. 3. When you transfer to MCC [Massey Combines], pay levels and benefit programmes will remain unchanged. There will be no loss of seniority or pensionable service.

"Q. 4. Do you expect the terms and conditions of employment to change?

"A. 4. Employment conditions in the future will depend on our ability to make Massey Combines Corporation a success and if changes are considered necessary or appropriate, they will be made.

. . .

"Q. 8. Are the pensions protected under MCC?

"A. 8. Responsibility for pension benefits earned by employees transferring to Massey Combines Corporation is being assumed by the Massey Combines Corporation Pension Plan.

"The assets which are held in the Massey Ferguson Pension Plan to fund such benefits as determined by actuarial calculations, are being transferred to the Massey Combines Corporation Plan. Such benefits and assets will be protected by the same legislation that protect the Massey Ferguson Pension Plan.

"There will be no change in pension benefits as a result of your transfer to Massey Combines Corporation."

(c) The transcript of the 90-second videotape message repeated much of the information in the question-and-answer sheet, adding assurances about Massey Combines' viability:

"This financial restructuring created Massey Combines Corporation and will provide the funds necessary to ensure its future viability. I believe that with the continued help and support of you we can make Massey Combines Corporation the kind of successful business enterprise which we all want to work for.

" . . . . When you transfer your employment to the Massey Combines Corporation, pay levels and benefit programs will remain unchanged. There will be no loss of seniority or pensionable service. Employment conditions in the future will depend on the success of the Massey Combines Corporation and should changes be deemed appropriate or necessary, they will be made . . . .

"Finally, despite the depression which persists in the North American economy, I am excited about the future of Massey Combines Corporation." *Id.* at 80.

(d) The cover letter, in five short paragraphs, repeated verbatim these benefit-related assurances:

> "To enable us to accept you as an employee of Massey Combines Corporation and to continue to process the payment of benefits to you, we require that you complete the information below and return this letter . . . .
>
> "When you accept employment with Massey Combines Corporation, pay levels and benefit programs will remain unchanged. There will be no loss of seniority or pensionable service. Employment conditions in the future will depend on our ability to make Massey Combines Corporation a success, and if changes are considered necessary or appropriate, they will be made.
>
> "We are all very optimistic that our new company, has a bright future, and are excited by the new challenges facing all of us . . . .
>
> "In order to ensure uninterrupted continuation of your pay and benefits, please return this signed acceptance of employment . . . ."

Given this record material, the District Court determined, as a factual matter, that the key meeting, to a considerable extent, was about benefits, for the documents described them in detail, explained the similarity between past and future plans in principle, and assured the employees that they would continue to receive similar benefits in practice. The District Court concluded that the basic message conveyed to the employees was that transferring from Massey-Ferguson to Massey Combines would not significantly undermine the security of their benefits. And, given this view of the facts, we believe that the District Court reached the correct legal conclusion, namely, that Varity spoke, in significant part, in its capacity as plan administrator.

To decide whether Varity's actions fall within the statutory definition of "fiduciary" acts, we must interpret the statutory terms which limit the scope of fiduciary activity to discretionary acts of plan "management" and "administration." ERISA § 3(21)(A). These words are not self-defining, and the activity at issue here neither falls clearly within nor outside of the common understanding of these words. The dissent looks to the dictionary for interpretive assistance. Though dictionaries sometimes help in such matters, we believe it more important here to look to the common law, which, over the years, has given to terms such as "fiduciary" and trust "administration" a legal meaning to which, we normally presume, Congress meant to refer. The ordinary trust law understanding of fiduciary "administration" of a trust is that to act as an administrator is to perform the duties imposed, or exercise the powers conferred, by the trust documents. The law of trusts also understands a trust document to implicitly confer "such powers as are necessary or appropriate for the carrying out of the purposes" of the trust. 3 A. Scott & W. Fratcher, *Law of Trusts* § 186, 6 (4th ed. 1988). Conveying information about the likely future of plan benefits, thereby permitting beneficiaries to make an informed choice about continued participation, would seem to be an exercise of a power "appropriate" to carrying out an important plan purpose. After all, ERISA itself specifically requires administrators to give beneficiaries certain information about the plan. And administrators, as part of their administrative responsibilities, frequently offer beneficiaries more than the minimum information that the statute requires — for example, answering beneficiaries' questions about the meaning of the terms of a plan so that those beneficiaries can more easily obtain the plan's benefits. To offer beneficiaries detailed plan information in order to help them decide whether to remain with the plan is essentially the same kind of plan-related activity.

Moreover, as far as the record reveals, Mr. Porter's letter, videotape, and the other documents came from those within the firm who had authority to communicate as fiduciaries with plan beneficiaries. Varity does not claim that it authorized only special individuals, not connected with the meeting documents, to speak as plan administrators.

Finally, reasonable employees, in the circumstances found by the District Court, could have thought that Varity was communicating with them both in its capacity as employer and in its capacity as plan administrator. Reasonable employees might not have distinguished consciously between the two roles. But they would have known that the employer was their plan's administrator and had expert knowledge about how their plan worked. The central conclusion ("your benefits are secure") could well have drawn strength from their awareness of that expertise, and one could reasonably believe that the employer, aware of the importance of the matter, so intended.

We conclude, therefore, that the factual context in which the statements were made, combined with the plan-related nature of the activity, engaged in by those who had plan-related authority to do so, together provide sufficient support for the District Court's legal conclusion that Varity was acting as a fiduciary.

Varity raises three contrary arguments. First, Varity argues that it was not engaged in plan administration because neither the specific disclosure provisions of ERISA, nor the specific terms of the plan instruments, required it to make these statements. But that does not mean Varity was not engaging in plan administration in making them, as the dissent seems to suggest. There is more to plan (or trust) administration than simply complying with the specific duties imposed by the plan documents or statutory regime . . . . Indeed, the primary function of the fiduciary duty is to constrain the exercise of discretionary powers which are controlled by no other specific duty imposed by the trust instrument or the legal regime. If the fiduciary duty applied to nothing more than activities already controlled by other specific legal duties, it would serve no purpose.

Second, Varity says that when it made the statements that most worried the District Court — the statements about Massey Combines' "bright future" — it must have been speaking only as employer (and not as fiduciary), for statements about a new subsidiary's financial future have virtually nothing to do with administering benefit plans. But this argument parses the meeting's communications too finely. The ultimate message Varity intended to convey — "your benefits are secure" — depended in part upon its repeated assurances that benefits would remain "unchanged," in part upon the detailed comparison of benefits, and in part upon assurances about Massey Combines' "bright" financial future. Varity's workers would not necessarily have focused upon each underlying supporting statement separately, because what primarily interested them, and what primarily interested the District Court, was the truthfulness of the ultimate conclusion that transferring to Massey Combines would not adversely affect the security of their benefits. And, in the present context, Varity's statements about the security of benefits amounted to an act of plan administration. That Varity intentionally communicated its conclusion through a closely linked set of statements (some directly concerning plan benefits, others concerning the viability of the corporation) does not change this conclusion.

We do not hold, as the dissent suggests, that Varity acted as a fiduciary simply because it made statements about its expected financial condition or because "an ordinary business decision turn[ed] out to have an adverse impact on the plan." Instead, we accept the undisputed facts found, and factual inferences drawn, by the District Court, namely, that Varity intentionally connected its statements about Massey Combines' financial health to statements it made about the future of benefits, so that its intended communication about the security of benefits was rendered materially misleading. And we hold that making intentional representations about the future of plan benefits in that context is an act of plan administration.

Third, Varity says that an employer's decision to amend or terminate a plan (as Varity had the right to do) is not an act of plan administration. How then, it asks, could conveying information about the likelihood of termination be an act of plan administration? While it may be true that amending or terminating a plan (or a common-law trust) is beyond the power of a plan administrator (or trustee) — and, therefore, cannot be an act of plan "management" or "administration" — it does not follow that making statements about the likely future of the plan is also beyond the scope of plan administration. As we explained above, plan administrators often have, and commonly exercise, discretionary authority to communicate with beneficiaries about the future of plan benefits.

The second question — whether Varity's deception violated ERISA-imposed fiduciary obligations — calls for a brief, affirmative answer. ERISA requires a "fiduciary" to "discharge his duties with respect to a plan solely in the interest of the participants and beneficiaries." ERISA § 404(a). To participate knowingly and significantly in deceiving a plan's beneficiaries in order to save the employer money at the beneficiaries' expense is not to act "solely in the interest of the participants and beneficiaries." As other courts have held, "[l]ying is inconsistent with the duty of loyalty owed by all fiduciaries and codified in section 404(a)(1) of ERISA," *Peoria Union Stock Yards Co. v. Penn Mut. Life Ins. Co.*, 698 F.2d 320, 326 (7th Cir. 1983). Because the breach of this duty is sufficient to uphold the decision below, we need not reach the question whether ERISA fiduciaries have any fiduciary duty to disclose truthful information on their own initiative, or in response to employee inquiries.

We recognize, as mentioned above, that we are to apply common-law trust standards "bearing in mind the special nature and purpose of employee benefit plans." H.R. Conf. Rep. No. 93-1280, at 302, 3 Leg. Hist. 4569. But we can find no adequate basis here, in the statute or otherwise, for any special interpretation that might insulate Varity, acting as a fiduciary, from the legal consequences of the kind of conduct (intentional misrepresentation) that often creates liability even among strangers.

. . .

JUSTICE THOMAS, with whom JUSTICE O'CONNOR and JUSTICE SCALIA join, dissenting.

To determine whether an employer acts as a fiduciary under ERISA, I begin with the text of § 3(21)(A)(iii). To "administer" a plan is to "manage or supervise the execution . . . or conduct of" the plan. *Webster's Ninth New Collegiate Dictionary* 57 (1991). Essentially, to administer the plan is to implement its provisions and to carry out plan duties imposed by the Act. The question in this case is whether Varity was carrying out discretionary responsibilities over management or implementation of the plan, when, as respondents argued below, it "made misrepresentations to the class plaintiffs about MCC's business prospects and about the anticipated effect of the employment transfers on plaintiffs' benefits." Although representations of this sort may well affect plan participants' assessment of the security of their benefits, I disagree with the majority that such communications qualify as "plan administration" under the Act.

In the course of running a business, an employer that administers its own benefits plan will make countless business decisions that affect the plan. Congress made clear in § 3(21)(A), however, that " 'ERISA does not require that "day-to-day corporate business transactions, which may have a collateral effect on prospective, contingent employee benefits, be performed solely in the interest of plan participants."'" *Adams v. Avondale Industries, Inc.*, 905 F.2d 943, 947 (6th Cir. 1990). Thus, ordinary business decisions, such as whether to pay a dividend or to incur debt, may be made without fear of liability for breach of fiduciary duty under ERISA, even though they may turn out to have negative consequences for plan participants. Even business decisions that directly affect the plan and plan participants, such as the decision to modify or terminate welfare benefits, are not governed by ERISA's fiduciary obligations because they do not involve discretionary administration of the plan. In contrast, the discretionary interpretation of a plan term, or the discretionary determination that the plan does not authorize a certain type of procedure, would likely qualify as plan administration by a fiduciary. There is no claim in this case, however, that Varity failed to implement the plan according to its terms, since respondents actually received all of the benefits to which they were entitled under the plan, as the courts below found.

An employer will also make countless representations in the course of managing a business about the current and expected financial condition of the corporation. Similarly, an employer may make representations that either directly or impliedly evince an intention to increase, decrease, or maintain employee welfare benefits. Such communications simply are not made in the course of implementing the plan or executing its terms. Rather, they are the necessary incidents of conducting a business, and Congress determined that employers would not be burdened with fiduciary obligations to the plan when engaging in such conduct.

Because an employer's representations about the company's financial prospects or about the possible impact of ordinary business transactions on the security of unvested welfare benefits do not involve execution or implementation of duties imposed by the plan or the Act, and because these are the types of representations employers regularly make in the ordinary course of running a business, I would not hold that such communications involve plan administration. The untruthfulness of a statement cannot magically transform it from a nonfiduciary representation into a fiduciary one; the determinative factor is not truthfulness but the capacity in which the statement is made.

The remainder of the opinion is reproduced in Chapter 7 as *Varity Part II.*

6-2 QUESTIONS AND PROBLEMS

1. Why was Varity a fiduciary?

2. What did Varity do that violated ERISA?

3. When Varity informed the employees about the proposed corporate reorganization, was it acting in the capacity of an employer or a fiduciary?

4. Was there any way that Varity could have informed the employees about the reorganization plans without being considered a fiduciary?

5. The dissent begins by looking in a dictionary to determine whether Varity was acting as a fiduciary. Is that helpful?

6. As pointed out by the dissent, it is legal for an employer to lie to its employees about how the entity is doing and its future prospects. May a fiduciary ever lie to plan participants about the prospects of their pensions?

7. *Varity* suggests that an employer might be better off not to be a plan fiduciary. Are there reasons why an employer might prefer to be a plan administrator and fiduciary despite the holding in *Varity*?

Just what degree of disclosure is owed to employees by a fiduciary engaged in "internal deliberations" is not clear. While *Varity* requires employers who are plan fiduciaries to be more forthcoming, the exact parameters of that duty remain in debate. A fiduciary's obligations to disclose information to plan participants is examined in later in this Chapter.

[3] Third Parties as Plan Fiduciaries

Every plan must a have a plan administrator who is responsible for the day-to-day operations of the plan. In many instances, the plan sponsor also serves as the plan administrator. In such cases, the sponsor acting as plan administrator is a fiduciary. Often the sponsor hires a third party to act as plan administrator. Whether the third party administrator is a fiduciary depends upon how much discretion it exercises.

BOARD OF TRUSTEES OF BRICKLAYERS v. WETTLIN ASSOC.
237 F.3d 270 (3d Cir. 2001)

WEIS, CIRCUIT JUDGE. The issue in this case is whether ERISA's definition of "fiduciary" includes an entity that receives contributions from employers and awards benefits to participants pursuant to an agreement with trustees of a union welfare fund. We conclude that the allegations in plaintiff's complaint were sufficient to preclude a ruling that no fiduciary status existed as a matter of law. Accordingly, we will reverse the District Court's ruling that the complaint failed to state a claim.

Plaintiff is the Board of Trustees of Bricklayers and Allied Craftsman Local 6 of New Jersey Welfare Fund, an employee benefit plan within the meaning of ERISA, § 3(3). The members of the Board of Trustees have the discretionary authority to manage and control the Local 6 Fund and are fiduciaries under ERISA, § 3(21)(A). They meet only four to six times a year.

In 1988, the Board entered into an agreement providing that defendant Wettlin Associates, Inc. would provide administrative services to Local 6 Fund. The Board delegated to Wettlin the day-to-day responsibility to control, manage, hold, safeguard, and account for the fund's assets and income. Wettlin determined the legitimate expenses of the fund, wrote checks, and disbursed assets from the fund's bank account in accordance with such determinations. That conduct was within Wettlin's discretion and it was not required to seek approval from the Trustees in advance.

Wettlin was also required to collect contributions from employers under the terms of collective bargaining agreements, deposit them in Local 6 Fund's bank account, and make payments in accordance with the fund's obligations under the plan. As stated in the agreement, Wettlin would receive the following monthly compensation:

Welfare Fund	$2,208.33
Pension Fund	$833.33
Annuity Fund	$833.33
Apprentice Training Fund	$41.67

TOTAL $3,916.66

According to the complaint, "effective as of January, 1996, the [Local 6] Fund also collected fringe benefit funds from contributing employers which, in turn, were to be transferred by the Fund for deposit to the New Jersey Bricklayers and Allied Craftworkers Health Fund [('state-wide fund')]." In carrying out this arrangement, Wettlin was to transfer ninety-eight percent of the employer contributions earmarked for the state-wide fund to that entity. The amended complaint alleges that the two percent not transferred became an asset of Local 6 Fund.

In February 1998, the Board notified Wettlin that its services would terminate on April 1, 1998. Beginning on March 1 and continuing through March 31, Wettlin paid itself $42,743.71 from the Local 6 Fund account, the amount representing the two percent withheld from payments to the state-wide fund.

Upon learning of this series of payments, the Board demanded reimbursement, and when this was refused, filed suit in the District Court of New Jersey. The Board alleged that Wettlin was a fiduciary under ERISA and had breached its duty to the fund. The complaint also pleaded various state law claims.

Relying on Federal Rule of Civil Procedure 12(b)(6), the District Court dismissed plaintiff's complaint because it failed to offer any factual basis to support its allegation that defendant was a fiduciary under ERISA. Plaintiff then proffered an amended complaint, which was rejected by a magistrate judge on the ground that it failed to state a claim that would survive a motion to dismiss. The District Judge agreed and dismissed the case, observing that Wettlin's role was "nothing more than ministerial." The Board appealed.

. . .

The Board of Trustees argues that Wettlin can be a fiduciary under ERISA because discretion is not always a prerequisite for such a role. Even if discretion is required, the Board contends that the amended complaint sets forth a factual basis for concluding that Wettlin did function in that manner. Wettlin contends that it was not a fiduciary because it acted in a ministerial capacity, exercised no discretion, and additionally asserts that the money in question was not an asset of Local 6 Fund.

The ERISA provision at the heart of this case sets out the description of a fiduciary:

> "[A] person is a fiduciary with respect to a plan to the extent (i) he exercises any discretionary authority or discretionary control respecting management of such plan or *exercises any authority or control respecting management or disposition of its assets*, (ii) he renders investment advice for a fee . . . or has any authority or responsibility to do so, or (iii) he has any discretionary authority or discretionary responsibility in the administration of such plan."

[ERISA] § 3(21)(A) (emphasis added).

This statutory definition requires that a fiduciary "must be someone acting in the capacity of manager, administrator, or financial advisor to a 'plan.'" *Pegram v. Herdrich*, 530 U.S. 211, 222 (2000). The statute uses differing criteria in imposing fiduciary obligations for each of these roles. For plan financial advisors, Congress assigned a fiduciary duty in subsection (ii) both to those who actually render advice and those who simply have the authority to do so. [ERISA] § 3(21)(A)(ii). For plan administrators, subsection (iii) limits fiduciary status to those who have discretionary authority or discretionary responsibility. [ERISA] § 3(21)(A)(iii). For managers, subsection (i) sets the criteria. Subsection (i) of [ERISA] § 3 (21)(A) differentiates between those who manage the plan in general, and those who manage the plan assets. These functions are set out in two clauses under subsection (i) separated by the conjunction "or." A significant difference between the two clauses is that discretion is specified as a prerequisite to fiduciary status for a person managing an ERISA plan, but the word "discretionary" is conspicuously absent when the text refers to assets. "This distinction is not accidental — it reflects the high standard of care trust law imposes upon those who handle money or other assets on behalf of another." *FirsTier Bank, N.A. v. Zeller*, 16 F.3d 907, 911 (8th Cir. 1994).

This distinction was emphasized in *IT Corp. v. General American Life Insurance Co.*, 107 F.3d 1415 (9th Cir. 1997). In that case, the administrator had check-writing authority over the money received from the employer that was deposited in the plan's bank account. *Id.* at 1417. Noting that the "statute treats control over the cash differently from control over administration," the Court concluded that " '[a]ny' control over disposition of plan money makes the person who has the control a fiduciary." *Id.* at 1421.

The Court of Appeals noted that because the employer had the responsibility to keep an amount in a bank account sufficient to cover checks validly issued by the administrator, "as a practical matter, a substantial amount of money would [have been] under the control of [the administrator], in the form of a bank account which it could deplete by writing checks." *Id.* Where there is such "authority or control," the District Court could not hold that the administrator was a non-fiduciary as a matter of law. *Id.*

In *Yeseta v. Baima*, 837 F.2d 380, 386 (9th Cir. 1988), the same Court of Appeals held that a corporate officer who withdrew plan funds for the company's benefit was a fiduciary, despite authorization for the withdrawal from other officers. Noting that section 3(21)(A) establishes that a person can be a fiduciary on the basis of control of a plan's assets, the Court concluded it was unnecessary to sort through the disputed facts to determine authority because control could decide the issue. *Id.*

A corporate officer in *LoPresti v. Terwilliger*, 126 F.3d 34, 40 (2d Cir. 1997), commingled company assets with benefit funds, and used them to pay company debts. Hinting that the District Court had apparently failed to appreciate the significance of the second clause of subsection (i), the Court of Appeals reversed. *Id.* It held that an individual may also become an ERISA fiduciary by exercising any authority or control in connection with the management or disposition of plan assets. *Id.*

We come then to *Confer v. Custom Engineering Co.*, 952 F.2d 34 (3d Cir. 1991), on which the District Court relied in the present case. Confer, a participant in an employee health benefit plan, alleged a breach of fiduciary duty when he was denied medical benefits following an accident. He sued his employer, Custom Engineering Co., which was the plan's administrator and fiduciary, as well as the officers of that company. He also named as a defendant Self-Funded Plans, Inc., which had been delegated day-to-day administrative tasks for the plan. We affirmed summary judgment in favor of the company officers, concluding that corporate officers acting on behalf of a corporation are not themselves fiduciaries unless they have individual discretionary roles in plan administration.

More important to the case before us, we also held that Self-Funded, the day-to-day administrator, was not responsible for wrongfully denying benefits to the plaintiff. "Since discretionary authority, responsibility or control is a prerequisite to fiduciary status, it follows that persons who perform purely ministerial tasks, such as claims processing and calculation, cannot be fiduciaries because they do not have discretionary roles. Self-Funded had no discretion to deny or allow [plaintiff]'s claim." *Id.* The plaintiff's assertion to the contrary had "no basis in the plan document, in Self-Funded's contract with Custom Engineering, or anywhere else in the record." *Id.*

There are important distinctions between *Confer* and the case at hand. Self-Funded's alleged breach was with regard to its responsibilities in the administration of benefits under the plan; therefore, its fiduciary status under ERISA was determined by subsection (iii) of [ERISA] § 3(21)(A). Plaintiff in that case never alleged mismanagement of assets. Thus, *Confer* concluded only that plaintiff had not demonstrated that Self-Funded had discretionary authority or discretionary responsibility in the administration of the plan. *Confer*, 952 F.2d at 39.

Wettlin does not argue that subsection (iii) applies in the present case. Although *Confer* addressed subsection (iii). Wettlin contends that the statements in that opinion linking fiduciary status and discretion apply to all ERISA fiduciaries. We reject this argument as contrary to the statutory text. "Discretionary" authority or responsibility is required to confer fiduciary status for plan administration under subsection (iii), and "discretionary" authority or "discretionary" control is required for plan management under subsection (i). As noted earlier, however, the adjective "discretionary," so carefully selected for plan administration and management, is omitted in subsection (i) when dealing with authority or control over the management or disposition of plan "assets." "The statute treats control over the cash differently from control over administration." *IT Corp.*, 107 F.3d at 1421.

That Congress established a lower threshold for fiduciary status where control of assets is at stake is not surprising, given that "[a]t common law, fiduciary duties characteristically attach to decisions about managing assets and distributing property to beneficiaries." *Pegram*, 530 U.S. at 231 ("[T]he common law trustee's most defining concern historically has been the payment of money in the interest of the beneficiary.") . . . .

. . .

This is not the first case in which we have noted that the structure of subsection (i) is significant in its interpretation. In *Curcio v. John Hancock Mutual Life Insurance Co.*, 33 F.3d 226, 233 (3d Cir. 1994), we observed that although the party in that case was not a fiduciary under the second half of subsection (i), separate analysis was necessary to determine whether the first clause did give the party that status.

Unlike the defendant in *Confer*, Wettlin's potential liability is created by subsection (i), which addresses fund assets and directs that fiduciary status be assigned to the extent that a person "exercises any authority or control respecting management or disposition of its assets." [ERISA] § 3(21)(A)(i). To the extent it applied *dicta* in *Confer* to the analysis of subsection (i), the District Court erred.

The contract attached to the plaintiff's amended complaint lists the functions to be performed by Wettlin. Most of these appear to be purely ministerial and are specifically subject to the direction of the trustees. The provisions directing Wettlin to collect contributions and write checks on Local 6 Fund's account, however, are quite general in scope. Wettlin would have us construe these terms narrowly, in effect establishing it as a mere depository of Local 6 Fund assets.

We are inclined to agree that ERISA does not consider as a fiduciary an entity such as a bank when it does no more than receive deposits from a benefit fund on which the fund can draw checks. The allegations in the amended complaint, however, do not describe Wettlin's role as so circumscribed. Rather, the amended complaint alleges that the Board delegated to defendant the "day to day responsibility to control, manage, hold, safeguard, and account for the Fund's assets and income."

Moreover, the contract provides that Wettlin is to "[r]eceive request for benefits from employees and take appropriate action thereon." Notably lacking in the record is a description of the various benefits that are available and what actions the parties have considered to be "appropriate."

At this stage we are left with substantial doubt that there exist no facts that might establish that Wettlin did indeed exercise such authority and control over the management and disposition of Local 6 Fund assets so as to come within the statutory definition of a fiduciary. Further development is required and on this record we cannot say that, as a matter of law, Wettlin is not a fiduciary. The amended complaint does state a claim and the case should not have been dismissed at the pleading stage.

The Order of the District Court will be reversed and the case will be remanded for further proceedings in accordance with this Opinion.

6-3 QUESTIONS AND PROBLEMS

1. What is the holding of the court?

2. Has the court articulated a convincing reason to distinguish the outcome in *Confer*?

3. Why did Congress not make the existence of discretion a necessary prerequisite for labeling a party, who has authority or control over plan assets, a fiduciary?

HAROLD IVES TRUCKING COMPANY v. SPRADLEY & COKER, INC.

178 F.3d 523 (8th Cir. 1999)

ARNOLD, CIRCUIT JUDGE.

The events that led to this lawsuit are not in dispute and may be briefly summarized. In early October 1994, Kenneth Elliott was involved in an automobile accident. Mr. Elliott, a former employee of Harold Ives Trucking Company (Harold Ives) and a participant in the company's health benefits plan, sustained serious head injuries and was hospitalized at the University of Arkansas for Medical Sciences (UAMS). Several days after the accident, Mr. Elliott was transferred to Baptist Rehabilitation Institute, where he remained for more than a month. Later, Mr. Elliott's doctor recommended that he be moved again, this time to the Timber Ridge Ranch Neuro Rehabilitation Center. Before he was moved, however, Spradley & Coker, Inc., the third-party administrator of the Harold Ives plan, determined that charges incurred at Timber Ridge could not be paid by the plan because Timber Ridge was not a "covered facility." Spradley & Coker notified Timber Ridge of this decision on October 26, after consulting with Jefferson Pilot Life Insurance Company, the excess loss carrier for the plan. (Mr. Elliott's medical expenses were approaching $50,000, the excess loss policy's deductible.) Mr. Elliott's attorney objected to Spradley & Coker's denial of coverage, and, on November 17, Spradley & Coker reversed its decision, notifying Timber Ridge that Mr. Elliott's hospitalization at Timber Ridge would be covered. This decision was made despite the fact that Jefferson Pilot had not changed its mind about coverage. That day, Mr. Elliott was moved to Timber Ridge, where he stayed until April of 1995, incurring almost $73,000 in additional medical expenses.

A representative of Spradley & Coker testified that, although Jefferson Pilot was "adamant" that charges at Timber Ridge would not be covered by its excess loss policy, Spradley & Coker never informed Harold Ives of Jefferson Pilot's position. Two representatives of Spradley & Coker testified that, at the time Spradley & Coker reversed its decision, Jefferson Pilot had not changed its original position that Timber Ridge was not a "covered facility." One of these witnesses testified that Spradley & Coker should have provided written notification to Harold Ives Trucking of Jefferson Pilot's position because it was something the company would "need to know."

At the direction of Spradley & Coker, the plan paid Timber Ridge $72,942.23. By that time, Mr. Elliott's treatment at UAMS and Baptist had exhausted the $50,000 deductible under the Jefferson Pilot excess loss policy. Spradley & Coker submitted its first claim to Jefferson Pilot in early 1995, and Jefferson Pilot formally denied coverage of all of the Timber Ridge charges later that year.

Harold Ives, as sponsor of the plan, and the plan itself, brought an action against Jefferson Pilot for wrongfully denying the Timber Ridge claims. Harold Ives also sued Spradley & Coker and its successor, HealthSource Arkansas, Inc., for violating its duty as a fiduciary under ERISA, and for breach of the claims-administration contract that governed the parties' relationship . . . .

As we have noted, the District Court held that Spradley & Coker, as third-party administrator of the plan, functioned as a fiduciary, and violated its duty "when it failed to advise [the plaintiffs] that Timber Ridge Ranch was not a 'covered facility' under the Plan." We agree. First, the definitions section of [ERISA] § 3 provides that "a person is a fiduciary with respect to a plan to the extent (i) he exercises any discretionary authority or discretionary control respecting management of such plan or exercises any authority or control respecting management or disposition of its assets . . . ." [ERISA] § 3(21)(A). As Spradley & Coker argues, the administration contract provides expressly that it would have no discretionary authority as third-party administrator, and that it would provide only ministerial services. But the contract is controlling only to the extent that Spradley & Coker actually carried out its responsibilities in a manner consistent with its provisions. In other words, Spradley & Coker was not a fiduciary so long as it performed only ministerial duties. However, when a third-party administrator assumes discretionary authority, as occurred here when Spradley & Coker reversed its original decision that Mr. Elliott's hospitalization at Timber Ridge would not be covered by the plan, without consulting the plaintiffs, and in the face of Jefferson Pilot's "adamant" view that the charges would not be covered, it must be held to have acted as a fiduciary.

Second, ERISA requires that a fiduciary carry out its responsibilities "with the care, skill, prudence, and diligence under the circumstances then prevailing that a prudent man acting in a like capacity and familiar with such matters would use in the conduct of an enterprise of like character and with like aims." [ERISA] § 404(a)(1)(B). Spradley & Coker knew that Mr. Elliott's expenses were approaching $50,000, and that Harold Ives would expect Jefferson Pilot to reimburse the plan for claims paid on Mr. Elliott's behalf in excess of that deductible. Had Spradley & Coker disclosed the information, Harold Ives, as the plan sponsor and named administrator, could have filed a declaratory judgment action to determine its rights under the Jefferson Pilot policy, or it could have made other arrangements for Mr. Elliott's medical care. Spradley & Coker had an obligation to disclose the information to Harold Ives, and it violated its duty when it failed to do so.

. . .

6-4 QUESTIONS AND PROBLEMS

1. Did Spradley & Coker think it was a plan fiduciary? Would it have accepted the responsibility if asked?

2. How could Spradley & Coker have protected itself from being classed as a fiduciary?

3. Kay Co provides its employees with a self-insured comprehensive health plan. The plan is administered by Acme, a professional health care plan administrator. Acme negligently paid an expensive claim of an employee, Sarah, for a procedure not covered by the plan. Kay Co sued Acme for violating fiduciary obligations to the plan. Kay Co conceded that Acme, as plan administrator, had only ministerial duties. Kay Co insisted, however, that Acme exercised discretion when it improperly paid Sarah's claim. Acme did not agree that the claim was wrongly paid, but if it was, Acme argues that it is not a fiduciary and so cannot be sued under ERISA. What result?

Despite their administrative responsibilities, individuals and entities, who merely process plan claims and disburse funds, are not fiduciaries because they lack sufficient discretion. They are considered to have mere ministerial authority.

LAMPEN v. ALBERT TROSTEL & SONS EMPLOYEE WELFARE PLAN

832 F. Supp. 1287 (E.D. Wis. 1993)

REYNOLDS, SENIOR DISTRICT JUDGE.

At all times relevant to this case, plaintiff Jim Lampen was an hourly employee of Albert Trostel Packing, Ltd. ("Trostel Packing") and was a participant in defendant Albert Trostel & Sons' company employee welfare plan (the "Trostel Plan"), which is a self-funded employee health benefit trust organized and maintained under the Employee Retirement Income Security Act of 1974 ("ERISA"). Defendant Travelers Plan Administrators of Illinois, Inc. ("TPA"), is the claims administrator, an "independent contractor appointed by the Fiduciary to perform administrative services" pursuant to the claims administration agreement in effect at the time of the denial of benefits (the "Agreement"). The Agreement names Albert Trostel & Sons Co. (the "Trostel Company") as the plan administrator and the plan sponsor, which is also the fiduciary.

On November 3, 1991, Lampen suffered injuries in an automobile accident in Walworth County, Wisconsin. The sheriff's deputy who investigated the accident cited Lampen for inattentive driving in violation of Walworth County Ordinance No. 346.89(1). The deputy did not cite Lampen for driving while intoxicated; however Lampen's records from his hospitalization after the accident indicated a blood alcohol level of.2 percent.

The Trostel Plan in effect at the time of the accident excluded payment for health claims resulting from "*the commission of an act of crime.*" (emphasis added). The plan does not define what constitutes a crime. Ms. Lisa Myers, the TPA employee who handled the plaintiff's claim, denied benefits after seeing the hospital records indicating a blood alcohol concentration above Wisconsin's legal limit for driving an automobile, because she concluded that the plaintiff was injured during the commission of a crime. In order to do so, Myers relied on Wisconsin law, which prohibits driving a motor vehicle with a blood alcohol level of.1 percent or higher. She also relied on one or more telephone conversations with the controller for the Trostel Company, whose duty it is to oversee the administration of the Trostel Plan and who told her that anything that was not considered to be legal would not be covered under the plan.

. . .

Ms. Myers' initial and final denial of Mr. Lampen's claim for benefits was not subjected to any further review. However, under the Agreement, the plan administrator (the Trostel Company) possesses the "ultimate authority to decide all questions of eligibility . . . for the payment of benefits to Participants under the Plan." Further, the employer or trustee has "absolute authority with respect to the control, management, investment, disposition or utilization of Plan assets," but may instruct the TPA as claims administrator to "utilize Plan assets in any manner the Employer and Trustee deem proper." The Agreement authorizes the TPA to "do all acts necessary and proper to carry out" its enumerated function. The TPA adjusts and settles all claims for benefits "in accordance with the terms and conditions of the Plan" and subject to the ultimate decisional authority of the plan administrator.

Paragraph 4.01 of the Agreement specifically states that the TPA is only the administrative agent of the fiduciary and is not a fiduciary of the Trostel Plan in its own right . . . . Under the Agreement, the TPA is not the insurer or underwriter of the liability of the Trostel Company, nor does it have discretion regarding the control or management of Plan assets.

Both the TPA and the Plan have moved for summary judgment against Mr. Lampen, and Mr. Lampen has moved for summary judgment against each of the defendants for coverage of his medical expenses incurred as a result of the accident.

. . . The plaintiff has brought this action against the defendants for wrongful refusal of benefits pursuant to [ERISA] § 502(a)(1)(B) under which a participant or beneficiary may bring a civil action against the plan entity to recover benefits due or to enforce rights under the terms of his or her plan.

Under [ERISA] § 409 a participant or beneficiary may also sue fiduciaries to employee benefit plans for breaches of ERISA's fiduciary provisions. The plaintiff has argued that the TPA in this case acted as a plan fiduciary, that it breached its responsibilities when denying Lampen benefits, and that Lampen can recover personally for that breach. The TPA has moved for summary judgment stating that it is not a fiduciary and cannot therefore be sued, and that even if it were a fiduciary it would only be subject to a suit for breach of fiduciary duty brought on behalf of the plan and not by an individual seeking to recover a denied benefit. The court will address the TPA's summary judgment motion first.

Because the TPA is not the plan entity, it may not be sued under [ERISA] § 502(a)(1)(B). The claims against the TPA must be restricted to breach of fiduciary duty, and therefore this court must grant summary judgment for the TPA if it is not a fiduciary.

. . .

It is undisputed that TPA was the Trostel Plan Claims Administrator. The parties disagree, however, as to whether or not TPA is a fiduciary as defined in

ERISA, and therefore subject to suit. [ERISA] § 409(a). The TPA argues that it has not taken on a fiduciary role in this case as defined under ERISA and applied in this circuit. Even taking each of the plaintiff's assertions regarding the nature of the discretion exercised by the TPA as true, the governing document in this case — the plan — makes it abundantly clear that the TPA is bound to follow guidelines and cannot make its own.

Under ERISA, only those with discretionary authority are fiduciaries. A plan or claims administrator does not hold a fiduciary duty if its powers are merely "clerical, mechanical [and] ministerial." Seventh Circuit cases and the bulk of authority in this area indicate that when, as in this case, the claims administrator's decision-making authority falls only within the ambit of implementing rules established by another entity and is subject to the "ultimate decisional authority" of that entity, the claims administrator is not a fiduciary.

. . .

A plan administrator may be a fiduciary under ERISA if it exercises discretion over the plan, but it is not a fiduciary when merely following the guidelines of the plan. The Agreement authorizes the TPA to settle claims for benefits in accordance with the terms and conditions of the Trostel Plan and subject to the ultimate authority of the plan administrator. It expressly denies the TPA any discretion over the disposition of Plan assets, and states that the TPA is not liable for payment of claims, and that it is merely the administrative agent of the fiduciary and not the fiduciary. The plaintiff argues that the terms of the Trostel Plan should be ignored and that the actions of Lisa Myers show that the TPA had discretionary power and fiduciary duties. She made the initial denial of benefits, and also the final denial upon a request for review by the plaintiff. In doing so, however, she relied upon plan policy of denying benefits for injuries sustained during any act that was not considered to be legal. She was merely doing all that the TPA was allowed to do — implementing the policies of the plan, be they correct or not.

The TPA is not a fiduciary under the facts of this case. The TPA may only disburse benefits pursuant to the plan and does not have the discretion necessary to be a fiduciary, and is therefore not a correct party to this suit.

SAMARITAN HEALTH CENTER v. SIMPLICITY HEALTH CARE PLAN

459 F. Supp. 2d 786 (E.D. Wis. 2006)

Clevert, District Judge.

In October 1995, Mary Ann Bowe was admitted to plaintiff Samaritan Health Center's skilled nursing facility. Initially, defendants paid for Bowe's stay, but after about three weeks of care they denied further claims for payment. Samaritan, as assignee, brought this lawsuit under the Employee Retirement Income Security Act (ERISA) to recover welfare benefits allegedly owed to Bowe . . . .

* * *

UNDISPUTED FACTS

Simplicity established a welfare benefit plan, subject to ERISA, which provided medical benefits as well as prescription drug, dental, vision, and sickness and accident benefits. The plan was named "The Simplicity Health Care Plan." All benefits under the Plan were "self-funded and paid directly from the general assets of the plan sponsor."

Simplicity was the named "Plan Sponsor" and "Plan Administrator" in the "Medical Plan Document" dated January 1, 1994. The Medical Plan Document defined the term "Plan Administrator" as follows:

> Simplicity Manufacturing, Inc. is the named fiduciary of the plan, and is the Plan Administrator with the authority to control and manage the operation and administration of the plan . . .

Simplicity "engaged the services of certain organizations to provide claims administration services." First Health was a named third-party claims administrator in the Medical Plan Document. The Medical Plan Document defined "Claims Administrator" as follows:

> The *claims administrator* for the plan is First Health Strategies, Inc., the organization retained by the *plan administrator* to provide claims administration services to the plan. Although claims determinations will routinely be performed by the *claims administrator*, the *plan administrator* retains ultimate authority to interpret plan terms and make determinations regarding eligibility and benefits.

* * *

Simplicity, as plan sponsor and administrator of the Plan, and First Health entered into a Master Services Agreement (MSA), effective from January 1, 1996, to December 31, 1999. The MSA provided that First Health was to perform its services "in accordance with the terms of the Plan." It stated further:

> FIRST HEALTH is engaged to perform the services under this Agreement as an independent contractor and not as a fiduciary of the Plan or as an employee or agent of [Simplicity]. FIRST HEALTH shall have no final discretionary authority or control over the management or disposition of Plan assets, and no authority over or responsibilities for Plan administration. Because FIRST HEALTH is neither the Plan Sponsor or Administrator, nor a provider of health care services to Plan participants or beneficiaries (collectively "claimants"), FIRST HEALTH shall have no responsibility for: (a) any funding of Plan benefits . . .

* * *

The MSA's Services and Fees Exhibit provided that First Health was to conduct the claims review and appeals procedures "in accordance with Plan provisions" and that First Health was to advise the plan administrator, i.e., Simplicity, of all appeals of denied claims for the plan administrator to make the final benefits determinations . . .

* * *

MOTION FOR SUMMARY JUDGMENT AGAINST SAMARITAN

Against Samaritan's claim for payment of benefits under ERISA § 502(a)(1)(B), First Health argues that it is not a proper party defendant. According to First Health, Samaritan may sue the Plan and possibly the employer, but not a third-party claims administrator.

* * *

First Health argues in its initial brief that because it is not the Plan it cannot be sued for ERISA benefits, citing *Jass, Riordan v. Commonwealth Edison Co.*, 128 F.3d 549 (7th Cir. 1997), and *Lampen v. Albert Trostel & Sons Co. Employee*

Welfare Plan, 832 F. Supp. 1287 (E.D. Wis. 1993). Those cases do suggest that a plan is the only suable entity . . .

However, *Jass* and *Riordan* do not provide the bright-line rule First Health desires. Notwithstanding the *Jass* language quoted above, the Seventh Circuit has not mandated that the plan *alone* can be sued . . .

. . . The Seventh Circuit noted that the proposition that the plan alone can be sued "is much less firmly established than the defendants would have us believe." *Mein v. Carus Corp.*, 241 F.3d 581, 584 (7th Cir. 2001). The court found that when a plan and employing company are "closely intertwined," the employer may be sued instead of or in addition to the plan . . .

* * *

In *Penrose v. Hartford Life & Accident Insurance Co.*, No. 02-C-2541, 2003 W L 21801214, *3 (N.D. Ill. Aug. 4, 2003), District Judge Lefkow commented that the "*Jass* dictum is no longer good law if it ever was." She ruled that an insurer was a proper defendant in an ERISA benefits lawsuit where the identity of the plan was unclear and the insurer administered the plan, was the final decision-maker regarding benefits, and paid for benefits. Judge Lefkow noted that the Congressional purpose behind § 502(a)(1)(B) was that a party legally responsible for paying benefits governed by ERISA can be sued to pay for them. Therefore, the key to whether First Health may be sued in this case is not simply whether First Health is a third-party claims administrator, but whether it is "closely intertwined" or interchangeable with the Plan and whether it controls benefits determinations and payments.

A review of the Medical Plan Document shows that First Health cannot be sued for benefits under the Plan. Simplicity, not First Health, was the named Plan Sponsor and Plan Administrator and was given the authority to control administration of the plan. Although as claims administrator First Health did make routine benefits determinations, the Medical Plan Document stated that "the *plan administrator* retains ultimate authority to interpret plan terms and make determinations regarding eligibility and benefits." Consequently, First Health's control over benefits determinations was circumscribed. Further, although appeals of benefit denials were to be mailed to First Health, nothing in the Medical Plan Document indicates that First Health rather than Simplicity decided the appeals.

Importantly, the plan was self-funded and benefits were to be "paid directly from the general assets of the plan sponsor," from Simplicity rather than First Health. Participants were directed to contact the Plan Administrator with any questions about the plan. Further, Simplicity was the designated agent for service of legal process.

* * *

Thus, although First Health may have made routine determinations regarding whether benefits would be paid, Simplicity, not First Health, paid benefits, retained ultimate authority regarding benefits determinations, and was the designated agent. First Health was not so "closely intertwined" or in control of the Plan such that it is interchangeable with the Plan for lawsuit purposes.

. . .

6-5 QUESTIONS AND PROBLEMS

1. In *samaritan Health,* why does the Court conclude that the plaintiff cannot sue First Health Strategies? Why was it important that the plan was self-funded and benefits were paid directly from the assets of the plan sponsor?

2. What arguments can be made to support the claim by Lampen that the third party administrator was a fiduciary?

3. How significant was it that the plan administrator contacted the controller of the employer to ask whether Lampen's injuries would be covered by the plan?

4. Is the term "crime" as used in the employee benefit plan self-defining?

5. Suppose Lampen was the victim of a drive-by shooting while attempting to buy cocaine on a street corner. The shooter admits to having aimed at the drug dealer, not Lampen. Should Lampen's medical bills be paid by the Trostel benefit plan?

6. While crossing the street to the post office to file his federal income tax return that falsely fails to report substantial income from his successful gambling spree in Las Vegas, Lampen is run over by a hit-and-run driver who is never found. The medics who come to aid Lampen place his federal income tax return in a mail box. Subsequently, Lampen is charged with the crime of filing a false federal income tax return. Can Lampen collect medical benefits from the Trostel benefit plan?

Plan participants frequently claim that insurance companies, health, life or disability providers, who administer welfare benefit are plan fiduciaries. Courts have not reached consensus on the fiduciary status of insurance companies that provide services to a plan. All courts agree that the question is whether the insurer has discretionary authority that would trigger the fiduciary provisions of ERISA § 3(21)(A). Department of Labor regulations state that an insurer is a fiduciary if it retains discretion to review denied claims. 29 C.F.R. § 2560.503-1(g). But an agent who merely passed on policy applications was not a fiduciary. *Johnston v. Paul Revere Life Insurance Co.*, 241 F.3d 623 (8th Cir. 2001). In *Pegram v. Herdrich*, 530 U.S. 211 (2000), the Court held that treatment decisions made by HMOs acting through its physician employees are not fiduciary acts under ERISA § 409(a). The Court found that the decisions made by the physicians were mixed treatment and eligibility decisions. Since such decisions are the essence of an HMO, the Court did not believe that Congress intended ERISA to subject decisions by HMO physicians to a federal fiduciary standard of review. The Court found that state medical malpractice laws were adequate and proper as the means of policing physician mixed treatment and eligibility decisions.

The definition of fiduciary in ERISA § 3(21)(A)(i) includes those who exercise "authority or control" over the "disposition of plan assets." The application of that section is the demonstrated in the following case.

CHAO v. DAY

436 F.3d 234 (D.C. Cir. 2006)

SENTELLE, CIRCUIT JUDGE.

The A & D Insurance Agency and its President, Brittian P. Day (collectively, "Day"), appeal the District Court's grant of summary judgment in favor of the Secretary of the Department of Labor, Elaine L. Chao (the "Secretary"), under the Employee Retirement Income Security Act of 1974. Day contends that he is not a "fiduciary" within the meaning of ERISA § 3(21)(A)(i), and thus not covered by the statute. We agree with the District Court and affirm.

I

The Secretary filed a complaint in the United States District Court for the District of Columbia against Day, alleging that he violated his fiduciary responsibilities through an illegal scheme to misappropriate insurance assets. *See* ERISA § 409 (imposing civil liability for the breach of a fiduciary duty); *id.* § 502(a)(2) (empowering the Secretary of Labor to bring enforcement actions for the breach of a fiduciary duty). Specifically, the Secretary alleged that Day accepted hundreds of thousands of dollars from twenty-nine ERISA-covered employee benefit plans for the purpose of purchasing insurance for the plans. Under his brokerage scheme, Day sent invoices to the plans for various insurance policies, the plans paid the bills by sending checks to Day, and Day deposited the checks into his corporate account. Instead of using the plans' checks to purchase insurance, however, Day kept the money and provided the plans with fake insurance policies.

Day filed a motion to dismiss the Secretary's complaint, arguing that he did not fall within ERISA's definition of a "fiduciary." The District Court denied Day's motion and held "Defendants, by using plan funds for personal use, plainly exercised 'control' over the 'disposition' of plan assets . . . . [T]he court finds that the factual circumstances of the present case bring Defendants within the reach of the ERISA statute." Thereafter, the Secretary filed a motion for summary judgment, along with a statement of material facts and numerous exhibits. In response, Day filed a memorandum in opposition to the Secretary's motion, but Day did not file a separate statement of material facts. Taking the Secretary's statement of facts as undisputed, the District Court granted the Secretary's motion for summary judgment and ordered Day to pay almost $1 million in damages. The only issue on appeal is whether Day is a "fiduciary" under ERISA.

II

Our analysis begins, as always, with the text of the statute. Where, as here, it is plain and unambiguous, our analysis ends with the text as well.

The relevant section of ERISA defines two classes of fiduciaries:

> a person is a fiduciary with respect to a plan to the extent he [(a)] exercises any discretionary authority or discretionary control respecting management of such plan *or* [(b)] exercises any authority or control respecting management or disposition of its assets.

ERISA § 3(21)(A)(i) (emphasis added). In the Secretary's view, Day falls within the scope of the second clause because he exercised "authority or control" over the "disposition of [the plans'] assets." In response, Day argues that fiduciaries under both the first and second clauses-hereinafter referenced as the "discretionary" and "disposition" clauses, respectively-require some element of *discretionary* "authority or control." Day contends he was simply an insurance salesman, and he did not exercise any discretion over the plans' assets-he was under strict instructions to use the plans' funds to purchase insurance coverage for the plans' members. Therefore, Day concludes, he cannot qualify as a "fiduciary" under ERISA.

We reject Day's interpretation of § 3(21)(A)(i) because it does violence to the statutory text. The plain language of that text connects the two classes of "fiduciaries" with the disjunctive "or"-*not* the conjunctive "and." Congress plainly framed § 3(21)(A)(i) in the *alternative*, and it further bifurcated the subsection with the parallel inclusion of the verb "exercises" at the beginning of both the discretionary and disposition clauses. We therefore cannot commingle the textually distinct provisions of the two clauses.

Our conclusion is further buttressed by the structure of the statute. The "discretion" requirement-which is repeated twice in the discretionary clause-is conspicuously omitted altogether from the disposition clause. Instead, in order to qualify as a "fiduciary" with respect to a plan's "assets," a person must simply exercise "*any* authority or control" over their management or disposition. § 3(21)(A)(i) (emphasis added) . . . Day points to nothing-in either ERISA or the caselaw interpreting it-to overcome this reluctance. Day undeniably had "authority or control" over the "disposition" of the plans' "assets." The plans sent to Day checks made payable to him. Day then deposited the plans' funds into his account. Day was obligated to "control" the "disposition" of those funds for paying the plans' insurance premiums. Instead, Day absconded with the funds. Because the disposition clause contains no "discretion" requirement, it is irrelevant whether Day exercised "discretion" in his thievery. "[A]ny authority or control" is enough.

Therefore, in light of ERISA's statutory text and structure, we conclude Day was a "fiduciary," regardless of whether he possessed "discretionary authority or discretionary control" over the disposition of the plans' assets. Our conclusion comports with the results reached by every Court of Appeals that has considered the issue. *See David P. Coldesina, D.D.S., P.C., Empl. Profit Sharing & Trust v. Estate of Simper*, 407 F.3d 1126, 1132-35 (10th Cir. 2005) (holding an accountant is a "fiduciary" under the disposition clause where he wrongfully disbursed the plans' funds); *Srein v. Frankford Trust Co.*, 323 F.3d 214, 220-22 (3d Cir. 2003) (holding a bank is a "fiduciary" under the disposition clause where it wrongfully disbursed the plans' funds); *LoPresti v. Terwilliger*, 126 F.3d 34, 40 (2d Cir. 1997) (holding that insurance premiums deducted from employees' paychecks and commingled with corporate assets were plan assets in accordance with Department of Labor regulations, *see* 29 C.F.R. § 2510.3-102(a), and therefore that president of employer corporation acted as a fiduciary when he failed to separate those assets for payment to the funds and instead used them to pay company creditors); *IT Corp. v. Gen. Am. Life Ins. Co.*, 107 F.3d 1415, 1421 (9th Cir. 1997) (holding a plan administrator is a "fiduciary" under the disposition clause where it wrongfully disbursed the plan's funds).

* * *

We hasten to emphasize the limited scope of today's holding. Our interpretation of the disposition clause does not-as Day fears-extend fiduciary status to every person who exercises "mere possession, or custody" over the plans' assets. Day was far more than a mere custodian; he was a broker who solicited, accepted, and then pilfered the plans' assets by reneging on his promise to purchase insurance for the plans' members. On the facts presented here, we hold simply that Day exercised sufficient "authority or control" over the "disposition" of the plans' assets to qualify as a "fiduciary" under the disposition clause.

III

For the reasons set forth above, the District Court's entry of summary judgment in favor of the Secretary is

Affirmed.

[4] Investment Advisors and Managers

ERISA § 3(21)(A)(ii).

The definition of fiduciary in ERISA § 3(21)(A) includes anyone who "renders investment advice for a fee or other compensation." A broker who merely places orders for the plan is not a fiduciary. 29 C.F.R. § 2510.3-21(d). Distinguishing between an investment advisor and a broker can prove difficult.

THOMAS, HEAD & GREISEN EMPLOYEES TRUST v. BUSTER

24 F.3d 1114 (9th Cir. 1994)

HUG, CIRCUIT JUDGE.

Thomas, Head & Greisen Employees Trust ("Trust") is an employee trust fund subject to the Employee Retirement Income Security Act ("ERISA"). The Trust was established by Thomas, Head & Griesen, a professional corporation of certified public accountants. Jack Buster developed a business relationship with the trustees of the Trust, Henry Head and Ronald Greisen ("Trustees"), whereby Buster would locate and investigate deed of trust notes for investment by the Trust. Buster earned a commission from the sale of these notes.

In 1983, Buster joined Terry Parks and formed a general partnership, Northern Financial. Northern Financial continued to provide investment services to the Trust, and the Trust continued to purchase notes secured by deeds of trust. During 1986, the Trust purchased four such notes from Northern Financial, referred to as the Bergin, Kern, Falkenstein and Smith notes. Subsequent to the purchase, the Trust discovered that Northern Financial had made numerous misrepresentations with respect to each of those notes.

On February 24, 1989, the Trust filed suit in federal district court alleging losses in excess of $142,000 on the Bergin, Kern and Falkenstein notes . . . .

The primary issue in this appeal concerns Buster's status as a fiduciary within the meaning of ERISA. Buster challenges the district court's finding that he was a fiduciary and its ultimate conclusion that he was liable for breach of fiduciary duty . . . .

ERISA provides three ways in which one can acquire fiduciary status: (1) exercising discretionary authority or control over management of the plan or disposition of its assets; (2) rendering investment advice for a fee or other compensation; or (3) exercising discretionary authority in the administration of the plan. [ERISA] § 3(21)(A). The district court determined that Buster fell within the second definition of fiduciary, which states that a person acquires such status if "he renders investment advice for a fee or other compensation, direct or indirect, with respect to any moneys or other property of such plan, or has any authority or responsibility to do so." [ERISA] § 3(21)(A)(ii).

The Department of Labor issued regulations that further define "rendering investment advice" within the meaning of ERISA. The relevant provision states:

> (c) *Investment advice.* (1) A person shall be deemed to be rendering "investment advice" to an employee benefit plan, within the meaning of [ERISA] § 3(21)(A)(ii) only if:
>
> (i) Such person renders advice to the plan as to the value of securities or other property, or makes recommendation as to the advisability of investing in, purchasing, or selling securities or other property; and

> (ii) Such person either directly or indirectly . . . .
>
> . . .
>
> (B) Renders any advice . . . on a regular basis to the plan pursuant to a mutual agreement, arrangement or understanding, written or otherwise, between such person and the plan . . . that such services will serve as a primary basis for investment decisions with respect to plan assets, and that such person will render individualized investment advice to the plan based on the particular needs of the plan regarding such matters as, among other things, investment policies or strategy, overall portfolio composition, or diversification of plan investments. 29 C.F.R. § 2510.3-21(c)(1) (1992).

The district court made factual findings to support its conclusion that Buster was a fiduciary within the meaning of ERISA. Specifically, the court found that (1) Buster provided individualized investment advice; (2) the advice was given pursuant to a mutual understanding; (3) the advice was provided on a regular basis; (4) the advice pertained to the value of the property or consisted of recommendations as to the advisability of investing in certain property; and (5) the advice was rendered for a fee. All five factors are necessary to support a finding of fiduciary status. [ERISA] § 3(21)(A); 29 C.F.R. § 2510.3-21(c)(1)(i), 21(c)(1)(ii)(B).

Buster asserts that no evidence exists to support the district court's finding that he provided individualized investment advice. Rather, he argues that he was merely selling a product to the Trust. We disagree.

. . . The evidence presented at trial established that Buster engaged in regular meetings with the Trustees, during which they discussed investment strategies, the need for diversification, and the criteria used by Buster to determine which investments were suitable for the Trust.

Buster was providing investment advice to sophisticated customers, but this does not affect the finding that he was rendering individualized investment advice nonetheless. Moreover, Buster's assertion that he was unable to provide individualized investment advice because he had not been given the investment portfolio or trust documents similarly lacks merit. The relationship of the parties, which developed over the course of nine years, coupled with the evidence of regular meetings between Buster and the Trustees to discuss investment strategy, provided Buster with sufficient information about the Trust to enable him to render individualized investment advice.

. . .

Buster asserts that he never agreed to serve in a fiduciary capacity to the Trust as part of Northern Financial. The appellees acknowledge that there was not a written document memorializing their agreement, and that Buster was never added to the trust agreement as a fiduciary. Although a mutual agreement must be found to exist between the parties, the agreement need not be in writing nor must it specify that the party was to act as a fiduciary. Rather, the party need only agree to provide advice that is the primary basis for the Plan's investment decisions.

. . .

A finding that the investment advisor rendered advice on a "regular basis" is essential to a determination that a fiduciary relationship existed. We agree with the district court that the facts support a finding that Buster rendered investment advice to the Trust on a regular basis. The fact that the Trust purchased 61 deed of trust notes from Buster over a nine and one-half-year period, as a result of regular meetings, reflects the regularity of the advice.

. . .

Buster made recommendations as to the advisability of investing in certain deed of trust notes. Specifically, he provided information to the Trustees as to the value of various deed of trust notes by virtue of the yield calculations, mortgage analyses, and price information. He also provided descriptions of the property, and information pertaining to the payor's payment history and the payor's employment. We conclude that these details clearly relate to the value of the notes because they reflect the likelihood that the notes would be paid in full.

ERISA provides that a person is a fiduciary if "he renders investment advice for a fee or other compensation, direct or indirect." [ERISA] § 3(21)(A)(ii). Buster typically received a 10 percent commission on the sale of deed of trust notes to the Trust. On the particular notes at issue in the present case, Buster purchased various deed of trust notes, and subsequently resold them to the Trust at a higher price. Thus, Buster's compensation amounted to the difference between the amount at which he purchased the deed of trust notes, and the price at which he was able to resell them to the Trust. Buster asserts that this compensation is not a fee for investment advice, but rather represents the profit earned by a salesperson for the sale of his product. We disagree. The commission earned on the sales and the profit earned by the spread represent "fees or other compensation" for the rendering of investment advice. The court's conclusion is not clearly erroneous.

Our review of the five requisite elements leads us to conclude that Buster rendered individualized investment advice for a fee within the meaning of ERISA. We find that the existence of a fiduciary relationship in the present case is not affected by the fact that deed of trust notes were bought by Buster, and subsequently resold to the Trust. In serving as an investment adviser to the Trust for a nine and one-half-year period, Buster operated as a fiduciary. This status carries with it the responsibility to act in the best interest of the client at all times, and to serve with scrupulous good faith. Buster's conduct in this case clearly violated this standard, regardless of how the various transactions were structured. We will not permit a fiduciary to avoid his responsibilities merely by structuring a financial transaction so as to achieve that goal. The district court's conclusion that Buster served the Trust as a fiduciary was proper.

The Department of Labor promulgated the regulation at issue in *Thomas, Head & Greisin* more than thirty-five years ago when defined benefit plans were the most common type of retirement plan and plan sponsors typically hired a professional investment manager to decide how to invest plan assets. As the retirement plan world has shifted toward self-directed 401(k) plans, where individual plan participants are responsible for making investment decisions, plan investment services have changed dramatically. The types of products and services available to investors have increased greatly and become much more complex. As a result, in October 2010, the Department of Labor issued a proposed regulation setting forth a new, broader interpretation of fiduciary under ERISA § 3(21)(A)(ii). The proposed regulation met with a great deal of public resistance so the Department of Labor withdrew it in September 2011. The Department of Labor was expected to re-propose a revised version of the regulation in early 2012.

6-6 QUESTIONS AND PROBLEMS

1. Rho Corp. adopted a defined contribution pension plan and hired ABX Inc., an insurance company, to administer it. Under the plan, Rho Corp. deposits an amount equal to five percent of each employee's wages with ABX Inc. who accepts the funds, credits the amounts to each employee's account, and administers the plan. Upon the employee's retirement, ABX Inc. will supply him or her with a lifetime annuity, with the value of the annuity depending upon the value in the plan participant's account at the time of retirement. ABX Inc. commingles the Rho plan funds with funds in ABX's general account, and uses its investment expertise to seek a maximum return on the funds. ABX regularly credits each individual account with interest reflecting the return from its general commingled investment account. The three factors affecting the amount of benefits a participant will receive at retirement are the amount of the contributions to the retiree's account, the amount of return credited to the account from the commingled investment account, and the price at which the accumulated funds in the account are converted into an annuity at retirement. Is ABX Inc. a plan fiduciary?

2. Phi Inc. sponsors a defined benefit plan. The plan fiduciaries are three corporate officers appointed by the President of Phi Co. During the ten years the plan has been in existence, the fiduciaries have invested the plan assets in three mutual funds. Unhappy with the investment results, the fiduciaries hire Star Investment Advisors (SIA) to help the plan achieve better results. SIA agrees to advise the fiduciaries as to the percentage of assets invested in bonds and stocks and then to recruit six independent investment agents who will each control 1/6 of the plans assets. The agents will have authority to buy and sell stocks and bonds for the plan. SIA will not recommend or buy any particular stocks, but will advise the plan fiduciaries as to whether the investment agents are performing well or poorly and whether the fiduciaries should fire any investment agents and hire a replacement recommended by SIA will locate. Is SIA a plan fiduciary?

While an investment adviser is a fiduciary, a mutual fund operator is usually not. ERISA § 3(21)(B). The common practice of plans to invest pension assets in mutual funds does not make the operator of the fund a fiduciary to the plan, even though the mutual fund operator is making investment choices for the plan by virtue of selecting the stocks in which the mutual fund invests. The exclusion offered by ERISA § 3(21)(B) applies only to securities offered by investment companies registered under the Investment Company Act of 1940.

ERISA § 402(c)(3) permits the appointment of an investment manager(s) to manage the plan assets. The investment manager is defined as a fiduciary by ERISA § 3(38), and the manager must acknowledge "in writing that he is a fiduciary with respect to the plan." ERISA § 3(38)(C). The advantage of appointing an investment manager is found in ERISA § 405(d)(1), which relieves the trustee of liability for "the acts or omissions of such investment manager." Of course, the trustees must exercise prudent care in the selection of the investment manager.

[5] Other Professionals

Plans routinely employ accountants, actuaries, attorneys and various consultants. Under Department of Labor Regulations these professionals are not considered fiduciaries when performing "their usual professional functions" unless they have sufficient discretionary authority to bring them within the ERISA § 3(21)(A) definition of a fiduciary. *See* 29 C.F.R. § 2509.75-5, D-1. The stakes for professionals such as lawyers and accountants are high. If considered a fiduciary, they can be personally liable for the money damages to the pension trust attributable to their activities in their capacity as fiduciary. ERISA §§ 409, 502. As stated by one court, "imposing fiduciary status willy-nilly would make banks and law firms extremely wary of ERISA plans as customers and clients." *Chapman v. Klemick*, 3 F.3d 1508, 1511 (11th Cir. 1993). The power to distribute plan assets to plan participants upon severance of service, however, creates fiduciary status regardless of the degree of discretion. *Blatt v. Marshall & Lassman*, 812 F.2d 810 (2d Cir. 1987).

[6] Directed Trustees

ERISA § 403(a)(1).

ERISA § 403(a) requires that all assets of an employee benefit plan be held in trust by a trustee. The employer will normally appoint as a plan trustee(s), either a committee of company officers or employees, or an institutional trustee, typically a bank or insurance company, to manage the plan assets and make directed distributions to plan beneficiaries. While the thrust of ERISA is that the trustee will have discretionary control over the plan assets and thus qualify as a fiduciary, ERISA § 403(a)(1) permits the use of a trustee who does not have discretionary authority. Known as a "directed" or "custodial" trustee, such a trustee is not a fiduciary. Institutional entities such as banks and insurance companies often act as a nonfiduciary directed trustee who takes directions from the plan fiduciary, and whose directions in turn are subject to the fiduciary responsibilities and duties detailed in ERISA Part 4, §§ 401–414.

Some particularly plaintiff's attorneys, believe that the courts have been too willing to relieve directed trustees of any responsibility for their acts on the theory that they are merely agents of the plan and the fiduciary. Directions must be in accord with terms of the plan as required by ERISA § 403(a)(1)." Yet a directed trustee has no duty to inquire into the propriety of the fiduciary's directions absent actual knowledge that the directions violate the fiduciary's duties. As a practical matter, the directed trustee, who is hired by the fiduciary, has little incentive to uncover violations by the fiduciary of its obligations to the plan participants and beneficiaries.

On December 17, 2004, the Employee Benefits Security Administration (EBSA) published guidance regarding the Department of Labor's views on the responsibilities of directed trustees under the Employee Retirement Income Security Act of 1974 (ERISA). Among the points made in the bulletin:

- When a directed trustee knows or should know that a direction from a named fiduciary is not proper (*i.e.*, is not made in accordance with the terms of the plan or is contrary to ERISA), the directed trustee may not, consistent with its fiduciary responsibilities, follow the direction.
- The nature and scope of a directed trustee's fiduciary responsibility does not change merely because the directed trustee, in carrying out its duties, raises questions concerning whether a direction is "proper" or declines to follow a direction that the directed trustee does not believe is a proper direction.
- A directed trustee does not have an independent obligation to determine the prudence of every transaction. The directed trustee does not have an obligation to duplicate or second-guess the work of the plan fiduciaries that

have discretionary authority over the management of plan assets and does not have a direct obligation to determine the prudence of a transaction.

- If a directed trustee knows a named fiduciary is failing to discharge its obligations in accordance with ERISA's requirements, the directed trustee may not simply follow directions from the breaching fiduciary.

U.S. Department of Labor, Field Assistance Bulletin 2004-03 (Dec. 17, 2004).

IN RE WORLDCOM, INC. ERISA LITIGATION

354 F. Supp. 2d 423 (S.D.N.Y. 2005)

Cote, District Judge.

This Opinion addresses the circumstances in which a directed trustee of a 401(k) plan may be liable under the Employee Retirement Income Security Act of 1974, as amended for its failure to refuse on its own initiative to invest employee funds in the company's stock. Because plaintiffs have not shown that the trustee had non-public information regarding the company's stock that would warrant the trustee taking such an extraordinary action, and because the plaintiffs have not shown that the unusual circumstances that would otherwise require that action existed, the trustee's motion for summary judgment is granted.

BACKGROUND

Following the collapse of WorldCom, Inc. ("WorldCom"), this consolidated class action was brought by WorldCom employees who invested in WorldCom stock through the WorldCom 401(k) Salary Savings Plan (the "Plan"). Litigation in the aftermath of WorldCom's collapse revolves around accusations that the company disseminated materially false and misleading information about the company's financial health, using illegitimate accounting techniques in order to hide expenses and inflate reported earnings to meet increasingly unrealistic earnings projections. On June 25, 2002, WorldCom admitted that it had improperly treated over $3.8 billion in ordinary costs as capital expenditures, and consequently would have to restate its publicly-reported financial results for 2001 and the first quarter of 2002. WorldCom filed for bankruptcy on July 21, 2002. Criminal and civil litigation proliferated, with guilty pleas by WorldCom executives to violations of the securities laws, state government and congressional investigations, and numerous lawsuits against WorldCom officers, directors, its auditor, underwriting syndicates, and principal outside analyst.

. . .

On June 30, 2004, the named plaintiffs in the *ERISA Litigation* and all of the defendants except Merrill Lynch and Sullivan (the "Settling Defendants" and "Non-Settling Defendants," respectively) as well as the issuers of certain WorldCom insurance policies executed a Settlement Agreement that, *inter alia*, established a settlement fund of $47.15 million. . . .

The competing summary judgment motions address, *inter alia*, the following arguments by the parties. The plaintiffs contend that Merrill Lynch violated the fiduciary duty of prudence contained in Section 404(a) of ERISA. They seek to prove that Merrill Lynch was not a directed trustee, but owed a general duty of prudence with respect to Plan investments. In the alternative, they contend that as a directed trustee, Merrill Lynch breached its more limited fiduciary duty when it failed, based on publicly available information about WorldCom's financial difficulties, and its intimate knowledge of WorldCom's administration of the Plan, to suspend the acquisition of WorldCom common stock through the Plan by at least March 13, 2002, and failed to begin a liquidation of WorldCom holdings in the Plan by April 24, 2002.

Merrill Lynch argues that it was only a directed trustee, and as such, that it owed no fiduciary duty of prudence with respect to Plan investments. It posits that a directed trustee only has statutory duties and must always follow the investment instructions of plan participants and the administrator, except for limited circumstances not at issue here.

. . .

The Plan

As noted, this action is brought by and on behalf of participants in the Plan. Beginning in 2000, the Plan absorbed several predecessor plans, including the MCI Plan, the IDB Communications Group, Inc. 401(k) Savings and Retirement Plan, the Western Union International, Inc. 401(k) Plan for Collectively Bargained Employees, and the SkyTel Communications, Inc. Section 401(k) Employee Retirement Plan (together, the "Predecessor Plans").

The Plan gave participants the opportunity to choose to invest their account balances in a number of different funds, including a collective trust, a mortgage-backed securities fund, a bond fund, various equity funds, and one or more funds invested in WorldCom stock. Under the terms of the Plan, "[c]ontributions will be invested by the Trustee *pursuant to written direction from Participants*, each of whom has the right to choose among the investment alternatives selected by the Investment Fiduciary." Plan § 9.02. The Plan was funded by payroll contributions from employees and matching contributions from WorldCom in the form of cash. Participants were told through the Plan's Summary Plan Descriptions that investment decisions were up to them, and encouraged them to "learn as much as [they] can about the investment choices and consult [their] professional advisors, such as [their] accountant, financial consultant or attorney." Enrollment brochures accompanying the Plan nevertheless dispensed basic investment advice, such as the suggestion that "[o]ne way to balance risk and reward is to diversify your funds, or allocate your assets."

WorldCom was the sponsor of the Plan, the Plan Administrator, and the Investment Fiduciary. Plan §§ 1.02 & 1.32. Because the Plan designated the Plan Administrator and the Investment Fiduciary as "named fiduciaries," WorldCom could give directions to a directed trustee under ERISA. While WorldCom had the power to appoint others to carry out the roles of Administrator and Investment Fiduciary, it never did so.

As the named fiduciary, WorldCom had the authority to delegate its fiduciary responsibilities and to rely upon information or analysis provided by persons performing ministerial functions under the Plan. It was WorldCom's responsibility to choose the menu of investment options available for its employees' investments in the Plan. . . .

The Trust Agreement

On October 10, 1994, Merrill Lynch and LDDS Communications, Inc., which later became WorldCom, executed a Trust Agreement ("Agreement") in order to implement a 401(k) Salary Savings Plan. The Agreement provides that the

"Named Investment Fiduciary" and the "Named Administrative Fiduciary" are the same as those identified in the Plan, *i.e.*, WorldCom. The Agreement provides that the Named Investment Fiduciary shall manage the investment of the trust fund except to the extent that such authority is delegated to a designated Investment Manager, or that the Plan provides for participant or beneficiary direction of the investment of assets. WorldCom never appointed an Investment Manager, although the Plan did provide for participant direction of the investment of the participant's assets, and required Merrill Lynch to follow those directions. In this context, the Agreement states:

> Except as required by ERISA, the Trustee *shall invest* the Trust Fund *as directed by the Named Investment Fiduciary*, an Investment Manager *or a Plan participant* or beneficiary, as the case may be, and the Trustee *shall have no discretionary control* over, nor any other discretion regarding, the investment or reinvestment of any asset of the Trust. *The Trustee may limit the categories of assets in which the Trust Fund may be invested.* (Emphasis supplied).

The Agreement also explicitly limits the liability of Merrill Lynch as Trustee, for instance, but excluding liability for following directions and for failing to act "in the absence of" directions. It also relieved Merrill Lynch of any obligation to review the investments. It provides:

> *Directions for the investment* or reinvestment of Trust assets . . . from the Employer, the Named Investment Fiduciary, an Investment Manager or a Plan participant or beneficiary, as the case may be, *shall . . . be* communicated to and *implemented by . . . the Trustee . . . . The Trustee shall have no liability for* its or any other person's *following such directions or failing to act in the absence of such directions.* The Trustee shall have no liability for the acts or omissions of any person directing the investment or reinvestment of Trust Fund assets or making or failing to make any direction [regarding voting rights]. *Neither shall the Trustee have any duty or obligation to review any such investment or other direction,* act or omission or, except upon receipt of a proper direction, to invest or otherwise manage any asset of the Trust which is subject to the control of any such person. . . .

The Agreement also provides direction regarding Merrill Lynch's duties in carrying out its responsibilities as Trustee:

> *The Trustee shall have no duty to inquire whether directions* by the Employer, the Named Administrative Fiduciary, the Named Investment Fiduciary or any other person *conform to the Plan,* and the Trustee shall be fully protected in relying on any such direction communicated in accordance with procedures acceptable to the Trustee from any person who the Trustee reasonably believes is a proper person to give the direction. . . . (Emphasis supplied).

Merrill Lynch

As directed trustee for the Plan, Merrill Lynch staffed its client engagement with a financial advisor, a client relationship manager, a client service manager, and an investment strategist. Although the individuals fulfilling these roles changed over time, the client relationship manager for most of the Class Period was Thomas Eckert ("Eckert"), and the financial advisor was Michael Ryan ("Ryan"). Eckert was the primary liaison from Merrill Lynch to WorldCom on a day-to-day basis.

There is no dispute that in its role as directed trustee, Merrill Lynch assumed the burden of carrying out a number of administrative tasks, some of which included providing financial data and other information in order to assist WorldCom in its decisionmaking regarding the Plan. . . .

Merrill Lynch also prepared the narrative information provided to Plan participants in their enrollment materials that discussed the available investment options. Merrill Lynch helped WorldCom with its investment "mapping," which took place after each corporate acquisition, whereby investments in Predecessor Plans were converted into investments in the Plan. Additionally, at various points Merrill Lynch answered questions by WorldCom Plan officials about requests those officials had received from employees about offering other investment options.

At the direction of WorldCom, starting in September 2001, Merrill Lynch also provided a diversification service for Plan participants called "GoalManager." This enabled WorldCom to select up to five different portfolio models to offer to Plan participants based on personal risk tolerance levels ranging from "conservative" to "aggressive." WorldCom was responsible for selecting which funds offered in its Plan investment lineup would be included in which GoalManager model, and what percentage of each GoalManager model each of those mutual funds would represent. . . .

Merrill Lynch also gave Plan participants access to an internet website called "Benefits Online" that provided participants with, among other things, online access to their retirement accounts for inquiries, transactional activities such as transferring investments among the available options in the Plan, and investment educational materials. . . .

Merrill Lynch also answered questions from WorldCom officials regarding legal compliance issues. . . .

The Rise and Fall of WorldCom

There is no dispute that Merrill Lynch had, or could have had, the following public information at its disposal as the Class Period proceeded. WorldCom and MCI completed their corporate merger on September 14, 1998, when WorldCom's stock price closed at $47.75 per share. On June 21, 1999, WorldCom stock closed at its all-time high of $96.75 per share. When adjusted for a three-for-two stock split on December 20, 1999, the closing price of WorldCom stock as of June 21, 1999 was $62.

. . .

By March 2001, the economy had entered a downturn that was being labeled as a "recession" by many economists. This recession became more severe following the events of September 11, 2001. The recession was marked by significant declines in stock market indices, including the Nasdaq composite index that included WorldCom stock. . . .

By February 15, news articles began to report on an internal investigation being conducted by WorldCom into an order-booking scheme that may have boosted sales commissions in three of its branch offices. Some analyst reports continued to give reassuring opinions about WorldCom, . . .

On March 11, WorldCom announced that it had received a confidential request for the production of documents and information from the SEC with respect to certain aspects of its accounting. . . .

By the beginning of April, news reports focused on WorldCom's announcement of job cuts, as well as WorldCom stock's dip below the $5 per share value mark. On April 19, WorldCom revised downwards its earnings estimates and forecasts for the year 2002, although it reported that it still expected to earn an overall profit during the year, and anticipated revenues of $21–21.5 billion. The plaintiffs claim that in the five days following this announcement, at least eleven analysts downgraded their ratings of WorldCom stock. Among these reports, Quinton downgraded his rating of WorldCom stock to "reduce/sell" on April 22, 2002.

. . .

At the beginning of June, press reports concentrated on WorldCom's announcement of plans for another, more substantial, round of job cuts. On June 25, WorldCom announced that it would restate its 2001 and first quarter 2002 financial statements, because it had failed to comply with "Generally Accepted Accounting Principles" (GAAP). It announced that its reported EBITDA (earnings before interest, taxes, depreciation and amortization) for 2001 would be $6.34 billion, and for the first quarter 2002 would be $1.37 billion, representing a total reduction in EBITDA of almost $3.8 billion. That same day, WorldCom announced the termination of Sullivan's employment and the resignation of Myers. As a result of WorldCom's restatement, Nasdaq suspended the trading of WorldCom's stock and its MCI tracking stock. WorldCom filed for bankruptcy protection on July 21 in what some have reported as the largest bankruptcy in the history of the United States.

As of June 25, a large number of sophisticated institutional investors held substantial positions in WorldCom stock. For example, the California Public Employees Retirement System (CalPERS) held nearly 11 million shares of WorldCom stock at that time. The Ohio Public Employees Retirement System held almost 10 million shares of WorldCom stock at that time. Other public pension plans such as the California State Teachers Retirement System and the New York State Common Retirement Fund each held over 8 million shares of WorldCom stock at the end of June 2002.

. . .

DISCUSSION

Summary judgment may not be granted unless the submissions of the parties taken together "show that there is no genuine issue as to any material fact and that the moving party is entitled to a judgment as a matter of law." Rule 56(c), FED. R. CIV. P. The moving party bears the burden of demonstrating the absence of a material factual question, and in making this determination the court must view all facts in the light most favorable to the non-moving party. . . .

In addressing Merrill Lynch's summary judgment motion, there are essentially two issues to resolve. The first issue is whether Merrill Lynch was a directed trustee. Having answered that question in the affirmative, the second is the scope of Merrill Lynch's duties under ERISA as a directed trustee.

1. Merrill Lynch's Status as a Directed Trustee

Merrill Lynch contends that it was a directed trustee pursuant to ERISA § 403(a). The plaintiffs contend that Merrill Lynch was not a fiduciary because of its role as a directed trustee, but instead was simply an ERISA Plan fiduciary, apparently pursuant to ERISA § 3(21)(A)(i). The resolution of this dispute will affect the scope of Merrill Lynch's responsibilities under ERISA.

ERISA is a "comprehensive and reticulated statute" that governs employee benefit plans. *Mertens v. Hewitt Assocs.*, 508 U.S. 248 (1993) (citation omitted). ERISA is designed to protect employee pension and benefit plans by, among other things, "setting forth certain general fiduciary duties applicable to the management" of those plans. *Varity Corp. v. Howe*, 516 U.S. 489, 496 (1996).

ERISA allows a plan to designate what courts have labeled a "directed trustee." Section 403(a), the directed trustee provision ("Section 403(a)"), states in pertinent part,

> [A]ll assets of an employee benefit plan shall be held in trust by one or more trustees. . . . [T]he trustee . . . shall have exclusive authority and discretion to manage and control the assets of the plan, except to the extent that —
>
> (1) the plan expressly provides that the trustee . . . [is] subject to the direction of a named fiduciary who is not a trustee, in which case the *trustees shall be subject to proper directions* of such fiduciary which are made in accordance with the terms of the plan and *which are not contrary to this chapter* . . . . § 403(a) (emphasis supplied).

The Plan documents establish that Merrill Lynch was a directed trustee. WorldCom, as the Investment Fiduciary of the Plan, had the power and discretion to establish and change the options among which participants could choose to invest their 401(k) contributions. The Plan allows the Plan Administrator, again WorldCom, to appoint a Trustee who will invest contributions pursuant to participants' directions. WorldCom appointed Merrill Lynch as the Plan Trustee. Under the Agreement between WorldCom and Merrill Lynch, Merrill Lynch was required to invest funds as directed. Merrill Lynch was not obliged to review the soundness of any investment or direction it received, and it was explicitly relieved of liability for following directions. These undisputed facts are sufficient to establish that Merrill Lynch was a directed trustee under the terms of Section 403(a).

The plaintiffs argue that Merrill Lynch is not a directed trustee because Section 403(a) requires that trustees "shall be subject to proper directions" from a named fiduciary. The plaintiffs point out (1) that under the Plan, it was participants, and not WorldCom or another fiduciary, who gave Merrill Lynch directions regarding where to invest the 401(k) contributions, and (2) that two provisions of the Agreement can be read to give Merrill Lynch more discretion than Section 403(a) permits.

Even though it was the participants who gave Merrill Lynch specific instructions regarding the allocation of funds among 401(k) accounts, the Plan and Agreement required Merrill Lynch to follow WorldCom's instructions in every other material way. Among other things, it was WorldCom that chose which investment alternatives were available to Plan participants, and that gave Merrill Lynch the orders it needed to set up the accounts through which participants could invest in the alternatives selected by WorldCom. In hiring Merrill Lynch and executing the Agreement, WorldCom required Merrill Lynch to follow participants' directions when they made their choices among the investment options. Merrill Lynch was subject to WorldCom's directions in every aspect of the relationship that is relevant to an analysis under Section 403(a).

. . .

2. Fiduciary Duty of Directed Trustee To Act

The parties also dispute the standard that applies under ERISA to Merrill Lynch's obligations as a directed trustee. Merrill Lynch argues that a directed trustee is not a fiduciary with respect to investments in the Plan, and therefore does not owe a fiduciary duty of prudence with respect to those investments. It contends that Section 403(a) of ERISA creates statutory, not fiduciary duties for directed trustees. In the alternative, Merrill Lynch argues that if a directed trustee has a fiduciary duty with respect to the Plan's investments, the duty is only to inquire into the prudence of an investment fiduciary's direction to invest in a publicly traded stock if the trustee knows of non-public information that could significantly affect the value of the stock or public information of the impending dissolution of the company, or if it has reasonable grounds to question the trustworthiness of the fiduciary giving it directions. Under that standard, Merrill Lynch argues, it did not breach any fiduciary duty.

The plaintiffs dispute Merrill Lynch's contention that a directed trustee is not a fiduciary with respect to Plan investments, and they further dispute Merrill Lynch's description of the scope of a directed trustee's fiduciary duty. The plaintiffs argue that a directed trustee breaches its fiduciary duty if it fails to act when it knows or ought to know because of the existence of red flags (1) that the directions it receives from a named fiduciary are imprudent, disloyal, or otherwise violate ERISA, or (2) that a co-fiduciary is breaching its own fiduciary duty to a plan.

According to the plaintiffs, Merrill Lynch should have suspended the acquisitions of WorldCom common stock by March 13, 2002, insisted that WorldCom immediately commence a review of the prudence of the continued holding of such securities, and begun a liquidation of WorldCom securities by April 24. . . . The plaintiffs contend that as of those dates, Merrill Lynch was on notice that WorldCom, a named fiduciary, was the subject of an investigation of corporate wrongdoing; that there were "serious" questions about WorldCom's future prospects and accounting practices; that WorldCom, a "mammoth" corporation, was "unraveling" and in "serious" trouble; and that WorldCom was not reviewing the prudence of the Plan's investment in WorldCom securities. According to the plaintiffs each of these facts constituted red flags that required Merrill Lynch to act.

In ruling on Merrill Lynch's motion to dismiss, this Court held that a directed trustee is an ERISA fiduciary. *In re WorldCom, Inc. ERISA Litig.*, 263 F. Supp. 2d at 761–62. While a directed trustee is deprived of discretion to manage and control plan assets, it has responsibility over ERISA assets and is obliged to follow only those directions of a named fiduciary that are "proper" and not "contrary to" ERISA. Since that decision, an interpretive bulletin issued by the Department of Labor has advised that a "trustee, therefore, will, by definition, always be a 'fiduciary' under ERISA as a result of its authority or control over plan assets." U.S. Department of Labor, Field Assistance Bulletin 2004-03 (Dec. 17, 2004). In addition, other courts considering the issue have also held that directed trustees are ERISA fiduciaries. Nothing presented by Merrill Lynch on this motion suggests that the earlier ruling in this litigation, which is in any event the law of this case, should be revisited.

A directed trustee breaches its fiduciary duty when it breaches the "prudent man standard of care" that applies to all ERISA fiduciaries pursuant to Section 404(a). Since a person is a fiduciary to a plan only "to the extent" the person functions as a fiduciary, ERISA § 3(21)(A), the fiduciary obligations of directed trustees are circumscribed by the parameters of their duties pursuant to Section 403(a). A directed trustee must discharge its own duties in conformity with the prudent man standard of care, and avoid prohibited transactions. It may not comply with a direction from a named fiduciary that it knows or ought to know is violating that fiduciary's obligations to plan beneficiaries. And, it must attempt to remedy known breaches of duty by other plan fiduciaries. In this latter connection, every ERISA fiduciary, regardless of the parameters of its duties, is subject to the co-fiduciary liability provision of Section 405(a). . . .

In addition to any liability which he may have under any other provisions of this part, a fiduciary with respect to a plan shall be liable for a breach of fiduciary responsibility of another fiduciary with respect to the same plan in the following circumstances:

> (1) *if he participates knowingly in*, or knowingly undertakes to conceal, *an act or omission of such other fiduciary, knowing such act or omission is a breach*;
>
> (2) *if, by his failure to comply with section 1104(a)(1) of this title* [the prudent man standard of care] *in the administration of his specific responsibilities which give rise to his status as a fiduciary, he has enabled such other fiduciary to commit a breach*; or
>
> (3) *if he has knowledge of a breach by such other fiduciary, unless he makes reasonable efforts under the circumstances to remedy the breach.*

ERISA § 405(a) (emphasis supplied). Under this standard, a directed trustee may not follow the directions of a named fiduciary in circumstances where it has "knowledge" that such directions represent a breach of the named fiduciary's duties. As the Eighth Circuit has observed, "an ERISA trustee who deals with plan assets in accordance with proper directions of another fiduciary is not relieved of its fiduciary duties . . . to attempt to remedy known breaches of duty by other fiduciaries." *FirsTier Bank, N.A. v. Zeller*, 16 F.3d 907, 911 (8th Cir. 1994).

The Department of Labor recently addressed those circumstances in which a directed trustee has a duty to make an inquiry of a named fiduciary before investing plan assets as directed. *See* U.S. Department of Labor, *In the Context of Publicly Traded Securities, What Are the Fiduciary Responsibilities of a Directed Trustee?*, Field Assistance Bulletin 2004-03 (Dec. 17, 2004) ("Bulletin"). . . .

The Bulletin acknowledges that Section 403(a) of ERISA does not "eliminate the fiduciary status or duties that normally adhere to a trustee with responsibility over ERISA assets," but that by virtue of the limited responsibilities of directed trustees, their fiduciary duties are "significantly narrower than the duties generally ascribed to a discretionary trustee under common trust principles." The Bulletin endorses the proposition that a directed trustee's duty to act arises from its *knowledge*, stating that a directed trustee may not follow a direction that the trustee "knows or should know" is contrary to ERISA or the terms of an ERISA plan.

The Bulletin opines that the scope of a directed trustee's duty to determine the prudence of a particular investment is "significantly limited." The Bulletin posits two situations in which the duty of prudence may be breached: where the directed trustee has a duty to act based on possession of material non-public information, and based on possession of publicly available information.

In circumstances where a directed trustee possesses material non-public information that is necessary to evaluate the prudence of an investment decision,

> the directed trustee, prior to following a direction that would be affected by such information, *has a duty to inquire about the named fiduciary's knowledge and consideration of the information* with respect to the direction . . .

According to the Bulletin, when a directed trustee does not possess material non-public information, it will "*rarely* have an obligation under ERISA to question the prudence of a direction to purchase publicly traded securities at the market price solely on the basis of publicly available information." The Bulletin bases its conclusion on four well-settled principles. First, financial markets are assumed to be efficient, such that the prices of securities reflect all publicly available information and known risks. Second, in the case of employer securities, the securities laws impose substantial obligations and deterrence costs on the company, its officers, and its accountants to state their financial records accurately. Third, Section 404 of ERISA requires the instructing fiduciary to adhere to a stringent standard of care. Fourth, because stock prices "fluctuate as a matter of course, even a steep drop in a stock's price would not, in and of itself, indicate that a named fiduciary's direction to purchase or hold such stock is imprudent and, therefore, not a proper direction."

. . .

Having considered the prevailing law regarding the scope of an ERISA fiduciary's duties, the statutory imposition of such duties only "to the extent" a person functions as a fiduciary, ERISA § 3(21)(A), the limited discretion allowed "directed" trustees under Section 403(a), the standard of knowledge for co-fiduciary liability contained in Section 405(a), and the Department of Labor's careful and persuasive analysis in the Bulletin, including its thoughtful articulation of the policies underlying its analysis, it is possible to describe the standard that applies to trustees when they receive directions to invest in particular securities. The choice of investment options remains in the hands of the named investment fiduciary. A directed trustee has no duty to investigate the wisdom of those choices or any obligation to render advice regarding the choices.

. . . Knowledge that a company's fortunes are declining does not impose a duty of inquiry. For instance, a directed trustee's knowledge that a company's "stock price and profits were declining and that the company was undergoing a restructuring" is not sufficient to find a breach of a fiduciary duty where the trustee continued to invest plan funds in the company's stock as directed. . . .

Applying this standard, Merrill Lynch is entitled to summary judgment. The plaintiffs have not shown that there are questions of fact as to whether reliable public information existed that called into serious question the short-term viability of WorldCom as a going concern. Although WorldCom's financial fortunes appeared to be declining, particularly from January to June 2002, its decline was not generally out of step with the other large companies in its industry. Analyst recommendations to sell WorldCom securities do not represent reliable information regarding the company's viability. WorldCom's April 19, 2002 revised earnings announcement did not contain the type of fundamental perspective-shifting information that would disclose the impending collapse of the company. That kind of information did not appear until June 25 at the earliest, when the company made its stunning announcement of the need to restate its financial statements. . . .

In sum, the plaintiffs have not shown that this is one of those rare cases in which a directed trustee had a duty under ERISA to investigate whether the continued investment of Plan assets in company stock was imprudent. The publicly available information regarding WorldCom did not create at any time before June 25, 2002, a reliable picture of serious concerns regarding the short-term viability of WorldCom.

CONCLUSION

Merrill Lynch's summary judgment motion is granted.

D. FIDUCIARY OBLIGATIONS

Identification of the fiduciaries leads to the question: what are their duties? The answer is found in ERISA Part 4, Fiduciary Responsibility, which contains 14 sections relating to the obligations and responsibilities of plan fiduciaries. A glance at the titles of those sections reveals the extent of fiduciary responsibility and explains why many parties would prefer to avoid that designation.

[1] Fundamental Obligations

ERISA § 404(a).

The fundamental fiduciary obligations are listed in ERISA § 404(a). That section creates four basic statutory fiduciary obligations, similar to the common law obligations imposed on trustees of decedent's trusts, executors of wills, and directors of corporations. Under § 404(a), a fiduciary has:

(1) The duty to act for the exclusive benefit of the plan participants or beneficiaries, also known as the duty of loyalty. § 404(a)(1)(A)

(2) The duty to act with the care, skill, prudence and diligence of the prudent man. § 404(a)(1)(B)

(3) The duty to diversify the plan investments so as to minimize risks. § 404(a)(1)(C)

(4) The duty to act in accord with the plan "documents and instruments." § 404(a)(1)(D)

These fundamental fiduciary duties have their origin in the basic law of trusts. As stated in *Waller v. Blue Cross of California*, 32 F.3d 1337, 1344 (9th Cir. 1994):

> This interpretation of ERISA's fiduciary provisions comports fully with the common law of trusts, a body of law on which court[s] should draw when deciding ERISA cases. *Firestone Tire & Rubber Co. v. Bruch*, 489 U.S. 101, 110 (1989) ("ERISA's legislative history confirms that the Act's fiduciary responsibility provisions, [ERISA] §§ 401–414, 'codif[y] and mak[e] applicable to [ERISA] fiduciaries certain principles developed in the evolution of the law of trusts.' " (quoting H.R. Rep. No. 93-533, 11 (1973))); *Central States, Southeast & Southwest Areas Pension Fund v. Central Transport, Inc.*, 472 U.S. 559, 570, 105 (1985) ("[R]ather than explicitly enumerating all of the powers and duties of trustees and other fiduciaries, Congress invoked the common law of trusts to define the general scope of their authority and responsibility."). *See also Donovan v. Mazzola*, 716 F.2d 1226, 1231 (9th Cir. 1983) (explaining that "in enacting ERISA Congress made more exacting the requirements of the common law of trusts relating to employee benefit trust funds"). The common law bestows upon a trustee of a terminating trust all "such duties and powers as are appropriate for the winding up of the trust." 4 A. Scott & W. Fratcher, *The Law of Trusts* § 344 at 542 (4th ed. 1989). In performing these duties, the trustee remains obligated to act solely in the interest of the beneficiaries. *Restatement (Second) of Trusts*, § 170 (1959). In addition, "[t]he trustee has the duty to carry out this phase of the trust administration with reasonable care and prudence." G.G. Bogert & G.T. Bogert, *The Law of Trusts and Trustees* § 1010 at 450 (rev. 2d ed. 1983).

Although ERISA fiduciary obligations are similar to those under traditional trust law, acts by a fiduciary are only actionable if they violate the statute. ERISA fiduciary law, however, has been interpreted, illuminated, and even created by the courts who have been called upon to determine just what constitutes a violation of § 404 and the other ERISA sections that impose duties upon plan fiduciaries.

JAY CONISON, SUITS FOR BENEFITS UNDER ERISA

54 U. Pitt. L. Rev. 1, 9–14 (1992)

Fiduciary obligation under ERISA differs from conventional trustee obligation. Unlike a conventional trustee, an ERISA fiduciary is generally allocated only a part of the total responsibility for managing and administering the plan and its assets, and is a fiduciary only with respect to the areas of his managerial or administrative responsibility. ERISA makes its fiduciary duties second-order duties that regulate the manner in which a fiduciary is to carry out his primary or first-order duties relating, for example, to plan management or administration.

. . .

A recurring problem in this fiduciary structure is determining what conduct and responsibilities are part of plan management, plan administration, and plan asset management, and thus subject to ERISA's fiduciary rules. ERISA gives little express guidance.

. . .

The recognition that ERISA's fiduciary duties are owed to the plan, rather than to individual participants and beneficiaries, helps clarify some important features of the statute. It helps one to understand both the interrelationships and differences between suits for benefits and suits for breach of fiduciary duty. Section 502(a)(1)(B) provides for enforcement of a first-order duty owed to participants and beneficiaries. The remedy for a breach is an award of benefits due. Breach of this first-order duty is not itself a breach of fiduciary duty owed to the plan.

Breach of the duty to pay benefits, however, may be accompanied by a breach of fiduciary duty. If so, the appropriate remedy for the latter would be something very different from an individual award of benefits. For example, an administrator surely has a fiduciary obligation to the plan not to deny benefits that ought to be paid. Proper remedies for breach of this duty might include, in an appropriate case, compensation to the plan for litigation expenses incurred because of an improper denial. But there may be breaches of the fiduciary duties involved in benefit payment activity without there being a breach of the non-fiduciary duty to pay benefits. For example, a plan administrator surely is under a fiduciary obligation to the plan not to pay benefits that are not owed. Proper remedies for this breach may include reimbursement of the amount wrongfully paid and even, in extreme cases, removal of the fiduciary.

. . .

Thus, in the context of benefit administration, three varieties of duty, and three concomitant types of remedy, potentially are involved in any given case: (1) the duty owed to individual participants and beneficiaries to pay benefits, which is enforced through section 502(a)(1)(B); (2) the statutory fiduciary duties owed to the plan, which are enforced through sections 409(a) and 502(a)(2); and (3) other, non-statutory duties owed by fiduciaries (and others) to individual participants and beneficiaries, which are enforced under federal common law. These duties are distinct, and the principles governing them are not necessarily the same.

ERISA § 404(a)(1)(A) requires that a fiduciary must act "solely in the interest" of plan participants and beneficiaries and this duty of loyalty is not met by claims of "good faith." *Leigh v. Engle*, 727 F.2d 113, 124 (7th Cir. 1984). Yet this duty of loyalty provides less protection for the plan and its participants than might be expected, because the trustee's duty of loyalty to the plan is counterbalanced by the reality that the trustee is appointed by the employer who created the plan. If the trustee's actions seem too favorable to the plan participants and too expensive for the employer, the trustee can be replaced with a more accommodating trustee.

O'NEIL v. RETIREMENT PLAN FOR SALARIED EMPLOYEES OF RKO GENERAL, INC.

37 F.3d 55 (2d Cir. 1994)

ALTIMARI, CIRCUIT JUDGE.

. . .

Pension benefits under the RKO Plans were calculated based on a participant's pensionable "Earnings." The RKO Plans defined such "Earnings" as follows:

> "Earnings" means *the regular salary paid to a Participant by the Employer during the calendar year, excluding* severance pay or any special payments associated with termination of employment or retirement and contributions by the Employer to this or any other benefit plan and any imputed income due to any Employer provided group life insurance benefits, but *including* (A) overtime pay, (B) bonuses, so-called *Incentive or Additional Compensation paid to the Employee during the calendar year,* (C) amounts contributed by the Employer on behalf of a Participant to an employee pension plan pursuant to Section 401(k) of the Code, (D) in the case of Participants regularly employed outside of the United States of America, such Participant's regular salary paid by any subsidiary or affiliated company of RKO, whether or not an Employer, and (E) in the case of Participants regularly employed by the Employer who derive a substantial part or all of their total Earnings from commissions, the total amount of such commissions paid in the calendar year. (Emphasis added.)

The RKO Plans did not define "so-called Incentive or Additional Compensation," language that was added to the RKO Plans in 1963. The RKO Plans also provided that the Committee had the power "[t]o interpret the Plan, and to resolve ambiguities, inconsistencies and omissions, which findings shall be binding, final and conclusive."

In 1983, GenCorp adopted the SICP, a deferred compensation plan that tied the interests of its participants to the interests of GenCorp's shareholders. The purpose of the SICP was to reward key executives for contributing to the growth and profits of GenCorp. At the discretion of GenCorp's Board of Directors, certain executives of GenCorp and its subsidiaries, including RKO, would receive awards of "units" representing a quantity of GenCorp's publicly-traded stock. The awards had no value when conferred. Instead, their value was based on the difference between the fair market value of GenCorp's stock at the time of the award and when the award vested. As such, an award would have value only if GenCorp stock increased in value prior to vesting.

. . .

Prior to 1987, SICP payments were not included in "Earnings," although the Committee had never considered the issue. On September 24, 1987, the Committee, which at that point was composed entirely of RKO executives, addressed the issue for the first time and reached a consensus that SICP payments were incentive compensation includible in "Earnings." In reaching this conclusion, the Committee relied in part on advice from its outside ERISA counsel. The Committee, however, did not formally resolve the issue in the context of an actual claim; instead, the Committee decided to discuss the issue with GenCorp, which previously asserted that such payments were not "Earnings."

On November 30, 1987, shortly after the Committee expressed its view to GenCorp, the RKO Board of Directors replaced all of the members of the Committee with GenCorp personnel. According to the minutes of the November 30 meeting, the purpose of the change in Committee composition was to ensure oversight of employee benefits by GenCorp. Subsequently, Robert Johnson and Jeffrey Ruthizer, both RKO employees, formally requested that the Committee authorize the inclusion of SICP payments received during their employment in "Earnings."

The Committee denied Johnson's claim on June 30, 1988, and denied Ruthizer's claim on September 8, 1988. The minutes of the June 30 meeting set forth the factors upon which the Committee relied in making its determination, including the provisions of the RKO Plans and the intent, objective, history, and prior interpretations of the RKO Plans. On September 26, 1988, the Committee formally amended the definition of "Earnings" under the RKO Plans to expressly exclude payments received under the SICP.

We believe that the district court correctly regarded the plan language as ambiguous. First, "so-called Incentive or Additional Compensation" should be interpreted in light of the core definition of "Earnings," which was regular salary paid to a participant during the calendar year. Because of the deferred vesting and contingent valuation of SICP awards, it is not clear that such payments were regular salary. Second, unlike other terms under "Earnings," the phrase "so-called Incentive or Additional Compens ation" was capitalized, implying that it referred to a specific type of payment. As su ch, the SICP payments did not fall unambiguously within the scope of "Earnings." Therefore, we find that the district court correctly denied plaintiffs' motion for summary judgment.

Assuming that the relevant terms in the RKO Plans were ambiguous, plaintiffs next challenge the judgment of the district court upholding the Committee decision. The threshold issue is the appropriate standard of review applicable to the Committee decision. Courts should review a denial of benefits challenged under ERISA de novo, unless the plan itself grants the fiduciary discretion to construe the terms of the plan, in which event the court should apply the arbitrary and capricious standard.

Therefore, on appeal we must simply determine whether the Committee decision was arbitrary and capricious, not, as the district court determined, whether we would reach a different conclusion if considering the issue anew.

Plaintiffs' second argument is that the Committee's decision was contrary to ERISA's mandate that plan fiduciaries act "solely in the interest of the participants and beneficiaries," and for the "exclusive purpose of providing benefits to participants and their beneficiaries." [ERISA] § 404(a)(1). Plaintiffs contend that because the RKO Plans' liabilities were limited and the plans were comfortably overfunded, there was no reason to exclude the SICP payments from "Earnings." We disagree.

The fiduciary duty of loyalty imposed by ERISA is designed to ensure that fund assets are held and administered for the sole and exclusive benefit of plan participants. ERISA does not require, however, that a fiduciary resolve every issue of interpretation in favor of the plan beneficiaries. Indeed, a fiduciary must discharge its duties with respect to a plan in accordance with the documents and instruments governing the plan. In this case, the Committee decided that, based on the plan documents and extrinsic evidence, SICP payments were not "Earnings." The fact that the SICP participants would have preferred a contrary result does not render the Committee's action arbitrary and capricious.

6-7 QUESTIONS AND PROBLEMS

1. Is *O'Neil* consistent with ERISA § 404(a)(1), which states the fiduciary "shall discharge his duties with respect to a plan solely in the interest of the participants and beneficiaries" and IRC § 401(a)(2), which requires a qualifying pension trust to be for the "exclusive benefit" of the employees?

2. Is it reasonable or even possible for a fiduciary or trustee to act solely for the benefit of the plan and its participants and beneficiaries if the fiduciary or trustee is also a high-ranking officer or administrator of the employer?

3. Why does ERISA permit the appointment of a fiduciary who has a conflict of interest because obligations owed to the plan sponsor?

4. Should ERISA mandate independent fiduciaries who are not employees of the plan sponsor?

ERISA § 404(a)(1)(D) requires the fiduciary to act in accordance with the plan document. Woe unto the fiduciary who fails to do so.

BUSE v. VANGUARD GROUP

1996 U.S. Dist. Lexis 9152 (E.D. Pa. 1996)

DITTER, J.

The facts of this case are undisputed. Donald Buse played professional basketball in both the American Basketball Association and the National Basketball Association from 1972 until 1985. Around 1974, Robert R. Skinner began to serve as Buse's investment manager. Three years later Skinner established Donald R. Buse Enterprises, Inc., as a holding company for Buse's professional earnings. Buse was the president, treasurer, and only shareholder of Buse Enterprises. The incorporation papers designated Skinner's business address as the registered office of Buse Enterprises, and Skinner was named secretary of the corporation.

In 1978, Buse Enterprises established with Vanguard a Corporate Money Pension Plan. The plan application, executed on behalf of Buse Enterprises by Skinner as "Vice President & Secretary" of the corporation, identifies Buse as the sole participant and beneficiary of the plan.

In September of 1986, the parties amended their arrangement to create a qualified retirement program for Donald R. Buse Enterprises, Inc., identified in the plan documents as the employer and plan administrator, while Vanguard Fiduciary Trust Company was listed as plan trustee. The parties' purpose was to protect Buse's accumulated capital and provide for the reinvestment of income, while minimizing his taxes. Under the terms of the agreement, funds paid by Buse Enterprises to the trustee would be held for the exclusive purpose of providing benefits to plan "Participants and their Beneficiaries." Buse was named as the only participant and his wife and son the only beneficiaries. Buse and Skinner were each permitted to act on behalf of the plan administrator — Buse Enterprises.

On July 31, 1989, Skinner wrote Vanguard requesting that Vanguard "liquidate one-half" of the Buse Enterprises pension plan. The address Skinner used for Buse Enterprises was different than the address shown on Vanguard Fiduciary's records, the account number he used was incorrect, and the letterhead was typed rather than printed. Skinner signed himself as "Trustee & Plan Manager," titles he did not hold under the 1986 plan. A few days later, a Vanguard employee concluded that Skinner, as the agent of Buse Enterprises (the plan administrator), was authorized to take this action. Vanguard contacted Skinner making certain that Buse Enterprises was aware that the transaction might have possible tax consequences. In response, Skinner sent Vanguard a second letter, dated August 3, 1989, in which he indicated that he was aware "that there are penalties for a premature distribution" and he stated that Buse Enterprises was "planning to roll this into another qualified plan." In the letter, Skinner, again purporting to act on behalf of the plan administrator, Buse Enterprises, instructed Vanguard not to withhold any taxes in view of the fact that the disbursement was going to be placed in another qualified plan.

Following review of this second letter, "Vanguard processed the transaction as a withdrawal by the plan administrator." It issued a check on August 7, 1989, payable to "Donald R. Buse Enterprises, Inc." and "Robert R. Skinner, TR." Shortly after it issued the check, Vanguard sent Buse a confirmation statement. The statement was the first Buse had heard of the disbursement. Alarmed over why half of his retirement fund had just been withdrawn, Buse contacted Vanguard which informed him that the disbursement had been made at Skinner's request. Buse did not object to the transaction during this initial conversation with Vanguard.

Following his conversation with Vanguard, Buse contacted Skinner. Skinner told Buse that he had deposited Vanguard's check into an account for Buse Enterprises Pension Trust at Liquid Green Trust, a bank in Indianapolis. In response to Buse's request, Skinner sent Buse a deposit slip which confirmed that the funds were in Buse's Liquid Green account. Buse took no further action at that time.

In late August or early September of 1989, Skinner sent Buse a transaction summary for the Liquid Green account which indicated that a substantial portion of the money in that account had been withdrawn. Buse asked Skinner about these withdrawals. Skinner told Buse that the money was in a certificate of deposit.

Sometime in the spring of 1990, Skinner told Buse that the money withdrawn from the Liquid Green account was not invested in a certificate of deposit but was instead in a pension trust account at Ameritrust National Bank. Skinner told Buse that he needed the money in that account for some personal reasons. Buse permitted the money to stay in the Ameritrust account for up to two months in order "to help" Skinner.

In June of 1990, however, Buse learned that his money was not in the Ameritrust account. Skinner told Buse that the money that had been withdrawn from the Liquid Green account had actually been "loaned" to various individuals and entities.

On May 10, 1990, nine months after Vanguard had issued its check, Buse revoked Skinner's authority to act on behalf of the plan administrator. In June of 1994, Skinner was indicted in a criminal action. He pled guilty and agreed to make restitution to Buse for $300,000. To date, Buse has not been able to reclaim any of his money.

Buse's contention is simple and taken from a literal reading of the 1986 agreement. He asserts that Vanguard was a trustee and that under the terms of the trust it was only permitted to make payments to plan participants or their beneficiaries. Such payments could take the form of distributions or withdrawals; the payment Skinner requested and received was neither. The plan's terms did not authorize Skinner to "liquidate" any of the account. Moreover, the plan documents explicitly prohibited the trustee from permitting the plan's assets to inure to the employer's benefit, except under very limited circumstances that are not applicable here. Therefore, Vanguard breached its duty when it released the funds to Skinner even though he was purporting to act for Buse Enterprises. Finally, any payment that would inure to the benefit of the employer, here Buse Enterprises, Inc., would violate the Internal Revenue Code.

Vanguard does not argue that the disbursement was either a distribution or a withdrawal, or that it should not have permitted the funds to inure to the employer's benefit but instead focuses on section 5.1 of the Trust Agreement which provides that:

> Whenever the Trustee is permitted or required to act upon the instruction of the Plan Administrator . . . the Trustee shall be fully protected in all actions taken in good faith in reliance upon any instructions, directions, certifications and communications believed to be genuine and to have been signed or communicated by the proper person.

Vanguard contends that this language authorized it as trustee to follow Skinner's written instructions.

As it is clear that Skinner was not authorized to "liquidate" any of Buse's retirement fund, the question becomes whether section 5.1 of the trust agreement justifies Vanguard Fiduciary's reliance on Skinner's instructions. Put differently, did Vanguard act "in good faith" when, with little inquiry, it honored Skinner's unauthorized instruction contained in an error-laden letter, disregarded the trust agreement, and paid half the amount it held in trust to someone not authorized to receive that money. I find that it did not. Simply stated, a trustee does not act in good faith when it follows a fraudulent instruction that requires it to violate both its own trust agreement and the law. Section 5.1 of the trust agreement might conceivably be invoked where the plan administrator fraudulently instructed the trustee to pay a plan participant or beneficiary. However, the section has no application where the underlying instruction requires the trustee to violate every known concept of fiduciary duty.

6-8 QUESTIONS AND PROBLEMS

1. Should Vanguard have asked Buse for permission prior to making the distribution to Skinner? If it had, would that have changed the outcome of the case?

2. Suppose Skinner would have been able to repay the money to Buse. Would that have changed the outcome of the case?

3. Did the court hold Vanguard liable merely because it had "deep pockets," or was there a sound legal reason for doing so?

[2] Liability for Breaches by a Cofiduciary

ERISA § 405.

Fiduciaries must not only act with care, they must also be diligent about the acts of their cofiduciaries as ERISA § 405 makes fiduciaries potentially liable for breaches caused by a cofiduciary.

MAZUR v. GAUDET

826 F. Supp. 188 (E.D. La. 1992)

Clemen, District Judge. The New Orleans Sheet Metal Workers' "Health and Welfare" and "Pension and Retirement" Funds are administered by a board of trustees consisting of three employee trustees and three employer trustees. Defendant Stanley Gaudet was an employee trustee of the Funds from 1974 until 1989. In 1989, Gaudet pled guilty to embezzling $2,593,903.37 from the Funds before October, 1988. In April, 1991, Gaudet pled guilty to federal charges of theft and embezzlement.

As part of the embezzlement scheme, Gaudet would make withdrawals from the Funds' checking or EF Hutton accounts. Instead of purchasing CDs for the Funds with this money, Gaudet would take the check to a bank and obtain a certified check with which he would either purchase a CD or deposit the check into a bank account he maintained for himself. Gaudet would draft false safekeeping receipts to give to the Funds' administrator as a record of investments he supposedly made on behalf of the Funds.

Plaintiffs are current trustees of the Funds and, on behalf of the Union and the Funds, have sued Gaudet, the other trustees who served with Gaudet, Aetna (the trustees' insurer from October 1987 to October 1988), and ULICO (the trustees' insurer from December 1988 to December 1989) for the trustees' alleged breaches of fiduciary duty, and the trustees' accountant, John Chancellor, for malpractice. The trustee defendants filed third party claims against ULICO, who was an insurer of the trustees from December 1988 to December 1989. ULICO has filed a counter-claim for recision, reformation and cancellation of its insurance contract with the trustees.

Plaintiffs have moved for summary judgment, or, in the alternative, partial summary judgment on the issues of the trustees' liability, John Chancellor's liability and coverage under the ULICO policy. ULICO has moved for summary judgment dismissing all claims against it.

ERISA provides for the liability of fiduciaries for permitting a breach of fiduciary responsibility of another fiduciary in certain circumstances. [ERISA] § 405(a). Those circumstances are:

> (1) if he participates knowingly in, or knowingly undertakes to conceal, an act or omission of such other fiduciary, knowing such act or omission is a breach;
>
> (2) if, by his failure to comply with [ERISA] section 404(a)(1) in the administration of his specific responsibilities which give rise to his status as a fiduciary, he has enabled such other fiduciary to commit a breach; or
>
> (3) if he has knowledge of a breach by such other fiduciary, unless he makes reasonable efforts under the circumstances to remedy the breach. *Id.*

In this case, the plaintiffs have not alleged that any of the trustee defendants either participated in or knew about Gaudet's crimes. Thus, any liability on the part of the trustee defendants to be liable will be under subsection (2) above. [ERISA] § 405(a)(2).

Liability under [ERISA] § 405(a)(2), in turn, is based upon a breach of duty by the defendants themselves which enabled the co-fiduciary to commit a breach. For purposes of this case, that means that the defendant trustees, to be liable, would have had to have breached their fiduciary duties under [ERISA] § 404(a)(1), thus allowing Gaudet to embezzle funds. The relevant portions of [ERISA] § 404(a)(1) are §§ 404(a)(1)(B) and (D), which provide that "a fiduciary shall discharge his duties with respect to a plan solely in the interest of the participants and beneficiaries and —

> (B) with the care, skill, prudence, and diligence under the circumstances then prevailing that a prudent man acting in a like capacity and familiar with such matters would use in the conduct of an enterprise of a like character and with like aims, and
>
> (D) in accordance with the documents and instruments governing the plan insofar as such documents and instruments are consistent with the provisions of this title or title IV."

For purposes of plaintiffs' summary judgment motion, the question is whether, looking at the evidence in a light most favorable to the defendants, the evidence establishes that the defendant trustees breached their fiduciary duty to the beneficiaries, thus enabling Gaudet to commit his misdeeds.

Plaintiffs have established that the trustees had very little involvement in the management of the Funds. For example, none of the trustees never conducted an independent investigation to verify whether the Funds' assets were protected. There was also no procedure implemented in which to review checks the Fund had issued.

Plaintiffs also note that Section 5.1 of the trust document for each fund required two signatures on all instruments executed on behalf of the fund, one of an employer trustee and one of an employee trustee. It is undisputed that Gaudet used a signature stamp bearing the name of Charles Leysath, an employer trustee, even after Leysath had left the board, in violation of Section 5.1. There was no procedure in place to verify whether the two signature rule was being followed.

Four of the eight trustee defendants testified that they never saw an original certificate of deposit, an original safekeeping receipt, an original bond, original stock certificate nor any other documentation regarding investments. Another trustee defendant testified that he never saw an original certificate of deposit and never saw an original certificate of deposit safekeeping receipt between the late 1970s and 1988, when his term ended. Two defendants testified that they did nothing but attend the meetings. One defendant testified that, while he was on the board, Gaudet was the only one who took care of the Funds' investments. One trustee defendant, Mr. Holzer, was aware that Gaudet was managing the investments by himself, even though Gaudet had no authority to act alone. Holzer was also aware of a 1978 board resolution requiring an annual inspection of the Funds' securities and bank accounts, a practice which was later abandoned even though the resolution was never rescinded. Holzer testified that he wanted an independent money manager because he did not want Gaudet handling the investment transactions alone, but this was never done. The trustee defendants were also ignorant about the Pension and Retirement Fund's "401(h)" retirement plan, which plaintiffs allege was underfunded from 1985 through 1989. Seven of the trustee defendants testified that they had heard of the plan, but played no role in managing it. The eighth trustee defendant, Mr. Williams, had not even heard of it.

The defendants deny a number of these factual assertions in their opposition to plaintiffs' summary judgment motion, but do not present any evidence in support of these denials. The Court finds this practice bothersome. The defendants provide no affirmative evidence contradicting plaintiffs' assertions that the trustees did nothing personally to oversee Gaudet.

The only affirmative evidence presented by the defendants in support of the proposition that the trustees did satisfy their fiduciary duty is evidence indicating reliance upon experts. The defendants cite deposition excerpts indicating that the trustees, as individuals with little business or finance experience, relied on the annual audits performed by accountant John Chancellor and on the legal advice provided by attorney Philip Schuler. For example, employer trustee Charles Leysath testified that he thought that Chancellor's audits were "certified and verified," which indicated tha t "the CD's were actually in the bank, that they were actually there, that the money was there. And I [Leysath] accepted that." The defendants argue that there is a factual question as to whether this reliance upon Chancellor and Schuler constitutes satisfactory performance of the trustees' fiduciary duty.

Defendants are correct in their assertion that reliance upon experts is [relevant] . . . .

Plaintiffs note that reliance on experts cannot be a complete defense to a charge of imprudence. Plaintiffs also note that ERISA trustees have a duty to conduct their own independent investigation of the Funds' investments, even where experts have been consulted.

Although it is not a complete defense, the defendants are correct that reliance upon experts is a factor to be taken into consideration by the factfinder in making the factual determination of whether the trustees acted prudently. However, the existence of one (arguably) unanswered factual question does not mean that summary judgment is precluded. The question before the Court, then, is whether "a rational trier of fact," in light of all the evidence presented, could reasonably find that the trustees acted both prudently and in accordance with the rules of the Funds.

The defendants have taken the position that a rational factfinder could find that the trustees acted prudently, despite the fact that none of them ever played a significant role in managing the funds assets. Under § 404(a)(1)(B), an ERISA trustee is obligated to do more than simply attend the meetings and rely on the accountant's annual audits. The trustees have an independent duty to comply with ERISA. For purposes of ERISA § 404(a)(1)(B), "a pure heart and an empty head are not good enough." *Donovan v. Cunningham*, 716 F.2d 1455, 1467 (5th Cir. 1983). Furthermore, the trustees violated § 404(a)(1)(D) by not complying with Section 5.1 of the Fund rules which requires two signatures on all instruments executed on behalf of the Funds.

The Court is aware that summary judgment for the plaintiff in this context is unusual. However, courts have granted plaintiffs' summary judgment motions in exceptional ERISA fiduciary cases where the factfinder could not reasonably find that the trustees were prudent or had not violated the rules of the trust. Accordingly, plaintiffs' summary judgment motion on the issue of the trustees' liability must be granted.

ERISA § 410(a) states that "any provision in an agreement or instrument which purports to relieve a fiduciary from responsibility or liability for any responsibility, obligation, or duty under this part shall be void as against public policy." That section also states that if the plan purchases insurance to cover acts or omissions by a fiduciary, the insurer must have the right of recourse against the fiduciary (though the fiduciary is permitted to purchase insurance to cover any losses resulting from liability as a fiduciary). Moreover a fiduciary cannot exonerate itself from its fiduciary duties to the participants and beneficiaries of an ERISA plan, because the participant/employees were not signatories to any contract between the plan and its fiduciary or the plan and the employer. *IT Corporation v. General American Life Insurance Company*, 107 F.3d 1415 (9th Cir. 1997). The possible need for fiduciary insurance arises from ERISA § 409, which imposes personal liability upon a fiduciary to make good to all losses to the plan for any breach of the fiduciary obligations and responsibilities.

6-9 QUESTIONS AND PROBLEMS

1. In *Mazur*, the plaintiffs are looking to the trustees' insurer to pay the damages. Does trustee insurance create a moral hazard, i.e., the trustees are less diligent in fulfilling their duties?

2. The court concedes that granting summary judgment for the plaintiffs is unusual. What facts or actions by the defendants led the court to grant summary judgment?

3. What could the defendants have done to preclude liability?

4. Why should unsophisticated individuals be permitted to act as trustees? Should plans be required to at least hire a directed trustee with experience in financial affairs to manage the fund assets?

5. Delta Inc. sponsors defined contribution plan. The trustees are LaVern, the company Vice President of Personnel, and Pearl, the company Treasurer. Unbeknownst to LaVern, Pearl is the sister of Paul who acts as the accountant for the pension plan. Pearl steals $100,000 from the plan. Hoping that Pearl will pay back the money, Paul lies to LaVern and covers up the theft. Pearl never pays back the money. LaVern and Pearl are replaced as trustees. The new trustees sue LaVern under ERISA § 405(a)(2). Does the fact that Paul lied to LaVern relieve her of liability?

[3] Duty to Inform and Disclose Plan Amendments

Just what information a plan fiduciary must disclose to plan participants and beneficiaries has been frequently litigated. In response, the courts have developed a common law duty of disclosure that goes beyond the explicit language of ERISA.

KROHN v. HURON MEMORIAL HOSPITAL

173 F.3d 542 (6th Cir. 1999)

DAUGHTREY, CIRCUIT JUDGE.

PROCEDURAL AND FACTUAL BACKGROUND

The parties do not dispute the relevant facts. Margaret Krohn was employed as a registered nurse by Huron Memorial Hospital at the time of a March 1992 automobile accident that caused a closed-head injury and resulted in her permanent disability. At the time of Krohn's injury, she was eligible for both short-term and long-term disability benefits through Huron Memorial Hospital's disability policies. Under the short-term disability plan, a participant became eligible for benefits on the 15th day of an injury or illness in the amount of 60 percent of weekly earnings, up to a maximum of $200.00 per week, for up to 26 weeks. Under the long-term disability policy, a participant became eligible for benefits on the 180th day of an injury or illness in the amount of 60 percent of monthly earnings, up to a maximum of $3,000 per month. Based on Krohn's age at the time of the accident (42), she would have been entitled to disability benefits until age 65, for a total of 23 years.

When the long-term benefits first became available in 1988, some four years before Krohn's injury, Frances Neville, a personnel assistant at Huron Memorial, met individually with each nurse to provide them with a booklet regarding the long-term disability policy and orally explain the plan. Krohn later testified that she did not recall receiving the book, but conceded that it was "very possible" that she did receive it.

Within two weeks of Krohn's accident, her husband, James Krohn, had a conversation with Nancy Stanton, a personnel assistant at Huron Memorial Hospital, and inquired about the benefits to which his wife was entitled as a result of her injury and inability to work. According to Stanton's deposition testimony regarding that conversation, she

> . . . would have told him [Krohn] that — if she was going to be out for more than 14 days, that she would have been eligible for short-term disability, and that it would be 60 percent of her gross weekly wage up to a max of $200 for 26 weeks . . . . And I had told him that based on my handling of short-term disability, that employees that were involved in automobile accidents normally would opt for the car insurance, and that they normally paid a higher rate. I also told him in the abstract that you cannot collect any money from the short-term disabilities if you're collecting it from other companies.

At the conclusion of this meeting, Stanton gave James Krohn a form entitled Initial Application For Disability Benefits, which he took with him.

James Krohn completed and returned the application for disability benefits form that Stanton had given him. He filled in the "employee's statement" section and had his wife's physician complete the section for the "physician's statement." The doctor indicated on the form that he anticipated that Margaret Krohn could return to work within five months. Although James Krohn testified in deposition that he had no recollection of completing the application or returning it to Stanton, the parties nonetheless agree that it is his handwriting. Stanton testified that James Krohn returned the application form to her on or around April 8, 1992, and informed her at that time that Margaret Krohn had decided to collect the lost-wages benefits provided under her car insurance policy. Stanton said that she then placed the application, which had been completed except for the employer verification statement, in Krohn's employee file and did not submit the application form to Huron Memorial's long-term disability insurance provider, UNUM Life Insurance Company of America, as a claim for benefits.

Three years later, Krohn's benefits under her auto insurance policy expired, and she applied for the long-term disability benefits provided by UNUM. UNUM denied her claim as untimely, pointing out that its long-term disability policy required that notice of a claim be given to it or its authorized agents within 30 days of the occurrence of a loss covered by its policy, or as soon thereafter as reasonably possible. Under the terms of the UNUM policy, a claimant had to provide UNUM with proof of disability, including the occurrence, the character, and the extent of loss, within 90 days of the completion of the 180-day elimination period that had to elapse before benefits became payable. Failure to provide such proof within the 90-day time period "w[ould] not invalidate nor reduce any claim if it was not reasonably possible to give proof within such time, provided that proof [wa]s furnished as soon as reasonably possible and in no event later than one year from the time proof [wa]s otherwise required." Instructions provided by the insurer to the plan administrator instructed the plan administrator to complete and submit a long-term disability claim form "four to six weeks before the end of the employee's elimination period or earlier if possible."

Based on these provisions, UNUM denied Krohn's application for long-term disability benefits, insisting that the elimination period for an injury on March 21, 1992, would have been satisfied on September 17, 1992. Thus, because UNUM did not receive Krohn's application for benefits until April 28, 1995, UNUM concluded that the claim was not timely submitted under its policy.

This action was originally filed in state court against both UNUM and Huron Memorial Hospital. With Huron Memorial's consent, UNUM removed the suit to federal court, on the ground that plaintiff's claims were preempted by ERISA, and secured a grant of summary judgment in its favor, leaving Huron Memorial as the sole defendant. The district court also dismissed the plaintiff's state law claims.

Krohn and Huron Memorial then filed cross-motions for summary judgment on Krohn's ERISA breach-of-fiduciary-duty claim, in which she alleged that various acts and omissions by Huron Memorial caused her injury. The district court granted Huron Memorial's motion and entered summary judgment in its favor. From that order, Krohn now appeals.

DISCUSSION

The parties agree that the UNUM long-term disability policy qualifies as an employee welfare benefit plan under ERISA and that Huron Memorial was the plan administrator and ERISA fiduciary. Plaintiff Krohn raises two arguments on appeal. First, she contends that the district court erred in concluding that Huron Memorial did not breach its fiduciary duty under ERISA by failing to disclose the availability of long-term disability benefits to her spouse when a request for benefit information was made on her behalf. Second, she contends that the district court erred in holding that Huron Memorial did not breach its fiduciary duty by failing to notify UNUM, its long-term-disability insurer, of her claim for benefits after her husband completed and returned the form entitled Initial Application for Disability Benefits.

A. The Duty to Inform

ERISA imposes high standards of fiduciary duty upon administrators of an ERISA plan. *See* [ERISA] § 404(a)(1). As we have previously explained, ERISA's fiduciary duty encompasses three components. *See Berlin v. Michigan Bell Telephone Co.*, 858 F.2d 1154, 1162 (6th Cir. 1988). The first is a "duty of loyalty" which requires that "all decisions regarding an ERISA plan 'must be made with an eye single to the interests of the participants and beneficiaries.' " *Id.* (quoting *Donovan v. Bierwirth*, 680 F.2d 263, 271 (2d Cir. 1982)); *accord* [ERISA] § 404(a)(1) (requiring a plan fiduciary to "discharge his duties with respect to a plan solely in the interest of the participants and beneficiaries"). Second, ERISA imposes a "prudent person" fiduciary obligation, which is codified in the requirement that a plan fiduciary exercise his duties "with the care, skill, prudence, and diligence under the circumstances then prevailing that a prudent man [sic] acting in a like capacity and familiar with such matters would use in the conduct of an enterprise of like character and with like aims." [ERISA] § 404(a)(1)(B). The prudent person standard, in combination with the duty of loyalty, "imposes an unwavering duty on an ERISA trustee to make decisions with single-minded devotion to a plan's participants and beneficiaries and, in so doing, to act as a prudent person would act in a similar situation." *Berlin*, 858 F.2d at 1162 (quoting *Morse v. Stanley*, 732 F.2d 1139, 1145 (2d Cir. 1984)). Finally, ERISA requires that a fiduciary "act 'for the exclusive purpose' of providing benefits to plan beneficiaries." *Id.* (quoting *Donovan*, 680 F.2d at 271).

Although the United States Supreme Court has expressly declined to reach the question of whether ERISA imposes a duty on fiduciaries to disclose truthful information on their own initiative, or in response to employee inquiries, *see Varity Corp. v. Howe*, 516 U.S. 489, 506 (1996), we have previously held that "[a] fiduciary must give complete and accurate information in response to participants' questions . . . ." *Drennan v. General Motors Corp.*, 977 F.2d 246, 251 (6th Cir. 1992); *accord Electro-Mechanical Corp. v. Ogan*, 9 F.3d 445, 451 (6th Cir. 1993) ("ERISA imposes a duty upon fiduciaries to respond promptly and adequately to employee-initiated inquiries regarding the plan or any of its terms."). We have also held that "[m]isleading communications to plan participants 'regarding plan administration (for example, eligibility under a plan, the extent of benefits under a plan) will support a claim for breach of fiduciary duty.' " *Drennan*, 977 F.2d at 251 (quoting *Berlin*, 858 F.2d at 1163). Furthermore, a fiduciary breaches its duties by materially misleading plan participants, regardless of whether the fiduciary's statements or omissions were made negligently or intentionally. *See Berlin*, 858 F.2d at 1163–64. In the present context, a misrepresentation is material if there is a substantial likelihood that it would mislead a reasonable employee in making an adequately informed decision in pursuing disability benefits to which she may be entitled.

Many of our sister circuits have held, more specifically, that once an ERISA beneficiary has requested information from an ERISA fiduciary who is aware of the beneficiary's status and situation, the fiduciary has an obligation to convey complete and accurate information material to the beneficiary's circumstance, even if that requires conveying information about which the beneficiary did not specifically inquire. *See, e.g., Shea v. Esensten*, 107 F.3d 625, 629 (8th Cir. 1997) (health maintenance organization had fiduciary duty to disclose financial incentive structure intended to reward primary care physicians who minimized referrals to specialists); *Anweiler v. American Elec. Power Service Corp.*, 3 F.3d 986, 991 (7th Cir. 1993) (fiduciary duty to communicate material facts affecting interests of beneficiaries "exists when a beneficiary asks fiduciaries for information, and even when he or she does not"); *Eddy v. Colonial Life Ins. Co.*, 919 F.2d 747, 750 (D.C. Cir. 1990) ("At the request of a beneficiary (and in some circumstances upon his own initiative), a fiduciary must convey complete and correct material information to a beneficiary."). ERISA's fiduciary duty provisions incorporate the common law of trusts, which governed benefit plans before ERISA's enactment. *See Varity*, 516 U.S. at 496. As set out in the Restatement (Second) of Trusts, a trustee "is under a duty to communicate to the beneficiary material facts affecting the interest of the beneficiary which he knows the beneficiary does not know and which the beneficiary needs to know for his protection in dealing with a third person." Restatement (Second) of Trusts § 173, comment d (1959). Moreover, we have been admonished by the Supreme Court to interpret the trust-like fiduciary standards ERISA imposes "bearing in mind the special nature and purpose of employee benefit plans." *Varity*, 516 U.S. at 497. Accordingly, we agree with the conclusion of our sister circuits that the "duty to inform is a constant thread in the relationship between beneficiary and trustee; it entails not only a negative duty not to misinform, but also an affirmative duty to inform when the trustee knows that silence might be harmful." *Bixler v. Central Pa. Teamsters Health & Welfare Fund*, 12 F.3d 1292, 1300 (3d Cir. 1993).

These fiduciary duties to disclose and to inform govern the case before this court. First, Krohn claims that Huron Memorial, as a plan administrator, breached its fiduciary duty by failing to provide information about her entitlement to long-term disability benefits when her husband requested general information about the benefits to which she was entitled. Stanton concedes that she told plaintiff's husband only about short-term disability benefits. Huron Memorial argues that it was not required to provide information about long-term benefits for three reasons: (1) plaintiff did not specifically request information regarding long-term disability benefits; (2) all of the parties expected plaintiff to return to work before she would have become eligible for long-term disability benefits; and (3) Huron Memorial had already informed plaintiff of the availability of long-term disability benefits by providing her with a summary plan description and an employee handbook four years earlier. The district court agreed, focusing particularly on the fact that the physician's statement included on the application for disability benefits form indicated his expectation that the plaintiff would be able to return to work in less than five months, at which point she would not yet be entitled to long-term disability benefits because the 180-day elimination period would not have run. In reaching this conclusion, it is clear to us, the district court was not focusing on the "big picture" presented by this case. Other courts have employed broader vision in similar cases.

The facts in *Eddy*, for example, are analytically quite similar to those in the case at bar. There, the plaintiff faced termination of his benefits in a group health insurance plan just as he was approaching costly medical expenses resulting from his HIV-positive status. Eddy testified that when he called his insurer and inquired about his conversion rights under the policy, a representative of the insurer advised him that he had no rights under the policy to continue his coverage. Based on this representation, he did not apply for conversion and therefore lost his health insurance coverage. Witnesses for the insurer later testified that Eddy did have the right to "convert" his insurance coverage, which would have enabled him to retain his health and life insurance benefits. The district court held that Eddy had not demonstrated that he asked whether he could "convert" his coverage, to which he was entitled, as opposed to "continuing" his coverage, to which he was not entitled because his employer had canceled the group plan. The District of Columbia Circuit reversed, holding that "[r]egardless of the precision of his questions, once a beneficiary makes known his predicament, the fiduciary 'is under a duty to communicate . . . all material facts in connection with the transaction which the trustee knows or should know.'" *Eddy*, 919 F.2d at 751 (quoting Restatement (Second) of Trusts § 173, comment d (1959)).

Similarly, the Third Circuit in *Bixler* held that "while the beneficiary may, at times, bear a burden of informing the fiduciary of her material circumstance, the fiduciary's obligations will not be excused merely because she failed to comprehend or ask about a technical aspect of the plan." *Bixler*, 12 F.3d at 1300.

Like Eddy, Krohn's failure to specifically request information from Huron Memorial about long-term disability benefits did not relieve the hospital of its fiduciary duty to provide complete information about her disability insurance options. When James Krohn made the request for information, less than two weeks had elapsed since the plaintiff's car accident, and no one knew how long it would be before plaintiff could work again. Huron Memorial argues that it was unforeseeable that the plaintiff would need long-term disability benefits, because her physician later indicated on the application for disability benefits form — received by Huron Memorial after it had given Krohn's husband information about her benefits options — that he anticipated that plaintiff would be able to return to work within five months. We are simply unpersuaded by that argument. When James Huron first requested information about benefits, a complete prognosis had not been made, let alone an estimation about the duration of his wife's disability. Even when the hospital received the form on April 8, 1992, indicating that plaintiff would miss five months of work, they had merely an estimate made less than two weeks after a serious injury, which certainly did not preclude the possibility that plaintiff's injury would require six or more months of absenteeism from work.

Furthermore, two weeks later, on April 22, 1992, Krohn's physician provided Huron Memorial with an additional written statement indicating that Krohn would be unable to work for six months from that date, or until late October 1992, which was seven months after her initial injury. Based on this information, Huron Memorial knew that Krohn would probably be eligible for long-term disability benefits for at least one month. Perhaps anticipating her lengthy absence, the hospital hired a nurse to replace Krohn approximately two weeks after receiving the new prognosis. Thereafter, the plaintiff's prognosis got worse rather than better. Some seven months after Krohn's accident, her physician provided Huron Memorial with a statement indicating that the plaintiff would be unable to return to work for at least another year, or a total of 19 months after her accident. As it turned out, the plaintiff was so severely disabled that she was never able to resume work.

Our review of the record thus reveals that Huron Memorial received notice repeatedly that the plaintiff would be eligible for and would need long-term disability benefits. Furthermore, Huron Memorial knew that in order to secure her right to long-term disability benefits, Krohn was required by the UNUM policy to submit a claim within 30 days of the occurrence of a loss covered by its policy, or as soon thereafter as is reasonably possible, and to provide proof of disability within 90 days of September 17, 1992, the date on which the 180-day elimination period ended. A prudent fiduciary acting in the best interest of its beneficiary would have advised Krohn that failure to submit a claim and proof of loss to UNUM in a timely fashion would render her ineligible to receive long-term disability benefits.

Huron Memorial stresses its belief that the information Stanton conveyed to the plaintiff and her husband regarding the superiority of car insurance benefits was true. That argument is unpersuasive for two reasons. First, based on the fiduciary duties outlined above, the information provided by a fiduciary in response to a beneficiary's request for information need not be false to constitute a breach of fiduciary duty. Instead, Huron Memorial's failure to provide information about the availability of long-term benefits breached its duty to disclose and inform because it failed to "give complete and accurate information in response to participants' questions . . . ." *Drennan v. General Motors Corp.*, 977 F.2d 246, 251 (6th Cir. 1992). Second, it is clear, based on the facts before us, that Huron Memorial's statements regarding the general superiority of car insurance lost-wages benefits, as opposed to the disability benefits provided by Huron Memorial, were misleading, incomplete, and, for many potential beneficiaries such as Krohn, inaccurate. Although benefits available under the plaintiff's car insurance policy were ostensibly more generous than those provided by UNUM, her entitlement to lost-wage benefits under the auto policy terminated three years after her accident, whereas the UNUM benefits would have continued until she reached age 65 — some 23 years, based on her age at the time of the accident. The predicament in which plaintiff now finds herself, unable to work and without disability benefits, illustrates the short-coming of choosing her car insurance benefits over UNUM's long-term disability benefits.

In what we perceive to be its weakest argument, Huron Memorial contends that it had already informed plaintiff of the availability of long-term disability benefits by providing her with a summary plan description, an employee handbook, and an individual meeting with Frances Neville, who explained the long-term disability plan. True, we have previously held that an ERISA plan fiduciary may satisfy its obligation to provide employees with a comprehensive explanation of the contents of the plan by distributing to employees an explanatory booklet which adequately explains the plan and its terms. *See Electro-Mechanical Corp. v. Ogan*, 9 F.3d 445, 451 (6th Cir. 1993). However, in *Electro-Mechanical* we also noted that ERISA additionally "imposes a duty upon fiduciaries to respond promptly and adequately to employee-initiated inquiries regarding the plan or any of its terms." *Id.*; *see also Eddy*, 919 F.2d at 750 ("A fiduciary's duty, however, is not discharged simply by the issuance and dissemination of these [summary plan descriptions] and notices."). Hence, Sixth Circuit precedent is directly contrary to Huron Memorial's contention. Providing a summary plan description several years before the request for information does not excuse the hospital from its duty to respond fully and accurately to later inquiries regarding benefits. Indeed, it would have been preferable for Huron Memorial to refer the plaintiff to her summary plan description or employee handbook to find the answer to her questions, and to have given her an additional copy if she had lost her own, than to have undertaken to provide such information and to have done so in such a careless and incomplete manner. Instead, Huron Memorial did not mention to plaintiff or her husband that a thorough explanation of benefits could be found in those documents, even though her husband's questions revealed his, and perhaps the plaintiff's, lack of awareness of where to find Krohn's benefit information. Accordingly, we reject Huron Memorial's argument that provision of a summary plan description discharged or fulfilled its obligation to provide complete material information upon plaintiff's inquiry.

Moreover, we conclude that Stanton's communication with plaintiff's husband was a materially misleading response to his inquiry about benefits, in that there was a substantial likelihood that it would mislead a reasonable employee in the process of making an adequately informed decision regarding disability benefits to which she might be entitled. Significantly, Huron Memorial continued to breach its fiduciary duties to plaintiff by remaining silent in the face of subsequent notification that plaintiff would need and be eligible for long-term disability benefits. We conclude that a plan administrator has "an affirmative duty to inform when [it] knows that silence might be harmful." *Bixler*, 12 F.3d at 1300.

Had the hospital adequately informed plaintiff about the availability of long-term disability benefits through its insurer, it is likely that she would have chosen a different course of action. In fact, a review of the UNUM policy suggests that if Krohn had timely applied for UNUM's long-term disability benefits, she might have been able to receive the higher auto insurance lost-wage benefits for three years and then received the lower UNUM long-term disability benefits after the other benefits were no longer available. The UNUM policy states, although not clearly, that the amount to which a beneficiary is entitled under its policy, the "gross monthly benefit," is to be offset by any "other income benefits," which in this case undoubtedly would have included the plaintiff's auto insurance benefits. Thus, it appears that Krohn could have made a timely application for long-term benefits under UNUM's policy, received her benefits under the auto insurance policy for three years, which would have constituted an offset against any benefits to which she was entitled from UNUM, and then received benefits from UNUM after she was no longer entitled to car insurance benefits, until she reached 65 years of age. At the very least, if fully informed of her options, Krohn might have opted to forego three years' worth of the slightly higher benefits provided by her car insurance, knowing that there was a chance that her disability might extend more than three years from the date of her accident, in favor of the long-term benefits available under the UNUM policy. In either case, knowledgeable about Krohn's situation and armed with periodic updates about her disability status, Huron Memorial owed Krohn a duty to inform her — carefully, completely, and accurately — of the long-term disability benefits to which she was entitled through her employer, so that she could weigh her options and make informed decisions. This the hospital failed to do. We conclude, therefore, that the defendant is liable for the lost benefits that the plaintiff has sustained.

B. The Duty to File

Krohn also claims that Huron Memorial breached its fiduciary duty by failing to take action on her application for benefits form. The district court disagreed, holding that James Krohn's comment at the time he returned the form — to the effect that the plaintiff intended to file for benefits under her auto insurance policy rather than the hospital's medical policy — rendered his return of the form a nullity. Thus, the court concluded, Huron Memorial was under no duty to notify its long-term disability insurer that Krohn had submitted the form. We conclude that in making this call, the district court was plainly in error.

We first consider the provisions of the long-term disability policy issued by UNUM to Huron Memorial, which is the written instrument pursuant to which this employee benefit plan was established and maintained, as required by ERISA. *See* [ERISA] § 402(a)(1). The UNUM policy provides that the insurer must receive written notice of a claim within 30 days after the occurrence of a loss covered by the policy, at which time UNUM would furnish the client with forms for filing proof of loss. UNUM further instructed the plan administrator to file a completed long-term disability benefits claim form with UNUM at least four to six weeks before the end of the claimant's elimination period. Thus, under the terms of the plan, Huron Memorial was obligated to file plaintiff's application for benefits with UNUM without second-guessing her intentions in returning the form or her eligibility for benefits. In essence, Huron Memorial did not send plaintiff's application because it assumed that plaintiff would be ineligible for long-term benefits, given her decision to receive benefits from her auto insurer. As noted above, however, that assumption is irrelevant because, based on the language of UNUM's policy, it appears that any benefits received from another source, such as the plaintiff's car insurance, would simply reduce the UNUM plan benefits. In any event, it was not Huron Memorial's prerogative to make such an eligibility determination. The hospital's obligation was clear from the terms of the policy and as a matter of its fiduciary status.

Furthermore, in that fiduciary status, Huron Memorial had a duty either to send UNUM the application for benefits, which plaintiff's husband and physician had taken the time to complete and return, or to clarify the plaintiff's intentions in returning the form. Instead, the hospital carelessly assumed that the completion and return of the application form was meaningless and, therefore, rendered it meaningless in fact by failing to send it to UNUM. Huron Memorial's inaction was particularly egregious in light of its previous incomplete, misleading, and potentially erroneous response to James Krohn's request for information about his wife's disability benefits options. Had Huron Memorial taken the appropriately cautious approach by sending the plaintiff's application to UNUM, UNUM undoubtedly would have sent her forms for submitting proof of loss, which might have prompted her to submit such proof or, at least, to obtain further information from her employer or UNUM, which in turn might have remedied the inadequate information Huron Memorial had previously given her husband. For this reason, too, we find that the district court erred in granting summary judgment to the hospital.

CONCLUSION

ERISA imposes substantial duties upon fiduciaries of employee benefit plans, including the duty to respond fully and adequately to inquiries about employee benefits and to act in accordance with written plan instruments. We hold that Huron Memorial breached these duties by failing to provide plaintiff with pertinent information about the availability of long-term disability benefits and by failing to submit her application for disability benefits to its long-term disability insurer. We therefore REVERSE the order of the district court granting summary judgment to the defendant and REMAND the case to the district court to determine the extent of plaintiff's damages and to enter judgment in her behalf in that amount.

In light of *Varity*, courts have found false and misleading statements by a plan sponsor who is also a plan fiduciary to be grounds for suits by plan participants.

PFAHLER v. NATIONAL LATEX PRODUCTS COMPANY

517 F.3d 816 (6th Cir. 2007)

Before Guy, Rogers, and McKeage, Circuit Judges.

Plaintiffs are former employees of the National Latex Products Company ("NLP") and former participants in and beneficiaries of the National Latex Products Company Employee Welfare Benefit Plan ("Plan"). They brought suit under § 502(a)(2) and § 502(a)(3) of the Employee Retirement Income Security Act ("ERISA") against several parties after those parties allegedly breached fiduciary duties that they owed to the Plan. Among the parties named as defendants to the suit were NLP; Ross Gill, the president and Chief Executive Officer ("CEO") of NLP; Glass & Associates, a business consultant to NLP; and Jay AuWerter, an agent for Glass & Associates. . . .

The primary issues before this court are whether (1) NLP, Ross Gill, Glass & Associates, and AuWerter breached any fiduciary duties to the Plan and could consequently be held liable under §§ 502(a)(2) or (a)(3). . . .

We reverse because plaintiffs are permitted to seek relief from NLP, Ross Gill, Glass & Associates and AuWerter pursuant to § 502(a)(2). . . .

I.

NLP was a latex balloon and ball manufacturing company located in Ashland, Ohio. Members of the Gill family owned and operated NLP. Harry R. Gill, Jr. served as chairman of the board of directors; his wife, Patricia R. Gill, was a board member; and his son, H. Ross Gill III, was president, CEO, and also a board member.

NLP began to experience serious financial difficulties in the mid-1990s, and by December 1998 it was forced to seek outside financing from General Electric Capital Corporation ("GECC"), a lending company specializing in commercial loans. GECC provided NLP with a revolving credit account as well as outright loans, the proceeds of which were to be used for refinancing indebtedness, working capital, and other general business uses. In return, NLP granted GECC a security interest in all of its present and future assets and agreed to open a "lock box" account into which all of NLP's receivables were to be sent and held for repayment of the loans.

When it became evident that the financing arrangement was not solving NLP's financial problems, GECC requested that NLP retain a "turn around" consultant to assist with salvaging, or, if necessary, selling, the company. NLP and GECC selected Glass to fill this position, with AuWerter serving as Glass's primary on-site agent.

. . .

Upon assessing NLP's financial state, Glass and AuWerter, who took the title of NLP Executive Vice President, became increasingly involved in the management of NLP's day-to-day operations. . . .

Despite efforts to revitalize the company, Glass ultimately concluded that NLP was unlikely to rebound financially and should consequently be sold. The Gills agreed, and, on December 6, 1999, Pioneer National Latex, Inc. purchased NLP for $4.25 million in an asset-purchase sale. The proceeds of this sale were used to pay off the secured loan from GECC. All NLP employees were terminated at this time.

Until its sale, NLP sponsored a self-insured welfare benefit plan to provide health care benefits to its employees. The Plan was funded by both employee and employer contributions. NLP employees contributed to the Plan via deductions from their paychecks.

. . .

Great West Life & Annuity Insurance Company ("Great West") served as a third-party administrator for the Plan until September 1999. In this capacity, Great West was responsible for processing claims that were submitted by healthcare providers, paying those claims, and then seeking reimbursement for such payments from Plan assets. Effective September 1, 1999, Great West terminated its relationship with NLP due to NLP's alleged failure to fund the Plan. According to a subsequent letter sent by Great West, NLP was delinquent in its reimbursements in the amount of $162,273.

On September 22, 1999, AuWerter, writing under the title of Executive Vice President, sent a memorandum to NLP employees informing them that Stateline TPA had taken over as third-party administrator for the Plan. In the memorandum, AuWerter stated that "we have recently encountered difficulty getting our health claims paid through our carrier, Great West." AuWerter advised employees, however, that their health benefits would not be altered as a result of the switch to Stateline, writing "***your medical, prescription drug and dental benefits are not changing***" and that "all claims that have recently been submitted to Great West for payment, but have not been paid, ***will be paid*** once those claims have been resubmitted." [Ed. — emphasis in original.] AuWerter repeated these pledges in a September 30, 1999 memorandum to NLP employees, in which he wrote "[p]lease be assured that, although we are changing carriers, your group benefit plan coverage remains unchanged with the same entitlements. . . . Your weekly group benefit contribution that is deducted from your paycheck will remain the same."

On November 22, 1999, NLP transferred $230,091 into a trust account created by Stateline for the payment of claims. NLP employees continued to contribute to the Plan via payroll deductions during this period. There are no records showing that these employee contributions were ever sent to the Plan or held in trust.

When NLP was sold on December 6, 1999, $87,000 remained in the trust account. Stateline determined in early 2000 that the funds in the trust account were insufficient to cover all of the claims submitted prior to the sale of NLP. Accordingly, Stateline notified NLP employees that their benefits were denied due to inadequate funding and advised them to contact the Plan's administrator. According to a report prepared by Stateline's Chief Operating Officer ("COO"), NLP owed Stateline $312,072 in reimbursements.

II.

. . . Plaintiffs' amended complaint alleged that defendants conspired to, and did in fact, breach fiduciaries duties owed to the Plan, and requested, among other things, the "restitution of all damages suffered by the Plan and its participants."

. . .

A. ERISA § 502(a)(2)

Plaintiffs are entitled to seek relief from NLP, Ross Gill, and the Glass defendants under § 502(a)(2) because plaintiffs seek recovery for the Plan and have established that factual disputes exist as to whether these parties breached their fiduciary duties. Section 502(a)(2) authorizes plan participants and beneficiaries to bring derivative actions against fiduciaries who violate ERISA § 409 by breaching their duties to a plan. *Mass. Mut. Life Ins. Co. v. Russell*, 473 U.S. 134, 140 (1985). Pursuant to § 409, a breaching fiduciary "shall be personally liable to make good to such plan any losses to the plan resulting from each such breach. . . ." 29 U.S.C. § 1109.

1. Derivative Relief

Plaintiffs properly assert a claim under § 502(a)(2), as they seek to recover on behalf of the Plan, rather than individually. Because a § 502(a)(2) suit is a derivative action, a plaintiff bringing suit under this provision cannot obtain personal monetary relief, but must instead seek relief for the plan. . . .

That plaintiffs do, indeed, aim to recover on behalf of the Plan is evident from their amended complaint and supplemental briefing to the district court. In their amended complaint, plaintiffs requested that the district court "find and declare that defendants breached their fiduciary duties under ERISA and *are liable to the Plan* and its participants and beneficiaries as a result" and accordingly "order restitution of all damages *suffered by the Plan* and its participants." (emphasis added). Although plaintiffs explicitly sought relief for "the Plan *and its participants*," they acknowledge on appeal that they are only attempting to recover on the Plan's behalf.

. . . The plaintiffs submit that under ERISA Section 502(a)(2) when a breach of fiduciary duty is proven, then *the Plan is entitled to relief from the breaching fiduciaries, sufficient to make the plan participants whole*. . . .

Defendants argue that it is evident from the nature of the claimed fiduciary breaches that plaintiffs are seeking individual relief, not relief for the Plan. This is not true. First, a claim based on the purported material misrepresentations of fiduciaries is a classic breach-of-fiduciary-duty claim under ERISA. The Supreme Court has, for instance, stated that "[t]o participate knowingly and significantly in deceiving a plan's beneficiaries in order to save the employer money at the beneficiaries' expense is not to act 'solely in the interest of the participants and beneficiaries.'" *Varity Corp. v. Howe*, 516 U.S. 489, 506 (1996) (quoting ERISA § 404(a)). Second, plaintiffs' claims that the fiduciaries neglected their duty to enforce the Plan's right to employee and employer contributions are also breach-of-fiduciary duty claims, since the relief for these purported breaches would inure to the benefit of the Plan, not plaintiffs.

. . .

2. Breaches of Fiduciary Duties

. . .

"A fiduciary breaches his duties by providing plan participants with materially misleading information," even when he does so negligently, rather than intentionally. *James v. Pirelli Armstrong Tire Corp.*, 305 F.3d 439, 449 (6th Cir. 2002). To establish a breach of fiduciary duty claim based upon misrepresentations regarding coverage under an ERISA plan, a plaintiff must show:

(1) that the defendant was acting in a fiduciary capacity when it made the challenged representations; (2) that these constituted material misrepresentations; and (3) that the plaintiff relied on those misrepresentations to [his] detriment. *Id.*

With respect to the second element, there are genuine issues of material fact as to whether statements made by AuWerter in memoranda to NLP employees constituted material misrepresentations. In a September 22, 1999 memorandum, AuWerter told NLP employees that the company had "encountered difficulty getting our health claims paid through . . . Great West" and that "after several weeks of trying to resolve our differences with Great West, but making no progress, we have decided to change carriers." AuWerter advised employees, however that "***your medical, prescription drug and dental benefits are not changing***" and that "all claims that have recently been submitted to Great West for payment, but have not been paid, ***will be paid*** once those claims have been resubmitted to our new network provider." [Ed. — emphasis in original.] AuWerter provided similar assurances in a September 30, 1999 memorandum to NLP employees, in which he stated "[p]lease be assured that, although we are changing carriers, your group benefit plan coverage remains unchanged with the same entitlements . . . Your weekly group benefit contribution that is deducted from your paycheck will remain the same."

A reasonable juror could conclude that several of these representations were materially misleading when made. AuWerter's assurance that all claims would be paid could be found to be deceptive in light of NLP's financial woes. At the time that he made this statement, Great West had already terminated its relationship with NLP because of NLP's inability to fund the Plan properly. Moreover, in an August 27, 1999 memorandum to GECC, Glass expressed a belief that NLP's finances were not likely to improve. Given AuWerter's knowledge and beliefs, a reasonable juror could find that it was deceitful for him to state unequivocally that all claims would be paid. The insinuation that claims processing problems were the fault of Great West could similarly be found to be misleading based on these facts. Finally, because the record suggests that Great West ended its relationship with NLP, there are factual disputes concerning the truthfulness of AuWerter's statement in the September 22 memorandum that NLP initiated the change in claims administrators.

. . .

Further, there is evidence from which a reasonable juror could find that any misrepresentations were material and were relied upon by plaintiffs. A misrepresentation will be deemed material "if there is a substantial likelihood that it would mislead a reasonable employee in making an adequately informed decision." *Id.* (quotation omitted). A promise that all claims would be paid would plainly affect a beneficiary's decision as to whether to seek health care. Had plaintiffs been aware of the possibility of their benefits' being denied, they likely would have forgone some procedures.

. . .

Defendants did not breach their fiduciary duties by failing to collect employer contributions because the employer, NLP, was not obligated to fund the Plan. One of the duties that ERISA imposes upon fiduciaries is to take action to ensure that "a plan receives all funds to which it is entitled." *Cent. States, Se. & Sw. Areas Pension Fund v. Cent. Transp., Inc.*, 472 U.S. 559, 571 (1985). "ERISA does not," however, "create any substantive entitlement to employer-provided health benefits or any other kind of welfare benefits." *Curtiss-Wright Corp.*, 514 U.S. at 78. "Nor does ERISA establish any minimum participation, vesting or funding requirements for welfare plans." *Id.* Because ERISA does not require an employer to fund a plan, a plan fiduciary "is not duty-bound to bring suit to collect contributions from an employer unless an employer is bound contractually to . . . make those contributions." See *Bagsby v. Cent. States, Se. & Sw. Areas Pension Fund*, 162 F.3d 424, 431 (6th Cir. 1998). The district court concluded that NLP was not required under Plan documents to contribute to the Plan and that the fiduciaries were consequently not required to collect delinquent employer contributions. . . .

The district court properly determined that NLP did not obligate itself to fund the Plan. Nothing in the record indicates that NLP was contractually bound to contribute specific amounts to the Plan. . . .

6-10 QUESTIONS AND PROBLEMS

Troy, age 57, is a participant in the Zeta Co. benefit plan, which provides disability benefits and early retirement benefits at age 60. The normal retirement age of the plan is 65. Troy injured his arm when he fell down the stairs at his home. Despite therapy, his arm hurts severely when he performs his job as a fork lift operator. Troy called Hanna of Zeta's Benefit Office. He explained that, "I'm not feeling so good these days. Maybe I should retire. How old do I have to be to get that early retirement deal?" Hanna explained that he was not eligible until age 60. She said nothing about the possibility that he might qualify for disability payments if he was unable to perform his job. Troy listened to Hanna, did not ask any more questions, and a week later quit his job and took up work as a ticket seller at a local movie theater. His pay as a ticket seller was the same as he would have received had he applied for disability under the Zeta plan, for which he would have qualified, but he could have received disability and still worked as a ticket seller with no loss of benefits. One year later Troy learned that he should have applied for disability, but by then he was ineligible because he failed to apply within 90 days of terminating employment.

Can Troy successfully sue the fiduciary of the Zeta plan for violations of its fiduciary obligations?

An employer has no obligation to reveal its plans concerning possible plan amendments. Of course, once adopted, plan amendments must be communicated to the plan participants. But what if the employer is also a plan fiduciary? Is it then under an obligation as a fiduciary to reveal inchoate plans to the participants? Presumably the participants would benefit from advance knowledge about plan amendments. The following, which is considered a landmark case, addresses the duty of an employer who is a plan fiduciary to disclose possible plan amendments.

FISCHER v. PHILADELPHIA ELECTRIC CO.

96 F.3d 1533 (3d Cir. 1996)

ROTH, CIRCUIT JUDGE. In this appeal, we must review the application of a decision we reached when this case first came before us. In *Fischer v. Philadelphia Elec. Co.*, 994 F.2d 130 (3d Cir. 1993) ("*Fischer I*"), we reversed the district court's grant of summary judgment to defendant Philadelphia Electric Co. ("PECo"), holding that there were genuine issues of material fact as to whether PECo, acting in its role as fiduciary under the Employee Retirement Income Security Act ("ERISA"), had made affirmative material misrepresentations to its employee-beneficiaries. The misrepresentations alleged were that PECo had denied, or failed to disclose when asked, that it was seriously considering an early retirement program. We remanded the case to the district court to determine when PECo began to give serious consideration to an early retirement program. *Id.* at 135.

On remand, the district court concluded that PECo was seriously considering an early retirement program as of March 12, 1990. Applying *Fischer I*, the district court held that any employee who sought information about retirement benefits during the period from March 12, 1990, until the announcement of the plan on April 19, 1990, and who was told that no change was under consideration, had received material misinformation.

We find that the district court misunderstood the concept of "serious consideration." We will therefore reverse the decision of the district court, and we will enter judgment for defendants.

I.

This action arises out of PECo's efforts to cut costs and reduce its payroll by implementing an early retirement plan. On April 19, 1990, Joseph Paquette, PECo's President and Chief Operating Officer, announced in a letter to all employees that he would recommend to PECo's Board of Directors that the company cut its payroll through early retirement. On April 26, 1990, PECo sent a letter to all employees who had announced an intent to retire, suggesting that they delay their retirement until the company's early retirement package was finalized. On May 25, 1990, PECo's Board of Directors approved a plan, which included inducements such as a five year time-in-service credit, a five year age credit, and severance pay. These events caused much consternation among employees sponsor who had retired in the months preceding the plan's announcement. Various pre-plan retirees filed suit in the U.S. District Court for the Eastern District of Pennsylvania, alleging that PECo had long known of its intent to offer an early retirement package, or at least that it was considering a package, and had breached its fiduciary duty under ERISA § 404, by providing material misinformation. The district court certified a class, then entered summary judgment for PECo. In *Fischer I*, we reversed, holding that PECo could be liable for breach of fiduciary duty if the company represented that no early retirement plan was being considered at a time when the plan was in fact under serious consideration. We remanded for a trial on the merits; a bench trial followed. The facts we recite here were found by the district court; the vast majority were stipulated.

PECo had long engaged in a practice of reviewing its retirement and pension benefits packages as part of its ordinary course of business. During one such review, on March 21, 1988, Fred Beaver, an Administrative Assistant in the Benefits Division of Human Resources, prepared a memorandum for Charles Fritz, Vice President of Personnel and Industry Relations, on the possibility of reducing the size of PECo's work force. The memorandum suggested that a modest "sweetener" could induce approximately 50% of a target group of workers to retire. During the same period, on May 5, 1988, Michael Crommie, PECo's Director of Benefits, contacted William Murdoch, a consultant with Towers, Perrin, Forster & Crosby ("TPF & C"), to discuss various early retirement options. Discussions between management and TPF & C continued into June. Beaver's memorandum and the TPF & C consultations occurred roughly contemporaneously with Joseph Paquette's arrival at PECo as president and chief of operations. Paquette had a long term goal of reducing the number of PECo employees, and he would ultimately recommend the 1990 early retirement package. In June, 1988, however, Paquette decided against an early retirement plan. At trial, Paquette testified that PECo was then in the process of completing one nuclear plant and restarting another. He did not want to risk an early retirement program because personnel vital to the nuclear effort might leave. He believed that PECo could not legally institute an early retirement plan that excluded nuclear plant personnel. After deciding that no early retirement package would be considered, Paquette shifted his attention to promoting operational excellence at the company.

In July, 1989, PECo requested a rate increase from the Public Utility Commission ("PUC"). PUC staff made a preliminary recommendation that PECo be granted less than half its requested increase . . .

On December 13, 1989, Paquette held three meetings with employees to discuss the importance of the rate increase to the company. In response to questions, Paquette stated that an early retirement plan might be considered if the rate request was denied. He explained that the company had no plans for such a program because the outcome of the rate increase was in doubt. Paquette stated that PECo's first option in the event the increase was denied would be to appeal the decision but that the company would also consider cutting costs and reducing its stock dividend. On March 1, 1990, an Administrative Law Judge issued an interim decision recommending that PECo receive 21% of the rate increase it had requested. Events accelerated rapidly following the ALJ's decision. On March 12, 1990, Kenneth Lefkowitz, Manager of Compensation & Benefits, contacted Murdoch at TPF & C. Lefkowitz stated PECo's concern about its rate case before the PUC and the need to reduce costs quickly. The question of an early retirement sweetener was mentioned as a possible method. TPF & C had done no work for PECo on early retirement plans since June, 1988, nor had TPF & C been asked to prepare contingency plans in case PECo's rate request was denied. On March 20, 1990, Lefkowitz asked TPF & C to develop a set of early retirement alternatives. On March 28, 1990, Murdoch proposed three alternative programs, the first of which resembled the 1988 program in some respects, although it targeted a different group of eligible employees and contained different severance provisions. On April 2, 5, and 6, Murdoch had further discussions with PECo personnel about the details of the early retirement sweetener. On April 7, senior PECo executives attended a corporate strategy meeting. Notes from the meeting indicated a statement by Paquette that on April 20 he would issue a letter announcing a $100 million cost cutting program. On April 13, 1990, TPF & C provided PECo with a survey of early retirement plans used by other utilities. On April 19, 1990, the PUC granted less than 50% of PECo's rate request. Paquette then sent the letter to PECo employees announcing his intent to recommend an early retirement package.

Based on these findings, the district court held that PECo began seriously considering an early retirement plan on March 12, 1990. The district court entered judgment for those retirees who asked about an early retirement plan and retired after March 12. It entered judgment for PECo on the claims of those retirees who asked about retirement and retired before that date. Both PECo and the plaintiff class appealed. The plaintiff class appeals the district court's determination that serious consideration of the early retirement plan did not begin before March 12, 1990. PECo, on the other hand, asserts that serious consideration did not begin until after March 12, 1990.

Our analysis proceeds within the confines of *Fischer I*. In that decision, we established the general rule that governs interactions between a company-as-fiduciary and its employee-beneficiaries regarding changes in benefits: "A plan administrator may not make affirmative material misrepresentations to plan participants about changes to an employee pension benefits plan. Put simply, when a plan administrator speaks, it must speak truthfully." 994 F.2d at 135. This overarching duty of truthfulness forms an important part of our ERISA jurisprudence.

. . . .

In the current case, as in any case where the misrepresentation in question is the statement that no change in benefits is under consideration, the only factor at issue is the degree of seriousness with which the change was in fact being considered. This factor controls the materiality test: "[T]he more seriously a plan change is being considered, the more likely a misrepresentation . . . will pass the threshold of materiality." *Id.* Serious consideration forms the crux of the inquiry.

Although the test we set out in *Fischer I* ultimately turned on "serious consideration," we paid little attention to the details of that term. We offered nothing in the way of a definition, standard, or even factors to consider. We simply remanded the case to the district court, leaving to the district judge the task of determining when PECo's consideration became serious. We commend his efforts to apply this amorphous concept. We will now provide further guidance on the meaning of "serio us consideration." The concept of "serious consideration" recognizes and moderate s the tension between an employee's right to information and an employer's need to operate on a day-to-day basis. Every business must develop strategies, gather information, evaluate options, and make decisions. Full disclosure of each step in this process is a practical impossibility. Moreover, as counsel for PECo emphasized at oral argument, large corporations regularly review their benefit packages as part of an on-going process of cost-monitoring and personnel management. The various levels of management are constantly considering changes in corporate benefit plans. A corporation could not function if ERISA required complete disclosure of every facet of these on-going activities.

Consequently, our holding in *Fischer I* requires disclosure only when a change in benefits comes under *serious* consideration. Equally importantly, serious consideration protects employees. Every employee has a need for material information on which that employee can rely in making employment decisions. Too low a standard could result in an avalanche of notices and disclosures. For employees at a company like PECo, which regularly reviews its benefits plans, truly material information could easily be missed if the flow of information was too great. The warning that a change in benefits was under serious consideration would become meaningless if cried too often. . . . .

An ERISA fiduciary is under no obligation to offer precise predictions about future changes to its plan. Rather, its obligation is to answer participants' questions forthrightly, a duty that does not require the fiduciary to disclose its internal deliberations nor interfere with the substantive aspects of the collective bargaining process. Other courts of appeals have likewise emphasized the absence of any "duty of clairvoyance," as well as the fact that disclosure does not extend to internal deliberations.

In light of these concerns, we believe that the following formulation of serious consideration is appropriate: Serious consideration of a change in plan benefits exists when (1) a specific proposal (2) is being discussed for purposes of implementation (3) by senior management with the authority to implement the change. Consistent with our decision in *Fischer I*'s companion case, this formulation does not turn on any single factor; the determination is inherently fact-specific. Likewise, the factors themselves are not isolated criteria; the three interact and coalesce to form a composite picture of serious consideration. For purposes of discussion, we address each in turn.

The first element, a specific proposal, distinguishes serious consideration from the antecedent steps of gathering information, developing strategies, and analyzing options. A company must necessarily go through these preliminary steps before its deliberations can reach the serious stage. This factor does not mean, however, that the proposal must describe the plan in its final form. A specific proposal can contain several alternatives, and the plan as finally implemented may differ somewhat from the proposal. What is required, consistent with the overall test, is a specific proposal that is sufficiently concrete to support consideration by senior management for the purpose of implementation.

The second element, discussion for implementation, further distinguishes serious consideration from the preliminary steps of gathering data and formulating strategy. It also protects the ability of senior management to take a role in the early phases of the process without automatically triggering a duty of disclosure. This factor recognizes that a corporate executive can order an analysis of benefits alternatives or commission a comparative study without seriously considering implementing a change in benefits. Preliminary stages may also require interaction among upper level management, company personnel, and outside consultants. These discussions are properly assigned to the preliminary stages of company deliberations. Consideration becomes serious when the subject turns to the practicalities of implementation.

The final element, consideration by senior management with the authority to implement the change, ensures that the analysis of serious consideration focuses on the proper actors within the corporate hierarchy. As noted, large corporate entities conduct regular or on-going reviews of their benefit packages in their ordinary course of business. These entities employ individuals, including middle and upper-level management employees, to gather information and conduct reviews. The periodic review process may also entail contacting outside consultants or commissioning studies. During the course of their employment, the employees assigned these tasks necessarily discuss their duties and the results of their studies. These discussions may include issues of implementation. The employees may also make recommendations to upper level management or senior executives. As a general rule, such operations will not constitute serious consideration. These activities are merely the ordinary duties of the employees. Until senior management addresses the issue, the company has not yet seriously considered a change. Consideration by senior management is also limited to those executives who possess the authority to implement the proposed change. This focus on authority can be used to identify the proper cadre of senior management, but it should not limit serious consideration to deliberations by a quorum of the Board of Directors, typically the only corporate body that in a literal sense has the power to implement changes in benefits packages. It is sufficient for this factor that the plan be considered by those members of senior management with responsibility for the benefits area of the business, and who ultimately will make recommendations to the Board regarding benefits operations. At the risk of redundancy, we stress that these factors do not establish a bright-line rule.

. . . .

The elements that we have outlined limit serious consideration to the latter stages of corporate decision-making, but they remain flexible and fact-specific. We believe that our explanation of serious consideration maintains the balance struck in *Fischer I*. Our formulation respects the division of responsibility in corporate entities and the day-to-day realities of running a business. Even more importantly, it protects the right of employees to material information. Characterizing serious consideration in this fashion ensures that disclosures to employees about potential changes in benefits will be meaningful. Employees will learn of potential changes when the company's deliberations have reached a level where an employee should reasonably factor the potential change into an employment decision. This guarantees that employees will have the information they need, while avoiding a surfeit of meaningless disclosures. Finally, as a matter of policy, we note that imposing liability too quickly for failure to disclose a potential early retirement plan could harm employees by deterring employers from resorting to such plans. . . . Our formulation avoids forcing companies into layoffs, the primary alternative to retirement inducements. This further protects the interests of workers.

III.

Having explained our understanding of serious consideration, we now apply it to the case at bar. Although we would ordinarily remand to allow the district court to apply our standard in the first instance, we see no need in the current case. Judge Weiner's thoughtful opinion has set out clearly the necessary factual findings, and we can simply apply the law to reach the requisite conclusion. Based on our three factor test, we find that serious consideration began on April 7, 1990. We will therefore reverse the district court to the extent that it found serious consideration as of March 12, 1990.

The district court correctly dismissed events prior to March 12, 1990, as failing to rise to the level of serious consideration. Any potential consideration of an early retirement program prior to June, 1988, was conclusively ended by Paquette's decision to forego an early retirement option and focus on operational excellence. These events had no bearing on the subsequent decision to implement an early retirement plan in August, 1990.

The district court was equally correct to dispose of Paquette's statements during his speeches to employees on December 13, 1989. Paquette responded truthfully to employee questions regarding PECo's potential responses to an adverse decision in the rates case. Paquette explained that PECo would first appeal the decision but might also have to consider cutting costs by reducing its stock dividend or other methods. This is the type of frank response to employee concerns that should be encouraged. Paquette's statements will not support an inference that an early retirement plan was then under serious consideration.

The district court then concluded that PECo began seriously considering a plan sometime between December and April. Citing Lefkowitz's March 12, 1990, telephone call to TPF & C as the earliest example of affirmative action to implement the plan, the district court marked the start of serious consideration on that date. Under our three factor inquiry, this is incorrect. As we have explained, serious consideration requires (1) a specific proposal (2) discussed for purposes of implementation (3) by senior management with the authority to implement the change. In the case at bar, these three factors did not coincide until April 7, 1990, when senior PECo management met to discuss the TPF & C report on staff reduction options. The TPF & C report is an excellent example of a specific proposal. This document outlined various early retirement alternatives and served as the basis for management's deliberations. Senior management was present at the meeting. The subject of the meeting was corporate strategy, and meeting notes indicate that Paquette disclosed his intent to announce $100 million in cost cuts. Both facts suggest that an early retirement plan was discussed for purposes of implementation at the April 7 meeting.

Events prior to April 7, by contrast, do not rise to the level of serious consideration. The March 12 Lefkowitz telephone call is clearly insufficient. First, the substance of the March 12 call involved nothing more than a general discussion of early retirement options. Lefkowitz was reestablishing contact on a subject where TPF & C had done no work since 1988. The subject matter of the contact was therefore preliminary. Second, Lefkowitz was a middle management employee in PECo's benefits department. His official duties entailed monitoring PECo's benefits package and exploring potential changes. Nothing in the record indicates that, when Lefkowitz made his March 12 telephone call to TPF & C, he was doing anything more than acting within the scope of his normal duties. This type of action by a middle management employee is preliminary. Third, even if Lefkowitz were acting on orders from senior management, his call to TPF & C would still fall under the rubric of gathering information. Senior management is free to start the process of exploration and evaluation without immediately triggering a duty of disclosure. For each of these reasons, the March 12 phone call took place prior to serious consideration. The district court was therefore incorrect.

The March 20 contact between Lefkowitz and TPF & C confirms this conclusion. It was on March 20 that Lefkowitz asked TPF & C to develop a set of options for staff reduction, including various early retirement plans. This is crucial. Serious consideration can only begin after information is gathered and options developed. The record indicates that the March 20 phone call assigned TPF & C the task of developing options. This contact therefore preceded serious consideration. Events between March 20 and April 7 can similarly be categorized under preliminary stages such as information gathering and strategy formulation. The record indicates that Murdoch, a partner at TPF & C, met with Lefkowitz and other PECo executives during this period. These meetings are consistent with TPF & C's efforts to develop a report for PECo, the very task it had been assigned on March 20. The fact that TPF & C submitted its report on April 2 removes any lingering doubt. It was only after April 2 that a specific proposal existed.

Given that TPF & C submitted its report on April 2, the meetings that occurred on April 2, 5, and 6 between Murdoch, Paquette, and other PECo management present a closer question. A proposal had been developed and PECo management was involved in the meetings. However, details of the proposals were still being discussed. On April 7, a corporate strategy meeting was held. Paquette stated at the meeting that he would announce targets and programs on April 20. Based on this clear example of a meeting of senior PECo executives to address the early retirement issue at a time when a specific proposal had been submitted, we conclude that serious consideration began on April 7, 1990.

Under the rule established in *Fischer I*, any employee who asked about a potential early retirement plan after serious consideration began on April 7, 1990, but before the plan's formal announcement on April 19, 1990, received material misinformation. Such an employee would have established a claim for breach of fiduciary duty under ERISA. However, all of the members of the plaintiff class retired before this period. We will, therefore, enter judgment for PECo on the plaintiff's breach of fiduciary duty claim.

Under the rule in *Fischer I*, PECo's liability turns on the point at which serious consideration began. Applying our understanding of serious consideration, we find that serious consideration began on April 7, 1990. Because all the members of the plaintiff class retired before this date, none were provided with material misinformation. The class's alternative theories of recovery likewise fail. We will reverse the holding of the district court and enter judgment on behalf of all defendants.

6-11 QUESTIONS AND PROBLEMS

1. What is the legal basis for the court holding that a duty to disclose potential plan amendments arises at the point of "serious consideration"?

2. Does the "serious consideration" rule confuse the sponsor function with the fiduciary's obligations?

3. Is the "serious consideration" rule consistent with ERISA's requirement that the plan be in writing?

4. Can a plan sponsor avoid the rule by periodically informing the plan participants that it has the right to amend the plan, that it may amend the plan at any time, and that it will not give any notice of such amendments nor reveal whether it is considering a plan amendment?

5. Tau Inc., a large telecommunications company, operates a pension plan whose trustee is Vince, the director of personnel for Tau. The plan's normal retirement age is 65.

On April 10, the President of Tau instructed Vince to amend the existing defined benefit plan by creating an early retirement plan in order to reduce the size of its workforce. On May 1, Vince sent a "Preliminary Proposal" to the President, who on June 1st returned it to Vince with the note, "Good plan, but you need to reduce the expected costs by 20 percent."

On July 1, Vani, age 60, a Vice President for product development with no knowledge of the possibility of an enhanced early retirement program, said to Vince in the company cafeteria, "I am thinking of taking early retirement at the end of this month. Do you know of any reason that I should delay my retirement?" Vince replied, "Not that I know of." On July 2, Vani submitted her early retirement effective July 20.

On July 25, Vince submitted a revised early retirement plan to the company President, who presented it without revision on August 1 to the Board of Directors for approval. The plan was approved by the Board on August 5, announced to the employees on August 6, and went into effect September 1. It provided a substantial bonus to anyone age 60 or older who took early retirement.

Vani sued Tau Inc. alleging that Vince, as the plan fiduciary, violated his duty of loyalty by not informing her of the possible enhanced retirement plan before she retired. What result?

A plan sponsor is not required to volunteer information absent an employee inquiry. But what if an employee makes an inquiry before the employer has entered into serious consideration? The employer answers truthfully that no plan amendment is under consideration. Later, the employer does consider a plan amendment similar to that about which the employee inquired. Must the sponsor notify the employee that it is now considering such a plan amendment? Two circuits, the Fifth and the Second, have held that they have a duty of disclosure even before the amendment is under "serious consideration."

In *Martinez v. Schlumberger*, Ltd, 338 F.3d 407 (5th Cir. 2003), the court stated that it agreed that an ERISA plan administrator who speaks in its fiduciary capacity must speak truthfully but "Although we join our sister circuits in recognizing this duty, we cannot agree that misrepresentations are actionable only after the company has seriously considered the plan change. . . . When an employer speaks to the future of a plan, employees are justified in concluding that it is backed by the authority of the plan administrator, and should therefore be entitled to trust in those representations." *Id.* at. 425.

In *Ballone v. Eastman Kodak Co.*, 109 F.3d 117 (2d Cir. 1997) the court reached a similar conclusion: "Regardless of whether the employer is seriously considering altering its retirement plan, the employer's false assurance that future enhancements have been ruled out for some specific period can be decisive in inducing an employee to hasten retirement, rather than delay in the hope of receiving enhanced future benefits. This aspect of the assurance can render it material regardless of whether future changes are under consideration at the time the misstatement is made. *Id.* at 124.

. . . Plaintiffs contend that Kodak told them that it definitely would not implement a new retirement program in the near future. If Kodak had not actually made such a decision, this could be a material misrepresentation since Plaintiffs also allege that they would have delayed retiring if they had known that no such decision had been made. *Id.* at 125.

. . . Kodak need not be prescient, an employer does not enjoy carte blanche to make statements that the employer knows to be false, or that have no reasonable basis in fact, simply because the statements concern the future. *Id.* at 126."

What if the employer is considering a new plan, rather than a plan amendment? Does the employer have any duty of disclosure to its employees?

BEACH v. COMMONWEALTH EDISON COMPANY

382 F.3d 656 (7th Cir. 2004)

EASTERBROOK, CIRCUIT JUDGE.

After 31 years on the job, Randall Beach retired from Commonwealth Edison in June 1997 and moved to Idaho. He was 52 at the time. By leaving before age 55, Beach gave up entitlement to future health benefits, though he retained his vested pension. Before taking this extra-early retirement, Beach asked his supervisor, plus ComEd's human resources staff, whether there was any immediate prospect that the firm would offer a voluntary separation package in his department, the Transmission and Distribution Organization. Beach knew that ComEd was reorganizing department by department and that it sometimes offered sweeteners, such as severance pay and health benefits, to those who agreed to depart. As Beach remembers these conversations, "everybody said absolutely it's not going to happen. You're not going to get the package. The company is not going to offer your department a package. It just will not happen. That was the essence of everything I got." Six weeks after Beach's retirement, however, ComEd did offer a separation package to 240 of the 4,700 employees in his department. Had he been employed on August 7, 1997, Beach would have been eligible for these benefits. When ComEd declined to treat him as if he had departed in August or September rather than May (when he gave notice and stopped working) or June (when he left the payroll), Beach filed this suit under the Employee Retirement Income Security Act. After a bench trial on stipulated facts, the district judge concluded that ComEd had violated its fiduciary duty to a participant in an ERISA plan by giving incorrect advice. Even though no one had intended to deceive Beach — ComEd's senior managers did not begin to consider separation benefits for the Transmission and Distribution Organization until after Beach's retirement, and no one in the human resources staff knew what was coming — the district judge held that ComEd must treat Beach as if he had stayed through August and qualified for all benefits then on offer.

The district court's major premise is that ComEd owed Beach a fiduciary duty with respect to future fringe-benefit plans, because he was a participant in the firm's pension plan. . . . The district court's major premise is mistaken.

Duties under ERISA are plan-specific. The statute defines a "fiduciary" as a person who exercises authority or discretion over the administration of a plan, but only when performing those functions. Thus an employer is not a fiduciary when considering whether to establish a plan in the first place, or what specific benefits to offer when creating or amending a plan. . . . Beach was (and is) a participant in ComEd's pension plan but does not contend that he has received less than his due under it. He also was a participant in some welfare-benefit plans, such as ComEd's health-care plan; once again, however, he does not complain that ComEd wrongfully denied him any of those benefits or misled him in any way about them. He knew that if he left before age 55 those benefits would end; that decision was made with eyes open. What he wants- and what the district court gave him- is benefits under a separate plan that was not established until after he quit.

Throughout his briefs, Beach proceeds as if the separation incentives were created by amendment of a plan in which he was already a participant. That enables him to invoke *Varity Corp. v. Howe*, 516 U.S. 489 (1996), which held that ERISA prohibits a plan fiduciary from deceiving participants in an existing pension plan about the value of its benefits compared with those under a successor or substitute plan. Yet the plan under which Beach wants (and was awarded) benefits does not amend or modify any of ComEd's other plans — nor did Beach have to choose between its benefits and those of the plans in which he was a participant. The "Voluntary Separation Plan for Designated Transmission and Distribution Management Employees of Commonwealth Edison Company" dated August 7, 1997, is in the record: it is a stand-alone welfare-benefit plan that does not amend, supplement, or replace any other plan. As it did not come into existence until after Beach's retirement, ComEd did not owe him any fiduciary duty concerning its benefits.

. . .

A number of decisions address the question whether ERISA requires plan sponsors to give accurate information about potential amendments to existing plans. *Varity* shows that candid and complete information is required if two plans are in existence, and the sponsor tries to persuade employees to give up benefits under one in exchange for benefits under the other. These follow-on decisions conclude that a similar approach governs when a single plan is in the process of amendment. The majority view is that a duty of accurate disclosure begins "when (1) a specific proposal (2) is being discussed for purposes of implementation (3) by senior management with the authority to implement the change." *Fischer v. Philadelphia Electric Co.*, 96 F.3d 1533, 1539 (3d Cir. 1996). At that point details of the amendment become material; until then there is only speculation. Two circuits conclude that the duty of disclosure arises sometime before the change is under "serious consideration" — though just what must be disclosed, and when, these circuits have struggled to pin down. See *Ballone v. Eastman Kodak Co.*, 109 F.3d 117 (2d Cir. 1997).

. . .

The majority rule, reflected in *Fischer*, has the better of this debate. Giving firms a duty to forecast accurately, if the benefits staff says anything at all, could not help plan participants. It would just induce employers to tell the human resources staff to say nothing at all — to make no predictions and to refer employees to the printed plan descriptions. Yet chancy predictions may be better than silence; think of the 95% of the employees in ComEd's Transmission and Distribution Organization who would have received exactly the right advice, which could have facilitated their retirement planning. The alternative to enforced silence would be a declaration in the employee handbook that no one should rely on any oral information about the plans. That might or might not curtail legal risks — some workers would be bound to ask why the firm even had a benefits advisory staff, if it was insisting that everything the staff said was worthless — but again would do little to help people in Beach's position. It does not take familiarity with Bayes's Theorem to see that even potentially fallacious news may be better than no news. If the benefits staff must clam up, then rumor and office scuttlebutt come to the fore, and it is likely to be less accurate than the staff's educated guesses. So we are not persuaded by *Ballone* or *Martinez*.

ComEd did not amend any of its plans. We need not decide whether *Fischer*'s approach would apply to the establishment of a new plan, because none was under consideration when Beach resigned. There was no proposal at all, let alone a specific proposal under review by senior managers. It is undisputed that ComEd did not begin internal discussion of the details about the Transmission and Distribution Organization's reorganization until mid-June 1997, a month after Beach had given notice (and about the same time as his last day on the payroll). ComEd concluded that a small net reduction in staff would be required — about 30 of the 4,700 positions were to be eliminated. At a meeting on July 22 or 23, 1997, managers began to discuss whether it would make sense to use separation incentives, as opposed to other means, to achieve this reduction. Sometime late in July or early in August, Howard Nelson, ComEd's "Strategic Staffing Director," drafted a separation-incentives plan covering only 5% of the division's staff (240 employees, in the hope that 30 would take the bait). This plan was approved by Paul McCoy, Vice President for the Transmission and Distribution Organization, on August 6, and was announced to employees the next day. None of the circuits following the *Fischer* approach would conclude that this plan was under "serious consideration" before Beach retired. So even if we were to apply this approach to new plans — a question that we do not resolve today — Beach could not benefit.

Beach was not the victim of fraud, and ComEd did not have a duty of accurate disclosure in the period preceding the plan's adoption. The human relations staff might have been careless, but it did not violate any duty of loyalty owed to Beach. Accordingly, the judgment of the district court is reversed.

RIPPLE, CIRCUIT JUDGE, dissenting.

A single principle controls this case. "[A] fiduciary may not materially mislead those to whom the duties of loyalty and prudence described in 29 U.S.C. § 1104 are owed." *Berlin v. Michigan Bell Tel. Co.*, 858 F.2d 1154, 1163 (6th Cir. 1988). Mr. Beach was a participant in ComEd's retirement pension plan and its health-care plan; ComEd and Mr. Beach were in a fiduciary relationship with respect to these plans. See *supra* at 658. The Voluntary Severance Plan ("VSP"), in essence, supplemented the retirement pension plan and the health-care plan. Therefore, when ComEd misrepresented the status of the VSP and its future plan-related benefits, it was "administer[ing]" these plans under the rationale of *Varity Corporation v. Howe,* 516 U.S. 489 (1996). Because, in its administration, ComEd made material misrepresentations in violation of its fiduciary duties, I would affirm the judgment of the district court.

1.

My colleagues hold that ComEd's misrepresentations were not made in a fiduciary capacity and thus are not actionable. Their view rests on the conclusion that ERISA's fiduciary duties are plan-specific. That proposition is unassailable, as far as it goes. . . .

ComEd submits that ERISA's plan-specific nature means that an employer-administrator speaks as a fiduciary *only* when it speaks about new benefits that come in the form of an *amendment* to an established plan under which the employer and employee have a preexisting fiduciary relationship, as opposed to when that employer-administrator speaks about benefits in a *new* plan. At times, the majority appears inclined to that view. Such a limited review, however, is at odds with *Varity Corporation,* 516 U.S. 489, 116. In *Varity,* officials deliberately misled Varity employees, who were participants in an existing ERISA plan and in a fiduciary relationship with Varity regarding that plan (Plan 1), to transfer out of Plan 1 and into a new plan (Plan 2); this new plan was established in an undercapitalized subsidiary, which eventually went into receivership. . . .

At the least, *Varity* stands for the proposition that, when a company such as ComEd becomes a fiduciary to an employee as to an ERISA "plan" (e.g., Plan 1), then its fiduciary duties of loyalty and care can attach to representations made regarding new plans under which the employer and employee do not have a preexisting fiduciary relationship (e.g., Plan 2). *Varity* gave no hint, and neither have subsequent cases, that the critical distinction a court must draw in determining whether an employer-administrator spoke in a fiduciary status is whether the employer spoke about an "amendment" to an existing plan or to a "new" plan.

This interpretation also makes good sense. It would be intolerable to allow an employer-administrator to avoid the ramifications of its fiduciary status by simply attaching the label "new plan" — as opposed to "plan amendment" — to the subject of its misrepresentations. . . .

[4] Duty to Provide Plan Information

ERISA §§ 102, 104(b).

As discussed in Chapter 4, ERISA § 104(b) mandates that each participant and each beneficiary receiving benefits under the plan be furnished with an accurate and adequate summary plan description. The following case addresses whether the plan fiduciaries have met that obligation.

ESTATE OF BECKER v. EASTMAN KODAK CO.

120 F.3d 5 (2d Cir. 1997)

Leval, Circuit Judge.

The estate of Carol W. Becker and Frederick R. Becker (collectively, "plaintiffs") appeal from a decision granting summary judgment in favor of defendants Eastman Kodak Company and Kodak Retirement Income Plan Committee (collectively "Kodak") and dismissing plaintiffs' claims under the Employee Retirement Income Security Act ("ERISA"). The complaint alleges that Kodak violated ERISA by issuing a faulty Summary Plan Description ("SPD") and providing Carol Becker ("Becker") with inadequate information about her retirement benefits options. The district court held that Kodak's SPD complied with ERISA's disclosure requirements and that Kodak did not give Becker incomplete or misleading information.

Plaintiffs contend that (1) Kodak's SPD did not adequately describe the consequences of dying before the "effective date" of retirement, (2) Kodak did not timely update its SPD to describe the addition of a new "lump sum" retirement benef it, and (3) during an individual meeting in March 1991, a Kodak benefits counselor (Jean Ticen) gave Becker incomplete and misleading information about her retirement options.

Becker worked for Kodak for sixteen years and participated in the Kodak Retirement Income Plan (the "Plan"). On January 1, 1989, she became eligible for early retirement under the Plan's "55/10" rule, which allows employees who have reached the age of 55 with at least ten years service to retire before the normal retirement age of 65.

Prior to 1990, the Plan paid retirement benefits only in the form of an annuity. On April 19, 1990, Kodak announced in its internal newsletter, Kodakery, that as of September 1, 1990, retiring employees could elect to receive their retirement benefits in a one-time "lump sum."

In August 1990, Kodak mailed personalized estimates of retirement benefits to all employees eligible for retirement, including Becker. These estimates set forth the amount that each employee was then entitled to receive, calculated both as an annuity and as a lump sum.

Suffering from cancer, Becker took short-term disability leave on April 20, 1990. Kodak provided short-term disability benefits for up to one year. When it became apparent that Becker could not return to work before the expiration of her short-term benefits, she and her daughter, Elizabeth Ann Bryce, met on March 15, 1991 with benefits counselor Jean Ticen to discuss Becker's options and whether she should retire or take long-term disability status. Bryce tape recorded a portion of this meeting because her mother had difficulty concentrating on account of her illness, and wished to hear it again at home.

Ticen told Becker that the monthly benefit under long-term disability would be larger than the monthly retirement benefit to which she was then entitled, and that her retirement benefit would grow if she deferred retirement. She also told Becker that "[t]here may be some point at which the retirement income may be higher than what you receive on disability, so that would be an appropriate time for you to switch from disability to retirement." In short, Ticen's advice seemed to suggest that it was to Becker's advantage to elect disability status rather than retirement.

During this meeting, Ticen never mentioned the option of retiring with the lump sum benefit. Becker did not tell Ticen that she was suffering from a terminal illness. On several occasions, Ticen referred to decisions and benefits that would arise several years in the future. At one point, Becker asked Ticen: "If I take long term, can I take retirement any time I feel like it?" Ticen responded "Right."

After the meeting, Becker elected to postpone her retirement and take long-term disability benefits. The election form, signed by Becker on March 15, 1991, contains an explicit comparison of the monthly benefits available under the disability and retirement packages, but does not mention the lump sum option.

Around October 20, 1991, after her condition had deteriorated, Becker decided to retire and asked Ticen for information about the lump sum option. Ticen told her that she would not receive her lump sum if she died before the effective date of her retirement. Becker then tried to make her retirement retroactive to October 1, 1991. Ticen told her that the Plan did not permit retroactive retirement, but agreed to expedite her papers and to make her retirement effective November 1, 1991, the earliest possible date.

Becker died on October 29, 1991. As a result, she and her husband were ineligible to receive her lump sum payment, which would have amounted to about $212,620. Instead, on November 1, 1991, Mr. Becker became eligible for "Survivor Income Benefits," available to surviving spouses of "vested" Plan participants who die before retiring, which are monthly payments equal to 20–30% of the amount that would have b een payable as a retirement annuity. These benefits give Mr. Becker a monthly payment of $103.42, a far smaller benefit than the plaintiffs would have received had Becker retired before her death.

Plaintiffs brought this action alleging that Kodak violated three sections of the ERISA statute. The complaint alleged that Kodak violated [ERISA] § 102(a) by providing an inadequate SPD, violated § 104 by failing to issue a statement of material modification ("SMM") describing the lump sum option, and violated § 404 by failing to provide Becker with complete and correct information about her options under the Plan. The complaint also alleged that Kodak's failure to explain its benefits adequately caused Becker's failure to retire before her death and the consequent loss of vested benefits. The parties filed cross-motions for summary judgment.

The district court granted Kodak's motion for summary judgment. Although noting that the SPD, unlike the Plan itself, did not state explicitly that "[t]he lump sum will not be paid if the Participant dies before the date on which the lump sum would be payable," the court found that, read as a whole, the SPD "sufficiently apprise[s] plan participants and beneficiaries that an employee who dies before the effective date of his or her retirement will not receive vested pension benefits." The court thus held that the SPD did not violate § 102 because it provided Becker reasonable notice that her estate would receive no retirement benefits if she died before retiring.

Finally, the court ruled that Ticen had not given Becker incomplete or misleading information about her benefits options and that Kodak had not breached its fiduciary duty under ERISA. Finding that Ticen was under no obligation to inquire about Becker's condition or to provide personalized advice based on what she knew or suspected about that condition, the court held that Ticen had met her sole duty by explaining to Becker the "available options under the applicable Kodak benefit plan." As Becker "was provided with all the pertinent information required to make an informed decision regarding which benefits option to select," the court granted Kodak's motion for summary judgment.

As noted above, the arguments advanced by plaintiffs on appeal include (1) that the SPD did not reasonably describe the circumstances under which retirement benefits might be lost, and (2) that Ticen gave Becker misleading advice about the retirement option. Finding that the SPD and the advice given by Ticen, taken together, amounted to materially misleading information, we reverse the district court's ruling on that ground alone, and therefore do not consider whether either the SPD or Ticen's advice, taken separately, would justify relief.

An ERISA plan administrator must furnish its participants and beneficiaries with an SPD "written in a manner calculated to be understood by the average plan participant" and "sufficiently accurate and comprehensive to reasonably apprise such participants and beneficiaries of their rights and obligations under the plan." [ERISA] § 102(a)(1). An SPD "shall contain . . . the plan's requirements respecting eligibility for participation and benefits" and "circumstances which may result in disqualification, ineligibility, or denial or loss of benefits." [ERISA] § 102(b). In assessing the adequacy of an SPD, we consider the document as a whole.

ERISA also requires a plan fiduciary to "discharge his duties with respect to a plan solely in the interest of the participants and beneficiaries." [ERISA] § 404(a).

Plaintiffs argue that Kodak's SPD was deficient because it did not explain properly that a participant who dies before the "effective date" of her retirement is ineligible for the lump sum payment. They note that the complete Plan document states plainly in § 11.08(a) that "[t]he lump sum will not be paid if the Participant dies before the date on which the lump sum would be payable." They contend that the SPD did not make sufficiently clear that the Plan will not pay the retirement benefit if a participant dies before the "effective date" of her retirement.

Plaintiffs are correct in their assertion that the documents circulated by Kodak to announce the lump sum payment option do not state explicitly that the lump sum will not be paid if the participant dies before retirement. Moreover, the SPD itself does not contain a single, distinct announcement that a participant loses vested pension benefits if she dies before retirement, or that an employee's retirement election has no effect if she dies before the "effective date" of her retirement.

Although the SPD perhaps implies that an employee "retires" only by filling out a retirement election form and surviving until the effective date of retirement, it does not state this explicitly. The SPD does not make clear that the effective date is always the first of the month following the employee's election. Thus, an employee electing to retire on March 2 might think that the effective date of her retirement was March 1, rather than April 1. Under these circumstances, the employee might reasonably believe that she had retired — and was thus eligible for retirement benefits — upon submitting an election to retire.

In short, the SPD does not explain that an employee has not "retired," within the meaning of the Plan, until after she has made her election, complied with necessary formalities, and survived until the "effective date" of retirement. Nor does the SPD explicitly define that term to mean the first day of the month after an employee's election to retire. As a result, it is questionable whether the SPD clearly alerts participants to the fact that an employee who elects to retire but dies before the first day of the next month loses her vested retirement benefits. For this reason, we question whether the SPD adequately informs an "average plan participant" of an important circumstance "which may result in loss of benefits."

Nevertheless, because the deficiencies of the SPD do not stand alone in this case, we need not — and expressly do not — rule that the SPD was insufficient as a matter of law.

Regardless whether the SPD was, by itself, so ambiguous and incomplete as to violate § 102(b), we find that benefits counselor Ticen exacerbated the lack of clarity inherent in the SPD and thereby provided Becker with materially misleading information. During their meeting, Becker asked: "If I take long term, can I take retirement anytime I feel like it?" Ticen responded "Right." Particularly given the SPD's confusing message concerning the mechanics and timing of the election to retire, Ticen's response could easily have led Becker to believe mistakenly that she could retire at any time, effective immediately or retroactive to the first of the month.

Taking these circumstances together, we conclude that Kodak breached its fiduciary duty to provide Becker with complete and accurate information about her retirement options. Plaintiffs are entitled to a finding in their favor on that issue. We therefore vacate the judgment of the district court. We do not, however, direct the entry of judgment for plaintiffs because there remains the question of causation. We remand for the district court to determine whether the misleading communication resulting from Ticen's answer and the SPD caused Becker to delay electing her retirement.

6-12 QUESTIONS AND PROBLEMS

1. The facts in *Becker* are very compelling. Because Carol Becker died just two days before her "retirement date," her husband lost out on a substantial lump-sum distribution. Perhaps her mistake, however, was in looking for advice from a representative of the Pension Plan, rather than seeking out independent advice. With several hundred thousand dollars at stake, is it not reasonable to expect plan participants who are unsure of their rights to hire an attorney or private pension planner to help them decide how and when they should take their pension?

2. The district court held that the Plan "was under no obligation to inquire about Becker's condition or to provide personalized advice based on what she knew or suspected about that condition . . ." Is the court correct? What if a pension plan does not offer individual consultation. Is a Plan under any obligation to furnish anything more than a copy of the plan and a Summary Plan Description?

3. Does a plan incur greater potential liability if it offers individual advice to the plan participants.

E. REQUIREMENT OF WRITING AND ESTOPPEL CLAIMS

ERISA §§ 402(a)(1), 402(b)(3).

ERISA § 402(b)(3) requires that every plan provide a procedure for amending a plan, although no plan may be amended to reduce benefits already accrued. ERISA § 204(g) (discussed in Chapter 10). Though ERISA § 402(a)(1) requires all plans to be in writing plan participants assert that when they are orally given incorrect information about the plan, that information is an amendment to the plan, and binding upon the employer. In response, the employer contends that the alleged plan amendment is invalid because it was not in writing. The participant then argues that the employer who provided the false information upon which the participant detrimentally relied should be estopped from asserting that the information provided to the participant was an invalid plan amendment. At other times, the participant asks for an interpretation of plan benefits, such as is this particular medical procedure "x" covered by the plan, is told, yes, the plan will cover procedure "x," and undergoes the procedure. Later, when the participant seeks reimbursement, the plan refuses to pay, claiming that the earlier interpretation was not correct. Naturally these instances of alleged oral plan amendments and plan interpretations have engendered significant litigation.

Most courts have taken a very firm position that oral modifications are not valid plan amendments, and so reject the plaintiff's claim of estoppel, under which the plaintiff asserts that the defendant is estopped from raising the claim that the defendant's oral statements were inoperative as a plan amendment.

> . . . Under [ERISA] § 402(a)(1) "every employee benefit plan shall be established and maintained pursuant to a written instrument." We find that oral agreements or modifications to a pension plan are contrary to the express provisions of ERISA. Therefore, we conclude that any oral agreements or modifications relied on by the appellant cannot support his claim for recovery herein.
>
> The policy behind the "written instrument" clause in ERISA is to prevent collusive or fraudulent side agreements between employers and employees. But for the "written instrument" clause, employees could discriminate in favor of certain plan participants to the detriment of others. In addition, the writing requirement gives the plan's participants and administrators a clear understanding of their rights and obligations. Employees who rely on a written benefit plan should not have their benefits eroded by oral modifications to the benefit plan. Furthermore, the writing requirement protects the plan's actuarial soundness by preventing plan administrators from contracting to pay benefits to persons not entitled to such under the express terms of the plan. The statutory language of [ERISA] § 402(a)(1) is clear and concise and must be enforced as written. To hold otherwise would not only thwart congressional purpose and intent, but would afford less protection to employees and their beneficiaries.
>
> Thus, we hold that an oral agreement cannot be the basis of a cause of action under ERISA . . . .
>
> We conclude, in light of the foregoing principles, that we should not create federal common law in this case because ERISA specifically and clearly addresses the issue before this Court. ERISA expressly requires that employee benefit plans be "established and maintained pursuant to a

> written instrument." Thus, [ERISA] § 402(a)(1) precludes the creation of a cause of action based on an oral contract under ERISA The validation and enforcement of oral agreement or modifications to pension plans through estoppel also conflicts with [ERISA] § 402(a)(1). *Cefalu v. B.F. Goodrich Company*, 871 F.2d 1290 (5th Cir. 1989).

Other courts have permitted the application of estoppel, but have not permitted it to override the requirement that all plan amendments be in writing. "For estoppel to apply, the plaintiff must show the following: (1) knowing misrepresentation by the defendant; (2) in writing; (3) with reasonable reliance by the plaintiff on the misrepresentation; (4) to the plaintiff's detriment. Thus, [the plaintiff] cannot rely on the oral statements by [the plan sponsor] because the estoppel doctrine does not override the aforementioned rule proscribing oral modification of an ERISA plan." *Downs v. World Color Press*, 214 F.3d 802 (7th Cir. 2000).

The judicial refusal to apply the doctrine of estoppel to oral modifications, if not overruled, was at least distinguished in one case when the court concluded that the oral representations were an "interpretation" rather than a modification of the plan, and as such were enforceable. *Kane v. Aetna Life Insurance*, 893 F.2d 1283 (11th Cir. 1990).

Because ERISA preempts state law under which the plan participant might plead fraud or invoke the doctrine of equitable estoppel, some courts have been willing to craft a federal common law of estoppel that is applicable in an ERISA suit if: (1) the employer or plan administrator knew the facts, (2) intended that its conduct would be relied upon by the plan participant, (3) who is ignorant of the true facts, and (4) the participant relied on the employer's or plan administrator's conduct to his or her detriment. *Ellenburgh v. Brockway, Inc.*, 763 F.2d 1091 (9th Cir. 1985).

Estoppel is not permitted, however, if the oral representations conflict with the written plan document as explained in the following case.

MELLO v. SARA LEE CORPORATION

431 F.3d 440 (5th Cir. 2005)

EDITH CLEMENT BROWN, CIRCUIT JUDGE.

The appellant, Sara Lee Corporation, appeals the district court's grant of summary judgment for the appellee, Frank Mello. The district court applied ERISA-estoppel and found that because Mello, a Sara Lee employee, relied on the oral assurances of a company executive and on non-binding monthly pension statements to determine the value of his pension, Sara Lee was estopped from correcting a clerical error that reduced the amount of his expected benefits significantly. Because Mello could not have reasonably relied on informal communications to modify or supersede unambiguous Plan terms, we reverse the district court's grant of summary judgment for Mello and dismiss the cause of action as a matter of law.

I. FACTS AND PROCEEDINGS

On September 17, 1984, Dr. Frank Mello began working for Bil Mar Foods, Inc. In 1987, Sara Lee acquired Bil Mar Foods, which became an operating division of Sara Lee. Although Sara Lee had a benefit pension plan, Bil Mar Foods' executives, including Mello, were not permitted to join Sara Lee's pension plan until 1994. Until that time, Bil Mar maintained its own retirement plan, in which Mello participated from 1984 to 1994 and from which he remains entitled to receive benefits. In October of 1994, Sara Lee asked Mello to transfer from Bil Mar Foods to Bryan Foods, another division of Sara Lee.

A disagreement arose between Mello and Sara Lee over whether Mello's pension benefits should be calculated using a hire date of September 17, 1984 or October 31, 1994. If the former date is used, Mello is entitled to $6500 each month in pension benefits; if the latter date is used, he will only receive $950 a month. Mello avers that Lee Kramer, a Sara Lee vice-president, encouraged him to transfer and repeatedly assured him that his credited service date would remain September 17, 1984.

Bryan Foods recorded Mello's hire date on the rate card in his personnel file as October 31, 1994. However, the "original hire date" on his personnel forms was September 17, 1984. From 1995 to 2000, Mello received six annual benefit statements from Sara Lee. Each benefit estimate included a disclaimer regarding the accuracy of the content therein, and instructed the recipient to defer to the terms of Sara Lee's pension plan. Each statement listed Mello's "hire date" and "credited service date" as September 17, 1984. The statements reflected monthly benefits ranging from $5,378 in 1996 to $6,581 in 2000. In December 2001, Mello's wife, who also works at Sara Lee, received an electronic version of her annual benefits while Mello did not. When Mello inquired about his missing statement, he received a "pension estimate" letter, which stated that his credited service date was October 31, 1994 and his monthly benefits were approximately $950.

Mello spoke with several Sara Lee officials in hopes of reinstating his previously quoted monthly benefits amount. Sara Lee's Human Resources Department explained that under the terms of Sara Lee's pension plan, his credited service date was the date he transferred to Bryan: October 31, 1994. . . . On April 11, 2002, Mello appealed to the ERISA Appeal Committee, which denied his petition. The Committee found that Mello was not entitled to credited service for his years of employment with Bil Mar Foods.

In October 2002, Mello filed suit against Sara Lee and the Sara Lee Pension Plan (collectively "Sara Lee") for benefits under ERISA § 502(a)(1)(B). Both parties filed cross-motions for summary judgment. On May 27, 2004, the district court granted summary judgment against Sara Lee. It reasoned that "because the Fifth Circuit has not soundly rejected the applicability of ERISA estoppel . . . , and because allowing ERISA estoppel's use in the instant case would best comport with the basic policies undergirding ERISA itself (i.e., to ensure the security of employee income and retirement benefits), the doctrine of ERISA estoppel . . . is applicable in this cause of action." Applying the three elements of ERISA estoppel, the court found that (1) the erroneous benefits estimates qualified as material misrepresentations, (2) Mello "reasonably and detrimentally relied" on these representations in making his employment and retirement decisions, and (3) Mello's claim involved extraordinary circumstances in that his employer, through written benefit statements and officers' oral statements, repeatedly assured Mello over a six-year period that he was entitled to a monthly amount that was an "extraordinary" overstatement. . . .

This circuit has yet to explicitly adopt ERISA-estoppel as a cognizable legal theory.[1] In the past, we have considered that the theory could be cognizable given

---

[1] The majority of other circuits, however, have adopted the theory of ERISA estoppel. *See* Bonovich v. Knights of Columbus, 146 F.3d 57, 62–63 (2d Cir. 1998); Smith v. Hartford Ins. Group, 6 F.3d 131, 137 (3d Cir. 1993); Marks v. Newcourt Credit Group, Inc., 342 F.3d 444, 456 (6th Cir. 2003); Vallone v. CNA Fin. Corp., 375 F.3d 623, 639 (7th Cir. 2004); Jensen v. SIPCO, 38 F.3d 945, 953 (8th Cir. 1994); Pisciotta

the right set of facts. We now join other circuits in explicitly adopting ERISA-estoppel as a cognizable theory. To establish an ERISA-estoppel claim, the plaintiff must establish: (1) a material misrepresentation; (2) reasonable and detrimental reliance upon the representation; and (3) extraordinary circumstances.

A. Material Misrepresentation

Sara Lee concedes that it erred as to the amount Mello's benefit statements reflected that he was due upon retirement. Sara Lee argues, however, thatthese errors do not constitute material misrepresentations because the benefit statements are informal communications that cannot be used to amend the Plan. In other words, Sara Lee contends that representations are material only if they are in an official plan document. Sara Lee also argues that materiality is not in reference to "[w]hat is material to Mello" but rather "whether the Benefit Estimates are 'material' to the interpretation of the Plan."

Contrary to Sara Lee's assertions, material misrepresentations can be made in informal documents. For example, in *Curcio*, the Third Circuit concluded that statements in an audio-visual presentation and pamphlet were material representations. 33 F.3d at 237 (noting, however, that the company announced its new benefit through a pamphlet rather than by formally amending the summary plan description). As to whether materiality refers to the representation's importance to the plan or to the plaintiff, a " 'misrepresentation is material if there is a substantial likelihood that it would mislead a reasonable employee in making an adequately informed decision.' "

Plaintiffs are able to satisfy the material misrepresentation element if their employers misrepresented any pertinent information. Because there was a substantial likelihood that a reasonable employee would be misled about making adequately informed decisions by Sara Lee's benefit statements' undisputed errors, the district court correctly concluded that the benefits statements were material misrepresentations.

B. Reasonable and Detrimental Reliance

Mello must demonstrate reliance upon the representations made by Sara Lee. The reliance must be both reasonable and detrimental. Contrary to the district court's conclusion, it was unreasonable for Mello to rely on Sara Lee's informal material misrepresentations regarding his benefits and Mello cannot establish his estoppel claim.

ERISA's policy against informal modifications of plan terms precludes a finding that Mello reasonably relied on the benefit statements' pension amounts. Mello does not argue that he relied on the benefit statements and Kramer's oral representations to help him interpret an ambiguous or unclear term in the Plan. Rather, he contends that he was reasonable to rely on the benefit statements and Kramer's assertions *rather than* the unambiguous credited service definition in the Plan. Mello's claim therefore amounts to an argument that informal written and oral statements amended or modified the terms of the Plan.

The district court found that despite the benefit statements' disclaimer that they were "for illustrative purposes only" and "[t]he Plan documents will govern the determination of any benefits you are eligible to receive," "the substance and implications of the written misrepresentations are enough in and of themselves to warrant a finding of reasonable detrimental reliance on material

v. Teledyne Indus., Inc., 91 F.3d 1326, 1331 (9th Cir. 1996) (per curiam); Jones v. Am. Gen. Life & Accident Ins. Co., 370 F.3d 1065, 1069 (11th Cir. 2004).

misrepresentations." In reaching this conclusion, the district court took into account "the repeated oral assurances made by Sara Lee via its Vice President Lee Kramer that Mello would retain his credited service date of September 17, 1987 [sic] upon transfer within Sara Lee."

However, ERISA-estoppel is not permitted if "based on purported oral modifications of plan terms." Such claims are precluded because ERISA provides that " 'every employee benefit plan shall be established and maintained pursuant to a written instrument.' " *Cefalu*, 871 F.2d at 1296 (quoting 29 U.S.C. § 1102(a)(1)); *Rodrigue*, 948 F.2d at 971. . . .

In *Sprague v. GMC*, the Sixth Circuit noted that a "party's reliance can seldom, if ever, be reasonable or justifiable if it is inconsistent with the clear and unambiguous terms of plan documents available to or furnished to the party." 133 F.3d 388, 404 (6th Cir. 1998). The court held that allowing "estoppel to override the clear terms of plan documents would be to enforce something other than the plan documents themselve s. That would not be consistent with ERISA." In *In re Unisys Corp. Retiree Med. Benefit "ERISA" Litigations*, which applies the Third Circuit's estoppel test used in this circuit, the court emphasized that a basic principle of ERISA is that a plan cannot be modified or superceded by extrinsic evidence. 58 F.3d 896, 902 (3d Cir. 1995). In *Unisys*, a company engaged in a "systematic campaign of confusion" which led the plaintiff-employees to believe mistakenly that their benefits continued for life. The court "acknowledge[d] that many retirees may have relied to their detriment on their interpretation of the summary plan descriptions as promising vested or lifetime benefits." However, because the summary plan descriptions contained "unambiguous reservation of rights clauses," the plaintiffs' interpretation of the plans as providing lifetime benefits was unreasonable and their estoppel claim was precluded. The court summarized:

> While our decisions have not required an express finding of plan ambiguity as an element for establishing an estoppel claim, we have required that reliance be reasonable. Because our decisions require that any detrimental reliance on plan language also be "reasonable," our finding that the [terms of the Plan] are unambiguous undercuts the reasonableness of any detrimental reliance by the retirees. Accordingly, we hold that the district court did not err in concluding, on summary judgment, that the retirees' estoppel claim failed as a matter of law.

Id. at 908. Mello's claim cannot surmount the clear and consistent case law forbidding recognizing reasonable reliance on informal documents in the face of unambiguous Plan terms.

. . .

Because Mello's reliance on the informal benefit statements and oral representations was unreasonable, we need not consider whether the reliance was detrimental or if extraordinary circumstances existed.

Because Mello has not satisfied the reasonable reliance, he cannot establish that ERISA-estoppel should be applied to preclude Sara Lee from correcting the amount of his pension benefits. Therefore, the opinion of the district court is REVERSED and this case is remanded for further proceedings.

6-13 QUESTIONS AND PROBLEMS

1. Is a plan fiduciary not responsible if the individuals who perform "ministerial functions" mislead the plan participants and cause them financial harm?

2. Why was it unreasonable for Mello to rely on the oral representations made to him?

3. Why does the court ignore the fact that Mello claims that he transferred from one division of Sara Lee to another in reliance on the statement by the Sara Lee vice-president that he would be credited with service back to 1984?

4. Shanda works for Kappa Corp., which has a defined benefit plan managed by the named plan fiduciary, Pension Management Co. (PMC). At age 60, Shanda is offered a position by Iota Inc. with a substantial pay raise but no pension. Shanda asks the PMC representative to compare her pension at age 65 if she remains with Kappa for another five years with the alternative that she quits at age 60 and begins her pension at age 65. The PMC representative miscalculates Shanda's pension and tells her if she works until she is age 65, her pension will be 25% higher. In fact, it will be only 10% higher than if she quits at age 60 and defers beginning the pension until age 65. Based on this inaccurate advice, Shanda turns down the Iota job offer. One year later, reading the plan SPD, she realizes that she was misled and would have been much better off financially if she had taken the Iota offer. She sues PMC for the value of the lost opportunity with Iota. What result?

F. PROHIBITED TRANSACTIONS

ERISA §§ 406, 408(e).

ERISA § 406 provides a sweeping prohibition against:

(a) transactions with a party in interest as defined in § 3(14) (§ 406(a)), and

(b) self-dealing by fiduciaries (§ 406(b)).

Section § 406 prohibits the plan fiduciary from permitting the plan to engage in certain transactions defined as "prohibited transactions." Essentially, § 406 is an attempt to prevent fiduciaries from engaging in "sweetheart deals," and so bars transactions, such as the sale, leasing of property or loans, between the plan and any "party in interest." § 406(a).

The term "party in interest" is defined in great detail in ERISA § 3(14), and includes among others any fiduciary, counsel, person providing services to the plan, an owner of 50 percent of the stock of the employer, and relatives (spouses, ancestors, descendants and their spouses) of fiduciaries and persons providing services to the plan. §§ 3(14) & (15).

The judicial interpretation of § 406 is instructive. "Congress adopted specific prohibitions in Section 406 to 'prevent categories of transactions which offer a high potential for insider abuse of plans or for loss of plan assets.' " *Freund v. Marshall & Ilsley Bank*, 485 F. Supp. 629, 637 (W.D. Wis. 1979). The rules are designed to prevent a trustee "from being put into a position where he had dual loyalties and therefore he cannot act exclusively for the benefit of a plan's participants and beneficiaries." *N.L.R.B. v. Amax Coal Co., a Division of Amax, Inc.*, 453 U.S. 322, 329 (1981).

> We note that the national public interest in safeguarding anticipated employee benefits by establishing *minimum* standards to protect em-

> ployee benefit plans. The substantial growth of plans affecting the security of millions of employees and their dependents, as well as the limited resources of the Department of Labor in the enforcement of ERISA, leads us to believe that Congress intended to create an easily applied per se prohibition of the type of transaction in question.

Cutaiar v. Marshall, 590 F.2d 523, 529 (3d Cir. 1979).

The legislative history of § 406(b) and relevant case law indicate that Congress sought to prevent "kickbacks," making "illegal *per se* the types of transactions that experience had shown to entail a high potential for abuse." *Donovan v. Cunningham*, 716 F.2d 1455, 1465 (5th Cir. 1983).

The *per se* nature of the prohibition is underscored by the fact that whether one of the provisions has been violated does not depend on whether the prohibited act caused harm to the plan. *McDougall v. Donovan*, 552 F. Supp. 1206, 1215 (N.D. Ill. 1982). "Absent a statutory or administrative exemption, plan fiduciaries are forbidden to cause a fund to engage in specified deals regardless of whether any harm actually results from the transaction." *Donovan v. Walton*, 609 F. Supp. 1221, 1246 (S.D. Fla. 1985).

Examples of litigation invoking violations of the prohibited transaction doctrine of ERISA § 406 help illustrate the types of abuses targeted by the section. A § 406(a)(1)(C) violation was found when a union operated pension fund trustee had the fund hire two cooks from a restaurant operated by his son, who was the pension fund counsel, so that the cooks would be paid during winter months when the son's restaurant was not operating. The court held that the § 408(b)(2) exemption from prohibited transactions did not apply because the plan had no need to employ the cooks as "maintenance men" and did so only to benefit the restaurant operated by the son of the trustee of the plan. *N.Y. State Teamsters Council v. Estate of DePerno*, 816 F. Supp. 138 (N.D.N.Y. 1993). In 1978, the Central Conference of Teamsters union wanted to purchase a new jet from Falcon (the manufacturer) and trade in its old one, which it had purchased in 1975 for approximately $2.6 million. To facilitate the union's purchase of a new jet, the union operated pension plan agreed to purchase the old jet from the Falcon at a cost of $2.9 million. The Department of Labor sued the pension plan trustees, claiming that the indirect sale of the jet from the union to the pension plan was a prohibited transaction. The court agreed that an indirect sale could not be used to circumvent what would have been a *per se* violation of the prohibited transaction statute had the union sold the jet directly to the pension plan. *McDougall v. Donovan*, 552 F. Supp. 1206 (N.D. Ill. 1982). Section 406 was successfully invoked against a trustee of a union-operated pension fund who was the sole owner of two companies that sold insurance to the pension plan. As trustee, he alone set and approved the fees and commissions paid to his insurance companies. He, in turn, was compensated by the companies. The trustee was found to have violated the § 406(b)(1) prohibition against dealing with the assets of the plan "in his own interest or own account." *In re Consolidated Welfare Fund ERISA Litigation*, 839 F. Supp. 1068 (S.D.N.Y. 1993).

The harsh application of § 406 is tempered by § 408, which lists specific exemptions from the prohibited transaction doctrine and also permits the Secretary of Labor to grant additional exemptions to a class of fiduciaries or transaction. Fiduciaries can also apply to the Department of Labor for an individual exemption. IRC § 4975(c)(2). The exceptions under § 408 include contracting or making reasonable rents for office space, investment of the fund assets in bank deposits (at reasonable rates of interest), and the provision of ancillary services to the fund by a bank or other similar financial entity even though it is a plan fiduciary.

The rule that a fiduciary cannot engage in transactions involving securities or property of the employer is waived if the plan receives adequate consideration. ERISA § 408(e). The most blatant forms of self-dealing, however, are not saved by that rule.

LASCALA v. SCRUFARI

479 F.3d 213 (2d Cir. 2007)

RAKOFF, DISTRICT JUSTICE.

Plaintiffs Salvatore J. LaScala, Douglas A. Janese, and Richard J. Marino appeal from so much of a judgment of the United States District Court for the Western District of New York, entered after a bench trial, as found defendant Santo S. Scrufari not liable for certain breaches of fiduciary duties imposed by the Employee Retirement Income Security Act of 1974 ("ERISA"), 29 U.S.C. § 1001 *et seq.*, and as held that damages based on certain other fiduciary breaches that the district court found Scrufari did commit would stop accruing on December 31, 2003, and not be based on the pension benefits Scrufari would receive in the future. For the reasons that follow, we grant the appeal in all essential respects.

The underlying action, commenced in 1993, charged several violations of federal labor law and ERISA. By 2004, the primary issue remaining in the case was whether Scrufari, as the Plan Manager of the Niagara-Genesee & Vicinity Carpenters Local 280 Welfare and Pension Funds (the "Funds"), breached his fiduciary duties under ERISA by unilaterally increasing without trustee approval his compensation and benefits and the compensation of his son, who was also employed by the Funds.

The Funds were established pursuant to trust agreements among the Fund Trustees, Carpenters Local 280, and the Building Industry Employers Association of Niagara County, New York, Inc. These trust agreements provide for five union-designated trustees and five employer-designated trustees, all of whom are fiduciaries of the Funds. The agreements further give the trustees the power to "designate a salaried Fund Manager" and the power to "incur and pay the ordinary and necessary expenses of administration," including the Fund Manager's salary. The trustees may exercise these powers only "by majority vote of the quorum."

In the Fall of 1982, Scrufari had been a union-designated trustee of the Funds for some ten years and wanted to be appointed Plan Manager of the Funds. Scrufari met with his fellow union-designated trustee Sarkee Sanoian, who was the General Business Agent of Local 280, to seek Sanoian's help in obtaining this position. Sanoian apparently agreed to help Scrufari, because at a trustees' meeting in September 1982, Sanoian suggested that the current Plan Manager, Lorelei Collins, be replaced by a union member trained in collection procedures (Scrufari), and asked her when she expected to retire. Although Collins said she planned to stay another seven years, she suddenly (and somewhat mysteriously) resigned on October 10, 1983.

Shortly thereafter, at a trustee meeting held on October 21, 1983, a union-designated trustee made a motion to appoint Scrufari as the new Plan Manager. Two votes were taken and both resulted in a deadlock, with the five union-designated trustees (including Scrufari) voting for Scrufari and the five employer-designated trustees voting against Scrufari.

At a subsequent trustees meeting held on December 15, 1983, Sanoian raised again the possibility of appointing Scrufari as the Plan Manager of the Funds and noted that "Scrufari was qualified for the job and should be paid journeyman's wages for it." After a vote to reconsider the motion to appoint Scrufari once more resulted in a deadlock, the trustees agreed to refer the question to an already-scheduled arbitration of an unrelated dispute over a pension benefit increase.

At still a further trustees meeting held on March 9, 1984, several union members expressed dissatisfaction with the acting Plan Manager, Kathy Vance. A motion was made to put Scrufari in the Fund office along with Vance and a separate motion was made to fire Vance. The votes on both motions deadlocked. Shortly after the meeting, however, Vance resigned. The trustees held an emergency meeting on March 20, 1984 and a motion was again made to appoint Scrufari as acting Plan Manager. Once again, the vote deadlocked. Instead, the trustees voted to appoint the Funds' actuary, the firm of Maloney & O'Sullivan, as acting Plan Manager. Shortly thereafter, however, without consulting the trustees, Maloney & O'Sullivan hired Scrufari to supervise the Plan office. Scrufari subsequently acknowledged that he was effectively the Plan Manager while he was Maloney & O'Sullivan's employee.

. . .

While he was a Maloney . . . O'Sullivan employee, Scrufari was paid the "General Foreman" rate on the Carpenters Union scale, which the trustees had "generally agreed" would govern the Plan Manager's salary. . . .

At a meeting on March 7, 1985, the trustees finally made Scrufari the Plan Manager by passing the following resolution: "Motion by Sarkee Sanoian seconded by Merton Marshall to appoint Santo Scrufari as Plan Manager as opposed to the present arrangement with Maloney & O'Sullivan. *His present rate of pay as a salaried employee will remain.*" Scrufari himself was not present at the meeting and only one person at the meeting — O'Sullivan, of Maloney & O'Sullivan — knew what Scrufari's "present rate of pay" was. But nobody asked O'Sullivan what the rate was. Subsequently, at trial, Sanoian, who was present at the March meeting but who was subsequently alienated from Scrufari, testified that his understanding was that the reference to Scrufari's "present rate of pay" referred to a salary based on the "Journeyman" rate, i.e., the very lowest rate of pay on the Carpenters Union scale and well below what Maloney & O'Sullivan was actually paying him. At the other extreme, Thomas Hartz, a union-designated trustee who had remained friendly to Scrufari, testified that his understanding was that Scrufari was being paid at "the same rate that the general business agent [i.e., Sanoian] was making."

In any event, Scrufari unilaterally concluded that he was authorized to be paid at the same rate as Sanoian. Further, he concluded that he was authorized to match Sanoian's salary, increase by increase, for the remainder of his tenure as Plan Manager. In accordance with this understanding, on July 1, 1985, just three months after he became Plan Manager, Scrufari gave himself a raise without trustee approval from $18.47 an hour (roughly the General Foreman's rate) to $20.52 an hour (roughly the General Agent's rate, which was also Sanoian's rate). Between 1985 and 1989, Scrufari raised his salary five additional times, each time without trustee approval.

. . .

During the same period that Scrufari was Plan Manager, Scrufari's son Russell, who had been employed in the Funds office since 1984, asked his father for pay increases, and received same. Initially, this was done with trustee approval. Thus, in 1989, when Russell asked his father for a salary raise on the ground that the salary he was receiving — $9.95 per hour — was not commensurate with his experience, Scrufari instructed his son to clear it with Sanoian first and then to submit a letter to the trustees. Accordingly, Russell prepared a letter asking for a raise to $11.50 an hour, cleared it with Sanoian, and submitted it to the trustees, who approved Russell's request. In 1990, Russell went through the same process and received a raise to $12.50 an hour. Thereafter, however, between 1990 and 1992, Scrufari gave Russell four additional raises without trustee approval. Scrufari purported to justify these raises on the grounds that he had discretion to set the salaries of Plan-office employees and that the raises were commensurate with Russell's experience.

As noted, plaintiffs commenced the present action in 1993 alleging several causes of action against Scrufari and others. In particular, plaintiffs contended that Scrufari breached his fiduciary duties of loyalty and care, in violation of ERISA §§ 404(a)(1), and his fiduciary duty to avoid self dealing, in violation of ERISA § 406(b)(1), by (1) raising his own salary multiple times without trustee approval, (2) paying himself four hours of weekly overtime between 1989 and 1992 without trustee approval, (3) paying himself weighted fringe benefits based on this inflated salary and awarding himself retroactive weighted fringe benefits from 1984 to 1989, without trustee approval, and (4) raising his son Russell's compensation multiple times without trustee approval. Following a bench trial, the district courtfound that Scrufari had not breached these duties in awarding salary increases to himself and his son, chiefly because the trustees knew or should have known of the increases but did not object, but that Scrufari did breach these duties with respect to the overtime, of which the trustees were ignorant. . . .

On appeal, plaintiffs principally contend that the district court erred in concluding that Scrufari did not breach his fiduciary duties under ERISA when he gave himself and his son salary increases without trustee approval. ERISA § 404(a)(1) states that a fiduciary must discharge his duties "solely in the interest of the [ERISA plan] participants and beneficiaries and"

> (A) for the exclusive purpose of:
>
> (i) providing benefits to participants and their beneficiaries; and
>
> (ii) defraying reasonable expenses of administering the plan;
>
> (B) with the care, skill, prudence, and diligence under the circumstances then prevailing that a prudent man acting in a like capacity and familiar with such matters would use in the conduct of an enterprise of a like character and with like aims;
>
> . . . and
>
> (D) in accordance with the documents and instruments governing the plan . . . .

In the instant case, as noted, the district court found that Scrufari did not breach his fiduciary duties under ERISA §§ 404(a)(1) or 406(b)(1) by "taking regular salary increases without express Trustee approval" because "the Trustees knew, or in the exercise of their fiduciary duties should have known, that . . . Scrufari was being compensated at the same rate as Sanoian." But the fact that the trustees knew, or should have known, that Scrufari was being compensated at the same rate as Sanoian is irrelevant to whether Scrufari breached his fiduciary duties. The trustees, along w ith Scrufari, were fiduciaries of the Funds, and one fiduciary's knowledge of anot her fiduciary's breach does not excuse that breach; to the contrary, pursuant to ERISA § 405(a)(3), one fiduciary's knowledge of another's breach can make the first fiduciary liable for the other's breach.

. . .

Thus, the question of whether Scrufari breached his fiduciary duties does not turn, as the district court found, on whether the trustees knew or should have known of Scrufari's actions and acquiesced therein, but rather on whether Scrufari himself acted in accordance with the duties imposed by ERISA § 404(a)(1) and ERISA § 406(b)(1). As Plan Manager, Scrufari was a fiduciary bound by "the highest" duty "known to the law," to exercise his authority as Plan Manager "in accordance with the documents and instruments governing the plan," ERISA § 404(a)(1)(D). The "documents and instruments governing the plan" here do not give the Plan Manager the power to increase his compensation unilaterally; rather, the trust agreements provide, in effect, that only the trustees may increase the Plan Manager's salary, and then only by a majority vote. A prudent person in Scrufari's position, bound by the highest duty known to the law, would have known that he could not raise his compensation without a majority vote of the trustees and further would have known that no majority vote had taken place. And Scrufari clearly did know this, for when his son Russell initially asked Scrufari for salary increases in 1989 and 1990, Scrufari directed Russell "to submit a letter to the Trustees" for their approval.

In these circumstances, when Scrufari unilaterally awarded himself a series of salary raises, Scrufari was not acting "solely in the interest of the [ERISA plan] participants and beneficiaries," as ERISA § 404(a)(1) requires, and was "deal[ing] with the assets of the plan in his own interest," as ERISA § 406(b)(1) prohibits. Accordingly, the district court erred as a matter of law in holding that Scrufari did not breach his fiduciary duties under ERISA § 404(a)(1) and ERISA § 406(b)(1) each time he raised his own salary without trustee approval.

Scrufari also violated his fiduciary duties by giving his son Russell raises without trustee approval. The district court concluded that plaintiffs had "failed to establish any breach of the Plan Manager's fiduciary duties under ERISA §§ 404(a) or 406(b) as a result of his authorization of salary increases for his son, Russell," but offered no reason for this conclusion other than that "the preponderance of the evidence shows that the Funds did not suffer any loss as a result of Russell's employment." The fact that the Funds may not have suffered any loss as a result of Russell's salary increases may bear on the question of damages, but has no bearing on whether Scrufari breached his fiduciary duties in the first place. To the contrary, Scrufari's actions in giving his son raises without trustee approval, where a prudent person in his position would have known that the trust agreements did not authorize this, violated ERISA § 404(a)(1) and ERISA § 406(b)(1). Accordingly, the district court erred as a matter of law in holding that Scrufari did not breach his fiduciary duties each time he increased his son's compensation without trustee approval.

. . .

We have considered the parties' other arguments and find them to be without merit. We reverse the district court's determination that Scrufari did not breach his fiduciary duties when he gave himself and his son salary raises without trustee approval and conclude that he did so. . . . We remand to the district court to calculate damages on the salary claims and to recalculate damages on the overtime pay and fringe benefit claims.

6-14 QUESTIONS AND PROBLEMS

Mario is the President of Delta Co., a supplier of hospital equipment that sponsors the Delta Profit Sharing Plan. The Plan Trustees are Mario, Norris, the Vice President of Delta, and Odette, the treasurer of Delta. The Plan has $23 million in assets including $2 million in cash as a result of the sale of some of its corporate bond holdings. It also owns $15 million in corporate stocks and $6 million in corporate bonds. The Trustees believe the Plan should invest in real estate as a means of diversifying the Plan investment portfolio. Mario owns several thousand acres of ranch land in Montana. Mario wishes to sell half his land holdings, worth about $2 million, to create liquidity to finance a new internet based retailer that he has organized. The new company has nothing to do with Delta. How can Mario sell his land to the Plan without violating ERISA § 406? Are Norris and Odette at any risk of violating ERISA fiduciaries obligations if they approve the purchase of Mario's land?

In addition to the prohibition on self-dealing, § 406(b)(2) prohibits a fiduciary from acts in which there is a conflict of interest and from accepting "kickbacks." Note that § 406(a) prohibits certain transactions by the fiduciary with "a party in interest who is defined in § 3(14) as among others as "a person providing services to such plan." § 3(14)(B). Section 406(b) prohibits certain transactions between a fiduciary and a plan. However, § 408 provides a list of exemptions from the prohibitions under § 406.

6-15 QUESTIONS AND PROBLEMS

Look carefully at the interplay of § 406 and 408 and consider the following problems.

1. The Operating Engineers Local 675 Pension Fund makes mortgage loans at two percent below the prevailing community mortgage rates to Fund participants if they satisfy the following requirements: (1) proof of financial stability and credit-worthiness, (2) secure the loan by a first mortgage on the principal residence of the mortgagor, (3) title to the mortgaged property must be marketable and insurable, (4) the loan does not exceed 95 percent of the apprised value of the property, (5) mortgage insurance is required if the down payment is less than 20 percent of the appraised value, and (6) the borrower assigns all of his or her accrued pension rights to the Plan as additional security. Each loan had to be approved by the Trustees of the Plan. Do such loans constitute prohibited transactions?

2. The Zeta Co. Plan offers participants loans with the minimum loan amount of $25,000, with the only security for the loan the participant's vested accrued benefit? Are the loans prohibited transactions?

3. Taylor is the Trustee of Alpha Profit-Sharing Plan. His nieces, Anna and Bridget, are participants in the Plan. Under the Plan, the Trustee is permitted to establish a participant loan program if it meets certain specified criteria. Taylor creates a loan program, but before he notifies the other participants in the Plan, he notifies Anna and Bridget of the new loan program. Anna and Bridget borrow substantially all the funds set aside for the loan program. Taylor then tells the other participants about the loan program, but by then the program has almost no funds to lend. Are the loans to Anna and Bridget prohibited transactions?

4. The Carpenters Union Local 919 Pension Fund ("Fund") is a multi-employer trust fund. It provides pension benefits to retired members of the Union and is funded by contributions by the employers. The Fund has four trustees, two appointed by the Union leadership and two appointed by a committee representing the various employers who contribute to the Fund. In 2001, the Fund purchased 50

acres of land near the town of Athens. The land was purchased as an investment, in part because th e Fund was disappointed with the rate of return it had achieved in its investments in stocks. The Fund paid $1,000,000 cash for the land. The Fund then built a modest sized office building on the site, occupied about 20 percent of it, and attempted to rent out the remaining space. The building cost $2,000,000. The Fund paid for the building with $200,000 in cash and borrowed $1.8 from Beta Bank who took back a mortgage on the property.

The Beta loan was contingent upon the Fund preleasing at least 75 percent of the remaining space. The Fund was able to lease one-half of the remaining space, at a rate of $20 per square foot, to Delta Consulting Co., but because of the downturn in the economy, the Fund could not locate another lessee. Finally the Union, whose headquarters was located in a building that was sharply raising its rental rates from $15 a square foot to $22, agreed to rent the remaining space in the building at a rate of $18 a square foot. With that agreement, Big Bank agreed to the mortgage. The building was constructed, and the Fund and the Union moved in.

The Department of Labor (DOL) is investigating whether the lease between the Union and the Fund is a prohibited transaction. The DOL believes that the lease may violate ERISA § 406(a)(1)(A). The Fund cites ERISA § 408(b)(2) claiming that the lease is not a prohibited transaction.

Look at the cited sections. What additional facts are required to determine whether the DOL should sue the Fund for a prohibited transaction?

Some actions by fiduciaries violate both § 406(a) and (b).

MARTIN v. NATIONAL BANK OF ALASKA

828 F. Supp. 1427 (D. Alaska 1992)

HOLLAND, CHIEF JUDGE. The Secretary [of Labor] alleges that NBA invested the assets of plans within the meaning of ERISA Section 3(3), as to which NBA was a fiduciary, in mortgage loans (hereinafter "take-out loans") used to retire construction loans made to the mortgagors by NBA. The Secretary alleges that this practice is a violation of NBA's fiduciary duties as established by ERISA.

The Secretary also alleges that, in connection with the "take-out" loans, NBA received loan origination fees from the borrowers and loan servicing fees from the plans. The Secretary alleges that receipt of such fees is a violation of NBA's fiduciary duties as established by ERISA.

At issue is:

(1) whether the claims based on "take-out loans," origination fees, and servicing fees are barred by the statute of limitations;

(2) whether common trust funds, the source of one of the loans, is subject to the fiduciary duties established by ERISA; and

(3) whether the complained of transactions are prohibited by ERISA.

The loans at issue are long-term mortgage loans originated by [National Bank of Alaska] NBA on behalf of its Profit-Sharing Trust and Common Trust Fund "A." Borrowers would apply for a permanent loan and a construction loan at the same time. Before a permanent loan could be made, all secured debts on the property had to be paid. If there were a construction loan on the property, NBA would obtain a commitment to the permanent loan from the plan before, or at the same time, the construction loan was made. In relation to these permanent loans, NBA received origination fees from the borrowers. In return for these fees, NBA fulfilled a range of services, including but not limited to, helping borrowers fill out mortgage applications, doing credit checks to ensure borrowers could meet payments, obtaining an appraisal of the real estate, and helping to resolve the problems that might arise in the borrowers' credit worthiness.

In its first amended complaint, the Secretary alleges that NBA invested assets of plans as to which it was a fiduciary in mortgage loans used to retire construction loans made to the mortgagors by NBA and that such a practice is a violation of ERISA Section 404(a)(1)(A), 406(a)(1)(D), 406(b)(1), and 406(b)(2). NBA has moved for summary judgment in its favor as to the Secretary's claim that "take-out" loans violate ERISA. The Secretary has moved for summary judgment in its favor on the same claims.

. . .

Both parties have moved for summary judgment on the issue of whether NBA violated provisions of ERISA Section 406. While Section 404 deals with fiduciary standards, Section 406 addresses express prohibited transactions. Section 406(a) provides:

> (1) A fiduciary with respect to a plan shall not cause the plan to engage in a transaction, if he knows or should know that such transaction constitutes a direct or indirect —
>
> . . . .
>
> (D) transfer to, or use by or for the benefit of, a party in interest, of any assets of the plan . . . .

[ERISA § 406.] The Secretary asserts that NBA is a party in interest as defined in ERISA Section 3(14), and that the bank received plan assets when the borrower repaid the bank on the construction loan with the proceeds of the mortgage loan. The issue here is whether the take-out financing is an "indirect" transfer of assets of the plan to NBA, a party in interest.

NBA knew, at the time the permanent loans were made, that the borrowers would use the mortgage loan proceeds to satisfy the construction loans made by NBA. They were arranged by NBA as a package deal. These were not sham loans; but NBA knew that the mortgage loans from the plan assets would indirectly benefit a party in interest — the bank itself

There is no genuine issue as to whether NBA received plan assets. The construction loans and the permanent loans were arranged at the same time, and the plan assets used to fund the permanent loans were intended to go directly to NBA to satisfy the construction loans made by NBA. The Secretary's motion for summary judgment is granted as to Section 406(a)(1)(D).

. . .

There is no genuine issue as to whether NBA represented a party with interests adverse to the plan. NBA received origination fees from the borrowers of the loans at issue in exchange for NBA's help in obtaining the permanent loans from the plans. The interests of the lender and the borrower are inherently adverse, and to represent other sides creates a conflict. Does NBA act on behalf of the plan, to which it is a fiduciary, or does it act on behalf of the borrower who is paying NBA to obtain the permanent loan? This conflict is only aggravated by the fact theat NBA itself had an economic interest in the transactions in that the proceeds of the permanent loan would be used to retire the construction loans made by NBA to the borrowers.

The Secretary's motion summary judgment is granted as to ERISA Section 406(b)(2).

6-16 QUESTIONS AND PROBLEMS

1. What actions of NBA violated ERISA? Which sections of ERISA did it violate?

2. Is NBA creating investment opportunities for the retirement plan or is it shifting the risks of its loans to the plan?

3. Suppose the loans made by the plan were considered prudent investments. Would that change the outcome of the case?

In 1993, the Supreme Court held that the transfer by the plan sponsor of property (five truck terminals) in payment of its minimum funding obligation was a prohibited transaction, even though the assessed valuation of the properties was not in dispute and was sufficient to meet the funding obligation. The Court stated:

> We note, too, that this construction of the statute's broad language is necessary to accomplish Congress' goal. Before ERISA's enactment in 1974, the measure that governed a transaction between a pension plan and its sponsor was the customary arm's — length standard of conduct. This provided an open door for abuses such as the sponsor's sale of property to the plan at an inflated price or the sponsor's satisfaction of a funding obligation by contribution of property that was overvalued or nonliquid.
>
> Congress' goal was to bar categorically a transaction that was likely to injure the pension plan. The transfer of encumbered property may jeopardize the ability of the plan to pay promised benefits. Such a transfer imposes upon the trust the primary obligation to pay the encumbrance, and thus frees cash for the employer by restricting the use of cash by the trust. Overvaluation, the burden of disposing of the property, and the employer's substitution of its own judgment as to investment policy, are other obvious considerations. Although the burden of an encumbrance is unique to the contribution of encumbered property, concerns about overvaluation, disposal of property, and the need to maintain an independent investment policy animate any contribution of property that satisfies a funding obligation, regardless of whether or not the property is encumbered. This is because as long as a pension fund is giving up an account receivable in exchange for property, the fund runs the risk of giving up more than it is getting in return if the property is either less valuable or more burdensome than a cash contribution would have been.
>
> These potential harmful effects are illustrated by the facts of the present case, even though the properties at issue were unencumbered and not overvalued at the times of their respective transfers. There were exclusive sales-listing agreements respondent had made with respect to two of the truck terminals; these agreements called for sales commissions. The presence of this requirement demonstrates that it is neither easy nor costless to dispose of such properties. The Chicago truck terminal, for example, was not sold for 31/2 years after it was listed for sale by the Pension Trust.

Commissioner v. Keystone Consolidated Industries, Inc., 508 U.S. 152, 160 (1993).

The prohibited transaction doctrine is so broadly worded that it has the potential for very widespread application. As a result, the courts have taken care to limit its use. For example, Lockheed Corporation was faced with the need to reduce its workforce. It amended its pension plan and established an early retirement program that offered increased pension benefits to employees who would retire early, with benefits payable out of the surplus assets of the plan's pension fund. The effect of the early retirement plan was to use the plan surplus to promote the needs of Lockheed rather than the interests of the plan participants except for those who were willing to take early retirement As a condition of receipt of the benefits, the early retirees had to sign a release of any employment related claims they might have against Lockheed. Spink, an employee of Lockheed, refused to sign the waiver and so retired without the extra benefits. He later sued Lockheed, claiming that the signing of the release in exchange for higher pension benefits paid out of the plan was a prohibited transaction under ERISA § 406(a).

The Supreme Court held that the payment of benefits conditioned upon the signing of a release was not a "transaction" within the meaning of ERISA § 406(a)(1). It was merely a quid pro quo between the plan and the participants pursuant to the terms of the amended plan. *Lockheed Corp. v. Spink*, 517 U.S. 882 (1996). Moreover, when Lockheed amended the plan, it did so as plan sponsor, not as a plan fiduciary, and so did not trigger any of ERISA's fiduciary provisions such as the duty of loyalty. Therefore, Lockheed did not violate ERISA by using the plan assets to further corporate goals rather than "solely in the interest of the participants." ERISA § 404(a)(1).

Section 404 creates a basic duty of loyalty for a plan fiduciary and lists various actions necessary to comply with meeting the duty of the fiduciary to act solely for the benefit of the plan. The fiduciary, inter alia, must act with the "care, skill prudence, and diligence under the circumstances then prevailing that a prudent man" would act an d must diversify the plan investments in order to minimize the risk of "large losses." The broad, generalized standards of care contained in § 404 seem to encompass the more specific prohibitions of § 406. Some commentators believe that § 406 provides no greater protection against fiduciary fraud, abuse or mismanagement than does § 404.

G. INVESTMENT OF PLAN ASSETS

ERISA §§ 404(a)(1), 407(a).

Pension plans control trillions of dollars that must eventually be paid to the plan participants and other beneficiaries. While the security of the fund assets is paramount, beyond mere preservation of assets all plan fiduciaries seek to increase the value of the fund assets by successful investing. The only restrictions on investments are found in ERISA §§ 404 and 407. Section 404(a)(1)(B) and (C) requires that the fiduciary act with the prudence that is demanded by the circumstances, and that the fiduciary diversify investments in order to minimize the risk of large losses. Section 407(a)(2) limits to 10 percent the percentage of plan assets that can be invested in the securities of the plan sponsor. Interestingly, no similar limitation applies to § 401(k) plan accounts if the participant directs the investments. § 407(b)(2)(B).

Trustees of plans have the option of investing plan funds in annuities sold by insurance companies (such annuities are commonly purchased to finance the pensions for retirees of defined benefit plans), but the majority of pension assets are invested in corporate securities and bonds As a result, it is estimated that 40 percent of all the equities in United States companies are owned by pension plans.

Some plans invest directly in the stock and bond markets, while others invest through mutual funds or pooled funds operated by a bank or investment company.

Of course, not all investments rise in value. But as one court pointed out, ". . . the ultimate outcome of an investment is not proof of its imprudence." *DeBruyne v. Equitable Life Assurance Soc.*, 920 F.2d 457, 465 (7th Cir. 1990). ERISA does not require that pension plan investments be risk free since every investment entails some degree of risk. *Marshall v. Glass/Metal Association & Glaziers & Glassworkers Pension Plan*, 507 F. Supp. 378 (D. Haw. 1980).

Since 1979, investment managers have been held to the standard of prudence of the modern portfolio theory by the Secretary's regulations. 29 C.F.R. 2550.404a-1." The following material explains modern portfolio theory.

W. BRANTLEY PHILLIPS, JR., NOTE, CHASING DOWN THE DEVIL: STANDARDS OF PRUDENT INVESTMENT UNDER THE RESTATEMENT (THIRD) OF TRUSTS

54 Wash. & Lee L. Rev. 335, 348–350 (1997)

Acceptance of modern portfolio theory came slowly. Given that, in part, the theory combines speculative and "safe" investments in an effort to generate consistent portfolio gains, it can appear counterintuitive when compared with previous standards of prudence. Nevertheless, decades of empirical research now support modern portfolio theory and establish it firmly in the mainstream.

Current economic thinking broadly defines risk as the potential for an investment to underperform its expected rate of return. The focus of this thinking is the relationship between the risk of an individual investment and the entire investment portfolio. Modern portfolio theory recognizes that managing an asset's potential for under performance can reward prudent investors. By dividing risk into its various components, the theory seeks to aid an investor in understanding how to balance the opportunity for gain against the degree of risk undertaken.

Essentially, two types of risk threaten most investments. The first type of risk rises and falls in direct response to general economic conditions that affect the entire market. Modern portfolio theory describes this type of risk as "systematic" or "market" ri sk. Because market risk mirrors the fluctuations in the overall market, such risk is unavoidable. Nevertheless, because a rising market compensates an investor in the form of higher returns, incurring greater market risk is not inherently detrimental to an investment strategy.

Modern portfolio theory describes the second form of risk as "specific" or "residual" risk. This type of risk represents those market forces that negatively affect a specific investment or industry. Specific risk also measures how the variability in the rate of return for an individual investment impacts the whole portfolio. However, given that specific risk does not precisely imitate market fluctuations, increases in the market do not necessarily compensate an investor with higher returns when he assumes the additional specific risk because of a particular asset. Nevertheless, investors can take steps to avoid specific risk. Diversification effectively ties portfolio returns to general market conditions and thereby dilutes the volatility associated with any one investment. Therefore, by maintaining a broad portfolio, one can better hold specific risk to a relatively low level.

In addition to comparing risks, modern portfolio theory also suggests that the investment markets are reasonably efficient. This means that, at any given time, the price of an investment reflects virtually all information available for that investment. More importantly, however, a reasonably efficient market means that the price of an investment closely corresponds to its degree of specific risk. As a result, attempts to identify undervalued investments in order to earn above average returns are rarely successful because the market correctly prices every investment. The fact that the majority of professional investment managers consistently fail to match the performance of the market supports this view.

The ultimate goal of modern portfolio theory is to balance portfolio risks and returns through diversification of the assets held. Relying on efficient market principles, the theory concludes that, by using a wide range of investments to build a portfolio that more closely resembles the overall market, higher returns are possible. A diversified portfolio is prudent because, by incurring mostly market risk, it minimizes the specific risk associated with any one investment. Using a broad spectrum of investments, including those once regarded as speculative, an investor can improve the portfolio's expected rate of return without inherently increasing its exposure to uncompensated risks. Thus, under modern portfolio theory, the use of more volatile investments becomes prudent. Obviously, modern portfolio theory stands in sharp contrast to the notions of safe investment followed under the prudent person standard.

A lack of diversified investments does not necessarily lead to poor returns nor is it always evidence that the investments were not prudent.

REICH v. KING

867 F. Supp. 341 (Dist. Ct. Md. 1994)

NICKERSON, DISTRICT JUDGE.

Secretary of Labor brought suit against trustees of pension plan, alleging that trustees violated the Employee Retirement Income Security Act (ERISA) by investing a disproportionate percentage of plan assets in residential mortgages in one county. The District Court, Nickerson, J., held that trustees carried burden of showing that plan's investments, though not diversified, were otherwise clearly prudent, and thus they did not violate ERISA's diversification requirement.

Judgment for defendant.

MEMORANDUM

NICKERSON, DISTRICT JUDGE.

. . .

I. BACKGROUND

The Secretary of Labor has brought this action under the Employee Retirement Income Security Act ("ERISA"), ERISA § 502(a)(2) and (5), as amended, against Walter W. King Plumbing & Heating Contractor, Inc. ("King Plumbing"); the King Plumbing Money Purchase Plan, the King Plumbing Profit Sharing Plan, and the King Plumbing Benefit Trust (collectively the "Plan"); and Walter W. and Evelyn R. King as trustees of the plans (collectively, "the Kings"). The original complaint alleged that the Kings had invested a disproportionate percentage of plan assets in residential mortgages, and that the mortgages were made to the Kings' customers, who then allegedly used the proceeds to buy land and services from the Kings. The Secretary claimed that these activities were in violation of ERISA in that they constituted self-dealing, failure to diversify, and violation of the fiduciary obligation. Defendants answered the complaint and filed two counterclaims.

Before trial, by order or stipulation, all claims but one were either dismissed or withdrawn. The only issue remaining is whether the Kings' activities violated ERISA's diversification requirement.

The essential facts of this case are as follows. In 1976, King Plumbing established a profit-sharing plan and pension plan for its employees, known as the Profit Sharing Plan and Money Purchase Plan. Walter and Evelyn King were trustees of the Plan, and King Plumbing was the Plan's sponsor. In 1990, the Profit Sharing Plan and the Money Purchase Plan were merged into one Plan, the Benefit Trust. In the early 1980's, Walter King, who has substantial knowledge and experience in the real estate market in western Maryland, began investing the Plan's assets in residential real estate mortgages, primarily in Frederick County. King personally met with each borrower, reviewed each application, and visited each property. King patterned his interest rates after those charged by local banks. The loans typically had a loan to value ratio of 80% or less.

The number of assets invested in mortgages increased gradually, peaking in 1990 at 77%. In total, the number of mortgages hovered around 30 and most were for $100,000, or less. All of the mortgages were secured by residential real estate. Seventy-two percent, which equals 70% of all the Plan's investments, are secured by real estate located in Frederick County.

The Plan's loans are unique in that the vast majority are 5 year "balloon loans" amortized over 30 years. Testimony elicited at trial explained that the loans had to be paid off (refinanced through another lender), or renewed after 5 years. This arrangement is significant because it allowed the Plan to confine its exposure to certain risks (e.g., interest rate fluctuation) to the initial 5 year period. Of the 83 loans made from 1985 to the end of 1993, only 2 defaulted and required foreclosure proceedings. Even so, the Plan did not suffer any losses as a result of those 2 foreclosures. The average rate of return for all the Plan's mortgage loans is 8.93%.

In 1990, the Department of Labor targeted the King Plan as having more than 53% of its assets invested in real estate mortgages in 1987. The Department of Labor then opened an investigation of the Plan in October 1990. As a result of the investigation, the Secretary brought this civil action in July 1992.

II. DISCUSSION

The relevant ERISA provision requires a fiduciary to: "[diversify a plan's investments] so as to minimize the risk of large losses, unless under the circumstances it is clearly prudent not to do so." ERISA § 404(a)(1)(C).[2]

In cases brought by the Secretary, the initial burden is on the Secretary to show a violation of the diversification requirement. If the Secretary is successful in

---

[2] The 1974 Conference Report on ERISA explains that the reason for the diversification requirement of § 404(a)(1)(C) is to eliminate the risk of large losses.

> A fiduciary usually should not invest the whole or an unreasonably large proportion of the trust property in one type of security or in various types of securities dependent upon the success of one enterprise or upon conditions in one locality, since the effect is to increase the risk of large losses.

H.R. Rep. No. 1280, 93d Cong., 2d Sess. 304, *reprinted in* 1974 U.S. Code Cong. & Admin. News, 5038, 5085.

meeting that burden, then Defendants must demonstrate that their actions were "clearly prudent." In this case, Defendants concede that by concentrating in upwards of 70% of the Plan's assets in real estate mortgages, they have not met § 404's diversification requirement. Thus, Defendants bear the "heavy burden" of showing that their decision not to diversify was clearly prudent.

A fiduciary's subjective, good faith belief in his prudence will not insulate him from liability. Rather, the prudent person standard has been determined by the courts to be an objective standard, requiring the fiduciary to (1) employ proper methods to investigate, evaluate and structure the investment; (2) act in a manner as would others who have a capacity and familiarity with such matters; and (3) exercise independent judgment when making investment decisions.

Thus, the Kings' decision not to diversify must be measured by an objective standard — that of a prudent investor similarly situated.

Both parties put forth substantial expert testimony comparing the King Plan's investment portfolio to others in the industry. Richard Hinz, the Chief Economist and Director in the Office of Research and Economic Analysis for the Pension and Welfare Benefits Administration of the Department of Labor testified for the Secretary. In summary, Hinz was of the opinion that the Plan's lack of diversification was imprudent. Hinz conclusion was based on the premise that the Plan's returns could have been realized with a more diversified portfolio facing fewer risks, and that the Plan was not compensated for the significant risks that it faced. Hinz testified that the Plan could suffer large losses due to the following risks: default risk, interest rate risk, inflation risk, and liquidity risk. On cross-examination Hinz stated, however, that he had not investigated any of the particular loans in the Plan's portfolio. Rather, his analysis was based on general economic and investment theories. In addition, Hinz admitted that he had never managed an investment portfolio, and that his only experience with residential mortgages resulted from the purchase of his own home.

Defendants put forth the opinions of three experts: David E. Brock, president of the Bank of Brunswick, which does business in the area where the Plan's investments are based; Alfred J. Morrison, a private investment management consultant; and William G. Psillas, an employee benefit consultant.

Mr. Brock analyzed each of the loans in the Plan's portfolio. In many instances Brock personally visited the properties that served as collateral for the loans. Brock concluded that there is no risk of large losses due to the Plan's heavy concentration in residential mortgages, and that the loans were made in a prudent manner. Brock based his opinion on the loans' low loan to value ratios, their status as 5 year "balloons," the good payment histories of the borrowers, and Walter King's knowledge of the local rea l estate market. Brock further stated that at least 60% of his bank's assets are invested in similar mortgage loans in the same geographic area as the Plan's, and that the Plan's loans are marketable.

Morrison testified that, in general, mortgage-backed investments are a relatively low-risk form of investment. He based his opinion on nationwide data that included a wide array of mortgage investments, including pooled mortgages such as Ginnie and Fannie Maes. The Secretary correctly noted, however, that the residential mortgages in this case form only a small subset of the data group that Morrison relied on; thus, whether residential mortgages enjoy the same low-risk as mortgages in general, could not be determined to a "statistical certainty."

Psillas' offered a statistical comparison of the Plan's returns to the returns of 31 companies that his firm advises. The 31 companies' assets ranged from $250,000 to $10 million (the Plan's assets are around $5,000,000). Psillas testified that from

1984 to 1992, the Plan's average annual returns were better than the returns of the companies in his data base. On cross-examination Psillas acknowledged, however, that his comparison was "statistically invalid" given the small number of plans in his sampling.

This Court concludes from the evidence presented, concerning the time frame encompassed by the complaint, that the Kings have carried their burden of showing that the Plan's lack of diversification was clearly prudent and hence not violative of ERISA § 404(a)(1)(C). The Kings offered convincing and credible evidence that the Plan does not face the risk of large losses due to non-diversification. The fact that the loans were short term (5 year "balloons"), as well as the testimony of David Brock were particularly compelling in regard to the conclusion reached. Mr. Brock was the only expert that analyzed each of the particular loans at issue, and given his extensive experience in making residential mortgages in Frederick County, his testimony was given considerable weight. On the other hand, the Secretary's expert based his opinions on textbook type theories that appeared far removed from the actual realities of mortgages in Frederick County. In this regard, the Secretary simply failed to put forth sufficiently credible proof to refute the King's substantial presentation that the Plan's investments were clearly prudent.

V. CONCLUSION

For the reasons stated above, the Court determines that the Defendant has carried his burden of showing that the Plan's investments, though not diversified, were otherwise clearly prudent. Therefore, the Plaintiff's claims against the Defendant are dismissed in their entirety.

METZLER v. GRAHAM

112 F.3d 207 (5th Cir. 1997)

EDITH H. JONES, CIRCUIT JUDGE:

The Secretary of the United States Department of Labor alleges that Jack V. Graham violated his fiduciary duties under the Employee Retirement Income Security Act ("ERISA") as plan administrator of the Graham Associates, Inc. ("GAI") pension plan by failing to diversify the plan investments and by self-dealing. Specifically, the Secretary complains that Graham failed to diversify the plan assets by investing 63% of them in a single tract of undeveloped real estate, and he sacrificed the plan's best interests by buying land near other parcels in which he owned an interest. We agree with the district court's conclusion that under the circumstances before us, Graham did not violate ERISA § 404(a)(1)(A) and (C), and we therefore affirm.

I. Background

Graham is the president and sole owner of GAI. He also serves as the sole trustee and administrator of a defined contribution benefit plan established in 1975 to provide retirement, death and disability benefits to the employees of GAI. At the end of 1984, the plan had 123 participants and $2,740,735 in assets. Graham owned approximately 20% of the plan assets.

Before 1985, Graham invested the plan assets in a mixture of short-term certificates of deposit in denominations of less than $100,000, short-term U.S. Treasury Securities, cash and cash equivalents.

In April 1985, Graham paid $1,743,011 ($1.65 per square foot) on behalf of the plan for 24.251 acres of undeveloped land (the "Property") in the Great Southwest Industrial District in Grand Prairie, Texas, a suburb of Dallas. The Property is zoned for light industrial use. GAI had done civil engineering work on the property for the prio r owners. Graham personally owned an interest in two parcels adjacent to the property and in another parcel nearby. The investment in the Property represented 63% of the plan assets. The remaining 37% was invested as before.

At the time of the purchase, Graham obtained an independent appraisal valuing the Property at $2,154,000 ($2.00 per square foot). At the end of 1985, an independent appraiser valued the property at $2,900,000 ($2.75 per square foot). Graham envisioned selling the Property within a short period of time, but this did not transpire. Instead, since acquiring the Property, the plan has paid maintenance and taxes but has earned no income from it. The court found, however, that the Property has at least maintained its value and that no plan participants had lost benefits as a result of the purchase.

The Secretary brought this suit under Sections 502(a)(2) and (5) of ERISA. The Secretary alleged that the investment of 63% of the plan's assets in one piece of real estate violated Graham's duty to diversify plan assets. The Secretary also alleged that Graham violated his duty of loyalty by purchasing the land without taking precautions to ensure the purchase was in the best interests of the plan beneficiaries. After a bench trial, the district court entered findings of fact and concluded that Graham did not violate his duty to diversify or his duty of loyalty. The Secretary now appeals.

II. Duty to Diversify

> ERISA requires a plan fiduciary to discharge his duties with respect to a Plan solely in the interest of the participants and beneficiaries . . . by diversifying the investments of the Plan so as to minimize the risk of large losses, unless under the circumstances it is clearly prudent not to do so.

ERISA § 404(a)(1)(C). No statute or regulation specifies what constitutes "diversifying" plan investments, but the legislative history provides this guidance:

> The degree of investment concentration that would violate this requirement to diversify cannot be stated as a fixed percentage, because a fiduciary must consider the facts and circumstances of each case. The factors to be considered include (1) the purposes of the plan; (2) the amount of the plan assets; (3) financial and industrial conditions; (4) the type of investment, whether mortgages, bonds or shares of stock or otherwise; (5) distribution as to geographical location; (6) distribution as to industries; (7) the dates of maturity.

H.R. Rep. No. 1280, 93d Cong., 2d Sess. (1974), *reprinted in* 1974 U.S. Code Cong. & Admin. News 5038, 5084–85 (Conference report at 304). Without minimizing the importance of the usual need for diversification of a plan's portfolio, however, the foregoing open-ended "facts and circumstances" list ought to caution judicial review of investment decisions. It is clearly imprudent to evaluate diversification solely in hindsight — plan fiduciaries can make honest mistakes that do not detract from a conclusion that their decisions were prudent at the time the investment was made.

To establish a violation, a plaintiff must demonstrate that the portfolio is not diversified "on its face." Once the plaintiff has established a failure to diversify, th e burden shifts to the defendant to show that it was "clearly prudent" not to diversify. Prudence is evaluated at the time of the investment without the benefit of hindsight.

. . .

The district court credited Graham's testimony that, in purchasing the Property, he was attempting to increase the return on the plan's investments which previously had been entirely in short-term monetary or cash equivalent investments. The court found Graham knowledgeable in industrial-warehouse property, particularly those sites located in Grand Prairie. Before purchasing the Property, Graham discussed the purchase with the Plan's accountant, lawyer and actuary, as well as the Plan's major participants. The major plan participants also had considerable experience in commer cial real estate development in the area. A contemporaneous independent appraisal valued the property significantly higher than its purchase price. Graham believed the property was undervalued and anticipated selling it by 1986. The court concluded that Mr. Graham "exercised proper due diligence and prudence."

The court ultimately concluded that Mr. Graham had not violated his duty to diversify so as to minimize risk of large loss by investing 63% of the Plan's assets in one parcel of real property. The court found that "at no time relevant has there been a 'risk of large loss. . . . ' "

The Secretary contends that, as a matter of law, purchasing the Property constituted a failure to diversify on its face and that Graham did not prove at trial that it was clearly prudent not to diversify under the circumstances. We disagree. Even assuming *arguendo* that the plan's purchase of the property meant that the plan was not diversified on its face, we affirm the district court's decision because its findings demonstrate that, under the circumstances, it was clearly prudent not to diversify.

Both the diversification requirement and the clearly prudent exception to diversification must be analyzed from the perspective of what both parties acknowledge as their purpose: to reduce the risk of large loss. Several factors specific to this case indicate that Graham did not imprudently introduce a risk of large loss by purchasing the Property. First, the plan was not required to make payments to beneficiaries until age 65, death, or disability, and the average age of the plan participants was 37 years when the Property was purchased. Accordingly, the cash then remaining in the plan was sufficient to cover projected Plan payouts for the next 20 years. The relative youth of the participants made it appropriate to evaluate the risk of the plan investments over an extended time frame, thus minimizing the risks associated with short-term fluctuations in asset values.

Second, at the time of the purchase, an important concern to Graham, and an ominous "risk of large loss," was the prospect that high inflation would return. According to Graham's expert William Allbright, when the plan's holdings consisted solely of cash and short term instruments, there was little hedge against inflation. The purchase of real estate historically had provided excellent protection against inflation and could reasonably have been seen as an effort to diversify the portfolio to offset that risk. The purchase of the Property achieved *greater* diversity in plan assets than had existed.

Third, the significant cushion between the purchase price and the contemporaneous independent appraisal, and fourth, Graham's expertise in the development of this type of industrial property further support the conclusion that the investment in the Property was a prudent one.

The district court did not clearly err in crediting all this evidence and finding that the investment did not carry a "risk of large loss" at any relevant time. We reject the secretary's criticism of this finding. Under the circumstances of this case, irrespective whether the purchase of the Property in 1985 meant that the plan was not diversified on its face, it was clearly prudent not to diversify.

. . .

III. Duty of Loyalty

The Secretary also alleged that Graham violated his duty of loyalty as plan trustee by not appointing a neutral fiduciary or taking other precautions before purchasing the Property. ERISA § 404(a)(1) provides that

> a fiduciary shall discharge his duties with respect to a plan solely in the interest of the participants and beneficiaries and —
>
> (A) for the exclusive purpose of:
>
> (i) providing benefits to participants and their beneficiaries; and
>
> (ii) defraying reasonable expenses of administering the plan . . .

The Secretary contends that Graham did not discharge his duties solely in the interest of the participants because he owned interests in nearby parcels of land. Graham's other investments were allegedly enhanced in value by the plan's purchase of the Property, and the other parcels were in competition with the Property for potential buyers. The conflict was particularly evident, the Secretary urges, because Graham used a single agent to market the Property along with the other parcels in which he had an interest; this situation allegedly created the temptation to prefer Graham's personal property investments over the plan's Property marketing process.

Nevertheless, the district court concluded that Graham did not breach his fiduciary duty of loyalty, stating that:

> merely because Graham was a partner in other real estate investments in the area it was not a breach of his fiduciary duty to acquire the land on behalf of the Plan, nor was it, under the specific facts of this case, a breach of his fiduciary duty to try to market the Plan's Property in a package along with the property he had an interest in, since doing so provided a larger market of potential purchasers.

The court further found that Graham's control of the adjacent parcels "actually inured to the benefit of the Plan."

On appeal, the Secretary contends that there is no evidence that Graham took necessary steps to alleviate the potential conflict before purchasing the property. Specifically, the Secretary argues that given the potential conflict, Graham should have either appointed a neutral fiduciary to administer the plan or taken "every feasible precaution to see that [he] had carefully considered the other side, to free [himself], if indeed this was humanly possible, from any taint." *Donovan v. Bierwirth*, 680 F.2d 263, 271–72 (2d Cir.).

Graham counters that he at all times acted solely in the interests of the plan in making the purchase of the Property. . . .

. . . The level of precaution necessary to relieve a fiduciary of the taint of a potential conflict should depend on the circumstances of the case and the magnitude of the potential conflict. Furthermore, even under those decisions, the district court's findings that Graham reasonably believed he was acting in the participants' best interests, that Graham acted prudently in his decision to purchase the property, and that Graham's decisions inured more to the plan's benefit than to his own would support affirmance of the verdict. . . .

. . . We agree with the district court's conclusion that "clearly Graham did not breach his fiduciary duty of loyalty."

IV. Conclusion

For the foregoing reasons, we AFFIRM the decision of the district court that the Secretary take nothing in this action.

6-17 QUESTIONS AND PROBLEMS

1. Although in both cases the defendant conceded that the plan investments were not diversified, the defendant was held not to have violated ERISA. Why?

2. Are you satisfied in *Metzler* that the purchase of a single piece of property that did not produce income was a "prudent" investment? Why?

3. The increase in the value of the property in *Metzler* can only be realized by the sale or development of the land. Does that economic reality support or undermine the holding of the court?

4. If the parties had agreed that the property in *Metzler* has declined in value, would that have changed the outcome of the case?

5. Regis, Dewayne, and Sheena are partners in an public relations firm. The only employee is Charleen, the administrative assistant/secretary. Regis, Dewayne, and Sheena created a defined contribution plan with four participants: the three partners and Charleen. Dewayne was named plan fiduciary and trustee. After years of the plan being invested only in corporate bonds, the plan had an investment yield of six percent. Regis and Sheena complained to Dewayne that they knew other retirement plans with much higher yields. They suggested that Dewayne, as plan trustee, invest in commodity futures, a very risky but potentially very lucrative investment strategy. Dewayne agreed. On May 1, Dewayne invested all the plan funds in commodity futures. Unfortunately, in just six months of commodity trading the plan lost most of its value.

On November 1, Charleen turned age 65, the normal retirement age of the plan, and asked for a lump-sum distribution of her retirement account as provided for by the plan. She was shocked to learn that the value of her account declined from $60,000 on May 1 to $20,000 on November 1.

Charleen sued Dewayne for violating ERISA §§ 404 and 406 and asked that he make good the $40,000 loss. Is Dewayne liable?

Beyond diversification is the issue of whether a retirement plan should invest in the stock or other securities of the plan sponsor. Some observers say no. The employees, they argue, should not have their retirement benefits invested in the same enterprise for which they work because they are then doubly dependent on the success of their employer. Both their jobs and their retirement benefits are at risk should the employer fail. Perhaps in recognition of this observation, ERISA § 407(a)(2) bars most retirement plans from investing more than 10 percent of the value of plan assets in securities issued by the employer. That section, however, does not prohibit plans from allowing employees with 401(k) plan accounts to invest more than 10 percent of the account's assets in the stock of the employer. When employees invest their 401(k) assets in the stock of the employer, the results can be disastrous.

6-18 QUESTIONS AND PROBLEMS

What is more important: participant autonomy to freely invest a 401(k) plan or the need to protect participants from their own ineptness and lack of prudence in order to assure more value in the 401(k) at retirement?

ESOPs present a special problem as to diversification of the plan assets since by definition an ESOP is created with the intent of investing in the equities of the employer.

MOENCH v. ROBERTSON

62 F.3d 553 (3d Cir. 1995)

GREENBERG, CIRCUIT JUDGE.

This case requires us to decide the following difficult question: To what extent may fiduciaries of Employee Stock Ownership Plans (ESOPs) be held liable under the Employee Retirement Income Security Act (ERISA) for investing solely in employer common stock, when both Congress and the terms of the ESOP provide that the primary purpose of the plan is to invest in the employer's securities. The district court held that fiduciaries cannot be liable in such cases, and therefore it granted the fiduciaries' motion for summary judgment. Because we conclude that in limited circumstances, ESOP fiduciaries can be liable under ERISA for continuing to invest in employer stock according to the plan's direction, we will vacate the district court's grant of summary judgment in favor of the plan fiduciaries and will remand the case to the district court for further proceedings. In this opinion we will refer to the plaintiff-appellant Charles Moench, a plan beneficiary, as "Moench," and the defendants-appellees, the Plan Committee, the fiduciaries with investment responsibilities, singularly as the "Committee."

I. Introduction

A. Statewide's Demise

Statewide Bancorp was a bank holding company with its principal office in Toms River, New Jersey. During the time relevant to this appeal, it operated through two wholly owned subsidiaries, The First National Bank of Toms River, New Jersey (FNBTR), and The First National Bank of New Jersey/Salem County.

Statewide began experiencing financial difficulties in 1989. "Between July 1989 and December 1989, the market value of Statewide Bancorp common stock fell from $18.25 per share to $ 9.50 per share." Dist. Ct. op. at 2. During the next year, the price fell even more precipitously — to $6.00 per share in July 1990, to $2.25 per share in December, and finally to less than 25 cents per share in May 1991. During this period — from 1989 through 1991 — federal regulatory authorities repeatedly expressed concern to Statewide's Board of Directors over problems with Statewide's portfolio and financial condition . . . . A March 1990 report of an off-site review of FNBTR revealed "lack of depth and quality of management, unsafe and unsound credit practices, the resulting rapid deterioration in the quality of the loan portfolio, unreliable regulatory and management reports on loans, the inadequacy of the Allowance for Loan and Lea se Losses, and the adverse impact of asset quality upon earnings and capital adequacy." Ultimately, on May 22, 1991, the Federal Deposit Insurance Corporation took control of FNBTR and on May 23, 1991, Statewide filed a voluntary petition under Chapter 11 of the Bankruptcy Code.

B. Statewide's ESOP Plan

This case involves not so much Statewide's demise but the fate during the period of its decline of funds invested in its ESOP. Beginning on January 1, 1986, Statewide offered its employees the opportunity to participate in the ESOP, which was designed to invest primarily in Statewide common stock. The ESOP named various entities and gave them specific administrative and fiduciary duties. First, an ESOP Committee was set up "to administer the Plan." The plan provided that the Committee "shall adopt rules for the conduct of its business and administration of the Plan as it considers desirable, provided they do not conflict with the Plan. The documents authorized the Committee to "construe the Plan, correct defects, supply omissions or reconcile inconsistencies to the extent necessary to effectuate the Plan, and such action shall be conclusive." To allow the Committee fully and adequately to perform its duties, the plan authorized it to "contract for legal, actuarial, investment management . . . and other services to carry out the Plan." According to the Trust Agreement implementing the plan, the Committee:

> shall have responsibility and authority to control the operation and administration of the Plan in accordance with the terms of the Plan and of this Agreement, including . . . (i) establishment, in its discretion, of investment guidelines which shall be communicated to the Trustee in writing.

The Trustee of the plan had "exclusive responsibility for the control and management of the assets of the Trust Fund."

The plan provided that:

> Except as otherwise provided in this Section, the Trustee shall invest the Fund as directed by the Committee. Generally, within 30 days of receipt, the Trustee shall invest all contributions received under the terms of the plan not applied to the repayment of principal and interest on any Acquisition Loan in ESOP stock, except that the Trustee shall be authorized to invest a portion of the contributions received in other securities as a reserve for the payment of administrative expenses and cash distributions.

The plan documents gave Statewide, as the plan sponsor, "the authority and responsibility for . . . the design of the Plan, including the right to amend the Plan." The plan documents also required Statewide to exercise "all fiduciary functions provided in the Plan or in this [Trust] Agreement or necessary to the operation of the Plan except such functions as are assigned to other fiduciaries pursuant to the Plan or this Agreement."

The ESOP created and governed by these documents worked as follows: Employees became eligible to participate in the plan after one year of service. Employees who chose to participate had their contribution deducted from their salary; the employer then would match up to 50% of the employee's voluntary contribution. The plan also provided for an Employer Profit Sharing Contribution, to be made at the end of the Plan year, though only at the option of the Statewide Board of Directors.

Throughout the relevant time period, the Committee regularly invested the

ESOP fund in Statewide common stock, despite the continual and precipitous drop in its price and despite the Committee's knowledge of Statewide's precarious condition by virtue of the members' status as directors. Yet the record reflects that several Statewide insiders began to have misgivings regarding the investment. Jack Breda, FNBTR's Director of Personnel, testified that when the price of Statewide stock started to drop, he began thinking it would be inappropriate to continue such investments. He further testified that he relayed to Statewide's chief executive officer (CEO) the pension committee's recommendation that "we [should] look for other vehicles to invest money in," and that the CEO should relay that advice to the executive committee or the Board of Directors. Apparently, the CEO reported back that the Board of Directors had rejected the proposal because "the original intent of the plan was to invest [in] Statewide Bancorp stock." On May 13, 1991, C.T. Bjorklund, Statewide's Benefits and Compensation Manager, wrote a memorandum to Breda stating the following:

> The Statewide [ESOP] permits employees to voluntarily suspend contributions at any time during the year. The Bank can also cease contributions at any time without notice. Such discontinuance would not trigger a full vesting situation. Only a complete plan termination would cause immediate full vesting of all participants.
>
> Although the ESOP gives us a beginning bias to hold Statewide Stock and the plan says that amounts contributed are to be invested in company stock, the trustee has the power to invest in other vehicles. Potentially the trustee should consider investing in short term money market instruments with current and future contributions.

A notation from Breda to Bjorklund at the bottom of the memorandum states "I have been notified by [the CEO] on 5/21/91 that the Executive Committee of Statewide Bancorp voted not to accept the revised or restated ESOP plan . . . ."

Kevin William Bless, Assistant Vice President and Senior Pension Trust Officer of FNBTR testified that as Statewide's stock price fell, FNBTR's Trust Division held general discussions "about the permissibility of investing moneys in ESOP in a stock that had potential problems." The Trust Division decided that since the Committee's knowledge of Statewide's precarious state was based on confidential reports issued by the OCC, it would be inappropriate to use the information in making investment decisions. Thus, Bless testified that "the nature of the ESOP dictated that we invest solely in [Statewide] securities absent any public knowledge that it would be an imprudent investment." In these discussions, then, the ESOP was not seen as absolutely requiring investment in Statewide stock. Indeed, in early 1991 the Trustee decided to cease investing in Statewide stock and to place all of the ESOP assets in money market accounts.

The Committee has not directed our attention to anything in the record to suggest that while the stock price was falling and the OCC was issuing its warning letters, the Committee met to discuss any possible effects on the ESOP or any actions that it should take and we have not found any indication that there was such a meeting. Moreover, although on June 12, 1990, investors filed a class action securities fraud suit against Statewide and certain of its directors (the Lerner action), which eventually settled for $3,200,000.00, the Committee did not participate on behalf of the ESOP and therefore the ESOP did not share in the settlement. Ultimately, Statewide's descent rendered the employees' ESOP accounts virtually worthless.

C. The Litigation

On November 16, 1992, Moench, a former Statewide employee who participated in the ESOP plan, brought this action against the members of the Committee. These defendants were also members of Statewide's Board of Directors . . . .

On July 18, 1994, Moench filed a motion for a partial summary judgment declaring that the individual Committee members were fiduciaries governed by the standard of care provided in ERISA. The Committee did not oppose Moench's motion, and thus it admitted that its members were ERISA fiduciaries. The Committee nevertheless filed a cross-motion for summary judgment dismissing the complaint on the ground that it did not breach its ERISA obligations. The district court issued an opinion and order on September 21, 1994, granting both motions.

Noting that the Committee had conceded its fiduciary status, the court granted Moench's motion without analysis. The court then held that the Committee had no discretion under the terms of the plan to invest the ESOP funds in anything other than Statewide common stock. And since the plan complied with ERISA, "[Moench] has failed to establish that [the Committee's] actions in directing the purchases of stock for the Plan were other than in accordance with the requirements of the Plan or otherwise in violation of ERISA." The court found no merit in Moench's allegations that the Committee gave inaccurate, incomplete and false information about the plan. Rather, it observed, "the Plan specifically provides that it 'is a capital accumulation Plan [and therefore] . . . does not provide for a guaranteed benefit at retirement,' " and that "the very nature of ESOP plans contemplates that the value and security of the employees' retirement fund will necessarily fluctuate with the fortunes of the employer because ESOPs invest primarily in employer stock."

Moench timely filed this appeal. He argues that the district court erred in deciding that the plan documents absolved the Committee from any liability resulting from investing the ESOP funds in Statewide stock.

II. Discussion

. . .

C. The Committee's Duties Under ERISA

The first issue we address is the one on which the district court focused — the requirements of the Statewide ESOP and ESOPs generally. This inquiry raises the following questions: (1) Did the district court err in concluding that the Committee was required by the plan to invest the plan assets in Statewide stock; (2) If so, was the Committee nevertheless constrained by the nature of ESOPs themselves to invest solely in Statewide stock?; (3) If the plan required the Committee to invest in Statewide stock, did its fiduciary responsibilities under ERISA nevertheless require it to ignore the provisions of the plan and to diversify the plan's investments?

. . .

[A]pplying a de novo interpretation of the plan, we have no hesitation concluding that the Statewide ESOP, while designed with the primary purpose of investing in Statewide securities, did not absolutely require the Committee to invest exclusively in Statewide stock. We therefore believe that the district court erred in determining that the Committee had no latitude but to continue investing in Statewide stock.

The Committee nevertheless argues that it cannot be liable under ERISA because, consistent with the nature of ESOPs themselves, it cannot be accountable for investing the assets solely in Statewide stock. We turn to that argument now, which again requires a detailed inquiry into the standard of review over an ESOP fiduciary's decisions.

4. ESOPs and ERISA

a. General policies and the developed caselaw

ERISA contains specific provisions governing ESOPs. While fiduciaries of pension benefit plans generally must diversify investments of the plan assets "so as to minimize the risk of large losses," *see* [ERISA] § 404(a)(1)(C), fiduciaries of ESOPS are exempted from this duty. Specifically, "the diversification requirement . . . and the prudence requirement (only to the extent that it requires diversification) . . . is not violated by acquisition or holding of . . . qualifying employer securities . . . ." [ERISA] § 404(a)(2). In other words, under normal circumstances, ESOP fiduciaries cannot be taken to task for failing to diversify investments, regardless of how prudent diversification would be under the terms of an ordinary non-ESOP pension plan. ESOPs also are exempted from ERISA's "strict prohibitions against dealing with a party in interest, and against self-dealing, that is, 'dealing with the assets of the plan in his own interest or for his own account.' "

The reason for these specific rules arises out of the nature and purpose of ESOPs themselves. "Employee stock ownership plan[s are] designed to invest primarily in qualifying employer securities." [ERISA] § 407(d)(6)(A). Thus, unlike the traditional pension plan governed by ERISA, ESOP assets generally are invested "in securities issued by [the plan's] sponsoring company." In keeping with this, ESOPs, unlike pension plans, are not intended to guarantee retirement benefits, and indeed, by its very nature "an ESOP places employee retirement assets at much greater risk than does the typical diversified ERISA plan." The summary plan description in this case, for example, explicitly stated that the plan "does not provide for a guaranteed benefit at retirement."

Rather, ESOPs serve other purposes. Under their original rationale, ESOPS were described "as . . . devices for expanding the national capital base among employees — an effective merger of the roles of capitalist and worker." Thus, the concept of employee ownership constituted a goal in and of itself. To accomplish this end, "Congress . . . enacted a number of laws designed to encourage employers to set up such plans." The Tax Reform Act of 1976 was one of those statutes, and in passing it, Congress explicitly stated its concern that courts should refrain from erecting barriers that would interfere with that goal:

> The Congress is deeply concerned that the objectives sought by [the series of laws encouraging ESOPs] will be made unattainable by regulations and rulings which treat employee stock ownership plans as conventional retirement plans, which reduce the freedom of the employee trusts and employers to take the necessary steps to implement the plans, and which otherwise block the establishment and success of these plans.

Notwithstanding all of this, ESOPs are covered by ERISA's stringent requirements, and except for a few select provisions like the ones we quote above, ESOP fiduciaries must act in accordance with the duties of loyalty and care. In other words, "Congress expressly intended that the ESOP would be both an employee retirement benefit plan and a 'technique of corporate finance' that would encourage employee ownership." ESOP fiduciaries must, then, wear two hats, and are "expected to administer ESOP investments consistent with the provisions of both a specific employee benefits plan and ERISA."

All of this makes delineating the responsibilities of ESOP trustees difficult, because they "must satisfy the demands of Congressional policies that seem destined to collide." As the Cunningham court explained:

> On the one hand, Congress has repeatedly expressed its intent to encourage the formation of ESOPs by passing legislation granting such plans favorable treatment, and has warned against judicial and administrative action that would thwart that goal. Competing with Congress' expressed policy to foster the formation of ESOPs is the policy expressed in equally forceful terms in ERISA: that of safeguarding the interests of participants in employee benefit plans by vigorously enforcing standards of fiduciary responsibility.

So with the goals of ESOPs on the one hand, and ERISA's stringent fiduciary duties on the other, the courts' "task in interpreting the statute is to balance these concerns so that competent fiduciaries will not be afraid to serve, but without giving unscrupulous ones a license to steal." The goals of the two statutes often serve consistent ends — ensuring that the fiduciary acts in the interest of the plan — and in those cases the nature of a plaintiff's claim will not create tension. But when the plaintiff claims that an ESOP fiduciary violated its ERISA duties by continuing to invest in employer securities, the conflict becomes particularly stark.

Nevertheless, cases addressing the duties of ESOP fiduciaries in this area generally have allowed ERISA's strict standards to override the specific policies behind ESOPs. In *Eaves v. Penn*, 587 F.2d 453 (10th Cir. 1978), for example, an ESOP fiduciary argued that he was bound by both the terms of the ESOP plan and ERISA itself to invest the plan assets in employer securities. The court, relying extensively on the legislative history underlying ERISA, interpreted the statutory exception as only prohibiting per se liability based on failure to diversify. It justified this conclusion by reasoning that "the structure of the Act itself requires that in making an investment decision of whether or not a plan's assets should be invested in employer securities, an ESOP fiduciary, just as fiduciaries of other plans, is governed by the 'solely in the interest' and 'prudence' tests . . . ."

Other decisions are more specific and have held that notwithstanding ERISA's diversification provisions, an ESOP fiduciary must diversify if diversification is in the best interests of the beneficiaries. The Court of Appeals for the District of Columbia Circuit has stated:

> "[T]he requirement of prudence in investment decisions and the requirement that all acquisitions be solely in the interest of plan participants continue to apply. The investment decisions of a profit sharing plan's fiduciary are subject to the closest scrutiny under the prudent person rule, in spite of the 'strong policy and preference in favor of investment in employer stock.' "

Fink v. National Sav. and Trust Co., 772 F.2d 951, 955-56, 249 U.S. App. D.C. 33 (D.C. Cir. 1985).

Notwithstanding the fact that none of these decisions specifically delineate a standard of review, Moench and his amici read these cases as requiring that a court not be deferential when reviewing an ESOP fiduciary's actions in investing in employer securities. There are numerous problems with their argument. First, by subjecting an ERISA fiduciary's decision to invest in employer stock to strict judicial scrutiny, we essentially would render meaningless the ERISA provision excepting ESOPs from the duty to diversify. Moreover, we would risk transforming ESOPs into ordinary pension benefit plans, which then would frustrate Congress' desire to encourage employee ownership. After all, why would an employer establish an ESOP if its compliance with the purpose and terms of the plan could subject it to strict judicial second-guessing? Further still, basic principles of trust law require that the interpretation of the terms of the trust be controlled by the settlor's intent. That principle is not well served in the long run by ignoring the general intent behind such plans in favor of giving beneficiaries the maximum opportunities to recover their losses.

In short, the sheer existence of ESOPs demonstrates that there is some value in employee ownership per se, even though participants inevitably run some risk in terms of their financial gain. Therefore, the policies behind ERISA's rules governing pension benefit plans cannot simply override the goals of ESOPs, and courts must find a way for the competing concerns to coexist. Indeed, the position taken by Moench and the Secretary of Labor leaves numerous questions unanswered: How is an ESOP fiduciary to determine when diversification is in the best interest of the beneficiaries? Is the fiduciary always to seek the return-maximizing investment, or is there some non-tangible loyalty interest served by retaining ESOP investments in employer stock? Additionally, to what extent should ESOPs be considered retirement plans, notwithstanding the qualification contained in most of them, including Statewide's, that they are not designed to guarantee retirement income? We are uneasy with the answers Moench and the Secretary would give to these questions. Both seem ready and willing to sacrifice the policies behind ESOPs and employee ownership in order to make "ESOP fiduciaries virtual guarantors of the financial success of the [ESOP] plan." That we cannot, should not and will not do.

In this regard, we point out that the participants in the plan effectively became investors in Statewide and thus should have expected to run risks inherent in that role. The Statewide plan was voluntary and the summary plan description provides that "each individual Employee's account will experience gains or losses according to the performance of the investments held by the Plan. The primary investment of the Plan shall be Statewide Bancorp Common Stock." Therefore, the participants should have recognized that the value of their interests was dependent on Statewide's performance.

b. Developing a standard

We again look to trust law for guidance in determining the standard of review. We can formulate a proper standard of review of an ESOP fiduciary's investment decisions by recognizing that when an ESOP is created, it becomes simply a trust under which the trustee is directed to invest the assets primarily in the stock of a single company. More than that, the trust serves a purpose explicitly approved and encouraged by Congress. Therefore, as a general matter, "ESOP fiduciaries should not be subject to breach-of-duty liability for investing plan assets in the manner and for the . . . purposes that Congress intended." And while trustees — of both ordinary trusts and pension benefit plans — are under a duty to "diversify the investments of the trust," *see* Restatement (Third) § 227(b), that duty is waivable by the terms of the trust. Section 227(d) ("The trustee's duties under this Section are subject to the rule . . . dealing with contrary investment provisions of a trust or statute."). Seen in light of these principles, the provision in ERISA exempting

ESOPs from the duty to diversify is simply a statutory acknowledgement of the terms of ESOP trusts. And the common law of trusts in fact guides us in this difficult area.

The Restatement of Trusts provides that in investing trust funds, "the trustee . . . has a duty to the beneficiaries to conform to the terms of the trust directing . . . investments by the trustee." Restatement (Third) § 228. Thus, "as a general rule a trustee can properly make investments in such properties and in such manner as expressly or impliedly authorized by the terms of the trust." *Id.* comment (d). However, trust law distinguishes between two types of directions: the trustee either may be mandated or permitted to make a particular investment. If the trust requires the fiduciary to invest in a particular stock, the trustee must comply unless "compliance would be impossible . . . or illegal" or a deviation is otherwise approved by the court. *Id.* comment (e). When the instrument only allows or permits a particular investment, "the fiduciary must still exercise care, skill, and caution in making decisions to acquire or retain the investment."

In a case such as this, in which the fiduciary is not absolutely required to invest in employer securities but is more than simply permitted to make such investments, while the fiduciary presumptively is required to invest in employer securities, there may come a time when such investments no longer serve the purpose of the trust, or the settlor's intent. Therefore fiduciaries should not be immune from judicial inquiry, as a directed trustee essentially is, but also should not be subject to the strict scrutiny that would be exercised over a trustee only authorized to make a particular investment. Thus, a court should not undertake a de novo review of the fiduciary's actions similar to the review applied in *Struble*. Rather, the most logical result is that the fiduciary's decision to continue investing in employer securities should be reviewed for an abuse of discretion.

In light of the analysis detailed above, keeping in mind the purpose behind ERISA and the nature of ESOPs themselves, we hold that in the first instance, an ESOP fiduciary who invests the assets in employer stock is entitled to a presumption that it acted consistently with ERISA by virtue of that decision. However, the plaintiff may overcome that presumption by establishing that the fiduciary abused its discretion by investing in employer securities.

In attempting to rebut the presumption, the plaintiff may introduce evidence that "owing to circumstances not known to the settlor and not anticipated by him [the making of such investment] would defeat or substantially impair the accomplishment of the purposes of the trust." Restatement (Second) § 227 comment g. As in all trust cases, in reviewing the fiduciary's actions, the court must be governed by the intent behind the trust — in other words, the plaintiff must show that the ERISA fiduciary could not have believed reasonably that continued adherence to the ESOP's direction was in keeping with the settlor's expectations of how a prudent trustee would operate. In determining whether the plaintiff has overcome the presumption, the courts must recognize that if the fiduciary, in what it regards as an exercise of caution, does not maintain the investment in the employer's securities, it may face liability for that caution, particularly if the employer's securities thrive.

In considering whether the presumption that an ESOP fiduciary who has invested in employer securities has acted consistently with ERISA has been rebutted, courts should be cognizant that as the financial state of the company deteriorates, ESOP fiduciaries who double as directors of the corporation often begin to serve two masters. And the more uncertain the loyalties of the fiduciary, the less discretion it has to act. Indeed, " 'when a fiduciary has dual loyalties, the prudent person standard requires that he make a careful and impartial investigation of all investment decisions.' " *Martin v. Feilen*, 965 F.2d at 670 (citation omitted). As the *Feilen* court stated in the context of a closely held corporation:

> This case graphically illustrates the risk of liability that ESOP fiduciaries bear when they act with dual loyalties without obtaining the impartial guidance of a disinterested outside advisor to the plan. Because the potential for disloyal self-dealing and the risk to the beneficiaries from undiversified investing are inherently great when insiders act for a closely held corporation's ESOP, courts should look closely at whether the fiduciaries investigated alternative actions and relied on outside advisors before implementing a challenged transaction.

And, if the fiduciary cannot show that he or she impartially investigated the options, courts should be willing to find an abuse of discretion.

When all is said and done, this is precisely the argument Moench makes in this case: that the precipitous decline in the price of Statewide stock, as well as the Committee's knowledge of its impending collapse and its members' own conflicted status, changed circumstances to such an extent that the Committee properly could effectuate the purposes of the trust only by deviating from the trust's direction or by contracting out investment decisions to an impartial outsider.

Because the record is incomplete, we cannot determine whether the Committee is entitled to summary judgment. Therefore, we will remand the matter to the district court for further proceedings in which the record may be developed and the case may be judged on the basis of the principles we set forth.

6-19 QUESTIONS AND PROBLEMS

1. What is the purpose of ESOPs? Who are they intended to benefit? How?

2. Why would an employer adopt an ESOP?

3. Are ESOPs, which necessarily concentrate the plan investments in securities of the plan sponsor, consistent with ERISA protection of participants?

When the Third Circuit decided *Moench*, it broke new ground when it found that a fiduciary's action "should be presumed to be reasonable" if the terms of a retirement plan "require or strongly encourage" the fiduciary to take such an action. Five other circuit courts have expressly adopted the *Moench* presumption. To date, no Circuit Court has rejected the presumption. *Moench* involved an ESOP, but fiduciaries quickly sought to apply the defense in the context of other "eligible individual account plans," that is, 401(k) plans. In In re *Citigroup ERISA Litigation*, 662 F.3d 128 (2d Cir. 2011), the Second Circuit joined the Third, Fifth, Sixth and Ninth Circuits in extending the *Moench* presumption to employer stock in 401(k) plans.

Diversification is not the only contentious investment issue. The use of the pension plan assets to indirectly promote the interests of the plan participants is controversial. In 1982, the trustees of the Grumman Corporation Pension Plan, which held a significant number of shares of the Grumman Corporation, refused to tender the stock to the LTV Corporation, which was trying unsuccessfully to mount a hostile takeover of Grumman. Not only did the trustees refuse to sell the Grumman stock at above-market prices, but they used the pension assets to purchase additional Grumman shares in order to block the takeover. The trustees, officers of Grumman, argued that it was not in the best interests of the Grumman employees to have the firm taken over by LTV. A hostile takeover, they believed, put the future of Grumman and the jobs of the plan participants at risk. The Court of Appeals held that trustees appeared to have violated ERISA § 404(a)(1)(A) and (B) even though they were "honestly convinced" that the acquisition of Grumman by the debt-ridded LTV posed significant risks to the plan participants. *Donovan v. Bierwirth*, 680 F.2d 263 (2d Cir.), *cert. denied*, 459 U.S. 1069 (1982).

Union operated trust funds are also faced with whether it is prudent and in accordance with ERISA to use the pension funds to encourage economic activity such as construction projects that will create jobs for union members. The objection is that the trustees have a duty to the plan participants as beneficiaries of the plan, not as employees. Thus the pension trust funds should be invested solely with an eye to investment return and risk of investment and not to promoting employment of the union members.

6-20 QUESTIONS AND PROBLEMS

1. Beta Inc. wants to take over Gamma Co. In order to do so, it must purchase 51% of the outstanding Gamma stock. The trustees of the Beta Inc. Pension Plan were appointed by the President of Beta Inc. She asks the trustees to use some of the funds of the multi-million dollar pension trust to purchase shares of Gamma to aid in its takeover. Should they? Would your answer vary if the Beta Inc. Pension Plan was a defined benefit plan? A defined contribution plan?

2. Half of the trustees of the Construction Workers Multiemployer Pension Plan (Plan) are Construction Union members. The Plan is a defined benefit plan. The Union asks the trustees to lend the Union enough funds from the Plan to finance the construction of a new Union meeting hall. The construction of the hall would result in the employment of Construction Union members. The Plan is asked to loan 95% of the cost of the hall at current rates for a mortgage on an office building. Should the trustees loan the money? What if the Union asks that the loan be at mortgage rates that are 20% below commercial office rates, but comparable to the interest rate for a home purchase mortgage? What if the Union President owns the land on which the proposed hall would be built?

H. FIDUCIARY DUTIES ARISING IN CONNECTION WITH 401(k) PLANS

As part of the operation of the plan, a 401(k) plan must pay a variety of fees. The administration of the plan requires record-keeping, transaction processing, and trustee services, all of which must be paid for by the plan. Because of the plan participant's right to determine whether to participate, how much to participate and how to invest the amounts in the plan, communication with participants is vital. Consequently the plan must pay for communications with participants on a regular basis. The plan must also pay for the management of the funds including the right of participants to buy and sell securities and the right of employees to borrow money from the plan. Fees for audits, accounting and legal services are also incurred to comply with statutory and regulatory requirements. Typically the plan sponsor and the plan participants share these costs.

The most notorious fees are related to the investment of the plan funds. These include sales charges such as commissions, management fees, and record-keeping fees. The investment related fees average about 1 percent per year of the plan assets though they vary considerably, with smaller plans usually paying higher fees than larger plans. These fees are usually paid for by the plan participants.

[1] 401(k) Fees

The Department of Labor (DOL) and plaintiffs' attorneys have taken increasing interest in the fees charged to 401(k) plans. The DOL announced that beginning in 2008, on forms filed with the DOL, employers must fully disclose all expenses incurred with plans including indirect compensation that service providers receive from others in connection with the provision of plan services. The following case describes what is known as "revenue sharing" between the plan service provider and the mutual funds that it recommends to the 401(k) plan. Another term for "revenue sharing" would be "kickback."

HADDOCK v. NATIONWIDE FINANCIAL SERVICES, INC.

419 F. Supp. 2d 156 (D. Conn. 2006)

UNDERHILL, DISTRICT JUDGE.

A. *Structure of Plan Investments*

The plaintiffs are trustees of five employer-sponsored retirement plans ("Plans"). The Plans are participant-directed 401(k) retirement savings plans. The employers who sponsor the Plans used service providers to create the Plans and to provide the administrative services necessary to run them. Those service providers, sometimes known as Pension Plan Administrators or PPA's, persuaded the Plans to use Nationwide as their "investment providers."

Nationwide offers the Plans various investment options, including insurance products such as variable annuities. The variable annuities are fund vehicles that provide the Plans and their participants means for investing the retirement contributions.

The variable annuities include two types: group and individual. Pursuant to the group variable annuity contracts, Nationwide contracts with the Plans, while each participant holds an individual account. Pursuant to the individual variable annuity contracts, Nationwide contracts separately with each participant. The variable annuity contracts permit the Plans and participants to invest in a variety of mutual funds.

Nationwide plays a role in the selection of mutual funds that are available for investment by the Plans and participants. The process for selecting mutual funds available for investment has several steps. First, for group annuity contract-holders, Nationwide offers a selection of funds and the Plans choose a subset from among those funds to be available to their participants. The participants then make investment decisions, choosing from among that subset of funds. For individual annuity contract-holders, Nationwide offers a selection, and the participants choose to invest from among that selection.

In addition, Nationwide retains the authority to delete and substitute mutual funds from the list of available investment options "if, in the judgment of [Nationwide], further investment in the shares of a Fund should become inappropriate in view of the purposes of the Contract, [Nationwide] may substitute shares of another Fund or Fund shares already purchased or to be purchased in the future." . . .

The Plans and participants do not invest in the mutual funds directly. Rather, they invest their pension contributions and any employer-matching contributions in one of two Nationwide "variable accounts," unit investment trusts that hold assets from multiple Plans and participants. Those variable accounts are, in turn, divided into numerous "sub-accounts." Each sub-account corresponds to a particular investment option available under the group and individual annuity contracts. The investment options are largely mutual funds.

From among the selection of mutual funds offered by Nationwide, Plans and participants choose the mutual funds in which to invest their pension contributions.

Nationwide then allocates the funds to the appropriate sub-accounts. The sub-accounts receive allocations from multiple Plans and participants, and Nationwide purchases or sells a designated mutual fund to reflect the sub-accounts' combined allocations by the Plans and their participants. When the mutual funds receive funds from the sub-accounts, those funds are pooled with funds from investors other than the plaintiffs.

To reflect the amounts contributed to a particular mutual fund, Nationwide allocates "accumulation units," *i.e.*, shares, of the corresponding sub-account to the Plans and participants. The accumulation units reflect the total amount of money that the Plans and participants have invested in the variable account or sub-account. The value of the accumulation units fluctuates according to the value of the mutual fund shares held within the sub-accounts.

Pursuant to the governing contractual provisions, Nationwide cancels the accumulation units as necessary to pay its fees and to pay taxes. Nationwide also transfers accumulation units for use as collateral for loans, and cancels them to purchase annuities and make cash payments at the request of Plans and participants.

B. *Nationwide's Arrangements with Mutual Funds*

In the early to mid-1990's, Nationwide was concerned about the competitiveness of its pricing of certain annuity contracts. Accordingly, Nationwide investigated and ultimately implemented a system under which mutual funds make payments to it based on a percentage of the assets that Plans and participants invested in the mutual funds through Nationwide. Nationwide now refers to that source of income as "service contract payments" or "competitive pricing," although Nationwide previously used language similar to that adopted by the plaintiffs in this case: "mutual fund revenue" and "sharing."

The mutual funds have contracted with various service providers for the latter to provide investment, administrative, and other services. Some of those service providers are affiliated with the mutual funds. Some of those mutual fund affiliates have in turn contracted with Nationwide. Nationwide's contracts with the mutual funds are fashioned as "service contracts."

Although Nationwide contends that it contracted with the mutual funds to provide services to the funds, a fact-finder viewing the evidence in the light most favorable to the Trustees could conclude that the contracts were a guise for making payments to Nationwide or that Nationwide provided only nominal services and that the payments were not in consideration for those services. Prior to the implementation of the so-called service contracts, Nationwide's internal documents do not refer to services or service contracts; rather, they discuss generating additional revenue from the mutual funds or encouraging the mutual funds to "share" their revenue with Nationwide. For example, in one internal memorandum, dated April 4, 1995, "discussion issues" for an upcoming meeting included:

1. Status of mutual fund negotiations
   a) Funds that have agreed to share
   b) Funds that have refused to share
   c) Funds still in negotiation
2. What is the strategy for mutual funds that refuse to share?
   a) Current funds
   b) New Funds

Although the contracts have been dubbed service contracts, a reasonable fact-finder could infer that Nationwide does not perform additional services in consideration for payments under the contracts. Rather, pursuant to the service contracts, Nationwide provides mutual funds the same services that it had historically provided to the Plans and PPA's as a necessary part of its business and in exchange for payment from the Plans and PPA's. . . .

The amounts of the payments to Nationwide were based on how much the Plans and participants invested in the mutual funds. Nationwide has disclosed to the Plans and participants the fact that it receives payments from mutual funds.

In sum, viewing the evidence in the light most favorable to the Trustees, a reasonable jury could find that the purported service contracts were a means for Nationwide to collect payments from mutual funds in exchange for offering the mutual funds as investment options to the Plans and participants.

V. Conclusion

A rational fact-finder, viewing the evidence in the light most favorable to the Trustees, could find that Nationwide's ability to select, remove, and replace the mutual funds available for the Plans' investment constituted discretionary authority or discretionary control respecting disposition of plan assets, and thus that Nationwide is an ERISA fiduciary. The Trustees have also raised triable issues concerning whether the challenged payments constitute plan assets under a functional approach and whether, even if the revenue-sharing payments do not constitute plan assets, Nationwide's service contracts constitute prohibited transactions. Accordingly, Nationwide's motion for summary judgment is DENIED.

It is so ordered.

In 1998, the Department of Labor issued a report entitled "Study of 401(k) Plan Fees and Expenses" that noted:

> Assume that you are an employee with 35 years until retirement and a current 401(k) account balance of $25,000. If returns on investments in your account over the next 35 years average 7 percent and fees and expenses reduce your average return by 0.5 percent, your account balance will grow to $227,000 at retirement, even if there are no further contributions to your account. If fees and expenses are 1.5 percent, however, your account balance will grow to only $163,000. The 1 percent difference in fees and

expenses would reduce your account balance at retirement by 28 percent.

. . .

The SEC report "Staff Report Concerning Examinations of Select Pension Consultants" released in 2005 concluded that:

> [c]oncerns exist that pension consultants may steer clients to hire certain money managers and other vendors based on the pension consultant's (or an affiliate's) other business relationships and receipt of fees from those firms, rather than because the money manager is best-suited to the clients' needs. Such a conflict of interest can compromise the fiduciary duty that investment advisers owe to their clients. . . . With respect to the pension consultants that . . . provide disclosure, it does not clearly indicate that providing products/services to money managers may create a conflict of interest for the consultant, or it is not specific enough for a reasonable person to discern the potential harm of the conflict of interest.

The Joint Committee on Taxation Staff released a report entitled, "Present Law and Background Relating to Qualified Retirement Plan Fees" (Oct. 30, 2007), which stated:

MAGNITUDE OF FEES AND SOURCES OF VARIANCE

Several studies have been conducted on the amount of retirement plan fees paid by retirement plans. A recent benchmarking survey of 830 section 401(k) plan sponsors revealed an average expense ratio of 75 basis points (bps) (or 0.75 percent) for fund assets. The expense ratio represents total expenses as a fraction of total plan assets. Thus, 75 bps is equivalent to 0.75 percent of plan assets (or $7.50 for every $1,000 of assets invested). Plan fees can vary dramatically across certain plans. Larger companies and larger plans tend to have smaller expense ratios in part because certain fixed charges can be spread over more participants and more plan assets. Expense ratios may also vary because some employers may choose to subsidize certain fees that plan participants would otherwise pay. Some plans may have higher fees because they offer additional services, such as financial planning, which may be bundled with the typical investment management and recordkeeping functions. Individual participant accounts with high investment turnover may also have higher expenses (e.g.,, the participant frequently redirects the investment composition of the participant's account balance), leading some plans to charge additional fees on frequent traders in an effort to reduce costs on other participants.

According to another survey of defined contribution plans in 2005, total expense ratios ranged from 6 bps (or 0.06 percent) to 154 bps (or 1.54 percent). Key factors that contribute to this variation in plan costs include overall plan size, individual account size, and asset composition. Under this survey, large plans benefited from economies of scale, and plans with more than $10 billion in assets had costs less than half that of those plans with less than $500 million in assets (28 bps (or 0.28 percent) versus 71 bps (or 0.71 percent)). For a given overall plan size, a plan with fewer, but larger individual accounts may have lower expenses than a plan with many, but smaller accounts, in part due to lower administrative and recordkeeping costs since there are less participants in the plan and the spread of such costs over larger account balance and aggregate plan asset amounts. For accounts with an average balance below $55,000, costs are 4 bps (or 0.04 percent) higher than for accounts over $55,000 (19 bps (or 0.19 percent) versus 15 bps (or 0.15 percent) that the latter incurs).

Some question whether the regulation of fees charged with respect to retirement plans is an appropriate issue for regulation under the Code. Others respond that

Code-based regulation is appropriate given the significant tax expenditure associated with qualified retirement plans. Such individuals observe that the amount of the subsidy for qualified retirement plans is limited and thus Code-based regulation is appropriate because maximization of the subsidy is at issue.

A second issue that arises is over the type of fees that should be regulated and the scope of the regulation. Some assert that there is less need for regulation of administrative type fees and more need for regulation of fees relating to investment services. Such proponents argue that administrative fees are often more easily understood by plan sponsors and are more clearly disclosed by plan service providers. Others assert that all types of plan fees should be subject to more stringent regulation because it may be difficult to determine the amount of fees that relate to administrative services and those that relate to investment services.

A third set of issues arises as to whether additional regulation should be limited to special disclosure rules with respect to fees, or whether there should be additional regulation as to the amount of fees that are charged. With respect to disclosure, some advocate for uniform fee disclosure rules that allow plan sponsors and participants to easily compare information regarding various types of fees on the basis of uniform disclosure rules applicable to plan service providers or plan investment alternatives. Others are concerned that such rules will result in significant increases in plan administration costs or may overwhelm participants with too much information focused on one of the many factors relevant in selecting an investment alternative. With respect to limits on the amount of fees, some argue that plans should be required to offer participants one or more low-fee investment alternatives.

A fourth set of issues arises as to who should be the beneficiary of fee regulation and what types of plans should be subject to regulation. Some believe that only defined contribution plans should be subject to additional rules, while others believe that additional regulation should only apply to defined contribution plans in which the investments are directed by plan participants.

As the following cases illustrate, the courts have not decided fee dispute cases in a consistent manner.

HECKER v. DEERE & COMPANY

556 F.3d 575 (7th Cir. 2009)

WOOD, CIRCUIT JUDGE.

Even before the stock market began its precipitous fall in early October 2008, litigation over alleged mismanagement of defined contribution pension plans was becoming common. This type of litigation received a boost when, in *LaRue v. DeWolff, Boberg & Associates, Inc.*, 552 U.S. 248, 128 S. Ct. 1020, (2008), the Supreme Court held that "a participant in a defined contribution pension plan [may] sue a fiduciary whose alleged misconduct impaired the value of plan assets in the participant's individual account." 128 S. Ct. at 1022. Section 502(a)(2) of the Employee Retirement Income Security Act of 1974 ("ERISA"), 29 U.S.C. § 1132(a), provides the basis for such an action.

The present case requires us to look further into two questions: first, how broadly does the concept of actionable misconduct sweep, and second, does someone who serves as the manager and investment advisor for a 401(k) plan, or for some of the plan's investment options, owe fiduciary duties to the sponsor's employees. These questions arise in a lawsuit brought by some employees of Deere & Company, which sponsors two 401(k) plans relevant to this case. Fidelity Management Trust Company ("Fidelity Trust") is the directed and recordkeeper for the Deere plans; it also manages two of the investment vehicles available to plan participants. Fidelity Management & Research Company ("Fidelity Research") is the investment advisor for the mutual funds offered as investment options under Deere's plans.

Named plaintiffs Dennis Hecker, Jonna Duane, and Janice Riggins ("the Hecker group"), seeking to sue both on their own behalf and for a class of plan participants, asserted in their second amended complaint ("Complaint") that Deere violated its fiduciary duty under ERISA by providing investment options that required the payment of excessive fees and costs and by failing adequately to disclose the fee structure to plan participants. The Hecker group also sued Fidelity Trust and Fidelity Research on the theory that they were functional fiduciaries for the class and thus they too were liable under § 502(a). All three defendants moved to dismiss for failure to state a claim, see FED. R. CIV. P. 12(b)(6). The district court concluded that the case could be resolved at that preliminary stage, granted the motions to dismiss without resolving the class certification motion, and entered judgment for the defendants. Later, the court also denied plaintiffs' motion under Rule 59(e). We conclude that the district court correctly found that plaintiffs failed to state a claim against any of the defendants, and we therefore affirm the district court's judgment.

I

A

In 1990, Deere engaged Fidelity Trust to serve as trustee of two of the 401(k) plans ("the Plans") it offers to its employees. The Plans, everyone agrees, are subject to ERISA, and the three named plaintiffs are participants in them. Under its arrangement with Deere, Fidelity Trust was required to advise Deere on what investments to include in the Plans, to administer the participants' accounts, and to keep records for the Plans.

Each Plan offered a generous choice of investment options for Plan participants: the menu included 23 different Fidelity mutual funds, two investment funds managed by Fidelity Trust, a fund devoted to Deere's stock, and a Fidelity-operated facility called BrokerageLink, which gave participants access to some 2,500 additional funds managed by different companies. Fidelity Research advised the Fidelity mutual funds offered by the Plans. Each plan participant decided for herself where to put her 401(k) dollars; the only limitation was that the investment vehicle had to be one offered by the Plan. Each fund included within the Plans charged a fee, calculated as a percentage of assets the investor placed with it. The Hecker group alleges that Fidelity Research shared its revenue, which it earned from the mutual fund fees, with Fidelity Trust. Fidelity Trust in turn compensated itself through those shared fees, rather than through a direct charge to Deere for its services as trustee. As the Hecker group sees it, this led to a serious — in fact, impermissible — lack of transparency in the fee structure, because the mutual fund fees were devoted not only to the (proper) cost of managing the funds, but also to the (improper) cost of administering Deere's 401(k) plans.

Distressed primarily by the fee levels, the Hecker group filed this suit individually and on behalf of a class against Deere, Fidelity Trust, and Fidelity Research, asserting that all three defendants had breached their duties under

ERISA. The second amended complaint is the version on which the district court based its ruling. Paragraph 11 summarizes the plaintiffs' theory as follows: ". . . the fees and expenses paid by the Plans, and thus borne by Plan participants, were and are unreasonable and excessive; not incurred solely for the benefit of the Plans and the Plans' participants; and undisclosed to participants. By subjecting the Plans and the participants to these excessive fees and expenses, and by other conduct set forth below, the Defendants violated their fiduciary obligations under ERISA."

As we have already noted, Deere appointed Fidelity Trust to be trustee of the Plans. Fidelity Trust also performed administrative tasks for the Plans and managed two of the investment options available to the participants. Deere and Fidelity Trust agreed that Deere would limit the selections available to Deere's employees to Fidelity funds, with the exception of the Deere Common Stock Fund and some other minor guaranteed investment contracts. Fidelity Research served as the investment advisor for 23 out of the 26 investment options in the Plans. None of the Fidelity Research funds operated exclusively for Deere employees; all were available on the open market for the same fee. The Complaint alleges that Fidelity Research "maintains an active Revenue Sharing program, charging more for its services than it expects to keep in order to have additional monies with which to pay its affiliates and business partners." Those charges, plaintiffs allege, were excessive and unreasonable. Deere, in their view, failed to monitor Fidelity Trust's actions properly and failed to keep the participants properly informed.

A few more details about the Plans themselves are helpful. One plan was called the Savings & Investment Plan, or SIP, and the other was the Tax Deferred Savings Plan, or TDS. For all practical purposes, they operated the same way. Qualified employees could contribute up to a certain amount of their pre-tax earnings, and Deere would match those contributions in varying percentages up to 6%. Deere also made profit-sharing contributions on behalf of some participants. All participants were fully vested from the start with respect to their own contributions and were vested after three years' service with respect to the Deere contribution. By the end of 2005, the SIP had more than $2 billion in assets; more than $1.3 billion of that was held in Fidelity retail mutual funds. The TDS had more than $500 million in assets by that time, $244 million of which were held in Fidelity retail mutual funds.

B

Almost twenty years ago, the Supreme Court observed that "ERISA abounds with the language and terminology of trust law." *Firestone Tire and Rubber Co. v. Bruch*, 489 U.S. 101, 110 (1989). The Act's fiduciary responsibility provisions, found at ERISA §§ 401–14, are central to the Hecker group's case. Plaintiffs begin with § 403(c)(1), which says that, except as provided in certain other parts of the statute, "the assets of a plan shall never inure to the benefit of any employer and shall be held for the exclusive purposes of providing benefits to participants in the plan and their beneficiaries and defraying reasonable expenses of administering the plan." Plan fiduciaries must discharge their duties "solely in the interest of the participants and beneficiaries." ERISA § 404(a)(1). Section 404 recognizes an exception to that duty, however, for plans that delegate control over assets directly to the participant or beneficiary. The key language reads as follows:

> (c) Control over assets by participant or beneficiary
>
> (1)(A) In the case of a pension plan which provides for individual accounts and permits a participant or beneficiary to exercise control over

the assets in his account, if a participant or beneficiary exercises control over the assets in his account (as determined under regulations of the Secretary)—

(i) such participant or beneficiary shall not be deemed to be a fiduciary by reason of such exercise, and

(ii) no person who is otherwise a fiduciary shall be liable under this part for any loss, or by reason of any breach, which results from such participant's or beneficiary's exercise of control, except that this clause shall not apply in connection with such participant or beneficiary for any blackout period during which the ability of such participant or beneficiary to direct the investment of the assets in his or her account is suspended by a plan sponsor or fiduciary.

ERISA § 404(c)(1). Finally, the Hecker group relies on ERISA § 405(a), which provides that one fiduciary may be liable for breaches of fiduciary duty committed by another fiduciary under specified circumstances.

C

The district court disposed of the case on the pleadings, as we noted above. In evaluating the case, the court had to decide whether the Complaint included "enough facts to state a claim to relief that is plausible on its face." *Khorrami v. Rolince*, 539 F.3d 782, 788 (7th Cir. 2008) (quoting *Bell Atl. Corp. v. Twombly*, 550 U.S. 544 (2007)); see *Davis v. Indiana State Police*, 541 F.3d 760, 763–64 (7th Cir. 2008). Even after *Twombly*, courts must still approach motions under Rule 12(b)(6) by "constru[ing] the complaint in the light most favorable to the plaintiff, accepting as true all well-pleaded facts alleged, and drawing all possible inferences in her favor." *Tamayo v. Blagojevich*, 526 F.3d 1074, 1081 (7th Cir. 2008).

Looking first at plaintiffs' claims against Deere, the district court found that the company had complied with all applicable disclosure requirements found in ERISA. It saw nothing in the statute or regulations that required Deere to disclose the fact that Fidelity Research was sharing part of the fees it received with its corporate affiliate, Fidelity Trust. Materials furnished to plan participants did disclose the expenses actually paid to the fund managers, as plaintiffs implicitly conceded by alleging that the same fees were charged to all retail fund customers. The district court found it unremarkable that those fees included some profit margin for Fidelity Research. It also thought it "unlikely" that the fund sponsor (Deere) would be able to control the way in which the fund manager distributed its profits, particularly among related corporations. The court also noted that there were proposals to amend the regulations so that revenue sharing arrangements would be disclosed. See Proposed Rules, Department of Labor, Employee Benefits Security Administration, 71 Fed. Reg. 41,392, 41,394 (July 21, 2006). This, it thought, made it apparent that the present rules imposed no such obligation. Finally, the court rejected the plaintiffs' argument that disclosure was required as a general matter of ERISA law.

The Hecker group also asserted that Deere and the Fidelity companies breached their fiduciary obligations by selecting for the Plans investment options with unreasonably high fees. ERISA, the court acknowledged, requires a fiduciary to discharge its duties "with the care, skill, prudence, and diligence under the circumstances then prevailing that a prudent man acting in a like capacity and familiar with such matters would use in the conduct of an enterprise of a like character and with like aims." ERISA § 404(a)(1)(B). But (as we already have observed) the statute also provides a "safe harbor" for plans that permit the participant to exercise control over his or her own assets. ERISA § 404(c). Assuming that the "safe harbor" provision establishes an affirmative defense, the court held that the defendants could take advantage of the defense only if the facts asserted in the Complaint established all of its necessary elements, as set forth in 29 C.F.R. § 2550.404c 1. It then concluded that the defendants had met that burden, explaining itself as follows:

> Participants could choose to invest in twenty primary mutual funds and more than 2500 others through BrokerageLink. All of these funds were also offered to investors in the general public so expense ratios were necessarily set to attract investors in the marketplace. The expense ratios among the twenty primary funds ranges from just over 1% to as low as.07%. Unquestionably, participants were in a position to consider and adjust their investment strategy based in part on the relative cost of investing in these funds. It is untenable to suggest that all of the more than 2500 publicly available investment options had excessive expense ratios. The only possible conclusion is that to the extent participants incurred excessive expenses, those losses were the result of participants exercising control over their investments within the meaning of the safe harbor provision.

Last, the district court held that since plaintiffs had failed to state a claim against Deere for breach of fiduciary duty either for failure to disclose or for the selection of investment options, Fidelity could not be held liable either. Moreover, it added, neither Fidelity defendant had fiduciary responsibilities with respect to either of the tasks plaintiffs targeted. Under the trust agreements, Deere had the sole responsibility for the selection of plan investment funds. Thus, even if the Fidelity defendants were fiduciaries for some purposes, they were not fiduciaries for the purpose of making plan investment decisions.

After the court dismissed their case, plaintiffs moved for reconsideration under FED. R. CIV. P. 59(e), asserting that they had new evidence that would establish (1) the defendants' breach of duty in assessing fees and choosing investment options, (2) the fact that the defendants' failure to provide information about revenue sharing was an independent violation of ERISA, and (3) the impropriety of the court's evaluating the "safe harbor" defense on a motion to dismiss. Finding nothing new in their arguments or evidence, the court denied the motion. Later, it awarded costs in the amount of $54,396.57 for Deere and $163,814.43 for the two Fidelity defendants. This appeal followed. In addition to briefs from the parties, the court has had the benefit of *amicus curiae* briefs filed by the Secretary of Labor (supporting plaintiffs) and by a consortium composed of the ERISA Industry Committee, the National Association of Manufacturers, and the American Benefits Council (supporting defendants).

II

The Hecker group has offered numerous reasons for sending this case back to the district court. For convenience, we have organized the issues as follows: (1) did the district court commit a procedural error warranting reversal by considering documents outside the pleadings; (2) were the Fidelity defendants "functional" fiduciaries of the Plans with respect to the selection of investment options, the structure of the fees, or the provision of information regarding the fee structure; (3) did Deere or the Fidelity defendants breach any fiduciary duties toward plaintiffs, and if so, are they protected by the § 404(c) affirmative defense; (4) did the district court abuse its discretion in denying plaintiffs' Rule 59(e) motion; and (5) did the court err in its costs award to the defendants, either by giving excessive costs or by including items that are not authorized by 28 U.S.C. § 1920?

* * *

2. Functional Fiduciaries

Before we delve into the question whether any of the defendants breached a fiduciary duty, we must identify who owed such duties to plaintiffs with respect to the actions at issue here. Deere does not contest the fact that it owed some fiduciary duties to the plan participants; it argues instead that plaintiffs have too expansive a concept of its fiduciary responsibilities and, in any event, that it did not breach any fiduciary duty. Fidelity Trust and Fidelity Research, in contrast, argue that they were not fiduciaries at all. The Hecker group appears to concede that neither Fidelity entity was a named fiduciary under the Trust Agreement. It argues, however, that one or both of the Fidelity entities functioned as a fiduciary under ERISA § 3(21)(A). In order to find that they were "functional fiduciaries," we must look at whether either Fidelity Trust or Fidelity Research exercised discretionary authority or control over the management of the Plans, the disposition of the Plans' assets, or the administration of the Plans.

The Hecker group first argues that Fidelity Trust exercised the necessary control to confer fiduciary status by its act of limiting Deere's selection of funds through the Trust Agreement to those managed by Fidelity Research. But what if it did? Plaintiffs point to no authority that holds that limiting funds to a sister company automatically creates discretionary control sufficient for fiduciary status. To the contrary, as Fidelity points out, there are cases holding that a service provider does not act as a fiduciary with respect to the terms in the service agreement if it does not control the named fiduciary's negotiation and approval of those terms. *Chi. Dist. Council of Carpenters Welfare Fund v. Caremark, Inc.*, 474 F.3d 463 (7th Cir. 2007); *Schulist v. Blue Cross of Iowa*, 717 F.2d 1127 (7th Cir. 1983). In any event, the Trust Agreement gives Deere, not Fidelity Trust, the final say on which investment options will be included. The fact that Deere may have discussed this decision, or negotiated about it, with Fidelity Trust does not mean that Fidelity Trust had discretion to select the funds for the Plans.

Plaintiffs retort that, notwithstanding the language of the Trust Agreement, Fidelity Trust exercised *de facto* control over the selection of the funds and Deere rubber-stamped its recommendations. That is not, however, what the Complaint alleges. It asserts instead that Fidelity Trust "played a role in the selection of investment options," and it concedes that Deere had "final authority," *id.* Merely "playing a role" or furnishing professional advice is not enough to transform a company into a fiduciary. *Pappas v. Buck Consultants, Inc.*, 923 F.2d 531, 535 (7th Cir. 1991); *Farm King Supply, Inc. Integrated Profit Sharing Plan & Trust v. Edward D. Jones & Co.*, 884 F.2d 288, 292 (7th Cir. 1989). Many people help develop and manage benefit plans — lawyers and accountants, to name two groups — but despite the influence of these professionals we do not consider them to be Plan fiduciaries. This is not a case like *Johnson v. Georgia*, 19 F.3d 1184, 1189 (7th Cir. 1994), on which plaintiffs rely, because in that case the fiduciary both managed a defined-benefits plan and had ultimate authority over the selection of funds. Nor do we find plaintiffs' reference to the district court's decision in *Haddock v. Nationwide Fin. Servs.*, 419 F. Supp. 2d 156 (D. Conn. 2006), helpful or persuasive, since the service provider in that case had the authority to delete and substitute mutual funds from the plan without seeking approval from the named fiduciary.

There is an important difference between an assertion that a firm exercised "final authority" over the choice of funds, on the one hand, and an assertion that a firm simply "played a role" in the process, on the other hand. The Complaint on which the Hecker group proceeded made the latter allegation, not the former. It gave no notice to the defendants that they would be required to defend on the former basis. For that reason, we reject plaintiffs' tardy effort to present the *de facto* fiduciary argument, and we make no comment on the possible scope of the "functional fiduciary" concept.

Plaintiffs also argue that Fidelity Research, and possibly Fidelity Trust, exercised discretion over the disposition of the Plans' assets by determining how much revenue Fidelity Research would share with Fidelity Trust. The Fidelity defendants (with the support in this instance of the Department of Labor) respond that the fees that Fidelity Research collected were not Plan assets under ERISA § 401(b)(1). The fees were drawn from the assets of the mutual funds in question, which, as the statute provides, are not assets of the Plans:

> In the case of a plan which invests in any security issued by a [mutual fund], the assets of such plan shall be deemed to include such security but shall not, solely by reason of such investment, be deemed to include any assets of such [mutual fund].

Id. Once the fees are collected from the mutual fund's assets and transferred to one of the Fidelity entities, they become Fidelity's assets-again, not the assets of the Plans. *See also Caremark*, 474 F.3d at 476 n.6.

We conclude that the Complaint fails to state a claim against either Fidelity Trust or Fidelity Research based on the supposition that either one is a "functional fiduciary." Plaintiffs' effort to proceed against these companies thus fails at the threshold.

3. Fiduciary Duties and the Safe Harbor Defense

a. Violation of Fiduciary Duty

We are thus left with the claim against Deere. Plaintiffs' allegations can be distilled into two assertions: (1) Deere breached its fiduciary duty by not informing the participants that Fidelity Trust received money from the fees collected by Fidelity Research, and (2) Deere imprudently agreed to limit the investment options to Fidelity Research funds and therefore offered only investment options with excessively high fees. We analyze each claim in turn, beginning with the fee distribution.

Critical to plaintiffs' case is the proposition that Deere and Fidelity had a duty to disclose the revenue-sharing arrangements that existed between Fidelity Trust and Fidelity Research. They point to a number of facts in support of their theory. From 1991 through 2007, Deere and Fidelity Trust amended their agreement 27 times to add new Fidelity services and products and to adjust the administrative costs that Deere paid up front to Fidelity Trust. Those costs decreased over time, as Fidelity Trust shifted to a system whereby it recovered its costs from the Deere participants in the same way as it did from outside participants — that is, Fidelity Research would assess asset-based fees against the various mutual funds, and then transfer some of the money it collected to Fidelity Trust.

The Hecker group's case depends on the proposition that there is something wrong, for ERISA purposes, in that arrangement. The district court found, to the contrary, that such an arrangement (assuming at this stage that the Complaint accurately described it) violates no statute or regulation. We agree with the district court. Plaintiffs feel misled because the SPD supplements left them with the impression that Deere was paying the administrative costs of the Plans, even though in reality the participants were paying through the revenue sharing system we have described. But, as Deere and Fidelity both point out and the Complaint acknowledges, the participants were told about the total fees imposed by the various funds, and the participants were free to direct their dollars to lower-cost funds if that was what they wished to do. The SPD supplements told participants to look to the fund prospectuses for detailed information on fund-level expenses, and the prospectuses in fact furnished that information. In its brief, Deere points to the Magellan Fund Prospectus as an example. That prospectus broke down the Fund's total annual operating expenses paid from fund assets (0.59%) as follows: management fee, 0.39%; distribution or service fees, none; other expenses, 0.20%.

The fact that there were no *additional* fees borne by Deere is immaterial. While Deere may not have been behaving admirably by creating the impression that it was generously subsidizing its employees' investments by paying something to Fidelity Trust when it was doing no such thing, the Complaint does not allege any particular dollar amount that was fraudulently stated. How Fidelity Research decided to allocate the monies it collected (and about which the participants were fully informed) was not, at the time of the events here, something that had to be disclosed. It follows, therefore, that the Hecker group failed to state a claim against Deere based on the revenue-sharing arrangement and the lack of disclosure about it.

These conclusions go a long way toward disposing of plaintiffs' claims that the non-disclosure of the revenue-sharing breached the general fiduciary duty imposed on Deere by § 404(a)(1). Before such a violation can be found, there must be either an intentionally misleading statement, see *Varity Corp. v. Howe*, 516 U.S. 489, 505 (1996), or a material omission, see *Anweiler v. American Elec. Power Serv. Corp.*, 3 F.3d 986, 992 (7th Cir. 1993). The Complaint does not allege that the representation in the SPD supplement-that Deere paid the administration expenses for the Plans-was an intentional misrepresentation. To the contrary, plaintiffs have since submitted evidence with their Rule 59(e) motion showing that Deere believed that Fidelity Trust's services were free.

The only question is thus whether the omission of information about the revenue-sharing arrangement is material. Deere disclosed to the participants the total fees for the funds and directed the participants to the fund prospectuses for information about the fund-level expenses. This was enough. The total fee, not the internal, post-collection distribution of the fee, is the critical figure for someone interested in the cost of including a certain investment in her portfolio and the net value of that investment. Plaintiffs argue that some investors may have expected better management from a fund with a higher fee, but, as the Magellan Fund Prospectus illustrates, participants had access to information about management expenses as a percentage of fund assets. The later distribution of the fees by Fidelity Research is not information the participants needed to know to keep from acting to their detriment. See *Bowerman v. Wal-Mart Stores, Inc.*, 226 F.3d 574, 589 91 (7th Cir. 2000). The information is thus not material, and its omission is not a breach of Deere's fiduciary duty.

We turn next to plaintiffs' contention that Deere violated its fiduciary duty by selecting investment options with excessive fees. In our view, the undisputed facts leave no room for doubt that the Deere Plans offered a sufficient mix of investments for their participants. Thus, even if, as plaintiffs urge, there is a fiduciary duty on the part of a company offering a plan to furnish an acceptable array of investment vehicles, no rational trier of fact could find, on the basis of the facts alleged in this Complaint, that Deere failed to satisfy that duty. As the district court pointed out, there was a wide range of expense ratios among the twenty Fidelity mutual funds and the 2,500 other funds available through Brokerage Link. At the low end, the expense ratio was .07%; at the high end, it was just over 1%. Importantly, all of these funds were also offered to investors in the general public, and so the expense ratios necessarily were set against the backdrop of market competition. The fact that it is possible that some other funds might have had even lower ratios is beside the point; nothing in ERISA requires every fiduciary to scour the market to find and offer the cheapest possible fund (which might, of course, be plagued by other problems).

As for the allegation that Deere improperly limited the investment options to Fidelity mutual funds, we find no statute or regulation prohibiting a fiduciary from selecting funds from one management company. A fiduciary must behave like a prudent investor under similar circumstances; many prudent investors limit themselves to funds offered by one company and diversify within the available investment options. As we have noted several times already, the Plans here directly offered 26 investment options, including 23 retail mutual funds, and offered through BrokerageLink 2,500 non-Fidelity funds. We see nothing in the statute that requires plan fiduciaries to include any particular mix of investment vehicles in their plan. That is an issue, it seems to us, that bears more resemblance to the basic structuring of a Plan than to its day-to-day management. Compare *Hughes Aircraft Co. v. Jacobson*, 525 U.S. 432, 443-44 (1999); *Lockheed Corp. v. Spink*, 517 U.S. 882, 890 (1996). We therefore question whether Deere's decision to restrict the direct investment choices in its Plans to Fidelity Research funds is even a decision within Deere's fiduciary responsibilities. On the assumption that it is, however, we nonetheless conclude that taking the allegations in the Complaint in the light most favorable to plaintiffs, no breach of a fiduciary duty on Deere's part has been described.

b. Safe Harbor Defense

Even if we have underestimated the fiduciary duties that Deere had to its plan participants, the district court's judgment in favor of the defendants must stand if that court correctly decided that the safe harbor provided in § 404(c) is available to them. This was the ground on which the district court primarily relied. If the defense is available, it provides an alternate ground for affirmance.

Although ERISA normally imposes a fiduciary duty on plan managers, the statute modifies that rule for plans that provide for individual accounts and allow a participant or beneficiary "to exercise control over the assets in his account." ERISA § 404(c)(1). First, the participant must have the right to exercise independent control over the assets in her account and in fact exercise such control. Next, the participant must be able to choose "from a broad range of investment alternatives," 29 C.F.R. § 2550.404c-1(b)(1)(ii). As we noted in *Jenkins v. Yager*, 444 F.3d 916 (7th Cir. 2006), "prominent among [the conditions a plan must meet] is that it must provide at least three investment options and it must permit the participants to give instructions to the plan with respect to those options at least once every three months. 29 C.F.R. § 2550.404c 1(b)(2)(c)." 444 F.3d at 923. Third, the participant must be given or have the opportunity to obtain "sufficient information to make informed decisions with regard to investment alternatives available under the plan." 29 C.F.R. § 2550.404c 1(b)(2)(i)(B) . . .

* * *

Plaintiffs would like us to decide whether the safe harbor applies to the selection of investment options for a plan, but in the end we conclude that this abstract question need not be resolved to decide this case. Even if § 404(c) does not always shield a fiduciary from an imprudent selection of funds under every circumstance that can be imagined, it does protect a fiduciary that satisfies the criteria of § 404(c) and includes a sufficient range of options so that the participants have control over the risk of loss. *Cf. Langbecker v. Electronic Data Sys. Corp.*, 476 F.3d 299, 310 11 (5th Cir. 2007); and *Unisys*, 74 F.3d at 445 (holding that a fiduciary that committed a breach of duty in making an investment decision for a Plan may nevertheless take advantage of the § 404(c) defense). The regulation addresses the investment options by stipulating that the § 404(c) defense is available only if the plan offers "a broad range of investment alternatives." 29 C.F.R. § 2550.404c–1(b)(3). The necessary broad range exists "only if the available investment alternatives are sufficient to provide the participant or beneficiary with a reasonable opportunity to" accomplish three goals: the ability materially to affect potential return and degree of risk in the investor's portfolio; a choice from at least three investment alternatives each of which is diversified and has materially different risk and return characteristics; and the ability to diversify sufficiently so as to minimize the risk of large losses. *Id.* §§ 2550.404c1(b)(3)(i)(A) — (C).

Interestingly, in light of the inclusion of the BrokerageLink facility in the plans available to the Deere participants, the regulation also notes that "[w]here look-through investment vehicles are available as investment alternatives to participants and beneficiaries, the underlying investments of the look-through investment vehicles shall be considered in determining whether the plan satisfies the requirements of [the regulation]." *Id.* § 2550.404c–1(b)(3)(ii). The 2,500 mutual funds available through BrokerageLink had fees ranging from.07% to 1%. Any allegation that these options did not provide the participants with a reasonable opportunity to accomplish the three goals outlined in the regulation, or control the risk of loss from fees, is implausible, to use the terminology of *Twombly.* Plaintiffs complain that non-Fidelity funds were available only through BrokerageLink, but that is immaterial under this regulation. If particular participants lost money or did not earn as much as they would have liked, that disappointing outcome was attributable to their individual choices. Given the numerous investment options, varied in type and fee, neither Deere nor Fidelity (assuming for the sake of argument that it somehow had fiduciary duties in this respect) can be held responsible for those choices.

* * *

The judgment of the district court is AFFIRMED.

HECKER v. DEERE & COMPANY

569 F.3d 708 (7th Cir. 2009)

ORDER

Appellants filed their Petition for Panel Rehearing and Petition for Rehearing En Banc on March 9, 2009. Appellee Deere & Company and Appellees Fidelity Management Trust Company and Fidelity Management & Research Company filed their Answers to the Petition on April 6, 2009. In addition, three *amicus curiae* briefs in support of rehearing or rehearing *en banc* were filed in conjunction with the Petition: one from the Secretary of Labor (filed March 20,2009), one from the AARP and other groups (filed March 18, 2009), and one from a group of law professors (filed March 20, 2009). No judge asked for a vote on the petition for rehearing *en banc*, and all members of the panel have voted to deny the petition for rehearing, with the following addition to the original opinion, *Hecker v. Deere & Co.*, 556 F.3d 575 (7th Cir. 2009):

The Secretary of Labor has made a number of points in her *amicus* brief that deserve a brief response. First, she argues that the panel has erred by failing to give appropriate deference to her interpretation of the regulation implementing ERISA § 404(c), 29 C.F.R. § 2550.404c–1. But, as the Secretary herself acknowledges, the panel did not ignore any language in the regulation proper. Instead, it did not give the weight that the Secretary believes is due to some language in a footnote to the preamble to the regulation. (We are speaking here of the version of the regulation that was in force at the time relevant to this suit; it should go without saying that the Secretary is free to propose and enact new regulations addressed more specifically to the way in which choice of investment options in a plan relates to the safe harbor provision, if she believes that this would be appropriate.) In her brief, the Secretary explains that she presently "interprets her regulation to mean that, even if the plan otherwise qualifies as a section 404(c) plan, the fiduciary is not relieved by 404(c) from liability for plan losses resulting from the imprudent selection and monitoring of an investment option offered by the plan . . . " As support for that statement, she cites 56 Fed. Reg. 10724, 10732 n.21 (Mar. 13, 1991); DOL Opinion Letter No. 98–04A, 1998WL 326300 at *3 n.1 (May 28,1998); DOL Information Letter to Douglas O. Kant, 1997WL 1824017 at *2 (Nov. 26, 1997) (Kant Letter). This is enough, she asserts, to make that proposition a rule, entitled to deference under *Chevron USA Inc. v. Natural Resources Defense Council, Inc.*, 467 U.S. 837, 842–43 (1984), rather than a more informal statement of administrative practice, entitled only to respect under the standards of *United States v. Mead Corp.*, 533 US. 218, 229–30 (2001), which in turn relies on *Skidmore v. Swift & Co.*, 323 US. 134 (1944).

With respect, we cannot agree with the Secretary that the footnote in the preamble is entitled to full *Chevron* deference. The panel did defer to the Secretary's concerns, to the extent that it refrained from making any definitive pronouncement on "whether the safe harbor applies to the selection of investment options for a plan." *Hecker*, 556 F.3d at 589. Instead, as we explain further in this order, we left this area open for future development, whether on the basis of a different set of pleadings, or on the basis of a regulation directed to this issue. The Secretary admits that the panel's primary holding - that there was no duty to scour the market to find the fund with the lowest imaginable fees, and that the fees themselves in the Funds identified in the complaint could not be deemed imprudent because they were offered at the same prices to the general public - does not call into question the validity of even the preamble to the Secretary's regulation, much less the regulation taken as a whole. Thus, her real quibble is with the panel's alternate holding that the complaint the court was evaluating contained enough information to warrant the conclusion that Deere was entitled to the safe harbor defense. In our view, the Secretary's concern is more hypothetical than real. She fears that some case in the future may arise in which a Plan fiduciary acts imprudently by selecting an overpriced portfolio of funds, and that this opinion will somehow immunize the fiduciary from accountability for that decision.

The panel's opinion, however, stands for no such broad proposition. It was limited to the complaint before the court, as supplemented by the materials the panel found were properly before the district court. Applying the pleading standards enunciated in *Bell Atlantic Corp. v. Twombly*, 550 US. 544 (2007), we concluded that these plaintiffs failed to state a claim for the kind of fiduciary misfeasance the Secretary describes. At the time we wrote, the Court had not yet handed down *Ashcroft v. Iqbal*, 129 S. Ct. 1937 (2009). *Iqbal* reinforces *Twombly*'s message that "[a] claim has facial plausibility when the plaintiff pleads factual content that allows the court to draw the reasonable inference that the defendant is liable for the misconduct alleged." *Id.* at 1949. The Court explained further that "where the well-pleaded facts do not permit the court to infer more than the mere possibility of misconduct, the complaint has alleged — but it has not 'show[n]' — 'that the pleader is entitled to relief.' Fed. Rule Civ. Proc. 8(a)(2)." *Id.* at 1950.

The Secretary also fears that our opinion could be read as a sweeping statement that any Plan fiduciary can insulate itself from liability by the simple expedient of including a very large number of investment alternatives in its portfolio and then shifting to the participants the responsibility for choosing among them. She is right to criticize such a strategy. It could result in the inclusion of many investment alternatives that a responsible fiduciary should exclude. It also would place an unreasonable burden on unsophisticated plan participants who do not have the resources to pre-screen investment alternatives. The panel's opinion, however, was not intended to give a green light to such "obvious, even reckless, imprudence in the selection of investments" (as the Secretary puts it in her brief). Instead, the opinion was tethered closely to the facts before the court. Plaintiffs never alleged that any of the 26 investment alternatives that Deere made available to its 401(k) participants was unsound or reckless, nor did they attack the BrokerageLink facility on that theory. They argued — and especially in their Petition for Rehearing they continue to argue — that the Plans were flawed because Deere decided to accept "retail" fees and did not negotiate presumptively lower "wholesale" fees. The opinion discusses a number of reasons why that particular assertion is not enough, in the context of these Plans, to state a claim, and we adhere to that discussion.

We add another point that was raised earlier but that we did not mention in the opinion: the complaint is silent about the services that Deere participants received from the company sponsored plans. It would be one thing if they were treated exactly like all other retail market purchasers of Fidelity mutual fund shares; it would be quite another if, for example, they received extra investment advice from someone dedicated to the Deere accounts, or if they received other extra services. If the Deere participants received more for the same amount of money, then their effective cost of participation may in fact have approached wholesale levels. We return, therefore, to the general point made in the opinion: *this* complaint, alleging that Deere chose *this* package of funds to offer for its 401(k) Plan participants, with this much variety and this much variation in associated fees, failed to state a claim upon which relief can be granted.

We therefore DENY the Petition for Rehearing and Petition for Rehearing *En Banc.*

The reasoning in the *Hecker* case was not fully accepted by the Eight Circuit when it reviewed a case involving 401(k) fees.

JEREMY BRADEN v. WAL-MART STORES, INC.

588 F.3d 585 (8th Cir. 2009)

MURPHY, CIRCUIT JUDGE.

Jeremy Braden, an employee of Wal-Mart and participant in its employee retirement plan (Plan), brought this putative class action against appellees — Wal-Mart and various executives involved in the management of the Plan. Braden alleges that they violated fiduciary duties imposed by the Employee Retirement Income Security Act (ERISA). Appellees moved for dismissal under Federal Rules of Civil Procedure 12(b)(1) and 12(b)(6). The district court granted the motion, concluding that Braden lacked constitutional standing to assert claims based on breaches of fiduciary duty prior to the date he first contributed to the Plan and that he otherwise failed to state any plausible claim upon which relief could be granted. Braden timely appealed. We reverse and remand for further proceedings.

I.

Wal-Mart's "Profit Sharing and 401(k) Plan" is an "employee pension benefit plan" covered by ERISA. ERISA § 3(2)(A). It is also an "individual account plan," ERISA § 3(34), establishing an individual profit sharing and 401(k) account for each participating employee. Wal-Mart is the Plan's sponsor and administrator under ERISA § 3(16). Merrill Lynch & Co., Inc. is the Plan's trustee, holding its assets in trust and providing various administrative services necessary to the maintenance of participants' accounts.

At the end of 2007, the Plan had over one million participants and nearly $10 billion in assets. Individual participants directed investment of the assets in their Plan accounts by selecting from a menu of investment options. During the period relevant to Braden's claims, the available options included ten mutual funds, a common/collective trust, Wal-Mart common stock, and a stable value fund. These options were selected by Wal-Mart's Retirement Plans Committee, the Plan's named fiduciary and the entity responsible for the operation, investment policy, and administration of the Plan.

Jeremy Braden began working for Wal-Mart in May 2002. He became eligible to participate in the Plan in June 2003 and made his first contribution on October 31, 2003 . . .

Braden filed his complaint on March 27, 2008, alleging five causes of action against Wal-Mart and the individual appellees, executives serving on or responsible for overseeing the Retirement Plans Committee. The gravamen of the complaint is that appellees failed adequately to evaluate the investment options included in the Plan. It alleges that the process by which the mutual funds were selected was tainted by appellees' failure to consider trustee Merrill Lynch's interest in including funds that shared their fees with the trustee. The result of these failures, according to Braden, is that some or all of the investment options included in the Plan charge excessive fees. He estimates that these fees have unnecessarily cost the Plan some $60 million over the past six years and will continue to waste approximately $20 million per year.

Braden alleges extensive facts in support of these claims. He claims that Wal-Mart's retirement plan is relatively large and that plans of such size have substantial bargaining power in the highly competitive 401(k) marketplace. As a result, plans such as Wal-Mart's can obtain institutional shares of mutual funds, which, Braden claims, are significantly cheaper than the retail shares generally offered to individual investors. Nonetheless, he alleges that the Plan only offers retail class shares to participants. Braden also avers that seven of the ten funds charge 12b-1 fees, which he alleges are used to benefit the fund companies but not Plan participants.

Braden alleges further that the relatively high fees charged by the Plan funds cannot be justified by greater returns on investment since most of them underperformed lower cost alternatives. In support of this claim, he offers specific comparisons of each Plan fund to an allegedly similar but more cost effective fund available in the market. In comparison to an investment in index funds, Braden estimates that the higher fees and lower returns of the Plan funds cost the Plan some $140 million by the end of 2007.

Finally, the complaint also alleges that the mutual fund companies whose funds were included in the Plan shared with Merrill Lynch portions of the fees they collected from participants' investments. This practice, sometimes called "revenue sharing," is used to cover a portion of the costs of services provided by an entity such as a trustee of a 401(k) plan, and is not uncommon in the industry. Braden alleges, however, that in this case the revenue sharing payments were not reasonable compensation for services rendered by Merrill Lynch, but rather were kickbacks paid by the mutual fund companies in exchange for inclusion of their funds in the Plan. The Plan's trust agreement requires appellees to keep the amounts of the revenue sharing payments confidential.

* * *

The district court dismissed all claims . . .

III.

A.

* * *

With these principles in mind, we turn to Braden's complaint. Count I alleges that appellees breached the fiduciary duties of prudence and loyalty imposed upon them by ERISA § 404. In order to state a claim under this provision, a plaintiff must make a prima facie showing that the defendant acted as a fiduciary, breached its fiduciary duties, and thereby caused a loss to the Plan. Only the issue of breach is disputed here.

* * *

Focusing on this standard of liability, the district court found the complaint inadequate because it did not allege sufficient facts to show how appellees' decision making process was flawed. We conclude that the district court erred in its application of Rule 8. Accepting Braden's well pleaded factual allegations as true, he has stated a claim for breach of fiduciary duty.

The district court erred in two ways. It ignored reasonable inferences supported by the facts alleged. It also drew inferences in appellees' favor, faulting Braden for failing to plead facts tending to contradict those inferences. Each of these errors violates the familiar axiom that on a motion to dismiss, inferences are to be drawn in favor of the non-moving party . . .

* * *

. . . The complaint alleges that the Plan comprises a very large pool of assets, that the 401(k) marketplace is highly competitive, and that retirement plans of such size consequently have the ability to obtain institutional class shares of mutual funds. Despite this ability, according to the allegations of the complaint, each of the ten funds included in the Plan offers only retail class shares, which charge significantly higher fees than institutional shares for the same return on investment. The complaint also alleges that seven of the Plan's ten funds charge 12b-1 fees from which participants derive no benefit. The complaint states that appellees did not change the options included in the Plan despite the fact that most of them underperformed the market indices they were designed to track. Finally, it alleges that the funds included in the Plan made revenue sharing payments to the trustee, Merrill Lynch, and that these payments were not made in exchange for services rendered, but rather were a quid pro quo for inclusion in the Plan.

The district court correctly noted that none of these allegations directly addresses the process by which the Plan was managed. It is reasonable, however, to infer from what is alleged that the process was flawed. Taken as true, and considered as a whole, the complaint's allegations can be understood to assert that the Plan includes a relatively limited menu of funds which were selected by Wal-Mart executives despite the ready availability of better options. The complaint alleges, moreover, that these options were chosen to benefit the trustee at the expense of the participants. If these allegations are substantiated, the process by which appellees selected and managed the funds in the Plan would have been tainted by failure of effort, competence, or loyalty. Thus the allegations state a claim for breach of fiduciary duty. See *Roth*, 16 F.3d at 918-19.[3]

These are of course only inferences, and there may well be lawful reasons appellees chose the challenged investment options. It is not Braden's responsibility to rebut these possibilities in his complaint, however . . .

* * *

B.

ERISA and its associated regulations impose upon fiduciaries extensive and specific obligations of disclosure . . .

* * *

Braden claims that appellees breached their duty of loyalty by failing to disclose to participants complete and accurate material information about the Plan funds and the process by which they were selected. His nondisclosure claims can be separated into two groups. One group relates to the performance of and fees charged by the Plan funds and the other to the revenue sharing payments to Merrill Lynch. With respect to the former, Braden alleges that appellees should have disclosed that (1) the funds charged higher fees than readily available alternatives designed to track the same market indices; (2) the funds underperformed readily available and more cost effective alternatives; (3) all of the fees were paid from Plan assets and they consequently depleted participants' retirement savings; (4) all of the Plan funds offered retail shares despite the fact that Wal-Mart had access to institutional shares; (5) the 12b-1 fees charged by several of the funds did not

---

[3] In concluding that Braden has stated a claim, we do not suggest that a claim is stated by a bare allegation that cheaper alternative investments exist in the marketplace. It is clear that "nothing in ERISA requires every fiduciary to scour the market to find and offer the cheapest possible fund." *Hecker*, 556 F.3d at 586.

benefit participants, and comparable alternatives charged no such fees; and (6) appellees did not select the Plan funds or continually evaluate them based on the reasonableness of the fees they charged. In connection with the revenue sharing payments, Braden alleges that appellees should have disclosed (1) the amounts of the payments; (2) that they were retained by Merrill Lynch and not in turn paid to the Plan; and (3) that the payments were made in exchange for inclusion of certain funds in the Plan.

The district court dismissed these claims, concluding that ERISA does not require disclosure of revenue sharing arrangements and that the other information Braden sought was not material. We disagree.

Information is material if there is a substantial likelihood that nondisclosure "would mislead a reasonable employee in the process of making an adequately informed decision regarding benefits to which she might be entitled." *Kalda*, 481 F.3d at 644 (quoting *Krohn v. Huron Mem'l Hosp.*, 173 F.3d 542, 551 (6th Cir. 1999) (alteration omitted)). In the context of this case, materiality turns on the effect information would have on a reasonable participant's decisions about how to allocate his or her investments among the options in the Plan.

* * *

Braden's nondisclosure claim relating to fees parallels his claim for breach of fiduciary duty. He alleges, for example, that appellees had a duty to disclose to participants that Plan funds charged higher fees than comparable funds, that Wal-Mart had access to more cost effective institutional shares, and that appellees did not select or evaluate the funds on the basis of the fees they charged. A reasonable trier of fact could find that failure to disclose this information would mislead a reasonable participant in the process of making investment decisions under the Plan. See *Kalda*, 481 F.3d at 644. For example, participants might conclude in light of this information that Plan funds were not selected using appropriate criteria and might therefore direct their investments toward other options. Accordingly, Braden has stated a claim under ERISA § 404.

By the same token, Braden's allegations are sufficient to state a claim that appellees breached their duty of loyalty by failing to disclose details about the revenue sharing payments. Braden alleges that those payments corrupted the fund selection process — that each fund was selected for inclusion in the Plan because it made payments to the trustee, and not because it was a prudent investment. If true, this information could influence a reasonable participant in evaluating his or her options under the Plan . . . ERISA's duty of loyalty may require a fiduciary to disclose latent conflicts of interest which affect participants' ability to make informed decisions about their benefits.

* * *

C.

Section 406(a)(1) of ERISA, "supplements the fiduciary's general duty of loyalty to the plan's beneficiaries . . . by categorically barring certain transactions deemed 'likely to injure the pension plan.' " *Harris Trust & Sav. Bank v. Salomon Smith Barney Inc.*, 530 U.S. 238, 241-42 (2000) . . .

Braden alleges that appellees violated these sections of the statute by causing the Plan to engage in prohibited transactions with the trustee, Merrill Lynch. As trustee and as an entity "providing services to" the Plan, Merrill Lynch was a "party in interest" within the meaning of § 406. ERISA § 3(14). Braden alleges that the revenue sharing payments made by the Plan funds to Merrill Lynch were "kickbacks" in exchange for inclusion in the Plan, rather than reasonable compensation for actual services performed. Accordingly, he argues that these payments were prohibited by §§ 406(a)(1)(C) and (D) and not exempted by § 408(b)(2).

* * *

We conclude that Braden has stated a claim under § 406(a)(1)(C). The complaint alleges that appellees caused the Plan to enter into an arrangement with Merrill Lynch, a party in interest, under which Merrill Lynch received undisclosed amounts of revenue sharing payments in exchange for services rendered to the Plan . . .

For the reasons discussed, we vacate the judgment of the district court and remand for further proceedings consistent with this opinion.

Plaintiffs continue to claim that because of excessive fees fiduciaries of 401(k) plans have failed to meet their duties of loyalty and prudence when selecting the funds available to the plan participants.

TIBBLE v. EDISON INTERNATIONAL

2010 U.S. Dist. LEXIS 69119
(C.D. Cal. July 8, 2010)

STEPHEN V. WILSON, DISTRICT JUDGE.

I. INTRODUCTION AND PROCEDURAL BACKGROUND

Plaintiffs filed this class action on August 16, 2007 on behalf of the Edison 401(k) Savings Plan ("the Plan") and all similarly-situated participants and beneficiaries of the Plan, against Defendants Edison International ("Edison"), Southern California Edison Company ("SCE"), the Southern California Edison Company Benefits Committee ("Benefits Committee"), the Edison International Trust Investment Committee ("TIC"), the Secretary of the SCE Benefits Committee, SCE's Vice President of Human Resources, and the Manager of SCE's Human Resources Service Center (collectively, "Defendants"). Plaintiffs sought to recover damages pursuant to ERISA § 502(a), for alleged financial losses suffered by the Plan, in addition to injunctive and other equitable relief based on alleged breaches of Defendants' fiduciary duties. ERISA §§ 404, 406.

On June 30, 2009, the Court granted Plaintiffs' motion for class certification . . .

. . .

After the ruling on the summary judgment motions, two issues remained for trial: (1) whether the Defendants violated their duty of loyalty by selecting for the Plan certain retail mutual funds that provided for favorable revenue-sharing arrangements but charged higher fees to Plan participants than other funds; and (2) whether the Defendants violated their duty of prudence by selecting for the Plan a money market fund that allegedly charged excessive management fees. In preparing for (and during) trial, the Plaintiffs amended their first theory of liability to conform to proof. Specifically, as to the mutual funds, Plaintiffs argued that Defendants violated both their duty of loyalty and their duty of prudence by investing in the retail share classes of six mutual funds instead of the institutional share classes of those same funds. The retail share classes of the six mutual funds offered more favorable revenue-sharing arrangements to SCE but charged the Plan participants higher fees than the institutional share classes . . .

. . .

Having thoroughly examined the evidence, considered the arguments of both sides, and made the following factual findings, the Court concludes that Defendants violated their duty of prudence under ERISA § 404(a) by choosing to invest in the retail share class rather than the institutional share class of the William Blair Small Cap Growth Fund, the MFS Total Return Fund, and the PIMCO (Allianz) RCM Global Tech Fund. The Court awards damages accordingly, as set forth below.

The Court concludes that Defendants did not breach their fiduciary duties of loyalty or prudence by failing to switch into the institutional share classes of the Berger (Janus) Small Cap Value Fund, the Allianz CCM Capital Appreciation Fund, and the Franklin Small-Mid Cap Value Fund upon the occurrence of certain events within the limitations period.

Finally, the Court finds that Defendants did not breach their fiduciary duty of prudence by investing in the Money Market Fund managed by State Street Global Advisors or by failing to negotiate a lower management fee.

II. FINDINGS OF FACT

A. Background

. . .

Defendant SCE Benefits Committee ("Benefits Committee") and its members are among the named fiduciaries of the Plan. The Benefits Committee is the Plan Administrator and is responsible for the overall structure of the Plan. Members of the Benefits Committee are chosen by the SCE Chief Executive Officer and are required to report to the SCE Board of Directors . . .

. . .

C. Investment Selection Process

As stated above, the TIC and the Sub-TIC (collectively, "the Investment Committees") have the authority to decide whether to select, maintain or replace the investment options in the Plan, so long as such choices are consistent with the overall structure of the Plan as described above . . .

. . .

D. Mutual Funds

[T]he Plan began offering a mutual fund window to Plan participants in March 1999 in response to collective bargaining negotiations. At any given time, the Plan's mutual fund window consisted of approximately 40 retail mutual funds for participants to choose from.

1. Revenue Sharing

Before the addition of the mutual funds to the Plan in 1999, SCE paid the entire cost of Hewitt Associates' record-keeping services. These services include things such as mailing prospectuses, maintaining individual account balances, providing participant statements, operating a website accessible by Plan participants that allows participants to conduct transactions and obtain information about the Plan's investment options, and answering inquiries from Plan participants regarding their investment options. The fees for these services were paid by SCE, not the Plan participants.

With the addition of the mutual funds to the Plan, however, certain "revenue sharing" was made available to SCE that could be used to offset the cost of Hewitt Associates' record-keeping expenses. "Revenue sharing" is a general term that refers to the practice by which mutual funds collect fees from mutual fund assets and distribute them to service providers, such as recordkeepers and trustees-services the mutual funds would otherwise provide themselves . . . Each type of fee is collected out of the mutual fund assets, and is included as a part of the mutual fund's overall expense ratio. The expense ratio is the overall fee that the mutual fund charges to investors for investing in that particular fund, which includes 12b 1 fees as well as other fees, such as management fees. These fees are deducted from the mutual fund assets before any returns are paid out to the investors.

In 1999, when retail mutual funds were added to the Plan, some of the mutual funds offered revenue sharing which was used to pay for part of Hewitt Associates' record-keeping costs. Hewitt Associates then billed SCE for its services after having deducted the amount received from the mutual funds from revenue sharing. In short, revenue sharing offsets some of the fees SCE would otherwise pay to Hewitt Associates.

The use of revenue sharing to offset Hewitt Associates' record-keeping costs was discussed with the employee unions during the 1998 99 negotiations. Specifically, the unions were advised that revenue sharing fees would result in some of the administrative costs of the Plan being partially offset from mutual funds' revenue sharing payments to Hewitt Associates. Additionally, this arrangement was disclosed to Plan participants on approximately seventeen occasions after the practice began in 1999.

. . .

a. Overall trend toward reduced revenue sharing

From July 2002 to October 2008, the investment selections for the Plan demonstrate a general trend toward selecting mutual funds with reduced revenue sharing. During this period, Defendants made 39 additions or replacements to the mutual funds in the Plan's investment line-up. In 18 out of 39 instances, Defendants chose to replace an existing mutual fund that offered revenue sharing with a mutual fund that provided less revenue sharing or no revenue sharing at all . . .

. . .

Additionally, there is no evidence that Defendants were motivated by revenue sharing when deciding to add or retain the six specific mutual fund share classes at issue in this case, as discussed further below.

3. Mutual Fund Share Classes

Certain mutual funds offer their investors retail and institutional share classes. Institutional share classes are available to institutional investors, such as 401(k) plans, and may require a certain minimum investment. Institutional share classes often charge lower fees (i.e., a lower expense ratio) because the amount of assets invested is far greater than the typical individual investor. The investment management of all share classes within a single mutual fund is identical, and managed within the same pool of assets. In other words, with the exception of the expense ratio (including revenue sharing), the retail share class and the institutional share class are managed in identical fashion.

4. The Six Mutual Funds At Issue

Plaintiffs contend that Defendants violated their fiduciary duties of loyalty and prudence by investing in the retail share classes rather than the institutional share classes of the following six mutual funds: (1) Janus Small Cap Value Fund ("Janus Fund"); (2) Allianz CCM Capital Appreciation Fund ("Allianz Fund"); (3) Franklin Small-Mid Cap Growth Fund ("Franklin Fund"); (4) William Blair Small Growth Fund ("William Blair Fund"); (5) PIMCO RCM Global Tech Fund ("PIMCO Fund"); and (6) MFS Total Return A Fund ("MFS Total Return Fund"). The retail share classes of each of these funds had higher expense ratios than the institutional share classes; the higher fees were directly related to the fact that the retail share classes offered more revenue sharing.

. . .

C. Legal Standard: Breach of Fiduciary Duty

ERISA is intended to "promote the interests of employees and their beneficiaries in employee benefit plans." *Shaw v. Delta Air Lines, Inc.*, 463 U.S. 85, 90, (1983). In enacting ERISA, "the crucible of congressional concern was misuse and mismanagement of plan assets by plan administrators." *Mass. Mut. Life Ins. Co. v. Russell*, 473 U.S. 134, 140 n.8, (1985) (citations omitted). To effectuate this concern, Congress imposed a number of detailed duties on plan fiduciaries. *DiFelice v. U.S. Airways, Inc.*, 497 F.3d 410, 417 (4th Cir. 2007). ERISA § 404, codifies the duties of loyalty and care owed by a plan fiduciary:

> (a) (1) . . . [A] fiduciary shall discharge his duties with respect to a plan solely in the interest of the participants and beneficiaries and—
>
> (A) for the exclusive purpose of:
>
> (i) providing benefits to participants and their beneficiaries; and
>
> (ii) defraying reasonable expenses of administering the plan;
>
> (B) with the care, skill, prudence, and diligence under the circumstances then prevailing that a prudent man acting in a like capacity and familiar with such matters would use in the conduct of an enterprise of a like character and with like aims;

. . .

ERISA § 404(a)(1)(A) and (B). Subsection (a)(1)(A) codifies the duty of loyalty, while subsection (a)(1)(B) articulates the duty of prudence. These duties are "the highest known to the law." *SEC v. Capital Consultants, LLC*, 397 F.3d 733, 751 (9th Cir. 2005).

1. Duty of Loyalty

The duty of loyalty requires a fiduciary to "discharge his duties with respect to a plan solely in the interest of the participants and beneficiaries." ERISA § 404(a)(1)(A). A fiduciary must "act with complete and undivided loyalty to the beneficiaries of the trust," and must make any decisions in a fiduciary capacity "with an eye single to the interests of the participants and beneficiaries." *Leigh v. Engle*, 727 F.2d 113, 123 (7th Cir. 1984) (quotations omitted); *see Donovan v. Bierwirth*, 680 F.2d 263, 272 n.8 (2d Cir. 1982); *DiFelice*, 497 F.3d at 418 –19. These responsibilities have their source in the common law of trusts. *Pegram v. Herdrich*, 530 U.S. 211, 224, (2000). As Judge Cardozo famously stated: "Many forms of conduct permissible in a workaday world for those acting at arm's length are forbidden to those bound by fiduciary ties. A trustee is held to something stricter than the morals of the marketplace. Not honestly alone, but the punctilio of an honor the most sensitive, is then the standard of behavior." *Meinhard v. Salmon*, 249 N.Y. 458, 464, 164 N.E. 545 (Ct. App. 1928).

Although ERISA's duty of loyalty gains definition from the law of trusts, there is an important distinction provided for by the statute's provisions. *See Variety Corp. v. Howe*, 516 U.S. 489, 497 (1996) ("We also recognize . . . that trust law does not tell the entire story."); *DiFelice*, 497 F.3d at 417 ("The common law of trusts, therefore, 'will inform, but will not necessarily determine the outcome of, an effort to interpret ERISA's fiduciary duties.' ") (quoting *Variety Corp.*, 516 U.S. at 497). Under ERISA, "a fiduciary may have financial interests adverse to beneficiaries, but under trust law a trustee is not permitted to place himself in a position where it would be for his own benefit to violate his duty to the beneficiaries." *Bussian v. RJR Nabisco, Inc.*, 223 F.3d 286, 295 (5th Cir. 2000). Thus, unlike in trust law, ERISA contemplates that in many circumstances a plan fiduciary will "wear two hats," and may have conflicting loyalties . . .

Consistent with this rule, a fiduciary does not breach his duty of loyalty by pursuing a course of conduct which serves the interests of the plan's beneficiaries while at the same time "incidentally benefitting" the plan sponsor or even the fiduciary himself . . .

2. Duty of Prudence

ERISA requires that a fiduciary act with the "care, skill, prudence, and diligence under the circumstances then prevailing that a prudent man acting in a like capacity and familiar with such matters would use in the conduct of an enterprise of a like character and with like aims." ERISA § 404(a)(1)(B). Like the duty of loyalty, the duty of prudence is "the highest known to the law." *Howard v. Shay*, 100 F.3d 1484, 1488 (9th Cir. 1996) (quoting *Donovan v. Bierwirth*, 680 F.2d 263, 272 n.8 (2d Cir.1982).

. . .

The prudence standard is not that of a prudent lay person, but rather that of a prudent fiduciary with experience dealing with a similar enterprise. *Whitfield*, 682 F. Supp. at 194 (citing *Mazzola*, 716 F.2d at 1231–21). To determine whether the fiduciary has met the prudence standard, "the court focuses not only on the merits of the transaction, but also on the thoroughness of the investigation into the merits of the transaction." *Howard*, 100 F.3d at 1488. The question is whether, "at the time they engaged in the challenged transactions, [the fiduciaries] employed the appropriate methods to investigate the merits of the investment and to structure the investment." *Mazzola*, 716 F.2d at 1232 . . .

. . .

D. Challenged Conduct by the Plan Fiduciaries

1. Mutual Fund Investments

Plaintiffs contend that Defendants violated both their duty of loyalty and their duty of prudence when they invested in the retail share classes rather than the institutional share classes of . . . the mutual funds . . .

a. Duty of Loyalty

As to the duty of loyalty, Plaintiffs contend that, when deciding to invest in the retail share classes rather than the cheaper institutional share classes of these funds, Defendants were improperly motivated by a desire to capture more revenue sharing for SCE even though doing so increased the fees charged to Plan participants. Plaintiffs contend that Defendants put the interests of SCE in offsetting the record-keeping costs to Hewitt Associates above the interests of the Plan participants in paying lower fees.

. . .

. . . With regard to each of the . . . funds added to the Plan in 2003, the Investment Committees chose to invest in the fund share class with the lowest expense ratio and the lowest revenue sharing, with the exception of one fund, the Vanguard Mid-Cap Index Fund, which had no revenue sharing in either share class. Thus, the decisions made by the fiduciaries at the 2003 meetings clearly were not motivated by a desire to increase revenue sharing.

. . .

In sum, the Court concludes that there is no evidence that the Plan fiduciaries engaged in actual disloyal conduct. The Plan fiduciaries did not make fund selections with an eye toward increasing revenue sharing and did not put the interests of SCE above those of the Plan participants. For these reasons, Plaintiffs' duty of loyalty claim fails.

b. Duty of Prudence

Plaintiffs' duty of prudence argument is simple: Plaintiffs contend that, even if the Plan fiduciaries were not improperly motivated by revenue-sharing benefits, it was objectively imprudent for the Plan fiduciaries to decide to invest (or to continue to invest) in retail share classes of the six mutual funds where identical investments were available in the institutional share classes for lower fees. In other words, a prudent person managing his own funds would invest in the cheaper share class, all else being equal, because doing so saves money.

. . .

In sum, the Plan fiduciaries simply failed to consider the cheaper institutional share classes when they chose to invest in the retail share classes of the William Blair, PIMCO, and MFS Total Return funds. Defendants have not offered any credible explanation for why the retail share classes were selected instead of the institutional share classes. In light of the fact that the institutional share classes offered the exact same investment at a lower fee, a prudent fiduciary acting in a like capacity would have invested in the institutional share classes. Defendants violated their duty of prudence when selecting the retail share classes of the William Blair Fund, the PIMCO Fund, and the MFS Total Return Fund. Damages resulting from the breach are discussed *infra* at Section IV.

. . .

2. Fees of the Money Market Fund

Plaintiffs' final argument is that Defendants breached their duty of prudence by requiring Plan participants to pay excessive investment management fees for the Money Market Fund. Plaintiffs contend that Defendants either: (1) should have negotiated lower fees with the investment manager of the Money Market Mutual Fund, State Street Global Advisers ("SSgA"), and that had they done so, Defendants could have secured lower fees, or (2) Defendants should have invested in a similar money market fund with another investment manager that charged lower fees. Plaintiffs contend that Defendants' failure to take either of these actions resulted in the Plan participants paying fees that were, at times, twice the amount of a reasonable fee.

. . . [Ed. According to the court the evidence showed that the fees charged were well within the range of competitive, reasonable money market funds.]

. . . For the reasons stated above, Plaintiffs cannot show that the fees for the Money Market Fund exceeded the reasonable range of fees for comparably performing money market funds or that the decision to select and maintain the Money Market Fund was otherwise objectively imprudence. Thus, Plaintiffs' prudence claim fails with regard to the Money Market Fund.

IV. DAMAGES AND OTHER RELIEF

Defendants' decisions to invest in the retail share classes rather than the institutional share classes of the William Blair Fund, the PIMCO Fund, and the MFS Total Return Fund caused the Plan participants substantial damages . . .

. . .

. . . Plaintiffs should identify and measure the difference in investment fees between the retail share classes included in the Plan and the less expensive institutional share classes that were available but not selected for the Plan . . .

Finally, damages should account for the fact that had the Plan fiduciaries not invested in the more expensive retail share classes, the Plan participants would have had more money invested and therefore would have earned more money over the course of time, so called "lost investment opportunity." In calculating lost investment opportunity, Plaintiffs should use the returns of the funds in which the assets actually are (and have been) invested . . .

. . .

V. CONCLUSION

For the reasons stated above, the Court rules as follows:

. . .

Defendants breached their duty of prudence under ERISA by investing in retail share classes rather than institutional share classes of the William Blair Fund, the PIMCO Fund, and the MFS Total Return Fund . . .

. . .

Defendants did not breach their duty of prudence by investing in the Money Market Fund managed by SSgA or by failing to negotiate a different management fee for the Money Market Fund at any point from 1999 to the present.

A single law firm, Schlicter Bogard & Denton, filed complaints in about dozen cases alleging that 401(k) plan fiduciaries breached their fiduciary duties by paying excessive plan fees for plan investments. To date, three of the cases have reached multimillion dollar settlements. In one case awarding the firm \$5.05 million, or one-third of the \$15.15 million settlement, plus almost \$700,000 in costs, the judge declared, "Since filing this action, Class Counsel has devoted very substantial costs and attorney time to pursuing this case and several other 401(k) fee cases which were the first of their kind. The record reflects that these cases, collectively, have brought sweeping changes to fiduciary practices within 401(k) plans and have changed the 401(k) industry for the benefit of employees and retirees throughout the country." Will v. General Dynamics Corp., 2010 U.S. Dist. LEXIS 123349, at *8 (S. D. Ill. Nov. 22, 2010). The court also noted that the firm's work illustrated "an exceptional" example of a firm acting as "a private attorney general risking large sums of money and investing many thousands of hours for the benefit of employees and retirees." *Id.*

[2] Investment Options

Another point of contention for 401(k) plans is how the employer's selection of investment options for the employees' 401(k) plan accounts affects the investment risk and rate of return. Recall that the employer can limit the investment options open to the participant. Once the employer has designated the options, the question arises as to whether the employer may be liable if an approved investment option falls sharply in value after the employee invests 401(k) assets in it. Suppose, for example, that the employer knew at the time that it approved a mutual fund "X" that the fund was publishing false information as to its investment success. If employees invest 401(k) assets in mutual fund "X" and suffer significant financial losses, is the employer liable for failure to warn the employees of the potential risk? What if the employer permits its employees to purchase its own stock and is simultaneously falsifying its accounting to mask serious financial problems? Has the employer violated a fiduciary obligation to the employees by permitting them to purchase stock whose value is based on false financial statements? Or, what if the employer knows that the company is likely to go into bankruptcy and nevertheless continues to permit its employees to purchase company stock for their 401(k) accounts?

DIFELICE v. U.S. AIRWAYS, INCORPORATED

497 F.3d 410 (4th Cir. 2007)

Diana Gribbon Motz, Circuit Judge.

In August 2002, following a period of severe financial stress exacerbated by the September 11th attacks, U.S. Airways, Inc. (U.S. Airways), the principal operating subsidiary of U.S. Airways Group (Group), filed for relief under Chapter 11 of the Bankruptcy Code. As a consequence, all Group stock was cancelled without distribution to stockholders. Vincent DiFelice then brought this action seeking recovery under the Employee Retirement Income Security Act of 1974 (ERISA) on behalf of U.S. Airways employees (the Employees) who held Group stock from October 1, 2001 to June 27, 2002 through a U.S. Airways 401(k) plan. The district court certified a class, permitting DiFelice to represent these employees, and, after a bench trial, granted judgment to U.S. Airways. *DiFelice v. U.S. Airways, Inc.*, 436 F. Supp. 2d 756 (E.D. Va. 2006). For the reasons explained within, we affirm.

. . .

A.

Throughout the class period, U.S. Airways maintained a defined contribution § 401(k) plan for qualified employees, administered through a trust agreement (collectively the Plan). U.S. Airways, the named administrator of the Plan for tax and ERISA purposes, delegated its duties to the Pension Investment Committee (PIC), a group of high-ranking company officers, including the Chief Financial Officer, who reported, through the Human Resources Committee of the Board of Directors, to the full Board. The PIC, which had both the responsibility and the authority to make decisions regarding investment options under the Plan, met regularly to review the performance of the Plan's investment options and to confer with outside financial advisors and investment consultants. During the nine-month class period, the PIC held several informal meetings and four formal meetings, at which it circulated agendas and written materials.

U.S. Airways intended the Plan " 'to provide retirement income' " and " 'to operate for the exclusive benefit of eligible employees and their beneficiaries.' " The Plan "permitted participants to contribute up to 15% of their salaries . . . on a pre-tax basis"; U.S. Airways matched certain employee contributions up to a specified level. Each employee who chose to invest through the Plan had his own individual account; the balance in a participant's account consisted of his contributions and any matched funds, "plus any earnings and less any losses or allocated expenses."

The Plan granted U.S. Airways the authority to " 'determine the number and type of Investment Funds and select the investments for such Investment Funds.' " " '[I]n its discretion,' " U.S. Airways could " 'terminate any . . . Investment Fund.' " The Plan stated that the menu of Investment Funds could, but need not, include a Fund consisting of Group stock. If the Plan did include such a Fund, it required that U.S. Airways " 'continually monitor the suitability . . . of acquiring and holding Company Stock.' "

During the class period, the Plan offered twelve diversified Investment Funds, including a money market fund, a fixed income fund, various mutual funds, and several diversified portfolio funds. The Plan also offered a Company Stock Fund ("Company Fund"), which held Group stock and sufficient cash to meet transfer and payment needs, usually amounting to approximately 10% of Fund assets. Within this thirteen-Fund menu, participants had an almost unlimited ability to allocate their investments. Even after participants had elected to invest in a particular Fund or Funds, they could transfer any prior investments, and direct any new investments, to other Plan Funds. In this way, the onus was on the participants to manage their investments.

U.S. Airways, however, did provide participants with a Summary Plan Document (SPD), as well as other brochures and pamphlets, which provided general information about the Plan's mechanics, descriptions of the various Fund options, and specific warnings about the Company Fund. The materials identified the Company Fund as the riskiest, most volatile offering, and stated that investment in this Fund was appropriate for " '[s]omeone who does not rely on this fund for his/her entire portfolio.' " At least two Plan brochures included a graphic showing the thirteen investment options on a spectrum from lower risk and lower return potential to higher risk and higher return potential; the graphics showed the Company Fund as the highest risk (and highest return potential) Fund. These materials explained that this was so because " '[i]nvesting in a non-diversified single stock fund involves more risk than investing in a diversified fund.' "

In the same vein, the Plan literature emphasized the importance of spreading investment dollars among three basic asset types — stocks, bonds, and short-term investments — and among three basic strategies — growth, income, and preservation of principal — in order to minimize the risk of significant losses in one particular investment or investment type. The SPD informed participants that

U.S. Airways did not " 'guarantee the performance of the [Company] Fund,' " *id.* at 765, or any other Fund, and that participants alone were responsible for any losses which resulted from their Plan selections. The SPD also stated, in bold print, that Plan participants should consider seeking professional advice when deciding how to allocate their contributions.

B.

Throughout the class period, U.S. Airways remained an embattled company "facing serious hurdles, with its long-term success, and indeed viability, in doubt." Even before the attacks of September 11th, U.S. Airways confronted liquidity problems. Plans for a merger with United Airlines ended after the Department of Justice indicated its intent to file a lawsuit to block the merger. U.S. Airways then announced a three-phase restructuring plan, through which it hoped to reduce costs and improve its financial position.

The company's situation declined markedly after September 11, 2001. Although all airlines struggled then, U.S. Airways faced particular challenges. It had the highest cost structure of any major United States airline, confronted significant competitive threats from low-fare carriers in its primary markets, and suffered from a decrease in what had been substantial operations at Ronald Reagan National Airport in Washington, D.C. On September 10, 2001, the Group stock price closed at $11.62 per share. In the days after the September 11th attacks, Group stock never closed lower than $4.10 per share, its closing price on September 27, 2001. By October 1, 2001, the share price had rebounded very slightly to $4.48. The value of the Company Fund decreased in similar fashion over the same period.

. . . At the end of the 2001 calendar year, the Group stock price had rebounded to $6.34 per share. . . . in mid-April, the Group stock price was largely unchanged from four months earlier, trading at $6.25 per share on April 15th.

Over this same seven-month period — from September 2001 to April 2002 — as U.S. Airways's financial situation, and liquidity, generated both cautious optimism and cause for concern, the PIC not only met internally, but also sought outside advice from U.S. Airways's Associate General Counsel, and later from outside legal counsel, about whether it should retain the Company Fund as an option under the Plan. All parties — the PIC, the Associate General Counsel, and the outside legal counsel, O'Melveny & Myers, LLP — believed it unnecessary, at that time, to cease offering the Company Fund. The Human Resources Committee of the Board of Directors and, later, the full Board considered and approved the PIC's decision to retain the Fund.

In May 2002, U.S. Airways filed a required Form 10-Q with the Securities and Exchange Commission, which indicated that although U.S. Airways believed it could restructure successfully with liquidity assistance from the government, a judicial reorganization was also a possibility. Around the same time, the PIC recommended the appointment of an independent fiduciary to assume U.S. Airways's duties vis-à-vis the Company Fund. . . . By June 27, 2002, after an initial false start, U.S. Airways had retained Fiduciary Counselors, an independent third-party, to serve as an independent fiduciary for the Company Fund and had notified participants of this selection. This marked the end of the class period, which had begun on October 1, 2001. At this point, the stock price was $3.72 per share.

Once appointed, Fiduciary Counselors moved immediately to increase the cash component of the Company Fund from 10% to 20%, which required selling some Group stock. Shortly thereafter, on July 3, 2002, Fiduciary Counselors halted the purchase of additional shares of Group stock for the Company Fund, although it continued to allow participants to move freely in and out of the Company Fund.

By July 10, the ATSB had approved U.S. Airways's application for a loan guarantee, conditioned on U.S. Airways obtaining significant concessions from its employees and creditors. U.S. Airways was unable to obtain these concessions, and so the company voluntarily filed for bankruptcy on August 11, 2002. On that date, Fiduciary Counselors directed that the Company Fund be closed.

. . . On December 20, 2002, Fiduciary Counselors advised participants that existing Group stock would be cancelled and stockholders would receive no distribution under the Plan. This suit followed.

II.

. . .

The parties agree that during the class period the Plan authorized U.S. Airways to act as Plan fiduciary with discretion to select investment options and a duty to monitor their continued suitability. They also agree that U.S. Airways permissibly exercised that discretion to provide Plan participants the option of investing in a Company Fund.

. . .

Unquestionably, fiduciaries must exercise prudence in administering a plan. A fiduciary like U.S. Airways — that is, a fiduciary of a defined contribution, participant-driven, 401(k) plan created to provide retirement income for employees who is given discretion to select and maintain specific investment options for participants — must exercise prudence in selecting and retaining available investment options. In determining whether U.S. Airways has done so here we examine the totality of the circumstances, including, but not limited to: the plan structure and aims, the disclosures made to participants regarding the general and specific risks associated with investment in company stock, and the nature and extent of challenges facing the company that would have an effect on stock price and viability.

The district court concluded that U.S. Airways fulfilled its duties as a fiduciary, by acting both prudently and with loyalty toward the Plan participants. The Employees, however, challenge the district court's judgment on a variety of grounds. . . .

III.

The Employees contend that in its factual findings the district court failed to give adequate consideration to the Employees' evidence of U.S. Airways's precarious financial position during the class period. Furthermore, according to the Employees, the company's economic peril rendered its decision to offer the Company Fund to Plan participants a violation of its fiduciary duties to select and hold prudent investments and to monitor those investments prudently. The Employees also assert that the district court erred in failing to find that, in offering the Company Fund during the class period, U.S. Airways acted under an improper conflict of interest.

A.

Beyond the bare allegation of a conflict based on the corporate position of the plan fiduciary, the Employees have provided no evidence that U.S. Airways continued to offer the Company Fund based on anything other than the best interests of the Plan participants — those who had already invested in the Company Fund as well as those who might elect to do so in the future. The district court found no evidence of other indicators of a breach of a duty of loyalty, e.g., that high-ranking company officials sold company stock while using the Company Fund to purchase more shares, or that the Company Fund was being used for the purpose of propping up the stock price in the market. Indeed, the court found that, throughout the class period, the PIC had a "well-founded" belief that the company would avoid bankruptcy. If the PIC had been correct, holding Group stock could have been a very profitable venture and one that would have been in the best interest of participants. Furthermore, if U.S. Airways had closed the Company Fund prematurely, and Group stock had rebounded further, the PIC would have succeeded only in locking in participant losses and *precluding* Plan participants from benefitting from the increase in stock price.

On the basis of these findings, the district court did not err in concluding that the Employees had not demonstrated any breach of the duty of loyalty by U.S. Airways.

. . .

. . . "Under ERISA, the prudence of investments or classes of investments offered by a plan must be judged individually." That is, a fiduciary must initially determine, and continue to monitor, the prudence of *each* investment option available to plan participants. Here the relevant "portfolio" that must be prudent is *each* available Fund considered on its own, including the Company Fund, not the full menu of Plan funds.

This is so because a fiduciary cannot free himself from his duty to act as a prudent man simply by arguing that other funds, which individuals may *or may not* elect to combine with a company stock fund, could theoretically, in combination, create a prudent portfolio. To adopt the alternative view would mean that any single-stock fund, in which that stock existed in a state short of certain cancellation without compensation, would be prudent if offered alongside other, diversified Funds. Any participant-driven 401(k) plan structured to comport with section 404(c) of ERISA would be prudent, then, so long as a fiduciary could argue that a participant could, and should, have further diversified his risk. This result would be perverse in light of the Department of Labor's direction that selection of prudent plan *options* falls within the fiduciary duties of a plan administrator.

. . . For the reasons stated earlier, even considered individually the Company Fund was a viable and prudent option for investment over the class period.

V.

At the heart of the Employees' case seems to be the view that, given their losses and U.S. Airways's undisputed knowledge of its uncertain financial condition over the class period, U.S. Airways *must* have violated ERISA's "prudent man" duty when it continued to offer the Company Fund as a Plan option. Although we are not unsympathetic to the Employees' losses, such a contention is not tenable.

First and foremost, whether a fiduciary's actions are prudent cannot be measured in hindsight, whether this hindsight would accrue to the fiduciary's detriment or benefit. Put another way, an investment's diminution in value is neither necessary, nor sufficient, to demonstrate a violation of a fiduciary's ERISA duties.

Furthermore, although placing retirement funds in *any* single-stock fund carries significant risk, and so would seem generally *imprudent* for ERISA purposes, Congress has explicitly provided that qualifying concentrated investment in *employer* stock does not violate the "prudent man" standard per se. . . .

Apparently, Congress considered the possible benefits to employees and employers from undiversified investments in employer stock and found them to out-weigh the risks inuring from such strategy.

As more employers shift toward participant-driven, defined-contribution plans, and participant-driven 404(c) plans in particular, Congress may reconsider the necessity of more safeguards for participants. For example, ERISA already limits the amount of employer stock that can be held in any defined-benefit pension plan to 10% of total plan assets. ERISA § 407(a)(2). In light of the losses that have accrued to the Employees here, and others similarly situated, Congress may well decide that a similar limitation is appropriate for participant-driven, non-ESOP, defined-contribution plans. However, this policy decision is one for Congress and not for the courts. Accordingly, the Employees cannot succeed in this lawsuit simply by demonstrating that U.S. Airways offered the Company Fund during a time of grave uncertainty for the company, no matter how significant the Employees' ultimate financial losses.

VI.

For the foregoing reasons, the judgment of the district court is

AFFIRMED.

In *Edgar v. Avaya, Inc.*, 503 F.3d 340 (3d Cir. 2007), a 401(k) participant sued alleging that the employer breached its fiduciary duty under ERISA § 404 by offering the plan participants the option of investing in Avaya common stock, which dropped by 20 percent in value. The court noted that fiduciaries of individual account plans are entitled to judicial deference when they permit investments in the sponsoring company's stock, citing *Moench v. Robertson*, 62 F.3d 553 (3d Cir. 1995). The court held that the fiduciary is entitled to a presumption that it acted consistently with ERISA. That presumption was not overridden when the fiduciary permitted participants to purchase Avaya stock merely because of the downward trend in its market price given that Avaya was still profitable at the time and paying substantial dividends.

6-21 QUESTIONS AND PROBLEMS

1. Can you articulate why the 401(k) self-directed investment scheme is desirable or undesirable from:

- the employees's point of view?
- the employer's perspective?
- the interest of the larger society?

2. In *DiFelice*, just what actions or nonactions by the fiduciary were alleged to have violated ERISA fiduciary duties?

3. The plaintiffs argued in *DiFelice*, that:

> The mere possibility for "significant gain" cannot make an investment a "legitimate option" for participants investing for retirement. A lottery

> ticket also offers its purchaser an opportunity for "significant gain" but it is hardly a "legitimate" option for retirement savings.

Is that analogy correct? How should a court define or identify "legitimate investment options"?

4. Were the plan fiduciaries operating under a conflict of interest? If so, how should that affect the outcome of the case?

5. Do you agree with the court that the offering to participants of the right to invest in a fund that invests only in the stock of one company to be proper?

6. Did the fiduciaries, knowing of the perilous financial condition of U.S. Airways, have a duty to recommend to the plan participants that they sell their stock holdings in the company fund? If not, should the law be amended to impose such a duty?

Chapter 7

ENFORCEMENT ISSUES

The ERISA protections for plan participants would mean little without adequate enforcement mechanisms. Although the Secretary of Labor has the authority to enforce ERISA, overwhelmingly it is litigation brought by private litigants that puts the proverbial "teeth" into the statute. This chapter will examine this largely private enforcement of a public law, beginning with who may sue to enforce ERISA, the allocation of ERISA jurisdiction between federal and state courts, and the degree of deference that courts must give to decisions made by plan administrators. While plan fiduciaries can clearly be sued under appropriate ERISA sections, what about other parties who may have dealings with the plan? This chapter addresses their potential liability. Next the chapter covers the extensive litigation resulting from attempts to interpret the extent and form of the remedies afforded by ERISA. Finally, the chapter addresses various procedural issues, such as statutes of limitations and the need to exhaust plan remedies, and concludes with an examination of the right of the parties to attorney's fees and the lack of a right to a jury trial under ERISA.

A. CAUSES OF ACTION

ERISA § 502(a) provides for civil actions to enforce the proper administration of a plan. Section 502(a)(1)(B) permits participants or beneficiaries to sue to recover benefits due to them under the terms of the plan. Under § 501(a)(2), a plan participant, beneficiary, fiduciary or the Secretary of Labor can sue a plan fiduciary seeking relief for breaches of ERISA § 409 breaches of fiduciary duty (discussed in Chapter 6). Section 502(a)(3) authorizes a plan participant, beneficiary or fiduciary to enjoin any act or practice that violates either Title I of ERISA or the terms of the plan or to obtain other appropriate equitable relief to remedy such violation.

B. STANDING TO SUE

ERISA § 502(a).

ERISA § 502(a) lists who may bring claims: participants, beneficiaries, fiduciaries, and the Secretary of Labor. Other persons are typically left without standing to sue under ERISA. *See Franchise Tax Board v. Construction Laborers Vacation Trust for So. Cal.*, 463 U.S. 1, 27 (1983) ("ERISA carefully enumerates the parties entitled to seek relief under § 502; it does not provide anyone other than participants, beneficiaries, or fiduciaries with an express cause of action . . .").

[1] Plan Participants and Beneficiaries

ERISA §§ 3(7), 3(8), 502(a)(1)(B).

Under ERISA § 502(a)(1)(B), a plan participant or beneficiary may sue "to recover benefits due to him under the plan, or to clarify his rights to future benefits." ERISA § 3(7) defines a participant as "any employee or former employee . . . who is or may become eligible to receive a benefit of any type from an employee benefit plan" which covers that employee. Beneficiary is defined in ERISA § 3(8) to mean "a person designated by a participant, or by the terms of an employee benefit plan, who is or may become entitled to a benefit. . . ." Spouses who receive or who are eligible to receive a joint annuity from an employee pension plan are beneficiaries. A child, for example, as a secondary beneficiary under a defined contribution plan, is also an ERISA beneficiary.

Plan participants or beneficiaries may sue as individuals or as members of a class. Their claims against pension plans may allege a variety of misdeeds, including miscalculation of the amount of their pension benefit, claims about whether they were eligible for particular pension benefits, claims that they were duped into retiring and so losing financial incentives to retire, and complaints that the plan administrator mishandled or fraudulently invested funds in a defined contribution account.

Claims against welfare benefit plans depend upon the nature of the benefit. Disability benefit claims are often litigated when the plan participant or beneficiary believes that he or she is disabled as defined under the terms of the plan, and the plan administrator disagrees. Medical care benefits are frequently litigated, particularly as to whether the plan is obligated to reimburse the participant or beneficiary for a particular medical procedure.

[2] Former Employees

ERISA §§ 3(7), 502(a)(1)(B), 502(a)(9).

FIRESTONE TIRE & RUBBER CO. v. BRUCH

489 U.S. 101 (1989)

JUSTICE O'CONNOR delivered the opinion of the Court.

This case presents two questions concerning the Employee Retirement Income Security Act of 1974 (ERISA), as amended. First, we address the appropriate standard of judicial review of benefit determinations by fiduciaries or plan administrators under ERISA. Second, we determine which persons are "participants" entitled to obtain information about benefit plans covered by ERISA.

Late in 1980, petitioner Firestone Tire and Rubber Company (Firestone) sold, as going concerns, the five plants composing its Plastics Division to Occidental Petroleum Company (Occidental). Most of the approximately 500 salaried employees at the five plants were rehired by Occidental and continued in their same positions without interruption and at the same rates of pay. At the time of the sale, Firestone maintained three pension and welfare benefit plans for its employees: a termination pay plan, a retirement plan, and a stock purchase plan. Firestone was the sole source of funding for the plans and had not established separate trust funds out of which to pay the benefits from the plans. All three of the plans were either "employee welfare benefit plans" or "employee pension benefit plans" governed (albeit in different ways) by ERISA. By operation of law, Firestone itself was the administrator, ERISA § 3(16)(A)(ii), and fiduciary, § 3(21)(A), of each of these "unfunded" plans. At the time of the sale of its Plastics Division, Firestone was not aware that the termination pay plan was governed by ERISA, and therefore had not set up a claims procedure, § 503, nor complied with ERISA's reporting and disclosure obligations, §§ 101–111, with respect to that plan.

Respondents, six Firestone employees who were rehired by Occidental, sought severance benefits from Firestone under the termination pay plan. In relevant part, that plan provides as follows:

> If your service is discontinued prior to the time you are eligible for pension benefits, you will be given termination pay if released because of a reduction in work force or if you become physically or mentally unable to perform your job.
>
> The amount of termination pay you will receive will depend on your period of credited company service.

Several of the respondents also sought information from Firestone regarding their benefits under all three of the plans pursuant to certain ERISA disclosure provisions. *See* §§ 104(b)(4), 105(a). Firestone denied respondents severance benefits on the ground that the sale of the Plastics Division to Occidental did not constitute a "reduction in work force" within the meaning of the termination pay plan. In addition, Firestone denied the requests for information concerning benefits under the three plans. Firestone concluded that respondents were not entitled to the information because they were no longer "participants" in the plans.

Respondents then filed a class action on behalf of "former, salaried, non-union employees who worked in the five plants that comprised the Plastics Division of Firestone." The action was based on §§ 502(a)(1) . . . .

The District Court granted Firestone's motion for summary judgment. With respect to Count I, the District Court held that Firestone had satisfied its fiduciary duty under ERISA because its decision not to pay severance benefits to respondents under the termination pay plan was not arbitrary or capricious . . . . The District Court concluded that respondents were not entitled to damages under § 502(c) because they were not plan "participants" or "beneficiaries" at the time they requested information from Firestone.

. . . .

We granted certiorari to resolve the conflicts among the Courts of Appeals as to the appropriate standard of review in actions under § 502(a)(1)(B) and the interpretation of the term "participant" in § 3(7). We now affirm in part, reverse in part, and remand the case for further proceedings.

II

[The Court's analysis of the standard of review is deleted.]

III

Respondents unsuccessfully sought plan information from Firestone pursuant to ERISA § 104(b)(4), one of ERISA's disclosure provisions. That provision reads as follows:

> The administrator shall, upon written request of any participant or beneficiary, furnish a copy of the latest updated summary plan description, plan description, [sic] and the latest annual report, any terminal report, the bargaining agreement, trust agreement, contract, or other instruments under which the plan is established or operated. The administrator may make a reasonable charge to cover the cost of furnishing such complete copies. The Secretary [of Labor] may by regulation prescribe the maximum amount which will constitute a reasonable charge under the preceding sentence.

When Firestone did not comply with their request for information, respondents sought damages under ERISA § 502(c)(1) . . . . Respondents have not alleged that they are "beneficiaries" as defined in ERISA § 3(8). The dispute in this case therefore centers on the definition of the term "participant," which is found in § 3(7):

> The term "participant" means any employee or former employee of an employer, or any member or former member of an employee organization who is or may become eligible to receive a benefit of any type from an employee benefit plan which covers employees of such employer or members of such organization, or whose beneficiaries may be eligible to receive any such benefit.

The Court of Appeals noted that ERISA § 502(a)(1) allows suits for benefits "by a participant or beneficiary." Finding that it would be illogical to say that a person could only bring a claim for benefits if he or she was entitled to benefits, the Court of Appeals reasoned that ERISA § 502(a)(1) should be read to mean that "a civil action may be brought by someone who claims to be a participant or beneficiary." It went on to conclude that the same interpretation should apply with respect to § 104(b)(4): "A provision such as that one, entitling people to information on the extent of their benefits, would most sensibly extend both to people who are in fact entitled to a benefit under the plan and to those who claim to be but in fact are not."

The Court of Appeals "concede[d] that it is expensive and inefficient to provide people with information about benefits — and to permit them to obtain damages if information is withheld — if they are clearly not entitled to the benefits about which they are informed." It tried to solve this dilemma by suggesting that courts use discretion and not award damages if the employee's claim for benefits was not colorable or if the employer did not act in bad faith. There is, however, a more fundamental problem with the Court of Appeals' interpretation of the term "participant": it strays far from the statutory language. Congress did not say that all "claimants" could receive information about benefit plans. To say that a "participant" is any person who claims to be one begs the question of who is a "participant" and renders the definition set forth in § 3(7) superfluous. Indeed, respondents admitted at oral argument that "the words point against [them]." In our view, the term "participant" is naturally read to mean either "employees in, or reasonably expected to be in, currently covered employment, or former employees who "have . . . a reasonable expectation of retur ning to covered employment" or who have "a colorable claim" to vested benefits, *Kuntz v. Reese*, 785 F.2d 1410, 1411 (CA9). In order to establish that he or she "may become eligible" for benefits, a claimant must have a colorable claim that (1) he or she will prevail in a suit for benefits, or that (2) eligibility requirements will be fulfilled in the future. "This view attributes conventional meanings to the statutory language since all employees in covered employment and former employees with a colorable claim to vested benefits 'may become eligible.' A former employee who has neither a reasonable expectation of returning to covered employment nor a colorable claim to vested benefits, however, simply does not fit within the [phrase] 'may become eligible.' "

We do not think Congress' purpose in enacting the ERISA disclosure provisions — ensuring that "the individual participant knows exactly where he stands with respect to the plan," H.R. Rep. No. 93-533, 11 (1973) — will be thwarted by a natural reading of the term "participant." Faced with the possibility of $100 a day in penalties under § 502(c)(1)(B), a rational plan administrator or fiduciary would likely opt to provide a claimant with the information requested if there is any doubt as to whether the claimant is a "participant," especially when the reasonable costs of producing the information can be recovered. *See* 29 C.F.R. § 2520.104b-30(b) (1987) (the "charge assessed by the plan administrator to cover the costs of furnishing documents is reasonable if it is equal to the actual cost per page to the plan for the least expensive means of acceptable reproduction, but in no event may such charge exceed 25 cents per page").

The Court of Appeals did not attempt to determine whether respondents were "participants" under ERISA § 3(7). We likewise express no views as to whether respondents were "participants" with respect to the benefit plans about which they sought information. Those questions are best left to the Court of Appeals on remand.

For the reasons set forth above, the decision of the Court of Appeals is affirmed in part and reversed in part, and the case is remanded for proceedings consistent with this opinion.

So ordered.

The *Firestone* court stated that a participant whose account had been liquidated cannot have "a colorable claim to vested benefits" and so had no standing to sue. That pronouncement has not been rigidly enforced.

IN RE POLAROID ERISA LITIGATION

240 F.R.D. 65 (S.D.N.Y. 2006)

PAULEY, DISTRICT JUDGE.

Plaintiffs Robert Correia ("Correia"), Bradford Pires ("Pires") and Otis Powers ("Powers") (collectively, "Plaintiffs") bring this putative class action alleging various breaches of fiduciary duty concerning the Polaroid Retirement Savings Plan (the "Plan"). On March 31, 2005, this Court issued a Memorandum and Order denying Defendants' motion to dismiss except with respect to Plaintiffs' claim that Defendants breached their fiduciary duties by failing to avoid conflicts of interest (the "March 31 Order"). *In re Polaroid ERISA Litigation*, 362 F. Supp. 2d 461 (S.D.N.Y. 2005). Plaintiffs now move to certify a class pursuant to Fed. R. Civ. P. 23. For the reasons set forth below, Plaintiffs' motion is granted.

BACKGROUND

I. *Summary of Plan Terms*

The Plan comprised various components, of which only the 401(k) and Employee Stock Ownership Plan ("ESOP") are relevant for purposes of this motion. Participants in the 401(k) portion of the Plan could direct a portion of their compensation into any of 38 investment funds, including the Polaroid Stock Fund, which consisted of Polaroid stock. Participants in the 401(k) had no obligation to invest in the Polaroid Stock Fund. The Employee Stock Ownership Plan ("ESOP") portion of the Plan was funded entirely by Polaroid and was to invest "primarily" in Polaroid common stock. Nonetheless, three categories of ESOP participants could fully diversify and/or liquidate their ESOP accounts: (1) participants who had left the company; (2) participants on disability; and (3) participants over 59.5 years old.

II. *The Parties' Relationships*

Plaintiffs are former Polaroid employees and former Plan participants.

III. *The Deterioration of Polaroid's Stock Price*

At the beginning of the Class Period, Polaroid stock traded at $25.88 per share. However, throughout the Class Period, Polaroid's financial position deteriorated and its stock price declined. By November 2001, Polaroid stock traded at $0.24 per share. In December 2001, State Street divested the ESOP of Polaroid stock for an average price per share of $.0946. The Polaroid Stock Fund was liquidated in December 2002 for an average price per share of approximately $.01. The scale of these losses was massive — at the end of 1999, the Plan held over seven million shares of Polaroid common stock, valued at $138,346,897. By the end of 2000, the number of Polaroid shares held by the Plan had increased slightly, but the total value of those shares had plummeted to $45,745,761.

On August 15, 2002, Polaroid's Board of Directors passed a resolution to terminate the Plan and all Plan assets were distributed.

DISCUSSION

Plaintiffs' basic allegation is that Defendants breached their fiduciary duties by maintaining the Plan's investments in Polaroid common stock despite (1) their knowledge of certain accounting irregularities; and (2) the precipitous decline in price that the stock had taken. Plaintiffs also claim that DiCamillo failed to monitor other Plan fiduciaries, that Defendants made misleading statements to Plan participants and failed to keep them adequately informed, and that all Defendants are liable for the actions of their co-fiduciaries. Plaintiffs move to certify the following class:

> All persons who were participants in or beneficiaries of the Plan at any time between October 1, 1999 and January 15, 2003 (the "Class Period") and whose accounts included investments in Polaroid Stock.

Defendants argue that Plaintiffs lack standing to sue under ERISA and, in any event, cannot satisfy the requirements of Fed. R. Civ. P. 23. This Court considers each of these issues in turn.

I. *Statutory Standing Under ERISA*

ERISA actions seeking damages for breach of fiduciary duty can be brought only by certain parties under specified conditions. ERISA § 502 (titled "Persons empowered to bring a civil action") provides, in relevant part: "A civil action [for breach of fiduciary duty] may be brought . . . (2) by the Secretary, or by a participant, beneficiary, or fiduciary for appropriate relief under Section 1109 of this title." ERISA § 409 provides, in relevant part:

> Any person who is a fiduciary with respect to a plan who breaches any of the responsibilities, obligations, or duties imposed . . . by this subchapter shall be personally liable to make good to such plan any losses to the plan resulting from each such breach, and to restore to such plan any profits of such fiduciary which have been made through use of assets of the plan by the fiduciary . . . .

In *Mass. Mut. Life Ins. Co. v. Russell*, 473 U.S. 134 (1985), the Supreme Court stated that claims brought under §§ 502(a)(2) and 409 may not be made for individual relief, but instead are "brought in a representative capacity on behalf of the plan." *Russell*, 473 U.S. at 142 n.9. Thus, to determine whether Plaintiffs have statutory standing under § 502(a)(2), this Court must determine: first, whether

Plaintiffs are "participant[s][or] beneficiar[ies]" of the Plan for purposes of § 502(a)(2); and second, whether Plaintiffs are truly suing "in a representative capacity on behalf of the plan." *Russell*, 473 U.S. at 142 n.9.

A. *Plaintiffs' Status as Plan Participants*

ERISA § 3(7) defines a "participant" as "any employee or former employee of an employer . . . who is or may become eligible to receive a benefit of any type from an employee benefit plan . . . ." In *Firestone Tire & Rubber Co. v. Bruch*, 489 U.S. 101, 117 (1989), the Supreme Court expanded on the statutory definition: "[T]he term 'participant' is naturally read to mean either employees in, or reasonably expected to be in, currently covered employment . . . or former employees who have . . . a reasonable expectation of returning to covered employment or who have a colorable claim to vested benefits."

Plaintiffs admit that they have no reasonable expectation of returning to Polaroid as employees. Thus, Defendants argue that former Plan participants whose accounts have been liquidated by definition cannot have "a colorable claim to vested benefits" and thus may not bring suit under § 502(a)(2). *Firestone*, 489 U.S. at 117.

The Second Circuit has declined to apply the *Firestone* standard rigidly in the context of defining a "participant." *See Mullins v. Pfizer, Inc.*, 23 F.3d 663 (2d Cir. 1994). While acknowledging a circuit split on the issue of whether former employees qualify as "participants," *Mullins* suggested that "the basic standing issue is whether the plaintiff is '*within the zone of interests ERISA was intended to protect.*'" *Mullins*, 23 F.3d at 668 (emphasis in original) (quoting *Vartanian v. Monsanto Co.*, 14 F.3d 697, 701 (1st Cir. 1994)). Applying the "zone of interests" standard, the Court of Appeals concluded that a former employee had standing as a plan participant because he alleged that "but for the fact that [the defendant] misled him, he would have been a participant." *Mullins*, 23 F.3d at 667 (internal quotation marks omitted). The court reasoned that it would reap an "anomalous effect" to "allow[ ] a fiduciary through its own malfeasance to defeat the employee's standing." *Mullins*, 23 F.3d at 668 (internal quotation omitted).

The issue in *Mullins* was whether a defendant could take advantage of its own wrong to avoid suit under ERISA where it had fraudulently induced a plaintiff to liquidate his plan account in order to deprive him of benefits to which he would otherwise have been entitled. However, where the alleged misconduct is less directly linked to plaintiff's decision to terminate his involvement with the plan, the weight of authority in this circuit still allows former employee claims to proceed.

Moreover, although the Second Circuit recently declined to address the issue of whether former employees have standing to sue under § 502(a)(2), *see Coan v. Kaufman*, 457 F.3d 250, 255 (2d Cir. 2006), in doing so it noted in dicta that a former employee's claim that a lump sum distribution of a defined contribution account balance would have been greater absent the defendants' breach of fiduciary duty is "[a]rguably . . . [a claim] for benefits — which, if colorable, means that she may become eligible for benefits and thus qualif[y] as a participant under ERISA." *Coan*, 457 F.3d at 255 56.

In this action, Plaintiffs do not allege that they would still be Plan participants but for defendants' misconduct. However, they do allege that the distributions they received under a defined contribution plan were reduced because of defendants' breaches of fiduciary duty and that the defendants engaged in numerous misrepresentations and non-disclosures prior to the liquidation of their accounts. Accordingly, this Court finds that Plaintiffs have standing to sue as Plan "participants" under § 502(a)(2) despite their status as former employees.

LEUTHNER v. BLUE CROSS AND BLUE SHIELD OF NORTHEASTERN PENNSYLVANIA

454 F.3d 120 (3d Cir. 2006)

ROTH, CIRCUIT JUDGE.

If the beneficiary of an ERISA plan has lost her status as a beneficiary, due to what she claims is the plan administrator's breach of fiduciary duty, does she then have standing to sue the administrator under ERISA § 502(a)? Appellant Jean Mikulis retired early from Blue Cross, relying on what she claims was a promise from Blue Cross to provide her with 100% lifetime health benefits. Appellant Elizabeth Melley is the widow of a Blue Cross retiree. Both women lost their lifetime health benefits when the Blue Cross Plan was retroactively changed on January 1, 2001. After their benefits had been terminated, they intervened in a class action that had been brought by other Plan participants and beneficiaries to challenge the retroactive changes. The District Court dismissed Mikulis and Melley's suits under FED. R. CIV. P. 12(b)(6) for lack of statutory standing. Although appellants may have made retirement decisions based on a belief that their retirement medical benefits would continue for their lifetimes, we agree with the District Court's determination that they do not have statutory standing to bring this action. We will, therefore, affirm.

I. Background

Blue Cross Blue Shield of Northeastern Pennsylvania (Blue Cross) administers the Blue Cross of Northeastern Pennsylvania Retiree Health Insurance Plan (the Plan), a welfare benefits plan for Blue Cross retirees. The Plan is subject to the Employee Retirement Income Security Act of 1974 (ERISA), 29 U.S.C. § 1001, *et seq.* Blue Cross is a Plan fiduciary under ERISA § 3(21)(A). Originally, the Plan provided Blue Cross retirees with 100% lifetime health insurance coverage. Blue Cross altered the Plan in 1993, and then again in 1999 and 2001. Starting in 1993, the Plan's coverage changed to a formula that provided a percentage of the cost of the health care plan, based on the number of years of service that an employee had on retirement. The formula required a minimum of 10 years of service. The formula was changed in 1999 to require a minimum of 15 years of service. The 1993 and 1999 changes were applied prospectively to new retirees; the benefits of former retirees were not changed. On January 1, 2001, Blue Cross again amended the Plan (1) to provide for a graduated dollar contribution toward health insurance coverage for retirees with at least 15 years of service and (2) to eliminate coverage for surviving spouses of retirees. Blue Cross applied the 2001 Plan Amendment retroactively to all retirees.

Retired Blue Cross employees have brought a class action against Blue Cross for breach of fiduciary duty stemming from various changes made in the Plan's coverage. Elizabeth Melley and Jean Mikulis are intervenors in the action. Mikulis was an employee of Blue Cross for almost 13 years. She retired at age 62 on February 27, 1993, after being notified by Blue Cross that, unless she retired by April 1, 1993, her future retirement health benefits would no longer be guaranteed at 100% lifetime but would be subject to a percentage formula based on years of employment. As a result of early retirement, Mikulis received a smaller pension from Blue Cross and reduced Social Security benefits. Mikulis received 100%

benefits under the Plan until January 1, 2001, when she ceased to be eligible for any benefits under the amended Plan. She claims to have relied on having 100% lifetime health coverage in her savings and spending decisions.

Melley is the widow of a Blue Cross retiree. The record does not indicate when Melley's late husband retired from Blue Cross, what his age was at retirement, or if he had other employment thereafter. Melley received benefits under the Plan until January 1, 2001, when she ceased to be eligible for any benefits under the amended Plan.

Mikulis and Melley claim that Blue Cross knowingly made various material misrepresentations and omissions about Plan benefits and amendments. In particular, they maintain that they had no notice before the 1993 Plan amendment that Blue Cross could alter the Plan. They also allege that Blue Cross's pre-2001 practice of applying Plan changes only prospectively led them to believe that any future changes would be prospective. They further claim that they relied upon Blue Cross's misrepresentations and omissions to their detriment. Mikulis contends that, but for Blue Cross's misrepresentations and omissions, she would not have taken early retirement. Melley alleges that her late husband made retirement and insurance decisions based upon the promise of continuing lifetime health benefits for his spouse, even in the event of his death.

Mikulis and Melley brought an action under ERISA § 502(a)(3), in which they allege that Blue Cross breached its fiduciary duties under ERISA § 404(a), by failing to disseminate accurate information about the terms of retiree medical benefits under the Plan. They are seeking either reinstatement in the Plan as it existed prior to the 2001 amendments, comparable coverage, or its monetary equivalent.

Blue Cross moved to dismiss . . . . The District Court found that Mikulis and Melley did not have standing because they were neither Plan participants nor beneficiaries at the time they commenced their suit. Accordingly, the District Court dismissed both complaints for lack of standing. This appeal followed.

III. Discussion

ERISA's statutory standing requirements provide in § 502(a)(1) and (3) that a civil action may only be brought:

> (1) by a participant or beneficiary . . . (B) to recover benefits due to him under the terms of his plan, to enforce his rights under the terms of the plan, or to clarify his rights to future benefits under the terms of the plan . . . .
>
> (3) by a participant, beneficiary, or fiduciary (A) to enjoin any act or practice which violates any provision of this subchapter or the terms of the plan, or (B) to obtain other appropriate equitable relief (i) to redress such violations or (ii) to enforce any provisions of this subchapter or the terms of the plan.

The terms "participant" and "beneficiary" are defined in ERISA § 3(7) (8):

> (7) The term "participant" means any employee or former employee of an employer, or any member or former member of an employee organization, who is or may become eligible to receive a benefit of any type from an employee benefit plan which covers employees of such employer or members of such organization, or whose beneficiaries may be eligible to receive any such benefit.

> (8) The term "beneficiary" means a person designated by a participant, or by the terms of an employee benefit plan, who is or may become entitled to a benefit thereunder.

The Supreme Court has held that:

> the term "participant" is naturally read to mean either "employees in, or reasonably expected to be in, currently covered employment," or former employees who "have . . . a reasonable expectation of returning to covered employment" or who have "a colorable claim" to vested benefits. In order to establish that he or she "may become eligible" for benefits, a claimant must have a colorable claim that (1) he or she will prevail in a suit for benefits, or that (2) eligibility requirements will be fulfilled in the future. "This view attributes conventional meanings to the statutory language since all employees in covered employment and former employees with a colorable claim to vested benefits 'may become eligible.' "

Firestone Tire & Rubber Co. v. Bruch, 489 U.S. 101, 118 (1989) (internal citations omitted).

Thus, to bring a civil action under ERISA, Melley and Mikulis must have a colorable claim to Plan benefits as the result of their suit. We have interpreted the colorable claim requirement as a lower burden of persuasion than showing likelihood of success on the merits.

Mikulis and Melley have raised four arguments as to why they fall within the definition of participant or beneficiary and have statutory standing. First, they maintain that they have standing because they are within the zone of interest protected by ERISA. Second, they claim that they have standing because they have a colorable claim to receive Plan benefits in the future as part of an equitable remedy. Third, they argue that they have standing because they formerly received Plan benefits and they detrimentally relied on Blue Cross's misrepresentations. Finally, Mikulis contends that she has standing because, but for Blue Cross's misrepresentations and omissions, she would not have retired when she did.

For the reasons stated below, we reject these arguments.

1. Zone of Interest

To bring a civil action under ERISA, a plaintiff must have constitutional, prudential, and statutory standing. There is no question of Mikulis and Melley's constitutional standing in this case. They argue, however, that they have prudential standing because they are within the "zone of interest" that ERISA was created to protect and that prudential standing gives them statutory standing.

Whether a party has prudential standing depends on whether "a plaintiff's grievance . . . arguably fall[s] within the zone of interest protected or regulated by the statutory provision or constitutional guarantee invoked in the suit." *Bennett v. Spear*, 520 U.S. 154, 162 (1997). As a general matter, we have found that statutory standing requirements can eliminate prudential standing restrictions but are presumed not to:

> Because prudential standing doctrine is judge-made and not the product of constitutional restraints on the power of the federal courts to hear claims, Congress can eliminate prudential restrictions on standing if it so desires. As a matter of statutory interpretation, however, Congress is presumed to incorporate background prudential standing principles, unless the statute expressly negates them.

We extensively addressed the interplay of prudential and statutory standing in ERISA cases in *Rite Aid.* We remarked there that in past decisions we had stated that "[f]ar from abrogating the prudential standing doctrine . . . ERISA § 502(a)(1) . . . *restricts* civil actions brought against a plan administrator to actions brought by a 'participant or beneficiary.' " 334 F.3d at 340. In other words, the language of § 502(a)(1) sets forth the standing requirements to bring such an action — both prudential and statutory standing:

> In that sense, the "zone of interest" inquiry in the prudential standing analysis for § 502(a)(1) claims is inextricably tied to the question of whether a plaintiff can meet the definitions of either a "participant" or "beneficiary".

Rite Aid, 334 F.3d at 341.

* * *

When we stated in Rite Aid that "the 'zone of interest' inquiry in the prudential standing analysis for § 502(a)(1) claims is inextricably tied to whether a plaintiff can meet the definitions of either 'participant' or 'beneficiary'," 334 F.3d at 341, we meant that statutory standing requirements in ERISA § 502(a)(1) were essentially a codification of ERISA's "zone of interest" — we did not mean the inverse, *i.e.*, that prudential standing suffices for statutory standing. Indeed, it would make little sense for Congress to have enacted ERISA § 502(a)(1) to define who may bring suit against a plan administrator if standing to sue were to be determined by the traditional "zone of interest" prudential standing test.

Moreover, despite the citation to *Vartanian*, we did not undertake a "zone of interest" analysis in *Rite Aid.* Instead, we focused solely on whether the plaintiff met the ERISA § 3(7) definition of "participant." This focus is consistent with the conclusion that ERISA's statutory standing requirements are a codification of the "zone of interest" analysis. Mikulis and Melley's "zone of interest" argument does not prevail.

2. Colorable Claim to a Remedy Under ERISA

ERISA §§ 3(7) and 3(8) define participants and beneficiaries as those "who [are] or may become eligible to receive a benefit of any type from an employee benefit plan . . . ." Tracking this language, Mikulis and Melley's second argument is that they have standing because they are Plan participants/beneficiaries and they qualify as participants/beneficiaries because they have a colorable claim to receive Plan benefits in the future via equitable relief ordering the restoration of the Plan to its pre-January 1, 2001, status or enjoining the retroactive application of the January 1, 2001, Amendment.

* * *

Turning to the merits of the colorable claim to benefits argument, Blue Cross made four objections to it. First, Blue Cross contends that Mikulis and Melley have not asserted any claim for reinstatement in the Plan under ERISA § 502(a)(1)(B) but have merely requested monetary damages. Blue Cross is incorrect. Mikulis and Melley's joint Amended Class Action Complaint specifically requested that the Court "order the Defendant to reinstitute the Plan as it was in existence prior to the change complained of, and/or enjoin Defendant from implementing the revised Plan", not to mention award "such other legal and equitable relief as the Court may deem just and necessary." Mikulis's Second Amended Complaint only requests "Any other legal and equitable relief as the Court may deem just and necessary."

Although this is boilerplate, it tracks the language of ERISA § 502(a)(3)(B), which provides for participants and beneficiaries to bring suit "to obtain other appropriate equitable relief (i) to redress [ERISA violations] or (ii) to enforce any provisions of this subchapter or the terms of the plan".

Second, Blue Cross argues that under our decision in *Daniels*, 263 F.3d at 78, equitable relief is not a plan benefit. Thus, the right to equitable relief cannot give standing. This is not a correct reading of *Daniels. Daniels* merely determined that monetary damages are not plan benefits. It did not address the question of whether equitable relief could constitute a benefit under a plan. Here, Mikulis and Melley are requesting equitable relief including reinstatement of the Plan "as it was in existence prior to the changes complained of." The *sine qua non* of benefits of the Plan is to be covered by the Plan.

Third, Blue Cross remonstrates that Mikulis and Melley cannot have standing as a result of possible equitable relief because standing must exist at the time a suit is commenced, not at the time of judgment. For constitutional and prudential standing it is well established that standing must exist at the time the suit is commenced and throughout the suit. We have not addressed this issue in regard to statutory standing; moreover, because a decision on this issue is not necessary for the outcome of this case, we do not express an opinion on it now.

Fourth, Blue Cross maintains that because the amendment of ERISA plans is not a fiduciary act, equitable relief is not available. ERISA § 502(a)(3), authorizes equitable relief only for violations of ERISA's provisions. The amendment of an ERISA plan is not a fiduciary act governed by ERISA. Therefore, as the District Court correctly noted, Blue Cross did not violate ERISA by amending the Plan.

Mikulis and Melley, however, alleged breaches of fiduciary duty that included not only the amendment of the Plan, but also misrepresentations about future plan benefits and coverage. Unlike the amendment of the Plan, the provision of information about Plan benefits and coverage is a fiduciary act. Therefore, "[a]n employee may recover for a breach of fiduciary duty if he or she proves that an employer, acting as a fiduciary, made a misrepresentation that would confuse a reasonable beneficiary about his or her benefits, and the beneficiary acted thereupon to his or her detriment." In re *Unisys Corp. Retiree Med. Benefit "ERISA" Litig.*, 242 F.3d 497, 505 (3d Cir. 2001). If Mikulis and Melley raised a colorable claim of such a breach and detrimental reliance, then they would have standing because they would have a colorable claim to be eligible for equitable relief under § 502(a)(3).

As the District Court noted, however, Blue Cross' alleged misrepresentations did not divest Melley of her status as a plan beneficiary. It was the January 1, 2001, amendment of the Plan that did so. Melley's status was determined by her situation as surviving spouse of a retired Blue Cross employee. The alleged misrepresentations had no effect on that status nor was Melley in a position to make any changes to her status based on them. Her medical benefits were not a vested benefit, and the Plan contained language, inserted in the 1993 amendment, that it could be changed and that health benefits could be discontinued at any time. Thus, we find no basis to conclude that Melley's status as a beneficiary was affected by the alleged misrepresentations.

Mikulis is in the same situation as Melley in regard to the alleged misrepresentations made since the time of her retirement. Mikulis was not in a position to change her status of retired employee. Mikulis has, however, raised a related argument — "but for" Blue Cross's misrepresentations she would have retired later and would currently be a Plan participant.

Since the Supreme Court's ruling in *Firestone*, we have not had occasion to rule on the issue of whether a claimant, who is a former plan participant, has standing when it is the alleged breach of fiduciary duty that has caused the claimant to lose status as a plan participant.

ERISA's legislative history indicates that Congress intended the federal courts to construe the statutory standing requirements broadly in order to facilitate enforcement of its remedial provisions:

> The enforcement provisions have been designed specifically to provide both the Secretary [of Labor] and participants and beneficiaries with broad remedies for redressing or preventing violations of the [Act] . . . . The intent of the Committee is to provide the full range of legal and equitable remedies available in both state and federal courts and to remove jurisdictional and procedural obstacles which in the past appear to have hampered effective enforcement of fiduciary responsibilities under state law or recovery of benefits due to participants.

S. Rep. No. 127, 93d Cong., 2d Sess., 3 (1974), reprinted in 1974 U.S.C.C.A.N. 4639, 4871. Refusing to allow for "but for" standing would frustrate Congress's intention to remove jurisdictional and procedural obstacles to ERISA claims.

The majority of circuits that have addressed whether there is a "but for" exception for ERISA standing have adopted it. In *Christopher v. Mobil Oil Corp.*, 950 F.2d at 1221, the Fifth Circuit concluded that "it would seem more logical to say that but for the employer's conduct alleged to be in violation of ERISA, the employee *would* be a current employee with a reasonable expectation of receiving benefits, and the employer should not be able through its own malfeasance to defeat the employee's standing." Similarly, in *McBride v. PLM Int'l, Inc.*, 179 F.3d 737, 743 (9th Cir. 1999), the Ninth Circuit held that "[i]f an employee is a participant at the time of the alleged ERISA violation and alleges that he was discharged or discriminated against because of the protected whistleblowing activities, we hold that such an employee has standing to sue under ERISA."

A plan administrator's alleged ERISA violation should not be the means by which the plan is able to insulate itself from suits arising from the alleged violation. We will not read ERISA so myopically. As the Sixth Circuit observed, "ERISA should not be construed to permit the fiduciary to circumvent his ERISA-imposed fiduciary duty in this manner." *Swinney*, 46 F.3d at 518–519. Therefore, in the proper case, we may find that a plaintiff has statutory standing if the plaintiff can in good faith plead that she was an ERISA plan participant or beneficiary and that she still would be but for the alleged malfeasance of a plan fiduciary.

Turning to the case before us, in reviewing Mikulis's allegation that she would not have retired when she did had Blue Cross not made various misrepresentations and omissions, we must keep in mind that Mikulis retired on February 27, 1993, and any reliance on statements by Blue Cross that induced her to retire must have occurred before that time. More importantly, for Mikulis to prevail, her reliance must have been on "a material misrepresentation that would confuse a reasonable beneficiary about his or her benefits, and the beneficiary acted thereupon to his or her detriment." *Unisys*, 242 F.3d at 505.

Mikulis was instructed by the District Court in its Memorandum and Order of May 7, 2004, that in her Second Amended Complaint, she must set forth the specific actions she took or refrained from taking in reliance on Blue Cross's alleged misrepresentations and identify how she was harmed by the asserted action or forbearance. She has not done so except in generalities, as she did in her earlier complaint. Nor has she alleged how much longer she would have worked "but for" the alleged misrepresentations. In 1993, the 15 year cut-off of benefits, instituted in 2001, was not mentioned at all. There is no basis to conclude from the allegations in the complaint that, even if she had worked longer, she would still have qualified for benefits after the 2001 amendment.

In addition, Mikulis has not alleged that the statements made by Blue Cross prior to the 1993 amendment were false at the time that they were made. Without such an allegation, there is no ground to assert a breach of fiduciary duty. *Id.* A representation is not a misrepresentation if it is an accurate reflection of the plan administrator's intent when the statement was made.

We conclude therefore that Mikulis's "but for" claim is not a colorable claim for benefits and thus is insufficient to give her standing under *Firestone.*

IV. Conclusion

For the reasons discussed above, we will affirm the District Court's dismissal of Melley and Mikulis's claims.

Many courts have held that an employee has standing to sue an employer for fraudulently inducing the employee to retire in order to avoid paying certain benefits. As stated in *Jordan v. Tyson Foods*, 2007 FED App. 0868N (6th Cir.) "if the employer's breach of fiduciary duty causes the employee to either give up his right to benefits or to fail to participate in a plan, then the employee has standing to challenge that fiduciary breach. This exception exists in order to prevent employer from duping employees to give up their rights to participate in a plan."

Suppose a pension plan terminates and meets its obligations to participants and beneficiaries by purchasing annuities on their behalf from an insurance company. At that point, because there is no plan, there are apparently neither "participants" nor "beneficiaries." Later, the recipients of the annuities believe that the amount of the annuities was miscalculated by the former plan (it allegedly did not credit the plan participants with all their vested benefits). Can the beneficiaries sue the former trustees of the now defunct plan? Alternatively suppose that the insurance company that pays the annuities goes bankrupt. Do the annuitants have standing to sue the former plan fiduciary claiming that it violated its fiduciary obligations in its selection of the financially suspect insurance company? In 1994, Congress answered those questions by amending ERISA to add § 502(a)(9) that allows "any individual who was a participant or beneficiary at the time of the alleged violation" to sue for "appropriate relief" if the purchase of an annuity in connection with "the termination of an individual's status as a participant" violated ERISA. In short, ex-participants have standing to sue for alleged fiduciary violations that occurred in regards to their pension annuities.

7-1 QUESTIONS AND PROBLEMS

1. In *Firestone v. Brauch, supra*, the Supreme Court held that a "participant" meant either a currently covered employee or one with a "colorable" claim to benefits. Did the former employees have a colorable claim in *Firestone*?

2. Akira, a long-time employee of Beta Co., challenged the company's proposed termination of its defined benefit plan. Two weeks later, he was discharged. The

next day, the plan was terminated. One month ago, Akira sued in federal court, claiming that his discharge violated ERISA § 510. Does he have standing to sue?

[3] The Secretary of Labor

ERISA §§ 502(a)(2), 502(i), 504.

If a victim of a violation of ERISA lacks standing to sue or does not wish to individually pursue the cause of action, the Secretary of Labor is empowered by ERISA § 502(a)(2) to sue plan fiduciaries for the remedies provided by ERISA § 409. Similarly, ERISA § 502(i) authorizes the enforcement of ERISA §§ 406 and 502(a)(5) and permits the Secretary to enjoin any acts that violate any provision of ERISA or to "obtain other appropriate equitable relief. . . ." ERISA § 504 grants the Secretary broad investigative authority over pension and welfare benefit plans.

[4] The Plan Fiduciary

ERISA § 502(a)(3).

Under ERISA § 502(a)(3), the plan fiduciary can sue to enjoin any act that violates any aspect of ERISA or can sue for "other appropriate equitable relief." The fiduciary can sue to reclaim plan assets that have been mispaid, misappropriated, or otherwise diminished or lost due to the acts of the defendant.

C. FEDERAL JURISDICTION AND REMOVAL

[1] Complete Preemption and Removal

ERISA §§ 502(e), (f).

ERISA's enforcement provisions are found in § 502, which lists who may sue and the nature of available remedies. Sections 502(e) and (f) grant federal courts exclusive jurisdiction except for individual claims for benefits brought under § 502(a)(1)(B). Section 502(e) gives state and federal courts concurrent jurisdiction over § 502(a)(1)(B) suits to recover plan benefits or to enforce or clarify rights to future benefits. However, if the plaintiff files a § 502(a)(1)(B) claim in state court, the defendant has an absolute right to remove the case to federal court. Defendants often remove cases to federal court because of a perceived greater judicial sophistication and understanding of ERISA. Section 502(e) permits plaintiffs who wish to pursue both ERISA and state causes of action to file in state court, which will apply federal law to the ERISA claim and state law to the state law claims. As noted, however, the defendant can remove all claims to a federal district court. If, after removal, the ERISA claims are dismissed, the federal court may continue to exercise jurisdiction over the surviving state law claims, while applying appropriate state law to resolve the state law claims.

Even if the plaintiff purports to raise only state law causes of action, the defendant may seek to remove the case to federal court. By statute (28 U.S.C. § 1441(a)), any civil action brought in a state court over which federal district courts have original jurisdiction can be removed to federal district court by the defendant. Absent diversity jurisdiction, federal district courts have jurisdiction over cases that raise "federal questions"; that is, claims that arise under federal law. Under the "well-pleaded complaint" rule, a federal court has jurisdiction only if the federal cause of action appears on the face of the complaint. And although a claim by the defendant of ERISA preemption is federal *defense* to a state law cause of action, it does not create federal court jurisdiction because it is not a *cause of action* arising under federal law.

Nevertheless, Congress may so completely preempt an area of civil law that *any* claim in that area of law is necessarily federal in character and thus removable to federal court despite the complaint not alleging a federal cause of action. Any state cause of action that would be preempted by ERISA § 502(a) enforcement provisions is removable to federal court despite the complaint not stating a federal cause of action.

METROPOLITAN LIFE INS. CO. v. TAYLOR

481 U.S. 58 (1987)

Justice O'Connor, delivered the opinion of the Court.

By statute "any civil action brought in a State court of which the district courts of the United States have original jurisdiction, may be removed by the defendant or the defendants, to the district court of the United States for the district and division embracing the place where such action is pending." 28 U.S.C. § 1441(a). One category of cases over which the district courts have original jurisdiction are "federal question" cases; that is, those cases "arising under the Constitution, laws, or treaties of the United States." 28 U.S.C. § 1331. It is long settled law that a cause of action arises under federal law only when the plaintiff's well-pleaded complaint raises issues of federal law. The "well-pleaded complaint rule" is the basic principle marking the boundaries of the federal question jurisdiction of the federal district courts.

Federal pre-emption is ordinarily a federal defense to the plaintiff's suit. As a defense, it does not appear on the face of a well-pleaded complaint, and, therefore, does not authorize removal to federal court. *Gully v. First National Bank, supra.* One corollary of the well-pleaded complaint rule developed in the case law, however, is that Congress may so completely pre-empt a particular area that any civil complaint raising this select group of claims is necessarily federal in character. For 20 years, this Court has singled out claims pre-empted by § 301 of the LMRA for such special treatment. *Avco Corp. v. Machinists*, 390 U.S. 557 (1968).

> "The necessary ground of decision [in *Avco*] was that the pre-emptive force of § 301 is so powerful as to displace entirely any state cause of action 'for violation of contracts between an employer and a labor organization.' Any such suit is purely a creature of federal law, not-withstanding the fact that state law would provide a cause of action in the absence of § 301." *Franchise Tax Board of Cal. v. Construction Laborers Vacation Trust for Southern Cal., supra*, at 23 (footnote omitted).

There is no dispute in this litigation that Taylor's complaint, although pre-empted by ERISA, purported to raise only state law causes of action. The question therefore resolves itself into whether or not the *Avco* principle can be extended to statutes other than the LMRA in order to recharacterize a state law complaint displaced by § 502(a)(1)(B) as an action arising under federal law. In *Franchise Tax Board*, the Court held that ERISA pre-emption, without more, does not convert a state claim into an action arising under federal law. *Franchise Tax Board of Cal. v. Construction Laborers Vacation Trust for Southern Cal.*, 463 U.S. at 25–27. The court suggested, however, that a state action that was not only pre-empted by ERISA, but also came "within the scope of § 502(a) of ERISA" might fall within the *Avco* rule. *Id.* at 24–25. The claim in this case, unlike the state tax collection suit in

Franchise Tax Board, is within the scope of § 502(a) and we therefore must face the question specifically reserved by *Franchise Tax Board.*

In the absence of explicit direction from Congress, this question would be a close one. As we have made clear today in *Pilot Life Ins. Co. v. Dedeaux, ante*, at 54, "[t]he policy choices reflected in the inclusion of certain remedies and the exclusion of others under the federal scheme would be completely undermined if ERISA-plan participants and beneficiaries were free to obtain remedies under state law that Congress rejected in ERISA." Even with a provision such as § 502(a)(1)(B) that lies at the heart of a statute with the unique pre-emptive force of ERISA, *id.* at 24 n.26, however, we would be reluctant to find that extraordinary pre-emptive power, such as has been found with respect to § 301 of the LMRA, that converts an ordinary state common law complaint into one stating a federal claim for purposes of the well-pleaded complaint rule. But the language of the jurisdictional subsection of ERISA's civil enforcement provisions closely parallels that of § 301 of the LMRA. Section 502(f) says:

> "The district courts of the United States shall have jurisdiction, without respect to the amount in controversy or the citizenship of the parties, to grant the relief provided for in subsection (a) of this section in any action." 29 U.S.C. § 1132(f).

Cf. § 301(a) of the LMRA, 29 U.S.C. § 185(a). The presumption that similar language in two labor law statutes has a similar meaning is fully confirmed by the legislative history of ERISA's civil enforcement provisions. The Conference Report on ERISA describing the civil enforcement provisions of § 502(a) says:

> "[W]ith respect to suits to enforce benefit rights under the plan or to recover benefits under the plan which do not involve application of the title I provisions, they may be brought not only in U.S. district courts but also in State courts of competent jurisdiction. *All such actions in Federal or State courts are to be regarded as arising under the laws of the United States in similar fashion to those brought under section 301 of the Labor-Management Relations Act of 1947.*" H.R. Conf. Rep. No. 93 1280, p. 327 (1974) (emphasis added).

No more specific reference to the *Avco* rule can be expected and the rest of the legislative history consistently sets out this clear intention to make § 502(a)(1)(B) suits brought by participants or beneficiaries federal questions for the purposes of federal court jurisdiction in like manner as § 301 of the LMRA. See *Pilot Life Ins. Co. v. Dedeaux, ante*, at 54–55. For example, Senator Williams, a sponsor of ERISA, emphasized that the civil enforcement section would enable participants and beneficiaries to bring suit to recover benefits denied contrary to the terms of the plan and that when they did so "[i]t is intended that such actions will be regarded as arising under the laws of the United States, in similar fashion to those brought under section 301 of the Labor Management Relations Act." 120 Cong. Rec. 29933 (1974).

Taylor argues strenuously that this action cannot be removed to federal court because it was not "obvious" at the time he filed suit that his common law action was both preempted by § 514(a), and also displaced by the civil enforcement provisions of § 502(a). But the touchstone of the federal district court's removal jurisdiction is not the "obviousness" of the pre-emption defense but the intent of Congress. Indeed, as we have noted, even an "obvious" pre-emption defense does not, in most cases, create removal jurisdiction. In this case, however, Congress has clearly manifested an intent to make causes of action within the scope of the civil enforcement provisions of § 502(a) removable to federal court. Since we have found Taylor's cause of action to be within the scope of § 502(a), we must honor that intent whether pre-emption was obvious or not at the time this suit was filed.

Accordingly, this suit, though it purports to raise only state law claims, is necessarily federal in character by virtue of the clearly manifested intent of Congress. It, therefore, "arise[s] under the . . . laws . . . of the United States," 28 U.S.C. § 1331, and is removable to federal court by the defendants, 28 U.S.C. § 1441(b). The judgment of the Court of Appeals is

Reversed.

The application of complete preemption and removal under a § 502(a) claim is illustrated in the following case.

DUKES v. U.S. HEALTHCARE, INC.

57 F.3d 350 (3d Cir. 1995)

STAPLETON, CIRCUIT JUDGE:

The plaintiffs in these two cases filed suit in state court against health maintenance organizations ("HMOs") organized by U.S. Healthcare, Inc., claiming damages, under various theories, for injuries arising from the medical malpractice of HMO-affiliated hospitals and medical personnel. The defendant HMOs removed both cases to federal court, arguing (1) that the injured person in each case had obtained medical care as a benefit from a welfare-benefit plan governed by the Employee Retirement Income Security Act of 1974 ("ERISA"), (2) that removal is proper under the *Metropolitan Life Insurance Co. v. Taylor*, 481 U.S. 58 (1987), "complete preemption" exception to the "well-pleaded complaint rule," and (3) that the plaintiffs' claims are preempted by § 514(a) of ERISA. The district courts agreed with these contentions and dismissed the plaintiffs' claims against the HMOs. The plaintiffs appeal those rulings and ask that their claims against the HMOs be remanded to state court . . . .

. . .

The HMOs removed these cases to federal court pursuant to 28 U.S.C. § 1441, alleging that the district courts had original jurisdiction over the claims, because the claims "[arose] under the Constitution, treaties or laws of the United States." § 1441(b). To determine whether a claim "arises under" federal law — and thus is removable — we begin with the "well-pleaded complaint rule."

Under the well-pleaded complaint rule, a cause of action "arises under" federal law, and removal is proper, only if a federal question is presented on the face of the plaintiff's properly pleaded complaint. A federal defense to a plaintiff's state law cause of action ordinarily does not appear on the face of the well-pleaded complaint, and, therefore, usually is insufficient to warrant removal to federal court. Thus, it is well-established that the defense of preemption ordinarily is insufficient justification to permit removal to federal court. *Caterpillar Inc. v. Williams*, 482 U.S. 386, 398 (1987) ("The fact that a defendant might ultimately prove that a plaintiff's claims are pre-empted under [a federal statute] does not establish that they are removable to federal court.").

The Supreme Court has recognized an exception to the well-pleaded complaint rule — the "complete preemption" exception — under which "Congress may so completely pre-empt a particular area that any civil complaint raising this select group of claims is necessarily federal in character." *Metropolitan Life Insurance*

Co. v. Taylor, 481 U.S. 58, 63–64 (1987). The complete preemption doctrine applies when the pre-emptive force of [the federal statutory provision] is so powerful as to displace entirely any state cause of action [addressed by the federal statute]. Any such suit is purely a creature of federal law, notwithstanding the fact that state law would provide a cause of action in the absence of [the federal provision].

The Supreme Court has determined that Congress intended the complete-preemption doctrine to apply to state law causes of action which fit within the scope of ERISA's civil-enforcement provisions. . . . Thus, courts have found that the complete-preemption doctrine permits removal of state law causes of action in a host of different ERISA-related circumstances (holding that state common law causes of action asserting improper processing of a claim for benefits under an employee benefit plan are removable to federal court); (holding that removal was proper because state law claim alleging that plan fiduciary was demoted and terminated for refusing to violate ERISA fell within § 502(a)(2) & (3)); (plaintiff's state court rescission claim against a group insurance policy for the policy's refusal to reimburse plaintiff for medical treatment received was properly removed because plaintiff's claim was for a denial of benefits); (common law claim for breach of an oral promise to pay pension-related benefits properly removed to federal court); (plaintiff's state law claim challenging the calculation of his time of "uninterrupted service" for the purposes of calculating his pension benefits held removable).

That the Supreme Court has recognized a limited exception to the well-pleaded complaint rule for state law claims which fit within the scope of § 502 by no means implies that all claims preempted by ERISA are subject to removal. Instead, as the U.S. Court of Appeals for the Sixth Circuit wrote recently, "[r]emoval and preemption are two distinct concepts." *Warner v. Ford Motor Co.*, 46 F.3d 531, 535 (6th Cir. 1995). Section 514 of ERISA defines the scope of ERISA preemption, providing that ERISA "supersede[s] any and all State laws insofar as they may now or hereafter relate to any employee benefit plan described in [§ 4(a) of ERISA] and not exempt under [§ 4(b) of ERISA]." The complete-preemption exception, on the other hand, is concerned with a more limited set of state laws, those which fall within the scope of ERISA's civil enforcement provision, § 502. State law claims which fall outside of the scope of § 502, even if preempted by § 514(a), are still governed by the well-pleaded complaint rule and, therefore, are not removable under the complete-preemption principles . . .

The difference between preemption and complete preemption is important. When the doctrine of complete preemption does not apply, but the plaintiff's state claim is arguably preempted under § 514(a), the district court, being without removal jurisdiction, cannot resolve the dispute regarding preemption. It lacks power to do anything other than remand to the state court where the preemption issue can be addressed and resolved.

The district courts in these cases found that the plaintiffs' state law claims against the U.S. Healthcare HMOs fall within the scope of § 502(a)(1)(B) and that the *Metropolitan Life* complete-preemption doctrine therefore permits removal. We disagree.

To determine whether the state law claims fall within the scope of § 502(a)(1)(B), we must determine whether those claims, properly construed, are "to recover benefits due . . . under the terms of [the] plan, to enforce . . . rights under the terms of the plan, or to clarify . . . rights to future benefits under the terms of the plan." . . .

* * *

. . . We will assume, without deciding, that the medical care provided (and not merely the plaintiffs' memberships in the respective HMOs) is the plan benefit for the purposes of ERISA. We will also assume that the HMOs, either as a part of or on behalf of the ERISA plans, arrange for the delivery of those plan benefits. We thus assume, for example, that removal jurisdiction would exist if the plaintiffs were alleging that the HMOs refused to provide the services to which membership entitled them.

Given those assumptions, we nevertheless conclude that removal was improper. We are compelled to this conclusion because the plaintiffs' claims, even when construed as U.S. Healthcare suggests, merely attack the *quality* of the benefits they received: The plaintiffs here simply do not claim that the plans erroneously withheld benefits due. Nor do they ask the state courts to enforce their rights under the terms of their respective plans or to clarify their rights to future benefits. As a result, the plaintiffs' claims fall outside of the scope of § 502(a)(1)(B) and these cases must be remanded to the state courts from which they were removed.

Nothing in the complaints indicates that the plaintiffs are complaining about their ERISA welfare plans' failure to provide benefits due under the plan. Dukes does not allege, for example, that the Germantown Hospital refused to perform blood studies on Darryl because the ERISA plan refused to pay for those studies. Similarly, the Viscontis do not contend that Serena's death was due to their welfare plan's refusal to pay for or otherwise provide for medical services. Instead of claiming that the welfare plans in any way withheld some quantum of plan benefits due, the plaintiffs in both cases complain about the low quality of the medical treatment that they actually received and argue that the U.S. Healthcare HMO should be held liable under agency and negligence principles.

We are confident that a claim about the quality of a benefit received is not a claim under § 502(a)(1)(B) to "recover benefits due . . . under the terms of [the] plan."

Nor does anything in the legislative history, structure, or purpose of ERISA suggest that Congress viewed § 502(a)(1)(B) as creating a remedy for a participant injured by medical malpractice. When Congress enacted ERISA it was concerned in large part with the various mechanisms and institutions involved in the funding and payment of plan benefits. That is, Congress was concerned "that owing to the inadequacy of current minimum [financial and administrative] standards, the soundness and stability of plans with respect to adequate funds to pay promised benefits may be endangered." § 2, 29 U.S.C. § 1001(a). Thus, Congress sought to assure that promised benefits would be available when plan participants had need of them and § 502 was intended to provide each individual participant with a remedy in the event that promises made by the plan were not kept. We find nothing in the legislative history suggesting that § 502 was intended as a part of a federal scheme to control the quality of the benefits received by plan participants. Quality control of benefits, such as the health care benefits provided here, is a field traditionally occupied by state regulation and we interpret the silence of Congress as reflecting an intent that it remain such.

* * *

We recognize that the distinction between the quantity of benefits due under a welfare plan and the quality of those benefits will not always be clear in situations like this where the benefit contracted for is health care services rather than money to pay for such services. There well may be cases in which the quality of a patient's medical care or the skills of the personnel provided to administer that care will be so low that the treatment received simply will not qualify as health care at all. In such a case, it well may be appropriate to conclude that the plan participant or beneficiary has been denied benefits due under the plan. This is not such a case, however. While the *Dukes* complaint alleges that the Germantown Hospital committed malpractice when it decided not to perform certain blood tests, no one would conclude from that malpractice that Germantown Hospital was not acting as a health care provider when it made those decisions. Similarly, while the Viscontis claim that Dr. Wisniewski was incompetent, there is no indication that he was not performing health care services at the time he allegedly committed the malpractice charged.

* * *

7-2 QUESTIONS AND PROBLEMS

1. If a case is not subject to complete preemption under § 502, who decides if the case is preempted by § 514(a)?

2. If the case is preempted by § 514(a), is there a remedy for the plaintiff's claims?

3. What factors are a state court likely to take into account in deciding whether ERISA § 514(a) preemption is applicable?

[2] Limited Preemption and Removal

ERISA § 514(a).

The difference between "complete preemption" that provides a basis for removal from a state court under § 502(a) and the more limited preemption removal under § 514(a) is addressed in the following case excerpts.

> This case requires us to explore the difference between "conflict preemption" under § 514(a), and "complete preemption" under § 502(a). But in order to understand the importance of this distinction it is necessary to begin with the principles governing the removal jurisdiction of federal courts under 28 U.S.C. § 1441. Under that section "any civil action brought in a State court of which the district courts of the United States have original jurisdiction, may be removed by the defendant or the defendants, to the district court of the United States. . . ." 28 U.S.C. § 1441(b). Whether removal was proper in this case depends upon whether we have "federal question" jurisdiction under 28 U.S.C. § 1331, which gives federal courts jurisdiction over cases that "arise under the Constitution, laws, or treaties of the United States." 28 U.S.C. § 1331.
>
> Ordinarily a court determines whether there is federal question jurisdiction by examining the plaintiff's well-pleaded complaint, for "[i]t is long-settled law that a cause of action arises under federal law only when the plaintiff's well pleaded complaint raise issues of federal law."
>
> In contrast, "[t]he presence of a federal question . . . in a defensive argument does not overcome the paramount policies embodied in the well -pleaded complaint rule — that the plaintiff is the master of the complaint, that a federal question must appear on the face of the complaint, and that the plaintiff may, by eschewing claims based on federal law, choose to have the cause heard in state court."

Caterpillar Inc. v. Williams, 482 U.S. 386, 398–99 (1987).

> Put another way, federal preemption that merely serves as a defense to a state law action (sometimes called "conflict preemption") does not confer federal question jurisdiction. Thus the defendant cannot cause a transfer to federal court simply by asserting a federal question in his responsive pleading.
>
> The application of the complete preemption doctrine in the ERISA context originated in *Franchise Tax Board* where the Supreme Court observed that an action "that was not only preempted by ERISA but came within the scope of § 502(a)" might be subject to complete preemption. Later, the Court held that a plaintiff's common law claims were completely preempted by ERISA, because they were within the scope of § 502(a)(1)(B). These cases establish that, under ERISA, § 502(a) provides the basis for complete preemption whereas § 514(a) provides the basis for conflict preemption.
>
> The difference between complete preemption under § 502(a) and conflict preemption under § 514(a) is important because complete preemption is an exception to the well-pleaded complaint rule that has jurisdictional consequences. If a state law claim has been "displaced" and therefore completely preempted by § 502(a), then a plaintiff's state law claim is properly "recharacterized" as one arising under federal law. But state law claims that are merely subject to "conflict preemption" under § 514(a) are not recharacterized as claims arising under federal law; in such a situation, the federal law serves as a defense to the state law claim, and therefore, under the well-pleaded complaint rule the state law claims do not confer federal question jurisdiction. Thus, complete preemption under § 502(a) creates federal question jurisdiction whereas conflict preemption under § 514(a) does not. The difference in language between §§ 502(a) and 514(a) underscores the significant difference in the scope of the two sections. And if a claim is within the scope of § 502(a), then a participant's ability to recover damages is limited.

Rice v. Panchal, 65 F.3d 637 (7th Cir. 1995).

In *Dukes, supra*, the court held that claims for medical malpractice were not claims for plan benefits and so did not fall within § 502(a) complete preemption. Consequently, the case could not be removed to federal court and was remanded to the state court in which it was filed. Similarly, tax levies on the plan's trust fund are not subject to removal to a federal court because they do not raise claims that would be enforceable under any of ERISA's enforcement provisions. E.g., *Franchise Tax Board v. Construction Laborers Vacation Trust*, 463 U.S. 1 (1983).

The interplay of preemption and removal is demonstrated in the following case.

FELIX v. LUCENT TECHNOLOGIES, INC.

387 F.3d 1146 (10th Cir. 2004)

EBEL, CIRCUIT JUDGE.

Plaintiffs, a group of former employees of Defendant Lucent Technologies, Inc. ("Defendant"), sued Defendant in state court for fraud arising out of alleged misrepresentations made in encouraging Plaintiffs to take an early retirement benefits package. Defendant removed the case to federal court on the basis of complete preemption under the Employee Retirement Income Security Act . . . , and then moved to dismiss. Plaintiffs filed a motion to remand, which was denied by the distric t court on the basis of ERISA complete preemption. Plaintiffs appealed this order, and Defendant now asserts the same grounds for removal jurisdiction as it did below, in addition to arguing for complete preemption . . . .

. . . [W]e conclude that Plaintiffs' state law fraud claims are not completely preempted by ERISA, . . . Accordingly, we REVERSE and REMAND with instructions to remand to state court.

BACKGROUND

Plaintiffs, a group of former employees of Defendant Lucent Technologies, Inc., worked at a manufacturing facility in Oklahoma City known as the Oklahoma City Works ("OKCW"). In their Fourth Amended Petition ("FAP"), Plaintiffs alleged the following:

> Because of a series of substantial financial reversals Lucent determined to sell off its manufacturing facilities including OKCW. It communicated to its workforce at OKCW its intent to restructure and engaged in a series of highly-publicized attempts to sell its manufacturing plants or merge with other similar companies. In an effort to make it more attractive to purchasers/merging companies Lucent determined to reduce the number of long-term senior employees at the OKCW.
>
> On February 19, 2001, Lucent entered into a Memorandum of Agreement with the International Brotherhood of Electrical Workers ("IBEW") System Council EM-3 whereby OKCW employees that were retirement-eligible would retire in exchange for receipt of a payment equivalent to 110% of the amount of termination allowance to which the employee would be entitled if the employee was laid-off for lack of work up to a maximum of 32 years' service (under the applicable IBEW collective bargaining agreements) plus a "special pension benefit" in the amount of $11,000 . . . .
>
> . . .
>
> At each meeting attended by each individual plaintiff, it was stated by Lucent's authorized representatives that the offer being made by Lucent was a one-time, non-negotiable, final offer that was a take-it-or-leave-it proposal and that any delay by any employee in accepting the offer would not result in any additional benefit. To the contrary, it was emphasized at such meetings that failure to accept Lucent's offer was risking the benefits being offered since Lucent might file bankruptcy or merge with another company.
>
> . . .
>
> Subsequently, Lucent entered into an agreement with Celestica, Inc., a Canadian corporation involved in the manufacture of computer and telecommunications equipment whereby Celestica, Inc. was to act as a contract manufacturer and take over the operation of the OKCW and hire as its employees certain remaining OKCW Lucent employees on November 30, 2001.
>
> . . .
>
> Contrary to the representations made by Lucent, on October 1, 2001, Lucent agreed to pay retirement-eligible (and those made eligible by the 5+5 transitional offer) employees still on the OKCW roll benefits identical to those paid to the plaintiffs **plus** an additional payment of a "special one-time pension benefit" by Lucent of $15,000.

. . .

Plaintiffs requested as damages the additional $15,000 benefit that was later offered to the remaining employees, the value of an additional year of service that was lost by accepting the June 30 retirement date, and punitive damages.

Defendant removed the case to federal court on the basis of "complete preemption" under ERISA and the LMRA, and then moved to dismiss for failure to state a claim. . . .

Analysis:

I. Were Plaintiffs' fraud claims properly removed on the basis of "complete preemption" under ERISA?

Plaintiffs argue that the district court erred in denying their motion to remand and dismissing the case for failure to state a claim. Specifically, Plaintiffs argue that, contrary to the district court's holding, their state fraud claim was not "completely preempted" by ERISA. We agree with Plaintiffs.

Important to understanding the propriety of removing the instant case is the distinction between "conflict preemption" under § 514 of ERISA and "complete preemption" under § 502(a) of ERISA. Because these two concepts are often confused, as they were in the instant case, we provide an explanation of both before we analyze district court's denial of the motion to remand here.

A. ERISA § 514 Conflict Preemption

Section 514 of ERISA . . . contains an express preemption provision that provides that ERISA "shall supersede any and all State laws insofar as they may now or hereafter relate to any employee benefit plan" covered by ERISA. The Supreme Court has "observed repeatedly that this broadly worded provision is 'clearly expansive.'" *Egelhoff v. Egelhoff*, 532 U.S. 141 (2001). "But at the same time, [the Court has] recognized that the term 'relate to' cannot be taken 'to extend to the furthest stretch of its indeterminacy,' or else 'for all practical purposes pre-emption would never run its course.'" *Id.* (quoting *N.Y. State Conference of Blue Cross & Blue Shield Plans v. Travelers Ins. Co.*, 514 U.S. 645 (1995)).

The Court has held that a state law "relates to" an ERISA plan, and is thus preempted under § 514, "if it has a connection with or reference to such a plan." *Shaw v. Delta Airlines, Inc.*, 463 U.S. 85, 97 (1983). . . . This preemption provision does not apply "if the state law has only a tenuous, remote, or peripheral connection with covered plans, as is the case with many laws of general applicability." *District of Columbia v. Greater Wash. Bd. of Trade*, 506 U.S. 125 (1992). . . .

C. Distinction Between Preemption and Complete Preemption in the Context of ERISA

Although courts and parties often confuse § 514 preemption with § 502(a) complete preemption, the Supreme Court has held that the two are distinct concepts, with only the latter supporting removal. . . .

We have explained that ERISA preemption under § 514 is not sufficient for removal jurisdiction and that a state law claim is only "completely preempted" under Taylor if it can be recharacterized as a claim under § 502(a). . . .

To summarize:

> The difference between preemption and complete preemption is important. When the doctrine of complete preemption does not apply, but the plaintiff's state claim is arguably preempted under § 514(a), the district court, being without removal jurisdiction, cannot resolve the dispute regarding preemption. It lacks power to do anything other than remand to the state court where the preemption issue can be addressed and resolved.

Dukes v. U.S. Healthcare, Inc., 57 F.3d 350, 355 (3d Cir. 1995). . . .

D. Are Plaintiffs' state law fraud claims completely preempted so as to provide subject matter jurisdiction for removal?

The district court in the instant case found that Plaintiffs' state law claims were "related to" an ERISA plan and were thus preempted under the broad language in § 514. This finding may be correct. However, as discussed above, § 514 preemption is merely a federal defense that cannot provide the basis for removal jurisdiction. We thus turn to the separate question of whether Plaintiffs' claims fell within the scope of § 502(a) and were thus completely preempted. We ultimately conclude in this section that Plaintiffs could not have brought these fraud claims under f § 502(a) because their suit is not one to recover benefits due to them under the terms of their employee benefit plan. Accordingly, we reverse the district court's finding of complete preemption. . . .

1. Standing to Sue under ERISA

A plaintiff must have standing to sue under § 502(a) before his or her state law claim can be recharacterized as arising under federal law subject to federal jurisdiction under the doctrine of complete preemption. . . .

Here, Plaintiffs do not seek "to recover benefits due to [them] under the terms of [their] plan, to enforce [their] rights under the terms of the plan, or to clarify [their] rights to future benefits under the terms of the plan." [ERISA § 502(a)(1).] Neither Plaintiffs nor Defendants contend that Plaintiffs are entitled to the additional benefits under the plan. Rather, Plaintiffs claim that they were fraudulently induced to take early retirement, to their financial detriment; they seek monetary damages from their employer (not from the pension plan) for that alleged fraud. . . .

2. The "But For" Exception

Defendants contend, however, that Plaintiffs' claim is completely preempted because it is, in substance, a claim that "but for" Defendants' wrongful actions, they would have been entitled to the additional benefits under the plan. The circuits are split over whether plaintiffs have standing to sue under ERISA in such a case. Although the First, Second, Fifth, Sixth, and Eighth Circuits have held that former employees may sue under ERISA if they make a "but for" claim of this sort, we, along with the Fourth and Eleventh Circuits, have rejected this approach.

. . .

In sum, we have rejected a "but for" test for determining standing to sue under ERISA. We have found a lack of a "colorable claim to vested benefits" where the plaintiffs have already received full payment of all benefits entitled to them under their plan as it existed at the time of their retirement, where the plaintiff was not enrolled in the pension plan at issue, and where the plaintiff's medical condition was excluded by the terms of the ERISA health plan (notwithstanding defendant's misrepresentations to the contrary).

3. Do Plaintiffs Have ERISA Standing in the Instant Case?

In the instant case, because no party disputes that Plaintiffs are "former employees," we may only find they have standing to sue under ERISA if they have either a "reasonable expectation of returning to covered employment" or "a colorable claim for vested benefits." *Firestone*, 489 U.S. at 117–118. Plaintiffs do not assert any statutory or contractual right to reinstatement, nor do they even request reinstatement. Thus, they do not have a "reasonable expectation" of returning to such employment.

Nor have Plaintiffs asserted a "colorable claim to vested benefits," as they do not claim that they are entitled to benefits under the terms of their plan as it existed at the time of their retirement. Rather, they claim that they should receive damages for the loss of the additional benefits under the later package (*e.g.*, the $15,000 lump sum and the year of service) because they *would have been* participants under that package but for Defendant's misrepresentations. . . .

. . . The nature of their claim is not that Defendants improperly withheld vested benefits owed to them, but rather that they should receive damages for the fraud they suffered. As the Eleventh Circuit has held, ERISA provides no cause of action to non-participants who claim they were defrauded out of pension benefits in violation of common law fraud principles. Because Plaintiffs are not entitled to the additional benefits at issue "under the terms of [their] plan," their state law claims do not fall within the scope of ERISA § 502(a)(1), and our subject matter jurisdiction cannot be based upon the doctrine of complete preemption.

It is true that our opinion leaves open the uncomfortable possibility that Plaintiffs may lack standing to sue under ERISA, but will then be preempted in state court under § 514 from asserting a state claim, leaving them with no remedy. Although this is a valid concern, we have not found it to be a concern of the federal judiciary. . . .

We also point out that the policy gap here is smaller than it may first appear, as it is possible that some plaintiffs may be able to bring claims under other subsections of § 502 that are not at issue in the instant case. For example, there may be the possibility of claims, under proper factual circumstances, under § 510 of ERISA, or breach of fiduciary duty claims brought on behalf of the plan under § 502(a)(2), or claims for equitable relief brought under the catch-all provision of § 502(a)(3), see *Varity Corp. v. Howe*, 516 U.S. 489 (1996).

In conclusion, we refuse to second-guess Congress' policy choices in ERISA, and we hold that Plaintiffs are not "participants" so as to bring their fraud claims within the reach of § 502(a)(1). We thus hold that the district court erred in finding complete preemption. Upon remand, the state court will be free to consider dismissal under § 514's conflict preemption provision, but that issue is not properly before us.

CONCLUSION

For the foregoing reasons, we REVERSE and REMAND with instructions to remand this case to the state court.

7-3 QUESTIONS AND PROBLEMS

1. Why did Lucent try to remove the case to federal court?

2. If the defendant asserts in the sate court that the plaintiff's claims are preempted by ERISA § 514(a), how should the state court react?

3. Yolanda, now retired, sues the Rho Co. Pension Plan in state court, alleging that it failed to properly calculate her defined benefit. Can the Plan remove the case to a federal court?

4. Gavin works for Sigma Inc., which refuses to pay for his wife's operation under its health care plan. Sigma claims that the operation was unnecessary. Wayne sues Sigma in state court under the state's medical coverage act that would require Sigma to pay for the operation. Can Sigma remove to a federal court? Is the claim preempted by ERISA?

D. STANDARD OF REVIEW

[1] Basic Standard of Review

ERISA § 503.

Plan participants and beneficiaries whose claims or benefits are denied must be provided written notice of the reason for the denial. ERISA § 503. The Department of Labor regulations, 29 C.F.R. § 2560-503-1, require a full and fair claims procedure, including a written explanation for the reasons for the denial provided within 90 days of receipt of the claim. The regulations also require the plan to maintain a review procedure for denied claims. Only after the internal review procedures have been exhausted may the claimant file a lawsuit in state or federal court (*Amato v. Bernard*, 618 F.2d 559 (9th Cir. 1980)). Exhaustion will not be required if the plan's internal review procedure does not comply with the federal regulations or if the claimant was not permitted to present a claim to the plan. (*See infra*, Sec. G, 3.)

Assuming that the claimant has met the exhaustion standard, the question arises as to the judicial standard of review of the decisions made by the plan administrator. ERISA does not address this issue, and so the Supreme Court resolved the issue. In *Firestone Tire & Rubber Co. v. Bruch*, 489 U.S. 101 (1989) (*supra*) the Court held that:

> ". . . the validity of a claim to benefits under an ERISA plan is likely to turn on the interpretation of terms in the plan at issue. Consistent with established principles of trust law, we hold that a denial of benefits challenged under [ERISA] § 502(a)(1)(B) is to be reviewed under a de novo standard unless the benefit plan gives the administrator or fiduciary discretionary authority to determine eligibility for benefits or to construe the terms of the plan. *Id.* at 115.

The actual use of a de novo review, however, has been sharply diminished because the Court permitted the drafters of a plan to grant the plan administrator discretion in determinating eligibility for benefits or in interpreting the plan. If the administrator is granted such discretion, the proper standard of judicial review is limited to determining whether the plan administrator acted arbitrarily or capriciously. Because plan administrators would much prefer to limit judicial review to the arbitrary or capricious standard, most plan sponsors have inserted language that attempts to grant the plan administrator discretion and thus forestall de novo judicial review.

What language is necessary to confer the necessary degree of discretion? In *Sisters of the Third Order of St. Francis v. SwedishAmerican Group Health Benefit Trust*, 901 F.2d 1369 (7th Cir. 1990), the plan stated that the trustee had the authority to "construe and interpret the Plan, decide all questions of eligibility and determine the amount, manner and time of payment of any benefits hereunder." The court thought the language ambiguous. "This language might be taken as 'power to construe disputed or doubtful terms' within the meaning of Firestone. Because trustees may carry out their duty without language of this sort, its presence frequently signals the existence of discretion in implementation. Perhaps, though, it describes who shall decide (the Plan Committee, as opposed to other parties involved in the establishment and implementation of this complex welfare benefits plan) rather than the extent of the Committee's powers." (p. 1371)

For another court's interpretation of plan language and whether de novo review applies, consider this 1994 circuit court decision.

> This circuit has interpreted *Bruch* to mandate de novo review unless the plan expressly provides the administrator discretionary authority to make eligibility determinations or to construe the plan's terms. Thus, this court has applied the arbitrary and capricious standard when the plan provides that the administrators " 'determinations shall be final and conclusive' " so long as they are " 'reasonable determinations which are not arbitrary and capricious.' " This court has also applied the arbitrary and capricious standard when the plan confers upon the administrator " 'full and exclusive authority to determine all questions of coverage and eligibility' " and " 'full power to construe the provision' " of the plan. On the other hand, this court has applied the de novo standard when the plan confers upon the administrator the authority to make initial eligibility determinations " 'according to the terms of the Plan.' "
>
> The Plan at issue in this case provides that Marriott, as the Named Fiduciary, has "authority to control and manage the operation and administration of the Plan." Although the Plan does not specifically grant the Administrator the authority to deny claims, the benefit claim procedure described in the Plan contemplates that the Administrator will perform that function. Finally, para. 8.3 of the Plan provides:
>
> "The Administrator may promulgate such rules and regulations as deemed necessary and proper to interpret or administer the Plan. Such rules and regulations shall be communicated to Participants in compliance with ERISA requirements."
>
> The Administrator has not promulgated any rules or regulations.
>
> This language falls short of the express grant of discretionary authority necessary to trigger the arbitrary and capricious standard of review. Marriott may "control and manage" the Plan, but it must do so in accordance with the terms of the Plan, and there is no grant of authority to construe these terms. Faced with virtually identical language, the Seventh Circuit has applied the de novo standard of review. The Plan contemplates that the Administrator will determine whether a benefit is properly payable; however, there is no grant of discretion to accompany this mandatory function and no indication that the Administrator's determination is to be accorded deference.

> Although para. 8.3 permits the Administrator to promulgate rules to "interpret and administer" the Plan, we do not read this as a grant of authority to construe ambiguous terms in the Plan. The Plan is otherwise silent as to the Administrator's authority to construe terms. When a plan is silent or ambiguous as to an Administrator's discretionary authority, we will apply the de novo standard of review.

Kirwan v. Marriott Corp., 10 F.3d 784, 788–89 (11th Cir. 1994).

7-4 QUESTIONS AND PROBLEMS

1. Why doesn't ERISA contain an articulated standard of review?

2. How would you interpret the above quoted plan language in *Kirwan*? What do you think was the intent of the settlor who drafted the plan language?

3. Do you agree that the plan language in *Kirwan* is "ambiguous"? If so, where should the court look to discern the intent of the plan sponsor?

The following case illustrates the approach of most courts to whether a plan requirement of "proof of claim" creates the necessary degree of discretion to forestall de novo judicial review.

FITTS v. FEDERAL NATIONAL MORTGAGE ASSOCIATION AND UNUM LIFE INSURANCE COMPANY

236 F.3d 1 (D.C. Cir. 2001)

PER CURIAM.

Jane G. Fitts sued her former employer and the insurance company that administers claims under the employer's long-term disability plan, alleging that they violated the Americans with Disabilities Act of 1990 (ADA) and the Employee Retirement Income Security Act of 1974 (ERISA) by terminating her disability benefits after 24 months. The district court dismissed Fitts' ADA counts and granted summary judgment against her on the ERISA count. We affirm the dismissal of the ADA counts on the ground that the long-term disability plan comes within the safe harbor provisions of that statute. Because we conclude that the district court applied the wrong standard of review to the ERISA count, however, we reverse the grant of summary judgment and remand the case for further proceedings.

Under its employee welfare benefit plan, the Federal National Mortgage Association ("Fannie Mae") offers its employees the opportunity to select from an array of benefits, including a long-term disability insurance policy provided by Unum Life Insurance Company of America. In the event that an employee insured under the policy later becomes totally disabled, the policy pays a percentage of the employee's income until the age of 65. The policy, however, places a 24-month cap on benefits for disabilities due to mental illness, which it defines as "mental, emotional or nervous diseases or disorders of any type."

Jane Fitts, an attorney, was employed by Fannie Mae from 1982 to 1995 and paid the required premiums for the long-term disability policy. In 1995, Fitts became disabled by bipolar disorder, an illness characterized by cycles of depressive and manic episodes. Fitts applied to Unum for benefits under the policy, which Unum granted. Because Unum classified her disorder as a mental illness, however, it limited her benefits to 24 months. Fitts unsuccessfully protested Unum's decision, arguing that bipolar disorder is associated with changes in the physical structure of the brain and often runs in families, suggesting genetic causation. Unum asserts that it invited Fitts to submit additional medical information supporting her claims, but that she responded only with "conclusory" letters from her treating psychiatrist and two other psychiatrists. Fitts asserts that she signed a release permitting Unum to view her entire medical file, which contained data supporting her claim. Unum refused to alter its classification of bipolar disorder as a mental illness and ceased paying Fitts benefits after 24 months.

Fitts sued both Unum and Fannie Mae, contending that the termination of her benefits after 24 months violated Titles I and III of the ADA. Fitts also claimed that the termination of her benefits violated ERISA.

Fitts contends that Unum and Fannie Mae improperly classified her disability as mental rather than physical, and hence improperly terminated her long-term disability benefits after only 24 months. The district court concluded that the appropriate standard of review for that classification was whether it was arbitrary and capricious, determined that it was not, and granted summary judgment for defendants.

In *Firestone Tire & Rubber Co. v. Bruch*, 489 U.S. 101 (1989), the Supreme Court held that a denial of benefits challenged under [ERISA] § 502(a)(1)(B) is to be reviewed under a de novo standard — not under the more deferential arbitrary and capricious standard — "unless the benefit plan gives the administrator or fiduciary discretionary authority to determine eligibility for benefits or to construe the terms of the plan." Firestone's employee benefit plan provided severance benefits for employees "if released because of a reduction in work force or if . . . physically or mentally unable to perform [the] job." The Court held that those provisions did not require that the administrator's eligibility determinations be given deference.

Unum contends that, as the claims administrator of the long-term disability policy, it has discretionary authority to determine benefits eligibility because the policy requires the insured to submit proof of disability. Such a requirement, Unum asserts, necessarily gives the insurer discretion because it must evaluate the legitimacy of the proof submitted. As Unum conceded at oral argument, however, virtually all insurance policies require proof of eligibility before the dispensation of benefits — hardly a surprising fact, since insurance companies are not in the business of giving away money to anyone who requests it. Accordingly, if we were to regard any plan that requires proof of eligibility as conferring discretion, Firestone's exception would swallow its rule and render the standard of review deferential in almost every case. As Unum's argument would effectively circumvent the Supreme Court's decision, we cannot accept it.

Unum relies heavily on the Sixth Circuit's decision in *Perez v. Aetna Life Ins. Co.*, 150 F.3d 550 (6th Cir. 1998). The policy at issue there, however, did not simply require proof of eligibility but "satisfactory" proof. No such language appears in Unum's policy. Moreover, *Perez*'s view has been rejected by the [other] circuits.

For the foregoing reasons, we conclude that Unum's classification of Fitts' illness as mental rather than physical must be reviewed de novo. We do not, however, proceed with the de novo review ourselves, because numerous factual disagreements persist. Fitts contends that if Unum's classification is reviewed de novo, the record will demonstrate that her disability is physical; Unum asserts the contrary. Fitts contends that current medical research on bipolar disorder supports her claim; Unum argues that there is no such medical consensus. Unum asks us to rule on a motion to exclude certain items of evidence proffered by the plaintiff; Fitts argues that the evidence is admissible. Although the de novo standard might theoretically permit this court to perform the necessary review, the intensely factual nature of the record counsels that we return the case for the district court's examination. In light of the change in the standard of review, the parties will be free to supplement the existing record by, *inter alia*, submitting current medical evidence regarding bipolar disorder.

7-5 QUESTIONS AND PROBLEMS

1. In *Fitts*, just what is the nature of the "discretion" that Unum, the plan administrator, claims to have?

2. How should the plan have been written to grant sufficient discretion to avoid de novo review by the court?

3. What is the district court supposed to decide?

Many benefit claims to recover benefits that are brought under ERISA § 502(a)(1)(B) involve disputes over whether the employer-provided health care plan should pay for a particular medical treatment or whether the employer-provided disability plan has wrongfully denied that the claimant is disabled. Whether the issue is treatment coverage or if the claimant is disabled as defined by the plan, the plan settlor typically wants to grant the plan administrator sufficient discretion in order to preclude de novo review by a court of the decisions by the plan administrator. Discretionary decisions involving welfare benefit plans, such as reimbursement for medical expenses, are often made by an insurance company who provides the benefits. When an employer is seeking to contract with an insurer to set up a health care benefits plan, the insurer will encourage the employer to adopt a plan that grants the insurer, as plan administrator, broad discretionary powers to protect its decisions from de novo judicial review.

The employer, as the plan settlor, has an economic incentive to select a plan that grants discretionary authority to the insurance company when it determines benefits, because such discretion decreases the likelihood that a court will interpret the plan as granting greater benefits than were approved by the plan administrator. Limiting judicial review to an arbitrary and capricious standard should help limit or reduce benefit payments, and so reduce the cost of the insurance policy to the employer.

That tactic was successful in *Perez v. Aetna Life Insurance Co.*, 150 F.3d 550 (6th Cir. 1998), where the plan used the following language:

> "Written proof of total disability must be furnished to [Aetna] within ninety days after the expiration of the [first twelve months of disability]. Subsequent written proof of the continuance of such disability must be furnished to [Aetna] at such intervals as [Aetna] may reasonably require.
>
> . . .
>
> [Aetna] shall have the right to require as part of the proof of claim satisfactory evidence . . . that [the claimant] has furnished all required proofs for such benefits . . ."

The plaintiff, who had been denied disability coverage, argued that the plan language did not constitute a clear grant of discretion because it did not specify to whom the written proof of disability must be satisfactory. In response the court stated:

> "Although many of our prior cases finding a clear grant of discretion involved ERISA plans which explicitly provided that the evidence be satisfactory "to the insurer," "to the company" or "to us," it does not automatically follow that in the absence of such language discretion has not been granted to the plan administrator. Both parties acknowledge that the Plan allows for Aetna to request and receive satisfactory evidence of total disability before an individual is entitled to receive continued benefits. We agree with Aetna that this "right to require as part of the proof of claim satisfactory evidence" means, semantically, that the evidence must be satisfactory to Aetna, the only named party with the right to request such evidence. It naturally follows that Aetna, the receiver of the evidence, would review that evidence to determine if it constitutes satisfactory proof of total disability. *Id.* at 556."

The *Perez* decision is perhaps the most liberal judicial application of the *Bruch* discretion standard to a welfare benefit plan. The majority of the circuits have rejected *Perez*. Five circuits, the Second, Fourth, Seventh, Eighth, and Ninth, have held that merely requiring satisfactory written proof of a claim (such as the need for medical care) does not create the level of discretion necessary to limit judicial review to the arbitrary and capricious standard. These courts insist that the grant of discretion to the plan administrator be explicit in order to limit judicial review to the arbitrary and capricious standard. *See* Kathryn J. Kennedy, *Judicial Standard of Review in ERISA Benefit Claim Cases*, 50 Am. U. L. Rev. 1083, 1128 (2001).

The degree of deference to be given to a plan administrator is also at issue when the plan administrator makes a factual determination. In *Pierre v. Connecticut General Life Insurance Co.*, 932 F.2d 1552 (5th Cir. 1991), *cert. denied*, 502 U.S. 973 (1991), the Fifth Circuit held that the de novo standard of review applied only to plan interpretations and not to determinations of fact, pointing out that *Bruch* involved a plan interpretation. Other circuits have rejected the reasoning of *Pierre* and have held that factual determinations by plan administrators can be reviewed de novo.

Courts have also been asked to determine the deference that the plan administrator must give to the opinions of other expert, such as the treating physician. In 2003, the Supreme Court considered the issue of what degree of deference a plan administrator must give to the decision of a treating physician when the plan administrator determines if a participant is disabled and thus eligible for disability benefits under the plan. *The Black & Decker Disability Plan v. Nord*, 538 U.S. 822 (2003). The Court held that, although the plan administrator could not arbitrarily refuse to give credit to the opinion of a treating physician, the administrator could reject that opinion in the face of reliable conflicting evidence. The Court approved plan language that permitted the plan administrator to make a disability determination in its "sole and absolute discretion." According to the Court, the plan administrator could not be required to give special weight to the physician's opinion, nor could the administrator be required to have specific reasons backed by substantial evidence to justify the rejection of the physician's determination of disability. Conceding that the plan administrator might have an incentive not to find the participant to be disabled and thereby save the plan sponsor money, the Court nevertheless did not believe that the treating physician should always be assumed to be correct.

In response to the deference allowed by the federal courts to administrators acting under discretionary authority, a few states have taken steps to disallow nonreviewable discretionary clauses in certain insurance contracts. The right of states to regulate insurance even when provided as part of an ERISA plan was reinforced in *Rush Prudential HMO, Inc. v. Moran*, 536 U.S. 355 (2002), which upheld a state statute providing for independent review of medical necessity decisions made under health insurance plans. The Court held that states did not need to give deference to the claims decisions because such regulation does not conflict with the ERISA enforcement scheme. Following *Rush*, the Hawaii insurance commissioner, for example, declared that a discretionary review clause that attempts to deprive the insured of a *de novo* appeal is an unfair or deceptive insurance business practice. In 2004, the National Association of Insurance Commissioners voted to adopt model legislation banning the use of discretionary clauses in disability insurance policies, an expansion of the Model Act of 2002 that banned discretionary clauses in health insurance policies. A few states have adopted regulations that ban discretionary clauses in insurance policies.

[2] Standard of Review of Administrators Acting Under a Conflict of Interest

Because ERISA permits the employer to serve as plan administrator, conflicts of interest can arise. For example, a liberal reading of the plan's benefits can be costly to the employer; yet denying the requested benefits may violate the plan administrator's fiduciary duty of loyalty to the plan participants and beneficiaries. Of course, the plan administrator must also be concerned that if in borderline cases it rules against the employees too frequently, it risks undermining employee morale. Another conflict of interest can arise if an insurance company is both the administrator of a welfare benefit plan and the payor of benefit claims. In such cases, the profitability of the insurance company is affected by its decisions as a plan administrator.

If an employee's claim for benefits is denied, how is the court to determine whether the administrator is acting under a conflict of interest and, if it is, what is the proper standard of judicial review of the decision of the conflicted administrator?

METROPOLITAN LIFE INSURANCE COMPANY v. GLENN

128 S. Ct. 2343 (2008)

JUSTICE BREYER delivered the opinion of the Court.

The Employee Retirement Income Security Act of 1974 (ERISA) permits a person denied benefits under an employee benefit plan to challenge that denial in federal court. ERISA § 502(a)(1)(B). Often the entity that administers the plan, such as an employer or an insurance company, both determines whether an employee is eligible for benefits and pays benefits out of its own pocket. We here decide that this dual role creates a conflict of interest; that a reviewing court should consider that conflict as a factor in determining whether the plan administrator has abused its discretion in denying benefits; and that the significance of the factor will depend upon the circumstances of the particular case. See *Firestone Tire & Rubber Co. v. Bruch*, 489 U.S. 101, 115 (1989).

I

Petitioner Metropolitan Life Insurance Company (MetLife) serves as both an administrator and the insurer of Sears, Roebuck & Company's long-term disability insurance plan, an ERISA-governed employee benefit plan. See App. 182a 183a; ERISA § 4. The plan grants MetLife (as administrator) discretionary authority to determine whether an employee's claim for benefits is valid; it simultaneously provides that MetLife (as insurer) will itself pay valid benefit claims.

Respondent Wanda Glenn, a Sears' employee, was diagnosed with severe dilated cardiomyopathy, a heart condition whose symptoms include fatigue and shortness of breath. She applied for plan disability benefits in June 2000, and MetLife concluded that she met the plan's standard for an initial 24 months of benefits, namely, that she could not "perform the material duties of [her] own job." MetLife also directed Glenn to a law firm that would assist her in applying for federal Social Security disability benefits (some of which MetLife itself would be entitled to receive as an offset to the more generous plan benefits). In April 2002, an Administrative Law Judge found that Glenn's illness prevented her not only from performing her own job but also "from performing any jobs [for which she could qualify] existing in significant numbers in the national economy." The Social Security Administration consequently granted Glenn permanent disability payments retroactive to April 2000. Glenn herself kept none of the backdated benefits: three-quarters went to MetLife, and the rest (plus some additional money) went to the lawyers.

To continue receiving Sears plan disability benefits after 24 months, Glenn had to meet a stricter, Social Security-type standard, namely, that her medical condition rendered her incapable of performing not only her own job but of performing "the material duties of any gainful occupation for which" she was "reasonably qualified." App. 160a. MetLife denied Glenn this extended benefit because it found that she was "capable of performing full time sedentary work." *Id.* at 31a.

After exhausting her administrative remedies, Glenn brought this federal lawsuit, seeking judicial review of MetLife's denial of benefits. See ERISA § 502(a)(1)(B). The District Court denied relief. Glenn appealed to the Court of Appeals for the Sixth Circuit. Because the plan granted MetLife "discretionary authority to . . . determine benefits," the Court of Appeals reviewed the administrative record under a deferential standard. *Id.* at 666. In doing so, it treated "as a relevant factor" a "conflict of interest" arising out of the fact that MetLife was "authorized both to decide whether an employee is eligible for benefits and to pay those benefits." *Ibid.*

The Court of Appeals ultimately set aside MetLife's denial of benefits in light of a combination of several circumstances: (1) the conflict of interest; (2) MetLife's failure to reconcile its own conclusion that Glenn could work in other jobs with the Social Security Administration's conclusion that she could not; (3) MetLife's focus upon one treating physician report suggesting that Glenn could work in other jobs at the expense of other, more detailed treating physician reports indicating that she could not; (4) MetLife's failure to provide all of the treating physician reports to its own hired experts; and (5) MetLife's failure to take account of evidence indicating that stress aggravated Glenn's condition.

MetLife sought certiorari, asking us to determine whether a plan administrator that both evaluates and pays claims operates under a conflict of interest in making discretionary benefit determinations. The Solicitor General suggested that we also consider how any such conflict should be taken into account on judicial review of a discretionary benefit determination.

II

In *Firestone Tire & Rubber Co. v. Bruch,* 489 U.S. 101, this Court addressed "the appropriate standard of judicial review of benefit determinations by fiduciaries or plan administrators under" § 502(a)(1)(B), the ERISA provision at issue here. *Id.* at 105; see also *id.* at 108. *Firestone* set forth four principles of review relevant here.

(1) In "determining the appropriate standard of review," a court should be "guided by principles of trust law"; in doing so, it should analogize a plan administrator to the trustee of a common-law trust; and it should consider a benefit determination to be a fiduciary act (*i.e.*, an act in which the administrator owes a special duty of loyalty to the plan beneficiaries). *Id.* at 111 113.

(2) Principles of trust law require courts to review a denial of plan benefits "under a *de novo* standard" unless the plan provides to the contrary. *Firestone*, 489 U.S. at 115.

(3) Where the plan provides to the contrary by granting "the administrator or fiduciary *discretionary authority* to determine eligibility for benefits," *Firestone*, 489 U.S. at 115 (emphasis added), "[t]rust principles make a *deferential standard* of review appropriate," *id.* at 111 (citing Restatement § 187 (abuse-of-discretion standard); Bogert § 560, at 193–208; emphasis added).

(4) If "a benefit plan gives discretion to an administrator or fiduciary who *is operating under a conflict of interest*, that conflict must be *weighed as a 'factor* in determining whether there is an abuse of discretion.'" *Firestone, supra*, at 115 (quoting Restatement § 187, Comment *d*; emphasis added; alteration omitted).

The questions before us, while implicating the first three principles, directly focus upon the application and the meaning of the fourth.

III

The first question asks whether the fact that a plan administrator both evaluates claims for benefits and pays benefits claims creates the kind of "conflict of interest" to which *Firestone*'s fourth principle refers. In our view, it does.

That answer is clear where it is the employer that both funds the plan and evaluates the claims. In such a circumstance, "every dollar provided in benefits is a dollar spent by . . . the employer; and every dollar saved . . . is a dollar in [the employer's] pocket." *Bruch v. Firestone Tire & Rubber Co.*, 828 F.2d 134, 144 (C.A.3 1987). The employer's fiduciary interest may counsel in favor of granting a borderline claim while its immediate financial interest counsels to the contrary. Thus, the employer has an "interest . . . conflicting with that of the beneficiaries," the type of conflict that judges must take into account when they review the discretionary acts of a trustee of a common-law trust. Restatement § 187, Comment *d*; see also *Firestone, supra* at 115 (citing that Restatement comment); *cf.* Black's Law Dictionary 319 (8th ed. 2004) ("conflict of interest" is a "real or seeming incompatibility between one's private interests and one's public or fiduciary duties").

Indeed, *Firestone* itself involved an employer who administered an ERISA benefit plan and who both evaluated claims and paid for benefits. And thus that circumstance quite possibly was what the Court had in mind when it mentioned conflicted administrators. The *Firestone* parties, while disagreeing about other matters, agreed that the dual role created a conflict of interest of some kind in the employer.

MetLife points out that an employer who creates a plan that it will both fund and administer foresees, and implicitly approves, the resulting conflict. But that fact cannot change our conclusion. At trust law, the fact that a settlor (the person establishing the trust) approves a trustee's conflict does not change the legal need for a judge later to take account of that conflict in reviewing the trustee's discretionary decisionmaking. See Restatement § 107, Comment *f* (discretionary acts of trustee with settlor-approved conflict subject to "careful scrutiny").

MetLife also points out that we need not follow trust law principles where trust law is "inconsistent with the language of the statute, its structure, or its purposes." *Hughes Aircraft Co. v. Jacobson*, 525 U.S. 432, 447 (1999) (internal quotation marks omitted). MetLife adds that to find a conflict here is inconsistent (1) with ERISA's efforts to avoid complex review proceedings, see *Varity Corp. v. Howe*, 516 U.S. 489, 497 (1996); (2) with Congress' efforts not to deter employers from setting up benefit plans, see *ibid.*, and (3) with an ERISA provision specifically allowing employers to administer their own plans, see ERISA § 408(c)(3).

But we cannot find in these considerations any significant inconsistency. As to the first, we note that trust law functions well with a similar standard. As to the second, we have no reason, empirical or otherwise, to believe that our decision will seriously discourage the creation of benefit plans. As to the third, we have just explained why approval of a conflicted trustee differs from review of that trustee's conflicted decisionmaking. As to all three taken together, we believe them outweighed by "Congress' desire to offer employees enhanced protection for their benefits." *Varity, supra*, at 497 (discussing "competing congressional purposes" in enacting ERISA).

The answer to the conflict question is less clear where (as here) the plan administrator is not the employer itself but rather a professional insurance company. Such a company, MetLife would argue, likely has a much greater incentive than a self-insuring employer to provide accurate claims processing. That is because the insurance company typically charges a fee that attempts to account for the cost of claims payouts, with the result that paying an individual claim does not come to the same extent from the company's own pocket. It is also because the marketplace (and regulators) may well punish an insurance company when its products, or ingredients of its products, fall below par. And claims processing, an ingredient of the insurance company's product, falls below par when it seeks a biased result, rather than an accurate one. Why, MetLife might ask, should one consider an insurance company *inherently* more conflicted than any other market participant, say, a manufacturer who might earn more money in the short run by producing a product with poor quality steel or a lawyer with an incentive to work more slowly than necessary, thereby accumulating more billable hours?

Conceding these differences, we nonetheless continue to believe that for ERISA purposes a conflict exists. For one thing, the employer's own conflict may extend to its selection of an insurance company to administer its plan. An employer choosing an administrator in effect buys insurance for others and consequently (when compared to the marketplace customer who buys for himself) may be more interested in an insurance company with low rates than in one with accurate claims processing.

For another, ERISA imposes higher-than-marketplace quality standards on insurers. It sets forth a special standard of care upon a plan administrator, namely, that the administrator "discharge [its] duties" in respect to discretionary claims processing "solely in the interests of the participants and beneficiaries" of the plan, § 404(a)(1); it simultaneously underscores the particular importance of accurate claims processing by insisting that administrators "provide a 'full and fair review' of claim denials," *Firestone*, 489 U.S. at 113 (quoting § 503(2)); and it supplements marketplace and regulatory controls with judicial review of individual claim denials, see § 502(a)(1)(B).

Finally, a legal rule that treats insurance company administrators and employers alike in respect to the *existence* of a conflict can nonetheless take account of the circumstances to which MetLife points so far as it treats those, or similar, circumstances as diminishing the *significance* or *severity* of the conflict in individual cases.

IV

We turn to the question of "how" the conflict we have just identified should "be taken into account on judicial review of a discretionary benefit determination." In doing so, we elucidate what this Court set forth in *Firestone*, namely, that a conflict should "be weighed as a 'factor in determining whether there is an abuse of discretion.' " 489 U.S. at 115 (quoting Restatement § 187, Comment *d*; alteration omitted).

We do not believe that *Firestone*'s statement implies a change in the *standard* of review, say, from deferential to *de novo* review. Trust law continues to apply a deferential standard of review to the discretionary decisionmaking of a conflicted trustee, while at the same time requiring the reviewing judge to take account of the conflict when determining whether the trustee, substantively or procedurally, has abused his discretion. We see no reason to forsake *Firestone*'s reliance upon trust law in this respect.

Nor would we overturn *Firestone* by adopting a rule that in practice could bring about near universal review by judges *de novo* — *i.e.*, without deference — of the lion's share of ERISA plan claims denials. See Brief for America's Health Insurance Plans et al. as *Amici Curiae* 3-4 (many ERISA plans grant discretionary authority to administrators that combine evaluation and payment functions). Had Congress intended such a system of review, we believe it would not have left to the courts the development of review standards but would have said more on the subject. See *Firestone, supra*, at 109, 109 S. Ct. 948 ("ERISA does not set out the appropriate standard of review for actions under § 502(a)(1)(B)").

Neither do we believe it necessary or desirable for courts to create special burden-of-proof rules, or other special procedural or evidentiary rules, focused narrowly upon the evaluator/payor conflict. In principle, as we have said, conflicts are but one factor among many that a reviewing judge must take into account. Benefits decisions arise in too many contexts, concern too many circumstances, and can relate in too many different ways to conflicts — which themselves vary in kind and in degree of seriousness — for us to come up with a one-size-fits-all procedural system that is likely to promote fair and accurate review. Indeed, special procedural rules would create further complexity, adding time and expense to a process that may already be too costly for many of those who seek redress.

We believe that *Firestone* means what the word "factor" implies, namely, that when judges review the lawfulness of benefit denials, they will often take account of several different considerations of which a conflict of interest is one. This kind of review is no stranger to the judicial system. Not only trust law, but also administrative law, can ask judges to determine lawfulness by taking account of several different, often case-specific, factors, reaching a result by weighing all together.

In such instances, any one factor will act as a tiebreaker when the other factors are closely balanced, the degree of closeness necessary depending upon the tiebreaking factor's inherent or case-specific importance. The conflict of interest at issue here, for example, should prove more important (perhaps of great importance) where circumstances suggest a higher likelihood that it affected the benefits decision, including, but not limited to, cases where an insurance company administrator has a history of biased claims administration. It should prove less important (perhaps to the vanishing point) where the administrator has taken active steps to reduce potential bias and to promote accuracy, for example, by walling off claims administrators from those interested in firm finances, or by imposing management checks that penalize inaccurate decisionmaking irrespective of whom the inaccuracy benefits.

The Court of Appeals' opinion in the present case illustrates the combination-of-factors method of review. The record says little about MetLife's efforts to assure accurate claims assessment. The Court of Appeals gave the conflict weight to some degree; its opinion suggests that, in context, the court would not have found the conflict alone determinative. The court instead focused more heavily on other factors. In particular, the court found questionable the fact that MetLife had encouraged Glenn to argue to the Social Security Administration that she could do no work, received the bulk of the benefits of her success in doing so (the remainder going to the lawyers it recommended), and then ignored the agency's finding in concluding that Glenn could in fact do sedentary work. This course of events was not only an important factor in its own right (because it suggested procedural unreasonableness), but also would have justified the court in giving more weight to the conflict (because MetLife's seemingly inconsistent positions were both financially advantageous). And the court furthermore observed that MetLife had emphasized a certain medical report that favored a denial of benefits, had deemphasized certain other reports that suggested a contrary conclusion, and had failed to provide its independent vocational and medical experts with all of the relevant evidence. All these serious concerns, taken together with some degree of conflicting interests on MetLife's part, led the court to set aside MetLife's discretionary decision. We can find nothing improper in the way in which the court conducted its review.

Finally, we note that our elucidation of *Firestone*'s standard does not consist of a detailed set of instructions. In this respect, we find pertinent this Court's comments made in a somewhat different context, the context of court review of agency factfinding. In explaining how a reviewing court should take account of the agency's reversal of its own examiner's factual findings, this Court did not lay down a detailed set of instructions. It simply held that the reviewing judge should take account of that circumstance as a factor in determining the ultimate adequacy of the record's support for the agency's own factual conclusion. In so holding, the Court noted that it had not enunciated a precise standard. But it warned against creating formulas that will "falsif[y] the actual process of judging" or serve as "instrument[s] of futile casuistry." The Court added that there "are no talismanic words that can avoid the process of judgment." *Ibid.* It concluded then, as we do now, that the "[w]ant of certainty" in judicial standards "partly reflects the intractability of any formula to furnish definiteness of content for all the impalpable factors involved in judicial review."

We affirm the decision of the Court of Appeals.

It is so ordered.

Chief Justice Roberts, concurring in part and concurring in the judgment.

I join all but Part IV of the Court's opinion. I agree that a third-party insurer's dual role as a claims administrator and plan funder gives rise to a conflict of interest that is pertinent in reviewing claims decisions. I part ways with the majority, however, when it comes to *how* such a conflict should matter. See *ante*, at 2349 52. The majority would accord weight, of varying and indeterminate amount, to the existence of such a conflict in every case where it is present. See *ante*, at 2351 52. The majority's approach would allow the bare existence of a conflict to enhance the significance of other factors already considered by reviewing courts, even if the conflict is not shown to have played any role in the denial of benefits. The end result is to increase the level of scrutiny in every case in which there is a conflict — that is, in many if not most ERISA cases — thereby undermining the deference owed to plan administrators when the plan vests discretion in them.

I would instead consider the conflict of interest on review only where there is evidence that the benefits denial was motivated or affected by the administrator's conflict. No such evidence was presented in this case. I would nonetheless affirm the judgment of the Sixth Circuit, because that court was justified in finding an abuse of discretion on the facts of this case-conflict or not.

* * *

In the following case, the Supreme Court addressed what standard of review should apply to a plan administrator's decision after the administrator's prior decision was rejected as unreasonable.

CONKRIGHT v. FROMMERT

130 S. Ct. 1640 (2010)

Chief Justice Roberts delivered the opinion of the Court.

People make mistakes. Even administrators of ERISA plans. That should come as no surprise, given that the Employee Retirement Income Security Act of 1974 is "an enormously complex and detailed statute," *Mertens v. Hewitt Associates*, 508 U.S. 248, 262 (1993), and the plans that administrators must construe can be lengthy and complicated. (The one at issue here runs to 81 pages, with 139 sections.) We held in *Firestone Tire & Rubber Co. v. Bruch*, 489 U.S. 101 (1989), that an ERISA plan administrator with discretionary authority to interpret a plan is entitled to deference in exercising that discretion. The question here is whether a single honest mistake in plan interpretation justifies stripping the administrator of that deference for subsequent related interpretations of the plan. We hold that it does not.

I

As in many ERISA matters, the facts of this case are exceedingly complicated. Fortunately, most of the factual details are unnecessary to the legal issues before us, so we cover them only in broad strokes. This case concerns Xerox Corporation's pension plan, which is covered by ERISA. Petitioners are the plan itself (hereinafter Plan), and the Plan's current and former administrators (hereinafter Plan Administrator). Respondents are Xerox employees who left the company in the 1980's, received lump-sum distributions of retirement benefits they had earned up to that point, and were later rehired. The dispute giving rise to this case concerns how to account for respondents' past distributions when calculating their current benefits — that is, how to avoid paying respondents the same benefits twice.

The Plan Administrator initially interpreted the Plan to call for an approach that has come to be known as the "phantom account" method. Essentially, that method calculated the hypothetical growth that respondents' past distributions would have experienced if the money had remained in Xerox's investment funds, and reduced respondents' present benefits accordingly. After the Plan Administrator denied respondents' administrative challenges to that method, respondents filed suit in federal court under ERISA Sec. 502(a)(1)(B). The District Court granted summary judgment for the Plan, applying a deferential standard of review to the Plan Administrator's interpretation. The Second Circuit vacated and remanded, holding that the Plan Administrator's interpretation was unreasonable and that respondents had not been adequately notified that the phantom account method would be used to calculate their benefits.

The phantom account method having been exorcised from the Plan, the District Court on remand considered other approaches for adjusting respondents' present benefits in light of their past distributions. The Plan Administrator submitted an affidavit proposing an approach that, like the phantom account method, accounted for the time value of the money that respondents had previously received. But unlike the phantom account method, the Plan Administrator's new approach did not calculate the present value of a past distribution based on events that occurred after the distribution was made. Instead, the new approach used an interest rate that was fixed at the time of the distribution, thereby calculating the current value of the distribution based on information that was known at the time of the distribution. Petitioners argued that the District Court should apply a deferential standard of review to this approach, and accept it as a reasonable interpretation of the Plan.

The District Court did not apply a deferential standard of review. Nor did it accept the Plan Administrator's interpretation. Instead, after finding the Plan to be ambiguous, the District Court adopted an approach proposed by respondents that did not account for the time value of money. Under that approach, respondents' present benefits were reduced only by the nominal amount of their past distributions — thereby treating a dollar distributed to respondents in the 1980's as equal in value to a dollar distributed today. The Second Circuit affirmed in relevant part, holding that the District Court was correct not to apply a deferential standard on remand, and that the District Court's decision on the merits was not an abuse of discretion.

Petitioners asked us to grant certiorari on two questions: (1) whether the District Court owed deference to the Plan Administrator's interpretation of the Plan on remand, and (2) whether the Court of Appeals properly granted deference to the District Court on the merits. We granted certiorari on both, but find it necessary to decide only the first.

II

A

This Court addressed the standard for reviewing the decisions of ERISA plan administrators in *Firestone*, 489 U.S. 101. Because ERISA's text does not directly resolve the matter, we looked to "principles of trust law" for guidance. We recognized that, under trust law, the proper standard of review of a trustee's decision depends on the language of the instrument creating the trust. If the trust documents give the trustee "power to construe disputed or doubtful terms, . . . the trustee's interpretation will not be disturbed if reasonable." Based on these considerations, we held that "a denial of benefits challenged under section 502(a)(1)(B) is to be reviewed under a de novo standard unless the benefit plan gives the administrator or fiduciary discretionary authority to determine eligibility for benefits or to construe the terms of the plan."

We expanded *Firestone*'s approach in *Metropolitan Life Ins. Co. v. Glenn*, 554 U.S. 105 (2008). In determining the proper standard of review when a plan administrator operates under a conflict of interest, we again looked to trust law, the terms of the plan at issue, and the principles of ERISA-plus, of course, our precedent in *Firestone*. We held that, when the terms of a plan grant discretionary authority to the plan administrator, a deferential standard of review remains appropriate even in the face of a conflict.

It is undisputed that, under *Firestone* and the terms of the Plan, the Plan Administrator here would normally be entitled to deference when interpreting the Plan. The Court of Appeals, however, crafted an exception to *Firestone* deference. Specifically, the Second Circuit held that a court need not apply a deferential standard "where the administrator ha[s] previously construed the same [plan] terms and we found such a construction to have violated ERISA." Under that view, the District Court here was entitled to reject a reasonable interpretation of the Plan offered by the Plan Administrator, solely because the Court of Appeals had overturned a previous interpretation by the Administrator. *Cf. ibid.* (accepting the District Court's chosen method as one of "several reasonable alternatives").

B

We reject this "one-strike-and-you're-out" approach. As an initial matter, it has no basis in the Court's holding in *Firestone*, which set out a broad standard of deference without any suggestion that the standard was susceptible to ad hoc exceptions like the one adopted by the Court of Appeals. Indeed, we refused to create such an exception to Firestone deference in *Glenn*, recognizing that ERISA law was already complicated enough without adding "special procedural or evidentiary rules" to the mix. If, as we held in *Glenn*, a systemic conflict of interest does not strip a plan administrator of deference, it is difficult to see why a single honest mistake would require a different result.

Second, the Court of Appeals' exception to *Firestone* deference is not required by principles of trust law. Trust law is unclear on the narrow question before us. A leading treatise states that a court will strip a trustee of his discretion when there is reason to believe that he will not exercise that discretion fairly — for example, upon a showing that the trustee has already acted in bad faith.

* * *

This is not surprising — if the settlor who creates a trust grants discretion to the trustee, it seems doubtful that the settlor would want the trustee divested entirely of that discretion simply because of one good-faith mistake.

Here the lower courts made no finding that the Plan Administrator had acted in bad faith or would not fairly exercise his discretion to interpret the terms of the Plan. Thus, if the District Court had followed the trust law principles set out in Scott and Ascher, it should not have "act[ed] as a substitute trustee," *Eaton v. Eaton*, 82 N.H. 216, 218, 132 A. 10, 11 (1926), and stripped the Plan Administrator of the deference he would otherwise enjoy under *Firestone* and the terms of the Plan.

Other trust law sources, however, point the other way. For example, the Restatement (Second) of Trusts states that "the court will control the trustee in the exercise of a power where he acts beyond the bounds of a reasonable judgment." Restatement (Second) of Trusts § 187, Comment i, p. 406 (1957). Another treatise states that, after a trustee has abused his discretion, "[s]ometimes the court decides for the trustee how he should act, either by stating the exact result it desires to achieve, or by fixing some limits on the trustee's action and giving him leeway within those limits." G. Bogert & G. Bogert, Law of Trusts and Trustees § 560, p. 223 (2d rev. ed. 1980).

The unclear state of trust law on the question was perhaps best captured by the Texas Supreme Court:

> There is authority for ordering a dismissal of the case to afford the trustee an opportunity to exercise a reasonable discretion in arriving at the amount of payments to be made in the light of our discussion of the problem and after a proper consideration of the many factors involved. On the other hand, there is authority for remanding the case to the trial court to hear evidence and in the exercise of its supervisory jurisdiction to fix the amount of such payments. There is still other authority for remanding the case to the trial court to hear evidence and fix the boundaries of a reasonable discretion to be exercised by the trustee within maximum and minimum limits. *State v. Rubion*, 158 Tex. 43, 54-55, 308 S.W.2d 4, 11 (1957) (citations omitted).

While we are "guided by principles of trust law" in ERISA cases, *Firestone*, 489 U.S. at 111, we have recognized before that "trust law does not tell the entire story," *Varity Corp. v. Howe*, 516 U.S. 489, 497 (1996). Here trust law does not resolve the specific issue before us, but the guiding principles we have identified underlying ERISA do.

Congress enacted ERISA to ensure that employees would receive the benefits they had earned, but Congress did not require employers to establish benefit plans in the first place. *Lockheed Corp. v. Spink*, 517 U.S. 882, 887 (1996). We have therefore recognized that ERISA represents a "'careful balancing' between ensuring fair and prompt enforcement of rights under a plan and the encouragement of the creation of such plans." *Aetna Health Inc. v. Davila*, 542 U.S. 200, 215 (2004) (quoting *Pilot Life Ins. Co. v. Dedeaux*, 481 U.S. 41, 54 (1987)). Congress sought "to create a system that is [not] so complex that administrative costs, or litigation expenses, unduly discourage employers from offering [ERISA] plans in the first place." *Varity Corp., supra*, at 497. ERISA "induc[es] employers to offer benefits by assuring a predictable set of liabilities, under uniform standards of primary conduct and a uniform regime of ultimate remedial orders and awards when a violation has occurred." *Rush Prudential HMO, Inc. v. Moran*, 536 U.S. 355 (2002).

Firestone deference protects these interests and, by permitting an employer to grant primary interpretive authority over an ERISA plan to the plan administrator, preserves the "careful balancing" on which ERISA is based. Deference promotes efficiency by encouraging resolution of benefits disputes through internal administrative proceedings rather than costly litigation. It also promotes predictability, as an employer can rely on the expertise of the plan administrator rather than worry about unexpected and inaccurate plan interpretations that might result from de novo judicial review. Moreover, *Firestone* deference serves the interest of uniformity, helping to avoid a patchwork of different interpretations of a plan, like the one here, that covers employees in different jurisdictions — a result that "would introduce considerable inefficiencies in benefit program operation, which might lead those employers with existing plans to reduce benefits, and those without such plans to refrain from adopting them." *Fort Halifax Packing Co. v. Coyne*, 482 U.S. 1, 11 (1987).

Respondents and the United States as amicus curiae do not question that deference to plan administrators serves these important purposes. Rather, they argue that deference is less important once a plan administrator has issued an interpretation of a plan found to be unreasonable. But the interests in efficiency, predictability, and uniformity — and the manner in which they are promoted by deference to reasonable plan construction by administrators — do not suddenly disappear simply because a plan administrator has made a single honest mistake.

* * *

7-6 QUESTIONS AND PROBLEMS

1. Is the deeper problem not how to weigh the conflict, but the existence of the conflict that arises from permitting parties to make decisions in whose outcome they have a financial interest?

2. How would you respond to Chief Justice Robert's complaint in *Glenn* that the "majority is so imprecise about how the existence of a conflict should be treated"?

3. In *Conkright*, Justice Roberts repeatedly refers to "honest mistake." What does he mean by that? Do you agree that the interpretation was just "a single honest mistake?"

4. Explain what was at stake in *Conkright*, and why the Department of Labor intervened on behalf of the plaintiffs.

E. REMEDIES

ERISA §§ 409, 502.

ERISA does not have a single set of remedies. For example, each subsection of ERISA § 502(a) sets forth a cause of action and the available remedies. ERISA § 502(a)(1)(B) authorizes a plan participant to sue to recover benefits due under the terms of the plan. ERISA § 502(a)(2) authorizes participants, beneficiaries, the Secretary of Labor, and the plan fiduciary to sue for appropriate relief under ERISA § 409, which makes fiduciaries personally liable to the plan for any losses suffered by the plan due to the fiduciary breach of any duty to the plan. Section 409(a) authorizes removal of the fiduciary for malfeasance, provides that the fiduciary can be forced to repay the plan for any profits made by the fiduciary's self-dealing and finally, subjects the fiduciary who has breached any fiduciary obligation to "such other equitable or remedial relief as the court may deem appropriate." ERISA § 502(a)(3) authorizes "appropriate equitable relief" necessary to enforce ERISA or to redress violations of it, to enforce rights under a plan or to clarify rights under a plan. Plan administrators are also subject to fines up to $100 a day for failure to provide plan information in a timely manner or up to $1,000 a day for failure to file annual reports with the DOL. The section provides other fines up to $100 or $1,000 a day on employers or plan administrators for failure to give proper notice of the plan or to fail to file other required information. ERISA § 502(c)(1).

The extent and form of ERISA remedies under §§ 409 and 502 have given rise to extensive litigation and have been the subject of several Supreme Court decisions.

1. Claims Under ERISA § 502(a)(2).

MASSACHUSETTS MUTUAL LIFE INSURANCE CO. v. RUSSELL

473 U.S. 134 (1985)

JUSTICE STEVENS delivered the opinion of the Court.

The question presented for decision is whether, under the Employee Retirement Income Security Act of 1974 (ERISA), a fiduciary to an employee benefit plan may be held personally liable to a plan participant or beneficiary for extracontractual compensatory or punitive damages caused by improper or untimely processing of benefit claims.

Respondent Doris Russell, a claims examiner for petitioner Massachusetts Mutual Life Insurance Company (hereafter petitioner), is a beneficiary under two employee benefit plans administered by petitioner for eligible employees. Both plans are funded from the general assets of petitioner and both are governed by ERISA.

In May 1979 respondent became disabled with a back ailment. She received plan benefits until October 17, 1979, when, based on the report of an orthopedic surgeon, petitioner's disability committee terminated her benefits. On October 22, 1979, she requested internal review of that decision and, on November 27, 1979, submitted a report from her own psychiatrist indicating that she suffered from a psychosomatic disability with physical manifestations rather than an orthopedic illness. After an examination by a second psychiatrist on February 15, 1980, had confirmed that respondent was temporarily disabled, the plan administrator reinstated her benefits on March 11, 1980. Two days later retroactive benefits were paid in full.

Although respondent has been paid all benefits to which she is contractually entitled, she claims to have been injured by the improper refusal to pay benefits from October 17, 1979, when her benefits were terminated, to March 11, 1980, when her eligibility was restored. Among other allegations, she asserts that the fiduciaries administering petitioner's employee benefit plans are high-ranking company officials who (1) ignored readily available medical evidence documenting respondent's disability, (2) applied unwarrantedly strict eligibility standards, and (3) deliberately took 132 days to process her claim, in violation of regulations promulgated by the Secretary of Labor. The interruption of benefit payments allegedly forced respondent's disabled husband to cash out his retirement savings which, in turn, aggravated the psychological condition that caused respondent's back ailment. Accordingly, she sued petitioner in the California Superior Court pleading various causes of action based on state law and on ERISA.

Petitioner removed the case to the United States District Court for the Central District of California and moved for summary judgment. The District Court granted the motion, holding that the state-law claims were pre-empted by ERISA and that "ERISA bars any claims for extra-contractual damages and punitive damages arising out of the original denial of plaintiff's claims for benefits under the Salary Continuance Plan and the subsequent review thereof."

On appeal, the United States Court of Appeals for the Ninth Circuit affirmed in part and reversed in part. 722 F.2d 482 (1983). Although it agreed with the District Court that respondent's state-law causes of action were pre-empted by ERISA, it held that her complaint alleged a cause of action under ERISA. The court reasoned that the 132 days petitioner took to process respondent's claim violated the fiduciary's obligation to process claims in good faith and in a fair and diligent manner. The court concluded that this violation gave rise to a cause of action under § 409(a) that could be asserted by a plan beneficiary pursuant to § 502(a)(2). It read the authorization in § 409(a) of "such other equitable or remedial relief as the court may deem appropriate" as giving it "wide discretion as to the damages to be awarded," including compensatory and punitive damages.

According to the Court of Appeals, the award of compensatory damages shall "remedy the wrong and make the aggrieved individual whole," which meant not merely contractual damages for loss of plan benefits, but relief "that will compensate the injured party for all losses and injuries sustained as a direct and proximate cause of the breach of fiduciary duty," including "damages for mental or emotional distress." Moreover, the liability under § 409(a) "is against the fiduciary personally, not the plan."

The Court of Appeals also held that punitive damages could be recovered under § 409(a), although it decided that such an award is permitted only if the fiduciary "acted with actual malice or wanton indifference to the rights of a participant or beneficiary." The court believed that this result was supported by the text of § 409(a) and by the congressional purpose to provide broad remedies to redress and prevent violations of the Act.

We granted certiorari, to review both the compensatory and punitive components of the Court of Appeals' holding that § 409 authorizes recovery of extracontractual damages. Respondent defends the judgment of the Court of Appeals both on its reasoning that § 409 provides an express basis for extracontractual damages, as well as by arguing that in any event such a private remedy should be inferred under the analysis employed in *Cort v. Ash*, 422 U.S. 66, 78 (1975). We reject both arguments.

As its caption implies, § 409(a) establishes "LIABILITY FOR BREACH OF FIDUCIARY DUTY."

Specifically, it provides:

> "(a) Any person who is a fiduciary with respect to a plan who breaches any of the responsibilities, obligations, or duties imposed upon fiduciaries by this title shall be personally liable to make good to such plan any losses to the plan resulting from each such breach, and to restore to such plan any profits of such fiduciary which have been made through use of assets of the plan by the fiduciary, and shall be subject to such other equitable or remedial relief as the court may deem appropriate, including removal of such fiduciary. A fiduciary may also be removed for a violation of section 411 of this Act."

Sections 501 and 502 authorize, respectively, criminal and civil enforcement of the Act. While the former section provides for criminal penalties against any person who willfully violates any of the reporting and disclosure requirements of the Act, the latter section identifies six types of civil actions that may be brought by various parties . . . .

There can be no disagreement with the Court of Appeals' conclusion that § 502(a)(2) authorizes a beneficiary to bring an action against a fiduciary who has violated § 409. Petitioner contends, however, that recovery for a violation of § 409 inures to the benefit of the plan as a whole. We find this contention supported by the text of § 409, by the statutory provisions defining the duties of a fiduciary, and by the provisions defining the rights of a beneficiary.

The Court of Appeals' opinion focused on the reference in § 409 to "such other equitable or remedial relief as the court may deem appropriate." But when the entire section is examined, the emphasis on the relationship between the fiduciary and the plan as an entity becomes apparent. Thus, not only is the relevant fiduciary relationship characterized at the outset as one "with respect to a plan," but the potential personal liability of the fiduciary is "to make good to such plan any losses to the plan . . . and to restore to such plan any profits of such fiduciary which have been made through use of assets of the plan . . . ."

To read directly from the opening clause of § 409(a), which identifies the proscribed acts, to the "catchall" remedy phrase at the end — skipping over the intervening language establishing remedies benefiting, in the first instance, solely the plan — would divorce the phrase being construed from its context and construct an entirely new class of relief available to entities other than the plan . . . . A fair contextual reading of the statute makes it abundantly clear that its draftsmen were primarily concerned with the possible misuse of plan assets, and with remedies that would protect the entire plan, rather than with the rights of an individual beneficiary.

It is of course true that the fiduciary obligations of plan administrators are to serve the interest of participants and beneficiaries and, specifically, to provide them with the benefits authorized by the plan. But the principal statutory duties imposed on the trustees relate to the proper management, administration, and investment of fund assets, the maintenance of proper records, the disclosure of specified information, and the avoidance of conflicts of interest. Those duties are described in Part 4 of Title 1 of the Act, which is entitled "FIDUCIARY RESPONSIBILITY," *see* §§ 401(k)-414, whereas the statutory provisions relating to claim procedures are found in Part 5, dealing with "ADMINISTRATION AND ENFORCEMENT." §§ 502(a), 503. The only section that concerns review of a claim that has been denied — § 503 — merely specifies that every plan shall comply with certain regulations promulgated by the Secretary of Labor.

The Secretary's regulations contemplate that a decision "shall be made promptly, and shall not ordinarily be made later than 60 days after the plan's receipt of a request for review, unless special circumstances . . . require an extension of time for processing, in which case a decision shall be rendered as soon as possible, but not later than 120 days after receipt of a request for review." 29 C.F.R. § 2560.503-1(h)(1)(i) (1984). Nothing in the regulations or in the statute, however, expressly provides for a recovery from either the plan itself or from its administrators if greater time is required to determine the merits of an application for benefits. Rather, the regulations merely state that a claim may be treated as having been denied after the 60- or 120-day period has elapsed. *See* § 2560.503-1(h)(4) . . . . This provision therefore enables a claimant to bring a civil action to have the merits of his application determined, just as he may bring an action to challenge an outright denial of benefits.

Significantly, the statutory provision explicitly authorizing a beneficiary to bring an action to enforce his rights under the plan — § 502(a)(1)(B), quoted *supra*, at 140 — says nothing about the recovery of extracontractual damages, or about the possible consequences of delay in the plan administrators' processing of a disputed claim. Thus, there really is nothing at all in the statutory text to support the conclusion that such a delay gives rise to a private right of action for compensatory or punitive relief. And the entire text of § 409 persuades us that Congress did not intend that section to authorize any relief except for the plan itself. In short, unlike the Court of Appeals, we do not find in § 409 express authority for an award of extracontractual damages to a beneficiary.

Relying on the four-factor analysis employed by the Court in *Cort v. Ash*, 422 U.S. at 78, respondent argues that a private right of action for extracontractual damages should be implied even if it is not expressly authorized by ERISA. Two of the four *Cort* factors unquestionably support respondent's claim: respondent is a member of the class for whose benefit the statute was enacted and, in view of the pre-emptive effect of ERISA, there is no state-law impediment to implying a remedy. But the two other factors — legislative intent and consistency with the legislative scheme — point in the opposite direction. And unless this congressional intent can be inferred from the language of the statute, the statutory structure, or some other source, the essential predicate for implication of a private remedy simply does not exist." *Northwest Airlines, Inc. v. Transport Workers*, 451 U.S. 77, 94 (1981). "The federal judiciary will not engraft a remedy on a statute, no matter how salutary, that Congress did not intend to provide." *California v. Sierra Club*, 451 U.S. 287, 297 (1981).

The voluminous legislative history of the Act contradicts respondent's position. It is true that an early version of the statute contained a provision for "legal or equitable" relief that was described in both the Senate and House Committee Reports as authorizing "the full range of legal and equitable remedies available in both state and federal courts." But that language appeared in Committee Reports describing a version of the bill before the debate on the floor and before the Senate-House Conference Committee had finalized the operative language. In the bill passed by the House of Representatives and ultimately adopted by the Conference Committee the reference to legal relief was deleted. The language relied on by respondent and by the Court of Appeals below, therefore, is of little help in understanding whether Congress intended to make fiduciaries personally liable to beneficiaries for extracontractual damages.

The six carefully integrated civil enforcement provisions found in § 502(a) of the statute as finally enacted, however, provide strong evidence that Congress did not intend to authorize other remedies that it simply forgot to incorporate expressly. The assumption of inadvertent omission is rendered especially suspect upon close consideration of ERISA's interlocking, interrelated, and interdependent remedial scheme, which is in turn part of a "comprehensive and reticulated statute." *Nachman Corp. v. Pension Benefit Guaranty Corporation*, 446 U.S. 359, 361 (1980). If in this case, for example, the plan administrator had adhered to his initial determination that respondent was not entitled to disability benefits under the plan, respondent would have had a panoply of remedial devices at her disposal. To recover the benefits due her, she could have filed an action pursuant to § 502(a)(1)(B) to recover accrued benefits, to obtain a declaratory judgment that she is entitled to benefits under the provisions of the plan contract, and to enjoin the plan administrator from improperly refusing to pay benefits in the future. If the plan administrator's refusal to pay contractually authorized benefits had been willful and part of a larger systematic breach of fiduciary obligations, respondent in this hypothetical could have asked for removal of the fiduciary pursuant to §§ 502(a)(2) and 409. Finally, in answer to a possible concern that attorney's fees might present a barrier to maintenance of suits for small claims, thereby risking underenforcement of beneficiaries' statutory rights, it should be noted that ERISA authorizes the award of attorney's fees. *See* § 502(g).

We are reluctant to tamper with an enforcement scheme crafted with such evident care as the one in ERISA. "The presumption that a remedy was deliberately omitted from a statute is strongest when Congress has enacted a comprehensive legislative scheme including an integrated system of procedures for enforcement." *Northwest Airlines, Inc. v. Transport Workers*, 451 U.S. at 97 n.15.

In contrast to the repeatedly emphasized purpose to protect contractually defined benefits, there is a stark absence — in the statute itself and in its legislative history — of any reference to an intention to authorize the recovery of extracontractual damages. Because "neither the statute nor the legislative history reveals a congressional intent to create a private right of action . . . we need not carry the *Cort v. Ash* inquiry further." *Northwest Airlines, Inc. v. Transport Workers*, 451 U.S. at 94 n.31.

III

Thus, the relevant text of ERISA, the structure of the entire statute, and its legislative history all support the conclusion that in § 409(a) Congress did not provide, and did not intend the judiciary to imply, a cause of action for extracontractual damages caused by improper or untimely processing of benefit claims.

The judgment of the Court of Appeals is therefore Reversed.

[Concurring opinion of Justice Brennan deleted.]

7-7 QUESTIONS AND PROBLEMS

1. Should the plaintiff have sued under ERISA § 502(a)(3) rather than § 502(a)(2)? Why did she sue under § 502(a)(2)?

2. What are "extracontractual compensatory damages"?

3. Is § 502(a) as carefully crafted as the Court suggests?

4. Do you think that absent compensatory or punitive damages, plan administrators are likely to withhold or delay benefits?

5. Can you think of self-interested reasons that would discourage a plan administrator or fiduciary from deliberately withholding or delaying plan benefits?

6. What are the arguments — pro and con — of awarding compensatory damages? Punitive damages?

In 2008, the Supreme Court reconsidered the question first raised in *Russell* as to what is meant by the § 502(a)(2) requirement that any recovery must benefit the plan rather than the individual.

LARUE v. DeWOLFF, BOBERG & ASSOCIATES, INC.

552 U.S. 248 (2008)

JUSTICE STEVENS delivered the opinion of the Court.

In *Massachusetts Mut. Life Ins. Co. v. Russell*, 473 U.S. 134 (1985), we held that a participant in a disability plan that paid a fixed level of benefits could not bring suit under § 502(a)(2) of the Employee Retirement Income Security Act of 1974 (ERISA), to recover consequential damages arising from delay in the processing of her claim. In this case we consider whether that statutory provision authorizes a participant in a defined contribution pension plan to sue a fiduciary whose alleged misconduct impaired the value of plan assets in the participant's individual account. Relying on our decision in *Russell*, the Court of Appeals for the Fourth Circuit held that § 502(a)(2) "provides remedies only for entire plans, not for individuals. . . . Recovery under this subsection must 'inure[ ] to the benefit of the plan *as a whole*,' not to particular persons with rights under the plan." 450 F.3d 570, 572-573 (2006) (quoting *Russell*, 473 U.S. at 140). While language in our *Russell* opinion is consistent with that conclusion, the rationale for *Russell*'s holding supports the opposite result in this case.

I

Petitioner filed this action in 2004 against his former employer, DeWolff, Boberg & Associates (DeWolff), and the ERISA-regulated 401(k) retirement savings plan administered by DeWolff (Plan). The Plan permits participants to direct the investment of their contributions in accordance with specified procedures and requirements. Petitioner alleged that in 2001 and 2002 he directed DeWolff to make certain changes to the investments in his individual account, but DeWolff never carried out these directions. Petitioner claimed that this omission "depleted" his interest in the Plan by approximately $150,000, and amounted to a breach of fiduciary duty under ERISA. The complaint sought " 'make-whole' or other equitable relief as allowed by [§ 502(a)(3)]," as well as "such other and further relief as the court deems just and proper."

Respondents filed a motion for judgment on the pleadings, arguing that the complaint was essentially a claim for monetary relief that is not recoverable under § 502(a)(3). Petitioner countered that he "d[id] not wish for the court to award him any money, but . . . simply want[ed] the plan to properly reflect that which would be his interest in the plan, but for the breach of fiduciary duty." The District Court concluded, however, that since a fiduciary duty, [T]he District Court granted their motion.

On appeal petitioner argued that he had a cognizable claim for relief under §§ 502(a)(2) and 502(a)(3) of ERISA. The Court of Appeals stated that petitioner had raised his § 502(a)(2) argument for the first time on appeal, but nevertheless rejected it on the merits.

Section 502(a)(2) provides for suits to enforce the liability-creating provisions of § 409, concerning breaches of fiduciary duties that harm plans. The Court of Appeals cited language from our opinion in *Russell* suggesting that that these provisions "protect the entire plan, rather than the rights of an individual beneficiary." 473 U.S. at 142. It then characterized the remedy sought by petitioner as "personal" because he "desires recovery to be paid into his plan account, an instrument that exists specifically for his benefit":

The Court of Appeals also rejected petitioner's argument that the make-whole relief he sought was "equitable" within the meaning of § 502(a)(3). Although our grant of certiorari, 551 U.S. ___ (2007), encompassed the § 502(a)(3) issue, we do not address it because we conclude that the Court of Appeals misread § 502(a)(2).

II

As the case comes to us, we must assume that respondents breached fiduciary obligations defined in § 409(a), and that those breaches had an adverse impact on the value of the plan assets in petitioner's individual account. Whether petitioner can prove those allegations and whether respondents may have valid defenses to the claim are matters not before us. Although the record does not reveal the relative size of petitioner's account, the legal issue under § 502(a)(2) is the same whether his account includes 1% or 99% of the total assets in the plan.

As we explained in *Russell*, and in more detail in our later opinion in *Varity Corp. v. Howe*, 516 U.S. 489, 508-512 (1996), § 502(a) of ERISA identifies six types of civil actions that may be brought by various parties. The second, which is at issue in this case, authorizes the Secretary of Labor as well as plan participants, beneficiaries, and fiduciaries, to bring actions on behalf of a plan to recover for violations of the obligations defined in § 409(a). The principal statutory duties imposed on fiduciaries by that section "relate to the proper management, administration, and investment of fund assets," with an eye toward ensuring that "the benefits authorized by the plan" are ultimately paid to participants and beneficiaries. *Russell*, 473 U.S. at 142; see also Varity, 516 U.S. at 511-512 (noting that § 409's fiduciary obligations "relat[e] to the plan's financial integrity" and "reflec[t] a special congressional concern about plan asset management"). The misconduct alleged by the petitioner in this case falls squarely within that category.[1]

The misconduct alleged in *Russell*, by contrast, fell outside this category. The plaintiff in *Russell* received all of the benefits to which she was contractually entitled, but sought consequential damages arising from a delay in the processing of her claim. In holding that § 502(a)(2) does not provide a remedy for this type of injury, we stressed that the text of § 409(a) characterizes the relevant fiduciary relationship as one "with respect to a plan," and repeatedly identifies the "plan" as the victim of any fiduciary breach and the recipient of any relief. The legislative history likewise revealed that "the crucible of congressional concern was misuse and mismanagement of plan assets by plan administrators." Finally, our review of ERISA as a whole confirmed that §§ 502(a)(2) and 409 protect "the financial integrity of the plan," whereas other provisions specifically address claims for benefits. We therefore concluded:

> A fair contextual reading of the statute makes it abundantly clear that its draftsmen were primarily concerned with the possible misuse of plan assets, and with remedies that would protect the entire plan, rather than with the rights of an individual beneficiary.

Id. at 142.

Russell's emphasis on protecting the "entire plan" from fiduciary misconduct reflects the former landscape of employee benefit plans. That landscape has changed.

Defined contribution plans dominate the retirement plan scene today. Unlike the defined contribution plan in this case, the disability plan at issue in *Russell* did not have individual accounts; it paid a fixed benefit based on a percentage of the employee's salary. See *Russell v. Massachusetts Mut. Life Ins. Co.*, 722 F.2d 482, 486 (CA9 1983).

The "entire plan" language in *Russell* speaks to the impact of § 409 on plans that

---

[1] The record does not reveal whether the alleged $150,000 injury represents a decline in the value of assets that DeWolff should have sold or an increase in the value of assets that DeWolff should have purchased. Contrary to respondents' argument, however, § 502(a)(2) encompasses appropriate claims for "lost profits." Under the common law of trusts, which informs our interpretation of ERISA's fiduciary duties, trustees are "chargeable with . . . any profit which would have accrued to the trust estate if there had been no breach of trust," including profits forgone because the trustee "fails to purchase specific property which it is his duty to purchase." 1 Restatement (Second) Trusts § 205, and Comment *i*, § 211 (1957); see also 3 A. Scott, Law on Trusts §§ 205, 211 (3d ed. 1967).

pay defined benefits. Misconduct by the administrators of a defined benefit plan will not affect an individual's entitlement to a defined benefit unless it creates or enhances the risk of default by the entire plan. It was that default risk that prompted Congress to require defined benefit plans (but not defined contribution plans) to satisfy complex minimum funding requirements, and to make premium payments to the Pension Benefit Guaranty Corporation for plan termination insurance.

For defined contribution plans, however, fiduciary misconduct need not threaten the solvency of the entire plan to reduce benefits below the amount that participants would otherwise receive. Whether a fiduciary breach diminishes plan assets payable to all participants and beneficiaries, or only to persons tied to particular individual accounts, it creates the kind of harms that concerned the draftsmen of § 409. Consequently, our references to the "entire plan" in *Russell*, which accurately reflect the operation of § 409 in the defined benefit context, are beside the point in the defined contribution context.

Other sections of ERISA confirm that the "entire plan" language from *Russell*, which appears nowhere in § 409 or § 502(a)(2), does not apply to defined contribution plans. Most significant is § 404(c), which exempts fiduciaries from liability for losses caused by participants' exercise of control over assets in their individual accounts. This provision would serve no real purpose if, as respondents argue, fiduciaries never had any liability for losses in an individual account.

We therefore hold that although § 502(a)(2) does not provide a remedy for individual injuries distinct from plan injuries, that provision does authorize recovery for fiduciary breaches that impair the value of plan assets in a participant's individual account. Accordingly, the judgment of the Court of Appeals is vacated, and the case is remanded for further proceedings consistent with this opinion.

. . .

CHIEF JUSTICE ROBERTS, with whom JUSTICE KENNEDY joins, concurring in part and concurring in the judgment.

. . . I agree with the Court that the Fourth Circuit's analysis was flawed, and join the Court's opinion to that extent.

The Court, however, goes on to conclude that § 502(a)(2) does authorize recovery in cases such as the present one. It is not at all clear that this is true. LaRue's right to direct the investment of his contributions was a right granted and governed by the plan. In this action, he seeks the benefits that would otherwise be due him if, as alleged, the plan carried out his investment instruction. LaRue's claim, therefore, is a claim for benefits that turns on the application and interpretation of the plan terms, specifically those governing investment options and how to exercise them.

It is at least arguable that a claim of this nature properly lies only under § 502(a)(1)(B) of ERISA. That provision allows a plan participant or beneficiary "to recover benefits due to him under the terms of his plan, to enforce his rights under the terms of the plan, or to clarify his rights to future benefits under the terms of the plan." It is difficult to imagine a more accurate description of LaRue's claim. . . .

If LaRue may bring his claim under § 502(a)(1)(B), it is not clear that he may do so under § 502(a)(2) as well. Section 502(a)(2) provides for "appropriate" relief. Construing the same term in a parallel ERISA provision, we have held that relief is not "appropriate" under § 502(a)(3) if another provision, such as § 502(a)(1)(B), offers an adequate remedy. See *Varity Corp. v. Howe*, 516 U.S. 489 (1996). . . .

The significance of the distinction between a § 502(a)(1)(B) claim and one under § 502(a)(2) is not merely a matter of picking the right provision to cite in the complaint. Allowing a § 502(a)(1)(B) action to be recast as one under § 502(a)(2) might permit plaintiffs to circumvent safeguards for plan administrators that have developed under § 502(a)(1)(B). Among these safeguards is the requirement, recognized by almost all the Courts of Appeals, see *Fallick v. Nationwide Mut. Ins. Co.*, 162 F.3d 410, 418, n.4 (CA6 1998) (citing cases), that a participant exhaust the administrative remedies mandated by ERISA § 503 before filing suit under § 502(a)(1)(B).[2] Equally significant, this Court has held that ERISA plans may grant administrators and fiduciaries discretion in determining benefit eligibility and the meaning of plan terms, decisions that courts may review only for an abuse of discretion. *Firestone Tire & Rubber Co. v. Bruch*, 489 U.S. 101, 115 (1989).

These safeguards encourage employers and others to undertake the voluntary step of providing medical and retirement benefits to plan participants, see *Aetna Health Inc. v. Davila*, 542 U.S. 200, 215 (2004), and have no doubt engendered substantial reliance interests on the part of plans and fiduciaries. Allowing what is really a claim for benefits under a plan to be brought as a claim for breach of fiduciary duty under § 502(a)(2), rather than as a claim for benefits due "under the terms of [the] plan," § 502(a)(1)(B), may result in circumventing such plan terms.

I do not mean to suggest that these are settled questions. They are not. Nor are we in a position to answer them. LaRue did not rely on § 502(a)(1)(B) as a source of relief, and the courts below had no occasion to address the argument, raised by an *amicus* in this Court, that the availability of relief under § 502(a)(1)(B) precludes LaRue's fiduciary breach claim. I simply highlight the fact that the Court's determination that the present claim may be brought under § 502(a)(2) is reached without considering whether the possible availability of relief under § 502(a)(1)(B) alters that conclusion. . . .

Justice Thomas, joined by Justice Scalia, wrote in a concurrence that the main opinion was not required to justify its decision to modify *Russell* because the clear language of the statute allowed individual plan participants to bring claims under § 502(a)(2). Thomas wrote that §§ 409(a) and 502(a)(2) permit recovery of "all plan losses caused by a fiduciary breach," Thomas said that the assets allocated to LaRue's individual account were plan assets and therefore a claim under Section 502(a)(2) was clearly anticipated by the statute. "In short, the assets of a defined contribution plan under ERISA constitute, at the very least, the sum of all the assets allocated for bookkeeping purposes to the participants' individual accounts," Thomas concluded. "Because a defined contribution plan is essentially the sum of its parts, losses attributable to the account of an individual participant are necessarily 'losses to the plan' for purposes of § 409(a)."

7-8 QUESTIONS AND PROBLEMS

1. Has the Court awarded LaRue the $150,000 that he requested from his former employer?

2. How persuasive is the Court's distinction of *Russell*?

---

[2] Sensibly, the Court leaves open the question whether exhaustion may be required of a claimant who seeks recovery for a breach of fiduciary duty under § 502(a)(2).

2. Claims Under ERISA § 502(a)(3).

MERTENS v. HEWITT ASSOCIATES
508 U.S. 248 (1993)

JUSTICE SCALIA delivered the opinion of the Court.

The question presented is whether a nonfiduciary who knowingly participates in the breach of a fiduciary duty imposed by [ERISA] is liable for losses that an employee benefit plan suffers as a result of the breach.

I

According to the complaint, the allegations of which we take as true, petitioners represent a class of former employees of the Kaiser Steel Corporation (Kaiser) who participated in the Kaiser Steel Retirement Plan, a qualified pension plan under ERISA. Respondent was the plan's actuary in 1980, when Kaiser began to phase out its steelmaking operations, prompting early retirement by a large number of plan participants. Respondent did not, however, change the plan's actuarial assumptions to reflect the additional costs imposed by the retirements. As a result, Kaiser did not adequately fund the plan, and eventually the plan's assets became insufficient to satisfy its benefit obligations, causing the Pension Benefit Guaranty Corporation (PBGC) to terminate the plan pursuant to [ERISA § 4041]. Petitioners now receive only the benefits guaranteed by ERISA, *see* [§ 4022], which are in general substantially lower than the fully vested pensions due them under the plan.

Petitioners sued the fiduciaries of the failed plan, alleging breach of fiduciary duties. They also commenced this action against respondent, alleging that it had caused the losses by allowing Kaiser to select the plan's actuarial assumptions, by failing to disclose that Kaiser was one of its clients, and by failing to disclose the plan's funding shortfall. Petitioners claimed that these acts and omissions violated ERISA by effecting a breach of respondent's "professional duties" to the plan, for which they sought, *inter alia*, monetary relief. In opposing respondent's motion to dismiss, petitioners fleshed out this claim, asserting that respondent was liable (1) as an ERISA fiduciary that committed a breach of its own fiduciary duties, (2) as a nonfiduciary that knowingly participated in the plan fiduciaries' breach of their fiduciary duties, and (3) as a nonfiduciary that committed a breach of nonfiduciary duties imposed on actuaries by ERISA. The District Court for the Northern District of California dismissed the complaint and the Court of Appeals for the Ninth Circuit affirmed in relevant part.

Petitioners sought certiorari only on the question whether ERISA authorizes suits for money damages against nonfiduciaries who knowingly participate in a fiduciary's breach of fiduciary duty. We agree to hear the case.

II

ERISA is, we have observed, is a "comprehensive and reticulated statute," the product of a decade of congressional study of the Nation's private employee benefit system. The statute provides that not only the persons named as fiduciaries by a benefit plan, [ERISA] § 402(a), but also anyone else who exercises discretionary control or authority over the plan's management, administration, or assets, *see* [ERISA] § 3(21)(A), is an ERISA "fiduciary." Fiduciaries are assigned a number of detailed duties and responsibilities . . . . Section 409(a) makes fiduciaries liable for breach of these duties, and specifies the remedies available against them: The fiduciary is personally liable for damages ("to make good to [the] plan any losses to the plan resulting from each such breach"), for restitution ("to restore to [the] plan any profits of such fiduciary which have been made through use of assets of the plan by the fiduciary"), and for "such other equitable or remedial relief as the court may deem appropriate," including removal of the fiduciary. Section 502(a)(2) — the second of ERISA's "six carefully integrated civil enforcement provisions," *Russell*, allows the Secretary of Labor or any plan beneficiary, participant, or fiduciary to bring a civil action "for appropriate relief under section [409]."

The above described provisions are, however, limited by their terms to fiduciaries. The Court of Appeals decided that respondent was not a fiduciary, and petitioners do not contest that holding. Lacking equivalent provisions specifying *non*-fiduciaries as potential defendants, or damages as a remedy available against them, petitioners have turned to § 502(a)(3) which authorizes a plan beneficiary, participant, or fiduciary to bring a civil action:

> (A) to enjoin any act or practice which violates any provision of [ERISA] or the terms of the plan, or (B) to obtain other appropriate equitable relief (i) to redress such violations or (ii) to enforce any provisions of [ERISA] or the terms of the plan . . . .

See also § 502(a)(5) (providing, in similar language, for civil suits by the Secretary based upon violation of ERISA provisions). Petitioners contend that requiring respondent to make the Kaiser plan whole for the losses resulting from its alleged knowing participation in the breach of fiduciary duty by the Kaiser plan's fiduciaries would constitute "other appropriate equitable relief" within the meaning of § 502(a)(3).

We note at the outset that it is far from clear that, even if this provision does make money damages available, it makes them available for the actions at issue here. It does not, after all, authorize "appropriate equitable relief" at large, but only "appropriate equitable relief" for the purpose of "redress [ing any] violations or . . . enforc[ing] any provisions" of ERISA or an ERISA plan. No one suggests that any term of the Kaiser plan has been violated, nor would any be enforced by the requested judgment. And while ERISA contains various provisions that can be read as imposing obligations upon nonfiduciaries, including actuaries, no provision explicitly requires them to avoid participation (knowing or unknowing) in a fiduciary's breach of fiduciary duty. It is unlikely, moreover, that this was an oversight, since ERISA does explicitly impose "knowing participation" liability on cofiduciaries. *See* § 405(a). That limitation appears all the more deliberate in light of the fact that "knowing participation" liability on the part of both co-trustees and third persons was well established under the common law of trusts. In *Russell* we emphasized our unwillingness to infer causes of action in the ERISA context, since that statute's carefully crafted and detailed enforcement scheme provides "strong evidence that Congress did not intend to authorize other remedies that it simply forgot to incorporate expressly." 473 U.S. at 146–147. All of this notwithstanding, petitioners and their amicus the United States seem to assume that respondent's alleged action (or inaction) violated ERISA, and address their arguments almost exclusively to what forms of relief are available. And respondent, despite considerable prompting by its amici, expressly disclaims reliance on this preliminary point. Thus, although we acknowledge the oddity of resolving a dispute over remedies where it is unclear that a remediable wrong has been alleged, we decide this case on the narrow battlefield the parties have chosen, and reserve decision of that antecedent question.

Petitioners maintain that the object of their suit is "appropriate equitable relief" under § 502(a)(3). They do not, however, seek a remedy traditionally viewed as "equitable," such as injunction or restitution. (The Court of Appeals held that restitution was unavailable, and petitioners have not challenged that.) Although they often dance around the word, what petitioners in fact seek is nothing other than compensatory damages — monetary relief for all losses their plan sustained as a result of the alleged breach of fiduciary duties. Money damages are, of course, the classic form of legal relief. And though we have never interpreted the precise phrase "other appropriate equitable relief," we have construed the similar language of Title VII of the Civil Rights Act of 1964 (before its 1991 amendments) — "any other equitable relief as the court deems appropriate," to preclude "awards for compensatory or punitive damages."

Petitioners assert, however, that this reading of "equitable relief" fails to acknowledge ERISA's roots in the common law of trusts, *see Firestone Tire & Rubber v. Bruch*, 489 U.S. 101, 110–111 (1989). "[A]lthough a beneficiary's action to recover losses resulting from a breach of duty superficially resembles an action at law for damages," the Solicitor General suggests, "such relief traditionally has been obtained in courts of equity" and therefore "is, by definition, 'equitable relief.' " It is true that, at common law, the courts of equity had exclusive jurisdiction over virtually all actions by beneficiaries for breach of trust. It is also true that money damages were available in those courts against the trustee, and against third persons who knowingly participated in the trustee's breach.

At common law, however, there were many situations — not limited to those involving enforcement of a trust — in which an equity court could "establish purely legal rights and grant legal remedies which would otherwise be beyond the scope of its authority." 1 J. Pomeroy, *Equity Jurisprudence* § 181, 257 (5th ed. 1941). The term "equitable relief" can assuredly mean, as petitioners and the Solicitor General would have it, whatever relief a court of equity is empowered to provide in the particular case at issue. But as indicated by the foregoing quotation — which speaks of "legal remedies" granted by an equity court — "equitable relief" can also refer to those categories of relief that were typically available in equity (such as injunction, mandamus, and restitution, but not compensatory damages). As memories of the divided bench, and familiarity with its technical refinements, recede further into the past, the former meaning becomes, perhaps, increasingly unlikely; but it remains a question of interpretation in each case which meaning is intended.

In the context of the present statute, we think there can be no doubt. Since all relief available for breach of trust could be obtained from a court of equity, limiting the sort of relief obtainable under § 502(a)(3) to "equitable relief" in the sense of "whatever relief a common-law court of equity could provide in such a case" would limit the relief not at all. We will not read the statute to render the modifier superfluous. Regarding "equitable" relief in § 502(a)(3) to mean "all relief available for breach of trust at common law" would also require us either to give the term a different meaning there than it bears elsewhere in ERISA, or to deprive of all meaning the distinction Congress drew between "equitable" and "remedial" relief in § 409(a), and between "equitable" and "legal" relief in the very same section of ERISA, *see* [ERISA § 502(g)(2)(E)]; in the same subchapter of ERISA, *see* [ERISA § 104(a)(5)(C)]; and in the ERISA subchapter dealing with the PBGC. Neither option is acceptable. The authority of courts to develop a "federal common law" under ERISA, *see Firestone*, is not the authority to revise the text of the statute.

. . .

In the last analysis, petitioners and the United States ask us to give a strained interpretation to § 502(a)(3) in order to achieve the "purpose of ERISA to protect plan participants and beneficiaries." They note, as we have, that before ERISA nonfiduciaries were generally liable under state trust law for damages resulting from knowing participation in a trustees's breach of duty, and they assert that such actions are now pre-empted by ERISA's broad pre-emption clause, § 514(a). *Ingersoll-Rand Co. v. McClendon*, 498 U.S. 133, 139–140 (1990). Thus, they contend, our construction of § 502(a)(3) leaves beneficiaries like petitioners with *less* protection than existed before ERISA, contradicting ERISA's basic goal of "promot[ing] the interests of employees and their beneficiaries in employee benefit plans."

Even assuming (without deciding) that petitioners are correct about the pre-emption of previously available state-court actions, vague notions of a statute's "basic purpose" are nonetheless inadequate to overcome the words of its text regarding the *specific* issue under consideration. This is especially true with legislation such as ERISA, an enormously complex and detailed statute that resolved innumerable disputes between powerful competing interests — not all in favor of potential plaintiffs. *See, e.g., Pilot Life Ins. Co. v. Dedeaux*, 481 U.S. 41, 54–56 (1987). The text that we have described is certainly not nonsensical; it allocates liability for plan-related misdeeds in reasonable proportion to respective actors' power to control and prevent the misdeeds. Under traditional trust law, although a beneficiary could obtain damages from third persons for knowing participation in a trustee's breach of fiduciary duties, only the trustee had fiduciary duties. ERISA, however, defines "fiduciary" not in terms of formal trusteeship, but in *functional* terms of control and authority over the plan, *see* [ERISA] § 3(21)(A), thus expanding the universe of persons subject to fiduciary duties — and to damages — under § 409(a). Professional service providers such as actuaries become liable for damages when they cross the line from advisor to fiduciary; must disgorge assets and profits obtained through participation as parties-in-interest in transactions prohibited by § 406, and pay related civil penalties, *see* § 502(i), and (assuming nonfiduciaries can be sued under § 502(a)(3)) may be enjoined from participating in a fiduciary's breaches, compelled to make restitution, and subjected to other equitable decrees. All that ERISA has eliminated, on these assumptions, is the common law's joint and several liability, for *all* direct and consequential damages suffered by the plan, on the part of persons who had no real power to control what the plan did. Exposure to that sort of liability would impose high insurance costs upon persons who regularly deal with and offer advice to ERISA plans, and hence upon ERISA plans themselves. There is, in other words, a "tension between the primary [ERISA] goal of benefiting employees and the subsidiary goal of containing pension costs." *Alessi v. Raybestos-Manhattan, Inc.*, 451 U.S. 504, 515 (1981). We will not attempt to adjust the balance between those competing goals that the text adopted by Congress has struck.

The judgment of the Court of Appeals is Affirmed.

JUSTICE WHITE, with whom THE CHIEF JUSTICE, JUSTICE STEVENS and JUSTICE O'CONNOR join, dissenting.

The traditional "equitable remedies" available to a trust beneficiary included compensatory damages. Equity "endeavor[ed] as far as possible to replace the parties in the same situation as they would have been in, if no breach of trust had been committed." *Hill*. This included, where necessary, the payment of a monetary award to make the victims of the breach whole.

Given this history, it is entirely reasonable in my view to construe § 502(a)(3)'s reference to "appropriate equitable relief" to encompass what was equity's routine remedy for such breaches — a compensatory monetary award calculated to make the victims whole, a remedy that was available against both fiduciaries and participating nonfiduciaries.

. . .

Although the trust beneficiary historically had an equitable suit for damages against a fiduciary for breach of trust, as well as against a participating nonfiduciary, the majority today construes § 502(a)(3) as not affording such a remedy against any fiduciary or participating third party on the ground that damages are not "appropriate equitable relief." The majority's conclusion, as I see it, rests on transparently insufficient grounds. The text of the statute supports a reading of § 502(a)(3) that would permit a court to award compensatory monetary relief where necessary to make an ERISA beneficiary whole for a breach of trust. Such a reading would accord with the established equitable remedies available under the common law of trusts, to which Congress has directed us in construing ERISA, and with Congress' primary goal in enacting the statute, the protection of beneficiaries' financial security against corrupt or inept plan mismanagement. Finally, such a reading would avoid the perverse and, in this case, entirely needless result of construing ERISA so as to *deprive* beneficiaries of remedies they enjoyed prior to the statute's enactment. For these reasons, I respectfully dissent.

7-9 QUESTIONS AND PROBLEMS

1. Why didn't the plaintiffs sue under § 502(a)(1)(B) to recover the plan benefits due to them?

2. Why didn't the plaintiffs sue under § 502(a)(2) for appropriate relief under § 409?

3. Why wasn't the actuary a fiduciary? Can the plaintiffs recover against the actuary for the state law claim of professional malpractice?

4. Did the Supreme Court decide the question that it announced that was before it: is a nonfiduciary liable for losses of a pension plan suffered on account of the nonfiduciary's participation in the fiduciary's breach of its duties? What question did the Court decide?

5. Why did the Court address the common law of trusts? What relevance does it have to the interpreting ERISA remedies?

6. The failure of the actuary to adjust its calculation as to the proper funding of the pension trust resulted in injury to the petitioners. Did Congress intend that a party, such as an actuary, could negligently or intentionally injure plan participants or beneficiaries without there being any recourse for the injured parties?

7. Who has the better argument? Justice Scalia, who claims that under ERISA the term "equitable relief" means nonlegal, i.e. noncompensatory, relief, or Justice White, who writes that "equitable remedies" refers to the forms of relief, including legal relief, that a court sitting in equity could provide?

8. Is it sensible to refer to "Congressional intent," or is it more sensible to look at what will result depending on how the statute is interpreted?

In 1996, the Supreme Court reconsidered the scope of equitable remedies under ERISA § 502(a)(3).

VARITY CORP. v. HOWE (PART II)

516 U.S. 489 (1996)

[Factual aspects of the case are repeated from Part I of case found in Chapter 6, Plan Administration]

A group of beneficiaries of a firm's employee welfare benefit plan, protected by the Employee Retirement Income Security (ERISA), have sued their plan's administrator, who was also their employer. They claim that the administrator, through trickery, led them to withdraw from the plan and to forfeit their benefits. They seek, among other things, an order that, in essence, would reinstate each of them as a participant in the employer's ERISA plan. The lower courts entered judgment in the employees' favor, and we agreed to review that judgment.

In conducting our review, we do not question the lower courts' findings of serious deception by the employer, but instead consider three legal questions. First, in the factual circumstances (as determined by the lower courts), was the employer acting in its capacity as an ERISA "fiduciary" when it significantly and deliberately misled the beneficiaries? Second, in misleading the beneficiaries, did the employer violate the fiduciary obligations that ERISA § 404 imposes upon plan administrators? Third, does ERISA § 502(a)(3) authorize ERISA plan beneficiaries to bring a lawsuit, such as this one, that seeks relief for individual beneficiaries harmed by an administrator's breach of fiduciary obligations?

We answer each of these questions in the beneficiaries' favor, and we therefore affirm the judgment of the Court of Appeals.

The key facts, as found by the District Court after trial, include the following: Charles Howe, and the other respondents, used to work for Massey-Ferguson, Inc., a farm equipment manufacturer, and a wholly owned subsidiary of the petitioner, Varity Corporation. (Since the lower courts found that Varity and Massey-Ferguson were "alter egos," we shall refer to them interchangeably.) These employees all were participants in, and beneficiaries of, Massey-Ferguson's self-funded employee welfare benefit plan — an ERISA-protected plan that Massey-Ferguson itself administered. In the mid-1980's, Varity became concerned that some of Massey-Ferguson's divisions were losing too much money and developed a business plan to deal with the problem.

The business plan — which Varity called "Project Sunshine" — amounted to placing many of Varity's money-losing eggs in one financially rickety basket. It called for a transfer of Massey-Ferguson's money-losing divisions, along with various other debts, to a newly created, separately incorporated subsidiary called Massey Combines. The plan foresaw the possibility that Massey Combines would fail. But it viewed such a failure, from Varity's business perspective, as closer to a victory than to a defeat. Tha t is because Massey Combine's failure would not only eliminate several of Varity's poorly performing divisions, but it would also eradicate various debts that Varity would transfer to Massey Combines, and which, in the absence of the reorganization, Varity's more profitable subsidiaries or divisions might have to pay.

Among the obligations that Varity hoped the reorganization would eliminate were those arising from the Massey-Ferguson benefit plan's promises to pay medical and other nonpension benefits to employees of Massey-Ferguson's money-losing divisions. Rather than terminate those benefits directly (as it had retained the right to do), Varity attempted to avoid the undesirable fallout that could have accompanied cancellation by inducing the failing divisions' employees to switch employers and thereby voluntarily release Massey-Ferguson from its obligation to provide them benefits (effectively substituting the new, self-funded Massey

Combines benefit plan for the former Massey-Ferguson plan). Insofar as Massey-Ferguson's employees did so, a subsequent Massey Combines failure would eliminate — simply and automatically, without distressing the remaining Massey-Ferguson employees — what would otherwise have been Massey-Ferguson's obligation to pay those employees their benefits.

To persuade the employees of the failing divisions to accept the change of employer and benefit plan, Varity called them together at a special meeting and talked to them about Massey Combines' future business outlook, its likely financial viability, and the security of their employee benefits. The thrust of Varity's remarks was that the employees' benefits would remain secure if they voluntarily transferred to Massey Combines. As Varity knew, however, the reality was very different. Indeed, the District Court found that Massey Combines was insolvent from the day of its creation and that it hid a $46 million negative net worth by overvaluing its assets and underestimating its liabilities.

After the presentation, about 1,500 Massey-Ferguson employees accepted Varity's assurances and voluntarily agreed to the transfer. (Varity also unilaterally assigned to Massey Combines the benefit obligations it owed to some 4,000 workers who had retired from Massey-Ferguson prior to this reorganization, without requesting permission or informing them of the assignment.) Unfortunately for these employees, Massey Combines ended its first year with a loss of $88 million, and ended its second year in a receivership, under which its employees lost their nonpension benefits. Many of those employees . . . brought this lawsuit, seeking the benefits they would have been owed under their old, Massey-Ferguson plan, had they not transferred to Massey Combines.

. . .

The remaining question before us is whether or not the remedial provision of ERISA that the beneficiaries invoked, ERISA § 502(a)(3), authorizes this lawsuit for individual relief . . . .

> "Sec. 502. (a) A civil action may be brought — . . . .
>
> *"(3) by a participant, beneficiary, or fiduciary (A) to enjoin any act or practice which violates any provision of this title or the terms of the plan, or (B) to obtain other appropriate equitable relief (i) to redress such violations or (ii) to enforce any provisions of this title or the terms of the plan;*

The District Court held that the third subsection, which we have italicized, authorized this suit and the relief awarded. Varity concedes that the plaintiffs satisfy most of this provision's requirements, namely, that the plaintiffs are plan "participants" or "beneficiaries," and that they are suing for "equitable" relief to "redress" a violation of § 404(a), which is a "provision of this title." Varity does not agree, however, that this lawsuit seeks equitable relief that is "appropriate." In support of this conclusion, Varity makes a complicated, four-step argument:

> *Step One:* Section 502(a)'s *second* subsection says that a plaintiff may bring a civil action "for appropriate relief under section 409."
>
> *Step Two*: Section 409(a), in turn, reads:
>
> "Liability for Breach of Fiduciary Duty
>
> Sec. 409. (a) Any person who is a fiduciary with respect to a plan who breaches any of the responsibilities, obligations, or duties imposed upon fiduciaries by this title shall be personally liable to *make good to such plan any losses to the plan* resulting from each such breach, and to *restore to such plan any profits* of such fiduciary which have been made through use

of assets of the plan by the fiduciary, and shall be subject to such *other equitable or remedial relief* as the court may deem appropriate, including removal of such fiduciary . . . ."

Step Three: In *Massachusetts Mut. Life Ins. Co. v. Russell*, 473 U.S. 134 (1985), this Court pointed to the above-italicized language in § 409 and concluded that this section (and its companion remedial provision, subsection (2)) did not authorize the plaintiff's suit for compensatory and punitive damages against an administrator who had wrongfully delayed payment of her benefit claim. The first two italicized phrases, the Court said, show that § 409's "draftsmen were primarily concerned with the possible misuse of plan assets, and with remedies that would protect the *entire plan*, rather than with the rights of an individual beneficiary." *Id.* (emphasis added). The Court added that, in this context, the last italicized phrase ("other equitable or remedial relief") does not "authorize any relief except for the plan itself." *Id.* at 144.

Step Four: In light of *Russell*, as well as ERISA's language, structure, and purposes, one cannot read the third subsection (the subsection before us) as *including* (as "appropriate") the very kind of action — an action for individual, rather than plan, relief — that this Court found Congress *excluded* in subsection (2). It is at this point, however, that we must disagree with Varity. We have reexamined *Russell*, as well as the relevant statutory language, structure, and purpose. And, in our view, they support the beneficiaries' view of the statute, not Varity's.

First, *Russell* discusses § 502(a)'s *second* subsection, not its *third* subsection, and the language that the Court found limiting appears in a statutory section (§ 409) that the *second* subsection, not the *third*, cross-references. Russell's plaintiff expressly disavowed reliance on the third subsection, perhaps because she was seeking compensatory and punitive damages and subsection (3) authorizes only "equitable" relief. *See Mertens*, 508 U.S. at 255, 256–258 (compensatory and punitive damages are not "equitable relief" within the meaning of subsection (3)); ERISA § 409(a) (authorizing "other equitable or *remedial* relief"). Further, *Russell* involved a complicating factor not present here, in that another remedial provision (subsection (1)) already provided specific relief for the sort of injury the plaintiff had suffered (wrongful denial of benefits), but said "nothing about the recovery of extracontractual damages, or about the possible consequences of delay in the plan administrators' processing of a disputed claim." *Russell, supra* at 144. These differences lead us to conclude that *Russell* does not control, either implicitly or explicitly, the outcome of the case before us.

Second, subsection (3)'s language does not favor Varity. The words of subsection (3) — "appropriate equitable relief" to "redress" any "act or practice which violates any provision of this title" — are broad enough to cover individual relief for breach of a fiduciary obligation. Varity argues that the title of § 409 — "Liability for Breach of Fiduciary Duty" — means that § 409 (and its companion, subsection (2)) cover *all* such liability. But that is not what the title or the provision says. And other language in the statute suggests the contrary. Section 502(1), added in 1989, calculates a certain civil penalty as a percentage of the sum "ordered by a court to be paid by such fiduciary . . . to a plan *or its participants and beneficiaries*" under subsection (5). Subsection (5) is identical to subsection (3), except that it authorizes suits by the Secretary, rather than the participants and beneficiaries. Compare § 502(a)(3) with § 502(a)(5). This new provision, therefore, seems to foresee instances in which the sort of relief provided by both subsection (5) and, by implication, subsection (3), would include an award to "participants and beneficiaries," rather than to the "plan," for breach of fiduciary obligation.

Third, the statute's structure offers Varity little support. Varity notes that the *second* subsection refers specifically (through its § 409 cross-reference) to breaches of fiduciary duty, while the *third* subsection refers, as a kind of "catchall," to all ERISA Title One violations. And it argues that a canon of statutory construction, namely "the specific governs over the general," means that the more specific *second* (fiduciary breach) subsection makes the more general *third* (catchall) subsection inapplicable to claims of fiduciary breach. Canons of construction, however, are simply "rules of thumb" which will sometimes "help courts determine the meaning of legislation." *Connecticut Nat. Bank v. Germain*, 503 U.S. 249, 253 (1992). To apply a canon properly one must understand its rationale. This Court has understood the present canon ("the specific governs the general") as a warning against applying a general provision when doing so would undermine limitations created by a more specific provision. Yet, in this case, why should one believe that Congress intended the specific remedies in § 409 as a limitation?

To the contrary, one can read § 409 as reflecting a special congressional concern about plan asset management without also finding that Congress intended that section to contain the exclusive set of remedies for every kind of fiduciary breach. After all, ERISA makes clear that a fiduciary has obligations other than, and in addition to, managing plan assets. *See* § 3(21)(A) (defining "fiduciary" as one who "exercises any discretionary authority . . . respecting management of such plan *or* . . . respecting management or disposition of its assets") (emphasis added). For example, as the dissent concedes, a plan administrator engages in a fiduciary act when making a discretionary determination about whether a claimant is entitled to benefits under the terms of the plan documents. *See* § 404(a)(1)(D); . . . . And, as the Court pointed out in *Russell*, ERISA specifically provides a remedy for breaches of fiduciary duty with respect to the interpretation of plan documents and the payment of claims, one that is outside the framework of the second subsection and cross-referenced § 409, and one that runs directly to the injured beneficiary. § 502(a)(1)(B). Why should we not conclude that Congress provided yet other remedies for yet other breaches of other sorts of fiduciary obligation in another, "catchall" remedial section?

Such a reading is consistent with § 502's overall structure. Four of that section's six subsections focus upon specific areas, i.e., the first (wrongful denial of benefits and information), the second (fiduciary obligations related to the plan's financial integrity), the fourth (tax registration), and the sixth (civil penalties). The language of the other two subsections, the third and the fifth, creates two "catchalls," providing "appropriate equitable relief" for "any" statutory violation. This structure suggests that these "catchall" provisions act as a safety net, offering appropriate equitable relief for injuries caused by violations that § 502 does not elsewhere adequately remedy. And, contrary to Varity's argument, there is nothing in the legislative history that conflicts with this interpretation . . . .

Fourth, ERISA's basic purposes favor a reading of the third subsection that provides the plaintiffs with a remedy. The statute itself says that it seeks

> "to protect . . . the interests of participants . . . and . . . beneficiaries . . . by establishing standards of conduct, responsibility, and obligation for fiduciaries . . . and . . . providing for appropriate remedies . . . and ready access to the Federal courts." ERISA § 2(b).

Section 404(a), in furtherance of this general objective, requires fiduciaries to discharge their duties "solely in the interest of the participants and beneficiaries." Given these objectives, it is hard to imagine why Congress would want to immunize breaches of fiduciary obligation that harm individuals by denying injured beneficiaries a remedy . . . .

The plaintiffs in this case could not proceed under the first subsection because they were no longer members of the Massey-Ferguson plan and, therefore, had no "benefits due [them] under the terms of [the] plan." § 502(a)(1)(B). They could not proceed under the second subsection because that provision, tied to § 409, does not provide a remedy for individual beneficiaries. *Russell, supra* at 144. They must rely on the third subsection or they have no remedy at all. We are not aware of any ERISA-related purpose that denial of a remedy would serve. Rather, we believe that granting a remedy is consistent with the literal language of the statute, the Act's purposes, and pre-existing trust law.

For these reasons, the judgment of the Court of Appeals is Affirmed.

[Dissenting opinion of Justice Thomas joined by Justice O'Connor and Justice Scalia deleted.]

7-10 QUESTIONS AND PROBLEMS

1. Why didn't participants file suit under ERISA § 502(a)(2)?

2. Is the outcome in *Varity* consistent with *Russell* and *Mertens*?

3. What relief was granted to the plaintiffs?

4. Section 502(a)(3) permits a plan beneficiary to sue a fiduciary for alleged losses to the individual. May a plan beneficiary or participant sue a fiduciary for alleged losses to the plan?

The Supreme Court revisited the difference between equitable and legal relief in the following case.

GREAT-WEST LIFE & ANNUITY INS. CO. v. KNUDSON

534 U.S. 204 (2002)

JUSTICE SCALIA delivered the opinion of the Court.

The question presented is whether § 502(a)(3) of the Employee Retirement Income Security Act of 1974 (ERISA), authorizes this action by petitioners to enforce a reimbursement provision of an ERISA plan.

I

Respondent Janette Knudson was rendered quadriplegic by a car accident in June 1992. Because her then-husband, respondent Eric Knudson, was employed by petitioner Earth Systems, Inc., Janette was covered by the Health and Welfare Plan for Employees and Dependents of Earth Systems, Inc. (Plan). The Plan covered $411,157.11 of Janette's medical expenses, of which all except $75,000 was paid by petitioner Great-West Life & Annuity Insurance Co. pursuant to a "stop-loss" insurance agreement with the Plan.

The Plan includes a reimbursement provision that is the basis for the present lawsuit. This provides that the Plan shall have "the right to recover from the [beneficiary] any payment for benefits" paid by the Plan that the beneficiary is entitled to recover from a third party. Specifically, the Plan has "a first lien upon any recovery, whether by settlement, judgment or otherwise," that the beneficiary receives from the third party, not to exceed "the amount of benefits paid [by the Plan] . . . [or] the amount received by the [beneficiary] for such medical treatment. . . ." If the beneficiary recovers from a third party and fails to reimburse the Plan, "then he will be personally liable to [the Plan] . . . up to the amount of the first lien." *Id.* at 59. Pursuant to an agreement between the Plan and Great-West, the Plan "assigned to Great-West all of its rights to make, litigate, negotiate, settle, compromise, release or waive" any claim under the reimbursement provision.

In late 1993, the Knudsons filed a tort action in California state court seeking to recover from Hyundai Motor Company, the manufacturer of the car they were riding in at the time of the accident, and other alleged tortfeasors. The parties to that action negotiated a $650,000 settlement, a notice of which was mailed to Great-West. This allocated $256,745.30 to a Special Needs Trust to provide for Janette's medical care; $373,426 to attorney's fees and costs; $5,000 to reimburse the California Medicaid program (Medi-Cal); and $13,828.70 (the portion of the settlement attributable to past medical expenses) to satisfy Great-West's claim under the reimbursement provision of the Plan.

. . . .

Great-West . . . filed this action . . . seeking injunctive and declaratory relief under § 502(a)(3) to enforce the reimbursement provision of the Plan by requiring the Knudsons to pay the Plan $411,157.11 of any proceeds recovered from third parties . . . The District Court denied the temporary restraining order, a ruling that petitioners did not appeal. After the state court approved the settlement and the money was disbursed, the District Court granted summary judgment to the Knudsons. It held that the language of the Plan limited its right of reimbursement to the amount received by respondents from third parties *for past medical treatment*, an amount that the state court determined was $13,828.70. The United States Court of Appeals for the Ninth Circuit affirmed . . . it held that judicially decreed reimbursement for payments made to a beneficiary of an insurance plan by a third party is not equitable relief and is therefore not authorized by § 502(a)(3). We granted certiorari.

II

. . .

Section 502(a)(3) authorizes a civil action:

> "by a participant, beneficiary, or fiduciary (A) to enjoin any act or practice which violates . . . the terms of the plan, or (B) to obtain other appropriate equitable relief (i) to redress such violations or (ii) to enforce any provisions of . . . the terms of the plan." [ERISA] § 502(a).

As we explained in *Mertens*, " '[e]quitable' relief must mean something less than *all* relief.' " 508 U.S. at 258 n.8. Thus, in *Mertens* we rejected a reading of the statute that would extend the relief obtainable under § 502(a)(3) to whatever relief a court of equity is empowered to provide in the particular case at issue (which could include legal remedies that would otherwise be beyond the scope of the equity court's authority). Such a reading, we said, would "limit the relief *not at all*" and "render the modifier ['equitable'] superfluous." *Id.* at 257–258. Instead, we held that the term "equitable relief" in § 502(a)(3) must refer to "those categories of relief that were *typically* available in equity. . . ." *Id.* at 256.

Here, petitioners seek, in essence, to impose personal liability on respondents for a contractual obligation to pay money — relief that was not typically available in equity. "A claim for money due and owing under a contract is 'quintessentially an action at law.'" *Wal-Mart Stores, Inc. v. Wells*, 213 F.3d 398, 401 (C.A. 7 2000). "Almost invariably . . . suits seeking (whether by judgment, injunction, or declaration) to compel the defendant to pay a sum of money to the plaintiff are suits for 'money damages,' as that phrase has traditionally been applied, since they seek no more than compensation for loss resulting from the defendant's breach of legal duty." *Bowen v. Massachusetts*, 487 U.S. 879, 918–919 (1988). And "[m]oney damages are, of course, the classic form of *legal* relief." *Mertens, supra* at 255.

Nevertheless, petitioners, along with their *amicus* the United States, struggle to characterize the relief sought as "equitable" under the standard set by *Mertens.* We are not persuaded.

A.

First, petitioners argue that they are entitled to relief under § 502(a)(3)(A) because they seek "to enjoin a[n] act or practice" — respondents' failure to reimburse the Plan — "which violates . . . the terms of the plan." But an injunction to compel the payment of money past due under a contract, or specific performance of a past due monetary obligation, was not typically available in equity.[3] Those rare cases in which a court of equity would decree specific performance of a contract to transfer funds were suits that, unlike the present case, sought to prevent future losses that were either incalculable or would be greater than the sum awarded. For example, specific performance might be available to enforce an agreement to lend money "when the unavailability of alternative financing would leave the plaintiff with injuries that are difficult to value; or to enforce an obligor's duty to make future monthly payments, after the obligor had consistently refused to make past payments conceitedly due, and thus threatened the obligee with the burden of bringing multiple damages actions." *Bowen, supra* at 918. Typically, however, specific performance of a contract to pay money was not available in equity.

. . .

Second, petitioners argue that their suit is authorized by § 502(a)(3)(B) because they seek restitution, which they characterize as a form of equitable relief. However, not all relief falling under the rubric of restitution is available in equity. In the days of the divided bench, restitution was available in certain cases at law, and in certain others in equity. Thus, "restitution is a legal remedy when ordered in a case at law and an equitable remedy . . . when ordered in an equity case," and whether it is legal or equitable depends on "the basis for [the plaintiff's] claim" and the nature of the underlying remedies sought. *Reich v. Continental Casualty Co.*, 33 F.3d 754, 756 (C.A. 7 1994).

In cases in which the plaintiff "could *not* assert title or right to possession of particular property, but in which nevertheless he might be able to show just grounds for recovering money to pay for some benefit the defendant had received from him," the plaintiff had a right to restitution *at law* through an action derived from the common law writ of assumpsit. In such cases, the plaintiff's claim was considered legal because he sought "to obtain a judgment imposing a merely personal liability upon the defendant to pay a sum of money." Restatement of Restitution § 160, Comment *a*, pp. 641–642 (1936). Such claims were viewed essentially as actions at law for breach of contract (whether the contract was actual or implied).

---

[3] Here, of course, there is not only no contrary indication, but the positive indication in paragraph (B) that the injunction referred to in paragraph (A) is an equitable injunction.

In contrast, a plaintiff could seek restitution *in equity*, ordinarily in the form of a constructive trust or an equitable lien, where money or property identified as belonging in good conscience to the plaintiff could clearly be traced to particular funds or property in the defendant's possession. A court of equity could then order a defendant to transfer title (in the case of the constructive trust) or to give a security interest (in the case of the equitable lien) to a plaintiff who was, in the eyes of equity, the true owner. But where "the property [sought to be recovered] or its proceeds have been dissipated so that no product remains, [the plaintiff's] claim is only that of a general creditor," and the plaintiff "cannot enforce a constructive trust of or an equitable lien upon other property of the [defendant]." Restatement of Restitution, *supra*, § 215, Comment *a*, at 867. Thus, for restitution to lie in equity, the action generally must seek not to impose personal liability on the defendant, but to restore to the plaintiff particular funds or property in the defendant's possession.

Here, the funds to which petitioners claim an entitlement under the Plan's reimbursement provision — the proceeds from the settlement of respondents' tort action — are not in respondents' possession. As the order of the state court approving the settlement makes clear, the disbursements from the settlement were paid by two checks, one made payable to the Special Needs Trust and the other to respondents' attorney (who, after deducting his own fees and costs, placed the remaining funds in a client trust account from which he tendered checks to respondents' other creditors, Great-West and Medi-Cal). The basis for petitioners' claim is not that respondents hold particular funds that, in good conscience, belong to petitioners, but that petitioners are contractually entitled to *some* funds for benefits that they conferred. The kind of restitution that petitioners seek, therefore, is not equitable — the imposition of a constructive trust or equitable lien on particular property — but legal — the imposition of personal liability for the benefits that they conferred upon respondents.

Admittedly, our cases have not previously drawn this fine distinction between restitution at law and restitution in equity, but neither have they involved an issue to which the distinction was relevant. In *Mertens*, we mentioned in dicta that "injunction, mandamus, and *restitution*" are categories of relief that were typically available in equity. 508 U.S. at 256 (emphasis added). *Mertens*, however, did not involve a claim for restitution at all; rather, we addressed the question whether a nonfiduciary who knowingly participates in the breach of a fiduciary duty imposed by ERISA is liable to the plan for compensatory damages. *Id.* at 249–250. Thus, as courts and commentators have noted, "all the [Supreme] Court meant [in *Mertens* and other cases] was that restitution, in contrast to damages, is a remedy commonly ordered in equity cases and therefore an equitable remedy in a sense in which damages, though *occasionally* awarded in equity cases, are not." *Reich v. Continental Casualty Co.*, 33 F.3d at 756. *Mertens* did not purport to change the well-settled principle that restitution is "not an *exclusively* equitable remedy," and whether it is legal or equitable in a particular case (and hence whether it is authorized by § 502(a)(3)) remains dependent on the nature of the relief sought.

. . .

Justice Ginsburg's dissent finds it dispositive that *some* restitutionary remedies were typically available in equity. In her view, the touchstone for distinguishing legal from equitable relief is the "substance of the relief requested," — and since the "substantive" relief of restitution is typically available in equity, it is, she concludes, available under § 502(a)(3). It is doubtful, to begin with, that "restitution" — or at least restitution defined broadly enough to embrace those forms of restitution available at law — pertains to the *substance* of the relief rather than to the legal theory under which it is awarded. The "substance" of a money judgment is a compelled transfer of money; a money judgment *for restitution* could be thought to identify a particular *type* of relief (rather than merely the theory on which relief is awarded) only if one were to limit restitution to the return of identifiable funds (or property) belonging to the plaintiff and held by the defendant — that is, to limit restitution to the form of restitution traditionally available in equity.

In any event, Justice Ginsburg's approach, which looks only to the nature of the relief and not to the conditions that equity attached to its provision, logically leads to the same untenable conclusion reached by Justice Stevens's dissent — which is that § 502(a)(3)(A)'s explicit authorization of injunction, which it identifies as a form of equitable relief, permits (what equity would never permit) an injunction against failure to pay a simple indebtedness — or, for that matter, an injunction against failure to pay punitive damages. The problem with that conclusion, of course, is that it renders the statute's limitation of relief to "[injunction] . . . or other appropriate equitable relief' ' utterly pointless. It is easy to disparage the law-equity dichotomy as "an ancient classification," (opinion of Ginsburg, J.), and an "obsolete distinctio[n]," (opinion of Stevens, J.). Like it or not, however, that classification and distinction has been specified by the statute; and there is no way to give the specification meaning — indeed, there is no way to render the unmistakable limitation of the statute a limitation *at all* — except by adverting to the differences between law and equity to which the statute refers. The dissents greatly exaggerate, moreover, the difficulty of that task. Congress felt comfortable referring to equitable relief in this statute — as it has in many others — precisely because the basic contours of the term are well known. Rarely will there be need for any more "antiquarian inquiry," (opinion of Ginsburg, J.), than consulting, as we have done, standard current works such as Dobbs, Palmer, Corbin, and the Restatements, which make the answer clear . . . .

Justice Stevens finds it "difficult . . . to understand why Congress would not have wanted to provide recourse in federal court for the plan violation disclosed by the record in this case." It is, however, not our job to find reasons for what Congress has plainly done; and it *is* our job to avoid rendering what Congress has plainly done (here, limit the available relief) devoid of reason and effect. If, as Justice Ginsburg surmises, Congress meant to rule out nothing more than "compensatory and punitive damages," it could simply have said that. That Congress sought to achieve this result by subtle reliance upon the dissenters' novel and expansive view of equity is most implausible.

Respecting Congress's choice to limit the relief available under § 502(a)(3) to "equitable relief" requires us to recognize the difference between legal and equitable forms of restitution. Because petitioners seek only the former, their suit is not authorized by § 502(a)(3).

C

Third, the United States, as petitioners' amicus, argues that the common law of trusts provides petitioners with equitable remedies that allow them to bring this action under § 592(a)(3). Analogizing respondents to beneficiaries of a trust, the United States argues that a trustee could bring a suit to enforce an agreement by a beneficiary to pay money into a trust or to repay an advance made from the trustor to repay an advance made from the trust. These trust remedies are simply inapposite. In *Mertens*, we rejected the claim that the special equity-court powers applicable to trusts define the reach of § 502(a)(3). Instead, we held that the term "equitable relief" in § 502(a)(3) must refer to "those categories of relief that were *typically* available in equity. . . ." 508 U.S. at 256 . . . .

. . .

III

In the end, petitioners ask us to interpret § 502(a)(3) so as to prevent them "from being deprived of any remedy under circumstances where such a result clearly would be inconsistent with a primary purpose of ERISA," namely, the enforcement of the terms of a plan. We note, though it is not necessary to our decision, that there may have been other means for petitioners to obtain the essentially legal relief that they seek. We express no opinion as to whether petitioners could have intervened in the state-court tort action brought by respondents or whether a direct action by petitioners against respondents asserting state-law claims such as breach of contract would have been pre-empted by ERISA. Nor do we decide whether petitioners could have obtained equitable relief against respondents' attorney and the trustee of the Special Needs Trust, since petitioners did not appeal the District Court's denial of their motion to amend their complaint to add these individuals as codefendant.

"We need not decide these issues because, as we explained in *Mertens*, "[e]ven assuming . . . that petitioners are correct about the pre-emption of previously avai lable state-court actions" or the lack of other means to obtain relief, "vague notions of a statute's 'basic purpose' are nonetheless inadequate to overcome the words of its text regarding the *specific* issue under consideration." 508 U.S. at 261. In the very same section of ERISA as § 502(a)(3), Congress authorized "a participant or beneficiary" to bring a civil action "to enforce his rights under the terms of the plan," without reference to whether the relief sought is legal or equitable. [ERISA] § 502(a)(1)(B). But Congress did not extend the same authorization to fiduciaries. Rather, § 502(a)(3), by its terms, only allows for *equitable* relief. We will not attempt to adjust the "carefully crafted and detailed enforcement scheme" embodied in the text that Congress has adopted. *Mertens, supra* at 254. Because petitioners are seeking legal relief — the imposition of personal liability on respondents for a contractual obligation to pay money — § 502(a)(3) does not authorize this action. Accordingly, we affirm the judgment of the Court of Appeals.

It is so ordered.

[JUSTICE STEVENS' separate dissent deleted.]

JUSTICE GINSBURG, with whom JUSTICE STEVENS, JUSTICE SOUTER, and JUSTICE BREYER join, dissenting.

Today's holding, the majority declares, is compelled by "Congress's choice to limit the relief available under § 502(a)(3)." In the Court's view, Congress' placement of the word "equitable" in that provision signaled an intent to exhume the "fine distinction[s]" borne of the "days of the divided bench," to treat as dispositive an ancient classification unrelated to the substance of the relief sought; and to obstruct the general goals of ERISA by relegating to state court (or to no court at all) an array of suits involving the interpretation of employee health plan provisions. Because it is plain that Congress made no such "choice," I dissent.

The rarified rules underlying this rigid and time-bound conception of the term "equity" were hardly at the fingertips of those who enacted § 502(a)(3). By 1974, when ERISA became law, the "days of the divided bench" were a fading memory, for that era had ended nearly 40 years earlier with the advent of the Federal Rules of Civil Procedure . . . .

It is thus fanciful to attribute to members of the 93d Congress familiarity with those "needless and obsolete distinctions," much less a deliberate "choice" to resurrect and import them wholesale into the modern regulatory scheme laid out in ERISA. "[T]here is nothing to suggest that ERISA's drafters wanted to embed their work in a time warp. *Health Cost Controls of Ill. v. Washington*, 187 F.3d 703 (C.A. 7 1999) . . . .

It is particularly ironic that the majority acts in the name of equity as it sacrifices congressional intent and statutory purpose to archaic and unyielding doctrine. "Equity eschews mechanical rules; it depends on flexibility . . .

II

Unprepared to agree that Congress chose to infuse § 502(a)(3) with the recondite distinctions on which the majority relies, I would accord a different meaning to the term "equitable." Consistent with what Congress likely intended and with our decision in *Mertens*, I would look to the substance of the relief requested and ask whether relief of that character was "*typically* available in equity." *Mertens*, 508 U.S. at 256. Great-West seeks restitution, a category of relief fully meeting that measure even if the remedy was also available in cases brought at law. Accordingly, I would not oust this case from the federal courts.

Today's decision needlessly obscures the meaning and complicates the application of § 502(a)(3). The Court's interpretation of that provision embroils federal courts in "recondite controversies better left to legal historians" and yields results that are demonstrably at odds with Congress' goals in enacting ERISA. Because in my view Congress cannot plausibly be said to have "carefully crafted" such confusion, I dissent.

7-11 QUESTIONS AND PROBLEMS

1. To what extent is *Great-West* an extension or an affirmation of *Mertens*?

2. Why should relief be available when the employer deliberately misleads its employees as in *Varity*, but not when the employer is only guilty of negligence?

3. Is the court correct in stating that ERISA fails to provide a remedy and so it is for Congress to act or have the courts created a right without a remedy by virtue of how they have chosen to read the statute?

4. In October 2007, Susan began working for Kappa Co., which offered a long-term disability insurance policy, at no cost to its employees. On July 1, 2008, Martin, the Human Resource manager of Kappa, wrote to the policy carrier to cancel the policy. He mistakenly thought he had been instructed to terminate the policy.

On October 1, 2008, Susan was involved in an automobile accident and suffered serious injuries. Believing that she was covered under the disability policy, Susan submitted a claim for long-term disability benefits. But as the policy had already been cancelled, no benefits were paid.

On October 10, 2008, Ken, the President of Kappa, sent a letter informing all employees that the disability policy had been "cancelled inadvertently" "[b]ecause of some communication errors."

Susan filed suit in federal district court, alleging breach of fiduciary duty by Kappa under ERISA. She claimed that because she believed she was already covered she did not purchase outside disability insurance. She further claimed that Kappa had a fiduciary duty to "provide complete and accurate information about the status of the employee benefits plan," which included "providing notice of the discontinuation or suspension of coverage." According to her, Kappa violated its fiduciary duty to g ive adequate notice by concealing the fact that it had cancelled the policy. Susan sought either an order reinstating her disability benefits, or, in the alternative, other orders that would provide substantive relief equivalent to the reinstatement of the disability benefits.

Kappa moved for summary judgment claiming that Susan's request for a reinstatement of benefits or substantive relief equivalent to the reinstatement of benefits would be a compensatory monetary recovery not permitted under *Great-West Life & Annuity Insurance Co. v. Knudson*. What result?

If benefits are delayed, the lower court has the discretion to award prejudgment interest based upon general equitable principles, even though ERISA does not specifically provide for it. *Wells v. United States Steel & Carnegie Pension Fund*, 76 F.3d 731 (6th Cir. 1996). The rate of interest is left to the discretion of the district court. *Ford v. Uniroyal Pension Plan*, 154 F.3d 613 (6th Cir. 1998). The Third Circuit has held that a plan beneficiary may bring an action for interest on delayed benefit payments even though the beneficiary received the underlying benefits and therefore has no grounds to sue for unpaid benefits. *Fotta v. Trustees of United Mine Workers*, 165 F.3d 209 (3d Cir. 1998). By federal statute postjudgment interest is allowed on all money judgments (28 U.S.C. § 1961), with the rate based upon the interest rate for United States Treasury bills.

In 2006, the Supreme Court considered yet again the distinction between equitable and legal relief.

SEREBOFF v. MID ATLANTIC MEDICAL SERVICES, INC.

547 U.S. 356 (2006)

CHIEF JUSTICE ROBERTS.

In this case we consider again the circumstances in which a fiduciary under the Employee Retirement Income Security Act of 1974 (ERISA) may sue a beneficiary for reimbursement of medical expenses paid by the ERISA plan, when the beneficiary has recovered for its injuries from a third party.

I

Marlene Sereboff's employer sponsors a health insurance plan administered by respondent Mid Atlantic Medical Services, Inc., and covered by ERISA. Marlene Sereboff and her husband Joel are beneficiaries under the plan. The plan provides for payment of certain covered medical expenses and contains an "Acts of Third Parties" provision. This provision "applies when [a beneficiary is] sick or injured as a result of the act or omission of another person or party," and requires a beneficiary who "receives benefits" under the plan for such injuries to "reimburse [Mid Atlantic]" for those benefits from "[a]ll recoveries from a third party (whether by lawsuit, settlement, or otherwise)." The provision states that "[Mid Atlantic's] share of the recovery will not be reduced because [the beneficiary] has not received the full damages claimed, unless [Mid Atlantic] agrees in writing to a reduction."

The Sereboffs were involved in an automobile accident in California and suffered injuries. Pursuant to the plan's coverage provisions, the plan paid the couple's medical expenses. The Sereboffs filed a tort action in state court against several third parties, seeking compensatory damages for injuries suffered as a result of the accident. Soon after the suit was commenced, Mid Atlantic sent the Sereboffs' attorney a letter asserting a lien on the anticipated proceeds from the suit, for the medical expenses Mid Atlantic paid on the Sereboffs' behalf. On several occasions over the next 2½ years, Mid Atlantic sent similar correspondence to the attorney and to the Sereboffs, repeating its claim to a lien on a portion of the Sereboffs' recovery, and detailing the medical expenses as they accrued and were paid by the plan.

The Sereboffs' tort suit eventually settled for $750,000. Neither the Sereboffs nor their attorney sent any money to Mid Atlantic in satisfaction of its claimed lien which, after Mid Atlantic completed its payments on the Sereboffs' behalf, totaled $74,869.37.

Mid Atlantic filed suit in District Court under § 502(a)(3) of ERISA, seeking to collect from the Sereboffs the medical expenses it had paid on their behalf. Since the Sereboffs' attorney had already distributed the settlement proceeds to them, Mid Atlantic sought a temporary restraining order and preliminary injunction requiring the couple to retain and set aside at least $74,869.37 from the proceeds. The District Court approved a stipulation by the parties, under which the Sereboffs agreed to "preserve $74,869.37 of the settlement funds" in an investment account, "until the [District] Court rules on the merits of this case and all appeals, if any, are exhausted."

On the merits, the District Court found in Mid Atlantic's favor and ordered the Sereboffs to pay Mid Atlantic the $74,869.37, plus interest, with a deduction for Mid Atlantic's share of the attorney's fees and court costs the Sereboffs had incurred in state court. The Sereboffs appealed and the Fourth Circuit affirmed in relevant part. The Fourth Circuit observed that the Courts of Appeal are divided on the question whether § 502(a)(3) authorizes recovery in these circumstances. We granted certiorari to resolve the disagreement.

II

A

A fiduciary may bring a civil action under § 502(a)(3) of ERISA "(A) to enjoin any act or practice which violates any provision of this subchapter or the terms of the plan, or (B) to obtain other appropriate equitable relief (i) to redress such violations or (ii) to enforce any provisions of this subchapter or the terms of the plan." [ERISA § 502(a)(3).] There is no dispute that Mid Atlantic is a fiduciary under ERISA and that its suit in District Court was to "enforce . . . the terms of" the "Acts of Third Parties" provision in the Sereboffs' plan. The only question is whether the relief Mid Atlantic requested from the District Court was "equitable" under § 502(a)(3)(B).

This is not the first time we have had occasion to clarify the scope of the remedial power conferred on district courts by § 502(a)(3)(B). In *Mertens v. Hewitt Associates*, 508 U.S. 248 (1993), we construed the provision to authorize only "those categories of relief that were *typically* available in equity," and thus rejected a claim that we found sought "nothing other than compensatory *damages*." *Id.* at 255–256. We elaborated on this construction of § 502(a)(3)(B) in *Great-West Life & Annuity Ins. Co. v. Knudson*, 534 U.S. 204 (2002), which involved facts similar to those in this case. Much like the "Acts of Third Parties" provision in the Sereboffs' plan, the plan in *Knudson* reserved " 'a first lien upon any recovery, whether by settlement, judgment or otherwise,' that the beneficiary receives from [a] third party." *Id.* at 207. After Knudson was involved in a car accident, Great-West paid medical bills on her behalf and, when she recovered in tort from a third party for her injuries, Great-West sought to collect from her for the medical bills it had paid.

In response to the argument that Great-West's claim in *Knudson* was for "restitution" and thus equitable under § 502(a)(3)(B) and *Mertens*, we noted that "not all relief falling under the rubric of restitution [was] available in equity." 534 U.S. at 212. To decide whether the restitutionary relief sought by Great-West was equitable or legal, we examined cases and secondary legal materials to determine if the relief would have been equitable "[i]n the days of the divided bench." *Ibid.* We explained that one feature of equitable restitution was that it sought to impose a constructive trust or equitable lien on "particular funds or property in the defendant's possession." *Id.* at 213. That requirement was not met in *Knudson*, because "the funds to which petitioners claim[ed] an entitlement" were not in Knudson's possession, but had instead been placed in a "Special Needs Trust" under California law. *Id.* at 207, 214. The kind of relief Great-West sought, therefore, was "not equitable — the imposition of a constructive trust or equitable lien on particular property — but legal — the imposition of personal liability for the benefits that [Great-West] conferred upon [Knudson]." *Id.* at 214. We accordingly determined that the suit could not proceed under § 502(a)(3). *Ibid.*

That impediment to characterizing the relief in *Knudson* as equitable is not present here. As the Fourth Circuit explained below, in this case Mid Atlantic sought "specifically identifiable" funds that were "within the possession and control of t he Sereboffs" — that portion of the tort settlement due Mid Atlantic under the terms of the ERISA plan, set aside and "preserved [in the Sereboffs'] investment accounts." 407 F.3d at 218. Unlike Great-West, Mid Atlantic did not simply seek "to impose personal liability . . . for a contractual obligation to pay money." *Knudson*, 534 U.S. at 210. It alleged breach of contract and sought money, to be sure, but it sought its recovery through a constructive trust or equitable lien on a specifically identified fund, not from the Sereboffs' assets generally, as would be the case with a contract action at law. ERISA provides for equitable remedies *to enforce plan terms*, so the fact that the action involves a breach of contract can hardly be enough to prove relief is not equitable; that would make § 502(a)(3)(B)(ii) an empty promise. This Court in *Knudson* did not reject Great-West's suit out of hand because it alleged a breach of contract and sought money, but because Great-West did not seek to recover a particular fund from the defendant. Mid Atlantic does.

B

While Mid Atlantic's case for characterizing its relief as equitable thus does not falter because of the nature of the recovery it seeks, Mid Atlantic must still establish that the basis for its claim is equitable. Our case law from the days of the divided bench confirms that Mid Atlantic's claim is equitable. In *Barnes v. Alexander*, 232 U.S. 117 (1914), for instance, attorneys Street and Alexander performed work for Barnes, another attorney, who promised them "one-third of the contingent fee" he expected in the case. *Id.* at 119. In upholding their equitable claim to this portion of the fee, Justice Holmes recited "the familiar rul[e] of equity that a contract to convey a specific object even before it is acquired will make the contractor a trustee as soon as he gets a title to the thing." *Id.* at 121. On the basis of this rule, he concluded that Barnes' undertaking "create[d] a lien" upon the portion of the monetary recovery due Barnes from the client, *ibid.*, which Street and Alexander could "follow . . . into the hands of . . . Barnes," "as soon as [the fund] was identified," *id.* at 123.

Much like Barnes' promise to Street and Alexander, the "Acts of Third Parties" provision in the Sereboffs' plan specifically identified a particular fund, distinct from the Sereboffs' general assets — "[a]ll recoveries from a third party (whether by lawsuit, settlement, or otherwise)" — and a particular share of that fund to which Mid Atlantic was entitled — "that portion of the total recovery which is due [Mid Atlantic] for benefits paid." Like Street and Alexander in *Barnes*, therefore, Mid Atlantic could rely on a "familiar rul[e] of equity" to collect for the medical bills it had paid on the Sereboffs' behalf. Barnes, *supra*, at 121. This rule allowed them to "follow" a portion of the recovery "into the [Sereboffs'] hands" "as soon as [the settlement fund] was identified," and impose on that portion a constructive trust or equitable lien. 232 U.S. at 123.

. . .

Under the teaching of *Barnes* and similar cases, Mid Atlantic's action in the District Court properly sought "equitable relief" under § 502(a)(3); the judgment of the Fourth Circuit is affirmed in relevant part.

It is so ordered.

7-12 QUESTIONS AND PROBLEMS

1. Suppose the $257,000 allocated for future medical expenses had been paid to Ms. Knudson rather than to a trust. Would that have changed the outcome of the case? What if Ms. Knudson had been paid the $257,000 but spent it before Great-West sued her? What result?

2. In a footnote in *Great-West* Justice Scalia wrote:

> *Varity Corp. v. Howe*, upon which petitioners rely, is not to the contrary. In *Varity Corp.*, we explained that § 502(a)(3) is a " 'catchall' provisio[n]" that "act[s] as a safety net, offering appropriate equitable relief for injuries caused by violations that § 502 does not elsewhere adequately remedy." Thus, we concluded that § 502(a)(3) authorizes lawsuits by beneficiaries for individualized equitable relief for breach of fiduciary obligations, notwithstanding the petitioner's argument that such relief is not "appropriate" because § 502(a)(2) and § 409 of ERISA specifically address liability for breach of fiduciary duty and preclude individualized relief.
>
> In *Varity Corp.*, however, it was undisputed that respondents were seeking *equitable* relief, and the question was whether such relief was "appropriate" in light of the apparent lack of alternative remedies. *Varity Corp.* did not hold, as petitioners urge us to conclude today, that § 502(a)(3) is a catchall provision that authorizes all relief that is consistent with ERISA's purposes and is not explicitly provided elsewhere. To accept petitioners' argument is to ignore the plain language of the statute, which provides fiduciaries with only equitable relief.

Has the Court correctly interpreted the holding in *Varity*? Does *Great-West* limit or modify the holding in *Varity*?

3. In his dissent Justice Stevens wrote:

> In a response to this dissent that echoes Tennyson's poem about the Light Brigade — "Theirs not to reason why, Theirs but to do and die" — the Court states that it is "not our job to find reasons for what Congress has

> plainly done," Congress, of course, has the power to enact unreasonable laws. Nevertheless, instead of blind obedience to what at first blush appears to be such a law, I think it both prudent and respectful to pause to ask why Congress would do so.

Is Justice Stevens correct to claim that the majority interprets ERISA in a way that makes it an "unreasonable law"?

4. Is *Sereboff* new law or is it just an application of the holding in *Great-West*?

5. When the Court interprets the ERISA statute is it the duty of the Court to:

- attempt to read the language literally?
- interpret the statute in a common sense manner?
- interpret the statute with Congressional intent as its guide?
- attempt to interpret the statute in a manner that makes it internally consistent?
- attempt to interpret in a manner that promotes its general principals, goals and values?
- interpret it in a manner that fills in gaps or possible inconsistencies?

6. Phi Co. instituted an early retirement plan that included a sizeable lump-sum distribution. Leah accepted the proposal. After she retired, she learned that a significant amount of the lump-sum distribution that she received was taxable. In announcing the plan, Phi Co. had implied that the lump-sum was tax free and had not disclosed the adverse income tax consequences. Leah sued Phi Co. In federal court under ERISA under §§ 404 for violation of its fiduciary duty of loyalty and requested relief under § 409. Citing *Varity*, the court found that Phi Co. had violated its fiduciary duty of loyalty when it failed to deal fairly and honestly with Leah. In her complaint, Leah sought a remedy in the form of requiring Phi Co. to reimburse her for the taxes that she paid on the lump-sum distribution. Can the court award Leah these damages under § 502(a)(3)?

In 2011, the Supreme Court again considered what is meant by the term "equitable remedies" under ERISA § 502(a)(3).

CIGNA CORPORATION v. AMARA (PART III)

131 S. Ct. 1866 (2011)

Justice Breyer delivered the opinion of the Court.

In 1998, petitioner CIGNA Corporation changed the nature of its basic pension plan for employees. Previously, the plan provided a retiring employee with a defined benefit in the form of an annuity calculated on the basis of his preretirement salary and length of service. The new plan provided most retiring employees with a (lump sum) cash balance calculated on the basis of a defined annual contribution from CIGNA as increased by compound interest. Because many employees had already earned at least some old-plan benefits, the new plan translated already-earned benefits into an opening amount in the employee's cash balance account.

Respondents, acting on behalf of approximately 25,000 beneficiaries of the CIGNA Pension Plan (which is also a petitioner here), challenged CIGNA's adoption of the new plan. They claimed in part that CIGNA had failed to give them proper notice of changes to their benefits, particularly because the new plan in certain respects provided them with less generous benefits.

The District Court agreed that the disclosures made by CIGNA violated its obligations under ERISA. In determining relief, the court found that CIGNA's notice failures had caused the employees "likely harm." The Court then reformed the new plan and ordered CIGNA to pay benefits accordingly. It found legal authority for doing so in ERISA § 502(a)(1)(B), 29 U.S.C. § 1132(a)(1)(B) (authorizing a plan "participant or beneficiary" to bring a "civil action" to "recover benefits due to him under the terms of his plan").

We agreed to decide whether the District Court applied the correct legal standard, namely, a "likely harm" standard, in determining that CIGNA's notice violations caused its employees sufficient injury to warrant legal relief. To reach that question, we must first consider a more general matter — whether the ERISA section just mentioned (ERISA's recovery-of-benefits-due provision, § 502(a)(1)(B)) authorizes entry of the relief the District Court provided. We conclude that it does not authorize this relief. Nonetheless, we find that a different equity-related ERISA provision, to which the District Court also referred, authorizes forms of relief similar to those that the court entered. § 502(a)(3).

Section 502(a)(3) authorizes "appropriate equitable relief" for violations of ERISA. Accordingly, the relevant standard of harm will depend upon the equitable theory by which the District Court provides relief. We leave it to the District Court to conduct that analysis in the first instance, but we identify equitable principles that the court might apply on remand.

. . .

A

Under CIGNA's pre-1998 defined-benefit retirement plan, an employee with at least five years service would receive an annuity annually paying an amount that depended upon the employee's salary and length of service. Depending on when the employee had joined CIGNA, the annuity would equal either (1) 2 percent of the employee's average salary over his final three years with CIGNA, multiplied by the number of years worked (up to 30); or (2) 1 2/3 percent of the employee's average salary over his final five years with CIGNA, multiplied by the number of years worked (up to 35). Calculated either way, the annuity would approach 60 percent of a longtime employee's final salary. A well-paid longtime employee, earning, say, $160,000 per year, could receive a retirement annuity paying the employee about $96,000 per year until his death. The plan offered many employees at least one other benefit: They could retire early, at age 55, and receive an only-somewhat-reduced annuity.

In November 1997, CIGNA sent its employees a newsletter announcing that it intended to put in place a new pension plan. The new plan would substitute an "account balance plan" for CIGNA's pre-existing defined-benefit system. App. 991a (emphasis deleted). The newsletter added that the old plan would end on December 31, 1997, that CIGNA would introduce (and describe) the new plan sometime during 1998, and that the new plan would apply retroactively to January 1, 1998.

. . .

But what about the retirement benefits that employees had already earned prior to January 1, 1998? CIGNA promised to make an initial contribution to the individual's account equal to the value of that employee's already earned benefits. And the new plan set forth a method for calculating that initial contribution. The method consisted of calculating the amount as of the employee's (future) retirement date of the annuity to which the employee's salary and length of service already (*i.e.*, as of December 31, 1997) entitled him and then discounting that sum to its present (*i.e.*, January 1, 1998) value.

The new plan also provided employees a guarantee: An employee would receive upon retirement either (1) the amount to which he or she had become entitled as of January 1, 1998, or (2) the amount then in his or her individual account, whichever was greater.

. . .

B

1

The District Court found that CIGNA's initial descriptions of its new plan were significantly incomplete and misled its employees . . . .

* * *

The District Court concluded, as a matter of law, that CIGNA's representations (and omissions) about the plan, made between November 1997 (when it announced the plan) and December 1998 (when it put the plan into effect) violated:

. . .

(b) ERISA §§ 102(a) and 104(b), which require a plan administrator to provide beneficiaries with summary plan descriptions and with summaries of material modifications, "written in a manner calculated to be understood by the average plan participant," that are "sufficiently accurate and comprehensive to reasonably apprise such participants and beneficiaries of their rights and obligations under the plan."

* * *

For these reasons taken together we conclude that the summary documents, important as they are, provide communication with beneficiaries *about* the plan, but that their statements do not themselves constitute the *terms* of the plan for purposes of § 502(a)(1)(B). We also conclude that the District Court could not find authority in that section to reform CIGNA's plan as written.

B

If § 502(a)(1)(B) does not authorize entry of the relief here at issue, what about nearby § 502(a)(3)? That provision allows a participant, beneficiary, or fiduciary "to obtain other *appropriate equitable relief*" to redress violations of (here relevant) parts of ERISA "or the terms of the plan." 29 ERISA § 502(a)(3) (emphasis added). The District Court strongly implied, but did not directly hold, that it would base its relief upon this subsection were it not for (1) the fact that the preceding "plan benefits due" provision, § 502(a)(1)(B), provided sufficient authority; and (2) certain cases from this Court that narrowed the application of the term "appropriate equitable relief," see, *e.g.*, *Mertens*, 508 U.S. 248; *Great-West*, 534 U.S. 204. Our holding in Part II-A, *supra*, removes the District Court's first obstacle. And given the likelihood that, on remand, the District Court will turn to and rely upon this alternative subsection, we consider the court's second concern. We find that concern misplaced.

We have interpreted the term "appropriate equitable relief" in § 502(a)(3) as referring to " 'those categories of relief' " that, traditionally speaking (*i.e.*, prior to the merger of law and equity) " 'were *typically* available in equity.' " *Sereboff*, 547 U.S. at 361 (quoting *Mertens*, 508 U.S. at 256). In *Mertens*, we applied this principle to a claim seeking money damages brought by a beneficiary against a private firm that provided a trustee with actuarial services. We found that the plaintiff sought "nothing other than compensatory damages" against a nonfiduciary. *Id.* at 253, 255 (emphasis deleted). And we held that such a claim, traditionally speaking, was legal, not equitable, in nature. *Id.* at 255.

In *Great-West*, we considered a claim brought by a fiduciary against a tort-award-winning beneficiary seeking monetary reimbursement for medical outlays that the plan had previously made on the beneficiary's behalf. We noted that the fiduciary sought to obtain a lien attaching to (or a constructive trust imposed upon) money that the beneficiary had received from the tort-case defendant. But we noted that the money in question was not the "particular" money that the tort defendant had paid. And, traditionally speaking, relief that sought a lien or a constructive trust was legal relief, not equitable relief, unless the funds in question were "*particular* funds or property in the defendant's possession." 534 U.S. at 213 (emphasis added).

The case before us concerns a suit by a beneficiary against a plan fiduciary (whom ERISA typically treats as a trustee) about the terms of a plan (which ERISA typically treats as a trust). It is the kind of lawsuit that, before the merger of law and equity, respondents could have brought only in a court of equity, not a court of law. 4 A. Scott, W. Fratcher, & M. Ascher, Trusts § 24.1, p. 1654 (5th ed. 2007) (hereinafter Scott & Ascher) ("Trusts are, and always have been, the bailiwick of the courts of equity"); *Duvall v. Craig*, 4 L. Ed. 180, 2 Wheat. 45, 56 (1817) (a trustee was "only suable in equity").

With the exception of the relief now provided by § 502(a)(1)(B), Restatement (Second) of Trusts §§ 198(1)–(2) (1957) (hereinafter Second Restatement); 4 Scott & Ascher § 24.2.1, the remedies available to those courts of equity were traditionally considered equitable remedies, see Second Restatement § 199; J. Adams, Doctrine of Equity: A Commentary on the Law as Administered by the Court of Chancery 61 (7th Am. ed. 1881) (hereinafter Adams); 4 Scott & Ascher § 24.2.

The District Court's affirmative and negative injunctions obviously fall within this category. *Mertens*, *supra*, at 256 (identifying injunctions, mandamus, and restitution as equitable relief). And other relief ordered by the District Court resembles forms of traditional equitable relief. That is because equity chancellors developed a host of other "distinctively equitable" remedies — remedies that were "fitted to the nature of the primary right" they were intended to protect. 1 S. Symons, Pomeroy's Equity Jurisprudence § 108, pp. 139–140 (5th ed. 1941) (hereinafter Pomeroy). See generally 1 J. Story, Commentaries on Equity Jurisprudence § 692 (12th ed. 1877) (hereinafter Story). Indeed, a maxim of equity states that "[e]quity suffers not a right to be without a remedy." R. Francis, Maxims of Equity 29 (1st Am. ed. 1823). And the relief entered here, insofar as it does not consist of injunctive relief, closely resembles three other traditional equitable remedies.

First, what the District Court did here may be regarded as the reformation of the terms of the plan, in order to remedy the false or misleading information CIGNA provided. The power to reform contracts (as contrasted with the power to enforce contracts as written) is a traditional power of an equity court, not a court of law, and was used to prevent fraud.

Second, the District Court's remedy essentially held CIGNA to what it had promised, namely, that the new plan would not take from its employees benefits they had already accrued. This aspect of the remedy resembles estoppel, a traditional equitable remedy. Equitable estoppel "operates to place the person entitled to its benefit in the same position he would have been in had the representations been true." Eaton § 62, at 176. And, as Justice Story long ago pointed out, equitable estoppel "forms a very essential element in . . . fair dealing, and rebuke of all fraudulent misrepresentation, which it is the boast of courts of equity constantly to promote." 2 Story § 1533, at 776.

Third, the District Court injunctions require the plan administrator to pay to already retired beneficiaries money owed them under the plan as reformed. But the fact that this relief takes the form of a money payment does not remove it from the category of traditionally equitable relief. Equity courts possessed the power to provide relief in the form of monetary "compensation" for a loss resulting from a trustee's breach of duty, or to prevent the trustee's unjust enrichment. Restatement (Third) of Trusts § 95, and Comment *a* (Tent. Draft No. 5, Mar. 2, 2009) (hereinafter Third Restatement); Eaton §§ 211-212, at 440. Indeed, prior to the merger of law and equity this kind of monetary remedy against a trustee, sometimes called a "surcharge," was "exclusively equitable." *Princess Lida of Thurn and Taxis v. Thompson*, 305 U.S. 456 (1939).

The surcharge remedy extended to a breach of trust committed by a fiduciary encompassing any violation of a duty imposed upon that fiduciary. See Second Restatement § 201; Adams 59; 4 Pomeroy § 1079; 2 Story §§ 1261, 1268. Thus, insofar as an award of make-whole relief is concerned, the fact that the defendant in this case, unlike the defendant in *Mertens*, is analogous to a trustee makes a critical difference. See 508 U.S. at 262 263. In sum, contrary to the District Court's fears, the types of remedies the court entered here fall within the scope of the term "appropriate equitable relief" in § 502(a)(3).

III

Section 502(a)(3) invokes the equitable powers of the District Court. We cannot know with certainty which remedy the District Court understood itself to be imposing, nor whether the District Court will find it appropriate to exercise its discretion under § 502(a)(3) to impose that remedy on remand. We need not decide which remedies are appropriate on the facts of this case in order to resolve the parties' dispute as to the appropriate legal standard in determining whether members of the relevant employee class were injured.

The relevant substantive provisions of ERISA do not set forth any particular standard for determining harm. They simply require the plan administrator to write and to distribute written notices that are "sufficiently accurate and comprehensive to reasonably apprise" plan participants and beneficiaries of "their rights and obligations under the plan." § 102(a); see also §§ 104(b), 204(h). Nor can we find a definite standard in the ERISA provision, § 502(a)(3) (which authorizes the court to enter "appropriate equitable relief" to redress ERISA "violations"). Hence any requirement of harm must come from the law of equity.

Looking to the law of equity, there is no general principle that "detrimental reliance" must be proved before a remedy is decreed. To the extent any such requirement arises, it is because the specific remedy being contemplated imposes such a requirement. Thus, as CIGNA points out, when equity courts used the remedy of *estoppel*, they insisted upon a showing akin to detrimental reliance, *i.e.*, that the defendant's statement "in truth, influenced the conduct of" the plaintiff, causing "prejudic[e]." Eaton § 61, at 175; see 3 Pomeroy § 805. Accordingly, when a court exercises its authority under § 502(a)(3) to impose a remedy equivalent to estoppel, a showing of detrimental reliance must be made.

But this showing is not always necessary for other equitable remedies. Equity courts, for example, would reform contracts to reflect the mutual understanding of the contracting parties where "fraudulent suppression[s], omission[s], or insertion[s]," 1 Story § 154, at 149, "material[ly] . . . affect[ed]" the "substance" of the contract, even if the "complaining part[y]" was negligent in not realizing its mistake, as long as its negligence did not fall below a standard of "reasonable prudence" and violate a legal duty. 3 Pomeroy §§ 856, 856b, at 334, 340–341; see *Baltzer*, 115 U.S. at 645, 6 S. Ct. 216; Eaton § 307(b).

Nor did equity courts insist upon a showing of detrimental reliance in cases where they ordered "surcharge." Rather, they simply ordered a trust or beneficiary made whole following a trustee's breach of trust. In such instances equity courts would "mold the relief to protect the rights of the beneficiary according to the situation involved." Bogert § 861, at 4. This flexible approach belies a strict requirement of "detrimental reliance."

To be sure, just as a court of equity would not surcharge a trustee for a nonexistent harm, 4 Scott & Ascher § 24.9, a fiduciary can be surcharged under § 502(a)(3) only upon a showing of actual harm — proved (under the default rule for civil cases) by a preponderance of the evidence. That actual harm may sometimes consist of detrimental reliance, but it might also come from the loss of a right protected by ERISA or its trust-law antecedents. In the present case, it is not difficult to imagine how the failure to provide proper summary information, in violation of the statute, injured employees even if they did not themselves act in reliance on summary documents — which they might not themselves have seen — for they may have thought fellow employees, or informal workplace discussion, would have let them know if, say, plan changes would likely prove harmful. We doubt that Congress would have wanted to bar those employees from relief.

The upshot is that we can agree with CIGNA only to a limited extent. We believe that, to obtain relief by surcharge for violations of §§ 102(a) and 104(b), a plan participant or beneficiary must show that the violation injured him or her. But to do so, he or she need only show harm and causation. Although it is not always necessary to meet the more rigorous standard implicit in the words "detrimental reliance," actual harm must be shown.

We are not asked to reassess the evidence. And we are not asked about the other prerequisites for relief. We are asked about the standard of prejudice. And we conclude that the standard of prejudice must be borrowed from equitable principles, as modified by the obligations and injuries identified by ERISA itself. Information-related circumstances, violations, and injuries are potentially too various in nature to insist that harm must always meet that more vigorous "detrimental harm" standard when equity imposed no such strict requirement.

IV

We have premised our discussion in Part III on the need for the District Court to revisit its determination of an appropriate remedy for the violations of ERISA it identified. Whether or not the general principles we have discussed above are properly applicable in this case is for it or the Court of Appeals to determine in the first instance. Because the District Court has not determined if an appropriate remedy may be imposed under § 502(a)(3), we must vacate the judgment below and remand this case for further proceedings consistent with this opinion.

It is so ordered.

JUSTICE SCALIA, with whom JUSTICE THOMAS joins, concurring in the judgment.

I agree with the Court that § 502(a)(1)(B) of ERISA, does not authorize relief for misrepresentations in a summary plan description (SPD). I do not join the Court's opinion because I see no need and no justification for saying anything more than that.

Section 502(a)(1)(B) of ERISA states that a plan participant or beneficiary may bring a civil action "to recover benefits due to him under the terms of his plan, to enforce his rights under the terms of the plan, or to clarify his rights to future benefits under the terms of the plan." ERISA defines the word "plan" as "an employee welfare benefit plan or an employee pension benefit plan or a plan which is both," 29 U.S.C. § 1002(3), and it requires that a "plan" "be established and maintained pursuant to a written instrument," § 1102(a)(1). An SPD, in contrast, is a disclosure meant "to reasonably apprise [plan] participants and beneficiaries of their rights and obligations under the plan." § 1022(a). It would be peculiar for a document meant to "apprise" participants of their rights "under the plan" to be itself part of the "plan." Any doubt that it is not is eliminated by ERISA's repeated differentiation of SPDs from the "written instruments" that constitute a plan, see, *e.g.*, §§ 1029(c), 1024(b)(2), and ERISA's assignment to different entities of responsibility for drafting and amending SPDs on the one hand and plans on the other, see §§ 1002(1), (2)(A); 1021(a), 1024(b)(1). An SPD, moreover, would not fulfill its purpose of providing an easily accessible summary of the plan if it were an authoritative part of the plan itself; the minor omissions appropriate for a summary would risk revising the plan.

Nothing else needs to be said to dispose of this case. The District Court based the relief it awarded upon ERISA § 502(a)(1)(B), and that provision alone. It thought that the "benefits" due "under the terms of the plan," 29 U.S.C. § 1132(a)(1)(B), could derive from an SPD, either because the SPD is part of the plan or because it is capable of somehow modifying the plan. Under either justification, that conclusion is wrong. An SPD is separate from a plan, and cannot amend a plan unless the plan so provides. See *Curtiss-Wright Corp. v. Schoonejongen*, 514 U.S. 73 (1995). I would go no further.

* * *

7-13 QUESTIONS AND PROBLEMS

1 Does the Court eliminate the distinction between equitable and legal remedies in *Amara*?

2 Does *Amara* simplify the law governing remedies?

In a number of cases decided prior to *Amara*, lower courts denied participants remedies under ERISA § 502(a)(3) based on the Court's distinction between legal and equitable remedies. For example, in *Kerr v. Charles F. Vatterott & Co.*, 184 F.3d 938 (8th Cir. 1999), the plan administrator delayed making a lump sum distribution of the participant's account balance for 3½ years despite the participant's repeated requests for a distribution. The plan participant brought suit under ERISA § 502(a)(3) to recover the difference between the amount that he could have earned had the distribution between timely made and the "paltry" return the plan actually made. The court denied the plan participant's claim on the ground that the remedy he sought was not equitable in nature. In *Bast v. Prudential Insurance Company of America*, 150 F.3d 1003 (9th Cir. 1998),

Prudential, the third party administrator of a self-funded health plan, initially denied a claim for the treatment of breast cancer. After the participant's attorney protested, Prudential agreed to pay for the treatment, but it was too late; the cancer had spread and the woman died. Her heirs brought suit under ERISA § 502(a)(3) seeking restitution for the value of the denied medical benefits. The court denied relief on the basis that the claimed relief was money damages, not "equitable relief." The court contrasted cases in which a constructive trust, a form of equitable relief, was imposed upon the amount of money stolen from a pension trust. The court held that Prudential had not been unjustly enriched by its failure to pay the claim and so was not an appropriate target of a constructive trust.

7-14 QUESTIONS AND PROBLEMS

Does *Amara* compel a different result in *Kerr* and *Bast*?

F. LIABILITY OF PARTIES OTHER THAN FIDUCIARIES

Recall that in *Mertens*, the Court declared that the question presented to it was "whether a nonfiduciary who knowingly participates in the breach of a fiduciary duty imposed by [ERISA] is liable for losses that an employee benefit plan suffers as a result of the breach." *Mertens v. Hewitt Assocs.*, 508 U.S. 248, 249–50. The Court, however, did not answer that question. Instead, it addressed the availability of money damages under ERISA § 502(a)(3). Yet the question remained whether nonfiduciaries.

who participate in a breach of fiduciary duty or who participate in a transaction prohibited by the statute may be sued under ERISA's enforcement provisions.

. . . .

. . . .

In the following case, the Supreme Court addressed the question of whether a nonfiduciary party-in-interest who knowingly participates in a prohibited transaction is liable under ERISA.

HARRIS TRUST v. SALOMON SMITH BARNEY INC.
530 U.S. 238 (2000)

JUSTICE THOMAS delivered the opinion of the Court.

Section 406(a) of ERISA, bars a fiduciary of an employee benefit plan from causing the plan to engage in certain transactions with a "party in interest." [ERISA] § 406(a). Section 502(a)(3) authorizes a "participant, beneficiary, or fiduciary" of a plan to bring a civil action to obtain "appropriate equitable relief" to redress violations of ERISA. The question is whether that authorization extends to a suit against a nonfiduciary "party in interest" to a transaction barred by § 406(a). We hold that it does.

I

Responding to deficiencies in prior law regulating transactions by plan fiduciaries, Congress enacted ERISA § 406(a)(1), which supplements the fiduciary's general duty of loyalty to the plan's beneficiaries, § 404(a), by categorically barring certain transactions deemed "likely to injure the pension plan," *Commissioner v. Keystone Consol. Industries, Inc.*, 508 U.S. 152, 160 (1993),

Section 406(a)(1) provides, among other things, that "[a] fiduciary with respect to a plan shall not cause the plan to engage in a transaction, if he knows or should know that such transaction constitutes a direct or indirect . . . sale or exchange . . . of any property between the plan and a party in interest." [ERISA] § 406(a)(1)(A). Congress defined "party in interest" to encompass those entities that a fiduciary might be inclined to favor at the expense of the plan's beneficiaries. § 3(14). Section 406's prohibitions are subject to both statutory and regulatory exemptions. *See* §§ 408(a), (b).

This case comes to us on the assumption that an ERISA pension plan (the Ameritech Pension Trust (APT)) and a party in interest (respondent Salomon Smith Barney (Salomon)) entered into a transaction prohibited by § 406(a) and not exempted by § 408. APT provides pension benefits to employees and retirees of Ameritech Corporation and its subsidiaries and affiliates. Salomon, during the late 1980's, provided broker-dealer services to APT, executing nondiscretionary equity trades at the direction of APT's fiduciaries, thus qualifying itself (we assume) as a "party in interest." *See* § 3(14)(B) (defining "party in interest" as "a person providing services to [an employee benefit] plan"). During the same period, Salomon sold interests in several motel properties to APT for nearly $21 million. APT's purchase of the motel interests was directed by National Investment Services of America (NISA), an investment manager to which Ameritech had delegated investment discretion over a portion of the plan's assets, and hence a fiduciary of APT. *See* § 4(21)(A)(i).

This litigation arose when APT's fiduciaries — its trustee, petitioner Harris Trust and Savings Bank, and its administrator, petitioner Ameritech Corporation — discovered that the motel interests were nearly worthless. Petitioners maintain that the interests had been worthless all along; Salomon asserts, to the contrary, that the interests declined in value due to a downturn in the motel industry. Whatever the true cause, petitioners sued Salomon in 1992 under § 502(a)(3), which authorizes a "participant, beneficiary, or fiduciary" to bring a civil action "to enjoin any act or practice which violates any provision of [ERISA Title I] . . . or . . . to obtain other appropriate equitable relief . . . to redress such violations." [ERISA] § 502(a)(3).

Petitioners claimed, among other things, that NISA, as plan fiduciary, had caused the plan to engage in a per se prohibited transaction under § 406(a) in purchasing the motel interests from Salomon, and that Salomon was liable on account of its participation in the transaction as a nonfiduciary party in interest. Specifically, petitioners pointed to § 406(a)(1)(A), which prohibits a "sale or exchange . . . of any property between the plan and a party in interest," and § 406(a)(1)(D), which prohibits a "transfer to . . . a party in interest . . . of any assets of the plan." Petitioners sou ght rescission of the transaction, restitution from Salomon of the purchase price with interest, and disgorgement of Salomon's profits made from use of the plan assets transferred to it.

Salomon moved for summary judgment, arguing that § 502(a)(3), when used to remedy a transaction prohibited by § 406(a), authorizes a suit only against the party expressly constrained by § 406(a) — the fiduciary who caused the plan to enter the transaction — and not against the counterparty to the transaction. See § 406(a)(1). The District Court denied the motion, holding that ERISA does provide a private cause of action against nonfiduciaries who participate in a prohibited transaction, but granted Salomon's subsequent motion for certification of the issue for interlocutory appeal under 28 U.S.C. § 1292(b).

The Court of Appeals for the Seventh Circuit reversed. It began with the observation that § 406(a), by its terms and like several of its neighboring provisions, e.g., § 404, governs only the conduct of fiduciaries, not of counterparties or other nonfiduciaries. The court next posited that "where ERISA does not expressly impose a duty, there can be no cause of action," relying upon dictum in our decision in *Mertens v. Hewitt Associates*, 508 U.S. 248, 254 (1993), that § 502(a)(3) does not provide a private cause of action against a nonfiduciary for knowing participation in a fiduciary's breach of duty. The Seventh Circuit saw no distinction between the *Mertens* situation (involving § 404) and the instant case (involving § 406), explaining that neither section expressly imposes a duty on nonfiduciaries. Finally, in the Seventh Circuit's view, Congress' decision to authorize the Secretary of Labor to impose a civil penalty on a nonfiduciary "party in interest" to a § 406 transaction, *see* § 502(i), simply confirms that Congress deliberately selected one enforcement tool (a civil penalty imposed by the Secretary) instead of another (a civil action under § 502(a)(3)). Accordingly, the Seventh Circuit held that a nonfiduciary cannot be liable under § 502(a)(3) for participating in a § 406 transaction and entered summary judgment in favor of Salomon.

. . .

II

We agree with the Seventh Circuit's and Salomon's interpretation of § 406(a). They rightly note that § 406(a) imposes a duty only on the fiduciary that causes the plan to engage in the transaction. *See* § 406(a)(1). We reject, however, the Seventh Circuit's and Salomon's conclusion that, absent a substantive provision of ERISA expressly imposing a duty upon a nonfiduciary party in interest, the nonfiduciary party may not be held liable under § 502(a)(3), one of ERISA's remedial provisions. Petitioners contend, and we agree, that § 502(a)(3) itself imposes certain duties, and therefore that liability under that provision does not depend on whether ERISA's substantive provisions impose a specific duty on the party being sued.

[Court quotes ERISA § 502(a)(3)].

This language [ERISA § 502(a)(3)], to be sure, "does not . . . authorize 'appropriate equitable relief' at large, but only 'appropriate equitable relief' for the purpose of 'redress[ing any] violations or . . . enforc[ing] any provisions' of ERISA or an ERISA plan." But § 502(a)(3) admits of no limit (aside from the "appropriate equitable relief" caveat, which we address *infra*) on the universe of possible defendants. Indeed, § 502(a)(3) makes no mention at all of which parties may be proper defendants — the focus, instead, is on redressing the "act or practice which violates any provision of [ERISA Title I]." [ERISA] § 502(a)(3) (emphasis added). Other provisions of ERISA, by contrast, do expressly address who may be a defendant. *See* § 409(a), § 502(1), § 502(a)(3), and § 502(a)(5).

In light of Congress' precision in these respects, we would ordinarily assume that Congress' failure to specify proper defendants in § 502(a)(3) was intentional. But ERISA's " 'comprehensive and reticulated' " scheme warrants a cautious approach to inferring remedies not expressly authorized by the text. *Massachusetts Mut. Life Ins. Co. v. Russell*, 473 U.S. 134, 146 (1985) . . . . In this case, however, § 502(l) resolves the matter — it compels the conclusion that defendant status under § 502(a)(3) may arise from duties imposed by § 502(a)(3) itself, and hence does not turn on whether the defendant is expressly subject to a duty under one of ERISA's substantive provisions.

Section 502(l) provides in relevant part:

> "(1) In the case of —
>
> "(A) any breach of fiduciary responsibility under (or other violation of) part 4 of this subtitle by a fiduciary, or
>
> "(B) any knowing participation in such a breach or violation by any other person,
>
> "the Secretary shall assess a civil penalty against such fiduciary or other person in an amount equal to 20 percent of the applicable recovery amount.
>
> "(2) For purposes of paragraph (1), the term 'applicable recovery amount' means any amount which is recovered from a fiduciary or other person with respect to a breach or violation described in paragraph (1) —
>
> "(A) pursuant to any settlement agreement with the Secretary, or
>
> "(B) ordered by a court to be paid by such fiduciary or other person to a plan or its participants and beneficiaries in a judicial proceeding instituted by the Secretary under subsection (a)(2) or (a)(5) of this section."

Section 502(l) contemplates civil penalty actions by the Secretary against two classes of defendants, fiduciaries and "other person[s]." The latter class concerns us here. Paraphrasing, the Secretary shall assess a civil penalty against an "other person" who "knowing[ly] participat[es] in" "any . . . violation of . . . part 4 . . . by a fiduciary." And the amount of such penalty is defined by reference to the amount "ordered by a court to be paid by such . . . other person to a plan or its participants and beneficiaries in a judicial proceeding instituted by the Secretary under subsection (a)(2) or (a)(5)" (Emphasis added).

The plain implication is that the Secretary may bring a civil action under § 502(a)(5) against an "other person" who "knowing[ly] participat[es]" in a fiduciary's violation; otherwise, there could be no "applicable recovery amount" from which to determine the amount of the civil penalty to be imposed on the "other person." This § 502(a)(5) action is available notwithstanding the absence of any ERISA provision explicitly imposing a duty upon an "other person" not to engage in such "knowing participation." And if the Secretary may bring suit against an "other person" under subsection (a)(5), it follows that a participant, beneficiary, or fiduciary may bring suit against an "other person" under the similarly worded subsection (a)(3). *See Mertens*, 508 U.S. at 260. Section 502(l), therefore, refutes the notion that § 502(a)(3) (or (a)(5)) liability hinges on whether the particular defendant labors under a duty expressly imposed by the substantive provisions of ERISA Title I.

Salomon invokes *Mertens* as articulating an alternative, more restrictive reading of § 502(l) that does not support the inference we have drawn. In *Mertens*, we suggested, in dictum, that the "other person[s]" in § 502(l) might be limited to the "cofiduciaries" made expressly liable under § 405(a) for knowingly participating in another fiduciary's breach of fiduciary responsibility. *Id.* at 261. So read, § 502(l) would be consistent with the view that liability under § 502(a)(3) depends entirely on whether the particular defendant violated a duty expressly imposed by the substantive provisions of ERISA Title I. But the *Mertens* dictum did not discuss — understandably, since we were merely flagging the issue that ERISA defines the term "person" without regard to status as a cofiduciary (or, for that matter, as a fiduciary or party in interest), *see* § 3(9) . . . .

III

Notwithstanding the text of § 502(a)(3) (as informed by § 502(l)), Salomon protests that it would contravene common sense for Congress to have imposed civil liability on a party, such as a nonfiduciary party in interest to a § 406(a) transaction, that is not a "wrongdoer" in the sense of violating a duty expressly imposed by the substantive provisions of ERISA Title I. Salomon raises the specter of § 502(a)(3) suits being brought against innocent parties — even those having no connection to the allegedly unlawful "act or practice" — rather than against the true wrongdoer, i.e., the fiduciary that caused the plan to engage in the transaction.

But this reductio ad absurdum ignores the limiting principle explicit in § 502(a)(3): that the retrospective relief sought be "appropriate equitable relief." The common law of trusts, which offers a "starting point for analysis [of ERISA] . . . [unless] it is inconsistent with the language of the statute, its structure, or its purposes," *Hughes Aircraft Co. v. Jacobson*, 525 U.S. 432, 447 (1999), plainly countenances the sort of relief sought by petitioners against Salomon here. As petitioners and amicus curiae the United States observe, it has long been settled that when a trustee in breach of his fiduciary duty to the beneficiaries transfers trust property to a third person, the third person takes the property subject to the trust, unless he has purchased the property for value and without notice of the fiduciary's breach of duty. The trustee or beneficiaries may then maintain an action for restitution of the property (if not already disposed of) or disgorgement of proceeds (if already disposed of), and disgorgement of the third person's profits derived therefrom . . . .

Importantly, that a transferee was not "the original wrongdoer" does not insulate him from liability for restitution. It also bears emphasis that the common law of trusts sets limits on restitution actions against defendants other than the principal "wrongdoer." Only a transferee of ill-gotten trust assets may be held liable, and then only when the transferee (assuming he has purchased for value) knew or should have known of the existence of the trust and the circumstances that rendered the transfer in breach of the trust. Translated to the instant context, the transferee must be demonstrated to have had actual or constructive knowledge of the circumstances that rendered the transaction unlawful. Those circumstances, in turn, involve a showing that the plan fiduciary, with actual or constructive knowledge of the facts satisfying the elements of a § 406(a) transaction, caused the plan to engage in the transaction . . . .

But Salomon advances a more fundamental critique of the common-law analogy, reasoning that the antecedent violation here — a violation of § 406(a)'s per se prohibitions on transacting with a party in interest — was unknown at common law, and that common-law liability should not attach to an act that does not violate a common law duty. While Salomon accurately characterizes § 406(a) as expanding upon the common law's arm's-length standard of conduct, we reject Salomon's unsupported suggestion that remedial principles of the common law are tethered to the precise contours of common law duty.

We note, however, that our interpretation of § 502(a)(3) to incorporate common-law remedial principles does not necessarily foreclose accommodation of Salomon's underlying concern that ERISA should not be construed to require counterparties to transactions with a plan to monitor the plan for compliance with each of ERISA's intricate details. While we have no occasion to decide the matter here, it may be that such concerns should inform courts' determinations of what a transferee should (or should not) be expected to know when engaging in a transaction with a fiduciary.

For these reasons, an action for restitution against a transferee of tainted plan assets satisfies the "appropriate[ness]" criterion in § 502(a)(3). Such relief is also "equitable"in nature. [citing *Mertens*].

IV

. . .

Accordingly, we reverse the Seventh Circuit's judgment and remand the case for further proceedings consistent with this opinion.

7-15 QUESTIONS AND PROBLEMS

1. Where under ERISA does the duty of a party-in-interest arise? Is *Harris* congruous with *Mertens*, or has the Court modified its approach to construct an opinion more favorable to plan participants?

2. In *Harris*, the Court stated: ". . . we reject Salomon's unsupported suggestion that remedial principles of the common law are tethered to the precise contours of common law duty."

In *Mertens*, the Court stated: "The term 'equitable relief' can assuredly mean, as petitioners and the Solicitor General would have it, whatever relief a court of equity is empowered to provide in the particular case at issue . . . . But as indicated by the foregoing quotation — which speaks of 'legal remedies' granted by an equity court — 'equitable relief' can also refer to those categories of relief that were typically available in equity (such as injunction, mandamus, and restitution, but not compensatory damages). As memories of the divided bench, and familiarity with its technical refinements, recede further into the past, the former meaning becomes, perhaps, increasingly unlikely; but it remains a question of interpretation in each case which meaning is intended."

Are these statements consistent? If not, which should the Court adopt as its guide?

3. Look carefully at ERISA § 3(14) that defines a "party in interest." What advice would you give to parties who deal with ERISA plans after the *Harris* decision?

4. The Court held that § 502(a)(3) of ERISA provides a cause of action against nonfiduciary parties in interest who participate in a prohibited transaction. What if Solomon had not been found to be a party in interest. Would it have been held liable under ERISA?

5. Who bears the burden of proving that the participation was "knowing?" Does it matter?

6. Were the plaintiffs seeking equitable relief or is the claim for restitution merely a cover for a suit for money damages — a legal remedy?

G. PROCEDURAL ISSUES

As with all litigation, suing under ERISA raises a number of procedural issues, the resolution of which depends in part upon the nature of the plaintiff's cause of action.

[1] ERISA Statutes of Limitations

ERISA § 413.

Under ERISA different statute of limitations apply depending on the nature of the plaintiff's claim. If the claim is that the defendant breached a fiduciary duty, the statute of limitations found in ERISA § 413 applies.

BISHOP v. LUCENT TECHNOLOGIES, INC.

520 F.3d 516 (6th Cir. 2008)

McKeague, Circuit Judge.

This is an appeal from an order dismissing retirees' claims for breach of fiduciary duty against their former employer and its employment benefit plan. Plaintiff retirees allege they were misled into prematurely accepting early retirement. The district court dismissed the claims as time-barred. On appeal, plaintiffs contend the district court failed to construe the complaint liberally in their favor and misapplied the governing statute of limitations. For the reasons that follow, we affirm the judgment of the district court.

I

Plaintiffs Virginia Bishop, Gerald Deckard, Charles Himmelspach, Jr., James Kastet, Janet Koch, George Policello, Karen Staff, and Sharon Stratton were employees of defendant Lucent Technologies, Inc. in Ohio and Illinois. All eight plaintiffs retired from their employment with Lucent in late 2000 or early 2001. They allegedly retired in reliance on representations by Lucent officials that "there was no point in delaying their retirement in the hope that the company would offer special retirement incentives like those offered by Lucent in the past, because Lucent had decided not to offer packages again in the near future, a prospect the officials guaranteed the company had specifically ruled out." Yet, on June 11, 2001, within approximately six months after their retirements, Lucent publicly announced the offering of a lucrative severance package known as the 2001 Voluntary Retirement Program ("VRP"). Had they remained employed for several more months, plaintiffs allege, they would have been eligible for enhanced benefits. Feeling duped, they commenced this action under the Employee Retirement Income Security Act ("ERISA"), alleging under ERISA § 502(e)(1) [sic] that defendants Lucent Technologies and The Lucent Retirement Income Plan breached fiduciary duties owed them. Plaintiffs claim that defendants breached fiduciary duties "by actively misleading them into choosing to retire when they did with false information about the company's policy and intentions with respect to severance incentives." Amended complaint ¶ 1.

Plaintiffs filed their complaint in the District Court for the Southern District of Ohio on January 3, 2005. Defendants responded by moving to dismiss under Rule 12(b)(6) of the Federal Rules of Civil Procedure, contending the complaint fails to state a claim upon which relief can be granted because the claims are barred by the governing statute of limitations. In their motion to dismiss, defendants contended that plaintiffs had actual knowledge of the alleged breach of fiduciary duty on the date of the VRP announcement and that the three-year limitation period therefore expired on June 10, 2004, almost seven months before the complaint was filed.

Plaintiffs opposed the motion by contending that the VRP announcement itself did not necessarily disclose to plaintiffs that misleading representations earlier made by Lucent officials were untrue. They further insisted that the complaint does not allege *when* plaintiffs learned that they had been misled. Because the complaint does not reveal when plaintiffs acquired this actual knowledge, plaintiffs maintained that it could not be ascertained whether the complaint was untimely filed.

The district court rejected plaintiffs' argument, concluding they had actual knowledge of the facts or transactions that made out the alleged violation on June 11, 2001, even if they didn't then know all material facts necessary to understand that a breach of fiduciary duty occurred. This was held to be sufficient "actual knowledge" to trigger the running of the three-year period and the complaint was held to be time-barred.

II

Whether the district court properly dismissed the complaint pursuant to Rule 12(b)(6) is a question of law subject to *de novo* review. The reviewing court must construe the complaint in a light most favorable to plaintiffs, accept all well-pled factual allegations as true, and determine whether plaintiffs undoubtedly can prove no set of facts in support of those allegations that would entitle them to relief . . . .

In their motion to dismiss, defendants point out, with reference to the allegations of the complaint, that the violation complained of manifestly occurred on June 11, 2001, when the 2001 VRP was publicly announced. Because it appears from the complaint itself that plaintiffs knew they had been misled at that time, defendants reasonably deduced that the three-year period of limitation prescribed in ERISA § 413(2) began running at that time. The complaint not having been filed until January 3, 2005, more than three years after June 11, 2001, defendants contend that the complaint fails to state a claim upon which can be granted because it is time-barred. Defendants essentially contend . . . that the complaint fails to "contain either direct or inferential allegations respecting all material elements to sustain a recovery under some viable legal theory."

Pursuant to ERISA § 413(2), in relevant part, a claim for breach of fiduciary duty may not be brought after the earlier of

> (1) six years after (A) the date of the last action which constituted a part of the breach or violation, or (B) in the case of an omission, the latest date on which the fiduciary could have cured the breach or violation, or
>
> (2) three years after the earliest date on which the plaintiff had actual knowledge of the breach or violation.

The district court correctly determined that "actual knowledge" under ERISA § 413(2) is a term that has received a particular definition in the Sixth Circuit. "[T]he relevant knowledge required to trigger the statute of limitations under ERISA § 413(2) is knowledge of the facts or transaction that constituted the alleged violation; it is not necessary that the plaintiff also have actual knowledge that the facts establish a cognizable legal claim under ERISA in order to trigger the running of the statute." *Wright v. Heyne*, 349 F.3d 321, 330 (6th Cir. 2003). It follows that the question posed by the motion to dismiss is whether plaintiffs' complaint contains sufficient allegations, either direct or inferential, to facially support the conclusion that they first acquired actual knowledge of "the facts or transaction that constituted the alleged violation" at some point in time less than three years prior to the filing of their complaint.

Plaintiffs concede that their complaint does not affirmatively allege when they acquired actual knowledge of the facts or transaction that comprised the alleged breach of fiduciary duty. They maintain that the court, viewing the complaint in the light most favorable to them for purposes of Rule 12(b)(6) review, must resolve this ambiguity in their favor. Yet, the complaint certainly contains allegations which, on their face, give rise to the reasonable inference that they must have known, at the time of the public announcement of the 2001 VRP that they had been wronged. That is, the allegations indicate that plaintiffs: knew what representations had been made to them by Lucent officials, on which they allegedly relied in deciding to retire early; knew the offering of enhanced benefits in the 2001 VRP was inconsistent with the representations; and knew, in retrospect, that they had been misled by these representations into believing that something that did come to pass would not. It thus *appears* from the face of the complaint that plaintiffs had actual knowledge of the facts or transaction comprising the wrong complained of more than three years before the complaint was filed. In the words of *Wright*, 349 F.3d at 331: "Although the actions complained of in this case may not themselves 'communicate the existence of an underlying breach,' the extrinsic facts of which the Plaintiffs had actual knowledge demonstrate that Plaintiffs must have known that they had been wronged long before they consulted with an attorney."

Under these circumstances, it is not enough for plaintiffs to argue that the complaint, because it is silent as to when they first acquired actual knowledge, must be read in the light most favorable to them and construed as not precluding the possibility that they will be able to prove facts establishing their entitlement to relief. The obligation to plead facts in avoidance of the statute of limitations defense is triggered by the fact that "it is apparent from the face of the complaint that the time limit for bringing the claim[s] has passed." *Hoover v. Langston Equip. Assocs., Inc.*, 958 F.2d 742, 744 (6th Cir. 1992). "The Sixth Circuit has adopted the view, at least in cases where the face of the complaint discloses a failure to file within the time allowed, that the plaintiff may come forward with allegations explaining why the statute of limitations should be tolled." *Id.* When it affirmatively appears from the face of the complaint that the time for bringing the claim has passed, the plaintiff cannot "escape the statute by saying nothing." *Id.* at 745.

* * *

MEYER v. BERKSHIRE LIFE INS. CO.

128 F. Supp. 2d 831 (D. Md. 2001)

BLAKE, DISTRICT JUDGE.

Defendant Berkshire Life Insurance Company ("Berkshire") has moved for summary judgment on all claims brought by plaintiffs Paul D. Meyer and Jorge R. Ordonez (the "Doctors"). During the time relevant to this lawsuit, each doctor was the trustee for a Money Purchase Pension Plan and Trust which was administered by Berkshire and designed to provide life insurance and retirement benefits for the doctor and his employees. The Doctors now claim that Berkshire mismanaged the trust funds. Accordingly, they have filed suit alleging common law claims for professional negligence, negligent misrepresentation or omission, deceit, and breach of fiduciary duty. In the alternative, they claim damages under ERISA for breach of fiduciary duty. Now pending before this court are Berkshire's motions for summary judgment on all counts pursuant to Rule 56 of the Federal Rules of Civil Procedure. . . . Because those [state] claims are preempted by ERISA, the court will grant the defendant's motions as to Counts I, II, III, and IV. Summary judgment will be denied on Count V . . . .

Doctors Meyer and Ordonez are neurosurgeons. In 1980, they left the practice in which they were employed and opened separate, but affiliated, practices. At that time, the Doctors placed the money they received from their pension plans on deposit at a local bank. Over the next three years, the Doctors developed a relationship with the branch manager of that bank, Michael Meszaros. In 1983, Mr. Meszaros left the bank to work for Berkshire. At that time, he set up a meeting between himself, the Doctors, and Robert Walsh, the general agent for Berkshire in the Baltimore area. The purpose of that meeting was to acquaint the Doctors with the insurance and retirement services offered by Berkshire. The Doctors allege that, during this meeting or one subsequent, Mr. Meszaros told them that if each invested with Berkshire, their plans would be worth more than $2,000,000 by the time they were ready to retire.

Soon thereafter, the Doctors enrolled as employers in the "Berkshire Life Pension Plan." Each set up a separate plan, named himself as Trustee, and became a participant in the plan as an employee of the practice. Each doctor employed a secretary who was also a participant in his plan. The plans required each doctor to contribute $30,000 annually for himself and a smaller amount each year for his secretary. Of this amount, 25% was used as a premium on a life insurance policy and the remaining 75% was invested to provide a retirement fund.

The plans remained in existence until at least 1996. During that time, the Doctors were provided various reports and disclosures which purported to explain the status of their plans and the transactions that had been undertaken during the year. Further, the Doctors met annually with Mr. Meszaros and Mr. Walsh to discuss their plans. In addition, as trustees of their respective plans, each Doctor was required to approve and authorize all transactions that were made. These disclosures and approvals are the subject of significant debate. Berkshire claims they prove that the Doctors had knowledge sufficient to understand that a breach of fiduciary duty had occurred. In response, the Doctors contend that they relied almost entirely on Mr. Meszaros for investment advice. They claim to have simply "rubber-stamped" any transactions that he recommended and not to have read carefully the reports they were sent. Indeed, they claim that they looked at the reports only long enough to make sure that the value of the plans increased each year.

In the spring of 1996, Dr. Ordonez's secretary had a problem with a loan she had obtained from the plan through Mr. Meszaros. She contacted Mr. Meszaros and discovered that he was no longer employed by Berkshire. (*Id.*) Thereafter, she conveyed her concern to Dr. Ordonez, who met with Mr. Walsh and an insurance representative. That meeting worried Dr. Ordonez, he spoke to Dr. Meyer, and the two began looking for an attorney to investigate Berkshire's management of the pension funds.

That investigation led to the filing of this lawsuit in which the Doctors allege that Berkshire, through Mr. Meszaros and Mr. Walsh, mismanaged their pension funds. Specifically, they contend that "Meszaros provided grossly incompetent advice and defrauded the Plans by engaging in an investment strategy that significantly reduced the Plans' investment earnings." The Doctors claim that the mismanagement falls into two categories. First, they allege that Berkshire "churned" the plans' assets to produce commissions. That is, they claim that Meszaros traded among several investments unnecessarily in order to garner the commission that accompanies each transaction. Second, the Doctors contend that

Berkshire did not keep the plans appropriately diversified. In response, Berkshire argues that the common law claims are preempted by ERISA and that the ERISA claim is barred either by the statute of limitations or the Doctors' contributory negligence. It has also raised ratification, waiver, and estoppel as defenses.

In the first four counts of their complaint the Doctors assert common law claims for professional negligence, negligent misrepresentation or omission, deceit, and breach of fiduciary duty. Berkshire contends that these claims are preempted by ERISA. [The Court found the claims to be preempted and granted the defendant's motion for summary judgment] . . . .

In its motion, Berkshire presents three grounds on which it argues summary judgment should be granted on the Doctors' ERISA claim. First, it contends that the claim is barred by the statute of limitations. Second, Berkshire argues that the Doctors' negligence bars recovery. Finally, the company raises ratification, waiver, and estoppel as equitable defenses. The Doctors dispute each of these contentions; they will be examined in turn.

ERISA § [413] provides that

> [n]o action may be commenced under this subchapter with respect to a fiduciary's breach of any responsibility, duty, or obligation . . . after the earlier of —
>
> (1) six years after . . . the date of the last action which constituted a part of the breach or violation . . . , or (2) three years after the earliest date on which the plaintiff had actual knowledge of the breach or violation . . . ."

Cases involving "fraud or concealment" are exempt from this provision and may be filed up to six years after the violation is discovered.

Although this provision has been interpreted by several Courts of Appeal, it has not yet been the subject of an opinion in the Fourth Circuit. An analytic framework, however, has been developed by other circuits. The first step in the analysis is to "isolate and define the underlying violation." *Meagher v. International Ass'n of Machinists & Aerospace Workers Pension Plan*, 856 F.2d 1418, 1422 (9th Cir. 1988). Once it has been identified, the court must determine, first, when the breach or violation occurred and, second, when the plaintiff had actual knowledge of it. *See Ziegler v. Connecticut Gen. Life Ins. Co.*, 916 F.2d 548, 550 (9th Cir. 1990). *See also Maher v. Strachan Shipping Co.*, 68 F.3d 951, 954 (5th Cir. 1995) ("The statute specifies a two-step analysis of accrual of an ERISA action: first, when did the alleged breach or violation occur; and second, when did the plaintiff have actual knowledge of the breach or violation?") (citing *Ziegler*, 916 F.2d at 550); *Gluck v. Unisys Corp.*, 960 F.2d 1168, 1178 (3d Cir. 1992) (stating that once the breach has been identified, "two temporal determinations must then be made: the date of the last action which formed a part of the breach and the date of the plaintiff's actual knowledge of the breach").

In their complaint, the Doctors allege that Berkshire breached its fiduciary duty by failing to act "solely in the interest of the participants and beneficiaries of the Plans," by not exercising the required prudence in investing, and by "failing to diversify the investments of the plan." In their reply to Berkshire's motions for summary judgment, the Doctors refine these allegations by dividing "the conduct that caused the exceptional shortfall in earnings . . . into two general categories." First, they allege that Berkshire, through the actions of Mr. Meszaros, "churned" the plans' investments by making unnecessary trades and withdrawals so as to produce commissions. Specifically, the Doctors contend that Mr. Meszaros traded between annuity contracts. They argue that annuities are designed to be "long term, stable investments," and that, by moving money between the annuity fund and removing ten percent of the annuities annually, Meszaros breached the fiduciary duty he owed to the Doctors to invest prudently.

Second, the Doctors argue that Berkshire breached its fiduciary duty by failing to appropriately diversify the investments. Specifically, they allege that, rather than invest the plan funds in a diverse portfolio, Mr. Meszaros "loaded the plans with low yield, high fee annuities." This lack of diversification, the Doctors argue, cost the plans millions of dollars.

The next step in the analysis, determining when the breach occurred, is not as simple in this case. Neither churning nor lack of diversification is a discrete breach that easily could be limited to a specific time. Rather, each involves a series of transactions that, taken together, may constitute a breach. At this stage of the case, there has been no argument about when the transactions amounted to churning or at what point the portfolio was insufficiently diversified. Rather, both sides have focused on the next analytical step: determining when the Doctors had actual knowledge of the breaches they allege.

. . .

The question confronting the court is whether the documents provided to the Doctors and their acquiescence to the transactions are sufficient to establish actual knowledge for purposes of ERISA § [413]. Although the Fourth Circuit has not provided an interpretation of the actual knowledge standard, the courts of appeal that have faced the issue are in fairly close accord. First, the courts are adamant that § [413] requires actual, not constructive knowledge. *See, e.g.*, *Gluck v. Unisys Corp.*, 960 F.2d 1168, 1176 (3d Cir. 1992) ("Of course, a plaintiff may have constructive knowledge of a breach before he actually knows of the breach, but section 413 calls for actual knowledge."); *Radiology Center, S.C. v. Stifel, Nicolaus & Co.*, 919 F.2d 1216, 1222–23 (7th Cir. 1990) (finding that district court erred in using either constructive or actual knowledge because § 413 requires actual knowledge).

In addition, the Third Circuit has explained that "ERISA requires actual knowledge of all of the elements of the violation alleged . . . ." *Gluck*, 960 F.2d at 1176 . . . .

Beyond these rules, however, the analyses become very case-specific. Indeed, "[t]his inquiry into plaintiffs' actual knowledge is entirely factual, requiring examination of the record." *Ziegler*, 916 F.2d at 550 . . . .

In this case, Berkshire has attached as exhibits to its motions for summary judgment the annual reports and lists of transactions for each year the plans were in effect. The court has examined those documents and found them neither simple nor straightforward. By themselves, they do not provide sufficient information for the court to conclude that the Doctors had actual knowledge of an ERISA violation. Further, although the fact that the Doctors were required to approve each transaction weighs heavily in favor of finding actual knowledge, it is not apparent that the Doctors did so with adequate information. If the Doctors simply rubber-stamped Mr. Meszaros's recommendations without receiving a complete explanation, they may not have had actual knowledge of an ERISA violation.

Viewing the evidence in the light most favorable to the plaintiffs, it becomes apparent that an issue of material fact exists regarding the Doctors' knowledge. As they are described in the memoranda and exhibits, the reports and annual meetings are an insufficient basis on which to conclude that the Doctors had actual knowledge of an ERISA violation. For that reason, summary judgment will be denied . . . .

7-16 QUESTIONS AND PROBLEMS

1. In *Meyer* who is likely to prevail at trial? Why?

2. What exactly would the doctors have had to know to have actual knowledge?

3. Is the ERISA standard of "actual knowledge" a workable standard?

ERISA § 413 provides a six-year statute of limitations that begins to run after the discovery of the breach or violation in the case of "fraud or concealment." The meaning of those terms has been the subject of debate. The majority of courts have interpreted them to create a six year limit only when there has been "fraudulent concealment." The Second Circuit Court of Appeals has given the phrase a more expansive reading.

CAPUTO v. PFIZER

267 F.3d 181 (2d Cir. 2001)

McLaughlin, Circuit Judge.

[Plaintiffs were employed by Pfizer for many years. Pfizer made a decision to downsize by offering a generous severance package. Although the decision to offer the severance package had been made, employees were not told about the plan and, in fact, were falsely told that no such severance package was planned. The plaintiffs retired before the severance package was announced. The plaintiffs sued claiming that they would not have retired if they had known of the true state of affairs. Because of the passage of time, they claimed that because Pfizer was guilty of "fraud and concealment" the six year statute of limitations did not begin to run until they learned that they had, in the words of the court, been "snookered."] [Ed. summary]

. . . [P]laintiffs argue that their breach of fiduciary duty claims involve allegations of common-law fraud, and therefore earn the six-year "fraud or concealment" period rather than the three-year "actual knowledge" limitations period. Pfizer, however, contends that the "fraud or concealment" provision applies — not to actions for breach of fiduciary duty in which the underlying action itself sounds in fraud (i.e., looking to the nature of the factual allegations supporting the claim for breach of fiduciary duty) — but only to actions in which the plaintiff alleges that the defendant engaged in conduct intended to hide its breach of fiduciary duty, thereby preventing the plaintiff's discovery of the underlying breach. This issue was not placed before us in *Diduck I* and is, therefore, one of first impression in this Circuit.

In support of its argument, Pfizer cites various circuits that have held that the "fraud or concealment" provision does not automatically apply to fraud claims, but rather incorporates the federal concealment rule, also known as the "fraudulent concealment" doctrine. The concealment rule, established by the Supreme Court in *Bailey v. Glover*, 88 U.S. 342 (1874), grew from the soil of equitable estoppel. It provides that when a defendant's wrongdoing "has been concealed, or is of such character as to conceal itself, the statute [of limitations] does not begin to run until the [wrongdoing] is discovered" by the plaintiff. Therefore, to be entitled to the six-year "fraud or concealment" limitations period, these courts require that, in addition to alleging a breach of fiduciary duty (be it fraud or any other act or omission), the plaintiff must also allege that the defendant committed either: (1) a "self-concealing act" — an act committed during the course of the breach that has the effect of concealing the breach from the plaintiff; or (2) "active concealment" —

an act distinct from and subsequent to the breach intended to conceal it.

For a number of reasons, we decline to follow our sister circuits in fusing the phrase "fraud *or* concealment" into the single term "fraudulent concealment." First, the genesis of this uniformly adopted theory is a footnote in a district court opinion that cites no legal support for the proposition. Second, the "fraud or concealment" provi sion does not "toll" the otherwise applicable six or three-year statute of limitations established in § 413(1) or (2); rather, it prescribes a separate statute of limitations of six years from the date of discovery.

Third, principles of statutory interpretation counsel strongly against merging the two terms. Relying on the canon of statutory construction that "words grouped in a list should be given a related meaning," some courts have held that the term "fraud" cannot refer to the common-law cause of action because there is no such thing as a cause of action for "concealment." However, as the Supreme Court has recently held: "In interpreting a statute a court should always turn first to one, cardinal canon before all others. We have stated time and again that courts must presume that a legislature says in a statute what it means and means in a statute what it says there."

The plain language of the statute states that the six-year limitations period applies to "cases of fraud or concealment." When the statute was enacted, "fraud" was defined as "a false representation of a matter of fact, whether by words or conduct, by false or misleading allegations or by concealment of that which should have been disclosed, which deceives and is intended to deceive another so that he shall act upon it to his legal injury." *Black's Law Dictionary* 788 (Rev. 4th ed. 1968); compare *Black's Law Dictionary* 670 (7th ed. 1999) ("[a] knowing misrepresentation of the truth or concealment of a material fact to induce another to act to his or her detriment"). And "concealment" was defined as "[a] withholding of something which one knows and which one, in duty, is bound to reveal." *Black's Law Dictionary* 360 (Rev. 4th ed. 1968); compare *Black's Law Dictionary* 282 (7th ed. 1999) ("the act of refraining from disclosure; especially an act by which one prevents or hinders the discovery of something"). "Concealment of a cause of action" was similarly defined as follows: "To constitute it so as to prevent running of a limitations, some trick or artifice must be employed to prevent inquiry or elude investigation, or to mislead and hinder [a] party who has a cause of action from obtaining information, and acts relied on must be of an affirmative character and fraudulent." *Black's Law Dictionary* 361 (Rev. 4th ed. 1968).

Giving each term independent significance (as one must when terms are used in the disjunctive unless the context dictates otherwise, *Reiter v. Sonotone Corp.*, 442 U.S. 330, 339 (1979)) "the six-year statute of limitations should be applied to cases in which a fiduciary: (1) breached its duty by making a knowing misrepresentation or omission of a material fact to induce an employee/beneficiary to act to his detriment; or (2) engaged in acts to hinder the discovery of a breach of fiduciary duty. *In re Unisys Corp.*, 242 F.3d at 513–516. This interpretation is amply supported by the provision's legislative history.

A preliminary draft of § 413 provided:

> In the case of a willfully false or fraudulent statement or representation of a material fact or the willful concealment of, or willful failure to disclose, a material fact required by this Act to be disclosed, a proceeding in court may be brought at any time within ten years after such violation occurs.

S. 4, 93d Cong., 1st Sess. § 11 (draft, Jan. 4, 1973), reprinted, 1 Legislative History of the Employee Retirement and Income Security Act of 1974, at 315 (1976). Clearly, Congress intended to provide a lengthier statute of limitations where the fiduciary breached its duty by misrepresenting or failing to disclose a material fact that ERISA required the fiduciary to disclose, most likely because such violations would be difficult to discover. Although the final version of the statute adopted a six-year term and a discovery rule (i.e., the limitations period begins to run when the employee discovers or with due diligence should have discovered the breach) it retained the class of actions to which the exception applied. The pleonastic description of a cause of action for breach of fiduciary duty arising from the commission of a fraud (whether it be via affirmative misrepresentation, omission or concealment of a material fact) was replaced by the simpler term "fraud." The term "concealment" would thus be superfluous unless it be given its common, independent meaning with respect to causes of action. Therefore, in light of the adoption of the discovery rule, the term "concealment" arguably incorporates the "fraudulent concealment" doctrine.

Accordingly, our interpretation of ERISA § 413's "fraud or concealment" provision overlaps somewhat with that of our sister circuits as we construe it to apply "in cases of fraud or [fraudulent] concealment."

The United States District Court for the District of Columbia has defined the § 413 fraud or concealment provision as being something more than "substantive fraud." The fraudulent concealment doctrine requires that "the defendant engage in active concealment — it must undertake some trick or contrivance to exclude suspicion and prevent inquiry." It must be something more than merely a failure to disclose. *Harris v. Koenig*, 722 F. Supp. 2d 44, 57 (D.D.C. 2010).

7-17 QUESTIONS AND PROBLEMS

Carpenters Local 7 Fund is a collectively bargained, multi-employer pension fund. It was formed in 1960 to provide pension benefits to members of the Union. Participating employers make contributions to the Fund, as negotiated in the collective bargaining agreements. At one time, the Fund had more than 1,000 active participants. However, changing demographics and employment conditions in led to the severe contraction of the active membership. Today the Fund has only 500 active participants, while there are 900 retirees receiving pension benefits under the plan. As a result, the Fund is only able to meet its minimum funding requirements by "borrowing" future contributions and applying them to pay current pension obligations.

In 2011, the plaintiffs filed suit, alleging that, despite the continuous funding deficiencies, the trustees regularly approved increases of pension benefits for retired employees. Between 1990 and 2004, the trustees improved benefits payable on an almost annual basis, without fully evaluating whether or not the Fund could afford the improvements without recommending commensurate increases in the rates of employer contribution.

The defendants contend that plaintiffs' claims against them are time-barred because the claims are based on fiduciary conduct alleged to have occurred before 2005, six years prior to the filing of this action.

Plaintiffs cite ERISA's statute of limitations for claims of "fraud or concealment" that allows as timely claims brought within six years from the date of discovery of the breach. They argue that the trustees implemented regular pension benefit increases notwithstanding the precarious financial condition of the Fund, and in doing so knowingly concealed the true status of the Fund from participants. According to plaintiffs, it was not until 2009, with the election of new Union leadership, that the lack of prudent oversight on the part of the former trustees was discovered, and it is from that date the statute began to run.

Defendants move for summary judgment citing the lack of fraudulent concealment. Should the court grant the motion?

[2] Applicable State Statutes of Limitations

ERISA does not provide a specified statute of limitations if the complaint does not allege a fiduciary breach. In such instances, courts look at the state law claim that is the most analogous to the ERISA claim and then apply the state statute of limitations for that claim. (The federal court looks to the law of the state in which it sits.) For an action to recover benefits under § 502(a)(1)(B), the analogous state law claim is almost always held to be a contract claim because the existence of the plan crates contractual obligations upon the employer. Thus, the state statute of limitations for a contract claim is the applicable statute of limitations for the denial of plan benefits claim. Of course, state statute of limitations for contract claims vary considerably, including 15 years in Ohio six years in Georgia and four years in California. Selecting the correct state contract claim statute of limitations can be open to dispurte. In Delaware, for example, the statute of limitations is three years for an action on a promise, but only one year for contracts for labor. Del Code. Ann. tit. 10, §§ 8106, 8111. The Third Circuit, applied the Delaware one year statute of limitations for employment suits in an ERISA claim for long-term disability benefits. *Syed v. Hercules Inc.*, 214 F.3d 155 (3d Cir. 2000).

To avoid being governed by state statutes of limitations for contracts, a plan may provide a time limit for filing benefit claims if the limit is reasonable. A 90-day limitation period for filing benefit claims after completion of the plan's internal review of an employee's medical claims was held to be reasonable and enforceable. The court noted that the plaintiff had adequate time to file suit following a 10-month internal review and the additional 90-day period. As stated by the court, "An ERISA plan is nothing more than a contract, in which parties as a general rule are free to include whatever limitations they desire *Northlake Regional Medical Center v. Waffle House System Employee Benefit Plan*, 160 F.3d 1301, 1303 (11th Cir. 1998). Similarly, a 45-day limitation period was held to be reasonable. *Davidson v. Wal-Mart Associates Health & Welfare Plan*, 305 F. Supp. 2d 1059 (S.D. Iowa 2004).

7-18 QUESTIONS AND PROBLEMS

1. Does the *Northlake* court statement that a benefit plan is merely a contract "in which parties as a general rule are free to include whatever limitations they desire" comport with reality? Do nonunionized employees negotiate the terms of a benefit plan such as the time limits for filing a claim?

2. If employers are free to set "reasonable" limits on the filing of claims for benefits, is that not tantamount to delegating to employers the right to determine the statute of limitations? Is that consistent with the general goal of ERISA to create a uniform law of pensions?

3. How does the reliance upon state statutes of limitations comport with the Congressional intent to "federalize" pension and welfare benefit plan law? Is there

any justification for permitting plaintiffs to have a longer period of time to file a law suit than plaintiffs who live in another state with a shorter statute of limitations for contract claims?

4. Does the existence of concurrent state jurisdiction for ERISA claims under § 502(e) justify reliance upon varying state statutes rather than having a uniform time limit?

Not all ERISA claims are benefit claims that are analogous to a contract claim. For nonbenefit claims, the selection of the appropriate state law to determine the statute of limitations is both problematical and critical. Problematical, because ERISA preemption has insured that states will not have laws or case holdings that govern benefit plans. Consequently, the federal court must select the state analog to the ERISA cause of action. Critical, because the plaintiff may be non-suited if the court selects an analogous state law that has a statute of limitations that expired before the filing of the claim or lawsuit.

The ERISA § 413 statute of limitations does not apply to § 510 claims of interference with a protected plan right or benefit. The majority of courts have concluded that the state law most analogous to § 510 claims are causes of action for wrongful termination or retaliatory discharge. A minority have held that state causes of action for employment discrimination or breach of contract are more analogous.

For suits for claims under § 502(a)(3) to (9), courts adopt the analogous limitation period under state law. For a claim of restitution under § 503(a)(3), for example, the analogous Illinois limitation period is three years.

[3] Exhaustion of Internal Plan Remedies

ERISA § 503.

Although ERISA is silent as to the need of a claimant to exhaust any plan provided avenues of appeal, case law requires exhaustion of plan remedies before filing suit. ERISA § 503 and the Department of Labor's regulations, 29 C.F.R. § 2560.503-1, require that when a plan denies a benefit it must provide a clear written explanation of the specific reasons for the denial and a full and fair review of the claim by the appropriate fiduciary. Only after the internal "full and fair review" will courts permit the participant litigate the denied benefit.

The Tenth Circuit addressed the exhaustion requirement in *McGraw v. Prudential Insurance Co. of America*, 137 F.3d 1253 (10th Cir. 1998). It concluded that although ERISA contains no explicit exhaustion requirement, exhaustion of internal administrative remedies was an implicit prerequisite to seeking judicial relief. According to the court, "This proposition derives from the exhaustion doctrine permeating all judicial review of administrative agency action and aligns with ERISA's overall structure of placing primary responsibility for claim resolution on fund trustees. Otherwise, premature judicial interference with the interpretation of a plan would impede those internal processes which result in a completed record of decision making for a court to review. Nevertheless, "[b]ecause ERISA itself does not specifically require the exhaustion of remedies available under pension plans, courts have applied this requirement as a matter of judicial discretion." In exercising that discretion, district courts have eschewed exhaustion under two limited circumstances: first, when resort to administrative remedies would be futile; or, second, when the remedy provided is inadequate." *Id.* at 1263.

The issue of exhaustion of plan remedies by the plaintiff is the subject of the following case.

HARROW v. PRUDENTIAL INSURANCE CO. OF AMERICA

279 F.3d 244 (3d Cir. 2002)

Scira, Circuit Judge.

Stanley Harrow was insured under the Prudential HealthCare HMO Plan through his wife, Debra Harrow. In 1998, Mr. Harrow was prescribed Viagra, an FDA-approved drug, for diabetes-related impotence. On April 21, 1998, Mr. Harrow filled his prescription for Viagra at a local pharmacy. During this visit, his pharmacist informed him that his insurance did not cover Viagra, charged him $85.99 to fill the Viagra prescription, and instructed him to call Prudential. Upon returning home, Mr. and Mrs. Harrow reviewed the Prudential HealthCare HMO Plan handbook. On that same day, Mrs. Harrow called the claims department number listed on the back of the Prudential prescription card. She was informed by an unidentified person that the plan did not cover Viagra because it was a "new drug." She was also advised to save her receipts for future reimbursement in case Viagra became covered. The Harrows never contacted Prudential again about Viagra coverage and never refilled the prescription. On May 21, 1998, a month after being told Viagra was not covered, Mr. Harrow filed suit under ERISA. In June or July of 1998, Prudential announced in a press release that it would not provide coverage for Viagra.

. . .

The District Court granted summary judgment for the defendant on plaintiff's wrongful denial of benefits claim for failure to exhaust administrative remedies: "Making one step which could be construed as an initial complaint does not constitute exhaustion of all remedies, particularly when the Plan includes a concrete description of the appeal process available." . . . .

. . . .

This appeal followed.

. . . .

B. Summary Judgment was properly granted on plaintiff's benefits claim for failure to exhaust administrative remedies.

An ERISA beneficiary may bring a civil action to "recover benefits due to him under the terms of his plan, to enforce his rights under the terms of his plan, or to clarify his rights to future benefits under the terms of the plan . . . ." [ERISA] § 502(a)(1)(B). "Except in limited circumstances . . . a federal court will not entertain an ERISA claim unless the plaintiff has exhausted the remedies available under the plan." *Weldon v. Kraft, Inc.*, 896 F.2d 793, 800 (3d Cir. 1990). *See also Amato v. Bernard*, 618 F.2d 559, 567 (9th Cir. 1980) ("Sound policy requires the application of the exhaustion doctrine in suits under [ERISA]."). Courts require exhaustion of administrative remedies "to help reduce the number of frivolous lawsuits under ERISA; to promote the consistent treatment of claims for benefits; to provide a nonadversarial method of claims settlement; and to minimize the costs of claims settlement for all concerned." *Amato*, 618 F.2d at 567. Moreover, trustees of an ERISA plan "are granted broad fiduciary rights and responsibilities under

ERISA . . . and implementation of the exhaustion requirement will enhance their ability to expertly and efficiently manage their funds by preventing premature judicial intervention in their decision-making processes." *Id.*; *see also Zipf*, 799 F.2d at 892 ("When a plan participant claims that he or she has unjustly been denied benefits, it is appropriate to require participants first to address their complaints to the fiduciaries to whom Congress, in Section 503, assigned the primary responsibility for evaluating claims for benefits.").

A plaintiff is excused from exhausting administrative procedures under ERISA if it would be futile to do so . . . .

Whether to excuse exhaustion on futility grounds rests upon weighing several factors, including: (1) whether plaintiff diligently pursued administrative relief; (2) whether plaintiff acted reasonably in seeking immediate judicial review under the circumstances; (3) existence of a fixed policy denying benefits; (4) failure of the insurance company to comply with its own internal administrative procedures; and (5) testimony of plan administrators that any administrative appeal was futile. Of course, all factors may not weigh equally.

. . . .

Other courts of appeals have addressed whether the futility exception applies in circumstances that more closely mirror our case. These cases involve plaintiffs who, like Mr. Harrow, have requested plan benefits. Given the policies underlying the exhaustion requirement, these courts have been reluctant to grant the exception without clear evidence of futility . . . .

. . . .

Because the Harrows took no steps beyond an initial telephonic inquiry, the District Court held that plaintiff did not qualify for the futility exception.

We see no abuse of discretion in the District Court's refusal to apply the futility exception to the exhaustion doctrine. Mr. Harrow made one telephone call to Prudential before instituting an ERISA suit. Mr. and Mrs. Harrow reviewed the plan handbook outlining complaint procedures, but none were filed. The press release announcing Prudential's general policy of denying coverage was made at least one month after Mr. Harrow brought suit. Mrs. Harrow was told to save her receipts in the event Prudential did cover the drug, suggesting that internal administrative procedures would not necessarily be futile. Furthermore, Prudential administrators testified that the outcome of its internal appeal procedures was not predetermined, although as the District Court noted, there was conflicting testimony in this regard. Viewing the facts and weighing the relevant factors, we agree with the District Court that a plaintiff in these circumstances was obligated to do more than make one telephonic inquiry before instituting suit. In this sense, plaintiff did not act reasonably.

This case is difficult because at some point in the future — in this instance, only a few months — Prudential adopted a blanket policy denying coverage for Viagra. But at the time Mr. Harrow filed suit it was unclear and uncertain whether Prudential would automatically bar coverage. More importantly, the Harrows took no action after the initial phone call to an unidentified person to press their request. Under this set of facts, the exhaustion of remedies requirement demands more. For these reasons, we agree the futility exception does not apply and we will affirm the District Court's grant of summary judgment on the benefits claim for failure to exhaust administrative remedies.

C. Summary Judgment was properly granted on plaintiff's breach of fiduciary duty claim

The District Court also dismissed the claim alleging breach of fiduciary duty for failure to exhaust administrative remedies. Mrs. Harrow con tends the exhaustion requirement does not apply because she is asserting statutory rights under ERISA § 404. But the District Court held that the fiduciary duty claim merely recast the benefits claim in statutory terms and was still subject to the exhaustion doctrine. We agree.

As noted, courts require exhaustion of administrative remedies prior to hearing an action for a denial of ERISA benefits. We apply the exhaustion requirement to ERISA benefit claims, but not to claims arising from violations of substantive statutory provisions . . . .[4]

In *Zipf*, we explained why we do not apply the exhaustion doctrine to claims arising under substantive provisions like § 510:

> When a plan participant claims that he or she has unjustly been denied benefits, it is appropriate to require participants first to address their complaints to the fiduciaries to whom Congress, in Section 503, assigned the primary responsibility for evaluating claims for benefits . . . However, when the claimant's position is that his or her federal rights guaranteed by ERISA have been violated, these considerations are simply inapposite. Unlike a claim for benefits brought pursuant to a benefits plan, a Section 510 claim asserts a statutory right which plan fiduciaries have no expertise in interpreting. Accordingly, one of the primary justifications for an exhaustion requirement in other contexts, deference to administrative expertise, is simply absent. Indeed, there is a strong interest in judicial resolution of these claims, for the purpose of providing a consistent source of law to help plan fiduciaries and participants predict the legality of proposed actions.

Id. at 892–93.

To date, the cases applying the *Zipf* exception have primarily fallen in two categories: "(1) discrimination claims under § 510 of ERISA, or (2) failure to provide plaintiffs with summary plan descriptions, as required by ERISA." But the rationale articulated in *Zipf* is equally applicable to claims brought under ERISA §§ 404–406, for breach of fiduciary duty because these claims are also statutory.

Plaintiffs cannot circumvent the exhaustion requirement by artfully pleading benefit claims as breach of fiduciary duty claims. *Drinkwater v. Metro. Life Ins. Co.*, 846 F.2d 821, 826 (1st Cir. 1988) (exhaustion doctrine would be "rendered

---

[4] The circuits "are in sharp disagreement" as to whether plaintiffs must exhaust administrative remedies before bringing an action in federal court to assert a violation of substantive statutory provisions like ERISA § 510 (unlawful termination) and § 404 (breach of fiduciary duty). *Smith v. Sydnor*, 184 F.3d 356, 364 (4th Cir. 1999). *Compare id.* at 365 ("The judicially created exhaustion requirement does not apply to a claim for breach of fiduciary duty as defined in ERISA."); and *Horan v. Kaiser Steel Retirement Plan*, 947 F.2d 1412, 1416 n.1 (9th Cir. 1991) ("The exhaustion requirement applies to plaintiffs' benefits claim, but does not apply to the plaintiffs' fiduciary breach claim because this claim alleges a violation of the statute, ERISA, rather than the Plan."); and *Held v. Manf. Hanover Leasing Corp.*, 912 F.2d 1197, 1205 (10th Cir. 1990) (not requiring exhaustion for an unlawful termination claim); with *Perrino v. S. Bell Tel. & Tel. Co.*, 209 F.3d 1309, 1316 (11th Cir. 2000) ("We apply this exhaustion requirement to both ERISA claims arising from the substantive provisions . . . and ERISA claims arising from an employment . . . agreement."); and *Lindemann*, 79 F.3d at 650 (stating District Court has discretion to require exhaustion for ERISA § 510 claim).

meaningless" if plaintiffs were allowed to bypass exhaustion by artfully dressing contract claims in statutory clothing). When the facts alleged do not present a breach of fiduciary duty claim that is independent of a claim for benefits, the exhaustion doctrine still applies. *See Smith*, 184 F.3d at 363 (independent fiduciary duty claim established where plaintiffs alleged that defendants sold preferred stock at undervalued prices); *Diaz*, 50 F.3d at 1484–85 (discussing applicability of exhaustion where plaintiffs alleged that plan's failure to notify them in Spanish was a statutory breach). A claim for breach of fiduciary duty is "actually a claim for benefits where the resolution of the claim rests upon an interpretation and application of an ERISA-regulated plan rather than upon an interpretation and application of ERISA." *Smith*, 184 F.3d at 362.

Here, plaintiff's complaint states:

> In failing to insure that plaintiff and members of the class were furnished with coverage under the Plans for their Viagra prescriptions, defendants have failed to discharge their duties: (a) solely in the interest of the Plan participants and beneficiaries and for the exclusive purpose of providing benefits to the participants and beneficiaries; (b) with the requisite care and skill required of ERISA fiduciaries; and (c) in accordance with the documents and instruments governing the Plan.

Given this language, the District Court concluded plaintiff was recasting a benefits claim in statutory terms as a means of bypassing the exhaustion requirement. ("Although couched in terms of a statute, plaintiff's claim is based on the Plan itself and the failure of the defendant to provide benefits under the Plan.") The District Court explained:

> Plaintiff's breach of duty claim clearly involves some legal issues, [but] is premised on the fiduciaries' responsibilities under the Plan. This is a topic on which the Plan fiduciaries have expertise. In addition, this Court believes that a claim for breach of a duty to provide benefits should not be brought before giving the Plan fiduciaries an opportunity to provide those benefits. This could only occur through exhaustion of administrative remedies.

We agree that plaintiff is actually challenging a denial of benefits, and not conduct amounting to a statutory breach of fiduciary duty. Unlike the plaintiffs in Smith, Mrs. Harrow does not allege facts that, if proven, establish a breach of fiduciary duty independent of the denial of benefits (e.g., selling preferred stock at an undervalued price). As the District Court observed, the language of the complaint itself demonstrates that Mrs. Harrow's claim was actually premised on the plan administrators' failure to furnish plaintiff with insurance coverage for Viagra. Furthermore, Mrs. Harrow attempts to bolster her argument that the fiduciary duty claim is "independent" by arguing for the first time on appeal that Prudential failed to issue a written denial of benefits as required under [ERISA § 503(1)]. To be sure, "many employee claims for plan benefits may implicate statutory requirements imposed by ERISA . . . but that prospect does not give a claimant the license to attach a 'statutory violation' sticker to his or her claim and then to use that label as an asserted justification for a total failure to pursue the congressionally mandated internal appeal procedures." The Harrows made only one phone call to Prudential before instituting the present suit and cannot now excuse their failure to exhaust administrative remedies by draping a benefits claim in statutory language.

Having concluded that Mrs. Harrow's claim for breach of fiduciary duty constitutes a recasting of a claim for benefits, we hold that the District Court properly granted summary judgment for failure to exhaust administrative remedies.

7-19 QUESTIONS AND PROBLEMS

1. Is a withholding of benefits always a breach of fiduciary duty?

2. What legal options are now available to Mrs. Harrow and the class of plaintiffs that she represented? Can she now appeal the denial of benefits to the plan administrator as provided in the plan handbook?

3. Since ERISA is silent as to the need for the exhaustion of internal claim and appeal procedures, are the courts correct in creating an exhaustion requirement?

4. Does the lack of an express exhaustion requirement suggest that ERISA is not a "comprehensible" as suggested by the Supreme Court in the remedies cases?

5. What is the justification for the requirement of exhaustion when claiming a denial of benefits, but not for a breach of fiduciary duty?

The failure to exhaust administrative remedies can result in the loss of judicial review. In *Graham v. Federal Express Corp.*, 725 F. Supp. 429 (W.D. Ark. 1989), the court dismissed a lawsuit when the plaintiff failed to appeal a claim within the 60-day period allotted by the plan. Moreover, because the 60-day appeal period had long since elapsed by the time the action was brought, all further appeals were deemed untimely. *See also Tiger v. AT & T Technologies Plan for Employees' Pensions, Disability Benefits*, 633 F. Supp. 532 (E.D.N.Y. 1986).

H. ATTORNEY FEES

ERISA § 502(g)(1).

ERISA § 502(g)(1) provides that courts in their discretion may award reasonable attorney's fees and the costs of litigation to either party. The Supreme Court addressed the question whether a fee claimant must be the "prevailing party" in order to be entitled to an award of attorney's fees in the following case.

HARDT v. RELIANCE STANDARD LIFE INSURANCE CO.

130 S. Ct. 2149 (2010)

JUSTICE THOMAS delivered the opinion of the Court.

In most lawsuits seeking relief under the Employee Retirement Income Security Act of 1974 (ERISA) "a reasonable attorney's fee and costs" are available "to either party" at the court's "discretion." ERISA § 502(g)(1). The Court of Appeals for the Fourth Circuit has interpreted § 502(g)(1) to require that a fee claimant be a "prevailing party" before he may seek a fees award. We reject this interpretation as contrary to § 502(g)(1)'s plain text. We hold instead that a court "in its discretion" may award fees and costs "to either party," *ibid.*, as long as the fee claimant has achieved "some degree of success on the merits," *Ruckelshaus v. Sierra Club*, 463 U.S. 680, 694 (1983).

I

In 2000, while working as an executive assistant to the president of textile manufacturer Dan River, Inc., petitioner Bridget Hardt began experiencing neck and shoulder pain. Her doctors eventually diagnosed her with carpal tunnel syndrome. Because surgeries on both her wrists failed to alleviate her pain, Hardt stopped working in January 2003.

In August 2003, Hardt sought long-term disability benefits from Dan River's Group Long-Term Disability Insurance Program Plan (Plan). Dan River administers the Plan, which is subject to ERISA, but respondent Reliance Standard Life Insurance Company decides whether a claimant qualifies for benefits under the Plan and underwrites any benefits awarded. Reliance provisionally approved Hardt's claim, telling her that final approval hinged on her performance in a functional capacities evaluation intended to assess the impact of her carpal tunnel syndrome and neck pain on her ability to work.

Hardt completed the functional capacities evaluation in October 2003. The evaluator summarized Hardt's medical history, observed her resulting physical limitations, and ultimately found that Hardt could perform some amount of sedentary work. Based on this finding, Reliance concluded that Hardt was not totally disabled within the meaning of the Plan and denied her claim for disability benefits. Hardt filed an administrative appeal. Reliance reversed itself in part, finding that Hardt was totally disabled from her regular occupation, and was therefore entitled to temporary disability benefits for 24 months.

While her administrative appeal was pending, Hardt began experiencing new symptoms in her feet and calves, including tingling, pain, and numbness. One of her physicians diagnosed her with small-fiber neuropathy, a condition that increased her pain and decreased her physical capabilities over the ensuing months.

Hardt eventually applied to the Social Security Administration for disability benefits under the Social Security Act. Her application included questionnaires completed by two of her treating physicians, which described Hardt's symptoms and stated the doctors' conclusion that Hardt could not return to full gainful employment because of her neuropathy and other ailments. In February 2005, the Social Security Administration granted Hardt's application and awarded her disability benefits.

About two months later, Reliance told Hardt that her Plan benefits would expire at the end of the 24-month period. Reliance explained that under the Plan's terms, only individuals who are "totally disabled from all occupations" were eligible for benefits beyond that period, and adhered to its conclusion that, based on its review of Hardt's records, Hardt was not "totally disabled" as defined by the Plan. Reliance also demanded that Hardt pay Reliance $14,913.23 to offset the disability benefits she had received from the Social Security Administration. (The Plan contains a provision coordinating benefits with Social Security payments.) Hardt paid Reliance the offset.

Hardt then filed another administrative appeal. She gave Reliance all of her medical records, the questionnaires she had submitted to the Social Security Administration, and an updated questionnaire from one of her physicians. Reliance asked Hardt to supplement this material with another functional capacities evaluation. When Reliance referred Hardt for the updated evaluation, it did not ask the evaluator to review Hardt for neuropathic pain, even though it knew that Hardt had been diagnosed with neuropathy after her first evaluation.

Hardt appeared for the updated evaluation in December 2005, and appeared for another evaluation in January 2006. The evaluators deemed both evaluations invalid because Hardt's efforts were "submaximal."

Lacking an updated functional capacities evaluation, Reliance hired a physician and a vocation rehabilitation counselor to help it resolve Hardt's administrative appeal. The physician did not examine Hardt; instead, he reviewed some, but not all, of Hardt's medical records. Based on that review, the physician produced a report in which he opined that Hardt's health was expected to improve. His report, however, did not mention Hardt's pain medications or the questionnaires that Hardt's attending physicians had completed as part of her application for Social Security benefits. The vocational rehabilitation counselor, in turn, performed a labor market study (based on Hardt's health in 2003) that identified eight employment opportunities suitable for Hardt. After reviewing the physician's report, the labor market study, and the results of the 2003 functional capacities evaluation, Reliance concluded that its decision to terminate Hardt's benefits was correct. It advised Hardt of this decision in March 2006.

After exhausting her administrative remedies, Hardt sued Reliance in the United States District Court for the Eastern District of Virginia. She alleged that Reliance violated ERISA by wrongfully denying her claim for long-term disability benefits. See § 502(a)(1)(B). The parties filed cross-motions for summary judgment, both of which the District Court denied.

The court first rejected Reliance's request for summary judgment affirming the denial of benefits, finding that "Reliance's decision to deny benefits was based on incomplete information." . . . The court also found that Reliance had "improperly rejected much of the evidence that Ms. Hardt submitted," *id.* at 45a, and had "further ignored the substantial amount of pain medication Ms. Hardt's treating physicians had prescribed to her." Accordingly, the court thought it "clear that Reliance's decision to deny Ms. Hardt long-term disability benefits was not based on substantial evidence."

The District Court then denied Hardt's motion for summary judgment, which contended that Reliance's decision to deny benefits was unreasonable as a matter of law. In so doing, however, the court found "compelling evidence" in the record that "Ms. Hardt [wa]s totally disabled due to her neuropathy." Although it was "inclined to rule in Ms. Hardt's favor," the court concluded that "it would be unwise to take this step without first giving Reliance the chance to address the deficiencies in its approach." In the District Court's view, a remand to Reliance was warranted because "[t]his case presents one of those scenarios where the plan administrator has failed to comply with the ERISA guidelines," meaning "Ms. Hardt did not get the kind of review to which she was entitled under applicable law." Accordingly, the court instructed "Reliance to act on Ms. Hardt's application by adequately considering all the evidence" within 30 days; "[o]therwise," it warned, "judgment will be issued in favor of Ms. Hardt."

Reliance did as instructed. After conducting that review, Reliance found Hardt eligible for long-term disability benefits and paid her $55,250 in accrued, past-due benefits.

Hardt then moved for attorney's fees and costs under § 502(g)(1). The District Court assessed her motion under the three-step framework that governed fee requests in ERISA cases under Circuit precedent. At step one of that framework, a district court asks whether the fee claimant is a " 'prevailing party.' " If the fee claimant qualifies as a prevailing party, the court proceeds to step two and "determin[es] whether an award of attorneys' fees is appropriate" by examining "five factors." Finally, if those five factors suggest that a fees award is appropriate, the court "must review the attorneys' fees and costs requested and limit them to a reasonable amount."

Applying that framework, the District Court granted Hardt's motion . . . .

Reliance appealed the fees award, and the Court of Appeals vacated the District Court's order. According to the Court of Appeals, Hardt failed to satisfy the step-one inquiry — *i.e.*, she failed to establish that she was a "prevailing party." In reaching that conclusion, the Court of Appeals relied on this Court's decision in *Buckhannon*, under which a fee claimant qualifies as a "prevailing party" only if he has obtained an " 'enforceable judgmen[t] on the merits' " or a " 'court-ordered consent decre[e].' " The Court of Appeals reasoned that because the remand order "did not require Reliance to award benefits to Hardt," it did "not constitute an 'enforceable judgment on the merits' as *Buckhannon* requires," thus precluding Hardt from establishing prevailing party status.

II

Whether § 502(g)(1) limits the availability of attorney's fees to a "prevailing party" is a question of statutory construction. As in all such cases, we begin by analyzing the statutory language, "assum[ing] that the ordinary meaning of that language accurately expresses the legislative purpose." *Gross v. FBL Financial Services, Inc.*, 557 U.S. ___, ___ (2009).

Section 502(g)(1) provides:

> "In any action under this subchapter (other than an action described in paragraph (2)) by a participant, beneficiary, or fiduciary, the court in its discretion may allow a reasonable attorney's fee and costs of action to either party."

The words "prevailing party" do not appear in this provision. Nor does anything else in § 502(g)(1)'s text purport to limit the availability of attorney's fees to a "prevailing party." Instead, § 502(g)(1) expressly grants district courts "discretion" to award attorney's fees "to *either* party." (Emphasis added.)

That language contrasts sharply with § 502(g)(2), which governs the availability of attorney's fees in ERISA actions under § 515 (actions to recover delinquent employer contributions to a multiemployer plan). In such cases, only plaintiffs who obtain "a judgment in favor of the plan" may seek attorney's fees. § 502(g)(2)(D). The contrast between these two paragraphs makes clear that Congress knows how to impose express limits on the availability of attorney's fees in ERISA cases. Because Congress failed to include in § 502(g)(1) an express "prevailing party" limit on the availability of attorney's fees, the Court of Appeals' decision adding that term of art to a fee-shifting statute from which it is conspicuously absent more closely resembles "invent[ing] a statute rather than interpret[ing] one."

We see no reason to dwell any longer on this question. We therefore hold that a fee claimant need not be a "prevailing party" to be eligible for an attorney's fees award under § 502(g)(1).

III

We next consider the circumstances under which a court may award attorney's fees pursuant to § 502(g)(1). "Our basic point of reference" when considering the award of attorney's fees is the bedrock principle known as the " 'American Rule' ": Each litigant pays his own attorney's fees, win or lose, unless a statute or contract provides otherwise. Statutory changes to this rule take various forms. Most fee-shifting provisions permit a court to award attorney's fees only to a "prevailing party." Others permit a "substantially prevailing" party or a "successful" litigant to obtain fees. Still others authorize district courts to award attorney's fees where "appropriate," or simply vest district courts with "discretion" to award fees.

Of those statutory deviations from the American Rule, we have most often considered statutes containing an express "prevailing party" requirement. Our "prevailing party" precedents, however, do not govern the availability of fees awards under § 502(g)(1), because this provision does not limit the availability of attorney's fees to the "prevailing party."

. . . [w]e first look to "the language of the section," *id.* at 682, which unambiguously allows a court to award attorney's fees "in its discretion . . . to either party," § 502(g)(1). Statutes vesting judges with such broad discretion are well known in the law, particularly in the attorney's fees context.

Ruckelshaus lays down the proper markers to guide a court in exercising the discretion that § 502(g)(1) grants. As in the statute at issue in *Ruckelshaus*, Congress failed to indicate clearly in § 502(g)(1) that it "meant to abandon historic fee-shifting principles and intuitive notions of fairness." 463 U.S. at 686. Accordingly, a fees claimant must show "some degree of success on the merits" before a court may award attorney's fees under § 502(g)(1), *id.* at 694. A claimant does not satisfy that requirement by achieving "trivial success on the merits" or a "purely procedural victor[y]," but does satisfy it if the court can fairly call the outcome of the litigation some success on the merits without conducting a "lengthy inquir[y] into the question whether a particular party's success was 'substantial' or occurred on a 'central issue.' " *Id.* at 688.

Reliance essentially agrees that this standard should govern fee requests under § 502(g)(1), but argues that Hardt has not satisfied it. Specifically, Reliance contends that a court order remanding an ERISA claim for further consideration can never constitute "some success on the merits," even if such a remand results in an award of benefits. See *id.* at 34–50.

Reliance's argument misses the point, given the facts of this case. Hardt persuaded the District Court to find that "the plan administrator has failed to comply with the ERISA guidelines" and "that Ms. Hardt did not get the kind of review to which she was entitled under applicable law." Although Hardt failed to win summary judgment on her benefits claim, the District Court nevertheless found "compelling evidence that Ms. Hardt is totally disabled due to her neuropathy," and stated that it was "inclined to rule in Ms. Hardt's favor" on her benefits claim, but declined to do so before "first giving Reliance the chance to address the deficiencies in its" statutorily mandated "full and fair review" of that claim. Hardt thus obtained a judicial order instructing Reliance "to act on Ms. Hardt's application by adequately considering all the evidence" within 30 days; "[o]therwise, judgment will be issued in favor of Ms. Hardt." After Reliance conducted that court-ordered review, and consistent with the District Court's appraisal, Reliance reversed its decision and awarded Hardt the benefits she sought.

These facts establish that Hardt has achieved far more than "trivial success on the merits" or a "purely procedural victory." Accordingly, she has achieved "some success on the merits," and the District Court properly exercised its discretion to award Hardt attorney's fees in this case. Because these conclusions resolve this case, we need not decide today whether a remand order, without more, constitutes "some success on the merits" sufficient to make a party eligible for attorney's fees under § 502(g)(1).

We reverse the judgment of the Court of Appeals for the Fourth Circuit and remand this case for proceedings consistent with this opinion . . . .

In theory, a plan or fiduciary who has been unsuccessfully sued by a plan participant or beneficiary can collect its attorney fees and costs from the plaintiff. In practice, courts are willing to award attorneys fees and costs to victorious plaintiffs, but are very reluctant to assess the litigation expenses against losing plaintiffs. *Jones v. O'Higgins*, 736 F. Supp. 1243 (N.D.N.Y. 1990). Awards to defendants have occurred when the plaintiff's claims lacked substance or were abusive. Courts, however, do not want to punish a plaintiff whose lawsuit seemed reasonable when filed and only later was shown to lack merit. This asymmetrical treatment of attorney's fees has been criticized as being inconsistent with the language and the legislative history of ERISA. *Bittner v. Sadoff & Rudoy Industries*, 728 F.2d 820 (7th Cir. 1984).

Attorney fees are often calculated using the lodestar method, which multiplies the time spent by a reasonable hourly rate modified by a fee enhancement. First, the fee is estimated using a basic hourly rate. Next the fee is adjusted up or down depending on the particular circumstances of the case including the lawyers' "experience, skill, and reputation." *Blum v. Stenson*, 465 U.S. 886, 895 n.11 (1984). For class action lawsuits, a prevailing plaintiff may be awarded attorney fees based upon a court approved contingency fee, i.e. a percentage of the settlement or judgment.

I. RIGHT TO JURY TRIAL

ERISA is silent about whether claims are triable by a jury. Claims under § 502(a)(1)(B) to enforce benefits due under the terms of a plan have been held to be equitable in nature because they invoke the law of trusts (the pension being paid out of a trust) and thus not triable by jury. *Wardle v. Central States Pension Fund*, 627 F.2d 820 (7th Cir. 1980). Cases arising under § 510, interference with ERISA rights, have in the past been held to be in the nature of wrongful termination or breach of contract, thus legal in nature and so triable by a jury. *McDonald v. Artcraft Electric Supply Co.*, 774 F. Supp. 29 (D.D.C. 1991). But in 1993, the Ninth Circuit held a § 510 wrongful discharge, though a tort in nature, resulted in § 502(a)(3) equitable remedies and so precludes the use of a jury. *Spinelli v. Gaughan*, 12 F.3d 853 (9th Cir. 1993).

Chapter 8
NONDISCRIMINATION RULES

Almost since the inception of the federal income tax in 1913, Congress has encouraged the formation of private pension plans by affording them favorable income tax treatment. Indeed, as discussed in Chapter 1, the net exclusion of pension contributions and earnings for employer plans currently represents the second largest federal tax expenditure, estimated to be $515.4 billion of foregone income tax revenues from 2010 to 2014.

Sometimes described as a "carrot," this favorable income tax treatment does not affect all potential pension participants equally. Rather, because the value of a tax deferral is directly correlated to a taxpayer's marginal income tax rate, the higher an individual's income, the greater the tax incentive is. Thus, standing alone, this "carrot" might encourage employers to create pension plans that only benefit, or disproportionately benefit, highly paid workers. For example, a plan might solely benefit the doctors in a small office and exclude the nurses and receptionist. Or a plan for a Fortune 500 company might only benefit the company's executives and exclude all other employees from middle management down to hourly workers.

In order to prevent employers from using these tax benefits to create plans that solely, or disproportionately, benefit the highly paid, Congress has enacted nondiscrimination rules, sometimes referred to as a "stick." The nondiscrimination rules are intended to ensure that pension plans that receive favorable tax treatment provide meaningful benefits to employees at all income levels, not just the highly paid.

There are two key components to the nondiscrimination rules: (1) the IRC § 410(b) minimum coverage rules, and (2) the IRC § 401(a)(4) rule prohibiting discrimination in contributions or benefits. The minimum coverage rules are designed to ensure that the group of employees benefitting under a plan is an acceptable combination of highly compensated and non-highly compensated employees. The prohibition against discrimination in contributions or benefits is designed to ensure that the benefits provided to non-highly compensated employees for a year is roughly comparable to the benefits provided to the highly compensated employees for that year. In addition to these two key nondiscrimination requirements, IRC § 401(a)(26) also requires that defined benefit plans satisfy minimum participation standards.

The nondiscrimination rules can be quite simple to satisfy. For example, if Alpha Company establishes a profit-sharing plan that covers all ten of its employees, and contributes two percent of pay each year on behalf of each employee, the plan will easily satisfy the nondiscrimination requirements.

On the other hand, the nondiscrimination rules can be exceedingly difficult to apply. Some of this difficulty is due to the complexity of the modern corporate world. In the case of a vast corporate structure like Philip Morris or Daimler-Chrysler, it can be difficult to identify who exactly is the employer. More importantly, the rules do not mandate 100 percent coverage or absolute uniformity in contributions or benefits. Instead, the rules permit a limited amount of discrimination in favor of highly compensated employees. For example, the rules permit plans to exclude most part-time employees as well as employees covered by a collectively bargained agreement if pension benefits were an element of good faith bargaining.

As you read these materials, think about why the rules are so complex and whether — and how — they could be simplified. Remember, the rules only apply to qualified plans. An employer can avoid the rules by foregoing the tax benefits and establishing a non-qualified plan. In addition, an employer can avoid most of the complexity of the rules by establishing a plan that covers 100 percent of its employees and treats all of the employees in a uniform manner.

The Internal Revenue Code's prohibition against discrimination in favor of highly compensated employees runs throughout the Code. For example, the IRC § 411 vesting rules contain a nondiscrimination requirement, *see* IRC § 411(d), and IRC § 105(h) imposes a nondiscrimination requirement on benefits paid under a self-insured medical reimbursement plan. This chapter focuses on the principle nondiscrimination rules that apply to qualified retirement plans.

The chapter begins with a brief history of the nondiscrimination rules. It then discusses the preliminary issues that must be resolved before the rules may be applied. Those issues include identifying the entity and employees to be tested and determining which employees qualify as highly compensated. It then turns to the question of identifying the plan or plans to be tested. Finally, it addresses each of the nondiscrimination rules, beginning with the IRC § 401(a)(26) minimum participation requirement, then turning to the IRC § 410(b) minimum coverage requirement, and finally the IRC § 401(a)(4) prohibition against discrimination in contributions or benefits.

A. BRIEF HISTORY OF THE NONDISCRIMINATION RULES

JOSEPH BANKMAN, TAX POLICY AND RETIREMENT INCOME: ARE PENSION PLAN ANTI-DISCRIMINATION PROVISIONS DESIRABLE?

55 U. Chi. L. Rev. 790, 800–803 (1988)

The [anti-discrimination] rules appear to have originated in 1937 hearings before a specially convened Joint Committee on Tax Evasion and Avoidance. Pensions at that time were taxed in the same manner as they are taxed today: contributions were deductible to the employers, and employees were taxed on contributions and pension earnings, only upon withdrawal. These favorable provisions, then as now, made pensions particularly attractive to highly taxed employees and contributed to the development of plans designed exclusively for these employees. Noting this development, the Treasury argued that the original intent of the pension provisions — 'to encourage a sort of social security on the part of individual corporations' — had been 'twisted into a means of tax avoidance by the creation of pension trusts which include as beneficiaries only small groups of officers and directors who are in the high income brackets.'

The Treasury recommended that the then-current requirement that tax-qualified plans benefit 'some or all' employees be modified to require coverage of a 'reasonable number' of employees. The Treasury's recommendation was set forth in written supplemental materials offered to the Committee and was discussed only in passing in five days of hearings. The recommendation did not appear to provoke outside commentary and was not incorporated in the Committee's recommendations.

In 1942, the heart of the current anti-discrimination regimen was proposed by the Treasury and passed by Congress. In support of the legislation, the Treasury reiterated its belief that the subsidy inherent in the pension provisions had led to plans which gave too many benefits to highly compensated employees and too few benefits to rank-and-file employees. The legislation was also described as one of a number of necessary war-related revenue measures which would produce an estimated $100,000,000 in annual receipts.

The anti-discrimination proposals were noted in the press and discussed in hearings. Debate and commentary on the measure, however, centered on a side issue: whether the vesting provisions proposed by the Treasury (and ultimately rejected by Congress) would trigger the termination of the American Telephone and Telegraph Company pension plan. There was no discussion of the merits to a rule of proportionate equality of benefits or the effect of such a rule on wages rates. In a statement consistent with the position espoused by the Treasury but otherwise unilluminating, the House Committee Report explained that the measure was intended 'to insure that stock bonus, pension, or profit-sharing plans are operated for the welfare of employees in general, and to prevent the trust device from being used for the benefit of shareholders, officials, or highly paid employees . . . .'

Since 1942, the anti-discrimination rules have been strengthened through the enactment of vesting, aggregation, and top-heavy provisions, and through amendments to the coverage and integration provisions. However, the more recent legislative history says almost nothing about the purpose or efficacy of the anti-discrimination regimen.

8-1 QUESTIONS AND PROBLEMS

1. In general terms, what is the purpose of the nondiscrimination rules? To curtail the use of pension plans as tax shelters covering only key employees? To reserve the tax subsidy for pension plans that provide some social benefit — that is, benefits for the lower paid? To affirmatively encourage the formation of pension plans that provide benefits for the lower paid?

2. Given that qualified pension plans cover about half the workforce, and that half of the workforce tends to be the higher paid half, how successful are the nondiscrimination rules?

3. Why doesn't ERISA contain any nondiscrimination requirements like those contained in the Internal Revenue Code?

4. Why don't the nondiscrimination requirements apply to non-qualified plans?

5. Why doesn't Congress insist upon universal coverage and absolutely uniform treatment of all employees?

B. PRELIMINARY ISSUES

Determining whether a retirement plan satisfies the tax nondiscrimination requirements requires that a number of preliminary issues be resolved. First, the employer must be identified. In some instances, this may be simple and obvious. For example, in the case of a small company with a small workforce, the company is likely to be the employer. On the other hand, in the case of a complex corporate structure like General Electric or AOL Time Warner, it may be much more difficult to identify the employer.

Once the employer is identified, the employees must be identified. Again, in some instances this question may be easy to answer. For example, in the case of a small company with a few workers, those workers are likely to be the employees. On the other hand, if the company leases most of its employees from a separate agency, questions may arise as to who qualifies as employees of the company.

Finally, since the nondiscrimination rules prohibit discrimination in favor of "highly compensated employees," the highly compensated employees must be identified before the nondiscrimination requirements may be applied.

[1] Identification of Employer

Prior to the enactment of ERISA, the nondiscrimination rules applied separately to each entity. Consequently, an employer could circumvent the nondiscrimination rules by restructuring its business so that all of its highly compensated employees were employed in a single, separate, subsidiary and provide retirement benefits only to the employees in that subsidiary. To prevent employers from circumventing the nondiscrimination rules by structuring their businesses in this fashion, Congress added sections 414(b) and 414(c) to the Internal Revenue Code. These provisions require that entities that are directly or indirectly related be aggregated for purposes of applying the nondiscrimination rules.

Following the enactment of IRC §§ 414(b) and (c), taxpayers found new ways to structure their businesses so as to circumvent the nondiscrimination rules. For example, many professionals, such as doctors and lawyers, began to place their common law employees into separate partnerships composed of their professional corporations, and excluded those employees from their retirement plans. (Common law employees are discussed in Chapter 2.) Later, to get around the nondiscrimination rules, professional corporations began to "lease" their employees from separate leasing organizations. Congress added sections 414(m), (n), and ultimately (o) to the Internal Revenue Code to counteract taxpayers' creativity in avoiding the nondiscrimination rules.

This section examines the rules that govern the identification of the employer for purposes of the nondiscrimination rules. The rules may be thought of as a dance between taxpayers who seek to avoid the nondiscrimination rules and Congress who amends the Internal Revenue Code in response to taxpayer creativity.

[a] Employers under Common Control

IRC §§ 414(b) and (c).

For purposes of the nondiscrimination rules (as well as other purposes), employers with a sufficient degree of common ownership are treated as a single employer. IRC §§ 414(b) & (c). These provisions apply even if the related employers do not jointly maintain the same plan.

Pursuant to IRC § 414(b), employees of corporations who are members of a controlled group of corporations, as generally defined in IRC § 1563, will be treated as if employed by a single employer. IRC § 414(c) applies similar rules to employees of unincorporated trades or businesses under common control.

There are three basic types of controlled groups for purposes of IRC §§ 414(b) and (c): (1) a parent-subsidiary group, (2) a brother-sister group, and (3) a combined parent-subsidiary/brother-sister group.

A "parent-subsidiary group of trades or businesses under common control" is one in which one or more chains of organizations conducting trades or businesses are connected through ownership of a controlling interest by a common parent.

Treas. Reg. § 1.414(c)-2(b)(1). A controlling interest is generally defined as an 80 percent or more interest. Treas. Reg. § 1.414(c)-2(c)(i). In the case of a corporation, a controlling interest consists of 80 percent of the total combined voting power of all classes of stock entitled to vote, or at least 80 percent of the total value of all shares of all classes of stock of the corporation. Treas. Reg. § 1.414(c)-2(c)(i)(A). Common ownership can result from a chain of businesses linked by 80 percent ownership, or by a parent corporation with direct 80 percent ownership in any number of businesses.

A "brother-sister group of trades or businesses under common control" consists of two or more trades or businesses which satisfy two requirements: (1) the same five or fewer persons who are individuals, estates, or trusts, own a controlling interest (that is, 80 percent ownership as discussed above) in each organization, Treas. Reg. § 1.414(c)-2(c)(1)(i), IRC § 1563(a)(2)(A); and (2) taking into account the ownership of each such person only to the extent that it is identical with respect to each such organization, such 5 persons are in "effective control" of the organization, Treas. Reg. § 1.414(c)-2(c)(1)(ii), IRC § 1563(a)(2)(B). "Effective control" means the same thing as "controlling interest" except that effective control is more than 50 percent interest or ownership.

For example, suppose that Able owns 60 percent of the only class of stock of Alpha Corporation and 20 percent of the only class of stock of Beta Corporation. Brutus owns 20 percent of the stock of Alpha and 40 percent of the stock of Beta. Cody owns the remaining 20 percent of the stock of Alpha and the remaining 40 percent of the stock of Beta. Alpha and Beta are members of a brother-sister controlled group of corporations because (1) Able, Brutus, and Cody own a controlling interest in both Alpha and Beta, and (2) taking into account the ownership of Able, Brutus, and Cody only to the extent that it is identical with respect to each such organization, Able, Brutus, and Cody are in "effective control" of Alpha and Beta.

This relationship may be illustrated as follows:

	Alpha	Beta	For effective control, take into account:
Able	60%	20%	20%
Brutus	20%	40%	20%
Cody	20%	40%	20%
	100%*	100%**	60%***

A "combined group of trades or businesses under common control" is any group of three or more organizations, containing at least one parent-subsidiary group, the parent of which is a member of a brother-sister group.

* Able, Brutus, and Cody own a controlling interest in Alpha because they own at least 80 percent (in this case 100 percent) of Alpha.

** Able, Brutus, and Cody own a controlling interest in Beta because they own at least 80 percent (in this case 100 percent) of Beta.

*** Able, Brutus, and Cody have effective control of Alpha and Beta because, taking into account each individual's ownership only to the extent that it is identical with respect to each organization, they own more than 50 percent (in this case 60 percent) of Alpha and Beta.

8-2 QUESTIONS AND PROBLEMS

1. Alpha Corp. owns 90 percent of the only class of stock of Beta Corp. and Beta Corp. owns 85 percent of the only class of stock of Gamma Corp. Are Alpha, Beta, and Gamma members of a controlled group of corporations?

2. Danielle owns 90 percent of the only class of stock of Delta Corp. and 5 percent of the only class of stock of Epsilon Company. Ed owns 5 percent of the stock of Delta and 5 percent of the stock of Epsilon. Fatima owns the remaining 5 percent of the stock of Delta and 90 percent of the stock of Epsilon. Are Delta and Epsilon members of a controlled group of corporations?

3. Giovanna owns 30 percent of the only class of stock of Zeta Co., 20 percent of the only class of stock of Eta Corp., and 20 percent of the only class of stock of Theta Co. Hiroto owns 40 percent of the stock of Zeta, 20 percent of the stock of Eta, and 20 percent of the stock of Theta. Inez owns 30 percent of the stock of Zeta, 40 percent of the stock of Eta, and 20 percent of the stock of Theta. Jesse owns none of the stock of Zeta, 20 percent of the stock of Eta, and 40 percent of the stock of Theta. Are Zeta, Eta, and Theta members of a controlled group of corporations?

4. Parent Corp. owns 85 percent of Corp. A, which in turn owns 100 percent of Corp. B, which in turn owns 100 percent of Corp. 1. In addition, Parent Corp. owns 95 percent of Corp. Y, which in turn owns 95 percent of Corp. Z, which in turn owns 100 percent of Corp. 2. Are Corps. 1 and 2 members of a controlled group of corporations? How about Parent Corp., Corp. A, Corp. B, Corp. Y, and Corp. Z?

5. Kitaro owns 50 percent of the combined voting power of all classes of stock issued by Iota Corp. and 100 percent of the only class of stock of Kappa Corp. Lucas owns 50 percent of the stock of Iota and 100 percent of the only class of stock of Lambda Corp. Are Iota, Kappa, and Lambda members of a controlled group of corporations?

LLOYD M. GARLAND v. COMMISSIONER OF INTERNAL REVENUE

73 T.C. 5 (1979)

DAWSON, JUDGE:

This is an action for declaratory judgment pursuant to [IRC §] 7476(a). Respondent has determined that petitioner's pension plan does not qualify under [IRC §] 401 because it does not comply with the antidiscrimination provisions of [IRC §§] 401(a)(4) and 410(b)(1). Having exhausted all administrative remedies as required by [IRC §] 7476(b)(3), petitioner asks this Court to review respondent's adverse determination.

This case was submitted with a fully stipulated administrative record pursuant to Rule 122, Tax Court Rules of Practice and Procedure. The administrative record is incorporated herein by this reference. The pertinent facts are summarized below.

The petitioner, Lloyd M. Garland, M. D., F. A. C. S., P. A. (hereinafter the association), is a professional association organized under the laws of Texas and incorporated on February 1, 1973. The sole employee and shareholder of the association throughout its existence has been Dr. Lloyd M. Garland. Prior to the formation of the professional association, Dr. Garland had practiced medicine in partnership with Dr. Jack Dunn, Jr., in Lubbock, Tex. On February 1, 1973, their partnership was dissolved and the association and Dr. Dunn entered into a partnership known as the Neurosurgical Unit (hereinafter the partnership), in which each partner owned a 50-percent interest in profits.

The association adopted a pension plan which qualified under [IRC §] 401 on February 1, 1973. Thereafter, the association made contributions to a pension fund on behalf of Dr. Garland and the employees of the partnership. Subsequent to the enactment of the Employee Retirement Income Security Act of 1974 (ERISA), however, the association made a number of amendments to the plan. The amended plan did not cover the partnership employees,

. . . .

On March 15, 1977, the association submitted an application for determination of the plan's qualified status under [IRC §] 401. The District Director of the Dallas Key District subsequently issued a proposed adverse determination for the 1976 taxable year because the plan did not cover the partnership's employees. The Regional Office sustained this proposed determination, the National Office declined to reconsider the matter, and on August 15, 1978, the District Director issued a final adverse determination. The association has petitioned this Court for a review of that determination.

. . . .

The parties agree that [IRC §] 414(c) does not apply in this case. Section 414(c) [of the IRC] was enacted as part of ERISA and provides that the employees of two or more business entities which are under common control shall be treated as employed by a single employer for purposes of [IRC §] 401. Although Congress did not provide a statutory definition of "common control," it did require that the regulations under [IRC §] 414(c) be based on principles similar to those which are applicable in the case of [IRC §] 414(b). Section 414(b) states that all employees of corporations belonging to a controlled group (as defined in [IRC §] 1563(a)) must be treated as employed by a single employer for [IRC §] 401 purposes. Thus, the temporary regulations which define common control under [IRC §] 414(c) are modeled after the controlled group provisions in [IRC §] 1563(a).

. . . .

Section 11.414(c)-2, Income Tax Regs., lists three general situations when affiliated entities will, under certain circumstances, be deemed to be under common control: (1) A parent-subsidiary group, (2) a brother-sister group, (3) and a combined group. Petitioner clearly does not belong to any of these groups. Therefore, the employees of the partnership and the association are not required by [IRC §] 414(c) to be aggregated for purposes of [IRC §§] 401 and 410(b)(1).

Petitioner contends that [IRC §] 414(c) was intended to be the exclusive test for determining whether the employees of a related business entity should be considered in applying the antidiscrimination provisions. In the alternative, petitioner contends that even if [IRC §] 414(c) was not intended to supplant prior law on this point, the association nevertheless does not control the partnership employees under the principles set forth in *Thomas Kiddie, M.D., Inc. v. Commissioner*, 69 T.C. 1055, 1060–1061 (1978).

Respondent, on the other hand, maintains that [IRC §] 414(c) was not intended to be the exclusive test for determining whether the employees of affiliated entities should be aggregated for [IRC §] 401 purposes. He then asks us to overrule our opinion in *Thomas Kiddie, M.D., Inc. v. Commissioner*, *supra*, and hold that the employment relationship between the partnership and its employees must be attributed to each partner notwithstanding the possibility that his interest in partnership profits or capital may not exceed 50 percent. We agree with petitioner.

On brief, respondent repeatedly makes the assertion that [IRC §] 414(c) was not intended to be the exclusive test for employee attribution where affiliated entities are involved. Yet he is unable to advance a single cogent argument in support of that claim. The mere fact that the statute does not explicitly state that it is the exclusive test does not necessarily imply that the reverse is true. We think [IRC §§] 414(b) and 414(c) were intended to provide a definitive answer to the question of whether the employees of related entities should be aggregated for purposes of evaluating plan discrimination. The accompanying committee report states the following (H. Rept. 93-807, 1974-3 C.B. (Supp.) 285):

> Affiliated employers. — The committee bill also provides that in applying the coverage test, as well as the antidiscrimination rules, the vesting requirements, and the limitations on and benefits, employees of all corporations who are members of a "controlled group of corporations" (within the meaning of sec. 1563(a)) are to be treated as if they were employees of the same corporation. Thus, if two or more corporations were members of a parent-subsidiary, brother-sister, or combined controlled group, all of the employees of all of these corporations would have to be taken into account in applying these tests. A comparable rule is provided in the case of partnerships and proprietorships which are under common control (as determined under regulations), and all employees of such organizations are to be treated for purposes of these rules as though they were employed by a single person. The committee, by this provision, intends to make it clear that the coverage and antidiscrimination provisions cannot be avoided by operating through separate corporations instead of separate branches of one corporation. For example, if managerial functions were performed through one corporation employing highly compensated personnel, which has a generous pension plan, and assembly-line functions were performed through one or more other corporations employing lower-paid employees, which have less generous plans or no plans at all, this would generally constitute an impermissible discrimination. By this provision the committee is clarifying this matter for the future. . . . (Emphasis added.)

It is apparent from the committee report that Congress was aware that prior to the enactment of ERISA it was possible to circumvent the antidiscrimination provisions through the use of related business entities. To safeguard against this possibility, Congress enacted legislation which establishes a straightforward, objective test for determining whether the employees of affiliated entities should be treated as employed by a single employer. Under this test, the employees will be so treated if the business entities are found to be under common control as defined in regulations based on controlled group principles. In light of this direct congressional response to the employee attribution problem and the express statement of intent to clarify this matter for the future (*see* H. Rept. 93-807, *supra*), we see no reason to fortify the provisions of [IRC §] 414(c) with other, more stringent tests such as the one respondent has proposed in the present case. Accordingly, we hold that [IRC §§] 414(b) and 414(c) are the exclusive means for determining whether employees of related trades or businesses should be aggregated for purposes of applying the antidiscrimination provisions.

Assuming, arguendo, that [IRC §] 414(c) was not intended to be the exclusive test in this area, we nevertheless think the precedent established in *Thomas Kiddie, M.D., Inc. v. Commissioner*, *supra*, should govern our decision. The factual situation in Kiddie is virtually identical to the facts of this case, except that the taxable years in issue were pre-ERISA. In Kiddie, two professional medical corporations had formed a partnership in which each corporation held a 50-percent interest. Respondent issued an adverse determination as to the qualification of the pension plan of one of the corporations because it did not cover the employees of the partnership. We held, however, that for purposes of [IRC §] 401 the employment relationship between partnership and employee was not to be attributed to an individual partner unless it controlled the partnership. We further held that a partner has control only if he owns more than a 50-percent interest in the partnership (69 T.C. at 1060):

> Generally, attribution of partnership characteristics to a partner does not occur unless that partner controls the partnership. Although there is no universal definition, section 707(b) of subchapter K defines such control for two purposes. Thus, a partner owning more than a 50-percent interest may not recognize a loss which arose in dealings between such partner and the partnership; and gains realized in such dealings are treated as ordinary income if that partner owns more than an 80-percent interest in the partnership.
>
> These same percentage criteria are statutorily incorporated into the definition of control when dealing with section 179 additional depreciation allowances and section 38 investment credits. *Moradian v. Commissioner*, 53 T.C. 207, 209 (1969). In addition, section 707(b) has been used to elucidate the definition of section 1235(d) related persons when partnerships were involved. *Burde v. Commissioner*, 352 F.2d 995, 1000 (2d Cir. 1965). We find the greater than 50-percent interest test, when such interest is determined with reference to section 267(b) and (c), to be equally applicable in defining control of a partnership for purposes of section 401(a)(3).

We think the foregoing reasoning is sound and respondent's arguments to the contrary are unconvincing. Furthermore, we think the enactment of [IRC §] 414(c) provides additional support for the principle that a partner does not control a partnership unless he owns more than a 50-percent interest therein. The regulations under [IRC §] 414(c) are required by the statute to be based on the controlled group principles in [IRC §] 1563(a). As a result, respondent's own regulations under [IRC §] 414(c) variously define control insofar as partnerships are concerned as the ownership of an interest in profits or capital of either 80 percent or more than 50 percent. *See* secs. 11.414(c)-2(b)(2)(i)(C) and 11.414(c)-2(c)(2)(iii), Income Tax Regs. Therefore, we find no basis for attributing the employees of a partnership to an individual partner if his ownership interest is less than or equal to 50 percent.

Accordingly, we hold that the employees of the partnership are not to be treated as employees of the association for purposes of testing the association's pension plan under [IRC §§] 401(a)(4) and 410(b)(1). Therefore, the plan qualifies under [IRC §] 401(a).

An appropriate decision will be entered.

8-3 QUESTIONS AND PROBLEMS

1. Does the court focus on the purpose or language of the statute?
2. What role does legislative history play in the court's opinion?
3. What role should legislative history play in the court's opinion?

4. In light of *Garland*, how successful are IRC §§ 414(b) and (c) in preventing employers from creating and placing rank-and-file employees in a separate organization and providing pension benefits solely to highly compensated?

[b] Affiliated Service Groups

IRC § 414(m).

In the late 1970s, relying on *Garland* and *Kiddie* (cited in *Garland*), many professionals excluded their rank-and-file employees from participating in their qualified retirement plans by placing these common law employees into partnerships composed of their professional corporations. In 1980, Congress added section 414(m) to the Internal Revenue Code to curb this abuse.

In essence, IRC § 414(m) provides that the employees of a partnership and the corporate partners will be treated as having a single employer for nondiscrimination (and other) purposes. The section does not require that the employees of the partnership be included in their employer's plan. It simply requires that they be taken into account in determining whether the plan discriminates in favor of highly compensated employees.

The IRC § 414(m) rules are quite complex. The following examples briefly illustrate their application.

Anna, a partner in the Beta Law Firm, decides to become an independent contractor with respect to her firm. Anna and the Beta Law Firm will be treated as a single employer for purposes of the nondiscrimination rules if Anna remains an owner/shareholder in the Firm and continues to "regularly associate" with the Firm. *See* IRC § 414(m)(2)(A).

Brianna owns a hotel, and 75 of the hotel's 100 employees are members of the housekeeping staff. Brianna decides to spin off the housekeeping function to a new company, ThetaCo. Brianna owns a 20 percent interest in ThetaCo and 4 long term members of the housekeeping staff own the remaining 80 percent interest in ThetaCo. A significant portion of ThetaCo's work is performing housekeeping services for Brianna's hotel. Brianna's hotel company and ThetaCo will be treated as a single employer for purposes of the nondiscrimination rules. *See* IRC § 414(m)(2)(B).

Calvin, the CFO of a publicly traded corporation, resigns as an employee. He immediately incorporates himself and enters into a contract to provide all of his financial management services to his former employer. Calvin and his former employer will be treated as a single employer for purposes of the nondiscrimination rules. *See* IRC § 414(m)(5).

8-4 QUESTIONS AND PROBLEMS

1. Would IRC § 414(m) have been necessary if the court had taken a purposive approach in *Garland*?

2. Section 414(m) is very complex. Is there any way Congress could have avoided the complexity of IRC § 414(m) while still preventing professionals from excluding their rank-and-file employees from participating in their qualified retirement plans by placing these common law employees into partnerships composed of their professional corporations?

[c] Leased Employees

IRC § 414(n).

Employers sought to avoid IRC § 414(m) by leasing their employees from a separate leasing organization. In 1982, Congress added section 414(n) to the Internal Revenue Code to curb this perceived abuse of leasing, rather than hiring, employees solely to exclude the employees from coverage and participation in qualified plans. In essence, IRC § 414(n) treats the employees of certain leasing organizations as employed by the organization that leases their services (known as the "recipient") for nondiscrimination (as well as a number of other) purposes.

Under IRC § 414(n), a "leased employee" is defined as any person who is not an employee of the recipient but who provides services to the recipient where: (1) the services are provided pursuant to an agreement between the recipient and the leasing organization, (2) the person has performed such services for the recipient on a "substantially full-time" basis for a period of at least one year, and (3) the services are performed under the primary direction or control of the recipient. IRC § 414(n)(2).

Whether the services are performed under the primary direction or control of the recipient depends on the facts and circumstances. The House Ways and Means Committee Report explains:

> In general, primary direction and control means that the service recipient exercises the majority of direction and control over the individual. Factors that are relevant in determining whether primary direction or control exists include whether the individual is required to comply with instructions of the service recipient about when, where, and how he or she is to perform the services, whether the services must be performed by a particular person, whether the individual is subject to the supervision of the service recipient, and whether the individual must perform services in the order or sequence set by the service recipient. Factors that generally are not relevant in determining whether such direction or control exists include whether the service recipient has the right to hire or fire the individual and whether the individual works for others. House Ways and Means Committee Report on H.R. 3448, H. Rep. No. 104-586, 104th Cong. 2d Sess. 125 (1996).

Like IRC § 414(m), IRC § 414(n) does not require that employers include leased employees in their qualified plans. It only requires that such individuals be taken into account in determining whether the plan satisfies the nondiscrimination requirements. In addition, any qualified plan that intends to exclude such individuals must do so explicitly. IRS Notice 84-11, Q&A-16, 1984-2 C.B. 469, 471–72.

Section 414(n)(5) includes a safe harbor provision which permits a leased employee not to be treated as an employee of the recipient if: (1) the employee is covered by a money purchase plan that is maintained by the leasing organization that (a) provides for annual contributions by the employer equal to at least 10 percent of compensation, (b) admits employees to participate immediately, and (c) provides full and immediate vesting; and (2) leased employees, determined without regard to the safe harbor, constitute no more than 20 percent of the recipient's nonhighly compensated work force.

8-5 QUESTIONS AND PROBLEMS

Like IRC § 414(m), IRC § 414(n) is a very complex provision. Is there any way Congress could have avoided the complexity of IRC § 414(n) while still preventing employers from excluding employees from coverage and participation in qualified plans by leasing rather than hiring such employees?

MARK BERGER, THE CONTINGENT EMPLOYEE BENEFITS PROBLEMS

32 IND. L. REV. 301, 346–47 (1999)

If the employer is careful in his use of leased workers, the Internal Revenue Code's 'counting' requirement is likely to be of marginal significance. First, the employer can limit his use of leased workers to less than 1500 hours during the year. [This is because, as discussed later in this Chapter, part-time employees can be excluded in determining whether a plan discriminates in favor of highly compensated employees. Eds.] Alternatively, employers can utilize leasing agencies which provide supervision along with a staff of leased workers since the right of control in such an arrangement would not be vested in the employer. It is also generally true that leased professionals, such as attorneys, accountants, doctors, systems analysts, and engineers, who normally use independent judgment and discretion in performing their functions, are unlikely to be considered leased workers for purposes of determining a plan's eligibility for favored tax treatment. Furthermore, workers are not treated as countable leased employees if they participate in a "safe-harbor" pension plan provided by the leasing organization, and customers receive a credit for any benefits their leased workers receive from the leasing firm. In the final analysis, the system ensures limited applicability of the leased employee restrictions contained in the Internal Revenue Code. But in any event, the predominate judicial view of these provisions is that they only serve to determine the tax qualified status of a benefit plan, and do not encompass a leased employee right of participation.

Employers who do not use employee leasing agencies to create contingent employment arrangements in order to avoid benefit costs may achieve the same result through the use of independent contractors. There is a well-established principle in the common law which distinguishes between employees and independent contractors based upon the degree of control retained by the employer over the manner in which the work is performed. The distinction has become relevant for a number of employment law purposes. The relevance of the distinction for employee benefit programs is that service providers who fit within the independent contractor category will normally be deemed ineligible for participation in any plan provided by the employer for the exclusive benefit of his employees.

The common law distinction between employees and independent contractors is discussed in greater detail in Chapter 2.

[d] Anti-Avoidance Rule

IRC § 414(o).

Apparently tired of enacting specific legislation to prohibit perceived abuses of the rules defining employer, Congress added section 414(o) to the IRC. That section authorizes the Secretary of Treasury to prescribe such regulations as may be necessary to prevent the avoidance of any employee benefit requirement listed in IRC § 414(m)(4) or (n)(3) through the use of separate organizations, employee leasing, or other arrangements. To date, there is only one proposed regulation under this provision. Prop. Treas. Reg. § 1.414(o)–1.

[e] Separate Lines of Business

IRC § 414(r).

Sections 414(b), (c), (m), (n), and (o) of the Internal Revenue Code all expand the definition of employer and the number of employees that must be taken into account in determining whether a retirement plan satisfies the nondiscrimination rules. Section 414(r) of the Internal Revenue Code, in contrast, cuts back on the definition of employer and the number of employees that must be taken into account for nondiscrimination purposes. Specifically, if an employer maintains separate lines of business that qualify under IRC § 414(r), the separate lines of business are treated as separate employers for purposes of the IRC § 401(a)(26) minimum participation requirement, the IRC § 410(b) minimum coverage requirement, and the IRC § 401(a)(4) nondiscrimination in contributions or benefits requirement. Thus, the employees of each qualified separate line of business are treated as if they were the only employees of the employer.

PETER M. VAN ZANTE, MANDATED VESTING: SUPPRESSION OF VOLUNTARY RETIREMENT BENEFITS

75 NOTRE DAME L. REV. 125, 193 n.225 (1999)[1]

The controlled group rules cast an extremely broad net. In the case of a group that includes operations in different industries, each of which may have its own patterns for provision of retirement benefits, the controlled group rules could make it economically impossible to provide retirement benefits in one industry while leaving employees in another industry without benefits. In this circumstance, a controlled group would face a competitive disadvantage as compared with independently owned operations in each industry. Recognizing this problem, the Code provides relief from the controlled group rules for an employer than can establish that it operates "separate lines of business."

The IRC § 414(r) separate line of business rules are designed to permit an employer to divide its operations into separate lines for discrimination testing purposes if the employer is really engaged in different businesses. The regulations set forth a three part test to determine whether an employer satisfies the separate lines of business rules. First, the employer must be engaged in more than one "line of business." Second, the lines of business must be "separate." Finally, the separate lines of business must be "qualified."

A "line of business" is defined as "a portion of an employer that is identified by the property or services it provides to customers of the employer." Treas. Reg. § 1.414(r)-2(a). The regulations give employers a great deal of discretion in selecting

---

[1] Copyright 1999, *Notre Dame Law Review*. Reprinted with permission. Any errors in reprinting or editing are the responsibility of the publisher of this casebook.

their lines of business, so long as they are reasonable. For example, an employer may establish lines of business based upon geographic areas, levels of distribution (wholesale versus retail), or types of customer (governmental versus private). Treas. Reg. § 1.414(r)-2(b)(3)(iii).

Once the employer identifies its "lines of business," it must show that they are organized and operated "separately" from one another. "Separate" lines of business must satisfy four separate requirements. First, each line of business must be formally organized by the employer as a separate unit in the corporation, such as a division. Treas. Reg. § 1.414(r)-3(b)(2). Second, each line of business must have separate financial accountability; that is, each line of business must be a separate profit center or group of separate profit centers within the employer. Treas. Reg. § 1.414(r)-3(b)(3). Third, each line of business must have its own separate employee workforce. A line of business has its own separate employee workforce if at least 90 percent of the employees who provide services to the line of business, and who are not substantial service employees with respect to any other line of business, are substantial service employees with respect to the line of business. An employee is a substantial service employee if at least 75 percent of the employee's services are provided to that line of business for the testing year. Treas. Reg. § 1.414(r)-3(b)(4). Finally, a line of business must have its own separate management. A line of business has its own separate management if at least 80 percent of the employees who are top-paid employees with respect to the line of business are substantial-service employees with respect to the line of business. Treas. Reg. § 1.414(r)-3(b)(5). Because vertically integrated lines of business typically cannot meet the separate workforce and separate management requirements, the regulations provide an optional rule to assist them to satisfy the separate lines of business requirements. *See* Treas. Reg. § 1.414(r)-3(d).

Once an employer establishes that its lines of business are separate, the employer must show that the separate lines of business are "qualified." In order to be qualified, each line of business must have at least 50 employees, the employer must give appropriate notice to the Internal Revenue Service, and each line of business must satisfy an "administrative scrutiny" requirement designed to ensure that the highly compensated employees are not packed into a single unit. IRC § 414(r)(2)(A)–(C). Section 414(r)(3) exempts from this "administrative scrutiny" requirement lines of business that satisfy a safe harbor ratio percentage. A separate line of business satisfies the statutory safe harbor if the percentage of highly compensated employees with respect to the line of business is at least 50 percent, but not more than 200 percent, of the highly compensated employee percentage for the employer as a whole. IRC § 414(r)(3). If at least 10 percent of all highly compensated employees of the employer perform services solely for a single line of business, that line of business is deemed to satisfy the 50 percent requirement, but still must satisfy the 200 percent requirement. IRC § 414(r)(3).

The regulations set forth five regulatory safe harbors that satisfy the "administrative scrutiny" requirement: (1) the industry category safe harbor, (2) the mergers and acquisitions safe harbor, (3) the reportable business segments safe harbor, (4) the average benefits safe harbor, and (5) the minimum and maximum benefits safe harbor. Treas. Reg. § 414(r)-4(c)-(4)(g). If an employer's separate lines of business fails to satisfy the statutory safe harbor or one of the regulatory safe harbors, the employer may satisfy the "administrative scrutiny" requirement if it requests and receives an individual determination that the separate line of business satisfies administrative scrutiny. Treas. Reg. § 1.414(r)-6.

The flowchart on the following page from Treas. Reg. § 1.414(r)-0 illustrates the operation of these rules:

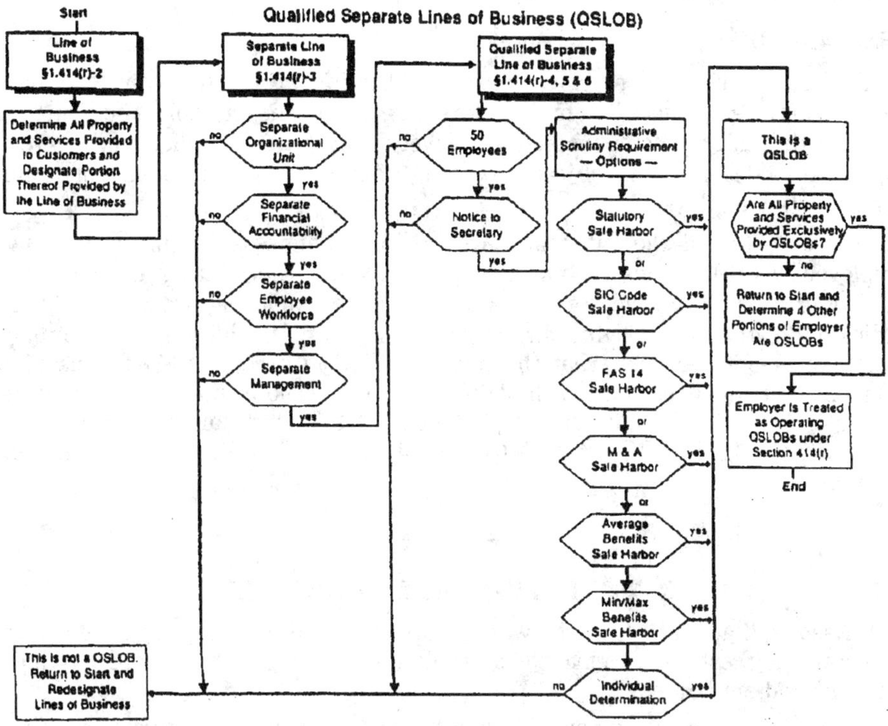

The Treasury Regulations governing IRC § 414(r), which are almost 50 pages long, have been described as "mind-numbingly complex," and difficult to satisfy in certain circumstances. *See* Michael J. Collins, *Reviving Defined Benefit Plans: Analysis and Suggestions for Reform*, 20 VA. TAX REV. 599, 618 (2001). In recent years, a number of bills have been introduced in Congress that would direct the Internal Revenue Service to modify the regulations to permit employees to be allocated among lines of business based on all the facts and circumstances. To date, none have been enacted.

8-6 QUESTIONS AND PROBLEMS

1. Should the regulations be replaced with a facts and circumstances test? If so, what are the relevant "facts and circumstances"?

2. Xi Corp. has 200 employees, 20 of whom are highly compensated. Suppose that 60 employees, 10 of whom are highly compensated, work for a line of business. Does that line of business satisfy the IRC § 414(r)(3) statutory safe harbor?

3. Omicron Industries has 400 total employees and three separate divisions: (1) a steel division, (2) a financial division, and (3) a plastics division. A total of 100 employees work for the steel division, 20 of whom are highly compensated. A total of 150 employees work for the financial division, 50 of whom are highly compensated. A total of 150 employees work for the plastics division, 30 of whom are highly compensated. Do Omicron Industries' three divisions satisfy the IRC § 414(r)(3) statutory safe harbor?

[2] Highly Compensated Employees

IRC § 414(q).

The nondiscrimination rules prohibit discrimination in favor of "highly compensated employees." Thus, before the nondiscrimination rules may be applied, the "highly compensated employees" must be identified. The Internal Revenue Code uses an objective, straightforward test to define a "highly compensated employee."

Section 414(q) of the Internal Revenue Code defines a "highly compensated employee" as (a) anyone who was a five percent owner during the current or preceding year or (b) had compensation from the employer in excess of $80,000 (adjusted for the cost of living) in the preceding year. In addition, if the employer elects, the employer may treat those who earned in excess of $80,000 as highly compensated employees only if they were in the top-paid group; that is, they were among the highest paid 20 percent of the employer's work force in the preceding year. As of 2012, the IRC § 414(q)(1)(B) limit, as adjusted for the cost of living, is $115,000.

8-7 QUESTIONS AND PROBLEMS

1. Assume that Alpha Co. has twenty employees and the following seven are the company's highest paid. Which, if any, of the following would qualify as highly compensated employees?

a. Anna, who has owned 50 percent of the company since its creation in 1995 and earned $160,000 last year.

b. Bernard, who earned $150,000 last year.

c. Corrine, who earned $120,000 last year.

d. Derek, who owned 50 percent of the company until 1999 when he sold his interest in the company and earned $90,000 last year.

e. Errol, who earned $75,000 last year and was recently promoted and expects to earn $120,000 this year.

f. Francois, who earned $75,000 from Alpha Co. and $55,000 from Beta Corporation, an unrelated company, last year.

g. Gunther, who has owned 50 percent of the company since 1999 and earned $60,000 last year.

2. Would any of the answers to problem 1 be different if the company had ten employees rather than twenty?

3. Suppose that last year a law firm had four partners who each earned more than $350,000, ten associates who earned between $150,000 and $175,000, and six support staff who earned between $30,000 and $50,000. Would the associates in that firm qualify as highly compensated employees? As a policy matter, should the associates qualify as highly compensated employees?

4. Suppose that a corporation has twenty-five employees, one of whom earns $140,000, three of whom earn $85,000, and the remainder of whom earn less than $25,000. How many highly compensated employees work for the corporation? How many employees should qualify as highly compensated?

5. Why is highly compensated employee status determined by compensation earned in the preceding year rather than the current year?

[3] Aggregation/Disaggregation of Plans

The nondiscrimination requirements mandate that a qualified "plan" not discriminate in coverage or the provision of contributions or benefits. Thus, the final issue that must be resolved before applying the nondiscrimination rules is identifying the "plan" that must be tested.

The Treasury regulations set forth detailed rules defining the term "plan" for purposes of the nondiscrimination rules. *See* Treas. Reg. § 1.410(b)-7. The regulations require that certain types of plans be disaggregated and tested separately. For example, the portion of a plan that is a 401(k) plan and the portion that is not a 401(k) plan must be treated as separate plans. *See* Treas. Reg. § 1.410(b)-7(c)(1). In addition, in some circumstances, the regulations permit employers to aggregate or combine two or more plans and treat the aggregated plan as a single plan for purposes of the nondiscrimination requirements. *See* Treas. Reg. § 1.410(b)-7(d).

Typically, an employer will elect to aggregate plans when one plan, viewed alone, does not satisfy the nondiscrimination rules. If plans are aggregated for purposes of the IRC § 410(b) coverage rule, however, they must also be aggregated for purposes of the IRC § 401(a)(4) nondiscrimination in contributions or benefits rule. Similarly, if plans are aggregated for purposes of the IRC § 401(a)(4) nondiscrimination in contributions or benefits requirement, they must also be aggregated for purposes of the IRC § 410(b) coverage rule.

If the plans being aggregated are all defined contribution plans, it is easy to determine the amount of contributions under the plans. Similarly, if all of the plans being aggregated are defined benefit plans, it is easy to determine the amount of benefits under the plans. If, however, the aggregated plans include both defined contribution plans and defined benefit plans, the contributions and benefits must be equated. The Treasury regulations provide a mechanism, called cross-testing, to do this. Treas. Reg. § 1.401(a)(4)-8. Under the complex cross-testing rules, the amounts allocated to employees under a defined contribution plan are converted to equivalent benefits or the amounts accrued for employees under a defined benefit plan are converted to equivalent contributions.

C. THE NONDISCRIMINATION REQUIREMENTS

The Internal Revenue Code has three separate nondiscrimination requirements. The first, the IRC § 401(a)(26) minimum participation requirement, only applies to defined benefit plans. It applies an objective test to determine whether the defined benefit plan actually covers enough employees. It is intended to address two concerns. First, it is designed to limit the extent to which employers may create different benefit formulas for different groups of employees and thus maximize benefits in favor of highly compensated employees. Second, it limits the extent to which a defined benefit plan can operate as an individual account for a single employee or small group of employees. It is always simple, straightforward, and easy to apply.

The second requirement, the IRC § 410(b) minimum coverage requirement, applies to all qualified plans. It looks at all of the employees of the employer to determine whether a sufficient percentage of nonhighly compensated employees, relative to highly compensated employees, participate in the plan. It too can be extremely simple, straightforward, and easy to apply. For example, if a plan covers all of the employer's employees, it easily satisfies the IRC § 410(b) minimum coverage requirement. On the other hand, it can be much more difficult to apply, because the IRC § 410(b) minimum coverage requirement does not require that a plan cover all of an employer's employees or that all of the employees be taken into account in testing the plan. For example, it permits employers to exclude certain part-time employees, nonresident aliens, and union workers in testing the plan. *See* IRC §§ 410(b)(3) & (4).

Finally, the IRC § 401(a)(4) nondiscrimination requirement applies to all qualified plans. It looks at the contributions or benefits actually provided by a plan to determine whether the plan discriminates in favor of highly compensated employees. The statutory mandate is quite brief, simple, and straightforward. "[T]he contributions or benefits provided under the plan [must] not discriminate in favor of highly compensated employees (within the meaning of section 414(q))." IRC § 401(a)(4). On the other hand, the Treasury regulations implementing the statutory mandate are almost 100 pages long and can be exceedingly technical and complicated. Remember, though, an employer can easily avoid much of the complexity of IRC § 401(a)(4) by providing all employees with identical benefits or contributions. The rules generally only become complicated when employers seek to provide greater benefits or contributions to highly compensated employees. The regulations permit some discrimination; that is, benefits or contributions for highly compensated employees can be somewhat higher than benefits or contributions for nonhighly compensated employees. They simply cannot exceed the benefits or contributions for nonhighly compensated employees by too great a percentage. Generally, an employer can exclude the same employees from testing a plan under IRC § 401(a)(4) as can be excluded in testing the plan under the IRC § 410(b) minimum coverage rules. *See* IRC § 401(a)(4).

There are two noteworthy adjustments to the general IRC § 401(a)(4) nondiscrimination requirement. First, for 401(k) plans, the IRC § 401(a)(4) nondiscrimination in contributions or benefits requirement is replaced with a special nondiscrimination test. IRC § 401(k)(3). This special test recognizes that contributions to a 401(k) plan depend principally on employee choice and may permit a higher level of discrimination in favor of highly compensated employees than does the regular IRC § 401(a)(4) nondiscrimination test. Generally, a plan must be tested each year to ensure that it satisfies the special IRC § 401(k)(3) nondiscrimination test. If an employer wishes to avoid the cost of testing (and perhaps correcting) the plan each year, it may do so by making certain contributions to the plan in accordance with statutory safe harbors set forth in IRC §§ 401(k)(12) or 401(k)(13).

Finally, IRC § 401(l) permits certain plans to have a higher level of discrimination in contributions or benefits than would be permitted under IRC § 401(a)(4). In essence, the rules permit Social Security benefits to be taken into account in determining whether a plan discriminates in favor of highly compensated employees. The rules generally permit contributions or benefits attributable to income above the Social Security taxable wage base (equal to $110,000 in 2012) to be higher than contributions or benefits below the Social Security taxable wage base. The rules increase the complexity of testing whether a plan's contributions or benefits discriminate in favor of highly compensated employees. Again, however, an employer can avoid this complexity by providing all employees with uniform benefits or contributions.

As should be clear, the nondiscrimination rules can be exceedingly technical and complex. The complexity, however, is due in large part to the fact that they sanction some level of discrimination in favor of highly compensated employees. An employer can avoid this complexity by providing all employees with uniform benefits. As you read these materials, consider whether they merit their complexity. Should they be replaced by a simple rule requiring that all plans provide all employees with uniform benefits?

[1] Minimum Participation Requirement

IRC § 401(a)(26).

Section 401(a)(26) of the Internal Revenue Code sets forth a threshold coverage rule that requires a defined benefit plan to satisfy a minimum participation standard in order for the plan to be eligible for favorable tax treatment. Specifically, IRC § 401(a)(26) requires that a defined benefit plan cover at least the lesser of (i) 50 employees, or (ii) the greater of 40 percent of the employer's employees or two employees (or one employee if there is only one employee).

The IRC § 401(a)(26) minimum participation requirement is intended to address two concerns. First, it is designed to limit the extent to which employers may create different benefit formulas for different groups of employees and thus maximize benefits in favor of highly compensated employees. Second, it limits the extent to which a defined benefit plan can operate as an individual account for a single employee, or a small group of employees.

The minimum participation standards must be met on each day of the plan year. IRC § 401(a)(26)(A). A plan, however, will be treated as satisfying this requirement if it meets the test on any single day during the plan year, provided that day is reasonably representative of the employer's workforce and the plan's coverage. Treas. Reg. § 1.401(a)(26)-7(b).

8-8 QUESTIONS AND PROBLEMS

1. Why does IRC § 401(a)(26) only apply to defined benefit plans, and not to defined contribution plans?

2. Suppose that an employer with 500 nonexcludable employees wishes to establish a defined benefit plan. How many employees must the defined benefit plan cover to satisfy IRC § 401(a)(26)?

3. Suppose that an employer with 50 nonexcludable employees wishes to establish a defined benefit plan. How many employees must the defined benefit plan cover to satisfy IRC § 401(a)(26)?

4. Why must an employer with a smaller workforce cover a much larger percentage of its workforce than an employer with a larger workforce?

[2] Minimum Coverage Tests

IRC § 410(b).

Section 401(a)(3) of the Internal Revenue Code requires that a retirement plan satisfy the minimum participation standards of IRC § 410 in order for the plan to be qualified and thus eligible for favorable tax treatment. Section 410(a) of the Internal Revenue Code duplicates the minimum participation standards set forth in ERISA § 202(a) and discussed in Chapter 4. In addition, IRC § 410(b) sets forth minimum coverage requirements that are only found in the Internal Revenue Code and are designed to ensure that a broad group of employees can participate in the plan.

Section 410(b) sets forth three alternative coverage tests: (1) the percentage test, (2) the ratio percentage test, and (3) the classification/average benefits test. A retirement plan must satisfy at least one of the three alternative coverage tests in order to be eligible for favorable tax treatment.

Under the percentage test, a retirement plan must benefit at least 70 percent of the employees who are not highly compensated. IRC § 410(b)(1)(A). Suppose, for example, Alpha's plan covers 800 of Alpha's 1,000 nonhighly compensated employees and 90 of its 100 highly compensated employees. The plan satisfies the IRC § 410(b)(1) percentage test because it benefits 800/1000 or 80 percent of its nonhighly compensated employees. For purposes of this test, it does not matter how many highly compensated employees the plan covers.

The ratio percentage test compares the percentage of highly compensated employees benefitting under the plan to the percentage of nonhighly compensated employees benefitting under the plan. Under the ratio percentage test, the percentage of nonhighly compensated employees benefitting under the plan must be at least 70 percent of the percentage of highly compensated employees benefitting under the plan. IRC § 410(b)(1)(B). Suppose, for example, Beta's plan covers 250 of its 500 nonhighly compensated employees and 70 of its 100 highly compensated employees. Beta's retirement plan does not satisfy the IRC § 410(b)(1)(A) percentage test because it only covers 250/500, or 50 percent, of its nonhighly compensated employees. It does, however, satisfy the IRC § 410(b)(1)(B) ratio percentage test, because the percentage of nonhighly compensated employees benefitting under the plan (50%) is 71 percent of the percentage of highly compensated employees benefitting under the plan (70/100 or 70%) [50%/70% = 71%]. If Gamma's plan covers 50 percent of its highly compensated employees, it must cover at least 35 percent of its nonhighly compensated employees [70% x 50% = 35%] to satisfy the ratio percentage test.

The classification/average benefit test has two parts: (1) the classification test and (2) the average benefit test. IRC § 410(b)(1)(C). Under the classification test, the plan must benefit such employees as qualify under a classification set up by the employer and found by the Secretary of the Treasury not to be discriminatory in favor of highly compensated employees. IRC § 410(b)(1)(C)(A)(i). Under the average benefit test, the average benefit percentage for nonhighly compensated must be at least 70 percent of the average benefit percentage for highly compensated employees. IRC § 410(b)(1)(C)(A)(ii).

Treasury Regulation § 1.410(b)-4(b) requires that the coverage classification established by the employer be reasonable and established under objective business criteria that identify the categories of employees who benefit under the plan, such as job categories, nature of compensation, or geographic location. To be nondiscriminatory, a reasonable classification must satisfy either a safe harbor or a facts and circumstances test.

A plan satisfies the safe harbor if the plan's ratio percentage is equal to or greater than the employer's safe harbor percentage. Treas. Reg. § 1.410(b)-4(c)(2). The employer's safe harbor percentage is 50 percent, reduced by 3/4 of a percentage point for each percentage point by which the nonhighly compensated employee concentration percentage exceeds 60 percent. The "nonhighly compensated employee concentration percentage" is the percentage of all the employees of the employer who are not highly compensated employees, excluding those who are not taken into account for purposes of the average benefit test. A table in the regulations sets forth the percentages. *See* Treas. Reg. § 1.410(b)-4(c)(4)(iv).

To apply the safe harbor test, first determine the plan's ratio percentage as described above for purposes of IRC § 410(b)(1)(B). Then determine the plan's nonhighly compensated employee concentration percentage; that is, the total number of nonhighly compensated employees divided by the total number of employees. The table in the regulations is then consulted to determine the safe harbor percentage for that nonhighly compensated employee concentration percentage.

For example, suppose that Delta's plan covers 110 of Delta's 350 nonhighly compensated employees and 75 of its 150 highly compensated employees. The plan's ratio percentage is 62.84 percent [(110/350)/(75/150) or 31.42%/50% or 62.84%]. The plan's nonhighly compensated employee concentration percentage is 70 percent [350 nonhighly compensated employees/500 total employees = 70%]. According to the table set forth in Treas. Reg. § 1.410(b)-4(c)(4)(iv), the safe harbor percentage for a nonhighly compensated employee concentration percentage of 70 percent is 42.50 percent. Since the plan's ratio percentage of 62.84 percent exceeds the safe harbor percentage of 42.50 percent, the plan satisfies the safe harbor test.

If a plan does not satisfy the safe harbor, but its ratio percentage is at least equal to its "unsafe harbor percentage," it may satisfy the facts and circumstances test. The unsafe harbor percentage is a percentage between 20 percent and 40 percent, depending on the nonhighly compensated employee concentration percentage. The unsafe harbor percentages are set forth in Treas. Reg. § 1.410(b)-4(c)(4)(iv). The facts and circumstances to be considered in determining whether a classification is nondiscriminatory include: (a) business reasons, (b) percentage of employees benefitting under the plan, (c) representation of employees benefitting at various salary ranges, (d) the difference between the plan's ratio percentage and the employer's safe harbor percentage, and (e) the extent to which the plan's average benefit percentage exceeds 70 percent. Treas. Reg. § 1.410(b)-4(c)(3).

If the plan's ratio percentage is less than the plan's unsafe harbor percentage, it does not satisfy IRC § 410(b) and is not eligible for favorable tax treatment. If the plan's ratio percentage is equal to or greater than the safe harbor percentage, or is less than its safe harbor percentage but equal to or greater than its unsafe harbor percentage and satisfies the facts and circumstances test, the plan must also satisfy an average benefit percentage test to satisfy IRC § 410(b)(1)(C).

The average benefit percentage test is met if the average benefit percentage for nonhighly compensated employees is at least 70 percent of the average benefit percentage for highly compensated employees. The "average benefit percentage" is determined by dividing the actual benefit percentage of all nonhighly compensated employees in the plan testing group by the actual benefit percentage of the highly compensated employees in the testing group. The testing group and "benefit percentage" are the same as would be used for purposes of applying the general nondiscrimination test for purposes of IRC § 401(a)(4) and are discussed in more detail in the following section.

Not all employees must be taken into account in determining whether a plan satisfies IRC § 410(b). For example, employees covered by a collective bargaining agreement may be excluded if retirement benefits were the subject of good faith bargaining. IRC § 410(b)(3)(A). Nonresident aliens may be excluded if they earned no U.S. source income. IRC § 410(b)(3)(C). Part-time employees may also be excluded if the plan prescribes minimum age or service requirements as a condition of participation. IRC § 410(b)(4). For example, employees who work less than 1,000 hours a year may be excluded if working more than 1,000 hours per year is a condition of participation in the plan. The employer may also exclude employees who do not work in the line of business being tested if the employer chooses to separate its lines of business under IRC § 414(r) and test each line separately. IRC § 410(b)(5). In addition, if an employer has no nonhighly compensated employees, the plan will automatically satisfy IRC § 410(b). IRC § 410(b)(6)(F).

The following chart summarizes the steps to be followed in determining whether a plan satisfies the IRC § 410(b) minimum coverage requirements.

BASICS OF COVERAGE TESTING

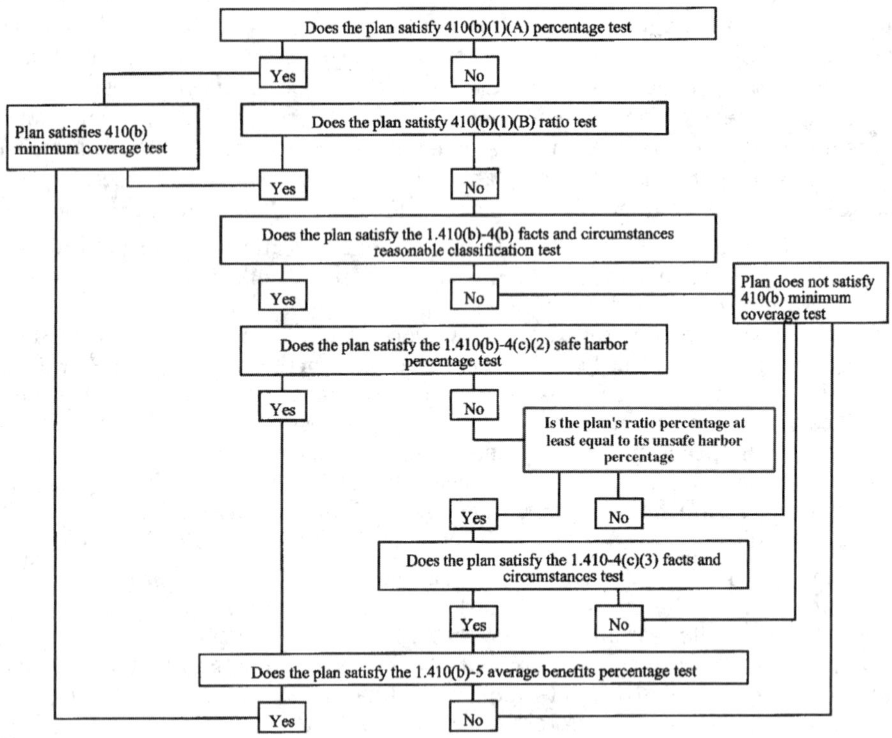

8-9 QUESTIONS AND PROBLEMS

1. Do the coverage rules benefit highly compensated employees, nonhighly compensated employees, or both?

2. Why doesn't ERISA impose minimum coverage requirements that are similar to those imposed by IRC § 410(b)?

3. For a plan year, Zeta's plan covers 750 of Zeta's 800 nonhighly compensated employees and 95 of its 100 highly compensated employees. Does the plan satisfy the IRC § 410(b)(1)(A) percentage test? Does the plan satisfy the IRC § 410(b)(1)(B) ratio percentage test?

4. For a plan year, Eta's plan covers 600 of Eta's 1,000 nonhighly compensated employees and 75 of its 90 highly compensated employees. Does the plan satisfy the IRC § 410(b)(1)(A) percentage test? Does the plan satisfy the IRC § 410(b)(1)(B) ratio percentage test?

5. For a plan year, Theta's plan covers 150 of its 1,000 nonhighly compensated employees and 5 of Theta's 50 highly compensated employees. Does the plan satisfy the IRC § 410(b)(1)(A) percentage test? Does the plan satisfy the IRC § 410(b)(1)(B) ratio percentage test?

6. For a plan year, Iota's plan covers 200 of Iota's 400 nonhighly compensated employees and 90 of its 100 highly compensated employees. Does the plan satisfy the IRC § 410(b)(1)(A) percentage test? Does the plan satisfy the IRC § 410(b)(1)(B) ratio percentage test? Does the plan fall within the Treas. Reg. § 1.410(b)-4(c)(4)(iv) nondiscrimination safe harbor?

7. For a plan year, Kappa's plan covers 45 of Kappa's 900 nonhighly compensated employees and 20 of its 100 highly compensated employees. Does the plan satisfy the IRC § 410(b)(1)(A) percentage test? Does the plan satisfy the IRC § 410(b)(1)(B) ratio percentage test? Does the plan fall within the Treas. Reg. § 1.410(b)-4(c)(4)(iv) nondiscrimination safe harbor?

8. For a plan year, Lambda's plan covers 288 of Lambda's 4,800 nonhighly compensated employees and 300 of its 1,200 highly compensated employees. Does the plan satisfy the IRC § 410(b)(1)(A) percentage test? Does the plan satisfy the IRC § 410(b)(1)(B) ratio percentage test? Does the plan fall within the Treas. Reg. § 1.410(b)-4(c)(4)(iv) nondiscrimination safe harbor?

9. For a plan year, Nu's plan Number 1 covers 15 of Nu's 215 nonhighly compensated employees and 20 of Nu's 20 highly compensated employees. All 200 of the nonhighly compensated employees excluded from Nu's plan Number 1 are included in a unit of employees covered by a collective bargaining agreement and are covered by a separate plan, Nu's plan Number 2. Does Nu's plan Number 1 satisfy IRC § 410(b). Would the answer be different if the excluded employees were not covered by a separate plan? Would Nu's plan Number 2 satisfy IRC § 410(b) if the plan only covered 100 of Nu's 200 nonhighly compensated employees included in the bargaining unit? *See* Treas. Reg. § 1.410(b)-2(b)(7).

10. For a plan year, Xi's plan covers 50 of Xi's 100 nonhighly compensated employees and all 20 of its highly compensated employees. The 50 nonhighly compensated employees who are excluded from the plan work fewer than 1,000 hours per year, and the plan requires employees to work at least 1,000 hours per year in order to be able to participate in the plan. Does the plan satisfy IRC § 410(b)(1)(A)? Would the answer be the same if the 5 of the 50 nonhighly compensated employees who participate in the plan worked fewer than 1,000 hours per year and thus the plan permitted some but not all employees who work fewer than 1,000 hours per year to participate in the plan?

[3] Nondiscrimination in Contributions or Benefits

IRC § 401(a)(4).

Section 401(a)(4) of the Internal Revenue Code requires that the contributions or benefits provided under a qualified retirement plan not discriminate in favor of highly compensated employees. This section of the Internal Revenue Code has been virtually unchanged since it was first enacted, but a large body of regulations, revenue rulings, and administrative procedures have been promulgated over the years to elaborate on the basic nondiscrimination requirement. Today, the Treasury regulations, which are almost 100 pages long, provide the exclusive means for determining whether a plan satisfies IRC § 401(a)(4). Treas. Reg. § 1.401(a)(4)-1(a). A plan must comply with the regulations in both form and in operation. Intent is irrelevant. Treas. Reg. § 1.401(a)(4)-1(a). This section gives a general overview of the Treasury § 401(a)(4) regulations.

The regulations contain three basic requirements. First, the core "amounts rule" requires that the amount of contributions or benefits not discriminate in favor of highly compensated employees. Treas. Reg. § 1.401(a)(4)-1(b)(2). Second, other benefits, rights, and features must not discriminate in favor of highly compensated employees. Treas. Reg. § 1.401(a)(4)-1(b)(3). Benefits, rights, and features include optional benefit forms, such as retirement annuities and lump sum payments, ancillary benefits, such as disability benefits, and other rights and features, such as plan loans and investment options. Treas. Reg. § 1.401(a)(4)-4(a). Finally, the plan must not discriminate in favor of highly compensated employees in special circumstances, such as plan amendments (including grants of past service credit) and terminations. Treas. Reg. § 1.401(a)(4)-1(b)(4).

[a] Amounts Rule

As noted, the Treasury regulations require that the "amount" of contributions or benefits provided by a qualified retirement plan not discriminate in favor of highly compensated employees. Typically, a defined contribution plan satisfies the nondiscriminatory amount requirement by showing that the *contributions* provided by the plan are not discriminatory in amount, while a defined benefit plan satisfies the requirement by showing that *benefits* provided under the plan are not discriminatory in amount. The regulations, however, permit a defined contribution plan to satisfy the requirement by showing that benefits are not discriminatory in amount while a defined benefit plan may satisfy the requirement by showing that contributions are not discriminatory in amount. Treas. Reg. § 1.401(a)(4)-1(b)(2)(ii)(A) & (iii).

A three step process may be used in determining whether a plan satisfies the amounts rule. First, does the plan pass muster under a "safe harbor?" The safe harbors are typically based on the contribution or benefit formula and do not look at the contributions or benefits provided to each individual employee. If the plan falls within a safe harbor, it satisfies IRC § 401(a)(4) and there is no need to go further. If, however, the plan does not satisfy a safe harbor, the "general test" must be applied. General testing looks at the actual benefits or contributions provided to each employee to determine whether the plan, as a whole, discriminates in favor of highly compensated employees. If the plan passes general testing, the plan satisfies IRC § 401(a)(4) and there is no need to go further. If, however, the plan does not satisfy general testing, the employer may use a variety of flexibility techniques to determine whether the plan discriminates in favor of highly compensated employees. These flexibility features include restructuring the plan into two halves or aggregating two plans and testing them together. If the plan is restructured, the restructured plan must satisfy IRC § 410(b) but does not need to independently satisfy IRC § 401(a)(26).

[i] Safe Harbors for Defined Contribution Plans

There are two safe harbors for defined contribution plans: (1) the uniform allocation formula and (2) the uniform points allocation formula. The uniform allocation formula safe harbor is the most common safe harbor. A defined contribution plan satisfies this safe harbor if all employer contributions and forfeitures for the plan year are allocated or treated as allocated under a single formula that provides all employees with: (1) the same percentage of plan year compensation, (2) the same dollar amount, or (3) the same dollar amount for each uniform unit of service (not to exceed one week) performed by the employee during the plan year. Treas. Reg. § 1.401(a)(4)-2(b)(2). Both contributions *and* forfeitures must be allocated under a uniform formula for purposes of this safe harbor. Forfeitures are money in account balances that do not vest. For purposes of this safe harbor, a plan can take into account permitted disparity under IRC § 401(l) if the plan follows IRC § 401(l) in form. The permitted disparity rules are discussed at the end of this chapter. This safe harbor is designed-based; that is, if a plan satisfies this safe harbor, it will always satisfy IRC § 401(a)(4) and does not have to be tested on an annual basis.

The second safe harbor, the uniform points allocation formula, is available to all defined contribution plans, other than ESOPs. Treas. Reg. § 1.401(a)(4)-2(b)(3). A plan satisfies this safe harbor if: (1) the plan allocates amounts under a uniform points allocation formula; and (2) for the plan year, the average of the allocation rates for the highly compensated employees does not exceed the average allocation rates for the nonhighly compensated employees. Uniform points plans must allocate the employer's contributions to each employee's account by multiplying the total employer contribution by a fraction. The numerator of the fraction is the employee's number of points, and the denominator is the total number of points for all participants. Points must be based on some combination of units of compensation, age, and service. The formula must award the same number of points for each year of service, year of age, and unit of compensation. For example, a plan could not award one point for each year of service up to 15 and two points for each year of service in excess of 15. The plan, however, may cap the number of points for years of service. Compensation points must be awarded on the same basis for all employees, and such points must be based on increments of single dollar amounts, not to exceed $200.

Unlike the uniform allocation formula safe harbor, the uniform points allocation safe harbor is not a design-based safe harbor. Each year, a plan falling within this safe harbor must be tested to ensure that the average allocation rate for the highly compensated employees does not exceed the average allocation rate for the nonhighly compensated. Allocation rates are calculated in the same manner as in general testing (which is described below), except that IRC § 401(l) permitted disparity may not be taken into account and the general testing allocation group rate method may not be used.

[ii] General Testing of Defined Contribution Plans

General testing of defined contribution plans involves a two-step process. First, the plan must be divided into rate groups. Then, after the plan is divided into rate groups, each rate group must be tested to see if it satisfies IRC § 410(b). Treas. Reg. § 1.401(a)(4)-2(c).

For general testing purposes, a rate group exists under a plan for each highly compensated employee in the plan and consists of the highly compensated employee and all other employees (both highly compensated and nonhighly compensated) who have an allocation rate greater than or equal to the highly compensated employee's allocation rate. An employee's allocation rate is based on the employer contributions and forfeitures that are allocated to the employee's account for the year. The allocation rate does not include amounts attributable to earnings, expenses, gains, and losses.

For example, suppose that a plan had the following employees with the following allocation rates:

A	HCE (Highly Compensated Employee)	5%
B	HCE	10%
C	NHCE (Nonhighly Compensated Employee)	5%
D	NHCE	5%
E	NHCE	5%
F	NHCE	5%
G	NHCE	10%
H	NHCE	10%

This plan has two rate groups, one for each of the two highly compensated employees. Rate group one consists of A and all employees with an allocation rate equal to or greater than A's allocation rate. Thus, rate group one consists of A, B, C, D, E, F, G, and H. Rate group two consists of B and all employees with an allocation rate equal to or greater than B's allocation rate. Thus, rate group two consists of B, G, and H.

Once the rate groups are determined, each rate group must be tested to see if it satisfies IRC § 410(b). The rules that apply in determining whether a rate group satisfies IRC § 410(b) are the same as those that apply in determining whether a plan satisfies IRC § 410(b) except that a rate group satisfies the Treas. Reg. § 1.410(b)-4 nondiscriminatory classification test if and only if the ratio percentage of the rate group is greater than or equal to the lesser of (A) the midpoint between the safe and the unsafe harbor percentages applicable to the plan and (B) the ratio percentage of the plan. Treas. Reg. § 1.401(a)(4)-2(c)(3)(ii).

Rate group one in the preceding example clearly satisfies IRC § 410(b) because the number of NHCEs benefitting/total number of NHCEs = 6/6 or 100 percent, which is greater than 70 percent and thus satisfies IRC § 410(b)(1)(A).

Unlike rate group one, rate group two does not satisfy IRC § 410(b)(1)(A). The number of NHCEs benefitting/total number of NHCEs = 2/6 or 33.3 percent, which is considerably less than 70 percent. Since rate group two does not satisfy IRC § 410(b)(1)(A), it should be tested to see if it satisfies IRC § 410(b)(1)(B). In this case,

$$\frac{\dfrac{\text{The number of NHCEs benefitting}}{\text{Total number of NHCEs}}}{\dfrac{\text{The number of HCEs benefitting}}{\text{Total number of HCEs}}} = \frac{\frac{2}{6}}{\frac{1}{2}} = \frac{33.3\%}{50\%} = 66.7\%$$

Since 66.7 percent is less than 70 percent, rate group two does not satisfy IRC § 410(b)(1)(B). Rate group two should then be tested to see if it satisfies IRC § 410(b)(1)(C).

To determine whether rate group two satisfies IRC § 410(b)(1)(C), it should first be tested to see if it satisfies the Treas. Reg. § 1.410(b)-4 nondiscrimination classification test. For these purposes, the rate group satisfies the Treas. Reg. § 1.410(b)-4 nondiscriminatory classification test (including the reasonable classification requirement) if and only if the ratio percentage of the rate group is greater than or equal to the lesser of (A) the midpoint between the safe and the unsafe harbor percentages applicable to the plan and (B) the ratio percentage of the plan.

To determine whether the rate group satisfies the nondiscrimination classification test, the plan's NHCE concentration percentage must be calculated. The plan's NHCE concentration percentage is the number of NHCEs/total number of employees or 6/8 or 75 percent. The safe harbor percentage for a NHCE concentration percentage of 75 percent is 38.75 percent, while the unsafe harbor percentage for a NHCE concentration percentage of 75 percent is 28.75 percent. Thus, the midpoint between the safe and unsafe harbor is 33.75 percent. In addition, the ratio percentage of the plan is 100% because it covers all of the employees. Since 66.7 percent is greater than 33.75 percent (the lesser of the 33.75 percent or 100 percent), rate group two satisfies the nondiscrimination classification test.

Finally, rate group two must be tested to see if satisfies the average benefits percentage test. Treas. Reg. § 1.401(a)(4)-2(c)(3)(iii). A rate group satisfies the average benefits percentage test if the *plan* of which it is a part satisfies the Treas. Reg. § 1.410(b)-5 average benefits percentage test. The average benefits percentage test is satisfied if the average benefit percentage of NHCEs divided by the average benefits percentage of HCEs is greater than or equal to 70 percent.

In this case, the average benefit percentage of the NHCEs is

$$\frac{5\% + 5\% + 5\% + 5\% + 10\% + 10\%}{6} = 6.67\%$$

while the average benefit percentage of HCEs is

$$\frac{5\% + 10\%}{2} = 7.5\%$$

Since the average benefit percentage of the NHCEs (6.67%) divided by the average benefit percentage of the HCEs (7.5%) or 6.67/7.5 = 88.9 percent, and 88.9 percent is greater than 70 percent, rate group two satisfies the average benefits percentage test. Because both rate groups satisfy IRC § 410(b), the plan satisfies the Treasury Regulation § 401(a)(4) amounts rule.

The following chart summarizes the basic general testing of defined contribution plans.

BASICS OF NONDISCRIMINATION TESTING OF DC PLANS

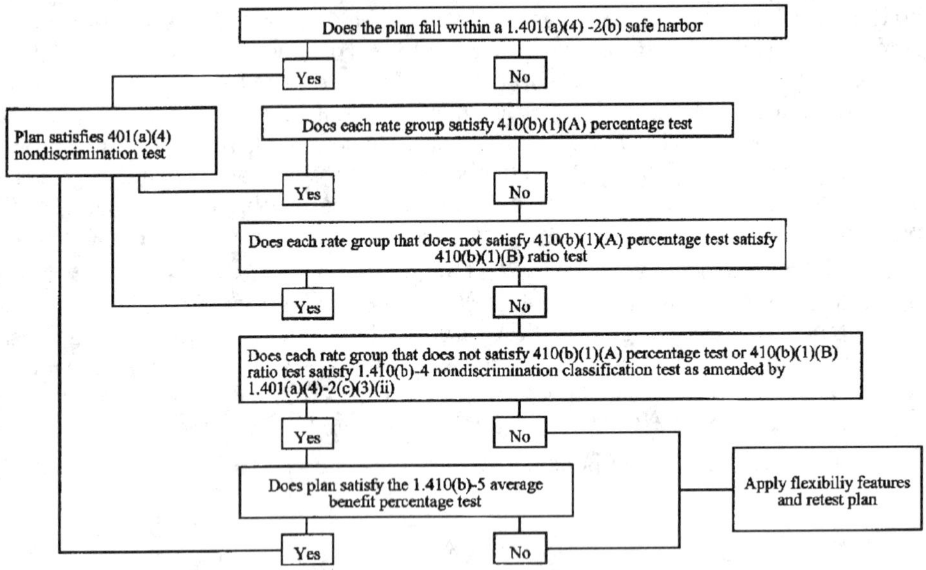

8-10 QUESTIONS AND PROBLEMS

1. What types of employers are likely to take advantage of the safe harbors? What types of employers are likely to rely on general testing? What are the advantages of general testing? What are the disadvantages?

2. Under the Gamma Co. Profit-Sharing Plan, each eligible employee receives an allocation each plan year equal to 3 percent of compensation. During the most recent plan year, all Gamma employees participated in and received an allocation under the plan. Does the plan satisfy the IRC § 401(a)(4) amounts rule for the most recent plan year?

3. Sigma Corp. has a defined contribution plan with a single allocation formula that applies to all employees, under which each employee's allocation for the plan year equals the product of Sigma's total contribution for the plan year and a fraction, the numerator of which is the employee's points for the plan year and the denominator of which is the sum of the points of all employees for the plan year. The plan grants each employee 10 points for each year of service and one point for each $100 of plan year compensation. For the most recent plan year, the total allocations are $85,200 and the total points for all employees are 8,520. Each employee's allocation for the most recent plan year is set forth in the table below. Does the plan satisfy the IRC § 401(a)(4) amounts rule for the most recent plan year? (Employee A owns 100 percent of Sigma Corporation.)

Employee	Years of Service	Plan Year Compensation	Points	Amount of Allocation
A	20	175,000	1,950	19,500
B	10	175,000	1,850	18,500
C	30	145,000	1,750	17,500

Employee	Years of Service	Plan Year Compensation	Points	Amount of Allocation
D	3	145,000	1,480	14,800
E	10	40,000	500	5,000
F	5	35,000	400	4,000
G	3	30,000	330	3,300
H	1	25,000	260	2,600

4. The following employer allocations were made pursuant to Beta's defined contribution plan during the most recent plan year:

Employee	Allocation Rate
H1	4%
H2	6%
H3	8%
N1	5%
N2	5%
N3	6%
N4	8%
N5	6%

Assume that H1, H2, and H3 are highly compensated employees, N1, N2, N3, N4, and N5 are nonhighly compensated employees, these are Beta's only employees, and none of the employees is excludable. Does the plan satisfy the IRC § 401(a)(4) amounts rule for the most recent plan year?

5. The following employer allocations were made pursuant to Alpha's defined contribution plan during the most recent plan year:

Employee	Allocation Rate
H1	5%
H2	5.5%
H3	7.5%
N1	8%
N2	7.5%
N3	5.5%
N4	5%
N5	2%
N6	2%

Assume that H1, H2, and H3 are highly compensated employees, N1, N2, N3, N4, N5, and N6 are nonhighly compensated employees, these are Alpha's only employees, and none of the employees is excludable. Does the plan satisfy the IRC § 401(a)(4) amounts rule for the most recent plan year?

6. The following employer allocations were made pursuant to Omega's defined contribution plan during the most recent plan year:

Employee	Allocation Rate
H1	4%
H2	8%
N1	5%
N2	5%
N3	5%
N4	5%

Assume that H1 and H2 are highly compensated employees, N1, N2, N3, and N4, are nonhighly compensated employees, these are Omega's only employees, and none of the employees is excludable. Does the plan satisfy the IRC § 401(a)(4) amounts rule for the most recent plan year?

[iii] Flexibility Features

If a defined contribution plan does not satisfy a safe harbor or general testing, an employer may use a variety of flexibility techniques to try to satisfy the nondiscrimination amounts rule. These flexibility features may permit the employer to adjust the size of the plan or the rates. There are four basic flexibility features: (1) plan aggregation, (2) plan restructuring, (3) rate grouping, and (4) "imputed" permitted disparity.

First, the Treasury regulations permit employers in some circumstances to aggregate or combine two or more plans and treat the aggregated plans as a single plan for purposes of the nondiscrimination rules. Treas. Reg. § 1.410(b)-7(d). Second, the Treasury regulations permit employers to restructure or divide a plan into separate component plans and test each component plan separately. Treas. Reg. § 1.401(a)(4)-9. Third, the Treasury regulations permit employers to group or "round" rates so that employees with similar allocation or accrual rates may be treated as having the same rates for testing purposes. Treas. Reg. § 1.401(a)(4)-2(c)(2)(v). Finally, the Treasury regulations permit employers to take into account permitted disparity in general testing; in essence, the permitted disparity rules permit an employer to take credit for Social Security benefits or contributions as if the employer provided them in determining whether a plan discriminates in favor of highly compensated employees. Treas. Reg. § 1.401(a)(4)-7.

[iv] Testing of Defined Benefit Plans

The IRC § 401(a)(4) nondiscrimination rules apply to defined benefit plans in much the same manner as they apply to defined contribution plans. Just as the regulations provide safe harbors for defined contribution plans, the regulations provide safe harbors for defined benefit plans. Treas. Reg. § 1.401(a)(4)-3(b). If a defined benefit plan satisfies one of the safe harbors, the plan satisfies the IRC § 401(a)(4) nondiscrimination rules. If the plan does not satisfy a safe harbor, the "general test" must be applied. As in defined contribution plans, the general test requires that the plan be divided into rate groups and each rate group satisfy IRC § 410(b). If the plan does not satisfy the general test, the employer may try to use the flexibility features and retest the plan. Collectively bargained plans automatically satisfy IRC § 401(a)(4). Treas. Reg. § 1.401(a)(4)-1(c)(5).

[b] Other Benefits, Rights, and Features

The Treasury § 401(a)(4) regulations' second basic requirement is that the other benefits, rights, and features of a qualified retirement plan be made available in a nondiscriminatory manner. Treas. Reg. § 1.401(a)(4)-1(b)(3). Benefits, rights, and features include optional benefit forms, such as retirement annuities and lump sum payments, ancillary benefits, such as disability benefits, and other rights and features, such as plan loans and investment options. According to the regulations, benefits, rights, and features provided under a plan are made available in a nondiscriminatory manner if, and only if, they satisfy current availability and effective availability requirements. Treas. Reg. § 1.401(a)(4)-4(b)(2).

In general, a benefit, right or feature satisfies the current availability requirement if the group of employees to whom it is available satisfies IRC § 410(b) without regard to the Treas. Reg. § 1.410(b)-5 average benefit percentage test. Treas. Reg. § 1.401(a)(4)-4(b)(1). Current availability is based on the facts and circumstances relating to the employee (e.g., current compensation, accrued benefit, position, or net worth). Treas. Reg. § 1.401(a)(4)-4(a).

In general, based on all the facts and circumstances, the group of employees to whom a benefit, right or feature is effectively available must not substantially favor highly compensated employees. Treas. Reg. § 1.401(a)(4)-4(c)(1). The regulations offer the following example of effective availability. An employer maintains a defined benefit plan that covers both of its highly compensated nonexcludable employees and nine of its twelve nonhighly compensated employees. The plan provides for a normal retirement benefit payable as an annuity and based on a normal retirement age of 65, and an early retirement benefit payable upon termination in the form of an annuity to employees who terminate from service with the employer on or after age 55 with 30 or more years of service. Both of the employers' highly compensated employees currently meet the age and service requirement or will have 30 years of service by the time they reach age 55. All but two of the nine nonhighly compensated employees who are covered by the plan were hired on or after age 35, and thus cannot qualify for the early retirement benefit. Even though the group of employees to whom the early retirement benefit is currently available satisfies IRC § 410(b), when age and service are disregarded, absent other facts, the group of employees to whom the early retirement benefits is effectively available substantially favors highly compensated employees. Treas. Reg. § 1.401(a)(4)-4(c)(2) Example 1.

[c] Nondiscrimination in Special Circumstances

The Treasury § 401(a)(4) regulation's final basic requirement is that the plan not discriminate in special circumstances. Specifically, plan amendments (including grants of past service credit) and terminations must not discriminate in favor of highly compensated employees. Treas. Reg. § 1.401(a)(4)-1(b)(4). Whether a plan amendment discriminates is determined at the time the plan amendment first becomes effective based on all the facts and circumstances. The regulations identify a number of relevant factors and provide safe harbor rules for certain grants of benefits for past service.

8-11 QUESTIONS AND PROBLEMS

1. Should the Treasury § 401(a)(4) regulations be replaced with a subjective facts and circumstances approach? What are the advantages of the highly detailed regulations? What are the disadvantages?

2. Do the highly detailed regulations encourage or discourage the formation of plans?

3. Do the highly detailed regulations encourage or discourage discrimination in favor of highly compensated employees?

[d] Special Nondiscrimination Rules for 401(k) Plans

IRC §§ 401(k)(3), 401(k)(12), 401(k)(13).

As discussed in Chapter 2, 401(k) plans are a unique kind of defined contribution plan that permit employees to elect whether and how much to contribute to their retirement plan. Contributions may consist solely of elective deferrals; that is, amounts that the employee elects to contribute to the plan rather than receive as cash compensation. In addition, employers may also contribute to such plans. Typically, contributions to a 401(k) plan vary from year to year and from employee to employee, with higher paid employees tending to make larger voluntary contributions than lower paid employees.

In order to be eligible for favorable income tax treatment, 401(k) plans must satisfy a host of requirements set forth in IRC § 401(k)(2). In addition, they must satisfy nondiscrimination rules contained in IRC § 401(k)(3).

Section 401(k)(3) establishes two separate nondiscrimination requirements. First, it requires that 401(k) plans satisfy the regular IRC § 410(b) minimum coverage requirements. IRC § 401(k)(3)(A)(i). Second, it sets forth a special nondiscrimination rule, applicable only to 401(k) plans, that is more liberal than the general IRC § 401(a)(4) nondiscrimination requirement. Plans that satisfy this special nondiscrimination rule are deemed to satisfy the IRC § 404(a)(4) core amounts rule discussed in section (C)(3)(a) above. Treas. Reg. § 1.401(a)(4)-1(b)(2)(ii).

Generally, employers must test their 401(k) plan each year to see if it satisfies the special IRC § 401(k)(3) nondiscrimination requirement. If a plan fails to satisfy the special IRC § 401(k)(3) nondiscrimination requirement, the plan may be corrected in one or a combination of three ways: (1) by returning the excess contributions, (2) by recharacterizing the excess contributions as after-tax contributions, or (3) by the employer making certain contributions to the plan. Treas. Reg. § 1.401(k)-1(f)(1).

If an employer wishes to avoid the cost of testing (and perhaps correcting) the plan each year, it may rely on one of the statutory safe harbors provided in IRC § 401(k)(12) and (13). The first set of safe harbors require that the employer either contribute 3 percent of compensation to all eligible nonhighly compensated employees under the plan regardless of how much, or whether, they voluntarily elect to contribute to the plan ("nonelective contributions") or make certain "matching" contributions to nonhighly compensated employees. The second set of safe harbors applies to plans that adopt automatic enrollment and also require that the employer provide either nonelective or matching contributions.

[i] Special IRC § 401(k)(3) Nondiscrimination Test

The special IRC § 401(k)(3) nondiscrimination test requires that the "actual deferral percentage" ("ADP") for eligible highly compensated employees satisfy one of two tests. Either the ADP for eligible highly compensated employees for the current plan year must not be more than the ADP of all other eligible employees for the preceding plan multiplied by 1.25 (the "125 percent test"), IRC § 401(k)(3)(A)(ii)(I), or the excess ADP for eligible highly compensated employees for the current plan year must not be more than 2 percentage points more than the ADP of all other eligible employees for the preceding plan year and must not be more than twice the ADP of all other eligible employees for the preceding plan year (the "alternative limitation"), IRC § 401(k)(3)(A)(ii)(II).

The ADP is defined as the average of the ratios (calculated separately for each employee in such a group) of the amount of employer contributions actually paid over to the trust on behalf of each such employee for such plan year to the employee's compensation for such plan year. IRC § 401(k)(3)(B). If the employer elects, it may apply the "alternative limitation" based on the ADP of the nonhighly compensated employees for the current year rather than the preceding plan year. If the employer so elects, however, it cannot change that election except as provided by the IRS. IRC § 401(k)(3)(a)(ii).

Applying the ADP test involves a four step process. First, identify the highly compensated employees. Second, calculate each individual highly compensated employee's actual deferral ratio for the current plan year and each individual nonhighly compensated employee's actual deferral ratio for the preceding year. Third, calculate the ADP for the highly compensated employees for the current plan year and the ADP for the nonhighly compensated employees for the preceding plan year. Finally, compare the ADP for highly compensated employees for the current plan year to the ADP for nonhighly compensated employees for the preceding plan year to determine whether the plan satisfies either of the IRC § 401(k)(3)(A)(ii) tests.

To illustrate, suppose that Omega Corporation has adopted a qualified profit-sharing plan with a 401(k) feature in which all four of its employees are eligible to participate. The plan permits employees to contribute up to 10 percent of their salary. The employer has elected to include salary reduction amounts in the definition of compensation. This is the only plan provided by the employer and no employees have any ownership interest in the corporation. The compensation and deferred amounts for the highly compensated employees for the current year and the nonhighly compensated employees for the preceding year are as follows:

Employee	Compensation	Elective Contribution
HCE 1	$160,000	$16,000
HCE 2	$150,000	$7,500
NHCE 1	$40,000	$3,000
NHCE 2	$20,000	$1,000

To determine whether the plan satisfies IRC § 401(k)(3)(A)(ii), begin by identifying which employees are highly compensated and which employees are nonhighly compensated. The facts state that HCE 1 and HCE 2 are highly compensated while NHCE 1 and NHCE 2 are nonhighly compensated. (*See* IRC § 414(q) and section B(2) of this Chapter for the rules defining highly compensated employees.)

Once the highly compensated employees and the nonhighly compensated employees are identified, calculate the actual deferral ratio for the individual highly compensated employees for the current plan year and the actual deferral ratio for the nonhighly compensated employees for the preceding plan year. The actual deferral ratio for each employee is the ratio of the amount of employer contributions actually paid over to the trust on behalf of each such employee for such plan year to the employee's compensation for the plan year. Thus, the actual deferral ratio for HCE 1 is 16,000/160,000 or 10 percent. The actual deferral ratio for HCE 2 is 7,500/150,000 or 5 percent. The actual deferral ratio for NHCE 1 is 3,000/40,000 or 7.5 percent. Finally, the actual deferral ratio for NHCE 2 is 1,000/20,000 or 5 percent.

Once the actual deferral ratio for each highly compensated employee for the current plan year and the actual deferral ratio for each nonhighly compensated employee for the preceding plan year are calculated, calculate the ADP for the highly compensated employees for the current plan year and the ADP for the nonhighly compensated employees for the preceding plan year. The ADP is the average of the actual deferral ratios for each group. Thus, the ADP for the highly compensated employees for the current plan year is (10% + 5%)/2 or 7.5 percent, while the ADP for the nonhighly compensated employees for the preceding plan year is (7.5% + 5%)/2 or 6.25 percent.

Finally, compare the ADP for highly compensated employees for the current plan year to the ADP for the nonhighly compensated employees for the preceding plan year to see whether either the IRC § 401(k)(3)(A)(ii)(I) 125 percent test or the IRC § 401(k)(3)(A)(ii)(II) alternative limitation is satisfied. In order to satisfy the IRC § 401(k)(3)(A)(ii)(I) 125 percent test, the ADP for the highly compensated employees for the current plan year must not be more than 125 percent of the ADP for the nonhighly compensated employees for the preceding plan year. In this case, the ADP for the highly compensated employees for the current plan year (7.5%) is less than 125 percent of the ADP for the nonhighly compensated employees for the preceding plan year (6.25%) (125% x 6.25% = 7.8%). Thus, the plan satisfies the 125 percent test.

In order to satisfy the IRC § 401(k)(3)(A)(ii)(II) alternative limitation, the excess ADP for the highly compensated employees for the current plan year must not be more than 2 percentage points more than the ADP for the nonhighly compensated employees for the preceding plan year and must not be more than twice the ADP for the nonhighly compensated employees for the preceding plan year. In this case, the ADP for the highly compensated employees for the current plan year (7.5%) is not more than 2 percentage points more than the ADP for the nonhighly compensated employees for the preceding plan year (6.25% + 2 = 8.25%) and is not more than twice the ADP for the nonhighly compensated employees for the preceding plan year (6.25% x 2 = 12.5%). Thus, the plan also satisfies the alternative limitation.

In testing the plan for its first year, the ADP for nonhighly compensated employees "for the preceding year" is either 3% or, if the employer elects, the actual ADP for nonhighly compensated employees for the plan's first year. *See* IRC § 401(k)(3)(E).

Generally, catch-up contributions, authorized under IRC § 414(v), may be disregarded in determining whether a 401(k) plan satisfies the ADP test. Prop. Treas. Reg. § 1.414(v)-1(d)(2)(i). Catch-up contributions are discussed in more detail in Chapter 9.

Employer matching contributions must satisfy an actual contribution percentage (ACP) test that is identical to the special IRC § 401(k)(3) nondiscrimination test for elective contributions. *See* IRC § 401(m)(2)(A).

8-12 QUESTIONS AND PROBLEMS

1. Why does IRC § 401(k)(3) permit some discrimination rather than requiring uniform contributions? Why does IRC § 401(k)(3) impose a special nondiscrimination rule for 401(k) plans?

2. Lamda Corp. has adopted a qualified profit-sharing plan with a 401(k) feature in which all six of its employees are eligible to participate. The plan permits employees to contribute up to 10 percent of their salary. The employer has elected to include salary reduction amounts in the definition of compensation. This is the only plan provided by the employer and no employees have any ownership interest in the corporation. The compensation and deferred amounts for the highly compensated employees for the current year and the nonhighly compensated employees for the preceding year are as follows:

Employee	Compensation	Elective Contribution
HCE 1	$160,000	$12,800
HCE 2	$150,000	$ 9,000
NHCE 1	$50,000	$3,000
NHCE 2	$40,000	$2,400
NHCE 3	$35,000	$1,750
NHCE 4	$30,000	$900

Does the plan satisfy the special IRC § 401(k)(3) nondiscrimination test?

3. Mu Corp. has adopted a qualified profit-sharing plan with a 401(k) feature in which all four of its employees are eligible to participate. The plan permits employees to contribute up to 10 percent of their salary. The employer has elected to include salary reduction amounts in the definition of compensation. This is the only plan provided by the employer, and no employees have any ownership interest in the corporation. The compensation and deferred amounts for the highly compensated employees for the current year and the nonhighly compensated employees for the preceding year are as follows:

Employee	Compensation	Elective Contribution
HCE 1	$160,000	$14,400
HCE 2	$150,000	$15,000
NHCE 1	$50,000	$3,000
NHCE 2	$20,000	$0

Does the plan satisfy the special IRC § 401(k)(3) nondiscrimination test?

4. Why does the special IRC § 401(k)(3) nondiscrimination test compare the ADP for the highly compensated employees for the current plan year with the ADP for the nonhighly compensated employees for the preceding plan year rather than with the ADP for the nonhighly compensated employees for the current plan year?

[ii] Safe Harbors

If an employer wants to avoid the cost and uncertainty of testing and correcting excess contributions, it may elect to satisfy one of the safe harbors set forth in IRC § 401(k)(12) or 401(k)(13).

Section 401(k)(12) provides that a 401(k) plan will be treated as meeting the nondiscrimination requirement if it satisfies either a matching contribution safe harbor or a nonelective contribution safe harbor and provides each employee with timely, written notice describing her rights and obligations under the plan.

Under the 401(k)(12) matching contribution safe harbor, a 401(k) plan will automatically satisfy the nondiscrimination requirement if the employer makes a matching contribution equal to 100 percent of each nonhighly compensated employee's elective 401(k) contribution in an amount up to 3 percent of the employee's compensation plus 50 percent of the amount the employee contributes that is greater than 3 percent but does not exceed 5 percent of compensation. IRC § 401(k)(12)(B)(i). An alternative matching contribution option is satisfied if (1) the rate of an employer's matching contribution does not increase as an employee's rate of contribution increases, and (2) the aggregate amount of the matching contributions at such rate of elective contribution is at least equal to the aggregate amount of matching contributions which would be made if the contributions were made on the basis of the general rule. IRC § 401(k)(12)(B)(iii). In order to satisfy the matching contribution safe harbor, the plan must not provide matching contributions to highly compensated employees at a higher rate than those provided to nonhighly compensated employees. IRC § 401(k)(12)(B)(ii).

Under the 401(k)(12) nonelective contribution safe harbor, a 401(k) plan will automatically satisfy the nondiscrimination requirement if the employer is required to make a contribution on behalf of each nonhighly compensated employee eligible to participate in the plan equal to at least 3 percent of the nonhighly compensated employee's compensation, regardless of whether the employee makes any contribution to the plan. IRC § 401(k)(12)(C).

In order to satisfy either safe harbor, the matching or nonelective contributions must also be fully vested at all times and must not be distributable earlier than separation from service, death, disability, an event described in IRC § 401(k)(10), or in the case of a profit-sharing or stock bonus plan, the attainment of age 59½. IRC § 401(k)(12)(E).

Section 401(k)(13) provides that a 401(k) plan will be treated as meeting the nondiscrimination requirement if it provides for certain minimum automatic salary deferrals, satisfies either a matching contribution safe harbor or a nonelective contribution safe harbor, and provides each employee with timely, written notice describing her rights and obligations under the plan.

To satisfy the IRC § 401(k)(13) automatic salary deferral requirement, the plan must provide for minimum automatic salary deferrals equal to at least 3 percent during the first year of participation, 4 percent during the second year, 5 percent during the third year, and 6 percent thereafter. IRC § 401(k)(13)(C). Although the automatic salary deferrals may exceed these minimum amounts, they may not exceed 10 percent. IRC § 401(k)(13)(C)(iii).

Under the IRC § 401(k)(13)(D) matching contribution safe harbor, the plan must provide matching contributions equal to 100 percent of elective deferrals up to 1 percent of compensation, plus 50 percent of elective deferrals between 1 percent and 6 percent of compensation. IRC § 401(k)(13)(D)(i)(I). In the alternative, the plan may use an alternative formula for matching contributions that is at least as generous for each rate of contribution as the basic method, so long as the rate of employer matching contributions does not increase an employee's rate of elective deferrals increases. IRC § 401(k)(13)(D)(ii).

Under the IRC § 401(k)(13)(D) nonelective contribution safe harbor, the plan must provide for an employer nonelective contribution of at least 3 percent of compensation of all nonhighly compensated employees eligible to participate in the plan, regardless of whether the employees make elective contributions. IRC § 401(k)(13)(D)(i)(II).

The matching and nonelective contributions must fully vest after two years of service. IRC § 401(k)(13)(D)(iii). In addition, each year the plan must notify employees of the amount to be deferred, the investments in which the deferrals will be deposited, and that the employee has the right to change the amount deferred, the investments into which the money is deferred, or to opt out of the arrangement altogether. IRC § 401(k)(13)(E).

8-13 QUESTIONS AND PROBLEMS

1. Why do IRC § 401(k)(12)(D) and IRC § 401(k)(13)(E) impose a notice requirement?

2. Which types of employers are likely to prefer having a safe harbor in their plan to testing their plan each year?

3. Which types of employers are likely to prefer IRC § 401(k)(12) matching contribution safe harbor?

4. Which types of employers are likely to prefer the IRC § 401(k)(12) nonelective contribution safe harbor?

5. Which types of employers are likely to prefer the IRC § 401(k)(13) automatic enrollment with matching contribution safe harbor?

6. Which types of employers are likely to prefer the IRC § 401(k)(13) automatic enrollment with nonelective contribution safe harbor?

7. Sigma Corp. maintains a 401(k) plan that provides a required matching contribution equal to 100 percent of each eligible employee's elective contributions up to 4 percent of compensation. Does the plan satisfy a 401(k)(12) safe harbor?

8. Tau Co. maintains a 401(k) plan that provides a required matching contribution equal to 150 percent of each eligible employee's elective contributions up to 3 percent of compensation. Does the plan satisfy a 401(k)(12) safe harbor?

9. Upsilon Inc. maintains a 401(k) plan with automatic salary deferrals equal to 2 percent during the first year of participation, 4 percent during the second year, 6 percent during the third year, and 8 percent thereafter and provides a required matching contribution equal to 100 percent of each eligible employee's elective contributions up to 2 percent of compensation and 50 percent of each eligible employee's elective contributions between 3 and 4 percent of compensation. Does the plan satisfy a 401(k)(13) safe harbor?

10. Phi Co. maintains a 401(k) plan with automatic salary deferrals equal to 3 percent during the first year of participation and 6 percent during the second year and thereafter and provides a required matching contribution equal 100 percent of each eligible employee's elective contributions up to 4 percent of compensation. Does the plan satisfy a 401(k)(13) safe harbor?

[iii] Methods for Correcting Excess Contributions

IRC § 401(k)(8).

If the plan does not satisfy one of the safe harbors or the special IRC § 401(k)(3) nondiscrimination test for a plan year, the plan may provide for the correction of excess contributions in one or a combination of three ways: (1) the excess contributions plus income allocated to those contributions may be distributed from the plan before the close of the following plan year, (2) the excess contributions may be recharacterized as after-tax contributions, or (3) the employer can make qualified nonelective or qualified matching contributions. Treas. Reg. § 1.401(k)-1(f)(1). Generally, if the excess contribution percentage is not corrected within two-and-a-half months after the end of the plan year, the employer will incur a 10 percent excise tax on the amount of the excess deferral percentage not corrected at that time. IRC § 4979; Treas. Reg. § 1.401(k)-1(f)(6). If the excess deferral percentage is not corrected within 12 months, the plan will be disqualified for the plan year in which the excess contributions were made and all subsequent plan years during which the excess contributions remain in the trust. Treas. Reg. § 1.401(k)-1(f)(6).

If a 401(k) plan with automatic contributions complies with the ERISA 404(c) requirements and meets other notice requirements, the plan may permit a participant to withdraw automatic contributions at any time during a 90-day window period without penalty. IRC § 414(w)(2). In addition, plans meeting these requirements may also make corrective distributions to satisfy the nondiscrimination tests within 6 months of year end, rather than 2½ months. IRC § 4979(f)(1). Amounts withdrawn or distributed are taxable in the year of receipt. IRC § 4979(f)(2).

[a] Distribution of Excess Contributions

The excess contribution of a highly compensated employee is the amount (if any) by which the employee's elective contributions must be reduced for the employee's actual deferral ratio to equal the highest permitted actual deferral ratio under the plan. Distributions are to be made on the basis of the amount of contributions by, or on behalf of, each highly compensated employee. IRC § 401(k)(8)(C).

The following procedure is to be used in making distributions:

Step 1: Calculate the dollar amount of excess contributions for each affected highly compensated employee.

Step 2: Determine the total of the dollar amounts calculated in Step 1. This total amount is then distributed in accordance with Steps 3 and 4.

Step 3: The elective contributions of the highly compensated employee with the highest dollar amount of elective contributions are reduced by the amount required to cause that highly compensated employee's elective contributions to equal the dollar amount of the elective contributions of the highly compensated employee with the next highest dollar amount. If, however, a lesser reduction, when added to the total dollar amount already distributed under this step, would equal the total excess contributions, the lesser reduction amount is distributed.

Step 4: If the total amount distributed is less than the total excess contributions, then step 3 is repeated.

The following example illustrates how excess contributions should be distributed:

Suppose that in 2011, the Theta plan's two highly compensated employees were to make contributions as follows:

HCE	Compensation	Deferral	Actual Deferral Ratio (ADR)
1	$180,000	$10,800	6%
2	$150,000	$10,500	7%

Suppose further that in the preceding plan year 2010, the ADP for the nonhighly compensated employees was 3 percent. Under the special IRC § 401(k)(3) nondiscrimination test, the ADP for the Theta plan's highly compensated employees for the following plan year of 2011 may not exceed 5 percent. (The ADP for the highly compensated employees can not exceed the greater of: (1) 3% + 1.25 or 3.75%, IRC § 401(k)(3)(A)(ii)(I), or (2) 3% + 2% or 5%, IRC § 401(k)(3)(A)(ii)(II).)

The total excess contributions for the highly compensated employees is determined as follows:

Step 1: The elective contributions of HCE 2 (the highly compensated employee with the highest ADR) are reduced by $1,500 in order to reduce the ADR of HCE 2 to 6 percent ($9,000/$150,000), which is the ADR of HCE 1. Because the ADP of the highly compensated employees (now 6%) still exceeds 5%, the special IRC § 401(k)(3)(A)(ii) nondiscrimination test is not satisfied and further reductions in elective contributions are necessary. The elective contributions of HCE 1 and HCE 2 are each reduced by one percent of compensation ($1,800 + $1,500, respectively). Because the ADP of the highly compensated employees now equal 5 percent, the special IRC § 401(k)(3)(A)(ii) nondiscrimination test is now satisfied and no further reductions in elective contributions are necessary.

Step 2: The total excess contributions for the highly compensated employees that must be distributed equal $4,800, the total reductions in elective contributions under step 1 ($1,500 + $1,800 + $1,500). Pursuant to IRC § 401(k)(8), the $4,800 in total excess contributions is distributed as follows:

Step 3: The plan distributes $300 to HCE 1 (the highly compensated employee with the highest dollar amount of elective contributions) in order to reduce the dollar amount of the elective contributions of HCE 1 to $10,500, which is the dollar amount of the elective contributions of HCE 2.

Step 4: Because the total amount distributed ($300) is less than the total excess contributions ($4,800), step 3 must be repeated. As the dollar amount of remaining elective contributions for both HCE 1 and HCE 2 are equal, the remaining $4,500 of excess contributions is then distributed equally to HCE 1 and HCE 2 in the amount of $2,250 each.

Under this example, HCE 1 must receive a total distribution of $2,550 of excess contributions and HCE 2 must receive a total distribution of $2,250 of excess contributions. This is true even though the ADR of HCE 2 exceeded the ADR of HCE 1. Moreover, the plan is now treated as satisfying the special IRC § 401(k)(3) nondiscrimination test regardless of whether the ADP would satisfy IRC § 401(k)(3), if recalculated after distributions.

A plan may only use this method (distributing excess contributions) to correct excess contributions if the plan expressly so provides. As a practical matter, most plans provide for this method of correction.

If excess contributions are distributed from the plan, the income allocable to the excess contributions must also be distributed. The income allocable to excess contributions is equal to the sum of the allocable gain or loss for the plan year and, if the plan so provides, the allocable gain or loss for the period between the end of the plan year and the date of distribution. A plan may use any reasonable method for allocating income on excess contributions so long as the method does not violate IRC § 401(a)(4) and is used consistently. The distributions must be made no later than 12 months after the end of the plan year. Treas. Reg. § 1.401(k)-1(f)(4)(i).

8-14 QUESTIONS AND PROBLEMS

1. What effect will returning excess contributions likely have on employee morale?

2. Why does IRC § 401(k)(8) require that excess contributions be distributed in order of dollar amount of elective contributions rather than in order of actual deferral ratios?

3. Suppose that in 2011, the Gamma plan's two highly compensated employees were to make contributions as follows:

HCE	Compensation	Deferral
1	$150,000	$15,000
2	$190,000	$11,400

Suppose further that in the preceding plan year 2010, the ADP for the nonhighly compensated employees was 4 percent. Assuming that the Gamma plan provides for correction of excess contributions through distributions, how should the plan's excess contributions be distributed?

4. Suppose that in 2011, the Delta plan's two highly compensated employees were to make contributions as follows:

HCE	Compensation	Deferral
1	$170,000	$17,000
2	$190,000	$15,200

Suppose further that in the preceding plan year 2010, the ADP for the nonhighly compensated employees was 5 percent. Assuming that the Delta plan provides for correction of excess contributions through distributions, how should the plan's excess contributions be distributed?

[b] Recharacterization of Excess Contributions

A plan may provide that excess contributions are to be corrected by recharacterizing the excess contributions as after-tax employee contributions. IRC § 401(k)(8)(A)(ii). Such recharacterizations must be made within 2½ months of the end of the plan year. Treas. Reg. § 1.401(k)-1(f)(3)(iii).

After-tax employee contributions must also meet a special nondiscrimination test that is similar to the special test under IRC § 401(k)(3). IRC § 401(m)(2).

Because highly compensated employees typically make greater after-tax contributions than do nonhighly compensated employees, recharacterizing excess contributions as after-tax contributions usually creates problems under IRC § 401(m) as it solves them under IRC § 401(k). Thus, recharacterizing excess contributions as after-tax employee contributions is a theoretical but often not a practical solution to correcting excess contributions.

[c] Employer Matching and Nonelective Contributions

If the plan so provides, an employer may correct excess contributions by making qualified nonelective contributions (QNECs) or qualified matching contributions (QMACs). Treas. Reg. § 1.401(k)-1(f)(1). Qualified matching contributions are contributions made on behalf of an employee on account of a contribution made by the employee and which are fully and immediately vested and subject to the special IRC § 401(k)(B)(2) distribution limitations for elective contributions. IRC §§ 401(k)(3)(D)(ii)(I); 401(m)(4)(A)(i). Qualified nonelective contributions are employer contributions (other than matching contributions) with respect to which the employee may not elect to have the contribution paid to the employee in cash instead of being contributed to the plan and which are fully and immediately vested and subject to the special IRC § 401(k)(B)(2) distribution limitations for elective contributions. IRC §§ 401(k)(3)(D)(ii)(II); 401(m)(4)(C).

QNECs and QMACs are treated as elective contributions for purposes of testing the plan under the special IRC § 401(k)(3) nondiscrimination test provided they satisfy certain conditions. IRC § 401(k)(3)(D)(ii). Treas. Reg. § 1.401(k)-1(b)(5). First, QNECs must satisfy the general nondiscrimination rules of Section 401(a)(4). Treas. Reg. § 1.401(k)-1(b)(5)(i). In addition, the employer's nonelective contributions, excluding QNECs that are treated as elective contributions for purposes of the special IRC § 401(k)(3) nondiscrimination test, must also satisfy the general nondiscrimination requirements of IRC § 401(a)(4). Treas. Reg. § 1.401(k)-1(b)(5)(ii). Second, QMACs that are not used for the special IRC § 401(k)(3) nondiscrimination must satisfy the similar IRC § 401(m)(2) nondiscrimination test. QNECs and QMACs must be actually paid to the trust no later than the end of the 12-month period immediately following the plan year. Treas. Reg. §§ 1.401(k)-1(b)(5)(v)& -1(b)(4)(i)(A)(2).

8-15 QUESTIONS AND PROBLEMS

1. Why might an employer prefer to correct excess contributions by the use of QNECs or QMACs rather than distributing the excess contributions?

2. Which are likely to be less costly, QNECs or QMACs?

[d] Permitted Disparity/Integration with Social Security

IRC §§ 401(a)(5)(C), 401(l).

A pension plan is not considered to be discriminatory within the meaning of IRC § 401(a)(4) if it discriminates in favor of highly compensated employees in a manner permitted by IRC § 401(l). IRC § 401(a)(5)(C). In essence, IRC § 401(l) permits Social Security benefits to be taken into account in determining whether a plan discriminates in favor of highly compensated employees. The rules generally permit contributions or benefits attributable to income above the Social Security taxable wage base (equal to $110,100 in 2012) to be higher than contributions or benefits below the Social Security taxable wage base. The rules add complexity to the nondiscrimination rules but can be avoided by providing all employees with identical benefits.

The following excerpt describes the permitted disparity/integration rules.

KATHRYN L. MOORE, THE EFFECTS OF PARTIAL PRIVATIZATION OF SOCIAL SECURITY UPON PRIVATE PENSIONS

NYU REVIEW OF EMPLOYEE BENEFITS AND EXECUTIVE COMPENSATION 5-1, 5-5–5-17 (2003)

Pamela Perun recently conducted a comprehensive study of the prevalence of integrated plans using data from Form 5500s filed during the period of 1993 to 1997. She found that about 24% of all plans were integrated, with defined benefit and defined contribution plans almost equally likely to be integrated. Specifically, she found that 27% of all defined benefit plans were integrated in 1997 while 24% of all defined contribution plans were integrated that year.

Some plans that are not expressly integrated with Social Security rely on integration to satisfy the nondiscrimination requirements. The Treasury regulations' "imputed permitted disparity" rules, which are based on the § 401(l) integration rules, permit plans that are not expressly integrated with Social Security to take Social Security benefits into account in determining whether the plan discriminates in favor of highly compensated employees in general testing of the plan. Unfortunately, there are no reliable statistics on how many plans rely on imputed disparity to satisfy the § 401(a)(4) non-discrimination requirement.

Commentators typically offer two justifications for the integration rules. First, at least nominally, employers are required to pay one-half of the Social Security payroll tax, and the integration rules allow employers to offset at least part of this cost. Second, because Social Security replaces a larger percentage of the pre-retirement earnings of the lower-paid than that of the higher-paid, some lower-paid workers might receive combined pension and Social Security benefits that exceed 100% of their pre-retirement earnings absent the integration rules.

. . .

There are two basic approaches to integration: the excess approach and the offset approach. Under the excess approach, which can apply to both defined benefit and defined contribution plans, the plan provides higher benefits (in the case of a defined benefit plan) or contributions (in the case of a defined contribution plan) with respect to compensation above the integration level than with respect to compensation at or below the integration level. Under the offset approach, which only applies to defined benefit plans, the plan provides that an employee's benefit is reduced or offset by a specified percentage of the employee's final average compensation up to the plan's offset level. "An offset plan may be thought of as a simple formula of A minus B equals C, where 'A' is the annual pension *accrual*, 'B' is the social security benefit *offset*, and 'C' is the amount of the pension *check*." Over the last twenty years, employers have shifted away from defined benefit offset plans to defined benefit excess plans.

Regarding excess plans, § 401(l) imposes limits on the amount by which benefits or contributions with respect to compensation above the integration level may exceed benefits or contributions with respect to compensation below the integration level. With respect to offset plans, § 401(l) imposes limits on the amount by which benefits below the offset level may be offset. The limits are related but not completely tied to Social Security benefits.

Specifically, with respect to defined contribution excess plans, § 401(l) provides that employer contributions with respect to compensation above the integration level may exceed contributions with respect to compensation below the integration level so long as contributions with respect to compensation above the integration level (the "excess contribution percentage") do not exceed contributions with respect to compensation below the integration level (the "base contribution level") by more than the lesser of the base contribution percentage or the greater of (a) 5.7 percentage points or (b) the percentage equal to the employer portion of the FICA tax attributable to old age insurance. Currently, the employer portion of the FICA tax attributable to old age insurance is about 5%, and "the Social Security Administration is to advise the IRS when the rate attributable to old age-insurance rises above 5.7 percent."

Thus, for example, the § 401(l) integration rules would permit a defined contribution plan to provide contributions equal to 4% of compensation below the integration level and 8% of compensation above the integration level because the excess contribution percentage of 8% would not exceed the base contribution percentage of 4% by more than the lesser of the base benefit percentage of 4% or 5.7%. On the other hand, the integration rules would not permit a defined contribution plan to provide contributions equal to 6 percent of compensation below the integration level and 12 percent of compensation above the integration level because the excess contribution level of 12% would exceed the base contribution percentage of 6% by more than the lesser of the base contribution percentage of 6% or 5.7%.

The 5.7% excess contribution allowance is tied directly to Social Security contributions: it equals the employer's share of contributions to Social Security old-age and survivors and disability insurance in 1986 (when § 401(l) was amended to include this provision). Similarly, "the percentage equal to the employer portion of the FICA tax attributable to old age insurance" is expressly tied to Social Security, although it is not yet in effect because the employer's share of FICA tax attributable to old age insurance is currently (as of 2003) less than 5.7%.

The Treasury regulations provide that if the integration level is less than the Social Security taxable wage base, then the 5.7% maximum excess contribution allowance is generally reduced. This reduction is designed to prevent discrimination in favor of highly compensated employees and not to reflect employer contributions to Social Security. Similarly, the alternative base contribution percentage limitation is not tied to Social Security but instead is designed to ensure that employers make some contribution on behalf of lower-paid employees. The limitation requires that employers provide contributions with respect to compensation below the integration level that are at least half the percentage of contributions made with respect to compensation above the integration level.

With respect to defined benefit excess plans, § 401(l) provides that the excess benefit percentage "may not exceed the base benefit percentage by more than the maximum excess allowance." It then provides that the maximum excess allowance with respect to benefits attributable to any year of service taken into account with respect to the plan is the lesser of the base benefit percentage or 0.75%. The maximum excess allowance with respect to total benefits is the lesser of the base benefit percentage or 0.75% times the participant's years of service (not to exceed thirty-five years) taken into account under the plan.

Thus, for example, the § 401(l) integration rules would permit a defined benefit excess plan to provide a benefit of 0.5% of the participant's average annual compensation up to the integration level for the plan year plus 1% of his average annual compensation for the plan year in excess of the integration level, for each year of service up to thirty-five years, because the excess benefit percentage of 1% does not exceed the base benefit percentage of 0.5% by more than the lesser of the base benefit percentage of 0.5% or 0.75%. On the other hand, the integration rules would not permit a defined benefit excess plan to provide a benefit of 0.5% of the participant's average annual compensation up to the integration level for the plan year plus 1.25% of his average annual compensation for the plan year in excess of the integration level, for each year of service up to thirty-five years, because the excess benefit percentage of 1.25% would exceed the base benefit percentage of 0.5% by more than the lesser of the base benefit percentage of 0.5% or 0.75%.

With respect to defined benefit offset plans, § 401(l) provides that a participant's accrued benefit in an offset plan may not be reduced by reason of the offset by more than the maximum offset allowance. The maximum offset allowance with respect to a participant for any year of service taken into account under the plan is the lesser of 50% of the benefit that would have accrued without regard to the offset reduction or 0.75% of the participant's final average compensation. The maximum offset allowance with respect to a participant's total benefits is the lesser of 50% of the benefit that would have accrued without regard to the offset allowance or 0.75% of the participant's final average compensation times the participant's years of service (not to exceed thirty-five) taken into account under the plan.

Thus, for example, the integration rules would permit a defined benefit offset plan to provide a normal retirement benefit equal to 1% of average annual compensation minus 0.5% of final average compensation up to the offset level, for each year of service up to thirty-five, because the offset percentage of 0.5% is not greater than the lesser of 50% of the benefit that would have accrued without regard to the offset allowance, which is 0.5%, or 0.75%. On the other hand, the integration rules would not permit a defined benefit offset plan to provide a normal retirement benefit equal to 1% of average annual compensation minus 0.75% of final average compensation up to the offset level for each year of service up to thirty-five because the offset percentage of 0.75% is greater than the lesser of 50% of the benefit that would have accrued without regard to the offset allowance, which is 0.5%, or 0.75%.

Just as the 5.7 percent limitation for defined contribution excess plans is designed to approximate the Social Security employer contribution rate, the 0.75% factor for defined benefit excess and offset plans is designed to approximate the Social Security benefit accrual rate. According to James Holland, then chief of the I.R.S. Pension Actuarial Branch, the 0.75% factor was derived from at least three different calculations [, each of which was designed to approximate the Social Security employer contribution rate.]

Treasury regulations provide that if the integration level exceeds covered compensation, defined as the average of the employee's taxable wage base in effect for each year of the thirty-five year period ending with the year in which the employee reaches the Social Security retirement age, the 0.75% factor is reduced. The reduction in the 0.75% factor is designed to reflect the fact that the Social Security replacement rate declines for compensation in excess of the covered compensation (because such compensation generates no additional old-age benefits) and to prevent discrimination in favor of highly compensated employees. Like the alternative base contribution percentage limitation for defined contribution excess plans, neither the alternative base benefit percentage limitation for defined benefit excess plans nor the alternative limitation of 50% of the benefit that would have accrued without regard to the offset for defined benefit offset plans are tied to Social Security. Instead, both are designed to ensure that employers make some contribution on behalf of lower-paid employees.

8-16 QUESTIONS AND PROBLEMS

1. Should employers be permitted to take Social Security benefits into account in determining whether their pension plans discriminate in favor of highly compensated employees? Do the integration/permitted disparity rules benefit nonhighly compensated employees or highly compensated employees or both?

2. Nu Co's profit-sharing plan provides that the account of each employee who has plan year compensation in excess of the Social Security taxable wage base in effect at the beginning of the plan year will receive an allocation for the plan year of 5.7 percent of plan year compensation in excess of the taxable wage base. The plan provides that no allocation will be made to the account of any employee for the plan year with respect to plan year compensation which is not in excess of the Social Security taxable wage base. Does Nu Co's profit-sharing plan satisfy IRC § 401(l)?

3. Xi Corp's profit-sharing plan provides that the account of each employee will receive an allocation of 3 percent of the employee's plan year compensation up to the Social Security taxable wage base in effect at the beginning of the plan year plus an allocation of 6 percent of the employee's plan year compensation in excess of the Social Security taxable wage base. Does Xi Corp's profit-sharing plan satisfy IRC § 401(l)?

4. Omicron Co's money purchase plan provides that the account of each employee will receive an allocation of 7 percent of the employee's plan year compensation up to the Social Security taxable wage base in effect at the beginning of the plan year plus 14 percent of the employee's plan year compensation in excess of the Social Security taxable wage base. Does Omicron Co's money purchase plan satisfy IRC § 401(l)?

5. Pi Corp. maintains a noncontributory defined benefit plan that provides a normal retirement benefit of 0.8% of the participant's average annual compensation up to the integration level for the plan year plus 1.6% of average annual compensation for the plan year in excess of the integration level, for each year of service up to 35. The plan's integration level does not exceed covered compensation. Does Pi Corp.'s defined benefit plan satisfy IRC § 401(l)?

6. Rho Inc. maintains a noncontributory defined benefit plan that provides a normal retirement benefit of 0.4% of the participant's average annual compensation up to the integration level for the plan year plus 0.8% of average annual compensation for the plan year in excess of the integration level, for each year of service up to 35. The plan's integration level does not exceed covered compensation. Does Rho Inc's defined benefit plan satisfy IRC § 401(l)?

7. Sigma Co. maintains a noncontributory defined benefit plan that provides a normal retirement benefit equal to 2% of average annual compensation minus 1% of final average compensation up to the offset level, for each year of service up to 35. Does Sigma Co's defined benefit plan satisfy IRC § 401(l)?

8. Tau Corp. maintains a noncontributory defined benefit plan that provides a normal retirement benefit equal to 1.5% of average annual compensation minus 0.5% of final average compensation up to the offset level, for each year of service up to 35. Does Tau Corp.'s defined benefit plan satisfy IRC § 401(l)?

Chapter 9

PLAN OPERATION

This chapter explores a variety of issues that arise in the day-to-day operation of a retirement plan. The Internal Revenue Code imposes a variety of limitations on plan operation. Some of those limitations, such as the IRC § 401(a)(17) limitation on compensation, apply in determining whether a plan discriminates in favor highly compensated employees. Other limitations, such as the IRC § 404 rules governing the deductibility of employer contributions, apply independently of the nondiscrimination rules. All of the limitations discussed in the first section of this chapter concern tax qualification and deductibility requirements that are contained solely in the Internal Revenue Code. ERISA does not impose parallel requirements.

ERISA and the Internal Revenue Code do, however, contain parallel funding rules. The requirements applicable to defined contribution plans are quite straightforward. Sponsors must contribute any amounts they promise to contribute to the plan. The funding rules for defined benefit plans, on the other hand, are quite complex. Although most of the actual calculations are made by actuaries, lawyers should be familiar with the basic rules.

Plan distributions are regulated in a number of ways. For example, IRC § 72(t) imposes a penalty on early distributions, and IRC § 401(a)(9) mandates certain minimum distributions. Although participants generally need not include contributions to qualified plans in income when the contributions are made, plan distributions are generally included in income when received; an exception to this rule is certain distributions rolled over to another qualified plan or IRA. In addition, plan loans are subject to special tax treatment.

A. INTERNAL REVENUE CODE LIMITATIONS ON PLAN OPERATION

As discussed throughout this book, the Internal Revenue Code encourages the formation of private pension plans by affording them favorable income tax treatment. This favorable tax treatment, however, is not without limitations. In addition to the Internal Revenue Code limits on the amount of contributions and benefits that may be provided on behalf of highly compensated employees, discussed in Chapter 8, the Internal Revenue Code imposes a number of other limitations.

First, IRC § 401(a)(17) imposes a limit on the amount of compensation that a qualified plan may take into account for purposes of determining benefits or contributions under the plan and for purposes of determining whether the plan discriminates in favor of highly compensated employees. IRC § 415 imposes a limit on the contributions and benefits a qualified plan may provide. IRC § 402(g) limits elective deferrals, although IRC § 414(v) provides an exception for "catch-up contributions." IRC § 404 imposes limits on the deductibility of employer contributions while IRC § 4972 imposes an excise tax on contributions that exceed the IRC § 404 limits.

Some of these limitations, such as the compensation limitation, are intended, like the nondiscrimination rules, to ensure that nonhighly compensated employees receive meaningful benefits from tax qualified plans. Other limitations, such as the limitations on the deductibility of employer contributions, are designed simply to limit the amount of the pension tax subsidy. Most of the limitations are objective dollar amounts. The dollar amounts, however, are not constant. Many are indexed to increases in the cost of living. More importantly, the limitations are often amended as part of the federal budget balancing process. In periods of budget deficits, the limitations are often reduced. In times of budget surplus, they are often increased. (*See* Colleen E. Medill, *Targeted Pension Reform*, 27 J. Legis. 1 (2001)).

[1] Compensation Limit

IRC § 401(a)(17).

Section 401(a)(17) of the Internal Revenue Code limits the amount of compensation that a qualified plan may take into account for purposes of determining benefits or contributions under the plan, and determining whether the plan discriminates in favor of highly compensated employees. Treas. Reg. § 1.401(a)(17)-1(a)(1). The limit is $200,000 for plan years beginning after December 31, 2001, and is adjusted for increases in the cost-of-living in $5,000 increments. In 2012, the IRC § 401(a)(17)(A) limit, as adjusted, is $250,000.

9-1 QUESTIONS AND PROBLEMS

1. Suppose that Ralph works for Nu Corporation and earns $350,000 in 2012. If the Nu Profit-Sharing Plan provides contributions equal to 5 percent of pay for each employee in 2012, how much will be contributed on behalf of Ralph in 2012?

2. Who benefits from the IRC § 401(a)(17) limitation on compensation? Who is harmed?

3. Prior to the enactment of the Economic Growth and Tax Relief Reconciliation Act of 2001, one commentator suggested that the IRC § 401(a)(17) compensation limit be increased for defined benefit plans but not for defined contribution plans. Was this a sound proposal?

[2] Limitations on Contributions and Benefits

IRC § 415.

In order for a plan to be qualified and thus eligible for favorable tax treatment, the plan must satisfy IRC § 415, which sets forth limitations on contributions and benefits under qualified retirement plans. IRC § 401(a)(16). Although IRC § 415 was added to the Internal Revenue Code with the enactment of ERISA, it is purely a tax qualification requirement and is not required by Title I of ERISA.

[a] Limitations on Contributions

IRC § 415(c).

Section 415(c) limits the "annual additions" which may be made to a defined contribution plan to the lesser of (a) $40,000, adjusted for increases in the cost-of-living, or (b) 100 percent of the participant's compensation. IRC § 415(c)(1). "Annual additions" are defined as (a) employer contributions, (b) employee contributions, and (c) forfeitures. IRC § 415(c)(2). Annual additions do not include rollover contributions. The participant's compensation means compensation as determined before any reduction for the participant's before-tax salary deferral contribution to a section 401(k) plan or a section 125 cafeteria plan. IRC § 415(c)(3)(D). In 2012, the IRC § 415(c)(1)(A) limit, as adjusted, is $50,000.

9-2 QUESTIONS AND PROBLEMS

1. Cameron, an employee of the Beta Corporation, earned $170,000 in 2012. What is the maximum annual addition that Beta can make to Cameron's individual account in the Beta Corporation's Profit-Sharing Plan without running afoul of Section 415?

2. Berta is a participant in her employer's 401(k) plan. For the plan year beginning 2012, Berta elects to have $5,000 in before-tax contributions contributed to the plan. Before this reduction, she had compensation of $20,000. What is Berta's annual addition limitation for 2012? What would her annual addition limitation be if her compensation were $20,000 after the reduction?

3. Why are rollover contributions not taken into account for purposes of IRC § 415(c)?

[b] Limitations on Benefits

IRC § 415(b).

Section 415(b) of the Internal Revenue Code limits the annual benefit that a participant may receive under a defined benefit plan to the lesser of (A) $160,000, adjusted for increases in the cost-of-living, or (B) 100 percent of the participant's average compensation for the 3 consecutive years during which the participant had his or her highest compensation. IRC § 415(b)(1); Treas. Reg. § 1.415-3(a)(3). This limitation applies to benefits payable at age 62 in the form of a straight life annuity or in the form of a joint and survivor annuity for the lives of the employee and spouse. IRC § 415(b)(2)(B). The permissible level of benefits is actuarially reduced if the benefits begin before age 62 or are paid in a different form and are actuarially increased if the benefits begin later than age 65. IRC § 415(b)(2)(B)–(D). In 2012, the IRC § 415(b)(1)(A) limit, as adjusted, is $200,000.

The limitations are reduced for employees with less than 10 years of participation in the plan. IRC § 415(b). The IRC § 415(b)(1)(A) maximum dollar benefit limitation is reduced by multiplying the dollar limitation by a fraction, the numerator of which is the employee's years of participation in the plan and the denominator of which is ten. IRC § 415(b)(5)(A). Thus in 2012, for an employee with three years of participation, the maximum dollar benefit limitation would be $200,000 x 3/10, or $60,000. The IRC § 415(b)(1)(B) highest three years of compensation limitation is also reduced by multiplying the limitation by a fraction, the numerator of which is the employee's years of service (as opposed to participation) and the denominator of which is ten. IRC § 415(b)(5)(B).

A defined benefit plan may provide an annual pension benefit of up to $10,000 without regard to the IRC § 415(b)(1)(B) highest three year of compensation limitation if the employer has never maintained a defined contribution plan in which the employee participated. IRC § 415(b)(4). This $10,000 de minimis allowance is also phased in over ten years of service. IRC § 415(b)(5)(B).

If the defined benefit plan provides for mandatory or voluntary employee contributions, the annual benefit attributable to those contributions is not taken into account for purposes of applying the defined benefit limitations. IRC § 415(b)(2)(B). Instead, the employee contributions are considered to be a separate defined contribution plan maintained by the employer and are subject to the limitations on defined contribution plans. Treas. Reg. § 1.415-3(d).

9-3 QUESTIONS AND PROBLEMS

1. Arnaud joined Xi Co. on January 2, 1995. For the last three years, he has earned $150,000, $155,000, and $160,000. What is the maximum annual benefit that the Xi Pension Plan may provide Arnaud this year under IRC § 415?

2. Brooke joined OmicronCo on January 2, 2009, and immediately began to participate in the OmicronCo Pension Plan. Brooke earned $95,000 in 2009, $110,000 in 2010, $125,000 in 2011, and $140,000 in 2012. What is the maximum annual benefit that the OmicronCo Pension Plan may provide Brooke for the year 2012 under IRC § 415?

3. A joint and survivor annuity paying $200,000 per year is much more valuable than a single life annuity paying $200,000 per year. Why does IRC § 415(b) not require that the benefit payable under a joint and survivor annuity for the lives of the employee and spouse be actuarially reduced to equal the actuarial value of a single life annuity of $200,000?

4. If an employer maintains both a defined benefit plan and a defined contribution plan, can an employee receive both the maximum defined benefit and the maximum annual addition? Should an employee be permitted to receive both?

[c] Purpose of IRC § 415

NORMAN P. STEIN, SIMPLIFICATION AND IRC § 415

2 FLA. TAX REV. 69, 82 (1994)

Prior to the enactment of ERISA, the Code placed no direct limitations on contributions or benefits for individual employees. It was thus possible for an employer to make exceedingly large contributions or to fund exceedingly large benefits for an employee. Congress, in enacting ERISA, believed that the law's failure to place limits on contributions and benefits represented a shortcoming. Senator Long expressed this view in comments before the Senate:

> Senate 415 makes the tax laws regarding pension plans fairer by limiting the amount of the contributions or benefits that can be provided to any individual under such a plan. The fact that present law does not provide such specific limitations has made it possible for extremely large contributions and benefits to be made under qualified plans for some highly paid individuals. While there is, of course, no objection to large retirement benefits in themselves, it is not appropriate to finance extremely large retirement benefits in part at public expense through the use of special tax treatment.

The purpose of Section 415 can be understood as limiting contributions and benefits under qualified plans to levels that are proportionate "to the reasonable needs of individuals for a dignified level of retirement income." Benefits and contributions in excess of these levels are not eligible for the tax deferral available under a qualified plan.

9-4 QUESTIONS AND PROBLEMS

1. How well does Section 415 effectuate its purpose?

2. Are the limits too high or too low?

[3] Limitation on Elective Deferrals

IRC § 402(g).

Section 401(a)(30) of the Internal Revenue Code provides that in order to be qualified any plan that accepts elective deferrals (e.g., 401(k) plans) must provide that the amount of such deferrals under the plan and all other plans maintained by the same employer will be limited to the extent required by IRC § 402(g). The IRC § 402(g) limit was set at $15,000 in 2006, and is adjusted for increases in the cost-of-living. In 2012, the IRC § 402(g) limit, as adjusted, is $17,000.

[a] Overview of IRC § 402(g)

Section 402(g) of the Internal Revenue Code sets forth a separate limit on the total amount of "elective deferrals" that an employee may make in a single year. It defines "elective deferrals" to include any elective contribution to a qualified 401(k) plan (to the extent the contributions are not taxed to the employee before applying the § 402(g) dollar limitation). IRC § 402(g)(3)(A).

9-5 QUESTIONS AND PROBLEMS

1. Suppose that Jamal works for Omicron Industries from January 1, 2012, until May 31, 2012, and contributes $8,500 to the Omicron Industries' 401(k) plan during that time. On June 1, 2012, he terminates employment with Omicron Industries and joins Pi Corp., an unrelated corporation.

   a. Assuming that Jamal may immediately begin to participate in the Pi Corp. 401(k) plan and that he files his tax returns on a calendar year basis, how much may he contribute to the plan between June 1, 2012, and December 31, 2012?

   b. Would the answer be different if the Omicron Industries' 401(k) plan year was the calendar year while the Pi Corp. 401(k) plan's year ran from June 1 through May 31?

   c. Would the answer be different if Omicron Industries and Pi Corp. were related companies?

2. If an employer elects to offer a 401(k) plan, must it permit employees to elect to defer amounts equal to the IRC § 402(g) limit?

3. How does an excess deferral differ from an excess contribution for purposes of IRC § 401(k)?

4. Why does IRC § 402(g) impose a separate limitation on elective deferrals? Why are elective deferrals not simply subject to the same IRC § 415(c) limitations as all other defined contribution plans?

[b] Treatment of Excess Deferrals

If an individual's elective deferrals exceed the IRC § 402(g) limit, the excess deferrals must be included in the individual's gross income for that year. IRC § 402(g)(1); Treas. Reg. § 1.402(g)-1(a). In addition, if the excess deferrals (and income) for a taxable year are not distributed by April 15 of the following year, the amounts will be includible in gross income again when distributed from the plan. Treas. Reg. § 1.402(g)-1(e)(8)(iii).

A plan, however, may provide for a correction method to avoid double taxation of excess deferrals. Specifically, a plan may provide that excess deferrals may be distributed by the first April 15 following the close of the individual's taxable year in which the excess deferrals were included in income. IRC § 402(g)(2)(A); Treas. Reg. § 1.402(g)-1(e)(2). In addition, a plan may provide that an individual who has excess deferrals for a taxable year may receive a corrective distribution of the excess deferrals during the same year provided that (1) the individual designates the distribution as an excess deferral, (2) the corrective distribution is made after the date on which the plan received the excess deferral, and (3) the plan designates the distribution as a distribution of excess deferrals. Treas. Reg. § 1.402(g)-1(e)(3).

A corrective distribution of excess deferrals made on or before April 15 of the year following the deferral is not includible in income for the year of distribution but is includible in income for the year of deferral. IRC § 402(g)(2)(C)(i); Treas. Reg. § 1.402(g)-1(e)(8). The income allocable to excess deferrals, however, is includible in the employee's income in the year in which the allocable income is distributed. IRC § 402(g)(2)(C)(ii); Treas. Reg. § 1.402(g)-1(e)(8). The corrective distribution of excess deferrals (and income) is not subject to the IRC § 72(t) early distribution tax. IRC § 402(g)(2)(C); Treas. Reg. § 1.402(g)-1(e)(8).

Even if distributed, excess deferrals must be treated as employer contributions for purposes of IRC §§ 401(a)(4), 401(k)(3), 404, 409, 411, 412, and 416. Excess deferrals of a nonhighly compensated employee, however, are not taken into account under the IRC § 401(k)(3) actual deferral percentage test to the extent the excess deferrals are prohibited under IRC § 401(a)(30). In addition, excess deferrals are treated as employer contributions for purposes of IRC § 415 unless distributed. Treas. Reg. § 1.402(g)-1(e)(1)(ii).

9-6 QUESTIONS AND PROBLEMS

1. Alina is a 45-year-old highly compensated employee who participates in the Pi Co. 401(k) plan. During the period of January through September 2012, she contributed $17,000 to the plan in elective deferrals. During the same period she also contributed $2,000 in elective deferrals to the 401(k) plan of an unrelated employer. May Alina exclude from income in 2012 the $19,000 she contributed to the two plans?

2. Suppose that Alina notifies the Pi Co. 401(k) plan that she had an excess deferral of $2,000 in 2012, and pursuant to the terms of the plan, the plan distributes the $2,000 plus $50 in earnings to Alina on February 1, 2013. How should that distribution be taxed? How much of Alina's deferrals must the Pi Co. plan take into account in applying the IRC § 401(k)(3) actual deferral percentage test?

3. Luis had excess deferrals of $1,000 in 2012. The income attributable to those excess deferrals is $100. Luis properly notified his employer and requested a distribution of the excess deferral (and income) on February 1, 2013. The plan distributed $1,000 to Luis by April 15, 2013. How should the distribution be taxed?

4. Margaret works for Rho Company from January through June and transfers to related Sigma Company for the next six months. Must Sigma Company take into account Margaret's elective deferrals into the Rho Company's 401(k) plan in accepting elective deferrals into the Sigma Company 401(k) plan? Suppose that Sigma Company were not related to Rho Company, would it be required to take

into account Margaret's elective deferrals into the Rho Company's 401(k) plan in accepting elective deferrals into its (the Sigma Company's) 401(k) plan?

5. Must a plan contain a correction method for excess deferrals? Why might an employer want to include a correction method in a plan? What happens to excess contributions if the plan does not include a correction method?

[4] Catch-up Contributions

IRC § 414(v).

Section 414(v) of the Internal Revenue Code authorizes plans to permit individuals who are age 50 or over to make "catch-up contributions"; that is, additional elective deferrals to 410(k) plans (and certain other plans that may allow elective deferrals). The plan may allow the individual to make a catch-up contribution equal to the lesser of (1) the "applicable dollar amount" or (2) the participant's compensation for the year reduced by any other elective deferrals of the participant for the year. IRC § 414(v)(1)(A). Generally, the "applicable dollar amount" was set at $5,000 in 2006 and is to be adjusted for increases in the cost-of-living. IRC § 414(v)(1)(B). In 2012, the IRC § 414(v)(2)(B)(i) limit, as adjusted, is $5,500.

Catch-up contributions are not subject to any other contribution limits that would otherwise apply, such as IRC § 402(g), and are not taken into account in applying these limitations to other contributions or benefits under the plan. IRC § 414(v)(3)(A). In order to satisfy IRC § 401(a)(4), however, if the plan offers catch-up contributions, they must be available to all eligible participants. IRC § 414(v)(4). "Eligible participants" are defined as participants who are age 50 or over and with respect to whom no other elective deferrals may (without regard to section 414(v)) be made to the plan for the plan year due to other statutory limitations or limitations contained in the terms of the plan. IRC § 414(v)(5).

9-7 QUESTIONS AND PROBLEMS

1. David, a 52-year-old participant in the Tau Co. 401(k) plan, has compensation of $50,000 in 2012. Without regard to IRC § 414(v), his maximum annual deferral limit for 2012 is $17,000 under IRC § 402(g). Under the terms of the plan, however, his maximum annual deferral limit is 10 percent of compensation. Assuming that the plan authorizes catch-up contributions, what is the maximum amount that David may contribute to the Tau Co. 401(k) plan in 2012?

2. Marguerite is a 53-year-old highly compensated employee who is a participant in the Upsilon Ltd. 401(k) plan. Without regard to IRC § 414(v), her maximum annual deferral limit for 2012 is $17,000 under IRC § 402(g). After application of the special nondiscrimination rules applicable to section 401(k) plans, the maximum elective deferral Marguerite may make in 2012 is $8,000 under IRC § 401(k)(3). Assuming that the plan authorizes catch-up contributions, what is the maximum amount that Marguerite may contribute to the Upsilon Ltd. 401(k) plan in 2012?

3. Nola is a 51-year-old participant in the Phi Co. 401(k) plan. Her compensation in 2012 is $30,000. Without regard to IRC § 414(v), her maximum annual deferral limit for 2012 is $17,000 under IRC § 402(g). Under the terms of the plan, the maximum permitted deferral is 10 percent of compensation. The plan also authorizes catch-up contributions. Nola elects to contribute $2,000 to the Phi Co.

401(k) plan in 2012. How much of that $2,000 is characterized as a catch-up contribution? Why might an employer want to characterize the entire $2,000 as a catch-up contribution?

4. Must a plan permit IRC § 414(v) catch-up contributions?

5. Does IRC § 414(v) distinguish between employees who contributed little or nothing to their 401(k) accounts in their early years of employment and employees who contributed the maximum amount permitted throughout their career? Should it?

6. The Conference Report categorizes the addition of IRC § 414(v) catch-up contributions as a pension provision that "enhance[s] fairness for women." *See* Economic Growth and Tax Relief Reconciliation Act of 2001, Conference Report as made available on May 26, 2001, 137 (CCH). How does IRC § 414(v) "enhance fairness for women?"

[5] Deductibility of Employer Contributions

IRC § 404.

One of the principal advantages of plan qualification is that an employer may deduct contributions to a qualified retirement plan when the contributions are made, regardless of when those contributions are included in the employee's income. The deductibility of those contributions, however, is subject to a variety of limitations, depending on the type of plan and number of plans the employer maintains.

In order for employer contributions to be deductible, they must satisfy two separate tests. First, they must be deductible under the general business deduction sections, IRC §§ 162 or 212. Determining whether a contribution is deductible under IRC §§ 162 or 212 is a factual question. In essence, IRC §§ 162 and 212 require that the employee's compensation, including contributions to the plan, be ordinary, necessary, and reasonable. Treas. Reg. § 1.404(a)-1(b).

Second, the deduction must satisfy the requirements of IRC § 404, which governs the deductibility of contributions to all pension plans, profit-sharing plans, annuity plans, stock-bonus plans, and plans of deferred compensation, regardless of whether the plan is tax qualified. Section 404 limits the amount of contribution that an employer may deduct. It does not prevent an employer from making contributions that exceed the deductible limitations; however, IRC § 4972 imposes an excise tax on contributions that exceed the limitations. In addition, IRC § 404 does not affect or otherwise restrict the maximum contribution or benefit which may be allocated or accrued for any individual participant. Instead, IRC § 415 (discussed above) governs restrictions on allocations or accruals for individual participants.

Under IRC § 404(a), contributions are generally deductible in the year paid. Section 404(a)(6), however, permits a limited retroactive deduction. Contributions made after the close of the taxable year, but not later than the due date (including extensions) of the employer's tax return, are eligible for deduction in the preceding year. In order to be eligible for such a retroactive deduction, however, the contributions must be made to a qualified retirement plan which was in existence by the end of the employer's taxable year, and the contributions must be attributable to compensation earned in the year of deduction.

9-8 QUESTIONS AND PROBLEMS

1. Suppose that Zeta Corporation is on a calendar-year basis and files for an extension so that its tax return for the tax year 2011 is due on September 15, 2012.

a. Can Zeta Corporation establish a profit-sharing plan on December 15, 2011, fund the plan by September 14, 2012, and take a deduction for the 2011 tax year?

b. Would the answer be different if the plan were established on March 14, 2012?

c. Would the answer be different if the employer had not received an extension to file its tax return?

2. Eta Corporation maintains a 401(k) plan. Eta Corporation's taxable year is the fiscal year ending June 30. The Eta 401(k) plan has a calendar plan year. By the last day of the Eta 401(k) plan's 2012 calendar plan year, Eta Corporation had contributed $40,000 to the Eta 401(k) plan in accordance with the terms of the plan. The $40,000 consisted of (a) $20,000 in elective deferral and matching contributions attributable to compensation earned by plan participants before the end of Eta's taxable year ending June 30, 2012 (Pre-Year End Contributions) and (b) $20,000 in elective deferral and matching contributions attributable to compensation earned by plan participants after the end of Eta's taxable year ending June 30, 2012 (Post-Year End Contributions). Eta received an extension of time to March 15, 2013, to file the income tax return for its taxable year ending June 30, 2012 (2012 Taxable Year). How much may Eta deduct of the contributions it made to the Eta 401(k) plan during the 2012 calendar year?

[a] Limitations on Defined Contribution Plans

IRC § 404(a)(3).

The maximum deductible contribution with respect to defined contribution plans is limited to the greater of (1) 25 percent of aggregate participant compensation, or (2) in the case of a safe-harbor 401(k) plan, the amount the employer is required to contribute under IRC § 401(k)(11) for the plan year. IRC § 404(a)(3)(A)(i). If an employer maintains two or more defined contribution plans, they are considered as a single plan for purposes of the limitations. IRC § 404(a)(3)(A)(iv).

To illustrate, suppose that Theta, Inc. maintains a qualified profit-sharing plan that operates on the calendar year. For the plan year ending December 31, 2012, the plan has three participants with the following compensation paid for the plan year: Anna — $100,000, Benita — $90,000, and Carter — $50,000. The maximum deductible contribution Theta, Inc. can make for the plan year is $60,000 (100,000 + 90,000 + 50,000 = 240,000 x 25% = $60,000).

In determining the 25 percent limit, only the compensation of employees who, in the relevant taxable year, are participants under the plan may be taken into account. Treas. Reg. § 1.404(a)-9(b). An employee must actually participate in the allocation of the employer's contribution to the plan in the year for which the contribution is made in order for the employee's compensation to be taken into account. Rev. Rul. 65-295, 1965-2 CB 148. An employer may not include the compensation paid to an employee who terminates service during the plan year if the employee does not share in the allocation of the employer's contribution for the year.

Compensation for purposes of the IRC § 404 limitation means all compensation paid or accrued other than that for which a deduction is allowable under a plan that qualifies pursuant to section 401(a). Treas. Reg. § 1.404(a)-9(b). Thus, an employer contribution made on behalf of an employee to a qualified defined benefit plan is not deemed to be compensation for this purpose. Compensation, however, includes elective deferrals under IRC § 415(c)(3)(D) and is subject to the IRC § 401(a)(17) limitation.

To illustrate, suppose that Iota Co. maintains a qualified profit-sharing plan that operates on the calendar year. For the plan year ending December 31, 2012, the plan has three participants with the following compensation paid for the plan year: Derek — $120,000, Evan — $100,000, and Franco — $80,000. The maximum deductible contribution Iota Co. can make for the plan year is $75,000 (120,000 + 100,000 + 80,000 = 300,000 x 25% = $75,000). If Iota Co. contributes the full $75,000, or any amount less than $75,000, the contribution is not taken into account in determining the limit. In addition, if Derek, Evan, and Franco elect to contribute $11,000 each of their compensation to a 401(k) plan maintained by Iota Co., Iota Co. can still include the compensation they elected to defer in calculating its maximum contribution.

9-9 QUESTIONS AND PROBLEMS

1. Kappa Corporation, whose taxable year is the calendar year, has a qualified profit-sharing plan and paid total compensation of $300,000 in 2012. What is the maximum deductible contribution Kappa Corporation can make in 2012?

2. Prior to December 31, 2001, IRC § 404(a)(3) limited the maximum deductible contribution with respect to profit-sharing and stock-bonus plans to 15 percent of aggregate participant compensation. The Economic Growth and Tax Relief and Reconciliation Act of 2001 increased the limit to 25 percent. Who benefits from the increased limit? Why do you think Congress increased the limit? Should Congress have increased the limit?

3. Prior to December 31, 2001, compensation for purposes of the IRC § 404 limitations excluded elective deferrals. The Economic Growth and Tax Relief Reconciliation Act of 2001 amended the definition of compensation for these purposes to include elective deferrals. *See* IRC § 404(a)(12). Why do you think Congress amended the term compensation to include elective deferrals? Who benefits from the amendment? Should Congress have amended the definition of compensation to include elective deferrals?

[b] Limitations on Deductible Contributions to Defined Benefit Plans

IRC § 404(o).

For plan years beginning after December 31, 2007, IRC § 404(o) sets forth the deduction limit for contributions to defined benefit plans, other than multi-employer plans. The limitation ensures that, at a minimum, plan sponsors are permitted to deduct an amount equal to any contribution required under the minimum funding rules. IRC § 404(o)(1). (The minimum funding rules are discussed in the following section of this Chapter.) Specifically, IRC § 404(o)(1) provides that the employer may deduct the greater of (1) the minimum required contributions for each plan year ending with or within the taxable year, or (2) the amount required for the plan to be 100 percent funded plus a "cushion" of 50 percent of the present value of accrued benefits plus amounts that reflect projected salary increases. IRC § 404(o).

[c] Limitations on Combined Plans

IRC § 404(a)(7).

Section 404(a)(7) of the Internal Revenue Code imposes an overall maximum limitation on the deductibility of contributions for employers that maintain both a defined contribution plan and a defined benefit plan. Specifically, if an employer maintains both types of plans and at least one employee is covered by both plans, the maximum deductible contribution is equal to the greater of (1) 25 percent of the aggregate compensation of all participants, or (2) the amount necessary to meet the minimum funding standard for the defined benefit plan. IRC § 404(a)(7). If no employee is covered by both plans, the regular deductible limitations apply. IRC § 404(a)(7)(C).

[d] Penalties for Excess Contributions and Deductions

IRC § 4972.

If an employer's contributions to a qualified plan exceed the deductible limit, the employer may carry the excess over and deduct it in succeeding years. IRC § 404(a)(3)(A)(ii). In the alternative, the excess contribution may be returned to the employer if the contribution was conditioned on its deductibility and the facts and circumstances indicate that a good faith mistake was made in determining the deductibility of the contribution. Rev. Rul. 91-4, 1991-1 C.B. 57. If an employer's contribution to a qualified plan exceeds the deductible limit and the excess contribution is not returned to the employer prior the employer's tax filing date, including extensions filed for and granted, the excess contribution is subject to an excise tax equal to 10 percent of the nondeductible contribution, determined as of the close of the taxable year of the employer. IRC § 4972. The excise tax applies regardless of whether or not the employer claimed a deduction with respect to the contribution.

The nondeductible contribution is equal to the sum of (1) the nondeductible contributions made for the current year and (2) the nondeductible contributions from the preceding year. IRC § 4972(c)(1). The statute provides an ordering rule pursuant to which amounts allowable as a deductible contribution for any plan year are deemed to come first from carryforwards from prior taxable years with the oldest contributions being deducted first and then from current contributions. IRC § 4972(c)(2). The effect of the rules is to subject the same nondeductible contribution to the excise tax until it is returned to the employer or allowed as a deduction pursuant to the carryover rules.

To illustrate, suppose that Lambda Corporation maintains a qualified profit-sharing plan that operates on the calendar year. For its first plan year, the year ending December 31, 2010, the plan has three participants with total compensation of $500,000, and Lambda Corporation contributes $150,000 to the plan. Of the $150,000 contributed to the plan, only $125,000 is deductible ($500,000 x .25 = $125,000). Accordingly, it is subject to an excise tax on the remaining $25,000 ($150,000 – $125,000 = $25,000) equal to $2,500 ($25,000 x .10 = $2,500) (assuming the excess contribution is not returned to Lambda Corporation). For the following plan year, the plan year ending December 31, 2011, the plan has three participants with total compensation of $600,000 and Lambda Corporation contributes $140,000 to the plan. Lambda Corporation is permitted a $150,000 deductible contribution for 2011 ($600,000 x.25 = $150,000). Lambda Corporation is first permitted to deduct the $25,000 carryforward from 2010. It is then permitted to deduct an additional $125,000 of the $140,000 it contributed ($150,000 – $25,000 = $125,000). Lambda Corporation is then subject to an excise tax on its excess contribution of $15,000 ($140,000 – $125,000 = $15,000). The excise tax is equal to $1,500 ($15,000 x .10 = $1,500). Finally, for its third plan year, the plan year ending December 31, 2012, the plan has four participants with total compensation of $700,000 and Lambda Corporation contributes $100,000 to the plan. Lambda Corporation is permitted a $175,000 deduction for 2012. Lambda Corporation is first permitted to deduct the $15,000 carryforward from 2011. It is then permitted to deduct the entire $100,000 contributed to the plan in 2012 ($15,000 + $100,000 < $175,000). Lambda Corporation is not subject to any excise tax in 2012 and has no nondeductible carryforward.

The following chart summarizes this illustration:

Year	Total Comp.	Amount Deductible	Actual Contribution	Amount Deducted	Amount Carried Forward	Excise Tax
2010	$500,000	$125,000	$150,000	$125,000	$25,000	$2,500
2011	$600,000	$150,000	$140,000	$150,000	$15,000	$1,500
2012	$700,000	$175,000	$100,000	$115,000	$0	$0

There are a few exceptions to the imposition of this excise tax. For example, it does not apply to contributions of up to six percent of compensation to a defined contribution plan for employer matching and elective contributions, IRC § 4972(c)(6)(A), nor does it apply to employer contributions that do not exceed the accrued liability full-funding limit, IRC § 4972(c)(7).

9-10 QUESTIONS AND PROBLEMS

1. Mu Corporation, whose taxable year is the calendar year, adopts a qualified profit-sharing plan. For the plan's first year, 2009, Mu Corporation pays total compensation to plan participants equal to $300,000 and contributes $100,000 to the plan. For 2010, Mu Corporation pays total compensation to plan participants equal to $500,000 and contributes $150,000 to the plan. For 2011, Mu Corporation pays total compensation to plan participants equal to $600,000 and contributes $190,000 to the plan. In 2012, Mu Corporation pays total compensation to plan participants equal to $800,000 and contributes $100,000 to the plan. Assume that no contributions are returned to Mu Corporation.

   a. How much, if anything, may Mu Corporation deduct each year?

   b. How much excise tax, if any, is imposed under IRC § 4972 each year?

   c. What, if anything, can Mu Corporation do to avoid any excise tax imposed under IRC § 4972?

2. Why do you think IRC § 4972 imposes an excise tax on nondeductible contributions? How valuable are the carryforwards of excess contributions in light of this excise tax?

B. FUNDING

ERISA §§ 302, 303; IRC §§ 412, 430.

As discussed in Chapter 2, there are two basic types of retirement plans, defined contribution plans and defined benefit plans. In a defined contribution plan, the employer typically promises to pay a certain amount to the plan each year, and the participant's ultimate benefit from the plan depends on the amount contributed to the plan and any earnings or losses on those contributions. In a defined benefit plan, in contrast, the employer does not promise to contribute a specific amount to the plan. Instead, the employer promises the participant a specific benefit. Typically, the benefit is a fixed amount per month to be paid for the life of the retired participant, with the fixed amount generally based on a formula that takes into account the participant's years of service and salary.

The cost to an employer of a defined contribution plan is quite straightforward; it constitutes the amount the employer promises to contribute to the plan. The cost of a defined benefit plan, in contrast, is much more complex. It depends on wide variety of factors, such as how long its participants live, the rate of turnover, future compensation levels, and investment earnings on plan assets.

Because of the differences between determining the costs of defined contribution plans and defined benefit plans, the rules governing the funding of such plans fundamentally differ. Generally, neither ERISA nor the Internal Revenue Code impose independent funding obligations on defined contribution plans. Instead, they simply require that all plans, including defined contribution plans, conform to the provisions of the plan, and thus indirectly require employers to contribute to defined contribution plans any amounts that they have agreed to contribute to such plans. On the other hand, in order to ensure the solvency of defined benefit plans, both ERISA and the Internal Revenue Code impose minimum funding requirements. *See* ERISA §§ 302, 303; IRC §§ 412, 430. (Technically, the minimum funding rules apply to certain defined contribution plans. Specifically, they apply to money purchase pension plans and target benefit plans. For these plans, however, the minimum funding rules are satisfied so long as the employer makes the contributions required by the plan document.)

Despite the minimum funding obligations set forth in ERISA and the Internal Revenue Code, defined benefit plans can still terminate with insufficient funds to pay all promised benefits. For example, in December 2002, the PBGC terminated Bethelehem Steel's pension plan with an estimated $4.3 billion in underfunding. More recently, in October 2007, the PBGC became trustee of the Easton Hospital Employees' Pension Plan which had a funding shortfall of $40 million. In 2006, Congress substantially revamped the minimum funding rules to reduce underfunding. Nevertheless, current law still does not completely eliminate underfunding. For example, a plan sponsor may apply for a funding waiver if the employer is unable to satisfy the minimum funding standard for the plan year without temporary substantial business hardship.

[1] Basic Methods of Funding of Defined Benefit Plans

Theoretically, defined benefit plans can be funded in one of three ways: (1) on a pay-as-you go basis, (2) on a terminal basis, or (3) on a prefunded basis. In a plan funded on a pay-as-you go basis, employers do not accumulate funds in advance to pay for the benefits, but instead, pay the benefits from current assets as they become due. Under the terminal funding method, when an employee retires a lump sum is set aside to finance that retiree's benefit. Finally, under a prefunded system, the employer sets aside funds during the employee's working life to fund the employee's future retirement benefit. Determining how much should be set aside involves complex actuarial calculations that take into account a variety of factors including the employee's life expectancy, likelihood of turnover, future compensation levels, and investment earnings on plan assets.

Plans funded on a pay-as-you go basis or terminal basis subject participants to a serious risk of default should the employer terminate the plan prior to the employee's receipt of benefits. Even prefunded plans can subject participants to such risk if they are inadequately funded. Prior to the enactment of ERISA, underfunding was a serious problem that led to many participants losing some or all of their retirement benefits. For example, when the Studebaker automobile plant in South Bend, Indiana, was closed in December, 1963, it terminated an underfunded defined benefit plan. Pursuant to an agreement with the United Automobile Workers, the employer divided its plan participants into three groups and paid their benefits as follows: (1) 3,600 retirees and active workers who had already reached the plan's normal retirement age of 60 received their full benefits in the form of a life annuity, (2) 4,000 employees between the ages of 40 and 59 who had at least 10 years of service with their employer received lump sum payments representing about 15 percent of the actuarial value of their accrued benefits, and (3) 2,900 workers who had no vested rights received nothing.

Believing that "it is essential for pension plans to be adequately funded in accordance with a contributions schedule which will produce sufficient pension funds to meet the obligations of the plan when they fall due," Congress enacted minimum funding requirements under ERISA. Private Pension Plan Reform, S. Rep. No. 93-383, at 22 (1973). These rules, which are contained in Title I of ERISA as well as section 412 (and now section 430) of the Internal Revenue Code, prohibit pay-as-you go and terminal financing and require that all covered pension plans be prefunded so as to satisfy minimum funding standards. Certain plans, primarily governmental and church plans, are not covered. *See* ERISA § 4(b); IRC § 412(h).

Traditionally, the minimum funding rules afforded a tremendous amount of discretion as to the level of funding. In the Pension Protection Act of 2006, however, Congress revamped the funding rules to eliminate many of the discretionary aspects of the rules.

[2] Actuarial Assumptions

The minimum funding rules require that the present value of future benefits be determined. The present value of future retirement benefits in turn depends on the terms of the plan and a number of actuarial assumptions.

Suppose, for example, that a defined benefit plan promises its participants an annuity equal to 3 percent of the average of the employee's three final years of compensation times the employee's years of service (not to exceed 30). Calculating the present value of this benefit depends on a number of factors, including the employee's estimated final three years of compensation, the expected interest the plan will earn on contributions to the plan prior to the employee's retirement, the employee's life expectancy, and the likelihood of the employee terminating service prior to reaching retirement age. Because none of these factors is currently certain, an actuary must make "actuarial assumptions" with respect to each of these factors to determine the present value of the retirement benefit.

There are two basic types of actuarial assumptions: demographic and economic. Demographic assumptions involve estimations about the various components of the plan's population, such as employee turnover, employee disability, employee mortality (both before and after retirement or termination of service), the age difference and mortality of the employee's spouse (in the case of a joint and survivor annuity), and the number of employees who will select early retirement. Economic assumptions are based on broad economic forces and reflect predictions about future economic behavior, such as the cost of living, salary progression, and interest rates.

In the past, ERISA and the Internal Revenue Code did not dictate the actuarial assumptions. The Pension Protection Act of 2006, however, amended the law with respect to two actuarial assumptions: interest rates and mortality tables. Current law requires the use of IRS-determined "segment" interest rates based on high quality corporate bond yields. ERISA § 303(h)(2); IRC § 430(h)(2). The three segments are for benefits expected to be payable (1) within the next five years, including the current plan year; (2) within 6-20 years; and (3) after 20 years. ERISA § 303(h)(2)(B)—(C); IRC § 430(h)(2)(B)—(C).

Current law also requires that plans use IRS-prescribed mortality tables. ERISA § 303(a); IRC § 430(a). The IRS is directed (1) to continue to update mortality tables for determining present value for funding purposes and certain other purposes for at least every 10 years, and (2) to develop two additional tables — for individuals becoming disabled before 1995 and after 1994. ERISA § 303(h)(3)(B) & (D); IRC § 430(h)(3)(B) & (D). Employers may request that the IRS approve plan-specific mortality tables for plans that have a sufficient number of participants and credible experience. ERISA § 303(h)(3)(C); IRC § 430(h)(3)(C). Unless the IRS determines otherwise, however, plan-specific tables can only be used if all of the plans maintained by the employer and any other member of the employer's controlled group use plan-specific tables, and each plan separately has credible experience. ERISA § 303(h)(3)(C)(iv); IRC § 430(h)(3)(C)(iv).

ERISA and the Internal Revenue Code do not dictate the other actuarial assumptions that must be made, but do require that (1) each of the assumptions be reasonable, taking into account the experience of the plan and reasonable expectations, and (2) the actuary certify that they represent the actuary's "best estimate" of future experience. ERISA § 303(h)(1); IRC § 430(h)(1).

9-11 QUESTIONS AND PROBLEMS

1. Why do ERISA and the Internal Revenue Code require the use of uniform "segment" interest rates?

2. Why do ERISA and the Internal Revenue Code require the use of IRS-prescribed mortality tables? Why are employers permitted to use plan-specific mortality tables if the plan has a sufficient number of participants and credible experience? Which types of employers are likely to use plan-specific mortality tables?

[3] Minimum Required Contributions

ERISA and the Internal Revenue Code require that a plan sponsor make a minimum contribution to a single-employer defined benefit plan that generally depends on a comparison of the plan's assets with the plan's funding target and target normal cost. ERISA § 303(h)(3)(A); IRC § 430(h)(3)(A). A plan's funding target is the present value of all benefits, including early retirement benefits, accrued or earned as of the beginning of the plan year. ERISA § 303(d)(1); IRC

§ 430(d)(1). A plan's target normal cost for a plan year is the present value of all benefits expected to accrue or be earned during the plan year. ERISA § 303(b); IRC § 430(b). If a plan's assets (less any credit balances) are less than the funding target, the plan has a funding shortfall. ERISA § 303(c)(4); IRC § 430(c)(4). Generally, funding shortfalls must be amortized over seven years. ERISA § 303(c); IRC § 430(c). Funding shortfalls for plan years beginning in 2008, 2009, 2010, and 2011 may be eligible for longer amortization periods under the Preservation of Access to Care for Medicare Beneficiaries and Pension Relief Act of 2010.

If the value of plan assets (reduced by any credit balances) is less than the funding target, the minimum contribution due is the sum of (1) the target normal cost, (2) the total of installments to amortize any shortfall, and (3) any waiver amortization charges for a plan that has obtained a funding waiver. ERISA § 303(a)(1); IRC § 430(a)(1). If the value of plan assets (reduced by any credit balances) equals or exceeds the funding target, the minimum contribution due is (1) the target normal cost minus (2) the amount by which the assets exceed the funding target, but not less than zero. ERISA § 303(a)(2); IRC § 430(a)(2). The 100 percent funding target is generally to be phased in over a four year period. ERISA § 303(c)(5)(B)(ii); IRC § 430(c)(5)(B)(ii).

The funding rules provide for two types of credit balances: (1) a "prefunding balance" and (2) a "funding standard carryover balance" that preserves prior law credit balances. A "funding standard carryover balance" is the positive balance in the plan's minimum funding standard account under IRC § 412(b) at the end of the plan's 2007 plan year. ERISA § 303(f)(7); IRC § 430(f)(7). If the employer's contributions for a year after the plan's 2007 plan year exceed the minimum required contribution for the year, the excess is credited to the "prefunding balance." ERISA § 303(f)(6)(B)(i); IRC § 430(f)(6)(B)(i). The total prefunding balance is the sum of such amounts plus interest minus (1) any amount applied to reduce the minimum required contribution, (2) any prefunding amount waived, and (3) any contributions required to avoid certain benefit limitations. ERISA § 303(f)(6)(B)&(C); IRC § 430(f)(6)(B)&(C). The two types of credit balances may be credited against a minimum required contribution at the employer's election. ERISA § 303(f)(1); IRC § 430(f)(1). The balances, however, generally reduce plan assets for purposes of determining a plan's funding shortfall and minimum required contributions and may even subject an otherwise well-funded plan to "at-risk status." Employers may waive the use of credit balances under certain circumstances.

The minimum funding rules are enforced by the imposition of an excise tax. IRC § 4971. The excise tax is 10 percent (for single-employer plans and 5 percent for multi-employer plans) of the amount by which the plan fails to pay its minimum required contribution for the year. IRC § 4971(a). The tax increases to 100 percent if the underfunding is not timely corrected after notification from the IRS. IRC § 4971(b).

9-12 QUESTIONS AND PROBLEMS

1. The minimum funding rules require that the plan's target normal cost, that is, the present value of all benefits expected to accrue or be earned during the plan year, be funded each year. How then is it possible for a plan to have a funding shortfall?

2. Why are credit balances excluded in determining whether a plan has a funding shortfall?

3. Underfunding of pension plans was a serious problem when ERISA was enacted. Despite the enactment of ERISA, underfunding continued to be a serious problem, so Congress revamped the minimum funding rules in the Pension Protection Act of 2006 to reduce underfunding. ERISA and the Internal Revenue Code require that funding shortfalls be amortized over a seven year period. What effect does the seven year amortization period have on the risk of underfunding of plans?

[4] At-Risk Plans and Limitations on Certain Benefits

"At-risk" plans are subject to additional funding requirements. A plan is at-risk if two conditions apply. First, the plan assets (generally reduced by credit balances) are less than 80 percent of the plan's funding target, computed using the generally applicable actuarial assumptions. ERISA § 303(i)(4)(A)(i); IRC § 430(i)(4)(A)(i). Second, the plan's assets (generally reduced by credit balances) are less than 70 percent of the plan's funding target, computed using special at-risk actuarial assumptions. ERISA § 303(i)(4)(A)(ii); IRC § 430(i)(4)(A)(ii). If the plan is determined to be at-risk, the at-risk actuarial assumptions must be used to calculate the plan's funding target for purposes of determining the amount of the funding shortfall, ERISA § 303(i)(1)(A); IRC § 430(i)(1)(A), which increases the shortfall and accelerates funding.

If a plan is underfunded by more than a specified percentage, the provision of certain benefits may be limited. First, plans may not provide shutdown or other unpredictable contingent event benefits if the plan is less than 60 percent funded or would be less than 60 percent funded taking into account the occurrence of the event. ERISA § 206(g)(1); IRC § 436(b). Second, an amendment to increase benefits is prohibited from taking effect if a plan is less than 80 percent funded or would be less than 80 percent funded taking into account the amendment. ERISA § 206(g)(2)(A); IRC § 436(c)(3). Third, a plan that is less than 60 percent funded, or less than 100 percent funded if the employer is in bankruptcy, is prohibited from paying benefits in a lump sum or other "accelerated form" or from purchasing an annuity as an irrevocable commitment to provide benefits. ERISA § 206(g)(3); IRC § 436(d). Finally, if a plan is less than 60 percent funded, benefit accruals must cease unless the employer contributes an amount sufficient to increase funding to 60 percent in addition to the minimum required contribution for the year. ERISA § 206(g)(4); IRC § 436(e).

9-13 QUESTIONS AND PROBLEMS

1. From a policy standpoint, does it make sense to require "at-risk" plans to use special actuarial assumptions for purposes of determining whether the plan has a funding shortfall?

2. Why do ERISA and the Internal Revenue Code prohibit plans that are less than 60 percent funded from providing shutdown or other unpredictable contingent event benefits?

3. Why do ERISA and the Internal Revenue Code prohibit amendments to increase benefits from taking effect if a plan is less than 80 percent funded?

4. Why do ERISA and the Internal Revenue Code prohibit a plan that is less than 60 percent funded (or 100 percent funded if the employer is in bankruptcy) from paying benefits in a lump sum?

5. Why do ERISA and the Internal Revenue Code require benefit accruals to cease if a plan is less than 60 percent funded?

[5] Funding Waivers

If a plan has a minimum funding standard deficiency, the employer may apply for a funding waiver. To obtain a waiver, the employer must be unable to satisfy the minimum funding standard for the plan year without temporary substantial business hardship and application of the standard must be adverse to the interests of plan participants in the aggregate. IRC § 412(c)(1)(A). If a funding deficiency in a single-employer plan is waived in whole or in part, the amount of the minimum required contribution will be reduced by the waived amount, and the amount of the waived funding deficiency will be amortized over five years. IRC §§ 412(c)(1)(B)(1), 430(e)(1).

Generally, a waiver may not be granted with respect to a plan for more than three of any fifteen consecutive plan years. IRC § 412(c)(1). Affected participants must be notified of the filing of an application for a funding waiver. IRC § 412(c)(6). If aggregated funding deficiencies, funding waivers, and the cumulative effect of amortization period extensions, if any, equal or exceed $1 million, an employer may be required to provide security to the plan, in the case of a single employer plan. IRC § 412(c)(4). In the case of plans potentially subject to the security requirement, the PBGC is to be given notice and the opportunity to comment and its comments, as well as those of any employee organization representing plan participants, is to be considered before a waiver or extension is granted or modified. IRC § 412(c)(4)(B).

The following factors are taken into account in determining whether there is a temporary substantial business hardship:

- The employer is operating at an economic loss.
- There is substantial unemployment or underemployment in the trade or business and in the concerned industry.
- The sales and profits of the concerned industry are depressed or declining; and
- It is reasonable to expect that the plan will be continued only if the waiver is granted. IRC § 412(c)(2).

9-14 QUESTIONS AND PROBLEMS

1. Why are funding waivers only available for temporary substantial business hardship and not available for any substantial business hardship?

2. How do funding waivers protect against the underfunding of plans?

3. Should funding waivers exist?

C. PLAN DISTRIBUTIONS

The law governing plan distributions can be exceedingly complex. Indeed, two commentators have noted:

> The rules governing distributions from tax-favored retirement arrangements are so complex that even tax practitioners who came of age with ERISA approach them with trepidation. Much of this complexity is attributable to the continued proliferation of different types of retirement plans, each with its own set of rules, and to the numerous special rules, most of which were enacted to achieve worthwhile goals, but many of which have outlived their original purpose and usefulness. David A. Pratt & Dianne Bennett, *Simplifying Retirement Plan Distributions*, New York University 57th Institute on Federal Taxation — Employee Benefits and Executive Compensation 5-3 (1999).

This section will not delve into all of the intricacies of the law governing distributions from tax-favored retirement vehicles. Instead, it will focus on a few basic rules.

First, it will begin with the IRC § 72(t) additional tax on early distributions. It will then turn to IRC § 402 which provides that distributions from qualified plans are generally taxable under IRC § 72 in the year in which they are actually distributed. Section 72 of the Internal Revenue Code in turn provides that distributions are generally taxable as ordinary income when received unless the participant has an "investment in the contract" or basis. If the participant has an investment in the contract, participants are permitted a pro rata recovery of the investment in the contract.

The chapter will then examine two important exceptions to the general rule that distributions from qualified plans are taxable in the year actually distributed. First, under IRC § 402(c), a participant who transfers all or any portion of an "eligible rollover distribution" to an eligible retirement plan may exclude the amount rolled over from gross income in the year distributed. The amount rolled over will be includible in the participant's income when it is later distributed from the plan to which it was rolled over. In addition, IRC § 72(p) permits plan loans to be excludible from income if the loan satisfies three general requirements: (1) the amount of the loan satisfies the limits imposed by IRC § 72(p)(2)(A); (2) the terms of the loan require the loan to be repaid within five years unless the loan is used by a participant to acquire a principal residence, IRC § 72(p)(2)(B); and (3) the loan repayments must be substantially level and made no less frequently than once each quarter. IRC § 72(p)(2)(C).

The chapter will conclude with the IRC § 401(a)(9) rules governing required minimum distributions.

[1] Additional Tax on Early Distributions

IRC § 72(t).

> The primary purpose of the tax subsidy for qualified plans is to encourage individuals to save for their retirement. An important aspect of this policy is to attempt to ensure that funds contributed to a retirement plan continue to be held in a retirement plan until the individual retires, rather than being used for current consumption. One way in which the social policy is enforced is the premature distribution penalty, a 10 percent additional income tax imposed on distributions before an individual reaches age 59½.

David A. Pratt & Dianne Bennett, *Simplifying Retirement Plan Distributions*, New York University 57th Institute on Federal Taxation — Employee Benefits and Executive Compensation 5-1, 5-9–5-10 (1999)

Section 72(t) of the Internal Revenue Code imposes this 10 percent "additional tax" on early distributions. The statute, however, does not define "early distributions" as distributions made to individuals before they reach age 59½. Instead, it provides that the additional tax applies to all distributions unless they fall within one of the exceptions set forth in the statute. IRC § 72(t)(A). Distributions "made on or after the date on which the employee attains age 59½" are simply the first of thirteen different exceptions enumerated in the statute. IRC § 72(t)(A)(i).

Other exemptions include distributions "made to a beneficiary (or to the estate of the employee) on or after the death of the employee," IRC § 72(t)(A)(ii), and distributions "attributable to the employee's being disabled within the meaning of subsection m(7)," IRC § 72(t)(A)(iii). In addition, IRC § 72(t)(2)(A)(iv) exempts distributions that are part of a series of substantially equal periodic payments made at least annually, for the life expectancy of the employee, or for the joint life expectancy of the employee and his or her beneficiary. In order to qualify for this exception, the payments must begin after the employee separates from service with the employer, unless the distributions are from an IRA. IRC § 72(t)(3)(B). If the series of payments is subsequently modified, other than by reason of death or disability, before the later of five years after the payments began or the date the employee attains age 59½, the additional tax will apply retroactively to the first payment. IRC § 72(t)(4).

All of these exceptions apply to distributions from individual retirement accounts (IRAs) as well as distributions from qualified retirement plans. The statute, however, also sets forth exceptions that apply solely to distributions from an IRA. For example, IRC § 72(t)(2)(E) exempts distributions from IRAs to pay for certain higher education expenses, and IRC § 72(t)(2)(F) exempts distributions from IRAs to pay for first home purchases.

In addition, the statute sets forth exceptions that apply to distributions from qualified retirement plans but not to distributions from IRAs. For example, IRC § 72(t)(2)(A)(v) exempts distributions made to an employee after separation from service after age 55, but the exemption does not apply to distributions from IRAs. *See* IRC § 72(t)(3)(A). Similarly, IRC § 72(t)(2)(C) exempts distributions made to an alternate payee under a qualified domestic relations order (QDRO), but the exemption does not apply to distributions from IRAs. *See* IRC § 72(t)(3)(A). (QDROs are discussed in more detail in Chapter 4.)

The "additional tax" only applies to taxable distributions; if the distributions are rolled over to an IRA or another qualified plan, the "additional tax" does not apply. In addition, other sections of the Internal Revenue Code clarify that certain other distributions are exempt from the IRC § 72(t) additional tax. For example, IRC § 402(g)(2)(C) clarifies that distributions of excess deferrals, and the income thereon, are exempt from the IRC § 72(t) additional tax.

9-15 QUESTIONS AND PROBLEMS

1. Kwasi, 50 years of age, retires from the Beta Corp. after having worked there for 10 years. Six years later (at age 56), he takes a lump sum distribution from the Beta Corp. Profit-Sharing Plan. Is the lump sum distribution subject to the IRC § 72(t) 10 percent additional tax on early distributions?

2. How does the IRC § 72(t) "additional tax" on "early distributions" further the primary purpose "of the tax subsidy for qualified plans [of] encourag[ing]

individuals to save for retirement?" Do some, none, or all of the IRC § 72(t) exceptions further this purpose?

3. Why does IRC § 72(t) distinguish between distributions from qualified plans and individual retirement accounts for purposes of the exceptions for distributions to pay for higher education expenses and first home purchases?

4. David Pratt and Dianne Bennett have proposed that IRC § 72(t) be substantially changed. First, they propose that all of the exceptions to the additional tax be eliminated, other than the exceptions for distributions after death, disability, and age 59½. Second, they propose that the age 59½ rule be modified to either age 55 or 60 or 62. Third, they suggest that the amount of the penalty (i.e. 10 percent) be increased significantly. *See* David A. Pratt & Dianne Bennett, *Simplifying Retirement Plan Distributions*, New York University — 57th Institute on Federal Taxation; Employee Benefits and Executive Compensation 5-1, 5-9 (1999). Is their proposal sound?

[2] Basic Taxation of Distributions

IRC §§ 402(a), 72(a)–(e).

Section 402 of the Internal Revenue Code, which governs the taxation of distributions, provides that distributions from a qualified retirement plan are generally taxable under IRC § 72 in the year in which they are actually distributed. IRC § 72 generally provides that such distributions are taxable as ordinary income when received unless the participant has an "investment in the contract," or basis. If the participant has an investment in the contract, IRC § 72 permits a pro rata recovery of that investment in the contract.

Under IRC § 72, the taxation of distributions from qualified retirement plans first depends on whether the distribution is an "amount received as an annuity," commonly referred to as a "periodic payment" or, "an amount not received as an annuity," commonly referred to a "nonperiodic payment." A distribution qualifies as an amount received as an annuity, or periodic payment, if (1) the distribution is received on or after the annuity starting date; (2) the distribution is one of a series of payments payable in periodic installments at regular intervals (e.g., annually, semiannually, quarterly, monthly, or weekly) over a period of more than one year; and (3) with certain exceptions, the total amount payable is determinable at the annuity starting date either directly under the terms of the contract, or indirectly by the use of mortality tables or compound interest calculations in accordance with sound actuarial theory. Treas. Reg. § 1.72-2(b)(2).

Common types of annuities, or periodic payments, include:

> *Single life annuities*, which pay a fixed amount at regular intervals for the lifetime of a single individual.
>
> *Joint and survivor annuities*, which pay a fixed amount at regular intervals for the lifetime of a single individual and, following the death of that individual, pay a fixed amount at regular intervals for the lifetime of another individual. The amount of payments to the survivor may or may not be different from the amount of payments to the first annuitant.
>
> *Term-certain annuities*, which pay a fixed amount at regular intervals over a specified period (for example, 10 years).

A nonperiodic payment or amount not received as an annuity is any payment to which IRC § 72 applies that is not an annuity or periodic payment. Treas. Reg. § 1.72-1(b)(1).

Taxation under IRC § 72 next depends on whether the participant has an investment in the contract. Generally, a participant has an investment in the contract if the participant made after-tax contributions to the plan. A participant's investment in the contract is defined as the aggregate premiums or other consideration paid (generally, the aggregate amount of after-tax contributions made to the plan), reduced by any amounts received before the annuity starting date that were excluded from gross income. IRC §§ 72(c)(1) & (f).

If the distribution is an annuity and the participant has no investment in the contract, or basis, IRC § 72(a) provides that the entire distribution is includible in gross income when received. Similarly, if the distribution is not an amount received as an annuity and the participant does not have an investment in the contract, IRC § 72(e) provides that the entire distribution is includible in gross income when received.

If the participant has an investment in the contract, taxation becomes more complex because IRC § 72 permits a pro rata recovery of that investment in the contract. If the participant has an investment in the contract and the participant receives distributions in the form of an annuity, IRC § 72(d) sets forth a "simplified method" pursuant to which the participant may recover the investment in the contract. If the participant has an investment in the contract and the participant receives distributions other than in the form of an annuity, IRC § 72(e) sets forth the method pursuant to which the participant may recover his or her investment in the contract.

Under the IRC § 72(d) simplified method, the participant recovers the investment in the contract in level amounts over an expected number of monthly payments. As noted above, the employee's investment in the contract is generally the aggregate amount of after-tax contributions made to the plan, reduced by any amounts received before the annuity starting date that were excluded from gross income. IRC § 72(c)(1) & (f).

Sections 72(d)(1)(B)(iii) and (iv) of the Internal Revenue Code set forth two tables pursuant to which the expected number of payments are to be determined. If the annuity is payable based on the life of a single individual, IRC § 72(d)(1)(B)(iii) provides that the number of anticipated payments is determined as follows:

If the age of the annuitant on the annuity starting date is:	Number of anticipated payments is:
Not more than 55	360
More than 55 but not more than 60	310
More than 60 but not more than 65	260
More than 65 but not more than 70	210
More than 70	160

If the annuity is payable based on the life of more than one individual, IRC § 72(d)(1)(B)(iv) provides that the number of anticipated payments is determined based on the combined ages of the annuitants at the starting date. Specifically,

If the combined ages of annuitants are:	The number is:
Not more than 110	410
More than 110 but not more than 120	360
More than 120 but not more than 130	310
More than 130 but not more than 140	260

If the combined ages of annuitants are:	The number is:
More than 140	210

If the annuity does not depend in whole or in part on the life expectancy of one or more individuals, the expected number of payments is the number of monthly annuity payments under the contract. IRC § 72(d)(1)(B)(i)(II).

To illustrate: upon retirement Ryan, age 65, begins receiving retirement benefits in the form of a joint and 50 percent survivor annuity to be paid for the joint lives of Ryan and Ryan's spouse, Emma, age 64. Ryan's annuity starting date is January 1, 2004. Ryan made $26,000 of after-tax contributions to the plan and has received no distributions prior to the annuity staring date. Ryan will receive a monthly retirement benefit of $1,000 and Emma will receive a monthly survivor benefit of $500 upon Ryan's death.

Ryan's investment in the contract is $26,000. The expected number of monthly payments is 310 for the two distributees whose combined ages are 129. The tax-free portion of each $1,000 annuity payment to Ryan is $83.87, determined by dividing Ryan's investment in the contract ($26,000) by the expected number of payments (310).

$$\frac{\$26{,}000 \text{ investment}}{310 \text{ monthly payments}} = \$83.87 \text{ return of investment per month}$$

Upon Ryan's death, if Ryan has not received the full $26,000 investment, Emma will also exclude $83.87 from each $500 monthly payment. Any annuity payments received after the 310 monthly payments have been made will be fully includible in gross income. If Ryan and Emma die before 310 monthly payments have been made, a deduction is allowed for the last income tax return in the amount of the unrecovered investment.

If the periodic payments are made on other than a monthly basis, adjustments are made to the simplified method. In addition, if the annuitant is over age 75 and there are five or more years of guaranteed payments under the annuity, the IRC § 72(d) simplified method does not apply.

If a participant receives a distribution that is not an amount received as an annuity (a nonperiodic payment), and the participant has an investment in the contract, taxation of the distribution depends on when the distribution is made in relation to the annuity starting date. If the nonperiodic payment is made on or after the annuity starting date, then generally all of the payment is includible in gross income when received. IRC § 72(e)(2)(A). On the other hand, if the nonperiodic payment is made before the annuity starting date, the participant can generally allocate part of distribution to the cost basis and exclude from gross income that part of the nonperiodic payment allocable to the cost basis.

9-16 QUESTIONS AND PROBLEMS

1. Upon retirement, Emily, age 63, begins receiving retirement benefits in the form of a single life annuity. Her annuity starting date is January 1, 2012, and she will receive a benefit of $750 per month.

   a. If Emily made no after-tax contributions to the plan, how will she be taxed on her monthly benefit of $750?

b. If Emily contributed $3,100 worth of after-tax contributions to the plan and received no distributions prior to the annuity starting date, how will she be taxed on her monthly benefit of $750?

2. Upon retirement, Natalie, age 63, and her husband, Jacob, age 64, begin receiving a joint and survivor annuity. Her annuity starting date is January 1, 2012, and she will receive a monthly retirement benefit of $750 per month and Jacob will receive a monthly survivor benefit of $750 upon Natalie's death.

a. If Natalie made no after-tax contributions to the plan, how will she and Jacob be taxed?

b. If Natalie contributed $9,300 worth of after-tax contributions to the plan and received no distributions prior to the annuity starting date, how will she and Jacob be taxed?

c. If the joint and survivor annuity is a joint and 50 percent survivor annuity and Natalie made no after-tax contributions to the plan, how will Natalie and Jacob be taxed if Natalie will receive a monthly retirement benefit of $750 and Jacob a monthly survivor benefit of $375 upon Natalie's death.

3. Upon retirement, Zachary, age 57, begins receiving retirement benefits in the form of a joint and 50 percent survivor annuity to be paid for the joint lives of Zachary and his wife, Olivia, age 57. Zachary contributed $36,000 worth of after-tax contributions to the plan. His annuity starting date is July 1, 2012. Zachary will receive a retirement benefit of $1,500 per month and Olivia will receive a monthly survivor benefit of $750 upon Zachary's death. How will Zachary and Olivia be taxed on these benefits?

4. How simple is the IRC § 72(d) "simplified method?"

5. The Staff of Joint Committee on Taxation has recommended that the IRC § 72(d) "simplified method" be replaced with an even simpler method. Under the staff's proposed method, distributions would be treated as attributable to the investment in the contract first, until the entire amount of the investment in the contract has been recovered. Once the investment in the contract is recovered, all distributions would be includible in income. As under current law, if the participant dies before recovering the investment in the contract, the amount of remaining investment in the contract would be allowed as a deduction on the final return. Study of the Overall State of the Federal Tax System and Recommendations for Simplification, Pursuant to Section 8022(3)(B) of the Internal Revenue Code of 1986, 107th Cong., 1st Sess., JCS-3-01 (2001). What are the advantages of this method? The disadvantages?

[3] Rollovers and Individual Retirement Accounts (IRAs)

[a] Rollover Distributions

IRC § 402(c).

Section 402(c) of the Internal Revenue Code sets forth an important exception to the general rule that distributions from a qualified retirement plan are generally taxable in the year in which they are actually distributed. Pursuant to IRC § 402(c), a participant who transfers all or any portion of an "eligible rollover distribution" to an eligible retirement plan may exclude the amount rolled over from gross income in the year distributed. The amount rolled over will not be included in the participant's income until it is distributed from the recipient retirement plan.

Section 402(c)(4) of the Internal Revenue Code defines an "eligible rollover distribution" as any distribution from a qualified plan to a participant with the exception of three specific types of distributions: (1) periodic payments, (2) distributions required by the IRC § 401(a)(9) minimum distribution rules, and (3) hardship distributions. IRC § 402(c)(4). For these purposes, a periodic payment is defined as any distribution that is one of a series of substantially equal periodic payments, payable in installments no less often than annually, and made over the life or life expectancy of the employee or joint lives or joint life expectancies of the employee and his or her beneficiary or for a specified period of ten years or more. IRC § 402(c)(4)(A).

Thus, every distribution from a qualified plan to a participant will be an eligible rollover distribution unless it is specifically excluded from the definition of eligible rollover distributions. The Treasury regulations also exclude certain other distributions, such as loans treated as deemed distributions under IRC § 72(p), from the definition of an eligible rollover distribution. *See* Treas. Reg. § 1.402(c)-2 Q&A-4.

"Eligible retirement plans," that is, plans that are eligible to receive eligible rollover distributions include (1) IRC § 408(a) individual retirement accounts ("IRAs"), (2) IRC § 408(b) individual retirement annuities (other than endowment contracts), (3) IRC § 401(a) qualified retirement plans, (4) IRC § 403(a) annuity plans, (5) IRC § 457 governmental plans, and (6) IRC § 403(b) tax-sheltered annuities. IRC § 402(c)(8)(B). Although each of these types of plans may be "eligible" to receive rollovers, they are not required to accept rollover contributions. Treas. Reg. § 1.401(a)(31)-1 Q&A-13. In fact, most defined contribution plans accept rollover contributions while few defined benefit plans accept such contributions.

There are two basic types of rollovers: actual rollovers and direct rollovers. An actual rollover distribution involves a two step process. First, the plan administrator makes an eligible rollover distribution to a plan participant. The participant then rolls the distribution over to an eligible retirement plan within 60 days of receipt to avoid taxation on the distribution. A direct rollover distribution occurs when the plan administrator transfers the eligible rollover distribution directly to the recipient retirement plan in a direct trustee-to-trustee transfer.

Section 401(a)(31) of the Internal Revenue Code requires that qualified plans offer participants the option of a direct rollover. Direct rollovers are strongly encouraged because any eligible rollover distribution that is not directly rolled over is subject to a 20 percent withholding tax. IRC § 3405(c).

Thus, if a plan makes a distribution directly to a participant, the distribution is subject to 20 percent mandatory withholding and is taxable to the participant in the year of distribution. If, however, the participant rolls the distribution into an eligible retirement plan within 60 days of receipt pursuant to an "actual rollover," the amount rolled over is not subject to tax. Nevertheless, the participant has to come up with the cash necessary to replace the tax withheld to avoid taxation on any part of the distribution. For example, suppose that Ariadna receives an eligible rollover distribution of $200,000 from the Chi Profit-Sharing Plan. Because the distribution is subject to mandatory withholding, she receives $160,000 ($200,000 - (20% x $200,000)) in cash from the plan. If she rolls the cash she received to an IRA within 60 days of receipt, she will not have to pay tax on the $160,000. She is, however, subject to tax on the $40,000 that was withheld. In order to avoid taxation on the $40,000 in the year in which the distribution was made, Ariadna must find an additional $40,000 in personal funds and roll the total eligible distribution of $200,000 to an eligible retirement plan within 60 days. In the alternative, Ariadna may avoid both withholding and taxation on the distribution by having the plan administrator roll the distribution directly to the IRA in a direct trustee-to-trustee transfer.

If an eligible rollover distribution is made in the form of property, such as stock, the actual property distributed must be rolled over, or the property must be sold and the proceeds rolled over. IRC §§ 401(c)(1)(C) & 401(c)(6)(A). An employee can not keep the distributed property and roll over cash or other property. If the distributed property is sold and the proceeds rolled over, no gain or loss is recognized on the sale. IRC § 402(c)(6)(D). The entire sale proceeds, (including any portion representing an increase in value) is treated as part of the distribution, and is not included in gross income. If only a portion of the proceeds is rolled over, the employee is taxed on the portion retained. The proceeds must be allocated between the part representing ordinary income from the distribution (its value upon distribution) and the part representing gain or loss from the sale (its change in value from its distribution to its sale). If an employee receives an eligible rollover distribution consisting of both cash and property and makes a rollover after selling part or all of the distributed property, the employee may designate the portions of such rollover to be treated as a contribution of sales proceeds and as cash received in the rollover distribution, respectively. IRC § 402(c)(6)(C).

9-17 QUESTIONS AND PROBLEMS

1. Which of the following distributions qualify as eligible rollover distributions under IRC § 402(c)?

a. Psi Inc. maintains the Psi Inc. Pension Plan, which meets the requirements of IRC § 401(a). On April 1, 2012, Carol, age 65, separates from service with Psi Inc. and begins to receive an annuity of $350 per month for life.

b. Same facts as (a) except that the annuity is $600 per month for 5 years.

c. Omega Co. maintains the Omega Co. Profit-Sharing Plan which meets the requirements of IRC § 401(a). On September 15, 2012, George, age 59, separates from service and receives a cash distribution of $5,000 which represents his entire interest in the Plan.

d. Same facts as (c) except that George only receives $2,500 which represents one-half of his interest in the Plan.

e. Same facts as (c) except that the distribution is made to George's former wife, Becky, pursuant to a qualified domestic relations order. *See* IRC § 402(e)(1)(B).

f. Same facts as (c) except that Becky receives the distribution after George's death (and Becky and George were not divorced at the time that George died). *See* IRC § 402(c)(9).

g. Same facts as (f) except that the distribution is made to George's daughter, Catherine, age 20. *See* IRC § 402(c)(II).

2. On September 6, 2012, Paula received an eligible rollover distribution from her employer's noncontributory qualified employee plan of $50,000 in nonemployer

stock. How much, if anything, must be withheld from this distribution? How is the withholding to be satisfied? *See* Treas. Reg. § 35.3405-1T Q&A-F-2.

a. Suppose that Paula sold the stock for $60,000 on September 27, 2012 and contributed $60,000 in cash to a traditional IRA on October 5, 2012. How much income must Paula recognize in 2012 as a result of this transaction?

b. Same facts as (a) above, except Paula sold the stock for $40,000 and contributed $40,000 to the IRA. How much income or loss must Paula recognize in 2012 as a result of this transaction?

c. Same facts as (a) above, except Paula rolled over only $45,000 of the $60,000 proceeds from the sale of stock. How much income must Paula recognize in 2012 as a result of this transaction?

d. Same facts as (b) above, except that Paula only rolled over $25,000 of the $40,000 proceeds from the sale of the stock. How much income or loss must Paula recognize in 2012 as a result of this transaction?

3. Why must distributees either roll over the actual property they receive in a distribution or sell the property and roll over the proceeds from the sale, rather than simply rolling over the cash equivalent of distributions made in the form of property?

4. Why are periodic payments, distributions required by the minimum distribution rules, and hardship distributions excluded from the definition of eligible rollover distributions?

5. The mandatory withholding requirement was included in the Unemployment Compensation Amendments of 1992 as a revenue raising measure to pay for an increase in unemployment benefits. Does the withholding rule make sense from a pension policy standpoint?

[b] IRAs

IRC §§ 408(a), 408A, 219.

Plan participants often roll eligible rollover distributions into an Individual Retirement Account or "IRA." IRAs, introduced with the enactment of ERISA in 1974, were created to enable individuals whose employers did not sponsor a retirement plan to save for retirement on a tax-favored basis. The taxation of conventional IRAs mirrors that of qualified retirement plans with neither contributions nor earnings subject to tax until the money is withdrawn from the IRA. IRC §§ 219(a), 408(d), 408(e).

The eligibility rules for IRAs have changed over the years. Originally, IRAs were limited to individuals who did not have an employer-sponsored retirement plan. For a brief period of time (from 1982 through 1986), IRAs were available to all individuals with earned income, including those with employer-sponsored retirement plans. In 1986, eligibility was restricted to individuals who did not participate in an employer-sponsored plan or who had relatively modest incomes.

In 1997 (and later in 2001), the eligibility rules were liberalized in three ways. First, the income ceiling for individuals with an employer-sponsored plan was raised so that in 2012, single taxpayers with an adjusted gross income of no more than $58,000 and married taxpayers with an adjusted gross income of no more than $92,000 are eligible to make tax deductible contributions to an IRA even if they participate in an employer-sponsored retirement plan. IRC § 219(g)(3)(B).

(Individuals with income that exceed these limits may make non-deductible contributions to IRAs. IRC §§ 408(o)(1), 408(o)(2)(A), 408(o)(2)(B).)

Second, the spouse of an individual participating in an employer-sponsored plan can set up his or her own IRA, even if the spouse has no earned income, as long as the couple's adjusted gross income is no more than $173,000. IRC § 219(g)(7). Finally, both an individual participating in an employer-sponsored retirement plan and the participant's spouse can set up a new variant of the IRA, called a Roth IRA, as long as the couple's adjusted gross income does not exceed $173,000 (or $110,000 for single taxpayers). IRC § 408A(c)(3)(C)(ii).

Roth IRAs, named for Senator William Roth of Delaware who was chairman of the Senate Finance Committee when this saving device was added to the Internal Revenue Code, differ fundamentally from traditional IRAs in that initial contributions to a Roth IRA are not deductible but earnings accrue tax free and no tax is due when the money is withdrawn from the IRA as long as it was in existence for at least 5 years prior to the withdrawal and the owner is at least 59½ years old. IRC §§ 408A(c)(1), 408A(d)(1), 408A(d)(2). Although this tax treatment may appear significantly different from that of a conventional IRA, as an economic matter, the value of a Roth IRA is virtually identical to that of a conventional IRA (assuming uniform tax rates). (*See* Chapter 2.)

Just as there are limits on how much can be contributed to qualified plans, there are limits on how much can be contributed to an IRA. The IRA limits, however, are significantly lower than the limits for qualified plans. The IRA limit is the lesser of (a) 100 percent of the individual's compensation or (b) $5,000 in 2008 and indexed for inflation thereafter. IRC § 219(b)(5)(A). In 2012, the IRA limit remains $5,000. (The IRA limits are phased out as earnings reach the applicable income ceiling. IRC § 219(g)(2)(A) & 408A(c)(3)(A).) Individuals who are 50 or older may also make "catch up" contributions of $1,000. IRC § 219(b)(5)(B).

Individuals can contribute to both a conventional IRA and a Roth IRA, but the total contribution in any given year cannot exceed the limits described above. IRC § 408A(c)(2). In addition, taxpayers can convert their conventional IRAs to Roth IRAs by withdrawing the money from the conventional IRA, paying income tax on the withdrawal as they would with any normal withdrawal, and depositing the after-tax amount into a Roth IRA. IRC § 408(C)(3)(b). Withdrawals from the converted Roth IRA will be treated like withdrawals from any other Roth IRA (that is, exempt from tax as long as the Roth owner is 59½ or older and the Roth IRA has been in existence for at least five years).

Like distributions from qualified plans, distributions from both conventional and Roth IRAs are subject to the IRC § 72(t) additional tax for early distributions. Thus, distributions to individuals who are younger than 59½ are generally subject to the IRC § 72(t) 10 percent additional tax. IRC § 72(t), however, creates two exceptions for early distributions from IRAs that do not apply to distributions from qualified plans. Those exceptions are for withdrawals made to pay for higher education costs or to pay for home purchases for first-time home buyers. IRC § 72(t)(E)&(F).

Taxpayers over age 70½ cannot contribute to a conventional IRA and must begin taking a minimum level of distributions from the conventional IRA or face substantial penalties. IRC §§ 219(d)(1), 408(a)(6), 401(a)(9). Roth IRAs, however, are not subject to these rules. An individual over age 70½ can continue to contribute a Roth IRA and is not required to commence withdrawals from the Roth IRA at any time. IRC §§ 408A(c)(4), 408A(c)(5). Thus, individuals can use Roth IRAs to build up the value of their estates.

Although IRAs were originally created to assist individuals with no employer-provided retirement plan to save for retirement, only about 5 percent of individuals who are eligible to make a tax-deductible contribution to an IRA do so each year. Instead, most IRAs consist of assets rolled over from qualified retirement plans.

9-18 QUESTIONS AND PROBLEMS

1. Why is the IRA limit so much lower than the IRC § 402(g) limit for 401(k) plans and the IRC § 415 limits for qualified plans? Should it be?

2. Congress' stated objective in creating Roth IRAs was to encourage and increase savings among Americans. How successful are Roth IRAs likely to be in increasing savings? In increasing retirement savings?

3. Hannah, a single woman, earns $20,000 a year and is covered by an employer-sponsored retirement plan. How much, if any, can Hannah contribute to a conventional IRA? A Roth IRA? Would the answers change if Hannah were married to Hunter, who also earns $20,000 and is covered by an employer-sponsored retirement plan?

4. Alexander, a single man, earns $45,000 and is covered by an employer-sponsored retirement plan. How much, if any, can Alexander contribute to a conventional IRA? A Roth IRA? Would the answers change if Alexander were married to Alyssa, who also earns $45,000 and is covered by an employer-sponsored retirement plan?

5. Madison, a single woman, earns $90,000 and is covered by an employer-sponsored retirement plan. How much, if any, can Madison contribute to a conventional IRA? A Roth IRA? Would the answers change if Madison were married to Matthew, who also earns $90,000 and is covered by an employer-sponsored retirement plan?

6. Nick, a single man, is a law student earning $1,500 a year. How much can he contribute to a conventional IRA? A Roth IRA? Would the answers change if Nick were married to Nina, who earns $120,000 and is covered by an employer-sponsored retirement plan?

[4] Plan Loans

IRC § 72(p).

Most 401(k) plans permit participants to borrow against their account balances at relatively low interest rates, although not many plan participants take advantage of them. At the end of 2009, only 21 percent of participants eligible for loans had loans outstanding at that time, with an average principal amount of about $7,300.

Plan loans have distinct advantages. They offer fast cash and a convenient procedure. Interest is paid back into the participant's 401(k) account, instead of to a third party. There is no credit check, and the borrower is qualified just by having a plan.

Plan loans, however, have distinct disadvantages. First, they may be viewed as contrary to the philosophy of retirement savings; that is, the philosophy that retirement savings should be used for retirement purposes. In addition, plan loans may reduce a participant's retirement savings. Because plans typically offer loans at a favorable interest rate, a borrower may earn less on the loan balance than on alternative investments. In addition, a participant may be subject to double taxation on the interest paid on plan loans. The interest paid to the plan is paid with after-tax dollars, and the participant is taxed again on the interest when it is distributed from the plan.

9-19 QUESTIONS AND PROBLEMS

1. Why do most 401(k) plans offer plan loans? Should they?

2. Who is most likely to benefit from plan loans and who is most likely to be harmed?

3. Does the availability of plan loans increase employees' willingness to contribute to 401(k) plans?

Three distinct sets of rules apply to plan loans: (1) plan qualification rules, (2) prohibited transaction rules, and (3) taxable distribution rules. If a plan fails to satisfy the plan qualification rules with respect to a plan loan, the plan can lose its qualified status. If the applicable prohibited transaction rules are violated, the plan may be subject to an excise tax and/or the plan fiduciaries may be subject to personal liability. Finally, if the tax rules are violated, the loan may be treated as a taxable distribution.

As discussed in Chapter 4, IRC § 401(a)(13) provides that a trust shall not be a qualified trust "unless the plan of which such trust is a part provides that benefits under the plan may not be assigned or alienated." IRC § 401(a)(13)(A). Section 401(a)(13) expressly excepts from this anti-alienation provision a plan loan if the "loan is secured by the participant's accrued nonforfeitable benefit and is exempt from the tax imposed by section 4975 by reason of section 4975(d)(1)." IRC § 401(a)(13)(A).

Section 4975 of the Internal Revenue Code imposes a tax on prohibited transactions. Section 406 of ERISA sets forth prohibited transaction rules that are substantially similar, though not identical to, the prohibited transaction rules contained in the Internal Revenue Code. Generally, loans to plan participants or beneficiaries are defined as prohibited transactions. ERISA § 406(a)(1)(B); IRC § 4975(c)(1)(B). Such loans, however, are exempted from the prohibited transaction rules if the loans (A) are available to all participants or beneficiaries on a reasonably equivalent basis, (B) are not made available to highly compensated employees in an amount greater than that made available to other employees, (C) are made in accordance with specific provisions regarding such loans set forth in the plan, (D) bear a reasonable rate of interest, and (E) are adequately secured. ERISA § 408(b)(1); IRC § 4975(d)(1). The prohibited transaction rules are discussed in Chapter 6.

Concerned that the widespread use of loans would diminish retirement savings, Congress enacted IRC § 72(p) in 1982. It begins by setting forth the general rule that a loan from a qualified employer plan will be deemed a taxable distribution. IRC § 72(p)(1). It then provides a carefully structured exception to the deemed distribution rule pursuant to which a loan will not be a deemed distribution if the loan satisfies three general requirements.

First, the amount of the loan must not exceed the limits set forth in IRC § 72(p)(2)(A). Second, the terms of the loan must require that the loan be repaid within five years unless the loan is used by a participant to acquire a principal residence. IRC § 72(p)(2)(B). Third, the loan repayments must be substantially level and made no less frequently than once each quarter. IRC § 72(p)(2)(C).

The amount of a loan, when added to the outstanding balance of all other loans from the plan, can not exceed the lesser of (a) $50,000 and (b) the greater of (i) one-half of the present value of the participant's or beneficiary's vested accrued benefit under the plan or (ii) $10,000. IRC § 72(p)(2)(A). The $50,000 limit is reduced by the excess of the highest outstanding loan balance during the one-year period ending on the day before the date on which a new loan is made over the outstanding loan balance on the date on which the new loan is made. IRC § 72(p)(2)(A)(i).

To illustrate the loan amount limit, suppose that Teeka, a participant in a profit-sharing plan maintained by her employer, has a vested benefit in the plan of $150,000. She may borrow a maximum of $50,000 from the plan because $50,000 does not exceed the lesser of (a) $50,000 or (b) the greater of (i) one-half of the present value of her vested accrued benefit (½ x $150,000 = $75,000) or (ii) $10,000. Suppose that Teeka borrows $50,000 from the plan as of January 15, 2010, and her balance on the loan is $40,000 as of January 15, 2011. Suppose further that as of January 15, 2012, the balance on her loan is $30,000, and she wishes to borrow additional money from the plan. The total of her new loan plus her outstanding balance ($30,000) cannot exceed the lesser of (a) $50,000 reduced by the highest outstanding loan balance on the day before the date on which such loan was made (or $40,000), over the outstanding balance of loans made from the plan on the date on which such loan was made (or $30,000), or ($50,000 – ($40,000 – $30,000) = $40,000) or (b) the greater of (i) ½ of the present value of her nonforfeitable accrued benefit (½ x $150,000 = $75,000) or (ii) $10,000. Thus, her new loan (plus her outstanding balance of $30,000) cannot exceed $40,000, and the maximum amount she may borrow from the plan is $10,000 ($40,000 – $30,000 = $10,000).

9-20 QUESTIONS AND PROBLEMS

1. Given Congress' concern that the widespread use of loans would diminish retirement savings, why didn't Congress simply prohibit such loans?

2. Alpha Inc. maintains the Alpha Inc. Money Purchase Pension Plan (the "Plan") which meets the requirements of Section 401(a) of the Code. In each of the parts below, determine how Alpha's employee is taxed. Assume that, except as indicated, there are no loans outstanding from the Plan and no employee contributions were made to the Plan.

a. Mitchell, who is age 40, borrows $50,000 from the Plan to buy a boat. Mitchell's account balance in the Plan is $200,000, and Mitchell is fully vested under the Plan. The loan term is five years, and the loan must be repaid in level quarterly installments.

b. Same as "a" except that the loan is for $70,000.

c. Same as "a" except that the loan term is 8 years.

d. Same as "c" except that Mitchell uses the loan to buy his new principal residence.

e. Same as "a" except that Mitchell's account balance is only $80,000.

f. Same as "a" except that after five years $10,000 of the loan remains outstanding.

g. Same as "a" except that Mitchell has $10,000 outstanding from a previous loan from the Plan and his highest outstanding loan balance in the previous 12 months was $40,000.

h. Brian, who is age 37, has a vested benefit in the plan equal to $300,000. On July 1, 2010, he borrows $40,000 from the plan. As of July 1, 2011, the balance on his loan is $30,000. As of July 1, 2012, the balance on his loan is $20,000. What is the maximum amount he can borrow from the plan as of July 1, 2012, without the loan being deemed a distribution?

3. Why does IRC § 72(p)(2)(A)(i) reduce the $50,000 limit by the excess of the highest outstanding loan balance during the one-year period ending on the day before the date on which a new loan is made over the outstanding loan balance on the date on which a new loan is made?

[5] Minimum Distribution Rules

IRC § 401(a)(9).

Section 401(a)(9) of the Internal Revenue Code sets forth minimum distribution rules for qualified retirement plans. The rules generally require that participants in qualified retirement plans begin receiving minimum distributions no later than age 70½. The rules are designed to ensure that retirement savings are used principally for retirement purposes and not as an estate planning device, and that income taxation is not postponed indefinitely. Given these purposes, it is hardly surprising that the rules are contained solely in the Internal Revenue Code and have no parallel in ERISA.

The minimum distribution rules begin by setting forth a "required beginning date," or "RBD." IRC § 401(a)(9)(A). The RBD is generally April 1st of the year following the year the participant reaches age 70½. IRC § 401(a)(9)(C)(i)(I). If the participant remains actively employed at age 70½ (and is not a 5 percent owner of the employer), the RBD is extended until April 1st of the year following the participant's retirement. IRC §§ 401(a)(9)(C)(i)(II) & 401(a)(9)(C)(ii)(I).

The rules require that, no later than the participant's RBD, the participant's benefits must either (1) be paid out in a lump sum or (2) begin to be paid out in substantially equal periodic payments over: (a) the life of the participant, (b) the joint lives of the participant and a designated beneficiary, (c) a period not extending beyond the participant's life expectancy, or (d) a period not extending beyond the joint and last survivor expectancy of the participant and a designated beneficiary. IRC § 401(a)(9)(A).

Because defined benefit plans typically distribute benefits in the form of a single life annuity (or joint life annuity, in the case of a married participant) and thus automatically spread payments evenly over the life of the participant (and his or her spouse), distributions from defined benefit plans typically have little trouble satisfying the minimum distribution rules. Distributions from defined contribution plans, in contrast, are not designed to automatically satisfy the minimum distribution rules, unless the benefits are paid out in the form of a lump sum by the RBD. Accordingly, the treasury regulations provide extensive guidance on how distributions from defined contribution plans may satisfy the minimum distribution rules. Once described as "byzantine," the proposed regulations were amended and greatly simplified in 2001, and final regulations were issued in 2002.

Pursuant to the treasury regulations, the amount of the minimum required distribution is determined by dividing the participant's account balance (revalued annually) by a life expectancy factor (the "divisor"). There are currently two methods for determining the appropriate divisor. One method applies to any participant whose sole beneficiary is his spouse who is more than ten years younger than he is. *See* Treas. Reg. § 1.401(a)(9)-5, A-4(b). The other method (the "Uniform Lifetime Table") applies to all other participants. *See* Treas. Reg. § 1.401(a)(9)-9, A-4(a).

The divisors in the Uniform Lifetime Table represent the joint life expectancy of a participant age 70 or older and a hypothetical beneficiary who is ten years younger than the participant. For a 70-year-old participant, the initial divisor under the Uniform Lifetime Table is 27.42 (the joint life expectancy of a 70-year-old and a 60-year old). The Uniform Lifetime Table is contained in Treas. Reg. § 1.401(a)(9)-9, A-2. The preamble to the proposed regulations explains that the Uniform Table "reflects the fact that an employee's beneficiary is subject to change until the death of the employee and ultimately may be a beneficiary more than 10 years younger than the employee." The Uniform Table thus permits lifetime distributions at a rate consistent with this possibility.

If the participant's only designated beneficiary is a spouse who is more than ten years younger than the participant, the divisor is based on the actual joint life expectancy of the participant and his or her spouse. Treas. Reg. § 1.401(a)(9)-5, A-4(b). The determination of whether the spouse is the sole beneficiary is made on a year by year basis, and the spouse must be the sole beneficiary for the entire distribution calendar year. *Id.*

To illustrate, suppose that Participant is 75, he has an account balance of $500,000, and he has named his wife, age 70, as his sole beneficiary. Participant will use the Uniform Table to calculate his minimum distribution for the year because his wife is less than 10 years younger than he is. The divisor for age 75 under the Uniform Table is 22.9. Thus, Participant's minimum distribution for the year is $21,834 ($500,000/22.9).

For years after the year of the participant's death, the distribution period is generally the remaining life expectancy of the designated beneficiary. *See* Treas. Reg. § 1.401(a)(9)-5, A-5(a). The beneficiary's remaining life expectancy is calculated using the age of the beneficiary in the year following the year of the participant's death, reduced by one for each subsequent year. *See* Treas. Reg. § 1.401(a)(9)-5, A-5(c)(1). If the participant's spouse is the participant's sole beneficiary at the end of the year following the year of the participant's death, the distribution period during the spouse's life is the spouse's single life expectancy (recalculated each year). *See* Treas. Reg. § 1.401(a)(9)-5, A-5(c)(2). For years after the year of the spouse's death, the distribution period is the spouse's life expectancy calculated in the year of death, reduced by one for each subsequent year. *Id.*

If the participant dies before his or her RBD and the sole designated beneficiary is the participant's spouse, distributions need not commence until the beneficiary would have reached age 70½. If the participant dies before his or her RBD and someone other than the participant's spouse is the designated beneficiary, distributions must begin no later than the end of the calendar year after the year of the participant's death. *See* Treas. Reg. § 1.401(a)(9)-3, A-3.

If the minimum distribution rules are not satisfied IRC § 4974(a) imposes a 50 percent excise tax on the difference between the minimum required distribution and the actual distribution made in any given year. The minimum distribution rules also apply to distributions from conventional IRAs.

9-21 QUESTIONS AND PROBLEMS

1. For the following fact patterns, determine the participant's RBD.

a. Arnold, a participant in the Beta Company Profit-Sharing Plan, was born on June 30, 1941, and retired from the Beta Company on March 15, 2008.

b. Same facts as (a), except that Arnold participates in the Beta Company (Defined Benefit) Pension Plan.

c. Same facts as (a) except that Arnold, who has no ownership interest in Beta, does not retire before his death on June 30, 2012.

d. Same facts as (c) except that Arnold owns 50 percent of Beta Company.

e. Bonita, a participant in the Beta Company Profit-Sharing Plan, was born on July 1, 1942, and retired from the Alpha Company on March 16, 2010.

f. Calvin, a participant in the Beta Company Profit-Sharing Plan, was born on January 1, 1965, and died on June 30, 2012. His wife, Nora, age 55, was designated as his sole beneficiary.

g. Same facts as (f) except that Calvin's 10-year-old son, David, was designated as his sole beneficiary.

2. For the following fact patterns, determine the amount of the participant's required minimum distribution.

a. Evan, a retired participant in the Zeta Company 401(k) Plan, is 77 years old and has an account balance of $422,000. He has designated his wife, Fran, 79 years old, as his sole beneficiary.

b. Same facts as (a) except Evan has designated his son, George, age 47, as his sole beneficiary.

c. Same facts as (a) except that Evan has designated both Fran and George as his beneficiaries.

d. Would your answer to (b) and (c) change if Fran were 59 years old rather than 79 years old?

Chapter 10

PLAN AMENDMENT AND TERMINATION

ERISA permits employee benefit plans to be amended or terminated subject to certain limitations. Plan sponsors cannot amend pension plans in a manner that reduces accrued benefits. ERISA § 204(g); IRC § 411(d)(6). The Internal Revenue Code imposes special accelerated vesting rules on qualified plans upon termination. *See* IRC § 411(d)(3). Defined benefit plans may be either underfunded, i.e., unable to pay all their obligations, or overfunded, i.e., have assets that exceed their obligations. To protect plan participants and beneficiaries of underfunded defined benefit plans, Congress created the Pension Benefit Guaranty Corporation (PBGC) to monitor plan terminations and operate an insurance program to insure plan benefits. ERISA §§ 4001 *et seq.* Conversely, both ERISA and the Internal Revenue Code regulate who is entitled to the plan surplus when an overfunded plan is terminated.

A. PLAN AMENDMENTS

ERISA §§ 104(b)(1), 204(h), 402(b)(3).

ERISA requires that every employee benefit plan provide a plan amendment procedure and identify the persons who have authority to amend the plan. ERISA § 402(b)(3). The formal plan language need not be a model of precision. Many employee benefits plans satisfy this requirement by including a provision that authorizes the employer to amend the plan at any time. In *Curtiss-Wright Corp. v. Schoonejongen*, 514 U.S. 73 (1995), the Court found that the clause, "The Company reserves the right at any time and from time to time to modify or amend, in whole or in part, any of all of the provision of the Plan," met the ERISA § 402(b)(3) requirement of identifying the persons who can amend the plan and provided an amendment "procedure" by stating that the plan could only be amended by "The Company." According to the Court, a plan amendment procedure does not have to specify the particular individuals or entities who may amend the plan.

Because the decision to amend a plan is a settlor function, it is not subject to ERISA's fiduciary rules as explained in these quotes from Supreme Court cases.

> Plan sponsors who alter the terms of a plan do not fall into the category of fiduciaries. As we said with respect to the amendment of welfare benefit plans, "[e]mployers or other plan sponsors are generally free under ERISA, for any reason at any to time, to adopt, modify, or terminate welfare plans." When employers undertake those actions, they do not act as fiduciaries, but are analogous to the settlors of a trust. *Lockheed Corp. v. Spink*, 517 U.S. 882, 890 (1996) (quoting *Curtiss-Wright Corp. v. Schoonejongen*, 514 U.S. 73, 78 (1995)).
>
> We made clear in *Spink* that our reasoning applied both to "pension benefit plans" and "welfare benefit plans" since "[t]he definition of fiduciary makes no distinction between persons exercising authority over" these different types of plans. [*Spinks*] at 890–891. Our conclusion applies with equal force to persons exercising authority over a contributory plan, a noncontributory plan, or any other type of plan. *Hughes Aircraft Co. v. Jacobson*, 525 U.S. 432, 443 (1999).

ERISA, § 104(b)(1), however, does require that participants and beneficiaries be informed of any material modifications to the plan, and that plan participants be given advance notice of any significant reduction in the rate of future benefit accruals under any defined benefit, money purchase, or target benefit plan. ERISA § 204(h).

[1] Anti-Cutback Rule

ERISA § 204(g); IRC § 411(d)(6)(A).

Both ERISA and the Internal Revenue Code contain an "anti-cutback rule" that prohibits pension plans from reducing accrued benefits. ERISA § 204(g); IRC § 411(d)(6)(A). The anti-cutback rule does not apply to ancillary or incidental benefits, but does protect early retirement benefits and retirement-type subsidies as well as optional forms of benefits. ERISA § 204(g)(2); IRC § 411(d)(6)(B). The regulations include as examples of retirement-type subsidies, a subsidized early retirement benefit and a subsidized qualified joint and survivor annuity. Treas. Reg. § 1.411(d)-3(g)(6)(iv).

The following two cases address the question of when a plan amendment violates the anti-cutback rule.

CENTRAL LABORERS' PENSION FUND v. HEINZ

541 U.S. 739 (2004)

JUSTICE SOUTER.

With few exceptions, the "anti-cutback" rule of the Employee Retirement Income Security Act of 1974 (ERISA) prohibits any amendment of a pension plan that would reduce a participant's "accrued benefit." [ERISA § 204(g).] The question is whether the rule prohibits an amendment expanding the categories of postretirement employment that triggers suspension of payment of early retirement benefits already accrued. We hold such an amendment prohibited.

I

Respondents Thomas Heinz and Richard Schmitt (collectively, Heinz) are retired participants in a multiemployer pension plan (hereinafter Plan) administered by petitioner Central Laborers' Pension Fund. Like most other participants in the Plan, Heinz worked in the construction industry in central Illinois before retiring, and by 1996, he had accrued enough pension credits to qualify for early retirement payments under a defined benefit "service only" pension. This scheme pays him the same monthly retirement benefit he would have received if he had retired at the usual age, and is thus a form of subsidized benefit, since monthly payments are not discounted even though they start earlier and are likely to continue longer than the average period.

Heinz's entitlement is subject to a condition on which this case focuses: the Plan prohibits beneficiaries of service only pensions from certain "disqualifying employment" after they retire. The Plan provides that if beneficiaries accept such employment their monthly payments will be suspended until they stop the forbidden work.[1] When Heinz retired in 1996, the Plan defined "disqualifying

[1] This suspension provision was adopted on the authority of ERISA § 203(a)(3)(B). In authorizing such suspensions, Congress seems to have been motivated at least in part by a desire "to protect participants against their pension plan being used, in effect, to subsidize low-wage employers who hire plan retirees to compete with, and undercut the wages and working conditions of employees covered by the plan." 120 CONG. REC. 29930 (1974) (statement of Sen. Williams regarding § 203(a)(3)(B)). That

employment" as any job as "a union or non-union construction worker." This condition did not cover employment in a supervisory capacity, however, and when Heinz took a job in central Illinois as a construction supervisor after retiring, the Plan continued to pay out his monthly benefit.

In 1998, the Plan's definition of disqualifying employment was expanded by amendment to include any job "in any capacity in the construction industry (either as a union or non-union construction worker)." The Plan took the amended definition to cover supervisory work and warned Heinz that if he continued on as a supervisor, his monthly pension payments would be suspended. Heinz kept working, and the Plan stopped paying.

Heinz sued to recover the suspended benefits on the ground that applying the amended definition of disqualifying employment so as to suspend payment of his accrued benefits violated ERISA's anti-cutback rule. On cross-motions for judgment on the pleadings under Federal Rule of Civil Procedure 12(c), the District Court granted judgment for the Plan, only to be reversed by a divided panel of the Seventh Circuit, which held that imposing new conditions on rights to benefits already accrued was a violation of the anti-cutback rule. 303 F.3d 802 (CA7 2002). We granted certiorari in order to resolve the resulting Circuit split, see *Spacek v. Maritime Ass'n*, 134 F.3d 283 (CA5 1998), and now affirm.

II

A

There is no doubt about the centrality of ERISA's object of protecting employees' justified expectations of receiving the benefits their employers promise them.

. . .

ERISA's anti-cutback rule is crucial to this object, and (with two exceptions of no concern here) provides . . . that "a plan amendment which has the effect of . . . eliminating or reducing an early retirement benefit . . . with respect to benefits attributable to service before the amendment shall be treated as reducing accrued benefits." [ERISA § 204(g).]

Hence the question here: did the 1998 amendment to the Plan have the effect of "eliminating or reducing an early retirement benefit" that was earned by service before the amendment was passed? The statute, admittedly, is not as helpful as it might be in answering this question; it does not explicitly define "early retirement benefit," and it rather circularly defines "accrued benefit" as "the individual's accrued benefit determined under the plan . . . ." [ERISA § 3(23)(A).] Still, it certainly looks as though a benefit has suffered under the amendment here, for we agree with the Seventh Circuit that, as a matter of common sense, "[a] participant's benefits cannot be understood without reference to the conditions imposed on receiving those benefits, and an amendment placing materially greater restrictions on the receipt of the benefit 'reduces' the benefit just as surely as a decrease in the size of the monthly benefit payment." Heinz worked and accrued retirement benefits under a plan with terms allowing him to supplement retirement income by certain employment, and he was being reasonable if he relied

explains why ERISA permits multiemployer plans to suspend a retiree's benefits only if he accepts work "in the same industry, in the same trade or craft, and the same geographic area covered by the plan." [ERISA § 203(a)(3)(B)(ii).]

on those terms in planning his retirement. The 1998 amendment undercut any such reliance, paying retirement income only if he accepted a substantial curtailment of his opportunity to do the kind of work he knew. We simply do not see how, in any practical sense, this change of terms could not be viewed as shrinking the value of Heinz's pension rights and reducing his promised benefits.

B

The Plan's responses are technical ones, beginning with the suggestion that the "benefit" that may not be devalued is actually nothing more than a "defined periodic benefit the plan is legally obliged to pay," Brief for Petitioner 28, so that § 204(g) applies only to amendments directly altering the nominal dollar amount of a retiree's monthly pension payment. . . .

The Plan also contends that, because § 204(g) only prohibits amendments that "eliminat[e] or reduc[e] an early retirement benefit," the anti-cutback rule must not apply to mere suspensions of an early retirement benefit. This argument seems to rest on a distinction between "eliminat[e] or reduc[e]" on the one hand, and "suspend" on the other, but it just misses the point. No one denies that some conditions enforceable by suspending benefit payments are permissible under ERISA: conditions set before a benefit accrues can survive the anti-cutback rule, even though their sanction is a suspension of benefits. Because such conditions are elements of the benefit itself and are considered in valuing it at the moment it accrues, a later suspension of benefit payments according to the Plan's terms does not eliminate the benefit or reduce its value. The real question is whether a new condition may be imposed after a benefit has accrued; may the right to receive certain money on a certain date be limited by a new condition narrowing that right? In a given case, the new condition may or may not be invoked to justify an actual suspension of benefits, but at the moment the new condition is imposed, the accrued benefit becomes less valuable, irrespective of any actual suspension.

C

. . .

III

In criticizing the Seventh Circuit's reading of § 204(g), the Plan and the United States rely heavily on an entirely separate section of ERISA § 203(a)(3)(B). Here they claim to find specific authorization to amend suspension provisions retroactively, in terms specific enough to trump any general prohibition imposed by § 204(g). Section 203(a)(3)(B) provides that

> [a] right to an accrued benefit derived from employer contributions shall not be treated as forfeitable solely because the plan provides that the payment of benefits is suspended for such period as [beneficiaries like respondents are] employed . . . in the same industry, in the same trade or craft, and the same geographic area covered by the plan, as when such benefits commenced.

The Plan's arguments notwithstanding, § 203(a)(3)(B) is irrelevant to the question before us, for at least two reasons.

First, as a technical matter, § 203(a) addresses the entirely different question of benefit forfeitures. This is a distinct concept: § 204(g) belongs to the section of ERISA that sets forth requirements for benefit accrual (the rate at which an employee earns benefits to put in his pension account), see 29 U.S.C. § 1054, whereas § 203(a)(3)(B) is in the section that regulates vesting (the process by which an employee's already-accrued pension account becomes irrevocably his property). It requires generally that a plan treat an employee's benefits, to the extent that they have vested by virtue of his having fulfilled age and length of service requirements no greater than those specified in § 203(a)(2), as not subject to forfeiture." To be sure, the concepts overlap in practical effect, and a single act by a plan might raise both vesting and accrual concerns. But it would be a non sequitur to conclude that, because an amendment does not constitute a prohibited forfeiture under § 203, it must not be a prohibited reduction under § 204. Just because § 203(a)(3)(B) failed to forbid it would not mean that § 204(g) allowed it.

Second, read most simply and in context, § 203(a)(3)(B) is a statement about the terms that can be offered to plan participants up front and enforced without amounting to forfeiture, not as an authorization to adopt retroactive amendments. . . . Congress wanted to allow employers to condition future benefits on a plan participant's agreement not to accept certain kinds of postretirement employment, and it recognized that a plan provision to this effect might be seen as rendering vested benefits improperly forfeitable. Accordingly, adding § 203(a)(3)(B) made it clear that such suspension provisions were permissible in narrow circumstances. But critically for present purposes, § 203(a)(3)(B) speaks only to the permissible substantive scope of existing ERISA plans, not to the procedural permissibility of plan amendments. The fact that ERISA allows plans to include a suspension provision going to benefits not yet accrued has no logical bearing on the analysis of how ERISA treats the imposition of such a condition on (implicitly) bargained-for benefits that have accrued already. Section 203(a)(3)(B) is no help to the Plan.

The judgment of the Seventh Circuit is affirmed.

10-1 QUESTIONS AND PROBLEMS

1. Can a plan be amended to eliminate early retirement benefits for current plan participants? Can a plan be amended to eliminate early retirement benefits for individuals who become participants in the plan after the effective date of the amendment?

2. The Delta Pension Plan provides that participants will accrue benefits at the rate of 3% of final average pay per year of service up to 30 years of service. Can the Delta Pension Plan be amended to provide that, effective one week after the amendment is adopted, participants will accrue benefits at the rate of 1.5% of final average pay per year of service up to 30 years of service? *See* Treas. Reg. § 1.411(d)-4 Q & A2(a)(1). *Cf.* ERISA § 204(h).

3. Does ERISA § 204(g) protection extend to ancillary life insurance protection or accident or health insurance? *Cf.* Treas. Reg. § 1.411(d)-4 A-1.

IN RE BATTONI

594 F.3d 230 (3d Cir. 2010)

Smith, Circuit Judge.

This appeal requires us to consider the scope of the Employee Retirement Income Security Act's ("ERISA") Anti-Cutback rule, ERISA § 302(d). Certain current and retired members of a union (the "Battoni Plaintiffs") challenged an amendment to their welfare plan (the "Disputed Amendment") as an unlawful cutback of their accrued benefits under their pension plan. We must determine whether the Disputed Amendment, which conditions receipt of healthcare benefits under a welfare plan on non-receipt of an accrued benefit under a pension plan, violates the Anti-Cutback rule. In light of ERISA's statutory text and our precedent, we conclude that the Disputed Amendment violated the Anti-Cutback rule by constructively amending the pension plan in a manner that decreased an accrued benefit under that plan. Accordingly, we will affirm the District Court's judgment in favor of the Battoni Plaintiffs.

I.

A.

In November 1999, the Local 675 and the Local 102 chapters of the International Brotherhood of Electrical Workers ("IBEW") merged. As a result of the merger, the Local 675 chapter was dissolved and its members were transferred to the Local 102 chapter. The chapters' pension and welfare plans were also combined.

Before the merger, the Local 675 Pension Plan permitted plan participants to choose between a lump sum pension benefit or a periodic monthly benefit. The Local 102 Pension Plan, on the other hand, provided only a periodic monthly benefit to its participants. After the merger, the two pension plans were combined into one-the Local 102 Pension Plan. To accommodate the lump sum pension benefit option that was included in the Local 675 Pension Plan, the Local 102 Pension Plan was amended to provide former Local 675 members the right to receive a lump sum benefit for pre-merger accruals. Post-merger accruals, however, could be applied only towards a periodic monthly benefit.

The chapters' welfare plans were combined by transferring the Local 675 members to the Local 102 Welfare Plan. That plan provided eligible retirees healthcare benefits for themselves and their spouses. To receive these benefits, a retiree was required to satisfy certain conditions outlined in the plan. Shortly after the merger, the Local 102 Welfare Plan was amended to include a new condition on the receipt of healthcare benefits. This amendment, the Disputed Amendment, conditioned a retiree's receipt of healthcare benefits on the retiree's not choosing the lump sum pension benefit offered under the Local 102 Pension Plan. The Disputed Amendment stated, in relevant part, that:

> Retired employees who elect a lump sum pension benefit in lieu of periodic monthly benefits from [the] IBEW Local 102 Pension Plan and/or from another Local Union IBEW Pension Plan shall not be eligible for continued [healthcare] coverage.

Before the addition of the Disputed Amendment, a former Local 675 member could elect to receive the lump sum pension benefit provided under the Local 102 Pension Plan and still receive healthcare benefits under the Local 102 Welfare Plan.

B.

A group of current and retired members of the Local 102 chapter who were formerly members of the Local 675 chapter, the Battoni Plaintiffs, challenged the Disputed Amendment, alleging, among other things, that it violated the Anti-

Cutback rule. The Battoni Plaintiffs filed suit in the United States District Court for the District of New Jersey, naming the Local 102 Pension and Welfare Plans and the current and former trustees of those plans (collectively, the "Union") as defendants.

After a bench trial, the District Court concluded that the Disputed Amendment violated the Anti-Cutback rule and entered judgment in favor of the Battoni Plaintiffs. The Union then filed this timely appeal.

. . .

III.

The Anti-Cutback rule states: "The accrued benefit of a participant under a plan may not be decreased by an amendment of the plan, other than an amendment described in section 302(d)(2) or 4281." ERISA § 204(g)(1). To state a claim for violation of ERISA's Anti-Cutback rule one must show (1) that a plan was amended and (2) that the amendment decreased an accrued benefit.

* * *

A.

The first question that must be resolved is whether the Disputed Amendment, by conditioning the receipt of welfare benefits on a retiree not exercising her right to receive a lump sum pension benefit under the Local 102 Pension Plan, constituted an amendment to the Local 102 Pension Plan. *See* ERISA § 302(d)(1). Because the Disputed Amendment constructively amended the right to receive a lump sum pension benefit under the Local 102 Pension Plan, we conclude that the first requirement of an Anti-Cutback claim was satisfied.

1.

Our view of what constitutes an "amendment" to a pension plan has been construed broadly to protect pension recipients. . . . According to the Union, the Disputed Amendment amended the welfare plan and thus was exempted from the Anti-Cutback rule. ERISA § 201(1). The Anti-Cutback rule, however, cannot be employed in such an overly simplistic, robotic fashion.

We must examine the Disputed Amendment closely to determine its true character before we declare it solely a welfare plan amendment and exempt from the Anti-Cutback rule. An evaluation of the amendment's benefit characteristics, which are independent of the formal placement of the amendment, is necessary. "The type of benefit provided, not other considerations, determines whether a plan [amendment amends a] pension plan or a welfare plan." *Id.; see Rombach v. Nestle USA, Inc.*, 211 F.3d 190, 193-94 (2d Cir. 2000).

As a general rule, an amendment amends a pension plan "to the extent that by its express terms or as a result of surrounding circumstances . . . [it] provide[s] retirement income to employees, or . . . results in a deferral of income by employees for periods extending to the termination of covered employment or beyond[.]" ERISA § 3(2)(A) (defining "pension plan"). "[T]he words 'to the extent that' rather than 'solely' clearly indicate that Congress intended to allow any plan or part of a plan," *McBarron*, 771 F.2d at 98, to be considered a pension plan or a welfare plan. As such, the "meaning and function" of the amendment determines whether it modifies a pension plan, a welfare plan, or both.

2.

The Disputed Amendment is part of the Local 102 Welfare Plan "to the extent" that it pertains to welfare benefits, ERISA § 3(1), and part of the Local 102 Pension Plan "to the extent" that it pertains to pension benefits. The Disputed Amendment constructively amended the pension plan by adding a condition to the receipt of a benefit accrued under that plan. If a retiree elects to receive the lump sum pension benefit under the Local 102 Pension Plan she loses healthcare benefits under the Local 102 Welfare Plan. Thus, the Disputed Amendment necessarily, "by its express terms or as a result of surrounding circumstances," ERISA § 3(2)(A) amended the Local 102 Pension Plan.

B.

Having determined that the Disputed Amendment amended the Local 102 Pension Plan, the next inquiry is whether the amendment decreased an accrued benefit. *See* ERISA § 302(d)(1). The Union argues that the Disputed Amendment merely restricts access to healthcare benefits and does not decrease any accrued benefit. But because the Disputed Amendment imposed a condition on the receipt of the lump sum benefit under the Local 102 Pension Plan, it decreased an accrued benefit. "[A]t the moment [a] new condition is imposed, the accrued benefit becomes less valuable[.]" *Cent. Laborers' Pension Fund v. Heinz*, 541 U.S. 739, 746 (2004) . . . .

In *Central Laborers' Pension Fund*, the Supreme Court considered "whether the [Anti-Cutback] rule prohibits an amendment expanding the categories of postretirement employment that triggers suspension of payment of early retirement benefits already accrued." 541 U.S. at 741. It held that such an amendment was prohibited in part because the imposition of a new condition on an accrued benefit decreased the value of that accrued benefit. *Id.* at 746.

* * *

The same reasoning applies here. The Local 102 Pension Plan, like Heinz's pension plan, imposed a new condition on the receipt of an accrued benefit. The Battoni Plaintiffs' lump sum pension benefits accrued before the Disputed Amendment was added to the Local 102 Welfare Plan. Yet the Disputed Amendment conditioned the receipt of those accrued benefits on forfeiting healthcare benefits. This "new condition," in and of itself, decreased the value of the lump sum pension benefit . . . .

* * *

IV.

The Disputed Amendment constructively amended the pension plan because it conditioned receipt of the lump sum pension benefit, an accrued benefit, on surrendering healthcare benefits provided by the welfare plan. This condition on the receipt of the lump sum pension benefit decreased the value of that benefit in violation of the Anti-Cutback rule. Thus, we will affirm the District Court's judgment that the Disputed Amendment violated ERISA's Anti-Cutback rule.

Whether ERISA § 204(g) protection extends to benefits that are contingent on the occurrence of an unpredictable benefit, such as a plant shutdown, is unclear.

Employers sometimes provide extra pension benefits to employees who, because of a plant shutdown, are terminated before they reach normal retirement age. Under such plans the terminated employee who meets age and service requirements when the plant closes gets an unreduced pension even though the benefits begin to be paid before his or her normal retirement age. Such a worker typically receives a greater pension than would be available had he or she taken early retirement.

Whether plant-shutdown benefits can be taken away depends on the question of whether the benefits are protected by ERISA § 204(g)(2). Courts who have considered the issue have come to quite different results. At least two federal appellate and one district court have supported the proposition that plant shutdown benefits are not protected. *Ross v. Pension Plan for Hourly Employees of SKF Industries*, 847 F.2d 329 (6th Cir. 1988), *Roper v. Pullman Standard*, 859 F.2d 1472, 1474 (11th Cir. 1988) and *Blank v. Bethlehem Steel Corp.*, 758 F. Supp. 697, 700 n.3 (M.D. Fla. 1990). Two other courts have concluded that plant-shutdowns are protected by ERISA § 204(g). *Bellas v. CBS, Inc.*, 221 F.3d 517 (3d Cir. 2000); *Richardson v. Pension Plan of Bethlehem Steel Corp.*, 67 F.3d 1462 (9th Cir. 1995), *modified on reh'g*, 112 F.3d 982 (9th Cir. 1997).

10-2 QUESTIONS AND PROBLEMS

Which interpretation of ERISA § 204(g) seems most consistent with the statutory language and the purposes of ERISA?

[2] Plan Amendments and Welfare Benefit Plans

Recall that in *Sprague v. General Motors Corporation* (discussed in Chapter 3), the court held that retiree medical benefits could be reduced or eliminated if the employer reserved the right to amend the plan providing those benefits. Suppose that the employer expressly reserves the right to amend or terminate the plan. Are there any limitations on the employer's right to amend or terminate a welfare benefit plan?

The following excerpt refers to *Wheeler v. Dynamic Engineering, Inc.*, 62 F.3d 634 (4th Cir. 1995). In that case the employer changed the coverage under its medical insurance plan and so no longer covered a breast cancer treatment that the plaintiff had commenced. Holding that the plan amendment, though valid, did not relieve the plan from paying for the plaintiff's cancer treatment, the court wrote:

> When an insured begins a particular multi-stage treatment, culminating in a final step within a fixed period of time and with the preliminary stages intended as preparation for the final step, she relies on the fact that the entire procedure will be covered. If her coverage terminated part way through the procedure, she would be required personally to pay the costs of the final stages or else lose all of the benefit of the preliminary stages. When the entire procedure terminates within a fixed and relatively short period of time, it poses little danger of imposing massive unforeseen costs on the employer. Finding coverage for such a procedure is entirely different from finding coverage for lifelong treatment of a particular illness, including potentially unforeseeable costs, simply because the illness was diagnosed while a policy was in force.
>
> In summary, Wheeler submitted a claim for, arranged for, and began HDC/PSCR, a well-defined procedure of limited duration, while she was covered under Dynamic's 1993 plan. Accordingly, the expenses associated with HDC/PSCR were incurred, and coverage for them vested under the

1993 plan, in December 1993. Dynamic's subsequent amendment may not apply retroactively to deny her coverage.

Blackshear v. Reliance Standard Life Ins. Co., 509 F.3d 634 (4th Cir.2007)

10-3 QUESTIONS AND PROBLEMS

1. Does the holding in *Blackshear* mean that the plan participants are vested in the insurance benefits?

2. Assume that the employer in *Blackshear* discovered a copy of the insurance policy that the company adopted that stated that there was a six month waiting period. The policy that was subsequently supplied to the company lacked that clause. Would the outcome of the case have been different?

3. Is the holding in *Wheeler* essentially the imposition of a substantive requirement upon a welfare benefit plan?

4. Did the *Wheeler* court draw a defensible distinction between its facts and those of *McGann v. H & H Music Co.*, (Chapter 3) in which an employer was permitted to unilaterally reduce the dollar value of the plan medical coverage of AIDS? Is the following language of the court convincing?

> Wheeler seeks coverage for a particular medical procedure whose scope is relatively short and well defined. We believe a meaningful distinction may be made between HDC/PSCR, a specific procedure terminating after several months, and treatment for AIDS, which continues throughout an employee's lifetime and may well involve a variety of unforeseeable future procedures.

5. Marquis, age 47, participates in the Nu Co. health care plan. He is diagnosed with colon cancer. He is operated on, apparently with success. He receives no further treatment for the cancer. One year after his Nu Co. amended its plan to limit lifetime cost coverage of colon cancer to $50,000. Marquis' treatment costs exceeded that amount. Two months after the plan amendment, Marquis' colon cancer reappears. The treating physician concedes that the operation did not remove all the cancer. Is the Nu Co. health plan liable for the cost of treating Marquis or is he subject to the $50,000 cost limit?

[3] Plan Amendments and Plan Surpluses

Suppose a defined benefit plan has a surplus. Can the plan sponsor amend the plan to use the surplus to fund early retirement benefits? The deeper question is whether plan surpluses effectively belong to the plan sponsor so that it can amend the plan to use those surpluses in ways that promote the goals of the plan sponsor or whether plan assets must be preserved for the benefit of the current participants.

HUGHES AIRCRAFT COMPANY v. JACOBSON

525 U.S. 432 (1999)

JUSTICE THOMAS. delivered the opinion of the Court.

Five retired beneficiaries of a defined benefit plan, subject to the terms of the Employee Retirement Income Security Act of 1974 (ERISA), as amended, filed a class action lawsuit against their former employer, Hughes Aircraft Company (Hughes), and the Hughes Non-Bargaining Retirement Plan (Plan). They claim that Hughes violated ERISA by amending the Plan to provide for an early retirement program and a noncontributory benefit structure. The Ninth Circuit held that ERISA may prohibit these amendments. We reverse.

I

According to the complaint, Hughes has provided the Plan for its employees since 1955. Prior to 1991, the Plan required mandatory contributions from all participating employees, in addition to any contributions made by Hughes. Section 3.1 of the Plan defines Hughes' funding obligations:

> "The cost of Benefits under the Plan, to the extent not provided by contributions of Participants . . . shall be provided by contributions of [Hughes] not less than in such amounts, and at such times, as the Plan Enrolled Actuary shall certify to be necessary, to fund Benefits under the Plan. . . . "

In addition, § 3.2 provides that Hughes' contributions shall not fall below the "amount necessary to maintain the qualified status of the Plan . . . and to comply with all applicable legal requirements." But § 6.2 of the Plan gives Hughes "the right to suspend its contributions to the Plan at any time," so long as doing so does not "create an 'accumulated funding deficiency' " under ERISA.

By 1986, as a result of employer and employee contributions and investment growth, the Plan's assets exceeded the actuarial or present value of accrued benefits by almost $1 billion. In light of this Plan surplus, Hughes suspended its contributions in 1987, which it has not resumed. Pursuant to the terms of the Plan, the employee contribution requirement remains operational.

Two amendments Hughes made to the Plan are the subject of the present litigation. In 1989, Hughes established an early retirement program that provided significant additional retirement benefits to certain eligible active employees. Subsequently, Hughes again amended the Plan to provide that, effective January 1, 1991, new participants could not contribute to the Plan, and would thereby receive fewer benefits. Existing members could continue to contribute or opt to be treated as new participants. The Plan obligations created by these amendments constitute the only use of the Plan's assets other than paying the pre-existing obligations under the original contributory benefit structure. The Plan's assets substantially exceed the minimum amount needed to fund all current and future defined benefits.

In January 1992, respondents filed this class action on behalf of all Plan participants who had contributed to the Plan and who are or may become eligible to receive benefits designated for contributing participants. The District Court granted Hughes' motion to dismiss the complaint for failure to state a claim. A divided panel of the Ninth Circuit reversed. The majority concluded that the 1991 amendment may have terminated the Plan and created two plans: one consisting of pre-existing members and the other consisting of new participants . . . . The majority also thought that the employees who were members of the contributory structure had a vested interest in the Plan's surplus.

. . .

The majority's decision is in tension with our decision in *Spink*, where we held that "the act of amending a pension plan does not trigger ERISA's fiduciary provisions," 517 U.S. at 891, and with other Circuits' decisions. We granted certiorari, and now reverse.

II

. . .

A

Respondents' vested-benefits and anti-inurement claims proceed on the erroneous assumption that they had an interest in the Plan's surplus, which, with respect to the anti-inurement claim, was used exclusively to benefit Hughes. These claims fail because the 1991 amendment did not affect the rights of pre-existing Plan participants and Hughes did not use the surplus for its own benefit.

To understand why respondents have no interest in the Plan's surplus, it is essential to recognize the difference between defined contribution plans and defined benefit plans, such as Hughes'. A defined contribution plan is one where employees and employers may contribute to the plan, and " 'the employer's contribution is fixed and the employee receives whatever level of benefits the amount contributed on his behalf will provide.' " *Nachman Corp. v. Pension Benefit Guaranty Corp.*, 446 U.S. 359, 364 n.5 (1980). A defined contribution plan "provides for an individual account for each participant and for benefits based solely upon the amount contributed to the participant's account." ERISA § 3(34). "Under such plans, by definition, there can never be an insufficiency of funds in the plan to cover promised benefits," *Nachman*, at 365 n.5, since each beneficiary is entitled to whatever assets are dedicated to his individual account.

A defined benefit plan, on the other hand, consists of a general pool of assets rather than individual dedicated accounts. Such a plan, "as its name implies, is one where the employee, upon retirement, is entitled to a fixed periodic payment."). *Commissioner v. Keystone Consol. Industries, Inc.*, 508 U.S. 152, 154 (1993). The asset pool may be funded by employer or employee contributions, or a combination of both. *See* ERISA § 204(c). But the employer typically bears the entire investment risk and — short of the consequences of plan termination — must cover any underfunding as the result of a shortfall that may occur from the plan's investments. Conversely, if the defined benefit plan is overfunded, the employer may reduce or suspend his contributions.

The structure of a defined benefit plan reflects the risk borne by the employer. Given the employer's obligation to make up any shortfall, no plan member has a claim to any particular asset that composes a part of the plan's general asset pool. Instead, members have a right to a certain defined level of benefits, known as "accrued benefits." That term, for purposes of a defined benefit plan, is defined as "the individual's accrued benefit determined under the plan [and ordinarily is] expressed in the form of an annual benefit commencing at normal retirement age." ERISA § 3(23)(A). In order to prevent a subsequent downward adjustment in benefits below a member's contribution amount, a defined benefit plan participant has a nonforfeitable right to the greater of (1) the benefits provided under the plan or (2) an amount derived from the employee's accumulated contributions, determined using an interest rate fixed by statute. *See* § 204(c)(2)(B); *see also* § 3(23)(A); § 204(c)(2)(c). Given this accumulated contribution floor, plan members generally have a nonforfeitable right only to their "accrued benefit," so that a plan's actual investment experience does not affect their statutory entitlement. Since a decline in the value of a plan's assets does not alter accrued benefits, members similarly have no entitlement to share in a plan's surplus — even is partially attributable to the investment growth of their contributions.

Therefore, Hughes could not have violated ERISA's vesting requirements by using assets from the surplus attributable to the employees' contributions to fund the noncontributory structure. ERISA's vesting requirement is met "if an employee's rights in his accrued benefit derived from his own contributions are nonforfeitable," assuming that such are not limited to a certain percentage of benefits depending on the employee's years of service. § 203(a)(1)–(2). The vesting provision "sets the minimum level of benefits an employee must receive after accruing specified years of service." *International Bhd. of Teamsters, Chauffeurs, Warehousemen and Helpers of America v. Daniel*, 439 U.S. 551, 569 (1979). Otherwise, the "level of benefits" is determined by "the private parties, not the Government." *Alessi v. Raybestos-Manhattan, Inc.*, 451 U.S. 504, 511 (1981). Hence, this provision does not concern items such as a return on investment that fall outside of the definition of "accrued benefit." ERISA §§ 3(23)(A), 203(a). Assuming that an employee's minimum accrued benefit is provided, this section is not implicated. Hughes never deprived respondents of their accrued benefits. Indeed, when it implemented the noncontributory structure, Hughes permitted the Plan's existing participants to switch into the new structure. Since respondents do not allege that Hughes has ever withdrawn accrued benefits or otherwise nonforfeitable interests from the pre-existing members, this vesting claim is meritless.

Respondents further contend that, even if they have no interest in the Plan's assets, the creation of the new contributory structure permitted Hughes to use assets from the surplus attributable to employer *and* employee contributions for its sole and exclusive benefit, in violation of ERISA's anti-inurement provision. This section provides, in relevant part:

> "The assets of a plan [except as otherwise provided in the statute] shall never inure to the benefit of any employer and shall be held for the exclusive purposes of providing benefits to participants in the plan and their beneficiaries and defraying reasonable expenses of administering the plan." § 403(c)(1).

As the language makes clear, the section focuses exclusively on whether fund assets were used to pay pension benefits to plan participants, without distinguishing either between benefits for new and old employees under one or more benefit structures of the same plan, or between assets that make up a plan's surplus as opposed to those needed to fund the plan's benefits. Respondents do not dispute that Hughes used fund assets for the sole purpose of paying pension benefits to plan participants. Furthermore, at all times, Hughes satisfied its continuing obligation under the provisions of the Plan and ERISA to assure that the Plan was adequately funded. *See* Plan § 6.2; ERISA § 302. In other words, Hughes did not act impermissibly by using surplus assets from the contributory structure to add the noncontributory structure to the Plan. The act of amending a pre-existing plan cannot as a matter of law create two de facto plans if the obligations (both preamendment and postamendment) continue to draw from the same single, unsegregated pool or fund of assets. ERISA provides an employer with broad authority to amend a plan, and nowhere suggests that an amendment creating a new benefit structure also creates a second plan. Because only one plan exists and respondents do not allege that Hughes used any of the assets for a purpose other than to pay its obligations to the Plan's beneficiaries, Hughes could not have violated the anti-inurement provision under ERISA § 403(c)(1).

B

Each of respondents' fiduciary duty claims must fail because ERISA's fiduciary provisions are inapplicable to the amendments. This conclusion follows from our decision in *Spink*, where we considered whether amending a plan to require the conditioning of benefit payments under an early retirement program on the participants' release of employment-related claims was a prohibited transaction under ERISA § 406(a). 517 U.S. at 885. We explained:

> "Plan sponsors who alter the terms of a plan do not fall into the category of fiduciaries. As we said with respect to the amendment welfare benefit plans, 'employers or other plan sponsors are generally free under ERISA, for any reason at any time, to adopt, modify, or terminate welfare plans.' When employers undertake those actions, they do not act as fiduciaries, but are analogous to the settlors of a trust." *Id.* at 890.

We made clear in *Spink* that our reasoning applied both to "pension benefit plans" and "welfare benefit plans," since "the definition of fiduciary makes no distinction between persons exercising authority over" these different types of plans. Our conclusion applies with equal force to persons exercising authority over a contributory plan, a noncontributory plan, or any other type of plan. Our holding did not turn, as the Court of Appeals below thought, on the type of plan being amended for the simple reason that the plain language of the statute defining fiduciary makes no distinction. ERISA § 404(a) (specifying duties of a "fiduciary . . . with respect to a plan"). Rather, it turned on whether the employer's act of amending its plan constituted an exercise of fiduciary duty. In *Spink*, we concluded it did not.

The same act of amending here also does not constitute the action of a fiduciary, although Hughes' Plan happens to be one to which employees contribute. In general, an employer's decision to amend a pension plan concerns the composition or design of the plan itself and does not implicate the employer's fiduciary duties which consist of such actions as the administration of the plan's assets. ERISA's fiduciary duty requirement simply is not implicated where Hughes, acting as the Plan's settlor, makes a decision regarding the form or structure of the Plan such as who is entitled to receive Plan benefits and in what amounts, or how such benefits are calculated. A settlor's powers include the ability to add a new benefit structure to an existing plan. Respondents' three fiduciary duty claims are directly foreclosed by *Spink*'s holding that, without exception, "plan sponsors who alter the terms of a plan do not fall into the category of fiduciaries." 517 U.S. at 890.

Respondents attempt to circumvent this conclusion by arguing that the amendments amounted to a sham transaction. Specifically, respondents argue that Hughes — by effectively increasing certain employees' wages through either providing increased retirement incentives or including those employees in the Plan's noncontributory structure — reduced its labor costs by spending down the Plan's surplus to cover its own obligations. In *Spink*, we noted in passing that if a transaction constituted "merely a sham transaction, meant to disguise an otherwise unlawful transfer of assets to a party in interest, . . . that might present a different question." *Id.* at 895 n.8. Even assuming that a sham transaction may implicate a fiduciary duty, the incidental benefits conferred upon Hughes when it amended the Plan are not impermissible under the statute. It is irrelevant whether Hughes received lower labor costs or other such incidental benefits from implementing the noncontributory structure under the 1991 amendment. As we noted in *Spink*:

> "Among the 'incidental' and thus legitimate benefits that a plan sponsor may receive from the operation of a pension plan are attracting and retaining employees, paying deferred compensation, settling or avoiding strikes, providing increased compensation without increasing wages, increasing employee turnover, and reducing the likelihood of lawsuits by encouraging employees who would otherwise have been laid off to depart voluntarily." *Id.* at 893–894.

Receipt of these types of benefits no more constitutes a breach of fiduciary duties than they would constitute improper inurement or otherwise violate ERISA. To find that such benefits somehow violated the statute would forestall employers' efforts to implement a pension plan. ERISA, by and large, is concerned with "ensuring that employees will not be left empty handed once employers have guaranteed them certain benefits," *id.* at 887, not with depriving employers of benefits incidental thereto. In sum, respondents have failed to show that Hughes labored under fiduciary duties or engaged in a sham transaction.

C

Finally, respondents allege that the 1991 amendment requires a court to order petitioners to terminate the Plan. ERISA itself plainly spells out the circumstances under which a plan terminates. In a section entitled, "exclusive means of plan termination," the statute provides:

> "Except in the case of a termination for which proceedings are otherwise instituted by the [Pension Benefit Guaranty Corporation] as provided in section 1342 of this title, a single-employer plan may be terminated only in a standard termination under subsection (b) of this section or a distress termination under subsection (c) of this section." § 4041(a)(1).

Subsections (b) and (c) concern the two ways by which an employer may voluntarily terminate a plan. Based on the language of the statute, these means constitute the sole avenues for voluntary termination.

Respondents concede that no voluntary termination has occurred, but nevertheless contend that the 1991 amendment worked an effective termination based on the common-law theory of a wasting trust. Under common law, a wasting trust is a trust whose purposes have been accomplished, such that the continuation of the trust would frustrate the settlor's intent. This claim also fails.

As an initial matter, because ERISA is a "comprehensive and reticulated statute," *Nachman*, 446 U.S. at 361, and is "enormously complex and detailed," *Mertens v. Hewitt Associates*, 508 U.S. 248, 262 (1993), it should not be supplemented by extratextual remedies, such as the common-law doctrines advocated by respondents . . . .Although trust law may offer a "starting point" for analysis in some situations, it must give way if it is inconsistent with "the language of the statute, its structure, or its purposes." *Varity Corp. v. Howe*, 516 U.S. 489, 497 (1996). Application of the wasting trust doctrine in this context would appear to be inconsistent with the language of ERISA's termination provisions.

Even assuming that the wasting trust doctrine might apply in certain circumstances — an extremely doubtful proposition — it is by its own terms inapplicable here. As respondents concede, since the date of the 1991 amendment, the Plan has been accepting new members and paying all the promised benefits to eligible Plan participants. Furthermore, thousands of active participants in the contributory benefit structure continue to accrue benefits. Simply put, these circumstances can in no way be construed to constitute an enfeebled plan whose membership has dwindled to a mere remnant that would no longer benefit from the Plan's administration. Therefore, the wasting trust doctrine cannot salvage respondents' termination claim.

The judgment of the Court of Appeals is therefore reversed.

It is so ordered.

A plan sponsor may terminate a plan in an attempt to cause a reversion of the plan surplus. Today that any reversion of a plan surplus is subject to a tax imposed by the Internal Revenue Code that was enacted in order to discourage terminations initiated to capture plan surpluses. See discussion in Part B, Plan Termination.

10-4 QUESTIONS AND PROBLEMS

1. The Court makes much of the claim that the risk of investment for a defined benefit plan is on the employer. How does this lead to the conclusion that the employer is free to use plan surpluses to fund benefits designed to further the interests of the employer rather than those of a plan participant?

2. How does the Court answer the claim that the plan amendments violate the anti-inurement provisions of ERISA § 403(c)(1)?

3. When the plan sponsor is also a plan fiduciary there appears to be a possible conflict of interest when the plan is amended in a manner that benefits the sponsor rather than the plan participants. How does the Court resolve that issue?

B. PLAN TERMINATION

[1] Vesting upon Termination

IRC § 411(d)(3).

Section 411(d)(3) of the Internal Revenue Code requires that upon termination or partial termination of a qualified retirement plan, all employees be fully vested in their plan benefits "to the extent funded." The Treasury regulations do not define the term "partial termination," but only state that whether there has been a partial termination depends on all the "facts and circumstances" in the particular case. Treas. Reg. § 1.411(d)-2(b)(1). This "facts and circumstances" approach has given rise to a great deal of litigation.

ADMINISTRATIVE COMMITTEE OF THE SEA RAY EMPLOYEE'S STOCK OWNERSHIP AND PROFIT SHARING PLAN v. ROBINSON

164 F.3d 981 (6th Cir. 1999)

COLE, CIRCUIT JUDGE. At issue in this appeal is whether the layoffs at Sea Ray Boats, Inc. between 1989 and 1991 constituted a partial termination of the company's stock ownership and profit sharing plan ("Plan"), governed by the Employee Retirement Income Security Act of 1974 ("ERISA"). Sea Ray's administrative committee ("Committee") concluded that the company had not terminated the Plan. Upon review, the district court granted summary judgment in favor of the Committee and a cla ss of Sea Ray employees ("Class II") who are current or fully vested participants in the Plan and their beneficiaries. Another class of former Sea Ray employees ("Class I"), non-vested former participants in the Plan and their beneficiaries, contends that the district court erred in applying an arbitrary and capricious rather than a de novo standard of review of the Committee's decision. Class I also contends that the Committee erred in determining that a partial termination of the Plan had not occurred. For the reasons that follow, we affirm the judgment of the district court.

I

Sea Ray manufactures sport boats, sport cruisers, and yachts — a particular line of boats known as pleasure crafts. Founded in the late 1950s by C.N. Ray in Oxford, Michigan, the company enjoyed steady growth from the late 1960s through the 1970s. During this time, it systematically opened new plants and renovated existing ones. During the 1980s, the company experienced unprecedented growth, enjoying an average annual growth of 35 percent from 1983 to 1986 and record sales from 1986 to 1988. In 1986, Brunswick Corporation purchased Sea Ray, but allowed it to operate as a separate entity.

As part of its employee benefits, Sea Ray offers employees membership in the Plan, a defined contribution stock bonus and profit-sharing plan established under the provisions of ERISA. The Committee, as a fiduciary under ERISA, acts as the administrator for the Plan. Sea Ray funds the Plan in its entirety; participating employees do not contribute to the Plan. The Plan's assets are allocated to the individual accounts of its participants, with the benefits of each participant based solely upon the amount contributed to the participant's account and any income, expenses, gains and losses, or forfeitures of accounts of other participants which may be allocated to such participant's account. Although membership in the Plan is voluntary, a majority of Sea Ray's employees participate.

Sea Ray begins contributing to the Plan on behalf of an employee after he or she has completed one full year of service. As permitted under ERISA, § [203(a)(1)(B)], the Plan adopts a gradual vesting formula . . .

Employees become fully vested in their account balances after they have worked at Sea Ray for seven full years. Under normal circumstances, if an employee leaves Sea Ray before completing seven years of service, the non-vested (or forfeitable) portion of his or her account balance is reallocated among the employees who remain at Sea Ray and are currently participating in the Plan.

The one exception to reallocation for non-fully vested employees, stated in § 19 of the Plan and codified in [IRC] § 411(d)(3), occurs if Sea Ray engages in a partial termination of the Plan. In this event, the terminated employees become fully vested and are entitled to retain their full account balances irrespective of the years they have actually served.

During Sea Ray's period of unprecedented growth, membership in the Plan grew from 1,501 employees in July 1985 to 3,832 employees in July 1989. Beginning in March 1989, however, Sea Ray began to experience serious declines in sales, affecting all boats except yachts. During many of the months during 1989 through 1991, Sea Ray laid off part of its work force; some layoffs began as temporary, but almost all became permanent. By June 1990, as the company reduced its number of employees, the number of participants in the Plan declined to 3,060 employees. In 1990, Congress passed a federal luxury tax targeting five high-priced consumer goods — private boats, private planes, cars, jewelry, and furs — as part of its annual budget agreement: effective January 1991, any boat was subject to a 10 percent tax for the amount above $100,000. In the aftermath of the luxury tax, sales of all boats continued to decline as did the number of participants in the Plan. By June 1991, membership in the Plan had shrunk to 1,968 participants and twelve of the thirteen plants had either reduced their workforce or closed altogether.

Between 1989 and 1991, decisions regarding hiring, firing, and dismissal of employees were not vested in any one centralized figure or manager but left to the discretion of each plant. Since each plant at Sea Ray was operated separately as a profit center, each plant's manager determined the plant's criteria for laying off employees at his or her plant. During the downsizing, however, Sea Ray's corporate headquarters issued written directions to affected plant managers on how to handle the layoffs.

In June 1992, prior to any litigation leading to the present case, the Committee convened to discuss the partial termination question and the governing legal standards, and made the following determinations:

> 1. The reductions in employees was motivated by unfavorable changes in the economy and not by targeted employment numbers.
>
> 2. Partial determinations were defined by the Internal Revenue Code and determined on the basis of all facts and circumstances.
>
> 3. The historic application of the partial termination rule focused primarily on whether the termination resulted in funds reverted to the employer or discrimination in favor of highly compensated employees; recently, however, the emphasis had shifted to percentage decline in employment.
>
> 4. Case law was unsettled on what constitutes a significant decline and the level of deference, if any, owed to employer or IRS determinations.
>
> 5. Lastly, the courts' determinations regarding partial terminations were binding on the IRS only if it joined the suit or the suit was an appeal of a final administrative determination by the IRS.

Later that month, the Committee reconvened and concluded that for the period between 1989 and 1991, "there were no facts or circumstances other than the layoff due to the cyclical business which would dictate a finding of a Partial Termination." In making that determination, the Committee decided to calculate the percentage of layoffs for each year separately. The Committee also decided that the company would retain legal counsel to commence a lawsuit on behalf of the plan to seek a judicial ruling upholding the Committee's determination that a partial termination did not occur. The Committee filed an action before the district court in August. Following pre-trial matters, Class I filed a motion for summary judgment on December 1995. The Committee and Class II each filed a cross-motion for summary judgment in March 1996. The district court referred the motion and cross-motions to a magistrate judge, who recommended that the district court grant the cross-motions by the Committee and Class II and deny the motion by Class I. Specifically, it recommended holding that 1) the Committee's determination that a partial termination had not occurred was subject to the arbitrary and capricious standard of review; 2) the layoffs, calculated as caused by two separate corporate events, were not at a level generally considered determinative of a partial termination; and 3) the Committee's determinations regarding partial termination were neither arbitrary nor capricious. Although Class I filed an objection to the magistrate judge's report and recommendation, the district court accepted it in its entirety. Class I filed a timely notice of appeal.

. . .

III

[Court finds that the Plan vests the Committee with discretionary authority and thus its decision is subject to arbitrary and capricious standard of review.]

IV

Having established the appropriate standard of review, we now evaluate whether the Committee's determination that a partial termination did not occur between 1989 and 1991 was arbitrary and capricious. The Committee contends that the percentage of terminations at Sea Ray during these years, in the absence of improper motive or bias on the part of Sea Ray, did not constitute a partial termination. Class I counters that the percentage of terminations was higher than the Committee calculated, and the real percentage was high enough in itself to be determinative of a partial termination. The differences in calculations stem from the Committee's decision to calculate the layoffs from each year separately and to exclude certain classes of former employees in its tally of terminated employees.

In determining whether a partial termination has occurred, this court has held that Treasury Regulation § 1.411(d)-2(b)(1) "directs us to consider all the facts and circumstances, of which the percentage of excluded plan participants is but one, albeit generally the most persuasive one." *Kreis v. Charles O. Townley, M.D. and Associates, P.C.*, 833 F.2d 74, 79 (6th Cir. 1987). In some cases, however, we have held that "the percentage may be so high or so low as to be determinative standing alone." *Id.* at 80.

Neither this court nor other circuits have established clear benchmarks for these high or low percentages. This court noted that one court has held 34 and 51 percent terminations of the work force constituted partial terminations, while other courts have held that termination rates of 16.7 percent, 13.0 percent, and 12.4 percent were insufficient to trigger a partial termination. *See id.* at 83 (citing *Tipton and Kalmbach, Inc. v. Commissioner*, 83 T.C. 154, 162 (1984) (34 and 51 percent); *Wishner v. St. Luke's Hosp.*, 550 F. Supp. 1016, 1019 (S.D.N.Y. 1982) (16.7 percent); *Taylor v. Food Giant, Inc. Salaried Employees Pension Plan*, 1984 U.S. Dist. LEXIS 21592 (N.D. Ga. Nov. 30, 1984) (13.0 percent); *Babb v. Olney Paint Co.*, 764 F.2d 240, 243 (4th Cir. 1985) (12.4 percent)). The United States Tax Court in *Halliburton Co. v. C.I.R.*, 100 T.C. 216 (1993) stated that a percentage exceeding 50 percent may be sufficient standing alone to establish a partial termination; conversely, a drop of less than 20 percent is significant only if accompanied by egregious abuse on the part of the employer. *See id.* at 236–37. A drop of at least than 20 percent is sufficient, if coupled with other circumstances, to suggest a partial termination. *See id.* at 237. We decline to establish rigid percentage parameters for partial terminations, and repeat our holding in Kreis that while the percentage of excluded plan participants is the most persuasive factor, we must generally consider all the facts and circumstances, "unless and until Congress or the Treasury Department provides otherwise." *Kreis*, 833 F.2d at 80.

Before evaluating the Committee's determination, we must first ascertain the percentage of participants involuntarily excluded from the Plan between 1989 and 1991 through actual or constructive discharge. Whether an actual or constructive discharge has occurred is a question of fact, and we must affirm the district court's findings on this question unless they are clearly erroneous . . . .

The district court first concluded that the layoffs at Sea Ray between 1989 and 1991 were caused by two separate events: a two-year downturn in the small boat industry and a downturn in the large boat business caused by the federal luxury tax.

It therefore decided to analyze the percentage of actual or constructive discharges as separate years. In deciding which terminated employees to count for the partial termination calculation, the court excluded classes of employees who left Sea Ray for the following reasons: death, normal retirements, terminations for cause, terminations due to disabilities, departure due to a transfer, and voluntary departures — even if the departure were influenced by the economic downturn at the company. Class I disagrees with the district court's findings, maintaining that the discharges should be considered as one event and that former employees who left in anticipation of an involuntary layoff should count as constructive discharges.

We see no occasion to disturb the factual findings of the district court. First, our review of the record does not firmly convince us that the district court erred in its conclusion that two events occurred. We agree that the economic downturn in 1989 and the federal luxury tax in 1990, while both leading to dire consequences at Sea Ray, stem from two independent factors. Second, while we do not dispute that some former Sea Ray employees felt compelled to leave in light of the economic downturn, a showing of constructive discharge requires more than dissatisfaction with the economic conditions at work. The record does not reflect that working conditions at Sea Ray were "so difficult or unpleasant that a reasonable person in the employee's shoes would have felt compelled to resign." *Held v. Gulf Oil Co.*, 684 F.2d 427, 432 (6th Cir. 1982). To characterize the conditions at Sea Ray as intolerable is to impute liability to the company simply because of broad economic conditions which were beyond the company's control. That imputation exceeds the scope of partial termination.

While adopting the findings of the Committee with the modifications noted by Class II, the district court generated three sets of calculations for the percentage of discharged employees at Sea Ray between 1989 and 1991, based on each party's interpretation of the layoffs.

Committee	Class II	Class I
1989-90: 16.1%	1989-90: 15.9%	(a) 1989-91: 32.9%
1990-91: 28.8%	1990-91: 27.9%	(b) 1989-91: 36.7%

Finding no clear error by the district court, we also adopt the percentages generated by Class II. Because we do not find the percentage for either 1989–90 or 1990–91 to be so high as "as to be determinative standing alone," *Kreis*, 833 F.2d at 80, we consider additional facts and circumstances.

This court in *Kreis* considered two additional factors to determine whether a partial termination has occurred: one, the effects on the plan of the exclusion of employees from participation; two, the employer's motives. *See id.* at 79. We similarly apply these factors in the present case. We quickly dismiss the first factor, as none of the parties allege that the layoffs at Sea Ray between 1989 and 1991 financially impaired the Plan. For the second factor, we look to see whether the Committee initiated the layoffs to generate profit from the forfeitures from non-vested employees, either for itself or a third party. Evidence of this type of profit "supports but is not sufficient for a finding of bad faith." *Id.* at 80. Nonetheless, we can similarly dismiss this factor, as Class I does not contend that Sea Ray was motivated by improper motives in terminating the employees.

We are left to decide whether the Committee's determination that a partial termination did not occur at Sea Ray between 1989 and 1991 was arbitrary and capricious . . .

We find that the Committee's determination regarding the partial termination issue was neither arbitrary nor capricious. The Committee made its decision only after carefully deliberating both the governing legal standards of partial terminations and Sea Ray's actions in light of these standards. Given its calculation of the percentage of terminations — both years were below 30 percent — and the absence of any damage to the Plan or improper motive for profit, the Committee was reasonable in concluding that the Plan had not been partially terminated.

V

For the reasons stated above, we affirm the district court's grant of summary judgment in favor of the Committee and Class II.

MATZ v. HOUSEHOLD INTERNATIONAL TAX REDUCTION INVESTMENT PLAN

388 F.3d 570 (7th Cir. 2004)

Posner, Circuit Judge.

The district judge, in this suit by participants in an ERISA pension plan, has asked us, and we have agreed, to entertain an interlocutory appeal from a ruling in which she answered in favor of the plaintiffs a potentially controlling question of law that had arisen in the course of the litigation. 28 U.S.C. § 1292(b). . . . The question is the correct approach to deciding whether an ERISA pension plan — in this case a defined-contribution plan in which the employer matched contributions that its employees made by means of payroll deductions to individual retirement accounts — has been partially terminated.

Provided that certain requirements are met, the interest or other earnings in an individual retirement account are not taxed as they accrue; see 26 U.S.C. §§ 402(a), 501(a). Suppose the employer terminates the plan. Were it not for the special rule on terminations that is the focus of this case, an employee whose pension entitlement had not yet fully vested would receive (i.e., would be deemed fully vested as to), over and above the vested portion of the employer's contribution, only the contributions he had made to his retirement account, plus the earnings on them. The portion of the employer's contributions that had not yet vested would revert to the employer, compare ERISA § 203(a)(2) with § 203(a)(1), yielding it a tax benefit because the amount by which its contributions had grown as a result of the pension plan's investing them would have escaped being taxed. But this is where the special rule clicks in: in the event of termination the rights of *all* the participants in the terminated plan vest in full, so that none of the money that the employer contributed is returned to it. 26 U.S.C. § 411(d)(3).

The purpose of the rule is to prevent plan terminations motivated by the prospect of a tax windfall. We are unconvinced by an alternative rationale sometimes suggested for the rule-to protect nonvested employees' expectations of receiving pension benefits. Until his pension benefits have vested, an employee at will, lacking as he does any job tenure, *has* no reasonable expectations of receiving benefits. The point of vesting is to create such an expectation.

To prevent evasion, the rule requiring immediate vesting of all participants' pension benefits applies to "partial" terminations as well as to complete ones. The statute does not define "partial termination." . . .

. . . The Supreme Court, however, vacated our decision, 533 U.S. 925 (2001) (per curiam), in light of the just-decided *United States v. Mead Corp.*, 533 U.S. 218

(2001), where the Court had ruled that informal agency actions are not to receive *Chevron* deference . . . .

On remand from the Supreme Court, . . . we "adopt[ed] the rule that only non-vested participants should be counted in determining whether partial termination of a pension plan has occurred." By "non-vested" we meant not *fully* vested . . . .

* * *

. . . The purpose of section 411(d)(3) of the Internal Revenue Code is to prevent an employer from obtaining a tax windfall at the expense of the not fully vested participants in his plan. But the statute does not provide that plan alterations which result in a tax windfall at the expense of such participants shall be deemed terminations and precipitate full vesting. It provides that terminations precipitate full vesting, and to prevent evasion adds that terminations include partial terminations.

The natural way to decide whether a partial termination has occurred is to see how close it is to a complete termination. On the one hand, clearly an employer shouldn't be able to get away with ejecting 99 percent of the plan's participants. On the other hand, no one is arguing that an employer should be forbidden to alter his plan in the slightest degree without forfeiting tax benefits. Such a rule would go far toward erasing the distinction between fully vested and not fully vested employees. For every time the plan was altered to remove even a small handful of not fully vested participants, there would be a case for treating the alteration as a partial termination, requiring immediate full vesting of all not yet fully vested participants.

So where to draw the line? The IRS, which is not famous for encouraging tax windfalls, draws it at 20 percent. As we look back upon the course of this litigation, now in its ninth year and its third *interlocutory* appeal to this court, we find ourselves drawn back to the IRS's position. Not because it is entitled to *Chevron* deference-we adhere to our holding that it is not-but because, having toyed with the alternatives, we think it is the best available and we respect the IRS's experience in formulating tax rules.

* * *

We acknowledge that even the 20 percent rule proposed in the IRS's amicus brief in *Weil* was not intended to be hard and fast despite its appearance of mathematical exactitude. And yet the following table, which summarizes the cases (treating cases involving distinct plans as multiple cases) and rulings on partial termination, reveals the surprising robustness of the 20 percent benchmark:

PARTIAL TERMINATION CASES AND RULINGS

Case or Ruling	*Total Participants*	*Number Who Lost Coverage*	*Percentage Who Lost Coverage*	*Partial Termination?*
Revenue Ruling 69-24, 1969 Cumulative Bulletin 110	224	220	98.2	Yes
Collignon v. Reporting Services Co., 796 F. Supp. 1136 (C.D. Ill. 1992)	6	5	83.3	Yes

Revenue Ruling 73-284, 1973-2 Cumulative Bulletin 139	15	12	80.0	Yes
Revenue Ruling 72-439, 1972-2 Cumulative Bulletin 223	170	120	70.6	Yes
Peter M. Boruta M.D., P.C. v. Commissioner, 55 T.C.M. 670 (1988)	3	2	66.7	Yes
Revenue Ruling 81-27, 1981-1 Cumulative Bulletin 228 (superseding Revenue Ruling 72-510, 1972-2 Cumulative Bulletin 223)	165	95	57.6	Yes
Tipton & Kalmbach, Inc. v. Commissioner, supra (1972 plan year)	43	22	51.2	Yes
In re Gulf Pension Litigation, supra	14,233	6,427	45.2	Yes
In re Gulf Pension Litigation, supra (alternative calculation)	24,599	8,534	34.7	Yes
Weil v. Retirement Plan Administrative Committee, 1988 U.S. Dist. Lexis 5802, at *5 (S.D.N.Y. June 15, 1988)	386	132	34.2	Yes
Tipton & Kalmbach, Inc. v. Commissioner, supra (1971 plan year)	65	22	33.8	Yes
Administrative Committee of Sea Ray Employees' Stock Ownership & Profit Sharing Plan v. Robinson, 1996 U.S. Dist. Lexis 22772, at *93 (E.D. Tenn. Oct. 30, 1996) (1991 plan year)	3,111	867	27.9	No
Halliburton Co. v. Commissioner, supra	19,598	3,891	19.9	No
Administrative Committee of the Sea Ray Employees' Stock Ownership & Profit Sharing Plan v. Robinson, supra (1990 plan year)	4,084	651	15.9	No

Morales v. Pan American Life Ins. Co., 718 F. Supp. 1297, 1303 (E.D. La. 1989), affirmed on other grounds, 914 F.2d 83 (5th Cir. 1990)	835	128	15.3	No
Kreis v. Townley, supra	20	3	15.0	No
Babb v. Olney Paint Co., 764 F.2d 240 (4th Cir. 1985)	109	16	14.7	No
Kreis v. Townley, supra (second plan)	22	3	13.6	No
Wishner v. St. Luke's Hospital Center, 550 F. Supp. 1016 (S.D.N.Y. 1982)	1,529	57	3.7	No
Ehm v. Phillips Petroleum Co., 583 F. Supp. 1113 (D. Kan. 1984)	16,444	415	2.5	No
Bruch v. Firestone Tire & Rubber Co., 640 F. Supp. 519, 530 (E.D. Pa. 1986)	10,500	228	2.2	No

In 20 of the 21 cases and rulings, if 20 percent or more of the participants lose coverage, there is a finding of a partial termination, and if fewer than 20 percent do, a partial termination is not found. The exception is the *Sea Ray* case, where a 27.9 percent loss of coverage was held not to be a partial termination because the loss was the consequence purely of economic conditions; the employer was not motivated by any desire to obtain a tax benefit or reallocate pension benefits to favored participants in the pension plan.

In an effort to make the law as certain as possible without opening up gaping loopholes, we shall generalize from the cases and the rulings a rebuttable presumption that a 20 percent or greater reduction in plan participants is a partial termination and that a smaller reduction is not. How rebuttable? One can imagine cases in which a somewhat smaller reduction in the percentage of plan participants would be tax-driven and might on that account be thought a "partial" termination, and other cases, like *Sea Ray*, in which the reduction is perhaps not so far above 20 percent that further inquiry is inappropriate. We assume in other words that there is a band around 20 percent in which consideration of tax motives or consequences can be used to rebut the presumption created by that percentage. A generous band would run from 10 percent to 40 percent. Below 10 percent, the reduction in coverage should be conclusively presumed not to be a partial termination; above 40 percent, it should be conclusively presumed to be a partial termination.

* * *

The range of possible reduction-of-coverage percentages in the present case-15.4 percent to 35.8 percent (treating the series of terminations as a single event-if on remand the district court rejects that treatment this will affect the range, perhaps decisively)-lies within the band, and so a remand will be necessary in which the district court will have to consider additional "facts and circumstances." But given that the statutory purpose is to prevent tax windfalls, it seems to us that the only relevant facts and circumstances should be the tax motives and tax consequences involved in the reduction in plan coverage.

VACATED AND REMANDED.

10-5 QUESTIONS AND PROBLEMS

1. Why is vesting on termination or partial termination only required of qualified plans? Why doesn't ERISA extend this requirement to all pension plans?

2. Suppose that the Zeta Pension Plan has 150 participants, 100 of whom are fully vested and 50 of whom are partially vested. A reduction in force causes the dismissal of 75 participant, 65 of whom are fully vested and 10 are partially vested. Has there been a partial termination?

3. Suppose that Rho Inc., the parent corporation of a varied group of businesses, has 1000 participants in its pension plan at the beginning of 2009. In November of 2009, it sells a business with 150 participants, in May 2010, it sells a business with 150 participants, and in January 2011, it sells yet another business with 150 participants. Should the sales in all three years be combined to determine whether there has been a partial termination or should each year be treated separately?

4. Should employees who transfer to successor plans be taken into account in determining whether there has been a partial termination of a plan?

5. What effect does a partial termination have on the benefits of partially vested participants in an underfunded defined benefit plan? *See* IRC § 411(d)(3).

6. Suppose that Delta Co. has 7 employees. Five of the employees each own 20% of the company and earn more than $100,000 per year while the remaining 2 clerical employees earn less than $30,000. Delta Co. maintains a qualified profit-sharing plan with a 5 year cliff vesting schedule. All 7 of the employees participate in the profit-sharing plan. Three years after the plan was adopted, the shareholders decide that business conditions require them to terminate the 2 clerical employees. At the time of the terminations, all 7 employees had completed 3 years of service with the company. Has there been a partial termination? Assuming there is no partial termination, what effect, if any, would the terminations have on the tax plan's qualification? *See* IRC § 411(d)(1). Could the clerical employees challenge the termination on any other grounds?

There are two types of partial terminations — vertical and horizontal. Vertical partial terminations result from a plant or division closing or employee turnover. Horizontal partial terminations may arise in two different ways. First, the cessation or decrease of future benefit accruals in a defined benefit plan which results in a potential reversion for the employer may cause a horizontal partial termination. *See* Treas. Reg. § 1.411(d)- 2(b)(2). Second, a horizontal partial termination may arise when plan amendments make vesting or eligibility more restrictive. Treas. Reg. § 1.411(d)-2(b)(1).

Horizontal partial terminations are infrequent and the law governing such terminations is not well-developed. In a rare case addressing the issue, the district court in the *In re Gulf Pension Litigation*, 764 F. Supp. 1149 (S.D. Tex. 1991), held that a partial termination occurred when benefits under an employer's plan, which merged into an acquiring corporation, were reduced and resulted in a potential reversion. The court stated that:

> [T]he horizontal partial termination rule, although not a model of clarity, is intended to deter employers from adopting plan amendments that lessen accruals of future benefits, including ancillary benefits, if the effect of such an amendment would be to create or increase the likelihood that the employer would receive a reversion of plan assets in the future. This is a broader goal than other provisions of § 411, which protect already accrued benefits.

Id. at 1177.

On appeal, the appellate court declined to consider the issue of whether there was a partial termination because it would not have affected its holding that the terminated employees were not entitled to share in the plan's surplus upon termination even if there had been a partial termination. *Borst v. Chevron Corp.*, 36 F.3d 1308 (1994).

[2] Pension Benefit Guaranty Corporation

Prior to the enactment of ERISA, there was little regulation of plan termination. The decision to terminate a plan was generally within the complete discretion of the employer. If an employer terminated an underfunded defined plan, the plan participants risked losing all or most of their benefits. The most famous example of this risk was the termination of the Studebaker automobile plant in 1963, which resulted in almost 7,000 employees losing all or most of their retirement benefits.

To reduce the likelihood of severe underfunding of defined benefit plans, ERISA created minimum funding requirements, *see* Chapter 9. To protect participants in defined benefit plans that terminate when underfunded, Title IV of ERISA created the Pension Benefit and Guaranty Corporation (PBGC), which operates an insurance program under ERISA § 4022 that guarantees benefits (up to certain limits) in the event of a termination of an underfunded defined benefit plan. ERISA §§ 4002–4003. (There is no insurance protection for defined contribution plans. All discussion of retirement plans in the remainder of this chapter refers to defined benefit plans.) The PBGC guarantees "the payment of all nonforfeitable benefits. § 4022(a). Title IV also regulates the manner of plan termination, grants the PBGC rights against an underfunded terminated defined benefit plan, and grants the PBGC powers to investigate plan solvency and to enforce measures designed to protect plan benefits. ERISA §§ 4002–4003. The PBGC is financed by premiums paid each year by plan sponsors, investment returns on assets held by the PBGC, assets the PBGC acquires from terminated plans, and recoveries obtained from employers responsible for underfunded terminated plans. ERISA § 4005(b)(1).

The PBGC administers two separate programs: a program for single-employer plans, and a program for multiemployer plans. (Multiemployer plans are established pursuant to collective bargaining agreements between several employers and one or more employee unions. ERISA § 4001(a)(3)). The PBGC is financed from three main sources: (1) insurance premiums that it receives from employers that sponsor insured pension plans, (2) assets it receives from terminated pension plans, and (3) investment income it earns from its assets. Single-employer plans pay a premium in 2011 of $35 per participant (indexed to increases in the national average wage index), plus underfunded plans pay an additional premium of $9 per $1,000 of unfunded vested benefits. ERISA § 4006(a)(3)(A)(i) & 4006(a)(3)(E)(ii). Multiemployer plans pay an annual premium of $9 per participant. ERISA § 4006(a)(3)(A)(iii).

The U.S. Government Accountability Office (GAO) has designated the PBGC's single-employer program a "high risk" program since 2003 when the program moved from having an accumulated surplus of $9.7 billion in 2000 to an accumulated deficit of $3.6 billion in 2002. In the Deficit Reduction Act of 2005 and the Pension Protection Act of 2006, Congress increased the PBGC's premiums and tightened the minimum funding standards in order to address the PBGC's deficit. These changes are expected to improve the PBGC's finances but not completely eliminate its difficulties. Among other things, the changes do not address the fact the PBGC, unlike private insurers, cannot decline to provide insurance coverage or adjust premiums to reflect actual or expected claims exposure. As of September 30, 2010, the PBGC held about $79.5 billion in assets and had about $102.5 billion in liabilities, for an accumulated deficit of about $23 billion. Proposals for higher premiums and to charge financially shakier companies higher fees than financially secure ones have yet to be adopted in part because of the fear that higher premiums might accelerate the decline in the number of defined benefit plans.

[a] Distribution of Assets Upon the Termination of Single-Employer Plan

ERISA § 4044(a).

Upon termination, a pension plan is supposed to have sufficient assets to pay all promised benefits. If it does not, ERISA § 4044(a) sets forth a priority of payment pursuant to which assets are to be paid upon termination of a single-employer plan:

(1) Benefits derived from voluntary employee contributions;

(2) Benefits derived from mandatory employee contributions;

(3) Benefits that were being paid as an annuity for at least three years prior to the plan termination or could have been paid as annuity for at least three years prior to plan termination had the participant elected to begin to receive benefits at that time;

(4) All other guaranteed benefits;

(5) All other nonforfeitable (vested) benefits;

(6) All other benefits, whether forfeitable or nonforfeitable.

If, after distribution of all of the plan assets, there remain unpaid vested benefits, the PBGC will take over the plan, become the plan trustee and make up the shortfall subject to certain limitations. For example, the PBGC does not guarantee benefits that become vested solely because the plan was terminated. ERISA § 4022(a). The PBGC phases in its guarantee of benefits that are created or increased within five years of the plan's termination. ERISA §§ 4022(b)(1); 4022(b)(7). In addition, the PBGC imposes a dollar limit, which is indexed to increases in the Social Security wage base, on its guarantee. ERISA § 4022(b)(3). In 2012, the limit was $54,840.92 a year for a single-life annuity beginning at age 65. The limit is higher for those who retire later than age 65 and the limit is lower if the annuity begins at a younger age or if the benefit is paid in the form of a joint-and-survivor annuity. Despite these limits, more than 90 percent of participants in PBGC-trusteed plans receive all of their promised benefits. If the plan has sufficient assets, the PBGC may pay benefits above the guaranteed amount.

[b] Types of Plan Terminations

ERISA §§ 4041, 4042.

The termination of a single-employer defined benefit plan can occur in one of three ways:

(1) A voluntary standard termination under ERISA § 4041(b);

(2) A voluntary distress termination under ERISA § 4041(c); or

(3) An involuntary termination initiated by the PBGC under ERISA § 4042.

A plan sponsor may undertake a voluntary standard termination if the plan has sufficient assets to satisfy all fixed and contingent benefit liabilities determined as of the termination date. ERISA §§ 4041(b)(1)(D); 4001(a)(16). The plan must fulfill a series of procedural requirements designed to ensure that both participants and the PBGC have adequate notice of the termination and that plan assets are properly distributed. For example, the plan must give all affected parties at least 60 days notice of the termination. ERISA § 4041(b)(1)(A).

A plan, which lacks sufficient assets to qualify for a voluntary standard termination, may be eligible for a voluntary distress termination if it (a) has sufficient assets to pay all of the benefits guaranteed by the PBGC; and (b) the plan sponsor (and each member of its controlled group) is in "distress." ERISA 4041(c). A plan sponsor is in distress if it is in liquidation, has filed a petition seeking reorganization under bankruptcy law, or will be unable to pay its debts and continue in business unless a distress termination occurs. A plan sponsor is also considered to be in distress if the cost of providing pension coverage has become unreasonably burdensome because of a decline in the number of covered employees. PBGC Reg. § 4041.41(c)(4). As with a voluntary standard termination, the plan must also satisfy a series of procedural requirements.

The PBGC may involuntarily terminate a plan if: (1) the plan fails to satisfy the minimum funding requirements, (2) the plan will be unable to pay benefits when due, (3) the plan makes certain distributions to a substantial owner, or (4) the long-run potential cost to the PBGC will unreasonably increase if the plan is not terminated. ERISA § 4042(a). The PBGC must involuntarily terminate a plan if the plan does not have sufficient assets to pay current benefits or if the plan has elected a distress termination but the plan lacks sufficient assets to pay guaranteed benefits. ERISA §§ 4041(c)(3)(B)(iii); 4042. If the PBGC institutes an involuntary termination, it may apply to the appropriate U.S. District Court to be appointed as the trustee to administer the plan. ERISA § 4042(b). In the fiscal year ending September 30, 2010, the PBGC assumed responsibility for 109,000 additional workers and retires in 172 failed plans. In December of 2011, the parent company of American Airlines filed for bankruptcy. The PBGC urged the company to fix its financial problems and preserve its pension plans. The company's plans covered almost 130,000 participants and had $8.3 billion in assets to cover about $18.5 billion in liabilities. If the plans were terminated, the PBGC would be required to cover about $17 billion of the plan's liabilities, and American Airlines employees could lose up to $1 billion in benefits that were promised but not guaranteed by the PBGC.

The PBGC has developed an "early warning program" for large underfunded plans pursuant to which it threatens involuntary termination in the event of major corporate transactions. For example, when Harvard Industries, the sponsor of eight pension plans that were underfunded by at least $25 million, proposed a $100 million debt offering to retire existing bank and trade debt and a portion of its preferred stock, the PBGC invoked its early warning program to convince Harvard Industries to contribute an extra $24 million to the plans over three years.

Through this early warning program, the PBGC has caused a number of companies to make significant one-time contributions to improve the funding of their plans.

Other times the PBGC has forced underfunded defined plans to terminate to limit the PBGC's exposure to additional liability. For example, in the early 2000s American steel companies came under intense competitive pressure from imported steel. Faced with severely declining profits that limited the ability of the companies to pay required contributions to their retirement plans, many of the plans became significantly underfunded. The funding problems were exacerbated when the plans suffered severe investment losses when the stock market declined 40 percent after 2001. Faced with a plan funding crisis of unprecedented proportions, in 2002, the PBGC assumed more than $7 billion of pension obligations owed by steel company retirement plans. Some plans voluntarily terminated, but many plans were involuntarily taken over by PBGC because of their underfunded status. The PBGC estimated that it avoided another $1 billion in liability by not delaying in taking over the plans. Unfortunately for plan participants, the PBGC takeover in many cases resulted in significantly reduced pension benefits in part because many plans promised additional benefits in the case of a plant shutdown. If the PBGC takes over the plan after a shutdown, it must pay the additional retirement benefits. If the PBGC takes over a plan before the plant is shutdown, however, no additional benefits will be paid on account of the shutdown of the plant. Attempts by unions to preserve plant shutdown benefits by overturning what they deem to be "premature" takeovers by the PBGC have generally proven unsuccessful.

A plan termination under the multiemployer program does not trigger the PBGC guarantee. Instead, a terminated plan must continue to pay full benefits so long as it has sufficient assets to do so. If a plan does not have enough assets to pay full plan benefits, it may reduce or suspend payment of that portion of the benefit that exceeds the PBGC guarantee level. Currently, the PBGC monthly benefit guarantee level is 100 percent of the first $11 of the plan-designated dollar amount multiplied by the participant's years of service under the plan plus 75 percent of the next $33 of the dollar amount multiplied by the participant's years of service. Thus, for a worker with 30 years of service in a multiemployer plan, the monthly benefit guarantee is $1,072.50 (or $12,870 per year). Unlike the guarantee in the single-employer program, the dollar levels in the multiemployer benefit guarantee formula are not indexed.

If a multiemployer plan becomes insolvent despite benefit cutbacks, the PBGC will provide the plan with financial assistance — typically in the form of a loan — in an amount necessary to pay guaranteed benefits and administrative expenses. Few plans that receive such financial assistance are likely to recover sufficiently to repay the monies lent to them.

10-6 QUESTIONS AND PROBLEMS

1. Why does the PBGC insurance cover defined benefit plans but not defined contribution plans?

2. In order to reduce the cost of operating defined benefit plans and thus encourage more employers to adopt such plans, should the PBGC mandatory insurance program be converted to a voluntary insurance program in which each participant would elect whether or not to participate? Alternatively, should each participant be mandatorily assessed the cost of the PBGC insurance?

3. Why are there limits on voluntary plan terminations?

4. Should the PBGC guarantee all promised plan benefits? Only retirement benefits?

[3] Tax on Reversions of Plan Surpluses

IRC § 4980.

Imagine a company, Alpha Inc., a family owned business which sponsors a defined benefit plan, the Alpha Pension Plan (Plan), which has been funded solely by employer contributions. The president of the company dies, and her children decide to end the business and sell its assets. The end of the company also means the end of the defined benefit plan. Upon termination, the Plan must meet its obligations to plan participants and beneficiaries. The retired beneficiaries are not an issue because the Plan has always purchased an annuity from a reliable insurance company for each employee (and spouse where applicable) upon retirement. As for the current participants, the Plan also purchases an annuity equal to the current value of the employee's pension with payment to commence upon the employee reaching age 65, the plan's normal retirement age. After buying annuities for all the participants from the safest available annuity provider (as required by the DOL Interpretive Bulletin 95) the Plan finds itself with substantial assets, the result of conservative actuarial projections, greater employee turnover than expected, and very successful investments of the fund assets. In short, the Plan is overfunded. What is to be done with the surplus?

Section 4044(d)(1) of ERISA permits the Plan to distribute any "residual" assets to Alpha, Inc. upon termination of the Plan once all plan liabilities have been satisfied. The surplus, however, is subject to income tax because the Alpha's Inc.'s contributions to the plan were tax deductible when made. In addition, the surplus may be subject to a hefty excise tax under IRC § 4980.

Congress added this tax on reversions to the Internal Revenue Code in 1986 in response to a wave of terminations of overfunded plans in the 1980s when corporate raiders targeted companies with overfunded defined benefit plans as an opportunity to terminate the target company's plan and recapture the excess cash. For example, in 1985, Ronald Perelman acquired Revlon and recaptured a surplus of more than $100 million. In another takeover, the acquisition costs of the Pacific Lumber Corporation were partly financed by a $55 million surplus in its defined benefit plan. As originally enacted, IRC § 4980 imposed a 10 percent excise tax on any reversion from a qualified plan. The rate was increased to 15 percent in 1988, and again in 1990 to the current rate of 50 percent.

The 50 percent rate falls to 20 percent if at least 25 percent of the surplus is transferred to a "qualified replacement plan" or is used to increase benefits before terminating the plan. To be a qualified replacement plan the new plan must cover at least 95 percent of the participants in the terminated plan who remain as employees after the termination and must receive at least 25 percent of the value of the reversion. Alternatively, the surplus can be rolled over to a defined contribution plan if the roll-over is allocated to the accounts of participants in the year of the transfer or credited to participant accounts over the next seven years. Amounts rolled over can be used as employer matching contributions. IRC § 4980. The 50 percent excise tax is also reduced to 20 percent if in connection with the plan termination the employer amends the plan, effective on the date of termination, to provide pro rata increases in accrued benefits equal to at least 20 percent of the amount of the reversion. IRC § 4980(d).

The combination of the income tax and excise tax can greatly reduce the value of any plan reversion. For example, assume that Gamma Co. terminates its defined benefit plan and recaptures the $10 million plan surplus. If Gamma neither creates a qualified replacement plan nor increases benefits for participants, the reversion is subject to the 50 percent excise tax. The reversion is also subject to income tax. If the income tax rate averages 34 percent, the income tax is $3.4 million (34% * $10,000,000). The excise tax is $5 million (50% * $10,000,000). The taxes total $8.4 million, leaving Gamma with only $1.6 million of after-tax reverted surplus. In order to avoid these excessive taxes, most employers establish a "qualified replacement plan" upon terminating an overfunded plan.

10-7 QUESTIONS AND PROBLEMS

1. Why are plan surplus reversions exempted from the exclusive benefit rule found in ERISA § 403(c)(1) and IRC § 401(a)(2) and permitted to revert to the employer?

2. What does the reversion of a defined benefit plan surplus say about who "owns" the pension funds?

3. Do employees have any reason to object to the termination of a defined benefit plan whose surplus is rolled over into replacement plan that is a defined contribution plan?

4. What of the erosion of the value of retiree benefits due to post-retirement inflation? Should the plan sponsor be required to apply any surplus on plan termination to increase benefits to retirees on the theory that inflation both lowered the value of the retirement benefits and helped in the growth of fund assets and the resulting surplus?

5. Do excise taxes on plan reversions discourage the formation and liberal funding of defined benefit plans?

[4] Insolvency of Annuity Provider

Typically when a plan terminates pursuant to a voluntary standard plan termination, the plan administrator enters into a contract with an insurance company, which makes an irrevocable promise to pay the participants their benefits in the form of a life annuity. The result is to move the risk of payment of the pension benefit from the plan to the insurance company that issued the annuity. What happens, however, if the insurance company becomes insolvent and unable to perform its obligation? This issue arose in the early 1990s, when in the wake of the collapse of several very large insurance companies pension annuitants turned to the PBGC for assistance. The PBGC took the position, however, that it did not guarantee the annuities because the PBGC's guarantee is triggered by the termination of a pension plan and an insurance company's default is unrelated to plan termination. Instead, the former plan participants' annuities were only guaranteed by state insurance guarantee laws which were not always as generous as the PBGC's guarantee. In many instances, once the insurance companies were taken over by state insurance departments, former plan participants only received about 70 percent of their promised annuity.

The Department of Labor and former participants in a number of plans filed lawsuits claiming that the plan's fiduciaries violated their fiduciary duties when they selected these insurers. Generally, the plaintiffs argued that the fiduciary selected the insurer without adequately analyzing its financial stability, creditworthiness, and claims-paying ability relative to those of other available insurers and their actions violated ERISA's anti-inurement, exclusive benefit, and prudence requirements.

A preliminary question that arose in these suits was whether the former plan participants even had standing to file the suits. Congress resolved that question with the enactment of the "Pension Annuitant Protection Act of 1994," which amended ERISA § 502 to expressly authorize former plan participants or beneficiaries and the Department of Labor to sue plan fiduciaries under these circumstances. *See* ERISA § 502(a)(9). The Act, however, did not impose liability upon the PBGC.

Most of these lawsuits were settled with the employers agreeing to make good any losses. For example, one of the longest and most hotly litigated suits against Pacific Lumber Company was settled in 1996 when the company agreed to pay $7 million into a settlement account. In that case, the former plan participants claimed that the company had improperly recovered about $62 million in surplus pension assets when it terminated its plan and purchased a contract with Executive Life Insurance Company in 1998. Executive Life, which was taken over by California regulators in 1991, had underbid all competitors by at least $2.7 million. Payments were suspended for a short time after Executive Life was taken over and then resumed at 70 percent of their previous levels. Pursuant to the settlement, Pacific Lumber agreed to pay the other 30 percent.

10-8 QUESTIONS AND PROBLEMS

1. How does a plan sponsor benefit when it purchases a less costly, but more risky, annuity for plan beneficiaries?

2. What standard of care should an employer, as plan administrator, be held to when deciding from whom to purchase annuities? Should an employer, as plan administrator, be permitted to make the decision as to which company it should purchase the annuity from or because of the inherent conflict of interest should it be required to have an independent, disinterested third party select the appropriate seller of the annuity?

3. Should the PBGC guarantee be extended to annuity contracts purchased upon the termination of a defined benefit plan?

[5] Restoration of Underfunded Plans

ERISA § 4047.

PENSION BENEFIT GUARANTY CORPORATION v. LTV CORPORATION

496 U.S. 633 (1990)

Justice Blackmun delivered the opinion of the Court.

In this case we must determine whether the decision of the Pension Benefit Guaranty Corporation (PBGC) to restore certain pension plans under § 4047 of [ERISA] was, as the Court of Appeals concluded, arbitrary and capricious or contrary to law, within the meaning of the Administrative Procedure Act (APA), 5 U.S.C. § 706.

I

Petitioner PBGC is a wholly owned United States Government corporation, *see* [ERISA § 4002], modeled after the Federal Deposit Insurance Corporation. The Board of Directors of the PBGC consists of the Secretaries of the Treasury, Labor, and Commerce. [ERISA § 4002(d).] The PBGC administers and enforces Title IV of ERISA. Title IV includes a mandatory Government insurance program that protects the pension benefits of over 30 million private-sector American workers who participate in plans covered by the Title. In enacting Title IV, Congress sought to ensure that employees and their beneficiaries would not be completely "deprived of anticipated retirement benefits by the termination of pension plans before sufficient funds have been accumulated in the plans." *Pension Benefit Guaranty Corporation v. R. A. Gray & Co.*, 467 U.S. 717, 720 (1984). *See also Nachman Corp. v. Pension Benefit Guaranty Corporation*, 446 U.S. 359, 361–362, 374–375 (1980).

When a plan covered under Title IV terminates with insufficient assets to satisfy its pension obligations to the employees, the PBGC becomes trustee of the plan, taking over the plan's assets and liabilities. The PBGC then uses the plan's assets to cover what it can of the benefit obligations. *See* [ERISA § 4044.] The PBGC then must add its own funds to ensure payment of most of the remaining "nonforfeitable" benefits, i.e., those benefits to which participants have earned entitlement under the plan terms as of the date of termination. [ERISA §§ 4001(a)(8), 4022(a) & (b).] ERISA does place limits on the benefits PBGC may guarantee upon plan termination, however, even if an employee is entitled to greater benefits under the terms of the plan. *See* 29 CFR § 2621.3(a)(2) and App. A (1989); [ERISA § 4022(b)(3)(B)]. In addition, benefit increases resulting from plan amendments adopted within five years of the termination are not paid in full. Finally, active plan participants (current employees) cease to earn additional benefits under the plan upon its termination and lose entitlement to most benefits not yet fully earned as of the date of plan termination. [ERISA §§ 4022(a) and (b), 4001(a)(8)]; 29 CFR § 2613.6 (1989).

The cost of the PBGC insurance is borne primarily by employers that maintain ongoing pension plans. Sections 4006 and 4007 of ERISA require these employers to pay annual premiums. The insurance program is also financed by statutory liability imposed on employers who terminate funded pension plans. Upon termination, the employer becomes liable to the PBGC for the benefits that the PBGC will pay out. Because the PBGC historically has recovered only a small portion of that liability, Congress repeatedly has been forced to increase the annual premiums. Even with these increases, the PBGC in its most recent annual report noted liabilities of $4 billion and assets of only $2.4 billion, leaving a deficit of over $1.5 billion.

As noted above, plan termination is the insurable event under Title IV. Plans may be terminated "voluntarily" by an employer or "involuntarily" by the PBGC. An employer may terminate a plan voluntarily in one of two ways. It may proceed with a "standard termination" only if it has sufficient assets to pay all benefit commitments. A standard termination thus does not implicate PBGC insurance responsibilities. If an employer wishes to terminate a plan whose assets are insufficient to pay all benefits, the employer must demonstrate that it is in financial "distress" as defined in [ERISA § 4041(c).] Neither a standard nor a distress termination by the employer, however, is permitted if termination would violate the terms of an existing collective-bargaining agreement. [ERISA § 4041(a)(3).]

The PBGC, though, may terminate a plan "involuntarily," notwithstanding the existence of a collective-bargaining agreement. *Ibid.* [Court quotes ERISA § 4042].

Termination can be undone by PBGC. [Court quotes ERISA § 4047].

When a plan is restored, full benefits are reinstated, and the employer, rather than the PBGC, again is responsible for the plan's unfunded liabilities.

II

This case arose after respondent The LTV Corporation (LTV Corp.) and many of its subsidiaries, including LTV Steel Company Inc. (LTV Steel) (collectively LTV), in July 1986 filed petitions for reorganization under Chapter 11 of the Bankruptcy Code. At that time, LTV Steel was the sponsor of three defined benefit pension plans (Plans) covered by Title IV of ERISA. Two of the Plans were the products of collective-bargaining negotiations with the United Steelworkers of America (Steelworkers). The third was for nonunion salaried employees. Chronically underfunded, the Plans, by late 1986, had unfunded liabilities for promised benefits of almost $2.3 billion. Approximately $2.1 billion of this amount was covered by PBGC insurance.

It is undisputed that one of LTV Corp.'s principal goals in filing the Chapter 11 petitions was the restructuring of LTV Steel's pension obligations, a goal which could be accomplished if the Plans were terminated and responsibility for the unfunded liabilities was placed on the PBGC. LTV Steel then could negotiate with its employees for new pension arrangements. LTV, however, could not voluntarily terminate the Plans because two of them had been negotiated in collective bargaining. LTV therefore sought to have the PBGC terminate the Plans.

To that end, LTV advised the PBGC in 1986 that it could not continue to provide complete funding for the Plans. PBGC estimated that, without continued funding, the Plans' $2.1 billion underfunding could increase by as much as $65 million by December 1987 and by another $63 million by December 1988, unless the Plans were terminated. Moreover, extensive plant shutdowns were anticipated. These shutdowns, if they occurred before the Plans were terminated, would have required the payment of significant "shutdown benefits." The PBGC estimated that such benefits could increase the Plans' liabilities by as much as $300 million to $700 million, of which up to $500 million would be covered by PBGC insurance. Confronted with this information, the PBGC, invoking § 4042(a)(4) of ERISA, determined that the Plans should be terminated in order to protect the insurance program from the unreasonable risk of large losses, and commenced termination proceedings in the District Court. With LTV's consent, the Plans were terminated effective January 13, 1987.

Because the Plans' participants lost some benefits as a result of the termination, the Steelworkers filed an adversary action against LTV in the Bankruptcy Court, challenging the termination and seeking an order directing LTV to make up the lost benefits. This action was settled, with LTV and the Steelworkers negotiating an interim collective-bargaining agreement that included new pension arrangements intended to make up benefits that plan participants lost as a result of the termination. New payments to retirees were based explicitly upon "a percentage of the difference between the benefit that was being paid under the Prior Plans and the amount paid by the PBGC." App. 181. Retired participants were thereby placed in substantially the same positions they would have occupied had the old Plans never been terminated. The new agreements respecting active participants were also designed to replace benefits under the old Plans that were not insured by the PBGC, such as early retirement benefits and shutdown benefits. With respect to shutdown benefits, LTV stated in Bankruptcy Court that the new benefits totaled "75% of benefits lost as a result of plan termination." *Id.* at 159. With respect to some other kinds of benefits for active participants, the new arrangements provided 100% or more of the lost benefits. *Id.* at 235.

The PBGC objected to these new pension agreements, characterizing them as "follow-on" plans. It defines a follow-on plan as a new benefit arrangement designed to wrap around the insurance benefits provided by the PBGC in such a way as to provide both retirees and active participants substantially the same benefits as they would have received had no termination occurred. The PBGC's policy against follow-on plans stems from the agency's belief that such plans are "abusive" of the insurance program and result in the PBGC's subsidizing an employer's ongoing pension program in a way not contemplated by Title IV. The PBGC consistently has made clear its policy of using its restoration powers under § 4047 if an employer institutes an abusive follow-on plan. In three opinion letters, two in 1981 and one in 1986, the PBGC stated: "[T]he termination insurance program of Title IV was not intended to subsidize an employer's ongoing retirement program." Accordingly, the PBGC has indicated that if an employer adopts a new plan that, "together with the guaranteed benefits paid by the PBGC under the terminated plan, provide[s] for the payment of, accrual of, or eligibility for benefit s that are substantially the same as those provided under the terminated plan," the PBGC will view the plan as an attempt to shift liability to the termination insurance program while continuing to operate the plan.

LTV ignored the PBGC's objections to the new pension arrangements and asked the Bankruptcy Court for permission to fund the follow-on plans. The Bankruptcy Court granted LTV's request. In doing so, however, it noted that the PBGC "may have legal options or avenues that it can assert administratively . . . to implement its policy goals. Nothing done here tonight precludes the PBGC from pursuing these options . . . ." *Id.* at 261.

In early August 1987, the PBGC determined that the financial factors on which it had relied in terminating the Plans had changed significantly. Of particular significance to the PBGC was its belief that the steel industry, including LTV Steel, was experiencing a dramatic turnaround. As a result, the PBGC concluded it no longer faced the imminent risk, central to its original termination decision, of large unfunded liabilities stemming from plant shutdowns. Later that month, the PBGC's internal working group made a recommendation, based upon LTV's improved financial circumstances and its follow-on plans, to the PBGC's Executive Director to restore the Plans under the PBGC's § 4047 powers. After consulting the PBGC's Board of Directors, which agreed with the working group that restoration was appropriate, the Executive Director decided to restore the Plans.

The Director issued a notice of restoration on September 22, 1987, indicating the PBGC's intent to restore the terminated Plans. The PBGC notice explained that the restoration decision was based on (1) LTV's establishment of "a retirement program that results in an abuse of the pension plan termination insurance system established by Title IV of ERISA," and (2) LTV's "improved financial circumstances." *See* App. to Pet. for Cert. 182a. Restoration meant that the Plans were ongoing, and that LTV again would be responsible for administering and funding them.

LTV refused to comply with the restoration decision. This prompted the PBGC to initiate an enforcement action in the District Court. The court vacated the PBGC's restoration decision, finding, among other things, that the PBGC had exceeded its authority under § 4047. *See In re Chateaugay Corp.*, 87 B.R. 779 (SDNY 1988).

The Court of Appeals for the Second Circuit affirmed, holding that the PBGC's restoration decision was "arbitrary and capricious" or contrary to law under the APA, 5 U.S.C. § 706(2)(A), in various ways. 875 F.2d 1008, 1015–1021 (1989). . . .

Because of the significant administrative law questions raised by this case, and the importance of the PBGC's insurance program, we granted certiorari. 493 U.S. 932 (1989).

III

[The Court held that PBGC was not required to consider the principles and policies of bankruptcy and labor law in making its restoration decision.]

The Court of Appeals also rejected the grounds for restoration that the PBGC *did* assert and discuss. The court found that the first ground the PBGC proffered to support the restoration — its policy against follow-on plans — was contrary to law because there was no indication in the text of the restoration provision, § 4047, or its legislative history that Congress intended the PBGC to use successive benefit plans as a basis for restoration. The PBGC argues that in reaching this conclusion the Court of Appeals departed from traditional principles of statutory interpretation and judicial review of agency construction of statutes. Again, we must agree.

In *Chevron U.S.A. Inc. v. Natural Resources Defense Council, Inc.*, 467 U.S. 837 (1984), we set forth the general principles to be applied when federal courts review an agency's interpretation of the statute it implements:

> "When a court reviews an agency's construction of the statute which it administers, it is confronted with two questions. First, always, is the question whether Congress has directly spoken to the precise question at issue. If the intent of Congress is clear, that is the end of the matter; for the court, as well as the agency, must give effect to the unambiguously expressed intent of Congress. If, however, the court determines Congress has not directly addressed the precise question at issue, the court does not simply impose its own construction on the statute, as would be necessary in the absence of an administrative interpretation. Rather, if the statute is silent or ambiguous with respect to the specific issue, the question for the court is whether the agency's answer is based on a permissible construction of the statute." *Id.* at 842–843, 104 S. Ct. at 2781–82 (footnotes omitted).

Here, the PBGC has interpreted § 4047 as giving it the power to base restoration decisions on the existence of follow-on plans. Our task, then, is to determine whether any clear congressional desire to avoid restoration decisions based on successive pension plans exists, and, if the answer is in the negative, whether the PBGC's policy is based upon a permissible construction of the statute. *See Mead Corp. v. Tilley*, 490 U.S. 714 (1989) (applying *Chevron* principles to the PBGC's construction of ERISA).

Turning to the first half of the inquiry, we observe that the text of § 4047 does not evince a clear congressional intent to deprive the PBGC of the ability to base restoration decisions on the existence of follow-on plans. To the contrary, the textual grant of authority to the PBGC embodied in this section is broad. As noted above, the section authorizes the PBGC to restore terminated plans "in any such case in which [the PBGC] determines such action to be appropriate and consistent with its duties under [Title IV of ERISA]." 29 U.S.C. § 1347. The PBGC's duties consist primarily of furthering the statutory purposes of Title IV identified by Congress. These are:

> "(1) to encourage the continuation and maintenance of voluntary private pension plans for the benefit of their participants,
>
> "(2) to provide for the timely and uninterrupted payment of pension benefits to participants and beneficiaries under plans to which this subchapter applies, and
>
> "(3) to maintain premiums established by [the PBGC] under section 1306 of this title at the lowest level consistent with carrying out the obligations under this subchapter." [ERISA § 4002(a)].

On their face, of course, none of these statutorily identified purposes has anything to say about the precise question at issue — the use of follow-on plans as a basis for restoration decisions.

Nor do any of the other traditional tools of statutory construction compel the conclusion that Congress intended that the PBGC not base its restoration decisions on follow-on plans . . . . We see no suggestion in the legislative history that Congress intended its list of examples to be exhaustive. Under these circumstances, we conclude that ERISA's legislative history does not suggest "clear congressional intent" on the question of follow-on plans.

The Court of Appeals also relied on the legislative history of the 1987 amendments to ERISA effected by the Pension Protection Act, Pub. L. 100-203, 101 Stat. 1330–333. *See* 875 F.2d at 1017. This history reveals that Congress in 1987 considered, but did not enact, a provision that expressly would have authorized the PBGC to prohibit follow-on plans . . . Despite Congress' awareness of the PBGC's belief that the adoption of follow-on plans was a ground for restoration, Congress did not amend § 4047 to restrict the PBGC's discretion. The conclusion that Congress thought the PBGC was properly exercising its authority is at least as plausible as any other. Thus, the legislative history surrounding the 1987 amendments provides no more support than the 1974 legislative history for the Court of Appeals' holding that the PBGC's interpretation of § 4047 contravened clear congressional will.

Having determined that the PBGC's construction is not contrary to clear congressional intent, we still must ascertain whether the agency's policy is based upon a "permissible" construction of the statute, that is, a construction that is "rational and consistent with the statute." *NLRB v. Food & Commercial Workers*, 484 U.S. 112, 123 (1987); *see also Sullivan v. Everhart*, 494 U.S. 83 (1990). Respondents argue that the PBGC's anti-follow-on policy is irrational because, as a practical matter, no purpose is served when the PBGC bases a restoration decision on something other than the improved financial health of the employer. According to respondents, "financial improvement [is] both a necessary and a sufficient condition for restoration. The agency's asserted abuse policy . . . is *logically irrelevant* to the restoration decision." Brief for Respondents LTV Corp. and LTV Steel 33 (emphasis added). We think not. The PBGC's anti-follow-on policy is premised on the belief, which we find eminently reasonable, that employees will object more strenuously to a company's original decision to terminate a plan (or to take financial steps that make termination likely) if the company cannot use a follow-on plan to put the employees in the same (or a similar) position after termination as they were in before. The availability of a follow-on plan thus would remove a significant check — employee resistance — against termination of a pension plan.

Consequently, follow-on plans may tend to frustrate one of the objectives of ERISA that the PBGC is supposed to accomplish — the "continuation and maintenance of voluntary private pension plans." [ERISA § 4002(a)(1).] In addition, follow-on plans have a tendency to increase the PBGC's deficit and increase the insurance premiums all employers must pay, thereby frustrating another related statutory objective — the maintenance of low premiums. *See* [ERISA § 4002(a)(3)]. In short, the PBGC's construction based upon its conclusion that the existence of follow-on plans will lead to more plan terminations and increased PBGC liabilities is "assuredly a permissible one." *Everhart*, 494 U.S. at 93. Indeed, the judgments about the way the real world works that have gone into the PBGC's anti-follow-on policy are precisely the kind that agencies are better equipped to make than are courts. This practical agency expertise is one of the principal justifications behind *Chevron* deference. *See* 467 U.S. at 865, 104 S. Ct. at 2793.

None of this is to say that financial improvement will never be relevant to a restoration decision. Indeed, if an employer's financial situation remains so dire that restoration would lead inevitably to immediate retermination, the PBGC may decide not to restore a terminated plan even where the employer has instituted a follow-on plan. For present purposes, however, it is enough for us to decide that where, as here, there is no suggestion that immediate retermination of the plans will be necessary, it is rational for the PBGC to disfavor follow-on plans.

. . .

IV

We conclude that the PBGC's failure to consider all potentially relevant areas of law did not render its restoration decision arbitrary and capricious. We also conclude that the PBGC's anti-follow-on policy, an asserted basis for the restoration decision, is not contrary to clear congressional intent and is based on a permissible construction of § 4047. Finally, we find the procedures employed by the PBGC to be consistent with the APA. Accordingly, the judgment of the Court of Appeals is reversed, and the case is remanded for further proceedings consistent with this opinion.

It is so ordered.

10-9 QUESTIONS AND PROBLEMS

1. How does restoration of the terminated plan help the PBGC? The plan participants?

2. Would the PBGC have reached the same result if LTV had not instituted a follow-on plan?

3. Can the PBGC base a restoration decision solely on the existence of a follow-on plan without considering any other factors such as the likelihood of retermination?

4. What effect is the Court's decision likely to have on an employer's post-termination collective bargaining or other post-termination arrangements?

TABLE OF CASES

[References are to pages]

A

B

C

[References are to pages]

D

E

F

G

[References are to pages]

[References are to pages]

N

O

P

[References are to pages]

[References are to pages]

V

W

Y

Z

INDEX

[References are to sections.]

[References are to sections.]

E

F

[References are to sections.]

[References are to sections.]

[References are to sections.]

[References are to sections.]